COMMENTARIES

ON THE

CONFLICT OF LAWS,

FOREIGN AND DOMESTIC,

IN REGARD TO

CONTRACTS, RIGHTS, AND REMEDIES,

AND ESPECIALLY IN REGARD TO

Marriages, Divorces, Wills, Successions, and Judgments.

BY JOSEPH STORY, LL.D.,

DANE PROFESSOR OF LAW IN HARVARD UNIVERSITY.

"Il régnera donc toujours entre les nations une contrariété perpétuelle de loix; peutêtre régnera-t-elle perpétuellement entre nous sur bien des objets. Delà la nécessité de s'instruire des régles, et des principes, qui peuvent nous conduire dans la décision des questions, que cette variété peut faire naître."—BOULLENOIS. *Traité de la Personalité, &c. des Loix, Préface.*

SECOND EDITION.

REVISED, CORRECTED, AND GREATLY ENLARGED.

THE LAWBOOK EXCHANGE, LTD.
Clark, New Jersey

ISBN 978-1-58477-145-6

Lawbook Exchange edition 2001, 2018

The irregular pagination is reproduced as it was found in the original work. Page 752 is followed by page 757. This is a typographical error in the original printing. No content is missing. The quality of this reprint is equivalent to the quality of the original work.

The Lawbook Exchange, Ltd.
33 Terminal Avenue
Clark, New Jersey 07066-1321

Please see our website for a selection of our other publications and fine facsimile reprints of classic works of legal history:
www.lawbookexchange.com

Library of Congress Cataloging-in-Publication Data

Story, Joseph 1779-1845.
Commentaries on the conflict of laws, foreign and domestic, in regard to contracts, rights, and remedies, and especiillly in regard to marriages, divorces, wills, successions, and judgments / by Joseph Story.
p. cm.
Originally published: 2nd ed., rev., con:, and greatly enl. London: A. Maxwell, 1841.
Includes bibliographical references and index.
ISBN 1-58477-145-3 (cloth: alk. paper)
1. Conflict of laws—United States. 2. Conflict of laws. I. Title.
KF411 .S76 2001
340.9—dc21 00-068897

Printed in the United States of America on acid-free paper

COMMENTARIES

ON THE

CONFLICT OF LAWS,

FOREIGN AND DOMESTIC,

IN REGARD TO

CONTRACTS, RIGHTS, AND REMEDIES,

AND ESPECIALLY IN REGARD TO

Marriages, Divorces, Wills, Successions, and Judgments.

BY JOSEPH STORY, LL.D.,

DANE PROFESSOR OF LAW IN HARVARD UNIVERSITY.

"Il régnera donc toujours entre les nations une contrariété perpétuelle de loix; peutêtre régnera-t-elle perpétuellement entre nous sur bien des objets. Delà la nécessité de s'instruire des régles, et des principes, qui peuvent nous conduire dans la décision des questions, que cette variété peut faire naître."—BOULLENOIS, *Traité de la Personalité, &c. des Loix, Préface.*

SECOND EDITION.

REVISED, CORRECTED, AND GREATLY ENLARGED.

LONDON:

REPRINTED UNDER THE DIRECTION AND SANCTION OF THE LEARNED AUTHOR,

BY A. MAXWELL, 32, BELL YARD, LINCOLN'S INN,

Law Bookseller to His late Majesty;

T. CLARK, EDINBURGH; AND A. MILLIKEN, DUBLIN.

MDCCCXLI.

LONDON:
W. M'DOWALL, PRINTER, PEMBERTON-ROW, GOUGH-SQUARE.

ADVERTISEMENT

TO THE

SECOND EDITION.

THE former edition of this Work being exhausted, I have availed myself, in the preparation of the present edition, of the opportunity of revising, correcting, and amending the text and notes throughout, and of adding such new materials, as have been furnished by the recent authorities at the common law, as well as by more diligent researches into foreign jurisprudence. For the opinions of some foreign jurists, I was obliged, in the former edition, (as the reader was informed in the notes,) to rely upon the citations from their works, which I found in other authors, not having access to the originals. With one or two unimportant exceptions, the originals of these foreign jurists are now in my possession, and have been consulted by me; so that I have been enabled to correct some errors in those citations, and also to furnish more complete and perfect statements of their respective opinions. Perhaps it may not be useless here to add, that in every case, where any authority for any position is cited at the bottom of the page, the reader may rest assured, that the very citation has been perused and diligently compared by me with the original.

As the works of foreign jurists, especially of those who lived before the middle of the eighteenth century, are rarely to be found in American Libraries, either public or private, and are becoming daily more scarce and difficult to be purchased abroad, I have made my extracts therefrom more copious, and often cited the words of the original, so that the reader might be spared the necessity of farther researches into the originals, and also might possess the means of ascertaining the accuracy of the expositions in the text.

These explanations may account for the fact, that the Work, unexpectedly to myself, has swelled to double its former size; a fact, which (as the pages and sections of the former edition are still preserved) might not readily occur to those, who are not accustomed to examine the signatures at the bottom of the different sheets*.

Since the publication of the former edition, Mr. Burge has published his very able and comprehensive Commentaries on Colonial and Foreign Law, mainly as applicable to the colonies of Great Britain, in which he has devoted a number of chapters to the consideration of many of the topics embraced in the present Work. The plan of his Work, however, essentially differs from my own in its leading objects. It exhibits great learning and research; and as its merits are not as yet generally known to the Profession on this side of the Atlantic, I have made many references to it, and occasional quotations from it, with the view of enabling the Profession to obtain many more illustrations of the doctrines than my own brief text would suggest, and also fully to appreciate his learned labors. Monsieur Fœlix, also, the accomplished Editor of the Revue Etrangere et Française, (a

* This passage applies only to the American Edition.

highly useful and meritorious periodical, published at Paris), has, in the volume of the year 1840, discussed, in a series of articles, many topics of the Conflict of Laws, and given the opinions of the leading foreign jurists on the subject. I have gladly referred to his very interesting and lucid expositions, that my own countrymen may more readily understand their great value and importance.

It is not probable, that, in the course of my own life, this Work will undergo any essential change from its present form. Other avocations and other pressing duties, judicial as well as professorial, will necessarily occupy all the time and attention, which I may hereafter be permitted to command for any juridical pursuits. I must, therefore, dismiss these Commentaries to the indulgent consideration of the reader, not as a work, which has surveyed the whole subject, or exhausted the materials; but as an essay towards opening the leading doctrines and inquiries belonging to private international jurisprudence, which the genius, and learning, and labors of more gifted minds may hereafter mould, and polish, and expand into an enduring system of public law. My own wishes will be fully satisfied, if (to use the language of my Lord Coke, in the close of his first Institute) any thing shall be found herein, which "may either open some windows of the law, to let in more light to the student, by diligent search to see the secrets of the law, or to move him to doubt, and withal to enable him to inquire, and learn of the sages, what the law, together with the true reason thereof, in these cases is."

JOSEPH STORY.

January, 1841.

TO THE HONORABLE

JAMES KENT, LL. D.

SIR,

IT affords me very sincere satisfaction to have the opportunity of dedicating this Work to you. It belongs to a branch of international jurisprudence which has been long familiar to your studies, and in which you have the honor of having been the guide and instructor of the American youth. I can trace back to your early labors in expounding the civil and the foreign law the motive and encouragement of my own far more limited researches. I wish the present Work to be considered as a tribute of respect to a distinguished Master from his grateful pupil.

It is now about thirty-six years since you began your judicial career on the Bench of the Supreme Court of the State of New York. In the intervening period between that time and the present, you have successively occupied the offices of Chief Justice and of Chancellor of the same State. I speak but the common voice of the Profession and the Public, when I say, that in each of these stations you have brought to its duties a maturity of judgment, a depth of learning, a fidelity of purpose, and an enthusiasm for justice, which have laid the solid foundations of an imperishable fame. In the full vigor of your intellectual powers, you left the Bench only to engage in a new task, which of itself seemed to demand by its extent and magnitude a whole life of strenuous diligence. That task has been accomplished. The "Commentaries on American Law" have already acquired the reputation of a juridical Classic, and have placed their Author in the first rank of the benefactors of the Profession. You have done for America what Mr. Justice Blackstone, in his invaluable Commentaries, has done for England. You have embodied the principles of our law in pages as attractive by the persuasive elegance of their style, as they are instructive by the fulness and accuracy of their learning.

You have earned the fairest title to the repose which you now seek, and which at last seems within your reach. It is, in the noblest sense, *Otium cum dignitate.* May you live many years to enjoy it! The consciousness of a life like yours, in which have been blended at every step public spirit and private virtue, the affections, which cheer, and the taste, which adorns the domestic circle, cannot but make the recollections of the past sweet, and the hopes of the future animating.

I am, with the highest respect,

Your obliged friend,

JOSEPH STORY.

CAMBRIDGE, MASSACHUSETTS,
January 1*st*, 1834.

PREFACE.

I now submit to the indulgent consideration of the Profession and the Public another portion of the labors appertaining to the Dane Professorship of Law in Harvard University. The subject is one of great importance and interest; and from the increasing intercourse between foreign States, as well as between the different States of the American Union, it is daily brought home more and more to the ordinary business and pursuits of human life. The difficulty of treating such a subject in a manner suited to its importance and interest can scarcely be exaggerated. The materials are loose and scattered, and are to be gathered from many sources, not only uninviting, but absolutely repulsive, to the mere Student of the Common Law. There exists no treatise upon it in the English language; and not the slightest effort has been made, except by Mr. Chancellor Kent, to arrange in any general order even the more familiar maxims of the Common Law in regard to it. Until a comparatively recent period, neither the English Lawyers nor the English Judges seem to have had their attention drawn towards it, as a great branch of international jurisprudence, which they were required to administer. And, as far as their researches appear as yet to have gone, they are less profound and satisfactory than their admirable expositions of municipal law.

The subject has been discussed with much more fulness,

learning, and ability, by the foreign jurists of continental Europe. But even among them there exists no systematical Treatise embracing all the general topics. For the most part, they have discussed it only with reference to some few branches of jurisprudence, peculiar to the civil law, or to the customary law (almost infinitely varied) of the neighboring States of Europe, or of the different Provinces of the same Empire. And it must be confessed, that their writings are often of so controversial a character, and abound with so many nice distinctions, (not very intelligible to Jurists of the school of the Common Law), and with so many theories of doubtful utility, that it is not always easy to extract from them such principles, as may afford safe guides to the judgment. Rodenburg, Boullenois, Bouhier, and Froland, have written upon it with the most clearness, comprehensiveness, and acuteness. But they rather stimulate than satisfy inquiry; and they are far more elaborate in detecting the errors of others, than in widening and deepening the foundations of the practical doctrines of international jurisprudence. I am not aware that the works of these eminent Jurists have been cited at the English Bar; and I should draw the conclusion, that they are in a great measure, if not altogether, unknown to the studies of Westminster Hall. How it should happen, that, in this age, English Lawyers should be so utterly indifferent to all foreign jurisprudence, it is not easy to conceive. Many occasions are constantly occurring, in which they would derive essential assistance from it, to illustrate the questions, which are brought into contestation in all their Courts.

In consulting the foreign Jurists, I have felt great embarrassment, as well from my own imperfect knowledge of the jurisprudence, which they profess to discuss, as from the remote analogies, which it sometimes bears to the rights, titles, and remedies, recognised in the Common Law. To give their opinions at large upon many topics would fill volumes; to omit all statements whatever of their opinions would be to withhold from the reader many most important lights, to guide his own studies, and instruct his own judgment. I have adopted an intermediate course; and have laid before the reader such portions of the opinions and reasonings of foreign Jurists, as seemed to me most useful to enable him to understand their doctrines and principles, and to assist him with the means of making more ample researches, if his leisure or his curiosity should invite him to the pursuit. Humble as this task may appear to many minds, it has been attended with a labor truly discouraging and exhausting. I dare not even now indulge the belief, that my success has been at all proportionate to my wishes or my efforts. I feel, however, cheered by the reflection (is it a vain illusion?), that other minds, of more ability, leisure, and learning, may be excited to explore the paths, which I have ventured only to point out. I beg, in conclusion, to address to the candor of the Profession my own apology in the language of Strykius:—" Crescit disputatio nostra sub manibus; unum enim si absolveris jus, plura se offerunt consideranda. At nos temporis, quod nimis breve nobis fit, rationem habentes, accuratius illa inquirere haud possumus. Hinc sufficerit, in presens sparsisse quædam saltem adhuc jura, quidque de iis statuamus, vel obiter dixisse*."

JOSEPH STORY.

CAMBRIDGE, MASSACHUSETTS,
January 1st, 1834.

---

* Strykii, Disputatio 1, ch. 2, § 92, tom. ii. p. 24.

CONTENTS.

LIST OF AUTHORS CITED.

THE following List of some of the more important Authors, whose works have been cited, may assist the Student in his researches:—

D'AGUESSEAU, HENRY FRANCIS, Chancellor of France, born at Limoges, 1668, and died 1751. His works are collected and published in 13 vols. 4to.

ALEXANDER AB ALEXANDRO, a Neapolitan lawyer, born 1461, and died at Rome about the age of 62.

D'ARGENTRÉ, BERTRAND, President of the *Présidial* of Rennes, born in 1519, and died in 1590. His works are entitled *Commentarii in Patrias Britonum Leges, seu Consuetudines generales Ducatûs Britaniæ.*

BALDUS, UBALDUS, born about 1324, died 1400. His works are comprised in 4 vols. fol.

BARTOLO, or BARTHOLUS, born at Sasse Ferrato, in the March of Ancona, 1313, and died in his 46th year. He was called "the star and luminary of lawyers, the master of truth, the lantern of equity, the guide of the blind," &c. His works were printed at Venice, 1499, in 4 vols. fol., according to Camus; in 1599, in 10 or 11 vols. fol., according to Watt.

BOUHIER, J., President of the Parliament of Dijon, born at that place 1673, and died 1746. His works, relating to the present subject, are published in two vols. fol., and entitled *Les Coutumes du Duché de Bourgogne avec les Observations du Président Bouhier.*

BOULLENOIS, LOUIS, advocate in the Parliament of Paris, born at Paris, 1680, and died 1762. There are two works by him on the present subject,—*Traité de la Personalité et de la Réalité des Lois, Coutumes, Statuts, par forme d'Observations,* in 2 vols. 4to., and *Dissertations sur des Questions, qui naissent de la Contrariété des Loix et des Coutumes,* 4to. This last was published first, and is the original outline of the larger work, which afterwards appeared.

BRETONNIER, BARTHOLEMEW JOSEPH, advocate of the Parliament of Paris, born at Montrotier, near Lyons, 1656, and died 1727. He is the author of a work in 2 vols. 12mo., entitled, *Recueil des principales Questions de Droit qui se jugent diversement dans les différens Tribunaux du Royaume, avec des Réflexions pour concilier la Diversité de la Jurisprudence.* He also edited the works of HENRYS.

BURGE, WILLIAM, Commentaries on Colonial and Foreign Laws generally, and in their Conflict with each other. 4 vols. 8vo. London, 1838.

BURGUNDUS, BURGUNDIUS, or BOURGOIGNE, NICOLAUS, jurisconsult, born at Enghien in Hainault, 1586. He is the author of a work entitled, *Tractatus Controversiarum ad Consuetudinem Flandriæ.*

BYNKERSHOEK, CORNELIUS VAN, born at Middlebourg, 1673, and died 1743. His works are well known.

CASAREGIS, JOSEPH LAURENTIUS DE, born at Genoa, 1670, and died 1737. His works are entitled, *Discursus legales de Commercio,* and are published in 2, 3, and 4 vols. fol.

CHRISTINÆUS, PAULUS, born at Malines, 1533, and died 1638. His works are,—*Practicarum Quæstionum Rerumque in Supremis Belgarum Curiis actarum et Observationum Decisiones;* and *Commentarii in Leges Municipales Mechlinienses.*

COCHIN, HENRY, advocate in Parliament, born at Paris, 1687, and died 1747. His works are collected in 6 vols. 4to.

COQUILLE, GUI, advocate of the Parliament of Paris, born at Decise in Nivernois, 1523, and died 1603. There is a work by him, *Des Coutumes des Nivernois.*

CUJAS, JAMES, born at Thoulouse, 1520, and died 1590. His voluminous works need not be particularly mentioned.

DENISART, J. B., jurisconsult, born 1712, and died 1765. He published *Collection de Décisions nouvelles relatives à la Jurisprudence.*

DOMAT, JOHN, born at Clermont in Auvergne, 1625, and died 1696. His *Civil Law in its Natural Order* is well known through the translation of Dr. Strahan.

DUMOULIN, (in Latin MOLINÆUS), CHARLES, born 1500, and died 1560. What he has written upon the present subject is to be found in his Commentary on the first book of the Code, verb. *Conclusiones de Statutis,* in his 53d *Consilium,* and in his notes on *Alexander, Decius,* and *Chasseneuz.*

DURANTON, A., Professor of Law at Paris. His works are, *Cours de Droit Français, suivant le Code civil,* in 16 vols. 8vo.

EMERIGON, BALTAZARD MARIE, advocate of the Parliament of Aix, born about 1725, and died 1784. His *Traité des Assurances,* 2 vols. 4to. is referred to in the present Commentaries.

ERSKINE, JOHN, Professor of Law at Edinburgh. His principal work is entitled. *Institutes of the Laws of Scotland.*

EVERHARD, NICHOLAS, born in the island of Walcheren, 1462, and died 1532. His works are *Topica Juris, sive Loci Argumentorum Legales;* and *Consilia, sive Responsa Juris.*

FŒLIX M., Editor of the *Review Etrangere et Française;* a learned periodical published at Paris, beginning in 1833 and still (1840) continued.

FROLAND, LOUIS, advocate of the Parliament of Rouen, died 1746. His works, relating to the present subject, in two 4to. vols., are entitled, *Mémoire concernant la Nature et la Qualité des Statuts.*

GAILL, ANDREW, born at Cologne, 1525, and died 1587. He was called the Papinian of Germany.

GROTIUS, HUGO, born at Delft, 1583, and died 1645. His works are well known.

HEINECCIUS, JOHANNES GOTLEIB, Professor of Philosophy and Law at Halle, born at Eisenberg, 1681, and died 1741. His works need not be particularly mentioned.

HENRYS, CLAUDE, juriconsult, born at Montbrison, 1615, and died 1662. His works are collected in four vols. fol.

HERTIUS, JOHANNES NICOLAUS, born near Giessen, 1651, and died 1710. His treatise, *De Collisione Legum,* is to be found in his select works in 2 vols. 4to.

HUBERUS, ULRICUS, a lawyer, historian, and philologer, born at Dockum, in the Dutch territories, 1635, and died 1694. His treatise, *De Conflictu Legum,* is to be found in his *Prælectiones Juris Civilis,* 3 vols. 4to.

KAIMS, LORD, (HENRY HOME), born at Kaims, in Berwickshire, 1696, and died 1782. The reader is referred to his *Principles of Equity.*

LE BRUN, DENIS, advocate, died 1708, before the publication of his principal work, *Traité de Communautés.*

LEEUWEN, SIMON VAN, born at Leyden, 1625, and died 1682. His work referred to, in the present Commentaries, is translated into English, with the title of *Commentaries on the Roman-Dutch Law.*

LIVERMORE, SAMUEL, of New Orleans, died 1833. He is the author of *Dissertations on the Contrariety of Laws.*

MASCARDUS, JOSEPHUS, an ecclesiastic and Italian juriconsult, born at Sarzana towards the end of the 16th century, and died about 1630. He is the author of an extensive work, entitled, *De Probationibus Conclusiones.*

MERLIN, M. (de DOUAI). His voluminous works are entitled, *Répertoire Universel et Raisonné de Jurisprudence;* and *Questions de Droit.*

MORNAC, ANTOINE, born near Tours, first appeared before the Parliament of Paris, in 1580, and died 1620. His works are comprised in 4 fols. fol.

PARDESSUS, J. M., *Cours de Droit Commercial.* 5 vols. 8vo. Paris.

PECK, PETER, born at Zirckzee, in Zealand, 1529, and died 1589. works are collected in one vol. fol.

POTHIER, ROBERT JOSEPH, born at Orleans, 1699, and died His works need not be particularly mentioned.

PUFFENDORF, SAMUEL, born in Upper Saxony, 1632, and died His works are well known.

RODENBURG, was a judge of the Supreme Court of Utrecht, and rished about the middle of the 17th century. His treatise, *De quod oritur ex Statutorum vel Consuetudinum Diversitate,* is found at the end of Boullenois's *Traité de la Personalité et Réalité des Loix.*

STOCKMANS, PETER, born at Antwerp, 1608, and died 1671. works are comprised in one vol. 4to.

STRYKIUS, SAMUEL, born 1640, and died 1710. His son, SAMUEL, was born 1668, and died 1715. Their works, with of RHETIUS, are collected in 14 vols. fol.

VOET, PAUL, (the father), born at Heusden, in Brabant, 1619, and 1677. His work on the present subject is entitled, *De Statu eorum Concursu.*

VOET, JOHN, (son of Paul), born at Utrecht, 1647, and died 1714. Commentary on the Pandects contains a short chapter, *De Stat*

TABLE OF CASES.

COMMENTARIES

ON

The Conflict

BETWEEN

FOREIGN AND DOMESTIC LAWS.

CHAPTER I.

INTRODUCTORY REMARKS.

§ 1. The Earth has long since been divided into distinct Nations, inhabiting different regions, speaking different languages, engaged in different pursuits, and attached to different forms of government[1]. It is natural, that, under such circumstances, there should be many variances in their institutions, customs, laws, and polity; and that these variances should result sometimes from accident, and sometimes from design, sometimes from superior skill and knowledge of local interests, and sometimes from a choice founded in ignorance, and supported by the prejudices of imperfect civilization. Climate, and geographical position, and the physical adaptations springing from them, must at all times have had a powerful influence in the organization of each society, and have given a peculiar complexion and character to many of its arrangements. The bold, intrepid, and hardy natives of the North of Europe, whether ci-

---

[1] Upon the subject of this chapter the learned reader is referred to Burge's Commentaries upon Colonial and Foreign Law, Vol. 1, Pt. 1, ch. 1, p. 1 to 32.

vilized or barbarous, would scarcely desire, or tolerate, the indolent inactivity and luxurious indulgences of the Asiatics. Nations, inhabiting the borders of the ocean, and accustomed to maritime intercourse with other nations, would naturally require institutions and laws, adapted to their pursuits and enterprises, which would be wholly unfit for those, who should be placed in the interior of a continent, and should maintain very different relations with their neighbours, both in peace and war. Accordingly we find, that, from the earliest records of authentic history, there has been (as far at least as we can trace them) little uniformity in the laws, usages, policy, and institutions, either of contiguous or of distant nations. The Egyptians, the Medes, the Persians, the Greeks, and the Romans, differed not more in their characters and employments from each other, than in their institutions and laws. They had little desire to learn, or to borrow, from each other; and indifference, if not contempt, was the habitual state of almost every ancient nation in regard to the internal polity of all others.

§ 2. Yet even under such circumstances, from their mutual intercourse with each other, questions must sometimes have arisen, as to the operation of the laws of one nation upon the rights and remedies of parties in the domestic tribunals, especially when they were in any measure dependent upon, or connected with, foreign transactions. How these questions were disposed of, we do not know. But it is most probable, that they were left to be decided by the analogies of the municipal code, or were abandoned to their fate, as belonging to that large class of imperfect rights, which rests wholly on personal confidence, and is left without any appeal to remedial justice. It is certain, that the nations of antiquity did not recognise the existence of any general or universal rights and obligations, such as among the moderns constitute, what is now emphatically called, the Law of Nations. Even among the Romans, whose jurisprudence has come down to us in a far more perfect and comprehensive shape than that of any other nation, there cannot be traced out any distinct system of principles, applicable to international cases of mixed rights. This has been in some measure accounted for by Huberus[1] upon the supposition, that at the time, to which the Roman jurisprudence relates, the Roman dominion extended over so great a portion of the habitable world, that frequent cases of contrariety or conflict of laws could scarcely occur[2]. But this is a very inadequate account of the matter; since the antecedent jurisprudence of Rome must have embraced many such cases at earlier periods; and if there had been any rules, even traditionally known, to govern them, they could scarcely have failed of being incorporated into the Civil Codes of Justinian. In many of the nations, over which the Romans extended their dominion, the inhabitants were left in possession of their local institutions, usages, and laws, to a large extent; and commercial, as well as political intercourse must have brought many diversities of laws and usages in judgment before the tribunals of justice[3]. We have the most abundant evidence on this head, in relation to the Jews, after they had submitted to the Roman yoke, who were still permitted to follow their own laws in the times of our Saviour, and down to the destruction of Jerusalem[4].

§ 2 *a*. When the Northern nations by their irruptions finally succeeded in establishing themselves in the Roman empire, and the dependent nations subjected to its sway,

---

[1] 2 Hub. lib. 1, tit. 3, p. 538.

[2] The language of Huberus is, "In jure Romano non est mirum nihil hac de re extare, cum populi Romani per omnes orbis partes diffusum, et æquabili jure gubernatum imperium, conflictui diversarum legum non æque potuerit esse subjectum."—Hub. lib. 2, tit. 3, sect. 1.

[3] See 1 Hertii Opera, § 4, de Collis. leg. p. 119, § 2; Id. p. 169, (edit. 1716).

[4] There are traces to be found in the Digest of the existence and operation of the Lex Loci. See Dig. lib. 50, tit. 1, l. 21, § 7; Id. lib. 50, tit. 6, l. 5, § 1; Id. tit. 4, l. 18, § 27; Id. tit. 3, l. 1; Livermore, Dissert. p. 1, n. (a.).

they seem to have adopted, either by design, or from accident, or necessity, the policy of allowing the different races to live together, and to be governed by and to preserve their own separate manners, laws, and institutions in their mutual intercourse. While the conquerors, the Goths, Burgundians, Franks, and Lombards, maintained their own laws and usages and customs over their own race, they silently or expressly allowed each of the races, over whom they had obtained an absolute sovereignty, to regulate their own private rights and affairs according to their own municipal jurisprudence. It has accordingly been remarked by a most learned and eminent jurist, that, from this state of society arose that condition of civil rights, denominated personal rights, or personal laws, in opposition to territorial laws [1].

---

1 Savigny's History of the Roman Law in the Middle Ages. The whole passage is exceedingly interesting and curious; and therefore I quote it at large from Mr. Catchcart's Translation, Vol. 1, ch. 3, p. 99 to 104.— "When the Goths, Burgundians, Franks, and Lombards, founded kingdoms in the countries, formerly subject to the power of Rome, there were two different modes of treating the conquered race. They might be extirpated, by destroying or enslaving the freemen; or, the conquering nations, for the sake of increasing their own numbers, might transform the Romans into Germans, by forcing on them their manners, constitution, and laws. Neither mode, however, was followed; for, although many Romans were slain, expatriated, or enslaved, this was only the lot of individuals, and not the systematic treatment of the nation. Both races, on the contrary, lived together, and preserved their separate manners and laws. From this state of society arose that condition of civil rights, denominated Personal rights, or Personal laws, in opposition to territorial laws. The moderns always assume, that the law, to which the individual owes obedience, is that of the country, where he lives; and that the property and contracts of every resident are regulated by the law of his domicile. In this theory, the distinction between native and foreigner is overlooked, and national descent is entirely disregarded. Not so, however, in the middle ages; where, in the same country, and often indeed in the same city, the Lombard lived under the Lombardic, and the Roman under the Roman law. The same distinction of laws was also applicable to the different races of Germans. The Frank, Burgundian, and Goth, resided in the same place, each under his own law, as is forcibly stated, by the Bishop Agobardus, in an Epistle to Louis le Debonnaire. 'It

§ 2 *b*. Still, however, this was but a mere arrangement in the domestic polity of each particular nation; and even

---

often happens,' says he, 'that five men, each under a different law, may be found walking or sitting together.'

"In the East-Gothic kingdom alone, this custom was not originally followed. There, an artificial and systematic plan was adopted, which belongs to the particular history of that nation, and cannot be brought within the general inquiry. All the other States followed the system of Personal laws: and, this universal practice could not have arisen from accidental reasons, but from common views, principles, and wants. These may be appropriately illustrated at present.

"According to the general opinion, the system of Personal laws prevailed among all the German nations, from the earliest times; and it is customary to explain this circumstance by the love of freedom, so peculiar to these races. In the first place, however, it is difficult to perceive, how such an institution could arise merely from regard to liberty. Such an attachment might, indeed, create a wish among nations, or individuals, to preserve their own laws, in a foreign country, or under a foreign yoke: but the question is, how were the predominant people induced to grant them this privilege? The benevolent and hospitable disposition of the victorious may have been partly the cause; but, their mere love of freedom affords no satisfactory explanation. This humane treatment of foreigners was not deeply seated in the character of the old Germans. It is probable, that among them every foreigner was, at first, a Wildfang, and belonged to the class of the Biesterfreien;—denied the advantages, arising from service in the national army, or from the obligations of fealty, and living as an alien, unprotected by any power, except the weak hand of the general government; who, while they excluded him from the rights of marriage, inherited his property, and exacted his composition, if slain. Further, the want of such an institution, as the Personal laws, could never have been felt, in a country without trade, and where few foreigners resided. In these circumstances, its introduction was impossible. If only a single Goth lived in the Burgundian Empire, none of his countrymen could be found to administer Gothic law, and the Burgundians themselves were entirely ignorant of it.

"The truth is, that the want of such an institution, and the possibility of introducing it, could occur only after the nations were blended together in considerable masses. The internal condition of each kingdom would then produce what could never have been brought about by mere benevolence towards individual foreigners. According to this account of the origin of the system of Personal laws, it prevailed in all the German States, settled in countries, formerly subject to Rome. At first, the validity of two Laws only was admitted: *e. g.* the Law of the victorious race, and of the vanquished Romans. Individuals, belonging to other German nations, did not at first enjoy the right of living under their own laws; but, when our supposed

then, it must often have involved serious embarrassments, whenever questions arose in regard to conflicting rights, and claims, and remedies, growing out of dealings, and acts, and contracts between individuals belonging to different races. But when the question assumed a more comprehensive character, and the point to be decided was, what rule should prevail, where there was a conflict of laws between different sovereignties, wholly independent of each other; and there were rights to be established of a private nature between some of the subjects of each sovereignty; there was no recognised principle or practice, which was promulgated by all, or submitted to by all. Such rights were probably left without any remedy, and became either the subject of private adjustment, or were silently disregarded.

§ 3. The truth is, that the Law of Nations, strictly so called, was in a great measure unknown to antiquity, and is the slow growth of modern times, under the combined

---

kingdom had extended its conquests, and spread out its dominion over other German tribes, then the laws of the conquered German races were acknowledged, in the same manner as the Roman formerly had been. Thus, also, every foreign law, prevailing in the empire of the conqueror, was admitted and considered as valid among all the vanquished. This practice ought to have produced the following results. At first, in the northern parts of France, the Frank and Roman laws must have been exclusively received: and, under the Carlovingian dynasty, it would become necessary to admit likewise the laws of the West Goths, Burgundians, Alemans, Bavarians, and Saxons; because, these, as nations, belonged to the empire. Italy, however, did not form a Province under the Franks, and there could not consequently be the same reason for admitting the validity of Lombardic Law within the Frank Empire. In Italy, also, under the Lombardic Kings, only Lombardic and Roman law could have prevailed to the exclusion of every other; but, after its conquest by the Franks, all the multifarious foreign laws, existing in the territory of the conquerors, must have been introduced. Now, these anticipated results are supported by history; and this accordance is a strong practical confirmation of that account of the origin of Personal laws, already established by general reasoning."—The same passage will be found in Mr. Guenoux's French translation of the same work, Vol. 1, ch. 3, p. 84 to 88, (edit. 1830); Id. ch. 3, § 30, (edit. 1839).

influence of Christianity and Commerce[1]. It is well known, that when the Roman Empire was destroyed, the Christian world was divided into many independent sovereignties, acknowledging no common head, and connected by no uniform civil polity. The invasions of the Barbarians of the North, the establishment of the feudal system in the middle ages, and the military spirit and enterprise cherished by the Crusades, struck down all regular commerce, and surrendered all private rights and contracts to mere despotic power. It was not until the revival of Commerce on the shores of the Mediterranean, and the revival of Letters and the study of the Civil Law by the discovery of the Pandects, had given an increased enterprise to maritime navigation, and a consequent importance to maritime contracts, that anything like a system of international justice began to be developed. It first assumed the modest form of commercial usages; it was next promulgated under the more imposing authority of royal ordinances; and it finally became by silent adoption a generally connected system, founded in the natural convenience, and asserted by the general comity of the commercial nations of Europe. The system, thus introduced for the purposes of commerce, has gradually extended itself to other objects, as the intercourse of nations has become more free and frequent. New rules, resting on the basis of general convenience, and an enlarged sense of national duty, have, from time to time, been promulgated by jurists, and supported by courts of justice, by a course of juridical reasoning, which has commanded almost universal confidence, respect, and obedience, without the aid, either of municipal statutes, or of royal ordinances, or of international treaties.

§ 4. Indeed, in the present times, without some general rules of right and obligation, recognised by civilized nations to govern their intercourse with each other, the most

---

[1] See 1 Ward, Law of Nations, ch. 6, p. 171 to 200; Id. ch. 3, p. 120 to 130.

serious mischiefs and most injurious conflicts would arise. Commerce is now so absolutely universal among all countries; the inhabitants of all have such a free intercourse with each other; contracts, sales, marriages, nuptial settlements, wills, and successions, are so common among persons, whose domicils are in different countries, having different and even opposite laws on the same subjects; that, without some common principles adopted by all nations in this regard, there would be an utter confusion of all rights and remedies; and intolerable grievances would grow up to weaken all the domestic relations, as well as to destroy the sanctity of contracts and the security of property[1].

§ 5. A few simple cases will sufficiently illustrate the importance of some international principles in matters of mere private right and duty. Suppose a contract, valid by the laws of the country where it is made, is sought to be enforced in another country, where such a contract is positively prohibited by its laws; or, *vice versâ*, suppose a contract, invalid by the laws of the country where it is made, but valid by that of the country where it is sought to be enforced; it is plain, that, unless some uniform rules are adopted to govern such cases, (which are not uncommon,) the grossest inequalities will arise in the administration of justice between the subjects of the different countries in regard to such contracts. Again; by the laws of some countries marriage cannot be contracted until the parties arrive at twenty-one years of age; in other countries not until they arrive at the age of twenty-five years. Suppose a marriage to be contracted between two persons in the same country, both of whom are over twenty-one

---

[1] Boullenois, in his Preface, (1 vol. p. 18,) says, "Il regnera donc toujours entre les nations une contrariété perpetuelle de loix; peut-être regnera-t-elle perpetuellement entre nous sur bien des objects. Delà la nécessité de s'instruire des règles et des principes, qui peuvent nous conduire dans la décision des questions, que cette variété peut faire naître."

years, but less than twenty-five, and one of them is a subject of the latter country. Is such a marriage valid, or not? If valid in the country, where it is celebrated, is it valid also in the other country? Or, the question may be propounded in a still more general form; is a marriage, valid between the parties in the place where it is solemnized, equally valid in all other countries? Or, is it obligatory only as a local regulation, and to be treated everywhere else as a mere nullity?

§ 6. Questions of this sort must be of frequent occurrence, not only in different countries, wholly independent of each other; but also in provinces of the same empire, which are governed by different laws, as was the case in France before the Revolution; and also in countries acknowledging a common sovereign, but yet organized as distinct communities, as is still the case in regard to the communities composing the British Empire, the Germanic Confederacy, the States of Holland, and the dominions of Austria and Russia[1]. Innumerable suits must be litigated in the judicial forums of these countries, and provinces, and communities, in which the decision must depend upon the point, whether the nature of a contract should be determined by the law of the place, where it is litigated; or by the law of the domicil of one or of both of the parties; or by the law of the place, where the contract is made; whether the capacity to make a testament should be regulated by the law of the testator's domicil, or that of the location (*situs*) of his property; whether the form of his testament should be prescribed by the law of the place of his domicil, or by that of the location of his property, or by that of the place where the testament is made; and in like manner, whether the law of the domicil, or what other law should govern in cases of succession to intestate estates[2].

§ 7. It is plain, that the laws of one country can have

---

[1] See 1 Froland, Mémoires sur les Statuts, P. 1, ch. 1, § 5 to 10.

[2] Livermore, Dissert. 3, 4; Merlin, Répert. Statut.

no intrinsic force, *proprio vigore,* except within the territorial limits and jurisdiction of that country. They can bind only its own subjects, and others, who are within its jurisdictional limits; and the latter only, while they remain therein. No other nation, or its subjects, are bound to yield the slightest obedience to those laws. Whatever extra-territorial force they are to have, is the result, not of any original power to extend them abroad, but of that respect, which, from motives of public policy, other nations are disposed to yield to them, giving them effect, as the phrase is, *sub mutuæ vicissitudinis obtentu,* with a wise and liberal regard to common convenience and mutual benefits and necessities. Boullenois has laid down the same exposition as a part of his fundamental maxims. "Of strict right," (says he,) "all the laws made by a sovereign have no force or authority, except within the limits of his domains. But the necessity of the public and general welfare has introduced some exceptions in regard to civil commerce." *De droit étroit, toutes les lois, que fait un souverain, n'ont force et autorité que dans l'étendue de sa domination; mais la nécessité du bien public et général des nations a admis quelques exceptions dans ce, qui regarde le commerce civil*[1].

§ 8. This is the natural principle flowing from the equality and independence of nations. For it is an essential attribute of every sovereignty, that it has no admitted superior, and that it gives the supreme law within its own dominions on all subjects appertaining to its sovereignty. What it yields, it is its own choice to yield; and it cannot be commanded by another to yield it as matter of right. And, accordingly, it is laid down by all publicists and jurists, as an incontestable rule of public law, that one may with impunity disregard the law pronounced by a magistrate beyond his own territory. *Extra territorium jus dicenti im-*

---

[1] 1 Boullenois, Prin. Gén. 6, p. 4.

pune non paretur, is the doctrine of the Digest[1]; and it is equally as true in relation to nations, as the Roman law held it to be in relation to magistrates. The other part of the rule is equally applicable; *Idem est, et si supra jurisdictionem suam velit jus dicere;* for he exceeds his proper jurisdiction, when he seeks to make it operate extra-territorially as a matter of power[2]. Vattel has deduced a similar conclusion from the general independence and equality of nations, very properly holding, that relative strength or weakness cannot produce any difference in regard to public rights and duties; that whatever is lawful for one nation, is equally lawful for another; and whatever is unjustifiable in one, is equally so in another[3]. And he affirms in the most positive manner, (what indeed cannot well be denied,) that sovereignty, united with domain, establishes the exclusive jurisdiction of a nation within its own territories, as to controversies, to crimes, and to rights arising therein[4].

§ 9. The jurisprudence, then, arising from the conflict of the laws of different nations, in their actual application to modern commerce and intercourse, is a most interesting and important branch of public law. To no part of the world is it of more interest and importance, than to the United States, since the union of a national government with already that of twenty-six distinct states, and in some respects independent states, necessarily creates very complicated private relations and rights between the citizens of those states, which call for the constant administration of extramunicipal principles. This branch of public law may, therefore, be fitly denominated private international law, since it is chiefly seen and felt in its application to the

---

1 Dig. lib. 2, tit. 1, l. 20; Pothier, Pand. lib. 2, tit. 1, n. 7.

2 Ibid.

3 Vattel, Prelim. § 15 to 20; Id. B. 2, ch. 3, § 35, 36; The St. Louis, 2 Dodson, R. 210.

4 Vattel, B. 2, ch. 7, § 84, 85.

common business of private persons, and rarely rises to the dignity of national negotiations, or of national controversies[1].

§ 10. The subject has never been systematically treated by writers on the common law of England; and, indeed, seems to be of very modern growth in that kingdom; and can hardly, as yet, be deemed to be there cultivated, as a science, built up and defined with entire accuracy and precision of principles. More has been done to give it form and symmetry within the last fifty years, than in all preceding time. But much yet remains to be done, to make it what it ought to be, in a country of such vast extent in its commerce, and such universal reach in its intercourse and polity[2].

§ 11. The civilians of continental Europe have examined the subject in many of its bearings with a much more comprehensive philosophy, if not with a more enlightened spirit. Their works, however, abound with theoretical distinctions, which serve little other purpose than to provoke idle discussions, and with metaphysical subtilties, which perplex, if they do not confound, the inquirer. They are also mainly addressed to questions intimately connected with their own provincial or municipal laws and customs, some of which are of a purely local, and others of a technical and peculiar character; and they do not always separate those considerations and doctrines, which belong to the elements of the general science, from those, which may be deemed founded in particular national interests and local ordinances. Pre-

---

[1] The civilians are accustomed to call the questions arising from the conflict of foreign and domestic laws mixed questions, *questions mixtes*. 1 Froland, Mémoires des Statuts, ch. 1, § 9, p. 13; Id. ch. 7, § 1, p. 155.

[2] Mr. Chancellor Kent has remarked, that these topics of international law were almost unknown in the English courts, prior to the time of Lord Hardwicke and Lord Mansfield; and that the English lawyers seem generally to have been strangers to the discussions on foreign law by the celebrated jurists of continental Europe. 2 Kent, Comm. Lect. 39, p. 455, (3rd edit.).

cedents, too, have not, either in the courts of continental Europe, or in the juridical discussions of its eminent jurists, the same force and authority, which we, who live under the influence of the common law, are accustomed to attribute to them; and it is unavoidable, that many differences of opinion should exist among them, even in relation to leading principles. But the strong sense and critical learning of the best minds among foreign jurists have generally maintained those doctrines, which at the present day are deemed entirely persuasive and satisfactory with us, who live under the common law, as well for the solid grounds, on which they rest, as for the universal approbation, with which they are entertained by courts of justice [1].

§ 12. In their discussions upon this subject the civilians have divided statutes into three classes: personal, real, and mixed. By statutes, they mean, not the positive legislation, which in England and America is known by the same name, viz. the acts of Parliament and of other legislative bodies, as contra-distinguished from the common law; but the whole municipal law of the particular state, from

---

[1] The late Mr. Livermore, (whose lamented death occurred in July, 1833,) in his learned Dissertations on the Contrariety of Laws, printed at New Orleans in 1828, has enumerated the principal continental writers, who have discussed this subject at large. I gladly refer the reader to these Dissertations, as very able and clear. There is also a catalogue of the principal writers in Boullenois, Traité des Statuts, Préface, Vol. 1, p. 29, note (1); in Dupin's edition of Camus, Profession d'Avocat, Vol. 2, tit. 7, § 5, art. 1561 to 1566; in Froland, Mémoires concernans les Qualités des Statuts, Vol. 1, P. 1, ch. 2, p. 15; in Bouhier, Coutum. de Bourg. Vol. 1, ch. 23, p. 450; and in Mr. Burge's recent Commentaries on Colonial and Foreign Law, Pt. 1, ch. 1, p. 6 to 32. In the preparation of these Commentaries I have availed myself chiefly of the writings of Rodenburg, the Voets (father and son,) Burgundus, Du Moulin (Molinaeus), Froland, Boullenois, Bouhier, and Huberus, as embracing the most satisfactory illustrations of the leading doctrines. My object has not been to engage in any critical examination of the comparative merits or mistakes of the different commentators; but rather to gather from each of them what seemed most entitled to respect and confidence.

whatever source arising[1]. Sometimes the word is used by them in contradistinction to the imperial Roman law, which they are accustomed to style, by way of eminence, the COMMON LAW, since it constitutes the general basis of the jurisprudence of all continental Europe, modified and restrained by local customs and usages, and positive legislation[2]. Paul Voet says; *Sequitur jus particulare, seu non commune, quod uno vocabulo usitatissimo* Statutum *dicitur, quasi statum publicum tuens*[3]. *Appellatur etiam* jus municipale. *Etiam in jure nostro dicta* lex, *seu* lex municipii, *quemadmodum in genere signat jus commune*[4]. And he defines it thus; *Est jus particulare ab alio legislatore quam Imperatore constitutum*[5]. *Dico,* jus particulare, *in quantum opponitur juri communi, non prout est gentium et naturale, sed prout est jus civile Romanorum, populo Romano commune, et omnibus, qui illo populo parebant*[6]. *Additur,* ab alio legislatore, *cum qui statuta condit, recte et suo modo legislator appelletur, ut ipsa statuta leges dicuntur municipiorum. Et quidem,* ab alio, *quia regulariter statuta non condit Imperator; excipe, nisi municipibus jura det, statuta præscribat, secundum quæ ipsi sua regant municipia*[7]. *Denique adjicitur,* quam imperatore, *quod licet Imperator solummodo dicatur legislator, id tamen, non alio sensu obtineat, quam quod suis legibus non hunc aut illum populum, verum omnes constringat, quos suæ clementiæ regit imperium*[8]. Merlin says; " This term, *statute,* is generally applied to all sorts

---

1 Bouhier, Coutum. de Bourg, Vol 1, p. 174 to 179, § 9 to 32; 1 Hertii Opera. De Collisione Legum, § 4, art. 5, p. 121; Id. p. 172, (edit. 1716).

2 Bouhier, Coutum. de Bourg. Vol. 1, p. 175, 178, § 16, 28, 29.

3 P. Voet, de Statut. § 4, ch. 1, § 1; Id. p. 123, (edit. 1661).

4 Ibid.

5 P. Voet, de Statut. § 4, ch. 1, § 2; Id. p. 124, (edit. 1661).

6 Ibid.

7 P. Voet, de Statut. § 4, ch. 1, § 2; Id. p. 125, (edit. 1661).

8 P. Voet, de Statut. § 4, ch. 1, § 2; Id. p. 125, (edit. 1661); Id. § 1, ch. 4; Id. p. 35, (edit. 1661); Liverm. Dissert. II., p. 21, n. (b), (edit. 1828).

of laws and regulations. Every provision of law is a statute, which permits, ordains, or prohibits anything." *Ce terme* (statut,) *s'applique en général à toutes sortes de lois et de réglémens. Chaque disposition d'une loi est un statut, qui permet, ordonne, ou défend quelque chose*[1].

§ 13. The civilians have variously defined the different classes of statutes or laws. The definitions of Merlin are sufficiently clear and explicit for all the purposes of the present work, and will therefore be here cited. The distinctions between the different classes are very important to be observed in consulting foreign jurists, since they have been adopted by them from a very early period, and pervade all their discussions. Personal statutes are held by them to be of general obligation and force everywhere; but real statutes are held to have no extra-territorial force or obligation[2]. "Personal statutes," (says Merlin,) "are those, which have principally for their object the person, and treat only of property (*biens*)[3] incidentally (*accessoirement*); such are those, which regard birth, legitimacy, freedom, the right of instituting suits, majority as to age, incapacity to contract, to make a will, to plead in proper person, &c.[4] Real statutes are those, which have principally for their object property (*biens*), and which do not speak of persons, except in relation to property; such are those, which concern the disposition, which one may make of his property, either while he is living, or by testament[5]. Mixed

---

1 Merlin, Répertoire, art. *Statut.* Vol. 31, (edit. 1828), Bruxelles; Saul *v.* His Creditors, 17 Martin, R. 569, 589.

2 Rodenburg, De Statut. Divers, c. 3, p. 7; 1 Froland, Mémoires des Statuts, ch. 7, § 1, 2.

3 The term "biens," in the sense of the civilians and continental jurists, comprehends not merely goods and chattels, as in the common law, but real estate. But the distinction between movable and immovable property is nevertheless recognised by them, and gives rise in the civil law, as well as in the common law, to many important distinctions as to rights and remedies.

4 See Pothier, Coutum. d'Orléans, ch. 1, § 1, art. 6.

5 See Pothier, Coutum. d'Orléans, ch. 1, § 2, art. 21.

statutes are those, which concern at once persons and property." But Merlin adds, "that in this sense almost all statutes are mixed, there being scarcely any law relative to persons, which does not at the same time relate to things[1]." He, therefore, deems the last classification unnecessary, and holds, that every statute ought to receive its denomination according to its principal object. As that object is real, or personal, so ought the quality of the statute to be determined[2]. But this distribution into three classes is usually adopted, precisely as it is stated by Rodenburg:—*Aut enim statutum simpliciter disponit de personis; aut solummodo de rebus; aut conjunctim de utrisque*[3]. And he proceeds to explain this division in the following manner: *Quæ ita constrictim dicta sic habentur explicatiùs: Aut universus personæ status, aut conditio in dispositione statuti vertitur, citra ullam rerum*

---

1 Merlin, Répertoire, Statut.; Id. Autorisation Maritale, § 10.

2 Ibid.

3 Rodenburg, De Statut. Diversitate, ch. 2, p. 4; Le Brun, Traité de la Communauté, Liv. 2, ch. 3, § 20 to 48; Bouhier, Coutum. de Bourg. ch. 21 to ch. 37; Voet, de Statut. § 4, ch. 2, p. 116 to p. 124; Id. p. 129 to p. 143, (edit. 1661;) Livermore, Dissert. § 65 to § 162; 1 Froland, Mémoires, Qualité des Statuts, Pt. 1, ch. 3, 25; Id. ch. 4, p. 49, ch. 5, p. 81, ch. 6, p. 114; Boullenois, Traité des Statuts, Vol. 1, Preface, p. 22; Pothier, Coutum. d'Orléans, ch. 1, § 1, art. 6, 7, 8.—Boullenois distributes all statutes into three classes: "Ou le statut dispose simplement des personnes; ou il dispose simplement des choses; ou il dispose tout à la fois des personnes et des choses." 1 Boullenois, Traité des Statuts réels et personnels, tit. 1, ch. 2, obs. 2, p. 25; Id. Princ. Gén. p. 4, 6. Mr. Henry, in his Dissertation on Personal, Real, and Mixed Statutes, has adopted the like distribution, without any acknowledgment of the source, (Boullenois,) from which he has drawn all his materials. See Henry on Personal and Real Statutes, ch. 1, § 2 to ch. 3, § 1, p. 2 to 33. See also Livermore's Dissert. 2, § 65 to § 162, p. 62 to 106; Id. § 168, p. 109. Mr. Justice Porter, in delivering the opinion of the Supreme Court of Louisiana, in the case of Saul *v.* His Creditors, (17 Martin, R. 569, 590,) said, that foreign jurists, by a personal statute, mean that, which follows, and governs the party subject to it, wherever he goes; and a real statute is that, which controls things, and does not extend beyond the limits of the country, from which it derives its authority. Is not this a description of the effect of such statutes, rather than a definition of their nature? See Id. 593.

adjectionem, adeoque de personis agitur in abstracto, absque ullâ consideratione rerum; ut, verbi gratiâ, quoto quis ætatis anno fui Juris sit, quando exeat parentum potestate; *de quibus et consimilibus exemplis mox fusiùs. Aut in solas nudasque res statuti dispositio dirigitur, ut nullum intervenire necesse sit actum hominis, aut aliquam concurrere personæ operam, cujusmodi sunt, quibus rerum successionibus ab intestato Jus ponitur; ut bona materna cedant maternis, paterna paternis, nothi succedant matribus, non succedant patribus; quando succedatur in stirpes, quando in capita: quæ Jura successionum ab intestato appellaveris. Aut permittit denique, vetat, aut ordinat, actum a personis circa res peragendum, ex utriusque complexu constructum Statutum, contra quod, ut queat committi quippiam, personæ actum intervenire necesse est. Quò pertinent. Sine indulto Principis de rebus suis nemo testator; conjuges sibi invicem non leganto; vir citra consensum uxorium res soli non alienato*[1].

§ 14. In the application of this classification to particular cases, there has been no inconsiderable diversity of opinion among the civilians. What particular statutes are to be deemed personal, and what real; when they may be said principally to regard persons, and when principally to regard things; these have been vexed questions, upon which much subtlety of discussion and much heat of controversy have been displayed. The subject is in itself full of intrinsic difficulties; but it has been rendered more perplexed by metaphysical niceties and over-curious learning[2].

---

1 Rodenburg, De Statut. Divers. ch. 2, p. 4, (2 Boullenois, Appendix, p. 4).

2 See 1 Boullenois, tit. 1, ch. 1, Observ. 2, p. 16, &c.; Id. ch. 2, Obs. 5, p. 114 to 122; 1 Froland, Mém. des Stat. ch. 2, p. 15; 2 Kent, Comm. Lect. 39, p. 453 to 457, (3rd edit.); Saul *v.* His Creditors, 17 Martin, R. 569 to 596; Henry on Foreign Law, ch. 3, p. 23, &c.—The Supreme Court of Louisiana have made some very just remarks on this subject. "We are led," (says Mr. Justice Porter, in delivering the opinion of the Court,) "into an examination of the doctrine of real and personal statutes, as it is called by the continental writers of Europe; a subject the most intricate and perplexed of any that has occupied the attention of lawyers and courts; one on which

Hertius admits, that these subtleties have so perplexed the subject, that it is difficult to venture even upon an explanation. His language is: *De collisu legum anceps, difficilis, et late diffusa est disputatio, quam nescio an quisquam explicare totam aggressus fuerit*[1]. And in another place he adds: *Cæterum Junioribus plerisque placuit distinctio inter statuta, realia, personalia, et mixta. Verum in iis definiendis mirum est, quam sudant Doctores*[2]. Bartolus has furnished a memorable example of these niceties. After remarking upon the distinction between personal and real statutes, and the mode of distinguishing the one from the other, and that in England the custom obtains of the eldest son's succeeding to all the property, he says: *Mihi videtur,*

---

scarcely any writers are found entirely to agree, and on which it is rare to find one consistent with himself throughout. We know of no matter in jurisprudence so unsettled, or none that should more teach men distrust of their own opinions, and charity for those of others." Saul *v.* His Creditors, 17 Martin, R. 569, 588. Chancellor D'Aguesseau has attempted a definition, or test, of real and personal laws. He says: "The true principle in this matter is, to examine if the statute has *property* directly for its object, or its destination to certain persons, or its preservation in families; so that it is not the interest of the person whose rights or acts are examined, but the interests of others to whom it is intended to assure the property, or the real rights which were the cause of the law. Or if, on the contrary, all the attention of the law is directed towards the person, to provide in general for his qualifications, or his general absolute capacity, as when it relates to the qualities of major or minor, of father or son, of legitimate or illegitimate, of ability or inability to contract, by reason of personal causes. In the first hypothesis, the statute is real; in the second it is personal." Cited in 17 Martin, R. p. 594; D'Aguesseau Œuvres, tom. 4, p. 660, (4to. edit.). How unsatisfactory is this description when applied in practice.

[1] 1 Hertii Opera, De Collis. Legum, § 1, n. 1, p. 91; Id. § 4, n. 3, pp. 121, 122; Id. p. 129, and p. 170, (edit. 1716).

[2] 1 Hertii Opera, § 4, n. 3, p. 120; Id. p. 170 (edit. 1716). See also 1 Froland, Mém. Qualité des Statut. ch. 3 to ch. 7; Bouhier, Coutum. de Bourg. ch. 23, §§ 58, 59.—Mr. Livermore has given a concise view of the various opinions of foreign jurists on this subject, which will well reward a diligent perusal. Liverm. Dissert. 2, § 65 to 162. His own opinions, which exhibit great acuteness, will also be found in the same work from § 163 to § 214. The subject is very amply discussed in Froland, Boullenois, Bouhier, Le Brun, and Rodenburg.

quod verba statuti seu consuetudinis sunt diligenter intuenda. Aut illa disponunt circa res; ut per hæc verba, "Bona decedentis, ut veniant in Primogenitum;" et tunc de omnibus bonis judicabo secundum usum et statutum, ubi res sunt situatæ, quia jus affecit res ipsas, sive possideantur à cive, sive ab advenâ. Aut verba statuti seu consuetudinis disponunt circa personas; ut per hæc verba: "Primogenitus succedat;" et tunc, aut ille talis decedens non erat de Angliâ, sed ibi haberet possessiones; et tunc tale statutum ad eum et ejus filios non porrigitur, quia dispositio circa personas non porrigitur ad forenses[1]. *Aut talis decedens erat Anglicus, et tunc filius primogenitus succederet in bonis quæ sunt in Angliâ, et in aliis succederet de jure communi.* So that, according to Bartolus, if a statute declares in words, that "The estate of the intestate shall descend to the eldest son," (*Bona decedentis ut veniant in primogenitum,*) it is a real statute; if it says, in words, "The eldest son shall succeed to the estate," (*Primogenitus succedat*), it is a personal statute[2]. This distinction has been justly exploded by other civilians, as the mere order and construction of the words of the statute, and not its objects, would otherwise decide its character[3].

---

1 Bartolus, ad Cod. Lib. 1, tit. 1, De Sum. Trinit. l. 1, Cunctos populos, n. 42; Liverm. Dissert. §§ 68, 69, pp. 63, 64; 1 Boullenois, Observ. 2, pp. 16, 17.—The text of Bartolus, in the only edition to which I have access, (Venet. 1602,) abounds exceedingly in abbreviations, so that in some few instances I am not perfectly sure that I have given the exact word.

2 1 Boullenois, tit. 1, ch. 1, Obs. 2, pp. 16, 17; Liverm. Dissert. § 3, pp. 22, 23; Id. §§ 67, 68, pp. 62, 63; Mr. Justice Porter in the case of Saul *v.* His Creditors, 17 Martin, R. 569, 590 to 595; Burgundus, Tract. 1, § 4, p. 16; Stockman, Decis. 125, § 8, p. 263.

3 Id. p. 19; Liverm. Dissert. 2, §§ 67, 68; Id. § 69 to 77; 1 Froland, Mém. Statut. P. 1, ch. 3, §§ 3, 4; Bouhier, Coutum. de Bourg. ch. 53, § 58 to 99.—The opinion of the Court by Mr. Justice Porter, in Saul *v.* His Creditors, 17 Martin, R., 569, 590 to 596, illustrates this subject in a very striking manner. "According to the Jurists" (says he) "of those countries, a personal statute is that which follows and governs the party subject to it, wherever he goes. The real statute controls things, and does not extend beyond the limits of the country from which it derives its authority.

§ 15. Le Brun says, that, in order to ascertain whether a statute is personal or not, it is necessary to examine

---

The personal statute of one country controls the personal statute of another country, into which a party once governed by the former, or who may contract under it, should remove. But it is subject to a real statute of the place where the person subject to the personal should fix himself, or where the property on which the contest arises may be situated. So far the rules are plain and intelligible. But the moment we attempt to discover from these writers what statutes are real and what are personal, the most extraordinary confusion is presented. Their definitions often differ, and when they agree on their definitions they dispute as to their application. Bartolus, who was one of the first by whom this subject was examined, and the most distinguished jurist of his day, established as a rule, that, whenever the statute commenced by treating of persons, it was a personal one; but if it began by disposing of things, it was real. So that if a law, as the counsel for the appellants has stated, was written thus: 'The estate of the deceased shall be inherited by the eldest son,' the statute was real; but if it said, 'The eldest son shall inherit the estate,' it was personal. This distinction, though purely verbal, and most unsatisfactory, was followed for a long time, and sanctioned by many whose names are illustrious in the annals of jurisprudence; but it was ultimately discarded by all. D'Argentre, who rejected this rule, to real and personal statutes added a third, which he called mixed. The real statute, according to this writer, is that which treats of immovables; In quo de rebus soli, id est immobilibus agitur. And the personal, that which concerns the person abstracted from things; Statutum personale est illud, quod afficit personam universaliter abstracte ab omni materia reali. The mixed he states to be one which concerns both persons and things. (D'Argentre, Comm. ad Leg. Brit. des Donat. art. 228, n. 5 to 9, tom. 1, p. 648.) This definition of D'Argentre of a personal statute has been adopted by every writer who has treated of this matter. A long list of them, amounting to twenty-five, is given by Froland, in his Mémoires concernans la Qualité des Statuts, among which are found Burgundus, Rodenburg, Stockmans, Voet, and Dumoulin. (Froland, Mémoires concernans la Qualité de Statuts, ch. 5, No. 1.) But the definition which he has given of a real statute does not seem to have been so generally adopted. It was, however, followed by Burgundus, Rodenburg, and Stockmans. Boullenois, who is one of the latest writers, attacks the definitions given by D'Argentre, and, as he supposes, refutes them; he adds others, which appear to be as little satisfactory as those he rejects. He divides personal statutes into personal particular, and personal universal; personal particular he subdivides again into pure personal, and personal real. (Boullenois, Traité de la Personalité et de la Realité des Lois, tit. 1, c. 2, Obs. 4, p. 44 to 52.) Voet has two definitions: one, that a real statute is that which affects principally things, though it also relates to persons; and the other, that a personal statute is that which affects

whether it universally governs the state of the person, independent of property. If it does not universally govern the

---

principally persons, although it treats also of things. It would be a painful and a useless task to follow these authors through all their refinements. President Bouhier, who wrote about the same time as Bullenois, and who has treated the subject as extensively as any other writer, after quoting the definitions just given, and others, says that they are all defective, and that he cannot venture on any, until the world are more agreed what statutes are real, and what are personal. While they remain so uncertain, he thinks the best way is to follow the second definition of Voet, which is, 'that a real statute is that which does not extend beyond the territory within which it is passed, and a personal is that which does.' (Bouhier, sur les Coutumes de Bourgogne, ch. 23, No. 59.) This last mode of distinguishing statutes, which teaches us what effect a statute should have, by directing us to inquire what effect it has, is quite as unsatisfactory as the rule given by Bartolus, who judged of it by the words with which it commenced. The rules given by Chancellor D'Aguesseau are perhaps preferable to any other. 'That,' says he, 'which truly characterizes a real statute, and essentially distinguishes it from a personal one, is not that it should be relative to certain personal circumstances, or certain personal events; otherwise, we should be obliged to say, that the statutes which relate to the paternal power, the right of wardship, the tenancy by courtesy, (droit de viduité,) the prohibition of married persons to confer advantages on each other, are personal statutes; and yet it is clear, in our jurisprudence, that they are considered as real statutes, the execution of which is regulated, not by the place of domicil, but by that where the property is situated. The true principle in this matter is, to examine if the statute has property directly for its object, or its destination to certain persons, or its preservation in families; so that it is not the interest of the person whose rights or acts are examined, but the interest of others, to whom it is intended to assure the property, or the real rights which were the cause of the law: or if, on the contrary, all the attention of the law is directed towards the person, to provide in general for his qualifications, or his general and absolute capacity; as when it relates to the qualities of major or minor, of father or of son, legitimate or illegitimate, ability or inability to contract by reason of personal causes.' 'In the first hypothesis the statute is real; in the second it is personal, as is well explained in these words of D'Argentre: "Cum statutum non simpliciter inhabilitat, sed ratione fundi aut juris realis alterum respicientis extra personas contrahentes, totas hanc inhabilitatem non egredi locum statuti."' (Œuvres, D'Aguesseau, Vol. 4, 660, cinquante-quatrième plaidoyer.) This definition is, we think, better than any of the rest; though even in the application of it to some cases, difficulty would exist. If the subject had been susceptible of clear and positive rules, we may safely believe this illustrious man would not have left it in doubt; for, if anything be more remarkable in him than his genius and his knowledge, it is the extraordinary

state of the person, but only particular acts of the person, it is not personal. Thus, a statute which prohibits married persons from making donations to each other, is purely real and local; because it regulates a particular act only. And a statute, to be personal, must regulate the state of the person without speaking of property (*biens*). Thus, a statute which excludes females from inheriting fiefs in favour of males, or which excludes a beneficiary heir from the succession in favour of the simple heir, or which excludes a daughter, who is endowed, from the succession, is real and local; for all these statutes speak of property. For the same reason he holds the *Senatûs-consultum Velleianum*, by which a married woman was prohibited from binding herself for the debt of another person[1], (and which was borrowed from the Roman Law into the customary jurisprudence of some of the French provinces,) to be a real statute; because it regulates a particular act of the person only[2]. And he adds, that the definition of a real statute results from that of a personal statute. In one word, a

---

fulness and clearness with which he expresses himself on all questions of jurisprudence. When he, therefore, and so many other men of great talents and learning are thus found to fail in fixing certain principles, we are forced to conclude that they have failed, not from want of ability, but because the matter was not susceptible of being settled on certain principles. They have attempted to go too far; to define and fix that which cannot, in the nature of things, be defined and fixed. They seem to have forgotten, that they wrote on a question which touched the comity of nations, and that that comity is, and ever must be, uncertain; that it must necessarily depend on a variety of circumstances which cannot be reduced within any certain rule; that no nation will suffer the laws of another to interfere with her own to the injury of her citizens; that, whether they do or not, must depend on the condition of the country in which the foreign law is sought to be enforced, the particular law of her legislation, her policy, and the character of her institutions; that, in the conflict of laws, it must be often a matter of doubt which should prevail; and that, whenever that doubt does exist, the court which decides will prefer the laws of its own country to that of the stranger."

1 Dig. lib. 16, tit. 1, l. 1; Id. l. 16, § 1.

2 Le Brun, Traité de la Communauté, Liv. 2, ch. 3, § 5, n. 20 to 48, p. 310 to 319.

statute is real which regulates a particular act of the person, or which speaks of property[1]. Other jurists of distinguished reputation (among whom is Boullenois) have denied this to be a sound distinction; and have especially held the *Senatûs-consultum Velleianum* to be a personal statute[2].

§ 16. It is not my design to engage in the controversy, as to what constitutes the true distinction between personal statutes and real statutes, or to examine the merits of the various systems propounded by foreign jurists on this subject. It would carry me too far from the immediate purpose of these commentaries, even if I felt myself possessed (which I certainly do not) of that critical skill and learning which such an examination would require, in order to treat the subject with suitable dignity. My object is rather to present the leading principles upon some of the more important topics of private international jurisprudence, and to use the works of the civilians, to illustrate, confirm, and expand the doctrines of the common law, so far, at least, as the latter have assumed a settled form. If, in referring to the authority of the civilians, I should speak of the personality of laws, (*personalité des statuts,*) and the reality of laws, (*réalité des statuts,*) let it not be attributed to a spirit of innovation upon the received usages of our language; but rather to a desire to familiarize expressions, which, in this peculiar sense, have already found their way into our juridical discussions, and are becoming daily more and more important to be understood by American lawyers, since they are incorporated into the very substance of the jurisprudence of some of the States in the Union[3]. By the personality of laws foreign jurists generally mean all laws which concern the condition, state, and capacity of persons;

---

[1] Le Brun, Traité de la Communauté, Liv. 2, ch. 3, § 5, n. 20 to 48, p. 310 to 319.

[2] 1 Boullenois, Princ. Gen. 5; Id. Observ. 3, p. 40; Id. Observ. 4, pp. 43, 49; Id. Observ. 5, pp. 78, 79, 82, 101, 103, 105, 106, 118; Henry on Foreign Law, 31, 50.

[3] See note to 2 Kent, Comm. Lect. 39, p. 446, (3rd edit.).

by the reality of laws, all laws which concern property or things; *quæ ad rem spectant*[1]. Whenever they wish to express that the operation of a law is universal, they compendiously announce that it is a personal statute; and whenever, on the other hand, they wish to express that its operation is confined to the country of its origin, they simply declare it to be a real statute.

---

[1] 1 Boullenois, Observ. 3, pp. 41, 42.—Mr. Livermore, in his Dissertations, used the words, *personality* and *reality;* Mr. Henry, in his work, the words *personalty* and *realty.* I have preferred the former, as least likely to lead to mistakes, as "personalty" is in our law confined to personal estate, and "realty" to real estate.

CHAPTER II.

GENERAL MAXIMS OF INTERNATIONAL JURISPRUDENCE.

§ 17. Before entering upon any examination of the various heads which a treatise upon the Conflict of Laws will naturally embrace, it seems necessary to advert to a few general maxims or axioms, which constitute the basis upon which all reasonings on the subject must necessarily rest; and without the express or tacit admission of which, it will be found impossible to arrive at any principles to govern the conduct of nations, or to regulate the due administration of justice.

§ 18. I. The first and most general maxim or proposition is that which has been already adverted to: that every nation possesses an exclusive sovereignty and jurisdiction within its own territory. The direct consequence of this rule is, that the laws of every state affect and bind directly all property, whether real or personal, within its territory; and all persons who are resident within it, whether natural-born subjects or aliens; and also all contracts made and acts done within it[1]. A state may therefore regulate the manner and circumstances under which property, whether real or personal, or in action, within it shall be held, transmitted, bequeathed, transferred, or enforced; the condition, capacity, and state of all persons within it; the validity of contracts and other acts done within it; the resulting rights and duties growing out of these contracts and acts; and the remedies and modes of administering justice in all cases calling for the

---

[1] Henry on Foreign Law, P. 1, ch. 1, § 1, p. 1; Huberus, Lib. 1, tit. 3, § 2; Hall *v.* Campbell, Cowp. R. 208; Ruding *v.* Smith, 2 Hagg. Consist. R. 383.

interposition of its tribunals to protect, and vindicate, and secure the wholesome agency of its own laws within its own domains.

§ 19. Accordingly, Boullenois has laid down the following among his general principles (*Principes généraux*). He says: (1.) He, or those who have the sovereign authority, have the sole right to make laws; and these laws ought to be executed in all places within the sovereignty where they are known, in the prescribed manner. (2.) The sovereign has power and authority over his subjects, and over the property which they possess within his dominions. (3.) The sovereign has also authority to regulate the forms and solemnities of contracts, which his subjects make within the territories under his dominions; and to prescribe the rules for the administration of justice. (4.) The sovereign has also a right to make laws to govern foreigners in many cases; for example, in relation to property which they possess within the reach of his sovereignty; in relation to the formalities of contracts which they make within his territories; and in relation to judiciary proceedings, if they institute suits before his tribunals. (5.) The sovereign may in like manner make laws for foreigners who even pass through his territories; but these are commonly simple laws of police, made for the preservation of order within his dominions, and these laws are either permanent, or they are made only for certain particular occurrences[1]. The same doctrine is either tacitly or expressly conceded by every other jurist who has discussed the subject at large, whether he has written upon municipal law or upon public law[2].

§ 20. II. Another maxim or proposition is, that no state or nation can, by its laws, directly affect or bind property out of its own territory, or bind persons not resident therein, whether they are natural-born subjects

---

[1] 1 Boullenois, Traité des Statuts, pp. 2, 3, 4.

[2] Vattel, B. 2, ch. 7, §§ 84, 85.

or others. This is a natural consequence of the first proposition; for it would be wholly incompatible with the equality and exclusiveness of the sovereignty of all nations, that any one nation should be at liberty to regulate either persons or things not within its own territory. It would be equivalent to a declaration, that the sovereignty over a territory was never exclusive in any nation, but only concurrent with that of all nations; that each could legislate for all, and none for itself; and that all might establish rules which none were bound to obey. The absurd results of such a state of things need not be dwelt upon. Accordingly Rodenburg has significantly said, that no sovereign has a right to give the law beyond his own dominions; and if he attempts it, he may be lawfully refused obedience; for wherever the foundation of laws fails, there their force and jurisdiction fail also. *Constat igitur extra territorium legem dicere licere nemini, idque si fecerit quis, impune ei non pareri; quippe ubi cesset statutorum fundamentum, robur et jurisdictio*[1]. P. Voet speaks to the same effect: *Nullum statutum, sive in rem sive in personam, si de ratione juris civilis sermo instituatur, sese extendit ultra statuentis territorium*[2]. Boullenois (as we have seen) announces the same rule: *De droit étroit, toutes les loix, que fait un souverain, n'ont force et autorité que dans l'étendue de sa domination*[3]; and, indeed, it is the common language of jurists[4]. Mr. Chief Justice Parker has recognised the doctrine in the fullest manner. "That the laws" (says he) "of any state cannot by any inherent authority be entitled to respect extra-territorially, or beyond the jurisdiction of the state which enacts them, is the necessary result of the independence of distinct sovereignties[5]."

---

1 Rodenburg, de Stat. ch. 3, § 1, p. 7.

2 Voet, de Stat. § 4, ch. 2, n. 7, p. 124; Id. 138, 139, (edit. 1661).

3 1 Boullenois, des Statut. Princip. Gén. 6, p. 4; Id. ch. 3, Observ. 10, p. 152.

4 Ibid.

5 Blanchard v. Russell, 13 Mass. R. 4.—The same doctrine is reasoned

§ 21. Upon this rule there is often engrafted an exception of some importance to be rightly understood. It is, that, although the laws of a nation have no direct binding force or effect, except upon persons within its own territories; yet that every nation has a right to bind its own subjects by its own laws in every other place[1]. In one sense this exception may be admitted to be correct, and well founded in the practice of nations; in another sense it is incorrect, or, at least, it requires qualification. Every nation has hitherto assumed it as clear that it possesses the right to regulate and govern its own native-born subjects everywhere; and, consequently, that its laws extend to and bind such subjects at all times, and in all places. This is commonly adduced as a consequence of what is called natural allegiance, that is, of allegiance to the government of the territory of a man's birth. Thus, Mr. Justice Blackstone says: "Natural allegiance is such as is due from all men, born within the king's dominions, immediately upon their birth." "Natural allegiance is, therefore, a debt of gratitude which cannot be forfeited, cancelled, or altered by any change of time, place, or circumstance. An Englishman who removes to France or to China, owes the same allegiance to the king of England there as at home, and twenty years hence as well as now[2]." And he proceeds to distinguish it from local allegiance, which is such as is due from an alien or stranger born, for so long a time as he continues within the dominions of a foreign prince. The former is universal and perpetual; the latter ceases the instant the stranger transfers himself to another country[3]; and it is therefore local and temporary. Vattel, on the other hand, seems to admit the right of allegiance

---

out with great ability in the opinion of Mr. Chief Justice Taney, in the case of the Bank of Augusta *v.* Earle, 13 Peters, R. 584 to 591.

1 Henry on Real and Personal Statutes, P. 1, ch. 1, p. 1.

2 1 Black. Comm. 369, 370; Foster, C. L. 184.

3 Ibid.

not to be perpetual even in natives; and that they have a right to expatriate themselves, and, under some circumstances, to dissolve their connexion with the parent country[1].

§ 22. Without entering upon this subject, (which properly belongs to a general treatise upon public law,) it may be truly said, that no nation is bound to respect the laws of another nation, made in regard to the subjects of the latter, who are non-residents. The obligatory force of such laws of any nation cannot extend beyond its own territories. And if such laws are incompatible with the laws of the country where such subjects reside, or interfere with the duties which they owe to the country where they reside, they will be disregarded by the latter. Whatever may be the intrinsic or obligatory force of such laws upon such persons, if they should return to their native country, they can have none in other nations wherein they reside. Such laws may give rise to personal relations between the sovereign and subjects, to be enforced in his own domains; but they do not rightfully extend to other nations. *Statuta suo clauduntur territorio, nec ultra territorium disponunt.* Nor, indeed, is there, strictly speaking, any difference in this respect, whether such laws concern the persons, or concern the property of native subjects. A state has just as much intrinsic right, and no more, to give to its own laws an extra-territorial force, as to the property of its subjects situated abroad, as it has in relation to the persons of its subjects domiciled abroad. That is, as sovereign laws, they have no obligation on either the person or the property. When, therefore, we speak of the right of a state to bind its own native subjects everywhere, we speak only of its own claim and exercise of sovereignty over them when they return within its own territorial jurisdiction, and not of its right to compel or require obedience to such laws on the part of other nations within their own terri-

---

[1] Vattel, B. 1, ch. 19, § 220 to 228.

torial sovereignty. On the contrary, every nation has an exclusive right to regulate persons and things within its own territory according to its own sovereign will and public polity.

§ 23. III. From these two maxims or propositions, there flows a third, and that is, that whatever force and obligation the laws of one country have in another, depend solely upon the laws and municipal regulations of the latter; that is to say, upon its own proper jurisprudence and polity, and upon its own express or tacit consent.[1] A state may prohibit the operation of all foreign laws, and the rights growing out of them, within its own territories. It may prohibit some foreign laws, and it may admit the operation of others. It may recognise, and modify, and qualify some foreign laws; it may enlarge or give universal effect to others. It may interdict the administration of some foreign laws; it may favour the introduction of others. When its own code speaks positively on the subject, it must be obeyed by all persons who are within the reach of its sovereignty. When its customary, unwritten, or common law speaks directly on the subject, it is equally to be obeyed; for it has an equal obligation with its positive code. When both are silent, then, and then only, can the question properly arise, what law is to govern in the absence of any clear declaration of the sovereign will. Is the rule to be promulgated by a legislative act of the sovereign power, or is it to be promulgated by courts of law, according to the analogies, which are furnished in the municipal jurisprudence? This question does not admit of any universal answer; or rather, it will be answered differently in different communities, according to the organization of the departments of each particular government[2].

§ 24. Upon the continent of Europe some of the principal states have silently suffered their courts to draw this portion of their jurisprudence from the analogies furnished

---

[1] Huberus, Lib. 1, tit. 3, § 2. [2] See post, § 38.

by the civil law, or by their own customary or positive code. France, for instance, composed, as it formerly was, of a great number of provinces, governed by different laws and customs, was early obliged to sanction such exertions of authority by its courts, in order to provide for the constantly occurring claims of its own subjects living and owning property in different provinces, and a conflict between the different provincial laws. In England and America the courts of justice have hitherto exercised the same authority in the most ample manner; and the legislatures have in no instance (it is believed) in either country interfered to provide any positive regulations. The common law of both countries has been expanded to meet the exigencies of the times as they have arisen; and so far as the practice of nations, or the *jus gentium privatum*, has been supposed to furnish any general principle, it has been followed out with a wise and manly liberality.

§ 25. The real difficulty is to ascertain what principles, in point of public convenience, ought to regulate the conduct of nations on this subject in regard to each other, and in what manner they can be best applied to the infinite variety of cases, arising from the complicated concerns of human society in modern times. No nation can be justly required to yield up its own fundamental policy and institutions, in favour of those of another nation. Much less can any nation be required to sacrifice its own interests in favour of another; or to enforce doctrines which, in a moral or political view, are incompatible with its own safety or happiness, or conscientious regard to justice and duty. In the endless diversities of human jurisprudence many laws must exist in one country which are the result of local or accidental circumstances, and are wholly unfit to be engrafted upon the institutions and habits of another. Many laws, well enough adapted to the notions of heathen nations, would be totally repugnant to the feelings as well as to the justice of those which embrace Christianity. A heathen nation might justify polygamy or incest, contracts of moral turpitude or exercises of despotic cruelty over persons, which would be repugnant to the first principles of Christian duty. The laws of one nation may be founded upon a narrow selfishness, exclusively adapted to promote its own peculiar policy, or the personal or proprietary interests of its own subjects, to the injury or even the ruin of those of the subjects of all other countries. A particular nation may refuse all reciprocity of commerce, rights, and remedies to others. It may assume a superiority of powers and prerogatives for the very purpose of crushing those of its neighbours who are less fortunate or less powerful. In these and in many other cases which may easily be put without any extravagance of supposition, there would be extreme difficulty in saying, that other nations were bound to enforce laws, institutions, or customs of that nation which were subversive of their own morals, justice, interest, or polity. Who, for instance, (not to multiply cases,) would contend, that any nation in Christendom ought to carry into effect, to its utmost range, the paternal power of the ancient Romans in their early jurisprudence, extending to power over the life and death of their children[1]? Or, who would now contend for that terrible power (if it ever really existed) under the law of the Twelve Tables, which enabled creditors to cut their debtor's body into pieces and divide it among them[2]?

§ 26. The jurists of continental Europe have, with uncommon skill and acuteness, endeavoured to collect principles which ought to regulate this subject among all nations. But it is very questionable, whether their success has been at all proportionate to their labour; and whether their principles, if universally adopted, would be found either convenient or desirable, or even just, under all cir-

---

[1] Laws of the Twelve Tables, Table 4, ch. 1; 1 Pothier, Pandects, and Id. §§ 1, 2, (8vo. edit. Paris, 1818,) pp. 386, 387; 1 Black. Comm. 452; Fergusson on Marriage and Divorce, 411; Grotius, B. 2, ch. 5, § 7.

[2] Table 3, ch. 4; 1 Pothier, Pandects, and Id. Comm. § 2, (8vo. edit. Paris, 1818,) pp. 372, 380, 381; 2 Black. Comm. 472, 473.

cumstances. Their systems, indeed, have had mainly in view the juridical polity, fit for the different provinces and states of a common empire, although they are by no means limited to such cases. It is easy to see, that, in a nation like France before the revolution, governed by different laws in its various provinces, some uniform rules might be adopted, which would not be equally fit for the adoption of independent nations, possessing no such common interests, or such a common basis of jurisprudence. The leading positions maintained by many of the French jurists are, that the laws of a country which concern persons who reside within, and are subject to its territorial jurisdiction, ought to be deemed of universal obligation in all other countries; that the laws which concern the property of such persons ought to be deemed purely local, and the laws of a mixed character, concerning such persons and property, ought to be deemed local or universal, according to their predominant character. Thus, Boullenois lays down these rules in pointed terms : *Les loix pures personelles, soit personelles universelles, soit personelles particuliéres, se portent partout ; c'est-à-dire, que l'homme est partout de l'état, soit universel, soit particulier, dont sa personne est affectée, par la loi de son domicil. Les loix réelles n'ont point d'extension directe, ni indirecte, hors la jurisdiction et la domination du legislateur. Le sujet et le materiel dominant direct et immediat du statut en determine la nature et qualité ; c'est-à-dire, que le sujet et le materiel le font être réel, ou personnel.*[1]

§ 27. Independent of the almost insurmountable difficulties in which the continental jurists admit themselves to be involved, in the attempt to settle the true character of these mixed cases of international jurisprudence, and about which they have been engaged in endless controversies with each other, there are certain exceptions to these rules,

---

1 1 Boullenois, Traité des Statuts, Prin. Gén. 18, 23, 27, pp. 6, 7.

generally admitted, which shake the very foundation on which they rest, and admonish us that it is far easier to give simplicity to systems, than to reconcile them with the true duties and interests of all nations in all cases. Take, for example, two neighbouring states, one of which admits, and the other of which prohibits, the existence of slavery, and the rights of property growing out of it; what help would it be to either, in ascertaining its own duties and interests in regard to the other, to say, that their laws, so far as they regard the persons of the slaves, were of universal obligation; and, so far as they regard the property in slaves, they were real, and of no obligation beyond the territory of the lawgiver?[1]

§ 28. There is, indeed, great truth in the remarks which have been judicially promulgated on this subject by a learned court:—"When so many men of great talents and learning are thus found to fail in fixing certain principles, we are forced to conclude that they have failed, not from want of ability, but because the matter was not susceptible of being settled on certain principles. They have attempted to go too far, to define and fix that which cannot, in the nature of things, be defined and fixed. They seem to have forgotten, that they wrote on a question which touched the comity of nations, and that that comity is, and ever must be, uncertain. That it must necessarily depend on a variety of circumstances, which cannot be reduced to any certain rule. That no nation will suffer the laws of another to interfere with her own to the injury of her citizens. That, whether they do or not, must depend on the condition of the country in which the foreign law is sought to be enforced; the particular nature of her legislation, her policy, and the character of her institutions. That, in the conflict of laws, it must often be a matter of doubt which should prevail; and that, whenever a doubt

---

[1] See Somerset's case, and Hargrave's note to Co. Lit. 79. b., note 44.

does exist, the court which decides will prefer the laws of its own country to that of the stranger[1]."

§ 29. Huberus has laid down three axioms, which he deems sufficient to solve all the intricacies of the subject. The first is, that the laws of every empire have force only within the limits of its own government, and bind all who are subjects thereof; but not beyond those limits[2]. The second is, that all persons who are found within the limits of a government, whether their residence is permanent or temporary, are to be deemed subjects thereof[3]. The third is, that the rulers of every empire from comity admit, that the laws of every people in force within its own limits, ought to have the same force everywhere, so far as they do not prejudice the powers or rights of other governments, or of their citizens[4]. "From this," he adds, "it appears, that this matter is to be determined, not simply by the civil laws, but by the convenience and tacit consent of different people; for since the laws of one people cannot have any direct force among another people, so nothing could be more inconvenient in the commerce and general intercourse of nations, than that what is valid by the laws of one place should become without effect by the diversity of laws of another; and that this is the true reason of the last axiom, of which no one hitherto seems to have entertained any doubt[5]."

---

1 Mr. Justice Porter, in delivering the opinion of the Court in the case of Saul *v.* His Creditors, 17 Martin, R. 569, 595, 596.

2 Huberus, Lib. 1, tit. 3, De Conflictu Legum, § 2, p. 538.

3 Ib.

4 Ib.

5 Ib.—These axioms of Huberus are so often cited, that it may be well to give them in his own words. "(1) Leges cujusque imperii vim habent intra terminos ejusdem reipublicæ, omnesque ei subjectos obligant, nec ultra. (2) Pro subjectis imperio habendi sunt omnes, qui intra terminos ejusdem reperiuntur, sive in perpetuum, sive ad tempus ibi commorentur. (3) Rectores imperiorum id comiter agunt, ut jura cujusque populi intra terminos ejus exercita teneant ubique suam vim, quatenus nihil potestati aut juri alterius imperantis ejusque civium prejudicetur." 2 Hub. Lib. 1, tit. 3; De Conflictu Legum, § 2.

§ 30. Hertius seems to have been dissatisfied with these rules, and especially with the last; and he doubts exceedingly, whether this comity of nations, founded upon the notion of mutual convenience and utility, can furnish any sufficiently solid basis of a system. *Ob reciprocam enim utilitatem, in disciplinam juris gentium abiise, ut civitas alterius civitatis leges apud se valere patiatur, adeoque exemplum hoc, ut evidentissimi argumenti ad probandum, quod jus gentium reverâ a jure naturæ distinctum sit, vult observari. Verum enim nos valde dubitamus, num res hæc ex jure gentium, sive mutuâ earum indulgentiâ, possit definiri, præsertim cum in unâ eâdemque civitate collisio sæpissime fiat. Norunt etiam periti ex solis exemplis jus gentium adstruere, quam sit fallax; tum si solâ populorum conniventiâ id niti dicamus, quæ juris erit efficacia*[1]*?* He adds, that he is disposed to search deeper into the matter: *Nobis paullo altius libet repetere*[2]*;* and he proceeds to enunciate his own views under the known distinctions of personal statutes and real statutes, and then lays down the following rules:—(1.) "When a law is directed, or has regard to the person, we are to look to (be governed by) the laws of the country to which he is personally subject." *Quando lex in personam dirigitur, respiciendum est ad leges illius civitatis, quæ personam habet subjectam*[3]. (2.) "If a law bears directly upon things it is local, in whatever place and by whomsoever the act is done." *Si lex directò rei imponitur, ea locum habet, ubicunque etiam locorum et a quocunque actus celebretur*[4]. (3.) "If a law gives the form (prescribes the form) to the act, then the place of the act, and not of the domicil of the party, or of the situation of the thing,

---

[1] 1 Hertii Opera, De Collis. Leg. § 4, nn. 3, 4, p. 120; Id. pp. 170, 171, (edit. 1716).

[2] Ibid.

[3] Hertii Opera, De Collis. § 4, art. 8, p. 123; Id. p. 175, (edit. 1716). post, § 238.

[4] Id. § 4, art. 9, p. 123; Id. p. 177, (edit. 1716); post, § 238.

is to be regarded." *Si lex actui formam dat, inspiciendus est locus actûs, non domicilii, non rei sitæ*[1]. Now, after the admission of Hertius himself, that the usage of nations must furnish a very fallacious guide on such a subject, it is not a little difficult to perceive what superior authority or value his own rules have over those of Huberus. The latter has at least this satisfactory foundation for his most important rule, that he is mainly guided in it by the practice of nations; and he thus aimed, as Grotius had done before him, to avail himself of the practice of nations, as a solid proof of the acknowledged law of nations[2].

§ 31. Some attempts have been made, but without success, to undervalue the authority of Huberus. It is certainly true that he is not often spoken of, except by jurists belonging to the Dutch School. Boullenois, however, has quoted his third and last axiom with manifest approbation[3]. But it will require very little aid of authority to countenance his works if his maxims are well founded; and if they are not, no approbation founded on foreign recognitions of them can disguise their defects. It is not, however, a slight recommendation of his works, that hitherto he has possessed an undisputed preference on this subject over other continental jurists, as well in England as in America. Indeed, his two first maxims will in the present day scarcely be disputed by any one; and the last seems irresistibly to flow from the right and duty of every nation to protect its own subjects against injuries resulting from the unjust and prejudicial influence of foreign laws; and to refuse its aid to carry into effect any foreign laws, which are repugnant to its own interests and polity.

---

1 1 Hertii Opera, De Collis. Leg. § 4, art. 10, p. 126; Id. p. 179, (edit. 1716); post, § 238.

2 The Scottish courts seem constantly to have held the doctrine of Huberus in his third axiom to be entirely correct. See Fergusson on Marr. and Div. 395, 396, 410.

3 1 Boullenois, Traité des Statuts, ch. 3, Observ. 10, p. 155.

§ 32. It is difficult to conceive upon what ground a claim can be rested, to give to any municipal laws an extra-territorial effect, when those laws are prejudicial to the rights of other nations, or to those of their subjects. It would at once annihilate the sovereignty and equality of every nation which should be called upon to recognise and enforce them; or compel it to desert its own proper interest and duty to its own subjects, in favour of strangers who were regardless of both. A claim, so naked of any principle or just authority to support it, is wholly inadmissible.

§ 33. It has been thought by some jurists, that the term "comity" is not sufficiently expressive of the obligation of nations to give effect to foreign laws, when they are not prejudicial to their own rights and interests. And it has been suggested, that the doctrine rests on a deeper foundation; that it is not so much a matter of comity or courtesy, as a matter of paramount moral duty[1]. Now, assuming that such a moral duty does exist, it is clearly one of imperfect obligation—like that of beneficence, humanity, and charity. Every nation must be the final judge for itself, not only of the nature and extent of the duty, but of the occasions on which its exercise may be justly demanded. And, certainly, there can be no pretence to say, that any foreign nation has a right to require the full recognition and execution of its own laws in other territories, when those laws are deemed oppressive or injurious to the rights or interests of the inhabitants of the latter, or when their moral character is questionable, or their provisions are impolitic or unjust[2]. Even in other cases, it is difficult to perceive a clear foundation in morals, or in natural law, for declaring that any nation has a right (all others being equal in sovereignty) to insist that its own positive laws shall be of superior obligation in a foreign

---

1 Liverm. Dissert. p. 26 to p. 30.

2 See Mr. Justice Porter, in the case of Saul *v.* His Creditors, 17 Martin, R. 569, 596 to 599.

realm to the domestic laws of the latter, of an equally positive character. What intrinsic right has one nation to declare, that no contract shall be binding which is made by any of its subjects in a foreign country unless they are twenty-five years of age, any more than another nation where the contract is made has a right to declare that such contract shall be binding if made by any person of twenty-one years of age? One should suppose, that, if there be anything clearly within the scope of national sovereignty, it is the right to fix what shall be the rule to govern contracts made within its own territories[1].

§ 34. That a nation ought not to make its own jurisprudence an instrument of injustice to other nations, or to their subjects, may be admitted. But in a vast variety of cases which may be put, the rejection of the laws of a foreign nation may work less injustice than the enforcement of them will remedy. And, here again, every nation must judge for itself, what is its true duty in the administration of justice in its domestic tribunals. It is not to be taken for granted, that the rule of the foreign nation which complains of a grievance is right, and that its own rule is wrong.

§ 35. The true foundation on which the administration of international law must rest, is, that the rules which are to govern are those which arise from mutual interest and utility; from a sense of the inconveniences which would result from a contrary doctrine; and from a sort of moral necessity to do justice, in order that justice may be done to us in return[2]. This is the ground upon which Rodenburg puts it. *Quid igitur* (says he) *rei in causâ est, quod personalia statuta territorium egrediantur? Unicum hoc ipsa rei natura ac necessitas invexit, ut cum de statu et conditione hominum quœritur, uni solummodo judici, et quidem domicilii,*

---

1 See post, § 75; and Mr. Justice Porter's opinion in Saul *v.* His Creditors, 17 Martin, R. 569, 596, 597, 598.

2 Liverm. Dissert. p. 28; Blanchard *v.* Russell, 13 Mass. R. 4.

universum in illâ jus sit attributum; cum enim ab uno certoque loco statum hominis legem accipere necesse est, quod absurdum, earumque rerum naturaliter inter se pugna foret, ut in quot loca quis iter faciens, aut navigans, delatus fuerit, totidem ille statum mutaret aut conditionem; ut uno eodemque tempore hic sui juris, illic alieni futurus sit; uxor simul in potestate viri, et extra eandem sit; alio loco habeatur quis prodigus, alio frugi[1]. President Bouhier expounds the ground with still more distinctness. *Mais avant toutes choses il faut se souvenir, qu'encore que le règle étroite soit pour la restriction des coutumes dans leurs limites, l'extension en a néanmoins été admise en faveur de l'utilité publique, et souvent même par une espéce de nécessité, &c. Ainsi, quand les peuples voisins ont souffert cette extension, ce n'est point qu'ils se soient vûs soumis à un statut étranger. C'est seulement, parcequ'ils y ont trouvé leur interêt particulier en ce, qu'en pareil cas leurs coutumes ont le même avantage dans les provinces voisines. On peut donc dire, que cette extension est sur une espéce de droit des gens, et de bienséance, en virtu duquel les différens peuples sont tacitement demeurés d'accord, de souffrir cette extension de coutume à coutume, toutes les fois que l'equité et l'utilité commune le demanderaient; à moins que celle, où l'extension seroit demandée, ne contînt en ce cas une disposition prohibitive*[2].

§ 36. But of the nature, and extent, and utility of this recognition of foreign laws, respecting the state and condition of persons, every nation must judge for itself, and certainly is not bound to recognise them, when they would be prejudicial to its own interests. The very terms, in which the doctrine is commonly enunciated carry along with them this necessary qualification and limitation of it. Mutual utility presupposes, that the interest of all nations is consulted, and not that of one only. Now, this demon-

---

[1] Rodenb. de Stat. Diversit. tit. 1, c. 3, § 4; 2 Boullenois, App. p. 8.

[2] Bouhier, Cout. de Bourg. ch. 23, §§ 62, 63, p. 457.

strates, that the doctrine owes its origin and authority to the voluntary adoption and consent of nations. It is, therefore, in the strictest sense, a matter of the comity of nations, and not of any absolute paramount obligation, superseding all discretion on the subject[1].

§ 37. Vattel has with great propriety said, "That it belongs exclusively to each nation to form its own judgment of what its conscience prescribes to it; of what it can, or cannot do; of what is proper or improper for it to do. And of course it rests solely with it to examine and determine, whether it can perform any office for another nation, without neglecting the duty which it owes to itself[2]." Lord Stowel has pointed out the same principle in his usual felicitous manner. Speaking with reference to the validity of a Scotch marriage in controversy before him, he remarked, "Being entertained in an English court, it (the cause) must be adjudicated according to the principles of English law applicable to such a case. But the only principle applicable to such a case by the law of England is, that the validity of the marriage rights must be tried by reference to the law of the country where, if they exist at all, they had their origin. Having furnished this principle, the law of England withdraws altogether, and leaves the legal question to the exclusive judgment of the law of Scotland[3]."

§ 38. There is, then, not only no impropriety in the use of the phrase "comity of nations," but it is the most appropriate phrase to express the true foundation and extent of the obligation of the laws of one nation within the territories of another[4]. It is derived altogether from the volun-

---

1 2 Kent, Comm. Lect. 39, pp. 457, 458, (3rd edit.).

2 Vattel, Prelim. Disc. pp. 61, 62, §§ 14, 16.

3 Dalrymple *v.* Dalrymple, 2 Hagg. Consist. R. 59. See Scrimshire *v.* Scrimshire, Id. 407, 416.

4 See Robinson *v.* Bland, 2 Burr. R. 1077, 1079; Blanchard *v.* Russell, 13 Mass. R. 4.

tary consent of the latter; and is inadmissible, when it is contrary to its known policy, or prejudicial to its interests. In the silence of any positive rule, affirming, or denying, or restraining the operation of foreign laws, courts of justice presume the tacit adoption of them by their own government, unless they are repugnant to its policy, or prejudicial to its interests. It is not the comity of the courts, but the comity of the nation, which is administered, and ascertained in the same way, and guided by the same reasoning, by which all other principles of the municipal law are ascertained and guided[1]. The doctrine of Huberus would seem, therefore, to stand upon just principles; and though, from its generality, it leaves behind many grave questions as to its application, it has much to commend it, in point of truth as well as of simplicity. It has accordingly been

---

[1] See this doctrine expressly recognised by the Supreme Court of the United States, in Bank of Augusta *v.* Earle, 13 Peters, R. 519, 589. Mr. Chief Justice Taney, in delivering the opinion of the Court, said: "It is needless to enumerate here the instances in which, by the general practice of civilized countries, the laws of the one will, by the comity of nations, be recognised and executed in another, where the rights of individuals are concerned. The cases of contracts made in a foreign country are familiar examples; and Courts of justice have always expounded and executed them according to the laws of the place in which they were made, provided that law was not repugnant to the laws or policy of their own country. The comity thus extended to other nations is no impeachment of sovereignty. It is the voluntary act of the nation by which it is offered; and is inadmissible when contrary to its policy, or prejudicial to its interests. But it contributes so largely to promote justice between individuals, and to produce a friendly intercourse between the sovereignties to which they belong, that Courts of justice have continually acted upon it as a part of the voluntary law of nations. It is truly said in Story's Conflict of Laws, 37, that 'In the silence of any positive rule, affirming, or denying, or restraining the operation of foreign laws, Courts of justice presume the tacit adoption of them by their own government; unless they are repugnant to its policy, or prejudicial to its interests. It is not the comity of the Courts, but the comity of the nation which is administered, and ascertained in the same way, and guided by the same reasoning, by which all other principles of municipal law are ascertained and guided.'"

sanctioned both in England and America by a judicial approbation, as direct and universal as can fairly be desired, for the purpose of giving sanction to it as authority or as reasoning[1].

---

[1] Out of the great variety of authorities, in which the rules of Huberus are directly or indirectly approved, the reader is referred to the following:— Co. Lit. 79. b., Hargrave's note 44; Robinson *v.* Bland, 2 Burr. R. 1077, 1078; Holman *v.* Johnson, Cowper, 341; 2 Kent, Comm. Lect. 39, p. 453 to p. 463, (3rd edit.); Pearsall *v.* Dwight, 2 Mass. R. 84, 90; Desesbats *v.* Berquier, 1 Binn. R. 336; Holmes *v.* Remsen, 4 John. Ch. R. 469; Mr. Cowen's note to 4 Cowen, R. 410; Saul *v.* His Creditors, 17 Martin, R. 569, 596, 597, 598; Greenwood *v.* Curtis, 6 Mass. R. 358; Bank of Augusta *v.* Earle, 13 Peters, R. 519, 588 to 591.

CHAPTER III.

NATIONAL DOMICIL.

§ 39. HAVING disposed of these preliminary considerations, it is proposed in the further progress of these Commentaries to examine the operation and effect of laws: first, in relation to persons, their capacity, state, and condition; secondly, in relation to contracts; thirdly, in relation to property, personal, mixed, and real; fourthly, in relation to wills, successions, and distributions; fifthly, in relation to persons acting *in autre droit*, such as guardians, executors, and administrators; sixthly, in relation to remedies and judicial sentences; seventhly, in relation to penal laws and offences; and eighthly, in relation to evidence and proofs.

§ 40. As, however, in all the discussions upon this subject perpetual reference will be made to the domicil of the party, it may be proper to ascertain what is the true meaning of the term "domicil;" or, rather, what constitutes the national or local domicil of a party according to the understanding of publicists and jurists[1].

§ 41. By the term "domicil," in its ordinary acceptation, is meant the place where a person lives or has his home. In this sense the place where a person has his actual residence, inhabitancy, or commorancy, is sometimes called his domicil. In a strict and legal sense that is properly the domicil of a person where he has his true fixed permanent home and principal establishment, and to which, whenever he is absent, he has the intention of returning (*animus revertendi*)[2].

---

[1] Upon the subject of this chapter the learned reader is referred to Burge's Comment. on Col. and Foreign Law, Vol. 1, P. 1, ch. 2, p. 32 to p. 57.

[2] Dr. Lieber's Encyc. Americ., art. *Domicil.*

§ 42. In the Roman law it is said, "There is no doubt, that every person has his domicil in that place which he makes his family residence and principal place of his business; from which he is not about to depart unless some business requires; when he leaves it he deems himself a wanderer; and when he returns to it he deems himself no longer abroad." *In eodem loco singulos habere domicilium, non ambigitur, ubi quis larem rerumque ac fortunarum summam constituit; unde rursus non sit discessurus, si nihil avocet; unde cum profectus est, peregrinari videtur: quod si rediit, peregrinari jam destitit*[1]. And in another place it is said, "If any one always carries on his business, not in a colony, but in a municipality or city, where he buys, sells, and contracts; where he makes use of, and attends the forum, the public baths, and public shows; where he celebrates the holidays, and enjoys all municipal privileges, and none in colony; he is deemed there to have his domicil, rather than in the place (colony), in which he sojourns for purposes of agriculture." *Si quis negotia sua non in coloniâ, sed in municipio, semper agit; in illo vendit, emit, contrahit; eo in foro, balneo, spectaculis utitur; ibi festos dies celebrat; omnibus denique municipii commodis, nullis coloniarum, fruitur; ibi magis habere domicilium, quam ubi colendi causâ diversatur*[2]. And again: "He is deemed an inhabitant, who has his domicil in any place, and whom the Greeks call πάροικον, that is to say, a neighbour, or person inhabiting near to a village. For those are not alone to be deemed inhabitants who dwell in a town; but those, also, who cultivate grounds near its limits, so that they conduct themselves as if their place of abode were there." *Incola est, qui aliquâ regione domicilium suum contulit; quem Græci πάροικον (id est,* juxta habitantem) *appellant. Nec tantum hi, qui in*

---

[1] Cod. Lib. 10, tit. 39, l. 7; Pothier, Pand. Lib. 50, n. 15; 1 Voet, ad Pand. Lib. 5, tit. 1, n. 92, p. 344; Id. n. 94, p. 345.

[2] Dig. Lib. 50, tit. 1, l. 27; Pothier, Pand. Lib. 50, tit. 1, n. 18; 2 Domat, Public Law, B. 1, tit. 16, § 3, art. 4.

oppido morantur, incolæ sunt; sed etiam, qui alicujus oppidi finibus ita agrum habent, ut in eum se, quasi in aliquam sedem, recipiant[1]. Some, at least, of these are more properly descriptions, than definitions of domicil. Pothier has generalized them in his own introduction to this title of the Pandects, and says, The seat of the fortune or property, which any person possesses in any place, constitutes his chief domicil. *Domicilium facit potissimum sedes fortunarum suarum, quas quis in aliquo loco habet*[2]. Voet says, *Proprie dictum Domicilium est, quod quis sibi constituet animo inde non decedendi, si non aliud avocet*[3].

§ 43. The French Jurists have defined domicil to be the place where a person has his principal establishment. Thus Denizart says, "The domicil of a person is the place where a person enjoys his rights, and establishes his abode, and makes the seat of his property." *Le domicile est le lieu où une personne, jouissant de ses droits, établit sa demeure et la siége de sa fortune*[4]. The Encyclopedists say, "That it is, properly speaking, the place where one has fixed the centre of his business." *C'est, à proprement parler, l'endroit où l'on a placé le centre de ses affaires*[5]. Pothier says, "It is the place where a person has established the principal seat of his residence and of his business." *C'est le lieu où une personne a etabli la siége principal de sa demeure et de ses affaires*[6]. And the modern French code declares, that the domicil of every Frenchman, as to the exercise of civil rights, is the place where he has his principal establishment, (*Est le lieu où il a son principal établissement*[7]). Vattel has defined domicil to be a fixed residence in any

---

1 Dig. Lib. 50, tit. 16, l. 239, § 2; Id. l. 203; Pothier, Pand. Lib. 50, n. 16.

2 Pothier, Pand. Lib. 50, tit. 1, Introd. art. 2, n. 18.

3 Voet, ad Pand. Lib. 5, tit. 1, n. 94.

4 Denizart, art. *Domicil.*

5 Encyclop. Moderne, art. *Domicil.*

6 Pothier, Introd. Gén. Cout. d'Orleans, ch. 1, § 1, art. 8.

7 Cod. Civ. art. 102. See also Merlin, Répert., art. *Domicil.*

place, with an intention of always staying there[1]. But this is not an accurate statement. It would be more correct to say, that that place is properly the domicil of a person in which his habitation is fixed, without any present intention of removing therefrom[2].

§ 44. Two things, then, must concur to constitute domicil: first, residence; and, secondly, the intention of making it the home of the party. There must be the fact, and the intent; for, as Pothier has truly observed, a person cannot establish a domicil in a place, except it be *animo et facto*[3]. Voet emphatically says, *Illud certum est, neque solo animo atque destinatione patris familias, aut contestatione solâ, sine re et pacto, domicilium constitui; neque solâ domus comparatione in aliquâ regione; neque solâ habitatione, sine proposito illic perpetuo morandi*[4]. So D'Argentre says: *Quamobrem, qui figendi ejus animum non habent, sed usus, necessitatis, aut negotiationis causâ alicubi sint, protinus a negotio discessuri, domicilium nullo temporis spatio constituent; cum neque animus sine facto, neque factum sine animo ad id sufficiat*[5]. However, in many cases actual residence is not indispensable to retain a domicil, after it is once acquired; but it is retained *animo solo*, by the mere intention not to change it, or to adopt another. If, therefore, a person leaves his home for temporary purposes, but with an intention to return to it, this change of place is not in law a change of domicil. Thus, if a person should go on a voyage to sea or to a foreign country for health, or for pleasure, or for business of a temporary nature, with an intention to return, such a transitory residence would not constitute a new domicil, or amount to an abandonment of the old one;

---

1 Vattel, B. 1, ch. 19, § 22.

2 Dr. Lieber's Encyc. Amer. *Domicil;* Putnam *v.* Johnson, 10 Mass. R. 488; Tanner *v.* King, 11 Louisiana Rep. 175.

3 Pothier, Cout. d'Orleans, ch. 1, § 1, art. 9. See Scrimshire *v.* Scrimshire, 2 Hagg. Ecc. R. 405, 406.

4 1 Voet, ad Pand. Lib. 5, tit. 1, n. 98, p. 346.

5 D'Argentre, ad Leg. Britonum, art. 9, n. 4, p. 26.

for it is not the mere act of inhabitancy in a place which makes it the domicil; but it is the fact, coupled with the intention of remaining there, *animo manendi*[1].

§ 45. It is sometimes a matter of no small difficulty to decide in what place a person has his true or proper domicil. His residence is often of a very equivocal nature; and his intention as to that residence is often still more obscure[2]. Both are sometimes to be gathered from slight circumstances of mere presumption, and from equivocal and conflicting acts. An intention of permanent residence may often be engrafted upon an inhabitancy originally taken for a special or fugitive purpose[3]. And, on the other hand, an intention to change the domicil may be fully announced, and yet no correspondent change of inhabitancy may be actually made[4]. *Domicilium re et facto transfertur, non nudâ contestatione*[5]. The Roman lawyers were themselves greatly puzzled upon this subject by cases of an equivocal nature; and Ulpian, and Labeo, and others, held different opinions respecting them[6]. Thus, to the question, where a person had his domicil, who did his business equally in two places, Labeo answered that he had no domicil in either place[7]. But other jurists, and among them was Ulpian, were of opinion that a man might in such a case have two domicils, one in each place[8]. Celsus seems to have thought that, in such a case, which place was the domicil of the party depended upon his own

---

1 Pothier, Cout. d'Orléans, ch. 1, § 1, art. 9; Encyclop. Amer, art. *Domicil;* Cochin, Œuvres, tom. 5, pp. 4, 5, 6, (4to. edit.).

2 Pothier, Cout. d'Orléans, ch. 1, art. 20; Merlin, Répert., *Domicil,* §§ 2, 6; Bouhier, Cout. de Bourg. ch. 22, § 196 to 206.

3 The Harmony, 2 Robinson, R. 322, 324; Pothier, Cout. d'Orléans, ch. 1, art. 15.

4 See Harvard College *v.* Gore, 5 Pick. R. 370.

5 Dig. Lib. 50, tit. 1, l. 20; Pothier, Pand. Lib. 50, tit. 1, n. 26.

6 Dig. Lib. 50, tit. 1, l. 5; Id. l. 27, §§ 1, 2, 3; Pothier, Pand. Lib. 50, tit. 1, n. 16; Id. nn. 18, 21, 22.

7 Dig. Lib. 50, tit. 1, l. 5; Pothier, Pand. Lib. 50, tit. 1, n. 18; post, § 47.

8 Dig. Lib. 50, tit. 1, l. 6, § 2; Pothier, Pand. Lib. 50, tit. 1, n. 18.

choice and intention[1]. And Julian doubted whether, if he had no fixed choice and intention, he could have two domicils[2].

§ 46. Without speculating upon all the various cases which may be started upon this subject, it may be useful to collect together some of the more important rules which have been generally adopted as guides in the cases which are of most familiar occurrence. First, the place of birth of a person is considered as his domicil, if it is at the time of his birth the domicil of his parents. *Patris originem unusquisque sequatur*[3]. This is usually denominated the domicil of birth or nativity, *domicilium originis*. But, if the parents are then on a visit, or on a journey, (*in itinere*), the home of the parents (at least if it is in the same country) will be deemed the domicil of birth or nativity[4]. If he is an illegitimate child, he follows the domicil of his mother. *Ejus, qui justum patrem non habet, prima origo à matre*[5]. Secondly, the domicil of birth of minors continues until they have obtained a new domicil. Thirdly, minors are generally deemed incapable, *proprio marte*, of changing their domicil during their minority; and, therefore, they retain the domicil of their parents; and if the parents change their domicil, that of the infant children follows it; and if the father dies, his last domicil is that of the infant children[6]. *Placet*

---

[1] Dig. Lib. 50, tit. 1, l. 27, § 2; Pothier, Pand. Lib. 50, tit. 1, n. 18.

[2] Ib.; Somerville *v.* Somerville, 5 Vesey, 750, 786, 790; 2 Domat, Public Law, B. 1, tit. 16, § 3, p. 462; Id. art. 6; Post, § 47.

[3] Cod. Lib. 10, tit. 31, l. 36; 2 Domat, Public Law, B. 1, tit. 16, § 3, art. 10; 1 Boullenois, Observ. 4, p. 53; Voet, ad Pand. Lib. 5, tit. 1, n. 91, 92, 100. See Scrimshire *v.* Scrimshire, 2 Hagg. Eccl. R. 405, 406; Cochin, Œuvres, Tom. 5, pp. 5, 6; Id. 698, (4to. edit.).

[4] Dr. Lieber's Encyc. Amer. art. *Domicil*; Pothier, Cout. d'Orléans, ch. 1, art. 10, 12; Somerville *v.* Somerville, 5 Vesey, 750, 787; 1 Boullenois, Observ. 4, p. 53.

[5] Dig. Lib. 50, tit. 1, l. 9; Pothier, Pand. Lib. 50, tit. 1, n. 3.

[6] Ib.; Pothier, Cout. d'Orléans, ch. 1, art. 12, 16; 2 Domat, Public Law, B. 16, tit. 16, § 3, art. 10; Guier *v.* O'Daniel, 1 Binn. R. 349, 351; Voet, ad Pand. Lib. 5, tit. 1, n. 91, 92, 100.

etiam filium-familias domicilium habere posse; non utique ibi, ubi pater habuit, sed ubicunque ipse constituit[1]. Fourthly, a married woman follows the domicil of her husband[2]. This results from the general principle, that a person who is under the power and authority of another, possesses no right to choose a domicil[3]. *Mulierem, quamdiu nupta est, incolam ejusdem civitatis videri, cujus maritus ejus est*[4]. Fifthly, a widow retains the domicil of her deceased husband until she obtains another domicil. *Vidua mulier amissi mariti domicilium retinet*[5]. Sixthly, *primâ facie*, the place where a person lives is taken to be his domicil until other facts establish the contrary[6]. Seventhly, every person of full age having a right to change his domicil, it follows, that, if he removes to another place with an intention to make it his permanent residence (*animo manendi*), it becomes instantaneously his place of domicil[7]. Eighthly, if

---

1 Dig. Lib. 50, tit. 1, l. 3, 4; Pothier, Pand. Lib. 50, tit. 1, n. 25.—Whether a guardian or father can change the domicil of a minor, or idiot, or insane person, under his charge, has been matter of doubt, upon which different opinions have been expressed by jurists. In the affirmative there may be found, among others, Bynkershoeck, Boullenois, Bretannier. In the negative, Pothier and Mornac. See Pothier, Cout. d'Orléans, ch. 1, art. 17; Bynker. Quæst. Privat. Juris. Lib. 1, ch. 16; Merlin. Répert. *Domicil*, § 5, art. 2, 3; Boullenois, Quest. de la Contrariété des Lois, Quest. 2, p. 40, (edit. 1732). See also Guier *v.* O'Daniel, 1 Binn. R. 349, note; Somerville *v.* Somerville, 5 Ves. 750, 787; Potinger *v.* Wightman, 3 Merivale, R. 67; Cutts *v.* Haskins, 9 Mass. R. 543; Holyoke *v.* Haskins, 5 Pick. R. 20.

2 Voet, ad Pand. Lib. 5, tit. 1, n. 101; Warrender *v.* Warrender, 9 Bligh, R. 89, 103, 104.

3 Dr. Lieber's Encyc. Amer. *Domicil;* Pothier, Cout. d'Orléans, ch. 1, art. 10; 2 Domat, Public Law, B. 1, tit. 16, § 3, art. 11, 13; Merlin, Répert. *Domicil*, § 5.

4 Dig. Lib. 50, tit. 1, l. 38, § 3; Id. Lib. 5, tit. 1. l. 65; Pothier, Pand. Lib. 50, tit. 1, n. 24; 2 Domat, Public Law, B. 1, tit. 16, § 3, art. 12; Voet, ad Pand. Lib. 5, tit. 1, n. 101.

5 Dig. Lib. 50, tit. 1, l. 22, § 1; Pothier, Pand. Lib. 50, tit. 1, n. 28.

6 Bruce *v.* Bruce, 2 Bos. & Pull. 228, note; Id. 230; Bempde *v.* Johnstone, 3 Ves. 198, 201; Stanley *v.* Bernes, 3 Hagg. Eccles. R. 374, 437.

7 Pothier, Cout. d'Orléans, ch. 1, art. 13.

a person has actually removed to another place with an intention of remaining there for an indefinite time, and as a place of fixed present domicil, it is to be deemed his place of domicil notwithstanding he may entertain a floating intention to return at some future period [1]. Ninthly, the place where a married man's family resides is generally to be deemed his domicil [2]. But the presumption from this circumstance may be controlled by other circumstances; for if it is a place of temporary establishment only for his family, or for transient objects, it will not be deemed his domicil [3]. Tenthly, if a married man has his family fixed in one place, and he does his business in another, the former is considered the place of his domicil [4].

§ 47. Eleventhly, if a married man has two places of residence at different times of the year, that will be esteemed his domicil which he himself selects or describes, or deems to be his home, or which appears to be the centre of his affairs, or where he votes or exercises the rights and duties of a citizen [5]. Twelfthly, if a man is unmarried, that is generally deemed the place of his domicil where he transacts his business, exercises his profession, or assumes and exercises municipal duties or privileges [6]. But this rule is of course subject to some qualifications in its application [7]. Thirteenthly, residence in a place, to produce a change of domicil, must be voluntary. If, therefore, it be by constraint or involuntary, as by banishment, arrest, or

---

1 Bruce *v.* Bruce, 2 Bos. & Pull. 228, note; Id. 230; Stanley *v.* Bernes, 3 Hagg. Eccles. R. 374.

2 Pothier, Cout. d'Orléans, ch. 1, art. 20; Bempde *v.* Johnstone, 3 Ves. 198, 201.

3 Pothier, Cout. d'Orléans, ch. 1, art. 15.

4 Ante, § 42, 43, 44.

5 Pothier, Cout. d'Orléans, ch. 1, art. 20; Somerville *v.* Somerville, 5 Ves. 750, 788, 789, 790; Harvard College *v.* Gore, 5 Pick. R. 370; Cochin, Œuvres, Tom. 3, p. 702, (4to. edit.).

6 Somerville *v.* Somerville, 5 Ves. 750, 788, 789.

7 Ib.

imprisonment, the antecedent domicil of the party remains[1]. Fourteenthly, the mere intention to acquire a new domicil, without the fact of an actual removal, avails nothing; neither does the fact of removal without the intention[2]. Fifteenthly, presumptions from mere circumstances will not prevail against positive facts which fix or determine the domicil[3]. Sixteenthly, a domicil once acquired remains until a new one is acquired[4]. It is sometimes laid down that a person may be without any domicil; as, if he quits a place with an intent to fix in another place, it has been said, that, while he is *in transitu* he has no domicil. Julian in the Roman law has so affirmed. *Si quis domicilio relicto naviget, vel iter faciat, quærens quo se conferat, atque ubi constituat; hunc puto sine domicilio esse*[5]. But the more correct principle would seem to be, that the original domicil is not gone until a new one has been actually acquired, *facto et animo*[6]. Seventeenthly, if a man has acquired a new domicil different from that of his birth, and he removes from it with an intention to resume his native domicil, the latter is re-acquired even while he is on his way, *in itinere,* for it reverts from the moment the other is given up[7].

§ 48. The foregoing rules principally relate to changes

---

1 2 Domat, Public Law, B. 1, tit. 16, § 3, art. 14; Merlin, Répertoire, *Domicil,* § 4, art. 3; Bempde *v.* Johnstone, 3 Ves. 198, 202.

2 Ante, § 44.

3 Dr. Lieber, Encyc. Amer. *Domicil;* Ante, § 42, 43, 44.

4 Somerville *v.* Somerville, 5 Ves. 750, 787; Merlin, Répertoire, *Domicil,* § 2; Harvard College *v.* Gore, 5 Mass. R. 370; Cochin, Œuvres, Tom. 5, pp. 5, 6, (4to. edit.).

5 Dig. Lib. 50, tit. 1, l. 27, § 2; Pothier, Pand. Lib. 30, tit. 1, n. 18; 2 Domat, Public Law, B. 1, tit. 16, § 3, art. 9; Ante, § 45.

6 See Jennison *v.* Hapgood, 10 Pick. R. 77; Bruce *v.* Bruce, 2 Bos. & Pull. 228; Cochin, Œuvres, Tom. 5, pp. 5, 6, (4to. edit.); Ante, § 44.

7 The Indian Chief, 3 Rob. 12; La Virginie, 5 Rob. 98.—On the subject of Domicil the learned reader is referred to Fergusson on Marriage and Divorce, Appendix, p. 277 to 362; and Henry on Foreign Law, Appendix A. p. 181, &c.; Cochin, Œuvres, Tom. 5, pp. 4, 5, 6, (4to. edit.); Ex parte Wrigby, 8 Wend. R. 134.

of domicil from one place to another within the same country or territorial sovereignty, although many of them are applicable to residence in different countries or sovereignties. In respect to the latter, there are certain principles which have been generally recognised by tribunals administering public law, or the law of nations, as of unquestionable authority. First, persons who are born in a country are generally deemed to be citizens and subjects of that country[1]. A reasonable qualification of the rule would seem to be, that it should not apply to the children of parents who were *in itinere* in the country, or who were abiding there for temporary purposes, as for health, or curiosity, or occasional business. It would be difficult, however, to assert, that, in the present state of public law, such a qualification is universally established. Secondly, foreigners who reside in a country for permanent or indefinite purposes, *animo manendi*, are treated universally as inhabitants of that country[2]. Thirdly, a national character acquired in a foreign country by residence, changes when the party has left the country *animo non revertendi*, and is on his return to the country where he had his antecedent domicil. And especially if he be *in itinere* to his native country, with that intent, his native domicil revives while he is yet *in transitu;* for the native domicil easily reverts[3]. The moment a foreign domicil is abandoned, the native domicil is re-acquired. But a mere return to his native country without an intent to abandon his foreign domicil, does not work any change of his domicil[4]. Fourthly, ambassadors and other foreign ministers retain their domicil in the country which they represent, and to which they

---

1 1 Black. Comm. 366, 369.

2 Vattel, Lib. 1, ch. 19, § 213.

3 The Venus, 8 Cranch, 278, 281; The Frances, 8 Cranch, 335; The Indian Chief, 3 Rob. 12; Bempde *v.* Johnstone, 3 Ves. 198, 202; The Friendschaft, 3 Wheaton, R. 14; Ommany *v.* Bingham, cited 5 Ves. jun. 756, 757, 765.

4 Ibid.

belong[1]. But a different rule generally applies to Consuls and to other commercial agents, who are presumed to remain in a country for purposes of trade, and who therefore acquire a domicil where they reside[2]. Fifthly, children born upon the sea are deemed to belong and to have their domicil in the country to which their parents belong[3].

§ 49. From these considerations and rules the general conclusion may be deduced, that domicil is of three sorts: domicil by birth, domicil by choice, and domicil by operation of law. The first is the common case of the place of birth, *domicilium originis;* the second is that which is voluntarily acquired by a party, *proprio marte.* The last is consequential, as that of the wife arising from marriage[4].

---

[1] Vattel, B. 1, ch. 19, § 217; The Indian Chief, 3 Rob. 13, 27; The Josephine, 4 Rob. 26.

[2] Ibid.

[3] Vattel, B. 1, ch. 19, § 216; Dr. Lieber's Encyc. Amer. art. *Domicil.*

[4] Pothier, Cout. d'Orléans, ch. 1, art. 12.—Whoever wishes to make more extensive researches upon this subject, may consult Denizart's Dictionary, art. *Domicil;* Encyclopédie Moderne, Tom. 10, art. *Domicil;* Merlin, Répertoire, *Domicil;* 2 Domat, (by Strahan), p. 484, Lib. 1, tit. 16, § 3, of Public Law; Dig. Lib. 50, tit. 1, per tot.; Cod. Lib. 10, tit. 30, l. 2 to l. 7; Voet, ad Pandect. Lib. 5, tit. 1, § 90 to 92; Bynkershoeck, Quæst. Priv. Juris. Lib. 1, ch. 11, and the authorities cited in Dr. Lieber's Encyclopedia Americana, *Domicil;* Henry on Foreign Law, Appendix A. on *Domicil,* p. 181, &c., to p. 209.

CHAPTER IV.

CAPACITY OF PERSONS.

§ 50. We now come to the consideration of the operation and effect of foreign laws in relation to persons, and their capacity, state, and condition[1].

§ 51. All laws which have for their principal object the regulation of the capacity, state, and condition of persons, have been treated by foreign jurists generally as personal laws[2]. They are by them divided into two sorts: those which are universal, and those which are special. The former (universal laws) regulate universally the capacity, state, and condition of persons, such as their minority,

---

[1] Upon the subject of this chapter the learned reader is referred to Burge's Comment. on Col. and Foreign Law, Vol. 1, P. 1, ch. 3, § 1, p. 52, &c.; Id. § 2, p. 92, &c.; Id. § 3, p. 101; and to Id. ch. 4, p. 113 to 135.—Cujaccius defines the condition of a party thus: Conditio pro statu accipitur; puta, pater-familias sit, an filius-familias, servus, an liber. Ætatem, valetudinem, facultates, mores non significat. Liverm. Dissert. § 26, p. 38, cites Cujaccii Observ. Lib. 7, cap. 36.

[2] See Saul v. His Creditors, 17 Martin, R. 569, 596.—Boullenois enumerates as personal all laws which regard majority or minority, emancipation, interdiction for lunacy or prodigality, subjection of married women to the marital power, subjection of minors to the power of their parents and guardians, legitimacy and illegitimacy, excommunication, civil death, infamy, nobility, foreigners and strangers, and naturalization. 1 Boullenois, Observ. 4, pp. 46, 51; Id. 78; Id. 800. See, also, Merlin, Répert. Statut. Pothier enumerates among personal laws those respecting the paternal power, the guardianship of minors, and their emancipation, the age required to make a will, and the marital authority. Pothier, Cout. d'Orléans, introd. ch. 1, art. 6. See, also, Rodenburg, De Div. Stat. tit. 2, ch. 5, § 16; 2 Boullenois, App. 48. Le Brun enumerates among personal statutes those respecting majority, legitimacy, guardianship, and the paternal power. Le Brun, Traité de la Communauté, Liv. 2, ch. 3, § 5, n. 25. See, also, Bouhier, Cout. de Bourg. ch. 23, § 64; 1 Boullenois, ch. 2, Observ. 5, p. 74 to 122; 1 Burge, Comment. on Col. and For. Law, ch. 3, § 1, p. 57, &c.

majority, emancipation, and power of administration of their own affairs. The latter (special laws) create an ability or a disability to do certain acts, leaving the party in all other respects with his general capacity or incapacity[1]. But whether laws purely personal belong to the one class or to the other, they are for the most part held by foreign jurists to be of absolute obligation everywhere, when they have once attached upon the person by the law of his domicil[2]. Boullenois has stated the doctrine among his general principles. Personal laws (says he) affect the person with a quality which is inherent in him, and his person is the same everywhere. Laws purely personal, whether universal or particular, extend themselves everywhere; that is to say, a man is everywhere deemed in the same state, whether universal or particular, by which he is affected by the law of his domicil. *Ces loix personelles affectent la personne d'une qualité, qui lui est inhérente, et la personne est telle partout*[3]. And again: *Les loix pures personnelles, soit personnelles universelles, soit personnelles particulières, se portent partout; c'est-à-dire, que l'homme est partout de l'état, soit universel, soit particulier, dont sa personne est affectée par la loi de son domicil*[4]. *L'état personnel du domicil se parte partout.—Habilis vel inhabilis in loco domicilii*

---

[1] See Henry on Foreign Law, 2, 3; 1 Froland, Mem. ch. 5, p. 81.

[2] How extensively this rule may operate, may be readily understood by simply referring to the different ages at which majority is attained in different countries. By the civil law full age was not attained uutil twenty-four. By the old law of France the age of majority was twenty-five. By the custom of Normandy the age of majority was twenty; by the law of Spain, the age of twenty-four; by that of Holland, twenty-five. In some parts of Germany the majority is attained at twenty-one; in others, at eighteen; in others, at twenty-five; in Saxony, at twenty-one; and so in England, Scotland, Ireland, and the United States of America. The present law of France, for all purposes except marriage, adopts the same age; but for marriage the rule is still twenty-five. 1 Burge, Comm. on Col. and For. Law, P. 1, ch. 4, pp. 113, 114, 115; Post, § 66, note, § 90.

[3] 1 Boullenois, Prin. Gén. p. 4.

[4] 1 Boullenois, Prin. Gén. 10, 18, pp. 4, 6; Observ. 4, 10, 12, 14, 46.

est habilis vel inhabilis in omni loco[1]. Rodenburg says: Whenever inquiry is made as to the state and condition of a person, there is but one judge, that of his domicil, to whom the right appertains to settle the matter. *Cum de statu et conditione hominum quæritur, uno solummodo judici, et quidem domicilii, universum in illâ jus sit attributum*[2]. Hence (says Hertius) the state and quality of a person are governed by the law of the place to which he is by his domicil subjected. Whenever a law is directed to the person, we are to refer to the law of the place to which he is personally subject. *Hinc status et qualitas personæ regitur a legibus loci, cui ipsa sese per domicilium subjecit*[3]. *Quando lex in personam dirigitur, respiciendum est ad leges illius civitatis quæ personam habet subjectam*[4].

§ 51 *a*. Froland, Bouhier, Rodenburg, Paul Voet, Pothier, and others, lay down a similar rule[5]. Froland lays down the doctrine in the following broad terms:—A personal statute not only exerts its authority in the place of the domicil of the party; but its provisions follow the party, and accompany his person in every place where he goes to contract; and it extends over all his property (*biens*), under whatever customs it may be situated: *Et qu'elle influe sur*

---

1 Boullenois, Dissert. sur Quæst. de Contrariété des Loix, (edit. 1732), Disc. Prél. p. 20, Régle. 10.

2 Rodenburg, De Div. Stat. tit. 1, ch. 3, § 4 to 10; 1 Boullenois, pp. 145, 146; Id. Obs. 14, p. 196; 2 Boull. App. pp. 7, 8, 9.

3 Hertius, De Collis. Leg. § 4, n. 5, p. 122; Id. pp. 173, 174, (edit. 1716).

4 Id.; Id. n. 8, p. 123; Id. n. 12, p. 128; Id. p. 175; Id. p. 182, (edit. 1716).

5 1 Froland, Mém. de Statut. ch. 7, § 2, p. 156; Id. Vol. 2, ch. 33, § 8, 9, 10, p. 1574; Bouhier, Cout. de Bourg. ch. 23, § 92, p. 461; Id. ch. 24, § 11, p. 463; Id. ch. 22, § 5 to 11, p. 418; Voet, De Statut. § 4, ch. 2, n. 6, pp. 137, 138; Henry on For. Law, ch. 4, p. 34; Pothier, Introd. Gén. Cout. d'Orléans, ch. 1, art. 7; 1 Hert. Opera, De Coll. § 4, n. 5, p. 121, n. 8, p. 123; Id. pp. 172, 173, 175, (edit. 1716). See also Foelix, Revue Etrangère et Française, &c., 1840, Vol. 7, p. 200 to 216. Since the present work was in the press, I have for the first time seen these Dissertations of Mr. Foelix, and I shall gladly avail myself of his learned labours.

tous ses biens, sous quelques coutumes qu'ils soient assis[1]. Bouhier adopts the very rule of Boullenois: *Quand le statut personnel du domicil est in concurrence avec le statut personnel de la situation des biens celui du domicil dont l'emporter sur celui de la situation des biens*[2]. And again he says: It is necessary constantly to hold, that the capacity or incapacity which the law of the domicil has impressed upon the person should follow the person into all places; so that it shall become utterly impossible that a person, being incapable in the place of his residence, should go to contract in another place where he would have been capable if he had been domiciled there. *Il faut donc tenir pour constant, que la capacité ou l'incapacité, que la loi du domicil a imprimée sur la personne, la suit en tous lieux. En sorte que ce seroit inutilement, que étant incapable au lieu de sa résidence, elle voudroit aller contracter dans un endroit, où il auroit été capable si elle y avoit été domiciliée*[3]. Abraham à Wesel uses language equally strong: *Quotiescunque enim de habilitate atque inhabilitate personæ quæritur, toties domicilii leges et statuta spectanda, ut quocumque persona abeat, id jus sit quod judex domicilii statuerit*[4]; and he applies the rule equally to moveable and immovable property[5]. Pothier says, that personal statutes exert their power upon the persons in relation to their property (*biens*), wherever it may be situated: *Au reste, ces statuts personnels exercent leur empire sur les personnes par rapport à tous leur biens, quelque part, qu'ils soient situés*[6]. Rodenburg says: *Quocumque modo se casus habuerit, contrahentium erit respicere ad suum cujusque domicilii locum, impressam ibidem*

---

[1] 1 Froland, Mém. ch. 7, § 2, p. 156; Id. ch. 5, § 4, p. 89; Post, § 84.

[2] Bouh. Cout. de Bourg. ch. 23, § 91 to 96, p. 461; Id. ch. 22, § 4 to 14, § 19.

[3] Bouhier, Cout. de Bourg. ch. 24, § 11, p. 463.

[4] Wesel, Comm. ad Novell. Constit. Ultraj. art. 18, § 23, pp. 169, 170.

[5] Id. § 25, 27, pp. 170, 173; Liverm. Diss. § 55, p. 56.

[6] Pothier, Introd. Gén. aux Cout. d'Orléans, ch. 1, art. 7; Post, § 69.

personæ qualitatem, aut adeptam domi conditionem cujus ignarus non sit oportet, qui cum alio volet contrahere. Quare Hollandiæ incola major Ultrajecti, minor apud suos, contrahit apud nostrates invalidè. Contra Ultrajectinus lege domicilii major contrahit in Hollandiæ efficaciter; ut maxime ex more regionis istius rerum suarum necdum habentur compos[1]. Stockmannus holds equally strong language: *Unde recte, eum qui inhabilis est in uno loco, etiam in alio inhabilem censeri; et si aliter statuamus, incertus et varius erit personarum status; cum tamen uti personam ubique eandem, ita qualitatem personæ inhærentem, velut ejus accidens, ubique uniformem esse conveniat*[2]. Merlin has expressed it in equally comprehensive terms[3], saying, that the law of the domicil, as to majority or minority, governs in respect even to property (*biens*) situate in another territory[4].

§ 51 *b*. Paul Voet, on the other hand, speaks in far more qualified language, and lays down several rules on the subject. (1.) That a personal statute only affects the subjects of the state or territory wherein it is promulgated, and not foreigners, although doing some business there. *Statutum personale tantum afficit subditos territorii ubi statutum conditum est; non autem forenses, licet ibidem aliquid agentes*[5]. (2.) That as a personal statute does not affect a person out of the territory, it cannot therefore be reputed to be the same without the territory as it is within. *Sta-*

---

1 Rodenburg, De Diversit. Statut. tit. 2, ch. 1, § 2; 2 Boullenois, App. p. 11.

2 Stockmann. Decis. 125, § 6, p. 262, cited also 1 Boullenois, Observ. 6, p. 131; Liverm. Dissert. § 22, p. 35. See also Abraham à Wesel, Comment. ad Nov. Constit. Ultraject. art. 13, n. 24, 25, p. 170 to 172; Liverm. Dissert. § 55, p. 56.

3 Merlin, Répert. Statut.; Id. Majorité, § 5; Id. Autorisation Maritale, § 10.—The like rule is maintained by Burgundus, Stockmans, and D'Argentre, as to personal property and covenants. See Liverm. Diss. pp. 34, 35, 50; Merlin, Répert. Majorité, § 5; Id. Autorisation Maritale, § 10.

4 Merlin, Répert. Majorité, § 5, (edit. Brux. 1827), p. 189.

5 Voet, de Statut. § 4, ch. 2, p. 137, (edit. 1661).

tutum personale non afficit personam extra territorium; sic ut pro tali non reputetur extra territorium, qualis erat intra[1]. (3.) That a personal quality cannot be added out of the territory to a person not a subject. *Personalis qualitas non potest extra territorium addi personæ non subjectæ*[2]. (4.) A personal statute accompanies the person everywhere, in respect to property (*biens*) situate within the territory of the state where the person affected by it has his domicil. *Statutum personale ubique locorum personam comitatur, in ordine ad bona intra territorium statuentis sita, ubi persona affecta domicilium habet*[3]. We shall also presently see that he distinguishes between the effect of a personal statute upon moveable and its effect upon immovable property[4].

§ 52. The result of the doctrine maintained by the jurists above named, except Paul Voet, is, that a person who has attained the age of majority by the law of his native domicil, is to be deemed everywhere the same, of age; and, on the other hand, that a person who is in his minority by the law of his native domicil, is to be deemed everywhere in the same state or condition[5]. Thus, for example, if by the law of the place of his original domicil a person cannot make a will of his property before he is twenty-one years of age, he cannot, if under that age, make a valid will, even of such property as is situate in a place where the law allows persons of the age of fourteen years to make a will of the like property[6]. So, if by the law of her original domicil a woman cannot dispose of her property, except with

---

1 Voet, de Statut. § 4, ch. 2, p. 137, (edit. 1661).

2 Id. p. 138.

3 Ibid.

4 Post, § 52.

5 1 Boullenois, p. 103, &c.; 1 Burge, Comment. on Col. and For. Law, P. 1, ch. 4, p. 113 to p. 135.

6 Pothier, Cout. d'Orléans, ch. 1, art. 7; 1 Boullenois, Prin. Gén. 19, p. 7; Id. Observ. 16, p. 205; 1 Froland, Mém. ch. 7, p. 156; Bouhier, Cout. de Bourg. ch. 22, § 5 to 11; ch. 24, § 7 to 13; Merlin, Répert. Majorité, § 5; Id. Autorisation Maritale, § 10; Rodenburg, De Divers. Statut. tit. 2, ch. 1, § 1; 2 Boullenois, App. p. 11.

the consent of her husband, she is equally prohibited from disposing of her property situate in another place where no such consent is requisite[1]. Many jurists apply this doctrine indiscriminately to moveable as well as to immovable property. Thus, Boullenois says, "If a man has immovable property situate in a place where the age of majority is fixed at twenty-five, and by the law of his own domicil he is of age at twenty, he may at twenty sell or alienate such immovable property. On the other hand, if, by the law of the place where the immovable property is situate, he is of age at twenty, but by the law of his domicil not until twenty-five, he cannot sell or alienate such property until the age of twenty-five[2]." But other jurists distinguish between moveable and immovable property, applying the law of *situs* to the latter, and the law of the domicil to the former[3]. Paul Voet insists throughout upon this distinction, and holds that no personal statute extends to immovable property situate elsewhere. *Non tamen statutum personale sese regulariter extendet ad bona immobilia, alibi sita*[4]. But he admits that such a statute will apply to moveable property, upon the ground, that, wherever it may be situate, it follows the domicil of the owner. *Quin tamen ratione mobilium, ubicunque sitorum, domicilium seu personam domini sequamur, ut tamen spectentur loca, quo destinata, nullus iverit inficias; idque propter expressos textus juris civilis, quibus mobilia certo loco non alligantur, verum secundum juris intellectum personam comitari, eique adhærere judicantur; id quod etiam mores ubique locorum sequuntur*[5]. Burgundus

---

1 Ibid.; Henry on Foreign Law, § 1, p. 31.

2 Boullenois, Dissert. des Quæst. de la Contrar. des Loix, Quest. I[me.] pp. 19, 20; Basnage, Coutum. de Normand. tom. 2, art. 431, p. 243. See also Merlin, Répert. Majorité, § 4, 5.

3 Voet, Burgundus, Stockmans, and Peckius, cited in Merlin, Répert. Majorité, § 5, p. 189, (edit. 1827); Ante, § 52 *a*.

4 P. Voet, ad Statut. § 4, ch. 2, n. 6, p. 138, (edit. 1661); Id. ch. 3, n. 4, p. 148.

5 P. Voet, ad Statut. § 4, ch. 2, n. 9, pp. 139, 140, (edit. 1661).

holds the same opinion: *Consequenter ea quæ sunt personalia, una cum persona circumferuntur, quocumque loco se transtulerit, et per universa territoria, viresque et effectum porrigunt. Realia situm rerum sic spectant, ut territorii limites non excedant; quia rebus ipsis sunt affixa*[1]. Many other jurists maintain the same distinction[2]; but it needs not to be here further insisted on, as it will hereafter come more fully under our consideration.

§ 53. The doctrine, as to the nature and operation of personal statutes, thus asserted by foreign jurists, even with the distinction in its application between moveable property and immovable property, is found attended with many difficulties; and many of these jurists are compelled to make exceptions in its application, which go far to limit, if not to impair, its real force and efficiency[3]. Indeed, the language held by some of them on this subject has not always such a precision, as to its actual extent and operation, as to free the mind from all doubt in regard to the true meaning. Merlin says[4], "The law of the domicil governs the state of the person, and his personal capacity or incapacity. It also governs personal actions, moveables, and moveable effects, in whatever place they may in fact be situated. The power of the law of the domicil extends everywhere, to every thing within its reach or jurisdiction; so that he who is of majority by the law of his domicil, is of the age of majority everywhere. The law of the place where the property (*biens*) is situate regulates the quality and disposition of it. When the law of the domicil, and that of the situation (*situs*), are in conflict with each other, if the question is respecting the state and condition of the person, the law

[1] Burgundus, Tract. 1, § 3, p. 15.

[2] See J. Voet, Stockmannus, and Peckius, cited post, § 54, and 1 Boullenois, Observ. 4, p. 57; Id. Obs. 6, p. 131; Sandius, Lib. 4, tit. 8, Definit. 7, p. 104.

[3] See Livermore, Diss. p. 62 to 106.

[4] Merlin, Répert. Statut. See also Id. Majorité, § 5; Id. Autorisation Maritale, § 10.

of the domicil ought to prevail; if it is respecting the disposition of property (*biens*), the law of the place where they are situate is to be followed[1]." "If several real statutes are found in conflict with each other, each one has its own effect upon the property (*biens*) which it governs[2]." Now, this language of Merlin is in some parts sufficiently broad to cover moveable property as well as immovable property; and yet it is very clear that the disposition of moveable property, and the capacity to dispose of it, are by many foreign jurists, and by Merlin himself, held to be governed by the law of the domicil of the owner[3], according to the maxim, that moveables follow the person: *Mobilia sequuntur personam*[4]. What, perhaps, Merlin intends here to assert may be, that, where a person is incapable by the law of his domicil, he cannot dispose of any of his property situate elsewhere, the incapacity extending even to places where he is not domiciled, and where, by the local law, he would otherwise have capacity to dispose of it. But that, where a person is capable by the law of his domicil, and the question does not respect his personal capacity to dispose of property, but only the extent to which it may be exercised by persons who are capable, there the law of the place where it is situate will govern. Yet he would seem also to intimate that there is or may be some distinction between personal property and real property, (between moveables and immovables,) as to the effect of the operation of the *lex domicilii*[5].

§ 54. In another place Merlin lays down the rule, that a

---

1 Merlin, Répert. Statut. See also Id. Majorité, § 5; Id. Autorisation Maritale, § 10.

2 Ibid.

3 Ibid.

4 Pothier, Cout. d'Orléans, ch. 1, art. 7; 1 Boullenois, Prin. Gén. 16, p. 7; Id. Observ. 19, p. 338, &c.; Rodenburg, ch. 3, § 4, 9, 10, p. 7 to 9; Id. ch. 2, p. 6; Voet, de Stat. § 4, ch. 2, p. 125, § 8; Pothier, De Choses, P. 2, § 3; Livermore, Dissert. 82.

5 See Merlin, Répert. Majorité, § 5, pp. 188, 189, (edit. Brux. 1827).

law which declares a person a major or a minor, who is born within its reach of jurisdiction, is personal, and extends to property (*biens*) situate out of the territory; or, in other words, that a statute respecting majority, full and entire, is personal, and extends to property (*biens*) situate out of the territory. *De statut de la majorité pleine et entière est personnel, et s'étend aux biens situés hors de son territoire*[1]. Thus, if by the law of the place where a person has his domicil, he is of majority at the age of twenty, and has the faculty of disposing of his property, situate there, the same faculty will extend to his property situate in another country, where he would not be capable of alienating until he was twenty-five years of age. And he applies this doctrine equally to moveables and immovables[2]. He admits that the Voets, Burgundus, Stockmans, and Peckius, while they deem such a law to be personal, insist that it does not extend to the disposal of immovables, situate in a foreign country where a different rule as to capacity or majority prevails[3]. Merlin in another place says: "If the law of the domicil declares a person incapable to sell, alien, contract, or to bind himself in any manner to another, it is impossible that his immovables, in whatever

---

1 Merlin, Répertoire, Majorité, § 5, pp. 188, 189, (edit. Brux. 1827).

2 Ibid.

3 See Merlin, Répert. Majorité, § 5, (edit. Brux. 1827), p. 188; Id. Autorisation Maritale, § 10. I do not find the citations from some of these authors accurately given by Merlin; but I believe that the following will be found to verify his statement. J. Voet, ad Pandect. Lib. 4, tit. 4, n. 8, Lib. 23, tit. 2, n. 60, 136; P. Voet, ad Statut. § 4, ch. 3, n. 10, p. 153; Burgundus, Tract. 1, n. 5, 6, 7, 8; Peck, De Testam. Conjug. Lib. 4, ch. 28, Introd. n. 5, 6, 7; Stockmans, Decis. 125, § 6, 9, pp. 262, 263; Christin. Tom. 2, Decis. 56, § 12; Livermore, Dissert. § 47 to 52, p. 50 to 54. Immobilia (says P. Voet) statutis loci ubi sita; mobilia loci statutis ubi testator habuit domicilium. P. Voet de Statut. § 4, ch. 3, n. 10, p. 153, (edit. 1661). Again he adds: Quid circa successionem. Spectabitur loci statuta ubi immobilium sita, non ubi testator moritur. Id. § 9, ch. 1, n. 3, p. 305. See 1 Burge's Comment. on Col. and For. Law, P. 1, ch. 3, § 3, p. 118 to 129.

country they may be situated, can be aliened, bound, or hypothecated by him. Who has ever doubted that the interdiction pronounced against a prodigal or a madman by the judge of his domicil was an obstacle to the alienation of his property (*biens*), which is situate within the reach of another jurisdiction? Who has ever doubted that the tutor (guardian) named by the judge of the domicil, has the right to administer the property (*biens*) which is within the territory of another judge[1]?" This is very bold and uncompromising language; but it will be very difficult to sustain it without many qualifications. It may be added, that the modern Civil Code of France expressly declares, that the laws concerning the condition and capacity of persons govern Frenchmen, even if residing in a foreign country[2]. In the progress of our inquiries it will be found that many exceptions are admitted to exist as to the operation of personal laws, and that the practice of nations by no means justifies the doctrine in the extent to which it is ordinarily laid down by many foreign jurists.

§ 54 *a*. John Voet, on the other hand, is one of the few jurists who insist that personal statutes of all sorts respecting capacity or incapacity, majority or minority, legitimacy or illegitimacy, have no extra-territorial operation, either directly or consequentially. *Verius est* (says he) *personalia non magis quam realia territorium statuentis posse excedere, sive directo, sive per consequentiam*[3]. And he goes on to add: *Ita nec ratio ulla est, cur magis qualitas et habilitas privato per statutum data vel denegata, vires extenderet per ea loca, in quibus diversum quid aut contrarium circa personarum qualitatem lege cautum est. Quod, si hæc cuiquam minus videantur sufficere, is velim mihi rationem modumve expediat, per quem legislator personam, domicilii intuitu sibi suppositam, habilem inhabilemve ad actus gerendos declarans, alte-*

1 Merlin, Répert. Autorisation Maritale, § 10, art. 2.
2 Code Civil of France, art. 3; Post, § 68.
3 Voet, ad Pand. Lib. 1, tit. 4, § 7, p. 40.

rius loci legislatorem, potestate parem cogeret, ut is alienis decretis statutisve pareret, aut rata irritave haberet, quæ judex domicilii talia esse jussit in personâ domicilium, illic fovente; maxime, si fateatur (ut fateri necesse est) pari in parem nullam competere cogendi potestatem. Exponat, obsecro, prodigo declarato, vel infamiâ notato, vel legitimato, vel in ipso pubertatis tempore habili ad testamentum condendum declarato per magistratum Hollandum, ac Ultrajectum se conferente vel immobilia possidente; exponat inquam, quâ juris viâ magistratus Ultrajectinus adstringi posset, ut istum ratione bonorum, in Ultrajectino solo sitorum, pro tali agnosceret; adeoque contractus prodigi Hollandici haberet irritos; dignitates Hollando infamato denegaret; successionem in bona Trajectina ad spurium Hollandum legitimatum pertinentia, tanquam in legitime nati patrimonium, pateretur proximis deferri; testamentum masculi, ante annum ætatis octavum et decimum conditum, juberet ratum esse[1].

§ 55. Hitherto we have been considering cases of the capacity or incapacity of persons, arising from the domicil of origin, where there has been no subsequent change of domicil; as to which, as we have seen, the doctrine of foreign jurists is, that the law of the original domicil is to prevail as to such capacity or incapacity; some of them holding, that it applies to all personal acts whatever, and to all alienation of property, whether moveable or immovable; and others apply it only to personal acts and moveable property where there is a conflict of personal laws. But, suppose that a person has had different domicils, a domicil by birth, and a subsequent domicil by choice when he is *sui juris*,—which is to prevail as to his capacity or incapacity[2]? Hertius does not hesitate to say, that the law of the new domicil is to prevail. *Hinc status et qualitas personæ regitur*

---

1 Voet, ad Pand. Lib. 1, tit. 4, § 7, p. 40.

2 See, on this subject, 1 Burge, Comment. on Col. and For. Law, P. 1, ch. 3, § 3, p. 102 to 106; Id. ch. 4, p. 113 to 125.

a legibus loci (says he) *cui ipsa sese per domicilium subjecit. Atque inde etiam fit, ut quis major hic, alibi, mutato scilicet domicilio, incipiat fieri minor*[1]. The like opinion appears to be held both by Paul Voet and by John Voet[2]. The former says: *Nullum statutum, sive in rem, sive in personam, si de ratione juris civilis sermo instituatur, sese extendit ultra statuentis territorium*[3]. The latter holds, that the change of domicil of a person gives him the capacity or incapacity of his new domicil; so that, if he is of majority by the law of the place of his birth, and he removes to another country, by whose laws he would, according to his age, be a minor, he will acquire the character of his new domicil. *Si quis ex lege domicilii derelicti anno forte vicesimo completo major factus fuerit, translato domicilio ad locum illum, ubi non nisi absoluto viginti quinque annorum curriculo quisque major habetur, non dubitem, quin ex novi domicilii jura incipiat iterum minorennis esse*[4].

§ 55 *a*. Froland thinks this question cannot be answered universally; and he puts a distinction. "If" (says he) "the question is purely as to the state of the person, abstracted from all consideration of property, or subject-matter (*abstractè ab omni materiâ reali*), in this case the law, which first commenced to fix his condition, (that is, the law of the domicil of his birth,) will preserve its force and authority, and follow him wherever he may go. Thus, if, by the law of the domicil of his origin, a person attains his majority at twenty years, and he goes to reside in another

---

[1] 1 Hertii Opera, § 4, n. 5, p. 122; Id. n. 8, p. 123; Id. pp. 173, 175, (edit. 1716).

[2] 2 Boullenois, App. p. 57; Merlin, Répert. Majorité, § 4, (edit. Brux. 1827), p. 186; Merlin, Rep. Retroactif, § 3, art. 9, n. 3; P. Voet, De Stat. § 4, ch. 2, n. 6, pp. 137, 138; Rodenburg, De Div. Stat. p. 2, ch. 1, § 5, 6; J. Voet, ad Pand. Lib. 4, tit. 4, n. 10; 1 Boullenois, Observ. 4, p. 58.

[3] P. Voet, ad Statut. § 4, ch. 2, n. 7, p. 138, (edit. 1661).

[4] 1 J. Voet, ad Pand. Lib. 4, tit. 4, n. 10; Id. Lib. 5, tit. 1, n. 101.

place, where the age of majority is twenty-five years, he is held to be of the age of majority everywhere; and, notwithstanding he is under twenty-five years, he may in his new domicil sell, alien, hypothecate, and contract as he pleases, and *vice versâ*[1]." "But" (he adds) "when the question is as to the ability or disability of a person, who has changed his domicil, to do a certain thing, (*à faire une certaine chose,*) then, that which had governed his power (that is, the law of his original domicil) falls, and fails entirely in this respect, and yields its authority to the law of his new domicil. Thus, if a married woman, by the law of the country of her birth, is not allowed to pass property by will without the consent of her husband, and she acquires a new domicil in another country where no such restriction exists, she has full liberty to dispose of her property in the latter country by will, without the consent of her husband; and *vice versâ*[2]. This is a very nice, if it be not in many cases an evanescent, distinction; and Froland admits that a different doctrine is held by many jurists[3]. But he is not singular in his opinion of the value and importance of this distinction[4]. Boullenois has given to it a qualified sanction[5]. Bouhier also cites the same distinction with approbation, declaring it to be judicious; and he insists, that, in

---

[1] Froland, Mém. ch. 7, § 13, 14, p. 171; Post, § 138, note. See 2 Boullenois, Observ. 32, p. 7 to 11; Bouhier, Cout. de Bourg. ch. 22, § 4 to 10.

[2] 1 Froland, Mém. ch. 7, § 15, p. 172; Post, § 138, note.

[3] Ibid.—Boullenois remarks on this distinction of Froland, that it contains some truth mixed up with much obscurity, and embarrassed with ideas liable to contradiction without being answered. 2 Boullenois, Observ. 32, pp. 8, 9.

[4] See Rodenburg, De Div. Stat. tit. 2, ch. 1, 2, 3, 4, tit. 3, ch. 1, 2, 3, 4, tit. 4, ch. 1, 2, 3, 4; 2 Boullenois, App. p. 1 to 33; Id. p. 1 to 79; Id. p. 84 to 95; 2 Boullenois, ch. 1, Observ. 32, p. 1 to 53; Merlin, Répert. Effet Retroactif, § 3, p. 2, art. 5, n. 3, (edit. Brux. 1827), p. 13 to 15; Id. Majorité, § 4, pp. 186, 187.

[5] 2 Boullenois, Observ. 32, p. 7 to 11.

case of a transfer of the domicil, the law of the original domicil ought in all cases to regulate the personal capacity, and he enlarges on the subject with much ability[1].

§ 56. On the other hand, Burgundus does not hesitate to hold, that the law of the new or actual domicil ought to prevail. After citing the opinion of Baldus and Gail and Imbertus, that the state of the person is to be decided by the place of his domicil: *Ideo, si status personæ inspici debeat, dumtaxat rationem haberi Baldus existimat; cujus opinionem Andreas Gail et Imbertus amplectuntur; adeo ego* (he adds) *nisi ex privilegio vel longissimo usu aliud sit introductum. Proinde ut sciamus uxor in potestate sit mariti necne, quâ ætate minor contrahere posset, et ejusmodi, respicere oportet ad legem cujusque domicilii. Hæc enim imprimit qualitatem personæ, atque adeo naturam ejus afficit, ut quocumque terrarum sit transitura, incapacitatem domi adeptam non aliter quam cicatricem in corpore foras circumferat. Consequenter dicemus, si mutaverit domicilium persona, novi domicilii conditionem induere*[2]. Rodenburg is of the same opinion, upon the ground that the state and condition of the person is wholly governed by the law of his actual domicil; and when that is changed his state and condition change with it: *Personæ enim status et conditio cum tota regatur a legibus loci, cui illa sese per domicilium subdiderit, utique mutato domicilio, mutari et necesse est personæ conditionem*[3]. And he applies the rule indiscriminately to the case of minors and to the case of married women[4]. D'Argentré is also of the same opinion, and says: *Quotiescunque de habilitate aut inhabilitate personarum quæratur, toties do-*

---

1 Bouhier, Cout. de Bourg. ch. 22, § 4 to 10; Id. § 22, cited Merlin, Répert. Autorisation Maritale, § 10, art. 4, (edit. Brux. 1827), p. 243.

2 Burgundus, Tract. 2, n. 5, 6, 7; Post, § 140 *a*. Cited also in Merlin, Repert. Effet Retroactif. § 3, p. 2, art. 5, p. 14, (Brux. edit. 1827).

3 Rodenburg, De Div. Stat. tit. 2, P. 2, ch. 1, n. 3; 2 Boullenois, Observ. 32, pp. 2, 5, 7; Id. App. pp. 56, 57; Post, § 71.

4 Rodenburg, De Div. Stat. tit. 2, P. 2, ch. 1; Id. n. 5, 6; 2 Boullenois, Observ. 32, pp. 2, 5, 7, 8; Id. App. pp. 56, 57; Post, § 71.

micilii leges et statuta spectanda. Ratio est, quia hic abstractù de habilitate personæ, et universali ejus statu quæratur, ideoque personæ a foro domicilii afficiatur. Nam originis locus nusquam in foro considerationem habet, cum aliud domicilium proponitur [1].

§ 57. Boullenois (whose opinions will be stated more fully hereafter [2]) admits the general principle to be as Rodenburg states it, and asserts, that the whole world acknowledges that the state of the person depends on his actual domicil, and that the natural consequence is, that, if a person changes his domicil, and the law of the new domicil is contrary to that of the old one, the state and condition of the person change accordingly [3]. But then he insists that it is necessary to make a distinction between the states and conditions of persons which arise from laws (*droits*) founded in public reasons, admitted by all nations, and which have a cause absolutely unconnected with domicil; so that the moment a man is affected with these states and conditions, the original domicil not having any influence upon them, the new domicil ought not to have any, but merely the public reasons superior to those of domicil, to which all nations pay respect; and other subordinate states and conditions which are in truth founded in public laws (*droits publics*), but for one nation only, or for certain provinces of that nation [4]. Among the former class he enumerates interdiction, or prohibition to do acts by reason of insanity or of prodigality, emancipation by royal authority,

---

[1] D'Argentré, De Leg. Briton. art. 218, n. 47, 49; 1 Boullenois, Obs. 4, p. 53; Post, § 84.—Yet, though the language of D'Argentré is thus explicit, Bouhier seems to suppose that he aided his own opinion, because he has added in another place: Affectâ quocunque modo personâ domicilii lege, aut jure, eo perpetuo sic tenetur, ut ne ullâ mutatione loci sese possit exercere. Bouhier, Cout. de Bourg. ch. 22, § 9. But it is plain that D'Argentré is here speaking of a mere change of place, without a change of domicil. D'Argentré, De Leg. Briton. art. 218, § 13, p. 603.

[2] Post, § 71.

[3] 2 Boullenois, Observ. 32, pp. 10, 13.

[4] 2 Boullenois, Observ. 32, pp. 10, 11, 13, 19; Post, § 71.

legitimacy of birth, nobility, infamy, &c. These, he contends, are never altered by any change of domicil; but that, having at first fixed the condition of the person, the change of domicil does not cause them to cease[1]. Among the latter class he enumerates the community of property between husband and wife; the state of the husband as to the marital power; the state of the father as to real rights of the paternal power, and other subordinate states. These, he contends, sometimes are affected by a change of domicil, and sometimes are not[2]. Some of this last class (he adds) affect the person, at least *in vim conventionis tacitæ;* and this, according to the opinion of a great number of jurists, is the case in respect to the law of the community of property between husband and wife[3]. Others of the same class affect the person *in vim solius legis:* such is the statute or law, *Senatus-consultum Velleianum,* which prohibits married women from making obligatory personal contracts with others[4]. Boullenois himself holds, that the capacity of married women is governed by the law of the actual or new domicil[5]; but that the capacity of minors is governed by the law of their domicil of birth[6]. He also holds that the paternal power is regulated by the domicil of birth[7]. But here again he distinguishes between moveable property and immovable property; holding, that the law of the

---

1 2 Boullenois, Observ. 32, p. 11; Post, § 71; 1 Boullenois, Observ. 4, pp. 59, 64.

2 2 Boullenois, Observ. 32, pp. 11, 12, 13; Post, § 71.

3 2 Boullenois, Observ. 32, p. 11; Post, § 143 to 171.

4 2 Boullenois, Observ. 32, pp. 11, 13; Ante, § 15; Post, § 71, 425.

5 2 Boullenois, Observ. 32, p. 13 to 19; 1 Boull. Obs. 4, p. 61; Post, § 71.

6 2 Boullenois, Observ. 32, pp. 19 to 31; 1 Boullenois, Obs. 4, pp. 53, 54; Id. Dissert. Mixtes, Quest. 2, p. 40 to 62; Id. Quest. 20, p. 406 to 447.

7 2 Boullenois, Observ. 32, p. 31 to 53; 1 Boull. Observ. 32, p. 68; Post, § 71.

domicil of birth governs as to the former, and the law of the situation (*situs*) as to the latter[1].

§ 58. Merlin, after citing the opinions of other jurists, formerly came to the conclusion, that the law of the place of birth, and not that of the new domicil, ought to govern equally in all these cases of minority, of paternal power, and of marital power after marriage; and he expressed surprise, and not without reason, that Boullenois should have attempted to distinguish between them[2]. It is certainly not for me to interfere in such grave controversies between these learned jurists, differing from each other, sometimes in leading principles, and sometimes in deductions and distinctions applicable to principles in which they agree. *Non nostrum inter vos tantas componere lites.* Yet Merlin himself, after having advocated this doctrine as best founded in principle, although involving some inconveniences, still insisted, that, upon such a removal to a new domicil, the capacity of a person to dispose of his moveable property by a testament, is to be governed by the law of the new domicil; because the state of a person has no influence as to the distribution of his moveable property after his death; and the capacity to make a will resulting from age, has nothing in common with what is properly called the state of the person; which is so true, that his state is governed by the domicil, and the situation decides solely concerning the age at which a person may dispose of moveable property upon his death[3]. It seems, however, that Merlin has since, upon farther reflection, come to a different conclusion; and he may be now numbered among those who

---

[1] 1 Boullenois, Observ. 32, p. 32 to 53; Id. Dissert. Mixtes, Quest. 20, p. 406 to 447.

[2] Merlin, Répert. Autorisation Maritale, § 10, art. 4, (edit. Brux. 1827), pp. 243, 244; Post, § 139.

[3] Merlin, Répert. Majorité, § 4; Id. Effet Retroactif, § 3, n. 2, art. 5, n. 3; Id. Autorisation Maritale, § 10, art. 4, (edit. Brux. 1827).

support the doctrine, that the law of the new domicil ought to govern in all cases, whether they respect capacity or minority, or the paternal power, or the marital power after marriage[1].

§ 59. Pothier holds the doctrine in the most unqualified terms, that the law of the new or actual domicil ought in all cases to govern; and that the change of domicil discharges the party from the law of his former domicil, and subjects him to that of his new domicil. *Le changement de domicile delivre les personnes de l'empire des lois du lieu du domicile qu'elles quittent, et les assujettit à celles du lieu du nouveau domicile qu'elles acquierent*[2]. Whatever doubts may be suggested of the correctness of his opinion in a juridical sense, it must be admitted to possess the strong recommendation of general convenience and certainty of application[3].

§ 60. Huberus, instead of relying upon the mere quality of laws as personal, or real, or mixed, lays down the following doctrine:—Personal qualities impressed by the laws of any place, surround and accompany the person, wherever he goes, with this effect, that in every place he enjoys and is subject to the same law which other persons elsewhere enjoy or are subject to. *Qualitates personales certo loco alicui jure impressas, ubique circumferri et personam comitari, cum hoc effectu, ut ubique locorum eo jure, quo tales personæ alibi gaudent vel subjecti sunt, fruantur et subjiciantur*[4]. Therefore, (he adds), those who with us are under tutelage

---

1 See Merlin, Répert. Effet Retroactif, § 3, n. 2, art. 5, p. 13, &c., (edit. Brux. 1827); Id. Autorisation Maritale, § 10, art. 4, pp. 243, 244; Id. Majorité, § 4, pp. 187, 188. See, also, Id. Testament, § 1, n. 5, art. 1, 2, p. 309 to 324; Post, § 139.

2 Pothier, Cout. d'Orléans, ch. 1, art. 1, n. 13.—We shall presently see that Lord Stowell holds the opinion, that a change of domicil may change the state and condition of the party; as, for example, if he be a slave. See The Slave Grace, 2 Hagg. Adm. R. 94, 113; Post, 96, § 96 *a*.

3 See 1 Burge, Comment. on Col. and For. Law, P. 1, ch. 3, § 3, pp. 118, 119.

4 Huberus, De Conflict. Leg. Lib. 1, tit. 3, § 12.

or guardianship, such as minors, prodigals, and married women, are everywhere deemed to be persons subject to such guardianship, and possess and enjoy the rights which the law of the place attributes to persons under guardianship[1]. Hence, he, who in Friezeland has obtained the privilege of age (*veniam ætatis*), contracting in Holland, will not there be entitled to restitution *in integrum*, as if he were a minor[2]. In other words, he, who in Friezeland has obtained the privilege of an exemption from the disabilities of his minority, will not, if he afterwards contracts in Holland, be deemed entitled to the privilege of being there held a minor, so as to exempt him from liability on his contract, (*Ibi non restituitur in integrum*[3]). He who is declared a prodigal here cannot enter into a valid contract or be sued in another place. *Hinc, qui apud nos in tutelâ curâve sunt, ut adolescentes, filii-familias, prodigi, mulieres nuptæ, ubique pro personis, curæ subjectis habentur, et jure, quod cura singulis in locis tribuit, utuntur,* [*et*] *fruuntur. Hinc, qui in Frisiâ veniam ætatis impetravit, in Hollandiâ contrahens, ibi non restituitur in integrum. Qui prodigus*

---

1 Huberus, De Conflict. Leg. Lib. 1, tit. 3, § 12.

2 Ibid. Under the Roman law the Prætor by his edict declared, that he would grant redress in regard to transactions with minors under twenty-five years of age. Quod cum minore quam viginti-quinque annos natu, gestum esse dicetur; uti quæque res erit, animadvertam. Dig. Lib. 4, tit. 4, l. 1; Pothier, Pand. Lib. 4, tit. 4, n. 1. But those persons who had obtained the privilege of age were not entitled to any such relief. Eos, qui veniam ætatis à principali clementiâ impetraverunt, etiamsi minus idoneè rem suam administrare videantur, in integrum restitutionis auxilium impetrare non posse, manifestissimum est; ne hi, qui cum eis contrahunt, principali authoritate circumscripti esse videantur. Cod. Lib. 2, tit. 45, l. 1; Pothier, Pand. Lib. 4, tit. 4, n. 4. The action thus given to minors was often called, Restitutio in integrum. Vicat. Vocab. voce Restitutio.

3 The Veniam Ætatis is a privilege granted by the prince or sovereign, whereby the party is entitled to act, and to have all the powers to act sui juris, as if he were of full age. See Vicat. Vocab. voce "Veniam Ætatis." Calvinus, Lex. Jurid. h. v.; Cod. Lib. 2, tit. 45, l. 1; Rodenburg, De Diversit. Statut. tit. 1, ch. 3, § 9; 2 Boullenois, App. 9; 1 Burge, Comment. on Col. and For. Law, P. 1, ch. 3, § 3, p. 116.

hic est declaratus, alibi contrahens valide non obligatur, neque convenitur[1]. Again, in some provinces those who are over twenty-one years of age are deemed of majority, and may alienate their immovable property, and exercise other rights less important, even in those places where no one is deemed of majority until he has attained twenty-five years; because all other governments give effect by comity to the laws and adjudications of other cities in regard to their subjects, so always that there be no prejudice to their own subjects or their own law[2].

§ 61. He goes on to remark, "There are some persons who thus interpret the effect of laws respecting the quality of persons—that he who in a certain place is a major or a minor, in puberty or beyond it, a son subject to paternal power, or a father of a family, under or out of guardianship, everywhere enjoys and is subject to the same law which he enjoys, and to which he is subject, in that place where he first becomes or is deemed such. So that whatever he could do or could not do in his own country, the same is allowed and prohibited to him to do[3]. This seems to me unreasonable, and would occasion too great a confusion of laws and a burthen upon neighbouring nations arising from the laws of others[4]. The importance of this thing will be made plain by a few examples. Thus, an unemancipated son (*filius-familias*), who cannot in Friezeland make a testament, goes into Holland and there makes a testament; it is asked whether it has any validity? I suppose it is valid in Holland, according to my first and second rule[5], because the laws bind all those who are within any territory; neither is it proper (*civile sit*), that Hollanders, in respect to business done among themselves, should, neglecting their

---

1 Huberus, De Conflict. Leg. Lib. 1, tit. 3, § 12.

2 Huberus, Lib. 1, tit. 3, § 12; Ante, § 29; Post, § 139, 145.

3 Huberus, Lib. 1, tit. 3, § 12.

4 Ibid.

5 Ante, § 29.

own laws, be governed by foreign laws[1]. But it is true that this testament would not have effect in Friezeland according to the third rule[2]; because in that way nothing would be more easy than for our citizens to elude our laws, as they might be evaded every day[3]. But such a testament would be of validity elsewhere, even where an unemancipated son could not make a will; for there the reason of evading the laws of a country by its own citizens ceases; for in such a case the fact (of evasion) would not be committed[4]."

§ 62. This doctrine of Huberus is not in its full extent maintainable, and especially in relation to immovable property; it is universally repudiated by the common law, and in many cases is also denied by foreign jurists[5]. Lord Stowell has expressly said, that he does not mean to affirm that Huberus is correct in laying down as universally true, that, being of age in one country, a man is of age in every other country, be the law of majority of the latter what it may[6].

§ 63. Without venturing further into the particular opinions maintained by foreign jurists on this subject, under all its various aspects, (a task, considering the great diversity of judgment among them, which would be almost endless), it may perhaps be useful to place before the reader some of the doctrines maintained by foreign jurists, which appear best established, or, at least, which seem to have the sanction of such authority as has given them a superior weight and recommendation in the jurisprudence of continental Europe[7].

---

1 Huberus, Lib. 1, tit. 3, § 13.

2 Ante, § 29.

3 Huberus, Lib. 1, tit. 3, § 13.

4 Ibid.

5 See the Authors cited by Merlin, Répert. Majorité, § 5; Post, § 363 to 373, § 474 to 479.

6 Ruding *v.* Smith, 2 Hagg. Ecc. Rep. 391, 392.

7 See 1 Burge, Comment. on Col. and For. Law, P. 1, ch. 3, § 3, p. 118 to 129.

§ 64. In the first place, the acts of a person done in the place of his domicil, in regard to property situated therein, are to be judged of by the laws of that place, and will not be permitted to have any other legal effect elsewhere than they have in that place[1]. There are exceptions to this rule, but they result from some direct or implied provisions of law in the customary or positive code of the country in which the act comes in judgment, applying to the very case; for it is competent for a country, if it pleases, to prescribe its own rule for all cases arising out of transactions in foreign countries, whenever any rights under them are brought into controversy, or one sought to be enforced in its own tribunals. If, therefore, a person has a capacity to do any act, or is under an incapacity to do any act by the law of the place of his domicil, the act, when done there, will be governed by the same law whenever its validity may come into contestation in any other country. Thus, an act done by a minor, in regard to his property situate in the place of his domicil, without the consent of his guardian, if valid by the law of the place of his domicil where it is done, will be recognised as valid in every other place; if invalid there, it will be held invalid in every other place. So, if a married woman, who is disabled by the law of the place of her domicil from entering into a contract, or from transferring any property therein without the consent of her husband, should make a contract, or transfer any property situated therein, the transaction will be held invalid and a nullity in every other country[2]. This seems to be a principle generally recognised by all nations in the absence of any positive or implied municipal regulations to

---

1 "Statutum personale," (says Paul Voet), "ubique locorum personam comitatur, in ordine ad bona intra territorium statuentis sita, ubi persona affecta domicilium habet." P. Voet, De Statut. § 4, ch. 2, § 6, p. 138, (edit. 1661). See 1 Burge, Comment. on Col. and For. Law, P. 1, ch. 4, p. 113.

2 1 Boullenois, Prin. Gén. 6; 1 Froland, Mém. des Statuts, ch. 7, p. 156.

the contrary; according to the maxim, *quando lex in personam dirigitur, respiciendum est ad leges illius civitatis quæ personam habet subjectam*[1].

§ 65. In the next place, another rule, directly connected with the former, is, that the personal capacity or incapacity attached to a party by the law of the place of his domicil, is deemed to exist in every other country, (*qualitas personam, sicut umbra, sequitur,*) so long as his domicil remains unchanged, even in relation to transactions in any foreign country where they might otherwise be obligatory[2]. Thus, a minor, a married woman, a prodigal, or a spendthrift, a person *non compos mentis,* or any other person who is deemed incapable of transacting business (*sui juris*), in the place of his or her domicil, will be deemed incapable

---

[1] 1 Hertii Opera, De Collis. Leg. § 4, art. 8, p. 123, (edit. 1737); Id. p. 175, (edit. 716).—The learned reader is referred for proofs to Huberus, De Conflict. Leg. Lib. 1, tit. 3, § 12, 13, 15; 1 Boullenois, Prin. Gén. 10, 12, 16, 17; Id. Observ. 8, tit. 1, ch. 3, p. 145, &c.; 2 Boullenois, Observ. 32, tit. 2, ch. 1, p. 1 to 53; Rodenburg, De Divers. Statut. ch. 3; 2 Boull. App. p. 7; Id. tit. 2, ch. 1; 2 Boull. App. p. 10; P. Voet, De Statut. § 4, ch. 2; Id. ch. 3, pp. 128, 143, (edit. 1661); 1 Hertii Opera, De Collis. Leg. § 4, 8, p. 123, (edit. 1737); Id. p. 175, (edit. 1716); Froland, Mém. des Statuts, P. 1, ch. 5, 7; Id. P. 2, ch. 33; Bouhier, Cout. de Bourg. ch. 22, 23, 24.

[2] "Ergo conditio personæ a causa domicilii tota regitur. Nam ut consentiunt Doctores, idem sunt forum sortiri et statutis subjici; et unusquisque talis esse præsumitur, qualis est dispositio statuti suæ patriæ. Proinde, ut sciamus, uxor in potestate sit mariti necne, quà ætate minor contrahere possit, et ejusmodi respicere oportet ad legem cujusque domicilii." Burgundus, Trac. 2, n. 6; 1 Boullenois, Observ. 4, p. 53. "C'est ainsi, (says Boullenois,) que la majorité et la minorité du domicil ont lieu partout, même pour les biens situés ailleurs." 1 Boullenois, Prin. Gén. art. 6; Id. Observ. 10, 12, and 46. "Celui qui est majeur (says Froland) suivant la coutume, où il a pris naissance, et sous laquelle il réside, est majeur partout, et peut comme tel, aliener, hypotequer, vendre ses biens, sans considérer, si suivant la loi de leur situation il seroit mineur." 1 Froland, Mém. des Statuts, ch. 7, p. 156. Rodenburg holds the same doctrine. Rodenburg, De Divers. Stat. tit. 2, ch. 1. So D'Argentré: "Quotiescunque de habilitate aut de inhabilitate personarum quæratur, toties domicilii leges et statuta spectanda." D'Argentré, de Briton. Leg. des Donations, art. 218, Gloss. 7, n. 48, 49. 1 Livermore, Diss. 34. So, John Voet: "Potius domicilii leges observandas

everywhere, not only as to transactions in the place of his or her domicil, but as to transactions in every other place[1].

§ 66. Thus, according to this rule, if an American citizen domiciled in an American State, as, for instance, in Massachusetts, where he would be of age at twenty-one years, should order a purchase of goods to be made for him in a foreign country, where he would not be of age until twenty-five years old, the contract will nevertheless be obligatory upon him[2]. On the other hand, a person domiciled in such foreign country, of twenty-one years of age only, who should order a like purchase to be made of goods in Massachusetts, will not be bound by his contract; for he will be deemed a minor and incapable of making such a contract[3]. The same rule will govern in relation to the disposition of personal or moveable property, by any person who is a minor or a major in the place of his domicil; for it will be valid or not, according to the law of the place of his domicil, wherever such property may be situate[4]. There are exceptions also made to this rule, but they stand upon peculiar grounds, as expounded by foreign jurists.

§ 66 *a*. The like rule will apply to the capacity and in-

---

existimem; quoties in quæstione, an quis minor vel majorennis sit, obtinuit, id dijudicandum esse ex lege domicilii; sic ut in loco domicilii minorennis, ubique terrarum pro tali habendus sit, et contra." J. Voet, ad Pand. Lib. 4, tit. 1, § 29. See also Fœlix, Conflict des Lois-Revue Etrang. et Fran. Tom. 7, 1840, p. 200 to 216.

1 1 Boullenois, Prin. Gén. 10, 19, et Observ. 4, 12, 16, p. 5; 1 Froland, Mém. des Stat. ch. 7, pp. 155, 156; Rodenburg, De Divers. Stat. tit. 2, ch. 1; 2 Boullenois, App. p. 10.

2 By the law of some commercial countries the age of twenty-five years is that of majority. This was the old law of France; but the modern code has changed the age of majority to twenty-one, except as to marriage without the consent of parents. Code Civil of France, art. 488; Id. art. 148. See also Rodenburg, De Diversit. Statut. tit. 2, ch. 1; 2 Boullenois, App. p. 10.

3 Huberus, De Conflictu Legum, Lib. 1, tit. 3, § 12.

4 1 Froland, Des Stat. Mém. ch. 7, pp. 157, 158; 1 Boullenois, Prin. Gén. 6, 19; Id. Observ. 4, 12; Rodenburg, De Divers. Stat. tit. 2, ch. 1; 2 Boullenois, App. p. 10.

capacity of married women. If, by the law of the place of the domicil of the husband, a married woman has a capacity to sue, or to make a contract, or to ratify an act, her acts so done will be held valid everywhere. On the contrary, if she is deprived of such capacity by the law of the domicil of her husband, that incapacity exists in relation to all the like acts and contracts, even when done in a foreign country, or with reference to property in a foreign country [1].

§ 67. The ground upon which this rule has been generally adopted by many eminent continental jurists, doubtless is that suggested by Rodenburg, viz. the extreme inconvenience which would otherwise result to all nations from a perpetual fluctuation of capacity, state, and condition, upon every accidental change of place of the person or of his moveable property [2]. The language of Rodenburg is: *Quid igitur rei in causa est, quod personalia statuta territorium egrediantur? Unicum hoc ipsa rei natura ac necessitas invexit, ut, cùm de statu ac conditione hominum quæritur, uni solummodo Judici, et quidem domicilii, universum in illa jus sit attributum: cùm enim ab uno certoque loco statum hominis legem accipere necesse esset, quod absurdum, earumque rerum naturaliter inter se pugna foret, ut in quot loca quis iter faciens, aut navigans delatus fuerit, totidem ille statum mutaret aut conditionem; ut uno eodemque tempore hîc sui Juris, illic alieni futurus sit; uxor simul in potestate viri, et extra eandem sit; alio loco habeatur quis prodigus, alio frugi; ac præterea quod persona certo loco non affigeretur, cùm res soli loco fixæ citra incommodum ejusdem legibus subjaceant, summâ providentiâ constitutum est, ut à loco domicilii, cui quis larem fovendo se subdiderit, statum ac conditionem induat: illis Legislatoribus, pro soli sui genio, optime omnium compertum habentibus, quâ judicii maturitate*

---

[1] Garnier *v.* Poydras, 13 Louis. R. 177.

[2] Rodenburg, De Divers. Stat. tit. 1, ch. 3, n. 4; 2 Boullenois, App. p. 8. See also 1 Boullenois, Observ. 4, pp. 48, 49.

polleant subditi, ut possint constituere, qui eorum, ac quando ad sua tuenda negotia indigeant autoritate. Hæc igitur personarum qualitas ac conditio, ubi venerit applicanda ad res aut actus alterius territorii, jam indirecte, ac per consequentiam vis illius personalis Statuti, extra statuentis pertinget locum: cùm et aliàs non insolitum sit multa indirecte permitti et per consequentiam, quæ directe et expressim non valerent. Nec est, quod quemquam turbet, quod et illa Statuta extra territorii limites diximus excurrere, quibus nominatim status hominum in universum non discutitur, quæ in incertos personales actus à persona exercendos, prohibendo eos aut permittendo, concepta sunt[1].

§ 68. The modern law of France, as it is laid down by Pardessus, is to the same effect[2]. "No act, whatsoever may be its nature," (says he), "can be stipulated except by persons capable of binding themselves; and the general consent of civilized nations has allowed, that, whatever concerns the capacity of a person should be regulated by the laws of the country to which he belongs. A person declared incapable by the law of the country of which he is a subject cannot be relieved of that incapacity, except by the law of that country, as well in regard to the acts which it permits him to do, as to the conditions which it prescribes in doing them. Thus, French minors, incapable of binding themselves by engagements of commerce, unless they are emancipated or authorized, cannot bind themselves in commercial transactions in a foreign country, even when the law of that country does not require the like conditions. So, French married women, who are not public traders, are not deemed to have contracted valid engagements, even in commerce, unless they should be authorized by their husbands. Their personal incapacity follows them everywhere. For the same reason the French tribunals will not consider as

---

[1] 2 Boullenois, App. p. 8; Fœlix, Conflict des Lois, Revue Etrang. et Fran. Tom. 7, 1840, p. 200 to 216.

[2] 5 Pardessus, De Droit Commercial, Vol. 5, art. 1482, p. 248.

valid any commercial engagements entered into in France by minors or persons of either sex, who, by the law of their own country, are rendered incapable, even though the law to which they are subject should require other conditions than those prescribed by the law of France. For it is the interest of one government to respect in favour of the subject of another government, when he is cited before its tribunals, the laws upon the faith of which that foreigner has contracted, and not to tolerate him in withdrawing himself by a mere change of jurisdiction from the laws which regulate his capacity, and to which he is bound by his allegiance wherever he may inhabit. Without this the government would expose its own subject to be treated with a like injustice by what is denominated the right of retaliation or reprisals [1]. So also a foreigner, born under a legislation which does not require certain formalities like those of France, by which a minor or other person of either sex may be authorized to engage in commerce, cannot avail himself of our laws to escape from his engagement. One has no right to invoke for the same object two different legislations; the law which regulates the capacity of the foreigner, regulates it everywhere. It would be unjust that he should derive from our legislation, to which he is not subjected, an advantage which is not granted to him by his own proper legislation." Yet Pardessus is compelled to admit that there may be exceptions to the doctrine. Thus, for example, he says, that certain particular prohibitions, such as the prohibition of persons who are nobles, or possessing a certain dignity, to sign bills of exchange or other engagements which carry with them a right to arrest the body, ought not to govern transactions of that sort in foreign countries. However, the modern Civil Code of France [2] lays down the general rule in the broadest terms, and declares that the laws concerning the

---

[1] 5 Pardessus, P. 6, tit. 7, ch. 2, § 1, art. 1482; Henry on Foreign Law, Appendix, pp. 221, 222. See Cochin, Œuvres, Tom. 1, p. 154, (4to. edit.).

[2] Pardessus, De Droit Commerc. Vol. 5, art. 1483, p. 250; Post, § 74.

state and capacity of persons govern Frenchmen, even if resident in a foreign country: *Les loix concernant l'état et la capacité des personnes régissent les François même résidant en pais étranger*[1].

§ 69. In the third place, another rule is, that, upon a change of domicil, the capacity or incapacity of the person is regulated by the law of the new domicil[2]. Pothier lays down this rule, as we have seen, in emphatic terms:—"The change of domicil" (says he) "delivers persons from the empire of the laws of the place of the domicil they have quitted, and subjects them to those of the new domicil they have acquired." *Le changement de domicile délivre les personnes de l'empire des lois du lieu du domicile qu'elles quittent, et les assujettit à celles du lieu de nouveau domicile qu'elles acquièrent*[3]. Burgundus adopts the same rule: *Consequenter dicemus, si mutaverit domicilium persona, novi domicilii conditionem induere*[4]. So Rodenburg: *Personæ enim status et conditio cum tota regatur a legibus loci, cui illa sese per domicilium subdiderit, utique mutato domicilio mutari et necesse est personæ conditionem*[5]. Froland, indeed, (as we have already seen,) maintains a different doctrine, in which to some extent he is followed by Bouhier and others[6]. The doctrine, however, which is most generally approved is

---

1 Code Civil of France, art. 3; Ante, § 54.

2 Consult 1 Burge, Comment. on Col. and For. Law, P. 1, ch. 3, § 3, pp. 102, 103; Id. P. 1, ch. 4, p. 118 to 128, where the principal authorities are collected.

3 Pothier, Coutum. d'Orléans, ch. 1, art. 1, n. 13; Ante, § 51.

4 1 Boullenois, Obs. 4, p. 53; Ante, § 51 *a*, § 56; Burgundus, Tract. 2, n. 7, p. 61.

5 Rodenburg, De Divers. Stat. tit. 2, P. 2, ch. 1, n. 3; 2 Boullenois, App. p. 56; 2 Boullenois, ch. 1, and Obs. 32; Ante, § 51 *a*.

6 1 Froland, Mém. ch. 7, § 13, 14, 15, pp. 171, 172; Id. ch. 33, § 4, 5, 6, 7, p. 1575 to 1582; Ante, § 55 *a*; Bouhier, Coutum. de Bourg. ch. 22, § 17 to 20, 31, p. 419 to 421. See also Henry on Foreign Law, Appendix A. p. 196. See 2 Boullenois, p. 1 to 53; Merlin, Répertoire, Majorité, § 5; Autorisation Maritale, § 10; Effet Retroactif, § 3, 2, art. 5; Ante, § 55, 55 *a*, 56.

that which has been maintained by Pothier, although it is contradicted by the modern Code of France[1].

§ 70. Having stated these rules, it may be proper to notice a distinction which in many cases may have a material operation. So far as respects the capacity or incapacity of the person, the law of the new domicil would probably prevail in the tribunals of the country of that domicil as to all rights, contracts, and acts done or litigated there. The same law would probably have a like recognition in every other country, except that of the original or native domicil. The principal difficulty which would arise would be, how far any rights, contracts, and acts would be recognised by the latter, where they were dependent upon the law of the new domicil, which should be in conflict with its own law on the same subject. It is precisely under circumstances of this sort that the third axiom of Huberus may be presumed to have a material influence, viz. that a nation is not under any obligation to recognise rights, contracts, or acts which are to its own prejudice, or in opposition to its own settled policy[2].

§ 71. Boullenois was sensible of this distinction, as we have already seen[3], and says: "On this point it is necessary to distinguish from others the states and conditions of persons which arise from laws (*qui sont des droits*) founded upon public reasons, admitted among all nations, and which have a foundation or cause absolutely foreign from the domicil; so that the domicil, from the moment a man is affected with these states or conditions, not influencing it in any manner, the new domicil ought not to influence it, but merely the public reasons superior to those of the domicil, to which all nations pay respect. Such are

---

1 Code Civil of France, art. 3. See also Cochin, Œuvres, Tom. 1, p. 154, (4to. edit.); Ante, § 51 *a*, 68.

2 See, on this subject, 1 Burge, Comment. on Col. and For. Law, P. 1, ch. 3, § 3, p. 129 to 134.

3 Ante, § 57; 2 Boullenois, Observ. 32, pp. 10, 11, 13, 19.

interdiction or incapacity from insanity or from prodigality, emancipation from the paternal power by royal authority, legitimacy of birth, nobility, infamy, &c. These states do not change with the change of domicil; and of these it is properly said, that, having at first fixed the condition of the person, the change of domicil does not put an end to them[1]." And he adds: "But there are states and conditions more subordinate, and which in truth arise from public laws, (*que sont, à la verité, des droits publics,*) but are for one nation only, or for some provinces of the same nation. Such are the state of community or noncommunity (of property), among married persons (*conjoints*); the state of the husband as to his marital power; the state of the father as to the rights of property from the paternal power; and these subordinate states are almost infinitely various[2]." In regard to these latter states, he admits the embarrassment of laying down any general rules as to the effect of a change of domicil[3]. And he concludes his remarks by saying: "In the occurrence of so great a number of laws, (having enumerated several) which have so different an effect, what ought one to do in the decision of the questions which may be presented by them? For myself, I do not see any other means than these[4]." He then proceeds to lay down these rules: (1.) First, to follow the general principles which declare that the person should be affected by the state and condition which his domicil gives him. (2.) Secondly, not to derogate from these principles, except when the spirit of justice and necessity of not injuring the rights of parties require that it should be departed from. (3.) Thirdly, not to impair these principles, when otherwise the law furnishes the means of remedying any wrong which the change of

---

1 2 Boullenois, Observ. 32, p. 10, 11, 19.

2 2 Boullenois, Observ. 32, p. 11.

3 Ibid.

4 2 Boullenois, Observ. 32, p. 12.

domicil might cause [1]. Or, in other words, he affirms: first, that the law of the domicil ought generally to be followed, as to the state and condition of the persons; secondly, that it ought not to be derogated from, except so far as the spirit of justice, and the necessity of not injuring the rights of parties, require a departure; thirdly, that the general rule ought not to be impaired when the law will otherwise furnish means to remedy any injury which the change of domicil may occasion [2]. He goes on to declare what he supposes to be perfectly consistent with this doctrine, that, when a person in the domicil of his birth (*domicilium originis*) has arrived at the age of majority, and he afterwards removes to another place, where at the same years he would still be a minor, the law of the domicil of his birth ought to prevail [3]. For instance, if a person, who, by the law of the domicil of his birth is of age at twenty, removes to another place after that age where the minority extends to twenty-five years, he does not lose his majority and become a minor in his new domicil [4]. And, on the other hand, if the same person is a minor by the law of the place of his birth, and not so by that of his new domicil, his state of minority continues, notwithstanding his removal [5]. He deduces the former from the injustice, which he supposes would follow from reducing a person of majority in the domicil of his birth, to a state of minority upon a change of domicil; so that thereby he is not of an age sufficiently mature to contract, or to sell, or to alienate property. The latter he seems to ground upon a like inconvenience of allowing a man thus to escape from the disabilities of a minority in the place of his birth by a mere change of domicil [6]. This, however, is but changing

---

1 2 Boullenois, Observ. 32, pp. 12, 13.

2 2 Boullenois, Observ. 32, pp. 11, 12, 13, 19; Ante, § 57.

3 2 Boullenois, Observ. 32, p. 12.

4 2 Boullenois, Observ. 32, pp. 12, 19, 20.

5 Ibid.

6 Ibid.

the postures of the case. For Boullenois himself does not hesitate to declare the general principle to be incontestable, that the law of the actual domicil decides the state and condition of the person; so that a person by changing his domicil changes at the same time his condition [1]. And he is compelled to admit, that, while he has Froland and Maillaud in support of his opinion, Lauterback, and Burgundus, and Rodenburg are against him [2]. Perhaps a better illustration of the intrinsic difficulties of laying down any general rules for all cases could not well be imagined; for Boullenois himself, as we have seen, holds laws respecting the majority and minority of age to be laws affecting the state and condition of persons, and, as such, governed by the law of the domicil; and yet, in this instance, he rejects the natural inference from this doctrine [3].

§ 72. The reason given by those civilians who hold the opinion, that the law of the domicil of birth ought in all cases to prevail over the law of the place of the actual domicil in fixing the age of majority, and that it remains unalterable by any change of domicil, is, that each State or Nation is presumed to be the best capable of judging, from the physical circumstances of climate or otherwise, when the faculties of its citizens are morally or civilly perfect for the purposes of society. And, with respect to cases of lunacy, idiocy, and prodigality, it is supported by them upon the general argument from inconvenience, and the great confusion and mischief which would arise from the same person being considered as capable to contract in one place, but incapable in another; so that he might change his civil character and capacity with every change of his domicil [4]. There may, perhaps, be a solid ground of argument in

---

[1] 2 Boullenois, Observ. 32, p. 13; Ante, § 57.

[2] 2 Boullenois, Observ. 32, pp. 19, 20.

[3] 1 Boullenois, Prin. Gén. 8, 10, 11, 17, 18; Id. Observ. 4, pp. 51, 52.

[4] Henry on For. Law, pp. 5, 6; Rodenb. tit. 1, ch. 3, n. 4; 2 Boull. App. p. 8.

favour of giving a universal operation in all other countries to certain classes of personal incapacities, created by the law of the domicil of the party; but it will be difficult to maintain that the same reasoning does or can apply with equal force in favour of all personal incapacities; or, that the law of the domicil of birth ought to prevail over the law of the actual domicil. And, even in relation to those personal incapacities which are supposed most easily to admit of a general application, it is by no means so clear that the argument from inconvenience is not equally strong on the other side [1].

§ 73. The truth, however, seems to be, that there are, properly speaking, no universal rules by which nations are, or ought to be, morally or politically bound to each other on this subject. Each nation may well adopt for itself such modifications of the general doctrine as it deems most convenient, and most in harmony with its own institutions, and interests, and policy. It may suffer the same rule as to the capacity, state, and condition of foreigners, to prevail within its own territory, as does prevail in the place of their own native or acquired domicil; and it may at the same time refuse to allow any other rule than its own law to prevail within its own territory, in respect to the capacity, state, and condition of its own subjects, wherever they may reside, at home or abroad. It may adopt a more limited doctrine, and recognise the law of the domicil, both as to foreigners and as to its own subjects, in respect to transactions and property in that domicil, whether native or acquired, and at the same time exclude any operation, except of its own law, as to the transactions and property either of foreigners or of its own subjects within its own territory. It may adopt the more general doctrine, and allow the rule of the actual domicil, as to capacity, state, and condition, to pre-

[1] See 1 Burge, Comment. on Col. and For. Law, P. 1, ch. 3, § 3, p. 129 to 134.

vail under every variety of change of domicil; or, on the other hand, it may adhere to the stricter doctrine, that the domicil of birth shall exclusively furnish the rule to govern in all such matters. But whatever rules it may adopt, or whatever it may repudiate, will be alike the dictate of its own policy and sense of justice; and whatever it may allow or withhold will always be measured by its own opinion of the public convenience and benefit, or of the public prejudice and injury, resulting therefrom. Probably the law of the actual domicil (*domicilium habitationis*) will be found in most cases to furnish the most safe, convenient, and least prejudicial rule; at least in regard to transactions and property out of the country of the birth of the party (*domicilium originis*[1]). As to transactions and property within the country of his birth, the policy of most nations will naturally incline them to hold their own laws conclusive over their own subjects, wherever they may be domiciled; so far as regards their minority and majority, and their other capacity or incapacity to do acts.

§ 74. Illustrations may be easily found to confirm these remarks in the actual jurisprudence of many countries. Thus (as we have seen[2]) Pardessus, while he contends that the law of France, as to personal capacity and incapacity generally, ought to prevail as to French subjects, wherever they reside, abroad or at home, at the same time admits that it ought not to govern in relation to certain particular disabilities. Thus, he thinks that the law of France, which forbids nobles or persons of official dignity to sign bills of exchange or other engagements, by which the bodies of the parties are liable to an arrest for a breach of the contract, ought not to extend to the like acts of the same persons done in other countries[3]. For, although it may be urged, that it

---

1 See 1 Burge, Comment. on Col. and For. Law, P. 1, ch. 3, § 3, p. 129 to 134.

2 Ante, § 68.

3 Pardessus, De Droit Comm. Vol. 5, art. 1483, p. 250.

is a personal law which follows the person everywhere, as in the case of a minor, or of a married woman under the marital power; and every person is bound to know the state and condition of the person with whom he contracts; yet, he contends that the rule ought not to be applied, except to the universal state of the person, such as that of a minor or a major, or of a woman subject to, or free from the marital power. For, he adds, all nations are agreed in fixing the capacity to contract to a certain age, and in placing women in dependence upon their husbands [1]. Every one will at once perceive how exceedingly loose the distinction is for which Pardessus contends, and how unsatisfactory his reasoning, by which this exception is attempted to be maintained. The objection to the reasoning is, that, if well founded, the argument from inconvenience would carry it much farther; and persons dealing with others may require proof of their majority, or of their special authority to contract if they are minors, or whether they are married or not; and in both cases may guard against false statements by requiring a guaranty. On the contrary, these special prohibitions, on account of a certain quality or dignity, are more arbitrary. They are founded less in general public utility, and ought not, therefore, to be invoked in aid of the party. At least the exception ought not to be admitted, except between subjects of the same State, or unless the incapacity of the person, and the nullity of the obligation by the law, were known at the time of the contract by the other party [2].

§ 75. Now, it so happens, that what Pardessus (and many other jurists are certainly of the same opinion) supposed to be very clear doctrine, has been directly overturned, and the contrary doctrine has been held by the Supreme Court of Louisiana. That Court, in a very learned

---

[1] 5 Pardessus, Vol. 5, P. 6, tit. 7, ch. 2, § 1, art. 1483, p. 250; Henry on Foreign Law, App. 222.

[2] Ibid.

opinion, have said: "The writers on this subject, with scarcely an exception, agree, that the laws or statutes which regulate minority and majority, and those which fix the state or condition of man, are personal statutes, and follow and govern him in every country. Now, supposing the case of our law fixing the age of majority at twenty-five, and the country in which a man was born and lived previous to his coming here, placing it at twenty-one; no objection could perhaps be made to the rule just stated. And it may be, and we believe would be, true, that a contract made here at any time between the two periods already mentioned would bind him. But reverse the facts of this case, and suppose, as is the truth, that our law placed the age of majority at twenty-one; that twenty-five was the period at which a man ceased to be a minor in the country where he resided; and that at the age of twenty-four he came into this state, and entered into contracts; would it be permitted that he should in our courts, and to the demand of one of our citizens, plead, as a protection against his engagements, the laws of a foreign country, of which the people of Louisiana had no knowledge? And would we tell them that ignorance of foreign laws in relation to a contract made here, was to prevent him from enforcing it, though the agreement was binding by those of their own state? Most assuredly we would not[1]."

---

1 Saul *v.* His Creditors, 17 Martin, R. 596 to 598. The opinion of the Court was delivered by Mr. Justice Porter. See also Andrews *v.* His Creditors, 11 Louis. R. 464, 476.—A like doctrine was held by the same Court in another case. The Court on that occasion said: "A foreigner coming into Louisiana, who was twenty-three years old, could not escape from a contract with one of our citizens, by averring, that, according to the laws of the country he left, he was not a major until he reached the age of twenty-five." Baldwin *v.* Grey, 16 Martin, R. 192, 193. See also Fergusson on Divorce, Appendix, p. 276 to 363; Post, § 82. Hertius, De Collisione, Tom. 1, § 4, n. 5, pp. 120, 121; Id. pp. 173, 174, (edit. 1716). Grotius seems to have been of opinion, that the *lex loci contractûs* ought to govern in cases of minority. Grotius, B. 2, ch. 11, § 5.

§ 76. The case first put seems founded upon a principle entirely repugnant to that upon which the second rests. In the former case, the law of the place of the domicil of the party is allowed to prevail, in respect to a contract made in another country; in the latter case, the law of the place where the contract is made is allowed to govern, without any reference whatsoever to the law of the domicil of the party. Such a course of decision certainly may be adopted by a government, if it shall so choose. But then it would seem to stand upon mere arbitrary legislation and positive law, and not upon principle. The difficulty is in seeing how a court, without any such positive legislation, could arrive at both conclusions. General reasoning would lead us to the opinion, that both cases ought to be decided in the same way; that is, either by the law of the domicil of the party, or by that of the place where the contract is actually made. Many foreign jurists maintain the former opinion[1]; some the latter[2]. Perhaps it is

---

1 See Livermore, Dissert. § 17, p. 32 to § 56, p. 57.—Mr. Livermore denies this doctrine of the Supreme Court of Louisiana to be correct, and has collected, in the place cited, the leading authorities in favour of the doctrine, which he contends is the true one, that the law of the domicil of the person ought universally to prevail, as to his personal capacity or incapacity. Among the authorities in its favour, he enumerates D'Argentré, Bartolus, Rodenburg, Jason, and Paulo de Castro. Liverm. Dissert. § 21, p. 34. D'Argentré (Comm. Leg. Briton. art. 218, Gloss. 6, n. 47, 48) says: Quotiescunque de habilitate aut inhabilitate personarum quæratur, toties domicilii leges et statuta spectanda. Nam de omni personali negotio, Judicis ejus cognitionem esse, cui persona subsit, ut quocunque persona abeat, ad jus sit, quod ille statuerit. Bartolus puts the case, whether, if a filius-familias (an unemancipated son) is allowed by the local law to make a testament, a foreign filius-familias can, in the same place, make a valid testament; and he answers in the negative. Dico quod non; quia statuta non possunt legitimare personam sibi non subditam, nec circa ipsam personam aliquid disponere. Bartolus, ad Cod. Lib. 1, tit. 1, l. 1, n. 25, 26. De Castro (as cited in D'Argentré, ubi supra) says, that a statute of Modena, permitting minors to contract at fourteen years of age, will not make valid a contract at Modena by a minor of that age belonging to Bologna. Ratio est, quia hîc abstractè de habilitate personæ, et universali ejus statu quæratur, ideoque persona a statuto domicilii efficiatur. Liverm. Diss. § 21, pp. 34, 35, § 25, p. 37. Burgundus, Chris-

not very easy to decide which rule would, on the whole, be most convenient for any nation to adopt. It may be said, that he who contracts with another, ought not to be ignorant of his condition: *Qui cum alio contrahit, vel est, vel esse debet, non ignarus conditionis ejus*[3]. But this rule, however reasonable in its application to the condition of a person, as fixed by the law of the country where he is domi-

---

tinaeus, Grotius, and De Wesel, appear to hold the same opinion. See Voet, ad Pand. Lib. 1, tit. 4, ps. 2, n. 7; Burgundus, Tract. 1, n. 8, 34. Rodenburg is still more full to the same point. Rodenb. De Diversit. Statut. tit. 2, ch. 1, n. 1; 2 Boullenois, App. p. 11, cited also Liverm. Diss. § 31, pp. 40, 41. See also Hertii Opera, Tom. 1, De Collis. § 4, n. 8.

[2] Mr. Livermore says, that Huberus alone is in favour of the latter opinion. I draw the conclusion, that P. Voet, (Voet, De Statut. § 4, ch. 2, n. 6, pp. 137, 138, edit. 1661,) and J. Voet, (Voet, ad Pand. Lib. 1, tit. 4, ps. 2, n. 7,) entertain the same opinion. There are probably many other jurists who are on the same side. It is very certain, that the rule, that either the law of the domicil of origin, or the law of the actual domicil, or even the law of the lex loci contractûs, is to govern in all cases, has never been adopted in the English courts. The rule of the actual domicil, or the place of the contract, has been admitted generally; but does not (as we shall presently see) universally govern. Mr. Burge has propounded the same doctrine as the Supreme Court of Louisiana, and said: "In a conflict between the personal law of the domicil and the personal law of another place at variance with it, that of the domicil prevails. But the preceding rule admits of some qualification. It is not to be applied, when it would enable a person to avoid a contract, which he was competent to make by the personal law of the place in which he made it, although he was incompetent by the personal law of his domicil. Thus, if a person, whose domicil of origin was in Spain, where he does not attain his majority until his twenty-fifth year, should, at the age of twenty-three, enter into a contract in England, or any other place where his minority ceases at twenty-one, he would not be permitted to avoid his contract by alleging that he was a minor, and incompetent to contract, according to the law of Spain. The maxim, that every man is bound to know the laws of a country in which he enters into a contract, is of universal application, and is perfectly just and reasonable; because, it is in his power to obtain that knowledge: but the maxim, 'Qui cum alio contrahit, vel est, vel debet esse, non ignarus conditionis ejus,' cannot be applied to those cases in which the condition depends on facts and law to which he is a perfect stranger." 1 Burge, Comm. on Col. and For. Law, R. 41, ch. 1, pp. 27, 28. See Post, § 79 to 82.

[3] Dig. Lib. 50, tit. 17, l. 19. See Livermore, Diss. p. 38.

ciled, is not so clear, in point of convenience or equity, when applied to the condition of a person, as fixed by the law of a foreign country. How are the inhabitants of any country to ascertain the condition of a stranger dwelling among them, as fixed by the law of a foreign country, where he was born, or had acquired a new domicil? Even courts of justice do not assume to know what the laws of a foreign country are; but require them to be proved. How then shall private persons be presumed to have better means of knowledge? On the other hand, it may be said with great force, that contracts ought to be governed by the law of the country where they are made, as to the competence of the parties to make them, and as to their validity; because the parties may well be presumed to contract with reference to the laws of the place where the contract is made, and is to be executed. Such a rule has certainty and simplicity in its application. It ought not, therefore, to be matter of surprise, if the country of the party's birth should hold such a contract valid or void, according to its own law, and that, nevertheless, the country where it is made and to be executed should hold it valid or void according to its own law. It has been well observed by an eminent Judge, that "with respect to any ignorance arising from foreign birth and education, it is an indispensable rule of law, as exercised in all civilized countries, that a man, who contracts in a country, engages for a competent knowledge of the law of contracts of that country. If he rashly presumes to contract without such knowledge, he must take the inconveniences resulting from such ignorance upon himself, and not attempt to throw them upon the other party, who has engaged under a proper knowledge and sense of the obligation which the law would impose upon him by virtue of that engagement[1]."

---

[1] Lord Stowell, in Dalrymple *v.* Dalrymple, 2 Hagg. Consist. R. 61; Ante, § 75; Post, § 82.

§ 77. In another case, decided at an earlier period, the Supreme Court of Louisiana adopted the doctrine, that the laws of the domicil of origin ought to govern the state and condition of the party, whether as major or as minor, into whatever country the party removes. But the decision may, perhaps, be thought to rest on its own peculiar circumstances. The case was this. The plaintiff in the suit (a female) was born in Louisiana in 1802, and the laws of the State at that time fixed the age of majority at twenty-five years. In the year 1808, the period of majority in the State was altered to twenty-one years. The plaintiff in 1827 (when the suit was brought) was, and for several years before had been, a Spanish subject, and a resident in Spain, where minority does not cease until twenty-five years. The suit having been brought by her to recover her share in the succession to her grandmother, in the Courts of Louisiana, before she was twenty-five, the question arose, whether she was competent to maintain the suit; and that turned upon another question, whether she was to be deemed a minor or not. The Court upon that occasion decided, that she was to be deemed a major, as she was then over twenty-one years of age, although not twenty-five. Mr. Justice Porter, in delivering the opinion of the Court, said: "The general rule is, that the laws of the domicil of origin govern the state and condition of the minor, into whatever country he removes. The laws of Louisiana, therefore, must determine at what period the plaintiff became of age; and by them she was a major at twenty-five. Admitting that her removal into another country, before the alteration of our law, would exempt her from its operation, and that her state and condition were fixed by the rules prevailing in the place where she was born, at the time she left it, a point by no means free from difficulty, no proof has been given that the plaintiff was taken out of Louisiana before the change made in 1808. And as the defendant by pleading the minority assumed the affirmative, it was her duty to establish the fact on which the exception could be sustained[1]." The question, therefore, did not here arise as to the effect of any contract made in Louisiana, (as in the preceding case,) but the simple question of the state of minority or majority, or the competency of the party to maintain a suit in her own name, as being *sui juris*. The Court seem to have acted upon the general doctrine, that the capacity of the party did not depend upon her actual domicil; but upon the law of her domicil of origin. But it is difficult to perceive why the same rule should not apply to a case of contract, arising under the like circumstances; since the capacity or incapacity to contract would depend upon the very point, whether the law of the actual domicil, or that of the domicil of origin, or that of the place of the contract, ought to govern in respect to capacity or incapacity. And if the same rule would apply, it is not easy to reconcile this with the preceding doctrine, unless upon the ground that the courts of the native domicil ought to follow their own law as to minority and majority, in all cases, in preference to any other.

§ 78. There is an earlier case in the same court, in which it seems to have been incidentally stated, that, according to the law of nations, "personal incapacities communicated by the laws of any particular place, accompany the person wherever he goes. Thus, he who is excused from the consequences of contracts for want of age in his country, cannot make binding contracts in another[2]." This doctrine is certainly at variance with that maintained by the same court at other and later periods[3]. It is somewhat curious, that it was avowed in the case of what is called a runaway marriage, celebrated at Natchez in Mississippi, between a young man and a young woman, a minor of thirteen years of age, both of them being at the time domi-

---

[1] Barrera *v.* Alpuente, 18 Martin, R. 69.

[2] Le Breton *v.* Fouchet, 3 Martin, R. 60, 70; S. C. Post, § 180.

[3] Saul *v.* His Creditors, 17 Martin, R. 597, 598; Baldwin *v.* Gray, 16 Martin, R. 192, 193.

ciled in Louisiana, without the consent of her parents; and which marriage would seem to have been void without such consent by the law of Louisiana, if celebrated in that State. It was not, however, the main point in the case; and the decision itself was placed (as we shall hereafter see) upon a far broader foundation[1].

§ 79. In respect to contracts of marriage, the English decisions have established the rule, that a foreign marriage, valid according to the law of the place where celebrated, is good everywhere else[2]. But these decisions have not *e converso* established, that marriages of British subjects, not good according to the law of the place where celebrated, are universally and under all possible circumstances to be regarded as invalid in England[3]. On the contrary, Lord Stowell has decided, that a marriage had under peculiar circumstances, at the Cape of Good Hope, during British occupation, was valid; although not in conformity to the Dutch law which was then in force there[4]. In that case the husband (an Englishman) was a person entitled by the laws of his own country to marry without the consent of parents or guardians, he being of the age of twenty-one; but by the Dutch law he could not marry without such consent until he was thirty years of age. The lady (an Englishwoman) was under the age of nineteen, her father was dead, her mother had married a second husband, and she had no guardian. Upon that occasion Lord Stowell said: "Suppose the Dutch law had thought fit to fix the age of majority at a still more advanced period than thirty, at which it then stood; at forty, it might surely be a ques-

[1] Post, § 180.

[2] Ryan *v.* Ryan, 2 Phill. Ecc. R. 332; Herbert *v.* Herbert, 3 Phill. Ecc. R. 58; S. C. 2 Hagg. Ecc. R. 263, 271; Lacon *v.* Higgins, 3 Starkie, R. 178; S. C. 1 Dowl. & Ryl. N. P. R. 38. See Ryan & Mood. R. 80.

[3] Ruding *v.* Smith, 2 Hagg. Consist. R. 390, 391; Harford *v.* Higgins, 2 Hagg. Consist. R. 432; Post, § 79, p. 79, n. 1; Post, § 118, 119.

[4] Ibid.

tion in an English court, whether a Dutch marriage of two British subjects, not absolutely domiciled in Holland, should be invalidated in England on that account; or, in other words, whether a protection intended for the rights of Dutch parents, given to them by Dutch law, should operate to the annulling a marriage of British subjects, upon the ground of protecting rights which do not belong in any such extent to parents living in England, and of which the law of England could take no notice but for the severe purpose of this disqualification. The Dutch jurists (as represented in this libel) would have no doubt whatever that this law would clearly govern a British court. But a British court might think that a question not unworthy of further consideration, before it adopted such a rule for the subjects of this country." "In deciding for Great Britain upon the marriage of British subjects, they (the Dutch jurists) are certainly the best and only authority upon the question, whether the marriage is conformable to the general Dutch law of Holland; and they can decide that question definitely for themselves and for other countries. But questions of a wider extent may lie beyond this: whether the marriage be not good in England, although not conformable to the general Dutch law; and whether there are not principles leading to such a conclusion. Of this question, and of those principles, they are not the authorized judges; for this question and those principles belong either to the law of England, of which they are not the authorized expositors at all, or to the *jus gentium*, upon which the courts of this country may be supposed as competent as themselves; and certainly, in the case of British subjects, much more appropriate judges[1]."

---

[1] Ruding *v.* Smith, 2 Hagg. Consist. R. 389, 390; Post, § 118, 119.—That there are other cases excepted from the operation of foreign law, seems to have been directly held by Sir George Hay in Harford *v.* Higgins, 2 Hagg. Consist. R. 423. He there said: "I do not mean that every domicil is to give jurisdiction to a foreign country, so that the laws of that country are necessarily to obtain and attach upon a marriage solemnized there.

§ 80. In another case, where two British subjects, being minors, and in France solely for purposes of education, intermarried, it was held by the court, that the marriage, being void by the law of France, was a mere nullity[1]. The Court (Sir Edward Simpson) said: "The question before me is not whether English subjects are to be bound by the law of France; for undoubtedly no law or statute in France can bind subjects of England who are not under its authority. Nor is the consequence of pronouncing for or against the marriage, with respect to civil rights in England, to be considered in determining this case. The only question before me is, whether this be a good or bad marriage by the law of England. On this point I apprehend, that it is the law of this country to take notice of the laws of France, or of any foreign country, in determining upon marriages of this kind; and I am inclined to think it is not good. The question being in substance, whether by the law of this country marriage contracts are not to be deemed good or bad according to the laws of the country in which they are formed; and whether they are not to be construed by that law. If such be the law of this country, the rights of English subjects cannot be said to be determined by the laws of France, but by those of their own country, which sanction and adopt this rule of decision. By the general law, all parties contracting gain a forum in the place where the contract is entered into. All our books lay this down for law: 'It is needless at present to mention more than one. Gayll, (Lib. 2, obs. 123,) says: *In contractibus locus contractûs considerandus sit. Quoties enim statutum principaliter habilitat vel inhabilitat contractum, quoad solemnitates, semper attenditur locus, in quo talis contractus celebra-*

For what would become of our factories abroad, at Leghorn, or elsewhere, where the marriage is only by the law of England, and might be void by the law of that country? Nothing will be admitted in this court to affect such marriages so celebrated, even where the parties are so domiciled." Id. 432.

[1] Scrimshire *v.* Scrimshire, 2 Hagg. Consist. R. 395.

tur, et obligat etiam non subditum.' And again, (Lib. 2, obs. 36), *Quis forum in loco contractûs sortitur, si ibi loci, ubi contraxit, reperiatur; non tamen ratione contractûs, aut ratione rei, quis subditus dicitur illius loci, ubi contraxit, aut res sita est; quia aliud est forum sortiri, et aliud subditum esse. Constat unumquemque subjici jurisdictioni judicis, in eo loco in quo contraxit.* This is according to the text law, and the opinion of Donellus and other commentators. There can be no doubt, then, that both the parties in this case obtained a forum by virtue of the contract in France. By entering into the marriage there, they subjected themselves to have the validity of it determined by the laws of that country [1]." And he afterwards proceeded to add: "This doctrine of trying contracts, especially those of marriage, according to the laws of the country where they were made, is conformable to what is laid down in our books, and what is practised in all civilized countries, and what is agreeable to the law of nations, which is the law of every particular country, and taken notice of as such [2]."

§ 80 *a.* The learned Judge proceeded to cite the opinions of civilians to the same precise effect; and he afterwards concluded with these remarks: "Why may not this Court then take notice of foreign laws, there being nothing illegal in doing it? From the doctrine laid down in our books—the practice of nations—and the mischief and confusion that would arise to the subjects of every country from a contrary doctrine, I may infer, that it is the consent of all nations, that it is the *jus gentium* that the solemnities of the different nations with respect to marriages should be observed, and that contracts of this kind are to be determined by the laws of the country where they are made. If that principle is not to govern such cases, what is to be the rule where one party is domiciled and the other not? The *jus gentium* is the law of every country, and is obliga-

---

[1] Scrimshire *v.* Scrimshire, 2 Hagg. Consist. R. 407, 408.

[2] Id. 2 Hagg. Consist. R. 412.

tory on the subjects of every country. Every country takes notice of it; and this Court, observing that law in determining upon this case, cannot be said to determine English rights by the laws of France, but by the law of England, of which the *jus gentium* is part[1]. All nations allow marriage contracts. They are *juris gentium;* and the subjects of all nations are concerned in them; and from the infinite mischief and confusion that must necessarily arise to the subjects of all nations with respect to legitimacy, successions, and other rights, if the respective laws of different countries were only to be observed as to marriages contracted by the subjects of those countries abroad, all nations have consented, or must be presumed to consent, for the common benefit and advantage, that such marriages should be good or not, according to the laws of the country where they are made. It is of equal consequence to all, that one rule in all these cases should be observed by all countries; that is, the law of the countries where the contract is made. By observing this law no inconvenience can arise, but infinite mischief will ensue if it is not[2]." Again—"If countries do not take notice of the laws of each other with respect to marriages, what would be the consequence if two English persons should marry clandestinely in England, and that should not be deemed a marriage in France? Might not either of them, or both, go into France and marry again, because by the French law such a marriage is not good? And what would be the confusion in such a case? Or again: suppose two French subjects, not domiciled here, should clandestinely marry, and there should be a sentence for the marriage; undoubtedly the wife, though French, would be entitled to all the rights of a wife by our law. But if no faith should be given to that sentence in France, and the marriage should be declared null, because the man was not domiciled,

---

1 Scrimshire *v.* Scrimshire, 2 Hagg. Consist. R. 416, 417.

2 Id. 2 Hagg. Consist. R. 416, 417, 418.

he might take a second wife in France, and that wife would be entitled to legal rights there, and the children would be bastards in one country and legitimate in the other." So that, in cases of this kind, the matter of domicil makes no sort of difference in determining them; because the inconvenience to society and the public in general is the same, whether the parties contracting are domiciled or not. Neither does it make any difference whether the cause be that of contract or marriage; for if both countries do not observe the same law, the inconveniences to society must be the same in both cases. And as it is of consequence to the subjects of both countries, and to all nations, that there should be one rule of determining in all nations on contracts of this kind, it is to be presumed, that all nations do consent to determine on these contracts by the laws of the country where they are made; as such a rule would prevent all the inconveniences that must necessarily arise from judging by different laws, and is attended by no manner of inconvenience, but is for the advantage of the subjects of all nations[1]."

§ 81. Here, then, we have a doctrine laid down as the rule of the *jus gentium*, at least, as it is understood and recognised in England in regard to contracts generally, and especially in regard to contracts of marriage, very different from the rule which we have seen laid down by many foreign jurists, that the law of the domicil of origin, or the law of the actual domicil, is of universal obligation as to the capacity, state, and condition of persons[2]. The same doctrine has been formally promulgated upon other occasions by the English Courts[3]. In a grave case of extraordinary interest[4], which turned upon the validity of a

---

1 Scrimshire *v.* Scrimshire, 2 Hagg. Consist. R. 418, 419. See Lord Meadowbank's opinion, Fergusson on Marr. and Div. Appendix, pp. 361, 362.

2 Ante, § 51 to 68.

3 Doe *d.* Birthwhistle *v.* Vardill, 5 Barn. & Cres. 438, 452, 453.

4 Dalrymple *v.* Dalrymple, 2 Hagg. Consist. R. 54.

Scotch marriage, where one of the parties was an English minor, Lord Stowell said: "Being entertained in an English court, it (the case then before him) must be adjudicated according to the principles of English law applicable to such a case. But the only principle applicable to such a case by the law of England is, that the validity of the marriage rites must be tried by reference to the law of the country where, if they exist at all, they had their origin[1]."

§ 82. In regard to other contracts made by minors, a similar rule has prevailed. In a case where money had been advanced for a minor during his stay in Scotland, (who seems to have had his general domicil in England), it was held by Lord Eldon, that the question, whether in an English Court a recovery could be had for the money so advanced, depended upon the law of Scotland; for the general rule was, that the law of the place where the contract is made must govern the contract[2]. This also seems to be a just inference from the doctrine maintained by Lord Stowell, in the case of a contract of marriage[3].

§ 82 *a*. Upon this point there is a diversity of opinion among foreign jurists[4]. Some of them are strongly inclined to act upon the doctrine of the Roman law as applicable to this subject. *Aut si non appareat quid actum est, erit consequens, ut id sequamur quod in regione in quâ actum est frequentatur*[5]. Dumoulin is supposed to have adopted this doctrine; but it is far from being certain that he intended by his language to embrace this case. *In concernentibus contractibus et emergentibus tempore contractûs inspici debet*

---

1 Dalrymple *v.* Dalrymple, 2 Hagg. Consist. R. 58, 59. See also Conway *v.* Beasley, 3 Hagg. Ecc. R. 639; Middleton *v.* Janverin, 2 Hagg. Consist. R. 437, 446.

2 Male *v.* Roberts, 3 Esp. N. P. R. 163. See also Thompson *v.* Ketcham, 8 John. R. 189; Grotius, Lib. 2, ch. 11, § 5. See, also, Dalrymple *v.* Dalrymple, 2 Hagg. Consist. R. 60, 61; Ante, § 21, 25, p. 34, § 75, n. (1), p. 37.

3 Dalrymple *v.* Dalrymple, 2 Hagg. Consist. R. 61; Ante, § 80.

4 Post, § 368.

5 Dig. Lib. 50, tit. 17, l. 34; Post, § 270.

locus in quo contrahitur[1]. Paul Voet puts the doctrine thus: *Quid, si de contractibus proprie dictis, et quidem eorum solemnibus contentio; quis locus spectabitur? An domicilii contrahentis, an loci ubi quis contrahit. Respondeo affirmate, Posterius. Quia censetur quis semet contrahendo, legibus istius loci ubi contrahit, etiam ratione solemnium subjicere voluisse. Ut quemadmodum loci consuetudo subintrat contractum, ejusque est declarativa; ita etiam loci statutum*[2]. From the other known doctrine of Paul Voet, that personal laws have no extra-territorial operation, we see at once that he meant to apply his statement to laws of personal capacity and incapacity[3]. It has been supposed, that Christinæus and Bartolus entertain a similar opinion. But their language does not necessarily lead to that conclusion, since the place of the contract, spoken of by them, may mean the place also of the domicil of origin of the minor[4]. Grotius, however, is more explicit to the purpose. *Leges civiles* (says he) *justa ratione motæ, quasdam promissiones pupillorum ac minorum irritas pronunciant. Sed hi effectus sunt proprii legis civilis, ac proinde cum jure naturæ ac gentium nihil habent commune; nisi quod quibus locis obtinent, ibi eas servare naturale est. Quæ etiam si peregrinus cum cive paciscatur, tenebitur illis legibus; quia qui in loco aliquo*

---

[1] Molin. Tom. 1, Tit. 1, De feud. § 12, gloss. 7, § 37.—In another place Dumoulin says, after adverting to the fact that personal laws affect subjects and not foreigners: Quamvis is, qui datus est tutor vel curator a suo competenti judice sit inhabilitatus propter tutelam et curam, ubique locorum pro bonis ubicumque sitis. Quia non est in vim statuti solius, sed in vim juris communis, et per passivam interpretationem legis, quæ locum habet ubique. Molin. In Cod. Lib. 1, tit. 1, tom. 3, p. 556. See 1 Burge, Comment. on Col. and For. Law, P. 1, ch. 3, § 3, pp. 129, 130; Post, § 294; 1 Boullenois, Observ. 23, pp. 463, 464.

[2] P. Voet, de Statut. § 9, ch. 2, n. 9, p. 323, (edit. 1661); Post, § 261.

[3] P. Voet, de Statut. § 4, ch. 2, n. 6, p. 137, (edit. 1661).

[4] See the passages cited from these Authors in 1 Burge, Comment. P. 1, ch. 4, p. 130; Christin. Decis. Vol. 1, Decis. 183, p. 155; Bartolus, ad Cod. Lib. 1, tit. 1, l. 1, n. 13, 20; 2 Boull. Observ. 46, pp. 455, 456; Post, § 299.

contrahit, tanquam subditus temporarius legibus loci subjicitur[1].

§ 83. On the other hand, many foreign jurists (as we have seen) entertain a very different opinion on this very point, of the capacity of a person to contract in another country, when he is disabled, as a minor, by the law of his own country and domicil[2]. Thus, it has been said by Di Castro, and approved by D'Argentré, that where the law of Modena enabled a minor of fourteen years of age to contract, that would not enable a minor of Bologna of the same age to make a valid contract at Modena[3]. And Rodenburg asserts the same doctrine in the most emphatic terms; in which he is followed by Boullenois[4].

---

1 Grotius, De Jure Belli, Lib. 2, ch. 11, § 5.

2 Ante, § 51 to 68.

3 D'Argentré, Comm. ad Leges Britonum, art. 218, gloss. 6, n. 47, 48, cited Ante, § 76, note, and also in Liverm. Dissert. p. 42, § 33 to 56; 1 Froland, Mém. des Statuts. 112, 156, 159.

4 Rodenburg, De Div. Stat. tit. 2, ch. 1, § 1; 2 Boull. App. p. 11; 1 Boullenois, Obs. 16, pp. 200, 201, 204, 205; Bouhier, ch. 23, n. 92; 1 Froland, Mém. pp. 112, 159; 2 Froland, Mém. p. 1576 to 1582.—The language of Rodenburg is: De quibus et consimilibus id Juris est, ut quocunque se transtulerit persona statuto loci domicilii ita affecta, habilitatem aut inhabilitatem ademptam domi, circumferat ubique, ut in universa territoria suum Statutum exerceat effectum. Apertius rem intuebimur in exemplis. Ultrajecti sui juris efficiuntur qui vigesimum ætatis annum impleverint, apud Hollandos contra, ante vigesimum quintum rebus suis nemo intervenit. Apud utrumque populorum nupta citra viri consensum à rebus gerendis arcetur. In Regionibus, quæ Jure Romanorum hîc utuntur, commerciis gaudet uxor liberrime, potestati virili non supposita. Fac autem Ultrajectinum, qui vigesimum quintum ætatis annum necdum habuerit, contrahere in Hollandia: aut è contra Hollandiæ incolam vigesimum jam annum egressum, Ultrajecti: aut nuptam nostratem contrahere in regione Juris scripti, aut è contra. Quocumque modo se casus habuerit, contrahentium erit respicere ad suum cujusque domicilii locum, impressamque ibidem personæ qualitatem, aut adeptam domi conditionem, cujus ignarus non sit oportet, qui cum alio volet contrahere. Quare Hollandiæ incola major Ultrajecti, minor apud suos, contrahit apud nostrates invalide. Contra, Ultrajectinus lege domicilii major contrahit in Hollandia efficaciter, ut maxime ex more regionis istius rerum suarum necdum haberetur compos. Uxores domi sub maritorum potestate ita constitutæ, ut sine iis nec alienent nec contrahant,

§ 84. Bouhier (as we have seen[1]) holds to the doctrine, that the capacity and incapacity by the law of the domicil extends to every other place[2]; but yet he is manifestly startled when it is applied to the case of marriages. He admits, that in such cases it is commonly held, that the law of the place where the marriage is celebrated ought to prevail[3]. But he insists, that such a rule ought not to be adopted in regard to persons who are both subjects of the same country, who designedly go to a foreign country and contract marriage there, in order to evade the law of the country of their own domicil[4]. He applies also similar considerations to the case of an unemancipated son or minor belonging to one country, who, finding a woman of his own country in a foreign country, marries her there without the knowledge of his parents, holding, that, under such circumstances, the marriage ought not to be held valid[5]. But he propounds, as a case of more difficulty, where such a person going into a foreign country, without any intention of marrying, finds there a woman of his own country to his liking, whom he seeks in marriage and espouses. For, if such a marriage is celebrated according to the usual formalities in that country, he deems it valid, as being done in good faith, and affirms that the parties are not bound to follow the laws of their own country[6]. D'Argentré states the general doctrine in the follow-

---

nullibi locorum hanc incapacitatem exuunt. Cùm mulieris contra Juri scripto obnoxiæ contractus, apud nos celebratus, consistat omnimodo. Et quidem si ad personales actus, contractus puta, personæ applicetur habilitas, Argentrei, Burgundique, (quos Jure præcipui hîc semper nomino,) cæterorumque scribentium placita sat consentiunt. See Ante, § 51. See also Liverm. Dissert. § 21, p. 34, to § 34, p. 43; 2 Boull. App. 11. See also Foelix, Conflict. des Lois, Revue Etrangère et Française, Tom. 7, § 24, p. 204, to § 26, p. 216.

1 Ante, § 57 *a*.

2 Bouhier, Cout. de Bourg. ch. 24, § 11, p. 463; Post, § 123.

3 Bouhier, Cout. de Bourg. ch. 28, § 59, 60, pp. 556, 557.

4 Bouhier, Cout. de Bourg. ch. 28, § 61, p. 557.

5 Bouhier, Cout. de Bourg. ch. 28, § 62, p. 557.

6 Bouhier, Cout. de Bourg. ch. 28, § 59 to 67, pp. 556, 557; Id. ch. 24, § 11, p. 463.

ing manner:—"When the question is, as to the right or capacity of any person to do civil acts generally, it is to be referred to the judge who exercises judicial functions in the place of his domicil; that is to say, to whom his person is subject, and who has authority so to pronounce respecting him, that whatever he shall promulgate, adjudge, or ordain respecting the rights of persons, ought to obtain and be of force in every place to which he may transfer himself, on account of this authority over the person." *Quare cum de personæ jure aut habilitate quæritur ad actus civiles, in universum ea judicis ejus potestas est, qui domicilio judicat, id est, cui persona subjicitur, qui sic de eo statuere potest, ut quod edixerit, judicârit, ordinârit de personarum jure, ubicumque obtineat, quocumque se persona contulerit, propter afficentium personæ*[1]. Froland asserts the same doctrine, and expressly extends it to cases of contract. *Le statut personnel n'exerce pas seulement son autorité dans le lieu du domicile de la personne, qui dispensation la suit, et l'accompagne en quelque lieu qu'elle aille contracter; et qu'elle influe sur tous les biens sous quelques coûtumes, quils soient assis*[2]. Mr. Henry, in his judicial capacity, has given the doctrine a like extent in the English colony of Demarara; for he declares, that, in the cases of prodigals, minors, idiots, and lunatics, the law of the domicil accompanies the party everywhere[3]. Cochin lays down the doctrine with great boldness, that a marriage contracted in a foreign country by French subjects, although contracted in the form prescribed by the foreign law, is void, if it violates the laws of France[4]. The subjects of the King of France (says he)

---

[1] D'Argentré, de Leg. Briton. art. 218, gloss. 6, n. 4, p. 647; Ante, § 56; 1 Froland, Mém. des Statuts, 112; Liverm. Dissert. § 21, p. 34.

[2] 1 Froland, Mém. des Statuts, 156 to 160; Id. 112; Ante, § 51 *a*. See also 1 Hertii Opera, § 4, n. 8, p. 123; Id. n. 5, p. 122, (edit. 1737); Id. pp. 171, 172, (edit. 1715).

[3] Henry on Foreign Law, pp. 38, 39; Odwin *v*. Forbes, Id. pp. 95, 96, 97.

[4] Cochin, Œuvres, Tom. 1, Cause § xii. pp. 153, 154, (4to. edit.); Id. Tom. 3, Cause xii. p. 136, (8vo. edit. 1821).

are always his subjects. And the parties contracting at a place in Brabant have only that capacity to contract which is given by the laws of their own country. It is a personal statute which follows them everywhere [1].

§ 85. Huberus seems in some places to affirm a doctrine in some respects quite as extensive, although it is liable to be modified in some measure by the local law; while in other places he deems it too broad and indiscriminate, and introduces several exceptions. Thus, as we have seen, he lays it down as a general rule: *Qualitates personales certo loco alicui jure impressas, ubique circumferri et personam comitari, cum hoc effectu, ut ubivis locorum eo jure, quo tales personæ alibi gaudent vel subjecti sunt, fruuntur, et subjiciantur*[2]. So that, according to Huberus, the state or condition of the party, as to capacity or incapacity in the place of his original domicil, accompanies him everywhere, so far, and so far only, that the law of the place, where he happens to be, attaches to him, so far as it touches rights or powers growing out of such capacity or incapacity. A minor, for example, in his own country, is subject in every other country to the laws of minority of the latter country. In regard to the contract of matrimony he holds, that it is to be governed by the law of the place where the marriage is celebrated, with the exception, however, of cases of incest. "If" (says he) "the marriage is lawful in the place where it is contracted and celebrated, it will be held valid and have effect everywhere, with this exception, that it does not create a prejudice to others. To which it may be added, if it is not of an evil example; as, if it should be a case of incest within the second degree according to the law of nations." *Si licitum est eo loco ubi contractum et celebratum est, ubique validum erit, effectumque habebit, sub eâdem exceptione prejudicii aliis non creandi. Cui licet addere, si exempli nimis sit abo-*

---

1 Cochin, Œuvres, Tom. 1, Cause § xii. pp. 153, 154, (4to. edit.); Id. Tom. 3, Cause xii. p. 136, (8vo. edit. 1821).

2 Huberus, De Conflictu Legum, Lib. 1, tit. 3, § 12, 13.

minandi, ut si incestum juris gentium in secundo gradu contingeret, alicubi esse permissum; quod vix est, ut usu venire possit[1]. Huberus also puts another exception, where persons belonging to one country go into another to be married, merely to evade the law of their own country, in which case he holds the marriage to be void, although it is good by the law of the place where it is celebrated[2]. *Sæpe fit, ut adolescentes sub curatoribus agentes, furtivos amores nuptiis conglutinare cupientes, abeant in Frisiam Orientalem, aliave loca, in quibus curatorum consensus ad matrimonium non requiretur, juxta leges Romanos, quæ apud nos hac parte cessant. Celebrant ibi matrimonium, et mox redeant in patriam. Ego ita existimo, hanc rem manifesto pertinere ad eversionem juris nostri; et ideo non esse Magistratus heic obligatos, è jure Gentium, ejusmodi nuptias agnoscere et ratas habere. Multoque magis statuendum est, eos contra Jus Gentium facere videri, qui civibus alieni imperii suâ facilitate, jus patriis Legibus contrarium, scientes, volentes, impertiuntur*[3].

§ 86. The latter doctrine has, upon the most solemn consideration, been overturned in England, as we shall hereafter see[4]; and such a marriage in evasion of the domestic laws has been held valid. But we are not, therefore, to conclude that every marriage by and between British subjects in foreign countries will be held valid, because it is celebrated according to the laws of such countries. On the contrary, where the laws of England create a personal incapacity to contract marriage, that incapacity has, in some cases, been held to have a universal operation, so as to make a subsequent marriage in a foreign country a mere nullity when litigated in a British court[5].

---

1 Huberus, Lib. 1, tit. 3, § 8; Post, 122.

2 Ibid.

3 Ibid.; Post, § 123.

4 See 2 Kent, Comm. Lect. 26, pp. 91, 92, (3rd edit.); Post, § 123, 124.

5 Conway *v.* Beasley, 3 Hagg. Ecc. R. 639, 647, 652; Lolley's Case,

§ 87. Indeed, the general principle adopted in England in regard to cases of this sort appears to be, that the *lex loci contractûs* shall be permitted to prevail, unless when it works some manifest injustice, or is *contra bonos mores*, or is repugnant to the settled principles and policy of its own laws. An illustration of the general principle, and of the exception, may be found in the known difference between the Scottish law and the English law on the subject of the legitimation of antenuptial offspring. By the law of Scotland illegitimate children become by the subsequent marriage of the parents legitimate, and may inherit as heirs. But the law of England is otherwise; and a subsequent marriage between the parents will not take away the character of illegitimacy. Upon a recent occasion the question arose in an English court, (the Court of King's Bench,) whether a person, born in Scotland of Scottish parents, who afterwards intermarried there, and thereby became legitimate in Scotland, could inherit real estate as a legitimate heir in England. It was held by the Court, that he could not[1]. On that occasion it was admitted by the Court, that a foreign marriage, however solemnized, if good by the foreign local law, ought to be held valid everywhere; but that it did not follow from this, that all the consequences of such a marriage by such foreign local law were to be adopted. On the other hand, that it was sufficient that all such consequences, as follow from a lawful marriage solemnized in England, were admitted to govern in such cases[2]. One of

---

1 Russell & Ryan, Cr. Cas. 236.—It will probably be found very difficult to maintain the doctrine in Lolley's case, and in subsequent discussions its authority has certainly been a good deal shaken. See Warrender *v.* Warrender, 9 Bligh, R. 89; and Post, § 117, 124, 221 to 231.

[1] Doe *d.* Birthwhistle *v.* Vardell, 5 Barn. & Cres. 438; S. C. 9 Bligh, R. 32 to 88.

[2] Doe d. Birthwhistle *v.* Vardell, 5 Barn. & Cres. 438; S. C. 9 Bligh, R. 32 to 88.—This case was carried to the House of Lords by a Writ of Error; and there the question was propounded to the judges, who returned an answer affirming the decision of the King's Bench. But the question has

the learned Judges on that occasion said: "The very rule that a personal *status* accompanies a man everywhere, is admitted to have this qualification, that it does not militate against the law of the country where the consequences of that *status* are sought to be enforced [1].

§ 87 *a*. Yet the law of foreign countries as to legitimacy is so far respected in England, that a person, illegitimate by the law of his domicil of birth, will be held illegitimate in England [2]. Thus, it has been decided by the House of Lords, as a general doctrine, that the courts of the country where the lands lie, in a question respecting the heirship to these lands, ought to govern themselves as to the question of legitimacy, not by the law of the country where the lands lie, but by that of the country where the marriage of the parents was contracted, and the child born; and if he is not the legitimate heir by that foreign law, his claim to the inheritance ought to be rejected [3]. The natural conclusion from this doctrine would seem to be, that, if he was the legitimate heir by that foreign law, his claim to the inheritance ought to be firmly established. Yet this conclusion has been pointedly repelled by the learned Judges in the case already alluded to [4], and which we shall have occasion to consider more fully hereafter [5].

---

since been re-argued, and the case has not as yet been finally decided by the House of Lords. See Post, § 93.

1 Per Littledale, J., 5 Barn. & Cres. 455.

2 See Munro *v.* Saunders, 6 Bligh, R. 468; Shedden *v.* Patrick, and The Strathmore Peerage, cited in 5 Barn. & Cres. 444; in 3 Hagg. Ecc. R. 652; in 6 Bligh, R. 474, 475, 487; and in 9 Bligh, R. 51, 52, 75, 76, 80; and reported in 4 Wils. & Shaw, R. App. 89 to 95.

3 See Shedden *v.* Patrick, and the case of The Strathmore Peerage, as cited in 9 Bligh, R. 51, 52, 75, 76, 80, 81.

4 Birthwhistle *v.* Vardell, 9 Bligh, R. 52, 53.—I confess myself wholly unable to reconcile these latter decisions with the former. The attempt to reconcile them seems to me more ingenious than satisfactory. Lord Brougham's comments on the subject, in Birthwhistle *v.* Vardell, 9 Bligh, R. 75, 80, 81, appear to me exceedingly forcible and difficult to be answered. Post, § 93.

5 Post, § 93, 94.

§ 88. Another illustration, touching the capacity of persons to contract marriage, may be stated from English jurisprudence. By the law of England marriage is an indissoluble contract, except by the transcendent power of Parliament. Hence it has been held that a marriage, once celebrated between British subjects in an English domicil, cannot be dissolved by a divorce obtained under the laws of a foreign country, to which the parties may temporarily remove[1]. Thus, for example, that an English marriage cannot be dissolved, under such circumstances, by a Scotch divorce regularly obtained according to the law of Scotland, by persons going thither for that purpose, who have their domicil in England[2]. And a second marriage in Scotland after such divorce will be held unlawful, and will subject the parties to the charge of bigamy[3]. This doctrine, however, seems open to much controversy; and can scarcely now be held firmly established, if indeed it has not been overthrown by recent adjudications[3]. Perhaps it yet remains an undecided question in the English law, (as we shall hereafter see,) whether a *bonâ fide* change of domicil, and a divorce subsequently obtained, would change the legal predicament of the parties in an English tribunal[3]. But it has been directly decided, that the mere fact that the marriage takes place in England between British subjects, will not, if the husband at that time has his domicil in Scotland, take away the right of the courts in Scotland to entertain jurisdiction to decree a divorce founded on such domicil[3]. But this subject will presently come more fully under consideration[4].

---

[1] Lolley's Case, 1 Russ. & Ryan's Cases, 236. But see Warrender *v.* Warrender, 9 Bligh, R. 89; Post, § 219 *a*.

[2] See Rex *v.* Lolley, 1 Russ. & Ryan, C. 236; Tovey *v.* Lindsay, 1 Dow, R. 124; Beazley *v.* Beazley, 3 Hagg. Ecc. R. 639. See also Fergusson on Marr. and Div. Appendix, 269; Warrender *v.* Warrender, 9 Bligh, R. 89; Post, § 219 *a*.

[3] Ibid. See Warrender *v.* Warrender, 9 Bligh, R. 89; Post, § 219 *a*.

[4] Post, ch. 7, from § 200 to 231.

§ 89. In the American courts the doctrine as to capacity or incapacity to marry, has been held to depend generally on the law of the place where the marriage is celebrated, and not on that of the place of domicil of the parties. An exception would doubtless be applied to cases of incest and polygamy [1]. But, in affirmance of the general principle, it has been held, that, if a person divorced from his first wife is rendered by the law of the place of the divorce incapable of contracting a second marriage, still if he contracts marriage in another state, where the same disability does not exist, the marriage will be held valid [2]. And a marriage celebrated in a foreign state, to evade the law of the place of domicil, is on the same account held valid [3]. Mr. Chancellor Kent formerly laid down the doctrine in regard to contracts generally, in terms which might admit of a different interpretation. He said: "The personal incompetency of individuals to contract, as in the case of infancy, and the general capacity of parties to contract, depend, as a general rule, upon the law of the domicil [4]. But he was then to be understood as referring to the law of the domicil, only when it is the place where the contract is made; for in the same paragraph he stated, that the *lex loci contractûs* governs in relation to the validity of contracts; and he applied it especially to nuptial contracts [5].

---

1 Post, § 113, 114.

2 2 Kent, Comm. 91 to 93, (3rd edit.); Id. 458, 459; Putman *v.* Putman, 8 Pick. 433; West Cambridge *v.* Lexington, 1 Pick. R. 504; De Couche *v.* Savatier, 3 John. Ch. R. 190; Post, § 123.

3 Ibid.

4 2 Kent, Comm. Lect. 39, p. 458, (2nd edit.); Post, § 123.

5 2 Kent, Comm. Lect. 39, p. 458, (2nd edit.,) and De Couche *v.* Savatier, 3 John. Ch. R. 190.—The English authorities, cited by Mr. Chancellor Kent, justify this conclusion. One is Male *v.* Roberts, in 3 Esp. R. 163, which was a case of a contract by a minor in Scotland, during his temporary residence there, and it was held to be governed by the law of Scotland. Another is, Ex parte Otto Lewis, 1 Ves. R. 298, where a lunatic heir of a mortgagee, who had been declared a *non compos* in Hamburg, and no commission of lunacy had been taken out in England, was ordered to convey the estate in payment of the mortgage in Hamburg, under statute, 4 Geo. 2,

§ 90. The difficulty of applying any other rule, as to the capacity and incapacity of the person, in respect to the class of nuptial contracts, will become still more clear by attending to the great extent of the parental power, recognised by the continental nations of Europe, and derived by them from the civil law. Parental restraints upon the marriages of minors exist to a very great extent in Germany, Holland, France, and other civil law countries; to so great an extent indeed, that the marriage of minors, without the consent of their parents, or at least of their father, is absolutely void; and the disability of minority is in these countries carried to a much greater age, than it is by the common law[1]. In some of these countries majority is not attained until thirty; and until a very recent period, even in France, the age of majority of males was fixed at twenty-five, and of females at twenty-one. It is now fixed at twenty-one in all other cases, except for the purpose of contracting marriage; and a marriage cannot even now be contracted in France by a man until twenty-five years of age, and by a woman until twenty-one, without the consent of their parents, or at least of their fathers if the parents differ in opinion[2]. Yet France

---

ch. 10. Here Lord Hardwicke manifestly acted upon the ground, that the mortgage money was personal property, and, the lunatic being domiciled in Hamburg, the Court would take notice of his disability to convey there, by the law of that place. The remaining authority is Pardessus. His doctrine is certainly more broad. But it could not have been intended by Mr. Chancellor Kent to overrule the English doctrine, and his own prior statement upon the authority of a foreign jurist. The ambiguity is corrected in the third edition; and the words "the law of the place of contract" are substituted for the words "the law of the domicil." 2 Kent, Comment. Lect. 39, p. 458, (3rd edit.). Pardessus is an authority in favour of the limited doctrine, that a person incapacitated by the law of his domicil cannot contract with validity there; but he carries his doctrine much farther. The cases of Saul *v.* His Creditors, 17 Martin, R. 596, 598, and Baldwin *v.* Gray, 16 Martin, R. 192, 193, already cited, established a like limited doctrine, and decided that a contract by a minor is to be governed by the *lex loci contractûs;* Ante, § 75.

[1] 2 Kent, Comm. Lect. 26, p. 86, (3rd edit.); 1 Black. Comm. 437; Ruding *v.* Smith, 2 Hagg. Consist. R. 372, 389; Id. 395; 1 Brown, Civ. and Adm. Law, 59.

[2] Code Civil of France, art. 148, 488.

has ventured upon the bold doctrine, that the marriages of Frenchmen in foreign countries shall not be deemed valid, if the parties are not by its own law competent to contract by reason of their being under the parental power[1]. There can be little doubt that foreign countries, where such marriages are celebrated, will follow their own law, and disregard that of France[2].

§ 91. If we pass from cases of minority to other disabilities, enforced by the law of the native domicil, or that of an after-acquired domicil, there will be still more reason to doubt, whether any rule of such law respecting personal capacity and incapacity, ought to be declared to be of universal obligation and efficacy. Let us take the case of a person declared infamous by the law of the place of his domicil. It is said, that under such circumstances he ought to be deemed everywhere infamous. *Hinc* (says Hertius) *in uno loco infamis, ubique infamis habetur*. Surely it will not be contended, that, if a Protestant should be declared a heretic in a Catholic country, and there rendered infamous and inhabilitated thereby, he is to be deemed under the like infamy and disability in all Protestant countries. That surely would be pressing the doctrine to a wanton extravagance[3]. Yet certainly many foreign jurists do press it to that extent[4].

§ 92. In like manner, let us consider the civil disabilities imposed by the English laws, in cases of outlawry, excommunication, civil death, and popish recusancy[5]. It would be difficult to maintain that these accompanied the person

---

1 2 Kent, Comm. Lect. 26, p. 93, note, (3rd edit.); Code Civil of France, art. 170; Id. art. 148; 1 Toullier, Droit Civil, art. 576, 577.

2 See Post, § 123, 124.

3 See 1 Hertii Opera, § 4, n. 8, p. 124, (edit. 1737); Id. 178, (edit. 1716); Liverm. Diss. pp. 30, 31.

4 See Henry on Foreign Law, p. 30; 1 Boullenois, Observ. 4, p. 52 to 67; 1 Voet, ad Pand. Lib. 1, tit. 4, n. 7, p. 40.

5 See 3 Black. Comm. 101, 102, 283; 1 Black. Comm. 132; 4 Black. Comm. 54, 319, 320.

to America, where no like disabilities exist, and where they are foreign to the whole genius of our institutions. Yet many foreign jurists strenuously maintain the doctrine[1]. We have no positive laws declaring that such foreign disabilities shall not be recognised. But an American court would deem them purely local, and incapable of being enforced here. Even the conviction of a crime in a foreign country which makes the party infamous there, and incapable of being a witness in their courts, has been held not to produce a like effect here[2]. The capacity or incapacity of any persons to do acts in their own country, would undoubtedly, under such circumstances, be judged by their own laws; but not their capacity or incapacity to do the like acts in any foreign territory, where different laws prevail.

§ 93. Foreign jurists, also, generally, although not universally, maintain that the question of legitimacy or illegitimacy is to be decided exclusively by the law of the domicil of origin. They assert the general maxim to be of universal obligation, *Pater est, quem justæ nuptiæ demonstrant*, applying it in its broadest sense[3]. They therefore hold, that if, by the law of a country, (as, for example, of Scotland,) a man born a bastard becomes legitimate by a subsequent marriage of his parents there, he ought to be deemed legitimate everywhere. And so, on the contrary, if a man would by the law of the country of his birth be deemed illegitimate, (as, for example, in England,) he ought to be deemed illegitimate everywhere, even in another country where he would by its law otherwise be deemed legitimate[4].

---

[1] 1 Boullenois, Observ. p. 59 to 67; 2 Boullenois, pp. 9, 10, 19. But see contra, J. Voet, De Statut. § 4, ch. 3, n. 17, 18, p. 130, (edit. 1737).

[2] Commonwealth *v.* Green, 17 Mass. R. 515, 540, 541.

[3] Post, § 93 *a* to 93 *m*.

[4] 1 Boull. Obs. 4, p. 62 to 64. But see Voet, De Statut. § 4, ch. 3, n. 15, p. 138, (edit. 1712); 1 Hertii Opera, § 4, n. 14, 15, p. 129, (edit. 1737).—Legitimation by a subsequent marriage is admitted, with different

§ 93 *a.* It has been above stated, that foreign jurists generally, although not universally, hold this opinion; for there is some diversity of opinion among them, if not as to the application of the rule *ex directo* to the persons, at least as to its application to property situate in a foreign country. Considering, therefore, the importance of the subject, and that it has already undergone a most elaborate discussion in England, in the case already adverted to, and which we shall have occasion to consider more fully hereafter[1], it is desirable that doctrines maintained by foreign jurists, as well as the reasoning of the English courts on the subject, should be here brought under review.

§ 93 *b.* It seems, then, generally admitted by foreign jurists, that, as the validity of the marriage must depend upon the law of the country where it is celebrated, the *status,* or state or condition of their offspring, as to legitimacy or illegitimacy, ought to depend upon the same law. So that if, by the law of the place of the marriage, (at all events, if the parents were then domiciled there,) the offspring, although born before the marriage, would be legitimated, they ought to be deemed legitimate in every other country for all purposes whatsoever, including heirship of immovable property[2].

§ 93 *c.* This is certainly the doctrine maintained by many, perhaps by a large majority of foreign jurists[3]. Vinnius says: *Item, jus personæ hic esse, quod statum et*

---

modifications, by the law of Scotland, France, Spain, Portugal, Germany, and most of the continental nations of Europe. The rule was imported into their jurisprudence from the Roman law. 1 Burge, Comment. P. 1, ch. 3, § 2, pp. 92, 93; Cod. Lib. 5, tit. 27, l. 5; Novell. 78, ch. 4; Id. 89, ch. 8. In some of the American states the same rule prevails. 1 Burge, Comment. on Col. and For. Law, ch. 3, § 3, p. 101; Griffith's Law Register.

[1] Birthwhistle *v.* Vardell, 5 Barn. & Cres. 438; S. C. 9 Bligh, R. 82; Ante, § 81.

[2] See 1 Burge, Comment. on Col. and For. Law, P. 1, ch. 3, p. 101 to 106.

[3] See 1 Burge, Comment. on Col. and For. Law, P. 1, ch. 3, § 3, p. 101 to 106.

conditionem personæ sequitur. Nam status ipse est personæ conditio, aut qualitas, quæ efficit, ut hoc vel illo jure utatur, ut esse liberum, esse servum, esse ingenuum, esse libertinum, esse alieni, esse sui juris[1]. Huberus also extends the rule, not only to the marriage itself, but also to all rights and effects flowing therefrom. *Porro, non tantum ipsi contractus ipsæque nuptiæ, certis locis ritè celebratæ, ubique pro justis et validis habentur, sed etiam jure et effecta contractuum et nuptiarum, in iis locis recepta, ubique vim suam obtinebunt*[2]. Stockmannus says: *Statuta, in personas directa, quæ certam iis qualitatem affigunt, transeunt quidem cum personis extra territorium statuentum, ut personæ ubique sit uniformis, ejusque unus status*[3].

§ 93 *d*. Bouhier adopts the doctrine in its fullest extent, and applies it to the very case of legitimacy. He says that the state of the child, whether legitimate or illegitimate, must be decided by the law of the domicil of his parents; and that this is an inviolable rule upon every question of his state or condition. And hence, he holds, that if he is at his birth illegitimate, and he is legitimated by a subsequent marriage in the same country between his parents, he is in all respects to be treated as legitimate everywhere[4]. Hertius holds a similar opinion[5]. Froland is of the same opinion[6]. Boullenois is very full on the same point. He holds that the general rule is, *Pater est, quem justæ nuptiæ demonstrant;* and that, if a person is

---

1 Vinnius, ad Inst. Lib. 1, tit. 3, Introd.

2 Huberus, De Conflict. Leg. Lib. 1, tit. 3, § 9.

3 Stockmann. Decis. 125, § 6, p. 262; also cited 1 Boullenois, Observ. 6, p. 131; Livermore, Dissert. § 50, p. 52.—John Voet, in the most explicit terms, admits that this rule is held to apply to questions of legitimacy by many jurists, and especially by D'Argentré, by Grotius, by Christinæus, and by Rodenburg. J. Voet, Comm. ad Pand. Lib. 1, tit. 4, n. 7, p. 40.

4 Bouhier, Cout. de Bourg. ch. 24, § 122, 123, p. 481.

5 Hertii, De Collis. Leg. Tom. 1, § 4, n. 15, p. 184, (edit. 1716); Id. p. 129, (edit. 1737).

6 1 Froland, Mém. ch. 5, § 4, p. 89; Id. ch. 7, § 2, p. 156, (edit. 1716); Ante, § 51 *a*.

legitimate or illegitimate by the law of the place of the marriage, he is to be held of the same state and condition wherever he may go, and whatever change of domicil may take place[1]. Hence he declares, that if, by the law of a country a man born a bastard is legitimated by the subsequent marriage of his parents, or *e contra,* if, by the law of the country such subsequent marriage does not legitimate him, he is in every other country affected by his original state or condition; that is to say, if, legitimated by the subsequent marriage, he is legitimate everywhere; if not so legitimated, he is held illegitimate everywhere[2]. Even Burgundus, and Stockmannus, and Christinæus, whose systems are founded upon a different theory, viz.—that personal statutes have no extra-territorial effect, admit that, so far as the person is concerned, though not as to immovable property, (as we shall presently see[3],) the original state or condition ought to govern everywhere[4]. The opinion of Paul Voet and John Voet on the same subject is far more limited and qualified, and will come under our review hereafter[5].

§ 93 *e.* The same general doctrine is avowedly adopted by the courts of England. Lord Stowell on one occasion in effect maintained that, by the law of England, the *status* or condition of a claimant must be tried by reference to the law of the country where that *status* originated[6]. The same doctrine was adopted by the Judges of England in giving their opinion to the House of Lords. They admitted in the most solemn form, that the legitimacy or illegitimacy

---

[1] 1 Boullenois, Observ. 4, pp. 62, 63; Post, § 93 *i.*

[2] Ibid.

[3] Post, § 93 *k.*

[4] Ante, § 52; Burgundus, Tract. 1, § 3, p. 15; Christinæus, Tom. 2, Decis. 3, § 3, p. 4; Id. Decis. 56, § 12, p. 55; Stockmann. Decis. 125, § 6, 9, pp. 262, 263; 1 Boullenois, Observ. 4, pp. 130, 131.

[5] Post, § 93 *l.*

[6] Dalrymple *v.* Dalrymple, 2 Hagg. Consist. R. 54, 59; S. C. 9 Bligh, R. 45, 46.

of a person must be decided by the law of the place where the marriage was celebrated; and that if, by the law of that place, (for example, Scotland,) a son born before the marriage of his parents, would by a subsequent marriage between them be legitimated, that *status* of legitimacy must be deemed equally true and valid everywhere else where the question might arise[1].

§ 93 *f*. Still, however, although the general doctrine is thus extensively admitted, there is some diversity of opinion as to the true nature and extent of its application in regard to different kinds of property, and also in regard to the circumstances of particular cases[2]. Thus, for example, although its positive application in regard to moveable property is generally admitted; yet, in regard to immovable property in a foreign country, there has been some contrariety of judgment. The circumstances, also, under which the question of legitimacy or illegitimacy may arise, may be very various, and admit of important distinctions in the application of the general doctrine. The birth may be in one country, the marriage be in another, and the domicil of the parents be in a third[3].

§ 93 *g*. Several cases may easily be put to illustrate this suggestion. The question of legitimacy or illegitimacy may arise, among others, in the following cases. (1.) Where a child is born before marriage in the domicil of his parents, who afterwards intermarry there, and by the law of that domicil the child is thereby legitimated. (2.) Where a child is born before marriage in the domicil of his parents, and by the law thereof a subsequent marriage would legitimate the child, and the parents are afterwards married in another country, by whose law no such legitimation would

---

1 Birthwhistle *v.* Vardill, 9 Bligh, R. 45, 46, 48; Id. 71; Post, § 93 *n*, § 93 *o*.

2 See 1 Burge, Comment. on Col. and For. Law, P. 1, ch. 3, § 3, pp. 105, 106, 109, 110.

3 See Lord Brougham's Remarks in Birthwhistle *v.* Vardill, 9 Bligh, R. 78.

follow. (3.) Where a child is born before marriage in the domicil of his parents, by whose law no legitimation would follow on their subsequent marriage, and they remove to a new domicil, where the law would upon such marriage legitimate the child, and they are there married. (4.) Where the child is born before marriage in the domicil of his parents, by whose law no legitimation would follow from a subsequent marriage, and they are there married, and subsequently remove to a new domicil, by the law whereof such subsequent marriage would legitimate the child. It is plain that these several cases may admit of, if they do not absolutely require, the application of different principles to resolve them; and different questions may be put in respect to them. Ought the law of the place of birth, or that of the place of the marriage, or that of the actual domicil of the parents, or that of the actual domicil of the child, to govern[1]?

§ 93 *h*. The most simple case, and that which has most frequently arisen for discussion, is the first stated; where the birth, domicil, and marriage of the parties took place in a country, by the laws whereof a subsequent marriage would legitimate the child. Suppose, then, the question to arise, whether in such a case the child so legitimated by such marriage could inherit lands in another country, by the laws whereof no such legitimation would follow upon such marriage. Or, in other words, let us put the very case as it actually occurred in the courts of England in the case above alluded to[2], the case of an illegitimate son born

---

[1] A case still more complicated is said to be now pending before the House of Lords on an appeal from Scotland. In effect it is this: A., a Scotchman, domiciled in Scotland, had an illicit connexion with B., an Englishwoman, domiciled in England, by whom he had a son born in England. The parents afterwards intermarried in England, the father retaining his Scotch domicil. They then returned to Scotland; and the question before the Court was, whether, under these circumstances, the son was legitimated by the subsequent marriage. The Court of Sessions of Scotland held that he was. From this decision the appeal is taken.

[2] Birthwhistle *v*. Vardill, 5 Barn. & Ald. 438; S. C. 9 Bligh, R. 51, 52; Ante, § 93 *a*, § 93 *e*; Post, § 93 *n*.

in Scotland, whose parents afterwards intermarried there, and dying, held lands in England; would such son be entitled to inherit the land as lawful heir under the law of England? We have already seen how this question has been decided by the English courts[1]; but as the question is still supposed to be unsettled there, and is also of very general application and importance, it may be well to give it a fuller consideration.

§ 93 *i*. It is plain from what has been already stated, and indeed is directly established by their positive declarations, that those of the foreign jurists already mentioned, who affirm the general doctrine of the universality of the rule, that capacity and incapacity depend upon the law of the domicil of birth, and that it equally applies to moveable property and immovable property situate in foreign countries, would hold the same rule applicable to the question of legitimacy and illegitimacy, in regard to the inheritance or real property in all foreign countries. This is certainly maintained by Vinnius, Huberus, Wesel, Froland, Rodenburg, Bouhier, Boullenois, Pothier, and Merlin[2], and probably by Baldus and Grotius[3]. Hertius puts the converse case: *An filius, quem pater ante legitimum connubium in Angliâ genuerat, succedere possit patri huic naturali in bonis ex Angliâ sitis?* And he holds that he could not; because the son being illegitimate in England, would be held illegitimate everywhere[4]. And this naturally flows from one of his rules: *Quando lex in personam dirigitur, respiciendum est ad leges illius civitatis quæ personam habet subjectam*[5]. Bouhier states this as the universal rule (as we have seen[6]); but he admits, that, if the law of a particular nation should

---

1 Ante, § 87.

2 Ante, § 51 *a*, 52, 53, 54, 93, 93 *d*.

3 J. Voet, ad Pand. Lib. 1, tit. 4, n. 7, p. 40; Liverm. Dissert. § 56, p. 57, § 109 to 114, p. 84 to 87.

4 1 Hertii Opera, De Collis. Leg. § 4, n. 15, p. 183, (edit. 1716); Id. p. 129, (edit. 1737).

5 Id. § 4, n. 8, p. 175; Id. p. 123, (edit. 1837).

6 Ante, § 93 *d*.

allow the inheritance only to a child born in lawful matrimony, (only in loyal marriage,) then as to land there situate, it ought to prevail, upon the ground that the law in such a case designated the condition of heirship. And this seems to have been also Dumoulin's opinion[1]. Boullenois (as we have seen[2]) holds the doctrine without any qualification whatever. He presses the doctrine further, and insists, that if a child is born before marriage in England, and his parents are afterwards naturalized in France, and subsequently intermarry there, the child becomes legitimate to all intents and purposes[3]. He adds, that if a child is so born illegitimately in England, and his parents marry there and then die, and he then takes up his domicil in France and is naturalized there, he will be entitled to succeed to their property in France to the exclusion of collaterals[4].

§ 93 *k*. Burgundus, Christinæus, and Stockmannus may be thought to hold the contrary doctrine upon the general foundation of their system, that personal laws have no operation as to immovable property situate elsewhere[5]. But I am not aware that they have ever directly discussed this question. And it may be, that while they hold that immovable property must, as to heirship, be decided by the *lex loci status*, they may deem the capacity of legitimacy as to that heirship as conclusively established by the law of the birth and domicil of the party. The one doctrine is certainly not necessarily inconsistent with the other[6].

---

1 Bouhier, Cout. de Bourg. ch. 24, § 124, p. 481.

2 Ante, § 93 *d;* 1 Boullenois, Observ. 4, pp. 62, 63; Id. Obs. 6, pp. 129, 130, 134 to 137.

3 1 Boullenois, Observ. 4, pp. 62, 63; Ante, § 93 *d*.

4 1 Boullenois, Observ. 4, p. 63.

5 See Burgundus, Tract. 1, n. 8, 10, 25, 26; Christinæus, Vol. 2, Lib. 1, Decis. 56; Stockmann. Decis. 125, n. 10; Livermore, Dissert. § 47, p. 50; Id. § 106, p. 81; Ante, § 93 *d*.

6 John Voet seems to have understood, that those jurists who hold that legitimacy by the law of domicil extended the same capacity everywhere, gave the effect to it here supposed. J. Voet, ad Pand. Lib. 1, tit. 4, n. 7, p. 40.

§ 93 *l.* Paul Voet and John Voet are, as far as my researches have gone, the only jurists who contend that the law of legitimacy of the domicil of the party, although a a personal statute, is exclusively, like all other personal statutes, confined to the territory, and has no operation, directly or indirectly, beyond it. *Verius est* (says John Voet) *personalia, non magis quam realia, territorium statuentis posse excedere, sive directo, sive per consequentiam;* and he goes on (as we have seen[1]) to deny, that a bastard who is legitimated by the law of his domicil, can inherit by succession property situate in another country where no such legitimation would take place. Paul Voet holds the same opinion. *Quid autem statuendum erit de legitimato in uno territorio; censebitur, ne, ratione bonorum alibi jacentium, ubi legitimatus, non erat statutum vires suos exercere; vel, an illa qualitas seu habilitas, eum ubique locorum comitabitur, quoad effectum consequendæ dignitatis, vel succedendi ab intestato? Respondeo, etsi per legitimationem habilitetur persona, ut velint D. D., qualitatem eam comitari ubique locorum, etiam ex comitate id servari possit; quia tamen potissimum illa legitimatio fit ad effectum vel honoris vel hereditatis consequendæ; in quam nihil juris habet is, quia in suo territorio legitimavit; existimarem illam legitimationem ad honores subeundos et hereditatem extra territorium capiendam non sufficere*[2].

§ 93 *m.* The weight of foreign authority would therefore, on the whole, seem decidedly to preponderate in favour of the rule, that an illegitimate person, who by the subsequent marriage of his parents becomes legitimated as heir by the law of his domicil, ought to be deemed such as to the inheritance of land in all other countries, at least, where it is not expressly prohibited by the terms of the local law that such a person born before marriage should

---

[1] Ante, § 54 *a;* Liverm. Dissert. § 51, 52, p. 54.

[2] Paul Voet, De Statut. § 4, ch. 3, § 15, p. 156, (edit. 1661); Liverm. Dissert. § 51, 52, p. 54.

inherit[1]. Indeed, the opinion of the Voets is perhaps less fairly maintainable, because it proceeds upon the ground that the *status* or condition of the person by the law of his domicil has no operation beyond the territory, either directly or consequentially. To this extent the doctrine has certainly never been carried in England[2].

§ 93 *n*. In the case already alluded to in the English courts, where the question was, whether a son born of Scottish parents in Scotland before marriage, but who afterwards intermarried there, could inherit lands in England as heir, there was much learned discussion on the point. The Court of King's Bench decided in the negative, and that opinion was afterwards, upon a writ of error to the House of Lords, held by all the Judges of England to be correct. But it not being satisfactory, the case has since been ordered to be re-argued, and is still pending. Lord Brougham upon this occasion expressed an opinion directly opposed to that of the learned Judges. It may, therefore, be well to present a summary of the reasoning on each side of the question, and thus to exhibit the grounds of difference.

§ 93 *o*. It was conceded on all sides, that the right to inherit lands in England must depend upon the laws of England; in other words, that the right of inheritance follows the law of the *rei sitæ*, and not that of the domicil of the parties. In every case, therefore, in which an inheritance is sought in England, the question is, whether the claimant is the heritable heir according to the law of England. The learned Chief Baron, Alexander, who delivered the opinion of the Judges against the Scottish claimant, (though legitimate in Scotland,) reasoned to this effect: He admitted that the *status* or condition of the claimant must be tried by the law of Scotland where that *status* originated; that by the law of Scotland the claimant

---

[1] Liverm. Dissert. § 57 to 59, pp. 58, 59.

[2] Ante, § 93 *e*.

was clearly legitimate, and must be held so everywhere. But he insisted that the question was not, whether the claimant was legitimate or not; but whether he was heir in England; that he might be legitimate and yet might not be heir. By the law of England no person could inherit lands there unless he was born within lawful wedlock. This was so expressly affirmed by the Statute of Merton, which declared, that "he is a bastard that is born before the marriage of his parents." In order, therefore, to see whether the claimant was entitled, it was not sufficient to ascertain whether he was legitimate; but also to ascertain whether he was born in lawful wedlock; for that circumstance is essential to heirship in England. Lord Coke has, indeed, said: "*Hæres*, in the legal understanding of the common law, implieth that he is *ex justis nuptiis procreatus;* for *Hæres legitimus est, quem nuptiæ demonstrant.*" But his expression would have been more accurate if, instead of saying *ex justis nuptiis procreatus,* he had said *ex justis nuptiis natus.* As to the argument used for the claimant, that he is deemed born in lawful wedlock, because by a presumption of the Scottish law, a presumption *juris et de jure,* there was a marriage anterior to the procreation, it is a mere fiction of that law; and cannot govern in England where the actual fact of birth after marriage decides the right. The cases alluded to, where illegitimacy in the place of birth settled the question against the heirship[1], are perfectly consistent with this doctrine; for both facts must concur to establish heirship in England, legitimacy, and birth after marriage. In these cases the first fact was entirely wanting, and in the first step, therefore, in the claimant's title, the ground sunk under him[2].

---

1 Ante, § 87.

2 His Lordship's opinion deserves here to be cited at large: "As to the first of these questions, I believe I express the opinion of the Judges, when I say, in the well-considered language of Lord Stowell, in the case of Dalrymple *v.* Dalrymple, 'The cause being entertained in an English court, must be adjudicated according to the principle of the English law applicable

§ 93 *p*. On the other hand, the reasoning of Lord Brougham was to this effect. The reasoning of the Judges

---

to such a case; but the only principle applicable to such a case by the law of England is, that the status or condition of the claimant must be tried by reference to the law of the country where the status originated: having furnished this principle, the law of England withdraws altogether, and leaves the question of status in the case put to the law of Scotland.' Such is the sentiment of that great Judge, and such is his language, varied only so far as to apply to a question of legitimacy what was said of a question respecting the validity of marriage. When the question of personal status has been settled upon these principles, when it has been ascertained what the claimant's character and situation are, it becomes then necessary to inquire what are the rules and maxims of inheritance, which the law of that country, where the inheritance is placed, and whose tribunals are to decide upon it, has stamped and impressed upon the land in debate. In order the more distinctly to explain what is meant, I will suppose a case in many circumstances resembling the present. In addition to the circumstances stated in the question, let it be further supposed, that the father and mother of the claimant had after their marriage one or more sons born to them. Suppose then the present claim to be made. The first inquiry having been satisfied, and it being upon that inquiry perfectly ascertained that the claimant is the eldest legitimate son of his deceased parent, for the purpose of taking land, and for every other purpose by the law of Scotland, it will next be requisite to inquire what are the rules and maxims of inheritance which the law of England has impressed upon that land, which is the subject of the claim. Let it further be supposed, that upon this inquiry it shall turn out that the land claimed is of that description which is called Borough English. This being proved, we think it clear that the claimant's legitimacy by the law of Scotland, his right to inherit by that law, will give the claimant no right whatever to the land in England held in Borough English. The comity between nations is conclusive to give to the claimant the character of the eldest legitimate son of his father, and to give him all the rights which are necessarily consequent upon that character: but what these rights are respecting English land must be left to the law of England; and the comity is totally ineffectual to alter, in the slightest degree, the rules of inheritance and descent which the law of England has attached to this English land. It would, unquestionably, descend upon the youngest son. I am anxious to mark clearly the distinction which I have pointed out, because it is upon that distinction that our opinion turns. I will therefore illustrate it by another example. Take the case of Ilderton *v.* Ilderton, (2 H. Black. 145); that is the case of a claim to dower by a foreign widow; whether she is a widow or not, that is, whether she was the lawful wife of the man who was during the coverture seised of the land, is a question which the law of England permits, upon a claim to English land, to be determined by the foreign

admitted the validity of the marriage, and the *status* of legitimacy of the claimant. But it was said that the ques-

---

law, the law of the country where the contract of marriage was made; there the comity stops. When her character of widow shall have been fixed according to these foreign rules, the law of England comes into action; and, proceeding inexorably by its own provisions and regulations, decides what are the interests in the English land which her character of widow has conferred upon her. It inquires, what are the rules which attach upon the particular land in favour of a widow. If, upon that inquiry, it appears that the land is subject to the common law, it will give her a third; if it appears to be gavelkind, one half while she remains casta et sola. If the land be customary land of any manor, the custom must be looked into; and she can have only what that custom shall bestow, however strange and capricious that custom may be. The distinction to which I am directing your Lordships' attention, is very familiar to foreign jurists, and is noticed by them as the difference between real and personal status; the last being those which respect the person and follow it everywhere; the first being those which are connected with the land and adhere to it, and are as immovable as the subject to which they are applied. My Lords, it appears to us, that the answer to the question which your Lordships have put, must be founded upon this distinction: while we assume that B. is the eldest legitimate son of his father, in England as well as in Scotland, we think that we have also to consider whether that status, that character, entitles him to the land in dispute as the heir of that father; and we think that this question, inasmuch as it regards real property situated in England, must be decided according to those rules which govern the descent of real property in that country, without the least regard to the rules which govern the descent of real property in Scotland. We have therefore considered, whether, by the law of England, a man is the heir of English land merely because he is the eldest legitimate son of his father. We are of opinion that these circumstances are not sufficient of themselves, but that we must look further, and ascertain whether he was born within the state of lawful matrimony; because by the law of England that circumstance is essential to heirship; and that this is a rule not of a personal nature, but of that class which, if I may use the expression, is sown in the land, springs out of it, and cannot, according to the law of England, be abrogated or destroyed by any foreign rule or law whatsoever. It is this circumstance which, in my judgment, dictates the answer we must give to your Lordships' question, viz. that in selecting the heir for English inheritance, we must inquire only who is that heir by the local law. It has appeared to us, that the vice of the appellant's argument consists in treating the question of who shall be heir to English land, as a question of personal status. So it is, no doubt, up to a certain point; but beyond that point becomes a question to be decided entirely by the local rules relating to real property in the realm of England.

tion was of heirship. That was true. But, then, who was the heir? Why, according to the law of England, the

---

That the rule of the English law is what I have represented, can hardly require proof. If the argument from the comity of nations be shaken off, no man will doubt that a person legitimated per subsequens matrimonium, is not the heir of English land. What my Lord Coke says in page 7 of the first Institute, affords the rule:—'Hæres, in the legal understanding of the common law, implieth that he is ex justis nuptiis procreatus; for Hæres legitimus est, quem nuptiæ demonstrant.' Perhaps my Lord Coke's expression would have been more precise and accurate, if, instead of saying 'ex justis nuptiis procreatus,' he had said 'ex justis nuptiis natus.' But this is what is meant, as all experience shews. It would be useless to follow this further; but it will be material to recollect, that this maxim which pervades all our books, and which is confirmed by all our practice, though it is in form a description of the person who shall be heir, is in substance, in our opinion, a maxim regarding the land, describes one of its most important qualities, traces out the course in which it shall descend, and is no more liable to be broken in upon by any foreign constitution, than are the degree of interest which the heir shall take in the land, the conditions on which he shall hold it, the proportion which a woman shall obtain as a widow, or the limitations and conditions attached to her estate. I have endeavoured to state the principles and to shew the course of reasoning which has conducted my learned brothers and myself to the conclusion, that B., the person designated by your Lordships, is not entitled to the property in question as the heir of A. Before I finish, I will notice two arguments used on behalf of the Appellant which merit particular attention. It is said for the Appellant, that, according to the rule we adopt, if he is born in lawful wedlock, he fulfils every condition required of him. Now they say he is born in lawful wedlock, because, by a presumption of the Scottish law, a presumption juris et de jure, there was a marriage anterior to his procreation. It is by force of this presumption that he is legitimate: by this fiction he is born within the pale of lawful matrimony. We know that this fiction is, by many respectable writers on the Scottish law, represented as accompanying the legitimation per subsequens matrimonium. But we do not concede the consequence deduced from it as applicable to the present question. The question is, what the law of England requires, and, as we are advised, the law of England requires that the claimant should actually and in fact be born within the pale of lawful matrimony; we cannot agree that the presumption of a foreign jurisprudence, contrary to the acknowledged fact, should abrogate the law of England, and that by such a fiction a principle should be introduced, which, upon a great and memorable occasion, the legislature of the kingdom distinctly rejected: your Lordships will perceive that I allude to the statute of Merton. It would seem strange to introduce indirectly, and from comity to a foreign nation, a rule of inheritance which may affect every

eldest legitimate son. Now the claimant answered to this very character. He was the eldest son, and he was legiti-

---

honour and all the real property of the realm; which rule, when proposed directly and positively to the legislature, they directly and positively negatived and refused: a refusal that in England has obtained the approbation of every succeeding age. Again, my Lords, it is said that two cases have been decided in this House which are nearly in point, and will prove that the claim of B. should be supported. These cases are the cases of Shedden *v.* Patrick, and the case of Lord Strathmore. These two cases are alike in principle, and establish the same proposition. In the one case the parents lived in a state of concubinage in America, and in the other in England. In both children were born to them. Afterwards, the parties married in their respective countries; by force of their marriages the American issue claimed Scottish land, and the English issue claimed Scottish honours: in both your Lordships decided against the claimants. Now, it is said, these authorities are exactly the converse of the present case. They establish the principle, that the courts of the country where the lands lie, in a question respecting the heirship to these lands or honours, inform themselves whether the claimant is heir, not by the law of the country where the lands lie, but in the country of the domicil where the marriage of the parents was contracted; and if he is not heir by that foreign law, his claim is rejected; from which they deduce this consequence, that if he is heir his claim should be sustained. This argument presents itself in a very plausible shape, and was pressed at the bar, as it seemed to me, with striking ingenuity and force. But if I have had the good fortune sufficiently to explain the principles which have conducted my learned brothers and myself to the opinion I have stated, you will soon perceive that these principles afford a conclusive answer to it. The first step to be taken in every case of this kind, as I have already explained, is to inquire into the status of the claimant. The status, it is argued, is to be determined by the law of the foreign country; with this the lex rei sitæ does not intermeddle, and intermeddles no more when that foreign law establishes the claimant's bastardy than when it proves his legitimacy. In both the cases the claimants were bastards; the laws of their own country, the laws of their domicil, the laws of the spot where the matrimonial contract was entered into, declared them to be illegitimate: the law which, by the acknowledged principles, ascertained their personal status, fixed upon these persons a character of illegitimacy fatal to their claims: on the first step the ground sunk under them, and it became impossible for them to advançe. It is obvious, that if, in the cases to which I am now referring, the claimants had been declared heirs by the Scottish law, the Scottish law admitting of no heirship without legitimacy, must have been called in aid to bestow upon them that personal character of legitimacy refused to them by their own law; in other words, a law foreign to their birth, to their domicil, and to the marriage of their parents, would have been held to bestow upon

mate. In truth, legitimate son means lawful son, and the rule of inheritance is, that the eldest lawful son shall succeed the father. But lawful or not depends upon the law which is to govern; and no other definition can be given of what is lawful than this, that he is the lawful son whom the law declares such. What law? There are two, it is said, in this case: the law of the place of the party's birth and of his parents' marriage, and the law of the place where the land lies. Then which law is to prevail? The law of the birth-place. Any other rule would involve great inconvenience, and be inconsistent with principle; for then a man would be legitimate in one place, and illegitimate in another; legitimate as to personal property, and illegitimate as to real property in the same country. And this would not only affect him, but all persons who after his death should claim through him; even purchasers claiming from him or them.

§ 93 *q*. Then as to the argument, that heir means he who is born in lawful wedlock, *ex justis nuptiis*. It is true. But what is lawful wedlock? It is that which is so by the law of the place of marriage; and there is no greater reason for being bound by that law as to marriage than there is as to legitimacy, as consequent upon the marriage. Why may not the Court look behind the marriage, and ascertain whether the parties were competent to marry by the law of England? It is not correct to say, that the law of the place of marriage governs, as to that alone: it must govern as to all the effects consequent thereon. So it was held by Huberus. So it was held in the cases of Crawford *v*. Pa-

them their personal status and character,—a decision certainly contrary to the acknowledged principles upon this subject. The character of illegitimacy attached to the persons of the English and American claimants by their own law, accompanied them everywhere, and would prevent their being received as heirs anywhere within the limits of the Christian world. This view, in our judgment, renders these decisions entirely consistent with the principles I have unfolded, and prevents our considering them as objections to the opinion I entertain, that B. is not entitled to the property in question as the heir of A." Birthwhistle *v*. Vardill, 9 Bligh, R. 45 to 53.

trick, and Strathmore *v.* Bowes, already alluded to [1]. In Scotland the child born before the marriage ceremony has been performed, is legitimate, not because of the subsequent act of his parents; but because he is considered as born in lawful wedlock. The marriage is held to have preceded his birth, and so he is deemed *non legitimatus, sed legitimus ab initio.* This is not a mere refinement or fiction; because in Scotland marriage is a consentient contract; and such consent and marriage before the birth are deemed to be evidenced by the subsequent open ceremony and celebration of the marriage. This is no more a fiction, than the English law as to this very point. If in England a child is born the day after the marriage, he is deemed legitimate, although procreated long before. The law will not inquire into the fact.

§ 93 *r.* As to the statute of Merton, it has no bearing on the subject. That statute applies only to children born in England. It is no authority for saying, that he only can inherit English lands, whom that statute declares legitimate. That statute can in no just sense apply to persons born out of England. Their *status,* as to legitimacy, depends not on that statute; but on the laws of the country of their birth. He is legitimate, whom the law of his birth declares to be so. He is lawful heir, whom the law of his birth declares to be born in lawful wedlock. We are necessarily driven to this conclusion; and we must resort to the foreign law to solve all such questions. If it is said, that he is the lawful heir in England who is the eldest son born within lawful wedlock, it is but changing the position of the point; for we may just as well say, that he who is the eldest son born in lawful wedlock, (and so the claimant is,) is the lawful heir in England. The real point of difficulty was not met nor considered by the learned Judges. The very question was, whether the law of England did not take the rule, as to legitimacy, the eldest son born within lawful

---

[1] Ante, § 87.

wedlock, from the very *status* as to these points recognised and held by the law of Scotland. The whole constituted his personal *status;* and that personal *status* travelled with him into England[1].

---

[1] It may be far more satisfactory to the learned reader to have his Lordship's reasoning at large in his own words: "In approaching this question, there are some things not disputed. It is admitted that the validity of a marriage must depend on the law of the country where it is had, and that consequently the parents of this party were validly married. It seems also to be agreed, that, generally speaking, legitimacy is a status, and must be determined by the law of the country to which the party belongs. But it is said by those who support this judgment, that, whether the party here is legitimate or not, is no question before us; the only question being, it is alleged, whether or not he is the heir to an English real estate. This distinction, I confess, appears to me founded on an inaccurate view of the subject. It is true that the question here arises upon the claim of an heir as such, and that therefore the only question may be said to be whether he is heir or not. But it is also very possible, that this question may turn wholly upon another, namely, whether or not the claimant is eldest legitimate son of his father, the person last seised? Nor do I well see how legitimacy can ever come in question in any other way than as connected with the claim to succession, either real or personal, in England or in Scotland either, unless in the case of a declarator of bastardy or of legitimacy,—a proceeding unknown in the English law. It is therefore by no means sufficient for deciding this case to say, that the question touches not legitimacy, but inheritance; not the personal status of the party, but his right to real property. It may touch both these matters, and the latter may wholly depend upon the former. In truth, legitimate son means lawful son; and the rule of inheritance is, that the eldest lawful son shall succeed to the father; but 'lawful' or 'not' depends upon the law which is to govern; and no other definition can be given of what is lawful than this, that he is lawful son whom the law declares to be such. What law? There are two, it is said, in this case—the law of the place of the party's birth, and of his parents' marriage, and the law of the place where the land lies. Then which of these two laws shall prevail? The whole inclination of every one's mind must be towards that law which prevails where each person is born, and where his parents were married, supposing the countries to be one and the same; and if they differ, I should then say certainly the law of the birth-place. Nor can anything be more inconvenient or more inconsistent with principle, than the inevitable consequence of taking the lex loci rei sitæ for the rule; because this makes a man legitimate or illegitimate according to the place where his property lies, or rights come in question; legitimate when he sues for distribution of personal estate; a bastard, when he sues for succession to real; nay, legitimate in one country, where part of his land may lie; and a bastard in some other, where

§ 93 *s*. Another question also has arisen in England, whether a child born before marriage in one country, of

---

he has the residue. So, in like manner, all who claim through him must have their rights determined by the same vague and uncertain canon; a circumstance which I nowhere find adverted to below. All the learned Judges proceed upon the case being one of an inheritance claimed by the party himself. But what if he were dead years ago, and another claimed an estate in England, to which he (the alleged bastard) never had been, and never could have been entitled: an estate, for example, descending from a collateral, who took it by purchase after the death of the alleged bastard? Then the pedigree of the claimant must be made out through legitimate persons; and the question of legitimacy is raised as to one, who is not himself claiming any land; who never did or could claim any land; and it is not raised in respect of any right in him to inherit; any right to be called the heir to any land. I apprehend this shews strongly the necessity of taking another view than the learned Judges seemed to have deemed sufficient for getting over the difficulty of the case; and of admitting that there is a status of legitimacy which is personal, and, travelling about with the individual, must be determined by the law of his country. In the argument for the judgment below, it is thought enough to say, that heir means he who is born in lawful wedlock—ex justis nuptiis. Then what is lawful wedlock? Is there any greater reason for being bound by the law of the country where the marriage contract was made, in deciding whether or not the wedlock was lawful, than there is for being governed in ascertaining the legitimacy of the issue of the marriage by the law of the country where that issue was born, more especially when it was also the country where the marriage was had? But can the Court stop short, according to its own principle, at the mere fact of the marriage being according to the lex loci contractûs? Do not the principles on which their decision proceeds demand this further inquiry—Were the parties able to marry by the lex loci rei sitæ? and thus a door is opened to the further examination of how far a preceding divorce of one of the parties was sufficient to dissolve a previous English marriage. All such difficulties are got rid of by holding the lex loci contractûs et nativitatis as governing the validity of the contract and legitimacy of its issue; but they are not to be got over in this way by any argument which does not with equal force apply to holding that the legitimacy of the issue is a question equally to be governed by the lex loci contractûs and the law of the birth-place. Nor is it correct to say, as the Judges below assumed, that the lex loci only influences the validity of the contract, and extends not to its effects. The highest authorities have held expressly the reverse. Huber, in the Treatise De Conflictu Legum, which forms part of his larger work, and is constantly cited as the greatest authority on this question, says, 'Non solum ipsi contractus ipsæque nuptiæ certis locis rite celebratæ ubique pro justis et validis habentur, sed etiam jura et effectus contractûm nuptiarumque in iis locis recepta ubique vim suam ob-

parents domiciled in that country, by whose laws a subsequent marriage would not legitimate him, would, by a mar-

---

tinebunt.' I. 3, 9. It would be difficult to state anything more clearly and properly the effect of the matrimonial contract than the legitimacy of the issue; it is, in fact, the main object, and therefore the principal effect of that contract. But to remove all doubt on this subject, and to extend the same rule also to the lex loci nativitatis, he adds: 'Qualitates personales certo loco alicui impressas ubique circumferri et personam comitari cum hoc effectu, ut ubivis locorum eo jure quo tales personæ alibi gaudent vel subjecti sunt, gaudeantur et subjiciantur.' This principle was adopted and acted on in two very remarkable cases by your Lordships then proceeding under the advice of Lord Eldon; I mean Crawford *v.* Patrick, and Strathmore *v.* Bowes. In the former, a child having been born before marriage in America, where the English law prevails, claimed a Scotch estate in respect of the subsequent marriage of his parents there, of whom the father was Scotch. He contended, that the question having arisen upon a real estate in Scotland, the Court of Session was bound to administer the law loci rei sitæ, and that law declared him legitimate. But the Court below and your Lordships held, that legitimacy is a status to be determined by the law of the party's birth-place, or at any rate by that of the country where the marriage of his parents was had, as well as himself born; and they held him bastard in Scotland, where the land lay, because he was bastard in America, where his birth and his parents' marriage took place. In Strathmore *v.* Bowes, a marriage, had in London after the birth of the child, was held not to legitimate the issue either as to Scotch honours or estate on the same grounds; and in both these cases one of the points made for the judgment was the absurdity of holding the same person to be bastard in one country and legitimate in another. It is plain that legitimacy has but one meaning, namely, born in lawful wedlock. Now, in Scotland the child born before the marriage ceremony has been performed is legitimate; not because of a subsequent act of his parents, but because he is considered as born in lawful wedlock. The marriage is held to have preceded his birth, and according to the doctrine and language of the civil law, from which Scotland and other countries have borrowed this principle, he is considered as non legitimatus, sed legitimus ab initio. Nor is this a mere fiction of law and a technical refinement. Marriage in Scotland is a consensual contract, and perfected by consent alone. But this may be given, and the contract made in two ways, either per verba de præsenti, or by a promise subsequente copulâ. Now in the latter case, the copula makes the previous promise a consent; it turns the promise touching the future into a present consent. A child then, born in the interval between the promise and the copula, would be legitimate, for the copula would shew that consent, and therefore a marriage, had preceded his birth. But so does a marriage after the birth, for that raises the legal presumption, that there was a consent before the birth and at the cohabitation. The cohabitation is

riage of his parents in another country, by whose laws such subsequent marriage would legitimate him, become legiti-

---

held to have been a consent and a marriage; the ceremony is only held as evidence of that previous consent and contract. So much is this the case, that, if either party was married to another at the time of the child's birth, or during the interval between that birth and the ceremony, no legitimation takes place; because no room exists for the presumption of law, that the consent or marriage took place before the birth. All this is certain and clear; but the learned Judges in the Court below appear not to have taken it into their consideration. The judgment is rested entirely upon the statute of Merton, and it is contended, that, by that famous Act, he is declared a bastard who is born before the marriage of his parents: no doubt, so he is in England; and no doubt bastardy, the status of bastardy, is what the English law is there dealing with. But is this an authority for saying that he only shall inherit English lands whom that statute declares legitimate? It is said, that the lex loci rei sitæ must govern the succession to real estate; undoubtedly it must; and if that law gives it in Kent to all the sons, and in Brentford to the youngest, and elsewhere to the eldest, these several sons are the heirs in those several places. But when it is said the lawful issue shall take, I agree: I too say only the legitimate son or sons shall inherit; but to find who are the legitimate sons, I must ask the law of the birth-place, which fixes the status of legitimacy; of the personal quality, according to Huber, that travels round everywhere with the party. But the argument assumes a narrower and apparently closer form still; for it is said that the statute declares those only inheritable, who are born in marriage, and that Lord Coke accordingly defines the heir to be him who is ex justis nuptiis procreatus. There is in this, however, a great fallacy: 'Born in marriage' or not; 'ex justis nuptiis procreatus' or not; is to be determined by some law or other; it is not a question that answers itself and in one way only. Then what law shall determine? Certainly either the law of the country where the party was born, or where the marriage was had; the law either of the country where the nuptiæ were had, or where the procreatio took place. A question might arise where the events happened in different countries; it might then be doubted which law should govern; which should be resorted to for an answer to the question. But where both events happened in the same country, as here, there seems no doubt at all in the matter. Now the law of the country where both the marriage and the birth took place, declares that the party was born in lawful wedlock; that he was ex justis nuptiis procreatus; and wholly denies that he was born before marriage, or out of wedlock. But it is said that this is a fiction, and that our law cannot import the fictions of a foreign system, though its principles we are allowed to import. This distinction I do not profess to comprehend; what is a fiction but a principle? It is only one particular view which the law takes, and one doctrine which it lays down. Suppose a Scotch Court were to deny the le-

mate, so as to inherit lands in the latter country. It has been held by the House of Lords, that the mere fact of

---

gitimacy of a child, who was born on the day after his parents married in England, should we not say that a gross absurdity was committed? Should we not say the child was born in lawful wedlock, and hold the doctrine absurd which should question his being lawfully begotten? Nay, suppose a gift, in the usual terms, to the heirs of the body lawfully begotten; we should let the child born the day after marriage take under such a gift, although it was clearly not lawfully begotten in point of fact. This is a fiction exactly analogous to the Scotch fiction. The Scotch law presumes, against the fact, the marriage to have been had before the birth of the child; our law presumes, against the fact, the marriage to have been had before the cohabitation of the parents. The fiction, or rather presumption, is parcel of the legal principle in both, and there can be no reason for importing the residue of the doctrine, and rejecting the presumption; there can be no reason for importing the English law presumption into Scotland, which does not justify and require us to import the Scotch law presumption into England. It must be recollected, too, that the special verdict finds as a fact the legitimacy of the party, and not his legitimation; it finds as a fact that he is legitimate; that is to say, lawfully born. Now we know this to mean, by the Scotch law, born in lawful wedlock; but the finding in the verdict is sufficient; for legitimate, as contradistinguished from legitimated, means born in lawful wedlock, and can mean nothing else. So in the civil law, from whence this doctrine is wholly taken, both in Scotland and Holland, and other countries, the child is legitimus, not legitimatus; as in the same system of jurisprudence, liber is a free man; libertinus, one of the condition of a freed man; ingenuus, one free born. If any person were found to be ingenuus by an inquisition, we should contend that he never had been a slave, though a finding of liber might leave it equivocal. In like manner, and by parity of reason, a person being found legitimate, or legitimus, and not legitimated or legitimatus, excludes the supposition of his ever having been a bastard, and shews him to be lawfully born and begotten. Suppose a Scotch estate devolved to one born before marriage, as it might by devise (or rather Scotch conveyance in the nature of devise) to the first son of A., I apprehend that A. marrying the mother the day after the devisor's death, the estate would be vested in the son, because he would become legitimate, though born before the death. But it is unnecessary to argue this, though it illustrates the principle; the fact found is, that the lessor of the plaintiff was born in Scotland legitimate, or in lawful wedlock. The cases of Crawford *v.* Patrick and Strathmore *v.* Bowes have been already referred to, but they require another remark. They were decided in this House by appeal, it is true, from Scotland, and respecting the Scotch real estate; but still by this House, and upon general principles of law. Those cases were the precise converse of this: they decided the bastardy of parties, and on the distinct ground, that, as Lord Redesdale said,

marriage in such country, where there was no change of the domicil of the parents, would not give him such a capa-

they were 'bastard by the law of their birth-place, and therefore bastard in Scotland, where the rights claimed respected real estate.' It is not more the rule of the English law, that children born out of wedlock shall not inherit, though their parents intermarry, than it is the rule of the Scotch law that such children shall inherit if their parents do intermarry. It is not more alien to the English law to adopt the fiction, that such children are born in wedlock, than it is alien to the Scotch law to exclude this principle. The English rule being statutory can make no difference. A fixed and known principle of common law has exactly the same force with statutory provision. How then can the opposite principle be adopted in two cases identically the same? The Court below says, that the English law gives not an estate to the bastard *eigne*, and that it treats him as bastard, although by the law of his birth-place he was legitimate. The Scotch law gives the estate to the bastard *eigne*, regarding him as legitimate, and this House adjudged that he should not take that estate only because he was illegitimate by the law of his birth-place. Your Lordships decided, that the lex loci rei sitæ should not be regarded when it differed from the lex loci contractûs et nativitatis; you decided that, when the former law declared for legitimacy, it should yield to the latter, which declared for bastardy. How can you be called upon here to decide that the lex loci rei sitæ shall not overrule the other law, and that again in favour of bastardy? I profess my inability to understand how these two decisions of the same question can in any way stand together; nor am I able to perceive that the least attention was paid by the Court below to those important decisions of your Lordships. I perceive that the whole argument in that Court turned upon a question not in dispute here. The learned Judges suppose that they decide the question when they prove that the English law is to govern the case, because the question relates to real property situated in England. Now undeniably the English law is to govern the case in one sense; the eldest lawful son is to succeed; but who that son is must be determined by the law of his birth-place, and by the fact found, that, under that law, the lessor of the plaintiff is eldest lawful son. Nay, even if we take the English law to be, that lawful son or heir is he who was born in wedlock, then we have here the fact found, and found as a fact, that in the country where he was born the party was born in wedlock. No one, it must be always borne in mind, pretends to say that the English law can in any way dispose of the whole question. Admitting that the rule cited from Lord Coke in reference to the statute of Merton is to govern us, hæres qui ex justis nuptiis procreatus est, no one contends that the question, what are justæ nuptiæ, can be determined otherwise than by a reference to the lex loci contractûs, or, it may be, loci nativitatis. To that foreign law, then, we must resort; and the only question is, at what period of our inquiry this recourse shall be had? No more needs be said to shew how very far from decisive of the present ques-

city to inherit land, and that the stain of illegitimacy by his birth was not wiped away by such a marriage[1]. And

tion that position is, which alone is argued or defended by the learned Judges, namely, that the law of England must govern. It does govern; but with the aid, through the ministry of the foreign law. The reference made to the dictum of the Master of the Rolls, in Brodie *v.* Barry, (2 Ves. & Bea. p. 127,) does not touch the case. All that his Honor there said was, that questions on real rights must follow the law of the country where the land lies. This is not denied; nor was it denied by this House when it refused to consider W. Sheddon, or J. Bowes, as legitimate in respect to Scotch estates, although the law of Scotland, where those estates lay, held them both to be so; or rather would so have held, had they been born in Scotland. But while this House and the Court of Session admitted that the Scotch law must decide, they also held, that the Scotch law refused estate to bastards, and that it regarded one as a bastard who was so by the law of his birthplace. That was the same case in principle with this in every material respect. It is not easy in such a question, a question raised on the conflictus legum, to omit all considerations of convenience; inasmuch as it is principally on views of convenience that the whole doctrine of what is generally called comitas turns. One should say that nothing can be more pregnant with inconvenience; nay, that nothing can lead to consequences more strange in statement, than a doctrine which sets out with assuming legitimacy to be not a personal status, but a relation to the several countries in which rights are claimed, and indeed to the nature of different rights. That a man may be bastard in one country and legitimate in another, seems of itself a strong position to affirm; but more staggering when it is followed up by this other, that in one and the same country he is to be regarded as bastard when he comes into one court to claim an estate in land, and legitimate when he resorts to another to obtain personal succession; nay, that the same Court of Equity (when the real estate happens to be impressed with a trust) must view him as both bastard and legitimate, in respect of a succession to the same intestate. Further still, should he happen to be next of kin to his uncle who had a mortgage upon the estate, he must be denied his succession to the land of the mortgagor in his quality of bastard, and be allowed to come in as an incumbrancer upon the selfsame estate, in his capacity of legitimate son to the same mortgagor. All this is assumed to be the law by the learned Judges who have decided below, and advised your Lordships here. They have not assumed, what however they cannot deny, that it is another consequence of their doctrine to enable a descendant of this same bastard to claim through him as if he were legitimate, while the alleged force of the statute of Merton,

[1] Munro *v.* Saunders, 6 Bligh, R. 468; Rose *v.* Ross, 4 Wils. & Shaw, 289. See Id. App. p. 33 to 89, where the opinions of the Scotch Judges are also given at large.

it was intimated, that, under the like circumstances, in other respects, the change of domicil of the parents to the country

---

and of Lord Coke's commentary thereupon, excludes him from taking it himself. In the same country, in the same Courts, in respect to the same land, he is both bastard and legitimate; bastard for the purpose of his own succession, legitimate when the succession of others is concerned. May I be permitted most respectfully to express a doubt, whether or not this question has received all the consideration which it deserves at the hand of those learned Judges? I know not that it carries the argument much further; but there is a proceeding well known to your Lordships sitting here as a Court of general jurisdiction over the whole United Kingdom, though unknown to the Courts of England; the process of declarator. Suppose a declarator of legitimacy had been brought in the Scotch Courts by the lessor of this plaintiff: the judgment would have been, and quite as a matter of course, that he was lawful son of Wm. Birthwhistle; and the present defendant being made a party to this suit, the judgment could be given in evidence before the Court where the ejectment now before us was brought. I agree that such a judgment does not conclusively bind; yet it would place the conflict of the two laws in a somewhat stronger light, if the English Court should pronounce him bastard whom the Scotch Court, sitting in the country of his birth, had pronounced lawful son. But if both judgments were brought here by appeal and writ of error, as might easily happen, your Lordships would be compelled to affirm the sentence of the Scotch Court, and yet you are now asked to affirm the opposite judgment of the King's Bench. Let it be observed, too, that all this anomaly is in England; it begins and ends here; for the Scotch Judges have decided in such cases with perfect consistency as well as entire uniformity. Those learned persons, whose familiarity with legal principle in its enlarged sense, is derived from a deep study of the feudal and of the civil law, as well as of the modern jurisprudence of Scotland, have been guided in all their determinations of such questions by simple, rational, and intelligible principles. If a declarator of legitimacy were brought before them by one born in England before marriage, and whose parents afterwards intermarried, their sentence would be that he was illegitimate; and even were he to claim a Scotch estate, the law would be the same. This has been ruled in Scotland in the cases more than once referred to, and affirmed upon appeal here. But you are now advised to take a different course when the same question arises in another part of the United Kingdom. It may be observed, that, in referring to those Scotch cases, the learned Chief Justice says, without discussing them, that it is satisfactory to him that the form of the proceeding (a special verdict) was such as to carry the question before the same tribunal which pronounced those decisions. In the advice, however, which has been given to this tribunal by the same learned Judges, I do not find that those decisions have been much considered." Birthwhistle *v.* Vardill, 9 Bligh, R. 71 to 86.

where the marriage was celebrated, would not have given any better title to inherit, as the stain of the illegitimacy would be indelible[1]. The converse case has been decided in France, where it has been held, that, if a child is born in a country (France) where he would become legitimate by a subsequent marriage, he will become legitimate by such subsequent marriage, although the marriage should take place in a country (England) where a different law prevails, and where a subsequent marriage would not have the effect of rendering him legitimate[2]. The result of these two cases seems to be, that the law of the place of birth of the child, and not the law of the place of the marriage of the parents, is to decide whether a subsequent marriage will legitimate the child or not[3].

§ 93 *t*. We have already seen, that the same doctrine upon these very points is maintained by Hertius, by Bouhier, and by Boullenois[4]. The latter puts the very case of a child born in England in concubinage, and whose parents afterwards become residents in France, and there intermarry without being naturalized, and says that the child is not legitimated by such subsequent marriage; but remains illegitimate as he was by the law of the country

---

1 Munro *v*. Saunders, 6 Bligh, R. 468; Rose *v*. Ross, 4 Wils. & Shaw, 289; Id. App. p. 33 to 89. See 1 Burge, Comment. on Col. and For. Law, P. 1, ch. 3, § 2, pp. 108, 109, 110.

2 The case of De Conty, 1668, cited by Lord Brougham in Munro *v*. Saunders, 6 Bligh, R. 478, and in Rose *v*. Ross, 4 Wils. & Shaw, R. 299. The same case is reported in Merlin, Quest. de Droit, art. *Legitimation*, § 2, note (1), p. 151, (4to. edit.,) Paris, 1828, who corrects the error into which Boullenois had fallen in stating the facts of the same case. See also 1 Burge, Comment. on Col. and For. Law, P. 1, ch. 3, § 2, pp. 102, 106, 107. May there not be room for a distinction in such a case, as to the state of the party or property in the country of his birth, and that of the party or the property in the country of the marriage; each country adhering to its own laws in regard to the property situate there?

3 But see the elaborate opinions of the Scottish Judges on the same questions in Rose *v*. Ross, 4 Wils. & Shaw, App. p. 33 to 89. The House of Lords reversed their judgment.

4 Ante, § 93 *d*, 93 *i*.

of his birth. The converse case of a child born in France, and the parents subsequently intermarrying in England, he holds equally clear, and that thereby the child will become legitimate[1]. Boullenois has, as we have also seen, pushed his doctrine much farther; farther, indeed, than seems consistent with any just principle, especially in giving a retroactive effect to a subsequent naturalization in another country[2].

§ 93 *u*. Merlin supports the same general doctrine, holding, that it is impossible to consider as legitimate in France a natural child born in England of English parents, who afterwards intermarry in England[3]. But that a natural child born in France of French parents, who should afterwards remove to England, and there intermarry without being naturalized, would, by such subsequent marriage, be made legitimate[4]. In each case he holds, that the law of the place of the birth of the child gives the rule as to legitimacy by a subsequent marriage.

§ 93 *v*. Merlin supposes that Hertius holds a different doctrine, and affirms that the law of the place of marriage gives the rule as to legitimacy, and not that of the place of the birth of the child. I do not so understand Hertius. To me, it seems clear that Hertius was only contemplating the case of a marriage and birth both in England. *In Anglia* (says he) *legitimationi per subsequens matrimonium locus non est. Quæstio est igitur: An filius, quem pater ante legitimum connubium in Anglia genuerat, succedere possit patri huic naturali in bonis extra Anglia sitis? Affirmatum hoc in Auditorio Parisiensi*[5]. *Rectius negatur, nisi lex alterius populi etiam illegitimos ad successionem admittat;*

---

1 Ante, § 93 *d*, § 93 *i*; 1 Boullenois, Observ. 4, pp. 62, 63.

2 Ibid.; Merlin, in his Quest. de Droit, art. *Legitimation*, § 2, n. 1, combats this doctrine of Boullenois.

3 Merlin, Quest. de Droit, art. *Legitimation*, § 1, n. 1.

4 Ibid. § 2, n. 1, 2.

5 Ante, § 39 *s*. The case of De Conty in 1668.

neque enim lex illa Anglorum pugnat cum æquitate naturali[1]. It is highly probable, that Hertius understood the case referred to, as Boullenois had, by mistake, as a case where the child was born in England; whereas he was born in France[2].

§ 94. These cases may suffice in relation to the question of legitimacy or illegitimacy. We may now pass to another class of disabilities imposed by foreign laws, in order to illustrate the difficulty of maintaining the doctrine as a universal rule, obligatory upon all countries, under all circumstances, that the capacity or incapacity of a person is to be governed solely by the laws of his birth and domicil; and that is the class of persons whose marriages are void or voidable by reason of their profession. Thus, by the law of England, until after the Reformation, monks and nuns were deemed incapable of contracting marriage, (as they still are in many parts of the continent of Europe,) and their contracts for this purpose were held nullities. The marriages of priests are also in some countries voidable in law, as contrary to their office at any time during their lives[3]. And to this very day in Catholic countries, marriages are prohibited to the priesthood and to persons in monastic orders. Yet it would be extremely difficult to maintain that the marriage of a nun, or a monk, or a priest, celebrated in America, where no such prohibition exists, ought, *causâ professionis*, to be held a mere nullity on account of such foreign prohibitions, especially where the other party is at the time of the marriage domiciled here, and as such is entitled to the protection of our laws.

§ 95. By the laws of some countries the subjects thereof are prohibited from intermarrying with foreigners, or with

---

[1] Hertii Opera, De Collis. Leg. § 4, n. 15, p. 129; Id. pp. 183, 184, (edit. 1716).

[2] Merlin, Quest. de Droit, § 2, n. 2, p. 151, (4to. edit.,) Paris, 1828; Ante, § 93 *s*, note 2.

[3] 2 Inst. 686, 687; Com. Dig. *Baron and Feme*, B. 2; 1 Woodes. Lec. 16, p. 422.

persons of another religious sect; and some civilians have held that such laws are of universal obligation, and accompany the person everywhere[1]. But it can hardly be supposed that any other nation would suffer a marriage celebrated in its own dominions, according to its own laws, between such persons, and especially where one of them was a citizen or subject thereof, to be deemed a nullity in its own courts. Such a narrow prohibition would justly be deemed odious, and be rejected.

§ 96. Another case may be put of even a more striking character. Suppose a person to be a slave in his own country, having no personal capacity to contract there, is he, upon his removal to a foreign country where slavery is not tolerated, to be still deemed a slave? If so, then a Greek or Asiatic, held in slavery in Turkey, would, upon his arrival in England, or in Massachusetts, be deemed a slave, and be there subject to be treated as mere property, and be under the uncontrollable despotic power of his master. The same rule would exist as to Africans and others held in slavery in foreign countries. But we know that no such general effect has in practice ever been attributed to the state of slavery. There is a uniformity of opinion among foreign jurists and foreign tribunals, in giving no effect to the state of slavery of a party, whatever it might have been in the country of his birth, or of that in which he had been previously domiciled, unless it is also recognised by the laws of the country of his actual domicil, and where he is found, and it is sought to be enforced. Christinæus states this as a clear rule affirmed by judicial decisions: *Propter libertatis personarum usum hic per aliquot sæcula continuè observatum*[2]. Groenewegen, speaking of slavery, says: *Ejusque nomen hodie apud nos exolevit. Adeo quidem, ut servi, qui aliunde huc adducuntur, simul ac imperii nostri*

---

[1] See Paul Voet, De Statut. § 5, ch. 2, n. 1, pp. 178, 179, (edit. 1661); Vattel, B. 2, ch. 8, § 115.

[2] Christinæus, Vol. 4, Decis. 80, pp. 114, 115, n. 4; 1 Burge, Comment. on Col. and For. Law, ch. 10, p. 739.

fines intrârunt, invitis ipsis dominis, *ad libertatem proclamare possint. Id, quod et aliorum Christianorum gentium moribus receptum est*[1]. In Scotland the like doctrine has been solemnly adjudged[2]. The tribunals of France have adopted the same rule, even in relation to slaves coming from and belonging to their own colonies. This is also the undisputed law of England[3]. It has been solemnly decided that the law of England abhors, and will not endure the existence of slavery within the nation; and consequently, as soon as a slave lands in England, he becomes *ipso facto* a freeman, and discharged from the state of servitude[4]. Independent of the provisions of the Constitution of the United States, for the protection of the rights of masters in regard to domestic fugitive slaves, there is no doubt that the same principle pervades the common law of the non-slave-holding states in America; that is to say, foreign slaves would no longer be deemed such after their removal thither[5].

---

[1] Groenewegen, ad Instit. Lib. 1, tit. 8, n. 3, p. 5; cited also in 1 Burge, Comment. on Col. and For. Law, ch. 10, p. 739. Groenewegen cites many authorities in support of his opinion.

[2] Knight *v.* Wedderburn, 1778, 20 Howell, State Trials, 1 to 15, note.

[3] See cases cited 20 Howell, State Trials, 12, 13, 14, note; and Causes Célébres, vol. 13, p. 492, (edit. 1747); 1 Burge, Comment. on Col. and For. Law, ch. 10, pp. 739, 740.

[4] Somerset's Case, Lofft, R. 1; S. C. 11 State Trials, Hargrave (edit 340); 20 Howell, State Trials, 1 to 79; Co. Lit. 79; Harg. note, 44; 1 Black. Comm. 424, 425, Christian's note, and Coleridge's note; Forbes *v.* Cochrane, 2 Barn. & Cres. 448; The Amedie, 1 Acton, R. 240; S. C. 1 Dodson, R. 84; Id. 91, 95; The St. Louis, 2 Dodson, R. 210; The Slave Grace, 2 Hagg. Adm. R. 94, 104, 105, 106, 107, 109, 110, 111, 118; 1 Burge, Comment. on Col. and For. Law, P. 1, ch. 10, p. 735 to 752.

[5] See the opinion of the Court delivered by Mr. Justice Porter, in Saul *v.* His Creditors, 17 Martin, R. 598; In re Francisco, 9 Amer. Jurist, 490; Butler *v.* Hooper, 1 Wash. C. C. R. 499; Ex parte Simmons, 4 Wash. C. C. R. 390. See also Butler *v.* Delaplaine, 7 Serg. & Rawle, R. 378; Commonwealth *v.* Holloway, 6 Binn. R. 213; S. C. 2 Serg. & Rawle, R. 305; Lumsford *v.* Coquillon, 14 Martin, R. 408; Louis *v.* Cabarrus, 7 Louis. R. 170, 172; 1 Burge, Comm. on Col. and For. Law, P. 1, ch. 10, p. 744 to 749.—In the recent case of Commonwealth *v.* Aves, 1836, before Mr. Chief Justice Shaw, in Massachusetts, it was expressly held, that a

§ 96 *a*. It is quite a different question, how far rights acquired, and wrongs done to slave property, or contracts

---

slave brought into Massachusetts voluntarily by his master, from a slave state of the United States, was free here, and could not be recovered or carried back as a slave. Upon that occasion the learned Judge said: "The question now before the court arises upon a return to a habeas corpus, originally issued in vacation by Mr. Justice Wilde, for the purpose of bringing up the person of a coloured child named Med, and instituting a legal inquiry into the fact of her detention, and the cause for which she was detained. By the provisions of the revised code, the practice upon habeas corpus is somewhat altered. In case the party complaining, or in behalf of whom complaint is made, on the ground of unlawful imprisonment, is not in the custody of an officer as of a sheriff or deputy, or corresponding officer of the United States, the writ is directed to the sheriff, requiring him or his deputy to take the body of the person thus complaining, or in behalf of whom complaint is thus made, and have him before the Court or magistrate issuing the writ, and to summon the party alleged to have or claim the custody of such person, to appear at the same time, and shew the cause of the detention. The person thus summoned is to make a statement under oath, setting forth all the facts fully and particularly; and in case he claims the custody of such party, the grounds of such claim must be fully set forth. This statement is in the nature of a return to the writ, as made under the former practice, and will usually present the material facts upon which the questions arise. Such return, however, is not conclusive of the facts stated in it; but the court is to proceed and inquire into all the alleged causes of detention, and decide upon them in a summary manner. But the court may, if the occasion require it, adjourn the examination, and in the meantime bail the party, or commit him to a general or special custody, as the age, health, sex, and other circumstances of the case may require. It is further provided, that when the writ is issued by one Judge of the Court in vacation, and in the meantime, before a final decision, the court shall meet in the same county, the proceedings may be adjourned into the court, and there be conducted to a final issue, in the same manner as if they had been originally commenced by a writ issued from the Court. I have stated these provisions the more minutely, because there have been as yet but few proceedings under the revised statutes, and the practice is yet to be established. Upon the return of this writ before Mr. Justice Wilde, a statement was made by Mr. Aves, the respondent: the case was then postponed. It has since been fully and very ably argued before all the Judges, and is now transferred to and entered in court, and stands here for judgment in the same manner as if the writ had been originally returnable in court. The return of Mr. Aves states, that he has the body of the coloured child described in his custody, and produces her. It further states that Samuel Slater, a merchant, citizen and resident in the city of New Orleans, and State of Louisiana, purchased the child with her mother in 1833, the mother

made respecting such property in countries where slavery is permitted, may be allowed to be redressed, or recognised

and child being then and long before slaves by the laws of Louisiana; that they continued to be his property, in his service, at New Orleans, till about the first of May last, when Mary Slater, his wife, the daughter of Mr. Aves, left New Orleans for Boston, for the purpose of visiting her father, intending to return to New Orleans after an absence of four or five months; that the mother of the child remained at New Orleans in a state of slavery, but that Mrs. Slater brought the child with her from New Orleans to Boston, having the child in her custody as the agent and representative of her husband, whose slave the child was by the laws of Louisiana. When the child was brought thence, the object, intent, and purpose of the said Mary Slater being to have the said child accompany her, and remain in her custody and under her care during her temporary absence from New Orleans, and that the said child should return with her to New Orleans, the domicil of herself and her husband; that the said child was confided to the custody and care of the said Aves by Mrs. Slater, during her temporary absence in the country for her health. The respondent concludes by stating, that he has exercised no other restraint over the liberty of this child, than such as was necessary to the health and safety of the child. Notice having been given to Mr. and Mrs. Slater, an appearance has been entered for them, and, in this state of the case and of the parties, the cause has been heard. Some evidence was given at the former hearing, but it does not materially vary the facts stated in the return. The fact testified, which was considered most material, was the declared intent of Mrs. Slater to take the child back to New Orleans. But as that intent is distinctly avowed in the return—that is, to take the child back to New Orleans, if it could be lawfully done, it does not essentially change the case made by the return. This return is now to be considered in the same aspect as if made by Mr. Slater. It is made in fact by Mr. Aves, claiming the custody of the slave in right of Mr. Slater, and that claim is sanctioned by Mr. Slater, who appears by his attorney to maintain and enforce it. He claims to have the child as master, and carry her back to New Orleans, and whether the claim has been made in terms or not, to hold and return her as a slave, that intent is manifest, and the argument has very properly placed the claim upon that ground. The case presents an extremely interesting question, not so much on account of any doubt or difficulty attending it, as on account of its important consequences to those who may be affected by it, either as masters or slaves. The precise question presented by the claim of the respondent is, whether a citizen of any one of the United States where negro slavery is established by law, coming into this state for any temporary purpose of business or pleasure, staying some time, but not acquiring a domicil here, who brings a slave with him as a personal attendant, may restrain such slave of his liberty during his continuance here, and convey him out of this state on his return against his consent. It is not contended that a master can exercise here any other of

in the judicial tribunals of governments which prohibit slavery[1]. And it is also a very different question, how far

the rights of a slave owner, than such as may be necessary to retain the custody of the slave during his residence, and to remove him on his return. Until this discussion, I had supposed that there had been adjudged cases on this subject in this Commonwealth; and it is believed to have been a prevalent opinion among lawyers, that, if a slave is brought voluntarily and unnecessarily within the limits of this state, he becomes free if he chooses to avail himself of the provisions of our laws; not so much, because his coming within our territorial limits, breathing our air, or treading on our soil, works any alteration in his status or condition as settled by the law of his domicil, as because, by the operation of our laws, there is no authority on the part of the master, either to restrain the slave of his liberty whilst here, or forcibly to take him into custody in order to his removal. There seems, however, to be no decided case on the subject reported. It is now to be considered as an established rule, that by the constitution and laws of this Commonwealth, before the adoption of the Constitution of the United States, in 1789, slavery was abolished as being contrary to the principles of justice and of nature, and repugnant to the provisions of the Declaration of Rights, which is a component part of the constitution of the state. It is not easy, without more time for historical research than I now have, to shew the course of slavery in Massachusetts. By a very early Colonial Ordinance (1641), it was ordered that there should be no bond slavery, villanage, or captivity amongst us, with the exception of lawful captives taken in just wars, or those judicially sentenced to servitude as a punishment for crime. And by an act a few years after, (1646), manifestly alluding to some transaction then recent, the General Court conceiving themselves bound to bear witness against the heinous and crying sin of man-stealing, &c., ordered that certain negroes be sent back to their native country (Guinea,) at the charge of the country, with a letter from the Governor expressive of the indignation of the Court thereabouts. See Ancient Charters, &c., 52, ch. 12, § 2, 3. But notwithstanding these strong expressions in the acts of the Colonial Government, slavery to a certain extent seems to have crept in; not probably by force of any law, for none such is found or known to exist; but rather, it may be presumed, from that universal custom prevailing through the European colonies in the West Indies, and on the continent of America, and which was fostered and encouraged by the commercial policy of the parent state. That it was so established is shewn by this, that by several provincial acts passed at various times in the early part of the last century, slavery was recognised as existing in fact, and various regulations were prescribed in

1 Madrazo *v.* Willes, 3 B. & Ald. 353; Forbes *v.* Cochrane, 2 B. & Cres. 448; The St. Louis, 2 Dodson, R. 210; The Antelope, 10 Wheaton, R. 66; Wharton, Digest, Servants and Slaves, A. D. See 1 Burge, Comm. on Col. and For. Law, P. 1, ch. 10, p. 735 to 752.

the original state of slavery might re-attach upon the party, if he should return to the country by whose laws he was

---

reference to it. The act passed June, 1703, imposed certain restrictions upon manumission, and subjected the master to the relief and support of the slaves, notwithstanding such manumission if the regulations were not complied with. The act of October, 1705, levied a duty and imposed various restrictions upon the importation of negroes, and allowed a drawback upon any negro thus imported, and for whom the duty had been paid, if exported within the space of twelve months, and bonâ fide sold in any other plantation. How, or by what act particularly, slavery was abolished in Massachusetts, whether by the adoption of the opinion in Somerset's case, as a declaration and modification of the common law, or by the Declaration of Independence, or by the Constitution of 1780, it is not now very easy to determine, and it is rather a matter of curiosity than of utility; it being agreed on all hands, that if not abolished before, it was so by the Declaration of Rights. In the case of Winchendon *v.* Hatfield, (4 Mass. R. 123,) which was a case between two towns respecting the support of a pauper, Chief Justice Parsons, in giving the opinion of the Court, states, that at the first action which came before the Court after the establishment of the constitution, the judges declared that, by virtue of the Declaration of Rights, slavery in this state was no more. And he mentions another case, Littleton *v.* Tuttle, (4 Mass. R. 128, note,) in which it was stated as the unanimous opinion of the Court, that a negro born within the state before the constitution, was born free, though born of a female slave. The Chief Justice, however, states that the general practice and common usage have been opposed to this opinion. It has recently been stated as a fact, that there were judicial decisions in this state prior to the adoption of the present constitution, holding that negroes born here of slave parents were free. A fact is stated in the above opinion of Chief Justice Parsons, which may account for this suggestion. He states, that several negroes born in this country of imported slaves, had demanded their freedom of their masters by suits of law, and obtained it by a judgment of Court. The defence of the master, he says, was faintly made; for such was the temper of the times, that a restless discontented slave was worth little; and when his freedom was obtained in a course of legal proceedings, his master was not holden for his support if he became poor. It is very probable, therefore, that this surmise is correct, and that records of judgments to this effect may be found; but they would throw very little light on the subject. Without pursuing this inquiry farther, it is sufficient for the purposes of the case before us, that, by the constitution adopted in 1780, slavery was abolished in Massachusetts, upon the ground, that it is contrary to natural right and the plain principles of justice. The terms of the first article of the Declaration of Rights are plain and explicit: 'All men are born free and equal, and have certain natural, essential, and unalienable rights, among which are the right of enjoying and defending their lives and liberties; that of acquiring, possessing, and protecting property.' It would

declared to be, and was held as a slave. Lord Stowell, in a case of this sort, held, that upon such a return of the

---

be difficult to select words more precisely adapted to the abolition of negro slavery. According to the laws prevailing in all the states where slavery is upheld, the child of a slave is not deemed to be born free; a slave has no right to enjoy and defend his own liberty, or to acquire, possess, or protect property. That the description was broad enough in its terms to embrace negroes, and that it was intended by the framers of the constitution to embrace them, is proved by the earliest contemporaneous construction, by an unbroken series of judicial decisions, and by a uniform practice from the adoption of the constitution to the present time. The whole tenor of our policy, of our legislation and jurisprudence from that time to the present, has been consistent with this construction, and with no other. Such being the general rule of law, it becomes necessary to inquire how far it is modified or controlled in its operation, either, 1. By the law of other nations and states, as admitted by the comity of nations to have a limited operation within a particular state; or, 2. By the constitution and laws of the United States. In considering the first, we may assume that the law of this state is analogous to the law of England in this respect; that while slavery is considered as unlawful and inadmissible in both, and this because contrary to natural right, and to laws designed for the security of personal liberty, yet in both the existence of slavery in other countries is recognised, and the claims of foreigners growing out of that condition are to a certain extent respected. Almost the only reason assigned by Lord Mansfield in Somerset's case, was, that slavery is of such a nature, that it is incapable of being introduced on any reasons, moral or political, but only by positive law; and it is so odious, that nothing can be suffered to support it but positive law. The same doctrine is clearly stated in the full and able opinion of Marshall, C. J., in the case of the Antelope, 10 Wheat. R. 120. He is speaking of the slave trade; but the remark itself shews that it applies to the state of slavery. 'That it is contrary to the law of nature will scarcely be denied. That every man has a natural right to the fruits of his own labour is generally admitted; and that no other person can rightfully deprive him of those fruits, and appropriate them against his will, seems to be the necessary result of the admission.' But although slavery and the slave trade are deemed contrary to natural right, yet it is settled by the judicial decisions of this country and of England, that it is not contrary to the law of nations. It has been too long and too extensively admitted by the laws of all modern civilized nations, and more explicitly by those who have had foreign colonies, to warrant any one independent community to say that it is opposed to the laws of nations. The authorities are cited in the case of the Antelope, and that case is itself an authority directly in point. The consequence is, that each independent community, in its intercourse with every other, is bound to act on the principle, that such other country has a full and perfect authority to make such laws, for the government of its own subjects, as its own

slave to his original domicil, the state of slavery would re-attach upon him. On that occasion he said: "The

---

judgment shall dictate, and its own conscience approve, provided the same are consistent with the law of nations; and no independent community has any right to interfere with the acts or conduct of another state within the territories of such state, or on the high seas, which each has an equal right to use and occupy; and that each sovereign state, governed by its own laws, although competent and well authorized to make such laws as it may think most expedient, to the extent of its own territorial limits, and for the government of its own subjects, yet beyond those limits, and over those who are not its own subjects, has no authority to enforce her own laws, or to treat the laws of other states as void, although contrary to its own views of morality. This view seems consistent with most of the leading cases on the subject. Somerset's case, 20 Howell, State Trials, 1, as already cited, decides that slavery, being odious and against natural right, cannot exist, except by force of positive law. But it clearly admits that it may exist by force of positive law. And it may be remarked, that by positive law in this connexion, may be as well understood customary law as the enactment of a statute; and the word is used to designate rules established by tacit acquiescence, or by the legislative act of any state; and which derive their force and authority from acquiescence or enactment, and not because they are the dictates of natural justice, and, as such, of universal obligation. The Louis, 2 Dodson, R. 238. This was an elaborate opinion of Sir Wm. Scott. It was the case of a French vessel seized by an English vessel in time of peace, whilst engaged in the slave trade. It proceeded upon the ground, that a right of visitation by the vessels of one nation of the vessels of another, could only be exercised in time of war, or against pirates, and that the slave trade was not piracy by the laws of nations, except against those by whose government it has been so declared by law or by treaty. And the vessel was delivered up. The Amedie, 1 Acton, R. 240. The judgment of Sir Wm. Grant in this case, upon the point on which the case was decided, that of the burden of proof, has been doubted. But upon the point now under discussion, he says: 'But we do not lay down as a general principle that this is a trade which cannot, abstractedly speaking, be said to have a legitimate existence. I say abstractedly speaking, because we cannot legislate for other countries; nor has this country a right to control any foreign legislature that may give permission to its subjects to prosecute this trade.' He, however, held, in consequence of the principles declared by the British government, that he was bound to hold primâ facie that the traffic was unlawful; and threw on the claimant the burden of proof, that the traffic was permitted by the law of his own country. The Diana, 1 Dodson, R. 95. This case strongly corroborates the general principle, that, though the slave trade is contrary to the principles of justice and humanity, it cannot with truth be said that it is contrary to the laws of all civilized nations; and that courts will respect the property of persons engaged in it under the sanction of the laws of their own

entire change of the legal character of individuals produced by the change of local situation, is far from being a novelty

---

country. Two cases are cited from the decisions of Courts of common law, which throw much light upon the subject. Madrazo *v.* Willis, 3 B. & Ald. 353. It was an action brought by a Spaniard against a British subject, who had unlawfully and without justifiable cause captured a ship with three hundred slaves on board. The only question was the amount of damages. Abbott, C. J., who tried the cause, in reference to the very strong language of the acts of Parliament, declaring the traffic in slaves a violation of right and contrary to the first principles of justice and humanity, doubted whether the owner could recover damages in an English Court of justice, for the value of the slaves as property, and directed the ship and the slaves to be separately valued. On further consideration, he and the whole Court were of opinion, that the plaintiff was entitled to recover for the value of the slaves. That opinion went upon the ground that the traffic in slaves, however wrong in itself, if prosecuted by a Spaniard between Spain and the coast of Africa, and if permitted by the laws of Spain, and not restrained by treaty, could not be lawfully interrupted by a British subject on the high seas, the common highway of nations. And Mr. Justice Bayley in his opinion, after stating the general rule, that a foreigner is entitled in a British Court of justice, to compensation for a wrongful act, added, that, although the language used by the statutes was very strong, yet it could only apply to British subjects. It is true, he further says, that if this were a trade contrary to the laws of nations, a foreigner could not maintain this action. And Best, J., spoke strongly to the same effect, adding, that the statutes speak in just terms of indignation of the horrible traffic in human beings; but they speak only in the name of the British nation. If a ship be acting contrary to the general law of nations, she is thereby subject to confiscation; but it is impossible to say that the slave trade is contrary to what may be called the common law of nations. Forbes *v.* Cochrane, 2 Barn. & Cres. 448; Dowl. & Ryl. 679. This case has been supposed to conflict with the one last cited; but I apprehend, in considering the principles upon which they were decided, they will be found to be perfectly reconcilable. The plaintiff, a British subject, domiciled in East Florida, where slavery was established by law, was the owner of a plantation, and of certain slaves who escaped thence, and got on board a British ship of war on the high seas. It was held that he could not maintain an action against the master of the ship for harbouring the slaves after notice and demand of them. Some of the opinions given in this case are extremely instructive and applicable to the present. Holroyd, J., in giving his opinion, said that the plaintiff could not found his claim to the slaves upon any general right, because by the English law such a right cannot be considered as warranted by the general law of nature; that, if the plaintiff could claim at all, it must be in virtue of some right which he had acquired by the law of the country where he was domiciled; that when such rights are recognised by law, they must be con-

in the law. A residence in a new country often introduces a change of legal condition, which imposes rights and obli-

---

sidered as founded not upon the law of nature, but upon the particular law of that country, and must be co-extensive with the territories of that state; that if such right were violated by a British subject within such territory, the party grieved would be entitled to a remedy; but that the law of slavery is a law in invitum; and when a party gets out of the territory where it prevails, and under the protection of another power, without any wrongful act done by the party giving that protection, the right of the master, which is founded on the municipal law of the place only, does not continue. So in speaking of the effect of bringing a slave into England, he says, he ceases to be a slave in England, only because there is no law which sanctions his detention in slavery. Best, J., declared his opinion to the same effect. Slavery is a local law; therefore, if a man wishes to preserve his slaves, let him attach them to him by affection, or make fast the bars of their prison, or rivet well their chains, for the instant they get beyond the limits where slavery is recognised by the local law, they have broken their chains, they have escaped from their prison, and are free. That slavery is a relation founded in force, not in right, existing where it does exist by force of positive law, and not recognised as founded in natural right, is intimated by the definition of slavery in the civil law: 'Servitus est constitutio juris gentium, quâ quis domino alieno contra naturam subjicitur.' Upon a general review of the authorities, and upon an application of the well-established principles upon this subject, we think they fully maintain the point stated, that though slavery is contrary to natural right, and to the principles of justice, humanity, and sound policy, as we adopt them, and found our own laws upon them, yet not being contrary to the laws of nations, if any other state or community see fit to establish and continue slavery by law, so far as the legislative power of that country extends, we are bound to take notice of the existence of those laws, and we are not at liberty to declare and hold an act done within those limits unlawful and void, upon our views of morality and policy, which the sovereign and legislative power of the place has pronounced to be lawful. If, therefore, an unwarranted interference and wrong is done by our citizens to a foreigner, acting under the sanction of such laws, and within their proper limits, that is, within the local limits of the power by whom they are thus established, or on the high seas, which each and every nation has a right in common with all others to occupy, our laws would no doubt afford a remedy against the wrong done. So in pursuance of a well-known maxim, that in the construction of contracts, the lex loci contractûs shall govern, if a person, having in other respects a right to sue in our courts, shall bring an action against another, liable in other respects to be sued in our courts, upon a contract made upon the subject of slavery in a state where slavery is allowed by law, the law here would give it effect. As, if a note of hand made in New Orleans were sued on here, and the defence should be that it was on a bad consideration, or without consideration, be-

gations totally inconsistent with the former rights and obligations of the same persons. Persons bound by particular

cause given for the price of a slave sold, it may well be admitted that such a defence could not prevail, because the contract was a legal one by the law of the place where it was made*. This view of the law, applicable to slavery, marks strongly the distinction between the relation of master and slave, as established by the local law of particular states; and in virtue of that sovereign power and independent authority which each independent state concedes to every other, and those natural and social relations which are everywhere and by all people recognised, and which, though they may be modified and regulated by municipal law, are not founded upon it, such as the relation of parent and child, and husband and wife. Such also is the principle upon which the general right of property is founded; being in some form universally recognised as a natural right, independently of municipal law. This affords an answer to the argument drawn from the maxim, that the right of personal property follows the person, and therefore, where, by the law of a place, a person there domiciled acquires personal property by the comity of nations, the same must be deemed his property everywhere. It is obvious, that if this were true in the extent in which the argument employs it, if slavery exists anywhere, and if by the laws of any place a property can be acquired in slaves, the law of slavery must extend to every place where such slaves may be carried. The maxim, therefore, and the argument, can apply only to those commodities which are everywhere and by all nations treated and deemed subjects of property. But it is not speaking with strict accuracy, to say that a property can be acquired in human beings by local laws. Each state may, for its own convenience, declare that slaves shall be deemed property, and that the relations and laws of personal chattels shall be deemed to apply to them; as for instance, that they may be bought and sold, delivered, attached, levied upon; that trespass will lie for an injury done to them, or trover for converting them. But it would be a perversion of terms, to say that such local laws do in fact make them personal property generally; they can only determine that the same rules of law shall apply to them as are applicable to property, and this effect will follow only so far as such laws proprio vigore can operate. The same doctrine is recognised in Louisiana. In the case of Lunsford *v.* Coquillon, 14 Martin, R. 404, it is thus stated:—The relation of owner and slave in the states of this Union, in which it has a legal existence, is a creature of the municipal law. See Story, Conflict of Laws, 92, 97. The same principle is declared by the Court in Kentucky, in the case of Rankin *v.* Lydia, 2 Marshall, R. 470. They say slavery is sanctioned by the laws of this state; but we consider this as a right existing by positive law of a municipal character, without foundation in the law of nature. The conclusion to which we come from this view of the law is this: That by the general and now well-established

* But see post, § 259.

contracts which restrain their liberty, debtors, apprentices, and others, lose their character and condition for the time

law of this Commonwealth, bond slavery cannot exist, because it is contrary to natural right, and repugnant to numerous provisions of the constitution and laws designed to secure the liberty and personal rights of all persons within its limits, and entitled to the protection of its laws. That though by the laws of a foreign state, meaning by 'foreign' in this connexion, a state governed by its own laws, and between which and our own there is no dependence one upon the other, but which in this respect are as independent as foreign states, a person may acquire a property in a slave: that such acquisition, being contrary to natural right, and effected by local law, is dependent upon such local law for its existence and efficacy; and, being contrary to the fundamental law of the state, such general right of property cannot be exercised or recognised here. That, as a general rule, all persons coming within the limits of a state become subject to all its municipal laws, civil and criminal, and entitled to the privileges which those laws confer; that this rule applies as well to blacks as whites, except the case of fugitives, to be afterwards considered; that if such persons have been slaves, they become free, not so much because any alteration is made in their status or condition, as because there is no law which will warrant, but there are laws, if they choose to avail themselves of them, which prohibit their forcible detention, or forcible removal. That the law arising from the comity of nations cannot apply; because, if it did, it would follow as a necessary consequence, that all those persons who, by force of local laws, and within all foreign places where slavery is permitted, have acquired slaves as property, might bring their slaves here, and exercise over them the rights and power which an owner of property might exercise, and for any length of time, short of acquiring a domicil: that such an application of the law would be wholly repugnant to our laws, entirely inconsistent with our policy and our fundamental principles, and is therefore inadmissible. Whether, if a slave voluntarily brought here, and with his own consent returning with his master, would resume his condition as a slave, is a question which was incidentally raised in the argument; but is one on which we are not called on to give an opinion in this case, and we give none. From the principle above stated, on which a slave brought here becomes free, to wit, that he becomes entitled to the protection of our laws, and there is no law to warrant his forcible arrest and removal, it would seem to follow, as a necessary conclusion, that, if the slave waives the protection of those laws, and returns to the state where he is held as a slave, his condition is not changed. In the case Ex parte Grace, 2 Hagg. Adm. R. 94, this question was fully considered by Sir Wm. Scott, in the case of a slave brought from the West Indies to England, and afterwards voluntarily returning to the West Indies; and he held that she was reinstated in her condition of slavery. A different decision, I believe, has been made of the question in some of the United States; but, for the reasons already given, it is not necessary to consider it further here. The question

when they reside in another country, and are entitled as persons totally free, although they return to their original

---

has thus far been considered as a general one, and applicable to cases of slaves brought from any foreign state or country; and it now becomes necessary to see how far this result differs, where the person is claimed as a slave by a citizen of another state of this Union; that is, how the question, as between citizens of different states, is affected by the provisions of the Constitution and laws of the United States. In Article 4, Sect. 2, the Constitution declares, that no person held to service or labour in one state under the laws thereof, escaping into another, shall, in consequence of any law or regulation therein, be discharged from such service or labour, but shall be delivered up on claim of the party to whom such service or labour may be due. The law of Congress made in pursuance of this article, provides, that when any person held to labour in any of the United States, &c., shall escape into any other of the said states or territories, the person entitled, &c., is empowered to arrest the fugitive; and upon proof made, that the person so seized, under the law of the state from which he or she fled, owes service, &c. Act of February 12, 1793. In regard to these provisions, the Court are of opinion, that as, by the general law of this Commonwealth, slavery cannot exist, and the rights and powers of slave owners cannot be exercised therein, the effect of this provision in the Constitution and laws of the United States is to limit and restrain the operation of this general rule, so far as it is done by the plain meaning and obvious intent and import of the language used, and no farther. The constitution and law manifestly refer to the case of a slave escaping from a state, where he owes service or labour, into another state or territory. He is termed a fugitive from labour; the proof to be made is, that he owed service or labour under the laws of the state or territory from which he fled, and the authority given is to remove such fugitive to the state from which he fled. This language can by no reasonable construction be applied to the case of a slave who has not fled from the state, but who has been brought into this state by his master. The same conclusion will result from a consideration of the well-known circumstances under which this Constitution was formed. Before the adoption of the Constitution, the states were, to a certain extent, sovereign and independent, and were in a condition to settle the terms upon which they would form a more perfect union. It has been contended by some over-zealous philanthropists, that such an article in the Constitution could be of no binding force or validity, because it was a stipulation contrary to natural right. But it is difficult to perceive the force of this objection. It has already been shewn that slavery is not contrary to the laws of nations. It would then be the proper subject of treaties among sovereign and independent powers. Suppose, instead of forming the present constitution, or any other confederation, the several states had become in all respects sovereign and independent, would it not have been competent for them to stipulate that fugitive slaves should be mutually restored, and to frame suitable regulations, under which such a stipulation should be carried into

servitude and obligations, upon coming back to the country they had quitted; and even in the case of slavery, slaves

---

effect? Such a stipulation would be highly important and necessary to secure peace and harmony between adjoining nations, and to prevent perpetual collisions and border wars. It would be no encroachment on the rights of the fugitive; for no stranger has a just claim to the protection of a foreign state against its will, especially where a claim to such protection would be likely to involve the state in war; and each independent state has a right to determine by its own laws and treaties who may come to reside or seek shelter within its limits. Now the Constitution of the United States partakes both of the nature of a treaty and of a form of government. It regards the states, to a certain extent, as sovereign and independent communities, with full power to make their own laws and regulate their own policy, and fixes the terms upon which their intercourse with each other shall be conducted. In respect to foreign relations, it regards the people of the states as one community, and constitutes a form of government for them. It is well known that, when this Constitution was formed, some of the states permitted slavery and the slave trade, and considered them highly essential to their interests, and that some other states had abolished slavery within their own limits, and, from the principles deduced and policy avowed by them, might be presumed to desire to extend such abolition further. It was, therefore, manifestly the intent and the object of one party to this compact to enlarge, extend, and secure, as far as possible, the rights and powers of the owners of slaves, within their own limits as well as in other states, and of the other party to limit and restrain them. Under these circumstances, the clause in question was agreed on, and introduced into the Constitution. And as it was well considered, as it was intended to secure future peace and harmony, and to fix, as precisely as language could do it, the limit to which the rights of one party should be exercised within the territory of the other, it is to be presumed that they selected terms intended to express their exact and their whole meaning; and it would be a departure from the purpose and spirit of the compact, to put any other construction upon it, than that to be derived from the plain and natural import of the language used. Besides this construction of the provision in the Constitution gives to it a latitude, sufficient to afford effectual security to the owners of slaves. The states have a plenary power to make all laws necessary for the regulation of slavery and the rights of slave-owners, whilst the slaves remain within their territorial limits; and it is only when they escape, without the consent of their owners, into other states, that they require the aid of other states to enable them to regain their dominion over the fugitives. But this point is supported by most respectable and unexceptionable authorities. In the case of Butler *v.* Hooper, 1 Wash. C.C.R. 499, it was held by Mr. Justice Washington, in terms, that the provision in the Constitution, which we are now considering, does not extend to the case of a slave, voluntarily carried by his master into another state, and there leaving him under the protection of some law declaring him free. In this case, however, the master claimed to hold the slave in virtue of a law of

themselves possess rights and privileges in one character, which they are not entitled to in another. The domestic

Pennsylvania, which permitted members of Congress and sojourners to retain their domestic slaves, and it was held, that he did not bring himself within either branch of the exception, because he had, for two years of the period, ceased to be a member of Congress, and so lost the privilege; and by having become a resident, could not claim as a sojourner. The case is an authority to this point, that the claimant of a slave, to avail himself of the provisions of the Constitution and laws of the United States, must bring himself within their plain and obvious meaning, and they will not be extended by construction; and that the clause in the Constitution is confined to the case of a slave escaping from one state and fleeing to another. But in a more recent case, the point was decided by the same eminent Judge. Ex parte Simmons, 4 Wash. C. C. R. 396. It was an application for a certificate under § 3 of the Act of Feb. 12, 1793. He held, that both the Constitution and the laws of the United States apply only to fugitives, escaping from one state and fleeing to another, and not to the case of a slave voluntarily brought by his master. Another question was made in that case, whether the slave was free by the laws of Pennsylvania, which, like our own, in effect liberate slaves voluntarily brought within the state; but there is an exception in favour of Members of Congress, Foreign Ministers and Consuls, and sojourners. But this provision is qualified as to sojourners and persons passing through the state in such manner as to exclude them from the benefit of the exception, if the slave was retained in the state longer than six months. The slave in that case, having been detained in the state more than six months, was therefore held free. This case is an authority to this point; the general rule being, that if a slave is brought into a state where the laws do not admit slavery, he will be held free; the person who claims him as a slave, under any exception or limitation of the general rule, must shew clearly that the case is within such exception. The same principle was substantially decided by the state court of the same state in the case of Commonwealth *v.* Holloway, 2 Serg. & Rawle, 305. It was the case of a child of a fugitive slave, born in Pennsylvania. It was held, that the Constitution of the United States was not inconsistent with the law of Pennsylvania; that as the law and Constitution of the United States did not include the issue of fugitive slaves in terms, it did not embrace them by construction or implication. The Court considers the law as applying only to those who escape.—Yet by the operation of the maxim, which obtains in all the states wherein slavery is permitted by law, Partus sequitur ventrem, the offspring would follow the condition of the mother, if either the rule of comity contended for applied, or if the law of the United States would be extended by construction. The same decision has been made in Indiana, 3 Amer. Jurist, 404. In Louisiana, it had been held, that if a person with a slave goes into a state to reside, where it is declared that slavery shall not exist for ever so short a time, the slave ipso facto becomes free, and will be so adjudged and considered afterwards in all other states; and a person moving

slave may, in that character, by law accompany his master or mistress to any part of the world. But that privilege

---

from Kentucky to Ohio to reside, his slaves thereby became free, and were so held in Louisiana. This case also fully recognises the authority of states to make laws dissolving the relation of master and slave; and considers the special limitation of the general power, by the Federal Constitution, as a forcible implication in proof of the existence of such general power. Lunsford *v.* Coquillon, 14 Martin, R. 465. And in the above-cited case from Louisiana, it is very significantly remarked that such a construction of the Constitution and law of the United States can work injury to no one, for the principle acts only on the willing, and Volenti non fit injuria. The same rule of construction is adopted in analogous cases in other countries; that is, where an institution is forbidden, but where, for special reasons and to a limited extent, such prohibition is relaxed, the exemption is to be construed strictly; and whoever claims the exemption, must shew himself clearly within it; and where the facts do not bring the case within the exemption, the general rule has its effect. By a general law of France, all persons inhabiting or being within the territorial limits of France are free. An edict was passed by Louis XIV., called 'Le Code Noir,' respecting slavery in the colonies. In 1716, an edict was published by Louis XV., concerning slavery in the colonies, and reciting, among other things, that many of the colonists were desirous of bringing their slaves into France to have them confirmed in the principles of religion, and to be instructed in various arts and handicrafts, from which the colonists would derive much benefit on the return of the slaves, but that many of the colonists feared that their slaves would pretend to be free on their arrival in France, from which their owners would sustain considerable loss, and be deterred from pursuing an object at once so pious and so useful. The edict then provides a series of minute regulations, to be observed both before their departure from the West Indies and on their arrival in France; and if all these regulations are strictly complied with, the negroes so brought over to France shall not thereby acquire any right to their freedom, but shall be compellable to return; but if the owners shall neglect to comply with the prescribed regulations, the negroes shall become free, and the owners shall lose all property in them. 20 Howell, State Trials, 15, note. The Constitution and laws of the United States then are confined to cases of slaves escaping from other states, and coming within the limits of this state, without the consent and against the will of their masters, and cannot by any sound construction extend to a case where the slave does not escape, and does not come within the limits of this state against the will of the master, but by his own act and permission. This provision is to be construed according to its plain terms and import, and cannot be extended beyond this, and where the case is not that of an escape, the general rule shall have its effect. It is upon these grounds, we are of opinion, that an owner of a slave in another state, where slavery is warranted by law, voluntarily bringing such slave into this state, has no authority to detain him against his will,

exists no longer than his character of domestic slave attaches to him; for, should the owner deprive him of the character of being a domestic slave, by employing him as a field slave, he would be deprived of the right of accompanying his master out of the colony [1]."

§ 97. Struck with the inconveniences of the doctrine of the ubiquity of the law of the domicil, as to the capacity, state, and condition of persons, as an absolute and general doctrine, a learned Judge in the Scottish courts[2] has not hesitated to hold that no such doctrine is recognised as of universal obligation in Scotland. "Would a marriage here" (says he) "be declared void because the parties were domiciled in England, and were minors when they married here, and of course incapable by the law of that country

---

or to carry him out of the state against his consent, for the purpose of being held in slavery. This opinion is not to be considered as extending to a case where the owner of a fugitive slave, having produced a certificate according to the law of the United States, is bonâ fide removing such slave to his own domicil, and in so doing passes through a free state; where the law confers a right or favour, by necessary implication it gives the means of executing it. Nor do we give any opinion upon the case, where an owner of a slave in one state is bonâ fide removing to another state, where slavery is allowed, and in so doing necessarily passes through a free state, or, arriving by accident or necessity, he is compelled to touch or land therein, remaining no longer than necessary. Our geographical position exempts us from the probable necessity of considering such a case, and we give no opinion respecting it. The child, who is the subject of the habeas corpus, being of too tender years to have any will or give any consent to be removed, and her mother being a slave, and having no will of her own, and no power to act for her child, she is necessarily left in the custody of the law. The respondent having claimed the custody of the child, in behalf of Mr. and Mrs. Slater, who claim the right to carry her back to Louisiana, to be held in a state of slavery, we are of opinion that his custody is not to be deemed by the Court a proper and lawful custody. Under a suggestion made in the outset of this inquiry, that a probate guardian would probably be appointed, we shall for the present order the child into a temporary custody, to give time for an application to be made to the Judge of Probate.

[1] The Slave Grace, 2 Hagg. Adm. R. 94, 113, 114. It seems that Christinæus and Gudelin held the same opinion as Lord Stowell. See Christinæus, Vol. 4, Decis. 80, n. 4, p. 115; cited also, 1 Burge, Com. on Col. and For. Law, P. 1, ch. 10, p. 749.

[2] Lord Meadowbank; Fergusson on Mar. and Divorce, App. 361, 362.

of contracting marriage? This category of law does not affect the contracting individuals only, but the public, and that in various ways. And the consequences would prove not a little inconvenient, embarrassing, and probably, even inextricable, if the personal incapacities of individuals, as of majors and minors, the competency to contract marriages and infringe matrimonial engagements, the rights of domestic authority and service, and the like, were to be qualified and regulated by foreign laws and customs, with which the mass of the population must be utterly unacquainted. Accordingly, the laws of this description seem nowhere to yield to those of foreign countries; and accordingly, it is believed, no nation has hitherto thought of conferring powers and forms on its courts of justice adequate for enabling them to execute over foreigners regular authority, for enforcing the observance of them of the laws of their own country, when expatriated. In fact, the very same principles which prescribe to nations the administration of their own criminal law, appear to require a like exclusive administration of law relative to the domestic relations. Hence, both in England and Scotland, the most regular constitution abroad of domestic slavery was held to afford no claim to domestic service in this country, though restrictions for only such service, and under such domestic authority, as our laws recognised. The whole order of society would be disjointed, were the positive institutions of foreign nations concerning the domestic relations, and the capacities of persons regarding them, admitted to operate universally, and form privileged castes living each under separate laws, like the barbarous nations during many centuries after their settlement in the Roman empire[1]."

§ 98. These diversities in the practical jurisprudence of

---

[1] Lord Meadowbank; Fergusson on Mar. and Divorce, App. 361, 362.

different countries, as to the effect of personal ability and disability, and personal capacity or incapacity, abundantly establish, in the first place, that there is no general rule on the subject, which is admitted by all nations; and, in the next place, that the very exceptions introduced or conceded by those who most strenuously contend for the universal operation of the law of the domicil of the party, either native or acquired, in cases of this nature, as satisfactorily established, that no general rules have been or can be established, which may not work serious inconvenience to the interests or institutions of some particular countries, or to some particular classes of capacities or incapacities. The proper conclusion, then, to be drawn from this review of the subject is, that the rule of Huberus is correct, that no nation is under any obligation to give effect to the laws of any other nation, which are prejudicial to itself or to its own citizens; that in all cases every nation must judge for itself what foreign laws are so prejudicial or not; and that, in cases not so prejudicial, a spirit of comity and a sense of mutual utility ought to induce every nation to allow full force and effect to the laws of every other nation. This is the doctrine asserted by Mr. Chancellor Kent; and it certainly has a most solid foundation in the actual practice of nations. "There is no doubt," says he, "of the truth of the general proposition, that the laws of a country have no binding force beyond its own territorial limits; and their authority is admitted in other states, not *ex proprio vigore*, but *ex comitate;* or in the language of Huberus, *Quatenus sine præjudicio indulgentium fieri potest.* Every independent community will judge for itself, how far the *comitas inter communitates* is to be permitted to interfere with its domestic interests and policy, &c. It is a maxim that *locus regit actum,* unless the intention of the parties to the contrary be clearly shewn. It is, however, a necessary exception to the universality of the rule, that no people are bound to enforce, or hold valid in their courts of justice, any contract which is injurious to their public rights, or offends their morals, or contravenes their policy, or violates a public law[1]."

§ 99. In discussing this subject, our attention has been more particularly drawn to the common cases of incapacity, resulting from minority, and marriage, and legitimacy. But the principles which apply to them, are not materially different from those which apply to cases of idiocy, insanity, and prodigality. The extent of the rights and authorities of guardians, curators, parents, and masters, over persons subjected to their control, or committed to their charge, may, in a general sense, be said to depend, so far as they are to be recognised, or enforced by and in foreign nations, upon the same common ground of international jurisprudence, that is to say, upon a general comity, founded in the sense of mutual interests, mutual benefits, and mutual obligations to cultivate peace and harmony. It was said on a recent occasion, with great force and propriety, by Mr. Chief Justice Taney, in delivering the opinion of the Supreme Court:—"The comity thus extended to other nations, is no impeachment of sovereignty. It is the voluntary act of the nation by which it is offered, and is inadmissible when contrary to its policy or prejudicial to its interests. But it contributes so largely to promote justice between individuals, and to produce a friendly intercourse between the sovereignties to which they belong, that courts of justice have constantly acted upon it as a part of the voluntary law of nations[2].

---

1 2 Kent, Comm. Lect. 39, pp. 457, 458, (3rd edit.); Post, § 244—259. See also Greenwood *v.* Curtis, 6 Mass. R. 378, 379.—This subject is a good deal discussed in the able work of Mr. Fergusson on Marriage and Divorce; and the opinions of the Judges in the case of Gordon *v.* Pye, in 1815, and that of Edmonstone and others, in 1816, before the Scottish courts, are particularly worthy of examination, from their comprehensive learning and ability. Fergusson, App. pp. 276—363. See also, Id. pp. 384—422.

2 Bank of Augusta *v.* Earle, 13 Peters, R. 589.

§ 100. In concluding this discussion, as to the operation of foreign laws on questions relating to the capacity, state, and condition of persons, it may be useful to bring together some of those rules which seem best established in the jurisprudence of England and America, leaving others of a more doubtful character and extent, to be decided, as they may arise, in the proper forum.

§ 101. First. The capacity, state, and condition of persons, according to the law of their domicil, will generally be regarded, as to acts done, rights acquired, and contracts made in the place of their domicil, touching property situate therein. If these acts, rights, and contracts have validity there, they will be held equally valid everywhere. If invalid there, they will be held invalid everywhere[1].

§ 102. Secondly. As to acts done, rights acquired, and contracts made in other countries touching property therein, the law of the country where the acts are done, the rights are acquired, or the contracts are made, will generally govern in respect to the capacity, state, and condition of persons[2]. In affirmance of this doctrine, the Supreme Court of Louisiana, in a case where the direct question came before them, expressly stated, that they had no difficulty in assenting to the proposition, that contracts entered in other states, as it relates to their validity, and the capacity of the contracting parties, are to be tried in Louisiana, by the *lex loci celebrati contractûs*. And that, if a contract was entered into in another state, in conformity to the local law, to have its effects and execution there, the Courts of Louisiana cannot declare it a nullity on the ground that it would not be valid according to the system

---

[1] See Male *v.* Roberts, 3 Esp. R. 63; Thompson *v.* Ketcham, 8 John. R. 189; Ante, § 64—68: Id. § 87. See Fœlix, Conflict des Loix Revue Etrang. et Franç. Tom. 7, 1840, § 38, pp. 342—344.

[2] Ante, § 69, 70—74; Id. § 80—82, 87.

of jurisprudence of that state, even if one or both of the contracting parties were not citizens of such foreign state[1].

§ 102 *a.* It has been well remarked by Mr. Burge,—"This doctrine promotes, whilst that to which it is opposed is inconsistent with, those principles of mutual convenience, which induce the recognition of foreign laws. The obstacles to commercial intercourse between the subjects of foreign states, would be almost insurmountable, if a party must pause to ascertain, not by the means within his reach, but by recourse to the law of the domicil of the person with whom he was dealing, whether the latter has attained the age of majority, and consequently, whether he is competent to enter into a valid and binding contract. If the country in which the contract was litigated, was also that in which it had been entered into, and if the party enforcing it were the subject of that country, it would be unjust, as well as unreasonable, to invoke the law of a foreign state for the benefit of the foreigner, and to deprive its own subject of the benefit of the law of his own state[2]."

§ 102 *b.* He adds:—"It has been hitherto assumed, that according to the law of the domicil, the person was a minor, and incapable of contracting, although he had attained the age which *in loco contractûs* constituted majority, and where, according to that law, he was competent to contract. In such a case, it has been submitted that the *lex loci contractûs* ought to be followed. It ought also to be followed, if the converse of that case occurred, and he had attained majority according to the law of his domicil, but was a minor according to that which prevailed *in loco contractûs.* It is true, in the latter case, the party was subject to no greater liability than he would have incurred in

[1] Mr. Justice Bullard, in Andrews *v.* His Creditors, 11 Louis. R. 464; Ante, § 95, n. 3, § 96 a.

[2] 1 Burge, Comm. on Col. and For. Law, P. 1, ch. 4, p. 132.

the place of his domicil. But, if the principle be correct, that the *lex loci contractûs* ought to determine the validity of a contract, when that validity depends on the capacity of the contracting party, it must be uniformly applied, whether the law prevailing in the domicil, be that which capacitates or incapacitates; for it would not be reasonable, that two different laws should be applied to one and the same contract, and that the liability of one of the parties should be decided by the *lex loci contractûs;* and that of the other, by the *lex loci domicilii*[1]."

§ 103. Thirdly. Hence we may deduce, as a corollary, that in regard to questions of minority or majority, competency or incompetency to marry, incapacities incident to coverture, guardianship, emancipation, and other personal qualities and disabilities, the law of the domicil of birth, or the law of any other acquired and fixed domicil, is not generally to govern; but the *lex loci contractûs aut actûs,* the law of the place where the contract is made, or the act done. Therefore, a person who is a minor until he is of the age of twenty-five years by the law of his domicil, and incapable, as such, of making a valid contract there, may nevertheless, in another country, where he would be of age at twenty-one years, generally make a valid contract at that age, even a contract of marriage[2].

§ 104. Fourthly. Personal disqualifications, not arising from the law of nature, but from the principles of the customary or positive law of a foreign country, and especially such as are of a penal nature, are not generally regarded in other countries where the like disqualifications do not exist[3]. Hence, the disqualifications resulting from heresy, excommunication, popish recusancy, infamy, and other penal disabilities, are not enforced in any other country, except

---

[1] 1 Burge, Comm. on Col. and For. Law, P. 1, ch. 4, p. 133.

[2] Ante, § 75, 79, 80—82.

[3] Ante, § 91—96.

that in which they originate. They are strictly territorial[1]. So, the state of slavery will not be recognised in any country, whose institutions and policy prohibit slavery[2].

§ 105. Fifthly. In questions of legitimacy or illegitimacy, the law of the place of the marriage will generally govern, as to the issue subsequently born. If the marriage is valid by the law of that place, it will generally be held valid in every other country, for the purpose of ascertaining legitimacy and heirship. If invalid there, it will generally (if not universally) be held invalid in every other country[3].

§ 105 *a*. Sixthly. As to issue born before the marriage, if, by the law of the country where they are born, they would be legitimated by the subsequent marriage of their parents, they will by such subsequent marriage (perhaps in any country, but at all events in the same country) become legitimate, so that this character of legitimacy will be recognised in every other country. If illegitimate there, the same character will belong to them in every other country[4].

§ 106. Seventhly. No nation being under any obligation to yield up its own laws, in regard to its own subjects to the laws of other nations, it will not suffer its own subjects to evade the operation of its own fundamental policy or laws, or to commit frauds in violation of them, by any acts or contracts made with that design in a foreign country; and it will judge for itself, how far it will adopt, and how far it will reject, any such acts or contracts. Hence, the acts of prodigals, of minors, of idiots, of lunatics, and of married women, escaping into foreign countries, are not to be deemed as, of course, absolutely obligatory, even if sanctioned by the foreign law, unless the laws of their own

---

1 Ante, § 91, 92, 94, 95.

2 Co. Litt. 79. b.; Harg. n. 44; Ante, § 96.

3 Ante, § 79, 80, 81, 86.

4 Ante, § 87, 87 a; Munro *v*. Saunders, 6 Bligh, R. 468.

country adopt such foreign law as a rule to govern in such cases[1]. Hence, too, a person born before wedlock, who in the country of his birth is deemed illegitimate, may not by a subsequent marriage of his parents in another country, by whose laws such a marriage would make him legitimate, cease to be illegitimate in the country of his birth[2]. Hence, also, if a marriage is by the laws of a country indissoluble when once contracted between its own subjects, they may not by a mere removal into another country, at least without a change of domicil, be deemed capable of contracting a new marriage after a divorce, lawful by the law of the place to which they have removed[3]. In short, every nation in these and the like cases will govern itself by such rules

---

1 An apt illustration of this rule may be found in the present law of France. By that law, a marriage contracted in a foreign country between Frenchmen, or a Frenchman and a stranger, is valid, if celebrated according to the forms used in that country; provided it is preceded by a proper publication of banns, and the Frenchman does not contravene the other provisions of the French law. Upon this law Toullier remarks, that the conditions required to be complied with, are those of the code respecting the contract of marriage; for, as the laws respecting the person follow a Frenchman everywhere, it results, that even in a foreign country, he is held to conform to the French laws, relative to the age of the contracting parties, their family, and the impediments to marriage. 1 Toullier, Droit Civil François, art. 576, p. 484. So that French minors, who are incapable of contracting a marriage in France, are disabled everywhere, even though the marriage would be good by the law of the place where the marriage is celebrated. The English and American Courts would hold such a marriage good. Code Civil, art. 144, 148, 170; Merlin, Répert. tit. Loi. § 6, n. 1. See also 2 Kent, Comm. Lect. 26, p. 93, note, 3rd edition. The doctrine of France in this respect, is but an illustration of the general rule prescribed by the Civil Code of France, (art. 3.), that the laws respecting the state and condition of Frenchmen govern them, even when resident in a foreign country. Ante, § 54.

2 Ante, § 79, 87, 87 a, 105 a.

3 See Rex *v.* Lolley, 1 Russ. & Ryan's Case, 236; Tovey *v.* Lindsay, 1 Dow. R. 124; Beazley *v.* Beazley, 3 Hagg. Eccl. R. 639; M'Carthy *v.* De Caix, 1831, 2 Russ. & Mylne, R. 620. But see Warrender *v.* Warrender, 9 Bligh, R. 89; Post, § 215—231.

and principles, as are best adapted in its own judgment to subserve its own substantial interests and fixed policy, and to uphold its own institutions, as well as to promote a liberal intercourse, and a spirit of confidence and reciprocal comity, with all other nations. But this subject will be more fully considered in the succeeding chapters.

CHAPTER V.

MARRIAGE.

§ 107. Having treated of the capacity and incapacity of persons as affected by foreign law, and especially in relation to their capacity or incapacity to contract marriage in a foreign country[1], we shall next proceed to consider more fully the nature and effect of the relation of marriage contracted by and between persons who are admitted to be *sui juris,* and to possess competent capacity everywhere[2]. We shall then discuss the manner in which that relation may be dissolved, and the effect of such dissolution.

§ 108. Marriage is treated by all civilized nations as a peculiar and favoured contract. It is in its origin a contract of natural law[3]. It may exist between two individuals of different sexes, although no third person existed in the world, as happened in the case of the common ancestors of mankind. It is the parent, and not the child, of society; *Principium urbis et quasi seminarium reipublicæ.* In civil society it becomes a civil contract, regulated and prescribed by law, and endowed with civil consequences. In many civilized countries, acting under a sense of the force of sacred obligations, it has had the sanctions of religion superadded. It then becomes a religious, as well as a natural and civil, contract; for it is a great mistake to suppose, that, be-

---

1 Ante, § 79—90.

2 On this subject consult 1 Burge, Comm. on Col. and For. Law, P. 1, ch. 5, § 1, 2, 3, pp. 135—201.

3 I have throughout treated marriage as a contract in the common sense of the word; because this is the light in which it is ordinarily viewed by Jurists, domestic as well as foreign. But it appears to me to be something more than a mere contract: it is rather to be deemed an institution of society, founded upon the consent and contract of the parties; and in this view it has some peculiarities in its nature, character, operation, and extent of obligation, different from what belong to ordinary contracts.

cause it is the one, therefore it may not likewise be the other[1]. The common law of England (and the like law exists in America) considers marriage in no other light than as a civil contract. The holiness of the matrimonial state is left entirely to ecclesiastical and religious scrutiny[2]. In the Catholic countries, and in some of the Protestant countries of Europe, it is treated as a sacrament[3].

§ 109. There are some remarks on this subject, made by a distinguished Scottish Judge, so striking, that they deserve to be quoted at large[4]:—"Marriage being entirely a personal consensual contract, it may be thought that the *lex loci* must be resorted to in expounding every question that arises relative to it. But it will be observed, that marriage is a contract *sui generis*, and differing, in some respects, from all other contracts; so that the rules of law, which are applicable in expounding and enforcing other contracts, may not apply to this. The contract of marriage is the most important of all human transactions. It is the very basis of the whole fabric of civilized society. The *status* of marriage is *juris gentium*, and the foundation of it, like that of all other contracts, rests on the consent of parties. But it differs from other contracts in this, that the rights, obligations, or duties, arising from it, are not left entirely to be regulated by the agreements of parties; but are, to a certain extent, matters of municipal regulation, over which the parties have no control, by any declaration of their will. It confers the *status* of legitimacy on children born in wedlock, with all the consequential rights, duties, and privileges thence arising; it gives rise to the relations of consanguinity and affinity; in short, it pervades the whole system of civil society. Unlike other contracts, it cannot, in general, amongst civilized nations, be dissolved

---

1 Dalrymple *v.* Dalrymple, 2 Hagg. Consist. R. 63; Linclo *v.* Belisario, 1 Hagg. Consist. R. 231.

2 1 Black. Comm. 433.

3 Dalrymple *v.* Dalrymple, 2 Hagg. Consist. R. 63—65.

4 Lord Robertson, in Fergusson on Marr. and Divorce, 397—399.

by mutual consent; and it subsists in full force, even although one of the parties should be for ever rendered incapable, as in the case of incurable insanity, or the like, from performing his part of the mutual contract.

§ 110. "No wonder that the rights, duties, and obligations, arising from so important a contract, should not be left to the discretion or caprice of the contracting parties, but should be regulated, in many important particulars, by the laws of every civilized country. And such laws must be considered as forming a most essential part of the public law of the country. As to the constitution of the marriage, as it is merely a personal consensual contract, it must be valid everywhere, if celebrated according to the *lex loci;* but, with regard to the rights, duties, and obligations, thence arising, the law of the domicil must be looked to. It must be admitted, that, in every country, the laws relative to divorce are considered as of the utmost importance, as public laws affecting the dearest interest of society.

§ 111. "It is said, that in every contract the parties bind themselves, not only to what is expressly stipulated, but also to what is implied in the nature of the contract; and that these stipulations, whether express or implied, are not affected by any subsequent change of domicil. This may be true in the general case; but, as already noticed, marriage is a contract *sui generis,* and the rights, duties, and obligations which arise out of it, are matters of so much importance to the well-being of the state, that they are regulated, not by the private contract, but by the public laws of the state, which are imperative on all who are domiciled within its territory. If a man in this country were to confine his wife in an iron cage, or to beat her with a rod of the thickness of the Judge's finger, would it be a justification in any court to allege, that these were powers which the law of England conferred on a husband; and that he was entitled to the exercise of them, because his marriage had been celebrated in that country?

§ 112. "In short, although a marriage, which is contracted according to the *lex loci,* will be valid all the world over, and although many of the obligations incident to it are left to be regulated solely by the agreement of the parties; yet many of the rights, duties, and obligations arising from it, are so important to the best interests of morality and good government, that the parties have no control over them; but they are regulated and enforced by the public law, which is imperative on all who are domiciled within its jurisdiction, and which cannot be controlled or affected by the circumstance, that the marriage was celebrated in a country where the law is different. In expounding or enforcing a contract entered into in a foreign country, and executed according to the laws of that country, regard will be paid to the *lex loci,* as the contract is evidence that the parties had in view the law of the country, and meant to be bound by it. But a party who is domiciled here, cannot be permitted to import into this country a law peculiar to his own case, and which is in opposition to those great and important public laws which our Legislature has held to be essentially connected with the best interests of society[1]."

§ 113. The general principle certainly is, (as we have already seen), that between persons *sui juris,* marriage is to be decided by the law of the place where it is celebrated[2]. If valid there, it is valid everywhere; it has a legal ubiquity of obligation. If invalid there, it is equally invalid everywhere[3]. The grounds of this doctrine we shall

---

[1] Lord Robertson in Fergusson on Marr. and Divorce, 397—399.

[2] Ante, § 80, 81.

[3] Ryan *v.* Ryan, 2 Phill. Eccl. R. 332; Herbert *v.* Herbert, 3 Phill. Eccl. R. 58; Dalrymple *v.* Dalrymple, 2 Hagg. Consist. R. 54; Ruding *v.* Smith, 2 Hagg. Consist. R. 390, 391; Scrimshire *v.* Scrimshire, 2 Hagg. Consist. R. 395; Munro *v.* Saunders, 6 Bligh, R. 473, 474; Ilderton *v.* Ilderton, 2 H. Bl. 145; Middleton *v.* Janverin, 2 Hagg. R. 437; Lacon *v.* Higgins, 3 Starkie, R. 178; 2 Kent, Comm. Lect. 26, pp. 91—93, (3rd edit.); Medway *v.* Needham, 16 Mass. R. 157; Putnam *v.* Putnam, 8 Pick. R. 433; West Cambridge *v.* Lexington, 1 Pick. R. 506; 1 Burge, Comm. on Col. and For. Law, ch. 5, § 3, p. 184 to 201; 2 Kaims on Eq. B. 3, ch. 8, § 1.

have occasion presently to consider[1]. It is only necessary here to state, that it has received the most deliberate sanction of the English and American Courts[2].

§ 113 *a*. The most prominent, if not the only known, exceptions to the rule are those marriages involving polygamy and incest; those positively prohibited by the public law of a country, from motives of policy; and those celebrated in foreign countries by subjects entitling themselves, under special circumstances, to the benefit of the laws of their own country[3]. Cases, illustrative of each of these exceptions, have been already alluded to[4].

§ 114. In respect to the first exception, that of marriages involving polygamy and incest, Christianity is understood to prohibit polygamy and incest; and therefore no Christian country would recognise polygamy or incestuous marriages[5]. But, when we speak of incestuous marriages, care must be taken to confine the doctrine to such cases, as, by the general consent of all Christendom, are deemed incestuous. It is difficult to ascertain exactly the point at which the law of nature or the authority of Christianity, ceases to prohibit marriages between kindred; and Christian nations are by no means generally agreed on this subject[6]. In most of the countries of Europe, in which the canon law has had any authority or influence, marriages are prohibited between near relations by blood, or by marriage, or in other words, by consanguinity, or by affinity; and the canon and the common law seem to have made no distinction on this point between consanguinity or relation

---

1 Post, § 121. See also Ante, § 80.

2 See Cases cited supra, § 113, note 1; Post, § 122—124.

3 1 Burge, Comm. on Col. and For. Law, ch. 5, § 3, p. 188.

4 Ante, § 89.

5 See Paley on Moral Phil. B. 3, ch. 6; 2 Kent, Comm. Lect. 26, p. 81, (3rd edit.); 1 Bl. Comm. 436. See Grotius, B. 2, ch. 5, § 9; Greenwood *v.* Curtis, 6 Mass. R. 378; 1 Burge, Comm. on Col. and For. Law, P. 1, ch. 5, § 3, pp. 188, 189, 190; Huberus, lib. 1, tit. 3, § 8.

6 Grotius, B. 2, ch. 5, § 12, 13, 14. See 1 Brown, Civ. Law, 61—65; 1 Burge, Comm. on Col. and For. Law, ch. 5, § 3, p. 188.

by blood, and affinity or relation by marriage; although there certainly is a very material difference in the cases [1]. Marriages between relations by blood, in the lineal ascending or descending line, are universally held by the common law, the canon law, and the civil law, to be unnatural and unlawful [2]. So are marriages between brother and sister in

---

[1] 2 Kent, Comm. Lect. 26, pp. 81, 82, (3rd edit.); 1 Bl. Comm. 434. See on this subject The London Quarterly Law Magazine for May, 1839, Vol. 21, pp. 371—382, The London Monthly Law Magazine for May, 1840, Vol. 7, pp. 330, 322, and the London Legal Observer for January, 1840.

[2] Wightman *v.* Wightman, 4 John. Ch. R. 343; 2 Kent, Comm. Lect. 26, pp. 81—84, (3rd edit.); Harrison *v.* Burwell, Vaughan, R. 206; S. C. 2 Vent. R. 9; Grotius, B. 2, ch. 5, § 12, n. 1, 2; Id. § 13, n. 4; Id. § 14, n. 1; 2 Heinecc. Elem. Juris Natur. B. 2, ch. 2, § 40, by Turnbull; 1 Burge, Comment. on Col. and For. Law, P. 1, ch. 5, § 1, pp. 137, 146, 147; Com. Dig. *Baron and Feme*, (B) 4; 2 Inst. 693.—Lord Brougham, in Warrender *v.* Warrender, (9 Bligh, R. 112, 113,) speaking on this subject, said: "But the rule extends, I apprehend, no further than to the ascertaining of the validity of the contract, and the meaning of the parties, that is, the existence of the contract and its construction. If indeed there go two things under one and the same name in different countries; if that which is called marriage is of a different nature in each; there may be some room for holding, that we are to consider the thing to which the parties have bound themselves, according to its legal acceptation in the country where the obligation was contracted. But marriage is one and the same thing substantially all the Christian world over. Our whole law of marriage assumes this; and it is important to observe, that we regard it as a wholly different thing, a different status, from Turkish or other marriages among infidel nations, because we clearly never should recognise the plurality of wives, and consequent validity of second marriages standing the first, which second marriages the laws of those countries authorize and validate. This cannot be put upon any rational ground, except our holding the infidel marriage to be something different from the Christian, and our also holding Christian marriage to be the same everywhere. Therefore, all that the Courts of one country have to determine is, whether or not the thing called marriage, that known relation of persons, that relation which those Courts are acquainted with and know how to deal with, has been validly contracted in the other country, where the parties professed to bind themselves. If the question is answered in the affirmative, a marriage has been had; the relation has been constituted; and those Courts will deal with the rights of the parties under it, according to the principles of the municipal law, which they administer." See also Id. 114.

the collateral line, whether of the whole blood or of the half blood[1]; and, indeed, such marriages seem repugnant to the first principles of social order and morality. It has been well remarked by Mr. Chancellor Kent, that it will be found difficult to carry the prohibition farther in the collateral line than the first degree, (that is, beyond brother and sister), unless where the legislature have expressly provided such a prohibition[2]. Grotius has expressed an equally strong

---

1 2 Kent, Comm. Lect. 26, pp. 83, 84, (3rd edit.). See also Butler *v.* Gastrill, Gilb. Eq. R. 156; 1 Burge, Comm. on Col. and For. Law, P. 1, ch. 6, § 1, p. 127; Id. § 3, p. 188; Grotius De Jure Belli, lib. 2, ch. 5, § 12, n. 2; Id. § 13, n. 3 to 7.

2 Wightman *v.* Wightman, 4 John. Ch. R. 343.—The whole remarks of the learned Chancellor on this occasion deserve to be cited at large: "Besides the case of lunacy now before me, I have, hypothetically, mentioned the case of a marriage between persons in the direct lineal line of consanguinity, as clearly unlawful by the law of the land, independent of any church canon, or of any statute prohibition. That such a marriage is criminal and void by the Law of Nature, is a point universally conceded. And, by the Law of Nature, I understand those fit and just rules of conduct, which the Creator has prescribed to man, as a dependent and social being; and which are to be ascertained from the deductions of right reason, though they may be more precisely known, and more explicitly declared by Divine Revelation. There is one other case in which the marriage would be equally void, causâ consanguinitatis, and that is the case of brother and sister; and since it naturally arises in the consideration of this subject, I will venture to add a few incidental observations. I am aware that when we leave the lineal line and come to the relation by blood or affinity in the collateral line, it is not so easy to ascertain the exact point at which the Natural Law has ceased to discountenance the union. Though there may be some difference in the theories of different writers on the Law of Nature, in regard to this subject, yet the general current of authority, and the practice of civilized nations, and certainly of the whole Christian world, have condemned the connexion in the second case, which has been supposed as grossly indecent, immoral, and incestuous, and inimical to the purity and happiness of families, and as forbidden by the Law of Nature." (Grotius de Jure, &c. lib. 2, c. 5, s. 13; Puffend. De Jure Gent. lib. 6, c. 1, s. 34; Id. de Off. Hom. lib. 2, c. 2, s. 8; Heinecc. Oper. tom. 8, pars 2, p. 203; Taylors' Elem. Civ. Law, 326; Montesq. Esp. des Loix, liv. 26, c. 14; Paley's Moral Philosophy, B. 3, p. 3, c. 5.) We, accordingly, find such connexions expressly prohibited in different Codes. (Dig. lib. 23, tit. 2, l. 18, lib. 23, tit. 2, l. 14, s. 2, lib. 45, tit. 1, l. 35, s. 1; Just. Inst. lib. 1, tit. 10; De Nuptiis, Vinnius, h. t; Heinecc. ubi supra. Code Civile de France, n. 161, 162, 163, 164; Inst. of Menu, by Sir William

opinion upon the intrinsic difficulty of the subject. *De conjugiis eorum, qui sanguine aut affinitate junguntur, satis gravis*

Jones, c. 3, s. 5; Staunton's Ta-Tsing-Leu-Lee, s. 107, 108; Sale's Koran, c. 4; Marsden's Sumatra, pp. 194, 221.) And whatever may have been the practice of some ancient nations originating, as Montesquieu observes, in the madness of superstition, the objection to such marriages is, undoubtedly, founded in reason and nature. It grows out of the institution of families, and the rights and duties, habits and affections, flowing from that relation, and which may justly be considered as part of the Law of our Nature, as retional and social beings. Marriages among such near relations would not only lead to domestic licentiousness; but, by blending in one object duties and feelings incompatible with each other, would perplex and confound the duties, habits, and affections proceeding from the family state, impair the perception, and corrupt the purity of moral taste, and do violence to the moral sentiments of mankind. Indeed, we might infer the sense of mankind, and the dictates of reason and nature, from the language of horror and detestation, in which such incestuous connexions have been reprobated and condemned in all ages. (Plato de Leg. lib. 8; Cic. Orat. pro Mil. 27; Hermion. in Eurip. Androm. *v.* 175; Byblis. Ovid. Met. lib. 9; Tacit. Ann. lib. 12, c. 4; Vell. Paterc. Hist. lib. 2, c. 45; Corn. Nep. Excel. Imp. Prefat.) The general usage of mankind is sufficient to settle the question, if it were possible to have any doubt on the subject; and it must have proceeded from some strong uniform and natural principle. Prohibitions of the Natural Law are of absolute, uniform, and universal obligation. They become rules of the Common Law, which is founded in the common reason and acknowledged duty of mankind, sanctioned by immemorial usage, and, as such, are clearly binding. To this extent, then, I apprehend it to be within the power and within the duty of this Court to enforce the prohibition. Such marriages should be declared void, as contra bonos mores. But as to the other collateral degrees, beyond brother and sister, I should incline to the intimation of the Judges in Harrison *v.* Burwell, (Vaugh. R. 206; S. C. 2 Vent. 9), that, as we have no statute on the subject, and no train of common law decisions, independent of any statute authority, the Levitical degrees are not binding as a rule of municipal obedience. Marriages out of the lineal line and in the collateral line, beyond the degree of brothers and sisters, could not well be declared void, as against the first principles of society. The laws or usages of all the nations to whom I have referred, do, indeed, extend the prohibition to remoter degrees; but this is stepping out of the family circle; and I cannot put the prohibition on any other ground than positive institution. There is a great diversity of usage on this subject. Neque teneo, neque dicta refello. The limitation must be left, until the legislature thinks proper to make some provision in the case, to the injunctions of religion, and to the control of manners and opinion." See also 2 Kent, Comm. Lect. 26, pp. 83, 84, (3rd edit.); 1 Burge, Comment. on Col. and For. Law, P. 1, ch. 5, § 1, p. 188.

est quæstio, et non raro magnis motibus agitata. Nam causas certas ac naturales, cur talia conjugia, ita ut legibus aut moribus vetentur, illicita sint, assignare, qui voluerit, experiendo discet, quam id sit difficile, imo præstari non possit[1].

§ 114 *a.* At all events, in other cases of consanguinity not in the lineal line, or in the first degree of the collateral line, there is much room for diversity of opinion and judgment among jurists, and of practice among nations. Grotius has taken notice of this distinction, and says, *Quæ manifesta expressio ostendere videtur discrimen, quod est inter hos et alios remotiores gradus*[2]. Thus, he says, that it is forbidden to marry an aunt on the father's side; but not the daughter of a brother, who is of the same degree. *Nam ducere amitam agnatam vetitum est. At filiam fratris, qui par est gradus, ducere vetitum non est*[3]. In England it has been declared by statute, that all persons may lawfully marry, but such as are prohibited by God's law, that is, such as are within the Levitical degrees[4]. Under this ge-

---

1 Grotius, de Jure Belli, lib. 2, c. 5, § 12.

2 Grotius, de Jure Belli, lib. 2, c. 5, § 14, n. 1.

3 Ibid.

4 Com. Dig. *Baron and Feme*, B. 2, B. 4; 1 Black. Comm. 435; Leviticus, ch. 18.—Mr. Burge states the prohibitions in England, arising from the Levitical law, in the following terms:—" Cognatio, consanguinity or relationship by blood, and affinitas, affinity or relationship by marriage, constitute impediments to a lawful marriage. Marriages between parties related by blood or by affinity, in the direct ascending or descending line ad infinitum, are prohibited by the civil and canon law. This prohibition prevents that confusion of civil duties, which would be the necessary results of such marriages. The codes of Europe concur in this prohibition. In the collateral line, the prohibition is confined to those who stand in certain degrees of consanguinity or affinity to each other. In the computation of these degrees there is a difference between the civil and canon law. Thus, those who, according to the civil law, are in the second degree, are placed by the canon law in the first degree; and those who are placed by the civil law in the fourth degree, are by the canon law placed in the second degree. The degrees prohibited by the Levitical law are all within the fourth degree of consanguinity, according to the computation of the civil law; all collaterals, therefore, in that degree, or beyond it, may marry. First cousins are in the

neral provision it has been held, that a marriage between an uncle and a niece by blood is incestuous, (it being in the third degree), upon the ground that it is against the law of God, and sound morals; that it would tend to endless confusion; and that the sanctity of private life would be polluted, and the proper freedom of intercourse in families would be destroyed, if such practices were not discouraged in the strongest manner[1]. Yet Grotius not only deems such a marriage perfectly unexceptionable; but adds, that there are examples of it among the Hebrews[2]. But marriages between first cousins by blood, or cousins german, (being in the fourth degree), are, according to English jurisprudence, lawful; so that the prohibitions in the collateral line stop at the third degree[3]. The same rule, as to the marriage of first cousins, has been adopted by the Protestant countries of Europe. But the canon law prohibited such marriages, although a dispensation might be obtained

---

fourth degree by the civil law, and, therefore, may marry. Nephew and great-aunt, or niece and great-uncle, are also in the fourth degree, and may intermarry; and though a man may not marry his grandmother, it is certainly true that he may marry her sister. All these fourth degrees in the civil law are second degrees in the canon law. By the civil law, persons in the fourth degree might intermarry with each other. Such is the law of England, Scotland, Ireland, and the colonies." 1 Burge, Comment. on Col. and For. Law, P. 1, ch. 5, § 1, pp. 146, 147. There seems to be a mistake of the press in one part of the passage of Mr. Burge's remarks as to the difference between the civil law and the canon law. The latter counted the degrees only up to the common ancestor; the former also down to the Propositus. So that the first degree in the canon law was the second in the civil law, and the second in the canon law was the fourth in the civil law. 2 Black. Comm. 224; Ersk. Instit. B. 1, tit. 6, § 8; 2 Burns, Eccles. Law, tit. *Marriage*, I. See also The London Monthly Law Magazine for Feb. 1840, Vol. 7, p. 44 to 46. Mr. Burge's Text reverses the statement. 1 Burge, Comment. on Col. and For. Law, P. 1, ch. 5, § 1, p. 147.

[1] Burgess *v.* Burgess, 1 Hagg. Consist. R. 384, 386; 1 Bl. Comm. 435; Butler *v.* Gastrill, Gilb. Eq. R. 156, 158; 2 Kent, Comm. Lect. 26, p. 84, (3rd edit.); Comm. Dig. *Baron and Feme*, B. 4.

[2] Grotius, De Jure Belli, lib. 2, c. 5, § 14, n. 1.

[3] 1 Black. Comm. 435; Burns, Eccles. Law, tit. *Marriage*, I.; Harrison *v.* Burwell, Vaughan, R. 219; S. C. 2 Vent. 9; 2 Instit. 684.

thereof[1]. Incestuous marriages by the English law are not, however, deemed by the common law absolutely void; but they are voidable only during the lives of the parties; and, if not so avoided during their lives, they are deemed valid to all intents and purposes[2].

§ 115. Hitherto we have been speaking of cases of relation by consanguinity, between which and cases of relation by affinity, there seems to be a clear and just moral difference. The English law, however, has treated both classes of cases as falling within the same predicament of prohibition by the Levitical law. Hence it has been there held, that a marriage between a father-in-law and the daughter of his first wife by a former marriage is incestuous and unlawful[3]; and, indeed, there seems something repugnant to social feelings in such marriages. The prohibition has also been extended in England to the marriages between a man and the sister of his former deceased wife; but upon what ground of Scriptural authority it has been thought very difficult to affirm[4]. In many, and indeed in most of the Ame-

---

[1] Burns, Eccles. Law, tit. *Marriage*, I.; 1 Burge, Comm. on Col. and For. Law, P. 1, ch. 5, § 1, pp. 147, 148.

[2] 1 Black. Comm. 434, 435.—By a recent Act of Parliament, Act of 5th and 6th William 4th, c. 54, (1835), all future incestuous marriages are declared to be utterly void, and not merely voidable.

[3] Blackmore and Thorpe *v.* Brider, 2 Hagg. Consist. R. 393, note; S.C. 2 Phill. Eccles. R. 359.

[4] Burns, Eccles. Law, tit. *Marriage*, I.; 1 Black. Comm. 434, 435, Christian's note (2), citing Gibson's Codex, 412; Harris *v.* Hicks, Salk. 548; Hall *v.* Good, Vaughan, R. 302, 312; Faremouth *v.* Watson, 1 Phill. Eccl. R. 355; Chick *v.* Rawsdale, 1 Curteis, R. 34; Com. Dig. *Baron and Feme*, B. 2, B. 4; 2 Inst. 683; Bac. Abridg. *Marriage*, A. Lord Chief Justice Vaughan, in delivering the opinion of the Court in Harrison *v.* Burwell, (Vaughan, R. 206; S.C. 2 Vent. R. 9), says, that a man is prohibited by the statute, 32 Henry, 8, [ch. 38], to marry his wife's sister. But within the meaning of Leviticus, (ch. 18, v. 14), and the constant practice of the Commonwealth of the Jews, a man was prohibited to marry his wife's sister only during her life; after he might. So the text is. Vaughan, R. 241; S. C. 2 Vent. 17. There seems a discrepancy between what is here said, and his judgment in the subsequent case of Hall *v.* Good, Vaughan, R. 302, 312, 320. The opinion of Lord Chief Justice Vaughan,

rican States, a different rule prevails: and marriages between a man and the sister of his former deceased wife are not only deemed in a civil sense lawful; but are deemed in a moral, religious, and Christian sense lawful, and exceedingly praiseworthy. In some few of the States, the English rule is adopted. Upon the continent of Europe, most of the Protestant countries adopt the doctrine, that such marriages are lawful[1].

§ 116. It would be a strong point to put, that a marriage, perfectly valid between a man and the sister of his former deceased wife in New England, should be held invalid in Virginia or in England, even though the parties originally belonged to, or were born in, the latter country or

---

in both cases, and the case of Butler *v.* Gastrill, Gilbert, Eq. R. 156, are full of learning and instruction on the subject of the canonical and ecclesiastical prohibitions of marriage. Dr. John H. Livingston, of New Jersey, has written an elaborate dissertation upon the subject of the marriage of a man with his sister-in-law (wife's sister), which was printed at New Brunswick, N. J., in 1816. It holds the doctrine, that such marriages are scripturally incestuous. The opposite doctrine has been maintained by many able writers. See also 2 Kent, Comm. Lect. 26, p. 85, (3rd edit.), note. There are some very able articles on this subject in the London Quarterly Law Magazine for May, 1839, Vol. 21, p. 371; in the London Legal Observer for January, 1840; and in the London Monthly Law Magazine for May, 1840. All these articles are designed to shew that the most learned writers have differed upon this subject, and to establish that the doctrine is ill-founded and ought to be abolished. Grotius maintains in strong terms, that there is no foundation for the prohibition. Certè, canonibus antiquissimis, qui apostolici dicuntur, qui duas sorores alteram post alteram duxisset aut *αδελφιδην*, id est, fratris aut sororis filiam, tantum à clero arcetur.—Grotius, De Jure Belli, lib. 2, c. 5, § 14, n. 2.

[1] This is certainly the law in all the New England States, and in New York. Greenwood *v.* Curtis, 6 Mass. R. 378, 379. In Virginia, the English rule prevails. Commonwealth *v.* Perryman, 2 Leigh, R. 717; 2 Kent, Comm. Lect. 36, p. 85, note (a). Dr. Jeremy Taylor and Sir Wm. Jones both contend, that the Levitical degrees do not, by any law of God, bind Christians to their observation. See London Quart. Law Magazine, Vol. 21, pp. 373, 374. In Prussia, Saxony, Hanover, Baden, Mechlenburg, Hamburg, Denmark, and in most other of the Protestant states of Europe, the rule prevails, that a man may lawfully marry the sister of his former wife. Id. p. 376. It is otherwise in Scotland. Ersk. Inst. B. 1, tit. 6, § 9.

state. But as to persons not so born or belonging, it would be of the most dangerous consequence to suppose, that the Courts of either of them would assume the liberty to hold such marriages a nullity, merely because their own jurisprudence would not, in a local celebration of marriage therein, uphold it. This distinction between marriages, incestuous by the law of nature, and such as are incestuous by the positive code or customary law of a state, has been fully recognised by one of our most learned American Courts. "If" (say the Court) "a foreign state allows of marriages incestuous by the law of nature, as between parent and child, such marriage would not be allowed to have any validity here. But marriages not naturally unlawful, but prohibited by the law of one state and not of another, if celebrated where they are not prohibited, would be holden valid in a state where they are not allowed. As, in this state, a marriage between a man and his deceased wife's sister is lawful; but it is not so in some states. Such a marriage celebrated here would be held valid in any other state, and the parties entitled to the benefits of the matrimonial contract [1]." Indeed, in the diversity of religious opinions in Christian countries, a large space must be allowed for interpretation, as to religious duties, rights, and solemnities [2]. In the Catholic countries of continental Europe, there are many prohibitions of marriage which are connected with religious canons and establishments; and in most countries there are some positive or customary prohibitions, which involve peculiarities of religious opinion, or of conscientious doubt. It would be most inconvenient to hold all marriages celebrated elsewhere void, which are not in scrupulous accordance with the local institutions of a particular country.

---

[1] Greenwood *v.* Curtis, 6 Mass. R. 378, 379; Medway *v.* Needham, 16 Mass. R. 157, 161. But see Huberus, lib. 1, tit. 3, § 8; Wightman *v.* Wightman, 4 John. Ch. R. 343.

[2] See on this point, 2 Kent, Comm. Lect. 26, p. 85, (3rd edit.); Harrison *v.* Burwell, Vaugh. R. 206; S. C. 2 Vent. R. 9; Co. Litt. 149; Grotius, lib. 2, c. 5, § 12, 13, 14; Rutherf. Inst. B. 1, ch. 15, § 10; Wightman *v.* Wightman, 4 John. Ch. R. 343.

§ 116 *a*. In the cases of incest hitherto discussed, it has been supposed, that the parties marrying were either natives of, or actually and *bonâ fide* domiciled in, the country where the marriage was celebrated. But, suppose the case of a marriage, incestuous by the law of the country where the parties are born, or are *bonâ fide* domiciled, and without changing their domicil for the purpose of evading that law, they go to a foreign country where a different rule prevails, and the marriage, which would not be incestuous by its laws, is there celebrated; and the parties afterwards return to their own country: ought such a marriage to be held valid in such country? Huberus has put the very case, and held, that it ought not there to be held valid. If (says he) a Brabanter, who should marry within the prohibited degrees, under a dispensation from the Pope, should remove here (into Holland), the marriage would be considered valid. Yet if a Frizian should marry the daughter of his brother in Brabant, and celebrate the nuptials there, returning here he would not be acknowledged as a married man; because in this way our laws might be evaded by the worst examples. *Brabantus uxore ductâ, dispensatione Pontificis, in gradu prohibito, si huc migret, tolerabitur. Attamen, si Frisius cum fratris filiâ se conferat in Brabantiam, ibique nuptias celebret, huc reversus non videtur tolerandus; quia sic jus nostrum pessimis exemplis eluderetur*[1].

---

[1] Huberus, Lib. 1, tit. 3, § 8; Post, § 123; 1 Burge, Comm. on Col. and For. Law, P. 1, ch. 5, § 1, p. 147; Id. § 3, p. 188 to 191.—Mr. Burge maintains this to be the true doctrine, and says: "The law, which prohibits persons related to each other in a certain degree from intermarrying, and declares their intermarriage to be null, imposes on them a personal incapacity quoad that act; and that incapacity must continue to affect them, so long as they retain their domicil in the country in which that law prevails. The resort to another country, where there was no such prohibitory law, for the mere purpose of evading the law of their own country, and with the intention of returning thither when their marriage had taken place, cannot be considered a change of their former domicil, or the acquisition of a domicil in the country to which they had resorted. They must, therefore, be regarded as still subject to the personal incapacity, imposed by the law of their real domicil." See Post, § 123, 124. There are certain parts of the opinion of

§ 117. In respect to the second exception, that of prohibitions depending upon positive law of a particular country[1], they, of course, can apply strictly only to the subjects of that country. An illustration of this nature may be found in the Civil Code of France, which annuls marriages by Frenchmen, in foreign countries, who are under an incapacity by the laws of France[2]. A law of a similar nature may be found in the Act of 12 Geo. 3, ch. 11, respecting the royal family, by which they are prohibited from contracting marriage, unless under special circumstances, pointed out in the act[3]; and the provisions of that act have been actually applied to the case of a foreign marriage, contracted by one of the royal princes. The doctrine of the English Courts, already alluded to[4], in regard to the indissolubility of English marriages celebrated in England, notwithstanding a subsequent divorce in a foreign country, affords a still more striking illustration; as, in its practical effects, it may render the issue of a second marriage illegitimate: so that a son, the issue of the second marriage in Scotland, may be legitimate there, and illegitimate in England; he may be a lawful Scotch Peer, and yet lose the English estates which support his peerage[5].

§ 118. In respect to the third exception, that of marriages contracted and celebrated in foreign countries by

---

Sir George Hay, in Harford *v.* Morris, 2 Hagg. Consist. R. 431, 432, 435, from which it may fairly be deduced as his opinion, that the law of the place of marriage was the rule only when the parties were domiciled there; and that, if they went from their own country merely to celebrate the marriage in a foreign country, and immediately to return home, the law of such country would not govern, but the law of the country of their domicil. Post, § 124, note.

1 Ante, § 113 *a*.

2 2 Kent, Comm. Lect. 26, p. 93, (3rd edit.); Code Civil of France, art. 170; Merlin, Répert. Loi, § 6, n. 1.

3 1 Black. Comm. 226.

4 Ante, § 88.

5 See Beazley *v.* Beazley, 3 Hagg. Ecc. R. 639; Rex *v.* Lolley, 1 Russ. & Ryan, C. C. 236; Tovey *v.* Lindsay, 1 Dow, 124; M'Carthy *v.* De Caix, cited 3 Hagg. 642, note; S. C. 2 Russ. & Mylne, R. 620.

subjects under peculiar circumstances[1], it has been deemed to arise in cases of a sort of moral necessity; and it has been held to apply to persons residing in foreign factories, in conquered places, and in desert or barbarous countries, or in countries of an opposite religion, who are, therefore, permitted from necessity, to contract marriage there, according to the laws of their own country. In short, wherever there is a local necessity from the absence of laws, or from the presence of prohibitions or obstructions, in a foreign country, not binding upon other countries, or from peculiarities of religious opinion and conscientious scruples, or from circumstances of exemption from the local jurisdiction, marriages will be allowed to be valid, according to the law of the native or of the fixed actual domicil[2].

§ 119. The doctrine upon which this exception from necessity is founded, will be best explained by a quotation from the opinion of Lord Stowell, in a case already referred to, in which the question of the validity of a marriage, celebrated at the Cape of Good Hope between English subjects, by a chaplain of the British forces then occupying that settlement under a capitulation recently made, came before him for decision[3]. After citing the rule, that the law and legislative government of every dominion equally affect all persons and all property within the limits thereof, and remarking, that, to such a proposition, expressed in very general terms, only general truth can be ascribed, (for it is undoubtedly subject to exceptions), he proceeded to say, that even the native and resident inhabitants are not all brought strictly within the pale of the general law. And, in illustration of this remark, he referred to the fact, that,

---

[1] Ante, § 113 *a*.

[2] See Ruding *v.* Smith, 2 Hagg. Consist. R. 371, 384, 385, 386; Ante, § 79; Lautour *v.* Teesdale, 8 Taunt. R. 830; S. C. 2 Marshall, R. 243; The King *v.* Inhab. of Brampton, 10 East, R. 282. See also Harford *v.* Morris, 2 Hagg. Consist. R. 432, where Sir George Hay, in delivering judgment, spoke of this exception of foreign English Factories. Ante, § 79, and Id. p. 79, note 1.

[3] Ante, § 79.

even in England, there is a numerous and respectable body (referring to the Jews), distinguished by great singularity of usages, who, though native subjects under the protection of the general law, are, in many respects, governed by institutions of their own; and particularly in their marriages, for, it being the practice of mankind to consecrate their marriages by religious ceremonies, the differences of religion, in all countries that admit residents professing religions essentially different, unavoidably introduce exceptions in that matter to the universality of the rule, which makes mere domicil the constituent of an unlimited subjection to the ordinary law of the country. He then added: "What is the law of marriage in all foreign establishments, settled in countries, professing a religion essentially different? in the English factories at Lisbon, Leghorn, Oporto, Cadiz, and in the factories in the East, Smyrna, Aleppo, and others? in all of which (some of these establishments existing by authority under treaties, and others under indulgence and toleration) marriages are regulated by the law of the original country to which they are still considered to belong. An English resident at St. Petersburg does not look to the ritual of the Greek Church, but to the Rubric of the Church of England, when he contracts a marriage with an English woman. Nobody can suppose that, whilst the Mogul empire existed, an Englishman was bound to consult the Koran for the celebration of his marriage. Even where no foreign connexion can be ascribed, a respect is shewn to the opinions and practice of a distinct people. The validity of a Greek marriage in the extensive dominions of Turkey, is left to depend, I presume, upon their own canons, without any reference to Mahometan ceremonies. There is a *jus gentium* upon this matter; a comity, which treats with tenderness, or, at least, with toleration, the opinion and usages of a distinct people, in this transaction of marriage. It may be difficult to say *à priori*, how far the general law should circumscribe its own authority in this matter. But practice has established the principle in several instances;

and where the practice is admitted, it is entitled to acceptance and respect. It has sanctioned the marriages of foreign subjects in the houses of the ambassadors of the foreign country to which they belong[1]. I am not aware of any judicial regulation upon this point; but the reputation which the validity of such marriages has acquired, makes such a recognition by no means improbable, if such a question was brought to judgment[2]." And again: "It is true, indeed, that English decisions have established this rule, that a foreign marriage, valid according to the law of the place where celebrated, is good everywhere else. But they have not *e converso* established, that marriages of British subjects, not good according to the law of the place where celebrated, are universally, and under all possible circumstances, to be regarded as invalid in England. It is, therefore, certainly to be advised, that the safest course is, always to be married according to the law of the country; for then no question can be stirred. But if this cannot be done on account of legal or religious difficulties, the law of this country does not say that its subjects shall not marry abroad[3]." And he accordingly held the marriage valid on the distinct British character of the parties; on their independence of the Dutch law in their own British transactions; on the insuperable obstacles of obtaining any marriage conformable to the Dutch law; on the countenance given by British authority and British administration to this transaction; and upon the whole country being under British dominion[4].

§ 120. In regard to marriages by British subjects in their own foreign settlements, the general rule is, that marriages, good by the laws of England, will be valid there; for they carry those laws with them into such settlements, and are not to be governed by the laws or customs of the natives. Thus, it has been held, that a marriage between British

1 See Pertreis *v.* Tondear, 1 Hagg. Consist. R. 136.

2 Ruding *v.* Smith, 2 Hagg. Consist. R. 385, 386.

3 Ibid.

4 Ibid. p. 371; Ante, § 79.

subjects at Madras is good, if conformable to the British laws, and not to the laws of the natives of India[1].

§ 121. The ground, however, upon which the general rule of the validity of marriages, according to the *lex loci contractûs,* is maintained, is easily vindicated. It cannot be better expressed than in the language of Sir Edward Simpson already cited[2]. All civilized nations allow marriage contracts. They are *juris gentium;* and the subjects of all nations are equally concerned in them. Infinite mischief and confusion must necessarily arise to the subjects of all nations, with respect to legitimacy, successions, and other rights, if the respective laws of different countries were only to be observed, as to marriages contracted by the subjects of those countries abroad; and therefore all nations have consented, or are presumed to consent, for the common benefit and advantage, that such marriages shall be good or not, according to the laws of the country where they are celebrated. By observing this rule, few, if any, inconveniences can arise; by disregarding it, infinite mischiefs must ensue[3]. Suppose, for instance, a marriage celebrated in France, according to the law of that country, should be held void in England, what would be the consequences? Each party might marry anew in the other country. In one country the issue would be deemed legitimate; in the other, illegitimate. The French wife would, in France, be held the only wife, and entitled as such to all the rights of property appertaining to that relation; in England, the English wife would hold the same exclusive rights and character. What, then, would be the confusion, in regard to the personal property of the parties, in its own nature transitory, passing alternately from one country to the other! Suppose there should be issue of both marriages, and then all the parties should become domiciled in England or

---

[1] Lautour *v.* Teesdale, 8 Taunt. R. 830; S. C. 2 Marsh. R. 243.

[2] Ante, § 80 *a.*

[3] Scrimshire *v.* Scrimshire, 2 Hagg. Consist. R. 417, 418, and Ante, § 79, 80, 80 *a.*

France; what confusion of rights, what embarrassments of personal and conjugal relations, must necessarily be created[1]!

§ 122. Foreign jurists in general as strenuously support the general rule, as the tribunals sitting to administer the common law; and undoubtedly from a common sense of the pernicious consequences which would flow from a different doctrine[2]. This subject is much discussed by Sanchez to the following effect: As to the maxim or general rule, *Ut non teneantur peregrini legibus et consuetudinibus loci, per quem transeunt,* this rule has exceptions; (1.) *Quoad contractuum solemnitatem; nam quicunque forenses et peregrini tenentur servare solemnitates in contractu requisitas legibus et consuetudinibus oppidi, in quo contrahunt. Ratione enim contractus quilibet forum sortitur in loco contractûs; hinc est contractum absolutè initum, censeri celebratum juxta consuetudines et statuta loci in quo initur. Quod ita provenit, quia contractus sequitur consuetudines et statuta loci in quo celebratur*[3]. And a case is put, as to inhabitants of a place where the decree of the Council of Trent, for avoiding clandestine marriages, is not received. Suppose they go from England to places *per modum transitûs, ubi obligat decretum,* and marry there according to the laws of their own domicil. Some think that such marriage is good in the case of strangers, as agreeable to their own laws, to the law of the country in which they are domiciled, though not to the law of the place where they are married. But Sanchez holds, that a marriage is void, where it wants the solemnities prescribed by the local law. "What" (says he) "the laws of the place require, where the contract is made, and what are to be followed in contracts, are to be decided solely by the laws of the place in which the contract is celebrated:" *Quæ petunt leges loci, ubi contractus initur, et quoad solemnitatem adhibendam in contractibus, solæ leges*

---

[1] Scrimshire *v.* Scrimshire, 2 Hagg. Consist. R. 417, 418; Ante, § 80 *a.*
[2] 1 Burge, Comm. on Col. and For. Law, P. 1, ch. 5, § 3, p. 184 to 188.
[3] Post, § 260.

loci, in quo contractus celebratur, inspiciuntur[1]. *Locus, autem, ubi hoc matrimonium initur, non petit eam parochi et testium solemnitatem ad matrimonii valorem, cum ibi decretum Tridentini non obliget*[2]. *Ea solemnitas adhibenda est, quam petunt leges loci, ubi contractus initur; cum ergo locus ubi celebratur matrimonium, ab his peregrinis exigat solemnitatem Tridentini in eo vigentis; aliter contractum nullum erit*[3].

§ 122 *a*. John Voet seems to affirm the same doctrine to be generally, but not universally true, and liable to exceptions. He puts the case of the marriage of an inhabitant of Holland with a female of Flanders or Brabant—in Flanders or Brabant, according to the laws of the latter, but not according to the laws of Holland—and asks, if it would be valid in Holland. To which he answers, that, *primâ facie*, it should seem that such marriages ought in Holland to be held valid; "because" (says he) "it is sufficient in contracts to follow the solemnities of the place in which the contract is celebrated, although the solemnities are not observed which are prescribed in the place of the domicil of the parties, or of the situation of the property in executing the act." *Primâ quidem specie videri posset, nuptias tales etiam in ipsâ Hollandiâ ratas habendas esse. Eo quod sufficit in contrahendo adhiberi solennia loci illius, in quo contractus celebratur, etsi non inveniantur observata solennia, quæ in loco domicilii contrahentium, aut rei sitæ, actui gerendo præscripta sunt*[4]. He adds, that, there had been different opinions given in Holland on this point. But he expresses his own opinion to be, that such marriage, so ce-

---

[1] I cite this whole passage from the case of Scrimshire *v.* Scrimshire, 2 Hagg. Consist. R. 412, 413. See also 1 Burge, Comment. on Col. and For. Law, P. 1, ch. 5, § 3, pp. 185, 186; Sanchez, De Matrim. Lib. 3, Disput. 18, § 10, n. 26, 28.

[2] Cited in Burge, Comment., ubi supra, pp. 185, 186.

[3] Cited Ibid.

[4] J. Voet, ad Pand. Lib. 23, tit. 2, § 4, Tom. 2, p. 20; cited also in Scrimshire *v.* Scrimshire, 2 Hagg. Consist. R. 415. See also Voet, ad Pand. Lib. 23, tit. 2, § 85, p. 55.

lebrated out of Holland, ought to be pronounced invalid in Holland, upon the very terms of the edict of Holland, by which marriages by Hollanders, without proper notifications thereof, published in the place of their domicil, are declared to be void. That the general rule, that it is sufficient in negotiations and contracts to follow the solemnities required by the law of the place where the business is transacted, does not apply in such a case; for that rule has its proper place only where the business is not so transacted in fraud of the law, or where no statute has positively declared that the act shall be void, when done by a subject according to the foreign solemnities. *Sed, eo non obstante, magis est, ut matrimonia, eo modo extra Hollandiam ab Hollando celebrata, infirma per Judicem Hollandicum pronunciari debeant, propter Edicti verba, quibus nuptiæ, per Hollandum sine denunciationibus publicis in domicilii loco interpositis contractæ, irritæ esse jussæ sunt. Nihil in contrarium faciente illo axiomate, quod sufficiat in negotiis contrahendis adhiberi solennia loci, in quo actus geritur: cum ista regula locum inveniat, si non in fraudem statuti quis alio se contulerit ad actum celebrandum, aut statutum nominatim irritum declaraverit actum, à suo subjecto peregrinâ solennitate gestum*[1].

§ 122 *b*. Paul Voet holds an opinion decidedly in favour of the general rule. *Quid si de contractubus proprie dictis, et quidem eorum solemnibus contentio; Quis locus spectabitur; an domicilii contrahentis an loci, ubi quis contrahit? Respondeo affirmanter. Posterius. Quia, censetur quis semet contrahendo, legibus istius loci ubi contrahit, etiam ratione solemnium subjicere voluisse*[2]. Huberus admits, that a marriage valid by the law of the place where it is celebrated, is binding everywhere, under the exception, which he generally applies, that it is not prejudicial to others, or that it is not incestuous. *Matrimonium pertinet etiam ad has re-*

---

[1] J. Voet, ad Pand. Lib. 23, tit. 2, § 4, p. 20.

[2] Voet, De Statut. § 9, ch. 2, n. 9, p. 267, (edit. 1715); Ibid. 323, (edit. 1661); Post, § 261.

gulas. Si licitum est eo loco, ubi contractum et celebratum est, ubique validum erit, effectumque habebit, sub eadem exceptione prejudicii aliis non creandi; cui licet addere, si exempli nimis sit abominandi, ut si incestum juris gentium in secundo gradu contigerit alicubi esse permissum[1]. Bouhier adopts the general rule, hesitating as to the nature and extent of the exceptions[2]. Hertius lays down the following axiom: If the law prescribes a form for the act, the place of the act, and not of the domicil of the parties, or of the situation of the property, is to be considered. *Si Lex actui formam dat, inspiciendus est locus actûs, non domicilii, non rei sitæ*[3]. And he puts the following as an example: A marriage contracted according to the solemnities of any place, where the married couple are commorant, cannot be rescinded upon the pretext, that, in the domicil or country of the husband, other solemnities are required. *Matrimonium juxta solennitates loci alicujus ubi sponsus et sponsa commorabantur, contractum non potest prætextu illo rescindi, quòd in domicilio aut patriâ mariti aliæ solennitates observentur*[4]. He afterwards puts exceptions to this general axiom; one of which is, that a contract between foreigners, both belonging to a foreign country, is to be governed by the law of their own country, and not by that of the *lex loci contractûs*[5]. In this exception, he has to encounter many distinguished adversaries[6]. The French jurists seem generally to support the doctrine, that marriage is to be held valid or not, according to the law of the place of celebration, except in cases positively prohibited by their own laws to their own subjects, or where it is in fraud of those

---

1 Huberus, Lib. 1, tit. 3, § 8; Ante, § 85.

2 Bouhier, Cout. de Bourg. ch. 27, § 59 to 66.

3 Post, § 242, 260; Hertii Opera, Tom. 1, De Collis. Leg. § 4, art. 10, p. 126, (edit. 1737); Id. p. 179, (edit. 1716).

4 1 Hertii Opera, De Collis. Leg. § 4, art. 10, (edit. 1737), p. 126; Id. p. 179, (edit. 1716); Id. art. 10, p. 128, (edit. 1737); Id. p. 182, (edit. 1716).

5 Id. p. 128, § 10, (edit. 1737); Non Valet (6).

6 Ibid.

laws[1]. And Merlin says, that it is a contract so completely of natural and moral law, that, when celebrated by savages in places where there are no established laws, it will be recognised as good in other countries[2].

§ 123. A question has been much discussed, how far a marriage regularly celebrated in a foreign country between persons belonging to another country, who have gone thither from their own country for that purpose, is to be deemed valid if it is not celebrated according to the law of their own country. Huberus, as we have seen[3], has put the very question, and has applied it as well to cases of minority as of incest; and he does not hesitate to pronounce such marriages invalid, because they are an evasion or fraud upon the law of the country to which the parties belong, and in which they are domiciled[4]. Bouhier has advocated the same opinion[5]; and it is also maintained by Paul Voet. He states it as an exception to the general rule, that the law of the place of the contract ought to govern. *Nisi quis, quo in loco domicilii evitaret molestam aliquam vel sumptuosam solemnitatem; adeoque in fraudem sui statuti nullâ necessitate cogente alio proficiscatur, et mox ad eorum domicilium, gesto alibi negotio, revertatur*[6]. John Voet (as we have seen) holds the same opinion[7]. Pothier puts the very case in the strongest terms. He says, that the conditions and ceremonies, prescribed by the French

1 Post, § 123.

2 Merlin, Répert. Mariage, § 1, p. 343. See also 2 Boullenois, Observ. 46, p. 458; 1 Froland, Mém. p. 177, ch. 1; Pardessus, Vol. 5, P. 6, tit. 7, ch. 2, art. 1481 to 1495; Pothier, Traité du Mariage, n. 263; Journal des Audiences, Tom. 1, ch. 24; S. C. cited Scrimshire *v.* Scrimshire, 2 Hagg. Consist. R. 413, 414.

3 Ante, § 85, 116 *a*.

4 Huberus, lib. 1, tit. 3, § 9. See Ante, § 85, 116 *a*, where the passages are cited at large.

5 Bouhier, Cout. de Bourg. ch. 28, § 60, 61, 62, p. 557; Ante, § 84.

6 P. Voet, De Statut. § 9, ch. 2, p. 268, (edit. 1715); Id. pp. 323, 324, (edit. 1661).

7 Ante, § 122 *b*; 1 Burge, Comm. on Col. and For. Law, Pt. 1, ch. 5, § 3, p. 196.

laws for the validity of marriages between French subjects are obligatory; even when the marriage has been celebrated between them in a foreign country, whenever it appears that they have gone thither in fraud of those laws, and that the marriage, under such circumstances, will be a nullity[1]. This doctrine turns upon the general principle, that an act done designedly in fraud or evasion of the law, by a mere change of locality, is utterly void.

§ 123 *a*. In opposition to this doctrine, it has, however, been settled, after some struggle, both in England and America, that such a marriage is good. The question in England was first solemnly decided by the High Court of Delegates in 1768[2]; and having been subsequently recognised, notwithstanding the doubts of Lord Mansfield, it may now be deemed settled there beyond controversy[3]. Lord Mansfield on the occasion alluded to, *arguendo*, said: "It has been laid down at the bar, that a marriage in a foreign country must be governed by the law of the country where the marriage was had; which in general is true. But the marriages in Scotland of persons going from hence for that purpose were instanced by way of example. They may

---

[1] Pothier, Traité du Mariage, n. 263.

[2] Compton *v.* Bearcroft, cited in Bull. N. P, 114, and in Harford *v.* Morris, 2 Hagg. Consist. R. 429, 430, 443, 444.—It has been said, that this decision may be explained upon the ground, that the English Marriage Act, under which that question arose, contained an express exception of marriages in Scotland; and that the marriage of the parties in that case, who were English, and had gone from England for the express purpose of celebrating the marriage in Scotland, was therefore good, as it was according to the law of Scotland. Admitting this to be the true construction of the English Marriage Act; yet the question directly raised by the libel was, whether a marriage in a foreign country by British subjects, domiciled in England, and not changing their domicil, who had gone there expressly to avoid and evade the laws of England, was good or not; and there is strong reason to believe that this point was deemed a material ingredient in the ultimate judgment of the case.—See the case of Compton *v.* Bearcroft, as commented on in 2 Hagg. Consist. R. 443, 444, and the Reporter's note in p. 444.

[3] See Harford *v.* Morris, 2 Hagg. Consist. R. 423; Robinson *v.* Bland, 2 Burr. R. 1077 to 1080; Fergusson on Marr. and Divorce, 63 to 65.

come under a very different consideration, according to the opinion of Huberus and other writers[1]." This is manifestly no more than the expression of a doubt upon a point not directly before the Court.

§ 123 *b*. In Massachusetts, upon full discussion, the doctrine has been firmly established[2]. It was admitted on that occasion by the Court, that the doctrine is repugnant to the general principles of law relating to contracts; for a fraudulent evasion of, or fraud upon, the laws of the country where the parties have their domicil, would not, except in the contract of marriage, be protected under the general principle[3]. But the exception in favour of marriages is maintained upon principles of public policy, with a view to prevent the disastrous consequences to the issue of such a marriage, which would result from the loose state in which persons so situated would live[4]. The doctrine has been carried even farther, so as to admit the legitimacy of the issue of a person who had been divorced *à vinculo* for adultery, and had been declared by the local law incompetent to marry again, but who had gone into a neighbouring State and there contracted a new marriage, and had issue by that marriage[5]. The like rule has been applied in favour of the widow by such second marriage, so as to entitle her to dower in the real estate of her deceased husband, situate in Massachusetts[6].

---

1 Robinson *v.* Bland, 2 Burr. R. 1079, 1080; Huber. lib. 1, tit. 3, § 8.

2 Medway *v.* Needham, 16 Mass. R. 157, 161; Putnam *v.* Putnam, 8 Pick. R. 433.

3 Ibid. The Court put the following case:—Thus, parties intending to make an usurious bargain cannot give validity to a contract, in which more than the lawful interest of their country is secured, by passing into another territory, where there may be no restriction of interest, or where it is established at a higher rate, and there executing a contract before agreed on. Medway *v.* Needham, 16 Mass. R. 160.

4 Medway *v.* Needham, 16 Mass. R. 160, 161.

5 West Cambridge *v.* Lexington, 1 Pick. R. 596; 2 Kent, Comm. Lect. 26, pp. 92, 93, (3rd edit.). See Fergusson on Marr. and Divorce, note R, p. 469; Ante, § 89.

6 Putnam *v.* Putnam, 8 Pick. R. 433.

§ 124. The English doctrine, in relation to Scotch marriages, by parties domiciled in England and going to Scotland to marry, though a plain violation of the real object and intent, even if not of the words of the English Marriage Act, seems to have proceeded mainly upon the ground of public policy[1]. It is the least of two evils in a political

[1] Mr. Burge does not deem it to be in fraud of the English laws, because the English Marriage Act does not in fact prohibit such Scottish marriages. This is true in terms; and if it did prohibit, the question of the conflict of laws in relation to such marriages would never have arisen in England; for the statute would have directly decided the matter. Nevertheless, the whole object of the parties in this class of marriages plainly is to evade the law of their own country by a marriage, valid by the law of the country where it is celebrated, without changing their own domicil, and thus getting rid of all the anxious provisions of the statute against ill-advised and clandestine marriages. In short, all the Gretna Green marriages in Scotland (as they are called) are intended by the parties to get rid of the solemnities of the English law. Mr. Burge says: "The decisions of the Courts in England, which have declared valid a marriage contracted in Scotland by English persons, who had resorted thither for the sole purpose of evading the prohibitions of the English Marriage Act, are perfectly consistent with the admission of this exception. Such a marriage is valid, because it is not prohibited by the English Marriage Act. It is a misapplication of terms to describe it as an evasion or in fraud of the Act; for, in fact, it is not prohibited. There is an express provision, that nothing in that Act shall extend to marriages in Scotland, or to any marriages beyond sea. The act, therefore, left English subjects at perfect liberty to resort to any country for the purpose of contracting and celebrating their marriage. So far from the act containing a general and absolute prohibition, and a declaration of the nullity of all marriages contracted otherwise than in conformity to its provisions, it confines such prohibition and declaration to marriages contracted in England. These decisions, therefore, are founded upon the right of the parties, consistently with the Marriage Act, to resort to the foreign country for the purpose of contracting their marriage, and upon the act itself containing no provision which renders void a marriage so contracted. It is upon this ground, and to this extent, that the argument of Sanchez must be understood, when he contends that a marriage is not void, because the parties have resorted to a country in which they have contracted it, for the purpose of avoiding ceremonies which are required in their own country. 'Displicet mihi hæc limitatio, et credo, licet adirent eo fine, ut possent liberè absque parocho et testibus contrahere, esse ratum matrimonium; nam qui jure suo utitur, non potest dici fraudem committere, ut eâ ratione effectus impediatur.' 'Nullus videtur dolo facere, qui jure suo utitur.' 'Est enim fraus licita, cùm contrahentes utantur jure suo: ergò, cùm adeuntes locum, ubi non viget

sense, a civil sense, and a moral sense. We have already seen, that the positive code of France has promulgated an

---

Trident. animo contrahendi absque parocho et testibus, utuntur jure suo; habent enim jus sic ibi contrahendi, erit fraus licita, nec eâ ratione effectus ac valor matrimonii impedietur.' The same jurist, in a subsequent passage, admits the distinction between a personal incapacity imposed by the law of the domicil which would accompany the party in whatever country he contracted, and a law which attached to the act only in respect of its taking place in the country in which that law prevailed. 'Dic quando inhabilitas est constituta absolutè et simpliciter, sequi personam quocumque euntem: secùs, quando est constituta per modum legis, sicut enim lex illa non obligat in illis locis, ita inhabilitas, et annullatio actus non obligat ibi, nec sequitur personam, nisi dum est in locis, in quibus ea lex vim obligandi habet......non enim ligatur lege ecclesiasticâ in loco, ubi ex voluntate ac dispositione ejusdem Ecclesiæ non habet robur eadem lex: ut contingit in locis, ubi aut non recepta aut non publicata fuit." 1 Burge, Comment. on Col. and For. Law, Pt. 1, ch. 5, § 3, pp. 192, 193. The decisions in the Supreme Court of Massachusetts, as they are stated in the Commentaries on American Law, carry the doctrine much further, and reject any exception founded on the purpose for which the parties resorted to the country where they contracted the marriage. The parties, in the case referred to, had left the State on purpose to evade its statute law, and to marry in opposition to it, and being married they returned again; yet their marriage was held valid, if it were valid according to the laws of the place where it was contracted, notwithstanding the parties went into the other State with an intention to evade the laws of their own." (Ibid.) In these remarks Mr. Burge is mainly borne out as to the effect of the English Marriage Act, by the language of Sir George Hay, in Harford *v.* Morris, (2 Hagg Consist. R. p. 428 to 432). He there said: "The next question is, whether by the law of England this marriage is valid. It is stated throughout, that it is a marriage without the consent of the natural mother of the party, and of the testamentary Guardians, and the Lord Chancellor; and that the parties went into a foreign country to evade the laws of this realm. Whether upon that account, or any of the accounts already mentioned, it is void by the law of England, is the first question. Parties may go out of England and marry by necessity or choice; in either way a foreign marriage is not void upon that account by the laws of England. But it is said, they go in violation of the order of the Chancellor, and without the consent of parents and guardians. What is the law of England that requires the consent of parents and guardians? It is the marriage act. One of the greatest magistrates that ever appeared in this country explains it, that the view of that act was to restrain the abuse that was so scandalous in this country from clandestine marriages, and to get proof of marriages, which otherwise might become uncertain; as it is, wherever you cannot have evidence of the fact of the marriage being rightly performed, legitimacy becomes uncertain. The principal view of that law was to affect such marriages. The law does, indeed, in one respect,

opposite doctrine with unrelenting severity[1]. The wisdom of such a course remains to be established; and it will be

put a restraint which was not known to the Common law upon the marriage of minors, without the consent of parents; but it does not make all the marriages of minors, even in England, void. Marriages by license only are void for want of consent of parents and guardians. If this marriage had been in England, and if, instead of going abroad, the parties had been married in any great parish of this town or country by banns, would that marriage have been good or not by the laws of England? No law says that it shall be void. It is a marriage by license only, that is void by the law of England for want of consent of the parents or guardians. It is observed also, that the act makes particular exceptions, without which the purpose of the marriage act, though an exceedingly good act, might have been questioned before this time, if there had not been so many ways to avoid the restraint put upon the marriage of minors. It is provided, that nothing in this act shall extend to marriages in Scotland, nor to any marriages solemnized beyond sea. Then marriages in Scotland and beyond sea by the law of England remain in the same state, as if the statute had not passed. Marriage in Scotland, if not contrary to the law of England, is good, and it has been so determined. That determination passed, not on the ground that the marriage was valid in Scotland, and that therefore it was good—nothing was laid before the Court to shew that the marriage was valid in Scotland—but because the Act of Parliament did not put any restraint upon English subjects being married in Scotland, with respect to the consent of parents. On that ground it is, that those marriages are held good, not being contrary to the law of England. The same holds as to marriages beyond sea. For English subjects going abroad, or to Scotland, to marry English subjects, have an exemption from that restraint in the act. What was the case before the marriage act? Will anybody say, that before the act, a marriage solemnized by persons going over to Calais, or happening to be there, was void in this country; because such a marriage might be void by the laws of France, as perhaps it was, if solemnized by a Protestant Priest, whom they do not acknowledge, or if in any way clandestine, or without consent; and that therefore it should be set aside by a court in England, upon account of its being void by the law of France? No. The laws of the state to which the parties are subject, must determine the marriage, unless you can shew that the law of the other country is that by which its validity is to be decided. That brings me to the other great consideration in this case, whether the validity of these marriages, being solemnized in Ypres and Denmark, are to be tried by the laws of those countries. If they are, the laws of those countries must be laid before the Court and proved in the best manner possible; not by the opinions of lawyers, which is the most uncertain way in the world; but by certificates, laying the ordinances of those countries before the Court. Without consider-

[1] Ante, § 84, 90, 123, and note.

no matter of surprise, if hereafter we shall find a Frenchman with two lawful wives; one according to the law of the

ing how far that law is capable of being proved in the present case, the previous question arises with respect to jurisdiction, whether the laws of that country, in which the marriage is celebrated should operate, merely because it was celebrated there? I conceive the law to be clear, that it is not the transient residence, by coming one morning and going away the next day, which constitutes a residence, to which the lex loci can be applied; so as to give a jurisdiction to the law, and cause it to take cognizance of a marriage celebrated there. It is certain that domicil, or established residence, (that is, such a kind of residence as makes the party subject to the laws of that country), may have that effect; and with respect to persons so domiciled, the laws of the country must be adhered to in contracts made there. This was the case of Scrimshire. All the proceedings of the Court of France were laid before the Court. I remember it, though it was a long time ago; and I was counsel for the lady. The mother of the young man was at Boulogne, where they had gone, animo morandi. It was stated in all the proceedings that they were domiciled in France; he went there to reside for purposes of education, and did reside there; and the mother continued to reside there till she obtained the sentence that was pleaded in the Consistory Court. I do not in the least call in question that determination in the Consistory Court. Every man has allowed the great and extensive knowledge of the Judge; but he founded his judgment upon the sentence given in that Court which had assumed jurisdiction, and had a right to assume it; he paid all respect to the judgment; and upon that he gave his opinion, that the party suing should be dismissed." A somewhat different account of the case of Compton *v.* Bearcroft (here referred to) is given by Sir W. Wynne, in Middleton *v.* Janverin, (2 Hagg. Consist. R. 443, 444.) On that occasion he said,—" It is, however contended, that, admitting the law to invalidate the marriage in those countries, yet that is not the law by which this case is to be decided in this court. It is not the lex loci where the marriage ceremony is performed, which is to determine the question; but you must find out some other law, and that is declared by the counsel for Mrs. Janverin to be the law of England. Now, in respect to the lex loci having been adopted as a rule, I think the case of Compton *v.* Bearcroft proves it very strongly. In that case the Court of Delegates affirmed the rejection of the libel which was given in against the marriage on different grounds, as I have understood, from those which were taken in the Court of Arches, and because the marriage was a good marriage in Scotland; and if all facts pleaded in the libel were proved, the marriage could not be pronounced void under the marriage act, in which it is expressly declared that it shall not extend to Scotland. On those grounds it was, as I have understood, that the Delegates rejected the libel. The case of that marriage was therefore determined by the lex loci. Those persons having gone to Scotland, and been married in a way not good in England but good in Scotland, and not affected by the marriage

place of the marriage, and the other according to that of his domicil of origin [1]. The doctrine in England has indeed

act, were considered to have contracted a valid marriage." The learned Reporter has added a very important note to 2 Hagg. Consist. R. 444, n. (*), on this point. It is certain that foreign jurists do not take any distinctions between a violation of the positive prohibition by the words of the laws, and the case of a mere evasion or fraud upon the known policy of the laws by a marriage in another country without any change of domicil by the parties. See also Fergusson on Marr. and Divorce, 417; Id. 223, 461. It has always appeared to me, that the true doctrine of international policy is, that a foreign marriage valid by the law of the place of marriage, is valid everywhere, notwithstanding the parties may be domiciled in another country where the marriage, if celebrated there, would by the laws thereof be void; and the parties have gone thither for the express purpose of evading the requisitions of the law of their domicil. A learned writer, in the London Legal Observer for January 1840, has commented on this subject with great acuteness and ability. The following extract may be gratifying to the learned reader, as it constitutes an opposite view to that of Mr. Burge:— "The idea of fraud on the law of a country is rather a favourite one with jurists. When examined, however, we think it will be found to have a very narrow foundation for the supposed countenance afforded to it by our law. By the courts of several American States it has been repeatedly over-ruled. It is principally grounded on an opinion of the jurist Huber, (Hub. De Confl. Leg. lib. 1, tit. 3, § 8,) supported by a dictum of Lord Mansfield in Robinson *v.* Bland. (1 W. Bl. 234, 256; 2 Burrows, 1077.) In the first place, it is at once met by the difficulty, that it has been over and over again decided, that Scotch and foreign marriages (between minors and others, who could not have contracted marriage here) undertaken expressly and admittedly to evade our law, are good, if good per legem loci; and vice versâ. But then, say the advocates of the in fraudem legis doctrine, these decisions are consistent; because the marriage act in terms excepts Scotch and foreign marriages. In this view, however, they at once throw over Lord Mansfield's authority; because, as Sir W. Blackstone, who was counsel in the case, notes it in the margin of his report, he threw out a 'query, whether stolen marriages in Scotland are valid.' However, as this case is really the only one in which, as far as we are aware, the idea of evasion of our law is set up, we must go more fully into it. The case was argued in 1760. The question was, whether a bill of exchange given in France by one English subject to another, but made payable in England, the consideration of which was a gambling debt, should be held recoverable in an English court. It was found not to be recoverable in France; but Lord Mansfield (though on this plain ground he afterwards said the case had after all come to nothing) had

[6] 1 Toullier, Droit Civil, art. 576; Code Civil, art. 144, 148, 170; Merlin, Répert. tit. Loi, § 6, n. 1, and Ante, note, § 84, 117.

stopped short of the moral mischief; if the decision promulgated in its courts can be maintained, (of which doubts

---

it argued twice, as bearing on international law. In his judgment he touched on the rules applicable to foreign personal contracts. He lays down the general rule as to the lex loci prevailing. But then he says: 'This rule admits of an exception where the parties had a view to a different kingdom. Contracts are to be considered according to the place where they are to be executed.' And Mr. Justice Wilmot said: 'The place where the money is to be paid must govern the law. This was determined as to usury on contracts in Ireland.' From this it is evident, that there is no ground in the decision for the wide principle contended for. The query thrown out, merely in answer to an illustrative argument used by counsel, comes more to the point; but is plainly overruled. Burrows, in his report, says, that Lord Mansfield referred to a case before Lord Hardwicke of a minor's stolen marriage at Ostend; the validity of which Lord Hardwicke doubted, and ordered to be tried before an ecclesiastical court; but the trial was stopped by the minor's marrying again on coming of age. We have looked carefully for this case, and have no doubt Butler and Freeman (Ambl. 302) is the one referred to. It had been decided in 1756, four years before. It was the case of a ward married at Antwerp. Lord Hardwicke said: 'This is the first case under the late marriage act. As to such a marriage (I was going to call it a robbery) there is a door open in the statute as to marriages beyond seas and in Scotland.' He afterwards goes on to question the validity of the marriage: 'It is said by witness, that he saw them married according to the rites and ceremonies of the Church of England. But it will not be valid here unless it was so by the laws of the country where it was had.' The father, it appears, instituted a suit in the ecclesiastical court to try the validity according to the foreign law. This case, therefore, so far from supporting Lord Mansfield's doubt, as stated in the margin of Blackstone's report, expressly overrules it. It is the more material for our present purpose, as being the first case under the marriage act. The marriage act was passed in 1753. If Lord Hardwicke had thought, that before that act there was a principle of law in operation, that a party going abroad to evade our laws could not set up the lex loci contractûs, but that the new act had altered this, he could hardly have failed to have said so. He treats it, that the new statute, by leaving the old principle of lex loci contractûs untouched, had left a door open to evade its new provisions of banns, rites, consent for minors, &c.; not had opened a new door. We find but one other case before Lord Hardwicke bearing on the subject. It is Roach *v.* Garvan, decided in 1748. (1 Ves. R. 158.) It is material, as shewing the principles of law as to foreign marriages, clearly laid down before the marriage act passed. It was the case of a ward of Court aged only eleven, married in France to a boy of seventeen, the son of a Frenchman. Lord Hardwicke laid down, that the infant being a natural-born subject, could not renounce her allegiance. He said: 'The most material consideration is the

may justly be entertained,) that a second marriage, after a divorce in Scotland from a marriage originally celebrated

---

validity of the marriage. It has been argued to be valid, from being established by the sentence of a court in France having proper jurisdiction. And it is true, that if so, it is conclusive, whether a foreign court or not, from the laws of nations in such cases; otherwise the rights of mankind would be very precarious and uncertain.' Now here, if Mr. Burge is right, Lord Hardwicke was called upon to fall back on the general principle Mr. Burge contends for, that the subject, though abroad, unless bonâ fide domiciled there, (which in Mr. Burge's sense of domicil was not the case,) could not avail himself of the lex loci to avoid the operation of our law. The girl here was only eleven years old. By our common law, as stated by Mr. Burge, a female under twelve could not contract matrimony. Indeed, according to Sir Matthew Hale, the attempt would have subjected the party to a conviction for rape. (1 Hale, P. C. 630; and 4 Bla. Comm. 212.) So far from doing this in committing unreservedly the jurisdiction as to validity to a foreign court, he lays down a principle quite destructive of all Mr. Burge's doctrines as to bonâ fide domicil; because, as we shall presently remark further, if that principle only means bonâ fide, so far as required by the foreign law, it amounts to nothing, and there is nobody who doubts it. It would then be by common consent one of the incidents bearing on the validity of the marriage according to the lex loci contractûs. There are few opinions which command higher respect than Mr. Jacob's. In his very learned notes appended to his edition of Roper's Husband and Wife he takes the same view. He says, as to the objection, that an intention to evade our law may affect the validity of the foreign contract; 'that, though apparently sanctioned by Lord Mansfield, it has not prevailed, either with respect to marriages in Scotland, or with respect to marriages in other places out of England; and there does not appear any exception to the rule, that a foreign marriage, valid according to the law of the place where celebrated, is good everywhere else.' (2 Roper, Husb. & Wife, (edit. by Jacob, p. 495).) It must be observed, that Mr. Jacob does not specifically advert to objections arising from affinity, or from any prohibitory rules not being in the marriage act. The rule, however, is evidently older than the marriage act, and is always found without a limitation from the first. Except the case of legal personal disqualification against marrying at all, such as Lolley's, to which we shall soon advert, we know but of one country (France), where the validity of a foreign marriage between its own subjects is tried by its own, and not the foreign law. French subjects who are required at home to obtain the consent of parents, &c., are required so equally if they marry out of France. Did such a broad personal rule obtain here, there would have been no room for the present article; and it is to such a result that we are addressing ourselves, unless the rules of restriction can be so narrowed as to approve themselves to the moral approbation of all the community, minority as well as majority; *i. e.* to those cases of affinity, which by the common consent of the country

in England between English subjects, is void; although such divorce and second marriage would be unquestionably

---

would be discountenanced, viz. affinities in one degree as step-father and step-daughter. We will now go on to examine the supposed second rule as to a foreign bonâ fide domicil being required. Our English supposed limitation of the general rule is not, as we have seen, treated by such of the civilians as have espoused these views as an absolute personal rule, but one merely in fraudem legis; and they therefore attach to the limitation this sub-limitation, that the disqualification will be removed by a sufficient domicil abroad. But sufficient by what law? The sufficiency according to the requirements of the foreign law is admitted on all sides. Our law as to domicil proceeds on quite different grounds. But supposing our law required a year's residence to make a domicil in any place, and the law of that place required two years, and also required domicil to ratify the contract of marriage within it; it is evident that we here, trying the validity of such a marriage, should require the two years' residence to be proved. These civilians admit this, and require us to fulfil the foreign law in all cases. But then they require a sufficient domicil by our law as well. They would split the unity of the contract, and determine it partly by one law and partly by the other. They require two sorts of domicil to make up the marriage contract—the one by the law abroad to get over the lex loci, the one by our law, not as essential to the contract, but as evidence of the bona fides of the contract, and to get over the quasi personal disability they suppose, *i. e.* the suspicion of intention to evade our supposed prohibitory law. It is clear the bonâ fide domicil they would exact must be by way of evidence, and evidence only. But if so, how can it be an essential? Parties may marry without any intended fraud on their own law, where not domiciled to the satisfaction of the civilians; or what is more likely, may become so domiciled with a positive intention to evade their own law. They may get naturalized abroad, move their property there, do every thing which would shew a domicil with regard to the laws about personal estate, and yet all the while it may be capable of clear proof, that they did this only because they chose to be married, and were not permitted to be married here, and that they intended and did all for evasion. They may intend a permanent residence also, and merely because they do not like the English law as to affinity. What would the civilians, who countenance these refinements, say to this case? Their notion seems to have arisen from viewing the law, as an individual whose honour is to be vindicated, and who is to be treated with at least outward shew of observance and respect. They make it, let it be observed, not a principle of English law merely, but of general law; though they can find no instance in any one country to support it, except Lord Mansfield's manifestly erroneous dictum in a bill of exchange case. To us the whole scheme seems altogether insupportable. A law, we should think, is either local or it is personal, and anything between we cannot comprehend. If it were the case of a foreigner's marriage here, would they ask if he came here in evasion of his own law?

good by the law of Scotland[1]. So that here there may be two lawful wives of the party living at the same time in different countries, and two families of children, one of which may be deemed legitimate by the law of the one country, and illegitimate by the law of the other[2]. It is easy to see what various difficulties may grow out of such a state of things. A son by the second marriage may be entitled to the whole real and personal estate of the father in Scotland, and incapable of touching either in England. The Massachusetts' doctrine escapes from these incongruities; and appears to be founded upon a liberal basis of international policy, which deems it far better to support marriages celebrated in a foreign country as valid, when in conformity with the laws of that country; although the rule may produce some minor inconveniences, than by introducing distinctions as to the designs, and objects, and motives of the parties to shake the general confidence in such marriages; to subject the innocent issue to constant doubts as to their own legitimacy; and to leave the parents themselves to cut adrift from their solemn obligations when they may become discontented with their lot.

§ 124 *a*. It is no answer to this reasoning to say, that every nation has a right, at its pleasure, to impose any restraints and prohibitions upon the marriages of its own subjects, whether they marry within or without its own territory. Admitting this to be true in the fullest extent,

---

Or would they not rather say with Fergusson, 'A party domiciled here cannot be permitted to import a law peculiar to his own case.' (Ferg. on Mar. and Div. 399.)"—See also Huberus, lib. 1, tit. 3, De Conflictu Legum. § 13; Paul Voet, De Statut. § 9, c. 2, n. 4, p. 263, (edit. 1715); Id. p. 319, (edit. 1661). Lord Brougham, in Warrender *v.* Warrender, 9 Bligh, R. 129, 130, manifestly considered that the doctrine, that a marriage in a foreign country was void if it was a fraud upon the law of the domicil of the parties, was not maintainable in point of law.

[1] Lolley's Case, 1 Russ. & Ryan, Cas. 236. See Warrender *v.* Warrender, 8 Bligh, R. 891; Ante, § 86, 88; Post, § 215—226.

[2] Beazley *v.* Beazley, 3 Hagg. Eccl. R. 639; Rex *v.* Lolley, 1 Russ. & Ryan, Cas. 236.

to which it can justly be claimed in virtue of national sovereignty, it must be quite as true and quite as obvious, that no other nation is bound to recognise those restraints, and those prohibitions as obligatory upon such subjects, while they are domiciled within its own territory, or when they have contracted marriages there according to the laws thereof. All such local municipal restraints and prohibitions, must, under such circumstances, necessarily tend to mutual embarrassment and confusion in the intercourse between such nations. The very object of the rule arising from the comity of nations, and a sense of the importance and public policy of giving to marriages everywhere the most solemn and binding obligation, is to secure all nations against such a conflict of laws. If France has chosen to declare that all marriages celebrated by its subjects in foreign countries, in conformity with their laws but not according to its own laws, shall be utterly void, every other country has an equal right to declare that such marriages shall be deemed valid, and refuse to submit to the dictation of France. France may at home enforce such laws upon her own subjects; and their property, when found within its territory. But every other nation by whose laws the marriages celebrated therein would be valid, would sustain such marriages, and treat the claims of France as a usurpation founded in injustice, and a disregard of the true duty and policy of all civilized nations in their intercourse with each other.

CHAPTER VI.

MARRIAGES—INCIDENTS TO.

§ 125. HAVING considered how far the validity of marriages is to be decided by the law of the place where they are celebrated, we are next led to consider the operation of foreign law upon the incidents of marriage. These may respect either the personal capacity and powers of the husband and wife, or the rights of each in regard to the property, personal or real, acquired or held by both or either of them during the coverture[1].

§ 126. The jurisprudence of different nations contains almost infinitely diversified regulations upon the subject of the mutual obligations and duties of husband and wife, their personal capacities and powers, and their mutual rights and interests in the property belonging to, or acquired by each during the existence of the marriage; and the task of enumerating all of them would be as hopeless as it would be useless. Before the Revolution, there were in France a multitude of such diversities in the local and customary law of her own provinces; and in Germany, and the States of Holland and Italy, and the vast domains of Austria and Russia, the like diversities existed, and probably still continue to exist. Froland has enumerated a few of these diversities, by way of illustrating the endless embarrassments arising from the conflict of laws of different provinces and nations[2]; and his ample work is mainly devoted to a consideration of the mixed questions arising from the conjugal relation, as affected by different laws in different provinces and nations. In some of the French

[1] See on the subject of this chapter, 1 Burge, Comm. on Col. and For. Law, Pt. 1, ch. 6, § 1, 2, pp. 201—262; Id. ch. 7, § 1, pp. 262—276.

[2] 1 Froland, Mémoires, ch. 1, § 7, 8.

provinces before the Revolution, a married woman had a separate power to contract; in others, she had not[1]. In Holland, under the old laws thereof, (for it is unnecessary to consider whether they have undergone any substantial alteration in more recent times), the husband had the sole power to dispose of all the property of his wife; and she was entirely deprived of any power over it[2]. In Utrecht, her consent was necessary if there were not children by the marriage; and in some other places, whether there were or were not children. In Utrecht, the husband and wife were disabled from making donations to each other; in Holland, they may or might make them[3]. In some states there is a community of property between husband and wife; in others, none; and in others again, mixed rights and qualified claims[4].

§ 127. Boullenois has put several cases, shewing the practical difficulties of this conflict of laws. Suppose a husband domiciled in a place where he cannot bind his wife, if he contracts alone and without her, although she is under his marital power and authority; and the husband should go to and contract in a place, where, by reason of

---

1 Id.; Henry on Foreign Law, 31. See also 1 Boullenois, ch. 1, p. 421; Id. pp. 467, 468; Merlin, Répert. Autoris. Maritale, § 10.

2 1 Burge, Comm. on Col. and For. Law, Pt. 1, ch. 7, § 2, pp. 276, 302.

3 Rodenburg, De Divers. Stat. tit. 2, c. 5, § 9; 2 Boullenois, App. p. 39.—It may be useful here to state, (once for all,) that, in referring to the laws of different countries, I generally state them as they formerly were, without any attention to the changes which they may actually have undergone. The reasoning of the foreign jurists upon this subject would be rendered exceedingly obscure, and sometimes incorrect in any other way; and the object of this work is not so much to shew what particular conflicts of laws may now arise from the present jurisprudence of a particular country, as to illustrate the principles which different jurists have adopted in solving questions relating to the conflicts of laws generally. See 1 Burge, Comm. on Col. and For. Law, Pt. 1, ch. 7, § 2, pp. 276—332, where there will be found a summary of the laws of Holland on the subject of this chapter.

4 1 Burge, Comm. on Col. and For. Law, ch. 7, § 1—8, pp. 262—561; Henry on Foreign Law, ch. 1, § 3, pp. 10, 36, note; Id. 95; 1 Boull. Obs. 15, p. 198; Id. Princ. Gén. 8, p. 8.

this authority, he can bind his wife by binding himself; will the latter contract bind her? He answers in the negative: because the obligation of the wife does not spring from the nature of the contract, nor from the place of the contract; but from the marital authority which has no such effect in the place of his domicil[1]. In Brittany formerly, when a husband and wife were each bound *in solido* for the same contract or debt, payment was to be first sought out of the effects of the husband. But in Paris, upon a like contract, the effects of the husband and wife were formerly indiscriminately bound. Suppose, then, that at that period married persons domiciled in Brittany, had gone to Paris and there contracted, or that married persons domiciled in Paris had gone to Brittany and there contracted, in what manner should the creditor seek payment? Boullenois seems to have held, that, in such a case the laws were to be followed which regulate the estate and condition of the wife; that is to say, the laws of her domicil[2].

§ 128. It is hardly possible to enumerate the different rules adopted in the customary law, or in the positive law of different provinces of the same empire, upon the subject of the rights of husband and wife. In some places, the laws which place the wife under the authority of her husband extend to all her acts, as well to acts *inter vivos* as to acts testamentary. In others the former only are prohibited. In some places, the consent of the husband is necessary to give effect to the contracts of the wife. In others the contract is valid, but is suspended in its execution during the life of the husband. In some places, the wife has no power over the administration of her own property. In others the prohibition is confined to property merely *dotal*, and she has the free disposal of her other property which is called *paraphernal*[3].

---

1 2 Boullenois, Obs. 46, p. 467.

2 Id. pp. 468, 469.

3 2 Boullenois, Observ. 32, p. 11; 1 Domat, B. 1, tit. 9, pp. 166, 167; Id. § 4, pp. 179, 180, &c. See also 1 Froland, Mém. per tot.; Merlin,

§ 129. But not to perplex ourselves with cases of a provincial and unusual nature, let us attend to the differences on this subject in the existing jurisprudence of two of the most polished and commercial states of Europe, in order to realise the variety of questions which may spring up, and embarrass the administration of justice in the tribunals of those countries.

§ 130. The present Code of France does not undertake to regulate the conjugal association as to property, except in the absence of any special contract, which special contract the husband and wife may, under certain limitations, make as they shall judge proper. When no special stipulations exist, the case is governed by what is denominated the rule of community, *le régime de la communauté.* This community, or nuptial partnership, generally extends to all the movable property of the husband and wife, and to the fruits, income, and revenues thereof, whether it is in possession or in action at the time of the marriage, or it is subsequently acquired. It extends also to all immovable property of the husband and wife acquired during the marriage; but not to such immovable property as either possessed at the time of the marriage, or which came to them afterwards by title of succession or by gift[1]. The property thus acquired by this nuptial partnership is liable to the debts of the parties existing at the time of the marriage; to the debts contracted by the husband during the community, or by the wife during the community with the consent of the husband; and to debts contracted for the maintenance of the family and other charges of the marriage. As in common cases of partnership, recompense may be claimed and had for any charges which ought to be borne exclusively by either party. The husband alone is entitled to administer the property of the community; and he may alien,

---

Répert. Autoris. Maritale, § 10; 1 Burge, Comm. on Col. and For. Law, Pt. 1, ch. 6, § 1, pp. 201—244; Id. ch. 7, § 1—7, pp. 262—561.

[1] Code Civil of France, art. 1387—1408; Id. art. 1497—1541.

sell, and mortgage it without the concurrence of the wife. He cannot, however, dispose *inter vivos* by gratuitous title, of the immovables of the community or of the movables, except under particular circumstances; and testamentary dispositions made by him cannot exceed his share in the community[1]. The community is dissolved by natural death, by civil death, by divorce, by separation of body, or by separation of property. Upon separation of body or of property, the wife resumes her free administration of her movable property, and may alien it. But she cannot alien her immovable property without the consent of her husband, or without being authorised by law upon his refusal. Dissolution of the marriage by divorce gives no right of survivorship to the wife; but that right may occur on the civil death or the natural death of the husband. Upon the death of either party, the community being dissolved, the property belongs equally to the surviving party, and to the heirs of the deceased, in equal moieties, after the due adjustment of all debts, and the payment of all charges and claims on the fund[2].

§ 131. Such is a very brief outline of some of the more important particulars of the French Code, in regard to the property of married persons in cases of community. The parties may vary these rights by special contract, or they may marry under what is called the *dotal* rule, *le régime dotal.* But it would carry us too far to enter upon the consideration of these peculiarities, as our object is only to point out some of the more broad distinctions between the English law and the French law, as to the effects of marriage.

§ 132. In regard to the personal rights and capacities, and disabilities of the parties, it may be stated, that independent of the ordinary rights and duties of conjugal fidelity, succour, and assistance, the husband becomes the

---

1 Code Civil of France, art. 1409—1440.

2 Id. art. 1441—1496.

head of the family; and the wife can do no act in law without the authority of her husband. She cannot, therefore, without his consent, give, alien, sell, mortgage, or acquire property. No general authority, even though stipulated by a marriage contract, is valid, except as to the administration of the property of the wife. But the wife may make a will without the authority of her husband. If the wife is a public trader, she may, without the authority of her husband, bind herself in whatever concerns her business; and in such case she also binds her husband, if there is a community between them [1].

§ 133. If we compare this nuptial jurisprudence, brief and imperfect as the outline necessarily is, with that of England, it presents, upon the most superficial examination, very striking differences. In the first place, as to personal rights, capacities, and disabilities, the law of England, with few exceptions, (which it is unnecessary here to mention,) places the wife completely under the guardianship and coverture of the husband. The husband and wife are, in contemplation of law, one person. He possesses the sole power and authority over the person and acts of the wife; so that, as Mr. Justice Blackstone has well observed, the very being, or legal existence of the wife, is suspended during the marriage, or at least is incorporated and consolidated into that of the husband [2]. For this reason, a man cannot grant any thing to his wife, or enter into a covenant with her during his life, though he may devise to her by will. She is incapable of entering into any contract, executing any deed, or doing any other valid act in her own name. All suits, even for personal injuries to her, must be brought in the name of her husband and herself, and with his concurrence. Upon the marriage, the husband becomes liable to all her debts; but neither the wife, nor her pro-

---

[1] Code Civil of France, art. 212—226, art. 1426; 2 Toullier, Droit Civ. art. 618—655.

[2] 1 Bl. Comm. 441; 2 Story, Eq. Jurisp. ch. 36, § 1366—1429.

perty, is liable for any of his debts. In the Roman law, and (as we have seen) in the French law, the husband and wife are, for many purposes, considered as distinct persons, and may have separate estates, contracts, rights, and injuries [1].

§ 134. In respect to property in England, the husband, by the marriage, independent of any marriage settlement, becomes *ipso facto* entitled to all her personal or movable property of every description, in possession and in action, and may dispose of it at his pleasure. He has also a freehold in her real estate during their joint lives; and if he has issue by her, and survives her, he has a freehold also during his own life in her real estate, and an exclusive right to the whole profits of it during the same period. There is not any community between them in regard to property, as in the French law. Upon his death she is simply entitled to dower of one-third of his real estate during her life; and he may, at his pleasure, by a testamentary disposition, deprive her of all right and interest in his personal or movable estate, although the whole of it came to him from her by the marriage. During the coverture she is also incapable of changing, transferring, or in any manner disposing of her real estate, except with his concurrence; and she is incapable of making an effectual will or testament [2].

§ 135. Now, these differences, (which are by no means all which exist,) exemplified in the French laws and in the English laws, are, for the most part, the very same as exist in America between the states settled under the common law, and those settled under the civil law, between those deriving their origin from Spain or France, and those deriving their origin from England [3]. We may see at once, then, upon a change of domicil, or even of temporary resi-

---

[1] 1 Bl. Comm. 441; 2 Story, Eq. Jurisp. ch. 36, § 1366—1429; 1 Brown, Civ. Law, 82; 2 Kent, Comm. Lect. 28, p. 129, &c. (3rd edit.).

[2] 2 Kent, Comm. Lect. 28, p. 129, &c. (3rd edit.); 2 Black. Comm. 433.

[3] 2 Kent, Comm. Lect. 28, p. 183, and note (3rd edit.). See 1 Domat, B. 1, tit. 9; Id. tit. 10. See Christy, Louisiana Digest, art. *Husband and Wife*, and Louisiana Code, art. 121—133.

dence, from a state or country governed by the one law, to another governed by the other law, what various questions of an interesting and practical nature may, nay must, grow up from this conflict of local and municipal jurisprudence.

§ 135 *a*. The subject naturally divides itself into two heads: first, the effect of the marriage upon the personal capacities and incapacities of the wife, or in other words, her disabilities and her powers consequent upon the marriage; and secondly, the effect of the marriage upon the rights and interests of the husband or wife, or of both of them, in the property belonging to them at the time of the marriage, or subsequently acquired by them. We will examine them under these two separate heads, although (as we shall presently see) some of the considerations applicable to them mutually run into each other.

§ 136. And in the first place, as to the capacities and disabilities of the wife. It is extremely difficult, upon the subject of the personal capacities and disabilities of the wife, to lay down any satisfactory rule as to the extent to which they are or ought to be recognised by foreign nations. In general, she is deemed to have the same domicil as her husband; and she can, during the coverture, acquire none other *suo jure*[1]. Her acts done in the place of her domicil will have validity or not, as they are or are not valid there; but as to her acts done elsewhere, there is much room for diversity of opinion and practice among nations. We have seen that many of the civilians and jurists of continental Europe hold, that the capacity and incapacity of married women, as in other cases of the personality of laws, accompany them every where, and govern their acts[2]. And Mr. Chancellor Kent has said, that as personal qualities and civil relations of a universal nature, such as infancy and coverture, are fixed by the law of the domicil, it becomes

---

[1] Ante, § 46. See on this subject 1 Burge, Comm. on Col. and For. Law, Pt. 1, ch. 6, § 2, pp. 244—262.

[2] See Ante, § 51, 55—58, 60; Henry on Foreign Law, p. 50; Fergusson on Marr. and Div. 334—336; Merlin, Répert. Autoris. Maritale, § 10.

the interest of all nations mutually to respect and sustain that law [1]. This is true in a general sense. But every nation will judge for itself what its own interest requires; and in framing its own jurisprudence, will often hold acts valid within its own territories which the laws of a foreign domicil might prohibit, or might disable the parties from doing.

§ 137. In considering this subject, it is material, at least so far as foreign jurists are concerned, to distinguish between cases where there has been a change of domicil of the parties, and where there has not been any such change of domicil. Where the domicil of marriage remains unchanged, the acts of the wife, and her power over her property in a foreign country, are held by many foreign jurists to be exclusively governed by the law of her domicil; in other words, her acts are valid, or not, as the law of her domicil gives her capacity or incapacity to do them [2]. And the rule is applied to her immovable property as well as to her movable property. Thus, if by the law of her domicil she cannot alien property, or cannot contract, except with the consent of her husband, she cannot alien her property, and cannot contract without such consent, in a foreign country, where no such restriction exists [3]. But suppose that the parties afterwards remove to a new domicil, where the consent of the husband is not necessary, is the law of the new domicil, as to the capacity of the wife, to prevail, or that of the matrimonial domicil? This is a question upon which foreign jurists have been greatly divided in opinion [4].

§ 138. We may illustrate this distinction by a few examples. Thus, for example, the law of England disables a

---

1 2 Kent, Comm. Lect. 39, p. 419 (3rd edit.).

2 Ante, § 51—55, 57, 64, 65; Post, § 141.

3 Merlin, Répert. Autoris. Maritale, § 10, art. 2; Pothier, Cout. d'Orléans, ch. 1, n. 7, 15; Ante, § 51—54, 64, 65, 69.

4 See Merlin, Répert. Effet Rétroactif, § 2, 3, art. 5; Autoris. Maritale, § 10; Ante, § 55—62. See also 1 Burge, Comm. on Col. and For. Law, Pt. 1, ch. 6, § 2, pp. 244—262.

married woman from making a will in favour of her husband, or any other person; the law of France allows it. Suppose a husband and wife, married in and subjects of England, should temporarily or permanently become domiciled in France; would a will of the wife in France, in regard to her property in England, made in favour of her husband or others, be held valid in England[1]? Many foreign jurists, among whom may be enumerated Hertius, Paul Voet, John Voet, Burgundus, Rodenburg, Pothier, and Merlin, hold the opinion, that the law of the new domicil must in all cases of a change of domicil govern the capacities and rights of property of married women, as well as their obligations, acts, and duties[2]. Froland (it should seem) would answer this particular question upon principle in the affirmative, as a mere question of capacity or incapacity, or *status* of the wife; for he holds, that the capacity or incapacity of married women to do things, changes with their domicil; and that acts, valid by the law of their original domicil, if done in a new domicil, by whose laws they are void, are to be deemed nullities[3]. Thus, he says that a married woman, who is incapable by the law of her domicil, where the Roman law *(droit écrit)* prevails, of entering into a suretyship for another, by the *Senatûs consultum Velleianum*, or of contracting with her husband, as in Normandy, if she goes to reside at Paris, where no such law exists, is there deprived of that exception. And, on the other hand, a woman married and living at Paris, and afterwards going to reside in Normandy, or in any other country, where the Roman law prevails *(droit écrit)*, loses her capacity to enter into any such contract, which she previously possessed[4]. Yet Froland has in some other places

---

[1] See Merlin, Répert. Testament, § 1, 5, art. 1, 2, pp. 309—319.

[2] Ante, § 55—62; Post, § 140, 141. See also 1 Burge, Comm. on Col and For. Law, Pt. 1, ch. 6, § 2, pp. 253—261.

[3] 1 Froland, Mém. 172; Ante, § 55.

[4] 1 Froland, Mém. 172; 1 Boullenois, Observ. 4, p. 61; 2 Boullenois, Observ. 32, pp. 7, 13.—Froland has some subtle distinctions on this subject,

made distinctions, and insisted on a different rule, as applicable to the rights of married women in the property of their husbands, holding, that those rights are governed by the law of the place of the marriage rather than by that of the subsequent actual domicil[1].

§ 139. Other foreign jurists, however, have given a different response to the general question; for we have already seen, that in regard to personal laws there is much conflict of opinion among them how far these laws are affected by any change of domicil[2]. Huberus (as we have seen) holds a somewhat modified opinion[3]. Bouhier maintains the opinion in the broadest terms, that in respect to the rights derived from the marital power *(puissance maritale)*, the law of the matrimonial domicil determines the state or condition of the wife, and by consequence the extent of the

---

which, to say the least of them, are not in a practical sense very clear. Lest I should misstate the purport of his remarks, I will quote them in the original, having already referred to them in another place:—"Quand il s'agit de l'état universel de la personne, abstraction faite de toute matière réelle, *abstractè ab omni materiâ reali*, en ce cas le statut, qui a commencé à fixer sa condition, conserve sa force et son authorité, et la suit par tout en quelque endroit, qu'elle aille.—Mais quand il est question de l'habileté ou inhabileté de la personne, qui a changé de domicile, *à faire une certaine chose*, alors le statut, qui avoit réglé son pouvoir, tombe entièrement à son égard, et céde tout son empire à celui dans le territoire duquel elle va demeurer." 1 Froland, Mém. 171, 172; Ante, § 55. See 2 Boullenois, Observ. 32, pp. 7—10; Bouhier, Cout. de Bourg. ch. 22, § 6—14; Id. § 30—38; Id. § 148, 149.

[1] 1 Froland, Mém. Pt. 2, ch.4, pp. 340—408; 2 Boullenois, Observ. 32, pp. 22, 23, 29.

[2] See Ante, § 55—62; 1 Boullenois, Observ. 13, pp. 187, 188—196; Id. p. 200; 2 Boullenois, Observ. 32, p. 2; Id. Observ. 32, pp. 14, 15, 17, 19 to Id. Observ. 37, p. 204; Rodenburg, De Div. Stat. tit. 2, ch. 1, § 3; Id. Pt. 2, ch. 1, § 1; 2 Boullenois, App. p. 12; Id. pp. 55, 56, and 2 Boullenois, Observ. 32, pp. 22—28; Henry on Foreign Law, pp. 50, 51; Merlin, Répert. Autoris. Maritale, § 10; Id Effet Rétroactif, § 3, n. 2, art. 3; Bouhier, Cout. de Bourg. ch. 22, § 4—108, and especially § 67, 68; 1 Burge, Comm. on Col. and For. Law, Pt. 1, ch. 6, § 2, pp. 253—262.

[3] Ante, § 60, 61; Post, § 145; Huberus, lib. 1, tit. 3, De Conflict. Leg. § 12, 13; Id. § 9.

marital authority; and this state or condition of the wife being once fixed, cannot be afterwards changed by any change of domicil[1]. Dumoulin seems to have entertained the same opinion[2]. Merlin also at one time bent the whole strength of his acknowledged ability to establish the doctrine, that the law of the matrimonial domicil, and not of the new domicil, as to the capacity and incapacity of the wife, ought to prevail. He reasoned it out principally in his examination of the subject of the marital power or the incapacity of the wife, according to certain local laws, to do any valid act, make any conveyance, or engage in any contract, without the consent and authorization of her husband. And he then held, that this incapacity is not changed by a change of domicil to a place, in whose laws it has no existence[3]. After maintaining this opinion (as he himself says) for forty years, he has recently changed it, and adhered to the doctrine, that the law of the new domicil ought to govern[4]. In discussing the nature and extent of the paternal authority, conferred by the domicil of birth, in regard to foreign property, he seems to have been aware of the difficulties of his early doctrine; and he has said, with great truth, that to put an end to all the difficulties of such cases, it is necessary to make a uniform law, not for France only, but for the world; for the settlement of a foreigner in France, or of a Frenchman in a foreign country, would at once raise them anew, notwithstanding all the regulations of the present Civil Code of France[5]. His reasoning upon the testamentary power, and the manner in which it is affected by the *situs* of the property, also affords very strong

---

1 Bouhier, Cout. de Bourg. ch. 22, § 22—27; Id. § 45—47; Id. § 48—66; Id. § 69, 70; Id. § 79, 80, 82, 83; Id. § 89, 90; Id. § 147.

2 Molin. Oper. Comment. ad Cod. Lib. 1, tit. 1, l. 1; Conclus. De Statutis. Tom. 3, p. 555, edit. 1681.

3 Bouhier, Cout. de Bourg, ch. 22, § 22—32, 45.

4 Merlin, Répert. Effet Rétroactif, § 3, 2, art. 5, p. 15; Id. Autoris. Maritale, § 10, art. 4, pp. 243, 244; Id. Majorité, § 5; Ante, § 58, 59.

5 Merlin, Répert. Puissance Paternelle, § 7, art. 1—3.

proof of the intrinsic infirmity of all general speculations on this subject[1].

§ 140. It has been already intimated, that the opposite opinion has been maintained by many jurists. Let us briefly refer to the opinions of a few of them. Hertius has put the following case. By the law of Utrecht married persons are incapable of making a will of property in favour of each other: not so in Holland. Is such a will of property in Utrecht, made by married persons in Holland, valid? Or, *è contra,* is such a will, made by married persons in Utrecht, of property in Holland, valid? He answers the former question in the negative, and the latter in the affirmative[2].

§ 140 *a*. The language of Burgundus is still more direct, he affirming in every case of this sort, as to the rights and powers of the husband and wife, that they are regulated by the law of the new domicil. *Proinde, ut sciamus, uxor in potestate sit mariti, necne, quâ ætate minor contrahere possit, et ejusmodi, respicere oportet ad legem cujusque domicilii. Hæc enim imprimit qualitatem personæ, atque adeo naturam ejus afficit, ut quocunque terrarum sit transitura, incapacitatem domi adeptam, non aliter quam cicatricem in corpore foras circumferat. Consequenter dicemus, si mutaverit domicilium persona, novi domicilii conditionem induere*[3].

§ 141. Rodenburg has distinguished the cases on this subject into two sorts: (1), those in which there is no change of domicil of the married parties; (2), and those in which there is a change of domicil. In the former case he holds, that the capacity and incapacity by the law of the domicil extend everywhere. In the latter case, that the capacity and incapacity of the new domicil attach[4]. So

---

1 Merlin, Répert. Testament, § 1, § v. art. 1, 2, pp. 309—319.

2 Hertii Opera, De Collis. Leg. § 4, p. 142, § 42, 43, (edit. 1737); Id. p. 201, (edit. 1716).

3 Burgundus, Tract. 2, n. 7, p. 61.

4 Rodenburg, De Div. Stat. tit. 2, ch. 1, § 1; Id. Pt. 2, ch. 1, § 1; Id. ch. 4, § 1; 2 Boullenois, App. pp. 10, 11; Id. pp. 55, 56; Id. p. 63.

that, according to him, the disabilities of a wife by the law of her domicil attach to all her acts, wherever done, at home or abroad, as long as the domicil exists [1]. But upon a *bonâ fide* change of domicil by her husband, she loses all disabilities not existing by the law of the new domicil, and acquires all the capacities allowed by the latter [2]. Hence, if a husband, who by the law of his domicil has his wife subject to his marital authority, changes his domicil to a place where no such law exists, or *è contra,* if he changes his domicil from a place where the wife is exempt from the marital power, to one where it exists; in each case the wife has the capacity or incapacity of the new domicil. *Fac, igitur, virum, qui per leges loci, ubi degit, uxorem habeat in potestate, collocare domicilium aliò, ubi in potestate virorum uxores non sunt; vel vice versâ. Dicendumne erit, induere uxorem potestatem quâ prius liberata, et exuere, cui alligata est? In affirmationem sententiam deduci videmur per tradita Burgundi. Et recte; personæ enim status et conditio, cum tota regatur à legibus loci, cui illa sese per domicilium subdiderit, utique mutato domicilio, mutari necesse est personæ conditionem* [3]. Boullenois holds on this point the same opinion [4]. Rodenburg puts another case. By the law of Holland, married persons may make a will in favour of each other; by the law of Utrecht, not. Suppose a man and wife, who are married in Holland, move to Utrecht, is the will between them previously made, good? and he decides in the negative [5].

§ 142. Boullenois, however, has himself put a case which

---

1 Rodenburg, De Div. Stat. tit. 2, ch. 1, § 1; Id. Pt. 2, ch. 1, § 1; Id. ch. 4, § 1; 2 Boullenois, App. pp. 10, 11; Id. pp. 55, 56; Id. p. 63.

2 Ibid.

3 Rodenburg, De Div. Stat. tit. 2, Pt. 2, ch. 1, § 1; 2 Boullenois, App. pp. 55, 56; Burgund. Tract. 2, n. 7.

4 1 Boullenois, Observ. 4, pp. 61, 62; Id. Observ. 16, p. 205; 2 Boullenois, Observ. 32, pp. 7—54; Id. pp. 81, 82; Id. Observ. 35, pp. 93—112.

5 Rodenburg, De Div. Stat. tit. 2, Pt. 2, ch. 4, § 1; 2 Boullenois, App. p. 63; Id. p. 81; Id. Observ. 35, pp. 93—112.

he seems to decide upon a ground which breaks in, in some measure, upon the general doctrine. He supposes the case of a woman domiciled and married in a country using the Roman law (*droit écrit*), to a man belonging to the same country. She has the right and capacity by that law to enjoy her *paraphernal* property there, and to alienate it independently of her husband[1], and without his being entitled to intermeddle in the administration of it in any manner. He then puts the question, whether, if her husband goes to reside at Paris, (where no such right exists), then she falls under his marital authority, so as to lose from that period the administration and alienation of her *paraphernal* property? Boullenois admits that she falls under the marital authority; but at the same time he contends that she has, notwithstanding, the right of administering and alienating her *paraphernal* property; because it was given to her by the contract of marriage, supported by the law of her matrimonial domicil; and that her husband cannot by a change of domicil extinguish her right, founded upon such authentic titles. And though she cannot act without the consent of her husband in such administration and alienation, yet he is bound to give such consent[2]. But Boullenois is compelled to admit other exceptions to the doctrine, where other considerations are mixed up in the case. Thus, he says:—Suppose a woman is married at Paris, and has a community of property with her husband there, and she has property at Aix or Toulouse, and her husband goes to reside at either of these places; the question is, whether she is at liberty to sell her property there without the authority or consent of her husband; and he holds, that she cannot sell her property there without the consent of her husband, although she was married at Paris. The reason he assigns is: because in the countries governed

---

[1] 1 Domat. B. 1, tit. 9, p. 167; Id. § 4, pp. 179, 180.

[2] 2 Boullenois, Observ. 32, pp. 20, 21; Id. pp. 22—28. See Bouhier, Cout. de Bourg. ch. 22, § 28—30; Id. § 40—45.

by their own customary law, the property of a married woman in community is deemed *dotal* property, and is presumed to have been brought there by the parties as such; and that such property, as *dotal* property, is less alienable at Aix and Toulouse, than in countries governed by their customary law; and that in those Provinces, as well as in Paris, the husband has the right of the administration of *dotal* property during the marriage: so that the change of domicil does not make the right of the husband to cease. But (he adds) if the woman, married at Paris, had no community of property, and having the administration thereof, came to reside at Aix or Toulouse, then she might sell her property without the authority of her husband, even if situate in Paris; because she is no longer under the authority of her husband, who has no interest in the sale. But, if there were no such community, then he holds that she might sell[1].

§ 143. Passing from the consideration of the personal capacities, disabilities, and powers of the wife, and of the examination of the different opinions of foreign jurists respecting them, in cases where there has been no change of domicil, and in cases where there has been such a change, let us in the next place examine into the effect of marriage upon the mutual property of the husband and wife, and their respective rights in and over it[2]. The marriage may have taken place with an express nuptial contract or arrangement, as to the property of the parties; or it may have taken place without any such contract or arrangement. The principal difficulty is not so much to ascertain what rule ought to govern in cases of an express nuptial contract, (at least, where there is no change of domicil), as what rule ought to govern in cases where there is no

---

[1] 2 Boullenois, Observ. 32, pp. 22—24. See 2 Froland, Mém. 1007—1064; Bouhier, Cout. de Bourg. ch. 22, § 5—10; Id. § 28—32; J. Voet, ad Pand. Lib. 5, tit. 1, § 101; 1 Burge, Comm. on Col. and For. Law, Pt. 1, ch. 6, § 2, pp. 244—262.

[2] See 1 Burge, Comm. on Col. and For. Law, Pt. 1, c. 7, § 8, pp. 599—640.

such contract, or no contract which provides for the emergency. Where there is an express nuptial contract, that, if it speaks fully to the very point, will generally be admitted to govern all the property of the parties, not only in the matrimonial domicil, but in every other place, under the same limitations and restrictions as apply to other cases of contract[1]. But where there is no express nuptial contract at all, or none speaking to the very point, the question, what rule ought to govern, is surrounded with more difficulty. Is the law of the matrimonial domicil to govern? Or is the law of the local situation of the property? Or is the law of the actual or new domicil of the parties? Does the same rule apply to movable property as to immovable property, when it is situated in different countries[2]? Boullenois has remarked, that even on the subject of marriage contracts the law of the place of the contract will not always decide all the questions arising from it[3]. Many of the questions touching it must be decided by the law of the domicil of the parties, and sometimes by the law of the domicil of one of them[4].

§ 144. Two classes of cases naturally present themselves in considering this subject. First, those where during the marriage there is no change of domicil; secondly, those where there is such a change[5].

---

1 See Le Brun, Traité de la Communauté, Liv. 1, ch. 2, § 2; Murphy *v.* Murphy, 5 Martin, R. 83; Lashley *v.* Hogg, Robertson's Appeal Cases, 4; Feaubert *v.* Turst, Preced. in Chan. 207, 208. This doctrine has been fully recognised in England, in the case of Anstruther *v.* Adair, 2 Mylne & Keen, 513; Post, § 184.

2 In some foreign codes, there are express provisions, that marriage contracts shall not fix the rights of the couple according to the law of foreign countries. In France, there is an effective prohibition of contracts regulating marriage rights by the old customs of the provinces, which it has abolished. Code Civil, art. 1390. See also Bourcier *v.* Lanusse, 3 Martin, R. 581.

3 1 Boullenois, Prin. Gén. 48, p. 11. See also Dig. Lib. 5, tit. 1, l. 65.

4 Ibid.

5 See 1 Burge, Comm. on Col. and For. Law, Pt. 1, ch. 7, § 8, pp. 599—640.

§ 145. And, first, in cases where there is no change of domicil, and no express nuptial contract. Huberus lays down the doctrine in broad terms, that not only the contract of the marriage itself, properly celebrated in a place according to its laws, is valid in all other places; but that the rights and effects of the marriage contract, according to the laws of the place, are to be held equally in force everywhere[1]. Thus, he says: in Holland, married persons have a community of all their property, unless it is otherwise agreed in their nuptial contract; and, that this will have effect in respect to property situate in Friezeland, although in that province there is only a community of the losses and gains, and not of the property itself. Therefore, (he adds,) a Frizian married couple remain after their marriage the separate owners, each of their own property situated in Holland. But whenever they remove into another province, the property, which afterwards comes to either of them, ceases to be in community, and is held in distinct proprietary rights. But their antecedent property, held in community, remains in the state of right in which they originally possessed it. *Porro, non tantum ipsi contractus ipsæque nuptiæ certis locis ritè celebratæ, ubique pro justis et validis habentur; sed etiam jura et effecta contractuum nuptiarumque, in iis locis recepta, ubique vim suam obtinebunt. In Hollandia conjuges habent omnium bonorum communionem, quatenus aliter pactis dotalibus non convenit. Hoc etiam locum habebit in bonis sitis in Frisia, licet ibi tantum sit communio quæstus et damni, non ipsorum bonorum. Ergo et Frizii conjuges manent singuli rerum suarum, etiam in Hollandia sitarum, domini; cum primum vero conjuges migrant ex una provinia in aliam, bona deinceps quæ, alteri adveniunt, cessant esse communia, manentque distinctis proprietatibus; sic ut res antea communes factæ, manent in eo statu juris, quem induerunt*[2]. The example he thus puts

[1] Huberus, lib. 1, tit. 3, § 9; Post, § 169; 1 Burge, Comm. on Col. and For. Law, Pt. 1, ch. 6, § 2, pp. 244—262.

[2] Huberus, lib. 1, tit. 3, De Conflict. Leg. § 9; Post, § 169.

obviously shews that his doctrine is applied to cases where there is no express contract.

§ 145 *a*. Mr. Chancellor Kent has applied the doctrine of Huberus, in the case of an express ante-nuptial contract between the parties; and has laid down the rule, that the rights dependent upon nuptial contracts are to be determined by the *lex loci contractûs*[1]. This may be generally correct in regard to cases of express or of implied nuptial contracts; and it is probable that none other were at the time in the mind of the learned Judge. But we shall presently see, that, as a general question, in regard to the universal operation of the *lex loci matrimonii*, there is much controversy upon the subject among foreign jurists.

§ 146. There are many distinguished jurists, who, in common with Huberus, maintain the opinion, that the incidents and effects of the marriage upon the property of the parties, wherever it is situate, are to be governed by the law of the matrimonial domicil, in the absence of all other positive arrangements between the parties[2]. Thus, if English subjects are married in England without any nuptial contract, the husband, being entitled by the law of England to all the personal or movable property of his wife, will be entitled to it wherever it may be situated, whether in England or in any foreign country. And his rights, it would seem, in her immovable property, wherever it may be situated, would, in the opinion of many of the foreign jurists, be exclusively regulated by the law of England[3]. So, on the other hand, French subjects married in

1 See De Couche *v*. Savatier, 3 John. Ch. R. 211; 2 Kent, Comm. Lect. 39, pp. 458, 459, (3rd edit.). See also Feaubert *v*. Turst, cited in Robertson's Appeal Cases, 1, and Lashley *v*. Hogg, 1804, cited Id. 4.

2 Merlin, Répert. Commun. de Biens, § 1, art. 3; 1 Boullenois, pp. 660—673; Id. Observ. 29, pp. 732—818; Rodenbourg. De Div. Stat. tit. 2, ch. 5, § 12—15; 2 Boullenois, App. pp. 41—46; 1 Burge, Comm. on Col. and For. Law, Pt. 1, ch. 6, § 2, pp. 244—253; Id. ch. 7, § 8, pp. 599—609.

3 Hertii Opera, De Collis. Leg. § 47, p. 143, (edit. 1737); Id. p. 204, (edit. 1716).—Many jurists make no distinction in the application of the doctrine of the tacit contract of marriage between movable and immovable

France, without any contract whatever, would hold their property in community generally; and this rule would apply, as well to the property situated in foreign countries, as to that situated in France.

§ 147. The grounds upon which this opinion has been maintained, are various. Some foreign jurists hold, that the law of the matrimonial domicil attaches all the rights and incidents of marriage to it, *proprio vigore,* and independent of any supposed consent of the parties[1]. Others hold, that there is in such cases an implied consent of the parties to adopt the law of the matrimonial domicil, by way of tacit contract; and then the same rule applies, as is applied to express nuptial contracts. Dumoulin was the author, or at least the most distinguished advocate of this latter doctrine[2]. *Quia per prædicta inest* (says he) *tacitum pactum, quod maritus lucrabitur dotem conventam, in casu, et pro proportione statuti illius domicilii, quod prævidetur, et intelligitur; et istud tacitum pactum, nisi conventum fuerit, intrat in actionem ex stipulatu rei uxoriæ, et illam informat. Itaque semper remanet forma ab initio impressa*[3]. And he adds, that

---

property, and consider both to be governed by the law of the domicil of marriage. Others, again, distinguish between them. Foreign jurists commonly in the term, "biens," include all sorts of property, movable and immovable, in their discussions on this subject. See Merlin, Répert. Autoris. Maritale, § 10, art. 2; Id. Majorité, § 5; Id. Communauté de Biens, § 1, art. 3; Voet, De Statut. § 4, ch. 2, n. 16; Rodenburg, De Div. Stat. Pt. 1, tit. 2, ch. 5, § 13—15; Id. Pt. 2, tit. 2, ch. 4, § 1; 2 Boullenois, App. pp. 41—46; Id. p. 63; 1 Boullenois, pp. 673, 683, 767; 2 Boullenois, pp. 81—88; Observ. 35, pp. 93, 94; Id. Observ. 37, pp. 266, 277; 1 Hertii Opera, De Collis. Leg. § 46, 47, pp. 143, 144, (edit. 1737); Id. pp. 203, 204, (edit. 1716); Livermore, Dissert. § 89, pp. 73, 74; Huberus, lib. 1, tit. 3, § 9; Bouhier, ch. 22, § 79, p. 429. See also 1 Burge, Comm. on Col. and For. Law, Pt. 1, ch. 7, § 8, pp. 599—609.

1 See 1 Boullenois, Observ. 29, pp. 741, 750, 757, 758; Huberus, lib. 1, tit. 3, De Confl. Leg. § 9.

2 1 Boullenois, Observ. 29, p. 757.

3 Molin. Comm. ad. Cod. lib. 1, tit. 1, l. 1, Opera, tom. 3, p. 555, (edit. 1681); 1 Froland, Mém. 62, 218; Livermore, Dissert. § 89, pp. 73, 74; 1 Boullenois, Observ. 29, pp. 756, 758.

it applies to all property, wherever situate, and whether movable or immovable: *Non solum inspiciatur statutum vel consuetudo primi illius domicilii pro bonis sub illo sitis. Sed locum habebit ubique etiam extra fines et territorium dicti statuti, etiam interim correpti; et hoc indistinctè, sive bona dotalia sint mobilia, sive immobilia, ubicunque sita, sive nomina. Ratio punctualis specifica procedat in vim taciti pacti ad formam statuti; veluti, quod tacitum pactum pro expresso habetur*[1].

§ 148. The opinion of Dumoulin, that the law of the place of the marriage constitutes the rule by which the rights of married persons are regulated, by a tacit contract of the parties, in the absence of any express contract, according to the maxim, *In contractibus tacitè veniunt ea, quæ sunt moris et consuetudinis,* has been adopted by Bouhier, Hertius, Pothier, Merlin, and other distinguished jurists[2]. It is opposed, however, by others of no small celebrity; and the doctrine of tacit contract in the case of marriage (as we shall see) is treated by some of them as a mere indefensible and visionary theory[3]. D'Argentré, and Froland, and Vander Meulin, are at the head of those who maintain that the law of the *situs* of the property constitutes the rule to

---

1 Molin. Comm. ad Cod. lib. 1, tit. 1, l. 1; Conclus. De Statutis, Opera, tom. 3, p. 555, (edit. 1681); 1 Froland, Mém. 61—63, 218; Livermore, Dissert. § 89, pp. 73, 74; 1 Boullenois, Observ. 29, pp. 757, 758.

2 Bouhier, Cout. de Bourg. ch. 23, § 69—75, pp. 458, 459; Id. ch. 26, per tot. pp. 462—490; 1 Froland, Mém. 61—63; Id. 178—211; Id. 214—222; Id. 274; Merlin, Répert. Communauté, de Biens, § 1, art. 3; Pothier, Traite de la Communauté, art. 1, n. 10; 1 Hertii Opera, De Collis. Leg. § 47, p. 143, (edit. 1737); Id. p. 204, (edit. 1716); Post, § 150—152; 1 Burge, Comm. on Col. and For. Law, Pt. 1, ch. 7, § 8, pp. 599—614.

3 Froland, in opposing the doctrine of tacit contracts, derived from the supposed operation of the Lex Loci Matrimonii, says: "Ce ne sont là que des paroles, et rien au-dela. Mirificum illud Molinæi acumen; des subtilitez d'Esprit; des Idées; des Chimères; Enfin des moyens, que la seule imagination échauffée produit. Hac grandiloquentiâ etiamsi Molinæus personat, tamen apertè non est verum, quod dicit. 1 Froland, Mém. 316; Post, § 167.

decide the rights of the marriage couple at all times, and under all circumstances[1]. D'Argentré says: *Primùm, quod Molinæus à simplici consuetudinis dispositione elicet partium conventionem et pactum, citra ullam conventionem partium adjectam consuetudini, rationem non habet. Alia enim vis et ratio, aliud et principium et causa obligationis, quæ à lege inducitur, alia ejus, quæ ab pacto et conventione partium proficiscitur*[2].

§ 149. It may be useful to bring together in this place, in a more exact form, the opinions of some other jurists of the highest reputation on this subject, for the purpose of exhibiting some of the differences, as well as some of the coincidences, in the doctrines respectively maintained by them.

§ 150. Cochin holds the doctrine, that if the contract of marriage contains no stipulation for community of property, the law of the place where the parties are domiciled, and to which they submit by the contract of marriage, must govern, not only as to property (*biens*) situate in that place, but as to property situate in all other places[3]. The rights of married persons (he adds) over the property which they then have, as well as over that which they afterwards acquire, ought to be regulated by a uniform rule. If they have established an express rule by the contract of marriage, that ought to decide their rights as to all their pro-

---

1 D'Argentré, In Briton. Leges. Des Donations, art. 218, Gloss. 6, n. 33, tom. 1, pp. 655—657; Livermore, Dissert. § 95, p. 77; 1 Froland, Mém. 192—200; Id. 220, 222; Id. 316; 1 Boullenois, pp. 673—690; Id. Observ. 29, pp. 732—736; Id. pp. 740—750; Id. pp. 757, 792; 2 Boullenois, Observ. 35, p. 110; Merlin, Répert. Communauté de Biens, § 1, art. 3, pp. 110, 111; Livermore, Dissert. § 92—106, pp. 75—82; 1 Froland, Mém. 61—64; Post, § 152 a, note 2, § 167, 168; 1 Burge, Comm. on Col. and For. Law, Pt. 1, ch. 7, § 8, p. 609.

2 D'Argentré, In Briton. Leges. Des Donations, art. 218, Gloss. 6, n. 33, om. 1, p. 656; Livermore, Dissert, § 92, p. 75, § 95, p. 77, § 106, p. 81. See also 1 Burge, Comm. on Col. and For. Law, Pt. 1, ch. 7, § 8, pp. 609—614; 1 Boullenois, Observ. 29, pp. 761—767.

3 Cochin, Œuvres, tom. 3, p. 703, (4to edit.)

perty. If they have made no stipulation, then the law of the place of their common domicil establishes a rule for them; since they are presumed to submit themselves to it, when they have not stipulated anything to the contrary.

§ 151. Le Brun is quite as explicit. After stating that the community of property may be formed by an express contract, or by a tacit contract, he gives, as a reason for the latter, that if the married couple have not made any express stipulation, and are domiciled in a place where the law of community exists when they are married, the conclusion is, that they have referred themselves to that law. And this presumption has its foundation in law, which often decides, that, as to things omitted in the contract, the parties have referred themselves to the usage or law of the place[1]. And he adds, that as in cases of express contracts for community of property, the contracts reach all the property of the parties, even in other countries, so in cases of tacit contracts, such as those resulting by operation of law, the same rule applies. If the law of the place of domicil and marriage of the parties creates such a community, it applies to all property, wherever it is situate. It has, in short, all the character and effect of a personal law or statute, although it regulates property[2].

§ 152. Hertius has put a number of cases to illustrate the general principle. At Liege, by law, the husband by marriage acquires the ownership of all the property of his wife, of every nature. At Utrecht it is otherwise. Is an inhabitant of Utrecht entitled, *jure connubii,* to take all the property of his deceased wife, situate in Liege? He answers in the negative; because the law of the place of marriage (Utrecht) does not confer it[3]. Again: A person, in whose domicil there is no community of property between married persons, possesses property in another territory where such commu-

---

1 Le Brun, Traité de la Communauté, liv. 1, ch. 2, § 2—4.

2 Id. liv. 1, ch. 2, § 6, 36—42.

3 Hertii Opera, De Collis. Leg. § 44, pp. 142, 143, (edit. 1737;) Id. p. 201 (edit. 17 16.)

nity of all property exists, and he contracts marriage in another country where a qualified community only exists. (*Ubi societas bonorum tantum, sive simpliciter, ita dicta, obtinet.*) What law is to prevail? Some jurists hold, that the law of the domicil shall prevail. Others are of a different opinion. Hertius himself holds, that as the case supposes the place of the marriage to be foreign to both parties, the law of the husband's domicil ought to prevail, as an implied contract between the parties[1]. Again: In the domicil of the husband, a community of property exists between married persons; will that community apply to immovable property, bought by either party in a territory where such a law does not exist? Many jurists decide in the negative. Hertius holds the affirmative, upon the ground of an implied contract, resulting from the marriage[2].

§ 152 *a.* Froland puts the case of a man domiciled at Paris, who goes and marries a woman in a country governed by the Roman law, as in Rheims, Auvergne, or Normandy, or *è contra;* and the marriage is without any express contract; and he then asks, in such a case, what law is to prevail as to future acquisitions (conquests)? The law of the domicil of the husband? Or that of the wife? Or that of the place of marriage? Or of the location of the property? And he decides in favour of the latter[3].

§ 153. Froland has stated the question in a more general shape; whether, if a community of property exists by the law of the place of domicil and marriage of the parties, it extends to all property situate elsewhere, where no such law prevails[4]? He gives the reasoning of different jurists,

---

[1] Hertii Opera, De Collis. Leg. § 46, 143, (edit. 1737); Id. p. 202. (edit. 1716).

[2] Id. p. 144, § 47, (edit. 1737); Id. p. 204; (edit. 1716).—The decision of Mr. Chancellor Kent in De Couche *v* Sabatier, 3 John. Ch. R. 190, 211, treating it as the case of an express or an implied contract, would lead to the same conclusion.

[3] 1 Froland, Mém. 321. See also Voet, De Stat. § 4, ch. 3, § 9, pp. 134, 135, (edit. 1715); Id. pp. 151, 152, (edit. 1661).

[4] 1 Froland, Mém. pp. 178—200; Id. pp. 211—271; Id. pp. 272—

maintaining opposite opinions on the point, and concludes by stating, that the opinion of Dumoulin in the affirmative has finally prevailed, in cases where there is an express contract for such community; and Dumoulin equally contends for it in cases of tacit contract, resulting from the *lex loci contractûs*[1]. From this latter point, however, Froland dissents in a qualified manner[2]. He deems the law of community, independent of an express contract, to be a real law; and therefore confined to the territory. As to acquests, or acquisitions, whether of movable or of immovable property, made in foreign countries, where the law of community exists, he agrees, that, in cases of an express contract, the law of the matrimonial domicil ought to prevail. But as to foreign countries, where the law of community does not exist, he thinks the right does not extend, *aut in vim consuetudinis, aut in vim contractûs:* for it is in vain to presume a tacit contract; and that, therefore, it ought to be governed by the law *rei sitæ*[3]. It would seem, however, from subsequent passages, that he applied his doctrine to the case of

340. See also 1 Boullenois, pp. 660—683; Id. Observ. 29, pp. 732—818. Dumoulin's words are: "Nullum habet dubium quin societas, semel contracta, complectatur bona ubicumque sita, sine ullâ differentiâ territorii, quemadmodum quilibet contractus, sive tacitus, sive expressus, ligat personam, et res disponentis ubique. Non obstat, quod hujusmodi societas non est expressa, sed tacita; nec oritur ex contractu expresso partium, sed ex tacito vel præsumpto contractu a consuetudine locali introducto." 1 Froland, Mém. 274. See also Livermore, Dissert. § 78—90, pp. 69, 71—74; Saul *v.* His Creditors, 17 Martin, R. 569, 599. The same doctrine is maintained by Bouhier. "Tout statut," says he, "qui est fondé sur une convention tacite et presumée des contractans, est personnel." Bouhier, Cout. de Bourg. ch. 23, § 69—74. And he expressly applies it to the case of tacit contracts of marriage, following out the reasoning of Dumoulin. Id. ch. 26, § 1—20. On the other hand, D'Argentré and Vander Muelen hold, that all laws respecting community are real and not personal; and therefore, that they are governed by the law *rei sitæ*. 1 Boullenois, Observ. 39, pp. 758, 759, 760—765.

[1] 1 Froland, Mém. pp. 178—200; 211—271, 272—300. See also 1 Boullenois, 660—683; Id. Observ. 29, pp. 732—818.

[2] 1 Id. 315—317.

[3] Id. 315—317, 321—323, 338, 341; 1 Boullenois, Observ. 29, pp. 758, 759.

immovables only, admitting that movables should be governed by the law of the domicil of the parties[1].

§ 154. Rodenburg seems to apply the same principle to cases where there is a nuptial contract, as to cases where there is none, holding, that in the latter cases, the law of the matrimonial domicil is adopted by a tacit contract. At the same time he asserts, that the law of community is not personal, but is real: and hence, that although it does not, or may not, directly act upon property *aliunde,* where no community exists; yet it will give a right of action, founded in the tacit contract, which may be enforced everywhere. And, therefore, the law of the matrimonial domicil, in such a case acts indirectly, and obtains universality of application, by reason of the tacit contract[2]. And he applies it equally to present and future acquisitions[3].

§ 155. Boullenois holds an opinion somewhat different. After having stated that jurists have entertained different views, as to the operation of the law of the matrimonial domicil upon the real property then possessed by the parties, and upon that afterwards acquired by them, he says, that they seem generally agreed in one point, that, so far as respects their property at the time of the marriage, of strict right the law of the *situs* ought to be followed. But as to their property, acquired after the marriage, they differed; some holding, that it was governed by the law of the *situs;* others, that it was not, and that the law of the place of the marriage, as to community or non-community, ought to govern. Boullenois holds, that this latter doctrine is not correct; because that all laws respecting property are real; and that those who adhere to this doctrine, are obliged to resort to a supposed tacit contract of the parties, to be governed by the law of the matrimonial domicil. He goes on

[1] Froland Mém. 315—317, 321—323, 338, 341; 1 Boullenois, Obs. 29, pp. 758, 759.

[2] Rodenburg, De Div. Stat. tit. 2, ch. 5, § 12—15; 2 Boullenois, App. pp. 41—47; 1 Boullenois, pp. 673—683; Id. Observ. 29, pp. 732—735; Id. pp. 754—757.

[3] Ibid.

to state, that, without aiming a blow against this system of tacit contract, which, on account of its equity, he highly approves, his own opinion is, that there is no necessity for deeming the law of community to be a personal law, in order to give full effect to the doctrine, as to property acquired after the marriage, upon another distinction. This distinction is, that the law of community or non-community, is one merely fixing the state or condition of the married couple; and therefore not a real, but a personal law[1]. Hence he holds, that the law of community or of non-community, existing in the matrimonial domicil, extends to all property of the parties, wherever it is situated; not upon the ground of any tacit contract, but, *proprio vigore*, as a law, binding both as to their present property, and as to their future acquisitions. But if, by the law of the *situs*, the law of community is prohibited, as to their present property, or as to their future acquisitions, or as to both, then he admits, that the law of the *situs* ought to prevail; for in all cases of this sort, the personal law yields to the real law of the *situs*. *Le statut personnel céde en cette occasion au statut réel de la situation*[2].

§ 156. Pothier has adopted the doctrine of tacit contracts maintained by Dumoulin; and therefore, in case there is no express nuptial contract, if the law of the matrimonial domicil creates a community, he holds, that it applies to all property, present and future, wherever situated, and even in provinces which do not admit of a community[3]. Grotius is also stated to have held the same opinion in a case where he was consulted[4].

§ 157. It has been remarked by the Supreme Court of

---

1 1 Boullenois, Observ. 29, pp. 736, 741, 751—770.

2 Id. pp. 750, 751—754; Id. pp. 754—757, 759, 760, 766, 769, 770; 2 Boullenois, Observ. 37, p. 277; Post, § 166.

3 Pothier, Traité de la Communauté, art. Prélim. n. 10—18; Post, § 166.

4 See Henry on Foreign Law, ch. 5, pp. 36, 37, note; 1 Burge, Comm. on Col. and For. Law, Pt. 1, ch. 7, § 8, p. 605.

Louisiana, that the greater number of the jurists of France and Holland are of opinion that, in settling the rights of the husband and wife, on the dissolution of the marriage, to the property acquired by them, the law of the place where the marriage was contracted, and not of that where it was dissolved by death, must be the guide. And that this opinion is by most of them founded on the idea first promulgated by Dumoulin, that, where the parties marry without an express nuptial contract, they must be presumed to contract with reference to the law of the country where the marriage took place, and that this tacit contract follows them wherever they go[1]. But that Court are of opinion, that the ground is unsatisfactory, especially when it is applied to cases of property acquired after a subsequent change of domicil of the parties. Their view of the subject is, that if the doctrine of a tacit contract be admissible at all, the contract is to be construed in the same way as if the laws of the country of the marriage were inserted in it; and that, so far as they are to be deemed real laws, and not to be personal laws, they are necessarily territorial, and can be construed to apply only to acquests or acquisitions within that particular country. The extent of the tacit agreement depends upon the extent of that law. If it has no force beyond the jurisdiction of the sovereign by which it is enacted; if it is real, and not personal; then the tacit consent of the parties cannot turn it into a personal statute. The parties have not said so; and they are presumed to have contracted in reference to the law, such as it was; to have known its limitations, as well as its nature; and to have had the one as much in view as the other. In one word, the parties have agreed that the law shall bind them, as far as that law extends, but no farther[2].

§ 158. The result of this reasoning (and it certainly has

---

1 Mr. Justice Porter in delivering the opinion of the Court in Saul *v.* His Creditors, 17 Martin, R. 599; Post, § 170.

2 Id. R. 569, 603—605; Post, § 187.

very great force) would seem to be, that in the case of a marriage without any express nuptial contract, the *lex loci contractûs* (assuming that it furnishes any just basis to imply a tacit contract) will govern, as to all movable property, and as to all immovable property within that country: and as to property in other countries, it will govern movables, but not immovables; the former having no *situs*, and the latter being governed by the *lex rei sitæ*.

§ 159. Perhaps the most simple and satisfactory exposition of the subject, or at least, that which best harmonizes with the analogies of the common law, is, that in the case of a marriage where there is no special nuptial contract, and there has been no change of domicil, the law of the place of celebration of the marriage ought to govern the rights of the parties, in respect to all personal or movable property, wherever acquired, and wherever it may be situate; but that real or immovable property ought to be left to be adjudged by the *lex rei sitæ*, as not within the reach of any extra-territorial law[1]. Where there is any special nuptial contract between the parties, that will furnish a rule for the case; and, as a matter of contract, ought to be carried into effect every where, under the general limitations and exceptions belonging to all other classes of contracts[2].

---

[1] See Henry on Foreign Law, ch. 7, pp. 48, 49; Post, § 454.

[2] Post, § 454.—Paul Voet lays down the following doctrine:—"Si statuto hujus loci inter conjuges *bona sint communia*, vel *pactis antenuptialibus* ita conventum sit, ut omnia, ubique locorum sita, communia forent, etiam ad illa, quæ in Frisiâ jacent, ubi non, nisi quæsitorum est communio, dabitur actio, ut communicentur." Voet, De Stat. § 4, ch. 2, § 16, p. 127, (edit. 1716); Id. p. 142, (edit. 1661); Id. ch. 3, § 9, p. 134, (edit. 1760); Id. pp. 140, 141. Yet he deems laws establishing a community of property to be real, and not personal laws. Id. § 4, ch. 3, § 9, pp. 134, 135, (edit. 1716.) See 1 Froland, Mém. 199, 200. This apparent discrepancy may be reconciled, by considering, that though the law of community be real, yet it may found a right of action for property situate elsewhere. See also Rodenburg, De Div. Stat. tit. 2, ch. 5, § 12—15; 2 Boullenois, App. pp. 41—46. A distinction of this sort seems not unknown in the Scottish law. 1 Rose, Cas. in Bank. 481. Lord Meadowbank, in a Scottish case of great importance, laid down the following doctrine as unquestionable: "In the ordinary case of transference by contract of marriage, when a lady of fortune, having a

§ 160. In the next place, what is the principle to be adopted in cases where there has been a change of domicil? And this admits of a double aspect; first, in relation to property acquired by the parties before the removal; and secondly, in relation to property acquired by the parties afterwards in the new domicil. In each instance, however, we are to be understood to speak of the mere operation of law, where there is no express nuptial contract between them[1].

§ 161. Upon this subject there is, as we have already seen, no small diversity of opinion among foreign jurists, as well in regard to the rights to property acquired after the change of domicil, as in regard to the rights to property antecedently acquired[2]. Bouhier lays down the rule in general terms, that in relation to the beneficial and pecuniary rights *(les droits utiles et pécuniaires)* of the wife, which result from the matrimonial contract, either express or tacit, the husband has no power by a change of domicil to alter or change them according to the rule, *Nemo potest mutare consilium suum in alterius injuriam;* and he insists, that this is the opinion of jurists generally[3]. Thus, if by the law of the matrimonial domicil there exists a community of property between the husband and the wife, and they remove to another place where no such community exists, the rights of neither party are changed; and the community applies

---

great deal of money in Scotland, or stock in the bank or public companies there, marries in London, the whole property is *ipso jure* her husband's. It is assigned to him. The legal assignment of a marriage operates, *without regard to territory,* all the world over." Royal Bank of Scotland, *v.* Smith, &c. 1 Rose, Cas. Bank. App. 481. Lord Eldon has affirmed this doctrine to be correct, in relation to personal property; but not in relation to real property. And in cases of bankruptcy to which he applied it, he added, that there was no legal obligation on a bankrupt to convey his real estate, situate in a foreign country, to the assignees. Selkrig *v.* Davies, 2 Rose, Bank. Cas. 99, S. C. 2 Dow, R. 230, 250.

1 See 1 Burge, Comm. on Col. and For. Law, Pt. 1, ch. 7, § 7, pp. 609—640; Ante, § 155; Post, § 449—454.

2 Ante, § 137—142; Id. § 143—159; 1 Burge, Comm. on Col. and For. Law, Pt. 1, ch. 7, § 8, pp. 609—640.

3 Bouhier, Cout. de Bourg. ch. 22, § 63—72.

in the same manner as in the original domicil[1]. And, on the other hand, if no such community exists in the matrimonial domicil, a transfer of domicil to a place where it does exist will not create it; for a change of domicil would not add anything to the marriage rights in the case of an express contract, and therefore ought not to do so in that of a tacit contract[2]. This also is Dumoulin's opinion. He says, that this is controverted by some authors; but it is so unjustly and falsely. *Sed controvertunt, si maritus postea cum uxore transtulerit domicilium, an debeat attendi illud, quod erat tempore contractus, an vero ultimum quod invenitur tempore mortis; et istud ultimum tenet Salicetus, et sequitur Alexander. Sed hoc non solum iniquum; quia maritus de loco, in quo nihil lucratur, vel tantum quartam, posset transferre domicilium ad locum in quo totam dotem lucraretur, præmoriente uxore sine liberis. Et quod sit falsum, probo per textem dictæ Legis, Exigere dotem*[3]. Bouhier makes no distinction whatsoever between movable property and immovable property[4]. Nor does he seem to recognise any distinction between property acquired before the change of domicil, and that acquired after the change of domicil[5].

§ 162. Le Brun supports the like opinion. He insists that, if there is no special contract of marriage, the law of the place where the marriage is celebrated, and in which the parties are domiciled, governs as a tacit contract; and that no subsequent change of domicil can change the legal rights of the parties, even as to after-acquired property[6]. And he puts the case of a marriage in Paris, and a subsequent change of domicil of the parties to the province of Bar, where the survivor is by custom entitled to the whole property in movables by survivorship; and holds, that if

---

1 Bouhier, Cout. de Bourg. ch. 22, § 63—72.

2 Ibid.

3 Dig. lib. 5, tit. 1, l. 65, De Judiciis; Ante, § 147; Molin. Comment. ad Cod. lib. 1, tit. 1, l. 1; Molin Opera, tom. 3, p. 555.

4 Bouhier, Cout. de Bourg. ch. 22, § 79, 80.

5 Id. ch. 22, per tot.

6 Le Brun, Traité de la Communauté, liv. 1, ch. 2, § 55, 56, p. 20.

either die, the movables, whether acquired before the removal, or after the removal, are governed by the law of community, and do not all remain to the survivor. *La raison est, qui ce seroit changer l'éstablissement de communauté fait par le contrat, ou par la coutume, selon lequel on a dû partager les meubles aussi bien que les conquêts*[1].

§ 163. Rodenburg puts the case of a marriage in a place where the law of community of property between husband and wife prevails, and a subsequent removal to another place where it has no existence; and he asks, if the community still subsists in the new domicil. He observes, that most of the Dutch jurists are of opinion that it does; and in this opinion he concurs to this extent, that the community will continue, until the parties have, by some overt act, discarded it; and then it will cease[2]. And he applies the same principle to cases of dowry by the customary law, holding, that the matrimonial domicil ought to prevail[3].

§ 164. Hertius puts the following question:—A marriage is contracted in a place where the civil law governs, (i. e. where there is no community), and afterwards the couple remove to a place where the law of community exists; and to the inquiry, whether in such a case there is a community in the acquisitions of the parties after the removal, he answers in the negative, adopting the doctrine of Rodenburg; and he gives this reason for his opinion, that it is not probable that the married couple, who did not agree to a community of goods in the beginning, intended to adopt it by a mere change of domicil. *Nam probabile non est, conjuges, qui pactis in societatem bonorum ab initio non consenserant, sola domicilii mutatione eam inducere voluisse*[4]. In the more

---

1 Le Brun, Traité de la Communauté, liv. 1. ch. 2, § 55, 56, p. 20. Ante, § 151.

2 Rodenburg, De Div. Stat. Pt. 2, tit. 2, ch. 4, § 3, 4; 2 Boullenois, App. pp. 66, 67; Id. pp. 85—87; Id. Observ. 36, p. 173; Ante, § 154.

3 Rodenburg, De Div. Stat. Pt. 2, tit. 2, ch. 4, § 5; 2 Boullenois, App. pp. 66, 67; Id. p. 87; Ante, § 154.

4 2 Hertii Opera, De Collis. Leg. § 49, p. 145, (edit. 1737); Id. p. 205, (edit. 1716).

general form in which the question may be presented, whether in the case of married persons removing from their matrimonial domicil where a community of property exists, to a place where it does not, they are to be governed by the law of the matrimonial domicil, he evidently adopts the affirmative, citing Rodenburg[1]. And he applies his doctrine to immovable property, as well as to movable property, making an exception, however, of the case where there is a prohibitory law of the country of the *situs*[2].

§ 165. Paul Voet appears to maintain the doctrine generally, that a change of domicil does not change the effect of the marriage contract, express or tacit. *Quid, si maritus alio domicilium postmodum transtulerit, eritne conveniendus, secundum loci statutum in quem postremum sese recepit? Non equidem. Quia non eo ipso, qui domicilium transferat, censetur voluntatem circa facta nuptialia mutasse, nisi eadem solemnitas in actu contrario intercesserit. Accedit, quod illa pacta solus mutare nequeat maritus, id quod tamen posset, si per emigrationem in alium locum ea mutarentur*[3]. Merlin maintains the like opinion, saying, that if a couple are married at Paris, meaning at the time to live there, and afterwards they remove to Lyons; in such a case the community formed at Paris will continue as to property acquired at Lyons[4].

§ 166. Boullenois holds the opinion, (as we have seen), that the law regulating the community affects the state or

---

[1] Hertii Opera, De Collis. Leg. § 48, p. 145, (edit. 1737); Id. p. 206, (edit. 1716).

[2] Id. § 47, 48, (edit. 1737), pp. 144, 145; Id. p. 205. (edit. 1716).

[3] Voet, De Stat. § 9, ch. 2, n. 5, 5, 7, pp. 264, 266, (edit. 1716); Id. pp. 319, 322, (edit. 1661); Id. § 4, ch. 2, n. 16, p. 127, (edit. 1716); Id. p. 142, (edit. 1661); Id. § 4, ch. 3, n. 9, pp. 134, 135, (edit. 1716); Id. pp. 151, 152, (edit. 1661); Post, § 168.—Paul Voet holds all such contracts, whether express or tacit, to be real and not personal laws; and therefore not directly affecting property out of the territory; but only indirectly, by a remedy to enforce the contract against ex-territorial property. Voet, ad Statut. § 4, ch. 3, § 9, pp. 134, 135, (edit. 1716); Id. pp. 151, 152, (edit. 1661); Post, § 168; Livermore, Dissert. § 115—123, pp. 87—92.

[4] Merlin, Repért. Communauté de Biens, § 1, p. 111.

condition of the parties, and is, therefore, a personal law; and accompanies them every where, and affects property, wherever situate[1]. He accordingly insists, that, if by the law of the matrimonial domicil a community of property exists, that community extends to all future acquisitions, whether movable or immovable, even in places to which the parties have afterwards removed, and where no such community exists[2]. Pothier has adopted the opinion of Boullenois, that the law of community is to be deemed a personal law, and not a real law; and he also adopts the doctrine of Dumoulin, as to tacit contracts[3]. So that he has no hesitation in declaring, as we have seen, that the law of the matrimonial domicil governs the property every where[4]. But he has omitted to put the case of a change of domicil, and the effects which it would produce. In another place he has laid down as a general principle, that a change of domicil delivers all persons from the empire of the laws of their former domicil, and subjects them to the new[5]. What, then, ought to be the effect of a removal, upon property acquired in the new domicil?

§ 167. Froland, after a good deal of hesitation, has given his own opinion on the subject to this effect. In cases where there is an express contract of community of property between the husband and the wife, he holds, that a change of domicil does not alter the rights of the parties; and that the community applies to property situate where the community is unknown, as well as where it exists[6]. But where there is no express contract, he deems the law of community as purely real, and therefore as not extending beyond the

---

1 Ante, § 155; 1 Boullenois, Observ. 29, pp. 736, 741, 750—754; Id. pp. 759—770; 2 Boullenois, Observ. 38, p. 277; 17 Martin, R. 607.

2 2 Boullenois, Observ. 38, pp. 277, 278, 283—285; Ante, § 155.

3 Pothier, Traité de la Communauté, art. Prélim. n. 10—13; Ante, § 156.

4 Ibid.; Ante, § 156.

5 Pothier, Cout. d'Orléans, ch. 1, n. 13; Ante, § 51 a, § 156.

6 1 Froland, Mém. Pt. 2, ch. 1, § 10, 11, pp. 200—210; Id. p. 341; Id. p. 190.

matrimonial domicil[1]. He treats the notion of Dumoulin, of a tacit contract in such a case, as a mere imaginary thing; words, and nothing else; a mere subtilty, phantom, and chimera. *Ce sont là, que des paroles, et rien au-delà. Mirificum illud Molinæi acumen; des subtilités d'esprit; des Idées; des Chimères; Enfin des moyens, que la seule imagination échauffée produit. Hac grandiloquentiâ etiam Molinæus personat, tamen apertè non est verum, quod dicit*[2]. The conclusion to which he arrives is, that, if two persons marry without any contract in a place where the law of community exists, and remove to another place where it does not exist, the change of domicil has no effect whatsoever; but the rights of each are the same, as if they had remained in their matrimonial domicil; and the acquisitions of immovable property, situate in the new domicil, do not fall into community, but are governed by the law *rei sitæ.* As to movables he holds, that the law of the actual domicil ought to govern[3].

§ 168. There are many other jurists, who maintain that the law of community among married persons is *real,* and not personal; and among these the most distinguished are D'Argentré, Dumoulin, Paul Voet, and Vander Meulin[4]. According to them, the law *rei sitæ* will govern in all cases where there is no express or tacit contract. But, then, we

---

[1] 1 Froland, Mém. Pt. 2, ch. 3, § 9—11, pp. 315—338; Id. p. 341; Ante, § 148, n. § 149.

[2] Id. p. 316.

[3] Id. § 9—11, pp. 315—323; Id. p. 341. I confess myself under some difficulty in reconciling what is here said with what Froland seems to decide in the next chapter (4th), § 3, p. 345, &c., where he appears to hold, that a woman marrying in a place where the law of community does not exist, does not, by removing with her husband to a place where it does exist, acquire any right of community to his acquisitions or movables in the latter.

[4] 1 Boullenois, Observ. 29, pp. 758—761, 765; P. Voet, De Stat. § 4, ch. 3, pp. 134, 135, § 9, (edit. 1716); Id. pp. 151, 152, (edit. 1661). See also J. Voet, ad Pand. lib. 5, tit. 1, n. 101; Merlin, Communauté de Biens, § 1, art. 3, pp. 104—110; Bouhier, Cout. de Bourg. ch. 23, § 34. See Saul *v.* His Creditors, 17 Martin, R. 598, 599; Id. 588; Ante, § 148—159, note.

must take this proposition with the accompanying qualification, that those of these jurists who admit of the doctrine of a tacit contract, adopting the law of the place of marriage, (among whom are Dumoulin and Paul Voet), also hold, that although the law of the place of the marriage does not directly act upon the property in a foreign country; yet, through the means of this tacit contract, it acts indirectly, and enables the parties to enforce it against that property by a proper suit *in rem*[1].

§ 169. Huberus (as we have seen) does not hesitate to assert the doctrine, that, in case of a change of domicil, future acquisitions of married persons are governed by the law of their actual domicil, and not of their antecedent matrimonial domicil[2]. Thus, after asserting that in Holland there is a community of property, and in Friezeland not, he says, if the married couple remove from the one province (Holland) to the other (Friezeland), whatever property is afterwards acquired, ceases to be common, and remains in distinct ownership *(distinctis proprietatibus)*; and the property before held in community remains clothed with the same legal character that it previously possessed[3]. And he applies this doctrine as well to immovable property as to movable property, relying upon the doctrine of tacit consent, or tacit contract[4]; and holding the opinion of Dumoulin, *Quia pactio bene extenditur ubique, sed non statutum merum, hoc est, solâ et merâ vi statuti*[5].

§ 170. It would be endless to recount the diversities of opinion among foreign jurists on this subject, following out the almost infinitely varied cases, which the customs and laws of different provinces and countries have brought before them. According to the opinion of the Supreme Court

---

1 P. Voet, De Statut. § 9, ch. 2, n. 5, 6, 7, pp. 264—266, (edit. 1716); Id. pp. 319—323, (edit. 1661); Ante, § 165, note; Ante, § 147; Post, § 169; 1 Burge, Comm. on Col. and For. Law, Pt. 1, ch. 7, § 8, pp. 612—614.

2 Ante, § 145.

3 Ibid.

4 Huberus, lib. 1, tit. 3, § 9; Ante, § 145.

5 Livermore Diss. § 89, pp. 73, 74; 1 Froland, Mém. 63.

of Louisiana, already cited [1], the greater number of foreign jurists are of opinion, that, in settling the rights of husband and wife, on the dissolution of marriage, to the property acquired by them, the law of the domicil of the marriage, and not of the place where it is dissolved by death, is to be the guide [2]. It is probably so; but there is more difficulty in affirming it where there has been a change of domicil, than where there has been no such change. It may be inferred, that the Scottish law has adopted the rule, that in cases of community where there is no written contract, the law of the domicil of the parties, at the death of either of them, regulates the disposal of the property of the parties [3].

---

1 Ante, § 157.

2 Mr. Justice Porter in delivering the opinion of the Court in Saul *v.* His Creditors, 17 Martin, R. 599; Ante, § 157.

3 Fergusson on Marr. and Divorce, 346, 347; Id. 361.—There are some remarks of Mr. Burge on this subject, which deserve to be cited in this place. "In hoc igitur (says he) conflictu quibus adstipulabimur? was the obvious question of one of the jurists, after he had been reviewing these discordant opinions. The following considerations will perhaps justify a concurrence with him in the answer given by himself:—'Mihi tutiùs videtur, adhærere secundæ sententiæ, (quæ negat prædia alibi sita communicari), quam non solùm ratio validissima munit, sed et præstantes auctores, et consensus aliquot municipiorum probant.' 1st. The law, which by its own force and operation, and independently of contract, gives an interest in immovable property, is a real law. 2d. Immovable property is not subject to the power of a real law, unless such law exists in the country where that property is situated. 3d. The joint interest, which the husband and the wife acquire under the community in the immovable property of each other, is conferred by the law alone, unless that law be controlled in its operation by a tacit agreement; such an interest, therefore, will not be acquired in immovable property situated in a country where the law of community does not exist. 4th. If a tacit agreement could be inferred for the purpose of giving to the law of community a more extensive operation than belongs to the quality of a real law, it might with equal propriety be inferred for a similar purpose in the case of other real laws, i. e., those which govern the succession to real property, &c. A preference of the law of the country, in which a man has passed his life, to that of another country, in which his real property may be situated, is as natural a presumption as that in favor of the law of the matrimonial domicil. 5th. It cannot be said, that, because the title is conferred by the law, as the consequence of the marriage, there is a ground peculiar to marriage for admitting the presumption of a tacit agreement; because no such

§ 171. No question appears to have arisen in the English courts upon the point which we have been discussing; that is, what rule is to govern in cases of matrimonial property, where there is no express nuptial contract, and there has been a change of domicil. But there is a case[1], which, Lord Eldon is reported to have said, was founded in a (nuptial) contract; and that if there had been no such contract, the law of England (notwithstanding the domicil of the parties at the time of their marriage was in France) would have regulated the rights of the husband and wife, who were domiciled in England at the dissolution of the marriage by death[2]. So that according to this doctrine, the law of the

---

presumption is admitted in respect of other titles conferred by law as the consequence of marriage, e. g., the titles to douaire and droit de viduité. 6th. The laws which confer douaire and le droit de viduité, are admitted by all jurists to be real laws; and consequently they attach on that property only which is situated in the country where they prevail, and they do not extend to that which is situated in another country, and no tacit agreement is presumed, in order to control their powers. 7th. The law establishing a community in immovable property is not essentially distinguished from the laws of douaire and viduité, in any one of those particulars which, in the opinion of jurists, determine the reality or personality of laws, and consequently the extent of their power. There does not, therefore, appear to be any substantial reason for allowing the law of community to have the effect of a personal law, and to attach an immovable property, in whatever country it may be situated. If this reasoning be admitted, the community when it prevails in the matrimonial domicil, will be confined to such immovable property as is situated either there, or in a country in which a similar law exists, but it will not extend to such property situated in a country where a similar law does not exist. In the preceding observations, the law of community has been considered only as it affected immovable property. Its effect on personal property is determined by other principles. According to a principle of international jurisprudence, the acquisition of movable or personal property by the operation of law, is, as will be presently shewn, governed by the law of its owner's domicil. The community, if it prevailed in the matrimonial domicil, would therefore attach on the movable property of the husband and wife, in whatever place it was situated." 1 Burge, Comment. on Col. and For. Law, Pt. 1, ch. 7, § 8, pp. 617—619; and Lashley *v.* Hogg. cited Id. pp. 623—625.

[1] Lashley *v.* Hogg, cited in Robertson's Appeal cases, 4, and in 1 Burge, Comm. on Col. and For. Law, Pt. 1, ch. 7, § 8, pp. 623—625; Feaubert *v.* Turst, Prec. Ch. 207.

[2] Ibid.

actual domicil will govern as to all property, without any distinction, whether it is property acquired antecedently, or subsequently, to the removal.

§ 171 *a*. In a more recent case, where the parties were inhabitants of Prussia, and domiciled there, a question arose in the Court of Exchequer, upon the distribution of an intestate's estate under the administration of the Court, whether the wife, being a distributee, was entitled in equity, upon a petition by her husband for the amount, to have any of the money settled on her, or whether the whole was to be paid to him. It appeared that, by the laws of Prussia, the whole of the personality of the husband and wife is, during the coverture, at the absolute disposal of the husband; but on the death of either it is divided between the survivor and the heirs of the deceased. The wife made no application to the Court; and the Court ordered the whole money to be paid over to the husband[1]. Here we see the Court adopted the law of their actual domicil, to regulate the rights of the parties to the movable property.

§ 172. In America there has been a general silence in the States governed by the common law. But in Louisiana, whose jurisprudence is framed upon the general basis of the Spanish and French law, the point has several times come under judicial decision. The law of community exists in that State[2]; and from the frequency of removals from and to that State, it is scarcely possible that some of the doctrines which have so much perplexed foreign jurists, should not be brought under review.

§ 173. We have already had occasion to take notice of some of the views entertained by the Supreme Court of Louisiana upon this subject[3]. It has been very properly remarked by that Court, that questions upon the conflict of

---

[1] Sawyer *v.* Shute, 1 Anstr. R. 63. See also Anstruther *v.* Adair, 2 Mylne & Keen, 513.

[2] Civil Code of Louisiana, (1809), 336, art. 63; New Code, (1825), art. 2369—2393.

[3] Ante, § 157, 170.

the laws of different States are the most embarassing and difficult of decision of any that can occupy the attention of courts of justice[1]. And it may be added, almost in their own language, that the vast mass of learning which the researches of counsel can furnish, leaves the subject as much enveloped in obscurity and doubt, as it would be, if one were called upon to decide, without the knowledge of what others had thought and written upon it[2].

§ 174. It is manifest, that the great body of foreign jurists, who maintain the universality and ubiquity of the operation of the law of the matrimonial domicil, notwithstanding any subsequent change of domicil, found themselves upon the doctrine of a tacit contract, which, being once entered into, is of legal obligation everywhere[3]. The remarks of the Supreme Court of Louisiana on this point have been already cited; and certainly they have a great tendency to shake its foundation[4]. If the law of community be a real law, and not a personal law, it would seem to follow, that it ought to regulate all things which are situate within the limits of the country wherein it is in force, but not elsewhere[5]. The most strenuous advocate for the doctrine of tacit contract must admit, that, if by the statute of any country community is prohibited as to property there, the law of the matrimonial domicil ought not to prevail in such country, in contradiction to its own. And the learned Court above referred to, have said, that they can perceive no solid distinction between the case of a real statute, and a prohibitory statute, as to property situate in that country[6].

§ 175. But if the law of community be personal, still there is strong ground to contend, that the personal laws of one

---

1 Ante, § 157, 170.

2 Mr. Justice Porter in delivering the opinion of the Court in Saul *v.* His Creditors, 17 Martin, R. 571, 572.

3 Ante, § 147—170.

4 Saul *v.* His Creditors, 17 Martin, R. 599—608; Ante, § 157, 170.

5 Mr. Justice Porter in Saul *v.* His Creditors, 17 Martin, R. 601, 602.

6 Ibid; See post, § 449—454.

country cannot control the personal laws of another country, *ipso facto*, where they extend to, and provide for, property within the jurisdiction of the latter. No one can doubt, that any country has a right to say, that contracts for community made in another country, shall have no operation within its own territory. The question, then, is reduced to the mere consideration, whether the law of the country does directly or indirectly provide for, or repudiate, the community as to property locally situate within it[1].

§ 176. Upon reasoning to this effect, after full consideration, the Supreme Court of Louisiana came to the conclusion, that the law of community must, upon just principles of interpretation, be deemed a real law, since it relates to things, more than to persons, and it has, in the language of D'Aguesseau, the destination of property to certain persons, and its preservation in view[2]. The Court, therefore, held, that where a married couple had removed from Virginia, (their matrimonial domicil), where community does not exist, into Louisiana, where community does exist, the acquests and gains acquired after their removal, were to be governed by the law of community in Louisiana[3].

§ 177. This doctrine appears to be in full accordance with the laws of Spain. Those laws apply the same rule to cases of express contract, and to cases of tacit contract, or customary law. Where there is an express contract, that governs as to all acquisitions and gains before the removal. Where there is no express contract, the customary law of

---

1 Saul *v.* His Creditors, 17 Martin, R. 573, 574—588; 1 Hertii Opera, De Collis Leg. § 47, pp. 143, 144, (edit. 1737); Id. p. 294, (edit. 1716). Post. § 449—454.

2 Mr. Justice Porter in Saul *v.* His Creditors, 17 Martin, R. 593, 594, 595, 606, 607; D'Aguesseau, Œuvres, tom. 4, Pl. 54, p. 660, 4to. edit.

3 The law of community existed in Louisiana under the Spanish law, and now exists under the civil code of that State. Bruneau *v.* Bruneau's Heirs, 9 Martin, R. 217; Code Civil of Louisiana, (1809), 336, art. 63; Revised Code, (1825), art. 2370; Saul *v.* His Creditors, 17 Martin, R. 573; 2 Kent, Comm. Lect. 28, p. 183, note, 3rd edit.

the matrimonial domicil governs in like manner. But, in both cases, all acquisitions and gains made after the removal, are governed by the law of the actual domicil[1]. The present revised code of Louisiana adopts a like rule; and declares, that a marriage contracted out of the State, between persons who afterwards come to live within the State, is subject to the community of acquests, with respect to such property as is acquired after their removal[2].

§ 178. This Code of course furnishes the rule for all future cases in Louisiana; but the discussions in that State have arisen upon antecedent cases, and have involved a general examination of the whole doctrine upon principle and authority. The doctrine which, with reference to public law, has been established in that State, resolves itself into two fundamental propositions:—First, Where there is an express nuptial contract, that there shall be a community of acquests and gains between the parties, even though they should reside in countries where different laws prevail, that agreement will be held obligatory throughout, as a matter of contract, in cases of the removal of the parties to another State; with this restriction, however, which is applicable to all contracts, that it is not to cause any prejudice to the citizens of the country to which they remove, and that its execution is not incompatible with the laws of that country[3]. Secondly, Where there is no such express nuptial contract, the law of the matrimonial domicil is to prevail, as to the antecedent property; but the property acquired after the removal, is to be governed by the law of the actual domicil[4]. This latter proposition has been laid down, in terms unusually strong, by the Supreme Court of that State. "Though

---

1 Saul v. His Creditors, 17 Martin, R. 576—581, 607, 608.

2 Code Civil of Louisiana, (1825), art. 2370.

3 Mr. Justice Derbigny in Murphy v. Murphy, 5 Martin, R. 83; Mr. Justice Porter in Saul v. His Creditors, 17 Martin, R. 605, 606.

4 Mr. Justice Derbigny in Gale v. Davis, 4 Martin, R. 645; Saul v. His Creditors, 17 Martin, R. 605, 606; Le Breton v. Nouchet, 3 Martin, R. 60,73.

it was *once* a question, (say the Court), it seems *now* to be a *settled* principle, that when a married couple emigrate from the country where the marriage was contracted, into another, the laws of which are different, the property which they acquire in the place to which they have removed, is governed by the laws of that place[1]." Upon these propositions the Court have accordingly decided, that, where a couple who were married in North Carolina where a community does not exist, had removed to Louisiana where it does exist, the property acquired after the removal was to be held in community[2]. And in another case, where the marriage was in Cuba, and there was a special contract that there should be a community according to the custom of Paris, in whatever country the parties might reside; and the parties removed to South Carolina, where no community exists, the contract was held to govern the property acquired in the latter State[3]. The same doctrine has been maintained in New York, in the case of a marriage between French subjects, under a similar stipulation of community, and of mutual donation in case of survivorship of either of the parties[4].

§ 179. An instance illustrative of the exception in cases of express contract, may be drawn from other decisions in Louisiana. Upon a marriage celebrated in that State, the parties stipulated, that the rights of the parties should be governed by the custom of Paris. The question was, whether the parties, residing in the country, were competent to enter into a nuptial contract stipulating, that the effects of it on their property should be governed by a foreign law. The Court held, that they had no such competency, and that the contract was void[5].

---

1 Mr. Justice Derbigny in Gale *v.* Davis's Heirs, 4 Martin, R. 645, 649.

2 Id. 645.

3 Id. 83; Mr. Justice Porter in Saul *v.* His Creditors, 17 Martin, R. 605; Mr. Justice Derbigny in Bourcier *v.* Lanusse, 3 Martin, R. 581, 583.

4 De Couche *v.* Savatier, 3 John. Ch. R. 190, 211.

5 Mr. Justice Derbigny in Bourcier *v.* Lanusse, 3 Martin, R. 581. See Code Civil of France, art. 1390.

§ 180. A still more striking case occurred in the same State, upon some of the doctrines of which, as stated by the Court, there may, perhaps, be reason to pause; but the grounds are nevertheless stated with great force. A man ran away with a young lady of thirteen years of age, both of them being then domiciled in Louisiana, without the consent of her parents or guardian, and they went together to Natchez, in Mississippi, and were there married, and soon after returned to New Orleans, the place of their original domicil. The wife afterwards died, while they were living in Louisiana; and after her death, her mother demanded her property, as it would descend by the Louisiana law. The Court sustained the demand[1]. From the elaborate opinion delivered for the Court by Mr. Justice Derbigny, the following extract is made, as highly interesting: "With respect (say the Court) to the law of nations, the principle recognised by most writers may be reduced to this; that although no power is bound to give effect, within its own territory, to the laws of a foreign country; yet by the courtesy of nations, and from a consideration of the inconveniences which would be the result of a contrary conduct, foreign laws are permitted to regulate contracts made in foreign countries. But, in order that they may have such effect, it must first be ascertained, that the parties really intended to be governed by those laws, and had not some other country in contemplation at the time of the contract. This being previously recognised, the government, within the bounds of which such foreign laws claim admission, has next to consider, whether the enforcing of these laws will cause no prejudice to its rights, or to the rights of its citizens.

§ 181. "Let us take the first exception, and apply it to this case. Did the parties really intend to be governed by the laws of the Mississippi Territory? and had they not in contemplation, at the time of contracting marriage, their return to this country? If we were to judge from their acts

[1] Le Breton *v.* Nouchet, 3 Martin, R. 60, 73.

alone, there could be no hesitation in saying, that they went to Natchez for the purpose only of contracting marriage, and intended to come back as soon as it could conveniently be done. Their remaining at Natchez only a few weeks, and that in a tavern, their return to New Orleans not long after, and the continuation of their residence there until the death of the wife, would amount to an irresistible proof, that they had this country in contemplation at the time of contracting their marriage. But it is alleged, that however evident their intention may appear from these facts, the appellant had really taken the resolution to settle at Natchez. Evidence has been furnished of his declarations to that purpose, both before his departure, and after his arrival in the Mississippi Territory. One of his brothers has sworn, that previously to his leaving New Orleans, he told him and his other brothers, that he intended to stay at Natchez. Other persons have deposed, that letters, expressive of the determination of the appellant to remain there, were by them received from him, shortly after their dates. Without questioning the propriety of the admission of such testimony, the Court is satisfied, that it is insufficient to counterbalance the weight of the facts which disclose the real intention of the parties.

§ 182. "But, should their intention still remain a subject of doubt, we have next to consider, whether, by permitting the laws of the Mississippi Territory to regulate this case, this government would not injure its own rights, or the rights of its citizens. For a foreign law having no other force than that which it derives from the consent of the government, within the bounds of which it claims to be admitted, that government must be supposed to retain the faculty of refusing such admission, whenever the foreign law interferes with its own regulations. A party to this marriage was one of those individuals over whom our laws watch with particular care, and whom they have subjected to certain incapacities, for their own safety. She was a minor. Has she, by fleeing to another country, removed those incapacities? Her mother is a citizen of this State; she herself was a girl of thirteen years, who had no other domicil than that of her mother. Did she not remain, notwithstanding her flight to Natchez, under the authority of this government? Did not the protection of this government follow her wherever she went? If so, this government cannot, without surrendering its rights, recognise the empire of laws, the effect of which would be, to render that protection inefficacious. But the laws of the Mississippi Territory, as stated by the parties, do not only interfere with our rights, but are at war with our regulations. By our laws, a minor who marries, cannot give away any part of his property, without the authorization of those whose consent is necessary for the validity of the marriage. By the laws of the Mississippi Territory, all the personal estate of the wife (that would embrace, in this case, everything which she had) is the property of the husband. Again; according to our laws, we cannot give away more than a certain portion of our property, when we have forced heirs. But what our laws thus forbid, is permitted in the Mississippi Territory. And shall our citizens be deprived of their legitimate rights, by the laws of another government, upon our own soil? Shall the mother of Alexandrine Dussuau lose the inheritance of her deceased child, secured to her by our laws; because her daughter married at Natchez? Shall our own laws be reduced to silence within our own precincts, by the superior force of other laws? If such doctrine were maintainable, it would be unnecessary for us to legislate. In vain should we endeavor to secure the persons and the property of our citizens. Nothing would be more easy than to render our precautions useless, and our laws a dead letter. But the municipal law of the Mississippi Territory, which is relied upon by the appellant, is not the law which would govern this case, *even there.* The law of nations is law at Natchez, as well as at New Orleans. According to the principles of that law, 'Personal incapacities, communicated by the laws of any particular place, accompany the person wherever he goes. Thus, he who is excused the consequences of contracts for want of age in his country, cannot make binding contracts in another.' Therefore, even if this case were pending before a tribunal of the Mississippi Territory, it is to be supposed that they would recognise the incapacity under which Alexandrine Dussuau was labouring when she contracted marriage, and decide, that such marriage could not have the effect of giving to her husband what she was forbidden to give. If that be sound doctrine in any case, how much more so must it be in one of this nature; where the minor, almost a child, has, in all probability, been seduced into an escape from her mother's dwelling, and removed in haste out of her reach? We cannot, here, hesitate to believe, that the Courts of our neighbouring Territory, far from lending their assistance to this infraction of our laws, would have enforced them with becoming severity. For, if when an appeal is made to those general principles of natural justice, by which nations have tacitly agreed to govern themselves in their intercourse with each other, while nations entirely foreign to one another, feel bound to observe them, how much more sacred must they be between governments who, though independent of each other in matters of internal regulation, are associated for the purposes of common defence and common advantage, and are members of the same great body politic[1]?"

§ 183. In general, the doctrines thus maintained in Louisiana, will, most probably, form the basis of the American jurisprudence on this subject. They have much to commend them in their intrinsic convenience and certainty, as well as in their equity; and they seem best to harmonize with the known principles of the common law in other cases. In concluding this topic, the following propositions may be laid down, as those which, although not universally estab-

---

[1] Mr. Justice Derbigny in Le Breton *v.* Nouchet, 3 Martin, R. 60, 66, 71.

lished or recognised in America, have much of domestic authority for their support, and have none in opposition to them.

§ 184. (1.) Where there is a marriage between parties in a foreign country, and an express contract respecting their rights and property, present and future, that, as a matter of contract, will be held equally valid everywhere, unless, under the circumstances, it stands prohibited by the laws of the country, where it is sought to be enforced. It will act directly on movable property everywhere. But as to immovable property in a foreign territory, it will, at most, confer only a right of action, to be enforced according to the jurisprudence *rei sitæ*[1].

§ 185. (2.) Where such an express contract applies in terms or intent only to present property, and there is a change of domicil, the law of the actual domicil will govern the rights of the parties as to all future acquisitions [2].

§ 186. (3.) Where there is no express contract, the law of the matrimonial domicil will govern, as to all the rights of the parties to their present property in that place, and as to all personal property everywhere, upon the principle that movables have no *situs*, or rather, that they accompany the person everywhere [3]. As to immovable property, the law *rei sitæ* will prevail[4].

§ 187. (4.) Where there is no change of domicil, the same rule will apply to future acquisitions, as to present property. (5.) But where there is a change of domicil, the law of the actual domicil, and not of the matrimonial domicil, will govern as to all future acquisitions of movable property; and, as to all immovable property, the law *rei sitæ* [5].

---

[1] See Henry on Foreign Law, 48, 49; Id. 95; Ante, § 143.

[2] Ante, § 171, § 171 *a*.

[3] See Stein's Case, 1 Rose, Bank. Cases, App. 481; Selkrig *v*. Davies, 2 Rose, Bank. Cas. 99; S. C. 2 Dow, 230, 250; 1 Burge, Comm. on Col. and For. Law, Part 1, ch. 7, § 8. p. 619.

[4] See Henry on Foreign Law, 48, 49; 1 Burge, Comm. on Col, and For. Law, Part 1, ch. 7, § 8, pp. 618, 619.

[5] 2 Ante, § 157, 158.—Mr. Burge, adverting to the different opinions on

§ 188. (6.) And here also, as in cases of express contract, the exception is to be understood, that the law of the place where the rights are sought to be enforced, do not prohibit

this subject, has remarked:—"According to the general doctrine of jurists, the property of the husband and wife, whether it be acquired before or after the change of domicil, continues subject to the law of community, notwithstanding they have removed to another domicil, where that law does not exist. The change of the domicil neither divests them of any right which they had acquired under the law o, their matrimonial domicil, nor confers on them any right which they could not aequire under that law. If the law of community existed in their matrimonial domicil, they will not cease to be in community, although they should have acquired another domicil in a country where no law of community was established; and, on the other hand, if there was no law of community in their matrimonial domicil, they will not become subject to the law of community, because they have taken up their domicil in a country where that law does exist. The concurrence of jurists in this doctrine is so general, that there are few who have dissented from it. This doctrine seems to result as a necessary and legitimate conclusion from the theory, that the community exists by force of the tacit agreement of the parties, and which is considered of the same weight as if it had been an express agreement; because, if the rights of the parties, either in their present property, or in their future acquisitions, had been conferred by an agreement, they could not be varied by a change of domicil. But if this theory be rejected, and the law of community has no greater operation than any other real law, it can never be necessary to consider the effect of a change of domicil on the interests of the husband and wife on their real property, because those interests in their present property, as well as in their future acquisitions, are determined by the lex loci rei sitæ. The application of this doctrine to the interests acquired by the husband and wife in the personal property of each other, under the law of their matrimonial domicil, so far as it regards property acquired before their removal from their matrimonial domicil, might, it seems, be maintained without the aid of this theory. The matrimonial domicil of the parties may be supposed to be in a country where, as in England, the marriage is an absolute gift to the husband of the wife's whole personal estate; the subsequent domicil may be in a country where, as in British Guiana, the wife, by virtue of the communio bonorum, retains an interest in her own, and acquires an interest in her husband's, personal property; or the matrimonial domicil may have been in British Guiana, and the subsequently acquired domicil in England. In the one case, the whole personal estate of the wife has become vested in the husband; the wife brings no personal property of her own into British Guiana, on which the law of community can attach. In the other case, the wife arrives in England, not only retaining an interest in her own, but having acquired an interest in the property of her husband. The law of the matrimonial domicil has, in this case, already made a disposition of

such arrangements. For if they do, as every nation has a right to prescribe rules for the government of all persons and property within its own territorial limits, its own law, in a case of conflict, ought to prevail[1].

---

the property of the husband and wife at a time when the parties and the property were subject to that law. In neither case could the law of the new domicil be admitted, without divesting rights which had been already legally acquired. But in the opinion of the greater number of jurists, not only the property which had been acquired by the husband and wife, before their removal from their matrimonial domicil, but even that acquired in their new domicil, is subject to the law of the matrimonial domicil; and their opinion has been sanctioned, even to this extent, by the decisions in France. A person was married and domiciled in L., where the civil law prevailed. He afterwards removed to Paris, and established his domicil there. On his death, his widow demanded a share of his movables, and of the *acquêts* made since the marriage. By an *arrêt* of the 29th March, 1640, her demand was rejected. A similar decision was given in the case of a person married and domiciled in Normandy ,who afterwards removed to, and established his domicil in Paris. A demand by his widow for a share of the *acquêts,* made since the removal from Normandy, was rejected. The application of this doctrine to the acquisitions of personal property made by the husband and wife in their new or actual domicil, can only be sustained by means of the theory of a tacit agreement. Even its advocates do not all concur in subjecting future acquisitions after a change of domicil, to the law of the matrimonial domicil. Thus, Huber was of opinion, that they are governed by the law of the new or actual domicil : 'Cùm primùm verò conjuges migrant ex unâ provinciâ, (where the community prevailed), in aliam, (where it does not prevail), bona quæ deinceps alteri adveniunt, cessant esse communia, manentque distinctis proprietatibus; sicut res antea communes factæ, manent in eo statu juris, quem induerunt.' But if the law of community be a real law, its power as to personal property cannot be more extensive than as to real property. As it affects only such real property as is actually situated in the country where it is established, so it affects personal property only, when its owner is actually domiciled in the country where such law is established, because the place of his domicil is the situs in fictione juris of his movable property. The real law as to personal property is that which prevails in the place of its owner's actual domicil. He acquires and holds it according to the disposition of that law, and it depends upon that law, whether he and his wife acquire it for their joint benefit or for his sole benefit." 1 Burge, Comm. on Col. and For. Law, Pt. 1, ch. 7, § 8. pp. 619—622. See also Lashley *v.* Hogg, cited Id. pp. 623—625; Id. p. 626.

[1] See Fergusson on Marr. and Divorce, 358—363; Id. 383, 392—422; Huberus, lib. 1, tit. 3, De Conflict. Leg. § 2; Ante, § 111.

§ 189. (7.) Although, in a general sense, the law of the matrimonial domicil is to govern in relation to the incidents and effects of marriage; yet this doctrine must be received with many qualifications and exceptions. No other nation will recognise such incidents or effects, when they are incompatible with its own policy, or injurious to its own interests. A marriage in France or Prussia may be dissolved for incompatibility of temper; but no divorce would be granted from such a marriage, for such a cause, in England, Scotland, or America[1]. "If (said a learned Scottish judge, in a passage already cited) a man in this country were to confine his wife in an iron cage, or beat her with a rod of the thickness of the judge's finger, would it be any justification in any court to allege, that these were powers which the law of England conferred on a husband, and that he was entitled to exercise them, because his marriage had been celebrated in that country[2]?" And he added, with great emphasis: "Marriage is a contract *sui generis;* and the rights, duties, and obligations, which arise out of it, are matters of so much importance to the well-being of the state, that they are regulated, not by the private contract, but by the public laws of the state, which are imperative upon all who are domiciled within its territory[3]."

§ 190. (8.) The doctrine of tacit contract to regulate the rights and duties of matrimony, in cases where there is no express contract, according to the law of the place where the marriage has been celebrated, is questionable in itself; and, even if admitted, must be liable to many qualifications and restrictions[4]. We have seen, that it has been much doubted in Louisiana[5]; and the Scottish Courts have utterly refused (as we shall fully see hereafter) to allow the doc-

---

[1] Fergusson on Marr. and Div. 398.

[2] Per Lord Robertson. See Fergusson on Marr. and Divorce, 399; Id. 361.

[3] Id. 361, 399.

[4] Ante, § 147—170.

[5] Saul *v.* His Creditors, 17 Martin, R. 598—607; Ante, § 157.

trine of such a tacit contract to regulate the right of divorce [1].

§ 191. But a question may sometimes occur, what is to be deemed in the proper sense of the rule the true matrimonial domicil? Is it the place where the actual marriage is celebrated? Or that where the contract of marriage is entered into? Or that where the parties are domiciled, if the marriage is celebrated elsewhere? Or, if the husband or wife have different domicils, whose is to be rgearded? These and many other perplexing inquiries may be raised; and foreign jurists have not passed them over without examination [2].

§ 192. Where the place of domicil of both the parties is the same with that of the contract and the celebration of the marriage, no difficulty can arise. The place of celebration is clearly then the matrimonial domicil. But, let us suppose, that neither of the parties has a domicil in the place where the marriage is celebrated; but it is a marriage *in transitu*, or during a temporary residence, or on a journey made for that sole purpose, *animo revertendi;* what is then to be deemed the matrimonial domicil?

§ 193. The principle maintained by foreign jurists, in such cases, is, that with reference to personal rights and rights of property, the actual or intended domicil of the parties is to be deemed the true matrimonial domicil; or, to express the doctrine in a still more general form, they hold, that the law of the place, where at the time of marriage the parties intend to fix their domicil, is to govern all the rights resulting from the marriage. Hence, they would answer the question proposed, by stating, that in such a case the law of the actual domicil of the parties is to govern, and not the place of the marriage *in transitu* [3].

---

1 Fergusson on Mar. and Divorce 358—363; Id. 382, 393—422.

2 See on this subject, 1 Burge, Comm. on Col. and For. Law, Pt. 1, ch. 6, § 2, pp. 244—261.

3 2 Boullenois, Observ. 36, p. 260; Pothier Traité de la Communauté, art. Prélim. n. 14—16; Voet, De Statut. § 9, ch. 2, § 5, 6, p. 264, (edit.

§ 194. But, suppose a man domiciled in Massachusetts, should marry a lady domiciled in Louisiana, what is then to be deemed the matrimonial domicil? Foreign jurists would answer, that it is the domicil of the husband, if the intention of the parties is to fix their residence there; and of the wife, if the intention is to fix their residence there; and if the residence is intended to be in some other place, as in New York, then the matrimonial domicil would be in New York. Rodenburg lays down the doctrine in explicit terms; and gives as a reason, that the marriage is presumed to be contracted according to the laws of the place where they intend to fix their domicil. *Quia per destinationem in locis illis domicilii matrimonium contractum esse intelligitur*[1]. Boullenois states the same doctrine; and says:—that ordinarily, where the domicil of the husband and that of the wife are not the same, the law of the husband's domicil is to prevail, unless he means to establish himself in that of his wife[1]. Dumoulin is equally expressive. *Hinc infertur* (says he) *ad questionem quotidianam de contractu dotis et matrimonii, qui censetur fieri non in loco, in quo contrahitur, sed in loco domicilii viri; et intelligitur, non de domicilio originis, sed de domicilio habitationis ipsius viri, de quo nemo dubitat, sed omnes consentiunt*[3]. This appears also to be the opinion of Mascardus, Bartholus, Bouhier, Pothier, Merlin, and other distinguished jurists[4].

1715); Id. pp. 319, 320, (edit. 1661); 1 Burge, Comm. on Col. and For. Law, Pt. 1, ch. 6, § 2, pp. 244—261.

[1] Rodenburg, tit. 2, ch. 5, § 15; 2 Boullenois, App. p. 47; 1 Boullenois, 11, 682, 683; Id. Observ. 29, p. 802; Voet, De Statut. § 9, ch. 2, § 5, p. 264, (edit. 1716); Id. pp. 319, 320, (edit 1661); Le Brun, Traité de la Communauté, Liv. 1, ch. 2, § 42—48.

[2] 1 Boullenois, Observ. 29, p. 802; 2 Boullenois, Observ. 37, pp. 259, 260, 265; Voet, De Statut. § 9, ch. 2, § 5, 6, pp. 264, 265, (edit. 1715); Id. pp. 319, 320, (edit. 1661).

[3] Molinæi, Comment. ad Cod. lib. 1, tit. 1, l. 1, Conclus. de Statut. Molin. Opera, tom. 3, p. 555; 2 Boullenois, Observ. 37, p. 261.

[4] 2 Boullenois, Observ. 37, pp. 260—265; Pothier, Traité de la Communauté, art. Prélim. n. 14—16; Bouhier, Cout. de Bourg. ch. 22, §

§ 195. Cujas affirms the same doctrine. *Sed ex eo contractu mulier migravit in alium locum, id est, talis est contractus, ut ex eo mulier statim migret in alium locum. Ergo non is locus spectatur, sed ille, in quem sit migratio. Hac ratione, mulier non agit ubi matrimonium contraxit; sed ubi ex matrimonio migravit, divertit, aut aget*[1]. And in so doing, he does no more than affirm the very doctrine of the Pandects. *Exigere dotem mulier debet illic, ubi maritus domicilium habuit, non ubi instrumentum dotale conscriptum est; nec enim id genus contractûs est, ut eum locum spectari oporteat, in quo instrumentum dotis factum est, quam eum, in cujus domicilium et ipsa mulier per conditionem matrimonii erat reditura*[2].

§ 196. Huberus holds very decisive language on the same subject. "But (says he) the place where a contract is made, is not so exactly to be looked at; but that if the parties have in contracting had reference to another place, that is rather to be regarded; *Contraxisse unusquisque in eo loco intelligitur, in quo, ut solveret, se obligavit*[3]. Therefore, the place of the marriage contract is not so much to be deemed the place where the nuptial contract is made, as that in which the parties, contracting matrimony, intend to live. Thus it daily happens, that men in Friezeland, natives or sojourners, marry wives in Holland, whom they immediately bring into Friezeland. If this be their intention at the time of the contract, there is no community of property, although the marriage contract is silent according to the law of Holland; but the law of Friezeland in

---

18—28; Merlin, Repert. Autoris. Maritale, § 10, art. 5, p. 244; Id. Communauté de Biens, § 1, p. 111; 1 Burge, Comm. on Col. and For. Law, Pt. 1, ch. 6, § 2, p. 241—261.

1 Cujas, ad Legem, Exigere dotem, Dig. Lib. 5, tit. 1, l. 65, Cujacii Opera, tom. 7, p. 164, (edit. 1758). See also Ford's Curators *v.* Ford, 14 Martin, R. 577; Le Brun, Traité de la Communauté, Liv. 1, ch. 2, § 41; Post, § 198.

2 Dig. Lib. 5, tit. 1, § 65; Pothier, Pand. Lib. 5, tit. 1, n. 38.

3 Dig. Lib. 44, tit. 7, l. 21; Pothier, Pand. Lib. 44, tit. 7, n. 21.

this case, is the law of the place of a contract[1]. *Proinde et locus matrimonii contracti non tam is est, ubi contractus nuptialis initus est, quam in quo contrahentes matrimonium exercere voluerunt; ut omni die sit, homines in Frisia indigenas aut incolas, ducere uxores in Hollandia, quas inde statim in Frisiam deducunt; idque si in ipso contractu ineundo propositum habeant, non oritur communio bonorum, etsi pacta dotalia sileant, secundum jus Hollandiæ, sed jus Frisiæ in hoc casu est loco contractûs*[2].

§ 197. Le Brun has discussed the question at considerable length, and has arrived at the same conclusion. And he puts the case of a person domiciled in Normandy where the law of community does not exist, who marries in Paris, without any contract, where the law of community does exist; and he holds, that, if he has not changed his domicil, but returns immediately to Normandy, the law of Normandy will govern, and no community of property will exist between himself and his wife[3].

§ 198. The same doctrine has been repeatedly acted on by the Supreme Court of Louisiana. In one case of a runaway marriage, (already alluded to), in another State by parties domiciled in Louisiana, who immediately afterwards returned, the Court held, as we have seen, that the law of Louisiana governed the marriage rights and property[4]. In another case, where the parties were married in one State, intending immediately to remove into another, which intention was consummated, the Court held, that the marriage rights and property were governed by the law of the place of the intended residence. On this last occasion, the Court said:—"We think that it may be safely laid down as a principle, that the matrimonial rights of a wife, who marries

---

1 Huberus, lib. 1, tit. 3, § 10; S. P. Fergusson on Mar. and Divorce, 174; Voet, De Statut. § 9, ch. 2, § 5, 6, pp. 264, 265, (edit. 1715); Id. pp. 319, 320, (edit. 1661).

2 Huberus, lib. 1, tit. 3, § 10.

3 Le Brun, Traité de la Communauté, liv. 1, ch. 2, § 46—51, 55.

4 Le Breton *v.* Nouchet, 3 Martin, R. 60; Ante, § 78, 180.

with the intention of an instant removal for residence into another State, are to be regulated by the laws of her intended domicil, when no marriage contract is made, or one without any provision in this respect[1]." In the same case, the Court also recognised the general rule; that where the husband and wife have different domicils, the law of that of the husband is to prevail; because the wife is presumed to follow her husband's domicil[2].

§ 199. Under these circumstances, where there is such a general consent of foreign jurists to the doctrine thus recognised in America, it is not, perhaps, too much to affirm, that a contrary doctrine will scarcely hereafter be established; for in England, as well as in America, in the interpretation of other contracts, the law of the place where they are to be performed, has been held to govern[3]. Treated, therefore, as a matter of tacit matrimonial contract, (if it can be so treated), there is the rule of analogy to govern it. And treated as a matter to be governed by the municipal law, to which the parties were, or meant to be, subjected by their future domicil, the doctrine seems equally capable of a solid vindication[4].

---

1 Ford's Curators *v.* Ford, 14 Martin, R. 574, 578.

2 Id. 577.

3 Robinson *v.* Bland, 2 Burr. R. 1077; Lanusse *v.* Barker, 3 Wheaton, R. 101; 4 Cowen, R. 513, n.; 2 Kent, Comm. Lect. 39, p. 459, (3rd edit.); Fergusson on Mar. and Divorce, 341, 342, 395, 396, 416.

4 See Fergusson on Mar. and Divorce, 339—346.

CHAPTER VII.

FOREIGN DIVORCES.

§ 200. Having thus considered the operation of marriage upon the personal capacity and the property of the parties, in the place of its celebration, and in foreign countries, we next come to the consideration of the important subject of divorce[1]. Marriage is not treated as a mere contract between the parties, subject, as to its continuance, dissolution, and effects, to their mere pleasure and intentions; but it is treated as a civil institution, the most interesting and important in its nature of any in society. Upon it the sound morals, the domestic affections, and the delicate relations and duties of parents and of children, essentially depend. On this account, it has, in many nations, the sanction and solemnity of religious obligation superadded to it[2]. And it may be truly said, that Christianity, by giving to it a more affecting and sublime morality, has conferred upon mankind new blessings; and has elevated woman to the rank and dignity of an equal, instead of being a humble companion, or a devoted slave of her husband.

§ 201. It is not my design to enter into any discussion, as to the general right of the legislative power to authorize directly or indirectly a dissolution of the matrimonial state, and to release the parties from all the future obligation thereof. It is deemed by all modern nations to be within the competency of legislation to provide for such a dissolu-

---

[1] See on this subject, 1 Burge, Comm. on Col. and For. Law, Pt. 1, ch. 8, § 1, pp. 640—668; Id. § 2, pp. 668—694.

[2] See Id. pp. 642, 643; Post, § 209.

tion and release, in some form, and for some causes. And there is no doubt, that a divorce regularly obtained, according to the jurisprudence of the country where the marriage is celebrated and where the parties are domiciled, will be held a complete dissolution of the matrimonial contract in every other country[1]. I say where the marriage is celebrated, and where the parties are domiciled; for both ingredients are, or may be material; and the presence of one and the absence of the other may change the legal predicament of the case, according to the jurisprudence of different countries, when the subject comes under consideration therein.

§ 202. The real difficulty is to lay down appropriate principles to govern cases where the marriage is celebrated in one place, and the parties are at the time domiciled in another; where afterwards there is a change of domicil by one party without a similar change by the other; where by the law of the place of celebration, the marriage is indissoluble, or dissoluble only under peculiar circumstances; and where by the law of another place, it is dissoluble for various other causes, and even at the pleasure of the parties. By the law of England, marriage is indissoluble, except by a special act of Parliament[2]. By the law of Scotland, a divorce may be had through the instrumentality of a judicial process, and a decree on account of adultery[3]. By the civil law, an almost unbounded license was allowed to divorces; and wives were often dismissed by their husbands, not only for want of chastity, and for intolerable temper, but for causes of the most frivolous nature[4]. In

---

1 2 Kent, Comm. Lect. 27, pp. 107, 108, (3rd edit.).

2 1 Black. Comm. 440, 441; 1 Burge, Comm. on Col. and For. Law, Pt. 1, ch. 8, § 1, pp. 654—660.

3 Fergusson on Mar. and Divorce, 1, 18; Erskine's Instit. B. 1, tit. 6, § 38, 43; 1 Burge, Comm. on Col. and For. Law, Pt. 1, ch. 8, § 1, pp. 670—680.

4 2 Kent, Comm. Lect. 27, pp. 102, 103, (3rd edit.); 1 Brown, Civ. Law, 89—92; 1 Black. Comm. 441; Justin. Novellæ, 117, ch. 8; Cod.

France, a divorce may be judicially obtained for the cause of adultery, excess, cruelty, or grievous injuries of either party; and in certain cases by mutual and persevering consent[1]. In America, an equal diversity of principle and practice exists. In some States, as in Massachusetts and New York, divorces are grantable by judicial tribunals for the cause of adultery[2]. In other States, divorces are grantable judicially for causes of far inferior grossness and enormity, approaching sometimes almost to frivolousness. In other States, divorces can be pronounced by the legislature only, and for such causes as in its wisdom it may choose from time to time to allow[3].

§ 203. Some of the most embarrassing questions belonging to international jurisprudence arise under the head of marriage and divorce. Suppose, for instance, a marriage celebrated in England, where marriage is indissoluble, and a divorce obtained in Scotland *a vinculo matrimonii*, as it may be for adultery under the laws thereof; will that divorce be operative in England, so as to authorize a new marriage there by either party? Suppose a marriage in Massachusetts, where a divorce may be had for adultery, will a divorce obtained in another State, for a cause unknown to the laws of Massachusetts, be held valid there? If, in each of these cases the divorce would be held invalid in the country where the marriage is celebrated, but it

lib. 5, tit. 17, l. 8; Merlin, Repertoire Divorce, § 2, pp. 149, 150; Pothier, Traité de Mariage, art. 463; Van Leeuwen, Comm. B. 1, ch. 15, § 1—3.

[1] Code Civil, art. 229—233; Id. 275, &c. See in Fergusson on Mar. and Divorce, Appendix, 448, the Prussian Code on the subject of Divorce; among others, incompatibility of temper, endangering life or health, is a good cause of divorce, art. 703.

[2] This also is the law in Holland, in Prussia, and in the Protestant states of Germany, in Sweden, Denmark, and Russia. Fergusson on Mar. and Divorce, 202.

[3] See 2 Kent, Comm. Lect. 27, pp. 106—110; Id. pp. 117, 118, (3rd edit.). See also 1 Burge, Comm. on Col. and For. Law, Pt. 1, ch. 8, § 1, pp. 640—668, where are brought together, in a general review, the laws of different nations on the subject of divorce.

would be held valid where the divorce is obtained, what rule is to govern in other countries as to such divorce? Is it to be deemed valid, or invalid there? Will a new marriage contracted there by either party be good, or be not good? These, and many other perplexing questions may be put; and it is difficult at the present moment to give any answer to them, which would receive the unqualified assent of all nations.

§ 204. Other most perplexing inquiries may grow out of the consideration of the national character of the parties; whether they are both citizens, or subjects, or both foreigners, or one a citizen and the other a foreigner; whether the marriage is celebrated at home, or celebrated abroad; whether the jurisdiction of any court to pronounce a decree of divorce is to be founded upon the national character of the parties, or upon the celebration of the marriage within the territorial jurisdiction, or upon the domicil of the parties within it, or upon the actual presence or temporary residence of one or both of them at the time when the process for divorce is instituted. And if, upon any of these grounds, the jurisdiction is sustained, another not less important inquiry is, whether the law of divorce of the place of the marriage, or that of the place where the suit is instituted, is to be administered by the Court before which the suit is pending.

§ 205. It seems to have been thought that, under the Scottish, law it is not necessary to found a jurisdiction for divorce in the courts of Scotland, that both the parties should at the time of the adultery committed, or at the time of the suit brought, have their actual domicil in Scotland. It seems to be sufficient, that the defendant against whom the suit is brought, is domiciled in that kingdom, so that a citation may be served upon him, and that a divorce under such circumstances may be granted, whether the adultery is committed at home, or in a foreign country. Undoubtedly this doctrine is to be understood with the limitation, that the domicil is real, and not pretended, and that it is *bonâ fide*, and not by collusion between the parties for the mere purpose of maintaining the suit and procuring the divorce[1].

---

[1] Fergusson on Mar. and Divorce, Introd. pp. 16, 17, 18; Id. p. 51; Id. pp. 114, 115, n. St. Aubyn *v.* Obrien, Id. App. p. 276; Id. note B, pp. 363—376; 1 Burge, Comm. on Col. and For. Law, Pt. 1, ch. 8, § 2, pp. 672, 674—679, 688, 689. See M'Carthy *v.* De Caix, cited in a note to 3 Hagg. R. 642, and in Warrender *v.* Warrender, 9 Bligh, R. 141, 142; Conway *v.* Beazley, 3 Hagg. Eccles. R. 639, 645, 646; S. C. reported at large in 2 Russ. & Mylne, 614, 618—620; Tovey *v.* Lindsay, 1 Dow, R. 115, 131, 135—137; S. C. 2 Clarke & Fin. 569, n.; Post, § 216—218. See also Warrender *v.* Warrender, 9 Bligh, R. 89, 144; Post, § 226, a.—226, c. Mr. Chief Justice Gibson, in delivering the opinion of the Supreme Court of Pennsylvania, in a case of divorce, used the following language:—"In constructing our international law of divorce, we naturally look for the materials of it in the jurisprudence of our ancestors, whose institutions are more congenial with our own, than those of their Continental neighbours, and whose process of forensic discussion is usually more exact. But we find an irreconcileable difference betwixt the decisions of the English and of the Scottish Courts. The English judges acknowledge the legitimacy of no jurisdiction which is not founded in the law of divorce at the place of the marriage, if it be an English one; while the Scottish, in the other extreme, are willing to found theirs even on a temporary residence of the complainant in the country of the forum. Of the latter pretension, I shall say little more than that it is, in truth, a usurpation of power, to intermmeddle in the domestic concerns of a neighbour. If a bonâ fide domicil, in the strictest sense of the word, were not essential to jurisdiction, there would be nothing to prevent the exhibition of a libel by a proctor, and without the presence even of the complainant. But the respondent's presence would be more essential still; for a sentence against one who was not subject to the jurisdiction, would be void on the plainest principles of natural law. Moreover, it is not perceived, how the actual presence of both of them could confer jurisdiction of a cause of divorce, which was not, in its inception, subject to the law of the forum. It seems to me the fallacy in the reasoning of the Scottish judges—plausible though it be—consists in their assumption, that divorce is a penalty every where annexed to a breach of the marriage contract, which, like a civil cause of action attendant on the person, may be enforced any where; thus forgetting, that, whether it be a penalty at all depends not on the Scottish law, as an interpreter or avenger, but on the law of the domicil, or else on the lex loci contractûs, which exclusively furnishes the original conditions. The English doctrine, on the other hand, is not more reconcileable to our principle of finite allegiance; for notwithstanding the doubt and manifest inclination of Doctor Lushington in Conway *v.* Beazley, (3 Hagg. Eccles. R. 369), I take it to be settled by Lolley's case, (1 Russ. & Ryan's Crim. Cas. 236) sanctioned in Tovey *v.* Lindsay, (1 Dow, R. 124), by the preponderating

§ 206. A learned Scottish jurist, in remarking upon the embarrassments arising out of this state of the law of Scotland, has made the following powerful observations:—"These conclusions evidently demonstrate, that, unless the remedy in this judicature shall be limited, either to that which the *lex loci contractûs* affords, or to that which the *lex domicilii* taken in the same fair sense as in questions of succession, might give, the public decrees of the only court of Scotland which is competent to pronounce one in such consistorial causes, become proclamations to invite all the married who incline to be free, not in the rest of the British empire alone, but in all countries where marriage is indissoluble by judicial sentence, to seek that object in this tribunal. Adultery and presence within our territory are the only requisites to found the jurisdiction by citation. What

---

weight of Lord Eldon's name, that the dissolution of an English marriage, for any cause whatever, can be effected so as to be acknowledged in that country, only by English authority. It was indeed intimated in Conway *v.* Beazley, that the question of jurisdiction in Lolley's case, perhaps, turned on the difference between temporary and permanent residence; but the report certainly does not indicate it, and besides, the conclusion attained was an unavoidable consequence of the British tenet of perpetual allegiance. Though an English subject acquire a foreign character from a foreign domicil, insomuch as to be treated as an alien for commercial purposes—though he formally renounce his primitive allegiance, and profess another—he is accounted but as a sojourner while abroad; and England, by the dogma of her government, is his home, and his country still. Holding this dogma, it would be strange did she tolerate foreign interference with her domestic relations within her pale. Insisting on jurisdiction of his person, absent or present, she necessarily regards an attempt to change any one of these as an invasion of her sovereignty; and in that aspect, it cannot be denied, that the matter is within her province and her power; for though the status of marriage is juris gentium, the institution is, undoubtedly, a subject of municipal regulation. And it is this perpetual allegiance to the country, its institutions, and its laws—not an indissolubility of the marriage contract from the presumptive will and reservation of the parties—which is the root of the English doctrine. It truly assumes, that marriage is contracted on the basis of the laws, and that these forbid a British subject to dissolve it by the authority of any other country; but take away the law of perpetual allegiance, and you take away the foundation of the presumptive pledge not to submit the duration of it to foreign action." (Dorsey *v.* Dorsey, 1 Chand. Law Reporter, pp. 288, 289).

numbers of foreign parties may accept such an offer, and may even commit the crime here, for the very purpose of affording ground for the action, it is impossible to conjecture. But it is manifest, that, in exact proportion to their number, injury to the morals of this country must follow; and, by setting at nought the laws of other nations, reproach must be brought upon our own; for all foreign parties, while matters stand upon this footing, have it in their power, with the help of evidence as easily provided as it may be disgusting and impure, to oblige the Scotch Consistorial Court to entertain the whole mass of their foreign causes, although there is no fair interest to insist that the municipal law of Scotland shall decide these by its own peculiar rules. To what extent, therefore, the good order of society may eventually be disturbed by this compulsory abuse and pollution of its jurisdiction, in consequence of the doubts and contests that must ensue, as to rights of legitimacy and succession, no calculation can be made[1]."

§ 207. Upon the point, what is the rule of divorce, a learned Scottish judge has made the following remarks, in a case depending before him in judgment[2]:—"With us, the laws relative to divorce are founded on Divine authority. How can a person withdraw himself from obedience to such laws? Are these laws relaxed as to a person domiciled in Scotland, because his marriage is contracted in a country where the law of divorce is different? If two natives of Scotland were married in France or Prussia, according to the laws of those countries, the marriage would no doubt be valid here. But would they be entitled to come into the Commissary Court, and insist for a dissolution *a vinculo matrimonii*, merely because their tempers were not suitable, which, in France, was a ground of divorce, or for any of the numberless reasons for dissolving a marriage, which are allowed by the laws of Prussia? But, if we would not listen

---

1 Fergusson on Mar. and Divorce Introd. pp. 18, 19.

2 Lord Robertson; The cases of Edmondstone, of Levett, and of Forbes, in Fergusson, App. 383; Id. 398. See also Id. 415.

to the *lex loci,* when it facilitates divorce to a degree which our law considers as inconsistent with the best interests of society, and as not warranted by the Divine law, on what principle are we to give effect to the *lex loci,* which prohibits divorce, even *adulterii causâ,* though permitted in this country under the sanction of the Divine law?"

§ 208. These passages are sufficiently significant, as to the intrinsic difficulties of the subject, looking only to the law of divorce of a single country. But, when we look at the almost endless diversities of foreign Continental jurisprudence on the same subject, and the little regard which is habitually paid in that jurisprudence to the decrees of foreign courts, especially in matters which concern persons belonging to any other Continental sovereignty; it ought not to surprise us, that one nation should hold its own law of divorce of universal obligation and authority, and that another should yield it up in favour ofthe law of the domicil of the parties.

§ 209. Upon the continent of Europe there has long existed a known distinction between the Catholics and the Protestants upon the subject of divorce. The former, according to the doctrine of the Romish Church, consider marriage as a sacrament, and in its effects to be governed by the Divine law; and according to their interpretation of that law it was formerly held to be indissoluble[1]. The Protestants, on the contrary, have not generally considered it as a sacrament; but many, if not all of them, have considered it mainly as a civil institution, and subject to the legislative authority, as matter of public police and regulation[2].

---

[1] See Fergusson on Mar and Divorce App. note M. p. 443; Heinecc. Elem. Juris. Germ. tit. 14, § 328—332; Dalrymple *v.* Dalrymple, 2 Hagg. Consist. R. 63, 64, 67; 1 Burge, Comm. on Col. and For. Law, Pt. 1, ch. 8, § 1, pp. 642, 643.

[2] 1 Black. Comm. 433; 2 Hagg. Consist. R. 63, 67; 1 Burge, Comm. on Col. and For. Law, Pt. 1, ch. 8, § 1, pp. 648, 649; Id. pp. 650—653.

§ 210. In Catholic France, we are informed, that until some time after the revolution, (until 1792), marriage was always treated as indissoluble [1]. "Our Church (says Merlin) never approved of divorce, properly so called. It has always regarded it as contrary to the precept, *Quod Deus conjunxit, homo non separet;* What God hath joined together, let not man put asunder [2]. It is, therefore, a perpetual maxim among us, that marriage cannot be dissolved by means of a divorce [3]." Pothier says, Marriage is not dissolved, but by the natural death of one of the parties; while they live it is indissoluble [4]. He adds, that though divorce was permitted by the Christian Emperors, the Church regarded it as prohibited by the Gospel; and that it is not permitted by the French law for any cause whatsoever [5].

§ 211. Protestants have dealt differently by it [6]. In Scotland, which proposes on this subject to be governed exclusively by the Scriptures, divorce is allowed for the Scriptural causes, for adultery, and for wilful desertion [7]. In many other Protestant countries, it is not treated as indissoluble, except for Scriptural causes; but it may be dissolved for other causes. In England, it is never dissolved, except by an act of Parliament, and for adultery [8]. In the

---

1 We have already seen, that by the Code Civil of France, art. 229—233, divorce is allowed in a variety of cases. Upon the restoration of the Royal Family, in 1816, it seems that the existing law of divorce was abolished. Merlin, Repertoire, Divorce, § 4, p. 161. Whether, since the revolution of 1830, it has been reinstated I am not at this moment able to say. See Duranton, Cours de Droit Français, Vol. 14, p. 535, n.

2 Matthew, ch. 19, v. 6.

3 Merlin Repertoire, Divorce, § 3, p. 151.

4 Pothier, Traité du Mariage, n. 462.

5 Id., n. 464.

6 Id., n. 465; Ante, § 209.

7 Erskine's Instit. B. 1, tit. 6, § 43, 44; Fergusson on Mar. and Divorce App. note H. p. 423.

8 Ante, § 202.

Protestant Continental nations of Europe many other causes of divorce are known; and in America, as we have seen, it is generally treated as a matter of civil regulation[1].

§ 212. The conflict of laws on the subject of divorce does not seem to have undergone much discussion among the Continental jurists; at least I have not been able to trace any systematic examination of the subject in those works which are within my reach, and in which almost all other topics of the conflict of laws are so amply treated. The silence of the French jurists may be accounted for, in a great measure, from the uniformity of operation of the Catholic religion and its canons over all the provinces of that kingdom; from the strong probability, that few cases of foreign divorces between French subjects were ever judicially examined; and from the natural conclusion, that, as in their view Christianity made the marriage union indissoluble, no earthly tribunal, either foreign or domestic, could rightfully pronounce a sentence of divorce. The silence of other Catholic countries may be accounted for in the same way. But it is not so easy to assign a satisfactory reason for the omission of the Protestant countries of the continent of Europe to discuss the subject at large. It is highly probable, that in those countries, the parties have been referred to their own matrimonial forum, either to furnish the true rule to expound the contract, or to administer the law of divorce, or for both purposes. This course has not been without example, even in our own country, upon cases bearing a close affinity[2].

§ 213. Merlin has treated the question purely as one arising under the French law, either with reference to the allowance of divorces under the legislation of 1792, or with reference to the prohibition of divorces after the restoration

[1] See 1 Black. Comm. 441; Code Civil of France, art. 229—233; Fergusson on Mar. and Divorce App. note N. p. 448; 2 Kent, Comm. Lect. 27, pp. 95—106, (3rd edit.); Van Leeuwen, Comm. B. 1, ch. 15, § 1—6.

[2] 2 Kent, Comm. Lect. 27, p. 108, (3rd edit.).

of the Bourbons in 1816[3]. He asks the question, whether, in virtue of the new law, (of 1792), which introduced divorce, a marriage celebrated under the old law, which prohibited divorce, could be dissolved; and *vice versa*, whether a marriage celebrated after the new law, which permitted divorce, could be dissolved after the promulgation of the law (of 1816), which prohibited divorce[1]. He says, that if divorce was, as the state of the parties, (*l'état des époux*), the immediate effect and simple consequence of the marriage, the question might be easily answered[2]. Upon this hypothesis, as the state of the parties, the right of divorce would depend altogether upon the law at the time when the marriage was celebrated; because then, in the first case put, the contract must be deemed one for an indissoluble union; and in the second case a contract dissoluble for the proper causes of divorce[3] But he goes on to state, that divorce does not depend upon the intention of the parties, nor is it a consequence or interpretation of it. The legislature, in allowing or prohibiting divorce, has regard only to considerations of public order, and not to the mere contract of the parties. They are not permitted by private agreement to change the laws, or to make a marriage dissoluble or indissoluble in contravention of the policy of the state[4]. He therefore comes to the conclusion, that in a French court, a divorce in such case would be granted or denied, according to the law of France at the time of the suit[5].

§ 214. The question, how a marriage in a foreign country, between French subjects or between foreigners, would be affected by a naturalization or domicil in France, is not here touched. In another work, however, treating of moot questions, he has recently discussed the point. He asks, whether French subjects, married in France since the re-

---

1 Ante, § 210.

2 Merlin, Repertoire, Effet Retroactif, § 3, n. 2, art. 6.

3 Id. p. 19. 4 Ibid. 5 Ibid. 6 Ibid.

pealing act of 1816, who have abandoned their country, and become naturalized in a country where divorce is allowed, could institute a suit there, and dissolve their marriage by a decree of divorce pronounced there by mutual consent. He supports the affirmative, upon the general reasoning by which he has sustained the doctrine in the preceding paragraph[1]. It would seem, however, from his own statement, that this is quite an open question in France.

§ 215. It is to the decisions of the English and Scottish Courts, however, that we must look for the most thorough and exact discussions of this subject. From the different nature of the respective laws of England and Scotland upon the subject of divorce, from their national union, and from their constant, easy, and familiar intercourse, the Courts of both countries have been frequently called upon to pronounce very elaborate judgments respecting the jurisdiction and law of divorce in suits and contestations before them.

§ 216. Several questions on this subject have been recently discussed in the Courts of Scotland. One is, whether a permanent domicil of the parties is indispensable to found a jurisdiction in cases of divorce in the Scottish tribunals; or whether a citation given formally to the party defendant, or left at his dwelling-place in Scotland, after he has been forty days there, is sufficient to subject him to the jurisdiction of those courts in a suit for divorce? In the case in which this question was principally discussed, the marriage was celebrated in England; the husband many years afterwards abandoned his wife, and went to Scotland to reside; and the wife commenced a suit for divorce against her husband in the Scottish Consistorial Court. The Court were of opinion, that as the parties were English, and never cohabited as husband and wife in Scotland, and there was no proof that the husband had taken up a fixed

---

[1] Merlin, Questions de Droit, Divorce, § 11, p. 350; Ante, § 213.

and permanent residence in Scotland, the suit ought to be dismissed upon the ground of a want of jurisdiction. Upon appeal, the decree was reversed by the superior tribunal, and a decree of divorce was ultimately pronounced[1].

§ 217. The leading grounds of the reversal were:—"That the relation of husband and wife is a relation acknowledged *jure gentium;* that the duties, obligations, and rights to redress wrongs incident to that relation, as recognised by the law of Scotland, attach on all married persons living within the territory, and subject to that law, wheresoever their marriage may have been celebrated; that jurisdiction, or the right and duty of the Courts of Scotland to administer justice in such matters, over persons not natural-born subjects, arises from the person sued being resident within the territory at the time of their citation and appearance, or being duly domiciled, and being properly cited accordingly, at the instance of a person having a sufficient interest and title, and proceeding in due form of law[2]." The result of this decision is, that permanent domicil, or the *animus remanendi,* is not necessary to found the jurisdiction. In several other succeeding cases, the Court have followed up the same doctrine, affirming that a temporary residence is sufficient to found the jurisdiction, notwithstanding the permanent jurisdiction of the parties is in another country[3].

§ 218. This doctrine has been maintained by the Scottish judges with great ability and learning, and no one can read their reasoning without admitting its force. It has not, however, been deemed satisfactory in England. In a very important case before the twelve judges, (Lolley's case),

---

1 Utterton *v.* Tewsh, Fergusson on Mar. and Divorce, pp. 1—55; Id. pp 56—67.

2 Ibid. pp. 1, 55, 56; Id. pp. 57—67.

3 Duntze *v.* Levett, Fergusson on Mar. and Divorce, pp. 68—167; Edmonstone *v.* Lockhart, Id. pp. 168—208; Butler *v.* Forbes, Id. pp. 209—225; Kibblewhite *v.* Rowland, Id. pp. 226—248; Gordon *v.* Pye, Id. pp. 276—362; Id. pp. 383—423.

where English subjects were married in England, and afterwards the husband went to Scotland, and procured a divorce *à vinculo* there, and then returned to England, and married another wife, it was decided, that the second marriage was void, and the husband was guilty of bigamy[1]. It has been commonly supposed, that this decision proceeded upon the broad and general ground, that an English marriage is incapable of being dissolved under any circumstances by a foreign divorce; and so it seems to have been understood by Lord Eldon on a later occasion[2]. It has

---

[1] Lolley's Case, 1 Russ. & Ryan's Cr. Cases, 236. See Warrender *v.* Warrender, 9 Bligh, R. 122, 123, 127—130, 139—143.

[2] Tovey *v.* Lindsay, 1 Dow. R. 117, 131. See also M'Carthy *v.* De Caix, 1831, cited 3 Hagg. Eccles. R. 642, n.; S. C. 2 Russ. & Mylne, 614, 620.—Lord Eldon, on this occasion, is reported to have used the following language:—"Here then we have a case, in which both parties were domiciled in England, and then the husband went to Scotland, where it was said he had a domicil by reason of origin, and his being heir of entail of an estate there, and instituted a suit against his wife, which she said did not affect her in England; and, if his domicil was at Durham, the answer would be sufficient, though the rule of law should be admitted, that the domicil of the wife followed that of the husband. But if the jurisdiction, by reason of the original domicil, could be maintained, it would be attended with the most important consequences to the law of marriage. The decision in the second case appeared rather singular, when connected with the decision in the first. They stated, as a main ground of the judgment in the second cause, that the respondent was confessedly domiciled in Scotland, and that therefore they had jurisdiction, which appeared to imply a doubt whether they had jurisdiction in the first cause. If the first cause could be supported, there was no occasion for the second. But, suppose the respondent were domiciled in Scotland at the time of the alleged acts of adultery there, the question still remained, whether in 1810 he could institute a suit against her with effect, unless she had changed her forum likewise, merely upon the ground of the fiction, which had been stated? This was a question of the very highest importance." Lord Brougham, in delivering his own judgment, in M'Carthy *v.* De Caix, 2 Russ. & Mylne, 614, 620, said:—"I find from the note of what fell from Lord Eldon on the present appeal, that his Lordship laboured under considerable misapprehension as to the facts in Lolley's case. He is represented as saying, he will not admit that it is the settled law, and that therefore he will not decide whether the marriage was or not prematurely determined by the Danish divorce. His words are, 'I will not, without other assistance, take upon myself to do so.' Now, if it has not validly and

been suggested, however, that Lord Eldon was not prepared to carry the doctrine to such a length; and certainly there was room in that case for a distinction, founded upon the fact, that neither of the parties at the time of the suit for the divorce in Scotland had a *bonâ fide* domicil there; but

---

by the highest authorities in Westminster Hall been holden, that a foreign divorce cannot dissolve an English marriage, then nothing whatever has been established. For what was Lolley's case? It was a case the strongest possible in favour of the doctrine contended for. It was not a question of civil right, but of felony. Lolley had bonâ fide, and in a confident belief, founded on the authority of the Scotch lawyers, that the Scotch divorce had effectually dissolved his prior English marriage, intermarried in England, living his first wife. He was tried at Lancaster for bigamy, and found guilty; but the point was reserved, and was afterwards argued before all the most learned judges of the day, who, after hearing the case fully and thoroughly discussed, first at Westminster Hall, and then at Serjeant's Inn, gave a clear and unanimous opinion, that no divorce or proceeding in the nature of divorce, in any foreign country, Scotland included, could dissolve a marriage contracted in England; and they sentenced Lolley to seven years' transportation. And he was accordingly sent to the hulks for one or two years; though, in mercy, the residue of his sentence was ultimately remitted. I take leave to say, he ought not to have gone to the hulks at all, because he had acted bonâ fide, though this did not prevent his conviction from being legal. But he was sent notwithstanding, as if to shew clearly, that the judges were confident of the law they had laid down; so that, never was there a greater mistake than to suppose, that the remission argued the least doubt on the judges. Even if the punishment had been entirely remitted, the remission would have been on the ground, that there had been no criminal intent, though that had been done which the law declares to be felony. I hold it to be perfectly clear, therefore, that Lolley's case stands as the settled law of Westminster Hall at this day. It has been uniformly recognised since; and in particular it was repeatedly made the subject of discussion before Lord Eldon himself, in the two appeals of Tovey *v.* Lindsay, in the House of Lords, when I furnished his Lordship with a note of Lolley's case, which he followed in disposing of both those appeals, so far as it affected them. That case then settled two points; first, that no foreign proceeding in the nature of a divorce in an ecclesiastical court could effectually dissolve an English marriage; and, secondly, that a Scotch divorce is not such a proceeding in an ecclesiastical court as to bring the case within the exception in the Bigamy Act, for which nothing less than the sentence of an English ecclesiastical court is sufficient." See also 2 Clarke & Finell. R. 567, n., and Warrender *v.* Warrender, 9 Bligh, R. 89, 121, 124, 127; Id. 141—143; Post, § 219, a.

that they both, at that very time in fact, had their domicil in England, where the marriage was had[1].

§ 219. It has been stated by another learned judge, on a very recent case, that Lolley's case turned upon the very distinction, in point of jurisdiction, between a temporary and fugitive residence for the purpose of a divorce, and a *bonâ fide* change of domicil by the husband and wife, *animo remanendi.* And upon the ground of that distinction, in a case where there was no change of domicil, and the parties were not at any time *bonâ fide* domiciled in Scotland, he declared a Scottish divorce from an English marriage utterly void[2]. The language of his opinion is so important, that it deserves to be quoted at large. "A case, (says he), in which all the parties are domiciled in England, and resort is had to Scotland (with which neither of them have any connexion) for no other purpose than to obtain a divorce *à vinculo,* may properly be decided on principles which would not altogether apply to a case differently circumstanced; as, where, prior to the cause arising, on account of which a divorce was sought, the parties had been *bonâ fide* domiciled in Scotland. Unless I am satisfied that every view of this question had been taken, the Court cannot from the case referred to (Lolley's case) assume it to have been established as a universal rule, that a marriage had in England, and originally valid by the law of England, cannot, under any possible circumstances, be dissolved by the decree of a foreign court. Before I could give my assent to such a doctrine, (not meaning to deny that it may be true), I must have a decision, after argument, upon such a case as I will now suppose, viz., a marriage in England, the parties resorting to a foreign country, becoming ac-

---

1 Lolley's Case, 1 Russ. & Ryan's Cr. Cases, 237; S. C. 2 Clarke & Finell. R. 557, n.

2 Dr. Lushington in Conway *v.* Beazley, 3 Hagg. Eccles. R. 639, 645—647, 653.

tually *bonâ fide* domiciled in that country, and then separated by a sentence of divorce pronounced by the competent tribunal of that country. I am not aware that that point has ever been distinctly raised; and, I think, I may say with certainty, that it has never received any express decision. I believe the course of decision in Scotland up to the present hour has been to consider, that the Scotch Courts have a right to entertain jurisdiction with respect to marriages had in England, after the parties have been residents for a certain period in Scotland, though that period had been infinitely too short to constitute what we should call a legal domicil; and that those courts have proceeded in such cases to divorce *à vinculo*. It is obvious, that many most important differences may arise in cases of this description. Two Scotch persons, married in England, may afterwards go to reside in Scotland. Again: one of the contracting parties may be English, and the other Scotch. If the law of Scotland continue such, as their courts have hitherto held it to be, and if the decision in Lolley's case be of universal application, the issue of the second marriage may be legitimate in Scotland, and illegitimate in England. The son may take the real estate in Scotland, and not the real estate in England. He might possibly be a Scotch peer, and lose his English title, and with it the English estates, the only support of his Scotch peerage[1]."

§ 220. Independent of the point of general jurisdiction, founded upon the fact of the domicil of both the parties, or at least of the party defendant in the suit for a divorce, which for a series of years was most elaborately discussed, and remained in a state of distressing uncertainty, as well as to the effect of a permanent domicil, as to that of a temporary domicil, to found a sentence of divorce, the Scottish Courts have been called on to decide other questions of a broader character, and involving more extensive conse-

---

[1] Conway *v.* Beazley, 3 Hagg. Eccles. R. 645—647, 653.

quences. In the first place, the general question already hinted at, whether an English marriage between English subjects, being indissoluble by the law of England, can under any possible circumstances be dissolved by a decree of divorce in Scotland? In the next place, whether a marriage in Scotland by English subjects, domiciled at the time in England, is dissoluble under any circumstances by a decree of divorce in Scotland? In the next place, whether, in case of a marriage in England, it will make any difference that the parties are both Scotch persons, domiciled in Scotland, or afterwards become *bonâ fide* and permanently domiciled there?

§ 221. Upon these questions, the highest tribunals in Scotland have come to the following conclusions. First, that a marriage between English subjects in England, and indissoluble there, may be lawfully dissolved by the proper Scottish Court for a cause of divorce, good by the law of Scotland, when the parties are within the process and jurisdiction of the Court; or, in other words, that it is not a valid defence against an action of divorce in Scotland for adultery committed there, that the marriage was celebrated in England. Secondly, that a Scotch marriage by persons domiciled at the time in England, is dissoluble in like manner by the proper Scottish Court; or, in other words, that it is not a valid defence, that the parties were domiciled in England when the marriage was celebrated in Scotland. Thirdly, that in case of a marriage in England, it will make no difference that the parties are Scottish persons, domiciled in Scotland, or are afterwards *bonâ fide* and permanently domiciled there; or, in other words, that it is not a valid defence, that the parties are Scottish persons, happening to be in England when their marriage was celebrated, but who afterwards returned to Scotland, and cohabited, and continued domiciled there. The result of these opinions (the unanimous opinions of the judges of the Court of Session) is, that the mere fact of the marriage having been celebrated in England, whether it is between English parties or Scottish parties, or both, is not *per se* a defence against a suit of divorce for adultery committed there[1].

§ 222. The reasoning by which these opinions are maintained, as it may be gathered from comparing the arguments of the different judges, is to the following effect. The relation of husband and wife, wherever it may have been originally constituted, and the parties thereto been connected, is entitled to the same protection and redress from the Courts of justice in Scotland, as to wrongs committed in Scotland, which belong of right to that relation by the law of Scotland[2]. By marrying in England the parties do not become bound to reside for ever in England, or to treat one another in every other country where they may afterward reside, according to the law of England. Their obligation is to fulfil the duties of husband and wife to each other in every country to which they may be called in the course of Providence; and they neither promise, nor have they power to engage, that they will carry the law of England along with them to regulate what the duties and powers shall be which they shall fulfil and exercise, or the redress, which the violation of those duties, or abuse of those powers, may entitle them to in all other countries. All these functions belong to the law of the country where they may eventually reside, and to which they unquestionably contract the duties of obedience and subjection, whenever they enter its territories. Even if it had been the will of the parties by any stipulation, however express, to make the *lex loci* the law of their marriage, it would derive no force from that circumstance. An action of divorce could not be dismissed, because the parties when intermarrying had in the most formal manner renounced the benefit of divorce, and had become bound that their marriage should be indissoluble. It would be no objection to a divorce at

[1] Cases of Edmonstone, Levett, and Forbes, Fergusson on Mar. and Divorce, pp. 383, 392, 393; Id. pp. 114, 115.

[2] Fergusson on Mar. and Divorce, p. 358.

the instance of a Roman Catholic, that his marriage was to him a sacrament, and therefore by its own nature indissoluble. These are all *facta privatorum,* and cannot impede or embarrass the steady, uniform course of the *jus publicum,* which, with regard to the rights and obligations of individuals affected by the three great domestic relations, enacts them from motives of political expediency and public morality; and in nowise confers them as public benefits, resulting from agreements concerning *meum et tuum,* which are capable of being modified and renounced at pleasure[1].

§ 223. If this supposed obligation of indissolubility, resulting from contract, can derive no force from the will of the parties, it cannot derive any from the dictates of the municipal law, where the relation of marriage originated, so as to give it efficacy *ultra territorium;* for the general rule is—*Extra-territorium jus dicenti impune non paretur*[2]. In the fulfilment of ordinary contracts, as to *meum et tuum,* the *lex loci contractûs* forms an implied condition of the contract, and is accordingly adopted as furnishing the means of construing it aright. But this is merely a proceeding in execution of the will of the parties, and not in the least a recognition of the authority of a foreign law. The case is, therefore, quite different where the will of the parties only constitutes, and does not modify the relation or its rights; and where of course the municipal law, deriving nothing from stipulation or agreement, is merely the positive institution of the sovereign, and cannot direct the decisions of foreign courts, or the circumstances occurring within their own jurisdiction. Matrimonial rights and obligations, so far as they are *juris gentium,* admit of no modification by the will of parties; and foreign courts are, therefore, in nowise called upon to inquire after that will, or after any municipal law, to which it may correspond[3].

---

1 Fergusson on Mar. and Divorce, pp. 359, 360; Id. pp. 398, 399, 402.

2 Ante, § 8; Dig. lib. 2, tit. 1, l. 20.

3 Fergusson on Mar. and Divorce, pp. 360, 361, 402, 410, 412, 414.

§ 224. Foreigners equally with natives, while residents, are subject to the law here, and of course are under the protection of the law. The relations in which they stand towards one another, and which have been duly constituted, before they came here, if they are relations recognised by all civilized nations, must be observed; and the obligations created by them must be fulfilled agreeably to the dictates of the law of Scotland. If the law refused to apply its rules to the relation of husband and wife, parent and child, master and servant, among foreigners in this country, Scotland could not be deemed a civilized country; as thereby it would permit a numerous description of persons to traverse it, and violate with utter impunity all the obligations on which the principal comforts of human life depend. If it assumed jurisdiction, but applied not its own rules, but the rules of the law of a foreign country, the supremacy of the law of Scotland within its own territories would be compromised; its arrangements for domestic comfort would be violated, confounded, and perplexed; and the powers of foreign Courts, unknown to its law and constitution, would be usurped and exercised[1]. In every country the laws relative to divorce are considered of the utmost importance, as positive laws affecting the domestic interests of society; and in some places they are treated as of divine authority[2]. A party domiciled here cannot be permitted to import into this country a law peculiar to his own case, and which is in opposition to those great and important public laws, which are held to be connected with the best interests of society[3].

§ 225. That there is great force in this reasoning, cannot well be denied. For a long time it did not obtain any positive sanction in England; but as far as judicial opinions went, they were against the doctrine, that an English mar-

---

[1] Fergusson on Mar. and Divorce, pp. 57, 58, 414, 418.
[2] Id. pp. 398, 402, 403; Ante, § 108, 210.
[3] Id. pp. 399, 400, 412, 418.

riage is dissoluble by a Scottish divorce[1]. The reasoning by which this latter view was sustained, was to the following effect. The law of the place where the marriage is celebrated, furnishes a just rule for the interpretation of its obligations and rights, as it does in the case of other contracts which are held obligatory according to the *lex loci contractûs*[2]. It is not just that one party should be able at his option to dissolve a contract by a law different from that under which it was formed, and by which the other party understood it to be governed. If any other rule than the *lex loci contractûs* is adopted, the law of marriage, on which the happiness of society so mainly depends, must be completely loose and unsettled[3]; and the marriage state, whose indissolubility is so much favoured by Christianity, and by the best interests of society, will become subject to the mere will, and almost to the caprice, of the parties as to its duration. The Courts of the nations, whose laws are most lax upon this subject, will be constantly resorted to for the purpose of procuring divorces; and thus, not only frauds will be encouraged, but the common cause of morality and religion be seriously injured, and conjugal virtue and parental affection become corrupted and debased[4]. Thus, a dissatisfied party might resort to one foreign country where incompatibility of temper is a ground of divorce; or to another which admits of divorce upon even more frivolous pretences, or upon the mere consent of both, or even of one of the parties.

§ 226. In this manner, a nation may find its own inhabitants throwing off all obedience to its own laws and

---

1 Lolley's Case, 1 Russ. & Ryan's Ca. p. 236; Tovey *v.* Lindsay, 1 Dow, R. 124; M'Carthy *v.* De Caix, 3 Hagg. Eccles. R. 642, n.; S. C. 2 Russ. & Mylne, 620; 2 Kent, Comm. Lect. 27, pp. 116, 117, (3rd edit.).

2 Fergusson on Mar. and Divorce, pp. 283—285, 311—313, 318, 325, 335, 339.

3 Id. pp. 283, 298, 312.

4 Id. pp. 103, 104, 283, 284, 318, 319, 353, 355, 356.

institutions, and subverting, by the interposition of a foreign tribunal, its own fundamental policy. Nay, a stronger case may be put of a marriage, deemed, as a sacrament, indissoluble by the public religion of a nation, which is yet dissolved at the will of a foreign nation, in violation of the highest of all human duties, a perfect obedience to the Divine law. There is no solid ground upon which any government can be held to yield up its own fundamental laws and policy, as to its own subjects, in favour of the laws or acts of other countries. Parties contracting in a country where marriage is indissoluble, voluntarily submit to the jurisdiction and laws of that country, if they are foreigners domiciled there. If they are natural subjects, they are bound by the laws of the country in virtue of the general duty of allegiance. Why then should England permit her subjects, by a foreign domicil, to escape from the indissolubility of a marriage contracted in England, and thus permit them to defeat a fundamental policy of the realm[1]? Such is a summary of the reasoning on each side of this vexed question.

§ 226 *a*. The whole subject, however, recently came before the House of Lords in England, upon an appeal from the Court of Session in Scotland, in which the direct question was, whether it was competent for the Scottish Courts to decree a divorce between parties domiciled in Scotland, who were married in England? The facts of the case in substance were these. A Scotchman domiciled in Scotland was married to an Englishwoman in England; and, by their marriage contract, a jointure was secured to her in his Scottish estates. After their marriage they went to Scotland, and resided there a short time, and then returned to England. They afterwards in England executed

---

[1] Mr. Chancellor Kent has given an excellent summary of the reasoning on each side in his Commentaries; 2 Kent, Comm. Lect. 27, pp. 110—117, (3rd edit.). My own duty required me to follow out his doctrine by some additional sketches.

articles of separation, by which a separate maintenance was secured to the wife during her separation. Immediately afterwards the wife went abroad, and had ever since resided abroad. The husband continued to be domiciled in Scotland, where he brought a suit for a divorce against his wife, founded upon the charge of adultery. The preliminary question presented was, whether, even assuming the parties to be domiciled in Scotland, the suit could be maintained in Scotland for a divorce from an English marriage, which was by the law of England indissoluble? The Court of Session affirmed the jurisdiction to decree the divorce; and this decree was upon the appeal confirmed by the House of Lords[1].

§ 226 *b*. Very elaborate judgments were delivered by Lord Brougham and Lord Lyndhurst upon this occasion. The direct point decided was, that the Courts of Scotland had by the laws of Scotland a clear jurisdiction to decree a divorce in such a case between parties actually domiciled in Scotland, notwithstanding the marriage was contracted in England, and that the House of Lords, sitting as a Court of Appeal in a case, coming from Scotland, was bound to administer the law of Scotland. The Court did not, however, decide what effect that divorce would have, or ought to have in England, if it should be brought in question in an English court of justice[2]. Lolley's case was a good deal discussed; and without being overturned as to its professed general doctrine, must be now deemed to be greatly shaken, except as a decision upon its own peculiar circumstances.

§ 226 *c*. But although the general question as to the indissolubility of an English marriage, so far at least as it could arise in England upon a litigation there, was left undecided, Lord Brougham, in delivering his judgment, went into an elaborate examination of the general principles of

---

[1] Warrender *v*. Warrender, 9 Bligh, R. 89; S. C. 2 Clarke & Finell. R. 488.

[2] Ibid.

international law upon this subject. It cannot, therefore, but be acceptable to the learned reader to have in the subjoined note a summary of the reasoning by which this distinguished judge maintained the opinion that, upon principles of public law, a divorce from an English marriage, made by a competent Court of a foreign country, where the parties are domiciled, ought to be deemed in England to dissolve the marriage, and to confer upon the parties all the rights arising from a lawful dissolution[1].

---

[1] His Lordship's reasoning was in substance to the following effect:—"The general principle is denied by no one, that the lex loci is to be the governing rule in deciding upon the validity or invalidity of all personal contracts. This is sometimes expressed, and I take leave to say inaccurately expressed, by saying, that there is a comitas shewn by the tribunals of one country towards the laws of the other country. Such a thing as comitas or courtesy may be said to exist in certain cases, as where the French Courts inquire, how our law would deal with a Frenchman in similar or parallel circumstances, and upon proof of it, so deal with an Englishman in those circumstances. This is truly a comitas, and can be explained upon no other ground; and I must be permitted to say, with all respect for the usage, it is not easily reconcilable to any sound reason. But when the Courts of one country consider the laws of another, in which any contract has been made, or is alleged to have been made, in construing its meaning, or ascertaining its existence, they can hardly be said to act from courtesy, ex comitate, for it is of the essence of the subject-matter to ascertain the meaning of the parties, and that they did solemnly bind themselves; and it is clear that you must presume them to have intended what the law of the country sanctions or supposes; and equally clear, that their adopting the forms and solemnities which that law prescribes, shews their intention to bind themselves; nay, more, is the only safe criterion of their having entertained such an intention. Therefore, the Courts of the country where the question arises, resort to the law of the country where the contract was made, not ex comitate, but ex debito justitiæ; and, in order to explicate their own jurisdiction by discovering that which they are in quest of, and which alone they are in quest of, the meaning and intent of the parties. But whatever may be the foundation of the principle, its acceptance in all systems of jurisprudence is unquestionable. Thus, a marriage, good by the laws of one country, is held good in all others, where the question of its validity may arise. For why? The question always must be, Did the parties intend to contract marriage? And if they did what, in the place they were in, is deemed a marriage, they cannot reasonably, or sensibly, or safely, be considered otherwise than as intending a marriage contract. The laws of each nation lay down the forms and

§ 227. If in any nation the doctrine shall ever be established, in regard to marriages, that the law of the place of

---

solemnities, a compliance with which shall be deemed the only criterion of the intention to enter into the contract. If those laws annex certain qualifications to parties circumstanced in a particular way, or if they impose certain conditions precedent on certain parties, this falls exactly within the same rule; for the presumption of law is in the one case, that the parties are absolutely incapable of the consent required to make the contract, and in the other case, that they are incapable until they have complied with the conditions imposed. I shall only stop here to remark, that the English jurisprudence, while it adopts this principle in words, would not, perhaps, in certain cases which may be put, be found very willing to act upon it throughout. Thus, we should expect that the Spanish and Portuguese Courts would hold an English marriage avoidable between uncle and niece, or brother and sister-in-law, though solemnized under papal dispensation, because it would clearly be avoidable in this country. But I strongly incline to think, that our Courts would refuse to sanction, and would avoid by sentence, a marriage between those relatives contracted in the Peninsula, under dispensation, although beyond all doubt such a marriage would there be valid by the lex loci contractûs, and incapable of being set aside by any proceedings in that country. But the rule extends, I apprehend, no further than to the ascertaining of the validity of the contract, and the meaning of the parties, that is, the existence of the contract and its construction. If, indeed, there go two things under one and the same name in different countries—if that which is called marriage is of a different nature in each—there may be some room for holding, that we are to consider the thing to which the parties have bound themselves, according to its legal acceptation in the country where the obligation was contracted. But marriage is one and the same thing substantially, all the Christian world over. Our whole law of marriage assumes this; and it is important to observe, that we regard it as a wholly different thing, a different status, from Turkish or other marriages among infidel nations; because we clearly never should recognise the plurality of wives, and consequent validity of second marriages, standing the first, which second marriages the laws of those countries authorize and validate. This cannot be put upon any rational ground, except our holding the infidel marriage to be something different from the Christian, and our also holding Christian marriage to be the same every where. Therefore, all that the Courts of one country have to determine is, whether or not the thing called marriage, that known relation of persons, that relation which those Courts are acquainted with, and know how to deal with, has been validly contracted in the other country where the parties professed to bind themselves. If the question is answered in the affirmative, a marriage has been had; the relation has been constituted; and those Courts will deal with the rights of the parties under it, according to the principles of the municipal law which they administer. But it is said,

its actual celebration shall prevail, not only as to its original validity, but also as to its mode of dissolution, some other

---

that what is called the essence of the contract must also be judged of according to the lex loci; and as this is a somewhat vague, and for its vagueness, a somewhat suspicious proposition, it is rendered more certain by adding that dissolubility or indissolubility is of the essence of the contract. Now I take this to be really petitio principii. It is putting the very question under discussion into another form of words, and giving the answer in one way. There are many other things which may just as well be reckoned of the essence as this. If it is said, that the parties marrying in England must be taken, all the world over, to have bound themselves to live, until death or an act of Parliament them 'do part;' why shall it not also be said, that they have bound themselves to live together on such terms, and with such mutual personal rights and duties, as the English law recognises and enforces? Those rights and duties are just as much of the essence as dissolubility or indissolubility; and yet all admit—all must admit—that persons married in England and settled in Scotland, will be entitled only to the personal rights which the Scotch law sanctions, and will only be liable to perform the duties which the Scotch law imposes. Indeed, if we are to regard the nature of the contract in this respect as defined by the lex loci, it is difficult to see why we may not import from Turkey into England a marriage of such a nature, as that it is capable of being followed by and subsisting with another, polygamy being there of the essence of the contract. The fallacy of the argument, 'that indissolubility is of the essence,' appears plainly to be this: it confounds incidents with essence; it makes the rights under a contract, or flowing from and arising out of it, parcel of the contract; it makes the mode in which judicatures deal with those rights, and with the contract itself, part of the contract; instead of considering, as in all soundness of principle we ought, that the contract and all its incidents, and the rights of the parties to it, and the wrongs committed by them respecting it, must be dealt with by the Courts of the country where the parties reside, and where the contract is to be carried into execution. But at all events this is clear, and it seems decisive of the point, that if on some such ground as this a marriage indissoluble by the lex loci is to be held indissoluble every where, so, conversely, a marriage dissoluble by the lex loci must be held every where dissoluble. The one proposition is in truth identical with the other. Now, it would follow from hence, or rather it is the same proposition, that a marriage contracted in Scotland, where it is dissoluble by reason of adultery, or of non-adherence, is dissoluble in England, and that at the suit of either party. Therefore, a wife married in Scotland might sue her husband in our courts for adultery, or for absenting himself four years, and ought to obtain a divorce à vinculo matrimonii. Nay, if the marriage had been solemnized in Prussia, either party might obtain a divorce on the ground of incompatibility of temper; and if it had been solemnized in France during the earlier period of the revolu-

interesting questions will still remain for decision. In the first place, will any foreign Court have a right to entertain

---

tion, the mere consent of the parties ought to suffice for dissolving it here. Indeed, another consequence would follow from this doctrine of confounding with the nature of the contract, that which is only a matter touching the jurisdiction of the courts, and their power of dealing with the rights and duties of the parties to it. If there were a country in which marriage could be dissolved without any judicial proceeding at all, merely by the parties agreeing in païs to separate, every other country ought to sanction a separation had in païs there, and uphold a second marriage contracted after such a separation. It may safely be asserted that so absurd a proposition never could for a moment be entertained; and yet it is not like, but identical with the proposition upon which the main body of the Appellant's argument rests, that the question of indissoluble or dissoluble must be decided in all cases by the lex loci. Hitherto we have been considering the contract as to its nature and solemnities, and examining how far, being English, and entered into with reference only to England, it could be dissolved by a Scotch sentence of divorce. But the circumstance of parties belonging to one country marrying in another (which is the case at bar) presents the question in another light. In personal contracts, much depends upon the parties having regard to the country where it is to be acted under, and to receive its execution—upon their making the contract—with a view to its execution in that country. The marriage contract is emphatically one which parties make with an immediate view to the usual place of their residence. An Englishman marrying in Turkey, contracts a marriage of an English kind, that is, excluding plurality of wives; because he is an Englishman, and only residing in Turkey, and under the Mahomedan law accidentally and temporarily, and because he marries with a view of being a married man, and having a wife in England, and for English purposes; consequently, the incidents and effects, nay, the very nature and essence (to use the languge of the Appellant's argument) must be ascertained by the English, and not by the Turkish law. So of an Englishman marrying in Prussia, where incompatible temper, that is, disagreement, may dissolve the contract. As he marries with a view to English domicil, his contract will be judged by English law, and he cannot apply for a divorce here upon the ground of incompatible tempers. In like manner, a domiciled Scotchman may be said to contract not an English, but a Scotch marriage, though the consent wherein it consists may be testified by English solemnities. The Scotch parties, looking to residence and rights in Scotland, may be held to regard the nature and incidents and consequences of the contract, according to the law of that country, their home; a connexion formed for cohabitation, for mutual comfort, protection, and endearment, appears to be a contract having a most peculiar reference to the contemplated residence of the wedded pair; the home, where they are to fulfil their mutual promises, and perform those duties which were the objects of the union; in

jurisdiction to decree a divorce for causes justified by the law of the matrimonial domicil? Will the like right exist

---

a word, their domicil; the place so beautifully described by the civilian—'Locus, ubi quisque larem suum posuit sedemque fortunarum suarum, unde cum proficiscitur peregrinare videtur, quo cum revertitur redire domum.' It certainly may well be urged, both with a view to the general question of lex loci, and especially in answering the argument of the alleged essential quality of indissolubility, that the parties to a contract like this must be held emphatically to enter into it with a reference to their own domicil and its laws; that the contract assumes, as it were, a local aspect; but that, at any rate, if we infer the nature of any mutual obligation from the presumed intentions of the parties, and if we presume those intentions from supposing that the parties had a particular system of laws in their eye, (the only foundation of the argument for the Appellant), there is fully more reason to suppose they had the law of their own home in their view, where they purposed to live, than the law of the stranger, under which they happened for the moment to be. Suppose we take now another, but a very obvious and intelligible view of the subject, and regard the divorce not as a remedy given to the injured party, by freeing him from the chain that binds him to a guilty partner, but as a punishment inflicted upon crime, for the purpose of preventing its repetition, and thus keeping public morals pure. The language of the Scotch acts plainly countenances this view of the matter, and we may observe how strongly it bears upon the present question. No one can doubt that every state has the right to visit offences with such penalties as to its legislative wisdom shall seem meet. At one time adultery was punishable capitally in England; it is so in certain cases still by the letter of the Scotch law. Whoever committed it must have suffered that punishment, had the law been enforced, and without regard to the marriage of which he had violated the duties, having been contracted abroad. Indeed, in executing such statutes, no one ever heard of a question being raised as to where the contract had been made. Suppose, again, that the proposition frequently made in modern times were adopted, and adultery were declared to be a misdemeanor, could any one, tried for it either here or in Scotland, set up in his defence, that to the law of the country where he was married there was no such offence known? In like manner, if a disruption of the marriage tie is the punishment denounced against the adulterer for disregarding its duties, no one can pretend that the tie being declared indissoluble by the laws of the country where it was knit could afford the least defence against the execution of the law declaring its dissolution to be the penalty of the crime. Whoever maintains that the Scotch Courts are to take cognizance of the English law of indissolubility, when called upon to inflict the penalty of divorce, must likewise be prepared to hold that, in punishing any other offence, the same courts are to regard the laws of the state where the culprit was born, or where part of the transaction passed; that, for example, a

where no divorce is grantable by the *lex loci* for a similar cause in case of a domestic marriage? For instance, could a

---

forgery being committed on a foreign bill of exchange, the punishment awarded by the foreign law is to regulate the visitation of the offence under the law of Scotland. It may safely be asserted, that no instance whatever can be given of the criminal law of any country being made to bend to that of any other in any part of its administration. When the Roman citizen carried abroad with him his rights of citizenship, and boasted that he could plead in all the courts of the world, 'Civis Romanus sum,' his boast was founded, not on any legal principle, but upon the fact that his barbarian countrymen had overrun the world with their arms, reduced all laws to silence, and annihilated the independence of foreign legislatures. Their orators regarded this very plea as the badge of universal slavery, which their warriors had fixed upon mankind. But if any foreigner had come to Rome, and committed a crime punishable with loss of civil rights, he would in vain have pleaded in bar of the capitis diminutio, that citizenship was indelible and indestructible in the country of his birth. The lex loci must needs govern all criminal jurisdiction, from the nature of the thing and the purpose of that jurisdiction. How then can we say that, when the Scotch law pronounces the dissolution of a marriage to be the punishment of adultery, the Scotch Courts can be justified in importing an exception in favour of those who had contracted an English marriage,—an exception created by the English law, and to the Scotch law unknown? But it may be said, that the offence being committed abroad, and not within the Scotch territory, prevents the application to it of the Scotch criminal law. To this it may, however, be answered, that where a person has his domicil in a given country, the laws of that country to which he owes allegiance, may visit, even criminally, offences committed by him out of its territory. Of this we have many instances in our own jurisprudence. Murder and treason committed by Englishmen abroad are triable in England, and punishable here. Nay, by the bill which I introduced in 1811, and which is constantly acted upon, British subjects are liable to be convicted of felony for slave-trading in whatever part of the world committed by them. It would, no doubt, be going far to hold the wife criminally answerable to the law of Scotland, in respect of her legal domicil being Scotch. But we are here not so much arguing to the merits of this case, which has abundant other ground to rest upon, as to the general principle; and at any rate the argument would apply to the case most frequently mooted, of English married parties living temporarily in Scotland, and adultery being there committed by one of them. To such a state of facts the whole argument now adduced is applicable in its full force; and without admitting that application, I do not well see how we can hold that the Scotch legislature ever possessed that supreme power, which is absolutely essential to the very nature and existence of a legislature. If we deny this application, we truly admit that the Scottish parliament had no right to

Consistory Court of England entertain a suit for a divorce *a vinculo* for the cause of adultery in case of a Scottish mar-

---

punish the offence of adultery by the penalty of divorce. Nay, we hold, that English parties had a right to violate the Scotch criminal law with perfect impunity in one essential particular; for, suppose no other penalty had been provided by the Scotch law, except divorce, all English offenders against that law must go unpunished. Nay, worse still, all Scotch parties, who chose to avoid the punishment, had only to marry in England, and then the law, the criminal law, of their own country became inoperative. The gross absurdity of this strikes me as bearing directly upon the argument, and as greater than that of any consequences which I remember to have seen deduced from almost any disputed position. It may further be remarked, that this argument applies equally to the case if we admit that the Scotch divorce is invalid out of Scotland, and consequently, that it stands well with even the principles of Lolley's case. In order to dispose of the present question, it is not at all necessary on the one side to support, or on the other to impeach, the authority of Lolley's case, or of any other which may have been determined in England upon that authority. This ought to be steadily borne in mind. The resolution in Lolley's case was, that an English marriage could not be dissolved by any proceeding in the courts of any other country, for English purposes; in other words, that the courts of this country will not recognise the validity of the Scotch divorce, but will hold the divorced wife dowable of an English estate, the divorced husband tenant thereof by the courtesy, and either party guilty of felony by contracting a second marriage in England. Upon the force and effect of such a divorce in Scotland, and for Scotch purposes, the judges gave, and indeed could give, no opinion; and as there would be nothing legally impossible in a marriage being good in one country, which was prohibited by the law of another, so, if the conflict of the Scotch and English law be complete and irreconcilable, there is nothing legally impossible in a divorce being valid in the one country, which the courts of the other may hold to be a nullity. Lolley's case, therefore, cannot be held to decide the present, perhaps not even to affect it in principle. In another point of view it is inapplicable; for, though the decision was not put upon any special circumstance, yet, in fairly considering its application, we cannot lay out of view that the parties were not only married, but really domiciled in England, and had resorted to Scotland for the manifest purpose of obtaining a temporary and fictitious domicil there, in order to give the Scotch Courts jurisdiction over them, and enable them to dissolve their marriage; whereas, here, the domicil of the parties is Scotch, and the proceeding is bonâ fide taken by the husband in the courts of his own country, to which he is amenable, and ought to have free access, and no fraud upon the law of any other country is practised by the suit. It must be added, that in Lolley's case, the English marriage had been contracted by English parties, without any view to the execution of the contract at any time in Scotland; whereas, the marriage now in question was had by a Scotchman and a woman, whom the contract made

riage? Or in such cases, is the remedy to be exclusively pursued in the domestic forum of the marriage? Whoever

---

Scotch, and therefore may be held to have contemplated an execution and effects in Scotland. But although for these reasons the support of my opinion does not require that I should dispute the law in Lolley's case, I should not be dealing fairly with this important question if I were to avoid touching upon that subject; and as no decision of this House has ever adopted that rule, or assumed its principle for sound, and acted upon it, I am entitled here to express the difficulty which I feel in acceding to that doctrine—a difficulty which much deliberation and frequent discussion with the greatest lawyers of the age, I might say both of this and of the last age—has not been able to remove from my mind. If no decision had ever been pronounced in this country, recognising the validity of Scotch marriages between English parties going to Scotland, with the purpose of escaping from the authority of the English law, I should have felt it much easier to acquiesce in the decision of which I am speaking; for then it might have been said, consistently enough, that whatever may be the Scotch marriage law among its own subjects, and for the government of Scotch questions, ours is in irreconcilable conflict with it, and we cannot permit the positive enactments of our statute-book, and the principles of our common law, to be violated or eluded by merely crossing a river, or an ideal boundary line. Nor could anything have been more obvious than the consistency of those who, holding that no unmarried parties, incapable of marrying here, can, in fraud of our law, contract a valid marriage in Scotland, by going there for an hour, should also hold the cognate doctrine that no married parties can dissolve an English marriage, indissoluble here, by repairing thither for six weeks. But upon this firm ground, the decision of all the English Courts have long since prevented us from taking our stand. They have held, both the Consistorial Judges in Compton *v.* Bearcroft, and those of the Common Law in Ilderton *v.* Ilderton, the doctrine uniformly recognised in all subsequent cases, and acted upon daily by the English people, that a Scotch marriage, contracted by English parties in the face and in fraud of the English law, is valid to all intents and purposes, and carries all the real and all the personal rights of an English marriage, affecting in its consequences land and honours, and duties and privileges, precisely as does the most lawful and solemn matrimonial contract entered into among ourselves, in our own churches, according to our ritual, and under our own statutes. It is quite impossible, after this, to say that we can draw the line, and hold a foreign law, which we acknowledge all-powerful for making the binding contract, to be utterly impotent to dissolve it. Were a sentence of the Scotch Court in a declarator of marriage to be given in evidence here, it would be conclusive that the parties were man and wife, and no exception could be taken to the admissibility, or the effect of the foreign evidence, upon the ground of the parties having been English, and repaired to Scotland for the purpose of escaping the provisions of the English law. A similar sen-

shall diligently consider these questions, will not find them without serious embarrassment. They are incidentally

---

tence of the same Court, declaring the marriage to be dissolved by the same law of Scotland, is now supposed to be given in evidence between parties who had married in England. Can it, in any consistency of reason, be objected to the reception, or to the force of this sentence, that the contract had been made, and the parties had resided here? In what other contract of a nature merely personal—in what other transaction between men—is such a rule ever applied—such an arbitrary and gratuitous distinction made—such an exception raised to the universal position, that things are to be dissolved by the same process whereby they are bound together; or rather, that the tie is to be loosened by reversing the operation which knit it, but reversing the operation according to the same rules? What gave force to the ligament? If a contract for sale of a chattel is made, or an obligation of debt is incurred, or a chattel is pledged in one country, the sale may be annulled, the debt released, and the pledge redeemed by the law and by the forms of another country in which the parties happen to reside, and in whose Courts their rights and obligations come in question, unless there was an express stipulation in the contract itself against such avoidance, release, or redemption. But at any rate, this is certain, that if the laws of one country and its courts recognise and give effect to those of another, in respect of the constitution of any contract, they must give the like recognition and effect to those same foreign laws when they declare the same kind of contract dissolved. Suppose a party forbidden to purchase from another by our equity, as administered in the Courts of this country (and we have some restraints upon certain parties, which come very near prohibition); and suppose a sale of chattels by one to another party, standing in this relation towards each other, should be effected in Sctoland, and that our Courts here should (whether right or wrong) recognise such a rule, because the Scotch law would affirm it; surely it would follow, that our Courts must equally recognise a rescission of the contract of sale in Scotland by any act which the Scotch law regards as valid to rescind it, although our own law may not regard it as sufficient. Suppose a question to arise in the Courts of England respecting the execution of a contract thus made in this country, and that the objection of its invalidity were waived for some reason; if the party resisting its execution were to produce either a sentence of a Scotch Court, declaring it rescinded by a Scotch matter done in païs, or were merely to produce evidence of the thing so done, and proof of its amounting by the Scotch law to a rescission of the contract—I apprehend that the party relying on the contract, could never be heard to say, 'The contract is English, and the Scotch proceeding is impotent to dissolve it.' The reply would be, 'Our English Courts have (whether right or wrong) recognised the validity of a Scotch proceeding to complete the obligation, and can no longer deny the validity of a similar but reverse proceeding to dissolve it—unumquodque dissolvitur eodem modo, quo colligatur.' Suppose,

treated in the Scottish decisions already alluded to; and the reasoning on each side is worthy of an exact perusal[1].

for another example, (which is the case), that the law of this country precluded an infant, or a married woman, from borrowing money in any way, or from binding themselves by deed, and that in another country those obligations could be validly incurred; it is probable that our law and our Courts would recognise the validity of such foreign obligations. But suppose a feme covert had executed a power, and conveyed an interest under it to another feme covert in England, could it be endured, that where the donee of the power produced a release under seal from the feme covert in the same foreign country, a distinction should be taken, and the Court here should hold that party incapable of releasing the obligation? Would it not be said, that our Courts, having decided the contract of a feme covert to be binding when executed abroad, must, by parity of reason, hold the discharge or release of the feme covert to be valid if it be valid in the same foreign country? Nor can any attempt succeed in this argument, which rests upon distinctions taken between marriage and other contracts, on the ground that its effects govern the enjoyment of real rights in England, and that the English law alone can regulate the rights of landed property. For, not to mention that a Scotch marriage between English parties gives English honours and estates to its issue which would have been bastard, had the parties married, or pretended to marry in England; all personal obligations may in their consequences affect real rights in England. Nor does a Scotch divorce, by depriving a widow of dower or arrears of pin-money, charged on English property, more immediately affect real estate here than a bond or a judgment released in Scotland according to Scotch forms, discharges real estate of a lien, or than a bond executed, or indeed a simple contract debt incurred in Scotland, eventually and consequentially charges English real estate. It appears to me quite certain, that those who decided Lolley's case, did not look sufficiently to the difficulty of following out the principle of the rule which they laid down. At first sight, on a cursory survey of the question, there seems no impediment in the way of a judge who would keep the English marriage contract indissoluble in Scotland, and yet allow a Scotch marriage to have validity in England; for it does not immediately appear how the dissolution and the constitution of the contract should come in conflict, though diametrically opposite principles are applied to each. But only mark how that conflict arises, and how, in fact and in practice, it must needs arise, as long as the diversity of the rules applied is maintained. When English parties are divorced in Scotland, it seems easy to say, 'We give no validity to this proceeding in England, leaving the Scotch law to deal with it in that country; and with its awards we do not in anywise interfere.' But the time speedily arrives when we can no longer refuse to interfere, and then see

[1] See Fergusson on Mar. and Divorce, App. pp. 383—422.

The attempt to engraft foreign remedial justice upon domestic institutions, has always been found extremely

---

the inextricable confusion that instantly arises, and involves the whole subject. The English parties are divorced—they return to England, and one of them marries again; that party is met by Lolley's case, and treated as a felon. So far all is smooth. But what if the second marriage is contracted in Scotland? and what if the issue of that marriage claims an English real estate by descent, or a widow demands her dower? Lolley's case will no longer serve the purpose of deciding the rights of the parties; for Lolley's case is confined to the effects of the Scotch divorce in England, and professes not to touch, as indeed they who decided it had no authority to touch, the validity of that divorce in Scotland. Then, the marriage being Scotch, the lex loci must prevail by the cases of Compton *v.* Bearcroft, and Ilderton *v.* Ilderton. All its consequences to the wife and issue must be dealt with by the English Courts, and the same judge who, sitting under a commission of gaol delivery, has in the morning sent Mr. Lolley to the hulks for felony, because he re-married in England, and the divorce was insufficient; sitting at Nisi Prius in the afternoon, must give the issue of Mr. Lolley's second marriage an estate in Yorkshire, because she re-married in Scotland, and must give it on the precise ground that the divorce was effectual. Thus the divorce is both valid and nugatory, not according to its own nature, or the law of any one state, but according to the accident, whether a transaction which follows upon it, and does not necessarily occur at all, chanced to take place in one part of the island or in the other; and yet the felony of the husband depended entirely upon his not having been divorced validly in Scotland, and not at all upon his not being divorced validly in England; and the title of the wife's issue to the succession, or of herself to dower, depends wholly upon the same husband having been validly divorced in that same country of Scotland. Nor will it avail to contend, that the parties marrying in Scotland after a Scotch divorce, is in fraud of the English rule, as laid down in that celebrated case. It may be so; but it is not more in fraudem legis Anglicanæ, than the marriage was in Compton *v.* Bearcroft, which yet has been held good in all our Courts. Neither will it avail to argue, that the indissoluble nature of the English marriage prevents those parties from marrying again in Scotland, as well as in England; for the rule in Lolley's case has no greater force in disqualifying parties from marrying in Scotland, where that is not the rule of law, than the English Marriage Act has in disqualifying infants from marrying without banns published, and yet these may, by the law of England, go and marry validly in Scotland. Indeed, if there be any purely personal disqualification or incapacity caused by the law, and which, more than any other, may be said to travel about with the party, it is that which the law raises upon a natural status, as that of infancy, and fixes on those who, by the order of nature itself, are in that condition, and unable to shake it off, or by an hour to accelerate its termination. If, in a matter

difficult; and, as we shall hereafter see, has led to the conclusion, that the safest and best rule is to give remedies

---

confessedly not clear, and very far from being unincumbered with doubt and difficulty, we find that manifest and serious inconvenience is sure to result from one view, and very little in comparison from adopting the opposite course, nothing can be a stronger reason for taking the latter. Now, surely it strikes every one, that the greatest hardships must occur to parties, the greatest embarrassment to their rights, and the utmost inconvenience to the Courts of justice in both countries, by the rule being maintained, as laid down in Lolley's case. The greatest hardship to parties—for what can be a greater grievance, than that parties living bonâ fide in England, though temporarily, should either not be allowed to marry at all during their residence here, or if they do, and afterwards return to their own country, however great its distance, that they must be deprived of all remedy in case of misconduct, however aggravated, unless they undertake a voyage back to England, ay, and unless they can comply with the parliamentary forms in serving notices;—the greatest embarrassment to their rights—for what can be more embarrassing than that a person's status should be involved in uncertainty, and should be subject to change its nature, as he goes from place to place; that he should be married in one country, and single, if not a felon, in another; bastard here, and legitimate there?—the utmost inconvenience to the Courts—for what inconvenience can be greater, than that they should have to regard a person as married for one purpose, and not for another;—single and a felon, if he marries a few yards to the southward—lawfully married, if the ceremony be performed a few yards to the north;—a bastard, when he claims land—legitimate, when he sues for personal succession;—widow, when she demands the chattels of her husband—his concubine, when she counts as dowable of his land? It is in vain to remind us of the opportunity which a strict adherence to the lex loci, with respect to dissolution of the contract, would give to violators of our English marriage law. This objection comes too late. Before the validity of Scotch marriages had been supported by decisions too numerous and too old for any question, this argument ab inconveniente, might have been urged and set against those other reasons which I have adduced, drawn from the same consideration. But we have it now firmly established, as the law of the land, and daily acted upon by persons of every condition, that, though the law of England incapacitates parties from contracting marriage here, they may go for a few minutes to the Scotch border, and be married as effectually as if they had no incapacity whatever in their own country, and then return, after eluding the law, to set its prohibitions at defiance, without incurring any penalty, and to obtain its aid without any difficulty in securing the enjoyment of all the rights incident to the married state. Surely there is neither sense nor consistency in complaining of the risk, infraction, or evasion arising to the English law from supporting Scotch divorces, after having thus given to the Scotch marriages the power of eluding, and break-

only to the extent, and in the manner which the *lex loci* justifies and approves[1].

§ 228. In America, questions respecting the nature and effect of foreign divorces upon domestic marriages, and *vice versâ*, have, as might be expected, not unfrequently been under discussion in our Courts. In Massachusetts, in some

---

ing and defying that law for so many years. I have now been commenting upon Lolley's Case on its own principle; that is, regarding it as merely laying down a rule for England, and prescribing how a Scotch divorce shall be considered in this country, and dealt with by its Courts. I have felt this the more necessary; because I do not see, for the reasons which have occasionally been adverted to in treating the other argument, how, consistently with any principle, the Judges who decided the case, could limit its application to England, and think that it did not decide also on the validity of the divorce in Scotland. They certainly could not hold the second English marriage invalid and felonious in England, without assuming that the Scotch divorce was void even in Scotland. In my view of the present question, therefore, it was fit to shew that the Scotch Courts have a good title to consider the principle of Lolley's case erroneous, even as an English decision. This, it is true, their Lordships have not done; and the judgment now under appeal is rested upon the ground of the Scotch divorce being sufficient to determine the marriage-contract in Scotland only. I must now observe, that, supposing (as may fairly be concluded), Lolley's case to have decided that the divorce is void in Scotland, there can be no ground whatever for holding, that it is binding upon the Scotch Courts on a question of Scotch law. If the cases and the authorities of that law are against it, the learned persons who administer the system of jurisprudence, are not bound to regard—nay, they are not entitled to regard—an English decision, framed by English Judges upon an English case, and devoid of all authority beyond the Tweed. Now, I have no doubt at all, that the Scotch authorities are in favour of the jurisdiction, and support the decision under appeal. But I must premise, that, unless it could be shewn that they were the other way, my mind is made up with respect to the principle, and I should be for affirming on that ground of principle alone, if precedent or dicta did not displace the argument. The principle I hold so clear, upon grounds of general law, that the proof is thrown, according to my view, upon those who would shew the Scotch law to be the other way." I have given his Lordship's reasoning at large; because it seemed difficult to omit particular passages which have been already cited, or will be cited hereafter in other connexions, without impairing its true force. Ante, § 115; Post, § 259 b.

[1] See in English Law Magazine, vol. 6, p. 32, a review of the English law as to divorces. See on this very point the judgment of Lord Brougham in Warrender *v.* Warrender, 9 Bligh, R. 115—118, cited ante, § 226 c, note.

early cases, the Supreme Court refused to interfere and grant a divorce, where the parties lived in another State at the time the adultery was charged to have been committed, and the libellant had since that time removed into the State. These decisions seem mainly to have proceeded upon the construction of the local statutes, which conferred jurisdiction upon the Court in matters of divorce; but it was admitted that the State to which the parties belonged, had jurisdiction, and could exercise it if it appeared expedient[1]. In a later case, where a marriage, celebrated in Massachusetts, had been dissolved in Vermont, upon a suit by the husband for a divorce, for the cause of extreme cruelty of his wife, (a cause inadmissible by the laws of Massachusetts to dissolve a marriage), it appearing that the parties had not at the time any permanent domicil in Vermont, but that the husband had gone there for the purpose of obtaining a divorce, the divorce was held a mere nullity, upon the ground that there was no real change of domicil. "If," said the Court, "we were to give effect to this decree, we should permit another State to govern our citizens, in direct contravention of our own statutes; and this can be required by no rule of comity[2]."

§ 229. In another case, the general question came before the Court, whether a marriage, celebrated in Massachusetts, could be dissolved by a decree of divorce of the proper State Court of Vermont, both parties being at the time *boná fide* domiciled in that State, and the cause of divorce being such as would not authorize a divorce *a vinculo* in Massachusetts. The Court decided in the affirmative, upon the ground that the law of the actual domicil must regulate the right. The reasoning of the Court was to the following effect:—"Regulations on the subject of marriage and

---

1 Hopkins *v.* Hopkins, 3 Mass. R. 158; Carter *v.* Carter, 6 Mass. R. 268.

2 Inhabitants of Hanover *v.* Turner, 14 Mass. R. 227, 231. See also Barber *v.* Root, 10 Mass. R. 265, 266.

divorce are rather parts of the criminal, than of the civil code, and apply not so much to the contract between the individuals, as to the personal relations resulting from it, and to the relative duties of the parties to their standing and conduct in the society of which they are members; and these are regulated with a principal view to the public order and economy, the promotion of good morals, and the happiness of the community. A divorce, for example, in a case of public scandal and reproach, is not a vindication of the contract of marriage, or a remedy to enforce it; but a species of punishment which the public have placed in the hands of the injured party to inflict, under the sanction and with the aid of the competent tribunal, operating as a redress of the injury, when the contract having been violated, the relation of the parties, and their continuance in the married state, have become intolerable or vexatious to them, and of evil example to others. The *lex loci*, therefore, by which the conduct of married persons is to be regulated, and their relative duties are to be determined, and by which the relation itself is to be in certain cases annulled, must be always referred, not to the place where the contract was entered into, but where it subsists for the time—where the parties have had their domicil, and have been protected in the rights resulting from the marriage contract, and especially where the parties are or have been amenable for any violation of the duties incumbent upon them in that relation[1]."

---

[1] Barber *v.* Root, 10 Mass. R. 265. By the Revised Statutes of Massachusetts, 1835, ch. 76, § 9, 10, 11, it is declared, that no divorce shall be decreed for any cause, if the parties have never lived together as husband and wife in this State. No divorce shall be decreed for any cause which shall have occurred in any other state or country, unless the parties had, before such cause occurred, lived together as husband and wife in this State. No divorce shall be decreed for any cause which shall have occurred in any other state or country, unless one of the parties was then living in this State. It is also by another section (§ 39) of the same chapter, provided, that when an inhabitant of this State shall go into any other state or country, in order to obtain a divorce for any cause which had occurred here, and whilst the parties resided here, or for any cause which would not authorize a divorce

§ 229 *a.* In another case, the question as to the jurisdiction to found a suit for a divorce also arose; and it was held, that ordinarily such a suit cannot be entertained, unless the parties are *bonâ fide* domiciled in the State in which the suit is brought; and that for this purpose the domicil of the husband must be treated as the domicil of his wife. Hence, if a husband should *bonâ fide* remove from Massachusetts to another State with his wife, and there a good cause for a divorce by law should occur, a suit could not be maintained therefor in the Courts of Massachusetts[1]. But the Court thought that cases might arise in which the change of domicil of the husband might not deprive the wife of her right to sue for a divorce in the State where they originally lived together[2].

---

by the laws of this State, a divorce so obtained shall be of no force or effect in this State.

[1] Harteau *v.* Harteau, 14 Pick. R. 181.

[2] Ibid.—On this occasion Mr. Chief Justice Shaw, in delivering the opinion of the Court, said:—" Much obscurity has, we think, been thrown on the subject by confounding the two questions, which are essentially different, viz.—1. In what cases a party is entitled to claim a divorce; and 2. In what county the libel should be brought. As it is a right conferred by statute, the one question may sometimes depend on the other; for if by the terms of the statute no suit can be instituted, it is very clear that no divorce can be had. But I think there may be cases where the statute confers a right to have a divorce, in which the statute gives a general jurisdiction to this Court; and yet where the parties do not live, that is, have their domicil, either at the time of the act done, or at the time of the suit commenced, in any county in this commonwealth. If so, there are cases where the statute cannot be literally complied with, and must be construed *cy pres* according to the intent. Suppose a husband commits adultery, and then purchases a house and actually takes up his domicil in another State; but before his wife has joined him she is apprized of the fact, and immediately files a libel for a divorce, and obtains an order to protect her from the power of her husband, as by law she may: he is an inhabitant of another State, and can in no sense be said to live in any county in this State; and yet it would be difficult to say that she is not entitled to have a divorce here. Supposing, instead of the last case, he has actually purchased a house and changed his domicil to another State, and there commits adultery; and the wife, not having joined him, and not having left her residence in this State, becomes acquainted with the fact, and libels and obtains a similar

§ 230. In New York, as far as decisions have gone, they coincide with those of Massachusetts. Thus in a case

---

order, could she not maintain it? Yet, in the latter case, at the time of the act done, and in the other, at the time of the suit instituted, the respondent, one of the parties, certainly did not live in any county of this commonwealth. This suggests another course of inquiry; that is, how far the maxim is applicable to this case, 'that the domicil of the wife follows that of the husband.' Can this maxim be true, in its application to this subject, where the wife claims to act, and by law, to a certain extent, and in certain cases, is allowed to act, adversely to her husband? It would oust the Court of its jurisdiction, in all cases where the husband should change his domicil to another State before the suit is instituted. It is in the power of a husband to change and fix his domicil at his will. If the maxim could apply, a man might go from this county to Providence, take a house, live in open adultery, abandoning his wife altogether, and yet she could not libel for a divorce in this State, where, till such change of domicil, they had always lived. He clearly lives in Rhode Island; her domicil, according to the maxim, follows his; she, therefore, in contemplation of law, is domiciled there too; so that neither of the parties can be said to live in this commonwealth. It is probably a juster view to consider that the maxim is founded upon the theoretic identity of person and of interest, between husband and wife, as established by law, and the presumption, that from the nature of that relation the home of the one is that of the other, and intended to promote, strengthen, and secure their interests in this relation, as it ordinarily exists, where union and harmony prevail. But the law will recognise a wife as having a separate existence, and separate interests, and separate rights, in those cases where the express object of all proceedings is to show that the relation itself ought to be dissolved, or so modified as to establish separate interests, and especially a separate domicil and home, bed and board being put, a part for the whole, as expressive of the idea of home; otherwise, the parties in this respect would stand upon very unequal grounds, it being in the power of the husband to change his domicil at will, but not in that of the wife. The husband might deprive the wife of the means of enforcing her rights, and, in effect, of the rights themselves, and of the protection of the laws of the commonwealth, at the same time that his own misconduct gives her a right to be rescued from his power, on account of his own misconduct towards her. Dean *v.* Richmond, 5 Pick., 461; Barber *v.* Root, 10 Mass. R. 260. The place where the marriage was had seems to be of no importance. The law looks at the relation of husband and wife, as it subsists and is regulated by our laws, without considering under what law or in what country the marriage was contracted. The good sense of the thing seems to be, if the statute will permit us to reach it, that where parties have *bonâ fide* taken up a domicil in this commonwealth, and have resided under the protection and subject to the control of our laws, and

where the marriage was in that State, and afterwards the wife went to Vermont, and instituted a suit for divorce there, for a cause not recognised by the laws of New York, against her husband, who remained domiciled in New York, the Supreme Court of the latter State refused to carry the decree into effect, in regard to alimony, notwithstanding the husband had appeared in the cause[1], upon the ground that there being no *boná fide* change of the domicil of the parties, it was an attempt fraudulently to evade the force and operation of the laws of New York[2]. The Court,

---

during the continuance of such domicil, one does an act which may entitle the other to a divorce, such divorce shall be granted, and the suit for it entertained, although the fact was done out of the jurisdiction, and whether the act be a crime which would subject a party to punishment or not; that after such right has accrued, it cannot be defeated, either by the actual absence of the other party, however long continued animo revertendi, or by a colourable change of domicil, or even by an actual change of domicil; and that it shall not be considered in law that the change of domicil of the husband draws after it the domicil of the wife to another State, so as to oust the Courts of this State of their jurisdiction, and deprive the injured wife of the protection of the laws of this commonwealth, and of her right to a divorce. But where the parties have bonâ fide renounced their domicil in this State, though married here, and taken up a domicil in another State, and there live as man and wife, and an act as done by one, which, if done in this State, would entitle the other to a divorce, and one of the parties comes into this State, the Courts of this commonwealth have not such jurisdiction of the parties, and of their relation as husband and wife, as to warrant them in saying that the marriage should be dissolved. The case of Barber *v.* Root is an authority for saying that such a divorce would not be valid in New York. It is of importance that such a question should be regulated, if possible, not by local law, or local usage, under which the marriage relation should be deemed subsisting in one State and dissolved in another, but upon some general principle, which can be recognised in all states and countries, so that parties who are deemed husband and wife in one shall be held so in all. So may interesting relations, so may collateral and derivative rights of property and of inheritance, so may correlative duties depend upon the subsistence of this relation, that it is scarcely possible to overrate the importance of placing it upon some general and uniform principle, which shall be recognised and adopted in all civilized states."

[1] This does not appear in the statement of facts; but it is averred by counsel to appear upon the exemplification of the record of the decree of Vermont. 1 John. R. 431.

[2] Jackson *v.* Jackson, 1 John. R. 424.

however, abstained from declaring what was the legal effect of the divorce so obtained. In another case, where the marriage was in Connecticut, and the husband afterwards went to Vermont, and instituted a suit there for a divorce against his wife, who never resided there, and never appeared in the suit; it was held, that the decree of divorce obtained in Vermont was invalid, being *in fraudem legis* of the State where the parties were married and had their domicil. It was further held, that the Courts of Vermont could not possess a proper jurisdiction over the case, both parties not being within the State, and the wife not having had any personal notice of the suit[1]. What would be the effect of a marriage in Connecticut, a subsequent *bonâ fide* change of domicil to New York, and then a divorce in Connecticut, both parties appearing in the suit, remains, as yet, undecided[2].

§ 230 *a*. Upon the whole, the doctrine now firmly established in America upon the subject of divorce is, that the law of the place of the actual *bonâ fide* domicil of the parties gives jurisdiction to the proper Courts to decree a divorce for any cause allowed by the local law, without any reference to the law of the place of the original marriage, or the place where the offence for which the divorce is allowed, was committed. Perhaps the doctrine cannot be stated with more clearness than in the reasoning of Mr. Chief Justice Gibson, in a recent case. "The law of the place (says he) is necessarily the law of the marriage, for its primitive obligation; but, except on the principle of perpetual submission to its supremacy in all things, it is not the law of the contract for the determination of its dissolubility. Is, then, a rule thus founded, adapted to the jurisprudence of a country whose law of allegiance is different, and whose asserted right of affiliation in respect to

---

[1] Borden *v.* Fitch, 15 John. R. 121. See 2 Kent, Comm. Lect. 27, pp. 108—118, 3rd edit. See also Bradshaw *v.* Heath, 14 Wend. R. 407.

[2] Pawling *v.* Bird's Executors, 13 John. R. 192, 208, 209.

those whom it admits on that ground to its civil and political privileges, divorce among the rest, concedes the same right to every other country? Framed on the basis of this law, the contract implies no perpetuity of municipal regulation. While the parties remain subject to our jurisdiction, the marriage is dissoluble only by our law; when they are remitted to another, it is incidentally remitted along with them. And that consequence must ensue, as well when they are remitted to a jurisdiction entirely foreign, as when they are remitted to that of a sister-state; for whatever ultra-territorial force a sentence of divorce, by a Court of competent jurisdiction, may have been thought to gain from the constitutional precept, that the judgment of a State Court is to receive the same faith and credit in every other State as in its own, nothing in the federal constitution or laws has been thought to touch the question of jurisdiction; and the members of the union, therefore, stand towards each other, in relation to it, as strangers. With what consistency, then, would naturalized citizens be allowed our law of divorce, if the validity of a divorce by the law of the domicil in a sister-state were disallowed, because the marriage had not the same origin? Transfer of allegiance and domicil is a contingency which enters into the views of the parties, and of which the wife consents to bear the risk. By sanctioning this transfer beforehand, we consent to part with the municipal governance incident to it; but with this limitation we part not with the remedy of past transgression [1]."

§ 230 *b*. The incidents to a foreign divorce are also naturally to be deduced from the law of the place where it is decreed. If valid there, the divorce will have, and ought in general to have, all the effects in every other country, upon personal property locally situate there, which are properly attributable to it in the forum where it is decreed. In respect to real or immovable property, the

---

[1] Dorsey *v*. Dorsey, 1 Chand. Law Reporter, 287, 289.

same effects would in general be attributed to such divorce as would ordinarily belong to a divorce of the same sort by the *lex loci rei sitæ*. If a dissolution of the marriage would there be consequent upon such a divorce, and would there extinguish the right of dower, or of tenancy by the courtesy, according to such local law, then the like effects would be attributed to the foreign divorce, which worked a like dissolution of the marriage[1].

---

[1] Warrender *v.* Warrender, 9 Bligh, R. 127; Ante, § 226, c. note.

CHAPTER VIII.

FOREIGN CONTRACTS.

§ 231. We next come to the consideration of the highly important branch of international jurisprudence arising from the conflict of laws in matters of contract generally[1]. This subject has been very much discussed, not only by foreign jurists and foreign courts, but in our own domestic tribunals. The general principles which regulate it have, therefore, acquired a high degree of certainty, although, upon so complex a topic, many intricate and difficult questions yet remain unsettled.

§ 232. It is easy to see, that, in the common intercourse of different countries, many circumstances may be required to be taken into consideration before it can be clearly ascertained what is the true rule by which the validity, obligation, and interpretation of contracts are to be governed. To make a contract valid, it is a universal principle, admitted by the whole world, that it should be made by parties capable to contract; that it should be voluntary; that it should be upon a sufficient consideration; that it should be lawful in its nature; and that it should be in its terms reasonably certain. But upon some of these points there is a diversity in the positive and customary laws of different nations. Persons capable in one country are incapable by the laws of another[2]; considerations good in one country are insufficient or invalid in another; the public policy of

1 See on the subject of this chapter, 1 Burge, Comm. on Col. and For. Law, pt. 1, ch. 1, pp. 23, 24, 29; Id. vol. 3, pt. 3, ch. 22, pp. 749—780; Fœlix, Conflict. des Lois, Revue Etrang. et Fran. tom. 7, (1840), § 39—51, pp. 344—365.

2 Ante, § 51—90.

one country permits or favours certain agreements which are prohibited in another; the forms prescribed by the laws of one country to insure validity and obligation of contracts, are unknown in another; and the rights acknowledged by one country, are not commensurate with those belonging to another. A person sometimes contracts in one country and is domiciled in another, and is to pay in a third; and sometimes the property which is the subject of the contract is situate in a fourth; and each of these countries may have different, and even opposite, laws affecting the subject-matter. What, then, is to be done in this conflict of laws? What law is to regulate the contract, either to determine the rights, or the remedies, or the defences growing out of it, or the consequences flowing from it? What law is to interpret its terms, and ascertain the nature, character, and extent of its stipulations? Boullenois has very justly said, that these are questions of great importance, and embrace a wide extent of objects[1].

§ 233. There are two texts of the civil law which treat of this subject, which have been supposed by civilians and jurists to involve an apparent antinomy. One seems to require that the place where the contract is entered into should alone govern the contract. *Si fundus venierit, ex consuetudine ejus regionis, in quâ negotium gestum est, pro evictione caveri oportet*[2]. If land shall be sold, it is to be warranted against eviction, according to the law of the country in which the business is transacted. The other, on the contrary, seems to require that the place where the contract is to be executed should govern it. *Contraxisse unusquisque in eo loco intelligitur, in quo ut solveret se obligavit;* Every one is understood to have contracted in

---

[1] 2 Boullenois, Obser. 46, p. 445.

[2] Dig. lib. 21, tit. 2, l. 6; Pothier, Pand. lib. 21, tit. 2, n. 7. See Everhardus, Concil. 178, p. 207; Post, § 300 *b*. See Bartolus's interpretation of this law. Bartolus, ad Cod. lib. 1, tit. 1, l. 1, n. 14—16; Post, § 301.

the place in which he has bound himself to perform the contract[1].

§ 234. Dumoulin has endeavoured to reconcile these texts, by supposing that the former law, *Si fundus*, truly and fundamentally presupposes that the contracting parties have their domicil in the place of the contract, and that the contract is there to be executed; but that the latter law, *Contraxisse*, applies to the case where the party has bound himself to execute the contract throughout in another place than that in which the contract is made. *Sed hic venditor eo ipso se obligat, solutionem et traditionem realem per se vel per alium facere in loco, in quo fundus situs est; ergo, ibi contraxisse, censetur. Et sic Lex, Si fundus, ex viva et radicale ratione præsupponit contrahentes habere domicilium in loco contractûs*[2]. Le Brun says, that when the Doctors say, in commenting on the law, *Si fundus,—Locus contractûs regit in contractibus*, they mean in every thing which concerns the manner of contracting the exterior form of the contract. But that the law of the domicil is to govern in whatever respects the substance and effects of the acts done[3]. However, the generality of French authors have reconciled these laws in a different manner, by considering that the place of a contract admits of a double meaning, viz. the place where the contract is entered into; (*ubi verba proferuntur*); and that there the contract is to be executed where payment is to be made (*ubi solutio destinatur*[4]). They think, therefore, that the law, *Si fundus*, is to be understood of the place where the contract is entered

---

1 Dig. lib. 44, tit. 7, l. 21; Pothier, Pand. lib. 5, tit. 1, n. 36. To the same effect is the text:—"Contractum autem non utique eo loco intelligitur, quo negotium gestum sit, sed quo solvenda est pecunia." Dig. lib. 42, tit. 5, l. 3; Pothier, Pand. lib. 42, tit. 5, n. 24.

2 Molin. Comment. In. Cod. lib. 1, tit. 1, l. 1, Conclusiones de Statutis, Molin. Opera, tom. 3, p. 554; Everhardus, Consil. 178, pp. 206, 207; 3 Burge, Comm. on Col. and For. Law, pt. 2, c. 20, pp. 851—853; 2 Boullenois, Observ. 46, pp. 445—447.

3 Le Brun, De la Communauté, liv. 1, ch. 2, § 46.

4 2 Boullenois, Observ. 46, pp. 446, 447; Post, § 299—304.

into, (*ubi verba prolata sunt*); and, that it properly applies to cases where it is necessary to decide upon the form, either of the proof, or the substance, or the constitution, or the mode of the contract, or of its extrinsic ceremonies or solemnities; and that the law, *Contraxisse,* applies to the case where the question is respecting the rights which spring from the contract, of which the execution and performance are referred to another place[1].

§ 235. Boullenois holds both interpretations unsatisfactory and insufficient for many occasions; for they suppose that two places only are to be examined in resolving all questions, the place of the making, and the place of the performance of the contract; and, in effect, they put aside the law of the place of the *situs* of the thing (*rei sitæ*), and that of the domicil of the parties, which are often imperative, and on many occasions deserve a preference[2]. He adds, that there is another difficulty which arises in these mixed questions, which is, that the laws in one place affix to certain clauses a certain sense and a certain effect, and the laws of another place give them a sense and an effect either more extensive or more restrained[3]. He also informs us that many foreign jurists have warned us against two errors, which constitute the quicksands of the law on this subject, and which are necessary to be avoided[4]. One of these errors is the confounding of those things which belong to the solemnities of the acts, and the effects which result from the nature of the acts on the one side, with those which belong to the charges, or liens, which spring up after the acts, purely as accidents; on the other side[5]. The other, the omission in a proper case to have a due regard or deference to the law of the *situs* or locality of the thing[6].

---

1 2 Boullenois, Observ. 46, pp. 446, 447; Post, § 229—304. See also Everhardus, Consil. 78, n. 18, 19, p. 207.

2 2 Boullenois, Observ. 46, p. 447.

3 Post, § 275.

4 2 Boullenois, Observ. 46, pp. 447, 449.

5 Id. pp. 447—449.

6 Id. pp. 449, 450.

§ 236. Mævius has given us a warning in this matter against confounding the solemnities of acts and contracts, as well as the effects caused by them, with the charges thereof, and extrinsic accidents which follow the contracts, but are not in the contracts themselves. *Cave, autem, in hæc materia, confundas actuum et contractuum solennia, nec non effectus ac ipsis causatos, cum eorum onere et accidenti extrinseco, quod contractus subsequitur, sed ex non ipsis contractibus est. Id, dum multi ignorant, aut non discernunt, forenses maximè lædunt, et gravantur* [1]. So that, according to Mævius, the law of the place of the contract is to govern, first, as to the solemnities of the act or contract; and, secondly, as to the effects caused thereby; but as to the charges (*onus*) and extrinsic accidents, that it is not to govern. *Forenses servare teneri statuta et consuetudines loci, ubi aliquid agunt, et contrahunt ad validitatem actus et contractus. Statutum enim actus seu contractus semper attenditur, cui disponentes vel contrahentes se alligare et conformare voluisse censetur* [2]. And speaking afterwards upon the charges and extrinsic accidents of acts and contracts, he adds: *In his enim, quia non spectant ad formam modumque contrahendi, contractum autem extrinsecus subsequuntur, non sectamur statuta loci contractus* [3]. In this system he is not generally followed; and Boullenois has observed, that it is very difficult to say what ought to be deemed to belong to the solemnities of contracts, what are the effects caused by them, and what are the charges and extrinsic accidents resulting from them [4].

§ 237. Burgundus has offered the following system. In relation to express contracts, two things are to be considered—the form and the matter of the contract. *Omnis autem obligandi ratio habeat, necesse est, rem et verba, hoc*

---

1 Mævius, ad Jus Lubecense, Quest. Prelim. 4, n. 18, p. 22.

2 Id. 4, n. 11, 13, 14, p. 22.

3 Id. 4, n. 18, p. 22: 2 Boullenois, Observ. 46, pp. 448—450.

4 2 Boullenois, Observ. 46, pp. 447—449.

est, formam et materiam[1]. But he adds, that it is not indiscriminately permitted to contract in all times and places; but it is very often material, with what persons we contract; and all these things will be unavailing, unless the contract is conformable to the laws. *Sed nec omni loco et tempore contrahere licet; plurimum quoque refert, cum quibus stipulemur. Et sane hæc omnia supervacua sint, nisi et secundum leges paciscamur*[2]. These things being premised, Burgundus lays down the following rules; first, in every thing which regards the form of contracts and the perfecting of them, the law of the place where the contract is entered into is to be followed. *Et quidem in scripturâ instrumenti, in solemnitatibus et ceremoniis, et generaliter in omnibus quæ ad formam ejusque perfectionem pertinent, spectanda est consuetudo regionis, ubi fit negotiatio*[3]. These he deems the substantials of the contract (*substantialia contractûs*); and among them he includes the necessity of giving a caution or security upon a sale against any eviction, according to the customary law[4]. So, the laws which determine the place and time when and where contracts ought to be made, belong to the perfection of the form. *Conditio loci et temporis perfectionem formæ quoque respiciunt; et ideo regione contractûs pariter diriguntur*[5]. In like manner, all special stipulations for a limited responsibility, as of particular heirs only, belong to the form[6]. And he concludes by observing, that in all questions touching the obligation of the contract or its interpretation, as, for example, whom it binds, and to what extent—what is included, what is excluded from it; also, in respect to all actions, and all ambiguities arising out of the contract—we are first to follow what has been done by the parties; or if it does not

---

1 Burgundus, Tract. 4, n. 1, p. 100.

2 Id. pp. 100, 101; 2 Boullenois, Observ. 46, pp. 450, 451; Post, § 300 *a*.

3 Id. n. 7, n. 29, p. 104, 105.

4 Id. n. 7, p. 105. 5 Ibid. 6 Ibid.

appear what has been done, the consequence will be, that we are to follow what is usual in the country where the act took place. For the law is the common instructor of the whole country, whose voice all hear; and therefore every one who contracts in another province, is not supposed to be ignorant of its customs; but whatever he does not express plainly, he refers to the interpretation of the law, and wills and intends that which the law itself wills and intends. And all these things may well be said of the solemnities of contracts. *Igitur, ut paucis absolvam, quoties de vinculo obligationis vel de ejus interpretatione quæritur, veluti, quos et in quantum obliget, quid sententiæ stipulationes inesse, quid abesse credi oporteat—item in omnibus actionibus, et ambiguitatibus, quæ inde oriuntur, primùm quidem id sequemur quod inter partes actum erit; aut si non paret, quid actum est, erit consequens, ut id sequamur, quod in regione in qua actum est, frequentatur. Imputandum enim ei est, qui dicit vel agit, quod apertiùs legem non dixerit, in cujus potestate erat cuncta complecti, et voluntatem suam verbis exprimere. Nec enim stipulator ferendus est, si ejus intersit aliter actum non esse, cùm scire debuerit, id quod à contrahentibus est omissum, suppleri legibus, quæ haud aliter dirigunt humanas actiones, quàm corpora nostra luna alternat. Lex enim communis est præceptrix civitatis, cujus vocem cuncti exaudiunt. Et ideo, qui in alienâ provinciâ paciscitur, non credendus est esse consuetudinis ignarus; sed id quod palam verbis non exprimit ad interpretationem legum se referre, atque idem velle, et intendere, quod lex ipsa velit. Et hæc quidem cuncta de solemnitate dicta sint*[1]. He then passes to the consideration of the matter of the contract, by which he means the things of which it disposes; and he affirms, in respect to the matter, that the law of the situation of the property ought to govern. *Cæterum, ut sciamus, contractus, ex parte materiæ utilis sit, vel inutilis, ad leges, quæ, de quibus tractatur, impressæ sunt, hoc est, ad consuetudinem situs respiciemus*[2]. He

---

[1] Burgundus, Tract. 4, n. 8, p. 105, 106. [2] Id. 4, 9.

applies the same rule to *quasi* contracts as to express contracts. *Idem in quasi contractibus, quod in contractibus obtinet*[1].

§ 238. Hertius has laid down three general rules upon the subject of the operation of foreign law[2]. The first is, that when the law respects the person, the law of the country to which the party is a subject is to be followed. *Quando lex in personam dirigitur, respiciendum est ad leges civitatis quæ personam habet subjectam*[3]. Secondly, when the law respects things, the law of the *situs* is to govern, wherever and by whomsoever the act may be celebrated. *Si Lex directò rei imponitur, ea locum habet, ubicunque etiam locorum et a quocunque actus celebretur*[4]. Thirdly, when the law imposes any form in the transaction of the business (*actus*), the law of the place where it is transacted is to govern, and not the law of the domicil of the parties, or of the place where the property is situate. *Si lex actui formam dat, inspiciendus est locus actus, non domicilii, non rei sitæ*[5]. This last rule, in an especial manner, he applies to contracts, even when they regard property situated in a foreign country. *Valet, etiamsi bona in alio territorio sunt sita*[6].

§ 239. Huberus lays down the following doctrine. All business and acts done in court, and out of court, (or, as we should say, in *païs*, or judicial), whether testamentary or *inter vivos*, regularly executed in any place according to the law of that place, are valid every where, even in countries

---

[1] Burgundus, Tract. 5, n. 1. See also 2 Boullenois, Observ. 46, pp. 450—454, where he has given a summary of the doctrine of Burgundus. Burgundus, in exemplifying what he means by the matter of the contract where the law of the situs governs, evidently confines himself to real estate, or immovable property. See Everhardus, Consil. 78, n. 18, 19, p. 207; Post, § 299 *c*.

[2] Ante, § 30.

[3] 1 Hertii Opera, De Collis. Leg. p. 123, § 8; Id. p. 175, (edit. 1716).

[4] Id. p. 125, § 9; Id. p. 177, (edit. 1716).

[5] Id. p. 126, § 10; Id. p. 179, (edit. 1716).

[6] Id. § 4, p. 126, § 10, (edit. 1737); Id. pp. 179, 180, (edit. 1716); Post, 371 *a*.

where a different law prevails, and where, if transacted in the like manner, they would have been invalid. On the other hand, business and acts, executed in any place contrary to the law of that place where they are executed, as they are in their origin invalid, never can acquire any validity. And this rule applies not only to persons who are domiciled in the place of the contract, but to those who are commorant there. There is this exception, however, to be understood; that if the rulers of another people would be affected with any notable inconvenience thereby, they are not bound to give any effect to such business and transactions. *Inde fluit hæc Positio: Cuncta negotia et acta tam in judicio, quam extra judicium, seu mortis causâ sive inter vivos, secundum jus certi loci rite celebrata, valent, etiam ubi diversa juris observatio viget, ac ubi sic inita, quemadmodum facta sunt, non valerent. E contra, negotia et acta, certo loco contra leges ejus loci celebrata, cum sint ab initio invalida, nusquam valere possunt. Idque non modo respectu hominum qui in loco contractus habent domicilium, sed et illorum qui ad tempus ibidem commorantur. Sub hac tamen exceptione; si rectores alterius populi exinde notabili incommodo afficerentur, ut hi talibus actis atque negotiis usum effectumque dare non teneantur, secundum tertii axiomatis limitationem*[1]. He applies the same doctrine indiscriminately to testamentary acts, to acts *inter vivos*, and to contracts. *Quod de testamentis habuimus, locum etiam habet in actibus inter vivos. Proinde contractus celebrati secundum jus loci, in quo contrahuntur, ubique tam in jure, quam extra judicium, etiam ubi hoc modo celebrati non valerent, sustinentur: idque non tantum de forma sed etiam de materia contractus affirmandum est*[2]. He adds, that the place where a contract is entered into, is not to be precisely regarded; that if the parties had another country in view in making the contract, that ought not rather to be consi-

---

[2] 2 Huberus, lib. 1, tit. 3, § 3.

[2] Huberus, De Confl. Leg. lib. 1, tit. 3, § 5, 7—9.

dered. *Verum tamen non ita præcise respiciendus est locus, in quo contractus est initus; ut, si partes alium locum respexerint, ille non potius sit considerandus*[1]. But here the same restriction is to apply, that no injury arise thereby to the citizens of the foreign country in regard to their own rights. *Datur et alia limitationis sæpe dictæ applicatio in hoc articulo; Effecta contractuum certo loco initorum, pro jure loci illius alibi quoque observantur, si nullum inde civibus alienis creetur præjudicium, in jure sibi quæsito; ad quod Potestas alterius loci non tenetur, neque potest extendere jus diversi territorii*[2]. And he deduces the following general conclusion: If the law of a foreign country is in conflict with the law of our own country, in which a contract is also entered into, conflicting with another contract which is entered into elsewhere, in such a case our own law ought to prevail, and not the foreign law. *Ampliamus hanc regulam tali extensione:—Si jus loci in alio imperio pugnet cum jure nostræ civitatis, in quâ contractus etiam initus est, confligens cum eo contractu qui alibi celebratus est, magis est, ut jus nostrum, quam jus alienum, servemus*[3].

§ 239 *a*. Bartolus, on the subject of contracts between foreigners in another country, has expressed himself to the following effect:—That we are to distinguish whether the question is (1.) as to the law or custom which regulates the solemnities of the contract; or (2.) as to the institution of the remedy; or (3.) as to those things which belong to the jurisdiction, in executing the contract. In the first case, the law of the place of the contract is to govern; in the second case, the law of the place where the suit is instituted; but in the third case, as to those things which arise from the nature of the contract at the time when it was made, or those which arise afterwards on account of negligence or delay, the law of the place of the contract is to govern. *Et primo, Quæro quid de contractibus? Pone*

---

[2] 2 Huberus, lib. 1, tit. 3, § 10; Post, § 281, 299.

[2] Id. tit. 1, § 11.

[3] Id. tit. 3, § 11.

contractum celebratum per aliquem forensem in hac civitate; litigium ortum est, et agitatur lis in loco originis contrahentis; cujus loci Statuta debent servari, vel spectari? Distingue, aut loquimur de Statuto, aut de consuetudine, quæ respiciunt ipsius contractus solemnitatem, aut litis ordinationem, aut de his quæ pertinent ad jurisdictionem ex ipso contractu evenientis executionis. Primo casu, inspicitur locus contractus. Secundo casu, aut quæris de his, quæ pertinent ad litis ordinationem, et inspicitur locus judicii. Aut de his quæ pertinent ad ipsius litis decisionem; et tunc, aut de his, quæ oriuntur secundum ipsius contractus naturam tempore contractus, aut de his, quæ oriuntur ex post facto propter negligentiam, vel moram. Primo casu, inspicitur locus contractus[1].

§ 240. Boullenois has discussed this subject in a most elaborate manner, and has laid down a number of rules which are entitled to great consideration[2]. First.—The law of the place where a contract is entered into, is to govern as to every thing which concerns the proof and authenticity of the contract, and the faith which is due to it; that is to say, in all things which regard its solemnities or formalities[3]. Secondly.—The law of the place of the contract is generally to govern in every thing which forms the obligation of the contract, (*le lien du contrat*), or what is called *vinculum obligationis*[4]. Thirdly.—The law of the place of the contract is to govern as to the intrinsic and substantive form of the contract[5]. Fourthly.—When the law has attached certain formalities to the things themselves which

---

1 Bartol. Comment. ad Cod. lib. 1, tit. 1, l. 1, n. 13, cited also 2 Boullenois, Observ. 46, pp. 455, 456.

2 Boullenois, Observ. 46, pp. 445—538. Mr. Henry has laid down the first eight rules of Boullenois as clear law, without the slightest acknowledgment of the source whence they are taken. In fact, his Treatise is, in substance, taken from Boullenois, whose name, however, occurs only once or twice in it.

3 2 Boullenois, Observ. 46, p. 458.

4 Ibid.

5 2 Boullenois, Observ. 46, p. 467.

are the subject of the contract, the law of their situation is to govern[1]. This rule is applicable to contracts respecting real estate. Fifthly.—When the law of the place of the contract admits of dispositions or acts which do not spring properly from the nature of the contract, but have their foundation in the state and condition of the person, there the law, which regulates the person, and upon which his state depends, is to govern [2]. Sixthly.—In questions whether the rights which arise from the nature and time of the contract are lawful or not, the law of the place of the contract is to govern [3]. Seventhly.—In questions concerning moveable property, of which the delivery is to be instantly made, the law of the place of the contract is to govern[4]. Eighthly. —If the rights which arise to the profit of one of the contracting parties in fact arise under a contract valid in itself, and not subject to recision, but they arise from a new cause, purely accidental, and *ex post facto;* in this case, the law of the place where these rights arise, is to govern, unless the parties have otherwise stipulated [5]. Ninthly.—These rules are to govern equally, whether the contestation be in a foreign tribunal, or in a domestic tribunal having proper jurisdiction over the controversy[6]. Tenthly.—In questions upon the true interpretation of any clauses in a contract or in a testament, the accompanying circumstances ought ordinarily to decide them[7].

§ 241. Without entering farther into the examination of the opinions and doctrines of foreign jurists[8], (a task which would be almost endless), we shall now proceed to the consideration of those doctrines, touching contracts made

---

[1] 2 Boullenois, Observ. 46, p. 467.

[2] Ibid; Post, § 437.

[3] 2 Boullenois, Observ. 46, p. 472.

[4] Id. Observ. n. 46, p. 475.

[5] 2 Boullenois, Observ. 46, p. 477.

[6] Id. Observ. 46, p. 489.

[7] 2 Boullenois, Observ. 46, p. 489. See also Fœlix, Conflict. des Lois, Revue Etrang. et Fran. tom. 7, (1840), § 39, pp. 344—346.

[8] The learned reader, who wishes for farther instruction as to the opinions of foreign jurists on all these points, will find many of them collected in 2 Boullenois, Observ. 46, pp. 458—538.

in foreign countries, which appear to be recognised and settled in the jurisprudence of the common law. The law which is to govern in relation to the capacity of the parties to enter into a contract, has been already fully considered[1]. It has been shewn that, although foreign jurists generally hold, that the law of the domicil ought to govern in regard to the capacity of persons to contract[2]; yet, that the common law holds a different doctrine, viz., that the *lex loci contractus* is to govern[3].

§ 242. (1). Generally speaking, the validity of a contract is to be decided by the law of the place where it is made. If valid there, it is, by the general law of nations, (*jure gentium*), held valid every where, by the tacit or implied consent of the parties[4]. The rule is founded, not merely in

---

[1] Ante, § 51—79.

[2] Ante, § 51—79. In addition to the foreign authorities already cited, we may add that of Cochin and D'Aguesseau. The former says, that the subjects of the king of France are always subjects, and they cannot break the bonds which attach them to his authority; and parties contracting in a foreign country cannot possess any capacity to contract, but according to the law of their own country. It is a personal law, which follows them everywhere. Cochin, Œuvres, tom. 1, pp. 153, 154; Id. 545, 4to. edit.; Id. tom. 4, p. 555, 4to. edit. "When," says D'Aguesseau, "the question is as to an act purely personal, we consider only the law of the domicil. That alone commands all persons who are subject to it. Other laws cannot make those capable or incapable who do not live within their reach. And this is what Bartolus intended to remark when he said, 'Statutum non potest habilitare personam sibi non subjectam.'" D'Aguesseau, Œuvres, tom. 4, p. 639, 4to. edit.

[3] See Ante, ch. 4, § 51—54; Id. § 100—106. See also Male *v.* Roberts, 3 Esp. R. 163; Thompson *v.* Ketcham, 8 John. R. 189; Liverm. Diss. p. 34, § 21, p. 35; Id. § 22—24, p. 38; Id. § 26, 27, p. 40; Id. § 31, p. 42; Id. § 33, p. 43, § 35; Andrews *v.* His Creditors, 11 Louis. R. 464, 476.

[4] Pearsall *v.* Dwight, 2 Mass. R. 88, 89. See Casaregis, Disc. 179, § 1, 2; Willing *v.* Conseequa, 1 Peters. R. 317; 2 Kent, Comm. Lect. 39, pp. 457, 458, 3rd edit.; De Sobry *v.* De Laistre, 2 Harr. & John. R. 193, 221, 228; Smith *v.* Mead, 3 Connect. R. 253; Medbury *v.* Hopkins, 3 Connect. R. 472; Houghton *v.* Page, 2 N. Hamp. R. 42; Dyer *v.* Hunt, 5 N. Hamp. R. 401; Erskine's Inst. B. 3, tit. 2, § 39—41, pp. 514—516; Trimbey *v.* Vignier, 1 Bing. New Cas. 151, 159; S. C. 4 Moore & Scott, 695; Andrews *v.* Pond, 13 Peters. R. 65; Andrews *v.* His Creditors,

the convenience, but in the necessities of nations; for otherwise it would be impracticable for them to carry on an extensive intercourse and commerce with each other. The whole system of agencies, of purchases and sales, of mutual credits, and of transfers of negotiable instruments, rests on this foundation; and the nation which should refuse to acknowledge the common principles, would soon find its whole commercial intercourse reduced to a state like that in which it now exists among savage tribes, among the barbarous nations of Sumatra, and among other portions of Asia washed by the Pacific. *Jus autem gentium* (says the Institute of Justinian) *omni humano generi commune est; nam, usu exigente et humanis necessitatibus, gentes humanæ jura quædam sibi constituerunt. Et ex hoc jure gentium, omnes pene contractus introducti sunt, ut emptio et venditio, locatio et conductio, societas, depositum, mutuum, et alii innumerabiles*[1]. No more forcible application can be propounded of this imperial doctrine than to the subject of international private contracts[2]. In this, as a general principle, there seems a universal consent of all courts and jurists, foreign and domestic[3].

---

11 Louis. R. 465; Post, § 316 *a*; Bayley on Bills, ch. (A), 5th edit. by F. Bayley, p. 78; Id. Amer. edit. by Phillips & Sewell, 1836, pp. 78—86; 1 Burge, Comment. on Col. and For. Law, Pt. 1, ch. 1, pp. 29, 30; Whister *v.* Stodder, 8 Martin, R. 95; Bank of U. States *v.* Donally, 8 Peters, R. 361, 372; Wilcox *v.* Hunt, 13 Peters, R. 378, 379.

[1] 1 Inst. lib. 1, tit. 2, § 2.

[2] 2 Kent, Comm. Lect. 39, pp. 454, 455, and note, 3rd edit.; 10 Toullier, art. 80 note; Pardessus, Droit Comm. vol. 5, art. 1482, Charters *v.* Cairnes, 16 Martin, R. 1.

[3] The cases which support this doctrine are so numerous, that it would be a tedious task to enumerate them. They may, generally, be found collected in the Digests of the English and American Reports, under the head of Foreign Law, or Lex Loci. The principal part of them are collected in 4 Cowen, R. 510, note; and in 2 Kent, Comm. Lect. 39, p. 457, et seq. in the notes. See also Fonblanque on Eq. B. 5, ch. 1, § 6' note (t.) p. 443; Bracket *v.* Norton, 4 Connect. R. 517; Medbury *v.* Hopkins, 3 Connect. R. 472; Smith *v.* Mead, 3 Connect. R. 253; De Sobry *v.* De Laistre, 2 Harr. & John. R. 193, 221, 228; Trasher *v.* Everhart, 3 Gill. &

§ 242 *a*. Illustrations of this general doctrine may be derived from cases which have actually occurred in judgment. Thus, for example, where a bill of exchange was made and indorsed in blank in France, and the holder afterwards sued the maker in England, a question arose whether, upon such an indorsement in blank, without following the formalities prescribed by the Civil Code of France, the indorsement passed the right of property to the holder; and it being found that it did not, by the law of France, the Court held, that no recovery could be had by the holder upon the note in an English Court. The Court on that occasion said, that the question as to the transfer, was a question of the true interpretation of the contract, and was therefore to be governed by the law of France, where the contract and indorsement were made[1].

§ 243. (2.) The same rule applies, *vice versâ*, to the invalidity of contracts; if void or illegal by the law of the place of the contract, they are generally held void and illegal everywhere[2]. This would seem to be a principle derived from the very elements of natural justice. The Code has expounded it in strong terms. *Nullum enim pac-*

John. R. 234. The foreign jurists are equally full, as any one will find upon examining the most celebrated of every nation. They all follow the doctrine of Dumoulin. "In concernentibus contractibus, et emergentibus tempore contractûs, inspici debet locus in quo contrahitur." Molin. Comment. ad Consuet. Paris. tit. 1, § 12, Gloss. n. 37, tom. 1, p. 224; Post, § 260, 300 *d*. See Bouhier, ch. 21, § 190; 2 Boullenois, Observ. 46, p. 458. Lord Brougham, in Warrender *v*. Warrender, 9 Bligh. R. 110, made some striking remarks on this subject, which have been already cited, ante, § 226 *b*, note.

[1] Trimbey *v*. Vignier, 1 Bing. New Cases, 151, 159; Post, § 267, 270.

[2] Huberus, lib. 1, tit. 3, De Confl. Leg. § 3, 5; Van Reimsdyk *v*. Keane, 1 Gallis. R. 375; Pearsall *v*. Dwight, 2 Mass. R. 88, 89; Touro *v*. Cassin, 1 Nott & M'Cord, R. 173; De Sobry *v*. De Laistre, 2 Harr. & John. R. 193, 221, 225; Houghton *v*. Page, 2 N. Hamp. R. 42; Dyer *v*. Hunt, 5 N. Hamp. R. 401; Van Schaick *v*. Edwards, 2 John. Cas. 355; Robinson *v*. Bland, 2 Burr. R. 1077; Burrows *v*. Jemino, 2 Str. 732; Alves *v*. Hodgson, 7 T. R. 237; 2 Kent, Comm. Lect. 39, pp. 457, 458, 3rd edit.: La jeune Eugenie, 2 Mason, R. 459; Andrews *v*. Pond, 13 Peters, R. 65, 78.

tum, nullam conventionem, nullum contractum, inter eos videri volumus subsecutum, qui contrahunt lege contrahere prohibente[1]. If void in its origin, it seems difficult to find any principle upon which any subsequent validity can be given to it in any other country.

§ 244. (3.) But there is an exception to the rule as to the universal validity of contracts; which is, that no nation is bound to recognise or enforce any contracts which are injurious to its own interests, or to those of its own subjects[2]. Huberus has expressed it in the following terms:—*Quatenus nihil potestati aut juri alterius imperantis ejusque civium prœjudicetur*[3]; and Mr. Justice Martin still more clearly, in saying, that the exception applies to cases in which the contract is immoral or unjust, or in which the enforcing it in a State would be injurious to the rights, the interest, or the convenience of such State or its citizens[4]. This exception results from the consideration that the authority of the acts and contracts done in other States, as well as the laws by which they are regulated, are not, *proprio vigore,* of any efficacy beyond the territories of that State; and whatever is attributed to them elsewhere is from comity, and not of strict right[5]. And every independent community will and ought to judge for itself how far that comity ought to extend[6]. The reasonable limitation is, that it shall not suffer prejudice by its comity[7].

---

[1] Cod. lib. 1, tit. 14, l. 5.

[2] Greenwood *v.* Curtis, 6 Mass. R. 378, 379; Blanchard *v.* Russell, 13 Mass. R. 1, 6; Whiston *v.* Stodder, 8 Martin, R. 95; De Sobry *v.* De Laistre, 2 Harr. & John. R. 193, 228; Trasher *v.* Everhart, 3 Gill. & John. R. 234; 3 Burge, Comm. on Col. and For. Law, Pt. 2, ch. 20, p. 779; Post, § 348—351; Andrews *v.* Pond, 13 Peters, R. 65, 78.

[3] Huberus, lib. 1, tit. 3, De Conflict. Leg. § 2.

[4] Whiston *v.* Stodder, 8 Martin, R. 95, 97.

[5] Ante, § 7, 8, 18, 20, 22, 23, 36.

[6] Ibid.

[7] Ante, § 25, 27, 29; Huberus, lib. 1, tit. 3, De Conflict. Leg. § 2, 3, 5; Trasher *v.* Everhart, 3 Gill. & John. R. 234; Greenwood *v.* Curtis, 6 Mass. R. 378; 2 Kent, Comm. Lect. 39, p. 457, 3rd edit.; Pearsall *v.* Dwight, 2 Mass. R. 88, 89; Eunomus, Dial. 3, § 67.

This doctrine has been on many occasions recognised by the Supreme Court of Louisiana. On a recent occasion it was said by the Court:—"By the comity of nations a practice has been adopted, by which Courts of justice examine into and enforce contracts made in other States, and carry them into effect according to the laws of the place where the transaction took its rise. This practice has become so general in modern times, that it may be almost stated to be now a rule of international law, and it is subject only to the exception, that the contract to which aid is required should not, either in itself or in the means used to give it effect, work an injury to the inhabitants of the country where it is attempted to be enforced[1]." Mr. Justice Best, (afterwards Lord Wynford), on another occasion, with great force said, that in cases turning upon the comity of nations, (*comitas inter communitates*), it is a maxim that the comity cannot prevail in cases where it violates the law of our own country, or the law of nature, or the law of God[2]. Contracts, therefore, which are in evasion or fraud of the laws of a country, or of the rights or duties of its subjects,—contracts against good morals, or against religion, or against public rights, and contracts opposed to the national policy or national institutions, are deemed nullities in every country affected by such considerations, although they may be valid by the laws of the place where they are made.

§ 245. Indeed, a broader principle might be adopted, and it is to be regretted that it has not been universally adopted by all nations, in respect to foreign contracts, as it has been in respect to domestic contracts, that no man ought to be heard in a Court of justice to enforce a contract founded in, or arising out of moral or political turpitude, or in fraud of the just rights of any foreign nation whatsoever[3].

---

[1] Mr. Justice Porter, in Ohio Insur. Company *v.* Edmondson, 5 Louis. R. 295, 299, 300.

[2] Forbes *v.* Cochrane, 2 Barn. & Cress. R. 448, 471.

[3] Armstrong *v.* Toler, 11 Wheaton R. 258, 260; Chitty on Bills, 8th

The Roman law contains an affirmation of this wholesome doctrine. *Pacta, quæ contra leges constitutionesque, vel contra bonos mores fiunt, nullam vim habere, indubitati juris est*[1]. *Pacta, quæ turpem causam continent, non sunt observanda*[2]. Unfortunately, from a very questionable subserviency to mere commercial gains, it has become an established formulary of the jurisprudence of the Common Law, that no nation will regard or enforce the revenue laws of any other country; and that the contracts of its own subjects, made to evade or defraud the laws or just rights of foreign nations, may be enforced in its own tribunals[3]. Sound morals would seem to point to a very different conclusion. Pothier has (as we shall presently see) reprobated the doctrine in strong terms, as inconsistent with good faith and the just duties of nations to each other[4].

§ 246. A few cases may serve to illustrate the exceptions under each of the foregoing heads[5]. First, contracts which are in evasion or fraud of the laws of a particular country[6]. Thus, if a contract is made in France, to smuggle goods into America in violation of our laws, the contract will be treated by our Courts as utterly void, as an intended fraud upon our laws[7]. And in such a case, brought into controversy in our Courts, it will be wholly immaterial whether the parties are citizens or are foreigners. So, if a collusive

---

(edit., 1833), p. 143, note; Boucher *v.* Lawson, Cas. Temp. Hard. 84, 89, 194; Planche *v.* Fletcher, Doug. R. 250; Post, § 255, 257.

1 Cod. lib. 2, tit. 3, l. 6.

2 Dig. lib. 2, tit. 14, l. 27, § 4. See also 1 Chitty on Comm. and Manuf. ch. 4, pp. 82, 83.

3 See Boucher *v.* Lawson, Cas. Temp. Hard. 85, 89, 194; Post, § 256, 257.

4 Post, § 257.

5 Many of the cases upon this subject will be found referred to in the argument of Armstrong *v.* Toler, 11 Wheaton R. 265, 266.

6 See 1 Bell, Comm. § 233—247, pp. 232—240, 4th edit.; Id. pp. 298—314, 5th edit.; Kaims on Eq. b. 3, ch. 8, § 1.

7 See Holman *v.* Johnson, Cowper, R. 341; Armstrong *v.* Toler, 11 Wheaton, R. 258; Cambioso *v.* Maffit, 2 Wash. Cir. R. 98.

capture and condemnation are procured in our Courts in fraud of our laws, by foreigners, who are even enemies at the time, their contract for the distribution of the prize proceeds will be held utterly void by our Courts, although the acts are a mere stratagem of war. And it will make no difference that the laws have since been repealed, or that the war has since ceased; for the contract being clearly in fraud of the laws existing at the time, the execution of it ought not to be enforced by the Courts of the country, whose laws it was designed to evade[1].

§ 247. The same principle applies not only to contracts growing immediately out of and connected with an illegal transaction, but also to new contracts, if they are in part connected with the illegal transaction, and grow immediately out of it[2]. Thus, for example, a man who, under a contract made in a foreign country, imports goods for another by means of a violation of the laws of his own country, is disqualified from founding any action in the Courts of that country upon such illegal transaction, for the value or for the freight of the goods, or for other advances made on them. He is thus justly punished for the immorality of the act, and a powerful discouragement from the perpetration of the act is thus provided[3]. And if the importation is the result of a scheme to consign the goods to a friend of the owner, with the security of the former, that he may protect or defend them for the owner, in case they should be brought into jeopardy; a promise afterwards made by the owner to such friend to indemnify him for his advances and charges on account of any proceedings against the property, although it purport to be a new contract, will be held utterly void, as constituting a part of the *res gesta*, or original transaction.

---

1 Hannay *v.* Eve, 3 Cranch, R. 242. See Jaques *v.* Withy, 1 H. Black. R. 65; The Springfield Bank *v.* Merrick, 14 Mass. R. 322.

2 Armstrong *v.* Toler, 11 Wheat. R. 261, 262. See Canaan *v.* Brice, 3 Barn & Ald. 179.

3 Ibid.

It will clearly be a promise, growing immediately out of and connected with the illegal transaction[1].

§ 248. But the principle stops here, and is not extended to new and independent transactions after the illegal act. If the new contract is wholly unconnected with the illegal act, and is founded on a new consideration, and is not a part of the original scheme, it is not tainted by the illegal act, although it may be known to the party with whom the contract is made[2]. Thus, if, after the illegal act is accomplished, a new contract (not being unlawful in itself) is made by the importer for a sale of the goods to a retail merchant, and the merchant afterwards sells the same to a tailor, or to a customer, who had no participation whatsoever in the original illegal scheme, such new contract will be valid, although the illegality of the original importation is known to each of the vendees at the time when he entered into the new contract[3].

§ 249. It will make no difference that such new and independent contract is made with the person, who was the contriver and conductor of the original illegal act, if it is wholly disconnected therefrom; for a new contract, founded on a new consideration, although in relation to property, respecting which there have been prior unlawful transactions between the parties, is not in itself unlawful[4]. Thus, if A. should, in a foreign country, during war, contrive a plan for importing goods from the country of the enemy on his own account, by means of smuggling, or of a collusive capture, and goods should be sent in the same vessel by B., and A. should, upon the request of B., afterwards become surety for the payment of the duties, or should afterwards undertake to become answerable for the expenses on account of a pro-

---

[1] Armstrong *v.* Toler, 11 Wheat. R. 261, 262. See Canaan *v.* Brice, 3 Barn. & Ald. 179.

[2] Armstrong *v.* Toler, 11 Wheat. R. 262, 268, 269. In this case the general principles applicable to the question of illegality, as well as the authorities, were fully discussed and considered by the Court.

[3] Toler *v.* Armstrong, 11 Wheat. R. 261.

[4] Armstrong *v.* Toler, 11 Wheat. R. 262, 268, 269.

secution for the illegal importation, or should afterwards advance money to B., to pay these expenses; any such act, if it constituted no part of the original scheme, and if A. was not concerned, nor in any manner instrumental in promoting the illegal importation of B., but he was merely engaged in a similar illegal transaction, devising the plan for himself, would be deemed a new contract upon a valid and legal consideration, unconnected with the original act, although remotely caused by it[1]. Hence, such new contract would not be so contaminated by the turpitude of the offensive act, as to turn A. out of Court, when seeking to enforce the new contract in the Courts of this country, although the illegal introduction of the goods into the country was the consequence of the scheme projected by himself, in relation to his own goods[2].

§ 250. The same principle may be illustrated by another example. If A. should become answerable for expenses on account of a prosecution for the illegal importation, or should advance money to B., to enable him to pay those expenses; these acts would constitute a new contract, on which an action might be maintained in our Courts, if it constituted no part of the original scheme for the illegal importation, but it was subsequent to and independent of it[3].

§ 251. The same general distinction has been asserted in many cases, which have undergone a legal adjudication. Thus, in a case where goods were sold in France by a Frenchman to an Englishman, for the known purpose of being smuggled into England, it was held, that the Frenchman could maintain a suit in England for the price of the goods, upon the ground that the sale was complete in France, and the party had no connexion with the smuggling transaction. The contract (said the Court) is complete, and nothing is left to be done. The seller, indeed, knows what

---

[1] Armstrong *v.* Toler, 11 Wheat. R. 262, 268, 269.

[2] Ibid.

[3] Id. 11 Wheat. R. 258, 260, 268—271. But see Canaan *v.* Brice, 3 Barn. & Ald. 179.

the buyer is going to do with the goods; but he has no concern in the transaction itself[1]. But if it enters at all, as an ingredient, into the contract between the parties, that the goods shall be smuggled, or that the seller shall do some act to assist or facilitate the smuggling, such as packing them in a particular way; there, the seller is deemed active, and the contract will not be enforced[2]. The same doctrine has accordingly been held in other cases[3].

§ 252. Huberus puts a case illustrative of the same doctrine. In particular places (says he) certain merchandise is prohibited. If sold there, the contract is void. But, if the same merchandise is sold in another place where there is no such prohibition, and a suit is brought upon the contract in the place where the prohibition exists, the buyer will be held liable (*condemnabitur*); because the contract therefor was in its origin valid. But if the merchandise is sold to be delivered in another place where it is prohibited, the buyer will not be held liable; because such a contract is repugnant to the law and interest of the country which made the prohibition[4].

§ 253. The result of these decisions certainly is, that the mere knowledge of the illegal purpose for which goods are purchased, will not affect the validity of the contract of sale of goods intended to be smuggled into a foreign country, even in the Courts of that country; but that there must be some participation or interest of the seller in the act itself. It is difficult, however, to reconcile this doctrine with the strong and masculine reasoning of Lord Chief Justice Eyre in an important case upon the same subject; reasoning which

---

[1] Holman *v.* Johnson, Cowp. R. 341. But see Pellicat *v.* Angell, 2 Cromp. Mees. & Rosc. 311; Post 254, and note.

[2] Waynell *v.* Reed, 5 T. R. 599; Lightfoot *v.* Tenant. 1 Bos. & Pull. 551; Biggs *v.* Lawrence, 3 T. R. 459; Clugas *v.* Penaluna, 4 T. R. 466; Holman *v.* Johnson, Cowp. R. 341; Post, § 254, and note.

[3] Ibid.

[4] Huber. lib. 1, tit. 3, § 5; S. P. Greenwood *v.* Curtis, 6 Mass. R. 378; Executors of Cambioso *v.* Assignees of Moffat, 2 Wash. Cir. R. 98.

has much to commend it in point of sound sense and sound morals. "Upon the principles of the Common Law, (said he,) the consideration of every valid contract must be meritorious. The sale and delivery of goods, nay, the agreement to sell and deliver goods, is, *primâ facie,* a meritorious consideration to support a contract for the price. But the man who sold arsenic to one who he knew intended to poison his wife with it, would not be allowed to maintain an action upon his contract. The consideration of the contract, in itself good, is there tainted with turpitude, which destroys the whole merit of it. I put this strong case, because the principle of it will be felt and acknowledged without further discussion. Other cases, where the means of transgressing a law are furnished, with the knowledge that they are intended to be used for that purpose, will differ in shade more or less from this strong case; but the body of the colour is the same in all. No man ought to furnish another with the means of transgressing the law, knowing that he intended to make that use of them [1]." The wholesome morality and enlarged policy of this passage make it almost irresistible to the judgment; and indeed the reasoning seems positively unanswerable.

§ 254. The doctrine of Lord Chief Justice Eyre has been expressly adopted in other cases. Thus, on one occasion [2], the Court of King's Bench in England, held, that a person who sold drugs to a brewer, knowing that they were intended to be used in the brewing of beer contrary to an Act of Parliament, was not entitled to recover the money due upon sale. Lord Ellenborough, on that occasion, said: "A person who sells drugs, with a knowledge that they are meant to be so mixed, may be said to cause or procure, *quantum in illo,* the drugs to be mixed. So, if a person sell goods with a knowledge, and in furtherance of the buyer's intention to convey them upon a smuggling adventure, he is

---

[1] Lightfoot *v.* Tenant, 1 Bos. & Pull. 351, 356.

[2] Langton *v.* Hughes, 1 Maule & Selw. 593.

not permitted by the policy of the law to recover such a sale[1]." And the other members of the Court concurred in that opinion. Mr. Justice Bayley added: "If a principal sell articles in order to enable the vendee to use them for illegal purposes, he cannot recover the price. The smuggling cases which were decided on that ground, are very familiar[2]." There are other cases which adopt the same general principle of enlightened justice[3]. It has, however, been directly denied in some later decisions[4]. Whether these last decisions will be sustained remains a question for the determination of other tribunals. It is difficult to perceive any just or solid ground, upon which a contract is maintainable, or ought to be enforced in the tribunals of a country, which is knowingly entered into in a foreign country, with the subjects of the former country, for the sale of goods, which are to be smuggled into it against its laws; for the sale thus made is the avowed means to accomplish the illegal end[5].

---

1 Langton *v.* Hughes, 1 Maule & Selw. 593.

2 Ibid.

3 Canaan *v.* Brice, 3 Barn & Adol. 179, 181; Catlin *v.* Bell, 4 Camp. R. 183.

4 Hodgson *v.* Temple, 5 Taunt. R. 183; Pellicat *v.* Angell, 2 Cromp. Mees. & Rosc. 311. See also Johnson *v.* Hudson, 11 East, R. 180.

5 In Pellicat *v.* Angell, 2 Cromp. Mees. & Rosc. 311, the case was of a bill of exchange, accepted in France by the defendant, a British subject, payable to the plaintiff, (a Frenchman), being for the price of goods sold by the plaintiff to the defendant in Paris for the avowed purpose of being smuggled into England. The bill was sued in the English Court of Exchequer. Lord Abinger on that occasion said: "It is perfectly clear, that, where parties enter into a contract to contravene the laws of their own country, such a contract is void; but it is equally clear, from a long series of cases, that the subject of a foreign country is not bound to pay allegiance or respect to the revenue laws of this; except, indeed, that where he comes within the act of breaking them himself, he cannot recover here the fruits of that illegal act. But there is nothing illegal in merely knowing that the goods he sells are to be disposed of in contravention of the fiscal laws of another country. It would have been most unfortunate if it were so in this country, where, for many years, a most extensive foreign trade was carried on directly in contravention of the fiscal laws of several other states. The distinction is, where he takes an actual

§ 255. There seems at present a strong inclination in the Courts of law to hold, that if a contract is made in foreign parts by a citizen or subject of a country for the sale of goods, which he knows at the time are to be smuggled in violation of the laws of his own country, he shall not be permitted to enforce it in the Courts of his own country; although the contract of sale is complete, and might be enforced in the like case of a foreigner[1]. The truer doctrine would seem to be, to make no distinction whatsoever

---

part in the illegal adventure, as in packing the goods in prohibited parcels or otherwise; there, he must take the consequences of his own act. But it has never been said, that merely selling to a party who means to violate the laws of his own country is a bad contract. If the position were true, which is contended for on the part of the defendant, that this appears upon the plea to have been a contract for the express purpose of smuggling the goods, it would follow, that it would be a breach of the contract, if the goods were not smuggled. But nothing of the kind appears upon the plea; it only states a transaction which occurs about once a week in Paris. The plaintiff sold the goods; the defendant might smuggle them, if he liked, or he might change his mind the next day; it does not at all import a contract, of which the smuggling was an essential part." It appears to me, that this reasoning is wholly unsatisfactory. The question is not, whether it is a part of the contract with the Frenchman, that the goods shall be smuggled; but whether he does not knowingly co-operate by the very sale, as far as in him lies to accomplish the illegal intention of a British subject to smuggle his goods contrary to the laws of his country. Can a British tribunal be called upon to enforce such a contract? Can it be called upon to aid a Frenchman to recover a debt, contracted for the purpose of violating British laws? Could a Frenchman, selling poison in France to an Englishman, for the avowed purpose of poisoning the King or Queen of England, recover on such a contract in England? In Wetherell *v.* Jones, (3 Barn. & Adol. R. 225,) Lord Tenterden said: "When a contract which a plaintiff seeks to enforce, is expressly or by implication forbidden by the statute or common law, no Court will lend its assistance to give it effect. And there are numerous cases in the Books, where an action on a contract has failed, because either the consideration for the promise, or the act to be done, was illegal, as being against the express provisions of the law, or contrary to justice, morality, or sound policy." Can a contract be fit to be entertained in a British Court, whose very object is to aid in a violation of British laws, and policy, and morals?

[1] Biggs *v.* Lawrence, 3 T. R. 454; Clugas *v.* Penaluna, 4 T. R. 466; Weymell *v.* Reed, 5 T. R. 599; Eunomus, Dial. 3, § 67; Executors of Cambioso *v.* Assignees of Moffat, 2 Wash. Cir. R. 98.

between the case of a sale between citizens or subjects, and the case of a sale between foreigners; but to hold the contract in each case to be utterly incapable of being enforced, at least in the Courts of the country whose laws are thus designedly sought to be violated. Sound morals and a due regard to international justice seem equally to approve such a conclusion [1].

§ 256. Pardessus has asked the question, whether, if Frenchmen have entered into a contract abroad, forbidden by the laws of the place where it is made, they can insist upon its execution in France; as, for example, a contract for contraband trade, or smuggling against the laws of that country. And he has answered, that he rather thinks they may; since this offence is only a violation of the law of the foreign state; and governments in this respect exercise a sort of mutual hostility; and, without openly favouring enterprises of a contraband nature, they do not proscribe them [2]. But this doctrine of Pardessus is certainly a departure from the general principle, that the validity of contracts depends upon the *lex loci contractûs;* for, in the case supposed, the contract is clearly void by the laws of the country where it is made.

§ 257. It might be different according to the received, although it should seem upon principle indefensible, doctrine of judicial tribunals, if the contract were made in some other country, or in the foreign country to which the parties belong; for (as has been seen [2]) it has been long laid down as a settled principle, that no nation is bound to protect, or to regard the revenue laws of another country; and, therefore, a contract made in one country by subjects or residents there to evade the revenue laws of another country, is not deemed illegal in the country of its origin [4].

---

1 Ante, § 244, 245.

2 5 Pardessus, art. 1492.

3 Ante, § 245.

4 See Boucher *v.* Lawson, Cas. Temp. Hard. 84, 89, 194; Holman *v.* Johnson, Cowper, R. 341; Biggs *v.* Lawrénce, 3 T. R. 454; Clugas *v.*

Against this principle Pothier has argued strongly, as being inconsistent with good faith and the moral duties of nations [1]. Valin, however, supports it; and Emérigon defends it, upon the unsatisfactory ground, that smuggling is a vice common to all nations [2]. An enlightened policy, founded upon national justice as well as national interest, would seem to favour the opinion of Pothier, in all cases where positive legislation has not adopted the principle as a retaliation upon the narrow and exclusive revenue system of another nation [3]. The contrary doctrine seems, however,

---

Peñaluna, 4 T. R. 466; Ludlow v. Van Rennsallaer, 1 John. R. 94; Lightfoot v. Tenant, 1 Bos. & Pull. 551, 557; Planché v. Fletcher, Doug. R. 251; Lever v. Fletcher, 1 Marsh. Insur. 58—61, 2nd edit.

[1] Pothier, Assur. n. 58.

[2] 2 Valin, Comm. art. 49, p. 127; 1 Emérig. ch. 8, § 5, p. 212, 215; (pp. 215—218, edité par Boulay-Paty,) and see note of Estrangin to Pothier, Assur. n. 58; 1 Marshall, Ins. ch. 3, § 1, pp. 59, 60, 2nd edit.

[3] It is gratifying to find that Mr. Marshall and Mr. Chitty have both taken side with Pothier on this point. The following passage from a work of the latter expounds the reasoning with considerable force: "There is something in these decisions to which a liberal mind cannot readily assent; and the impropriety of them seems to have been hinted at by Lord Kenyon in the before-mentioned case of Weymell v. Reed. It is impossible not to feel a greater inclination towards the opinion of Pothier, who observes, 'that a man cannot carry on a contraband trade in a foreign country, without engaging the subjects of that country to commit an offence against the laws which it is their duty to obey; and it is a crime of moral turpitude to engage a man to commit a crime; that a man, carrying on commerce in any country, is bound to conform to the laws of that country; and therefore to carry on an illicit commerce there, and to engage the subjects of that country to assist him in so doing, is against good faith; and consequently a contract made to favour or protect this commerce is peculiarly unlawful, and can raise no obligation. If our law be justifiable in protecting these transgressions, it can be only on the plea of necessity. But where is the necessity? Shall we be told, that it is impossible to ascertain in the English Courts the complex provisions of another country's revenue law? Surely this argument can avail but little, when it is recollected, that, in all cases where the argument is not convenient, the law of another country, however complex, is the rule by which contracts negotiated in that country are tried and construed. It may be true, that the rule of our law was adopted by way of retaliation for the illiberal conduct of other states, and is continued from a cautious policy. But a cautious policy in a great state is but too often a narrow policy; and, after all, the best

firmly established in the actual practice of modern nations, without any such discrimination, too firmly, perhaps, to be shaken, except by some legislative act abolishing it.

§ 258. (2.) The second class of excepted contracts comprehends those against good morals, or religion, or public rights[1]. Such are contracts made in a foreign country for future illicit cohabitation and prostitution[2]; contracts for the printing or circulation of irreligious and obscene publications; contracts to promote or reward the commission of crimes; contracts to corrupt or evade the due administration of justice; contracts to cheat public agents, or to defeat the public rights; and in short, all contracts which in their own nature are founded in moral turpitude, and are inconsistent

---

policy for a state, as well as for an individual, will perhaps be found to consist in honesty and honourable conduct. Indeed the system is so directly opposite to the clear principles of right feeling between man and man, that nothing could have withheld the states of Europe from concurring for its total abrogation, except the smallness of the gain or loss, that attends upon it." 1 Chitty on Commerce and Manuf., p. 83, 84; 1 Marshall Insur. 59—61, 2nd edit. Mr. Chancellor Kent has also added his own high authority in favor of the rule of Pothier. He has observed, "It is certainly matter of surprise and regret, that in such countries as France, England, and the United States, distinguished for a correct and enlightened administration of justice, smuggling voyages, made on purpose to elude the laws and seduce the subjects of foreign states, should be countenanced, and even encouraged, by the Courts of justice. The principle does no credit to the commercial jurisprudence of the age." 3 Kent, Comm. Lect. 48, pp. 266, 267, 3rd edit. See also La jeune Eugenie, 2 Mason, R. 459, 461.

[1] 1 Bell, Comm. § 232, pp. 232—242, 4th edit.; Id. pp. 297—314, 5th edit.

[2] See 1 Selwyn's Nisi Prius, Assumpsit, pp. 59, 60; Walker *v.* Perkins, 3 Burr. 1568; Greenwood *v.* Curtis, 6 Mass. R. 379; Birmington *v.* Wallis, 4 Barn. & Ald. 650; Lloyd *v.* Johnson, 1 Bos. & Pull. 340; Jones *v.* Randall, Cowp. R. 37; Appleton *v.* Campbell, 2 Carr. & P. 347; De Sobry *v.* De Laistre, 2 Harr. & John. R. 193, 228.—Lord Mansfield, in the case of Robinson *v.* Bland, 2 Burr. 1084, puts the very case. In many countries (says he) a contract may be maintained by a courtesan for the price of her prostitution; and one may suppose an action to be brought here; but that could never be allowed in this country. Therefore the lex loci cannot in all cases govern and direct.

with the good order and solid interests of society[1]. All such contracts, even though they might be held valid in the country where they are made, would be held void elsewhere, or at least ought to be, if the dictates of Christian morality, or even of natural justice, are allowed to have their due force and influence in the administration of international jurisprudence.

§ 259. (3.) The next class of excepted contracts comprehends those which are opposed to the national policy and institutions. For example, contracts made in a foreign country to procure loans in our own country, in order to assist the subjects of a foreign state in the prosecution of war against a nation with which we are at peace; for such conduct is inconsistent with a just and impartial neutrality[2]; contracts entered into with a foreign government, or its agents, (such as for a loan of money,) such government being a new government, unacknowledged by our own government, to which the party entering into the contract belongs[3]; for a like rule of public policy applies to such cases; contracts entered into by our own citizens or others in violation of a monopoly, granted by our own country to particular subjects thereof[4]; contracts by our own citizens or others to carry on trade with the enemy, or to cover enemy property, or to transport goods contraband of war[5]; contracts to carry into effect the African slave trade, or the

---

1 See Com. Dig. Assumpsit, (F. 7); Smith *v.* Stotesbury, 1 W. Bl. 204; S. C. 2 Burr. 924; Foxes *v.* Johnnes, 4 Esp. R. 97; Willis *v.* Baldwin, Doug. R. 450; Walcot *v.* Walker, 7 Vesey, R. 1; Southey *v.* Sherwood, 2 Merivale, 435, 441; Lawrence *v.* Smith, Jacob, R. 471, 474, note; Jones *v.* Randall, Cowp. R. 37; Furgusson on Marr. and Div. 396, 397.

2 De Weitz *v.* Hendricks, 9 Moore, R. 586; S. C. 2 Bing. R. 314.

3 Thompson *v.* Powles, 2 Simons, R. 194. See also Jones *v.* Garcia del Rio, 1 Turner & Russ. R. 299.

4 Pattison *v.* Mills, 1 Dow & Clarke, R. 342.

5 1 Marshall, Insur. B. 1, ch. 3, § 3, p. 78, § 4, p. 85, 2nd edit.; Griswold *v.* Waddington, 16 John. R. 438; 2 Wheaton, R. Appendix, 35; Richardson *v.* Maine Ins. Co., 6 Mass. R. 102, 110—113; Musson *v.* Fales, 16 Mass. R. 332; Coolidge *v.* Inglee, 13 Mass. R. 26.

rights of slavery in countries which refuse to acknowledge its lawfulness, at least if entered into by subjects of, or residents within, such countries[1]. In all such cases the contracts would, or might be, held utterly void, whatever might be their validity in the country where they are made; as being inconsistent with the duties, the policy, or the institutions of other countries where they are sought to be enforced[2].

§ 259 *a.* A case illustrative of the same principle, but of far less repugnancy to the policy and interests of the particular country where the rights under a contract are sought to be enforced, occurred in Louisiana. A debtor in another State made a contract, and transferred his property to certain creditors in preference to his general creditors, which was not deemed by the laws of that State fraudulent in regard to the latter creditors; he afterwards came to Louisiana, and was arrested there; and he then by petition sought the benefit of the insolvent laws of Louisiana, by whose laws such a preference would be fraudulent; and

---

[1] See Somerset's Case, Lofft's R. 1; 20 Howell's State Trials, 79; Fergusson on Marr. and Div. 396, 397; Madrazo *v.* Willes, 3 Barn. & Ald. 353; Forbes *v.* Cochrane, 2 Barn. & Cress. 448; and especially the opinion of Best, J.—I am not unaware of the bearing of the case of Greenwood *v.* Curtis, 6 Mass. R. 358, on this point; and without undertaking to examine its authority, it may be sufficient to say, that it is not without difficulty in its principles and application, as will abundantly appear from the elaborate argument of Mr. Justice Sedgwick in the same case (Id. 362, n.), and the later reasoning of Mr. Justice Best, in Forbes *v.* Cochrane, 2 Barn. & Cress. 448. I have given, in the text, what seems to me to be the just doctrine resulting from the modern cases, without meaning to assert, that the authorities cited are fully in point. Ante, § 96 *a.* Mr. Chief Justice Shaw, arguendo, in the case of Commonwealth *v.* Aves (Ante, § 96 *a*, p. 146, note,) held, that a suit brought here upon a note of hand, given in a State where slavery was allowed, for the price of a slave, might be maintainable in our Courts, and that the consideration would not be invalidated upon the ground of the consideration. It may be so here; but this doctrine, as one of universal application, may admit of question in other countries where slavery may be denounced as inhuman and unjust, and against public policy.

[2] 1 Bell, Comm. § 234—250, pp. 232—240, 4th edit.; Id. pp. 298—314, 5th edit.

would deprive the debtor of the benefit of a discharge under the insolvent acts of the State. The Court held, that as the debtor sought the benefit of the Louisiana laws, he could entitle himself to it only by shewing a compliance with all their provisions; and that the preference so given, being fraudulent by those laws, he was not entitled to the discharge. On that occasion the Court said,—" But it is said, that if we put such a construction upon the act, we give an extra-territorial operation to our law, by treating, as null, contracts sanctioned by the *lex loci,* and regarding as fraudulent those transactions which were in fact not only legal but meritorious. To this it may be answered, that we leave those contracts undisturbed, and take cognizance of them no further than as the voluntary disposition of property in reference to our own insolvent laws, when the insolvent seeks an extraordinary remedy, to which he would not be entitled by the law of his domicil; that of being declared exonerated from the payment of his remaining debts, on the assignment of the remainder of his effects. We look at them only so far as they form a condition, upon which depends his right to be discharged, and consequently as pertaining to the remedy sought for. It is further urged, that the acts spoken of in the statute must be shewn to have been done in contemplation of taking the benefit of the act, and that it cannot be supposed, that Andrews had in view the bankrupt laws of Louisiana when he made these assignments in Alabama. Taken in their literal sense, it is certainly difficult, if not impossible, to give any legal effect to these expressions, without resorting to the extravagant supposition, that the insolvent had procured his own arrest, by colluding with some one creditor, and that he had done other acts which would tend to defeat his own project. But the charge prayed for does not omit those expressions, and it is not now our duty to inquire in what sense they are to be understood, and whether, by the general principles of our law, all contracts of the kind spoken of, within three months preceding insolvency, between debtor and creditor, be not presumed to be in fraud of other creditors.[1]"

§ 259 *b*. A case of a more difficult character, if indeed it be not of a more questionable character, is one put by Lord Brougham, *arguendo*, in the course of one of his judgments. Speaking upon the point, that the *lex loci contractûs* is the governing rule in deciding upon the validity or invalidity of all personal contracts, he said:—"Thus, a marriage good by the laws of one country, is held good in all others where the question of its validity may arise. For why? The question always must be:—Did the parties intend to contract marriage? And if they did what in the place they were in is deemed a marriage, they cannot reasonably, or sensibly, or safely be considered otherwise than as intending a marriage contract. The laws of each nation lay down the forms and solemnities, a compliance with which shall be deemed the only criterion of the intention to enter into the contract. If those laws annex certain qualifications to parties circumstanced in a particular way, or if they impose certain conditions precedent on certain parties, this falls exactly within the same rule: for the presumption of law is in the one case, that the parties are absolutely incapable of the consent required to make the contract; and in the other case, that they are incapable until they have complied with the conditions imposed. I shall only stop here to remark, that the English jurisprudence, while it adopts this principle in words, would not, perhaps, in certain cases which may be put, be found very willing to act upon it throughout. Thus, we should expect that the Spanish and Portuguese Courts would hold an English marriage avoidable between uncle and niece, or brother and sister-in-law, though solemnized under papal dispensation; because it would clearly be avoidable in this country. But I strongly incline to think, that our Courts would refuse to sanction, and would avoid by sentence, a marriage

---

[1] Andrews *v*. His Creditors, 11 Louis. R. 464, 479.

between those relatives contracted in the Peninsula, under dispensation, although beyond all doubt such a marriage would there be valid by the *lex loci contractûs*, and incapable of being set aside by any proceedings in that country[1]."

§ 260. (4.) Another rule, naturally flowing from, or rather illustrative of, that already stated, respecting the validity of contracts, is, that all the formalities, proofs, or authentications of them, which are required by the *lex loci* are indispensable to their validity every where else[2]. And this is in precise conformity to the rule laid down on the subject by Boullenois[3]. *Il faut, par rapport à la forme intrinseque et constitutive des actes, suivre encore la loi du contrat. Quand la Loi exige certaines formalites, lesquelles sont attachées aux choses mêmes, il faut suivre la loi de la situation*[4]. Burgundus has expressed the same doctrine in very pointed terms. *Et quidem in scriptura instrumenti, in solemnitatibus, et ceremoniis, et generaliter in omnibus quæ ad formam ejusque perfectionem pertinent, spectanda est consuetudo regionis ubi fit negotiatio*[5]. Dumoulin says,— *Aut statutum loquitur de his quæ concernunt nudam ordinationem vel solemnitatem actus; et semper inspicitur statu-*

---

1 Warrender *v.* Warrender, 9 Bligh, R. 111, 112; Post, § 226 *c.*

2 See Ante, § 123; 1 Burge, Comm. on For. and Col. Law, Pt. 1. ch. 1, pp. 29, 30; 3 Burge, Comm. Pt. 2, ch. 20, pp. 752—764; Fœlix, Conflit des Lois, Revue Etrang. et Fran. tom. 7, (1840), § 40—51, pp. 346—360; Warrender *v.* Warrender, 9 Bligh, 111; Ante, § 259 *c.*

3 Erskine's Inst. B. 3, tit. 2, § 39—41, pp. 514, 515; Boullenois, Quest. Mixt. p. 5; Bouhier, Cout. de Bourg. ch. 21, § 205; 2 Boullenois, Observ. 46, p. 467; Ante, § 240; 1 Hertii Op. de Collis, Leg. § 4, n. 59, edit. 1737), Id, p. 209, (edit. (1716). See also Voet, ad Pand. lib. 5, tit. 1, § 51; 1 Boullenois, Observ. 23, p. 523; Id. pp. 446—466; Henry on Foreign Law, 37, 38; Id. 224; 5 Pardessus, Droit Comm. art. 1485; Mr. Justice Martin, in Depau *v.* Humphreys, 20 Martin, R. 1, 22; Ante, § 122, 259 *b.*; Post, § 299 *a.*

4 2 Boullenois, Observ. 46, p. 467; Ante, § 240; 1 Boullenois Observ. 23, pp. 491, 492.

5 Burgundus, Tract. 4, n. 7, n. 29; Post, § 300 *a*; 2 Boullenois, Observ. 46, pp. 450, 451.

tum vel consuetudinem loci ubi actus celebratur, sive in contractibus, sive in judiciis, sive in testamentis, sive in instrumentis, aut aliis conficiendis[1]. And again:—*In concernentibus contractum, et emergentibus, spectatur locus in quo contrahitur; et in concernentibus meram solemnitatem cujuscunque actus, locus in quo ille celebratur.*[2] Casaregis says,—*Communissima enim est distinctio, quod aut disseritur de modo procedendi in judicio, aut de juribus contractus, cui robur et specialis forma tributa est a statuto, vel a contrahentibus. Et in primo casu attendendum sit statutum loci in quo judicium agitatur; in secundo, vero, casu attendatur statutum loci in quo fuit celebratus contractus*[3]. Hertius is still more direct:—*Si lex actui formam dat, inspiciendus est locus actûs, non domicilii, non rei sitæ; id est, si de solemnibus quæratur, si de loco, de tempore, de modo actûs, ejus loci habenda est ratio ubi actus sive negotium celebratur*[4]. Christinæus, Everhardus, and other distinguished jurists, adopt the same doctrine[5]. And it seems fully established in the common law. Thus, if by the laws of a

---

[1] Molin. Opera, Comment. Cod. lib. 1, tit. 4, l. 1, Conclus. de Statut, tom. 3, p. 554, (edit. 1681); Post, § 441, § 479 *k*.

[2] Molin. Opera, tit. 1, De fiefs, § 12, Gloss. 7, n. 37, tom. 1, p. 224, (edit. 1681).

[3] Casaregis, Disc. Comm. 179, n. 59.

[4] Hertii Opera, Collis. Leg. § 4, n. 10, p. 126; Id. n. 59, p. 148, (edit. 1737); Id. p. 179, p. 209, (edit. 1716); Post, § 3, 8, 10, 11. See also Cochin, Œuvres, tom. 1, p. 72, 4to. edit.; Id. tom. 3, p. 26; Id. tom. 5, p. 697; D'Aguesseau, Œuvres, tom. 4, pp. 637, 722, 4to. edit.

[5] Everhard. Consil. 72, n. 11, p. 206; Id. n. 18, p. 207; Id. 27, p. 209; Post, § 300 *b*; Christin. Decis. 283, vol. 1, p. 355, n. 1, 4, 5, 8, 9, 10, 11; Post, § 300 *c*; Molin. Comment. ad Consuet. Paris. tit. 1, § 12, Gloss. 7, n. 37, tom. 1, p. 224; Post, § 300 *d*; 2 Boullenois, Observ. 46, pp. 460, 461; Ante, § 122.—Dumoulin pushes the doctrine further, and says:—Et est omnium Doctorum sententia, ubicumque consuetudo, vel statutum locale, disponit de solemnitate vel forma actus, ligari etiam exteros ibi actum illum gerentes, et gestum esse validum et efficacem ubique, etiam super bonis solis extra territorium consuetudinis. Molin. Consil. 53, § 9; Molin. Oper. tom. 2, p. 965, (edit. 1681); 2 Burge, Comm. on Col. and For. Law, Pt. 2, ch. 9, pp. 865, 866; Post, § 441.

country a contract is void, unless it is written on stamped paper, it ought to be held void every where; for unless it be good there, it can have no obligation in any other country[1]. It might be different if the contract had been

[1] Alves *v.* Hodgson, 7 T. R. 237; Clegg *v.* Levy, 3 Camp. R. 166. But see Chitty on Bills, (8th edit.), p. 143, n; and Wynne *v.* Jackson, 2 Russ., R. 351; 3 Burge, Comm. on Col. and For. Law, Pt. 2, ch. 20, p. 762.—The case of Wynne *v.* Jackson, 2 Russ. R. 351, is certainly at variance with this doctrine. It was a bill brought to stay proceedings at law on a suit brought in England by the holder, against the acceptor of bills of exchange, made and accepted in France, and which, in an action brought in the French courts, had been held invalid for want of a proper French stamp. The Vice-Chancellor held, "that the circumstance of the bills being drawn in France, in such a form that the holder could not recover on them in France, was no objection to his recovering on them in an English court." This doctrine is wholly irreconcilable with that in Alves *v.* Hodgson, 7 T. R. 241, and Clegg *v.* Levy, 3 Camp. R. 166; and if by the laws of France such contracts were void if not on stamped paper, it is equally unsupportable upon acknowledged principles. In the case of James *v.* Catherwood, 3 Dowl. & Ry. 190, where assumpsit was brought for money lent in France, and unstamped paper receipts were produced in proof of the loan, evidence was offered to shew, that by the laws of France such receipts required a stamp to render them valid; but it was rejected by the Court, and the receipts were admitted in evidence upon the ground that the Courts of England could not take notice of the revenue laws of a foreign country. But this is a very insufficient ground, if the loan required such receipt and stamp to make it valid as a contract. And if the loan was good per se, but the stamp was requisite to make the receipt good as evidence, then another question might arise, whether other proof than that required by the law of France was admissible of a written contract. This case also is inconsistent with the case in 3 Camp. R. 166. Can a contract be good in any country, which is void by the law of the place where it is made, because it wants the solemnities required by that law? Would a parol contract made in England, respecting an interest in lands, against the Statute of Frauds, be held valid elsewhere? Would any court dispense with the written evidence required upon such a contract? On a motion for a new trial, the Court refused it, Lord Chief Justice Abbott saying: "The point is too plain for argument. It has been settled, or at least considered as settled, ever since the time of Lord Hardwicke, that in a British Court we cannot take notice of the revenue laws of a foreign state. It would be productivè of prodigious inconvenience if, in every case in which an instrument was executed in a foreign country, we were to receive in evidence what the law of that country was, in order to ascertain whether the nstrument was or was not valid." With great sub-

made payable in another country, or if the objection were, not to the validity of the contract, but merely to the admissibility of other proof of the contract in the foreign court[1], where a suit was brought to enforce it; or if the contract concerned real or immovable property situate in another country whose laws are different, respecting which, as we shall presently see, there is a difference of opinion among foreign jurists, although in England and America the rule seems firmly established, that the law *rei sitæ*, and not that of the place of the contract, is to prevail[2].

§ 260 *a*. So, where the forms of public instruments are regulated by the laws of a country, they must be strictly followed, to entitle them to be held valid elsewhere. As, for example, if a protest of a bill of exchange, made in another State, is required by the laws of that State to be under

---

mission to his Lordship, this reasoning is wholly inadmissible. The law is as clearly settled as anything can be, that a contract void by the law of the place where it is made, is void every where. Yet, in every such case, whatever may be the inconvenience, Courts of Law are bound to ascertain what the foreign law is. And it would be a perfect novelty in jurisprudence to hold, that an instrument which for want of due solemnities in the place where it was executed was void, should yet be valid in other countries. We can arrive at such a conclusion only by overturning well-established principles. The case alluded to before Lord Hardwicke, was probably Boucher *v.* Lawson (Cases T. Hard. 85), Id. 194, which was the case of a contract between Englishmen to be executed in England, to carry on a smuggling trade against the laws of Portugal. Lord Hardwicke said, that such a trade was not only a lawful trade in England, but very much encouraged. The case is wholly distinguishable from the present case, and from that of any contract made in a country, and to be executed there, which is invalid by its laws. A contract made in Portugal by persons domiciled there, to carry on smuggling against its laws, would, or ought to be held void every where. See also 3 Chitty on Comm. and Manuf. ch. 2, p. 166.

[1] Ludlow *v.* Van Rensselaer, 1 John. R. 93; James *v.* Catherwood, 3 Dowl. & Ry. 190. See Clarke *v.* Cochran, 3 Martin, R. 358, 360, 361; Brown *v.* Thornton, 6 Adolph. & Ellis, R. 185; Yates *v.* Thomson, 3 Clarke & Fin. R. 544.

[2] Post, § 363—373, § 435—445; Fœlix, Confl. des Lois, Revue Etrang. et Fran. tom. 7, (1840), § 40—50, pp. 316—359.

seal, a protest not under seal will not be regarded as evidence of the dishonour of the bill [1].

§ 261. The ground of this doctrine, as commonly stated, is, that every person contracting in a country is understood to submit himself to the law of the place, and silently to assent to its action upon his contract. Paul Voet has expressed it in the following language: *Quid si de contractibus proprie dictis, et quidem eorum solemnibus contentio; quis locus spectabitur, an domicilii contrahentis, an loci ubi quis contrahit? Respondeo, affirmanter; Posterius. Quia censetur quis, semet contrahendo, legibus istius loci ubi contrahit, etiam ratione solemnium subjicere voluisse. Ut quemadmodum loci consuetudo subintrat contractum, ejusque est declarativa ita etiam loci statutum* [2]. It would, perhaps, be more correct to say, that the law of the place of the contract acts upon it, independently of any volition of the parties, in virtue of the general sovereignty possessed by every nation, to regulate all persons and property, and transactions

---

1 Ticknor *v.* Roberts, 11 Louis. R. 14.

2 P.Voet, De Stat. § 9, ch. 2, n. 9, p. 267; Id. p. 323, (edit. 1661); Cochin, Œuvres, tom. 5, p. 697, 4to edit.; Fergusson on Mar. and Divorce, p. 397; 2 Boullenois, Observ. 46, pp. 475, 476; Id. pp. 500—502; Casaregis Disc. 179, § 56; Ante, § 122.—Boullenois and some other jurists contest the universality of this presumed assent to the law of the place of the contract; and assert, that the principle generally and broadly taken, généralement et cruement (nuditer et indistincte), is not correct. But where no other place of performance is pointed out, it seems difficult to see what other law is to govern. See 2 Boullenois, Observ. 46, pp. 457—459; Id. 501, 502—518; Bouhier, Cout. de Bourg. ch. 21, § 191, 192; Voet, De Stat. § 9, ch. 2, § 10, p. 269; Id. p. 325, (edit. 1661). Hertius even goes so far as to say, that the law of the place of a contract does not govern where the party is a stranger, ignorant of its laws:—"Non valet, si exterus ignoravit statutum." 1 Hertii Opera, De Collis. Leg. § 4, pp. 126, 127, § 10, (edit. 1737); Id. p. 179, (edit. 1716). See also 2 Boullenois, Observ. 46, p. 502. Can a stranger, living in a country, plead ignorance of the laws of that country in his defence? Is he not bound by them, whether he knows them or not? Huberus, on the contrary, holds, that the law of the place of the contract governs, not only in respect to those who are domiciled, but those who are commorant there. Huberus, lib. 1, tit. 3, De Conflict. Leg. § 3.

within its own territory[1]. And in admitting the law of a foreign country to govern in regard to contracts made there, every nation merely recognises, from a principle of comity, the same right to exist in other nations which it demands and exercises for itself[2]. Some foreign jurists make an exception from the general rule, in cases of contract made in a foreign country by any persons, for the purpose of evading the revenue system or the local solemnities prescribed by the laws of their own country, respecting such contracts[3]. Thus, Paul Voet lays it down among his exceptions: *Nisi quis, quo in loco domicilii evitaret molestam aliquam vel sumptuosam solemnitatem, adeoque in fraudem sui statuti nullâ necessitate cogente alio proficiscatur, et mox ad locum domicilii, gesto alibi negotio, revertatur*[4]. *Nisi etiam extra locum domicilii velit uti statuto suæ patriæ favorabili, quoad solemnia; tu forte contractus alibi ita gestus, ubi alia solemnia erant adhibenda, ex æquo et bono in patria, sustineretur*[5].

§ 262. Illustrations of this rule might be easily multiplied. Thus, by the English and American law, contracts which fall within the purview of what is called the Statute of Frauds, are required to be in writing; such are contracts respecting the sale of lands, contracts for the debts of third persons, and contracts for the sale of goods beyond a certain value. If such contracts, made by parol (*per verba*) in a country by whose laws they are required to be in writing, are sought to be enforced in any other country, they will be held void, exactly as they are held void in the place where they are made. And the like rule applies, *vice versâ*, where parol contracts are good by the law of the place

---

1 See the opinion of Mr. Chief Justice Marshall, in Ogden *v.* Saunders, 12 Wheat. R. 332, 338—347.

2 Blanchard *v.* Russell, 13 Mass. R. 1, 4.

3 P. Voet, De Stat. § 9, ch. 2, n. 9, p. 268, Excep. 3, 4; Id. p. 324, (edit. 1661).

4 Id. Excep. 2, p. 268, (edit. 1715); Id. p. 324; (edit. 1661).

5 Ibid.

where they are made; but they would be void if originally made in another place where they are sought to be enforced, for want of certain solemnities, or for want of being in writing, as required by the local law[1]. It is a very different question, as we shall presently see, what rule is to prevail, where the contract respects real or immovable property, and the law of the place of the contract and that of the *situs rei* require different forms and solemnities to give validity to them[2].

§ 262 *a*. But suppose goods are bargained for by a merchant in one country, to be paid for on delivery by a merchant in another country who is domiciled there, and has given the order therefor; and the law of the country where the bargain is made, does not require that there should be any memorandum thereof in writing; but the law of the country where the delivery is to be made, does require such a memorandum in writing. By what law is the bargain to be governed;—by the law of the place of the bargain, or by that of the place of delivery? It seems to have been

---

[1] 2 Boullenois, Observ. 33, pp. 459—461; 1 Boullenois, Observ. 46, pp. 492—498; Id. 499; Id. 506; Id. 523; Erskine's Inst. B. 3, tit. 2, § 39, 40; Vidal *v.* Thompson, 11 Martin, R. 23; Casaregis, Disc. 179, n. 59, 60; 1 Hertii Opera, De Collis. Leg. p. 148, § 59, (edit. 1737); Boullenois, Quest. de la Contrar. des Loix, p. 5; Livermore Diss. p. 46, § 41; 1 Burge, Comm. Pt. 1, ch. 1, p. 29; 3 Burge, Comm. p. 2, c. 20, pp. 758—762, 769; Alves *v.* Hodgson, 7 T. R. 241; Clegg *v.* Levy, 3 Camp. 166. But see Wynne *v.* Jackson, 2 Russ. R. 251; and James *v.* Catherwood, 3 Dowl. & Ry. 190; Ante, § 260, and note, p. 216; Post, § 362—373. Hertius seems to think, that if foreigners in another country make a contract according to the law of their own country (both belonging to the same country), in such a case, the contract will avail in their own country, even if not made according to the lex loci contractûs. 1 Hertii Opera, De Collis. Legum, § 10, pp. 126, 128, (edit. 1737); Id. pp. 179—181, (edit. 1716.) So is Voet, De Statut. § 9, ch. 2, Excep. 4, p. 268, (edit. 1716); Id. p. 325, (edit. 1661). But Boullenois has observed, that he does not find any authors, who are of opinion, that such a contract made elsewhere, according to the law of their own country, ought to have place even beyond the country. 2 Boullenois, Observ. 46, p. 459.

[2] Post, § 363—373, § 435—445; 1 Boullenois, Observ. 23, pp. 448—472.

thought, that, in such a case, the law of the place of delivery is to govern[1].

§ 263. (5.) Another rule, illustrative of the same general principle, is, that the law of the place of the contract is to govern, as to the nature, the obligation, and the interpretation of the contract: *Locus contractûs regit actum*[2]. Again: *Quod si de ipso contractu quæratur* (says Paul Voet) *seu de naturâ ipsius, seu de iis, quæ ex naturâ contractûs veniunt, puta fidejussione, etc. etiam spectandum est loci statutum, ubi contractus celebratur; quod ei contrahentes semet accommodare præsumantur*[3]. First, as to the nature of the contract;

---

[1] The case of Acebal *v.* Levy, 10 Bing. R. 376, seems to have involved this very question, although it does not appear to have attracted the attention either of the Bar or of the Court. The case went off upon a supposed variance between the counts and the evidence. The statement of the facts in the body of the Report does not shew, whether the goods in the case, which were sold and shipped at Gigon, in Spain, by order of an agent of the defendants, and were to be sent to the defendants in England, were sold to be paid for in England after their arrival and delivery there, or were to be paid for on their shipment. But Lord Chief Justice Tindal, in delivering the opinion of the Court, said, that in point of fact the parol evidence at the trial established, that the price of the goods was to be the current shipping price at Gigon; and to be paid for on the delivery thereof in England. The defendants refused to receive them; and the agent of the plaintiff then sold them for account of the plaintiff, and the action was brought for the difference between the price of the purchase and the sale thus made. One of the objections taken was, that there was no memorandum in writing required by the English Statute of Frauds. The objection was not sustained, because the Court thought that there was a sufficient memorandum, but the memorandum varied from the counts in the declaration. But the Court and Bar seem to have supposed that the English Statute of Frauds did apply to the case; which is certainly a matter open to much discussion, and as we shall presently see (Post, § 285, 318) has been thought open to a very different conclusion. See Vidal *v.* Thompson, 11 Martin, R. 23—25.

[2] 1 Emér. Assur. ch. 4, § 8, pp. 122, 125, 128. See Casaregis, Disc. 179, § 60; Erskine's Inst. B. 3, tit. 2, § 39, 40, pp. 514, 515; Delvalle *v.* Plomer, 3 Camp. R. 444; Harrison *v.* Sterry, 5 Cranch, 289; Le Roy *v.* Crowninshield, 2 Mason, R. 15; Van Reimsdyke *v.* Kane, 1 Gallis. R. 371; 2 Kent, Comm. Lect. 37, p. 394, Lect. 39, p. 458—460, 3rd edit.

[3] P. Voet, De Stat. § 9, ch. 2, § 10, 269, (edit. 1737); Id. p. 325, (edit. 1661). J. Voet is still more full on the same point. Voet, Ad Pand. lib. 4, tit. 1, § 29, pp. 240, 241. Si adversus contractum (says he) aliudve negotium gestum factumve restitutio desideretur, dum quis aut metu, aut dolo,

by which is meant those qualities, which properly belong to it, and by law or custom always accompany it, or inhere in

aut errore lapsus, damnum sensit contrahendo, transigendo, solvendo, fidejubendo, hereditatem adeundo, aliove simili modo; recte interpretes statuisse arbitror, leges regionis in quâ contractum gestumve est id, contra quod restitutio petitur, locum sibi debere vindicare in terminandâ ipsâ restitutionis controversiâ, sive res illæ de quibus contractum est et in quibus læsio contigit, eodem in loco, sive alibi sitæ sint. Nec intererit, utrum læsio circa res ipsas contigerit, veluti pluris minorisve, quam æquum est, errore justo distractas, an vero propter neglecta solennia in loco contractûs desiderata. Si tamen contractus implementum non in ipso contractûs loco fieri debeat, sed ad locum alium sit destinatum, non loci contractûs, sed implementi leges spectandas esse ratio suadet: ut ita, secundum cujus loci jura implementum accipere debuit contractus, juxta ejus etiam leges resolvatur. Boullenois says, that Jurists distinguish four things in contracts. (1.) Substantialia contractuum; (2.) Naturalia contractuum; (3.) Accidentalia contractuum; (4.) Solemnia contractuum. He says: Ils appellent substantialia contractuum, tout ce qui sert à la composition intérieure des contrats; c'est-à-dire, tout ce qui est de l'essence déterminant la nature de chaque acte, et sans quoi il ne seroit pas un tel acte. Substantialia sunt, quæ ita formam et essentiam uniuscujusque actûs constituunt, ut sine iis talis actus esse non possit, cùm forma dat unicuique esse id, quod est. Suivant cette définition, le consentement des parties dans tous les contrats, la chose, et le prix de la chose dans un contrat de vente, pertinent ad substantialia contractuum et ad speciem contractûs constituendam; et elles sont tellement nécessaires, intrinseques et constitutives d'un contrat, que sine iis actus qui geritur, non valeat. Naturalia contractuum, ces sont les suites et les engagements qui fluent et dérivent de la nature et de l'espèce des contrats, dont il s'agit. Naturalia contractuum dicuntur ea, quæ pendent et manant à natura et potestate cujusque actûs; sed ejus formam non constituunt. Telle est la garantie dans la vente. Mais par rapport à ces engagements qui dérivent des contrats, on en distingue de deux sortes. Il y en a, quæ sunt interna, intrinseca, et inseparabilia; c'est-à-dire, qui sont liés et attachés à chaque espèce de contrats, et qui sont propres à chacun de ces contrats, suivant la différente nature, dont ils sont. Quæ naturæ contractûs cohærent, et sunt veluti propriæ possessiones, propriæ affectiones ab essentialibus cujusque contractûs principiis enatæ. Telle est, dans un contrat de vente, la nécessité que le domaine de la chose vendue, soit transféré à l' acquéreur; et à cet égard on ne peut se soustaire à ces choses; on ne pourroit pas en effet stipuler, que le domine de la chose vendue ne passeroit pas à l'acquéreur; et il y en a qui ne naissent que de l'usage ordinaire où on est d'en convenir, et qui, à raison de ce, sont toujours présumés être convenus par les parties. Quæ ex consuetudine etiam insunt contractibus, quæ consuetudo in naturam quasi contractûs transiit; et on les appelle, externa et separabilia. Telle est la garantie de fait dans une cession, et à cet égard on peut y déroges, les parties peuvent stipuler qu'il n'y aura d'autre

it[1]. Foreign jurists are accustomed to call such qualities *Naturalia contractus*[2]. *Ea enim, quæ autoritate legis vel con-*

---

garantie que celle que l'on appelle garantie de droit. Accidentalia contractûs, ce sont les choses, qui ne sont point de la substance constitutive de l'acte, qui ne fluent et ne dérivent point de sa nature et de son espèce, et ne tombent point en convention ordinaire; mais qui ne se recontrent dans les contrats que parce que les parties en conviennent. Accidentalia contractûs ea sunt, quæ neque substantiam contractuum constituunt, neque ex naturâ et potestate contractûs dimanant, sed pro voluntate contrahentium, adjici contractibus solent, veluti varia pacta. Je voudrois ajouter, et encore celles, qui ne sont requises que par des dispositions légales, à la vérité, mais pures locales, comme la nécessité de donner caution pour la garantie d'un contrat, laquelle a lieu dans certains endroits. Enfin, il y a, solemnia contractuum; et on en distingue de deux sortes, solemnia intrinseca, et solemnia extrinseca. Solemnia intrinseca sunt ea, quæ insunt in ipsâ formâ cujusque actûs, neque separari ab eâ possunt; telles sont les choses qui appartiennent à la preuve et à l'authenticité de l'acte, et qui comme telles sont partie de ce qui constitue l'être et l'existence de cet acte; aussi sont-elles appellées par quelques-uns substantialia contractuum. Solemnia extrinseca sunt ea, quæ actui per se formam habenti, et ultra conventionem contrahentium, sed ad ipsam conventionem roborandam, extrinsecus accedunt, et ce sont les choses, qui n'appartenant en rien à la composition intrinseque de l'acte, sont seulement requises, post actum originatum, pour lui procurer son exécution. La solemnité intrinseque est tellement nécessaire, que si on l'omet, l'acte n'est pas acte, il n'a nul être, nulle existence; l'omission vitiat et corrumpit actum; raison pour laquelle on la place volontiers inter substantialia contractuum. Mais à l'égard de la solemnité extrinseque, il n'en est pas toujours de même, aliquando obmissa impedit executionem ex omni parte. 1 Boullenois, Observ. 23, pp. 446—448. See also 2 Burge, Comm. on Col. and For. Law, Pt. 2, ch. 9, pp. 848—850; 3 Burge, Comm. on Col. and For. Law, Pt. 2, ch. 20, pp. 758—763; Don *v.* Lippman, 5 Clarke & Fin. 1, 12, 13.

[1] Pothier, as well as other jurists, distinguish between the essence, the nature, and the accidents of contracts: the former includes whatever is indispensible to the constitution of it; the next, whatever is included in it, without being expressly mentioned by operation of law, but is capable of a severance without destroying it; and the last, those things which belong to it only by express agreement. Without meaning to contest the propriety of this division, I am content to include the two former in the single word, nature, as quite conformable to our English idiom. Cujas also adopts the same course. See Pothier, Oblig. n. 5. See also 2 Boullenois, Observ. 46, pp. 460—462; Bayou *v.* Vavasseur, 10 Martin, R. 61; Merlin, Répertoire Convention, § 2, n. 6, p. 357; Rodenburg, De Div. Stat. tit. 2, ch. 5, § 16; 2 Boullenois, App. 50; 1 Boullenois, 688; 3 Burge, Comm. on Col. and For. Law, Pt. 2, ch. 20, pp. 848—851.

[2] 1 Boullenois, Observ. 23, p. 446; 2 Boullenois, Observ. 46, pp. 460

suetudinis contractum comitantur, eidem adherent, Naturalia à Doctoribus appellantur. Lex enim altera est quasi natura, et in naturam transit. Atque quoad naturalia contractuum etiam forenses statuta loci contractus observare debent[1]. Thus, whether a contract be a personal obligation or a real obligation; whether it be conditional or absolute; whether it be the principal or the accessary; whether it be that of principal or of surety; whether it be of limited or of universal operation; these are points properly belonging to the nature of the contract, and are dependent upon the law and custom of the place of the contract, whenever there are no express terms in the contract itself, which otherwise control them. By the law of some countries, there are certain joint contracts, which bind each party for the whole *in solido;* and there are other joint contracts, where the parties are, under circumstances, bound only for several and distinct portions[2]. In each case the law of the place of the contract regulates the nature of the contract, in the absence of any express stipulations[3]. These

---

461; Voet, De Stat. § 9, ch. 10, § 10, p. 287; Id. p. 325, (edit. 1661); Hertius, De Collis. Leg. tom. 1, § 10, p. 127; Id. pp. 179, 180, (edit. 1716); Post, § 301 *f.*

[1] Lauterback, Diss. 104, Pt. 3, n. 58, cited 2 Boullenois, Obs. 46, p. 460.

[2] 4 Burge, Comm. on Col. and For. Law, Pt. 2, ch. 15, § 4, pp. 722—735; Post, § 322.

[3] Pothier on Oblig. n. 261—268; Van Leeuwen, Comm. B. 4, ch. 4, § 1; Fergusson *v.* Flower, 16 Martin, R. 312; 2 Boullenois, Observ. 46, p. 463; Code Civil of France, art. 1197, 1202, 1220, 1222; Id. Code of Comm. art. 22, 140.—One may see, how strangely learned men will reason on subjects of this nature, by consulting Boullenois. He puts the case of a contract, made in a country where all parties would be bound in solido, and by the law of their own domicil they would be entitled to the benefit of a division, and vice versâ; and asks, What law is to govern? In each case he decides, that the law should govern which is most favourable to the debtor. "Ainsi, les obligês solidaires ont contracté sous une loi, qui leur est favorable; j'embrasse cette loi; elle leur est contraire, j'embrasse la loi de leur domicile." 2 Boullenois, Observ. 46, pp. 463, 464. See also Bouhier, ch. 21, § 198, 199.

may therefore be said to constitute the nature of the contract[1].

---

[1] See Henry on Foreign Law, 39.—Pothier on Obligations, n. 7, has explained the meaning of the words, the nature of the contract, in the following manner:—" Things which are only of the nature of the contract are those, which, without being of the essence, form a part of it though not expressly mentioned; it being of the nature of the contract, that they shall be included and understood. These things have an intermediate place between those which are of the essence of the contract, and those which are merely accidental to it, and differ from both of them. They differ from those which are of the essence of the contract, inasmuch as the contract may subsist without them, and they may be excluded by the express agreement of the parties; and they differ from things which are merely accidental to it, inasmuch as they form a part of it without being particularly expressed, as may be illustrated by the following examples. In the contract of sale, the obligation of warranty which the seller contracts with the purchaser, is of the nature of the contract of sale; therefore the seller, by the act of sale, contracts this obligation, though the parties do not express it, and there is not a word respecting it in the contract; but as the obligation is of the nature and not of the essence of the contract of sale, the contract of sale may subsist without it; and if it is agreed, that the seller shall not be bound to warranty, such agreement will be valid, and the contract will continue a real contract of sale. It is also of the nature of the contract of sale, that, as soon as the contract is completed by the consent of the parties, although before delivery, the thing sold is at the risk of the purchaser; and that, if it happens to perish, without the fault of the seller, the loss falls upon the purchaser, who is, notwithstanding the misfortune, liable for the price; but as that is only of the nature, and not of the essence of the contract, the contrary may be agreed upon. Where a thing is lent, to be specifically returned [commodatur], it is of the nature of the contract that the borrower shall be answerable for the slightest negligence in respect of the article lent. He contracts this obligation to the lender by the very nature of the contract, and without anything being said about it. But as this obligation is of the nature, and not of the essence of the contract, it may be excluded by an express agreement, that the borrower shall only be bound to act with fidelity, and shall not be responsible for any accidents merely occasioned by his negligence. It is also of the nature of this contract, that the loss of the thing lent, when it arises from inevitable accident, falls upon the lender. But as that is of the nature, and not of the essence of the contract, there may be an agreement to charge the borrower with every loss that may happen, until the thing is restored. A great variety of other instances might be adduced from the different kinds of contracts. Those things which are accidental to a contract are such as, not being of the nature of the contract, are only included in it by express agree-

§ 264. An illustration may be taken from a case often put by the civilians. By the law of some countries a warranty is implied in all cases of sale; by that of others, it is not. Suppose a contract of sale is made in any of the former countries, by parties domiciled in any of the latter countries: if the contract is to be executed in the country where it is made, a warranty will be implied, as an incident arising from the nature of the contract; if it is to be executed in the place of the domicil of the parties, for reasons which we shall presently see, no warranty will be implied[1]. By the civil law, there is an implied warranty, as to the quality and soundness of goods sold; by the common law, there is not[2]. A sale of goods in England would be governed by the common law; a sale in a foreign country, under the civil law, would be governed by that law, as to this implied warranty. Boullenois lays down this as one of his fundamental rules, in the interpretation of contracts. Whenever (says he) the controversy respects movables, of which an immediate delivery is made, the law of the place of the contract is to govern; adopting on this point the doctrine, although not the reasoning, of Colerus. *Consuetudo si quidem loci ubi negotium geritur, ita subintrat ipsum contractum; ut secundum leges loci intelligatur actus fuisse celebratus, quamvis ea de re nihil fuerit expressum*[3].

§ 265. Another illustration may be borrowed from an actual decision under the common law. By the law of England, an acceptance of a bill of exchange binds the

---

ment. For instance, the allowance of a certain time for paying the money due, the liberty of paying it by instalments, that of paying another thing instead of it, of paying to some other person than the creditor, and the like, are accidental to the contract; because they are not included in it without being particularly expressed."

1 Pothier, Oblig. n. 7; 2 Boullenois, Obs. 46, pp. 475, 476; Id. 460—463; Code Civil of France, art. 1135; Voet, De Statut, § 9, ch. 2, § 10, p. 269, (edit. 1715); Id. p. 325, (edit. 1661); 3 Burge, Comm. on Col. and For. Law, Pt. 2, ch. 20, pp. 769, 770.

2 Pothier, Pand. Lib. 19, tit. 1, art. 5, § 48—51; 2 Black. Comm. 451; 2 Kent Comm. Lect. 39, pp. 478—481, 3rd edition.

3 2 Boullenois, Observ. 46, pp. 475, 476.

acceptor to payment at all events. By the law of Leghorn, if a bill is accepted, and the drawer fails, and the acceptor has not sufficient effects of the drawer in his hands at the time of acceptance, the acceptance becomes void. An acceptance in Leghorn is governed by this latter law; and under such circumstances it has been held void, and not obligatory upon the acceptor[1].

§ 266. Secondly, the obligation of the contract, which, though often confounded with, is distinguishable from, its nature[2]. The obligation of a contract is the duty to perform it, whatever may be its nature. It may be a moral obligation or a legal obligation, or both. But when we speak of obligation generally, we mean legal obligation, that is, the right to performance which the law confers on one party, and the corresponding duty of performance to which it binds the other[3]. This is what the French jurists call *le lien du contrat* (the legal tie of the contract), *onus conventionis*, and what the civilians generally call, *vinculum juris* or *vinculum obligationis*[4]. The Institutes of Justinian have thus defined it: *Obligatio est juris vinculum, quo necessitate adstringimur alicujus rei solvendæ, secundum nostræ civitatis, jura*[5]. A contract may in its nature be purely voluntary, and possess no legal obligation. It may be a mere naked pact (*nudum pactum*). It may possess a legal obligation; but the laws may limit the extent and force of that obligation *personam*, or *in rem*. It may bind the party personally, but not bind his estate; or it may bind his estate, and not bind his person. The obligation may be limited in its operation or duration; or it may be revocable

---

[1] Burrows *v.* Jemimo, 2 Str. R. 733; 2 Eq. Abr. 526.

[2] See 2 Boullenois, Observ. 46, pp. 454, 460, 462, 463, 464; 3 Burge, Comm. on Col. and For. Law, Pt. 2, ch. 20, pp. 764, 765.

[3] See 3 Story, Comm. on Constitution, § 1372—1379; Ogden *v.* Saunders, 12 Wheaton, 213; Pothier on Oblig. art. 1, n. 1, pp. 173, 174, 175.

[4] 2 Boullenois, Observ. 46, pp. 458, 459, 460.

[5] Inst. lib. 3, tit. 14; Pothier, Pandect. lib. 44, tit. 7, Pt. 1, art. 1, § 1; Pothier, Oblig. n. 173, 174.

or dissoluble in certain future events, or under peculiar circumstances [1].

§ 266 *a*. An illustration may be readily seen in the common case of a Scotch heritable bond. It is well known, that by the common law of England, a bond, which is also a charge on land, as, for example, a bond accompanying a mortgage of land as a security, is primarily in a contest between the heir and the administrator, a charge on the personal estate, and of course the heir has a right in equity to be relieved therefrom, so far as there are personal assets to discharge the bond [2]. In the Scotch law the same rule prevails as to movable debts, which are primarily and properly chargeable upon the personal assets [3]. But, as to heritable bonds, a different rule prevails; and they are primarily a charge on the real estate of the debtor [4]. Now, suppose a question should arise in England, as, indeed, it has arisen, whether, in the case of a Scotch movable debt, the heir upon payment of it was entitled to be exonerated therefrom, and to receive the amount out of the personal assets in England. Upon principle it should seem clear, that he would be entitled to the relief and exoneration; for the heir, having by the law of the country where the land lies, a right to such relief and exoneration, would have the same right in regard to the same debt in every other country, since it properly belongs to the nature, obligation, and interpretation of the contract [5]. On the other hand, a Scotch heir paying a heritable

---

[1] See 2 Boullenois, Observ. 46, pp. 452, 454; Code Civil of France, art. 1168—1196.

[2] 1 Story on Eq. Jurisp. § 571, 574; Earl of Winchelsea *v.* Garetty, 2 Keen, R. 293, 309.

[3] Earl of Winchelsea *v.* Garetty, 2 Keen, R. 293, 309, 310; Post, § 487, 529.

[4] Post, § 486—489, § 529; Drummond *v.* Drummond, 6 Bro. Parl. R. by Tomlins, 550.

[5] Earl of Winchelsea *v.* Garetty, 2 Keen, R. 293, 308, 309, 310.—Upon this occasion Lord Langdale said: "By the law of England, the personal estate is the primary fund for the payment of all debts, contracted by the deceased person whose estate it was. By the law of Scotland, movable debts

bond, would be entitled to no such relief or exoneration, because the debt is primarily by the local law a charge on

---

are primarily and properly chargeable upon the personal estate. The creditor may, indeed, enforce payment against the real estate in the hands of the heir; but, if he does so, the heir is entitled to relief against the executors out of the personal estate: in other words, according to the law of Scotland, the real estate, though subject to the payment of movable debts, is only a subsidiary fund for the purpose of payment. Payment by the heir does not extinguish the debt, but vests in him a right to recover the amount against the personal estate, and constitutes him a creditor against the personal estate; and whether he can enforce payment against the personal estate, which is to be distributed according to the laws of another country, which makes the personal estate the primary fund for the payment of debts, is the question. Primâ facie, there would seem to be no difficulty; the heir, having by the law of the country in which the land lies, a right to relief or exoneration would seem to be at liberty to make that right available in a country where the personal estate is the primary fund for the payment of all debts. But it is objected, that, in all the opinions upon which the finding of the Master rests, it has been assumed that the law of domicil makes no difference; whereas it is clear that the domicil determines the law by which the personal estate is to be distributed; and that, although it be true that in England the personal estate must be applied in exoneration of the English heir of real estate, yet that the right of the heir to be exonerated is founded on the law peculiar to England, and that a foreign heir of foreign lands is not entitled to the same relief as an English heir of English lands. The law of England, it is said, affords no relief to foreign real estate out of English personal estate; and although the law of Scotland regulates the administration of the real estate, and provides that the real estate, if applied in payment of personal debts, shall be exonerated out of the personal estate, the proposition must be limited to personal estate, of which the distribution is regulated according to the law of Scotland, and consequently to the personal estate of debtors domiciled in Scotland. Several cases were cited. They sufficiently establish the propositions, which are not disputed on either side; and Drummond *v.* Drummond establishes, that a Scotch heir is ultimately liable to pay heritable debts, which have, in the first instance, been paid out of the personal estate distributable according to the law of England; but no case has occurred, in which it has been decided, that the Scotch heir having paid movable debts, is entitled to be relieved out of the personal estate distributable according to the law of England; and that is the question here. The personal estate is taken by the administrator, according to the law of England, subject to the payment of all the debts of the intestate. The real estate is taken by the heir, according to the law of Scotland, subject to the payment of all movable debts, but with a right of relief out of the personal estate, and subject to the payment of all heritable debts without such right of relief. As to the heri-

the real estate[1]; and if such heritable bond should be paid by an English administrator out of the personal assets, he would be entitled to reimbursement from the Scotch heir[2].

---

table debts, in respect of which there is no such right of relief, the heir is not entitled to the benefit of the English law, which makes the personal estate subject to the payment of all debts. The Scotch law, which makes the heir ultimately liable to the payment of such debts, and which governs the distribution of the real estate, prevails in favour of the persons entitled to the personal estate distributable according to the law of England. As to personal debts, in respect of which there is such right to relief, the English law subjects the personal estate to all debts; the Scotch law relieves the real estate, as far as it can consistently with the claims of the creditors. The heir, by paying, satisfies the creditor, but at the same time acquires for himself a right of demand against the executor; he may, if he pleases, take an assignation of the debt, and make it available; but that is not necessary, because, without any assignation, his own claim to relief subsists, and constitutes him a creditor against the personal estate. Under these circumstances the question does not appear to me to be fully stated, when it is said to be, whether a foreign heir of foreign lands is entitled to the same relief, as an English heir of English lands. The case is, that a foreign heir of foreign lands is, in respect of those lands, subsidiarily liable to pay debts, to which the personal estate distributable according to the law of England, is primarily liable; and that, having paid the debt, he is by the law of the country in which the land lies, constituted a creditor upon the personal estate distributable according to the law of that country. And it is under these circumstances, and without reference to English tenures, or the title to exoneration, which an English heir may possess, that the question arises, whether the subsidiary debtor, or the person, who by the law of a foreign country is constituted surety for the payment of debts primarily chargeable on another fund, and paying the debts by force of, and according to the law which constitutes him a creditor upon that other fund, is or is not entitled to make his title as to creditor available in another country, where the personal estate is distributable, and where the law makes the personal estate primarily liable to the payment of all debts. And upon consideration of the case, I am of opinion that the right of relief or demand against the personal estate, which in the administration of the real estate by the law of Scotland is vested in the heir who has paid movable debts, is capable of being made available in England, where the personal estate is the primary fund for the payment of all debts."

[1] Drummond *v.* Drummond, 6 Bro. Parl. R. by Tomlins, 550; Post, § 486—489, 529; Elliott *v.* Lord Minto, 6 Madd. R. 16; Earl of Winchelsea *v.* Garetty, 2 Keen, R. 293, 308—310.

[2] Robertson on Personal Succession, 209—214.

§ 267. It would be easy to multiply illustrations under this head. Suppose a contract by the law of one country to involve no personal obligation, (as was supposed to be the law of France in a particular case which came in judgment [1]), but merely to confer a right to proceed *in rem;* such a contract would be held every where to involve no personal obligation whatsoever. Suppose, by the law of a particular country, a mortgage for money borrowed, should, in the absence of any express contract to repay, be limited to a mere repayment thereof out of the land, a foreign Court would refuse to entertain a suit giving to it a personal obligation. Suppose a contract for the payment of the debt of a third person, in a country where the law subjected such a contract to the tacit condition, that payment must first be sought against the debtor and his estate; that would limit the obligation to a mere accessorial and secondary character; and it would not be enforced in any foreign country, except after a compliance with the requisitions of the local law. Sureties, indorsers, and guarantees are therefore liable every where only according to the law of the place of their contract. Their obligation, if treated by such local law as an accessorial obligation, will not any where else be deemed a principal obligation [2]. So, if by the law of the place of a contract, its obligation is positively and *ex directo* extinguished after a certain period by the mere lapse of time, it cannot be revived by a suit in a foreign country, whose laws provide no such rule, or apply it only to the remedy [3]. To use the expressive language of a learned Judge, it must be shewn in all such cases, what

---

[1] Melan *v.* Fitz-James, 1 Bos. & Pull. 138.

[2] See Pothier on Oblig. n. 407; Trimbey *v.* Vignier, 6 Carr. & Payne, 25; S. C. 1 Bing. N. C. 151, 159; 4 Moore & Scott, 695; Post, § 314, 316 *a;* 3 Burge, Com. on Col. and For. Law, Pt. 2, ch. 20, pp. 764—766.

[3] See Le Roy *v.* Crowninshield, 2 Mason, R. 151; Pothier, Oblig. n. 636—639; Voet, Ad Pand. lib. 4, tit. 1, § 29, ad finem.

the laws of the foreign country are, and that they create an obligation which our laws will enforce [1].

§ 267 *a*. This doctrine was fully recognised in a recent case, where the question was, as to the rights of parties growing out of various bonds, executed in a State which was governed by the common law, some of the bonds being designed as security or indemnity to a surety on the other bonds. The Court said: "These different bonds were entered into in States of the Union where the common law prevails, and consequently the rights and liabilities of the parties are to be measured by that system of jurisprudence; and whatever the plaintiff (the assignee of the surety) would be entitled to recover (upon the indemnity bond) in a Court of law or equity in the State where the transaction originated, he is entitled to in this Court in the present form of action [2].

§ 268. Let us take another case, which has actually passed into judgment. By the common law, heirs are not bound by the simple contracts of their ancestor, but only by instruments under seal, declaring them expressly bound. By the law of Louisiana, the heirs are *ipso facto* bound by such simple contracts of their ancestors [3]. If a simple con-

---

1 Lord Chief Justice Eyre, Melan *v.* Duke of Fitz-James, 1 Bos. & Pull. 141.

2 Mr. Justice Bullard in King *v.* Harman's Heirs, 6 Louis. R. 607, 617.

3 Brown *v.* Richardson, 13 Martin, R. 202.—Mr. Justice Porter, in delivering the opinion of the Court in this case, said: "We recognise the distinction made by the plaintiff's counsel between the right and the remedy, and agree with him, that contracts should be expounded according to the laws of the country where they are made, and enforced according to the regulations which prevail where the debtor is found. It is that distinction which gives the defendants immunity in this case. For, in order to ascertain who is debtor, we must recur to the laws of the country where the contract was made; and if these laws do not make persons standing in the character of the appellants liable, under the circumstances now in proof, they cannot be made so by a change of jurisdiction. It is true that, according to our jurisprudence, the heir is obliged to pay the debts of the ancestor if he accepts the succession unconditionally; but it does not follow that the same rule exists in other countries. An embarrassment is created in considering the case,

tract is made in a State governed by the common law, it cannot be enforced in Louisiana against the heirs of the debtor, although they are domiciled in Louisiana [1]. The remedy must be sought through the instrumentality of an administration of the assets there [2].

§ 268 *a*. To this head of the obligation of contracts, may also be appropriately referred the consideration of the nature and extent of the obligation of contracts in respect to their dissolubility or indissolubility in point of duration. This topic has been already incidentally discussed in examining the nature and obligation of the contract of marriage, which indeed is truly a contract; but, properly speaking, it is something more — an institution of civil society [3]. It has been often urged, especially in regard to the contract of marriage, that indissolubility is of its very essence; and that what is of the essence of a contract, must be judged of according to the *lex loci contractûs*. It has remarked by an eminent judge, that this is somewhat a vague, and for its vagueness a somewhat suspicious proposition, and that there are many other things which may just as well be reckoned of the essence of the contract as this. He afterward added: "The fallacy of the argument, 'that indissolubility is of the essence,' appears plainly to be this: it confounds incidents with essence; it makes the rights under a contract, or flowing from and arising out of it, parcel of the contract; it makes the mode in which judicatures deal with those rights and with the contract itself, part of the contract; instead of considering, as in all soundness of principle we ought, that the contract and all its

---

from a feeling, which it is difficult to check, that there exists something like a natural obligation on the child to pay the parent's debts, particularly if he takes any of his property. But that obligation is in fact nothing but the creature of positive law, and is of course subject to all the modifications which the policy of different States may induce them to adopt." Id. p. 208.

1 Brown *v*. Richardson, 13 Martin, R. 202.

2 Ibid.

3 Ante, § 108 *a*, 218—230; Id. § 226 *c*, note.

incidents, and the rights of the parties to it, and the wrongs committed by them respecting it, must be dealt with by the Courts of the country where the parties reside, and where the contract is to be carried into execution [1]." These considerations are certainly entitled to great weight; but they only shew the intrinsic difficulty of laying down any general rules on such complicated subjects which shall be of universal application. It will probably be found that the proposition, that a contract cannot be dissolved, except in the manner and under the circumstances prescribed by the law of the place where it was made, if true at all, must be asserted with many qualifications and exceptions. Contracts of marriage, and other contracts of a peculiar nature, may perhaps require a different exposition in this respect from other ordinary pecuniary contracts. And even if a contract be indissoluble by the *lex loci contractûs*, except in a special mode, it may nevertheless be thought reasonable that that rule should not prevail upon a change of domicil, as to an act of the parties done in the latter place where another mode is prescribed or allowed for its dissolution [2]. But of this we shall speak hereafter [3].

§ 269. Cases sometimes occur in which the tribunals of a foreign country are called upon to decide upon the law of another country where the contract is made; and they, by mistake, misinterpret that law. In such a case, if they discharge the parties from the obligation of the contract, in consequence of such misinterpretation of the foreign law, that discharge will not be held obligatory upon the Courts of the country where the contract was made [4]. A recent case has occurred on this subject. A bill of exchange drawn in France, and indorsed there, and accepted and payable

---

1 Lord Brougham, in Warrender *v.* Warrender, 9 Bligh, R. 114; Ante, § 226 *c*, note.

2 Ibid.

3 See Post, § 351 *a;* Ante, § 226 *a*, note.

4 Novelli *v.* Rossi, 2 Barn. & Adol. 757.

in England at a banker's, was passed by an indorsee in discharge of an antecedent debt; and upon presentment for payment it was dishonoured, and the banker's clerk by mistake cancelled the acceptance, and then wrote on it, "cancelled by mistake." Afterwards the indorser, who had so passed the bill in discharge of his debt, cited all the parties, and among others the creditor and holder of the bill, before the tribunals of France, who decreed that the cancellation operated as a suspension of legal remedies against the acceptor, and consequently discharged the other parties, the indorsers as well as the drawer. A suit was afterwards brought by the creditor against the debtor-indorser in England; and it was held, that the Courts of France had mistaken the law of England as to the effect of the cancellation; and that the plaintiff was entitled to recover against the defendant the full amount of the debt, notwithstanding the decree in the French Courts [1].

§ 270. Thirdly.—The interpretation of contracts. Upon this subject there would scarcely seem to be any room for doubt or disputation. There are certain general rules of interpretation, recognised by all nations, which form the basis of all reasoning on the subject of contracts. The object is to ascertain the real intention of the parties in their stipulations; and when the latter are silent or ambiguous, to ascertain what is the true sense of the words used, and what ought to be implied in order to give them their true and full effect [2]. The primary rule in all expositions of this

---

[1] Novelli *v.* Rossi, 2 Barn. & Adol. 757.

[2] See Lord Brougham's striking remarks on this subject already cited, ante, § 226 *c.* In Prentiss *v.* Savage, 13 Mass. R. 23, Mr. Chief Justice Parker said:—"It seems to be an undisputed doctrine, with respect to personal contracts, that the law of the place where they are made shall govern in their construction, except when made with a view to performance in some other country, and then the law of such country is to prevail. This is nothing more than common sense and sound justice, adopting the probable intent of the parties as to the rule of construction: for when a citizen of this country enters into a contract in another, with a citizen or subject thereof

sort is that of common sense, so well expressed in the Digest. *In conventionibus contrahentium voluntas, potius quam verba, spectari placuit*[1]. But in many cases the words used in contracts have different meanings attached to them in different places by law or by custom. And where the words are in themselves obscure or ambiguous, custom and usage in a particular place may give them an exact and appropriate meaning. Hence, the rule has found admission into almost all, if not into all, systems of jurisprudence, that if the full and entire intention of the parties does not appear from the words of the contract, and if it can be interpreted by any custom or usage of the place where it is made, that course is to be adopted. Such is the rule of the Digest. *Semper in stipulationibus, et in cœteris contractibus id sequimur, quod actum est. Aut si non appareat, quod actum est, erit consequens, ut id sequamur, quod in regione, in quâ actum est, frequentatur*[2]. *Conservanda est consuetudo regionis et civitatis* (says

---

and the contract is intended to be there performed, it is reasonable to presume that both parties had regard to the law of the place where they were, and that the contract was shaped accordingly. And it is also to be presumed when the contract is to be executed in any other country than that in which it is made, that the parties take into their consideration the law of such foreign country. This latter branch of the rule, if not so obviously founded upon the intention of the parties as the former, is equally well settled as a principle in the law of contracts." Mr. Chancellor Walworth, in Chapman *v.* Robertson, (6 Paige, R. 627, 630), used equally strong language :—"It is an established principle," said he, "that the construction and validity of personal contracts, which are purely personal, depend upon the laws of the place where the contract is made, unless it was made with reference to the laws of some other place or country, where such contract, in the contemplation of the parties thereto, was to be carried into effect and performed."—2 Kent, Comm. Lect. 39, pp. 457, 458, 3rd edit. ; 3 Burge, Comm. on Col. and For. Law, Pt. 2, ch. 20, pp. 752—764.

[1] Dig. lib. 50, tit. 16, l. 219. Many rules of interpretation are found in Pothier on Obligation, n. 91—102 ; in Fonblanque on Equity, B. 1, ch. 6, § 11—20, and notes; 1 Domat, Civil Law, B. 1, tit. 1, § 2; 1 Powell on Contracts, 370, et seq.; Merlin, Répertoire, Convention, § 7, p. 366.

[2] Dig. lib. 50, tit. 17, l. 34; 1 Domat, Civil Law, B. 1, tit. 1, § 2, n. 9; 2 Boullenois, Observ. 46, p. 490 ; 3 Burge, Comm. on Col. and For. Law, Pt. 2, ch. 20, pp. 775, 776.

J. à Sandè) *ubi contractum est. Omnes enim actiones nostræ (si non aliter fuerit provisum inter contrahentes) intrepretationem recipiunt a consuetudine loci, in quo contrahitur*[1]. Usage is, indeed, of so much authority in the interpretation of contracts, that a contract is understood to contain the customary clauses, although they are not expressed according to the known rule, *In contractibus tacite veniunt ea, quæ sunt moris et consuetudinis*[2]. Thus, if a tenant is, by custom, to have the outgoing crop, he will be entitled to it, although not expressed in the lease[3]. And if a lease is entirely silent as to the time of the tenant's quitting, the custom of the country will fix it[4]. By the law of England a month means ordinarily in common contracts, as in leases, a lunar month; but in mercantile contracts it means a calendar month[5]. A contract, therefore, made in England for a lease of land for twelve months, would mean a lease for forty-eight weeks only[6]. A promissory note to pay money in twelve months would mean in one year, or in twelve calendar months[7]. If a contract of either sort were required to be enforced in a foreign country, its true intepretation must be every where the same, that is, according to the usage in the country where the contract was made.

§ 271. The same word, too, often has different significations in different countries. Thus, the term *usance*, which is common enough in negotiable instruments, means in some countries a month, in others two or more months, and in

---

1 J. à Sandè, Op. Comm. de Reg. Jur. l. 9, p. 17.

2 Pothier, Oblig. n. 95; Merlin, Répertoire, Convention, § 7; 2 Kent, Comm. Lect. 39, p. 555, 3rd edit.

3 Wigglesworth *v.* Dallison, Doug. R. 201, 207.

4 Webb *v.* Plumer, 2 B. & Ald. 746.

5 2 Black. Comm. 141; Catesby's Case, 6 Coke, R. 62; Lacon *v.* Hooper, 3 T. R. 224; 3 Burge, Comm. on Col. and For. Law, Part 2, ch. 20, pp. 776, 777.

6 Ibid.

7 Chitty on Bills, (8th edit. 1833), p. 406; Lang *v.* Gale, 1 M. & Selw. 111; Cockell *v.* Gray, 3 B. & Bing. 187; Leffingwell *v.* White, 1 John. Cas. 99.

others half a month. A note payable at one usance must be construed every where according to the meaning of the word in the country where the contract is made[1]. There are many other cases illustrative of the same principle. A note made in England for £100 would mean £100 sterling. A like note made in America would mean £100 American currency, which is one-fourth less in value. It would be monstrous to contend, that on the English note, sued in America, the less sum only ought to be recovered; and on the other hand, on the American note, sued in England, that one-third more ought to be recovered[2].

§ 271 *a*. Another illustration may easily be suggested, which is not quite so simple in its circumstances. Suppose a contract is made in England between two Englishmen for the sale of lands situate in Jamaica; and the vendee agreed to give £20,000 for the lands, without specifying in what currency. The difference between Jamaica pounds currency and English sterling pounds currency, by the par of exchange, exclusive of any premium on bills of exchange on England, is forty per cent. Consequently, £28,000 Jamaica currency would constitute only £20,000 sterling. The question might then arise, according to which currency the purchase-money is to be paid. In the absence of all expressions and circumstances, from which a different intention may be inferred, the interpretation of the contract would be, that it was payable in the currency of the country where the contract was made, and not in that of the *situs* of the property[3]. Another illustration may be in case of a sale of lands situate in one country, and the contract made in another, and the sale to be of a certain number of acres

---

[1] Chitty on Bills, (8th edit. 1833), pp. 404, 405. See also 2 Boullenois. Observ. 46, p. 447.

[2] See also Powell on Contracts, 376; 2 Boullenois, Observ. 46, pp. 498, 503; Henry on Foreign Law, Appendix, 233; Pardessus, Droit Comm. art. 1492; 3 Burge, Comm. on Col. and For. Law, Pt. 2, ch. 20, pp. 772, 773; Post, § 272 *a*, § 307, 308.

[3] 2 Burge, Comm. on Col. and For. Law, Pt. 2, ch. 9, pp. 860, 861.

for a gross price, or at a specific price per acre, the mode of measuring an acre or the contents thereof being different in different countries. The question might arise, whether the acre was to be according to the measurement in the one country or in the other. Now, upon this very point different opinions and judgments have been held by different jurists and tribunals on the continent of Europe; some holding, that the *lex loci contractûs* ought to govern; and others, that the *lex situs* ought to govern the admeasurement[1]. Choppin has reported a case, where the highest tribunal of Orleans held, that the laws of the place of the contract should determine the admeasurement of the acre. But he disapproves of it, and says: *Justior tamen est diversa opinio, venditi agri mensuram ex lege petendam situs prædiorum non loci pactæ venditionis*[2]. John Voet holds the same opinion: *Si res immobilis ad certam mensuram debeantur, et ea pro locorum diversitate varia sit, in dubio solvi debent juxta mensuram loci, in quo sitæ sunt*[3]. In respect to movables he holds the opposite opinion, that they are governed by the law of the place of the contract. Dumoulin holds the same opinion as to immovables; that they are governed by the *lex situs. Unde stantibus mensuris diversis, si fundus venditur ad mensuram, vel affirmatur, vel mensuratur, non continuo debet inspici mensura, quæ viget in loco contractûs, sed in dubio debet attendi mensura loci, in quo fundus debet metiri, et tradi, et executio fieri*[4]. He admits, that other jurists differ from him, and that other circumstances may vary this interpretation. *Et ita tenendum, nisi ex aliis circumstantiis constet, de qua mensura senserint*[5]. Indeed he

---

1 2 Burge, Comm. on Col. and For. Law, Pt. 2, ch. 9, pp. 858, 859.

2 Choppini Opera, De Feudis Andeg. tom. 2, lib. 2, tit. 3, n. 10, pp. 132, 133, (edit. 1611); 2 Boullenois, Observ. 46, p. 497; 2 Burge, Comm. on Col. and For. Law, Pt. 2, ch. 9, pp. 858, 859.

3 J. Voet, lib. 46, tit. 3, n. 8, p. 949; 2 Burge, Comm. Pt. 2, ch. 9, p. 859; 2 Boullenois, Observ. 46, p. 497.

4 Molin. Oper. Comm. ad Cod. lib. 1, tit. 1, l. 1, tom. 3, Conclus. de Statut. p. 554.

5 Ibid.

denies that any universal rule can be established[1]. The same doctrine, that the *lex situs* ought to govern in the like cases, would seem to be favoured, if not positively established in the jurisprudence of England and America[2].

§ 272. The general rule, then, is, that, in the interpretation of contracts, the law and custom of the place of the contract is to govern in all cases, where the language is not directly expressive of the actual intention of the parties; but it is to be tacitly inferred from the nature, and objects, and occasion of the contract[3]. The rule has been fully recognised in the Courts of Common Law; and it has been directly decided by those courts, that the interpretation of the contract must be governed by the laws of the country where the contract is made[4]. And the rule is founded in wisdom, sound policy, and general convenience. Especially in interpreting ambiguous contracts, ought the domicil of the parties, the place of execution, the various provisions and expressions of the instrument, and other circumstances, implying a local reference, to be taken into consideration[5]. Thus, Gothofredus says: *Consuetudo regionis sequemur, et ideo conducere, concedere, contrahere, et quidvis agere pro modo regionis in dubio præsumitur. Nam*

---

1 Molin. Oper. Comm. ad Cod. lib. 1, tit. 1, l. 1, tom. 3; Conclus. de Statut. p. 354; Post, § 274 *a*.

2 Ante, § 270.

3 See the opinion of the Court, delivered by Mr. Justice Martin, in the case of Depau *v.* Humphreys, 20 Martin, R. 1, 8, 9, 13, 22, 23, 24; Mr. Justice Porter, in the case of Morris *v.* Eves, 11 Martin, R. 730; Courtois *v.* Carpenter, 1 Wash. Cir. R. 376.

4 Trimby *v.* Vignier, 1 Bing. New Cases, 151, 159; Post, § 316 *a*; De la Vega *v.* Vianna, 1 Barn. & Adol. R. 284; British Linen Company *v.* Drummond, 10 Barn. & Cress. 903; Bank of U. States *v.* Donally, 8 Peters, R. 361, 372; Wilcox *v.* Hunt, 13 Peters, R. 378, 379.—We shall presently see, that the same rule is adopted in the interpretation of wills. See Lansdowne *v.* Lansdowne, 2 Bligh, R. 60, 88, 89, 91, and cases there cited. Holmes *v.* Holmes, 1 Russ. & Mylne, 660, 662; Chapman *v.* Robertson, 6 Paige, R. 627, 630; Post, § 479 *a*—479 *n*.

5 Ante, § 237. See Lansdowne *v.* Lansdowne, 2 Bligh, Parl. R. 60, 87; Post, § 479 *m*—478 *n*.

sicut natura non separetur a subjecto, ita nec a consueto. Quod est de consuetudine habetur pro pacto[1]. Burgundus is more full and pointed to this point, as we have already seen[2]. John à Sandè expresses the same doctrine in these words: *Quando verba sunt dubia et ambigua, tunc inspicimus, quod verisimiliter a contrahentibus actum sit, aut quid testator senserit*[3].

§ 272 *a*. One of the simplest cases to illustrate the rule, is the case of a promissory note, made and dated in a particular country, payable in a currency which has the same name, but is of a different value in different countries. The question is, what currency is presumed to be intended by the parties. The answer would seem to be equally certain; the currency of the country where it is payable. Suppose, then, a promissory note is dated at Dublin, and thereby the maker promises to pay to the payee, or order, £100 in forty days after date, and the note is after sued in England; the question would arise, whether the note meant £100 English currency, or Irish currency. This would depend upon another question, whether the note was payable, as no place of payment was named, in England, or in Ireland. Now, by the rules of law in the interpretation of all such contracts, when no other place of payment is named, the contract is treated as a contract made in, and governed by the law of the place where it is made and dated, and therefore it would be interpreted to mean £100 Irish currency, because payable there, and, indeed, payable every where, where the maker should afterwards be found[4]. The converse rule would be applied, if the

---

1 Gothofred. Ad Pand. lib. 50, tit. 17, l. 34; Le Brun, Traité de la Communauté, liv. 1, ch. 2, § 46.

2 Ante, § 237; 2 Boullenois, Observ. 46, p. 451.

3 J. à Sandè, Op. Comm. De Reg. Juris. l. 9, p. 17.

4 Kearney *v*. King, 2 Barn. & Ald. R. 301; Sprowle *v*. Legge, 1 B. & Cress. 16.

note, though drawn in the same terms, and dated at Dublin, were upon its face made payable in London[1].

§ 273. Boullenois, while he admits the general propriety of the rule, *locus contractûs regit actum,* contests its universality[2]. He seems to think, and some other jurists have adopted the same opinion, that where a contract is made between foreigners belonging to the same country, who are not domiciled, but are merely transient persons in the place where the contract is made, it ought to be governed by the law of their own country; and that this rule applies *à fortiori,* where they are ignorant of the laws of the place where the contract is made[3]. Without undertaking to say, that the exception may not be well founded in particular cases, as to persons merely *in transitu,* it may unhesitatingly be said, that nothing but the clearest intention on the part of foreigners, to act upon their own domestic law, in exclusion of the law of the place of the contract, ought to change the application of the general rule[4]. And, indeed, even then, if the performance of the contract is to be in the same country where it is made, it seems difficult, upon principle, to sustain the exception. Huberus has applied

---

1 Ibid.; Ante, § 271; Post, § 317; 3 Burge, Comm. on Col. and For. Law, Pt. 2, ch. 20, pp. 772, 773; 2 Burge, Comm. Pt. 2, ch. 9, p. 860—862.

2 2 Boullenois, Observ. 46, pp. 456, 489, 490.

3 2 Boullenois, Observ. 46, pp. 455—458; Id. pp. 495—497, 501—503, and note.—Boullenois (in pp. 494, 495) says: To return to our question upon the interpretation of contracts or testaments, I think the sole rule which can be prescribed, is that of determining it according to the different circumstances. These different circumstances will lead us sometimes in favour of the law of the place of the contract, sometimes in favour of that of the situs, often in favour of that of the domicil, and often in favour of that where the payment is to be made. And hence he agrees to Dumoulin's opinion in his Commentary on the Code. Molin. Comment. ad Cod. lib. 1, tit. 1, l. 1, Conclus. de Statut. p. 554; Ante, § 263; Bartol. Comment. ad Cod. lib. 1, tit. 1, l. 1, n. 13; Post, § 279; 3 Burge, Comm. on Col. and For. Law, Pt. 2, ch. 20, pp. 775—777.

4 See Pardessus, Droit Comm. n. 182, 191; 1 Emérigon, ch. 4, § 8.

the same rule to those who are domiciled and to those who are merely commorant, in the place of the contract; that the law of the place of the contract is to govern[1].

§ 274. Grotius has also affirmed the doctrine in a general form. "If," says he, "a foreigner makes a bargain with a native, he shall be obliged by the laws of his state; because he who enters into a contract in any place, is a subject for the time being, and must be obedient to the laws of that place." *Quare etiamsi peregrinus cum cive paciscatur, tenebitur illis legibus; quia qui in loco aliquo contrahit, tanquam subditus temporarius legibus loci subjicitur*[2]. Emérigon follows Grotius, and adopts his very language. "A stranger," says he, "who contracts in the territories of a state, is held as a temporary subject of the state, subject to the laws thereof. *L'étranger qui contracte dans les terres d'un état, est tenu, comme sujet à temps de cet état, de se soumettre aux lois du pays*[3]. Lord Stowell, in a passage in one of his most celebrated judgments, has refused to acknowledge ignorance of the law of a foreign country, to be any foundation to release a party from the obligation of a contract made there[4].

§ 274 *a*. Dumoulin, while he admits the general rule to be, that the law and custom of the place where a contract is made, ought generally to govern in the interpretation of the contract, at the same time denies that it is of universal application. On the contrary, he holds, that there are cases, in which it ought to be disregarded. "*Et animadvertendum*," says he, "*quod doctores pessimè intelligunt, d. l., quia putant ruditer et indistinctè, quod debeat ibi inspici locus et consuetudo, ubi fit contractus, et sic jus in loco contractûs. Quod est falsum; quinimò jus est in tacita et veri*-

---

[1] Huberus, lib. 1, tit. 3, § 2, 3; Ante, § 261, note. See Livermore's Diss. p. 46, § 42.

[2] Grotius, lib. 2, ch. 11, § 5, n. 2.

[3] Emérigon, Assur. ch. 4, § 8, tom. 1, pp. 124, 125. See also Casaregis, Disc. 179, n. 60—62.

[4] Dalrymple *v.* Dalrymple, 2 Hagg. Consist, R. 60, 61.

similiter mente contrahentium. Fac, civem Tubingensem peregrè euntem per urbem Italiæ, vendere ibi domum suam Tubingæ vel Augustæ, an teneatur dare duos fidejussores evictionis, et de duplo, prout probat statutum loci contractus. Et omnes dicunt, quod sic, in quo errant, non intelligentes praxim, et hic non perspicientes mentem, d. l. quæ est practica. Ideò contrarium dicendum; quia venditor non est subditus statutis Italiæ, et statutum illud non concernit rem, sed personam, et sic non potest ligare exteros, qui non censentur sese obligare ad statutum, quod ineunt. Ideò non tenetur cavere, nisi secundùm morem sui domicilii, vel secundùm jus commune; nec verum est, quod istud statutum concernat solemnitatem et modum contrahendi. Quinimò respicit effectum, meritum, et decisionem, et dicta lex malè allegatur ad materiam primæ conclusionis. Faciamus civem Tubingensem hic vendere vicino domum Genevæ, vel Tiguri sitam, ubi sit statutum, quod venditor fundi tenetur de duplo cavere, per duos idoneos cives, ne teneantur litigare extra forum suum. Iste est proprius casus et verus, intellectus, d. l. in quâ dicitur; Venditorem teneri cavere secundùm consuetudinem loci contractus; quod est intelligendum non de loco contractus fortuiti, sed domicilii, prout crebrius usuvenit, immobilia non vendi peregrè, sed in loco domicilii. Lex autem debet adaptari ad casus vel hypotheses, quæ solent frequenter accidere: nec extendi ad casus rarò accidentes. Saltem quando contrarium apparet de ratione diversitatis, vel quandò sequeretur captio ingerentis. Quia quâ ratione dicta lex, excludit externum locum situs rei, in quo contrahentes non habent domicilium; multò fortius excluditur locus fortuitus contractus, in quo partes peregrè transeunt. Patet: Quia quis censetur potius contrahere in loco in quo debet solvere, quam in loco ubi fortuitò transiens contrahit. Sed hic venditor eo ipso se obligat, solutionem et traditionem realem, per se, vel per alium, facere in loco in quo fundus situs est: ergo ibi contraxisse censetur. Et tamen in dubio non attenditur consuetudo loci contractus. Quia venditor illi non subest, nec ejus notitiam habere præsumitur, ergo multo minus consuetudo loci fortuiti, quam magis ignorat" [1].

§ 275. Cases, illustrative of the importance of the general rule, may be easily found in the jurisprudence of modern nations. "In some countries," says Boullenois, "the laws give a certain sense and a certain effect to clauses in an instrument, while the laws of another country give a sense and effect more extensive, or more restrained. For example, at Toulouse, the clause, *si sine liberis*, added to a substitution, means a gradual substitution; and in other places, it means only a condition, if other circumstances do not concur [2]." The full effect of this example may be felt only by a civilian. But an analogous one may be put from the common law. A contract in England for an estate there situate, or a conveyance of such an estate to A., and the heirs of his body begotten, would, before the statute *de donis*, have been interpreted to mean a contract for, or a conveyance of, a conditional fee-simple; but since that statute, it would be construed to be a contract for or a conveyance of a fee-tail [3]. The rights growing out of these different interpretations are (as every common lawyer knows) exceedingly different; and to construe them otherwise than according to the common law, would defeat the intention of the parties and uproot the solid doctrines of law. The sense of the terms, and the legal effect of the instrument ought, and, it is to be presumed, would be

---

[1] Molin. Oper. Comm. ad Cod. lib. 1, tit. 1, l. 1, Conclus. de Statut. tom. 3, p. 554; 2 Burge, Comm. on Col. and For. Law, Pt. 2, ch. 20, pp. 851, 852; Id. pp. 858, 859.

[2] 2 Boullenois, Observ. 46, pp. 447, 518, 519. In the French Law substitution is either simple or gradual. It is called simple, when one person only is substituted for another in a donation; as a donation to A., and if he refuses or dies to B. It is called gradual, when there are several substitutes in succession; as a donation to A., and if he refuses or dies to B., and if B. refuses or dies to C., and if C. refuses or dies to D., &c. &c. Pothier, Traité des Substitutions, art. Prelim.; Id. § 3, art. 1. See also 2 Burge, Comm. on Col. and For. Law, pt. 2, ch. 20, pp. 855—857.

[3] 2 Black. Comm. 110—112.

every where ascertained by the same mode of interpretation, wherever the point should come, directly or indirectly, in judgment, in any foreign country.

§ 276. The language of marriage contracts and settlements must, in like manner, be interpreted according to the law of the place where they are contracted. A moment's consideration would teach us the inextricable confusion which would ensue from disregarding the habitual construction put by courts of law upon instruments of this sort, executed in England or in France, and brought into controversy in any other country. The whole system of interpretation of the clauses of marriage contracts and settlements in England, is, in a high degree, artificial; but it is built upon uniform principles, which could not now be swept away without leaving innumerable difficulties behind. What could a foreign Court do in interpreting the terms, *heirs of the body, children, issue,* connected with other words of limitation or description in a marriage settlement or a will made in England? The intricate branch of English jurisprudence, upon which the true exposition of such clauses depends, has tasked and exhausted the diligence and learning of the highest professional minds; and requires almost the study of a life to be thoroughly mastered[1]. Probably the system of interpretation in similar cases in France does not involve fewer difficulties, dependent upon the nice shades of meaning of words in different connexions, and the necessary complexity of matrimonial rights, and nuptial contracts, and prospective successions[2]. The general rule is in no cases more firmly adhered to, than in cases of nuptial contracts and settlements, that they are to be construed and enforced according to the *lex loci contractûs*[3].

---

[1] See Fearne on Contingent Remainders, passim.

[2] See 2 Boullenois, Observ. 46, pp. 489—494, 503—505, 513; Martyn *v.* Fabrigas, Cowper, R. 174.

[3] Feaubert *v.* Turst, Prec. Ch. 207; De Couche *v.* Savatier, 3 John. Ch. R. 190.

§ 276 *a*. The same doctrine was fully recognised in a recent case in England. In that case the parties were domiciled and married in Scotland, and executed a nuptial contract, containing mutual provisions for the benefit of the parties and their offspring. Afterwards the wife, upon the death of her mother in England, became entitled to certain stock; and the husband filed a bill in Chancery to have the stock conveyed to him by the trustee thereof, without a settlement being made upon his wife in regard thereto. The question was, whether the wife was entitled to the common equity to a settlement out of the stock, according to the English law. It appeared, that, by the law of Scotland, acting upon the interpretation and construction of the provisions of the nuptial contract, the wife was not entitled to any such equity to a settlement. The Lord Chancellor held, that the Court, in administering the rights of the parties under that nuptial contract, was bound to give the same construction and effect to it in England, as the Scottish law would give to it; and he therefore awarded the stock to the husband without any settlement[1].

§ 277. The same rule is also universally acknowledged in relation to commercial contracts[2]. Where the terms of an instrument executed by foreigners in a foreign country are free from obscurity, it will be construed according to the obvious import of those terms, unless there is some proof, that, according to the law of the foreign country, the true interpretation of them would be different[3]. But where a particular interpretation is established, that must be followed. Indeed, the Courts of every country must be presumed to be the best expositors of their own laws, and of

---

[1] Anstruther *v.* Adair, 2 Mylne & Keen, R. 513, 516. See also Breadalbane *v.* Chandos, cited in 4 Burge, Comm. on Col. and For. Law, App. 749, 755.

[2] Pardessus, Droit Comm. tom. 5, n. 1491, 1492; 2 Kent, Comm. Lect. 39, pp. 457, 458, (3rd edit.).

[3] King of Spain *v.* Machado, 4 Russ. R. 225; Post, § 286.

the terms of contracts made with reference to them. And no court on earth, professing to be governed by principle, would assume the power to declare, that a foreign court misunderstood the laws of their own country, or the operation of them on contracts made there[1].

§ 278. The remarks already suggested upon this rule cannot be better enforced, than by a quotation from an opinion of the late learned Mr. Chief Justice Parker. "That the laws of any State cannot, by any inherent authority, be entitled to respect extra-territorially, or beyond the jurisdiction of the State which enacts them, is the necessary result of the independence of distinct sovereignties. But the courtesy, comity, or mutual convenience of nations, amongst which commerce has introduced so great an intercourse, has sanctioned the admission and operation of foreign laws relative to contracts. So that it is now a principle generally received, that contracts are to be construed and interpreted according to the laws of the State in which they are made, unless from their tenor it is perceived, that they were entered into with a view to the laws of some other State. And nothing can be more just than this principle. For when a merchant of France, Holland, or England, enters into a contract in his own country, he must be presumed to be conusant of the laws of the place where he is, and to expect, that his contract is to be judged of and carried into effect according to those laws; and the merchant with whom he deals, if a foreigner, must be supposed to submit himself to the same laws, unless he has taken care to stipulate for a performance in some other country, or has in some other way excepted his particular contract from the laws of the country where he is[2]."

§ 278 *a*. Hence it is adopted by the common law, as a

---

1 Mr. Chief Justice Marshall in Elmendorf *v*. Tayler, 10 Wheaton, R. 159; Mr. Justice Porter in Saul *v*. His Creditors, 17 Martin, R. 587.

2 Blanchard *v*. Russell, 13 Mass. R. 1, 4, 5.

general rule in the interpretation of contracts, that they are to be deemed contracts of the place where they are made, unless they are positively to be performed or paid elsewhere. Therefore a note made in France, and payable generally, will be treated as a French note, and governed accordingly, by the laws of France, as to its obligation and construction. So, a policy of insurance, executed in England on a French ship for the French owner, on a voyage from one French port to another, would be treated as an English contract, and in case of loss, the debt would be treated as an English debt. Indeed, all the rights, and duties, and obligations, growing out of such a policy, would be governed by the law of England, and not by the law of France, if the laws respecting insurance were different in the two countries[1].

§ 279. It has sometimes been suggested, and especially by foreign jurists, that contracts made between foreigners in a foreign country, ought to be construed according to the law of their own country, whenever they both belong to the same country[2]. Where they belong to different countries, some controversy has arisen as to the point, whether the law of the domicil of the debtor or that of the creditor ought to prevail[3]. Where a contract is made in a country between a citizen and a foreigner, it seems admitted, that the law of

---

[1] Don *v.* Lippman, 5 Clarke & Fin. 1, 18, 19, 20; Post, § 317.

[2] Ante, § 273; 2 Boullenois, Observ. 46, pp. 455—458; Id. pp. 495—503. Hertius seems to make the following distinction. After having stated the general rule to be: Si lex actui formam dat, inspiciendum est locus actus, non domicilii, non rei sitæ; he adds: Nimirum valet hæc Regula, etiam in extero, qui actum celebrat, licet enim hic subjectus revera maneat patriæ suæ, tamen illud, de actu primo est intelligendum, quoad actum verò secundum subditus illius loci sit temporarius, ubi agit, vel contrahit, simulque ut forum ibi sortitur, ita statutis ligatur. Non valet si exterus ignoravit statutum. Hertii Opera, tom. 1, De Collis. Leg. § 4, n. 10, pp. 126, 128; Id. (edit. 1716), pp. 179—181.

[3] See Fœlix, Conflict des Lois, Revue Etrang. et Franç. 1840, tom. 7,

the place where the contract is made ought to prevail, unless the contract is to be performed elsewhere[1]. In the common law of England and America all these niceties are discarded. Every contract, whether made between foreigners, or between foreigners and citizens, is deemed to be governed by the law of the place where it is made, and is to be executed[2].

§ 279 *a*. Hertius has put a case where a contract made in a country is subject to a condition, and the performance of that condition takes place in another country, the laws of which are different; and the question is, whether the laws of the one, or those of the other ought to govern the contract. He answers, that the laws of the country where the contract was made; because the condition, when fulfilled, refers back to the time of the contract. *Quia conditio retrotrahitur ad tempus conventionis*[3]. J. à Sandè adopts the same doctrine almost in the same words[4].

§ 280. The rules already considered suppose, that the performance of the contract is to be in the place where it is made, either expressly or by tacit implication. But where the contract is either expressly or tacitly to be performed in any other place, there the general rule is, in conformity to the presumed intention of the parties, that the contract, as to its validity, nature, obligation, and interpretation, is to

---

§ 21—23, pp. 200—209; Id. § 40—50, pp. 46—49; 3 Burge, Comm. on Col. and For. Law, Pt. 2, ch. 20, pp. 775, 776.

1 See Livermore's Dissert., § 42, p. 46; 1 Hertii Opera, De Collis. Leg. § 10, pp. 126, 128; Id. pp. 179—181, (edit. 1716); Voet, De Statut. § 9, ch. 2, Excep. 4; Id. § 10, p. 268, (edit. 1715); Id. p. 325, (edit. 1661). But see contra, 2 Boullenois, Observ. 46, p. 459; Ante, § 263, 273, 274.

2 Smith *v*. Meade, 3 Connect. R. 253; De Sobry *v*. De Laistre, 2 Harr. & John. R. 193, 228.

3 Hertii Opera, De Collis. Leg. § 4, n. 54, p. 147, (edit. 1737); Id. p. 207, (edit. 1716).

4 J. à Sandè, Comm. ad Reg. Jur. l. 9, p. 18; Post, § 287.

be governed by the law of the place of performance[1]. This would seem to be a result of natural justice; and the Roman law has (as we have seen) adopted it as a maxim: *Contraxisse unusquisque in eo loco intelligitur, in quo ut solveret, se obligavit*[2]. And again, in the law, *Aut ubi quisque contraxerit. Contractum autem non utique eo loco intelligitur, quo negotium gestum sit; sed quo solvenda est pecunia*[3]. The rule was fully recognised, and acted on in a recent case by the Supreme Court of the United States, where the Court said, that the general principle, in relation to contracts made in one place to be executed in another, was well settled; that they are to be governed by the laws of the place of performance[4].

§ 281. Paul Voet has laid down the same rule. *Hinc, ratione effectûs et complimenti ipsius contractûs, spectatur ille locus, in quem destinata est solutio; id, quod ad modum, mensuram, usuras, &c. negligentiam, et moram post contractum initum accedentem, referendum est*[5]. He puts the question: *Quid si in specie, de nummorum aut redituum solutione difficultas incidat, si forte valor sit immutatus, an spectabitur loci valor, ubi contractus erat celebratus, an loci, in quem destinata erat solutio? Respondeo: Ex generali Regulâ, spectandum esse loci statutum, in quem destinata erat solutio*[6]. So that, according to him, if a contract is for money or goods, the value is to be ascertained at the place

---

[1] 2 Kent, Comm. Lect. 37, pp. 393, 394, and Lect. 39, p. 459, (3rd edit.); Casaregis, Disc. 179; 1 Emerigon, c. 4, § 8; Voet, De Stat. § 9, ch. 2, § 15, p. 270, (edit. 1715); Id. p. 328, (edit. 1661); Boullenois, Quest. Contr. des Lois, p. 330, &c.; 3 Burge, Comm. on Col. and For. Law, pt. 2, ch. 20, pp. 771, 772; Don *v.* Lippman, 5 Clarke & Fin. R. 1, 13, 19.

[2] Dig. lib. 44, tit. 7, l. 21; Ante, § 233.

[3] Id. 42, tit. 5, l. 3.

[4] Andrews *v.* Pond, 13 Peters, R. 65.

[5] P. Voet, De Stat. § 9, ch. 2, p. 270, § 12, 14—16, pp. 269—273, (edit. 1715); Id. pp. 326—329, (edit. 1661); Post, § 301 *f.*

[6] P. Voet, De Stat. § 15, 16, p. 271, (edit. 1715); Id. p. 328, (edit. 1661); Post, § 301 *f.*

of performance, and not at the place where the contract is made[1]. And the same rule applies to the weight or measure of things, if there be a diversity in different places[2]. Everhardus adopts the same doctrine:—*Quod, æstimatio rei debitæ consideratur secundum locum ubi destinata est solutio, seu deliberatio, non obstante quod contractus alibi sit celebratus*[3]. *Ut videlicet inspiciatur valor monetæ, qui est in loco destinatæ solutionis*[4]. Huberus adopts the same exposition:—*Verum tamen non ita præcisè respiciendus est locus in quo contractus est initus, ut si partes alium in contrahendo locum respexerint, ille non potius sit considerandus*[5]. Indeed, it has the general consent of foreign jurists[6]; although to this, as to most other doctrines, there are to be found exceptions in the opinions of some distinguished names. Thus, John à Sandè maintains that the law of the place where the contract is made is to govern, although the payment is to be made in another place:—*Denique inspicitur locus contractûs, etiamsi solutio in alium locum sit destinata. Et proinde mensura usurpanda est non loci, ubi frumentum vel vinum exigitur, sed ubi de eo conventum est*[7]. The general rule has however been adopted both in England and America. In one of the earliest cases, Lord Mansfield stated the doctrine with his usual clearness:—"The law of the place can never be the rule where the transaction is entered into with an express view to the law of another country, as the rule by

---

1 P. Voet, De Stat. § 15, 16, p. 271, (edit. 1715); Id. p. 328, (edit. 1661); Post, § 301 *f*.

2 P. Voet., De Stat. § 15, 16, p. 271, (edit. 1715); Id. p. 328, (edit. 1661).

3 Everhardus, Consil. 78, n. 9, p. 205; Post, § 300 *b*.

4 Ibid.

5 Huberus, lib. 1, tit. 3, § 10; Ante, § 239; Post, § 299.

6 2 Boullenois, Observ. 46, pp. 475, 476; Id. p. 488; 1 Hertii Oper. De Collis. Leg. § 4, n. 53, p. 147, (edit. 1737); Id. p. 207, (edit. 1716); Voet, Ad Pand. lib. 4, tit. 1, § 29; Post, § 300 *a*—300 *f*.

7 J. à Sandè, Opera, Comm. De Reg. Jur. l. 9, p. 18. See also Colerus, De Process. Exec. pt. 2, n. 79, cited 2 Boullenois, Observ. 46, pp. 475, 476.

which it is to be governed[1]." And this has uniformly been recognised as the correct exposition in the common law[2].

§ 282. But although the general rule is so well established, the application of it in many cases is not unattended with difficulties; for it is often a matter of serious question, in cases of a mixed nature, which rule ought to prevail, the law of the place where the contract is made, or that of the place where it is to be performed[3]. In general, it may be said, that if no place of performance is stated, or the contract may indifferently be performed anywhere, it ought to be referred to the *lex loci contractûs*[4]. But there are many cases where this rule will not be a sufficient guide; and as the subject is important in its practical bearings, it may be well to illustrate it by some cases[5].

---

1 Robinson *v.* Bland, 2 Burr. R. 1077, 1078; Post, § 308—314.

2 Ludlow *v.* Van Rensselaer, 1 John. R. 94; Thomson *v.* Ketcham, 8 John. R. 189; Fanning *v.* Conseequa, 17 John. R. 511; Powers *v.* Lynch, 3 Mass. R. 77; 4 Cowen, Rep. 510, n.; Van Reimsdyk *v.* Kane, 1 Gall. R. 371; Cox and Dick *v.* U. S., 6 Peters, 172, 203; 2 Fonbl. Eq. b. 5, ch. 1, § 6, and note; Prentiss *v.* Savage, 13 Mass. R. 20, 23, 24; Ante, § 270, 280; 3 Burge, Comm. on Col. and For. Law, pt. 2, ch. 20, pp. 752—754; Id. 771—773; Don *v.* Lippman, 5 Clarke & Fin. R. 1, 13, 19, 20.

3 See 2 Kaims, Eq. b. 3, ch. 8, § 4; Voet, De Stat. § 9, ch. 2, § 10.—Hertius puts some questions under this head. A condition is added to a contract in Belgium, which is performed by the debtor in Germany; if the laws of the countries are different, which are to prevail? Hertius says, those of Belgium; because the condition performed relates back to the time of making the contract. Again: a contract made in one place is confirmed in another; what laws are to govern? He answers, if the confirmation is to give greater credit to the contract, as putting it in writing for the sake of proof, the law of the place of the contract is to prevail; if to give validity to the contract, the law of the place of the confirmation. 1 Hertii Opera, De Collis. Leg. p. 147, § 54, 55; Id. pp. 207, 208, (edit. 1716).

4 Don *v.* Lippman, 5 Clarke & Fin. R. 1, 13, 19, 20; Post, § 317.

5 Mr. Burge has expressed the true sense of the general rule and its qualifications in the following terms: "It may be stated generally, that with respect to contracts of which movable property is the subject, the law of the place in which the contract is made will in some respects exclusively prevail, although the contract is to be performed in another; and that in those respects in which it does not prevail, the law of the place where the

§ 283. One of the most simple cases is, where two merchants doing business with each other, reside in different countries, and have mutual accounts of debt and credit with each other for advances and sales; what rule is to be followed as to the balance of accounts existing from time to time between them? Is it the law of the one country or of the other, if there is a conflict between their laws on the subject? If the business transactions are all on one side, as in case of sales and advances made by a commission merchant in his own country for his principal abroad; there the contracts may well be referred to the country of the commission merchant, and the balance be deemed due to him according to its laws[1]. For, although it may be truly said that the debt is due from the principal, and he is generally expected to pay it where he dwells, yet it is equally true that the debt is due where the advances are made, and that payment may be insisted upon there.

§ 284. But suppose the advances have been made in the country of the principal, and the goods sold in the other country,—is the same rule to prevail? or are the advances to be governed by the law of the place where they are advanced, and the sales of the goods by that of the place where they are received by the commission merchant? Suppose both the merchants in different countries sell goods and make advances mutually for each other, and upon the accounts a balance is due from one to the other; by the law of what place is such balance to be ascertained and paid? In these, and many other like mixed cases, the amount of the balance, the time and the manner, and the place of payment, and the true principle of the adjustment of the mutual accounts, may materially depend upon the

---

contract is to be performed must be adopted. But this conclusion is subject to some qualifications and exceptions." 3 Burge, Comm. on Col. and For. Law, pt. 2, ch. 20, pp. 778, 779.

1 Coolidge *v.* Poor, 15 Mass. R. 427; Conseequa *v.* Fanning, 3 John. Ch. R. 587, 610. See also Bradford *v.* Harvard, 13 Mass. R. 18; Milne *v.* Moreton, 6 Binn. R. 353, 359, 365.

operation of the *lex loci*, when the law of the one country conflicts with that of the other. The habits of business and trade between the parties may sometimes decide these points; but if no such governing circumstances are established, the cases must be reasoned out upon principle. Upon principle, it may, perhaps, be found most easy to decide that each transaction is to be governed by the law of the place where it originated; advances by the law of the place where they are advanced, and sales of goods by the law of the place where they are received[1]. The importance of the true rule is peculiarly felt, in all cases of interest to be paid on balances.

§ 284 *a*. This subject was a good deal discussed in a recent case, where goods had been consigned for sale in Trieste by a merchant of Boston, and advances were made by the agent of the consignees in Boston to an amount exceeding the amount of the proceeds of the goods when sold. A suit was brought by the consignees to recover the balance, and the question was, at what rate of exchange the balance was to be allowed; and that depended upon another question, where the balance was reimbursable—in Boston, or in Trieste. The Court held, that the balance was reimbursable at Boston, where the advances were made; but that if the advances had been made at Trieste, the balance would have been reimbursable there. The Court consequently allowed the par of exchange at Boston upon the balance, it being payable there[2].

§ 285. Another case may serve to illustrate the same doctrine. A merchant in America orders goods to be purchased for him in England; in which country is the contract to be deemed complete, and by the laws of which is it to be governed? Casaregis has affirmed, that in such a case the law of England ought to govern; for there the final assent

---

[1] See Conseequa *v*. Fanning, 3 John. Ch. R. 587, 610; 17 John. R. 511; Casaregis, Disc. 179.

[2] Grant *v*. Healey, 2 Chand. Law Reporter, 113. See Post, § 311 *a*, and note.

is given by the person who receives and executes the order of his correspondent. *Pro hujus materiæ declaratione præmittenda est regula ab omnibus recepta, quod contractus vel negotium inter absentes gestum dicatur eo loci, quo ultimus in contrahendo assentitur, sive acceptat; quia tunc tantum uniuntur ambo consensus*[1]. *Sic mandati contractus dicitur initus in loco quo diriguntur literæ missivæ alicujus mercatoris, si alter ad quem diriguntur, eas recipit, et acceptat mandatum*[2]. He goes on to illustrate the doctrine by putting the case of a merchant directing his correspondent in a foreign country to buy goods for him; in which case, he says, if the correspondent accept the order, and in the execution of it he buys the goods of a third person, two contracts spring up; the first, of mandate between the principal and his agent, and the second, of purchase and sale between the vendor and the agent, as purchaser in the name of the principal; and both are to be deemed contracts made in the place where the agent resides. His language is,—*Quando Mercator alteri suo Corresponsori mandat, ut aliquas merces pro se emat, easque sibi transmittat, quo casu si Corresponsor acceptet mandatum, et in illius executionem ab aliqua tertia persona merces commissas emat, duo perficiuntur contractus: Primus, mandati inter mandantem, et mandatarium, et alter, emptionis, et respective venditionis inter eundem mandatarium, uti emptorem nomine mandantis, et venditorem, et ambo perficiuntur in loco mandatarii: Nam, quoad mandati contractum, ratio est, quia consensus mandantis per literas unitur cum ultimo consensu mandatarii in loco, quo mandatarius reperitur, et acceptat mandatum, eoque magis quoad alterum venditionis, et respective emptionis, quia mandatarius vere emit in loco, in quo et ipse, et venditor existunt*[3]. This doctrine, so reason-

---

1 Casaregis, Disc. 179, § 1, 2. See 1 Hertii Opera, De Collis. Leg. § 56, p. 147; Id. p. 208, (edit. 1716); 1 Burge, Comm. on Col. and For. Law, pt. 2, ch. 20, p. 753.

2 Ibid.

3 Casaregis, Disc. 179, n. 10, p. 192.

able in itself, has been expressly affirmed by the Supreme Court of Louisiana[1]. It has also received a sanction in a recent case in the House of Lords, where the Lord Chancellor said:—"If I, residing in England, send down my agent to Scotland, and he makes contracts for me there, it is the same as if I myself went there and made them[2]." The same rule has been held to apply even to an English corporation contracting by its agent in Scotland; for the contract takes effect as a contract in Scotland[3].

§ 286. And if a like contract of purchase is made by an agent without orders, and the correspondent ratifies it, Casaregis says, that the contract is not to be deemed a contract in the country of the ratification, but of the purchase; because the ratification has reference back to the time and place of the purchase: *Ratio est, quia ille ratificationis consensus, licet emitatur in loco ratificantis, et ibi videatur se unire cum altero precedenti gerentis consensu, qui venit a loco gerentis ad locum ratificantis, retrotrahitur ad tempus et ad locum, in quo fuit per gestorem initus contractus emptionis; vel aliud negotium pro absente; et ratio rationis est, quia consensus ratificantis non unitur in loco suo ad aliquem actum seu contractum perficiendum, sed acceptandum contractum vel negotium pro se in loco gestoris jam factum; ac si eodem tempore et loco, in quo fuit per gestorem negotium gestum, ipsemet ratificans esset præsens, ibique contraxisset*[4]. So, a like

---

1 Mr. Justice Martin, in Whiston *v.* Stodder, 8 Martin, R. 93. See also Malpica *v.* M'Kown, 1 Louis. R. 248, 255.

2 Pattison *v.* Mills, 1 Dow. & Clarke, R. 342; Albion F. and L. Insur. Co. *v.* Mills, 3 Wils. & Shaw, 218, 233.—It is difficult to reconcile this doctrine with the views of the Court and Bar in Acebal *v.* Levy, 10 Bing. R. 376, 379—381, (Ante, § 262 *a*), where upon a sale of goods in Spain, to be delivered in England, the purchase having been made by an agent of the purchasers by orders sent to Spain, the Court and Bar seem to have thought that the contract was governed by the English Statute of Frauds. See Ante, § 262 *a;* Post, § 318, and note. Did the place of the delivery and payment make any difference? See Post, § 318, and note.

3 Albion F. and L. Insur. Co. *v.* Mills, 3 Wils. & Shaw, R. 218, 233, 234. See also 3 Burge, Comm. on Col. and For. Law, pt. 2, ch. 20, p. 753.

4 Casaregis, Disc. 179, § 20, 64, 76—80, 83.

rule applies if a merchant in one country agrees to accept a bill drawn on him by a person in another country. It is deemed a contract in the place where the acceptance is to be made [1]. Paul Voet adopts the same conclusion:—*Quid si de literis cambii incidat questio, Quis locus erit spectandus? Is spectandus est locus, ad quem sunt destinatæ, et ibidem acceptatæ* [2].

§ 286 *a*. Hertius takes a curious distinction on this subject. If, says he, a contract is made in one country and is ratified in another, it may be asked, if the laws of the different places vary, which is to govern? To which he answers: If the confirmation is made to add additional faith to the contract, as, for example, if the contract is reduced to writing for the sake of proof, then the law of the place where the contract is made is to be looked to. But, if to give validity to the contract itself, the law of the place of confirmation—*Contractus in alio loco fit, in alio confirmatur; quæritur, cujus loci leges, si discrepare eas usuveniat, intuer idebeamus? Si confirmatio accedat ad conciliandam contractui majorem fidem, v. g. contractus probationis gratiâ in scripturam redigatur, arbitramur, spectandam loci, ubi contrahitur legem. Sin, ut contractus sit validus, loci ubi confirmatur jura prævalebunt* [3]. So that Hertius seems to put the solution of the case upon the point of the supposed intention of the parties to give validity to a defective contract, or only to impart a better proof of its original validity.

§ 286 *b*. A question of a somewhat analogous nature, growing out of agency, and of very familiar occurrence, deserves notice in this place. It is well known, that, by the common law, the master of a ship has a limited authority to take up money in a foreign port, and give a bottomry bond

---

[1] Boyce *v*. Edwards, 4 Peters, R. 111.

[2] P. Voet, De Stat. § 9, ch. 2, § 14, p. 271, (edit. 1715); Id. p. 327, (edit. 1661).

[3] 1 Hertii Opera, De Collis. Leg. § 4, n. 55, p. 147 (edit. 1737); Id. p. 208 (edit. 1716); Ante, § 297.

in cases of necessary repairs, and other pressing emergencies. But he is not at liberty to give such a bond for mere useful supplies or advances, which are not strictly necessary. It is highly probable, that, in some maritime countries, the basis of whose jurisprudence is the civil law, a broader authority is allowed to the master, or at least a broader liability may attach upon the vessel and the owner [1]. In such a case, the question might arise, whether the liability of the ship or of the owner was to be decided by the authority of the master according to the law of the foreign place where the money was advanced, or by the law of the place of the domicil of the ship and owner. In England it would be held, (at least, such seems the course of the adjudications), that the master's authority to bind the ship or the owner in a foreign port would be governed by the law of the domicil of the owner; and that consequently, the master of an English ship could not bind the owner for advances or supplies in a foreign port, which were not justifiable by the English law [2]. But it is far from being certain, that foreign

---

[1] See 2 Emérigon, Contrats à la Grosse, ch. 4, § 2—6, 8, pp. 422—445.

[2] The Nelson, 1 Hagg. Adm. R. 169, 175, 176.—In the case of The Nelson, Lord Stowell said: "It is certainly the vital principle of this species of bonds, that they shall have been taken, where the owner was known to have no credit—no resources for obtaining necessary supplies. It is that state of unprovided necessity that alone supports these bonds. The absence of that necessity is their undoing. If the master takes up money from a person, who knows that he has a general credit in the place, or at least an empowered consignee or agent willing to supply his wants, the giving a bottomry bond is a void transaction,—not affecting the property of the owner, —only fixing loss and shame on the fraudulent lender; but where honourably transacted, under an honest ignorance of this fact, an ignorance that could not be removed by any reasonable inquiry, it is the disposition of this Court to uphold such bonds, as necessary for the support of commerce in its extremities of distress, and as such recognised in the maritime codes of all commercial ages and nations. To the bond exhibited here, some objections are taken respecting its form, but not affecting its validity. One objection is, that it binds the owners personally, as well as the ship and freight, which it cannot do. That is held in this Court to be no objection to the efficacy of what it is admitted it can do. Here we do not take this bond in toto, as is

courts, and especially the courts of the country where the

---

done in other systems of law, and reject it as unsound in the whole, if vicious in any part; but we separate the parts, reject the vicious, and respect the efficiency of those which are entitled to operate. The form of these bonds is different in different countries; so is their authority. In some countries they bind the owner or owners, in others not; and where they do not, though the form of the bond affects to bind the owners, that part is insignificant, but does not at all touch upon the efficiency of those parts which have an acknowledged operation. It is objected likewise, that this bond does not express the obligation to be on the sea risk, and it does not expressly, or in exact terms; but it does in terms amounting to the same effect. The money is to be paid at such a time 'after the ship arrives at her port.' If the ship never arrives at her port, or is lost upon the voyage, that is a sufficient description of sea risk. I take no notice of the other objections made to this bond: they are objections invariably paraded on these occasions, and as invariably overruled by the Court." Mr. Brodie, in his Notes on Lord Stair's Institutes, (Vol. ii. pp. 955, 956), has gone into a full examination of this subject, and said, "It may be laid down as a general, though not absolute principle, that people may be held to contract in reference to the law of the country under whose protection they happen to be at the time. Grant this, however, and the conclusion follows, that the lex loci contractûs becomes in reality a constituent quality of their agreements. Hence it may be argued, that if, on account of a vessel, a debt be contracted in a foreign country, which admits the principle of a tacit hypothecation for repairs, &c., such a jus in re ought to be implied, as the actual import and understanding of the transaction, and as therefore no less acquired ex lege loci, than if it had been constituted by a formal writing. But if in this way such a right do arise ex lege loci, then ex justicia and on principles of international law, ought it to be rendered effectual with us? a point which will be manifest, if we consider that the validity of even a written instrument must be tried by the law of the place in which it was executed. Still, however, must it be remembered, that it is merely as the presumed understanding and intention of parties, that the jus in re can so arise; as a right conceived in favour of the creditor, it can unquestionably be renounced by him; and then comes the question, whether circumstances do not exclude the presumption quoad a mutual understanding founded on the law of the place. When, not to speak of necessary advances, a foreign ship is repaired here, the shipwright, who parts with the possession without stipulating for, and obtaining in due form, a security over the thing, may be supposed to have, according to the principle of the common law, relied exclusively on the personal credit of his debtor; did, therefore, the other party even conceive that he had likewise bound the vessel, there would be wanting the mutual understanding to infer an agreement. So far, then, does the lex loci operate against the contraction of a jus in re for the debt; but it does not thence follow that elsewhere the lex loci should operate in favour of

advances or supplies were furnished, would adopt the same

---

a tacit hypothecation. A distinction is ever to be attended to between the case of a party casually entering a foreign country, and that of one who resides in it; and the distinction is particularly strong in regard to an individual who, as master, has the charge of a vessel in a foreign port. Well may such a person, when he orders repairs on personal credit, be presumed to be ignorant of any further condition which the law of his own country denies; and while, if the other party leave that unexplained, it may be argued with great plausibility, that he has consented to waive the additional security tacitly admitted in ordinary cases, ex lege loci, it must be considered that there would, at all events, be wanting the mutual assent which constitutes the basis of a contract. But this is not all. The contract in such cases is made with the shipmaster, who acts as the implied mandatory of the owners; and the effect of the transaction must greatly depend on the extent of his authority. Now, it is true, that, as a person who has been appointed to an office, must be presumed to be invested with the usual powers, so restrictions upon the ordinary authority will not be effectual against another party who has not been apprized of them; yet it will be observed, that, since it is the duty of those who deal with an agent to make themselves acquainted with the extent of his powers, whether expressed or fairly implied from his office, so the presumed mandate here must be measured, either by some general principle of maritime law, or by the law of the country to which the ship belongs. Such a general principle of maritime law would, of itself, though in a different way, tend, in my apprehension, to exclude the lex loci; but there is no such universally received principle, and the more positive exclusion of the principle of the lex loci is the consequence. Thus, the English law does not allow the master to hypothecate the vessel, at least expressly, unless in a foreign port, where personal credit is unattainable; but entitles him to pledge the absolute personal responsibility of his constituents for the amount of necessary repairs, furnishings, &c.; while, on the other hand, the French law authorizes him to hypothecate the vessel, &c., not bind his constituents personally, at least not beyond the eventual value of the ship and freight, &c., on her return. And it is quite clear, that the merchants and artisans of the respective countries must contract with the shipmasters of each other, according to the powers respectively inherent in those offices. It would be to no purpose for the English artizan or merchant to plead in France the law of his own country, in support of his action for absolute responsibility; and to allow the Frenchman to have the benefit of a privilege ex lege loci, while he has acquired the absolute personal liability of the owners, would, while an opposite measure of justice was awarded to the English, be to afford him a double advantage—the combined effect of the laws of both countries,—would give him a right, the opposite party never contracted for, nor himself could fairly anticipate. The clear result then is, that the transactions must be held to have reference to the master's implied mandate, according to the law of his own country—a mandate which it is the duty of those who deal with him as an agent, to ascertain the extent of; and,

rules, if the lender or supplier had acted with good faith, and in ignorance of the want of authority in the master [1].

§ 286 *c.* In a recent case in Louisiana, where the question arose as to the liability of the owner for the property on board, belonging to a passenger who died on the voyage, the property being afterwards lost, the point was made, whether, as the passenger and property were taken on board at a foreign port, the law of that port, or the law of the place where the vessel and owner belonged, ought to govern, as to the owner's liability. On that occasion the Court said: "We are of opinion, that the law of the place of the contract, and not that of the owner's residence, must be the rule by which his obligations are to be ascertained. The *lex loci contractûs* governs all agreements, unless expressly excluded, or the performance is to be in another country where different regulations prevail. What we do by another we do by ourselves; and we are unable to distinguish between the responsibility created by the owner sending his agent to contract in another country, and that produced by going there and contracting himself [2]. Perhaps the case itself did not require so broad an expression of opinion; since the Court seem to have assumed, that the law of the owner's domicil coincided with the law of the place of the contract, as to the owner's responsibility, and the authority of the master. But the same doctrine has been elaborately maintained by the same Court in another case [3].

---

that, while they never can justly complain of having their right limited by such a principle, the shipmaster cannot be supposed to intend an abuse of his powers—whence the very gist of all contracts, the understanding of parties, would be wanting to infer a right, ex lege loci contractûs, which the scope of his authority did not import. Thus much for the principle of the lex loci contractûs. We shall now proceed to inquire into the principles recognised in England."

1 Emérigon, Contrat. à la Grosse, ch. 4, § 8, pp. 441, 442; Malpica *v.* M'Kown, 1 Louis. R. 249, 254, 255.

2 Mr. Justice Porter in Malpica *v.* M'Kown, 1 Louis. R. 249, 254; Ante, § 285.

3 Arago *v.* Currell, 1 Louis. R. 528.—Mr. Justice Martin in delivering

§ 286 *d.* Another case may readily be suggested as to the conflict of laws in cases of agency. Let us

---

the opinion of the Court in this case said: "The first question it presents relates to the law by which the rights of the parties are to be governed. The defendant sent his vessel from New Orleans to Vera Cruz, to be employed in the transportation of passengers—and the master there entered into a contract for their passages, which being within the scope of his authority, must be as binding on the defendant as if it had been entered into by him personally. This proposition is, however, strenuously combated by his counsel, who contends, that the master had no authority to bind the owner absolutely, but only to the amount of the value of the vessel and freight; because the laws of the country in which the owner has his domicil, fix the measure of his responsibility on all contracts made by the master; that the question, whether an agent has exceeded his powers, must be solved by the laws of the place in which he received them. The admission of this position would still present the question, whether, according to the laws of Louisiana, the agent who contracted in Mexico, in the manner the master did in the present case, exceeded his powers; and the question would still remain open, as to the laws which ought to govern. So it would be under the provision of our code relied on, that the principal is bound only for the acts of his agent, which he could have prevented. So, if it be held, that the law of Mexico is to govern a contract directed to be made there, the question would not be, whether the agent exceeded his powers, but what responsibility the principal would have incurred, had he contracted personally. This has appeared to us the sole question for our examination and solution. The master was sent to Vera Cruz to take passengers on board of the vessel he commanded. He did so. It is not pretended that he made any other than the agreement usual on such an occasion. Whether the property was received and put on board by the owner or master, would make no difference. If the last was committed out of the presence of the owner, his liability would be the same. No question therefore arises as to the authority conferred being exceeded. The owner is sought to be made liable, not on the contract, but for a tort committed by the master, acting within the scope of his powers, in the execution of the contract. The law relied on, which furnishes the owner with an exemption on account of the misfeasance of the master and crew on the surrender of the vessel and freight, would cause the same immunity had the owner contracted personally. If we understand the matter rightly, the immunity is independent entirely of the agreement having been entered into by the agent. For example, in England, where such a rule prevails, we do not understand that there could be the slightest difference in the responsibility of the owner for the torts of the master; whether the contract was for passage or freight, whether the contract was entered into with one or the other. We repeat, therefore, that we cannot see how the question, whether the agent exceeded his powers, is at all involved in the inquiry before us. The moment it is admitted or established,

suppose that A., in Massachusetts, should, by a letter of attorney, duly executed in Boston, authorize B., his

---

that the master's agreement for carrying passengers was on terms such as he was authorized to make, its legal consequences must depend on other principles than those of the law of the contract of mandate. The agreement must have the same effect as if entered into with the owner personally. If then the defendant had gone himself to Vera Cruz, and entered into a contract with a man there, which was to be performed in the island of Cuba, would it have been governed by the law of Louisiana? Now, if there be a principle better established than any other on the subject of the conflict of laws, it is, that contracts are governed by the laws of the country in which they are entered into, unless they be so with a view to a performance in another. Every writer on that subject recognises it. Judicial decisions, again and again, through the civilized world, have sanctioned it. Why then should this form an exception? Why should the contract of affreightment, or for the conveyance of passengers, stand on different grounds than those of buying and selling merchandize? Whoever contracts in a particular place, subjects himself to its laws as a temporary citizen. The idea, that the law of a man's domicil follows him through the world, and attaches to all his contracts, is as novel as unfounded. The proposition was not, indeed, maintained in general terms; but that offered to the Court, in relation to the contract, is identical with it; and it is impossible for us not to feel, that, if the defendant and appellant is to have the contract decided by the laws of Louisiana, it will be equivalent to a declaration of this amount—that an inhabitant of this State carries its laws with him, wherever he goes, and they regulate and govern his contracts in foreign countries—that, whether a man contracts with him in Paris or London, our municipal regulations are the measure of the rights and duties of both parties to the contract. That the Legislature of Louisiana may have a right to regulate the contracts of her own citizens in every country, so long as they owe her allegiance, may or may not be true. But where the citizen contracts abroad with a foreigner, it is evident the rule must be limited in its operation. The Legislature may refuse permission to enforce the agreement at home; but abroad, and particularly where the agreement is entered into, it is valid. The general rule, however, is never to extend the prohibition to contracts made abroad, unless there be an express declaration of the legislative will. We therefore conclude, that, as the master was sent with the vessel to Vera Cruz, to take passengers; as he acted as the owner's agent n making the agreement, and this is admitted by the answer; and as the limitation to the responsibility is resisted on grounds which would have an equal force if the agreement had been made with him personally, we are bound, in our inquiry as to the law which governs the agreement, to consider it as made personally by the owner, and it is to be governed, not by the laws of his domicil, but by those of the country in which it was entered into and to be performed. But, although the case does not present the question of the

agent in New Orleans, to sell his ship, then lying in New Orleans, and to execute a bill of sale in his (A.'s) name,

---

owner's responsibility, in relation to the contract of mandate, the agent having confined himself within his powers; yet, as the argument has placed the immunity claimed by the defendant and appellant on that ground, it is well to notice it more particularly. If we understood the arguments correctly, it was contended, that the laws of Louisiana, having put some limitations to the power of the master to bind the owner, any contract of the former, in a foreign country, must be subject to the limitation; and if they be exceeded, there is an end to the latter's responsibility. Where a general power is confined to an agent, the party contracting with him is not bound by any limitation, which the principal may have affixed, at the time or since, by distinct instructions. Now, in the case before us, if instructions be supposed to have been given to the master, not to bind the owner beyond the value of the vessel and freight, or for any act which the latter could not prevent, would parties contracting with the former in a foreign country be bound by them? We think it is certain they would not. Every contract, which by the general maritime law the master can make, is binding on the owner. By putting the former in command, and sending him abroad, the latter invests him with the general powers masters have as such, and those who contract with him have nothing to do with any private instructions, by which the general power may have been limited. If the limitation arises, not from the owner's instructions, but from the particular laws of the country from which the vessel has sailed, must not the consequence be the same? Can these laws limit the master's power more effectually than the owner could, or can they extend farther? We think not. They have no force in a foreign country, where they are presumed to be equally unknown. Emérigon, treating of the case where the master was prohibited from taking des deniers à la grosse, during the voyage, examines the question, whether those who furnished them would have an action against the owner. He cites all the texts of the Roman laws on which the negative can be maintained; and concludes, that if the lender had no knowledge of the prohibitions, the owner would be responsible; that those who contract with him in a foreign country have a right to presume he is clothed with all the powers which belong to his station. Boulay Paty is of the same opinion, as to the responsibilities of the owner for the acts of the master appointed by him, whom they put in command, with a special prohibition from making a subrogation of his powers. (2 Emérig. Contrats à la Grosse, ch. 4, § 8; Boulay Paty, 289). In another part of his work, Emérigon treats of the power of a master to draw bills on his owners in a foreign port, contrary to the authority given by the ordinance, and he considers he cannot, because he exceeds the powers of his legal mandate. In support of this opinion he cites decisions in opposition to what, he says, was the former jurisprudence of France, founded on the authority of Valin. He seems to conclude the rule is firmly fixed as he un-

to the purchaser, and B. should accept the agency, and sell the ship after the death of A., but before he had received or could receive any notice thereof, and should execute a bill of sale in A.'s name to the purchaser. In such a case, the question might arise, (especially if A. died insolvent, or the money was invested in pursuance of other orders of A. in goods, which had perished by fire, or other accident), whether the bill of sale was valid or not valid. By the law of Massachusetts a letter of attorney is revoked by the death of the principal, whether known or unknown, and all acts done after his death under it are mere nullities [1]. By the law of Louisiana, if an attorney, being ignorant of the death, or of the cessation of the rights of his principal, should continue to act under his power of attorney, the transactions done by him during this state of

---

derstood it. But we find it was not generally adopted. Boulay Paty states, that opinions were divided; and the Chamber of Commerce of Nantz, in their observations on the Code of Commerce, observe, it is a question often agitated, and which had been decided in different ways. (2 Emérig. Contrats à la Grosse, ch. 4, § 11, pp. 441—458; 2 Boulay Paty, 71). The new Code adopted Valin's doctrine. But Emérigon, who is an author of distinction, in treating of the question, says, that although the master cannot abroad go beyond the legal mandate, provided that his contract (son raccord) or the general mercantile laws give him a more extensive power, à moins que son raccord ou le droit commune, en certant cas, ne lui donne un pouvoir plus étendu. (2 Emérig. Contrats à la Grosse, ch. 4, § 11, p. 452). The general rule, where there is no statute limiting the owner's responsibility, is, that he is responsible for all damages done by the master, while acting within the scope of his powers. Abbott states, that this is the doctrine of the common and civil law, and so do all the writers we have been able to consult. In Chancellor Kent's late work, and in Judge Story's edition of Abbott, it is stated, that the owner is bound for the whole amount of the injury done by the master or crew, unless where ordinances and statutes have established a different rule. (3 Kent Comm. 172; Abbott on Shipping (edit. 1829); 1 Pothier, Oblig. n. 451, 452). If this question turned on the master's having exceeded his powers, we are inclined to think, that, as the general rule authorized him to bind the owner to the extent contracted for, the plaintiff and appellant, who contracted with him, was unaffected by a limitation in a statute of another country, of which he could not be presumed to have any knowledge, and to the authority of which he was not subject."

[1] Story on Agency, § 488, 489.

ignorance would be valid[1]. Assuming that this provision covers all cases, not only when the transaction is executed in the name of the agent, but also when it is executed in the name of the principal, upon which some doubt may be entertained, (as a dead man cannot act at all[2]), still the question would be, by what law the letter of attorney, with reference to its revocability, duration, and effect, is to be governed. The general rule certainly is, that all the instruments made and executed in a country take effect, and are to be construed, as to their nature, operation, and extent, according to the law of the country where they are made and executed. *Locus regit actum*[3]. But the question here would be, whether, as the execution of the power was to be in another country, the power should not be construed and executed, and its nature, operation, and extent, ascertained by the law of the latter, as an exception to the general rule. There is no doubt, that where an authority is given to an agent to transact business for his principal in a foreign country, it must be construed, in the absence of any counter proofs, that it is to be executed according to the law of the place where the business is to be transacted[4]. But this may well be admitted to be the rule, while the authority is in full force, without making the law of that place the rule by which to ascertain whether the original power of attorney is still subsisting, or is revoked, or dead by operation of law in the place of its origin. The point has never, as far as my researches extend, been directly decided, either at home or abroad; and therefore it is submitted to the learned reader for his consideration. Some of the cases already alluded to, may be thought to furnish an analogy unfavourable to the validity of the sale[5].

---

1 Code Civil of Louisiana, art. 3001. The Civil Code of France contains a similar regulation. Code Civil of France, art. 2008; Pothier on Oblig. n. 81.

2 See Story on Agency, § 491—499.

3 Ante, § 263.

4 Owings *v.* Hull, 9 Peters, R. 607—627, 628.

5 Ante, § 286 *b*, 286 *c*.

§ 287. Another class of cases may be stated. A merchant in one country sends a letter to a merchant in another, requesting him to purchase goods, and to draw on him for the amount of the purchase-money by bills. In which country is the contract for the repayment of the advances, if the purchase is made, to be deemed to be made? Is it in the country where the letter is written, and on which the drafts are authorized to be drawn? or where the goods are purchased? The decision has been, that when such advances are made, the undertaking is to replace the money at the same place at which the advances are made; and, therefore, the party advancing will be entitled to interest on the advances according to the law of the place of the advances [1]. So, if advances are made for a foreign merchant at his request, or security is given for a debt, the party paying or advancing is in like manner entitled to repayment in the place where the advances are made, or the security is given, unless some other place is stipulated therefor [2].

§ 287 *a*. So, where a loan is made in one state, and security is to be given therefor in another state by way of mortgage; it may be asked, what law is to govern in relation to the contract and its incidents? The decision has been, that the law of the place where the loan is made is to govern; for the mere taking of a foreign security does not, it is said, necessarily alter the locality of the contract. Taking such security does not necessarily draw after it the consequence, that the contract is to be fulfilled where the security is taken. The legal fulfilment of a contract of loan on the part of the bondsman, is repayment of the money; and the security given is but the means of securing what he has contracted for, which, in the eye of the law, is to pay where he borrows, unless another place of

---

[1] Lanusse *v.* Barker, 3 Wheat. R. 101, 146; Grant *v.* Healey, 2 Chand. Law Reporter, 113; Ante, § 284 *a*. See also Hertii Opera, tom. 1, De Collis. Leg, § 4, n. 55, p. 147, (edit. 1737); Id. p. 208 (edit. 1716).

[2] Bayle *v.* Zacharie, 6 Peters, R. 635, 643, 644; Post, § 320 *a*.

payment be expressly designated by the contract[1]. But if the mortgage is actually to be executed in a foreign country, and the money is to be paid there, the loan will be deemed to be there completed, although the money may have been actually advanced elsewhere[2].

§ 288. A case somewhat different in its circumstances, but illustrative of the general principle, occurred formerly in England. By a settlement made upon the marriage of A. in England, a term of five hundred years was created upon estates in Ireland, in trust to raise £12,000 for the portions of daughters. The parties to the settlement resided in England; and a question afterwards arose, whether the £12,000, charged on the term of years, should be paid in England, without any abatement or deduction for the exchange from Ireland to England? It was decided, that the portion ought to be paid in England, where the contract was made, and the parties resided; and not in Ireland, where the lands lay, which were charged with the payment; for it was a sum in gross, and not a rent issuing out of the land[3].

§ 289. Let us take another case. A merchant, resident in Ireland, sends to England certain bills of exchange, with

---

[1] De Wolf *v.* Johnson, 10 Wheaton, R. 367, 383. See also Ranelagh *v.* Champant, 2 Vern. R. 395, and Raithby's note; Conner *v.* Bellamont, 2 Atk. 382; Post, § 293. See Chapman *v.* Robertson, 6 Paige, R. 627, 630; Post, § 293 *b.*

[2] De Wolf *v.* Johnson, 10 Wheaton, R. 367; Hosford *v.* Nichols, 1 Paige, R. 221; Lloyd *v.* Scott, 4 Peters, R. 211, 229.—Whether a contract, made in one state, for the sale of lands situate in another state, on credit, reserving interest at the legal rate of interest of the state where the lands lie, but more than that of the state where the contract is made, would be usurious, has been much discussed in the State of New York. In Van Schaick *v.* Edwards, 2 John. Cas. 355, the judges were divided in opinion upon the question. See also Hosford *v.* Nichols, 1 Paige, R. 220, and Dewar *v.* Span, 3 T. R. 425; Ante, § 279 *a.*

[3] Phipps *v.* Earl of Anglesea, cited 5 Vin. Abridg. 209, pl. 8; 2 Eq. Abridg. 220, pl. 1; Id. 754, pl. 3; 1 P. Will. 696; 2 Bligh, Parl. R. 88, 89. See also Lansdowne *v.* Lansdowne, 2 Bligh, Parl. R. 60; Stapleton *v.* Conway, 3 Atk. 727; S. C. 1 Ves. 427.

blanks for the dates, the sums, the times of payment, and the names of the drawees. These bills are signed by the merchant in Ireland, indorsed with his own name, and dated from a place in Ireland, and are transmitted to a correspondent in England, with authority to him to fill up the remaining parts of the instrument. The correspondent in England accordingly fills them up, dated at a place in Ireland. Are the bills, when thus filled up and issued, to be deemed English or Irish contracts? It has been held, that under such circumstances they are to be deemed Irish contracts, and of course to be governed, as to stamps and other legal requisitions, by the law of Ireland; and that, as soon as they are filled up, the whole transaction relates back to the time of the original signature of the drawer[1]. One of the learned judges on that occasion said, that if the drawer had died while the bills were on their passage, and afterwards the blanks had been filled up, and the bills negotiated to an innocent indorsee, the personal representatives of the drawer would have been bound[2].

§ 290. Bonds for the faithful discharge of the duties of office are often given with sureties, by public officers, to the government of the United States; and it sometimes happens, that the bonds are executed by the principals in one State, and by the sureties in a different State, or in different States. What law is in such cases to regulate the contract? The rights and duties of sureties are known to be different in different States. In Louisiana one system prevails, deriving itself mainly from the civil law; in other States a different system prevails, founded on the common law. It has been decided, that the bonds in such cases must be treated as made and delivered, and to be performed by all the parties, at the seat of the government of the Union, upon the ground, that the principal is bound to account there; and, therefore, by necessary implication, all the

---

1 Smith v. Mingay, 1 Maule & Selw. 87.

2 Mr. Justice Bayley, ibid. p. 95.

other parties look to that as the place of performance, by the law of which they are to be governed[1].

§ 291. The question also often arises in cases respecting the payment of interest. The general rule is, that interest is to be paid on contracts according to the law of the place where they are to be performed, in all cases where interest is expressly or impliedly to be paid[2]. *Usurarum modus ex*

---

1 Cox and Dick *v.* U. States, 6 Peters, R. 172, 202; Duncan *v.* U. States, 7 Peters, R. 435.

2 Post, § 292, 293, 293 *a*—§ 293 *e*, 304; Conner *v.* Bellamont, 2 Vern. R. 382; Cash *v.* Kennion, 11 Vesey, R. 314; Robinson *v.* Bland, 2 Burr. R. 1077; Ekins *v.* East India Company, 1 P. W. 395; Ranelagh *v.* Champant, 2 Vern. R. 395, and note, ibid. by Raithby; 1 Chitty on Comm. & Manuf. ch. 12, pp. 650, 651; 3 Chitty, Id. ch. 1, p. 109; Eq. Abridg. Interest, E.; Henry on Foreign Law, 43, n.; Id. 53; 2 Kaims, Equity, b. 3, ch. 8, § 1; 2 Fonbl. Eq. b. 5, ch. 1, § 6, and note; Bridgman's Equity Digest, Interest, vii.; Fanning *v.* Conseequa, 17 John. R. 511; S. C. 3 John. Ch. R. 610; Hosford *v.* Nichols, 1 Paige, R. 220; Houghton *v.* Paige, 2 N. Hamp. R. 42; Peacock *v.* Banks, 1 Minor, R. 387; Lapice *v.* Smith, 13 Louis. R. 91, 92; Thomson *v.* Ketchum, 4 John. R. 285; Healy *v.* Gorman, 3 Green, N. J. R. 328; 2 Kent, Comm. Lect. 39, pp. 460, 461, 3rd edit.—A case illustrative of this principle recently occurred before the House of Lords. A widow in Scotland entered into an obligation to pay the whole of her deceased husband's debts. It was held by the Court of Session in Scotland, that the English creditors, on contracts made in England, were entitled to recover interest in all cases where the law of England gave interest, and not where it did not. Therefore, on bonds and bills of exchange interest was allowed, and on simple contracts not. And this decision was affirmed by the House of Lords. Montgomery *v.* Budge, 2 Dow. & Clarke, Rep. 297. The case of Arnott *v.* Redfern (2 Car. & Payne, 88) may at first view seem inconsistent with the general doctrine. There, the original contract was made in London between an Englishman and a Scotchman. The latter agreed to go to Scotland as agent four times a-year, to sell goods and collect debts for the other party, to remit the money, and to guarantee one-fourth part of the sales; and he was to receive one per cent. upon the amount of sales, &c. The agent sued for a balance of his account in Scotland, and the Scotch Court allowed him interest on it. The judgment was afterwards sued in England; and the question was, whether interest ought to be allowed. Lord Chief Justice Best said: "Is this an English transaction? For, if it is, it will be regulated by the rules of English law; but, if it is a Scotch transaction, then the case will be different." He afterwards added—"This is the case of a Scotchman, who comes into England,

more regionis, ubi contractum est, constituitur, says the Digest.[1] Thus, a note made in Canada, where interest is six per cent., payable with interest in England, where it is five per cent., bears English interest only[2]. Loans made in a place bear the interest of that place, unless they are payable elsewhere[3]. And, if payable in a foreign country, they may bear any rate of interest not exceeding that which is lawful by the laws of that country[4]. And on this account a contract for a loan made and payable in a foreign country, may stipulate for interest higher than that allowed at home[5]. If the contract for interest be illegal there, it will

---

and makes a contract. As the contract was made in England, although it was to be executed in Scotland, I think it ought to be regulated according to the rules of the English law. This is my present opinion. These questions of international law do not often occur." And he refused interest, because it was not allowed by the law of England. The Court afterwards ordered interest to be given, upon the ground that the balance of such an account would carry interest in England. But Lord Chief Justice Best rightly expounded the contract as an English contract, though there is a slight inaccuracy in his language. So far as the principal was concerned, the contract to pay the commission was to be paid in England. The services of the agent were to be performed in Scotland; but the whole contract was not to be executed exclusively there by both parties. A contract made to pay money in England for services performed abroad, is an English contract, and will carry English interest.

[1] Dig. lib. 22, tit. 1, l. 1; 2 Burge, Comm. on Col. and For. Law, pt. 2, ch. 9, pp. 860—862.

[2] Scofield *v.* Day, 20 John. R. 102.

[3] De Wolf *v.* Johnson, 10 Wheaton, R. 367, 383; Conseequa *v.* Willing, Peters, Cir. R. 225; 2 Boullenois, Observ. 46, pp. 477, 478; Andrews *v.* Pond, 13 Peters, R. 65, 78.

[4] Ibid.; 2 Kent, Comm. Lect. 39, pp. 460, 461, 3rd edit.; Thomson *v.* Ketchum, 4 John. R. 285; Healy *v.* Gorman, 3 Green, N. J. R. 328.

[5] 2 Kent, Comm. Lect. 39, pp. 460, 461, 3rd edit.; Hosford *v.* Nichols, 1 Paige, R. 220; Houghton *v.* Paige, 2 N. Hamp. R. 42; Thompson *v.* Powles, 2 Simons, R. 194.—In this last case the Vice-Chancellor said:—"With respect to the question of usury, in order to hold the contract to be usurious, it must appear that the contract was made here, and that the consideration for it was to be paid here. It should appear, at least, that the payment was not to be made abroad; for if it was to be made abroad, it would not be usurious." See also Andrews *v.* Pond, 13 Peters, R. 65, 78; De Wolf *v.* Johnson, 10 Wheat. R. 383.

be illegal every where[1]. But if it be legal where it is made, it will be of universal obligation, even in places where a lower interest is prescribed by law[2].

§ 292. The question, therefore, whether a contract is usurious or not, depends, not upon the rate of the interest allowed, but upon the validity of that interest in the country where the contract is made and is to be executed[3]. A contract made in England for advances to be made at Gibraltar, at a rate of interest beyond that of England, would nevertheless be valid in England; and so a contract to allow interest upon credits given in Gibraltar at such higher rate, would be valid in favour of the English creditor[4].

§ 292 *a*. This, too, seems to be the doctrine propounded by Rodenburg, who says: *Status quidem aut conditio personarum dirigitur a loco domicilii: cæterum tamen in vinculo cujusque obligationis, ut sciamus, quos obliget conventio, spectamus leges reigionis ubi illa celebratur. Quemadmodum et in illicita stipulatione, quæ legibus est interdicta, ut puta; si debitum modum usurarum excedit, traditum est valere pactum, quo foris secundùm mores illius regionis stipulati sumus prohibitam domi usurarum quantitatem. Unde non longe abire videtur, quod memini nuper apud nos responsum esse, si*

---

1 2 Kaims, Equity, b. 3, ch. 8, § 1; Hosford *v.* Nichols, 1 Paige, R. 220; 2 Boullenois, Observ. 46, p. 477.—In the case of Thomson *v.* Powles, (2 Simons, R. 194), the Vice-Chancellor said: "In order to have the contract (for stock) usurious, it must appear that the contract was made here, and that the consideration for it was to be paid here." (See also Yrisarri *v.* Clement, 2 Car. & Payne, R. 223). In Hosford *v.* Nichols, (1 Paige, R. 220), where a contract was made for the sale of lands in New York, by citizens then resident there, and the vendor afterwards removed to Pennsylvania, where the contract was consummated, and a mortgage given to secure the unpaid purchase-money with New York interest, (which was higher than that of Pennsylvania), the Court thought the mortgage not usurious, it being only a consummation of the original bargain made in New York.

2 Ibid.

3 Harvey *v.* Archbold, 1 Ryan & Mood., R. 184; Andrews *v.* Pond, 13 Peters, R. 65, 78; Ante, § 243.

4 Ibid.

contracta sit eo loci obligatio ubi sortem liceat exigere cum usuris, ut maxime jam earum aliquæ essent persolutæ, Jure caput cum usuris et apud nos exigi, ubi usurarum solutione protinùs via petitioni sortis præcluditur, locumque sibi vindicat decantata adeo parœmia[1]. Burgundus is still more direct and positive[2].

§ 293. And in cases of this sort, it will make no difference, (as we have seen), that the due performance of the contract is secured by a mortgage, or other security, upon property situate in another country where the interest is lower[3]. For it is collateral to such contract; and the interest reserved being according to the law of the place where the contract is made and to be executed, there does not seem to be any valid objection to giving collateral security elsewhere, to enforce and secure the due performance of a legal contract[4]. But, suppose a debt is contracted in one country, and afterwards, in consideration of farther delay, the debtor in another country enters into a new contract for the payment of interest upon the debt at a higher rate than that allowed by the country where the original debt was contracted, but not higher than that allowed by the law of the country where it is so stipulated; it may be asked, whether such stipulation is valid? It has been decided that it is[5]. On the other hand, suppose the interest so stipulated is according to the rate of interest allowed in the country where the debt was contracted, but higher than that in the country where the new contract is made; is the

---

1 Rodenburg, De Diversit. Stat. tit. 4, Ps. 2, c. 2, p. 92.

2 Burgundus, tract. 4, n. 10, p. 109; Post, § 293 *e*, 300 *a*; 2 Burge, Comm. pt. 2, ch. 9, pp. 860—862.

3 Ante, § 287.

4 Conner *v*. Bellamont, 2 Atk. R. 382; Stapleton *v*. Conway, 3 Atk. R. 727; S. C. 1 Vesey, R. 427; De Wolf *v*. Johnson, 10 Wheaton, R. 367, 383.

5 Conner *v*. Bellamont, 2 Atk. R. 382. See also Hosford *v*. Nichols, 1 Paige, R. 220.

stipulation invalid? It has been decided that it is[1]. In each of these cases the *lex loci contractûs* was held to govern as to the proper rate of interest.

§ 293 *a*. In the cases hitherto stated, the transaction is supposed to be *bonâ fide* between the parties; for if the transaction is a mere cover for usury, as if the transaction is in form a bill of exchange drawn upon and payable in a foreign country, but in reality the parties resort to that as a mere machinery to disguise the usury in the transaction against the laws of the country where the contract is made, the form of the transaction will be treated as a mere nullity, and the Court will decide according to the real object of the parties. Thus, for example, where a bill of exchange was drawn in New York, payable in Alabama, and the bill was for an antecedent debt, and a large discount was made from the bill, greater than the interest in either State, for the supposed difference of exchange, the Court considered the real question to be as to the *bona fides* of the transaction. If a mere cover, it was usurious[2].

---

[1] Dewar *v.* Span, 3 T. R. 435. See also Stapleton *v.* Conway, 3 Atk. R. 382; S. C. 1 Vesey, R. 427. See Chapman *v.* Robertson, 6 Paige, R. 627, 631.

[2] Andrews *v.* Pond, 13 Peters, R. 65, 77, 78.—On this occasion Mr. Chief Justice Taney said: "Another question presented by the exception, and much discussed here, is, whether the validity of this contract depends upon the laws of New York, or those of Alabama. So far as the mere question of usury is concerned, this question is not very important. There is no stipulation for interest apparent upon the paper. The ten per cent. in controversy is charged as the difference in exchange only, and not for interest and exchange. And if it were otherwise, the interest allowed in New York is seven per cent., and in Alabama eight; and this small difference of one per cent. per annum, upon a forbearance of sixty days, could not materially affect the rate of exchange, and could hardly have any influence on the inquiry to be made by the jury. But there are other considerations which make it necessary to decide this question. The laws of New York make void the instrument when tainted with usury; and if this bill is to be governed by the laws of New York, and if the jury should find that it was given upon a usurious consideration, the plaintiff would not be entitled to recover, unless he was a bonâ fide holder, without notice, and had given for it a valuable consideration:

§ 293 *b*. Indeed in all cases of this sort we are to look to the real intentions of the parties, and their acts as expressive of them. Thus, where a citizen of New York applied in England to a British subject for a loan of money, upon the security of a bond and mortgage upon land in New York, at the legal rate of interest (seven per cent.) of that

---

while by the laws of Alabama he would be entitled to recover the principal amount of the debt, without any interest. The general principle, in relation to contracts made in one place to be executed in another, is well settled. They are to be governed by the law of the place of performance—and if the interest allowed by the laws of the place of performance is higher than that permitted at the place of the contract, the parties may stipulate for the higher interest, without incurring the penalties of usury. And in the case before us, if the defendants had given their note to H. M. Andrews and Co., for the debt then due to them, payable at Mobile in sixty days, with eight per cent. interest, such a contract would undoubtedly have been valid, and would have been no violation of the laws of New York, although the lawful interest in that State is only seven per cent. And if in the account adjusted at the time this bill of exchange was given, it had appeared that Alabama interest of eight per cent. was taken for the forbearance of sixty days given by the contract, and the transaction was in other respects free from usury, such a reservation of interest would have been valid and obligatory upon the defendants, and would have been no violation of the laws of New York. But that is not the question which we are now called on to decide. The defendants allege that the contract was not made with reference to the laws of either state, and was not intended to conform to either. That a rate of interest forbidden by the laws of New York where the contract was made, was reserved on the debt actually due; and that it was concealed under the name of exchange, in order to evade the law. Now, if this defence is true, and shall be so found by the jury, the question is not which law is to govern in executing the contract, but which is to decide the fate of a security taken upon a usurious agreement, which neither will execute? Unquestionably it must be the law of the State where the agreement was made, and the instrument taken to secure its performance. A contract of this kind cannot stand on the same principles with a bonâ fide agreement made in one place to be executed in another. In the last-mentioned cases the agreements were permitted by the lex loci contractûs; and will even be enforced there if the party is found within its jurisdiction. But the same rule cannot be applied to contracts forbidden by its laws, and designed to evade them. In such cases the legal consequences of such an agreement must be decided by the law of the place where the contract was made. If void there, it is void everywhere." See Chapman *v.* Robertson, 6 Paige, R. 627, 630, 631.

State; and it was agreed that the borrower should, upon his return to New York, execute the bond and mortgage, and duly record the same; and upon the bond and mortgage being received in England, the lender agreed to deposit the money loaned at the bankers of the borrower in London for his use; and the bond and mortgage were executed and received, and the money paid accordingly to the bankers; the question arose, whether the transaction was usurious or not; and that depended upon the law of the place by which it was to be governed, whether by the law of England (where interest is only five per cent.) or by the law of New York. It was held by the Court, that the contract was to be construed according to the laws of New York, and therefore, that a bill to foreclose the mortgage, filed in New York, was maintainable; and that the law of usury of England was no defence to the suit. On that occasion the learned Chancellor said, that as no place of payment was mentioned in the bond or mortgage, the legal construction of the contract was, that the money was to be paid where the obligee resided, or wherever he might be found; that the residence of the obligee being in England at the time of the execution of the bond, that must be considered the place of payment, for the purpose of determining the question, where that part of the contract was to be performed; and that the execution of the bond in New York did not make it a personal contract there, because it was inoperative until received there, and the money deposited with the bankers for the borrower. And he concluded by saying; "Upon a full examination of all the cases to be found upon the subject, either in this country or in England, none of which, however, appear to have decided the precise question which arises in this cause, I have arrived at the conclusion, that this mortgage, executed here, and upon property in this State, being valid by the *lex sitûs*, which is also the law of the domicil of the mortgagor, it is the duty of this Court to give full effect to the security, without reference to the usury laws of England, which neither party intended to evade or violate by the execution of a mortgage upon the lands here[1]."

§ 293 *c*. Whatever objections may be made to the reasoning of the learned Chancellor, and it is certainly open to some observation, the decision itself seems well supported in point of principle; for the parties intended that the whole transaction should be in fact, as it was in form, a New York contract, governed by the laws thereof, and the repayment of the debt was there to be made. It is easily reconcilable with other laws and principles, if viewed in this light; if viewed as the Chancellor interpreted the case, it is perhaps irreconcilable with other cases, and with general principles[2].

---

1 Chapman *v*. Robertson, 6 Paige, R. 627, 630—633.

2 Ibid. It appears to me, that the case was correctly decided; but, with the greatest deference for the learned Chancellor, upon principles and expositions, to which I cannot assent, and which appear to me inconsistent with the general reasoning of the authorities. It appears to me, that there being no place of payment designated in the bond and mortgage, which was executed at New York where the borrower was domiciled,—that although it was not operative until received by the lender; yet when received and adopted by him, the transaction related back to its origin, and it was valid, not as a bond and mortgage executed in England for the payment of money there, but as a bond and mortgage for the payment of the money in New York, as having originated there, and having its whole validity and operation from the law of New York. If an order for goods were sent from New York to England, and the order were complied with, and the goods received in New York, after the receipt of the goods the debt would be treated as an English debt; since the contract of purchase would there be deemed to be negotiated and perfected. Ante. § 285, 286. In truth, where no place of payment is mentioned, the law of the place where the contract is made fixes it in that place wherever the parties may be domiciled. The bond and mortgage took effect as contracts of the borrower executed at New York. If a negotiable note is made in one state, and is negotiated to an indorsee in another state, the contract with the indorsee by the maker takes effect as a promise in the state where the note was made, and not where it was indorsed. The payment of the money to the bankers of the borrower in London was merely for his accommodation, and it by no means made the money repayable there. The case of Stapleton *v*. Conway, 3 Atk. R. 727; S. C. 1 Ves. 427, is, as far as it goes, in opposition to the decision in 6 Paige, R. 627. It is not, however, my design in this place to enter upon the reasons of my dissent from the doctrines stated by the learned Chancellor in 6 Paige, R. 627. The

§ 293 *d.* John Voet, in his Commentaries on the Pandects, holds this very doctrine, which appears to me to be entirely in harmony with the received principles of international law. He considers, that the interest must be according to the law of the place where the contract is to be performed, whether that place be where the contract is made, or it be another place. If the interest is in either case stipulated for beyond that rate, he deems it usurious. *Si alio in loco graviorum usurarum stipulatio permissa, in alio vetita sit, lex loci in quo contractus celebratus est, spectanda videtur in quæstione, an moderatæ, an vero modum excedentes, usuræ per conventionem constitutæ sint. Dummodo meminerimus, illum proprie locum contractus in jure non intelligi, in quo negotium gestum est, sed in quo pecuniam ut solveret, se quis obligavit. Modo etiam bonâ fide omnia gesta fuerint, nec consulto talis ad mutuum contrahendum locus electus sit, in quo graviores usuræ, quam in loco, in quo alias contrahendum fuisset, probatæ inveniuntur. Etiamsi de cætero hypotheca, in sortis et usurarum securitatem obligata, in alio loco sita sit, ubi solæ leviores usuræ permissæ ; cum æquius sit, contractum accessorium regi ex loco principalis negotii gesti, quam ex opposito contractum principalem regi lege loci, in quo accessorius contractus celebratus est*[1].

§ 293 *e.* Burgundus adopts the same doctrine, and says : *Licita verò sit, an illicita, stipulatio, à formâ quoque videtur proficisi, et ideo ejusdem legibus dirigitur, quibus ipsa forma, et ad locum contractus collimare, oportet. Quare et usurarum modus is constituendus est, qui in regione in qua est contractum legitimè celebratur. Et cùm reditus duodenarius, in Galliâ stipulatus, in controversiam incidisset, patrocinante me judicatum est, in curia Flandriæ valere pactum: nec obesse, quod in Flandria, ubi reditus constitutus, sive hypothecæ im-*

---

principles stated fron § 280—321, sufficiently explain some of the grounds upon which that dissent may be maintained. See also 2 Kent, Comm. Lect. 39, pp. 460, 461, 3rd edit., and Andrews *v.* Pond, 13 Peters, R. 65; Ante, § 291; Post, § 304.

[1] J. Voet, Ad. Pand. lib. 22, tit. 1, § 6, p. 938; Post, § 304.

positus proponeretur, usuras semisse graviores stipulari non liceat; quia ratio hypothecæ non habetur, quæ hac in re nihil conferens ad substantiam obligationis, tantum extrinsecus accedit legitimæ stipulationi. Sed hoc intellige de usuris in stipulationem deductis, non autem de iis, quæ ex mora debentur, in quibus ad locum solutionis (ut docebimus posteà) respicere oportet[1].

§ 294. In cases of express contracts for interest, foreign jurists generally hold the same doctrine. Dumoulin, and after him Boullenois, says: *In concernentibus contractum, et emergentibus tempore contractus spectatur locus, in quo contrahitur*[2]. And hence the latter deduces the general conclusion, that the validity of contracts for rates of interest depends upon the laws of the place where the contract is made and payable, whether it be in the domicil of the debtor, or in that of the creditor, or in that where the property hypothecated is situated, or elsewhere[3]. He holds this also to be a just inference from the language of the Digest: *Cum judicio bonæ fidei disceptatur, arbitrio judicis usurarum modus ex more regionis, ubi contractum est constituitur*[4]; and that it applies where the parties have designedly contracted in the one place rather than in the other[5]. But, where there is no express contract, and interest is to be implied, foreign jurists are not so well agreed[6]. Some contend, that, if the contract is between foreigners, the law of interest of the domicil of the creditor ought to prevail; and others, that that of the domicil of the debtor ought to prevail[7].

---

1 Burgundus, Tract. 4, § 10, pp. 108, 109; Post, § 302.

2 Molin, Opera, Comm. ad Consuet. Paris, tit. 1, § 12, gloss. 7, n. 37, tom. 1, p. 224; 2 Boullenois, Observ. 46, p. 472; Henry on Foreign Law, p. 53; Boullenois, Quest. de la Contr. des Lois, pp. 330—338; Ante, § 82 *a*.

3 2 Boullenois, Observ. 46, p. 472.

4 Dig. lib. 22, tit. 1, l. 1.

5 2 Boullenois, Observ. 46, p. 472.

6 Id. 477—479, 496.

7 Ibid.; Bouhier, Cout. de. Bourg. ch. 21, § 194—199; Livermore, Dissert. § 42, pp. 46, 47.

§ 295 Boullenois is of opinion, that, where there is no express contract, the interest for which a delinquent debtor is tacitly liable on account of his neglect to pay the debt, is the interest allowed by the law of the place where the debt is payable; because it is there that the interest has its origin[1]. And, in this, he follows the doctrine of Everhardus, who says: *Quia, ubi certus locus solutionis faciendæ destinatus est, tunc non factâ solutione in termino et loco præfixo, mora dicitur contrahi in loco destinatæ solutionis, non in loco celebrati contractûs*[2]. Strykius holds the same opinion: *Si lis oritur ex post facto propter negligentiam et moram, consideratur locus, ubi mora contracta est*[3]. Boullenois puts a distinction which also deserves notice, between cases where the debt for money loaned is payable at a fixed day, and where no day is fixed for payment, but it is at the pleasure of the creditor when it shall be paid, and no place of payment is mentioned[4]. In the former case he holds, that the debtor is bound, in order to avoid default, to seek the creditor and pay him; and therefore the neglect to make payment arises in the domicil of the creditor, and interest ought to be allowed according to the law of that place[5]. In the latter case, the creditor is to demand payment of the debtor; and the neglect of payment is in the domicil of the debtor, and therefore interest ought to be allowed according to the law of his domicil[6]. And if between the time of contracting the debt, and the demand of the creditor, the debtor has changed his domicil, Boullenois is of opinion, that, if the demand is in the new domicil, interest for neglect of payment should be according to the law of the latter; especially if the change of domicil is known to the creditor[7]. And

---

1 2 Boullenois, Observ. 46, p. 477.

2 Everhard. Consil. 78, n. 10, p. 205.

3 2 Boullenois, Observ. 46, p. 477: Henry on Foreign Law, p. 53.—For the citation from Strykius I have been obliged to rely on Boullenois; as I have not been able, after considerable research in the voluminous works of Strykius, to find the particular passage.

4 2 Boullenois, Observ. 46, pp. 477, 478.

5 Ibid. 6 Ibid. 7 Ibid.

he applies the same rule to a case where, by the law of the old domicil, a simple demand only is required, and, by the law of the new domicil, a demand by judicial process is necessary[1]. The distinction does not appear to have any foundation in our jurisprudence; for, whether the debt be payable at a fixed day, or upon a demand of the creditor, if no place of payment is prescribed, the contract takes effect as a contract of the place where it is made; and being payable generally, it is payable everywhere; and after a demand and refusal of payment, interest will be allowed according to the law of the place of the contract[2].

§ 296. It may, therefore, be laid down as a general rule, that, by the common law, the *lex loci contractûs* will in all cases govern as to the rule of interest, following out the doctrine of the civil law already cited: *Cum judicio bonæ fidei disceptatur, arbitrio judicis usurarum modus, ex more regionis, ubi contractum, constituitur; ita tamen ut legi non offendat*[3]. But if the place of payment or of performance is different from that of the contract, then the interest may be validly contracted for at any rate not exceeding that which is allowed in the place of payment or performance. And in the absence of any express contract as to interest, the law of the same place will silently furnish the rule, where interest is to be implied or allowed for delay (*ex mora*) of payment or performance[4].

§ 297. But, clear as the general rule as to interest is,

---

1 2 Boullenois, Observ. 46, pp. 477—479.

2 Ante, § 272, 278 *a*; Post, § 317, 329.

3 Dig. lib. 22, tit. 1, l. 1; Id. l. 37; Ante, § 294; 1 Eq. Abr. Interest, E.; Champant *v.* Ranelagh, Prec. Ch. 128; De Sobry *v.* De Laistre, 2 Harr. & John. R. 193, 228. See 1 Burge, Comment. on Col. and For. Law, Pt. 1, ch. 1, pp. 29, 30.

4 Ante, § 291; 2 Kent, Comm. Lect. 32, pp. 460, 461, 3rd edit.; Robinson *v.* Bland, 2 Burr. R. 1077; Ekins *v.* East India Company, 1 P. W. 396; Royce *v.* Edwards, 4 Peters, R. 111: 2 Fonbl. Eq. B. 5, ch. 1, § 6; Fanning *v.* Conseequa, 17 John. R. 511; De Sobry *v.* De Laistre, 2 Harr. & John. R. 193, 228; Smith *v.* Mead, 3 Connect. R. 253; Winthrop *v.* Carlton, 12 Mass. R. 4; Foden *v.* Sharp, 4 John. R. 183; Henry on Foreign Law, p. 53.

there are cases in which its application has been found not without embarrassments. Thus, where a consignor in China consigned goods for sale in New York, and delivered them to the agent of the consignee in China, and the proceeds were to be remitted to the consignor in China, and there was a failure to remit, the question arose whether interest was to be computed according to the rate in China, or the rate in New York. Mr. Chancellor Kent held, that it should be according to the rate in China. But the Appellate Court reversed his decree, and decided in favour of the rate in New York. Each Court admitted the general rule, that the interest should be according to the law of the place of performance, where no express interest is stipulated. But the Court of Chancery thought that the delivery of the goods being in China, and the remittance being to be made there, the contract was not complete until the remittance arrived and was paid there. The Appellate Court thought, that the delivery of the goods in China, to be sold at New York, was not distinguishable in principle from a delivery at New York; and that the remittance would be complete, in the sense of the contract, the moment the money was put on board the proper conveyance in New York for China; and it was then at the risk of the consignor. The duty of remittance was to be performed in New York, and the failure was there; and consequently the rate of interest of New York only was due[1].

§ 298. Another case has arisen of a very different character. The circumstances of the case were somewhat complicated; but the only point for consideration there arose upon a note, of which the defendants were the indorsers, and with the amount thereof they had debited themselves in an account with the plaintiff; and which they sought now to avoid upon the ground of usury. The note was given in

---

[1] Conseequa *v.* Fanning, 3 John. Ch. R. 587, 610; S. C. 17 John. R. 511, 520, 521. See Grant *v.* Healey, 2 Chand. Law Reporter, 113; Ante, § 284 *a*.

New Orleans, payable in New York, for a large sum of money, bearing an interest of ten per cent., being the legal interest of Louisiana, the New York legal interest being seven per cent. only. The question was, whether the note was tainted with usury, and therefore void, as it would be if made in New York. The Supreme Court of Louisiana decided, that it was not usurious; and that, although the note was made payable at New York, yet the interest might be stipulated for, either according to the law of Louisiana, or according to that of New York. The Court seem to have founded their judgment upon the ground that, in the sense of the general rule, already stated[1], there are, or there may be, two places of contract; that in which the contract is actually made, and that in which it is to be paid or performed: *Locus, ubi contractus celebratus est; locus, ubi destinata solutio est;* and, therefore, that if the law of both places is not violated in respect to the rate of interest, the contract for interest will be valid[2]. In support of their decision the Court mainly relied upon the doctrines supposed to be maintained by certain learned jurists of continental Europe, whose language, however, does not appear to me to justify any such interpretation, when properly considered, and is perfectly compatible with the ordinary rule, that the interest must be, or ought to be, according to the law of the place where the contract is to be performed and the money is to be paid. It may not be without use to review some of the more important authorities thus cited, although it must necessarily involve the repetition of some which have been already cited.

§ 299. There is no doubt that the phrase *lex loci contractûs* may have a double meaning or aspect; and that it may indifferently indicate the place where the contract is

---

[1] Ante, § 280.

[2] Depau *v.* Humphreys, 20 Martin, R. 1.—Mr. Chancellor Walworth, in Chapman *v.* Robertson, 6 Paige, R. 627, 634, has expressed his entire concurrence in the decision in 20 Martin, R. 1. But see Van Schaike *v.* Edwards, 2 John. Ch. Cas. 355.

actually made, or that where it is virtually made, according to the intent of the parties; that is, the place of payment or performance[1]. We have seen that the rule of the civil law clearly indicates this. *Contractum autem non utique eo loco intelligitur, quo negotium gestum sit; sed quo solvenda est pecunia*[2]. Many distinguished Jurists refer to this distinction. Huberus, in the passage already cited, says: *Verum tamen non ita præcisè respiciendus est locus in quo contractus est initus, ut si partes alium in contrahendo locum respexerint, ille non potius sit considerandus*[3]. Everhardus (as we have seen) says: *Ubi certus locus solutioni faciendæ destinatus est, tunc non facta solutione in termino et loco præfixo mora dicitur contrahi in loco destinatæ solationis, et non in loco celebrati contractus. Nimirum, ergo, si inspiciatur valor rei debitæ secundum locum, ubi destinata est solutio. Tum etiam, quia locus contractus, conventio, sive obligatio, perficitur, seu verba proferuntur. Secundò, ubi solutio seu deliberatio destinatur*[4]. And he adds: *Quia dico, ut supra dixi; quod locus contractus dicitur duobus modis; primò, ubi contractus celebratus est; secundò, ubi solutio destinata est*[5]. And again: *Duplex est locus contractus, ut supra dixi, quo casu in tantum censetur contractus celebratus in loco destinatæ solutionis, quod nullo modo censetur celebratus in loco, ubi verba fuerunt prolata, quoad ea, quæ veniunt post contractum in esse productum*[6]. Paul Voet places it in a strong light: *Ne tamen hic oriatur confusio, locum contractûs duplicem facio; alium, ubi fit, de quo jam dictum; alium, in quem destinata solutio. Illud locum verum, hunc fictum appellat Salicetus*[7]. *Uterque tamen recte locus dicitur contrac-*

---

1 2 Boullenois, Observ. 46, p. 446; Ante, § 235.

2 Dig. lib. 42, tit. 5, l. 3; Pothier, Pand. lib. 42, tit. 5, n. 24; Ante, § 280.

3 Ante, § 239, 281; Huber. lib. 1, tit. 3, § 10.

4 Everhard. Consil, 78, nn, 10, 11, p, 205; Ante, § 295.

5 Everhard. Consil. 78, n. 18.

6 Id. n. 17; Id. n. 20.

7 Lib. 1, Cod. tit. 1. Summ. Trinit. n. 4.

tûs, etiam secundum leges civiles, licet postremus aliquid fictionis contineat[1].

§ 299 *a*. But for what purpose do these foreign jurists refer to the distinction? Is it, that the validity of the same contract is to be at the same time ascertained in part by the law of one country, and in part by that of another? By no means. They nowhere assert, that the validity of the contract is not to be judged of throughout by one and the same law; that is, by the law of the place where it is made, or by the law of the place where it is to be performed, according as, in a just sense, with reference to the nature and objects of the particular contract, the one or the other is properly to be deemed the place of the contract. They nowhere assert, that one and the same rule is not to apply throughout, to all the stipulations in the contract. That the contract is good, notwithstanding it does not conform either to the law of the place where it is made, or to that where it is to be performed. That the contract is to be treated, not as a whole, but is to be distributed into parts; so that, if in some of the stipulations it violates the law of each place, it shall still be good throughout, if it does not violate in the whole the law of both places. In many of the passages cited in support of the supposed mixed character, and mixed interpretation, and mixed operation of the contract, these learned jurists were considering questions of a very different nature. Some of them were considering the question as to the rule, which is to govern generally in regard to the formalities, solemnities, and modes of execution of contracts, where the place of execution is the same place where it was made; others again were considering the rule, as to the interpretation and extent of the obligation of contracts generally, under the like circumstances; and others again were con-

---

1 Voet, De Statut. § 9, c. 2, § 11, p. 270, (edit. 1715); Id. p. 326, (edit. 1661). See also 2 Boullenois, Observ. 46, p. 488; Boullenois, Quest. sur Contr. des Lois, pp. 330—338.

sidering the rule, where the contract is made in one place and is to be executed in another. We are, therefore, to understand their language according to the particular occasion, and the particular circumstances to which it is applied.

§ 300. Let us examine then the particular language which is used by these jurists in the passages cited. Thus Alexander is said to use the following passage[1]:—*In scriptura instrumenti, in ceremoniis, et solemnitatibus, et generaliter in omnibus quæ ad formam et perfectionem contractus pertinent, spectanda est consuetudo regionis, ubi fit negotium. Debet enim servari statutum loci contractus, quoad hæc quæ oriuntur secundum naturam ipsius contractus.* This language expresses only a general truth, and we have no means of knowing that the author intended to speak here of anything further than the general rule, applicable to all contracts made and to be performed in the same place[2].

§ 300 *a*. Burgundus says: *Et quidem in scriptura instrumenti, in solemnitatibus, et ceremoniis, et generaliter in omnibus quæ ad formam ejusque perfectionem pertinent, spectanda est consuetudo regionis, ubi fit negotiatio. Rationem assignant Doctores quod consuetudo influat in contractus, et convenientes ad eum respicere, ac voluntatem suam accommodare videantur. Et recte*[3]. Now we know upon what occasion this language was used. Burgundus was here considering the question solely with reference to the point when a contract is to be deemed lawful or not; or,

---

1 I cite the passage from Alexander, as I find it in 20 Martin, R. 22, 23, not having been able to obtain the works of Alexander. But I have some doubt, whether the first part of the passage is not copied by mistake from Burgundus, who uses almost the identical language. Burgundus, Tract. 4, n. 7, p. 104; Post, § 300 *a*.

2 From other passages cited by Everhardus from Alexander, and Bartolus, and Baldus, it seems clear that they all consider the locus solutionis to be the proper locus contractus, except so far as regards the solemnities and creation of the contract. (Solemnitatem et subsistentiam contractus). See Everhard. Consil. 78, n. 20, p. 207; Id. n. 24, p. 208.

3 Burgundus, Tract. 4, n. 7, p. 104.

in other words, by what law its validity is to be governed. *Illicita stipulatio est* (says he) *quæ legibus est interdicta, utputa, si debitum modum usararum excedat. Nunc ergo considerandum, cujus loci ratio haberi debeat*[1]. He does not even allude to a case where the contract is made in one place, and is to be performed in another place. He adds: *Igitur, ut paucis absolvam, quoties de vinculo obligationis, vel de ejus interpretatione quæritur, veluti, quos et in quantum obliget, quid sententiæ, stipulationis inessæ, quid abesse credi oporteat; item in omnibus actionibus, et ambiguitatibus, quæ inde oriuntur, primum quidem id sequemur, quod inter partes actum erit, aut si non apparet, quid actum est, erit consequens, ut id sequamur, quod in regione, in quâ actum est, frequentatur*[2]. And he concludes by saying: *Doctores toties ingerunt ea, quæ respiciunt solemnitatem actus, vel quæ tempore contractus ex natura ipsius adhibentur, oriunturque, ex more regionis, ubi contractum est, legem accipere. Ea vero, quæ ad complementum vel executionem contractus spectant, vel absoluto eo superveniunt, solere a statuto loci dirigi, in quo peragenda est solutio*[3].

§ 300 *b*. Everhardus says: *Quod quò ad perfectionem contractus seu ad solemnitatem ad esse seu substantiam ejus requisitam semper inspicitur statutum seu consuetudo loci celebrati contractus. Et est ratio, quia ex quo agitur de consuetudine contrahendi non mirum, si inspiciatur locus initæ conventionis, ubi contractus accepit perfectionem*[4]. But he immediately adds: *Sed ubi agitur de consuetudine solvendi, ut in casu presenti,* (that is, where a contract made in one place was payable in another,) *vel de his, quæ veniunt implenda diu post contractum, et in alio loco impletioni destinato, tunc inspicitur locus destinatæ solutionis.* Now, this

---

1 Id. n. 6, p. 104.

2 Burgundus, Tract. 4, n. 7, p. 105.

3 Id. n. 29, p. 116. See also Id. n. 10, p. 109; Ante, § 292 *a*, 293 *e*.

4 Everhard. Consil. 78, n. 11, p. 206; Id. n. 18, p. 207; Id. n. 27, p. 209.

latter passage would seem as strictly to apply to the case of payment of interest, as to the case of payment of principal. If the parties have not stipulated for a particular rate of interest, the usage of the place of payment ought constantly to govern. If they have stipulated for a particular rate of interest, inconsistent with that of the *lex loci solutionis*, the question will still remain, whether it can lawfully be done. Everhardus has not here discussed it; far less has he decided it. And he cites Baldus in support of his opinion, as saying: *Quod in expeditivis contractus non inspiciuntur ordinativa contractus, sed locus solutionis*[1]. He afterwards adds, that this rule, in regard to the forms and solemnities required in order to create and perfect any contract, equally applies to cases where the performance is to be in the same place, and where it is to be in another place. *Ubi vero in uno loco celebratus est contractus, et in alio loco destinata est solutio, tunc quoad ea, quæ concernunt solemnitatem actus, item ad esse et perfectionem contractus, inspicitur consuetudo loci celebrati contractus. Unde si ex statuto loci contractus requiratur certa solemnitas in ipso contractu, &c., tale statutum vel consuetudo debet observari, licet in loco destinatæ solutionis non sit simile statutum*[2]. How far this latter doctrine is correct and maintainable as a general rule, we have already had occasion in some measure to consider[3]. It is not material to the present discusssion, which turns upon another point, that is, whether the validity of a contract may depend partly upon the law of one place, and partly on the law of another place, some of its stipulations being contrary to the law of each place.

§ 300 *c*. Christinæus expressly professes to follow the doctrine of Everhardus on this subject. *Consuetudo loci* (says he) *ubi contrahitur spectanda est, scilicet quoad observantiam solemnitatum ipsius actus. Generalitur enim in omnibus, quæ*

---

[1] Everhard. Consil. 78, n. 11, p. 206; Id. n. 17, p. 207; Id. n. 27, p. 209.

[2] Id. n. 18, p. 207. [3] Ante, § 280.

ad formam ejusque perfectionem pertinent, spectanda est consuetudo regionis ubi fit negotiatio, quia consuetudo influit in contractus, et videtur ad eos respicere, et voluntatem suam eis accommodare. Idque rectè. Conditio quoque loci et temporis perfectionem formæ etiam respicit, et idcirco à regione contractus vicissim diriguntur[1]. He adds: *Sed quoad ejus executionem, utpote quoad solutionem faciendam, inspicienda venit consuetudo destinatæ solutionis*[2]. And again: *Quoad ea, quæ celebrato contractu veniunt facienda, inspicitur consuetudo loci, ubi ea debent fieri, puta, tradi, solvi*[3].

§ 300 *d.* Gregorio Lopez states only the general doctrine. *Quando contractus celebratur in uno loco, puta in Hispali, et destinata solutio in Cordubæ; tunc non inspicitur locus contractus, sed locus destinatæ solutionis; ut habetur in ista Lege ff. l. contraxisse*[4]. Dumoulin (Molinæus) says: *In concernentibus contractum, et emergentibus tempore contractus, spectatur locus, in quo contrahitur, et in concernentibus meram solemnitatem, cujus actus, locus, in quo ille actus celebratur*[5]. In another place he says: *Aut statutum loquitur de his, quæ concernunt nudam ordinationem et solemnitatem actus; et semper inspicitur statutum vel consuetudo loci, ubi actus celebratur, sive in contractibus, sive in judiciis, sive in testamentis, sive in instrumentis aut aliis conficiendis. Aut statutum loquitur de his, quæ meritum scilicet causæ, vel decisionem concernunt; et tunc, aut in his, quæ pendent a voluntate partium, vel per eas immutari possunt, et tunc inspiciuntur circumstantiæ, voluntatis, quarum una est statutum loci in quo contrahitur; et domicilii contrahentium antiqui vel recentis, et similes circumstantiæ*[6]. In another passage,

---

1 Christin. Decis. 283, Vol. 1, n. 1, 4, 5, 9, 10, 11, p. 355.

2 Id. n. 8, 9, p. 355.

3 Id. n. 10, 11, p. 355.

4 20 Martin, R. 9, 17; Ante, § 233; Dig. lib. 44, tit. 7, l. 21.

5 Dumoulin, cited in 20 Martin, R. 24; Molin. Comm. ad Consuet. Paris. tit. 1, § 12, gloss. 7, n. 37, tom. 1, p. 224, (edit. 1681); 2 Boullenois, Observ. 46, p. 472.

6 Molinæus, Comm. in Cod. lib. 1, tit. 1, tom. 3, p. 554, (edit. 1681).

he finds fault with those who exclusively look to the place where the contract is made in all cases. *Quia putant nuditer et indistinctè, quod debeat ibi inspici locus et consuetudo, ubi fit contractus, et sic jus in loco contractus*[1]. *Quod est falsum; quinimo jus est in tacita et verisimiliter mente contrahentium.* He adds: *Quia quis censetur potius contrahere in loco, in quo debet solvere, quam in loco, ubi fortuitò transiens contraxit*[2]. It is plain, that these passages do not justify the inference sought to be adduced from them. They import no more, than that the law which is to govern contracts is not, in all cases, to be exclusively the law of the place where they are made.

§ 300 *e.* Boullenois is also relied on in support of the doctrine. In one of the passages cited, he says: When the question is, whether, in contracts upon any subject, the rights which spring from the nature and time of the contract, (*natura et tempore contractus*), are lawful or not, it is necessary to follow the law of the place where the contract is made[3]. And in another passage, he says: When the question is, to determine the lawfulness of a rate of rent or annuity, (*taux de rentes*), and in the place where the contract is made, the rate is different from that which is to be paid, either in the country of the domicil of the debtor, or in that of the domicil of the creditor, or finally, in the place where the property hypothecated is situated; the rate will be adjudged lawful, if it conforms to the law of the place where the contract is made[4]. The context shews that Boullenois was only contemplating the case where the contract was made, in the place of its intended performance. For he adds: This is the provision of the law of the Digest, (De Usuris), where it is declared: *Cum judicio bonæ fide disceptatur, arbitrio judicis usurarum modus ex more regionis ubi contractum est, constituitur; ita tamen, ut legi non offen-*

---

1 Molinæus, Comm. in Cod. lib. 1, tit. 1, tom. 3, p. 554, (edit. 1681).
2 Ibid.
3 2 Boullenois, Observ. 46, p. 472. 4 Ibid.

dat[1]; and I believe it takes place whenever the parties designedly contract in one place rather than another[2]. The true meaning of Boullenois, in this citation, may be gathered from his own interpretation of the law of the Digest in another page, where he cites, with approbation, the opinion of Gothofredus, that the words "*Ubi contractum*" ought to be understood to mean the place where the payment ought to be made[3]. *Hæc verba, "Ubi contractum est," sic intellige, ubi actum est, ut solveret*[4].

§ 301. Bartolus has discussed the question somewhat at large, how far the law of the place of the contract is obligatory upon foreigners, and what effects the laws of the place of the contract have beyond the territory. And, first (he says) let us suppose a contract made by a foreigner in one place, and afterwards a suit is litigated thereon in another place, that of the origin of the contracting party; of which place ought the laws to be observed and followed in deciding it? He says, we should make a distinction. Either we speak of the statute, or custom which respects the solemnities of the contract, or of the process and proceedings in the suit, or of those things which appertain to the jurisdiction in the execution of the contract. In the first case, we are to look to the law of the place of the contract; in the second case, (as to the process and proceedings in the suit), to the place of the judgment[5]. Or else, we speak re specting those things which belong to the decision of the cause; and then the question is as to those things which arise from the very nature of the contract itself in its origin, or as to those things which arise afterwards, on account of

---

1 Dig. lib. 22, tit. 1, l. 1; Pothier, Pand. lib. 22, tit. 1, n. 52; Ante, § 296.

2 2 Boullenois, Observ. 46, p. 472; Id. p. 446.

3 Id. p. 446.

4 Gothofred. n. 10, Ad Dig. lib. 22, tit. 1, l. 1.

5 Everhardus manifestly understands Bartolus to speak with reference to contracts, where payment is to be made in loco celebrati contractûs. Everhard, Consil. 78, n. 26, 27, p. 208.

negligence or delay. In the first case, the law of the place of the contract is to be looked to, that is, the place where the contract is made, and not where it is performed. In the second case, either the payment is to be made in a fixed place, or alternately in several places, so that the plaintiff has his election; or it is to be made in no particular place, because the promise is simply made. In the first case, the custom of the place is to be looked to, in which the payment is to be made. In the second and third cases, the place is to be looked to where the suit is brought. His language is: *Et primo, utrum statutum porrigatur extra territorium ad non subditos; secundo, utrum effectus statuti porrigatur extra territorium statuentium. Et primo, quæro, quod de contractibus. Pone contractum celebratum per aliquem forensem in hac civitate; litigium ortum est, et agitatur lis in loco originis contrahentis, cujus loci statuta debent servari et spectari. Distingue. Aut loquimur de statuto, aut de consuetudine quæ respiciunt ipsius contractus solemnitatem, aut litis ordinationem, aut de his, quæ pertinent ad jurisdictionem ex ipso contractu evenientis executionis. Primo casu, inspicitur locus contractus. Secundo casu, aut quæris de his, quæ pertinent ad litis ordinationem, aut de his, quæ pertinent ad litis ordinationem; et inspicitur locus judicii. Aut de his, quæ pertinent ad ipsius litis decisionem; et tunc, aut de his, quæ oriuntur secundum ipsius contractus naturam tempore contractus, aut de his, quæ oriuntur ex post facto propter negligentiam, vel moram. Primo casu, inspicitur locus contractus, ubi est celebratus contractus; et intelligo locum contractus, ubi est celebratus contractus, non de loco, in quem collata est solutio. Secundo casu, aut solutio est collata in locum certum, aut in pluribus locis alternative, ita quod electio sit actoris; aut in nullum locum, quia promissio fuit facta simpliciter. Primo casu, inspicitur consuetudo, quæ est in illo loco, in quem est collata solutio; secundo et tertio casu, inspicitur locus, ubi petitur. Ratio prædictorum est, quia ibi est contracta negligentia vel mora*[1]. Now, taking this whole passage together, it is dif-

[1] Bartolus, Ad Cod. lib. 1, tit. 1, l. 1, n. 14—16, tom. 7, p. 4, (edit. 1602).

ficult to misunderstand the meaning of Bartolus. It is plain that he did not intend to repudiate the common distinction as to the *lex loci contractûs*, and the *lex loci solutionis*. He gives full effect to the latter, where a fixed place is prescribed for payment; and whether he is right or not, that where no place of payment is named, the payment is to be made according to the law of the place where it is demanded by the promisee; he goes no farther than to assert the general proposition, that the law of the place where the contract is made, is to govern in respect to its solemnities, and that the law of the place of payment is to be regarded in cases of payment[1]. He does not at all discuss the point which we have now under consideration.

§ 301 *a*. These are the principal passages adduced from foreign jurists, as authorities, in support of the docrine that a contract is, or may be valid, notwithstanding it does not in its entirety conform, either to the law of the place where the contract is made, or to that of the place where it is to be performed. Now, in the first place, it is manifest that many of these jurists, in the passages cited, speak exclusively as to the formalities and solemnities, and modes of execution of contracts; and they hold, that in these respects they must conform to the law of the place where they are made. Some of them make no distinction, in the application of this rule, between cases of contracts to be performed in foreign places, and cases of contracts to be performed in the place where they are made. And, perhaps, the generality of language used by most of them, even when they do not refer to this distinction, may be fairly applied indifferently to both classes of cases. But several, and, indeed, most of them, do expressly and directly recognise the rule, that, where the contract is made in one place, and is to be performed in another, not only may the law of the latter be properly called the *locus contractus;* but that it

---

1 Bartolus, Ad Cod. lib. 1, tit. 1, l. 1, n. 14—16, (edit. 1602). See Vidal *v.* Thompson, 11 Martin, R. 23.

ought in all respects, except as to the formalities, and solemnities, and modes of execution, to be deemed the rule to govern such cases.

§ 301 *b.* In the next place, when these foreign jurists speak of payment or performance, they all agree that the contract must be governed by the law of the place of payment or performance, and not by the law of the place where the contract is made. How, then, are we to distinguish between different parts of the payment? If principal and interest are both to be paid in a foreign place, how can the law of that place govern, as to the one, and not as to the other? As these jurists make no distinction in respect to the payment of principal, and that of interest, but say generally, that the payment must be according to the law of the place where the payment is to be made, it is certainly a reasonable inference that they did not intend to make any exception whatsoever, but deemed both the principal and the interest governed by the same rule. Indeed, it will be found exceedingly difficult to maintain any distinction between them, which is not purely artificial and arbitrary; for interest is but an incident or accessory to principal.

§ 301 *c.* But we need not rest entirely on the silence of foreign jurists in these passages; for the subject of interest will be found to be expressly treated by some of them; and, therefore, if any exception was intended by them, there the exception would naturally have found its appropriate place. The omission of any exception becomes, under such circumstances, peculiarly significant. Let us, therefore, review, in this connexion, some of the passages, in which the subject of interest is expressly or impliedly discussed.

§ 301 *d.* Everhardus says: *Aut quærimus, quis locus inspiciatur, quoad accessoria, utputa expensas et damna de jure canonico, et usuras de jure civili, si minores vel leviores sunt in uno loco, quam in alio, et similiter; certum est, quod inspicitur locus destinatæ solutionis; nedum quoad principalem obligationem, sed etiam quoad accessoria*[1]. And he insists, that the leading jurists whom he quotes hold the same opinion. This language would seem to be as direct as possible to the present inquiry; and it affirms that the *lex loci solutionis* must govern, as well to the interest as to the principal, the former being merely accessorial to the latter. It is no answer to suggest that he meant to speak of interest *ex mora,* or interest not expressly provided for; because there is no such qualification in his language, and it is positive as well as general as to the accessorial rights, under all circumstances.

§ 301 *e.* Christinæus avows the same doctrine: *Sic etiam inspicitur statutum loci destinatæ solutionis, si agatur de extinctione actionis per præscriptionem staturiam vigentem in uno loco, et non in alio. Item si agatur de accessoriis, ut de expensis, damnis, et interesse, aut denique usuris, si majores vel minores sint in uno loco, quàm in alio*[2].

§ 301 *f.* Paul Voet may fairly be deemed to hold the same opinion. After having said, in the passage already cited, that there may be a double place of the contract, one where it is made, and the other where it is to be paid or performed, he immediately adds: *Hinc ratione effectus, et complementi ipsius contractus, spectatur ille locus, in quem destinata est solutio, id, quod ad modum, mensuram, usuras, &c., negligentiam et moram post contractum initum accedentem referendum est*[3]; and he then refers to several authorities in support of this opinion. It seems plain from this language, in this connexion, that as to interest he deemed the true law by which the legality of the contract was to be adjudged, was the law of the place of payment.

§ 302. In one passage Burgundus says, that interest is to be allowed according to the place of the contract; and

---

1 Everhardus, Consil. 78, n. 24, pp. 208; Id. n. 27—29, pp. 208, 209.

2 Christin. Decis. 283, n. 12, 13, vol. 1, p. 355.

3 P. Voet, De Stat. § 9, c. 2, n. 12, p. 270, (edit. 1715); Id. p. 326, (edit. 1661); Ante, § 281.

that if the question comes under consideration in a foreign Court, the interest stipulated, though higher than what is lawful by the *lex fori*, ought to be allowed. But where no interest is stipulated, there the interest is to be *ex mora*, according to the law of the place of payment [1]. His language is: *Quare et usurarum modus is constituendus est, qui in regione, in qua est contractum, legitimè celebratur. Et cum redditus duodenarius in Gallia stipulatus, in controversiam incidisset, patrocinante me, judicatum est, in Curia Flandriæ, valere pactum; nec obesse, quod in Flandria, ubi redditus constitutus sive hypothecæ impositus proponeretur, usura semisse graviores stipulari non liceat. Quia ratio hypothecæ non habetur, quæ hac in re nihil conferens ad substantiam obligationis, tantum extrinsecus accedit legitimæ stipulationi. Sed, hoc intellige de usuris in stipulationem deductis, non autem de iis, quæ ex mora debentur, in quibus ad locum solutionis (ut docemus postea) respicere oportet* [2]. Now, if such be the rule where the contract is made in France, and to be performed there, the converse would seem equally to be correct, if the contract had been made in France to be performed in Flanders—that the contract would be void for usury as against the law of the latter. In another place he says: *Idem ergo de solutionibus dicendum, scilicet, ut in omnibus, quæ ex eâ sunt, aut inde oriuntur, aut circa illam consistunt, aut aliquo modo affinia sunt, consuetudinis loci spectemus, ubi eamdem implere convenit* [3]. He adds: *Itaque ex solutione sunt solemnia, valor rei debitæ, pretium monetæ; ex solutione oriuntur præstatio apochæ, antigraphæ, similiaque; circa solutionem consistunt pondera, mensuræ bonitas expensæ, mora, damna, interesse, usura ex mora debitæ, et*

---

[1] 20 Martin, R. 28; Burgundus, Tract. 4, n. 10, p. 109. See also Vidal v. Thompson, 11 Martin, R. 23.

[2] Burgundus, Tract. 4, n. 10, p. 109.

[3] Burgundus, Tract. 4, n. 25, 26, pp. 114, 115; Id. n. 10, p. 109; 2 Boullenois, Observ. 46, pp. 488, 498; Ante, § 293 *e*.

ejusmodi[1]. And he concludes by stating the reason of the doctrine, as given by all jurists: *Rationem mutuantur à Juris Consultis, qui unumquemque vult in eo loco contraxisse intelligi, in quo, ut solveret, se obligavit*[2]: So that, if this language is to be interpreted in its broad sense, the interest must, in all cases, be according to the law of the place of performance[3]. Burgundus's opinion may, perhaps, by some persons be thought of less value, however, because he applies the like rule to prescriptions: *Affinia solutioni sunt præscriptio, oblatio rei debitæ, consignatio, novatio, delegatio, et ejusmodi*[4].

§ 303. Boullenois has nowhere, to my knowledge, directly and positively treated the question, whether the interest may be stipulated for according to the place of the contract, when payment is to be made in another place where it would be illegal. The citations already referred to[5], which are supposed to countenance the affirmative, put the case only of a rate of interest, or of an annuity, good by the law of the place of the contract, (and for aught that appears payable there,) and hold that it will be good, although different from the law of the domicil of the creditor or debtor, or even from the law of the place where the property pledged for security is situate[6]. There is, however, a passage, which seems to indicate, although not directly, an opinion of Boullenois in the negative. After referring to, and approving the doctrine of Gothofredus, that interest is to be according to the law of the place of payment, he adds, that it is in this sense that Gothofredus is to be understood, in what he says of the Law 20, of the title of the Digest *de*

---

1 Burgundus, Tract. 4, n. 27, p. 115.

2 Id. n. 29, p. 116.

3 Id. n. 10, p. 109; Ante, § 293 *a*.

4 Burgundus, Tract. 4, n. 28, p. 116; 2 Boullenois, Observ. 46, pp. 488, 498; Ante, § 300 *e*.

5 Ante, § 300 *e*.

6 2 Boullenois, Observ. 46, pp. 472, 473.

Jurisdictione[1], where he supposes a Parisian, who has contracted at Rome (*Demus Romæ contractum esse*); and inquires, whether the Parisian, if sued at Paris, shall be condemned to pay the interest prescribed by the law of Rome for the delay; and he answers in the affirmative, saying: *Id videtur. Contractus enim istius initium vitio caret.* Boullenois says, that this decision is very just in effect, if we suppose that the Parisian has not only made the contract at Rome, but also has promised to pay at Rome[2]. The natural inference certainly would be, that if he expressly agreed to pay interest, that he should pay according to the rate of interest at the place of payment.

§ 304. It may then be affirmed with some confidence, that the foreign jurists who have been relied on, do not establish the asserted doctrine. On the other hand, there are other foreign jurists, whose doctrines lead to an opposite conclusion. Thus, John Voet says, if a stipulation for a high interest is allowed in one place, and in another it is prohibited, the law of the place where the contract is made, is to decide whether it is good, or whether it exceeds that which is allowable. Nevertheless, we must remember, that, in point of law, that is not properly to be deemed the place of the contract where the business is transacted, but where the money is by the contract to be paid. But good faith must also be observed; and the place of the contract, where higher interest is allowed, must not be sought for the purpose of evading the law. He adds; that an hypothecation of property, as security, situated in another place where the interest is lower, will not vary the rule; for the security will be treated as merely accessorial. And it is more equitable that the accessorial contract should be governed by the law of the place where the principal contract is made, than on the contrary, that the principal contract should be go-

---

[1] Dig. lib. 2, tit. 1, l. 20; Gothofred. n. 37.

[2] 2 Boullenois, Observ. 46, p. 446.

verned by the law of the place in which the accessorial contract is made.[1]

---

[1] Voet, Ad Pand. lib. 22, tit. 1, § 6, tom. 1, p. 938; Id. lib. 4, tit. 1, § 29, tom. 1, p. 241; Ante, § 293 *d.*—I have given the sense, although not a precisely literal translation, of the passage. The words are: Si alio in loco graviorum usurarum stipulatio permissa, in alio vetita sit, lex loci, in quo contractus celebratus est, spectanda videtur in quæstione, an moderatæ, an vero modum excedentes usuræ per conventionem constitutæ sint. Dummodo meminerimus, illum proprie locum contractus in jure non intelligi, in quo negotium gestum est, sed in quo, ut pecuniam solveret, se quis obligavit. Modo etiam bonâ fide omnia gesta fuerint, nec consulto talis ad mutuum contrahendum locus electus sit, in quo graviores usuræ, quam in loco, in quo alios contrahendum fuisset, probatæ convenientur. Etiamsi de cætero hypotheca in sortis et usurarum securitatem obligata, in alio loco sita sit, ubi solæ leviores usuræ permissæ; cum æquius sit, contractum accessorium regi ex loco principalis negotii gesti, quam ex opposito contractum principalem regi lege loci, in quo accessorius contractus celebratur. It appears to me, that the first part of the passage has been misunderstood, or at least mistranslated, in Depau *v.* Humphreys, 20 Martin, R. 32. The reasoning of the Court upon the passage will here be given, in justice to that learned tribunal. "The authority of the passage (says Martin, J. in delivering the opinion of the Court) from Voet remains to be examined. This author says: Si alio in loco graviorum usurarum stipulatio permissa, in alio vetita sit, lex loci, ubi contractus celebratus est, spectanda videtur, an moderatæ, an vero modum excedentes usuræ, per conventionem stipulatæ sint. If in a place the stipulation of higher interest be permitted, in another forbidden, the law of the place in which the contract was celebrated is to be resorted to, in order to ascertain whether the lesser or the greater rate of interest be stipulated by the contract. Thus far Voet teaches what we have seen Alexander, Bartolus, Burgundus, Everhard, Strykius, and Boullenois teach, and the contrary of which no other commentator positively asserts; what, in our opinion, every sound principle of law dictates. But the appellant's counsel urges, that Voet unsays, in the succeeding paragraph, what he appears to have so emphatically expressed. The words of the second paragraph are: Dummodo meminerimus, illum proprie locum contractus in jure non intelligi, in quo negotium gestum est, sed in quo, ut pecuniam solveret, se obligavit. In the argument which the appellee's counsel draws, in this respect, he is fully supported by what is said arguendo, by Lord Mansfield, in Robinson *v.* Bland, and in some degree by Judge Kent, in the same manner, in the case of Van Schaick *v.* Edwards, already cited. In endeavouring to ascertain the character of the rate of interest, stipulated in a note given in Massachusetts, Judge Kent says: 'Had the money, for instance, in this case been made payable at Albany, or elsewhere in this State, (New York), then perhaps the decision in Robinson *v.* Bland, would have applied.' If, in the second paragraph,

304 *a.* If to this doctrine, thus maintained by John Voet, (himself an author of distinguished weight and ability), we add the concurrent testimony of Huberus, Everhardus, Christinæus, and Paul Voet, already cited[1], on the same side, and the entire absence of any direct and absolute authority to the contrary, it is not perhaps too much to affirm, that the decision already alluded to of the Supreme Court of Louisiana[2], is not supported by the reasoning or the principles of foreign jurists. It is certainly also at variance with the doctrine maintained by Lord Mansfield and the Judges of the King's Bench, in a highly interesting case, (although not positively necessary to the judgment then pronounced), that the law of the place of payment or per-

---

Voet meant to introduce an exception to the rule laid down in the first; if he meant to teach, that the legality of a rate of conventional interest, arising, not ex mora, but tempore contractus, is exclusively to be tested by the law loci solutionis, even when it is different from the law loci celebrati contractûs; then, we cannot consider him as affording to us a legitimate rule of decision in the present case; because the weight of his authority is borne down by that of a crowd of the most respectable commentators of the law he cites. Perhaps, he must be understood, in the second paragraph, to convey to the student a warning, that by what he teaches in the first he must not be understood to impugn the proposition, that, in a great degree, the law loci solutionis, influences the obligation of the party who bound himself ut solveret pecuniam. Upon the whole, we must conclude, as we did in Norris *v.* Eves, and Vidal *v.* Thompson, that contracts are governed by the law of the country in which they were made, in every thing which relates to the mode of construing them, the meaning to be attached to the expressions by which the parties bound themselves, and the nature and validity of the engagement. But that, wherever the obligation be contracted, the performance must be according to the law of the place where it is to take place. In other words, that in a note executed here, on a loan of money made here, the creditor may stipulate for the legal rate of conventional interest authorized by our law, although such a rate be disallowed in the place at which payment is to be made." If I am right in the remarks in the text, it will be found that the authorities cited by the learned judge by no means justify the judgment. See Bouhier, Cout. de Bourg. vol. 1, ch. 21, p. 313; 3 Burge, Comm. on Col. and For. Law, pt. 2, ch. 20, pp. 773—775.

1 Ante, § 299, 300 *b*, 300 *c*.

2 Depau *v.* Humphreys, 20 Martin, R. 1.

formance constitutes the true test by which to ascertain the validity or invalidity of contracts[1]. And finally, in a very recent case the Supreme Court of the United States have adopted the doctrine, that, where a contract is made in one place to be executed in another, it is to be governed as to usury, by the law of the place of performance, and not by the law of the place where it is made. So, that, if the transaction is *bonâ fide,* and not with intent to evade the law against usury, and the law of the place of performance allows a higher rate of interest than that permitted at the place of the contract, the parties may lawfully stipulate for the higher interest[2]. But then the transaction must be *bonâ fide,* and not intended as a mere cover of usury. Bouhier, indeed, thinks, that every contract of this sort would almost from its very terms and nature import a design to evade the laws, and to cover usury[3]. But he manifestly presses the presumption far beyond its legitimate application; for the circumstances of the case may often establish, that the contract is perfectly innocent and praiseworthy.

§ 305. It has been said, that if the principle be that a contract valid in the place where the contract is celebrated, is void if it is contrary to the law of the place of payment, it must establish the converse proposition, that a contract void by the law of the place where it is made, is valid, if good by the law of the place of payment[4]. This would seem to be reasonable; and the doctrine is supported by the modern cases, notwithstanding the old cases have been supposed to lead to a contrary conclusion. In one case[5], a bond was executed in Ireland for a debt contracted in England; and because it constituted a security on lands in Ireland, Lord Chancellor Hardwicke held that it was valid,

---

1 Robinson, *v.* Bland, 2 Burr. 1077. See also Van Schaick *v.* Edwards, 2 John. Cas. 355.

2 Andrews *v.* Pond, 13 Peters, R. 65, 77, 78.

3 Bouhier, Cout. de Bourg. vol. 1, ch. 21, p. 413.

4 De Pau *v.* Humphreys, 20 Martin, R. 1, 30.

5 Connor *v.* Bellamont, 2 Atk. R. 381.

although it bore the Irish interest of seven per cent. But he thought it would have been otherwise if it had been a simple contract debt, or if the bond had been executed in England[1]. Mr. Chancellor Kent has correctly laid down the modern doctrine; and he is fully borne out by the authorities:—"The law of the place (says he) where the contract is made, is to determine the rate of interest, when the contract specifically gives interest; and this will be the case though the loan be secured by a mortgage on lands in another State, unless there be circumstances to shew that the parties had in view the law of the latter place in respect to interest. When that is the case, the rate of interest of the place of payment is to govern[2]."

§ 306. But it has been asked, if this be the established doctrine, of what use is it for any legislature to pass a law for the protection of the weak and necessitous[3]? And the case of minors has been mentioned, as exhibiting the inconvenience of the principle. But we have already seen that minors in one country may lawfully contract in another in which they are deemed of age[4]. The true answer to all such suggestions is, that no country can give to its own laws any extra-territorial authority, so as to bind other nations. If it undertakes to legislate in regard to acts done or contracts performed elsewhere, it can claim for its own laws no other validity than such as the comity of other nations may choose to allow towards them. It may, if it chooses, deem all such acts and contracts valid or invalid, according to its own laws; but it cannot impose a like obli-

---

[1] Stapleton *v.* Conway, 3 Atk. R. 727; S. C. 1 Ves. R. 427. See Dewar *v.* Span, 3 T. R. 425.

[2] 2 Kent, Comm. Lect. 39, pp. 460, 461, 3rd edit.; De Wolf *v.* Johnson, 10 Wheaton, R. 367; Scofield *v.* Day, 20 John. R. 102; Thompson *v.* Powles, 2 Simons, R. 194; Robinson *v.* Bland, 2 Bur. 1077; Boyce *v.* Edwards, 4 Peters, R. 111. But see Chapman *v.* Robertson, 6 Paige, R. 627, 630.

[3] De Pau *v.* Humphreys, 20 Martin, R. 1, 30.

[4] Saul *v.* His Creditors, 17 Martin, R. 596, 597; Ante, § 82.

gation on other nations so to treat them. The repose and common interest of all nations, therefore, require each to observe towards all others the principles of reciprocal justice and comity; and these, as we have seen, are best subserved by the adoption of the general rule, that the law of the place of the contract and payment shall govern [1].

§ 307. Analogous to the rule respecting interest, would seem to be the rule of damages in cases of contract, where damages are to be recovered for a breach thereof *ex mora*, or where the right to damages arises *ex delicto*, from some wrong or injury done to personal property. Thus, if a ship should be illegally or tortiously converted in the East Indies by a party, the interest there will be allowed by way of damages in a suit against him [2]. So, the rate of damages on a dishonoured bill of exchange will be according to the *lex loci contractûs* of the particular party [3]. So, if a bill of exchange be made in one State and indorsed in another State, and again indorsed by a second indorser in a third State, the rate of damages upon the dishonour of the bill will be against each party according to the law of the place where his own contract had its origin, either by making or by indorsing the bill [4]. So, if a note made in a foreign country is for the payment of a certain sum in sugar, and by the custom of that place the like notes are payable in sugar at a valuation, the law of the place is to govern in assessing the damages for a breach thereof [5].

§ 308. Where a contract is made in one country, and is payable in the currency of that country, and a suit is afterwards brought in another country to recover for a breach of the contract, a question often arises as to the manner in

---

1 Ante, § 242, 280.

2 Ekins *v.* East India Company, 1 P. Will. 394, 396; Conseequa *v.* Willing, Peters, Cir. R. 225; Id. 303.

3 Slacum *v.* Pomeroy, 6 Cranch, 221; Hazlehurst *v.* Kean, 4 Yates, R. 19; Pothier on Oblig. n. 171.

4 Post, § 314, 317.

5 Courtois *v.* Carpentier, 1 Wash. Cir. R. 370.

which the amount of the debt is to be ascertained, whether at the nominal or established par value of the currencies of the two countries, or according to the rate of exchange at the particular time existing between them. In all cases of this sort, the place where the money is payable, as well as the currency in which it is promised to be paid, are (as we shall presently see) material ingredients [1]. For instance, a debt of £100 sterling is contracted in England, and is payable there; and afterwards a suit is brought in America for the recovery of the amount. The present par fixed by law between the two countries is, to estimate the pound sterling at four dollars and forty-four cents [2]. But the rate of exchange on bills drawn in America on England, is generally at from eight to ten per cent. advance on the same amount. In a recent case it was held by the King's Bench, in an action for a debt payable in Jamaica, and sued in England, that the amount should be ascertained by adding the rate of exchange to the par value if above it; and so, *vice versâ,* by deducting it when the exchange is below the par [3]. Perhaps it is difficult to reconcile this case with the doctrine of some other cases [4] In a late American case, where the payment was to be in Turkish piastres, (but it does not appear from the Report where the contract was made or was made payable), it was held to be the settled rule, "where money is the object of the suit, to fix the value according to the rate of exchange at

---

[1] Post, § 310.

[2] This is the par for ordinary commercial purposes; but by the Act of Congress of 1832, ch. 229, § 16, the par, for the purpose of estimating the value of goods paying an ad valorem duty, and for that purpose only, is declared to be to estimate a pound sterling at four dollars and eighty cents.

[3] Scott *v.* Bevan, 2 Barn. & Adol. 78.—Lord Tenterden in delivering the opinion of the Court in favour of the rule, said: "Speaking for myself personally, I must say that I still hesitate as to the propriety of the conclusion." See Delegal *v.* Naylor, 7 Bing. R. 460; Ekins *v.* East India Company, 1 P. Will. 396.

[4] See Cockerell *v.* Barber, 16 Ves. 461; Post, § 312.

the time of the trial[1]." It is impossible to say that a rule laid down in such general terms ought to be deemed of universal application; and cases may easily be imagined which may justly form exceptions.

§ 309. The proper rule would seem to be, in all cases to allow that sum in the currency of the country where the suit is brought, which should approximate most nearly to the amount to which the party is entitled in the country where the debt is payable, calculated by the real par, and not by the nominal par of exchange[2]. This would seem to be the rule also which is adopted by foreign jurists[3]. In some countries there is an established par of exchange by law, as in the United States, where the pound sterling of England is now valued at four dollars and forty-four cents for all purposes, except the estimation of the duties on goods paying an *ad valorem* duty[4]. In other countries the original par has, by the depreciation of the currency, become merely nominal; and there we should resort to the real par. Where there is no established par, from any depreciation of the currency, there the rate of exchange may justly furnish a standard as the nearest approximation of the relative value of the currencies. And where the debt is payable in a particular known coin, as in Sicca rupees,

---

1 Lee *v.* Wilcocks, 5 Serg. & Rawle, 48. It is probable that in this case the money was payable in Turkey.

2 In Cash *v.* Kennion, (11 Vesey, R. 314), Lord Eldon held, that if a man in a foreign country agrees to pay £100 in London, upon a given day, he ought to have that sum there on that day. And if he fails in that contract, wherever the creditor sues him, the law of that country ought to give him just as much as he would have had if the contract had been performed. J. Voet says,—"Si major, alibi minor, eorundem nummorum valor sit, in solutione faciendâ; non tam spectanda potestas pecuniæ, quæ est in loco in quo contractus celebratus est, quam potius quæ obtinet in regione illâ in quâ contractûs implementum faciendum est." Voet, Ad Pand. lib. 12, tit. 1, § 25; Henry on Foreign Law, 43, n. See also Ante, § 281; 3 Burge, Com. on Col. and For. Law, Pt. 2, ch. 20, pp. 771—773.

3 Ante, § 281.

4 Ante, § 308, n. 2.

or in Turkish piastres, there the mint value of the coin, and not the mere bullion value in the country where the coin is issued, would seem to furnish the proper standard, since it is referred to by the parties in their contract by its descriptive name as coin.

§ 310. But in all these cases we are to take into consideration the place where the money is, by the original contract payable; for wheresoever the creditor may sue for it, he is entitled to have an amount equal to what he must pay, in order to remit it to that country[1]. Thus, if a note were made in England for £100 sterling, payable in Boston (Mass.), if a suit were brought in Massachusetts, the party would be entitled to recover 444 dollars and 44 cents, that being the established par of exchange by our laws. But if our currency had become depreciated by a debasement of our coinage, then the depreciation ought to be allowed for, so as to bring the sum to the real par, instead of nominal par[2]. But, if a like note were given in England for £100, payable in England, or payable generally (which in legal effect would be the same thing), there, in a suit in Massachusetts, the party would be entitled to recover in addition to the 444 dollars and 44 cents, the rate of exchange between Massachusetts and England, which is ordinarily from eight to ten per cent. above par. And if the exchange were below par, a proportionate deduction should be made; so that the party would have his money replaced

---

[1] See 1 Chitty on Comm. and Manuf. ch. 12, pp. 650, 651. See Ante, § 281, 308.

[2] Paul Voet has expressed an opinion upon this subject in general terms. "Quid si in specie de nummorum aut reddituum solutione difficultas incidat, si forte valor sit immutatus; an spectabitur loci valor, ubi contractus erat celebratus, an loci in quem destinata erat solutio? Respondeo, ex generali regulâ, spectandum esse loci statutum, in quem destinata erat solutio." P. Voet, De Stat. § 9, c. 2, § 15, p. 271; Id. p. 328, (edit. 1661). And he applies the same rule where contracts are for specific articles, the measures whereof are different in different countries. Id. § 16, p. 271; Id. p. 328, (edit. 1661).

in England at exactly the same amount which he would be entitled to recover in a suit there.

§ 311. This distinction may perhaps reconcile some of the cases, between which there might seem, at first view, to be an apparent contrariety. It was evidently acted on in an old case, where money payable in Ireland was sued for in England, and the Court allowed Irish interest, but directed an allowance to the debtor for the payment of it in England and not in Ireland[1]. It is presumable that the money was of less value in Ireland than in England. A like rule was adopted in a later case, where money payable in India was recovered in England, and the charge of remitting it from India was directed to be deducted[2].

§ 311 *a*. There is, however, an irreconcilable difference in some of the authorities on this subject. Thus, it has been held in New York, that where a debt is contracted in a foreign country, and is payable there, if the creditor afterwards sues the debtor here for the debt, he is entitled to recover only for the debt according to the par of exchange, and not according to the rate of exchange necessary to remit the amount to the foreign country. On that occasion the Court said: "The debt is to be paid according to the par, and not the rate of exchange. It is recoverable and payable here to the plaintiffs or their agent, and the Courts are not to inquire into the disposition of the debt after it reaches the hands of the agent. He may remit the debt to his principal abroad in bills of exchange, or he may invest it here on his behalf, or transmit it to some other part of the United States, or to other countries on the same account. We cannot trace the disposition which is to take place subsequent to the recovery, nor award special damages upon such uncertain calculations[3]. The same doctrine

[1] Dungannon *v.* Hackett, 1 Eq. Cas. Abr. 288, 289.

[2] Ekins *v.* The East India Company, 1 P. Will. 396; S. C. 2 Bro. Par. Cas. 382, edit. Tomlins.

[3] Martin *v.* Franklin, 4 John. R. 124, 125.

has been adhered to in subsequent decisions[1]. It has also been adopted by the Supreme Court of Massachusetts, as the proper rule in all cases, except bills of exchange[2]. On the contrary, in the Circuit Courts of the United States, the opposite doctrine has been maintained[3].

---

[1] Scofield *v.* Day, 20 John. R. 102.

[2] Adams *v.* Cordis, 8 Pick. R. 260, 266, 267.

[3] Smith *v.* Shaw, 2 Wash. Cir. R. 167, 168; Grant *v.* Healey, 2 Chand. Law Reporter, 113; Ante, § 284 *a*.—In this last case the subject was considered at great length; and the following remarks were made by the Judge, in delivering the opinion of the Court: "I take the general doctrine to be clear, that whenever a debt is made payable in one country, and it is afterwards sued for in another country, the creditor is entitled to receive the full sum necessary to replace the money in the country where it ought to have been paid, with interest for the delay; for then, and then only, is he fully indemnified for the violation of the contract. In every such case the plaintiff is, therefore, entitled to have the debt due to him first ascertained at the par of exchange between the two countries, and then to have the rate of exchange between those countries added to or subtracted from the amount, as the case may require, in order to replace the money in the country where it ought to be paid. It seems to me, that this doctrine is founded on the true principles of reciprocal justice. The question, therefore, in all cases of this sort, where there is not a known and settled commercial usage to govern them, seems to me to be rather a question of fact than of law. In cases of accounts and advances, the object is to ascertain where, according to the intention of the parties, the balance is to be repaid? In the country of the creditor or of the debtor? In Lanusse *v.* Barker, (3 Wheat. R. 101, 147), the Supreme Court of the United States seem to have thought, that where money is advanced for a person in another State, the implied understanding is to replace it in the country where it is advanced, unless that conclusion is repelled by the agreement of the parties or by other controlling circumstances. Governed by this rule, the money being advanced in Boston, so far as it was not reimbursed out of the proceeds of the sales at Trieste, would seem to be proper to be repaid in Boston. In relation to mere balances of account between a foreign factor and a home merchant, there may be more difficulty in ascertaining where the balance is reimbursable, whether where the creditor resides, or where the debtor resides. Perhaps it will be found, in the absence of all controlling circumstances, the truest rule and the easiest in its application, that advances ought to be deemed reimbursable at the place where they are made, and sales of goods accounted for at the place where they are made or authorized to be made. Thus, if a consignment is made in one country for sales in another country where the consignee resides, the true rule would seem to be, to hold the consignee bound to pay the balance there, if due from him;

§ 312. In one case, where, by a will made in India, a legacy was given of 30,000 Sicca rupees, and the testator

---

and if due to him on advances there made, to receive the balance from the consignor there. The case of Conseequa *v.* Fanning, (3 John. Ch. R. 587, 610), which was reversed in 17 John. R. 511, proceeded upon this intelligible ground, both in the Court of Chancery and in the Court of Errors and Appeals; the difference between these learned tribunals not being so much in the rule, as in its application to the circumstances of that particular case. I am aware, that a different rule in respect to balances of account and debts due and payable in a foreign country, was laid down in Martin *v.* Franklin, (4 John. R. 125), and Scofield *v.* Day, (20 John. R. 102); and that it has been followed by the Supreme Court of Massachusetts, in Adams *v.* Cordis, (8 Pick. R. 260). It it with unaffected diffidence that I venture to express a doubt as to the correctness of the decisions of these learned Courts upon this point. It appears to me that the reasoning in 4 John. R. 125, which constitutes the basis of the other decisions, is far from being satisfactory. It states very properly, that the Court have nothing to do with inquiries into the disposition which the creditor may make of his debt after the money has reached his hands; and the Court are not to award damages upon such uncertain calculations as to the future disposition of it. But that is not, it is respectfully submitted, the point in controversy. The question is, whether if a man has undertaken to pay a debt in one country, and the creditor is compelled to sue him for it in another country where the money is of less value, the loss is to be borne by the creditor who is in no fault, or by the debtor who, by the breach of this contract, has occasioned the loss? The loss of which we here speak is not a future contingent loss. It is positive, direct, immediate. The very rate of exchange shews that the very same sum of money paid in the one country, is not an indemnity or equivalent for it when paid in another country, to which by the default of the debtor the creditor is bound to resort. Suppose a man undertakes to pay another 10,000 dollars in China, and violates his contract; and then he is sued therefor in Boston, when the money if duly paid in China would be worth at the very moment 20 per cent. more than it is in Boston: what compensation is it to the creditor to pay him the 10,000 dollars at the par in Boston? Indeed I do not perceive any just foundation for the rule, that interest is payable according to the law of the place where the contract is to be performed, except it be the very same on which a like claim may be made as to the principal, viz., that the debtor undertakes to pay there, and therefore is bound to put the creditor in the same situation as if he had punctually complied with his contract there It is suggested, that the case of bills of exchange stands upon a distinct ground, that of usage, and is an exception from the general doctrine. I think otherwise. The usage has done nothing more than ascertain what should be the rate of damages for a violation of the contract generally, as a matter of convenience and daily occurrence in business, rather than to have a

afterwards died in England, leaving personal property both in England and in India; upon a suit in Chancery for the legacy the Master to whom it was referred,

---

fluctuating standard, dependent upon the daily rates of exchange; exactly for the same reason, that the rule of deducting one-third new for old is applied to cases of repairs of ships, and the deduction of one-third from the gross freight is applied in cases of general average. It cuts off all minute calculations and inquiries into evidence. But in cases of bills of exchange, drawn between countries where no such fixed rate of damages exists, the doctrine of damages applied to the contract is precisely that which is sought to be applied to the case of a common debt due and payable in another country; that is to say, to pay the creditor the exact sum which he ought to have received in that country. That is sufficiently clear from the case of Mellish *v.* Simeon, (2 H. Black. R. 378), and the whole theory of re-exchange. My brother, the late Mr. Justice Washington, in the case of Smith *v.* Shaw, (2 Wash. Cir. R. 167, 168, in 1808), which was a suit brought by an English merchant on an account for goods shipped to the defendants' testator,—where the money was doubtless to be paid in England, and a question was made, whether, it being a sterling debt, it should be turned into currency at the par of exchange, or at the then rate of exchange, held—that the debt was payable at the then rate of exchange. To which Mr. Ingersoll, at that time one of the ablest and most experienced lawyers at the Philadelphia bar, of counsel for the defendant, assented. It is said, that the point was not started at the argument, and was settled by the Court suddenly, without advancing any reasons in the support of it. I cannot but view the case in a very different light. The point was certainly made directly to the Court, and attracted its full attention. The learned Judge was not a Judge accustomed to come to sudden conclusions, or to decide any point which he had not most scrupulously and deliberately considered. The point was probably not at all new to him; for it must frequently have come under his notice in the vast variety of cases of debts due on account by Virginia debtors to British creditors, which were sued for during the period in which he possessed a most extensive practice at the Richmond bar. The circumstance, that so distinguished a lawyer as Mr. Ingersoll assented to the decision, is a farther proof to me, that it had been well understood in Pennsylvania to be the proper rule. If, indeed, I were disposed to indulge in any criticism, I might say that the cases in 4 John. R. 125, and 20 John. R. 101, 102, do not appear to have been much argued or considered; for no general reasoning is to be found in either of them upon principle, and no authorities were cited. The arguments and the opinion contain little more than a dry statement and decision of the point. The first and only case, in which the question seems to have been considered upon a thorough argument, is that in 8 Pick. R. 260. I regret that I am not able to follow its authority with a satisfied assent of mind."

estimated the Sicca rupees at 2*s.* 6*d.* per Sicca rupee, being the East India Company's rate of exchange between India and Great Britain, (*i. e.* on bills drawn in India on Great Britain), at the time the legacy became due. At the same time, the par or sterling value of the Sicca rupees in India and England was 2*s.* 1*d.* per Sicca rupee; and the East India Company's rate of exchange between Great Britain and India, (*i. e.* on bills drawn in England on India), was 2*s.* 3*d.* Upon exceptions taken to the Report, it was contended, that either the par of exchange or the rate of exchange between Great Britain and India ought to have been adopted[1]. Lord Eldon on that occasion said: "In all the cases reported upon the wills of persons in Ireland or Jamaica, and dying there, and *vice versâ* in this country, some legacies being expressed in sterling money, others in sums, without reference to the nature of the coin in which they are to be paid, the legacies are directed here to be computed according to the (real) value of the currency of the country to which the testator belonged, or where the property was; and I apprehend no more was done in such cases, than ascertaining the value of so many pounds in the current coin of the country, and paying that amount out of the funds in Court. On the other hand, I do not believe the Court have ever said they would not look at the value of the current coin of the country, but would take it as bullion. At the time of Wood's half-pence in Ireland, whatever was their actual worth, yet payment in England must have been according to their nominal current value, not the actual value. So whatever was the current value of the rupee at the time when this legacy ought to be paid, is the ratio according to which payment must be made here in pounds sterling. If twelve of Wood's half-pence were worth six pence in this Court, six pence must have been the sum paid. And in a payment in this Court, the cost of re-

---

[1] Cockerell *v.* Barber, 16 Ves. 461, 465.

mittance has nothing to do with it. So if the value of 30,000 rupees at the time the payment ought to have been made in India was £10,000, that is the sum to be paid here, without any consideration as to the expense of remittance." And he accordingly directed the Master to review his report, and the legacies to be paid according to the current value of the Sicca rupee in Calcutta[1].

§ 313. In considering this decision, it is material to observe, that the will was made in India, and, of course, the legacy payable there; and the testator died in England, leaving personal assets in both countries. Under these circumstances, the legatee was not compellable to resort to England for payment of the legacy; but he elected of his own mere choice to receive it there. He might have resorted to India if he had pleased[2]; and if so, he would have been entitled to the exact amount of 30,000 Sicca rupees, according to their current value there. He ought not, then, by resorting to a court in England, to oblige the estate to bear the charge of the remittance of the amount to England, with which it was charged by the Master's report. Nor ought the estate, upon his mere election to receive the amount in England, to pay for the remittance of the same from England to India. The decree of the Court was, therefore, manifestly right, and consistent with the principles above stated. The language of the Court, however, does not seem to put the case upon this clear ground; but to put it upon the ground, that the value, at the par of exchange, (not indeed the nominal, but the real par), without any reference to the place of payment or of remittance, was, in all cases, the true rule. It admits, however, of some doubt, whether the Court intended to make so general an application of its language, and did not intend to restrain it to the

---

1 Cockerell *v.* Barber, 16 Ves. 461, 465.

2 See Bourke *v.* Ricketts, 10 Ves. 332, and Raithby's Notes to Ranelagh *v.* Champant, 2 Vern. 395; Saunders *v.* Drake, 2 Atk. R. 466; Stapleton *v.* Conway, 1 Ves. 427.

circumstances of the particular case. Suppose the executor in India had remitted all the funds to England, and had become domiciled there, and the legatee had always lived in India; would not the latter, having no other means of getting payment but by a suit in England, have been entitled to the charge of remittance to India? Without expressing any opinion upon the subject, it may, perhaps, be thought worthy of further consideration. Some of the cases[1] already cited are certainly at variance with this decision, if it is to be deemed to assert a doctrine of universal application[2].

---

[1] Scott *v.* Bevan, 2 Barn. & Adol. 78. See also Delegal *v.* Naylor, 7 Bing. R. 460, which apparently supports the rule in Scott *v.* Bevan, and Ante, § 308, 309, 311, 311 *a.*

[2] In the case of mixed money, in Sir John Davies's Reports [28], 48, there is a curious discussion as to the nature and changes of English currency. A bond was given in England for the payment of "£100 sterling, current and lawful money of England," to be paid in Dublin, Ireland; and between the time of giving the bond and its becoming due, Queen Elizabeth, by proclamation, recalled the existing currency in Ireland, and issued a new debased coinage, (called mixed money), declaring it to be the lawful currency in Ireland. A tender was made in this debased coin, or mixed coin, in Dublin, in payment of the bond. The question, before the Privy Council of Ireland, was, whether the tender was good, or ought to have been in currency or value equal to the current lawful money then current in England. The Court held the tender good: first, because the mixed money was current lawful of England, Ireland being within the sovereignty of the British crown; and secondly, because the payment being to be in Dublin, it could be made in no other currency than the existing currency of Ireland, which was the mixed money. The Court do not seem to have considered that the true value of the English current money might, if that was required by the bond, have been paid in Irish currency, though debased, by adding so much more as would bring it to the par. And it is extremely difficult to conceive how a payment of current lawful money of England could be interpreted to mean current or lawful money of Ireland, when the currency of each kingdom was different, and the royal proclamation made a distinction between them, the mixed money being declared the lawful currency of Ireland only. Perhaps the desire to yield to the royal prerogative of the Queen a submissive obedience, as to all payments in Ireland, may account for a decision so little consonant with the principles of law in modern times. See also the comments on this case in the case of Pilkington *v.* Commissioners for Claims, 2 Knapp. R. 18—21; S. C. cited 2 Bligh, R. 98, n. See Kearney *v.* King, 2 Barn & Ald. 301; Sprowle *v.* Legg, 1 Barn. & Cres. 16.

§ 313 *a*. The question touching the effect of a depreciation of the currency between the time when the debt is contracted or it becomes due, and the subsequent payment thereof, which was hinted at in the preceding case, has since arisen in a more direct and solemn form, and undergone no inconsiderable discussion. The French government, during the war between England and France, had confiscated a debt, due from a French subject to a British subject; and subsequently an indemnity was stipulated for on the part of the French government; and there having been a great depreciation of the French currency after the time when the debt was confiscated, the question arose, whether the debt was to be calculated at the value of the currency at the time when the confiscation took place, or subsequently; and it was held, that it ought to be calculated according to the value at the time of the confiscation. On that occasion, the case in Sir John Davies's Reports, already alluded to [1], was referred to, as well as the opinions of foreign jurists on the same subject; and Sir William Grant, in delivering the opinion of the Court, said, "Great part of the argument at the bar would undoubtedly go to shew, that the Commissioners have acted wrong in throwing that loss upon the French government in any case; for they resemble it to the case of depreciation of currency, happening between the time that a debt is contracted and the time that it is paid; and they have quoted authorities for the purpose of shewing, that in such a case the loss must be borne by the creditor, and not by the debtor. That point it is unnecessary for the present purpose to consider, though Vinnius, whose authority was quoted the other day, certainly comes to a conclusion directly at variance with the decision in Sir John Davies's Reports. He takes the distinction, that if between the time of contracting the debt and the time of its payment, the currency of the country is depreciated by the State, that

---

[1] Ante, § 312, 313, note 2.

is to say, lowered in its intrinsic goodness, as if there were a greater proportion of alloy put into a guinea or a shilling, the debtor should not liberate himself by paying the nominal amount of his debt in the debased money; that is, he may pay in the debased money, being the current coin, but he must pay so much more as would make it equal to the sum he borrowed. But he says, if the nominal value of the currency, leaving it unadulterated, were to be increased, as if they were to make the guinea pass for 30*s.*, the debtor may liberate himself from a debt of 1*l.* 10*s.* by paying a guinea, although he had borrowed the guinea when it was but worth 21*s.* I have said it is unnecessary to consider whether the conclusion drawn by Vinnius, or the decision in Davies's Reports, be the correct one; for we think this has no analogy to the case of creditor and debtor. There is a wrong act done by the French government; then they are to undo that wrong act, and to put the party into the same situation as if they never had done it. It is assumed to be a wrong act, not only in the treaty, but in the repealing decree. They justify it only with reference to that which, as to this country, has a false foundation; namely, on the ground of what other governments had done towards them, they having confiscated the property of French subjects; therefore, they say, we thought ourselves justified at the time in retaliating upon the subjects of this country. That being destitute of foundation as to this country, the Republic themselves, in effect, confess that no such decree ought to have been made, as it affected the subjects of this country. Therefore it is not merely the case of a debtor paying a debt at the day it falls due; but it is the case of a wrong-doer, who must undo, and completely undo, the wrongful act he has done; and if he has received the assignats at the value of 50*d.*, he does not make compensation by returning an assignat, which is only worth 20*d.*; he must make up the difference between the value of the assignat at different periods. And that is the case stated by Sir John Davies, where *restitutio in integrum* is stated. He says, two cases were put by the Judges, who were called to the assistance of the Privy Council, although they were not positively and formally resolved. He says, it is said, if a man upon marriage receive £1000 as a portion with his wife, paid in silver money, and the marriage is dissolved *causâ precontractûs*, so that the portion is to be restored, it must be restored in equal good silver money, though the State shall have depreciated the currency in the meantime. So if a man recover £100 damages, and he levies that in good silver money, and that judgment is afterwards reversed, by which the party is put to restore back all he has received, the judgment-creditor cannot liberate himself by merely restoring £100 in the debased currency of the time; but he must give the very same currency that he had received. That proceeds upon the principle, that if the act is to be undone, it must be completely undone, and the party is to be restored to the situation in which he was at the time the act to be undone took place. Upon that principle, therefore, undoubtedly the French government, by restoring assignats at the end of thirteen months, did not put the party in the same situation in which he was when they took from him assignats that were of a very different value. We have said, that as this point is not directly or immediately before us, it can make no part of our decree. At the same time, it may not perhaps have been without some utility to have given an opinion upon it, inasmuch as it was argued and discussed at the bar. And we think, therefore, the Commissioners have proceeded on a perfectly right principle in those cases, in which we understand they have made an allowance for the depreciation of paper money; and considering that this case does not differ from those in which they have made that allowance, we are of opinion that the claimants ought to have the same equity administered to them in remunerating them for the loss they have sustained[1]."

---

[1] Pilkington *v.* Commissioners for Claims, 2 Knapp, R. 17—21.

§ 313 *b*. The opinions of Vinnius and Pothier, alluded to in the opinion of Sir Wm. Grant, fully confirm his statements. Vinnius is of opinion that the value of the money at the time when it ought to be paid, is the value which is to be allowed to the creditor. Of the same opinion, he adds, are Bartolus, and Baldus, and De Castro, and indeed of jurists generally, with the exception of Dumoulin, and Hotomannus, and Donellus, who think the value at the time of making the contract ought to govern. Hence, after having discussed the principle, he says, in conformity with the opinions of the former: *Hoc autem fundamento posito, siquidem neutri contrahentium injuriam fieri volumus, ita definiendum videtur, ut si bonitas moneta intrinseca mutata sit, tempus contractus, si extrinseca, id est valor impostitius, tempus solutionis in solutione facienda, spectari debeat*[1]. Po-

---

[1] Vinnius, Ad Instit. lib. 3, tit. 15; Textus De Mutuo. Comm. n. 12, p. 599, (edit. 1726). The whole passage deserves to be cited: Atque hinc pendet decisio nobilissimæ quæstionis, si post contractum æstimatio nummorum creverit aut decreverit, utrum in solutione facienda spectare oporteat valorem, quem habebant tempore contractus, an qui nunc est tempore solutionis: intellige si nihil, de ea re expresse dictum sit, neque mora intervenerit. Molinæus, Hotomannus, Donellus contendunt, tempus contractus inspiciendum esse, id est, ea æstimatione nummos reddendos, non quæ nunc est, sed quæ initio fuit, cum dabantur. Nimirum nihil illi in pecunia numerata præter æstimationem considerandum putant, totamque nummi bonitatem in hac ipsa æstimatione consistere: ac proinde creditori non facere injuriam, qui eandem æstimationem, quam accepit, reddit: tantum enim reddere eum, quantum accepit, quod ad solutionem mutui sit satis. Itaque secundum horum sententiam, si 100 aurei mutuo dati sint, cum aureus valebat asses 50 reddantur autem, cum singuli valent asses 55 debitor reddens creditori aureos 90 aut in singulos aureos 50 asses reddit, quantum accepit, et liberatur: et vicissim si imminuta sit ad eundem modum aureorum æstimatio, non liberatur, nisi reddat aureos 110 aut in singulos aureos asses 55. Bartolus vero (in l. Paulus 101 de solut). Baldus (in l. res in dotem. 24 de jur. dot.) Castro (in lib. 3, de reb. cred), et DD. comm. ut videre est apud Boër. decis. 327 contra censent, spectandum esse in proposito tempus solutionis, id est, aucto vel deminuto nummorum valore, ea æstimatione reddi eos oportere, non quæ tunc fuit, cum dabantur, sed quæ nunc est, cum solvuntur; neque aliud statui posse sine creditoris aut debitoris injuria. Quæ sententia, ut mihi videtur, et verior et æquior est. Nam quod contrariæ sententiæ auctores unicum urgent, in nummis non ma-

thier holds the opposite opinion, and says: "It remains to be observed, in regard to the price, that it may be rendered in a money different from that in which it is paid. If it is paid to the seller in gold, the seller may repay it in pieces of silver, or *vice versâ*. In like manner, though subsequent to the payment of the price, the pieces in which it is paid are increased or diminished in value; though they are dis-

-teriæ, sed solius æstimationis impositițiæ atque externæ, quam ob id vulgo extrinsecam nummi bonitatem vocant, rationem duci, nummumque nihil aliud esse, quam quod publicè valet, vereor, ut simpliciter verum sit. Utique enim materia numismatis fundamentum est et causa valoris: quippe qui variatur pro diversitate materiæ: oportetque valorem hunc justa aliqua proportione materiæ respondere: neque in bene constituta repub. nummo ea æstimatio imponi debet, quæ pretium materiæ, ex qua cuditur, superat, aut superet ultra modum expensarum, quæ in signanda pecunia fiunt; quod ad singularum specierum valorem parum addere potest. Sed hoc ad actus et præstationes privatorum non pertinet. Illud pertinet, quod si dicimus, creditis nummis nihil præter æstimationem eorum creditum intelligi, necessario sequitur, creditorem teneri in alia forma aut materia nummos accipere contra definitionem Pauli in d. l. 99, de solut. etiamsi damnum ex eo passurus sit: nam, qui recipit, quod credidit, nihil habet, quod conqueratur. Sequitur et hoc, si contingat mutari nummorum bonitatem intrinsecam, id est, si valore veteri retentio percutiantur novi nummi ex deteriore materia, quam ex qua cusi, qui dati sunt, puta, si qui dati sunt, cusi fuerint ex puro auro, postea alii feriantur ex auro minus puro et mixto ex ære, debitorem restituendo tot mixtos et contaminatos, quot ille puros accepit, liberari cum insigni injuria creditoris: et contra interpp. pene omnium doctrinam, qui hoc casu solutionem faciendam esse statuunt ad valorem intrinsecum monetæ, qui currebat tempore contractus, testibus Gail. 2, obs. 73, nn. 6 & 7. Borcholt. de feud. ad cap. un. quæ sunt regal. num. 62. Illud enim maxime in hac disputatione considerandum est, quoniam hic finis nummi principalis est, ut serviat rebus necessariis comparandis, auctore Aristotele 1. Polit. 6, quod mutata monetæ bonitate sive extrinseca, sive intrinseca, pretia rerum omnium mutentur, et pro modo auctæ aut imminutæ bonitatis nummorum crescant aut decrescant: quod ipsa docet experientia: eoque facit l. 2. C. de vet. num. pot. lib. 11. Crescunt rerum pretia, si deterior materia electa, aut manente eadem materia valor auctus sit: decrescunt electu materiæ melioris, aut si eadem bonitate materiæ manente valor imminutus fuerit. Fallitur enim imperitum vulgus, dum sibi persuadet, ex augmento valoris aurei aliquid sibi lucri accedere. Hoc autem fundamento posito, siquidem neutri contrahentium injuriam fieri volumus, ita definiendum videtur, ut si bonitas monetæ intrinseca mutata sit, tempus contractus, si extrinseca, id est, valor impositițius, tempus solutionis in solutione facienda spectari debeat. Atque ita sæpissimè judicatum est.

credited, and at the time of the redemption their place is supplied by new ones of better or worse alloy; the seller, who exercises the redemption, ought to repay, in money which is current at the time he redeems, the same sum or quantity which he received in payment, and nothing more nor less. The reason is, that in money we do not regard the coins which constitute it, but only the value which the sovereign has been pleased that they shall signify: *Eaque materia forma publica percussa, usum dominiumque non tam ex substantia præbet, quum ex quantitate;* D. 18, 1, 1. When the price is paid, the seller is not considered to receive the particular pieces, so much as the sum or value, which they signify; and, consequently, he ought to repay, and it is sufficient for him to repay, the same sum or value in pieces which are current, and which have the signs authorized by the prince to signify that value. This principle being well established in our French practice, it is sufficient merely to state it. It cuts off all the questions made by the Doctors concerning the changes of money[1]."

§ 314. Negotiable instruments often present questions of a like mixed nature[2]. Thus, suppose a negotiable bill of exchange is drawn in Massachusetts on England, and is indorsed in New York, and again by the first indorsee in Pennsylvania, and by the second in Maryland, and the bill is dishonoured; what damages will the holder be entitled to? The law as to damages in these States is different. In Massachusetts, it is ten per cent.; in New York and Pennsylvania, twenty per cent.; and in Maryland, fifteen per cent[3]. What rule, then, is to govern? The answer is, that, in each case, the *lex loci contractûs.* The drawer is liable on the bill according to the law of the place where the bill was drawn, and the successive indorsers are liable

1 Pothier, Traité du Contrat de Vente, n. 416. I quote from Mr. Cushing's excellent Translation, n. 416, pp. 264, 265.

2 See Post, § 344, § 353—361.

3 3 Kent. Comm. Lect. 44, pp. 116—120, 3rd edit.

on the bill according to the law of the place of their indorsement, every indorsement being treated as a new and substantive contract[1]. The consequence is, that the indorser may render himself liable, upon a dishonour of the bill, for a much higher rate of damages than he can recover from the drawer; but this results from his own voluntary contract, and not from any collision of rights arising from the nature of the original contract[2].

§ 315. It has sometimes been suggested that this doctrine is a departure from the rule, that the law of the place of payment is to govern[3]. But, correctly considered, it is entirely in conformity to the rule. The drawer and indorsers do not contract to pay the money in the foreign place on which the bill is drawn, but only to guarantee its acceptance and payment in that place by the drawee; and

---

[1] Ante, § 307; Post, § 317; Powers *v.* Lynch, 3 Mass. R. 77; Prentiss *v.* Savage, 13 Mass. R. 20, 23, 24; Slacum *v.* Pomeroy, 6 Cranch, 221; Depau *v.* Humphreys, 20 Martin, R. 1, 14, 15; Hicks *v.* Brown, 12 John. R. 142; Bayley on Bills, ch. A. p. 28, Phillips & Sewall's edition; Trimbey *v.* Vignier, 1 Bing. R. 151, 159, 160; Ante, § 267; Post, § 316 *a*, § 353—361; 3 Burge, Comm. on Col. and For. Law, pt. 2, ch. 20, pp. 771—774.

[2] Pardessus has discussed this matter at large: he adopts the general doctrine here stated, that the law of the place of each indorsement is to govern, as each indorsement constitutes a new contract between the immediate parties: and he applies the same rule to damages, and says, that if the law of the place where a bill of exchange is drawn admits of the accumulation of costs and charges on account of re-exchanges, (as is the law of some countries), in such a case each successive indorser may become liable to the payment of such successive accumulations, if allowed by the law of the place where they made their indorsement. He seems, indeed, to press his doctrine farther, and to hold, that if the law of the place of such indorsement does not allow such accumulation of re-exchanges, but the law of the place where the bill is drawn does, the indorsers will be liable to pay, as the drawer would. But his reasoning does not seem satisfactory; and it is certainly inconsistent with the acknowledged doctrines of the common law. Pardessus, Droit Commerc. art. 1500. See also Henry on Foreign Laws, 53 App. 239—242; 3 Kent, Comm. Lect. 44, p. 115, 3rd edit.

[3] 2 Kent, Comm. Lect. 39, pp. 459, 460, 3rd edit.; Chitty on Bills, pp. 191—194, 8th edit. London.

in default of such payment, they agree upon due notice to reimburse the holder, in principal and damages, at the place where they respectively entered into the contract[1].

§ 316. Nor is it any departure from the rule to hold, that the time when the payment of such a bill is to accrue is to be according to the law of the place where the bill is payable; so that the days of grace (if any) are to be allowed according to the law or custom where the bill is to be accepted and paid[2]; for such is the appropriate construction of the contract, according to the rules of law and the presumed intention of the parties[3].

§ 316 *a*. Another illustration of the general doctrine may be derived from the case of negotiable paper, as to the binding obligation and effect of a blank indorsement. It seems, that by the law of France an indorsement in blank of a promissory note does not transfer the property to the holder, unless certain prescribed formalities are observed in the indorsement, such as the date, the consideration, and the name of the party to whose order it is passed; otherwise, it is treated as a mere procuration[4]. Now, let us suppose a note made at Paris, payable to the order of the payee, and he should there indorse the same in blank without the prescribed formalities, and afterwards the holder should sue the maker of the note in another country, as for example in England, where no such formalities are prescribed; the question would arise, whether the holder could recover in such a suit in an English Court upon such an indorsement? It has been held that he cannot; and this decision seems to be founded in the true principles of international juris-

---

1 Potter *v.* Brown, 5 East, R. 123, 130; Hicks *v.* Brown, 12 John. R. 142; Powers *v.* Lynch, 3 Mass. R. 77; Prentiss *v.* Savage, 13 Mass. R. 20, 24; Pardessus, Droit. Comm. art. 1497.

2 See 2 Kent, Comm. Lect. 39, pp. 459, 460, 3rd edit.; Chitty on Bills, p. 191, 8th edit. London; Pothier, Contrat. de Change, n. 15, 155; 5 Pardessus, § 1495.

3 Mr. Justice Martin in Vidal *v.* Thompson, 11 Martin, R. 23, 24.

4 Code de Commerc. art. 137, 138; Trimbey *v.* Vignier, 1 Bing. N. Cas. 151, 158—160.

prudence; for it relates not to the form of the remedy, but to the interpretation and obligation of the contract, created by the indorsement, which ought to be governed by the law of the place of indorsement[1].

§ 316 *b*. Another illustration may be derived from the different obligations, which an indorsement creates in different States. By the general commercial law, in order to entitle the indorsee to recover against any antecedent indorser upon a negotiable note, it is only necessary that due demand should be made upon the maker of the note at its maturity, and due notice of the dishonour to the indorser. But by the laws of some of the American States, it is required, in order to charge an antecedent indorser, that not only due demand should be made and due notice given, but that a suit shall be previously commenced against the maker, and prosecuted with effect in the country where he resides; and then if payment cannot be obtained from him under the judgment, the indorsee may have recourse to the indorser. In such a case, it is clear upon principle that the indorsement, as to its legal effect and obligation, and the duties of the holder, must be governed by the law of the place where the indorsement is made. This very point has been recently decided in a case, where a note was made and indorsed in the State of Illinois. On that occasion Mr. Chief Justice Shaw in delivering the opinion of the Court, said: "The note declared on, being made in Illinois, both parties residing there at the time, and it also being indorsed in Illinois, we think that the contract created by that indorsement must be governed by the law of that State. The law in question does not affect the remedy, but goes to create, limit, and modify the contract effected by the fact of indorsement. In that which gives force and effect to the contract, and imposes restrictions and modifications upon it, the law

---

[1] Trimbey *v.* Vignier, 1 Bing. New Cases, 151, 158—160; § Ante, § 272.

of the place of contract must prevail when another is not looked to as a place of performance. Suppose it were shewn that by the law of Illinois the indorsement of a note by the payee merely transferred the legal interest in the note to the indorsee, so as to enable him to sue in his own name, but imposed no conditional obligation on the indorser to pay; it would hardly be contended, that an action could be brought here upon such an indorsement, if the indorser should happen to be found here, because by our law such an indorsement, if made here, would render the indorser conditionally liable to pay the note. By the law of Illinois, the indorser is liable only after a judgment obtained against the maker; and as no such judgment appears to have been obtained on this note, the condition upon which alone the plaintiff may sue is not complied with, and therefore the action cannot be maintained[1]".

§ 317. But, suppose a negotiable note is made in one country, and is payable there, and it is afterwards indorsed in another country, and by the law of the former country equitable defences are let in, in favour of the maker, and by the latter such defences excluded; what rule is to govern in regard to the holder, in a suit against the maker to recover the amount upon the indorsement to him? The answer is, the law of the place where the note was made, for there the maker undertook to pay; and the subsequent negotiation of the note did not change his original obligation, duty, or rights[2]. Acceptances of bills are governed by the same principles. They are deemed contracts of acceptance in the place where they are made, and where they are to be performed[3]. So, Paul Voet lays down the doctrine: *Quid si de literis Cambii incidat questio; quis locus erit spectandus? Is spectandus est locus, ad quem sunt destinatæ, et ibidem ac-*

---

1 Williams *v.* Wade, 1 Metcalf, R. 82, 83.

2 Ory *v.* Winter, 16 Martin, R. 277; Post, § 332, 343, 344.

3 Lewis *v.* Owen, 4 Barn. & Ald. 654; Ante, § 307; Post, § 333, 344, 345.

ceptatæ[1]. But suppose a negotiable acceptance, or a negotiable note made payable generally without any specification of place; what law is to govern in case of a negotiation of it by one holder to another in a foreign country, in regard to the acceptor or to the maker? Is it a contract by them to pay in any place where it is negotiated, so as to be deemed a contract of that particular place, and governed by its laws? The Supreme Court of Massachusetts have held, that it creates a debt payable any where, by the very nature of the contract; and it is a promise to whosoever shall be the holder of the bill or note[2]. Assuming this to be true, still it does not follow that the law of the place of the negotiation is to govern; for the transfer is not, as to the acceptor or the maker, a new contract; but it is under, and a part of the original contract, and springs up from the law of the place where that contract was made. A contract to pay generally is governed by the law of the place where it is made; for the debt is payable there, as well as in every other place[3]. To bring a contract within the general rule

---

[1] P. Voet, De Stat. § 9, ch. 2, n. 14, p. 270, (edit. 1713); Id. p. 327, (edit. 1661); Post, § 346, note.

[2] Braynard *v.* Marshall, 8 Pick. R. 194; Post, § 341, § 343—346.

[3] See Kearney *v.* King, 2 Barn. & Ald. 301; Sprowle *v.* Legge, 1 Barn. & Cres. 16; Ante, § 272 *a;* Post, § 329; Don *v.* Lippman, 5 Clark & Fin. 1, 12, 13.—In this last case a bill of exchange was drawn and accepted in Paris by a Scotchman domiciled in Scotland, and it was payable generally. It seems, that, by the law of Scotland, an acceptance is deemed payable at the place of the domicil of the acceptor, at the time when it becomes due. Lord Brougham on this occasion said: "It appears, that in Scotland—and it is rather singular that it should be so—where a bill is accepted payable generally, without any particular place being named, it shall be deemed payable at the place at which the acceptor is domiciled, when it becomes due. It becomes of some importance to know where the bills were payable, because this principle, which has been adopted of late years in many of the Scotch decisions, and towards which I admit the great leaning of the Scotch profession is, renders it material to consider whether this is a Scotch or a foreign debt. Yet sometimes this expression is used in the cases without affording any accuracy of description; for sometimes the debt is called English, or French, in respect of the place where the contract was made; sometimes it is the place of the

of the *lex loci*, it is not necessary that it should be payable exclusively in the place of its origin. If payable everywhere, then it is governed by the law of the place where it is made; for the plain reason, that it cannot be said to have the law of any other place in contemplation, to govern its validity, its obligation, or its interpretation. All debts between the original parties are payable everywhere, unless some special provision to the contrary is made; and therefore the rule is, that debts have no *situs;* but accompany the creditor everywhere [1]. The holder, then, takes the contract of the acceptor or maker, as it was originally made, and as it was in the place where it was made. It is there that the promise is made to him to pay everywhere [2].

§ 318. A case a little more difficult in its texture is when a contract is made in one country for payment of money in another country, and, by the laws of the latter, a stamp is required to make the contract valid, and it is not by those of the former; whether it is governed by the *lex solutionis*, or by the *lex loci contractûs*, as to the stamp. It has been held that a stamp is not required in such a case to give validity to the contract, upon the ground, that an instrument, as to its form and solemnities, is to be governed by the *lex loci contractûs*, and not by the law of the place of payment; and that therefore a stamp is not required by the principle [3]. On that occasion the Court said: "An instru-

---

origin, sometimes of the payment of the contract, and sometimes of the domicil of one of the parties. But, at all events, it becomes important to consider whether this was a foreign or a Scotch debt. In the present case it was held most properly to be a foreign debt. That is a fact admitted; it is out of all controversy. This, therefore, must now be taken to be a French debt; and then the general law is, that where the acceptance is general, naming no place of payment, the place of payment shall be taken to be the place of the contracting of the debt. I shall therefore deal with this bill as if it was accepted, payable in Paris."

1 Blanchard *v.* Russell, 13 Mass. R. 1, 6; Slacum *v.* Pomeroy, 6 Cranch, 221; Post, § 329, 362, 399, 400.

2 Post, § 343, 344.

3 Mr. Justice Martin in Vidal *v.* Thompson, 11 Martin, R. 23—25.

ment, as to its form and the formalities attending its execution, must be tested by the laws of the place where it is made; but the laws and usages of the place where the obligation, of which it is evidence, is to be fulfilled, must regulate the performance. A bill drawn out of London must be paid at the expiration of the days of grace, which the laws and usages of that place recognise; but need not have those stamps, which are by law required on a bill drawn there [1]."

§ 319. But a case more difficult to reconcile with established principles in its actual adjudication, has occurred in Massachusetts. A bill of exchange was drawn at Manchester, in England, upon a firm established at Boston, in Massachusetts, payable in London, and was accepted at Manchester by one of the firm, then there. The bill was, therefore, drawn in England, accepted in England, and payable in England. But upon its dishonour, it was held that it was to be deemed a bill accepted in Boston; because the domicil of the firm was there, and that damages were recoverable of ten per cent., as they would be upon a like bill, accepted in Boston [2]. There was nothing upon the face of the bill that alluded to an acceptance in Boston, and nothing in the circumstances that pointed in that direction. It was certainly competent for the firm to contract in England, and to accept in England; and, beyond all question, if the bill had been drawn solely on the person who accepted it, the acceptance must have been deemed to be made in

---

But see Ante, § 260 and note, § 262, 262 *a*; Wynne *v.* Jackson, 2 Russ. R. 351; Clegg *v.* Levy, 3 Camp. R. 166; James *v.* Catherwood, 3 Dowl. & Ryl. R. 190.

Ibid.

[2] Grimshaw *v.* Bender, 6 Mass. R. 157.—The case of Acebal *v.* Levy, 10 Bing. R. 376, 379, seems to have involved a question very nearly the same, arising under the Statute of Frauds of England, the contract having been made in Gijon in Spain for the delivery of the goods purchased in England. The Court and Bar seem to have thought, that the contract was to be governed by the English Statute of Frauds, although made in Spain. See Ante, § 262 *a*, and note.

England, notwithstanding his domicil was in Boston. Is there any difference between an acceptance by a firm, and an acceptance by a single person? Is not the general principle of law that which is affirmed by Casaregis, that a contract or acceptance is to be deemed made, where the contract or acceptance is perfected: *Eo loci, quo ultimus in contrahendo assentitur?* [1] It has certainly been put upon that ground in many modern authorities [2]. And, therefore, if the acceptor be an accommodation acceptor in one country, payments made by him of the bills drawn by the drawer in a foreign country, will be deemed payments under a contract, made with the drawer in the place of acceptance and payment [3].

§ 320. The doctrine maintained in Massachusetts, in this last case, is directly in conflict with that maintained under similar circumstances by the Supreme Court of New York. The latter Court has held, that the bill having been drawn in England, and made payable there, and accepted there, it was to be treated as an English contract; and that the English interest of five per cent. only was to be allowed for the delay of payment [4]. This decision being in entire harmony with the general principles on this subject, will probably obtain general credit in the commercial world [5].

§ 320 *a*. Many other cases might easily be put, to illustrate the law in relation to the conflict of the laws of different countries in cases of contract. In some countries there are limited or special partnerships, called in France partnerships *in commanditè*. In these partnerships the contract is between one or more partners, who are jointly and seve-

---

1 Casaregis, Disc. 179, n. 1; Ante, § 285.

2 Boyce *v*. Edwards, 4 Peters, R. 111; P. Voet, De Stat. § 9. ch. 2, § 14. See also M'Candish *v*. Cruger, 2 Bay, R. 377; Bain *v*. Ackworth, 1 S. Car. R. 107; Lewis *v*. Owen, 4 B. & Ald. 654.

3 Lewis *v*. Owen, 4 B. & Ald. 654.

4 Foden *v*. Thorp, 4 John. R. 183.

5 See Bayley on Bills, 5th edit., ch. A. pp. 72—86, Phillips & Sewall's n. edit.

rally responsible for the whole contracts and orders of the partnership, and one or more partners, who merely furnish a particular amount of funds, and are responsible only to the amount of such funds, and who are called *commandataires*, or partners *en commanditè*[1]. Similar limited partnerships are also authorized in some of the American States. Now, let us suppose an order given by the general partner in such a firm in one of such States, upon a house in England, for the purchase of goods there; and they were accordingly purchased in England on the credit of the firm. If the partnership became insolvent, the question might then arise whether the partner *in commanditè* was liable to pay for the goods beyond the amount of the funds which he had contributed, or was bound to contribute for the partnership. That question might essentially depend upon another, whether the contract is to be treated as made in the American States where the partnership was established, or in England, where the contract was consummated. And it might also be important in the case, whether the seller knew that the partnership was so limited or not. No point of this sort has as yet arisen for decision; and therefore it is left for the more full consideration of those who may be called upon to examine it in the case of a judicial controversy[2].

§ 321. In stating the foregoing rules, we have been necessarily led to the consideration of many of what are properly deemed the effects of contracts, which, like the validity of contracts, are dependent upon, and are to be governed by the *lex loci contractûs*. These effects are, the right conferred on the party for whose benefit the contract is made; the correspondent duty of the other party to fulfil it; the right of action which arises from the nonfulfilment of it; and the consequential right to interest or damages for the injury done by such non-fulfilment belong-

---

[1] Code of Commerce of France, art. 23—27.

[2] Ante, § 285—287.

ing to the injured party [1]. The manner in which remedies are to be administered, will fall under another and distinct head [2].

§ 322. But there are some other effects, which may be deemed accompaniments, effects, or incidents of contracts, which may here deserve a passing notice. They are properly collateral to them, and arise by operation of law or by the act of the parties. Among these may be placed the liability of partners and part owners for partnership debts. If, by the law of the place where the contract is made, they would be liable *in solido,* although by the law of the domicil of the partnership they might be liable only for a proportionate share, the law of the former will follow the debt everywhere; or in other words, the effect of the *lex loci* of the contract upon the liability of the partners and part owners will be of universal obligation [3]. By the law of some countries the acceptor of a bill of exchange is discharged from his acceptance, if, when he accepted, the drawer was bankrupt; and this effect of the acceptance regularly accompanies it everywhere as an incident [4].

§ 322 *a.* Another illustration may be found in the law of some countries, (as in Alost in Flanders), which allows to a debtor who has assigned or transferred a debt, the right of redemption of it upon payment back of the price. In such a case, according to Burgundus, the right of redemption will exist, notwithstanding the debt has been contracted in another country; for in such a case the right is for the benefit of the debtor, and the debts and the rights of action are judged of by the law of his domicil, without any consideration of the place where the debts were contracted. *Unde recte dici potest, consuetudinem Alostensem, quæ in-*

---

1 See Pothier, Oblig. n. 141—172; P. Voet, De Stat. § 9, ch. 2, § 12; Boullenois, Ques. de la Contr. des Lois, pp. 330—338.

2 Post, § 556—575.

3 Ferguson *v.* Flower, 16 Martin. R. 312. See also Carroll *v.* Waters, 9 Martin, R. 500; Pardessus, Droit Comm. art. 1495.

4 Pardessus, Droit Comm. art. 1495.

dulget debitori redemptionis cessi nominis, eo pretio, quod assionis auctori solutum est, etiam locum habere in œre alieno extra territorium Alostense contracto. Cum enim ejusmodi redemptio in favorem debitoris introducta, situm nominum, et actionum ex domicilio ejus metitur, sine consideratione qua regione contracta fuerint[1]. A more unexceptionable illustration is the incidental right of warranty, conferred by the civil law in cases of sales of merchandise, not merely as to title but as to quality[2].

§ 322 *b*. Of the like nature is the benefit of the right of discussion, as it is called. By the Roman law sureties were not primarily liable to pay the debt for which they became bound as sureties; but were liable only after the creditor had sought payment from the principal debtor, and he was unable to pay. This was called the benefit or right of discussion[3]. Under those systems of jurisprudence which adopt the Roman law, and under the present law of France, the rule is similar; and the obligation contracted by the surety with the creditor is, that the latter shall not proceed against him until he has first discussed the principal debtor, if he is solvent. This right the surety enjoys, as the *beneficium ordinis vel excussionis*[4]. And, again: if other persons are joined with him in the obligation as sureties, he is not in the first instance to be proceeded against for the whole debt, but only for his share of it, if his co-sureties and co-obligees are solvent[5]. This is commonly known as the benefit of division, or *beneficium divisionis*. If the suit should be brought in a different country from that where the contract or obligation is made, the right of discussion or divi-

---

1 Burgundus, Tract. 2, n. 24, 25.

2 Ante, § 264; Henry on Foreign Law, 51, 52; 2 Boullenois, Observ. 46, pp. 475, 476; P. Voet, De Stat. § 9, ch. 2, § 10.

3 1 Domat, b. 3, tit. 4, § 2, art. 1; Dig. lib. 46, tit. 1, l. 68; Novell. tit. 4, cap. 1.

4 Pothier on Oblig. n. 407—414; Code Civil of France, art. 2021—2026.

5 Pothier on Oblig. n. 415—427; Code Civil of France, art. 2026.

sion would still belong to the surety, as an incident to his contract, although it did not exist by the law of the place where the suit was brought (*lex fori*)[1]. The converse proposition would be equally true[2]. Such also is the lien of a vendor, upon a real estate sold for the payment of the purchase-money, according to the law of England; the lien given for the purchase-money upon goods or merchandise sold, by the civil law and by the law of some modern countries[3]; the right of stoppage *in transitu* of the vendor of goods, in case of the insolvency of the purchaser in the course of the transit[4]; the lien of a bottomry bond on the thing pledged; the lien of mariners on the ship for their wages; the priority of payment *in rem*, which the law sometimes attaches to peculiar debts or to particular persons. In these and like cases, where the lien or privilege is created by the *lex loci contractûs*, it will generally, although not universally, be respected and enforced in all places where the property is found, or where the right can be beneficially enforced by the *lex fori*[5]. And on the other hand, where the lien or privilege does not exist in the place of the contract, it will not be allowed in another country,

---

[1] 3 Burge, Comm. on Col. and For. Law, pt. 2, ch. 20, pp. 765, 766; Carroll *v.* Waters, 9 Martin, R. 500.

[2] Ibid.; Ante, § 316 *b*.

[3] 1 Domat, Civil Law, b. 4, § 2, n. 3; 3 Burge, Comm. on Col. and For. Law, pt. 2, ch. 20, pp. 770, 771. See, as to Lien of Vendor on Real Estate, Gilman *v.* Brown, 1 Mason, R. 219—221; Warrender *v.* Warrender, 9 Bligh, R. 127.—It seems that a lien created by the lex loci contractus may be dissolved and extinguished not only according to the law of that place, but also by any act done in a foreign country, which, according to the law of that country, would work such dissolution or extinguishment. See Post, § 351 *a*—§ 351 *d*.

[4] Post, § 401.

[5] See 3 Burge, Comm. on Col. and For. Law, pt. 2, ch. 20, pp. 770, 771, 779; Post, § 401; Fœlix, Conflit des Lois, Revue Etrang. et Fran. tom. 7, (1840), § 33, pp. 227, 228. The latter says,—"Nous avons vu, que la régle suivant laquelle les meubles sont régis par la loi du domicile de celui, à qui ils appartiennent, repose sur le rapport intime entre les meubles et la personne du propriétaire, sur une fiction légale, qui les répute exister au lieu

although the local law, where the suit is brought, would otherwise sustain it[1]. Thus, if goods are purchased in England by a citizen of Louisiana, no lien or privilege will exist for the unpaid price in case of his insovlency, although the law of Louisiana allows it in common cases; because it is not given by the law of the place of the contract, (England)[2]. Nor would there seem to be any just ground of doubt, that a bottomry bond would, generally, be held valid *in rem* in all commercial countries, if the lien is good by the law of the place of the contract[3].

§ 322 *c.* We have said that such liens will be generally, although not universally respected; for, although the foreign jurists generally assert the doctrine, they do not universally agree in it as to all kinds of property, or under all circumstances. Some of them take a distinction between personal

---

du domicile de ce dernier. De là il suit, que cette régle ne peut s'appliquer, qu'aux circonstances, ou actes dans lesquels les meubles n'apparaissent, que comme un accessoire de la personne; par exemple: en cas de succession ab intestat, de dispositions de dernière volonté ou entre-vifs (telles que les contrats de mariage exprès ou tacites). La régle est sans application à tous les cas où les meubles n'ont pas un rapport intime avec la personne du propriétaire: par exemple, lorsque la propriété de meubles est réclamée, et contestée, lorsqu'on invoque la maxime, qu'en fait de meubles possession vaut titre; lorsqu'il s'agit d'exercer des priviléges ou des voies d'exécution sur les meubles, d'en prohiber l'aliénation, d'en prononcer la confiscation, ou de déclarer une succession mobilière en déshérence au profit du fisc, ou enfin d'interdire l'exportation des meubles. Dans tous ces cas, il faut appliquer la loi du lieu, où les meubles se trouvent effectivement: car la dite fiction cesse par le fait. Par rapport aux priviléges sur les meubles, Hert soutient l'opinion contraire, en faisant observer, que toutes les questions de privilége sur les meubles doivent être décidées dans le lieu du domicile du débiteur, par suite de la connexité des causes. Cette opinion revient à celle, qui attribue à la loi du domicile son effet sur l'universalité des biens d'un individu. Nous réfuterons cette opinion au no 37 ci-après. Ce que nous venons de dire des meubles s'applique non-seulement aux meubles corporels, mais aussi aux meubles incorporels; il y a identité de raison." See Post, § 401—403.

[1] Ibid.

[2] Whiston *v.* Stodder, 8 Martin, R. 95, 134, 135.

[3] Post, § 323, note 2.

or movable property, and real or immovable property; giving effect to the former, according to the law of the place of the contract, and insisting, as to the latter, that no lien can exist except it is founded in the law of the place where the property is situated (*rei sitæ*). Others make no distinction whatsoever in respect to such lien or privilege between movable property and immovable property; some holding that in both cases the *lex loci contractûs* is equally to govern; and some that in both cases the *lex rei sitæ* is equally to govern[1].

§ 322 *d.* Rodenburg notices these distinctions, and says, that, although by the laws of some countries where a marriage is had, the wife has an hypothecation upon all the property of her husband, for her dotal portion, (*pro restitutione dotis*), yet a question may arise, whether this hypothecation can reach the property of the husband situate in another country where no such law exists, or the law is to the contrary. He remarks, also, that Christinæus has stated that the affirmative has been maintained in many decisions. But Rodenburg adds, that he dares not affirm that they have been rightly made. *Quæ tamen an recte se habeant, affirmare non ausim.* And he thinks that the hypothecation does not extend to the real property of the husband situate in a foreign country; because the statute is real, and cannot have an extra-territorial authority. *Consequenter non tacita seu legalis hypotheca adstringit bona alia, quam quibus lex poterit imperare; ea nimirum, quæ legislatoris territorio sunt supposita, cujus solius loci legis est, tanquam statuti realis, realem in rebus effectum producere, cum alterius judicis auctoritas non efficiat hypothecam*[2].

---

1 See some of these opinions cited in Rodenburg, De Divers. Stat. tit. 2, ch. 5, § 16; 2 Boullenois, App. pp. 49—51; Matthæus, De Auctionibus, lib. 1, ch. 21, nn. 35—41, pp. 294—299; 1 Boullenois, Observ. 30, pp. 833, 834, 838; Fœlix, Conflit des Lois, Revue Etrang. et Franç. 1840, tom. 7, § 32—34, pp. 222—228.

2 Rodenburg, De Divers. Stat. tit. 2, ch. 5, § 16; 2 Boullenois, App.

§ 323. But the recognition of the existence and validity of such liens by foreign countries is not to be confounded with the giving them a superiority or priority over all other liens and rights, justly acquired in such foreign countries under their own laws, merely because the former liens in the countries where they first attached, had there by law or by custom such a superiority or priority. Such a case would present a very different question, arising from a conflict of rights equally well founded in the respective countries[1]. This very distinction was pointed out by Mr. Chief Justice Marshall, in delivering the opinion of the Court in an important case. His language was: "The law of the place where a contract is made is, generally speaking, the law of the contract; *i. e.* it is the law by which the contract is expounded. But the right of priority forms no part of the contract. It is extrinsic, and rather a personal privilege, dependent on the law of the place where the property lies, and where the Court sits, which is to decide the cause[2]. And the doctrine was on that occasion expressly applied to the case of a contract made in a foreign country with a person resident abroad[3].

§ 324. Huberus has also laid down the same qualifying doc-

---

p. 47. See also Rodenburg, tit. 2, ch. 5, § 5—7; 2 Boullenois, App. pp. 37, 38. See also Post, § 324, 325; 1 Boullenois, 684, 685.

[1] Post, § 324, 327, 524—527, 582; Fœlix, Conflit des Lois, Revue Etrang. et Franç. tom. 7, 1840, § 33, pp. 227, 228.—This question might arise even in relation to a bottomry bond, which by the law of most maritime countries has a priority or preference over most other claims, in case of a deficiency of the proceeds to satisfy all claims. In such a case, if the local law of the country where the bond was sought to be enforced, differed as to such priority or preference from that of the place where the bond was made and executed, it might be a very nice question, which ought to prevail; and would therefore probably be disposed of upon consideration of local and municipal policy. But upon this subject we shall have occasion to speak hereafter. See Post, § 401—403.

[2] Harrison *v.* Sterry, 5 Cranch, 289, 298. See Ogden *v.* Saunders, 12 Wheaton, R. 361, 362.

[3] Ibid.

trine. Foreign contracts are to have their full effect here, provided they do not prejudice the rights of our own country or its citizens. *Quatenus nihil potestati aut juri alterius imperantes ejusque civium præjudicetur*[1]. Or, as he has more fully expressed it in another place: *Effecta contractuum certo loco initorum, pro jure loci illius alibi quoque observantur, si nullum inde civibus alienis creatur præjudicium in jure sibi quæsito; ad quod potestas alterius loci non tenetur, neque potest extendere jus diversi territorii*[2]. Hence he adds, that the general rule should be thus far enlarged. If the law of another country is in conflict with that of our own State, in which also a contract is made, conflicting with a contract made elsewhere, we should in such a case rather observe our own law than the foreign law[3]. *Ampliamus hanc regulam tali extensione. Si jus loci in alio imperio pugnet cum jure nostræ civitatis, in qua contractus etiam initus est, confligens cum eo contractu, qui alibi celebratus fuit; magis est, ut jus nostrum, quam jus alienum, servemus*[4]. And he puts several cases to illustrate the rule. By the Roman law, and the law of Friezeland, an express hypothecation of movable property, oldest in date, is entitled to a preference or priority even against a third possessor. But it is not so among the Batavians. And, therefore, if, upon such an hypothecation, the party brings a suit in Holland against such third possessor, his suit will be rejected; because the right of such third possessor cannot be taken away by the law of a foreign country[5].

§ 325. He also puts another case. In Holland, if a marriage contract is privately or secretly made, stipulating that the wife shall not be liable for debts contracted solely

---

1 Huberus, De Conflict. Leg. tom. 2, lib. 1, tit. 3, § 2.

2 Id. tom. 2, lib. 1. tit. 3, § 11; Post, § 525.

3 Ibid.

4 Ibid.; Ante, § 239.

5 Ibid. See also Rodenburg, De Divers. Stat. tit. 2, ch. 5; 2 Boullenois, App. p. 47; 1 Boullenois, pp. 683, 684.

by the husband, it is valid, notwithstanding it is to the prejudice of subsequent creditors. But in Friezeland such a contract is not valid, unless published; nor would the ignorance of the parties be an excuse, according to the Roman law and equity. If the husband should contract debts in Friezeland, on a suit there, the wife would be held liable for a moiety thereof to the Friezian creditors, and could not defend herself under her private dotal contract; for the creditors might reply, that such a private dotal contract had no effect in Friezeland, because it was not published. But the Batavian creditors, contracting in Holland, although suing in Friezeland, would not be entitled to a similar remedy; for, in such a case, the law of the place of their contract alone, and not the law of both countries, would come under consideration[1]. The author was probably here treating of a case where the debts were contracted in Friezeland, after the husband and wife had removed their domicil there; or, at least, if there was no change of domicil, where the property of the parties, to be affected by the marriage contract, was situate in Friezeland. Under any other aspect, it would be difficult to maintain the doctrine.

§ 325 *a.* Huberus in another place asserts a similar doctrine. A creditor (says he) on account of a bill of exchange, exercising his right in due time, has a preference in Holland to all other creditors against the movable property of his debtor. The debtor has property of the same kind in Friezeland, where no such law obtains. The question is, whether such a creditor will be preferred there to all other creditors? Certainly; not since, by the law there, the right

---

[1] Huberus, lib. 1, tit. 3, § 11.—Huberus adds: Et hoc prevalet apud nos, in contractibus heic celebratis, ut nuperrimè consultus respondi. The sense of this passage in Huberus is mistranslated in the note to 3 Dallas, R. 375. The translator has translated the words, *in contractibus heic celebratis,* "where the marriage was contracted here," and *jus loci contractûs,* "the law of the place where the marriage was contracted;" whereas the author in this clause is manifestly referring to the contracts (debts) of the respective creditors.

of the creditors is established. *Creditor ex causa Cambii, jus suum in tempore exercens, præfertur apud Batavos omnibus aliis creditoribus in bona mobilia debitoris. Hic habet ejusmodi res in Frisia, ubi hoc jus non obtinet. An, ibi, creditor etiam præferetur aliis creditoribus? Nullo modo; quoniam heic creditoribus vi legum hic receptarum jus pridem quæsitum est*[1].

§ 325 *b*. The same doctrine is adopted by Hertius. After remarking, that in this matter of preferences and privileges of creditors, the statute laws of particular countries have changed the common (the civil) law; in answer to the question, what law ought to govern in such cases, he says: If the controversy respects immovables, the law of the country of the *situs rei* is, without doubt, to govern. But in respect to movables, if the question arises in cases of contract, or of *quasi* contract, the law of the place of the contract is to be examined. But in as much as the preference arises from some peculiar law or privilege, it ought not to be extended to the prejudice of the State where the debtor resides, and his movables are deemed to be collected. In the conflict (*concursus*) of creditors, the law of the place of domicil of the debtor ought to be observed. *Enimvero, quia antelatio ex jure singulari vel privilegio competit, non debet in præjudicium illius civitatis, sub qua debitor degit, et res ejus mobiles contineri censentur, extendi. Ad jura igitur domicilii debitoris, ubi fit concursus creditorum, et quo omnes cujuscunque generis lites adversus illum debitorem propter connexitatem causæ traduntur, regulariter respiciendum erit*[2].

§ 325 *c*. Rodenburg has discussed this subject at large, in relation to the liens, the privileges, and the priorities of creditors in cases of insolvency, and in other cases, where his property, movable or immovable, is situated in different

---

[1] Hub. lib. J. P. Univer. cap. 10, § 44, cited 1 Hertii Opera, De Collis. Leg. § 4, n. 64, p. 150, (edit. 1737); Id. p. 211, (edit. 1716); Post, § 627.

[2] 1 Hertii Opera, De Collis. Leg. § 4, n. 64, p. 150, (edit. 1737); Id. p. 211, (edit. 1716).

countries, and is not sufficient to satisfy all his debts. This is commonly known by the name of *concursus creditorum*, and the privilege or priority itself by the name of the *jus prælationis*. It may be useful to present a brief sketch of the substance of his remark, and his conclusions on the subject. In respect to the property of debtors in different countries, he says, that jurists have distinguished between those things which concern the form and order of the suit, and those which concern the decision or matter of the suit. The suit is to be according to the law of the place where it is instituted. As for example, if the debtor's property is to be taken in satisfaction of a judgment, the execution and sale thereof are to be according to the law of the place where the goods are situated, or where they are taken upon the judgment. But if the debtor has become bankrupt, or notoriously insolvent, so that there is no further opportunity for the seizure of his movables, or for execution thereon, all the creditors being in the same condition, the question as to their rights and privileges should be discussed or litigated in the place of his domicil; for it is properly a question as to the proceedings in the suit, *de litis ordinatione*[1]. But a different rule prevails as to the decision and merits of a suit; and the rights of the creditors, in respect to the priority of their debts upon the property of the debtor, ought to be measured according to the law of the place where it is really situated, or is presumed to be situated[2].

§ 325 *d.* In respect to movable property, as it is always supposed to be in the place of the domicil of the debtor, (for all effects not having a fixed location are presumed to adhere to his person,) it is the law of his domicil which ought to decide the rights of creditors as to such movables. This rule will prevail where the goods are in his possession, unless

---

[1] Rodenburg, De Div. Stat. tit. 2, ch. 5, § 16; 2 Boullenois, App. pp. 47, 48; 1 Boullenois, 684, 685.

[2] Rodenburg, ibid; 2 Boullenois, App. p. 48; 1 Boullenois, 685; Post, § 524—527, 582.

indeed a creditor has by his diligence, according to the laws of the place, acquired a superior right by an execution over them; for he will then retain that privilege, since it is not so much founded in the quality of the debt, as that the creditor has by his diligence gained a priority; so that this privilege being attached to the formalities regulating the execution, it ought therefore to be regulated by the law of the place of execution. And besides, the Judge, who puts the creditor judicially in possession of property, seized within his jurisdiction, is regarded as acting in the name of the debtor; so that it may be deemed affected by the same reasoning, as if the debtor himself had given it in pledge to the creditor in the place where the property is seized[1].

§ 325 *e*. Rodenburg afterwards puts the case of a merchant, having different shops of trade in different places; and he says that the question has been put, whether in such a case the creditors in each place are entitled to be paid out of the property there in trade, or the whole property is to be divided among all the creditors. Some jurists maintain the affirmative. But others, with whom Rodenburg agrees, hold, that the whole should be distributed among the creditors generally, in cases of insolvency[2].

§ 325 *f*. Rodenburg then puts the case of a contract made in a foreign country, not being the domicil of the debtor, by whose laws a preference is granted to creditors by promissory notes of hand; and he says that it might seem, in such a case, that the law of the place where the contract is made, ought to govern; for that is the law by which the obligation of contracts is ordinarily expounded and governed[3]; *Eo quod obligationes dirigi soleant a loco, ubi contrahuntur*[4]. But after stating that Mascardus has

---

1 Rodenburg, Ibid.; 2 Boullenois, App. p. 48; 1 Boullenois, 685.

2 Rodenburg, De Div. Stat. tit. 2, c. 5, § 16; 2 Boullenois, App. p. 49, 50; 1 Boullenois, 687, 688.

3 Rodenburg, De Div. Stat. tit. 2, c. 5, § 16; 2 Boullenois, App., pp. 50; 1 Boullenois, 688.

4 Ibid.

expressed a similar opinion, following Decianus, he adds, that it is a nearer approach to the truth, to say that the law of the place of the contract ought not to govern; because that law can determine only the greater or less extent of the engagements of the debtor, and concerns only the contracting parties, who, having contracted in another place than that of their domicil, are presumed to have referred to the laws of that place, the form, the obligation, the mode, the condition, and whole nature of the contract. *Verum non esse respiciendum locum contractûs vero proprius est; utpote, qui eo duntaxat pertineat, quo vel arctius, vel remissius ex contractu suo teneatur ipse debitor, adeoque spectatur, quoad ipsos contrahentes, quod eo ipso, quod alio in loco contractum celebrant, ad ejusdem leges, formam, vinculum, modum, conditionem, totam denique negotii naturam, sui respectu, componunt*[1]. He proceeds to render the reasons of his opinion, that this preference of creditors constitutes no part of the law of the contract, obligatory in other countries, and says: Moreover, what does not arise from the act of man, but simply from the authority of the law, of which sort all privileges of preference among creditors are, it should be said that the authority of the legislator has no effect upon property not subjected to him when the controversy respects the interest of third persons, or of other creditors who have not contracted in that place, and who consequently have submitted themselves to the laws of that place. Besides, it is manifest that we do not exercise these sorts of privileges upon the persons of debtors; because, being directed upon the property, they have their place properly among all the creditors. *Cæterum, si quid non ab actu hominis, sed a potestate legis proficiscitur, cujusmodi sunt prælationis privilegia omnia, dicendum est vim legislatoris nullam esse in bona sibi non subjecta tertii respectu, seu cre-*

---

[1] Rodenburg, De Div. Stat. tit. 2, c. 5, § 16; 2 Boullenois, App. p. 50; 1 Boullenois, 688.

ditorum aliorum, qui inibi nullum gesserint negotium, nec legibus loci istius se submiserint. Ad hæc constat privilegiis istis non agi in debitoris personam, utpote quæ in res directa, locum habeant inter creditores[1].

§ 325 *g*. Rodenburg farther insists, that the same rule applies when the debtor has changed his domicil to another country. If, in the country of his original domicil where the contract is made, there would be a privilege thereby created upon the movables of the debtor, and he afterwards removes to another country where no such privilege exists, Rodenburg says, that although it might seem that the privilege ought still to continue on his movables in his old domicil, yet the true rule is, that the law of the new domicil is to prevail; for movables are governed by the law of the domicil. *Nec aliud de eo debitore dicendum est, qui in loco illo privilegii domicilium foverit tempore celebrati contractus; quamvis enim videri possit jus illud prælationis creditori per leges loci domicilii in rebus mobilibus legitime quæsitum, subsecutâ domicilii mutatione non debere amitti; mobilia tamen, in quibus prioris domicilii lege tenuit prælationis privilegium, traductis aliò domesticis laribus, traducuntur quoque in leges novi domicilii, eâque lege administrantur; mutatione enim domicilii mutatur et mobilium conditio eorum, quæ in manum aliis tradita non sunt, etiam dispendio tercii*[2].

§ 325 *h*. In regard to immovables, Rodenburg holds, that if there is either an express or tacit hypothecation or lien by the law of the domicil of the debtor, which is not equally allowed by the law of the *situs* thereof, the law of the *situs* or situation is to govern; and that the creditor will in vain seek to assert any right of priority or privilege; for, as no man has authority expressly to create such a charge under a foreign law by a judicial proceeding, so neither can the

---

[1] Rodenburg, De Div. Stat. tit. 2, c. 5, § 16; 2 Boullenois, App. p. 50; 1 Boullenois, 688; 3 Burge, Comm. on Col. and For. Law, Pt. 2, c. 20, pp. 770, 771.

[2] Ibid.

foreign law itself exert such an authority, since real statutes have no operation beyond the territory where they are enacted. *Tandem ut ad immobilia transeam. Fac, jus tacitæ seu legalis hypothecæ non obtinere idem in loco rei sitæ, quod obtinet in loco domicilii debitoris, dicendum frustra est esse creditorem, qui hujusmodi hypothecæ obtentu prioritatem sibi asseruerit; cum æque atque expressim facto hominis, coram uno judicio, hypothecæ nexu devinciri nequeunt alterius territorii bona, ita nec legis ullius potestas est afficere prædia extera; quod statuta realia territorium non egrediantur*[1]. The result, therefore, of the doctrine of Rodenburg, seems to be, that the proper *forum* to decide upon all questions of the priorities and preferences of creditors is the place of the domicil of the debtor; and that the law of that place, and not the law of the place of the contract, is to govern in all cases of such priorities and preferences, in respect to movables situated in his place of domicil. But as to movables situate elsewhere, as well as to immovables, the law *rei sitæ* is to govern; although, to prevent confusion and inconvenience, the administration and adjudication thereof in all cases, is to be by the *forum* or tribunal of the debtor's domicil[2].

---

[1] Rodenburg, De Div. Stat. tit. 2, c. 5, § 16; 2 Boullenois, App. pp. 50, 51; 1 Boullenois, 689, 690; Id. Observ. 30, pp. 818—875.

[2] 1 Boullenois, Observ. 30, pp. 818—820.—As the work of Rodenburg is rarely found in our libraries, and the subject here discussed is of great practical consequence, it may be useful to subjoin the whole passage in this note. "Pergamus quærere ulterius, creditoribus de prælatione contendentibus, quod jus cujusque loci oporteat inspicere. Primum utamur vulgatâ D D. distinctione, quâ separantur ea, quæ litis formam concernunt ac ordinationem, ab iis, quæ decisionem aut materiam. Lis ordinanda, secundùm morem loci, in quo ventilatur. Ut, si judicati exequendi causâ bona debitoris distrahantur, qui solvendo sit, executio peragatur eo loci, ubi bona sita sunt, aut in causam judicati capiuntur. Sin cesserit foro debitor, aut propalam desierit esse solvendo, ut isti mobilium capioni, aut ulli omninò executioni non sit ultra locus, factâ jam omnium creditorum conditione pari, disputatio de privilegiis, aut concursu creditorum veniat instituenda, ubi debitor habuerit domicilium. Unde cùm apud nos relictis fortunis solum vertisset debitor obæratus, ac res ejus sitas in Hollandia venum proscriberet curator, creditores Hollandi, apud Provinciæ suæ Curiam venditioni intercedentes, causâ ibidem

§ 325 *i*. Boullenois in commenting upon Rodenburg says, that every hypothecation or privilege upon property is to be

---

ventilatâ, tulerunt repulsam: audito in eo curatore, quod apud nos super universis debitoris facultatibus, adeoque et pretio ex venditione illa redigendo, ab uno eodemque Judice peragenda decidendaque sit creditorum contentio: ex communi scribentium placito. Ob manifestam quoque causæ continentiam, ne super creditorum Jure à diversis Judicibus dissonæ sententiæ pronuntientur. Hæc de litis ordinatoriis. Aliud fere à præcedentibus obtinere dixeris in ejusdem decisoriis: Jus enim creditorum super prioritate in bonis debitoris demetiri oportet à loco, ubi distracta bona sita sunt, vel esse, intelliguntur. Et quidem de mobilibus si quæratur, cùm semper ibi esse existimentur, ubi creditor [debitor] fovet domicilium, cujus ossibus vagæ hæ res intelliguntur adhærere, utique ex lege ejusdem domicilii discutienda causa creditorum est. Hæc ita nisi forsan executio directa sit in ejus debitoris mobilia, qui adhuc in possessione suorum bonorum sit, feret enim tum creditor diligentiæ ac vigilantiæ suæ prœmium, si quod eo nomine loci mores, ubi in causam judicati ceperit mobilia, præ aliis creditoribus ipsi indulserint; quod privilegium illud non tam proficiscatur ex credito, quàm ex actu ipso executionis, quâ alios creditor prævertit, adeoque hæc res tanquam concernens exequendi ordinem, legem accipiat à loco, ubi illa peragitur, ac præterea pignus illud judiciale ita constituens Judex in bonis, apud se in causam judicati captis, dicitur supplere vicem debitoris; ut perinde res habeatur, ac si ipse debitor bona illa eo loci pignori tradidisset. Hæc ita si in uno loco debitoris sit domicilium." Again; "Fac foris contractum celebratum, ubi per mores ejusdem loci Jus prælationis inter chiro-grapharios competit, locus videri posset attendendus esse contractæ obligationis: eo quod obligationes dirigi soleant à loco, ubi contrahuntur. Verùm non esse respiciendum locum contractûs vero proprius est: utpote qui eo duntaxat pertineat, quo vel arctiùs, vel remissiùs ex contractu suo teneatur ipse debitor, adeoque spectetur quoad ipsos contrahentes, quod *eo ipso, quod alio in loco contractum celebrent*, ad ejusdem leges, formam, vinculum, modum, conditionem, totam denique negotii naturam, sui respectu, componunt. Cæterùm si qui non ab actu hominis, sed à potestate legis proficiscitur, cujusmodi sunt prælationis privilegia omnia, dicendum est vim Legislatoris nullam esse in bona sibi non subjecta tertii respectu, seu creditorum aliorum, qui inibi nullum gesserint negotium, nec legibus loci istius se submiserint. Ad hæc constat privilegiis istis non agi in debitoris personam, utpote quæ in res directa, locum habeant inter creditores. Ecquid autem Juris est alieno Judici circa res sibi non suppositas, dispendio tertii, qui apud se non contraxit? Nec est, quod retorserit creditor suum non minus spectari oportere, atque debitoris domicilium. Constat quippe, qui cum alio contrahit, non esse vel debere esse conditionis ejus ignarum. Ut nihil imputetur ei, qui in mobilibus à loco domicilii debitoris sua mensus est privilegia, ad quem locum palam est mobilia pertinere: cùm culpa non vacent alii, qui privilegium sibi assumpserint à potestate Legislatoris alieni, cui de mobilibus disponendi

deemed a real right (*jus ad rem*, or *jus in re*). An action without any hypothecation or privilege is purely personal. The existence of a real right must depend either upon local ordinances, or upon the law of the *situs* of the property; and if the law of the *situs* differs from the ordinances of the place where the parties create the hypothecation or privilege, in allowing or disallowing such an hypothecation or privilege, the law of the *situs* must govern. In regard to movables, they are presumed to have their *situs* in the place of the domicil of the owner; and if the law of that domicil gives a privilege upon them, that privilege ought to be regarded in

---

nullum Jus est. Nec aliud de eo debitore dicendum est, qui in loco illo privilegii domicilium foverit tempore celebrati contractûs: quamvis enim videri possit Jus illud prælationis, creditori per leges loci domicilii in rebus mobilibus legitime quæsitum, subsecutâ domicilii mutatione non debere amitti; mobilia tamen, in quibus prioris domicilii lege tenuit prælationis privilegium, traductis aliò domesticis laribus, traducuntur quoque in leges novi domicilii, eâque lege administrantur: mutatione enim domicilii mutatur et mobilium conditio eorum, quæ in manum aliis tradita non sunt, etiam dispendio tertii: quo argumento, alia quanquam in specie, usus est Senatus Parisiensis, apud Chopin. Et huc spectat quod Burgundus tradit, mobilia sequi personam, hoc est (inquit) in domicilio ejus existere, et non aliter quàm cum domicilio transferri. Tandem ut ad immobilia transeam. Fac Jus tacitæ, seu legalis hypothecæ non obtinere idem in loco rei sitæ, quod obtinet in loco domicilii debitoris, dicendum frustra esse creditorem, qui hujusmodi hypothecæ obtentu prioritatem sibi asseruerit: cum æque atque expressim facto hominis, coram uno judicio, hypothecæ nexu devinciri nequeunt alterius territorii bona, ita nec legis ullius potestas est afficere prædia extera: quod Statuta realia territorium non egrediantur, ut supra tractatum est. Ita si Hollandus, cui generaliter bona debitoris coram quocunque Hollandiæ judicio, hypothecæ data sunt, apud nos cum reliquis creditoribus experiatur de prælatione, pro futura erit ei hypotheca in bonis, in quacunque Hollandiæ parte, extra districtum Amstelodamensem, sitis; non autem in bonis suppositis territorio nostratium, quibus nulla subsistit hypothecæ datio, nisi pacta coram judice rei sitæ. Contra cùm apud Hollandos hypotheca generalis extinguatur alienatione, non juvabitur creditor moribus nostris, quibus res ita obligata ad emptores transit cum suo onere. Consimilitèr, si teneat alibi consuetudo, ut in bonis debitoris concurrant creditores, nullâ habitâ ratione hypothecarum quale statutum profert Florentinum Straccha. Ex lege loci rei sitæ dirimenda creditorum contentio." Rodenburg, De Div. Statut. tit. 2, c. 5, § 16; 2 Boullenois, App. pp. 47—51.

every other place in which those movables may be found[1]. Boullenois in this respect adopts the language of Lautenburg. *In rebus mobilibus observari debent jura illius loci, in quo illorum dominus, vel creditor habet domicilium, etiam quando agitur de concursu et prælatione creditorum*[2]. In regard to immovables, Boullenois adopts the doctrine, that all preferences and privileges thereon are real, and are therefore governed by the law *rei sitæ*[3].

§ 325 *k*. John Voet has treated this question with great fulness. In respect to priorities and privileges in cases of hypothecations, he insists, that, as to movable property, the law of the domicil of the debtor ought to govern the order thereof, as well, because all movables are understood to be in the place where the owner lives, and are to be governed by the law of that place; as because all creditors who ought to bring their suit in the tribunal where the property is (*forum rei*), are deemed in their contracts to have had reference to the place of domicil of the debtor, since in that place the debtor, as the principal *forum*, ought to be sued; and also, because if the laws of the place where the contract is made, or of the *forum* in which the controversy respecting the conflict of rights and preferences between creditors, are to be observed, inexplicable difficulties will arise, or notorious absurdities will be fallen into; of which he proceeds to give some illustrations. But in respect to immovables, he holds, that the law of the place of the *situs* ought to govern in all questions of priorities and privileges. *Immobilia regenda esse jure loci, in quo sitæ sunt*[2].

---

1 1 Boullenois, Observ. 30, pp. 832—834.

2 Id. p. 834.

3 Ibid.

4 J. Voet, Ad Pand. lib. 20, tit. 4, n. 38, p. 904.—The whole passage deserves to be cited. "In questione, cujus loci statuta in prælatione tum hypothecariorum tum chirographariorum privilegio munitorum spectari debeant, dicendum videtur secundum fundamenta generalia in tit. de constitut. Princip. parte alterâ, de statutis proposita. In mobilibus debitoris bonis illum observari oportere prælationis ordinem, qui in loco domicilii debitoris probatus

§ 325 *l.* Matthæus holds, in a great measure, the same opinion, and has discussed the subject at large. The whole passage is too long for insertion in this place; but a moderate extract will present his views in a very clear manner.

---

est; tum quia mobilia omnia, ubicunque existentia, illic domino suo præsentia esse intelliguntur, ac propterea isto quoque jure regenda sunt; tum quia creditores omnes, qui sequi in agendo debent forum rei, etiam maxime locum domicilii in contrahendo respexisse videntur, quippe in quo præcipue debitor, velut in foro præprimis competente, conveniendus est; tum denique, quia, si leges vel loci in quo contractum est, vel fori in quo de creditorum prælatione ac concursu disputatur, observandas censueris, aut inexplicabilibus te difficultatibus implicaturus es, aut ad notabiles delapsurus absurditates. Etenim, si contractuum singulorum loca spectari debere contendas, explicari non poterit, quid fieri debeat, si in Hollandiâ, Frisiâ, Angliâ, Italiâ, Hispaniâ diversi per eundem debitorem contractus initi sint, quarum regionum unaquæque diversis ex parte, quin et subinde contrariis de protopraxiâ legibus utitur, dum in Angliâ aut Hollandiâ contrahens ex legibus Anglicanis aut Hollandicis præferri desiderabit ei, qui in Frisiâ contraxit; hic vero ex Frisiæ legibus contrariis potior esse velit eo, qui in Hollandiâ vel Angliâ effecit sibi devinctum debitorem. Quod si locum, ubi mobilia proscribuntur, et judicium concursus inter creditores agitatur, spectandum existimes, quasi distributio pecuniarum inter creditores pars et sequela executionis sit, (posito, quod alibi, quam in loco domicilii postremi debitoris obærati mobilia vendi et lis de protopraxiâ agitari possit, cujus contrarium apud nos nunc obtinere, supra x. t. num. 12. dictum est) absurdum illud inde sequeretur, quod tunc non mobilium tantum sed et immobilium intuitu leges loci, in quo judicium de protopraxiâ agitur, observandæ forent; cum non minus distributio pecuniæ ex immobilibus, quam ex mobilibus, redactæ dici deberet executionis sequela aut pars; atque ita fieret, immobilia non ex lege situs regi, sed incerti juris subesse dispositioni, prout in hoc vel illo loco, diversis juribus utente, contentio fuerit inter creditores instituta de prælatione. Quinimo, posito illo jure, quod judicium universale concursus creditorum in eo loco ventilari debeat, in quo debitor, cum moreretur aut foro cederet, domicilium habuit, esse in arbitrio debitoris positum, ut migrando de loco in locum creditores non privilegiatos efficeret privilegiatos, hypothecam legalem faceret aliis nasci, aliis interire, prout aliud atque contrarium domicilii prioris aut rei sitæ legibus jus in novissimi domicilii loco viguerit: quod in immobilibus loco certo alligatis, nec arbitrio domini situm mutantibus, ferendum non est; sed potius (cum jam ad immobilia nos deduxerit ratiocinium) in immobilium pretio inter creditores secundum cujusque privilegium distribuendo servandæ erunt leges locorum illorum, in quibus immobilia singula existunt, idque convenienter regulæ in tit. de constit. Princip. parte alterâ, de statutis num. 12. firmatæ, ac dictanti, immobilia regenda esse jure loci, in quo sita sunt."

Speaking of movables, he says: *Quantum igitur ad res mobiles attinet, tametsi omnes sint ejusdem generis atque naturæ, motu tamen et quiete discriminari possunt. Earum enim aliæ nullo certo loco dispositæ, huc illuc feruntur trahunturve; veluti merces in itinere deprehensæ, et ut hodie fieri solet, arresto retentæ: aliæ verò certo loco dispositæ quiescunt; veluti instrumentum et supellex, quam paterfam. prædiorum instruendorum gratia in provinciam misit: item feræ bestiæ, et pisces, et reliqua animalia, quæ in fundis habentur fœturæ et propagationis gratia. Quæcunque ejus generis deprehenduntur, ut certo loco prædiove affixæ non sint, in iis haud dubiè superior definitio observanda est. Cum enim maxime in motu sint, ac incertis quasi sedibus vagentur, nihil propius est, quam ut in disputatione de prærogativa creditorum spectemus domicilium debitoris. Quæ vero loco affixæ, aut certis possessionibus attributæ sunt, eæ naturam prædiorum sequuntur, ejusque provinciæ esse censentur, in quâ prædia sita sunt. Unde dicendum videbatur, in his rebus spectandas esse leges ejus loci, ubi prædia sita sunt, non ubi domicilium debitor habet*[1]. Again; referring to objections, which might made, he says: *Illud etiam objici poterat definitioni nostræ: In contractibus spectandas esse leges ejus loci, ubi contractum est, vel in quem solutio destinata est: his enim legibus contrahentes ultrò subjecisse se intelliguntur. Igitur in creditorum quoque contentione, non semper leges domicilii, sed si alibi contractum sit, loci contractûs sunt observandæ. Respondeo: Si ex contractu agatur, spectari quidem leges ejus loci, ubi contractum est, non tamen in omnibus controversiis. Etenim, si de solennibus quæratur, si de loco, de tempore, et modo obligationis, tum quidem locum contractûs observamus: sin de materia obligationis, seu de rebus, quæ in eam deducuntur, ejus loci habenda ratio est, ubi res sitæ sunt. Situm autem cum dicimus, prædia denotamus: hæc enim propriè sita dicuntur, non etiam res mobiles. In disputatione verò creditorum de*

---

[1] Matthæus, De Auctionibus, lib. 1, ch. 21, n. 35, 36, p. 295.

prærogativa, quo minus locum contractus spectemus, ipsa quodammodo rerum natura impedimento est. Quid enim si obæratus cum multis contraxerit, et variis quidem in locis, vario ac diverso jure utentibus: veluti Romæ, Lugduni, Antuerpiæ, Amstelodami, Dantisci, Genuæ, etc. qui poterit spectari locus contractûs, et cujus potissimum loci leges spectabis citra manifestam aliorum creditorum injuriam? At locum domicilii debitoris possis observare citra cujusquam injuriam, dum omnes cujuscunque gentis aut nationis cum aliquo debitore contrahentes, domicilium ejus spectasse, ac fortunam judiciorum ibidem experiri voluisse videantur. Postremò, opponi poterat, non tam domicilium debitoris spectandum esse, quam eum locum, ubi bona proscribuntur. Executionis enim seu pars, seu appendix, et sequela, videtur esse illa distributio pecuniarum inter creditores. Communi autem calculo doctorum traditur, in executione facienda spectandum eum locum ubi executio sit. Verùm hunc obicem ita facilè removebimus, si cogitaverimus communem illam sententiam de ordine et solennibus executionis duntaxat loqui, non etiam de ipsa creditorum contentione et causa, quæ inter eos vertitur: hæc enim incidit quidem in executionem, ab ordine tamen executionis separata est. In iis autem, quæ ad causæ decisionem pertinent, non illicò locum judicii, sed antiquiorem aliquem, puta domicilii, interdum contractus, aliquando situm rei spectamus. Instari poterat: Si ad decisionem causæ pertinet disputatio illa creditorum, jam sententia hæc premetur alio argumento: Nempe, quod in decisoriis litis observandæ sint leges ejus loci, ubi contractum est. Sed respondetur, hoc tum procedere, cum inter creditorem et debitorem lis vertitur: cum verò plures creditores ejusdem debitoris de prærogativa disputant, locum domicilii debitoris spectamus; quia locum contractus citra injuriam aliorum spectare per rerum naturam non possumus: nullo certe modo, cum idem debitor qui variis in locis negotiari solet, habuerit variarum gentium atque locorum creditores: puta Italos, Gallos, Belgas, Germanos, Hispanos, etc. Hic enim constituere non possis, cujus potissimum loci leges sint spectandæ: ut autem omnium simul locorum leges atque mores spectentur, rerum natura non patitur[1].

§ 325 *m.* And then, referring to immovables, he says: *Quantum ad res immobiles attinet, videndum, an rectè separaverimus hypothecam à privilegio: ita ut in æstimandis viribus hypothecæ spectemus eum locum, ubi prædium situm est; in privilegio inter hypothecarios exercendo, domicilium debitoris? Argumentum enim, quo usi sumus, infirmius videtur: Privilegium concernit personam: igitur domicilium debitoris in eo spectandum. Quasi verò non sit duplex privilegiorum ratio: ita ut alia quidem personæ, alia rei seu causæ data sint. Deinde, non videtur illa necessaria consecutio: privilegia personam concernunt: igitur personam comitantur, quocunque locorum commigraverit. Etenim illo duntaxat jura, quæ personæ qualitatem aliquam imprimunt, comitari personam solent: veluti si quis minor, fatuus, prodigus, infamis, declaretur: Vitium enim hoc perdurat, et quocunque locorum te contuleris, circumferes tecum notam illam et qualitatem in loco domicilii tibi impressam. At privilegium, quod personæ conceditur, nullam qualitatem personæ imprimit, nullam notam inurit: comitari ergò personam non poterit in eam provinciam, in qua fortè privilegium cessat. Sed imprimis illud obstat, quod privilegium detur quidem personæ, tamen in bonis debitoris exercendum. Ut autem in prædiis debitoris in alia provincia sitis exerceam privilegium, non possunt mihi tribuere ii, qui in loco domicilii debitoris jura condunt: quippe quorum jurisdictioni ager alterius territorii subjectus non sit. Mobilia duntaxat, quia personam comitantur, jurisdictioni eorum subjecta videntur, quocunque in loco reperiantur. Itaque si mulier nupserit in Frisia, ubi dotes sunt, dotiumque privilegia: distrahantur mariti prædia in Gelria, Hollandia, Trajecti, ubi ne dotes quidem veræ sunt, nedum dotium privilegia: non videtur mulier inter hypothe-*

---

[1] Matthæus, De Auctionibus, lib. 1, c. 21, n. 37—40, pp. 296—298.

carios habitura privilegium, quod haberet, si in Frisia sita prædia distraherentur. Valdè enim absurdum sit, velle hypothecariis eam præferri, quam ne numerant quidem Gelri inter hypothecarios. His de causis generalius concludendum, sive de viribus hypothecæ, sive de privilegio inter hypothecarios exercendo loquamur, in prædiis spectandas esse leges ejus loci, ubi prædia sita sunt[1].

§ 325 *n.* Mævius adheres to the same rule in cases of movables, that is to say, that the law of the domicil of the debtor is to govern in all cases of preferences and privileges[2]. D'Argentré adopts the same opinion: *Quare statutum de bonis mobilibus vere personale est, et loco domicilii judicium sumit; et quodcunque Judex domicilii de eo statuit, ubique locum obtinet*[3]. Burgundus may also fairly be presumed to hold the like opinion. *De cetero mobilia ibi esse dicemus, ubi quis instruxit domicilium; et ideo quodcumque Judex domicilii de iis statuerit, ubique locorum obtinet, sive, quod persona ibi est, aut esse, semper intelligitur, sive quod ibi rerum suarum summam collocavit. Et sic intelligendum est, quod dicimus mobilia sequi personam, hoc est, in domicilio ejus existere, et non aliter quam cum domicilio transferri. Nec refert, eadem bona in loco domicilii reperiantur, an non*[4]. Many other jurists assert the some doctrine[5]. Still, however, (as has been already intimated), all foreign jurists are not agreed in this doctrine, at least not without many modifications thereof[6].

§ 325 *o.* But whatever may be the differences of opinion among them, as to the operation of the rights of preference or privilege of creditors upon movable property, situate in fact in a foreign country, there seems to be a great pre-

---

[1] Matthæus, De Auctionibus, lib. 1, c. 21, n. 41, pp. 298, 299.

[2] Mævius, Ad Jus Lubesense, lib. 3, tit. 1. art. 11, n. 23—35.

[3] D'Argentré, De Briton. Leg. 218, gloss. 6, n. 30, p. 654.

[4] Burgundus, Tract. 2, n. 21, p. 113.

[5] 1 Boullenois, Observ. 30, pp. 834, 835, 840.

[6] Ante, § 322 *b*, 322 *c*.

ponderance of authority, although certainly not a universal agreement, in respect to immovable property, in favour of the doctrine, that the law of the place *rei sitæ* ought to prevail, as to the denial or allowance of such preferences and privileges [1]. Paul Voet expressed the general sense, when he said: *Vero immobilia reguntur locorum statutis, ubi sita; etiam quoad ea, si de æstimanda hypotheca, aut de privilegiis inter hypothecarios agatur, non inspiciendus erit locus domicilii, vel debitoris, vel creditoris, verum locus statuti, ubi jacent* [2]. An easy example may illustrate the importance of the distinction. Suppose a contract made in Massachusetts for the sale of lands lying in New York, by whose laws the vendor has a lien for the unpaid purchase-money, and by the laws of Massachusetts there would in such a case be no lien, if the land were in Massachusetts; the question would then arise, whether any lien attached on such a contract on the land. According to the opinions of the foreign jurists already referred to, the law of the *rei sitæ*, and not the law of the place of the contract, would attach upon the contract; and consequently, a lien for the unpaid purchase-money would exist on the lands in New York, although no such lien would exist in Massachusetts under, or in virtue of the contract [3].

§ 326. Lord Ellenborough has laid down a doctrine essentially agreeing with that of Huberus. "We always import (says he), together with their persons, the existing relations of foreigners, as between themselves, according to the laws of their own countries; except indeed where those laws clash with the rights of our own subjects here, and one or other of the laws must necessarily give way, in which case our own is entitled to the preference. This having been long settled in principle, and laid up among our ac-

---

1 Ante, § 322—325 *m*; Post, § 362—373.

2 P. Voet, De Stat. § 9, c. 2, n. 8, p. 267, (edit. 1715); Id. p. 322, (edit. 1661).

3 See Gilman *v.* Brown, 1 Mason, R. 219—221; S. C. 4 Wheat. R. 255.

knowledged rules of jurisprudence, it is needless to discuss it farther [1]." The Supreme Court of Louisiana have adopted a little more modified doctrine, coinciding exactly with that of Huberus: "That, in a conflict of laws, it must often be a matter of doubt which should prevail; and that, whenever that doubt does exist, the Court which decides will prefer the law of its own country to that of the stranger [2]. And, if the positive laws of a State prohibit particular contracts, from having effect according to the rules of the country where they are made, the former must prevail [3]."

§ 327. Mr. Chancellor Kent has laid down the same rule in his Commentaries, as is stated by Huberus and Lord Ellenborough, and has said: "But on this subject of conflicting laws it may be generally observed, that there is a stubborn principle of jurisprudence that will often intervene, and act with controlling efficacy. This principle is, that when the *lex loci contractûs* and the *lex fori*, as to conflicting rights acquired in each, come in direct collision, the comity of nations must yield to the positive law of the land. *In tali conflictu magis est, ut jus nostrum, quam jus alienum, servemus* [4]." Mr. Burge has expressed his own exposition of the same doctrine in the following terms: "It may be stated generally, that with respect to contracts of which movable property is the subject, the law of the place in which the contract is made, will in some respects exclusively prevail, although the contract is to be performed in another; and that in those respects in which it does not prevail, the law of the place where the contract is to be performed must be adopted. But this conclusion is subject to some qualifications and exceptions. If a right which is claimed as resulting from the contract, or if an act or dis-

---

1 Potter *v.* Brown, 5 East, R. 124, 130.

2 Mr. Justice Porter in the case of Saul *v.* His Creditors, 17 Martin, R. 596.

3 Id. pp. 586, 587.

4 2 Kent, Comm. Lect. 39, p. 461, 3rd edit.

position affect the interest of third parties as the creditors of the owner, resort must be had to the law of his domicil to determine whether that right exists, and whether he was competent to do the act or make the disposition. A preference claimed by a creditor on the estate of his debtor, by virtue of the contract, and a disposition made by a debtor which might be void against his creditors, are instances of this exception. The law of a foreign country is admitted, in order that the contract may receive the effect which the parties to it intended. No State, however, is bound to admit a foreign law, even for this purpose, when that law would contravene its own positive laws, institutions, or policy, which prohibit such a contract, or when it would prejudice the rights of its own subjects[1]."

§ 327 *a*. A question involving considerations of this nature, came recently before the Supreme Court of Louisiana. It was a suit brought in Louisiana upon a bottomry bond of a peculiar character, given by the owner of a steam-boat in Cincinnati (Ohio), and pledging the vessel for the repayment of a sum of money and interest lent to the owner for a year. The steam-boat had in the intermediate time been sold in Kentucky to a purchaser, with notice of the lien, and she was at New Orleans at the time of the suit brought; and the object thereof was to enforce the hypothecation or lien created by the bond. Various objections were taken in the defence, and among them was the objection that no lien was created in such a case, by the laws of Louisiana where the suit was brought. Mr. Justice Porter, in delivering the opinion of the Court on this occasion, said: "But a more formidable objection has been raised against the regularity of the proceedings. The statutes and jurisprudence of Louisiana, it is contended, only confer the privilege of sequestration to enforce liens given by its laws;

---

[1] 3 Burge, Comm. on Col. and For. Law, Pt. 2, ch. 20, pp. 778, 779; Id. p. 770. See also Fœlix, Conflit des Lois, Revue Etrang. et Fran. tom. 7, (1840), § 33, pp. 227, 228.

and that in aid of which this remedy was extended here, was not one that had any force, or conferred any privilege in our State, though it might have that effect in the country where it was made."....."The objection now taken raises a distinction in cases so circumstanced, between remedies before and after judgment; and we confess we are unable to see any solid grounds on which it can rest. If it be true, as we apprehend it is, that the Court can and should enforce the personal obligation which a party, not a citizen of the State, may have entered into in another country, and that on the judgment so rendered, the foreign creditor could obtain the benefit of all writs of execution which an inhabitant of Louisiana might resort to against a domestic debtor, then we can see no good ground for refusing the auxiliary process in the first instance; whether it be an order to arrest the person of the debtor and hold him to bail, or a writ to seize the property brought within the jurisdiction of a Court, if it be the subject of contest. Both seem to rest on the same principles. And a familiar illustration of the common received opinion on this subject, may be given in the case of attachments, which are almost every day resorted to in aid of the foreign creditor against the foreign debtor; and yet there is nothing in our law more expressly giving that remedy to the stranger than there is in the case of sequestration." After taking notice, that by the laws of Ohio it had been found that the bond created a lien on the steamboat, the learned Judge proceeded to say: "If the steamboat, then, had remained within the State of Ohio, the evidence satisfies us the plaintiffs could have had a lien on her. But the main difficulty in the cause still remains. She was sold in the State of Kentucky, under a decree of one of the Courts of that State, and purchased by the defendant at the sale. It is admitted on all hands that this sale was legal and regularly made, and the question is not, what was the effect of the lien in the country where the contract was made, nor in that where it is sought to be enforced; but what effect it had in the State where the defendant acquired title to the property." He then examined the laws of Kentucky on the subject, and concluded in the following words: "The State of Kentucky, we presume, gives effect to liens existing on property brought there from another country, on the principle of comity, which we have already noticed; and we must also presume, until the contrary be shewn, that she admits them with the same limitation which other States do; namely, that they shall not work an injury to her own citizens. To ascertain whether they do or not, recurrence must be had to her laws and policy in relation to contracts made within her limits; for we take the true principle in such cases to be, that the foreign creditor who has a lien, should have no greater or no less privilege than the domestic creditor. If, for example, the laws of Kentucky required no record to be made of liens given on personal properly within the State, she would not require registry on the part of the stranger who came there to enforce a mortgage on property on which he had a lien in another country; for if she did, she would neither carry the contract into effect according to the law of the country where it was made, nor according to her own. If this be true, whatever time is given to the domestic creditor to record his lien, should be given to him who comes from another State with one, if his lien be recognised as valid when enregistered, and his prayer to enforce it be admitted, as we are told by the testimony it could be." The Court accordingly enforced the lien against the steam-boat[1].

§ 327 *b*. Another case, which may serve to illustrate the difficulty of laying down any universal rule on the subject of contracts, as to the incidents and rights which may attach to or against third persons, residing in different countries, may readily be stated, as it is one which may not infrequently occur in practice. By the law of England, if two policies are underwritten on the same ship or cargo for the

---

[1] Ohio Insur. Company *v*. Edmondson, 5 Louis. R. 295—305; Ante, § 244.

same voyage, to the full amount of the property at risk, it is treated as a double insurance, and each policy is valid, without any reference to the respective dates thereof. And in case of a loss, the insured may recover the whole loss from the underwriters on either policy at his own election; and they are then entitled to a contribution *pro ratâ* from the underwriters on the other policy [1]. Now, in France, no such rule of contribution exists; but the policy prior in date is, in case of a double insurance, to be first exhausted, and if that is sufficient to pay the whole loss, there is no right to recover the loss, or to exact contribution from the underwriters on the policy of a later date [2]. This also seems to be the general rule among most of the maritime nations of continental Europe [3]. Now, let us suppose that two policies of different dates are underwritten on the same ship or cargo, the one in France and the other in England, for an American owner, on the same voyage, each policy being for a sum equal to the full value of the property at risk, and there should be a total loss on the voyage; the question might arise whether the English underwriters were liable at all, if the French policy was prior in date; and also, whether, if liable, they could claim contribution from the French underwriters: and, conversely, the question might arise, whether, if the English policy was prior in date, the French underwriters were liable at all, and if liable, whether they could claim contribution from the English underwriters. No such case seems as yet to have undergone any judicial decision. But probably it would be held, that each contract was to be exclusively construed according to the obligations and rights

---

1 Park on Insur. ch. 15, pp. 280, 281, 5th edit.; 3 Kent, Comm. Lect. 48, pp. 280, 281, 3rd edit.; 1 Marsh. on Insur. ch. 4, § 4, p. 146, 2nd edit.; 2 Phillips on Insur. pp. 59, 60; 2nd edit.

2 3 Kent, Comm. Lect. 48, pp. 280, 281, 3rd edit.; Code de Commerce, art. 359, Ordin. of Louis 14th, 1681; 2 Valin, Comm. lib. 3, tit. 6, art. 23—25, pp. 72, 73.

3 1 Emérigon, Assur. ch. 1, § 7, p. 23; 1 Marsh. on Insur. ch. 4, § 4, p. 146, 2nd edit., note *a*.

created by the *lex loci contractûs* between the parties themselves, without any regard to the collateral rights and obligations, which might arise between the underwriters, if both contracts were made in the same country. If a different rule were adopted, there might be an entire want of reciprocity in its operation. Thus, if the French policy were prior in date, and a recovery were had thereon against the French underwriters, they might have contribution from the English underwriters; and yet, if a recovery were had against the English underwriters, they could not have contribution from the French underwriters. On the other hand, if the English policy were prior in date, the French underwriters might be exempted from all liability for the loss, or, if liable, might recover a contribution from the English underwriters; at the same time, that if a recovery were had against the English underwriters, they would not be entitled to any contribution against the French underwriters. However, this case is merely propounded as one, on which the author professes to have no fixed opinion, and is designed rather to awaken inquiry than to satisfy doubts[1].

§ 328. This subject will be resumed hereafter under other heads[2]. But the remarks of a learned Scottish Judge[3] may here be properly introduced as exceedingly pertinent to the present discussion. "The application of the *lex loci* to contracts, although general, is not universal. It does not take place where the parties, at the time of entering into the contract, had the law of another kingdom in view, or where the *lex loci* is in itself unjust, or *contra bonos mores*, or contrary to the public law of the State, as regarding the

1 In some of the present American policies, there is now what is commonly called a priority clause, similar in effect to the French law. The very question, therefore, may arise in the case of a double insurance by different policies in England, and in a State using the priority clause, or in the latter State, and a State which uses the common English policy, and is governed by its laws.

2 Post, § 401, 402, 423 *a*, 524—527.

3 Lord Robertson in the case of Mrs. Levett in Fergusson on Marr. and Div. 385, 397.

interests of religion or morality, or the general well-being of society."

§ 329. It may also be stated, although the proposition has been already incidentally considered, that, when a debt is contracted in a foreign country, it is not to be deemed exclusively payable there, unless there is in the contract itself some stipulation to that effect[1]. On the contrary, a debt contracted in a particular country, and not limited to a particular place of payment, is, by operation of law, payable every where, and may be enforced wherever the debtor or his property can be found[2].

§ 330. Having considered the principles applicable to the nature, validity, interpretation, and incidents and effects of contracts, we are next led to the consideration of the manner in which they may be discharged, and what matters upon the merits will constitute a good defence to them. I say upon the merits, for the objections arising from the law of the State where the suit is brought, (*lex fori*), such as the limitation of remedies, and the forms and modes of suit, will constitute a separate head of inquiry[3].

§ 331. And here the general rule is, that a defence or discharge, good by the law of the place where the contract is made or is to be performed, is to be held of equal validity in every other place where the question may come to be litigated[4]. John Voet has laid down this doctrine in the

---

1 Ante, § 272 *a*, 278 *a*, 295, 317; Don *v.* Lippmann, 5 Clark & Fin. R. 1, 12, 13.

2 See Blake *v.* Williams, 6 Pick. R. 286, 315; Ante, § 272 *a*, 317; Don *v.* Lippmann, 5 Clark & Fin. 1, 12, 13.

3 Post, § 524—527.

4 2 Bell, Comm. B. 8, ch. 3, § 1267, p. 692, 4th edit.; Id. p. 688, 5th edit.; 3 Burge, Comm. on Col. and For. Law, Pt. 2, ch. 21, § 7, pp. 874—886; Id. ch. 22, pp. 924—929. As to what will constitute a discharge in foreign countries, and especially by novation, by confusion, by set-off or compensation, by payment or consignation, and by relapse, see 3 Burge, Comm. on Col. and For. Law, Pt. 2, ch. 21, § 1—6, pp. 781—880. See also Bartsch *v.* Atwater, 1 Connect. R. 409.

broadest terms. *Si adversus contractum aliudve negotium gestum factumve restitutio desideretur, dum quis aut metu, aut dolo, aut errore lapsus, damnum sensit contrahendo, transigendo, solvendo, fidejubendo, hereditatem adeundo, aliove simili modo ; recte interpretes statuisse arbitror, leges regionis in quâ contractum gestumve est, id, contra quod restitutio petitur, locum sibi debere vindicare in terminandâ ipsâ restitutionis controversiâ ; sive res illæ, de quibus contractum est, et in quibus læsio contigit, eodem in loco, sive alibi sitæ sint. Nec intererit utrum læsio circa res ipsas contigerit, veluti pluris minorisve, quam æquum est, errore justo distractas, an vero propter neglecta solennia in loci contractûs desiderata. Si tamen contractûs implementum non in ipso contractûs loco fieri debeat, sed ad locum alium sit destinatum, non loci contractûs, sed implementi, leges spectandas esse ratio suadet; ut ita secundum cujus loci jura implementum accipere debuit contractus, juxta ejus etiam leges resolvatur*[1]. Casaregis in substance lays down the same doctrine[2]; and Huberus throughout implies it[3], as indeed does Dumoulin[4].

§ 331 *a*. Burgundus says : *Idem ergo de solutionibus dicendum; scilicet, ut in omnibus quæ ex ea sunt, aut inde oriuntur, aut circa illam consistunt, aut aliquo modo affinia sunt, consuetudinem loci spectemus, ubi eandem implendam convenit. Itaque ex solutione sunt solemnia, valor rei debitæ, pretium monetæ; ex solutione oriuntur præstatio apochæ, antigraphi, similiaque. Affinia solutioni sunt, præscriptio, oblatio rei debitæ, consignatio, novatio, delegatio, et ejusmodi*[5]. *Ea, vero, quæ ad complementum vel executionem contractus spectant, vel absoluto eo superveniunt, sola a statuo*

---

[1] J. Voet, Ad Pand. lib. 4, tit. 1, § 29, p. 240.

[2] See Casaregis, Disc. 179, § 60, 61.

[3] Huberus, lib. 1, tit. 3, § 3, 7; J. Voet, De Statut. § 9, c. 2, § 20, p. 275, (edit. 1715); Id. pp. 332, 333, (edit. 1661).

[4] 2 Boullenois, Observ. 46, p. 462; Molin. Comm. ad. Cod. lib. 1, tit. 1, l. 1; Conclus. de Stat. tom. 3, p. 554, (edit. 1681).

[5] Burgundus, Tract. 4, n. 27, 28, pp. 114—116.

loci dirigi, in quo peragenda est solutio[1]. Many other foreign jurists maintain the same doctrine[2].

§ 332. In England and America the same rule has been adopted, and acted on with the most liberal justice[3]. Thus infancy, if a valid defence by the *lex loci contractûs*, will be a valid defence every where[4]. A tender and refusal good by the same law, either as a full discharge or as a present fulfilment of the contract, will be respected every where[5]. Payment in paper money, bills, or in other things, if good by the same law, will be deemed a sufficient payment every where[6]. And on the other hand, where a payment by negotiable bills or notes is, by the *lex loci*, held to be conditional payment only, it will be so held, even in States where such payment under the domestic law would be held absolute[7]. So, if by the law of the place of a contract (even although negotiable) equitable defences are allowed in favour of the maker, any subsequent indorsement will not change his rights in regard to the holder[8]. The latter must take it *cum onere*[9].

§ 333. The case of an acceptance of a bill of exchange in a foreign country affords another illustration. Although by our law it is absolute and binding in every event; yet if

---

[1] Burgundus, Tract. 4, n. 29, p. 116.

[2] 3 Burge, Comm. on Col. and For. Law, Pt. 2, ch. 21, § 7, pp. 874—876.

[3] 2 Kent, Comm. Lect. 39, p. 459, 3rd edit.; Potter *v.* Brown, 5 East, 124; Dwarris on Stat. Pt. 2, pp. 650, 651; 2 Bell, Comm. § 1267, pp. 691, 692, 4th edit.; Id. p. 688, 5th edit.

[4] Thomson *v.* Ketcham, 8 John. R. 189; Male *v.* Roberts, 3 Esp. R. 163.

[5] Warder *v.* Arell, 2 Wash. Virg. R. 282, 293, &c.

[6] Warder *v.* Arell, 2 Wash. Virg. R. 282, 293; 1 Brown, Ch. R. 376; Seabright *v.* Calbraith, 4 Dall. 325; Bartsch *v.* Atwater, 1 Connect. R. 409.

[7] Bartsch *v.* Atwater, 1 Connect. R. 409. See other cases cited, 3 Burge, Comm. on Col. and For. Law, Pt. 2, ch. 21, § 7, pp. 876—878.

[8] Ante, § 317.

[9] Ory *v.* Winter, 16 Martin, R. 277. See also Evans *v.* Gray, 12 Martin, R. 475; Chartus *v.* Cairnes, 16 Martin, R. 1.

by that of the foreign country it is merely a qualified contract, it is governed by that law in all its consequences[1]. Acceptances are deemed contracts in the country where they are made; and the payments are regulated by the law thereof[2].

§ 334. But although the general rule is clear as above stated, that a discharge by the law of a place where a contract is made, is a discharge every where; yet there are exceptions to the rule which every country will enforce or not, according to its own discretion and sense of justice[3]. Thus, where a contract was made in England between two Danish subjects, one of whom was domiciled in England; and afterwards, during a war between England and Denmark, the Danish government confiscated the debt, and required it to be paid by the debtor who was then in Denmark, and he paid it accordingly; the English Court of King's Bench, on a suit brought in England after the peace, by the creditor against the debtor, held that the payment to the Danish government was no discharge; although it would have been so by the laws of Denmark, upon the ground that such a confiscation was not justified by the law of nations[4].

§ 335. The most important, or at least most frequent, cases of discharges of contracts occurring in practice, are those of discharges arising from matters *ex post facto;* such

---

1 Burrows *v.* Jemimo, 2 Str. R. 733; S. C. 2 Eq. Abridg. 525. See Van Cleff *v.* Terasson, 3 Pick. R. 12.

2 Lewis *v.* Owen, 4 B. & Ald. 654; 5 Pardessus, § 1495; Ante, § 307, 317.

3 Post, § 337.

4 Wolf *v.* Oxholme, 6 M. & Selw. R. 92. See Post, § 348—351.—It is wholly unnecessary here to consider, whether the confiscation of debts by an enemy is conformable or not to the law of nations. That is a point belonging to the public law of nations, and underwent very grave discussions in England, in the case in 6 Maule & Selw. 92, as well as in the American courts, during the late war with Great Britain. See the Emulous, 1 Gallison, R. 563; S. C. on Appeal, Brown *v.* United States, 8 Cranch, R. 110.

as a discharge from the contract upon the subsequent insolvency or bankruptcy of the contracting party. And here the general rule is, that a discharge from the contract according to the law of the place where it is made, or where it is to be performed, is good every where, and extinguishes the contract[1]. This doctrine was fully recognised in the English law by Lord Mansfield (and it doubtless had a much earlier existence) in a formulary of language, which has been since often quoted as a general axiom of jurisprudence. "It is a general principle (said he) that where there is a discharge by the law of one country, it will be a discharge in another[2]." The expression is too broad, and should have the qualification annexed, which the case before him required, and which has been uniformly understood, viz. that it is a discharge in the country where the contract was made or was to be performed. And so it was interpreted by Lord Ellenborough in a much later case. "The rule (said he) was well laid down by Lord Mansfield, in Ballantine *v.* Golding, that what is a discharge of a debt in the country where it was contracted, is a discharge of it every where[3]." This doctrine is also firmly established, and generally recognised in America[4]. By some Judges the doctrine

---

1 2 Kent, Comm. Lect. 37, pp. 392, 393, 3rd edit.; 2 Bell, Comm. § 1267, pp. 691—695, 4th edit.; Id. p. 688, 5th edit.; 1 Chitty on Comm. and Manuf. ch. 12, p. 654.

2 Ballantine *v.* Golding, 1 Coop. Bank. Laws, p. 347, 5th edit., p. 515, 4th edit.; 13 Mass. R. 7; 2 Bell, Comm. § 1267, pp. 691, 692, 4th edit.; Id. p. 688, 5th edit.

3 Potter *v.* Brown, 5 East, 124, 130. See Hunter *v.* Potts, 4 T. R. 182; Quin *v.* O'Keefe, 2 H. Bl. 553.

4 See on this point, Smith *v.* Smith, 2 John. R. 235; Hicks *v.* Brown, 12 John. R. 142; Van Reimsdyk *v.* Kane, 1 Gallis. R. 371; Blanchard *v.* Russell, 13 Mass. R. 1; Baker *v.* Wheaton, 5 Mass. R. 511; Watson *v.* Bourne, 10 Mass. R. 337; 4 Cowen, Rep. note, p. 515; Green *v.* Sarmiento, Peter's Cir. R. 74; M'Menomy *v.* Murray, 3 John. Ch. R. 435, 440, 441; Walsh *v.* Nourse, 5 Binn. R. 381; Sturgis *v.* Crowninshield, 4 Wheaton, R. 122; Ogden *v.* Saunders, 12 Wheaton, R. 213, 358; 2 Kent, Comm. Lect. 27, pp. 392, 393; Id. Lect. 39, p. 459, 3rd edit.; Atwater *v.* Townsend, 4 Connect. R. 47; Hempstead *v.* Reed, 6 Connect. R. 480;

has been put upon the implied consent of the parties in making the contract, that they would be governed as to all its effects by the *lex loci contractûs*[1]. By others it has been put upon the more firm and solid basis of the sovereign operation of the local law upon all contracts made within its sovereignty; and the indispensable comity which all other nations are accustomed to exercise towards such laws whenever they are brought into question, either as to contracts or to rights, or to property[2].

§ 336. The doctrine has been stated in a more general form by a late learned American Judge, who said: "It may be assumed as a rule affecting all personal contracts, that they are subject to all the consequences attached to contracts of a similar nature by the laws of the country where they are made, if the contracting party is a subject of, or resident in that country where it is entered into, and no provision is introduced to refer to the laws of another country[3]." This is not, perhaps, in strictness of language, entirely correct. There are many consequences flowing from contracts in the place where they are made, which do not accompany them every where, and are not of universal obligation[4]. Remedies are a consequence of contracts, when broken; but, as we shall hereafter see, they are governed by different rules from rights[5]. And the rights given by the law of the place of the contract, are not always deemed of universal obligation or validity. Marriage, for instance, is admitted to be a valid contract every where, when it is

---

Houghton *v.* Page, 2 New Hamp. R. 42; Dyer *v.* Hunt, 5 New Hamp. R. 401; 2 Bell, Comm. § 1267, pp. 691—693, 4th edit.; Id. p. 688, 5th edit.

[1] See ante, § 261; Blanchard *v.* Russell, 13 Mass. R. 1, 4, 5; Prentiss *v.* Savage, 13 Mass. R. 20, 23.

[2] Potter *v.* Brown, 5 East, R. 124; Ante, § 261.

[3] Mr. Chief Justice Parker, in delivering the opinion of the Court in the case of Blanchard *v.* Russell, 13 Mass. R. 1, 5.

[4] Ante, § 325—327.

[5] Post, § 556—575.

valid by the law of the place where it is celebrated[1]. But, as we have seen, all the consequences attached to marriage in one country, do not follow it into other countries[2]. In Scotland, a subsequent marriage legitimates children antecedently born; but this consequence has not as yet been (as we have seen) finally adjudged in England, to the extent of making such antenuptial children legitimate, so as to be entitled to inherit lands of their parents situate in England. *Adhuc sub judice lis est*[3]. So the indissolubility of marriage by the law of one country will not attach to it every where[4].

§ 337. And even in regard to common contracts of a different nature, the general rule as to the consequences of them must receive many qualifications and limitations, resulting from the public policy or the domestic laws of other States where they are sought to be enforced, and the right and duty of self-protection against unjust foreign legislation[5]. If, for example, a country where a contract was made, should, under the pretence of a general bankrupt act, authorize a discharge from all contracts made with foreigners, and should at the same time exclude the latter from all participation with domestic creditors in the assets; it cannot be presumed that such an act would be held a valid discharge in the countries to which such foreigners belonged[6]. And certainly the priorities and privileges annexed by the laws of particular States to certain classes of debts contracted therein, are not generally admitted to have the

---

1 Ante, § 111, 113, 121—125.

2 See ante, § 145—190; Fergusson on Marr. and Div. 359—361, 397, —399, 402, 414; Conway *v.* Beazley, 3 Hagg. Ecc. R. 639.

3 Doe dem. Birtwhistle *v.* Vardill, 5 B. & Cress. 438; S. C. 9 Bligh, R. 468; Ante, § 87, 93, 94; 1 Hertii Opera, De Collis. Leg. § 4, 15, p. 129, (edit. 1737); Id. pp. 183, 184, (edit. 1716).

4 Ante, § 215—230.

5 § Ante, § 325—327, 334.

6 Blanchard *v.* Russell, 13 Mass. R. 1, 6; Huberus, De Conflict. Leg. lib. 1, tit. 3, § 11.

same pre-eminence over debts contracted in another country which is called upon to enforce them[1]. Nor are the courts of any State under any obligation to give effect to a discharge of a foreign debtor, where under its own laws the creditor has previously acquired a right to proceed against his property within its own territory[2].

§ 338. When we speak of the discharge of a debt in the country where it is contracted, being a discharge thereof everywhere, care must be taken to distinguish between cases, where by the *lex loci contractûs* there is a virtual or direct extinguishment of the debt itself; and where there is only a partial extinguishment of the remedy thereon. By the bankrupt laws of England, and by the corresponding insolvent laws of some of the United States, an absolute discharge from all rights and remedies of the creditors is provided for as part of the system; and, therefore, the whole obligation of the contract is deemed *ipso facto* extinguished[3]. But there are insolvent laws, and other special systems, both in Europe and America, which fall short of this extent and operation. In some cases, the person only is liberated from future imprisonment and responsibility; in others, particular portions of property only are exempted: and in others, again, a mixed system, embracing some postponed or modified liabilities both of the person and property prevails[4].

§ 339. Now, in all these cases, where there is not any positive extinguishment, or any virtual extinguishment of

---

[1] See ante, § 322—327; Huberus, De Conflict. Leg. lib. 1, tit. 3, § 11.

[2] Tappan *v.* Poor, 15 Mass. R. 419; Le Chevalier *v.* Lynch, Doug. R. 170. But see Hunter *v.* Potts, 4 T. R. 182; S. P. 2 H. Bl. 402; Ante, § 325—327.

[3] See 2 Kent, Comm. Lect. 37, pp. 389—402, 3rd edit.; 3 Burge, Comm. on Col. and For. Law, Pt. 2, ch. 22, pp. 886—929.

[4] See 1 Domat, Civ. Law, B. 4, tit. 5, § 1; Morris *v.* Eves, 11 Martin, R. 750. See Mather *v.* Bush, 16 John. R. 424, note; 2 Bell, Comm. ch. 5, § 1162—1164, pp. 563—567, 4th edit.; Id. pp. 580—597, 5th edit.; Phillips *v.* Allan, 8 B. & Cress. 477; 2 Kent, Comm. Lect. 37, pp. 389—404, 3rd edit.; 3 Burge, Comm. on Col. and For. Law, Pt. 2, ch. 22, pp. 886—904.

all rights and remedies of the creditors, the contract is not deemed to be extinguished; and, therefore, it may be enforced (as we shall hereafter more fully see) in other countries[1]. By the Roman law a *cessio bonorum* of the debtor was not a discharge of the debt, unless the property ceded was to the full sufficient for that purpose. It otherwise operated only as a discharge, *pro tanto,* and exonerated the debtor from imprisonment. *Qui bonis cesserint,* (says the Code), *nisi solidum creditor reciperit, non sunt liberati. In eo enim tantummodo hoc beneficium eis prodest, ne judicati detrahantur in carcerem*[2]. Huberus informs us, that in Holland, a *cessio bonorum* does not even exempt from imprisonment, unless the creditors assent. *Secundum jus nostrum cessio bonorum, invitis creditoribus, debitorem a carcere publico non liberat*[3]*;* and Heineccius proclaims the same as the law of some parts of Germany[4]. The Scottish

---

1 Post, § 340—352.

2 Cod. lib. 7, tit. 71, l. 1; 1 Domat, Civ. Law, B. 4, tit. 5, § 1, n. 1, 2. See Mather *v.* Bush, 16 John. R. 424, n. (b); 2 Bell, Comm. ch. 5, § 1162—1164, pp. 563—567, 4th edit.; Id. pp. 580—598, 5th edit.

3 Huberus, tom. 3, lib. 42, tit. 3, § 1—3, note; Ex parte Burton, 1 Atk. 255; M'Menomy *v.* Murray, 3 John. Ch. R. 442; Voet, Ad Pand. lib. 42, tit. 3, § 8; Le Roy *v.* Crowninshield, 2 Mason, R. 160.—Lord Mansfield is reported to have said in Ballantyne *v.* Golding, (1 Cooke, Bank. Laws p. 347, 5th edit., p. 515, 4th edit.) "That he remembered a case in Chancery, of a cessio bonorum in Holland, which is held a discharge in that country, and it had the same effect here." The case alluded to is most probably Ex parte Burton, (1 Atk. R. 255). The law of Holland is the reverse of what his lordship is here supposed to affirm, as the case in 1 Atk. R. 225, and the citations from Huberus and Voet establish. Whether the error is in the reporter, or in Lord Mansfield himself, may well be questioned. Mr. Henry has given a sketch of the present law of France, as to the cessio bonorum in cases of foreign contracts, which certainly has some peculiarities, not conforming to the general principles of international law adopted in other nations. Henry on Foreign Law, App. p. 250. See Pardessus, art. 1324—1328. The cessio bonorum of Scotland is (it seems) a mere discharge of the person. See 2 Bell, Comm. ch. 5, p. 563, &c. 4th edit.; Id. p. 580, &c. 5th edit.; Phillips *v.* Allan, 8 Barn. & Cress. 479.

4 Heinecc. Elem. Jur. Civ. Ad Pand. lib. 42, tit. 3, § 252, 254, p. 6; 3 John. Ch. R. 441, 442.

law conforms to the Roman Code in its leading outlines[1]; and the modern Code of France adopts the same system[2]. An Insolvent Act, or Bankrupt Act, or *cessio bonorum*, which only absolves the person of the debtor from imprisonment, but not his future property, or which only suspends remedies against either the one or the other for a limited period, is not to be deemed a discharge from the contract; and its operation is (as we shall presently see) purely intra-territorial[3].

§ 340. The general form in which the doctrine is expressed, that a discharge of a contract by the law of the place where it is made, is a discharge every where, seems to preclude any consideration of the question, between what parties it is made; whether between citizens or between a citizen and a foreigner, or between foreigners. The continental jurists recognise no distinction in the cases. The English decisions are understood to maintain the universality of the doctrine, whatever may be the allegiance or the country of the creditor[4]. And a like doctrine would seem generally to be maintained in America[5]. There are, how-

---

[1] Erskine, Inst. B. 4, tit. 3, § 26, 27; 2 Bell, Comm. ch. 5, § 1162—1164, pp. 563—567, 4th edit.; Id. p. 580, 5th edit.

[2] Code Civil of France, art. 1265 & 1270; Merlin, Répert. Cession de Biens.

[3] Tappan *v.* Poor, 15 Mass. R. 419; Morris *v.* Eves, 11 Martin, R. 730; Judd *v.* Porter, 7 Greenleaf, R. 337; Hinckley *v.* Morean, 3 Mason, R. 88; Titus *v.* Hobart, 5 Mason, R. 378; 1 Kent, Comm. Lect. 19, pp. 420, 422, 3rd edit.; 2 Bell, Comm. § 1162—1164, pp. 562, 567, 694, 4th edit.; Id. pp. 580—598, 5th edit.; Mason *v.* Haile, 12 Wheat. R. 370; 2 Kent, Comm. Lect. 37, pp. 394—401, 3rd edit.; Phillips *v.* Allan, 8 Barn. & Cress. 479; Ex parte Burton, 1 Atk. R. 255; Huberus, lib. 42, tit. 3, § 5; Heineccii Elem. ad Pand. tom. 3, Pt. 6, lib. 42, tit. 3, § 253; 3 Burge, Comm. on Col. and For, Law. Pt. 2, ch. 22, pp. 924—929; White *v.* Canfield, 7 John. R, 117; James *v.* Allen, 1 Dall. R. 188; Quin. *v.* O'Keefe, 2 H. Bl. 553; Le Roy *v.* Crowninshield, 2 Mason, R. 160; Wright *v.* Paton, 10 John. R. 300; Peck *v.* Hozier, 14 John. R. 346; Walsh *v.* Nourse, 5 Binn. R. 381.

[4] See Mason *v.* Haile, 12 Wheaton, R. 360; Potter *v.* Brown, 5 East, R. 124.

[5] See Robinson *v.* Bland, 1 W. Black. R. 258; Blanchard *v.* Russell, 13

ever, some cases in which a more limited doctrine would seem to be laid down; and which appear to confine it to cases of a discharge from contracts between citizens of the same State. Thus, in one case, it was laid down by the Supreme Court of Massachusetts, that if, when the contract was made, the promisee was not a citizen of the State where it was made, he would not be bound by the laws of such State in any other State; and, therefore, that a discharge there would not bind him or his rights[1]. In another case the same learned Court said, that a discharge of the contract can only operate where the law is made by an authority, common to the creditor and the debtor in all respects; where both are citizens and subjects[2]. But this qualification of the doctrine (which was only incidentally argued in those cases) was afterwards deliberately overruled by the same Court; and the general doctrine was established in its universality[3]. The qualification seems, however, again to have been asserted in a more recent decision of the same Court, upon grounds not very clearly defined, or perhaps not entirely satisfactory, unless the case is to be governed by the decisions of the Supreme Court of the United States upon the subject of discharges under insolvent laws, with reference to the Constitution of the United States[4]. It has been expressly

Mass. R. 1; 2 John. R. 235; 2 Kent, Comm. Lect. 37, p. 392, 393, 3rd edit.; Ory *v.* Winter, 16 Martin, R. 277; Sherill *v.* Hopkins, 1 Cowen, R. 103, 107.

1 Baker *v.* Wheaton, 5 Mass. R. 511.

2 Watson *v.* Bourne, 10 Mass. R. 337, 340.

3 Blanchard *v.* Russell, 13 Mass. R. 1, 10—12.

4 Braynard *v.* Marshall, 8 Pick. R. 194.—The case was a negotiable promissory note, made by A. in New York to B. or order; the note was afterwards indorsed to C. in Massachusetts, who sued A., the maker, there, and he pleaded his discharge under the insolvent laws of New York. On that occasion Mr. Chief Justice Parker, in delivering the opinion of the Court, declaring the discharge no bar to the suit, said: "The questions which arise out of the subject of state insolvent laws, and the effect of discharges under them, have been so long unsettled in this Commonwealth, owing to the unsatisfactory character of the decisions of the Supreme Court of the United States, which ought to govern cases of this nature, that we have waited with anxiety for a revision of all the cases by that high Court, and a final adjudication upon

denied by other learned State Courts[1]. In commenting upon some of the cases, in which, upon questions of discharge,

---

a subject so universally interesting, and hitherto involved in so much perplexity. The case of Ogden *v.* Saunders seemed, in its progress, to promise such a result; but, unhappily, on some of the points which the case presented, the law is left as uncertain as it was before. One thing, however, we understand to have been clearly decided by a majority of the justices of that court, and virtually by all, (as those, who admit no validity at all to such laws, may be considered as uniting with those who give them only a limited operation), which is, that discharges under such laws have no effect without or beyond the territory of the State where they are obtained, or against a party not a citizen of that State or where the suit shall be brought in a court of the United States, or of any state other than that in which the proceedings took place, notwithstanding the contract on which the discharge was intended to operate was entered into, and was to be performed in the State in which the discharge was granted. Now this law, thus settled, is binding upon this Court, as well on account of the nature of the question, which is peculiarly proper for the decision of the highest court of the nation, as because the case itself, unless restrained by the smallness of the sum in controversy, may be carried to that court by writ of error, and our judgment be reversed; it being a question, of which, by § 25 of the judiciary act of the United States (of September 24, 1789), that Court has jurisdiction. But even if we were not inclined to repose on the decision in Ogden *v.* Saunders, but considered ourselves at liberty to resort to general principles, we are disposed to think that the defence set up under the certificate in this case could not prevail. It does not come within the case of Blanchard *v.* Russell, in which the contract was made in New York by a citizen of that State, and was to be performed there, it not being transferable in its nature, being matter of account. A negotiable instrument made in New York and indorsed for a valuable consideration to a citizen of Massachusetts before an application for the benefit of the insolvent law, ought not to be discharged under the process provided by that law. It is a debt payable any where by the very nature of the contract, and it is a promise to whomsoever shall be the holder of the note. At the time of the defendant's application for a discharge, his creditor upon this note was a Massachusetts' man, and according to the case of Baker *v.* Wheaton, (5 Mass. R. 509), the certificate would be no bar to the action. The principle of this case was fully recognised and adopted in the case of Watson *v.* Bourne, (10 Mass. R. 337). Nor is there anything in the case of Blanchard *v.* Russell to controvert these decisions, whatever may have been said, arguendo, by the Judge who delivered the opinion. The contract in that case was in its nature to be performed in New York, and so was to be governed entirely by the laws of that State. The case before us is that of a negotiable promis-

---

[1] Ory *v.* Winter, 16 Martin, R. 277; Sherrill *v.* Hopkins, 1 Cowen, R. 103, 107.

considerable importance has been attached to the circumstance, that one or both of the parties were inhabitants of and domiciled in the state or country where the contract was made, the Supreme Court of New York have said: "All these cases stand upon a principle, entirely independent of that circumstance. It is that of the *lex loci contractûs*, that the place where the contract is made must govern the construction of the contract; and that, whether the parties to the contract are inhabitants of that place or not. The rule is not founded upon the allegiance due from citizens or subjects to their respective governments; but upon the presumption of law, that the parties to a contract are conusant of the laws of the country where the contract is made[1]."

§ 341. Under the peculiar structure of the Constitution of the United States, prohibiting the States from passing laws impairing the obligation of contracts, it has been decided that a discharge under the insolvent laws of the State where the contract was made, will not operate as a discharge of the contract, unless it was made between citizens of the same State. It cannot, therefore, discharge a contract made with a citizen of another State[2]. But this doctrine is wholly inapplicable to contracts and discharges in foreign countries, which must therefore be decided upon the general principles of international law.

§ 342. The converse doctrine is equally well established, viz. that a discharge of a contract by the law of a place

---

sory note, given in the first place by a citizen of New York to a person resident there, by whom it was immediately indorsed to a citizen of Massachusetts. The promisor became, immediately upon the indorsement, the debtor to the indorsee, who was not amenable to the laws of New York, where the application was made for relief under the insolvent law." See Ogden *v.* Saunders, 12 Wheaton, R. 213, 358; Post, § 341, 343, 344.

[1] Sherrill *v.* Hopkins, 1 Cowen, R. 102, 108.

[2] Ogden *v.* Saunders, 12 Wheaton, R. 358—369; Boyle *v.* Zacharie, 6 Peters, R. 348; 2 Kent, Comm. Lect. 37, pp. 392, 393, 3rd edit.; 3 Story, Comm. on Const. § 1384; 1 Kent, Comm. Lect. 9, pp. 418, 422, 3rd edit.

where the contract was not made or to be performed, will not be a discharge of it in any other country[1]. Thus it has been held in England, that a discharge of contract made there, under an insolvent act of the State of Maryland, is no bar to a suit upon the contract in the courts of England[2]. On that occasion Lord Kenyon said: "It is impossible to say that a contract made in one country is to be governed by the laws of another. It might as well be contended that, if the State of Maryland had enacted that no debts due from its own subjects to the subjects of England should be paid, the plaintiff would have been bound by it. This is the case of a contract lawfully made by a subject in this country, which he resorts to a court of justice to enforce; and the only answer given is, that a law has been made in a foreign country to discharge these defendants from their debts, on condition of their having relinquished all their property to their creditors. But how is that an answer to a subject of this country, suing on a lawful contract made here? How can it be pretended that he is bound by a condition to which he has given no assent, either express or implied[3]?" In America the same doctrine has obtained the fullest sanction[4]. It is also clearly established in Scotland[5].

---

1 See 2 Bell, Comm. § 1267, pp. 691—695, 4th edit.; Id. pp. 688—692, 5th edit.; Phillips v. Allan, 8 B. & Cress. 479; Lewis v. Owen, 4 Barn. & Ald. 654; 3 Burge, Comm. on Col. and For. Law, Pt. 2, ch. 22, pp. 924—929; Quelin v. Moisson, 1 Knapp, R. 265, note; Rose v. M'Leod, 4 S. & D. 311, cited 3 Burge, Comm. ubi supra, pp. 927, 928.

2 Smith v. Buchanan, 1 East, R. 6, 11.

3 Ibid; Lewis v. Owen, 4 Barn. & Ald. 654; Phillips v. Allan, 8 Barn. & Cress. 477.

4 Van Raugh v. Van Arsdaln, 3 Cain. R. 154; Frey v. Kirk, 4 Gill & John. R. 509; Green v. Sarmiento, Peters, Cir. R. 74; Le Roy v. Crowninshield, 2 Mason, R. 151; Smith v. Smith, 2 John. R. 235; Bradford v. Farrand, 13 Mass. R. 18; 2 Kent, Comm. Lect. 37, pp. 392, 393; Id. Lect. 39, pp. 458, 459, 3rd edit.; 2 Bell, Comm. § 1267, pp. 692, 693, 4th edit.; Id. pp. 688—692, 5th edit.; 3 Burge, Comm. on Col. and For. Law, pt. 2, ch. 22, pp. 924—929; Rose v. M,Leod, 4 S. & D. R. 311, cited in 3 Burge, Comm. 928, 929.

5 2 Bell, Comm. § 1267, pp. 692, 693, 4th edit.; Id. pp. 688—692, 5th edit.

§ 343. The subject of negotiable paper is generally governed by the same principles. Wherever the contract between the particular parties is made, the law of the place will operate, as well in respect to the discharge as to the obligation thereof. A nice question, however, has recently arisen on this subject, in a case already mentioned[1]. A negotiable note was made at New York between persons resident there, and was payable generally; and the payee subsequently indorsed the note to a citizen of Massachusetts, by whom a suit was brought in the State Court of the latter State against the maker. One point of the argument was, whether a discharge of the maker under the insolvent laws of New York operated as a bar to the suit? The case was decided upon another ground. But the Court expressed a clear opinion that it did not; and said: "It is a debt payable anywhere by the very nature of the contract; and it is a promise to whoever shall be the holder of the note." "The promisor became, immediately upon the indorsement, the debtor to the indorsee, who was not amenable to the laws of New York, where the discharge was obtained[2]."

§ 344. It is difficult (as has been already intimated) to perceive the ground upon which this doctrine can be maintained, as a doctrine of public law[3]. The Court admit that a debt contracted in New York and not negotiable, would be extinguished by such a discharge; although such a debt is by its very nature payable everywhere, as debts have no locality. As between the original parties, (the maker and the payee), the same result would follow. How then can the indorsement vary it? It does not create a new contract between the maker and the indorsee in the place of the indorsement. The rights of the indorsee spring from and

---

1 Ante, § 317, 340.

2 Braynard *v.* Marshall, 8 Pick. R. 194. See Ogden *v.* Saunders, 12 Wheaton, R. 358, 362—364; Ante, § 317—340.

3 Ante, § 340.

under the original contract, and are a component part of it. The original contract promises to pay the indorsee as much as the payee, and from the first of its existence. The indorsement is but a substitution of the indorsee for the payee; and it transfers over the old liability and creates no new liability of the maker [1]. If the indorsement created a new contract in the place where it was made, between the maker and the indorsee, then the validity, obligation, and interpretation of the contract would be governed by the law of the place of the indorsement, and not by that of the place where the note was originally made. It would not then amount to a transfer of the old contract, but to the creation of a new one, which, from a conflict of laws, not unusual in different States, would or might involve obligations and duties wholly different from, and even incompatible with, the original contract. Nay, the maker might, upon the same instrument, incur the most opposite responsibilities to different holders, according to the law of the different places where the indorsement might be made [2].

§ 345. Such a doctrine has never been propounded in any common law authority, nor ever been supported by the opinion of any foreign jurist. The same principle would apply to general negotiable acceptances, as to negotiable notes, for the maker stands in the same predicament as the acceptor. Yet, no one ever supposed that an indorsement after an acceptance ever varied the rights or obligations of the acceptor. It is, as to all persons who become holders, in whatever country, treated as a contract made by the acceptor in the country where such acceptance is made [3]. Yet, the acceptance being general, payment may be required in any place where the holder shall demand it. The other point, that the indorsement was to a citizen of another State, is equally inadmissible. The question is not whether he is

---

1 Pothier, De Change. art. 22; Ante, § 317.

2 Ante, § 314, 316, 317.

3 Id. 317.

bound by the laws of New York generally, but whether he can, in opposition to them, avail himself of a contract made under the sovereignty of that State, and vary its validity, obligation, interpretation, and negotiability, as governed by those laws. If the payee had been a citizen of Massachusetts, and the note had been made by the maker in New York, there could be no doubt that the contract would still be governed by the laws of New York in regard to the payee. What difference then can it make, that the indorsee is a citizen of another State, if he cannot shew that his contract has its origin there? In short, the doctrine of this case is wholly repugnant to that maintained by the same Court in another case, which was most maturely considered, and in which the argument in its favour was repelled. The Court there declared their opinion to be, that full effect ought to be given to such discharges, as to all contracts made within the State where they are authorized, although the creditor should be a citizen of another State [1].

§ 346. The Supreme Court of Louisiana have adopted the same reasoning, and held that, where a negotiable promissory note was made in one State, and was indorsed in another State to a citizen of the latter, the contract was governed by the law of the place where the note was made, and not by that of the place where the indorsement was made. "We see nothing," said the Court, "in the circumstance of the rights of one of the parties being transferred to the citizen of another State, which can take the case out of the general principle." "It is a demand made under an agreement (a note) entered into in a foreign State, and consequently the party claiming rights under it, must take it with all the limitations to which it was subject in the place where it was made, and that although he be one of our citizens [2]." This is certainly in conformity to what is deemed

---

[1] Blanchard v. Russell, 13 Mass. R. 1, 11, 12. See also Prentiss v. Savage, 13 Mass. R. 20, 23, 24; Ante, § 317, 340.

[2] Ory v. Winter, 16 Martin, R. 277; Sherrill v. Hopkins, 1 Cowen, R. 103; Ante, § 317, 340.

settled doctrine in England, as well as in some other States in America[1]. It was taken for granted by the Supreme Court of the United States to be the true doctrine in the case of a negotiable bill of exchange, in which the drawer's responsibility was supposed to be governed by the law of the place where the bill was drawn, notwithstanding an indorsement in another country[2]; and also by the Court of King's Bench in England, in a case in which the right to a Bank of England note was supposed to be governed by the law of England, notwithstanding a transfer of the same had been subsequently made in France[3].

§ 347. Pardessus has laid down a doctrine equally broad. He says, that it is by the law of the place where a bill of exchange is payable that we are to ascertain when it falls due, the days of grace belonging to it, the character of these delays, whether for the benefit of the holder, or of the debtor; in one word, everything which relates to the right of requiring payment of a debt, or the performance of any other engagement, when the parties have not made any stipulation to the contrary[4]. And it is of little consequence whether the person who demands payment is the creditor who made the contract, or an assignee of his right, such as the holder of a bill of exchange by indorsement. This circumstance makes no change in regard to the debtor. The indorsee cannot require payment in any other manner than the original creditor could[5]. And he applies this doctrine to the case of successive indorsements of bills of exchange

---

[1] See Blanchard *v.* Russell, 13 Mass. R. 12; Ogden *v.* Saunders, 12 Wheaton, R. 360; Potter *v.* Brown, 5 East, R. 123, 130.

[2] Slacum *v.* Pomeroy, 6 Cranch, R. 221.

[3] De la Chaumette *v.* The Bank of England, 9 Barn. & Cress. 208; S. C. 2 Barn. & Adol. 385; Post, § 353. See also 2 Bell, Comm. § 1267, pp. 692, 693, 4th edit.; Id. pp. 688—692, 5th edit. Quid si de literis cambii incidat questio, (says Paul Voet), quis locus spectandus? Is locus, ad quem sunt destinatæ, et ibidem acceptatæ. P. Voet, De Stat. § 9, c. 2, § 14, p. 271, (edit. 1715); Id. p. 327, (edit. 1661); Ante, § 317.

[4] Pardessus, Droit Comm. art. 1495, 1498—1500.

[5] Ibid.

made in different countries, stating that the rights of each holder are the same as those of the original payee against the acceptor [1]. He adds also, that the effects of an acceptance are to be determined by the law of the place where it has been made [2], that every indorsement subjects the indorser to the law of the place where it has been made, and that it governs his responsibility accordingly [3].

§ 348. Notwithstanding the principle, that a discharge of the *lex loci contractûs* is valid every where, and *vice versâ*, is generally admitted as a part of private international law; yet it cannot be denied, that any nation may by its own peculiar jurisprudence refuse to recognise it, and may act within its own tribunals upon an opposite doctrine [4]. But then, under such circumstances, its acts and decisions will be deemed of no force or validity beyond its own territorial limits. Thus, if a State should by its own laws provide that a discharge of an insolvent debtor under its own laws should be a discharge of all contracts, even of those made in a foreign country, its own courts would be bound by such provisions [5]. But they would or might be held mere nullities in every other country [6].

§ 349. And even in relation to a discharge acccording to the laws of the place where the contract is made, there are (as we have seen) some necessary limitations and exceptions engrafted upon the general doctrine which every country will enforce whenever those laws are manifestly unjust, or

---

1 Pardessus, Droit Comm. art. 1495, 1498—1500.

2 Id. art. 1495.

3 Id. art. 1499.

4 Ante, § 334; Post, § 349—351.

5 See Penniman *v.* Meigs, 9 John. R. 325; Babcock *v.* Weston, 1 Gallis. R. 168; Murray *v.* De Rottenham, 6 John. Ch. R. 52; Holmes *v.* Remsen, 4 John. Ch. R. 471.

6 See Blanchard *v.* Russell, 13 Mass. R. 6; Post, § 349; Van Raugh *v.* Van Ardaln, 3 Cain. R. 154; Smith *v.* Buchanan, 1 East, R. 6; Smith *v.* Smith, 2 John. R. 235; Green *v.* Sarmiento, Peters, Cir. R. 74; M'Menomy *v.* Murray, 3 John. Ch. R. 435; Wolff *v.* Oxholm, 6 Maule & Selw. R. 92; Ante, § 338.

are injurious to the fair rights of its own citizens[1]. It has been said by a learned Judge, with great force: "As the laws of foreign countries are not admitted *ex proprio vigore,* but merely *ex comitate,* the judicial power will exercise a discretion with respect to the laws which they may be called upon to sanction; for if they should be manifestly unjust, or calculated to injure their own citizens, they ought to be rejected. Thus, if any State should enact that its citizens should be discharged from all debts due to creditors living without the State, such a provision would be so contrary to the common principles of justice, that the most liberal spirit of comity would not require in adoption in any other State. So, if a State, under the pretence of establishing a general bankrupt law, should authorize such proceedings as would deprive all creditors living out of the State of an opportunity to share in the distribution of the effects of the debtor, such a law would have no effect beyond the territory of the State in which it was passed[2]".

§ 350. The same reasoning was again asserted by the same learned Judge in another case, calling for an exposition of the limitations of the doctrine: "This rule (said he) must, however, from its very nature, be qualified and restrained; for it cannot be admitted as a principle of law or justice, that when a valid personal contract is made, which follows the person of the creditor, and may be enforced in any foreign jurisdiction, that a mode of discharge manifestly partial or unjust, and tending to deprive a foreign creditor of his debt, while he is excluded from a participation with the domestic creditors in the effects of the debtor, should have force in any country to the prejudice of their own citizens. The comity of nations does not require it, and the fair principles of a contract would be violated by it[3]".

§ 351. "Thus, if a citizen of this State being in a foreign

---

1 Ante, § 339; Post, § 350, 351.

2 Mr. Chief Justice Parker, in Blanchard *v.* Russell, 13 Mass. R. 6.

3 Ibid.

country should, for a valuable consideration, receive a promise to pay money, or to perform any other valuable engagement from a subject of that country, and the law should provide for a discharge from all debts upon a surrender of his effects, without any notice which could by possibility reach creditors out of the country where such a law should exist; we apprehend that the contract ought to be enforced here, notwithstanding a discharge obtained under such law. For although the creditor is to be presumed to know the laws of the place where he obtains his contract, yet that presumption is founded upon another, which is, that those laws are not palpably partial and unjust, and calculated to protect the creditors at home at the expense of those who are abroad. Such laws would come within the well-known exception to the rules of comity, viz., that the laws which are to be admitted in the tribunals of a country where they are not made, are not to be injurious to the State, or the citizens of the State, where they are so received[1]".

§ 351 *a.* But although the general rule, that a contract, as to its dissolution and discharge, is to be governed by the law of the place where it is made, is thus, with few exceptions and limitations, admitted to be well established; yet we are not to understand that it thence follows, as a necessary consequence, that in no cases whatever can a contract be discharged or dissolved, except in the mode and by the process and formalities prescribed by the same law; or, in other words, that it must be discharged and dissolved *eo ligamine, quo ligatur*, or rather by reversing the operation, which knit it under the local law[2]. On the contrary, there are or may be circumstances under which an opposite rule may be maintainable; and the law of another country, prescribing different modes of proceeding, or different formali-

---

1 Mr. Chief Justice Parker in Prentiss *v.* Savage, 13 Mass. R. 23, 24. See also Fergusson on Marr. and Div. 396, 397; Wolff *v.* Oxholm, 6 Maule & Selw. 92; Ante, § 244.

2 See Warrender *v.* Warrender, 9 Bligh, R. 124, 125; Ante, § 226 *c*, note.

ties, or different acts which shall establish a dissolution thereof, may also well prevail to annul or discharge the contract. A change of domicil of the parties to the latter country, or an act done in that country which would there operate to dissolve or discharge the contract, may well produce the fullest effect, although the same act might not be recognised by the law of the place of the origin of the contract. Thus, for example, as we well know, the obligation of a bond or other sealed instrument, after a breach of the contract created thereby, cannot in England be discharged or released, except by a sealed instrument, or a release under seal, according to the known maxim of the common law: *Eodem modo, quo quid constituitur, eodem modo dissolvitur.* And yet by the law of most, if not of all, of the continental countries, whose jurisprudence is founded on the Roman law, a simple receipt or discharge not under seal would, if executed in such countries, be held to discharge the bond or other sealed instrument. Let us, then, suppose a bond executed in England for the payment of money, and, when it becomes due, there should be a default in payment, and afterwards the creditor should receive payment of the debtor in France, or otherwise should discharge him by a written unsealed instrument in France; such a discharge would in France be held valid and conclusive, if good by the law of France, notwithstanding it might be held invalid in an English court of common law. In short, any act done after such an obligation was created in a foreign country, by whose laws the act would operate as a dissolution thereof, would be treated in that country, at least, as a complete extinguishment thereof.

§ 351 *b*. It is not easy, therefore, upon principle, to say, why such an extinguishment of a contract, according to the *lex loci*, ought not everywhere else to have the same operation, even in the country of the origin of the contract. For if the contract derives its whole original obligatory force from the law of the place where it is made, it is but following out the same principle to hold, that any act subsequently done, touching the same contract by the parties, should have the same obligatory force and operation upon it, which the law of the place where it is done attributes to it. And in this respect there certainly is, or at least may be, a clear distinction between acts done by the parties in a foreign country, and which derive their operation from their voluntary consent and intention, and acts *in invitum*, deriving their whole authority and effect from the operation of the local law, independent of any such consent[1].

§ 351 *c*. Indeed, the reasonable interpretation of the general rule would seem to be, that while contracts made in one country are properly held to be dissoluble and extinguishable, according to the laws of that country, as natural incidents to the original concoction of such contracts, they are, and may at the same time also be equally dissoluble and extinguishable by any other acts done, or contracts made, subsequently in another country by the parties, which acts or contracts, according to the law of the latter country, are sufficient to work such a dissolution or extinguishment. It is to this double posture of a case that Lord Brougham referred in one of his judgments. "If a contract," said he, "for sale of a chattel is made, or an obligation of debt is incurred, or a chattel is pledged in one country, the sale may be annulled, the debt released, and the pledge redeemed, by the law and by the forms of another country, in which the parties happen to reside, and in whose courts their rights and obligations come in question, unless there was an express stipulation in the contract itself against such avoidance, release, or redemption. But at any rate this is certain, that if the laws of one country and its Courts recognise and give effect to those of another in respect to the constitution of any contract, they must give the like recognition and effect to those same foreign laws, when they declare the same kind of contract dissolved. Suppose a party forbidden to purchase from another by our equity, as adminis-

---

[1] Post, § 411.

tered in the Courts of this country, (and we have some restraints upon certain parties, which come very near prohibition); and suppose a sale of chattels by one to another party, standing in this relation towards each other, should be effected in Scotland, and that our Courts here should (whether right or wrong) recognise such a rule because the Scotch law would affirm it; surely it would follow, that our Courts must equally recognise a rescission of the contract of sale in Scotland by any act which the Scotch law regards as valid to rescind it, although our own law may not regard it as sufficient. Suppose a question to arise in the Courts of England respecting the execution of a contract thus made in this country, and that the objection of its invalidity were waived for some reason; if the party resisting its execution were to produce either a sentence of a Scotch Court, declaring it rescinded by a Scotch matter done in *pais,* or were merely to produce evidence of the thing so done, and proof of its amounting by the Scotch law to a rescission of the contract; I apprehend that the party relying on the contract could never be heard to say: 'The contract is English, and the Scotch proceeding is impotent to dissolve it.' The reply would be: 'Our English Courts have (whether right or wrong) recognised the validity of a Scotch proceeding to complete the obligation, and can no longer deny the validity of a similar, but reverse proceeding to dissolve it—*Unumquodque dissolvitur eodem modo, quo colligatur.*' Suppose, for another example, (which is the case), that the law of this country precluded an infant or a married woman from borrowing money in any way, or from binding themselves by deed; and that in another country those obligations could be validly incurred; it is probable that our law and our Courts would recognise the validity of such foreign obligations. But suppose a *feme covert* had executed a power, and conveyed an interest under it to another *feme covert* in England; could it be endured, that where the donee of the power produced a release under seal from the *feme covert* in the same foreign country, a distinction should be taken, and the Court here should hold that party incapable of releasing the obligation? Would it not be said, that our Courts having decided the contract of a *feme covert* to be binding, when executed abroad, must by parity of reason hold the discharge or release of the *feme covert* to be valid, if it be valid in the same foreign country[1]?"

§ 351 *d*. Nor does there seem to be in this respect any acknowledged distinction between contracts which are purely personal, and contracts which impose or may impose any charge on real estate; for, although in respect to immovable property, the law of the *situs* should be admitted (as certainly is the case at the common law) to regulate all the rights to immovable property, yet it does not thence follow, that an act which would operate as a dissolution or extinguishment of the contract creating such charge, according to the law of a foreign country where it is subsequently done, may not incidentally and indirectly work such a dissolution or extinguishment thereof, although it does not conform to the *lex rei sitæ*. Lord Brougham on the same occasion, referring to this topic, said: "All personal obligations may in their consequences affect real rights in England. Nor does a Scotch divorce, by depriving a widow of dower or arrears of pin-money charged on English property, more immediately affect real estate here, than a bond or a judgment released in Scotland according to Scotch forms, discharges real estate of a lien, or than a bond executed, or indeed a simple contract debt incurred in Scotland, eventually and consequently charges English real estate[2]."

§ 352. Before we quit this head of contracts, it may be well to bring together some principles applicable to negotiable instruments which have not been brought as distinctly under review in the preceding discussions as they deserve to be, and which afford important illustrations of the oper-

---

[1] Warrender *v*. Warrender, 9 Bligh, R. 125—127; Ante, § 226 *c*, note.

[2] Warrender *v*. Warrender, 9 Bligh, R. 127; Ante, § 226 *c*, note.

ation of foreign law upon contracts and their incidents. The subject of the assignments of debts and other *choses in action,* not negotiable by the general law merchant, or the laws of particular countries, will more properly find a place in our subsequent inquiries [1].

§ 353. Questions have arisen, whether negotiable notes and bills made in one country, are transferable in other countries, so as to found a right of action in the holder against the other parties. Thus, a question occurred in England, in a case where a negotiable note made in Scotland, and there negotiable, was indorsed, and a suit brought in England by the indorsee against the maker, whether the action was maintainable. It was contended, that the note, being a foreign note, was not within the statute of Anne, (3 & 4 Anne, ch. 9), which made promissory notes payable to order assignable and negotiable; for that statute applied only to inland promissory notes. But the Court overruled the objection, and held the note suable in England by the indorsee, as the statute embraced foreign as well as domestic notes [2]. In another case, a promissory note made in England, and payable to the bearer, was transferred in France; and the question was made, whether the French holder could maintain an action thereon in England, such notes being by the law of France negotiable; and it was held that he might [3]. But in each of these cases the decision was expressly put upon the provisions of the statute of Anne respecting promissory notes, leaving wholly untouched the general doctrine of international law.

---

[1] Post, § 355, 395—400, 566; 3 Burge, Comm. on Col. and For. Law, Pt. 2, ch. 20, pp. 777, 778.

[2] Milne *v.* Graham, 1 Barn. & Cress. 192.—It does not distinctly appear upon the Report, whether the indorsement was made in Scotland or in England; but it was probably in England. But see Carr *v.* Shaw, Bayley on Bills, p. 16, n. 5th edit.; Id. p. 22, American edit. by Phillips & Sewall, (1836).

[3] De la Chaumette *v.* the Bank of England, 2 Barn. & Adol. R. 385; S. C. 9 Barn. & Cress. 208; and see Chitty on Bills, pp. 551, 552, 8th edit.; Ante, § 346.

§ 353 *a*. In a more recent case, which has been already cited[1], a negotiable note was made in France and indorsed in France, and afterwards a suit was brought thereon by the indorsee against the maker in England. One question in the case was, whether a blank indorsement in France was, by the law of France, sufficient to transfer the property in the note without any other formalities. It was held that it was not sufficient. But it seems to have been taken for granted, that if the note was well negotiated by the indorsement, a suit might be maintained thereon in England by the indorsee in his own name. On that occasion the Court said: "The rule which applies to the case of contracts made in one country, and put in suit in the courts of law of another country, appears to be this: that the interpretation of the contract must be governed by the law of the country where the contract was made (*lex loci contractûs*); the mode of suing, and the time within which the action must be brought, must be governed by the law of the country where the action is brought. (*In ordinandis judiciis, loci consuetudo, ubi agitur.*) This distinction has been clearly laid down and adopted in the late case of De la Vega *v.* Vianna. See also the case of the British Linen Company *v.* Drummond, where the different authorities are brought together. The question therefore is, whether the law of France, by which the indorsement in blank does not operate as a transfer of the note, is a rule which governs and regulates the interpretation of the contract, or only relates to the mode of instituting and conducting the suit; for in the former case it must be adopted by our Courts; in the latter it may be altogether disregarded, and the suit commenced in the name of the present plaintiff. And we think the French law on the point above mentioned, is the law by which the contract is governed, and not the law which regulates the mode of suing. If the indorsement has not operated as a transfer, that goes directly to the point that there

---

[1] Ante, § 316 *a*.

is no contract upon which the plaintiff can sue. Indeed, the difference in the consequences that would follow, if the plaintiff sues in his own name, or is compelled to use the name of the former indorser as the plaintiff by procuration, would be very great in many respects, particularly in its bearing on the law of set-off; and with reference to those consequences, we think the law of France falls in with the distinction above laid down, that it is a law which governs the contract itself, not merely the mode of suing. We therefore think, that our courts of law must take notice that the plaintiff could have no right to sue in his own name upon the contract in the courts of the country where such contract was made; and that such being the case there, we must hold in our courts, that he can have no right of suing here[1]."

§ 354. Several other cases may be put upon this subject. In the first place, suppose a note negotiable by the law of the place where it is made, is there transferred by indorsement; can the indorsee maintain an action in his own name against the maker in a foreign country, (where both are found), in which there is no positive law on the subject of negotiable notes applicable to the case? If he can, it must be upon the ground, that the foreign tribunal would recognise the validity of the transfer by the indorsement according to the law of the place where it is made. According to the doctrine maintained in England, as choses in action are by the common law (independent of statute) incapable of being transferred over, it might be argued, that he could not maintain an action, notwithstanding the instrument was well negotiated, and transferred by the law of the place of the contract[2]. So far as this principle of the non-assignability of choses in action would affect transfers in England, it

---

[1] Trimbey v. Vignier, 1 Bing. N. Cas. 151, 159, 160; Post, § 565, 566.

[2] See 2 Black. Comm. 442; Jeffrey v. M'Taggart, 2 Barn. & Cress. 22, 23; Innes v. Dunlop, 8 T. R. 595. See also Jeffrey v. M'Taggart, 6 Maule & Selw. R. 126; Post, § 565, 566.

would seem reasonable to follow it. But the difficulty is in applying it to transfers made in a foreign country, by whose laws the instrument is negotiable, and capable of being transferred, so as to vest the property and right in the assignee. In such a case it would seem, that the more correct rule would be, that the *lex loci contractûs* ought to govern; because the holder under the indorsement has an immediate and absolute right in the contract vested in him, as much as he would have in goods transferred to him. Under such circumstances to deny the legal effect of the indorsement is to construe the obligation, force, and effect of a contract made in one place by the law of another place. The indorsement in the place where it is made, creates a direct contract between the maker and the first indorsee; and if so, that contract ought to be enforced between them every where. It is not a question as to the form of the remedy, but as to the right [1].

§ 355. The same view of the doctrine seems to have been taken in another case in England, much stronger in its circumstances, than the case of a foreign negotiable note, which may be thought to stand in some measure upon the custom of merchants. A suit was brought by the assignee of an Irish judgment against the judgment debtor in England, the judgment being made expressly assignable by Irish statutes; and the objection was taken, that no action could be maintained by the assignee, because it would contravene the general principle of the English law, that choses in action were not assignable. But the Court intimated a strong opinion against this ground of argument; and the cause finally was disposed of upon another point; but in such a manner as left the opinion in full force [2]. It is matter of surprise, that in some of the more recent discussions in England upon the negotiation of notes in foreign countries,

---

[1] See Trimbey *v.* Vignier, 1 Bing. New Cases, 159—161; Ante, § 353 *a*, where the same reasoning seems to have applied; Post, § 565, 566.

[2] O'Callaghan *v.* Thomond, 3 Taunt. R. 82; Post, § 565, 566.

this doctrine has not been distinctly insisted on. For, even in England, negotiable notes are not treated as mere choses in action, but they are deemed to have a closer resemblance to personal chattels on account of their transferability; so that the legal property in them passes upon the transfer, as it does in the case of chattels[1]. If so, no one could doubt that a title of transfer of personal property in a foreign country, good by the laws of the country where it is made, ought to be held equally good everywhere[2].

§ 356. In the next place, let us suppose the case of a negotiable note, made in a country by whose laws it is negotiable, is actually indorsed in another, by whose laws a transfer of notes by indorsement is not allowed. Could an action be maintained by the indorsee against the maker in the Courts of either country? If it could be maintained in the country whose laws do not allow such a transfer, it must be upon the ground that the original negotiability by the *lex loci contractûs*, is permitted to avail, in contradiction to the *lex fori*. On the other hand, if the suit should be brought in the country where the note was originally made, the same objection might arise, that the transfer was not allowed by the law of the place where the indorsement took place. But, at the same time, it may be truly said, that the transfer is entirely in conformity to the intent of the parties, and to the law of the original contract[3].

§ 357. In the next place, let us suppose the case of a note not negotiable by the law of the place where it is made, but negotiable by the law of the place where it is indorsed; could an action be maintained in either country

---

1 M'Neil *v.* Holloway, 1 Barn. & Ald. R. 218.

2 Ante, § 353 *a*.

3 See Chitty on Bills, ch. 6, pp. 218, 219, 8th Lond. edit. See Kaims on Equity, B. 3, ch. 8, § 4; Ante, § 353, 354.—In the cases of Milne *v.* Graham, 1 Barn. & Cress. 192; De la Chaumette *v.* Bank of England, 2 Barn. & Adol. 385; and Trimbey *v.* Vignier, 1 Bing. N. Cas. 151, the promissory notes were negotiable in both countries, as well where the note was made, as where it was transferred.

by the indorsee against the maker? It would seem, that in the country where the note was made it could not, because it would be inconsistent with its own laws. But the same difficulty would not arise in the country where the indorsement was made; and, therefore, if the maker used terms of negotiability in his contract capable of binding him to the indorsee, there would not seem to be any solid objection to giving the contract its full effect there. And so it has been accordingly adjudged in the case of a note made in Connecticut, payable to A., or order, but by the laws of that State not negotiable there, and indorsed in New York where it was negotiable. In a suit in New York by the indorsee against the maker, the exception was taken and overruled. The Court on that occasion said, that personal contracts just in themselves, and lawful in the place where they are made, are to be fully enforced, according to the law of the place and the intent of the parties, is a principle which ought to be universally received and supported. But this admission of the *lex loci contractûs* can have reference only to the nature and construction of the contract and its legal effect, and not to the mode of enforcing it. And the Court ultimately put the case expressly upon the ground, that the note was payable to the payee, or order; and therefore the remedy might well be pursued according to the law of New York against a party who had contracted to pay to the indorsee[1]. But if the words, "or order," had been omitted in the note, so that it had not appeared that the contract between the parties originally contemplated negotiability as annexed to it, a different question might have arisen, which would more properly come under discussion in another place; since it seems to concern the interpretation and obligation of contracts, although it has sometimes been treated as belonging to remedies[2].

---

[1] Lodge *v.* Phelps, 1 John. Cases, 139; S. C. 2 Caines, Cas. in Error, 321. See Kaims on Equity, B. 3, ch. 8, § 4.

[2] See Chitty on Bills, ch. 6, pp. 218, 219, 8th Lond. edit.; 3 Kent, Comm. Lect. 44, p. 77, 3d edit.; Ante, § 253 *a*.

§ 358. Another case may be put which has actually passed into judgment. A negotiable note was given by a debtor resident in Maine, to his creditor, resident in Massachusetts. After the death of the creditor, his executrix, appointed in Massachusetts, indorsed the same note in that State to an indorsee, who brought a suit as indorsee against the maker in the State Court of Maine. The question was, whether the note was, under the circumstances, suable by the indorsee; and the Court held that it was not; for the Court said, that the executrix could not herself have sued upon the note, without taking out letters of administration in Maine, and therefore she could not by her indorsement transfer the right to her indorsee[1].

§ 359. It does not appear by the report, whether the note was made in Massachusetts or in Maine. It is not, perhaps, in the particular case material, as, according to the law of both States, the note was negotiable by indorsement, whether made in the one or in the other State. If it had been different, it might have given rise to a different inquiry. But in either State the creditor might certainly, in his lifetime, by his indorsement have transferred the property in the note to the indorsee, and as clearly his executrix could do the same; for it is entirely well settled, that an executor or administrator can so transfer any negotiable security by his indorsement thereof[2]. If, then, by the transfer in Massachusetts the property passed to the indorsee, it is difficult to perceive why that transfer was not as effectual in Maine as in Massachusetts; and, by the law of both States, an indorsee may sue on negotiable instruments in his own name. In truth, such instruments are treated, not as mere choses in action, but rather as chattels personal[3]. Choses in action are not assignable by law; and actions must be brought

---

[1] Stearns *v.* Burnham, 5 Greenl. R. 261; S. P. Thompson *v.* Wilson, 2 N. Hamp. R. 291. But see Huthwaite *v.* Phaire, 1 Maun. & Grang. R. 159, 164; Post, § 516, 517.

[2] See Rawlinson *v.* Stone, 3 Wilson, R. 1; S. C. 2 Str. R. 1260.

[3] McNeilage *v.* Holloway, 1 Barn. & Ald. 218. But see Richards *v.* Richards, 2 Barn. & Adol. 447, 452, 453; Ante, § 355.

thereon in the name of the original parties. But negotiable notes are transferable by indorsement; and when transferred, the indorsee may sue in his own name. Upon the reasoning in the above case, the note would cease to be negotiable after the death of the payee, which is certainly not an inadmissible doctrine[1]. The decision in a recent case in the Supreme Court of the United States, is founded upon the doctrine, that an assignment by an executor of a chose in action in the State where he is appointed, and which is good by its laws, will enable the assignee to sue in his own name in any other State, by whose laws the instrument would be assignable, so as to pass the note to the assignee, and enable him to sue thereon[2].

§ 360. As to bills of exchange, it is generally required, in order to fix the responsibility of other parties, that, upon their dishonour, they should be duly protested by the holder, and due notice thereof given to such parties. And the first question which naturally arises, is, whether the protest and notice should be in the manner, and according to the forms of the place in which the bill is drawn, or according to the forms of the place in which it is payable. By the common law the protest is to be made at the time, in the manner, and by the persons prescribed in the place where the bill is payable[3]. But as to the necessity of making a demand and protest, and the circumstances under which notice may be required or dispensed with, these are incidents of the original contract, which are governed by the law of the place

---

[1] Rawlinson *v.* Stone, 3 Wilson, R. 1; S. C. 2 Str. R. 1260; Bayley on Bills, ch. 5, p. 78, 5th edit.—The effect of assignments of debts and other personal property will come more fully under review in the succeeding chapter, when we enter upon the subject of the law which regulates the transfer of personal property. Post, § 395—400.

[2] Harper *v.* Butler, 2 Peters, S. C. R. 239.—The case of Trimbey *v.* Vignier, 1 Bing. N. Cases, 151; Ante, § 353 *a*, seems to inculcate the doctrine as general, that a transfer of property, good by the lex loci of the transfer, will, at least in cases of negotiable instruments, be held good every where, so as to enable the indorsee to sue in his own name.

[3] Chitty on Bills, pp. 193, 506, 507, 508, 8th Lond. edit.

where the bill is drawn[1]. They constitute implied conditions, upon which the liability of the drawer is to attach according to the *lex loci contractûs;* and, if the bill is negotiated, the like responsibility attaches upon each successive indorser, according to the law of the place of his indorsement; for each indorser is treated as a new drawer[2]. The same doctrine, according to Pardessus, prevails in France[3].

§ 361. Upon negotiable instruments it is the custom of most commercial nations, to allow some time for payment beyond the period fixed by the terms of the instrument. This period is different in different nations; in some it is limited to three days, in others it extends as far as eleven days[4]. The period of indulgence is commonly called the *days of grace;* as to which, the rule is, that the usage of the place on which a bill is drawn, and where payment of a

---

1 Chitty on Bills, pp. 506—508 8th Lond. edit.; 1 Boullenois, Observ. 23, pp. 531, 532.

2 Bayley on Bills, ch. A. pp. 78—86, (5th edit. 1836), by Phillips & Sewall; Chitty on Bills, ch. 6, pp. 266, 267, 370, 8th Lond. edit.; Ballingalls *v.* Gloster, 3 East, R. 481; Ante, § 314 to—317.

3 Pardessus, Droit Comm. art. 1496—1499; Henry on Foreign Law, 53, App. pp. 239—248.—Boullenois admits, that the protest ought to be according to the law of the place where the bill is payable. But, in case of a foreign bill, indorsed by several indorsements in different countries, he contends, that the time, within which notice or recourse is to be had upon the dishonour, is to be governed by a different rule. Thus, he supposes, a bill drawn in England on Paris in favour of a French payee, who indorses it to a Spaniard, (in Spain), and he to a Portuguese, (in Portugal), and he to the holder; and then says, that the holder is entitled to have recourse against the Portuguese, within the time prescribed by the law of France, because the holder is there to receive payment; the Portuguese is to give notice to the Spaniard within the time prescribed by the law of Portugal, because that is the only law with which he is presumed to be acquainted, &c.; and so in regard to every other indorser, he is to have recourse within the period prescribed by the law of the place where the indorsement was made, and not of the domicil of the party indorsing. 1 Boullenois, Observ. 20, pp. 370—372; Id. Observ. 23, pp. 531, 532.

4 Bayley on Bills, (5th Amer. edit. by Phillips & Sewall), pp. 234, 235; Chitty on Bills, p. 407, (8th Lond. edit.); Id. p. 193.

bill or note is to be made, governs as to the number of the days of grace to be allowed thereon[1].

§ 362. This head, respecting contracts in general, may be concluded by remarking, that contracts, respecting personal property and debts, are now universally treated as having no *situs* or locality; and they follow the person of the owner in point of right; (*Mobilia inhærent ossibus domini*[2] *;*) although the remedy on them must be according to the law of the place where they are sought to be enforced. The common language is: *Mobilia non habent sequelam; Mobiliaos sibus inhærent; Actor sequitur forum Rei; Debita sequuntur personam debitoris*[3]. That is to say, they are deemed to be in the place, and are disposed of by the law of the domicil of the owner, wherever in point of fact they may be situate. *Quin tamen ratione mobilium,* (says Paul Voet, a strenuous opposer of the general doctrine of the extra-territorial operation of statutes), *ubicunque sitorum, domicilium seu personam domini sequamur*[4]. Burgundus says: *Sed tamen, ut existimem, bona moventia, et mobilia, ita comitari personam, ut extra domicilium ejus censeantur existere, adduci sane non possum*[5]. Rodenburg says the same: *Diximus, mobilia situm habere intelligi, ubi dominus instruxerit domicilium, nec aliter mutare eundem, quam unà cum*

---

1 Bank of Washington *v.* Triplett, 2 Peters, Sup. C. R. 30, 34; Chitty on Bills, p. 407, (8th Lond. edit.); Id. p. 193; S. P. 2 Boullenois, Observ. 23, pp. 531, 532, and Mascard. Conclus. 7, n. 72, there cited.

2 Thorne *v.* Watkins, 2 Ves. 35; 1Boullenois, Observ. 20, p. 348; Liverm. Diss. § 251, pp. 162, 163; P. Voet, de Stat. c. 2, § 4, n. 8, p. 126, (edit. 1715); Id. p. 139, (edit. 1661); Post, § 377, 378.

3 Kaims on Equity, b. 3, ch. 8, § 3, 4; Dwarris on Statutes, pt. 2, p. 650; Liverm. Diss. § 251, 252, 254, pp. 162, 163, 167; Fœlix, Conflit des Lois, Revue Etrang. et Fran. tom. 7, 1840, § 32, pp. 221—226; Id. § 33, pp. 227, 228; Christinæus, ad Cod. lib. 1, tit. 1, Decis. 5, n. 1—3, p. 7; 3 Burge, Comm. on Col. and For. Law, pt. 2, ch. 20, p. 777; Post, § 376—385, 395—400.

4 P. Voet, De Stat. § 4, ch. 8, n. 8, p. 126; Id. pp. 139, 140, (edit. 1661).

5 Burgundus, Tract. 2, n. 20, p. 71.

domicilio[1]. He goes on to assign the reasons founded upon the perpetually changeable location of movables. Pothier is equally expressive on the same point[2]. Indeed, the doctrine is so firmly established, that it would be a waste of time to go over the authorities;[3] and especially as the same

---

[1] Rodenburg, De Div. Stat. tit. 2, ch. 2, n. 1; 2 Boullenois, App. pp. 14, 15.

[2] Post, § 381.

[3] See Bouhier, Cout. de Bourg. ch. 21, § 172, p. 408; Id. ch. 22, § 79, p. 429; Id. ch. 25, § 5, 6, p. 490; Pothier, Des Choses, tom. 8, P. 2, § 3, pp. 109, 110; Id. Cout. d'Orléans, tom. 10, n. 24, p. 7; 2 Bell, Comm. 684, 685, 4th edit.; Bruce *v.* Bruce, 2 Bos. & Pull. 230; Sill *v.* Worswick, 1 H. Bl. 690, 691; In Re, Ewing, 1 Tyrwhitt, R. 91; Thorne *v.* Watkins, 2 Ves. R. 35; 4 Cowen, R. 517, note; Blanchard *v.* Russell, 13 Mass. R. 6; Liverm. Diss. 163, 164—171; Fœlix, Conflit des Lois, Revue Etrang. et Fran. tom. 7, 1840, § 31, p. 220, § 32, p. 221—§ 36, p. 229.—There are some few jurists, who seem to dissent from the doctrine, either in a qualified or absolute manner, who are cited by M. Fœlix. He enumerates Tittman, Muhlenbruch, and Eichhorn. Id. pp. 223, 224. John Voet has expounded this whole doctrine very fully. Atque ita (says he) evictum hactenus existimo, in omnibus statutis, realibus, personalibus, mixtis, aut quâcunque aliâ sive denominatione sive divisione concipiendis, verissimam esse regulam, perdere omnino officium suum statuta extra territorium statuentis; neque judicem alterius regionis, quantum ad res in suo territorio sitas, ex necessitate quâdam juris obstrictum esse, ut sequatur probetve leges non suas. In eo tamen forte scrupulus hæserit; si scilicet hæc ita sint, quì ergo fiat, quod vulgo reperitur traditum, in successionibus, testandi facultate, contractibus, aliisque, mobilia ubicunque sita regi debere domicilii jure, non vero legibus loci illius, in quo naturaliter sunt constituta; videri enim hâc saltem ratione jurisdictionem judicis domicilii non raro ultra statuentis fines operari in res dispersas per varia aliorum magistratuum, etiam remotissimis ad orientem occiduumque solem regionibus imperitantium, territoria. Sed considerandum, quâdam fictione juris, seu malis, præsumtione, hanc de mobilibus determinationem conceptam niti: cum enim certo stabilique hæc situ careant, nec certo sint alligata loco; sed ad arbitrium domini undiquaque in domicilii locum revocari facile ac reduci possint, et maximum domino plerumque commodum adferre soleant, cum ei sunt præsentia; visum fuit, hanc inde conjecturam surgere, quod dominus velle censeatur, ut illic omnia sua sint mobilia, aut saltem esse intelligantur, ubi fortunarum suarum larem summamque constituit, id est, in loco domicilii. Proinde si quid domicilii judex constituerit, id ad mobilia ubicunque sita non aliâ pertinebit ratione, quam quia illa in ipso domicilii loco esse concipiuntur. Si tamen has juris fictiones quis à ratione naturali, in hisce solum considerandâ, alienas putet, quippe desiderantes unum communem legislatorem, lege suâ fictiones tales introducentem

subject will occur, in a more general form, in the succeeding chapter[1].

§ 362 *a.* Debts, in the vocabulary of the civil law, are often known by the title of *Nomina debitorum*[2]; and they also follow the person of the owner; or, as Jason says: *Nomina infixa sunt ejus ossibus*[3]. Burgundus also says: *Nomina et actiones loco non circumscribuntur, quias unt incorporales; tamen et ibi per fictionem esse intelliguntur, ubi creditor habet domicilium. Nam, quod quidam ossibus creditoris, esse affixa putant, non magis movet, quam si dicamus, dominium fundi esse in proprietario; cum alioquin, si quis strictius interpretetur, aliud est fundus, aliud dominium; sicuti aliud est obligatio, aliud creditum*[4]. Dumoulin is

---

ac stabilientem; non equidem repugnaverim, atque adeo tunc hoc ipsum comitati, quam gens genti præstat, magis, quam rigori juris, et summæ potestati, quam quisque magistratus in mobilia, suo in territorio constituta, habet, adscribendum putem. Præsertim cum considero, subinde per magistratus loci, in quo mobilia vere existunt, de illis ea constitui sancirique, quæ domicilii judici displicere possent. Quid enim, si domicilii judex frumenta importari jubeat, penuriâ frugum vexatâ regione; incola spe lucri majoris frumenta sua, in aliâ regione horreis recondita inferre desideret; regioni vero isti imperans omnem vetuerit frugum exportationem, jure suo in sui territorii frumentis usus? Quis hic obsecro negare sustineat, mobilia regi lege loci, in quo vere sunt, non in quo ob domicilium domini esse finguntur. Nec minus id in rerum publicationibus ex delicto apparet, in quantum fisco loci, in quo reus condemnatus est, non sunt cessura bona omnia mobilia ubicunque sita, sed ea sola, quæ in loco condemnantis inveniuntur; nisi aliud ex comitate alicubi servetur. Nec dicam, variare de rebus quibusdam locorum plurimorum statuta, utrum mobilibus illæ, an immobilibus accensendæ sint; nec novum esse, ut quæ unâ in regione mobilia habentur, immobilium catalogo alibi adscripta inveniantur; annui, verbi gratiâ, reditus à Provinciâ debiti, in Hollandiâ mobiles, immobiles Trajecti: arbores grandiores solo hærentes passim immobiles, mobiles tamen in Flandriâ habitæ. Quo posito, necesse fuerit, ut, quæ in domicilii loco mobilia habentur, immobilia vero illic ubi sunt, regantur lege loci in quo vere sunt, magistratu ne ex comitate quidem permissuro, ut quasi mobilia domicilii dominici sequerentur jura. J. Voet. ad Pand. lib. 1, tit. 4, Post, 2, § 11, pp. 44, 45; Post, § 481, 482.

[1] Post, § 374—401.

[2] Ersk. Inst. b. 3, tit. 9, § 4; Cujaccii, Opera, tom. 7, p. 491, (edit. 1758); Dig. lib. 10, tit. 2, l. 2, § 6; Vicat. Vocab. Voce, Nomen.

[3] 1 Boullenois, Observ. 20, p. 348.

[4] Burgundus, Tract. 2, n. 33, p. 73.

equally explicit: *Nomina et jura, et quæcumque incorporalia, non circumscribantur loco; et sic non opus est accedere ad certum locum. Tum si hæc jura alicubi esse censerentur, non reputarentur esse in re pro illis hypothecata, nec in debitoris persona, sed magis in persona creditoris, in quo activè resident, et ejus ossibus inhærent*[1].

§ 362 *b*. The language of Hertius is: *Mobilibus interdum etiam κατ' ἀναλογίαν, (nam proprie neque mobiles sunt, nec immobiles), accensentur res incorporales*[2]. Huberus holds them to fall under the class of movables[3]. Paul Voet says: *Verum, quid de nominibus et actionibus statuendum erit? Respondeo, quia proprie loquendo, nec mobiliam nec immobiliam veniunt appellatione; Etiam vere non sunt in loco, quia incorporalia. Ideo non sine distinctione res temperari poterit. Aut igitur realis erit actio, tendens ad immobilia, et spectabitur statutum loci situs immobilium. Aut erit actio realis spectans mobilia, et idem servandum erit, quod de mobilibus dictum est. Aut erit actio personalis sive ad mobilia sive ad immobilia pertinens, quæ cum inhæreat ossibus personæ, statutum loci creditorum æstimari debebit*[4].

§ 363. But a question of a very different character may arise, as to executory contracts respecting real estate or immovables. Are they governed by the law of the place where the contract is made, or by the law of the place where the property is situate? Take, for instance, the case of a contract for the purchase or sale of lands in England or in America, arising under the Statute of Frauds, by which all contracts respecting real estate, or any interest therein, are required to be in writing, and otherwise they are void. If such a contract is made in France by parol or otherwise, in a manner not conformable to the law *rei sitæ*,

[1] Dumoulin, Comm. de Consuetud. Paris, tom. 1, De Fiefs. tit. 1, gloss. 4, n. 9, pp. 56, 57; Liverm. Dissert. § 251, pp. 162, 163; 3 Burge, Comm. on Col. and For. Law, pt. 2, ch. 20, p. 777; Post, § 392—400.

[2] Hertii, Opera, De Collis. Leg. § 4, n. 6, pp. 122, 123, (edit. 1737); Id. p. 174, (edit. 1716).

[3] Ibid.

[4] P. Voet. de Stat. § 9, ch. 1, n. 11, p. 256, (edit. 1715), pp. 312, 313, (edit. 1661).

for the purchase or sale of lands situate in England or in America, and the contract is conformable to the law of France on the same subject; is the contract valid in both countries? Is it valid in the country where the land lies, so as to be enforced there? If not, is it valid in the country where the contract was made[1]?

§ 364. If this question were to be decided exclusively by the law of England, it might be stated, that by the law of England such a contract would be utterly void; and it would be so held in a suit brought to enforce it in that realm, upon the ground that all real contracts must be governed by the *lex rei sitæ*[2]. Lord Mansfield took occasion, in a celebrated case, to examine and state the principle. "There is a distinction," said he, "between local and personal statutes. Local ones regard such things as are really upon the spot in England; as the Statute of Frauds, which respects lands situate in this kingdom. So stock-jobbing contracts, and the statutes thereupon, have a reference to our local funds. And so the statutes for restraining insurances upon the exportation of wool, respect our own ports and shores. Personal statutes respect transitory contracts, as common loans and insurances[3]." And in another report of the same case, after a second argument, he said: "In every disposition or contract, where the subject-matter relates locally to England, the law of England must govern, and must have been intended to govern. Thus, a conveyance or will of land, a mortgage, a contract concerning stocks, must all be sued upon in England; and the local nature of the thing requires them to be carried into execution according to the law here[4]."

---

[1] Ante, § 262; Post, § 435, 436—445. See 2 Burge, Comm. on Col. and For. Law, pt. 2, ch. 9, pp. 840—871; 4 Burge, Comm. pt. 2, ch. 5, § 11, p. 217.

[2] See 2 Dwarris on Stat. 648; Warrender *v.* Warrender, 9 Bligh, R. 127, 128; Ante, § 351 *d.*

[3] Robinson *v.* Bland, 1 W. Black, R. 234, 246; Post, § 383, and note.

[4] Robinson *v.* Bland, 2 Burr. R. 1079; S. P. 1 W. Black. R. 259. See

§ 365. The same doctrine has been laid down in equally emphatic terms in the Scottish Courts. Lord Robertson in a highly interesting case said: "Although the rule, as to the *lex loci contractûs,* is of very general application, particularly as to the constitution and validity of personal con-

---

also Ersk. Inst. b. 3, tit. 9, § 4; Henry on For. Law, pp. 12—15; Scott v. Alnutt, 2 Dow & Clarke, 404. See also Selkrig v. Davies, 2 Dow, R. 230, 250; Post, § 383, 435.—Mr. Burge, speaking on this subject, says: "There is an entire concurrence amongst them (jurists) in considering that the title to movables, or the validity of any disposition of them, is not governed by the law of their actual situs. This, which may be regarded as a general rule, is subject to this qualification, that the law of the country in which the movable may be actually situated, has not prescribed some particular mode by which alone the movable can be transferred. Thus, property in the public funds or stocks, shares in companies, joint stocks, &c., is a species of personal property, which as it is created so it is regulated by the law of the country in which it exists. Certain forms are prescribed, by which alone the holder of any share or interest can transfer it. Here the transfer is so far subject to the law of the place where the property is situated, that the legal title to it is not acquired unless those forms are observed. But although the contract may, in consequence of a non-compliance with those forms, fail in conferring the legal title on the disponee, yet it will give him a right to compel the disponer by action or suit to make a transfer in the manner required by the local law. To this limited extent the lex loci rei sitæ affects and controls the transfer by acts inter vivos of certain movables. But unless the local law gives to them the quality of immovable or real, as it may do, and has done in many instances, they still as subjects of succession are governed by the law of the owner's domicil. The rule is, that the title to movable property is governed by the law of the place of the owner's domicil; and this rule is uniformly applied in deciding on the title to movable property as a subject of succession. The law of the owner's domicil is not that which exclusively decides on the title to movable property, as a subject of transfer and acquisition by acts inter vivos. When contracts of purchase and sale, mortgage or pledge, are completed in a place which is not the domicil of the owner, the validity of such contracts, and the rights and obligations which they confer, are governed by the law of the country in which they are completed. 'Semper in stipulationibus, et in cæteris contractibus id sequimur, quod actum est; aut si non pareat, quid actum est, erit consequens, ut id sequamur, quod in regione, in quâ actum est, frequentatur.' 'Generaliter enim in omnibus, quæ ad formam ejusque perfectionem pertinent, spectanda est consuetudo regionis, ubi sit negotiatio, quia consuetudo influit in contractus, et videtur ad eos respicere, et voluntatem suam eis accommodare.'" 3 Burge, Comm. on Col. and For. Law, pt. 2, ch. 20, pp. 751, 752; 2 Burge, Comm. pt. 2, ch. 9, pp. 863—870. See Post, § 434.

tracts and obligations, it is not universal. In the first place, it does not apply to contracts or obligations relative to real estates[1]." Lord Bannatyne, on the same occasion, affirmed the like principle[2]. And it has received an unequivocal sanction in America; where it has been broadly declared to be a well-settled rule, that any title or interest in land, or in other real estate, can only be acquired or lost agreeably to the law of the place where the same is situate[3].

§ 365 *a*. Paul Voet has expressed the same opinion: *Quid si itaque contentio de aliquo jure in re, seu ex ipsâ se descendente? Vel ex contractu, vel actione personali, sed in rem scripta? An spectabitur loci statutum, ubi dominus habet domicilium, an statutum rei sitæ? Respondeo; Statutum rei sitæ. Ut tamen actio etiam intentari possit, ubi Reus habet domicilium. Idque obtinet, sive forensis sit ille, de cujus re controversia est, sive incola loci, ubi res est sita*[4].

§ 366. This doctrine may be farther illustrated by the case of Scotch heritable bonds. By heritable bonds in that law are meant bonds for the payment of money, which are

---

1 Fergusson on Marr. and Div. p. 395; Id. 397. See Ersk. Inst. b. 3, tit. 2, § 40, p. 515; Post, § 436, and note.

2 Fergusson on Marr. and Div. p. 401; 2 Kaimes on Equity, b. 3, ch. 2, § 2.—Erskine, in his Institutes, seems to assert a more modified doctrine. He says:—"All personal obligations or contracts entered into according to the law of the place where they are signed, or, as it is expressed in the Roman Law, secundum legem domicilii, vel loci contractus, are deemed effectual, when they come to receive execution in Scotland, as if they had been perfected in the Scotch form. And this holds even in such obligations as bind the grantor to convey subjects within Scotland; for where one becomes bound by a lawful obligation, he cannot cease to be bound by changing places." Yet Erskine afterwards adds, that if an actual conveyance of the property had been made, not according to the Scotch forms, the Courts of Scotland would not compel the party to convey, nor treat it as an obligation of the grantor to execute a more perfect conveyance. Ersk. Inst. b. 3, tit. 3, § 40, 41, p. 515. See Post, § 436.

3 Cutter *v*. Davenport, 1 Pick. R. 81; Hosford *v*. Nichols, 1 Paige, R. 220; Wills *v*. Cowper, 2 Hamm. R. 124; S. C. Wilcox, R. 278; Post, § 424, 427, 435.

4 P. Voet, de Stat. § 9, ch. 1, n. 2, p. 250, (edit. 1715); Id. p. 305, (edit. 1661); Post, § 426, 442.

secured by a conveyance or charge upon real estate. Such bonds usually contain not only a charge upon real estate, but a personal obligation to pay the debt. In general, by the Scotch law, mere personal bonds and other debts, on the decease of the creditor, pass to his personal representative; but heritable bonds belong to the heir; because the charge on the real estate, being *jus nobilius,* draws to it the personal right to the debt. According to the Scotch law, no contract or other act, disposing of a heritable bond, will be good, unless it is according to the law of Scotland; and no contract, intended to create such a heritable bond, will be valid, as such, unless it be made with the solemnities of the Scotch law [1]. There are other collateral consequences growing out of the same doctrine. Thus, if a Scotch heir should seek to be exonerated from a heritable bond by the application of the personal assets in England, his right would depend upon the law of Scotland, that is, the law of the place where the real estate was situate; and would not depend upon the law of the place where the personal estate happened locally to be [2].

§ 367. The same reasoning seems to have governed in the House of Lords in a recent case, where certain entailed estates in Scotland were sold for the redemption of the land-tax, and the surplus money of the proceeds of the sale was vested, according to a statute on the subject, in trustees who were required to pay the interest of it to the heir of entail in possession, until the money should be reinvested in

---

[1] Ersk. Inst. b. 2, ch. 2, § 9—20, pp. 198—204; Id. b. 3, tit. 2, § 39—41, pp. 514, 515; Jerningham *v.* Herbert, 1 Tamyn, R. 103; 2 Bell, Comm. § 668, pp. 7, 8; Id. § 1266, p. 690, 4th edit.; Id. p. 687, 5th edit.; Post, § 485—489.—Yet Mr. Erskine, in his Institutes, seems to admit that obligations to convey things in Scotland, although not perfected in the Scottish form, yet, if perfected according to the lex domicilii of the parties, are binding in Scotland, not as conveyances, but as contracts, under some circumstances. Ante, § 365, note 2.

[2] Elliott *v.* Lord Minto, 6 Madd. R. 16; Earl of Winchelsea *v.* Garetty, 2 Keen R. 293, 309, 310; Ante, § 266 *a.* See also 4 Burge, Comm. on Col. and For. Law, ch. 15, § 4, p. 722, et seq.

land. The heir of entail next entitled sold his reversionary and contingent right to the interest of this fund by a deed in the English form, and executed in England, where the parties were domiciled, but without the solemnities required by the law of Scotland. It was admitted, that the fund was to go to the heirs in entail, and that the principal thereof was consequently heritable, and could only be passed according to the solemnities of the law of Scotland. But the House of Lords adjudged the intermediate interest of the surplus, before the investment in lands, to be movable property, and alienable by the proprietor as such; and, therefore, they held the assignment of it according to the English law good [1].

§ 368. From what has been already stated in the preceding discussions, it will be seen that foreign jurists are by no means agreed in admitting the general doctrine [2]. On the contrary, some of them maintain that the validity of a contract is, in all cases, to be governed by the law of the place where it is made, whether it regards movables or immovables [3]. Thus, in respect to the capacity of persons to contract, their doctrine is, that if they are of age to contract in the place of their domicil, but are not in the place where their immovable property is situate, the contract to sell or alienate the latter will be valid everywhere; and so, *vice versâ* [4]. Others hold a different opinion, and insist that

---

1 Scott *v.* Allnutt, 2 Dow & Clarke, 404, 412.

2 Ante, § 260—263. See also Ante, § 82, 325—327; Post, § 369—373, 474—479. See 2 Burge, Comm. on Col. and For. Law, pt. 2, ch. 9, pp. 840—871.

3 Ante, § 52, 53, 60, 61, 62; Post, § 435—445. See also Fœlix, Conflit des Lois, Revue Etrang. et Fran. tom. 7, 1840, § 37, pp. 307—311; Id. pp. 352—360; Post, § 371 *f*, note. Mr. Burge has made a large collection of the various opinions of foreign jurists on this subject: 3 Burge, Comm. on Col. and For. Law, pt. 2, ch. 9, pp. 840—871.

4 Ante, § 51—54, 58—63; Post, § 430—435; Rodenburg, tit. 1, ch. 3; Id. tit. 2, ch. 3; Liverm. Diss. § 44—46, pp. 48, 49; Id. § 55, 56, p. 56; Id. § 58, 59, p. 58; 1 Boullenois, Observ. 2, p. 27; Id. p. 145; Id. Observ. 9, pp. 152—154; Id. Observ. 12, pp. 175—177; Id. Observ. 23,

whatever may be the law of the domicil as to capacity, and although it governs the person universally, yet it does not apply to immovable property in another country[1].

---

pp. 456—460; 1 Froland, Mém. 156, 160. See on this point Fœlix, Conflit des Lois, Revue Etrang. et Franç. (tom. 7, 1840), § 27—33, pp. 216—228; 2 Burge, Comm. on Col. and For. Law, pt. 2, ch. 9, pp. 840—870.

[1] Ante, § 54—62; Post, § 430—432, 435—445; Liverm. Diss. § 44, pp. 48, 49; Id. § 46—53, pp. 49—53; Id. § 59, p. 58. See 1 Boullenois, Observ. 6, pp. 127—130, 135; Id. Observ. 9, pp. 150—156; J. Voet, ad Pand. lib. 1, tit. 4, § 7, p. 40; 2 Froland. Mém. des Stat. 821.—There are some nice distinctions put by different authors upon this subject, which are stated with great clearness and force by Mr. Livermore, (Dissert. § 58, pp. 58—62), and upon which we may have occasion to comment more fully hereafter. At present it is only necessary to say, that Boullenois, Bouhier, and others hold, that while the law of the domicil, as to general capacity, governs as to contracts and property everywhere, the law of the situs of immovable property governs as to the quantity which the party, having full capacity, may sell, convey, or dispose of. See Livermore, Diss. § 58—63, p. 58; 1 Boullenois, Prin. Gen. 8, p. 7; Id. Observ. 6, pp. 127—133; Id. Observ. 12, pp. 172, 175—178; Id. Observ. 13, pp. 177, 183, 184, 188, 189; Bouhier, Cout. de Bourg. ch. 21, § 68—70; Id. § 81—84. See also 1 Boullenois, Observ. 5, pp. 101, 102, 107, 111, 112; 2 Henrys, Œuvres, lib. 4, ch. 6, quest. 105. Rodenburg seems to admit, that a contract respecting real property, which is entered into according to the forms of the lex loci contractus, may be good to bind the party personally, although it is not according to the forms prescribed by the lex rei sitæ. Rodenburg, tit. 2, ch. 3; 1 Boullenois, 414—416; 2 Boullenois, App. p. 19. M. Fœlix has enumerated many of the jurists on each side of this question in his Dissertation on the Conflict of Law: Fœlix, Conflit des Lois, Revue Etrang. et Fran. (1840, tom. 7), § 27—32, pp. 216—221; 2 Burge, Comm. on Col. and For. Law, pt. 2, ch. 9, pp. 840—870. Muhlenbruch, who is a very modern author, and is cited by Mr. Fœlix, has a single passage on the subject, which, from its generality, may serve to shew how difficult it is to obtain any certainty as to the exact opinion of foreign jurists on the various questions which may arise from the conflict of laws as to personal capacity, contracts, and rights to property. He lays down the following rules on the subject:—(1.) Jura atque officia ejusmodi, quæ hominum personis inhærent, et quasi sunt infixa, ex hisque apte pendentia, tum etiam ea, quæ ad universitatem patrimonii pertinent, ex legibus judicanda sunt, quæ in civitate valent, ubi is, de quo quæritur, larem rerumque ac fortunarum suarum summam constituit, scilicet non adversante exterarum civitatum jure publico. Enimvero mutato domicilio jura quoque hujusmodi mutantur, sic tamen, ut ne cui jus ex pristina ratione

§ 369. So, in respect to express nuptial contracts, we have seen that many foreign jurists hold them obligatory upon all property, whether movable or immovable, belonging to the parties in other countries, if they are valid by the law of the place of the nuptial contract[1]. And in respect to implied nuptial contracts, all those jurists who maintain

---

quæsitum, certisque suis terminis jamjam definitum eripiatur. (2.) Jura, quæ proxime rebus sunt scripta, velut quæ ad dominii causam spectant, vel ad vectigalium tributorumque onus, vel ad pignorum in judicati exsecutionem et capiendorum et distrahendorum, tum etiam rerum apud judicem petendarum persequendarumve rationem, et quæ sunt reliqua ex hoc genere, æstimantur ex legibus ejus civitatis, ubi sitæ sunt res, de quibus agitur, atque collocatæ, nullo rerum immobilium atque mobilium habito discrimine. (3.) Negotiorum rationem quod attinet, de forma quidem, quatenus non nisi ad fidem auctoritatemque negotio conciliandam valeat, nec in aliarum legum fraudem actum sit, non est, quod dubitemus, quin accommodate ad ejus loci instituta, ubi geritur res, dirigenda sit atque æstimanda. Nec est, quod non idem statuamus aut de personis, scilicet possintne omnino jure suo et velut arbitrio negotia instituere? Aut de negotiorum materia, atque vi et potestate, quæ iis cum per se insit, tum vero quoad agendi excipiendique facultatem, hac tamen itidem adscripta exceptione, ut ne quid in aliena civitate fiat contra ejusdem civitatis mores, leges, instituta, ad quæ immutanda prorsus nihil valet privatorum arbitrium. Quid? quod omnino sese, qui negotium aliquod instituerunt, tacite accommodasse videri possunt ad ejus regionis leges consuetudinesve, in qua ut exitum habeat res, de qua agitur, aut legum decreto, aut privatorum auctoritate certo constitutum est. (4.) Judex igitur, qui rem apud exteros natam judicabit, ea certe, quæ ad formam modumque litium instituendarum pertinent, ad jurium normas institutaque, quibus ipse paret, dirigat necesse est. In reliquis vero, quatenus aut idem illud servet jus domesticum, aut jus exteris scriptum, tamquam privatorum voluntate constitutum, in judicando sequatur, id ex principiis modo propositis quisque facile intelliget. Quibus etiam hæc esse consentanea videntur, ut præscriptio quidem acquisitiva, quam vocant, ex juribus rei sitæ, extinctiva vero ex judicii accepti legibus æstimanda sit, præterquam quod nihil hac quoque ratione juris detrahatur actori, si forte ingratiis suis loco haud condicto convenire reum cogatur; ut actiones, quæ vel ad rescindenda negotia, vel ad damna resarcienda comparatæ sunt, secundum leges loci, ubi res acta est, judicentur, nisi si ut alio loco fiat solutio, inter partes convenerit. Cæterum quæ de negotiorum alibi contractorum in alieno territorio vi diximus atque potestate, eadem sententiis quoque decretisque a judice prolatis apte convenient. Muhlenbruch, Doctrina Pandectarum, tom. 1, pp. 166—170. See also P. Voet, De Stat. § 4, ch. 2, n. 15, p. 127; Id. p. 142, (edit. 1661).

[1] Ante, § 143—160.

that the law of the domicil furnishes, in the absence of any express contract, the rule to ascertain the rights and intentions of the parties, by way of tacit contract, necessarily give to the doctrine the same universal operation[1].

§ 369 *a.* Dumoulin is most emphatic upon this matter. *Primo, in sano intellectu,* (says he), *nullum habet dubium, quin societas* (he is speaking of cases of marriage) *semel contracta, complectatur bona ubicunque sita, sine ulla differentia territorii, quam ad modum quilibet contractus, sive tacitus, sive expressus, ligat personam, et res disponentis ubique. Non obstat, quod hujusmodi societas non est expressa, sed tacita, nec oritur ex contractu expresso partium, sed ex tacito, vel præsumpto contractu a consuetudine locali introducto*[2].

§ 370. Merlin seems to think that, although in general the French law must govern in all cases of immovables in France, even when the owners are foreigners, yet that there are exceptions to the rule. As, for instance, if the foreign law, in the country where a contract is made respecting immovables, has been adopted by the contracting parties, and converted by them into an express contract; in such a case, he holds that the contract is binding, because the foreign law, as such, does not act upon the immovables in France; but it acts solely by way of contract[3]. And he applies the same principle to cases where there is no express adoption of the foreign law, but where it arises by way of tacit contract from the place of the contract[4].

§ 371. On the other hand, Pothier treats as real property, not only lands and houses and inheritable property, but also all rights in them and growing out of them; such as ground rents, or other rents annexed to lands and inherit-

---

1 Ante, § 57, 143—171: 1 Boullenois, Observ. 5, pp. 120, 121; Id. pp. 673, 674; Id. Observ. 29, pp. 757—767.

2 Dumoulin, Consil. 53, tom. 2, § 2, p. 964, (edit. 1681); 2 Burge, Comm. pt. 2, ch. 9, pp. 864, 865; Ante, § 260.

3 Merlin, Répert. Lois, § 6, n. 2, 3.

4 Ibid.

ances which fall under the denomination of *jus in re*; and also all rights to inheritances which fall under the denomination of *jus ad rem,* such as contracts or debts (*créances*) respecting the sale and delivery of immovable property, which are deemed to have the same situation as the things which are the object of them. *Les choses, qui ont une situation véritable, sont les héritages, c'est-à-dire, les fonds de terre, et maisons, et tout ce qui en fait partie. Les droits réels, que nous avons dans un héritage, qu'on appelle Jus in re, tels qu'un droit de rente foncière, de champart, &c. sont censés avoir la même situation que cet héritage. Pareilment, les droits que nous avons à un héritage, qu'on appelle Jus ad rem, c'est-à-dire, les créances que nous avons contre quelqu'un, qui c'est obligé à nous donner un certain héritage, sont censés avoir la même situation que l'héritage, qui en est l'objet*[1]. And he asserts the general principle, that all things which have a real or fictitious situation, are subject to the law of the place where they are situate, or are supposed to be situate. *Toutes ces choses, qui ont une situation réelle, ou feinte, sont sujettes à la loi ou coutume du lieu, où elles sont situées, ou censées d'être*[2]. This also is the doctrine maintained by Rodenburg and Boullenois[3].

---

1 Pothier, Cout. d'Orléans, ch. 1, § 2, n. 23, 24; Id. ch. 3, n. 51; Id. Traité des Choses, § 3; Post, § 382.

2 Pothier, Cout. d'Orléans, ch. 1, § 2, n. 24; Id. ch. 3, n. 51; Id. Traité des Choses, § 3.

3 1 Boullenois, Prin. Gén. 34—36, pp. 8, 9; Id. Observ. 5, pp. 121—129; Id. pp. 223—225; Id. Observ. 20, pp. 374, 381, 488; 2 Boullenois, Observ. 46, p. 472; Rodenburg, De Div. Stat. tit. 2, ch. 2, n. 2, p. 15; Henry on For. Law, 14 note; Id. 15.—Cochin lays down the following doctrine: "Les formalites, dont un acte doit être revêtu, se réglent par la loi, qui excerce son empire dans le leu, où l'acte a été passé; mais, quand il s'agit d'appliquer les clauses, qu'il renferme, aux biens des parties contractantes, c'est le lieu de la situation de ses biens, qui doit seule étre consultée." And he illustrates by reference to a donation in Paris, of property situated in places where donations inter vivos are prohibited, holding, that such donations, although clothed with all the proper Parisian formalities, are nullities. He then adds, "Ce n'est donc pas la loi du lieu, où l'acte a été passé, qui en détermine l'effet." Cochin, Œuvres, tom. 5, p. 697. See also 1 Boullenois, Prin. Gén. 31, p. 8.

Merlin, in a general view, assents to it[1]. Pothier further states, in relation to debts which are but *jus ad rem,* that they follow the nature of the thing, which is the object of the contract according to the maxim; *actio mobilis est mobilis; actio ad immobile est immobilis.* Hence, a debt due for money, or for any movable thing, belongs to the class of movable property. So also does a contract to do, or not to do any particular thing. He admits, that the same rule applies even when it is accompanied by an hypothecation of immovable property therefor. So that, when a debt is executed, and an hypothecation is made of immovable property, as collateral security, the debt is still to be deemed a movable debt, although the hypothecation might, *per se,* be an immovable debt; because the debt is the principal and the hypothecation the accessory; and, *accessorium sequitur naturam principalis*[2]. But he insists that contracts, which have for their objects any inheritable property or other immovable, are to be deemed immovable property; such as, for instance, in the case of a contract for the purchase of real estate, the right of the vendee against the vendor for the delivery of the same[3].

§ 371 *a.* D'Argentré says:—Whenever the question respects immovables or inheritances, situate in different places, where there are different modes of acquiring, transferring, and asserting ownership, and the question is, by what law they are to be governed,—the most certain rule in use is, that the law of the place where the property is situate is for the most part to be observed, and its laws, statutes, and customs, to be observed. He adds, that this rule prevails in contracts, in testāments, and in commercial matters. *Cum de rebus soli, id est immobilibus agitur, (qu'ils appellent*

---

1 Merlin, Répertoire, Meubles, § 5; Id. Biens, § 2, n. 2; Id. Loi. § 6, n. 3.

2 Pothier, Cout. d'Orléans, ch. 1, § 2, n. 24; Id. n. 50.

3 Pothier, Cout. d'Orléans, ch. 3, art. 2, n. 50, 51; Id. Traité des Choses, § 2. See Merlin, Répertoire, Biens, § 1, n. 13, § 2, n. 1; Id. Meubles, § 2, 3; Liverm. Diss. pp. 162, 163.

d'héritage), et diversa diversarum possessionum loca et situs proponuntur, in acquirendis, transferendis, aut asserendis dominiis, et in controversia est, quo jure regantur, certissima usu observatio est, id jus de pluribus spectari, quod loci est, et suas cuique loco leges, statuta, et consuetudines servandas, et qui cuique mores de rebus, territorio, et potestatis finibus sint recepti, sic ut de talibus nulla cujusquam potestas sit præter territorii legem. Sic in contractibus, sic in testamentis sic in commerciis omnibus, et locis conveniendi constitutum; ne contra situs legem in immobilibus, quidquam decerni privato consensu, et par est sic judicari[1].

§ 371 *b.* Christinæus adopts the very language of D'Argentré with seeming approbation[2], although there are other passages in which he seems to admit that a different rule prevails in respect to the acts which are done by a party which are to be governed by the *lex loci actûs.*—At least, he cites without disapprobation the doctrine of Baldus, (who certainly contradicts himself in the passages cited), that in the solemnities of testaments, the law of the place where the testament is made is to govern, even although the property is situate elsewhere[3]. However, he admits that in Belgium, by an express edict, the law of the *situs* in such cases prevails[4].

§ 371 *c.* John Voet has expressed a very different opinion. He holds, that it is sufficient in all cases, whether the contract respects movable property or immovable property, to follow the law of the place where the contract is made and the act done, whether it be a contract or a will. *Neque minus de statutis mixtis, actus cujusque solemnia respicientibus, percrebuit, insuper habitis de summo cujusque jure ac potestate ratiociniis, ad validitatem actus cujusque adhibitionem solemnitatum, quas lex loci, in quo actus geritur, præscrip-*

---

[1] D'Argent. ad Brit. Leg. Des Donat. art. 218, gloss. 6, n. 3, 1 vol. p. 647; Post, § 438.

[2] Christinæus, tom. 2, Decis. 3, n. 1, 2; Id. Decis. 4, n. 1, 4—6, pp. 4—6.

[3] Id. Decis. 3, n. 7.

[4] Id. Decis. 4, n. 1—3, p. 6.

serit observandas; sic ut quod ita gestum fuerit, sese porrigat ad bona mobilia et immobilia, ubicunque sita aliis in territoriis, quorum leges longè alium, longeque pleniorem requirunt solemnium interventum[1]. He assigns, as the principal reason, that otherwise, from ignorance or want of skill, it would be almost impossible for a man who possessed real property to make a valid disposition thereof by an act *inter vivos*, or by testament[2]. He adds, that this rule prevails in Belgium, in Spain, in Germany, and in France[3].

§ 371 *d.* Paul Voet holds a similar opinion, and puts several cases to illustrate it. If a testator in the place of his

---

1 J. Voet, ad Pand. lib. 1, tit. 4, Ps. 2, § 13, p. 45.

2 Ibid.

3 Ibid. citing authorities. His language is:—"Quod ita placuisse videtur, tum, ne in infinitum prope multiplicarantur et testamenta et contractus, pro numero regionum, diverso jure circa solennia utentium; atque ita summis implicarentur molestiis, ambagibus, ac difficultatibus, quotquot actum, res plures pluribus in locis sitas concernentem, expedire voluerint: tum etiam, ne plurima bonâ fide gesta nimis facile ac prope sine culpâ gerentis conturbarentur. Tum quia ne ipsis quidem in juris praxi versatissimis, multoque minus aliis simplicitate desidiâque laborantibus, ac juris scientiam haud professis, satis compertum est, ac vix per industriam exquisitissimam esse potest, quæ in unoquoque loco requisita sint actuum solennia, quid indies in hâc vel illâ regione novis legibus circa solennium observantiam mutetur: ut proinde, quæ ratio de militari testamento obtinuit Quiritium jure, milites nempe solennibus paganorum non fuisse adstringendos, dum in castris et expeditione occupati erant, quia et juris imperiti erant, et peritiores consulere in castris non poterant, etiam nunc suadeat, illum, qui actum gerit, ad alterius loci, quam in quo gerit, solennia non esse obligandum; quia et probabiliter aliorum locorum solennia ignorare potest, et in loco, in quo actum gerit, peritiores morum alienæ regionis non satis consulere; dum ita fere comparatum est, ut pragmatici, quibus auctoribus contractus celebrantur, aut conduntur testamenta, versati quidem plerumque satis sint in jure patrio, non item locorum omnium et universi orbis jure; atque insuper non raro moræ ad inquisitionem anxiam adhibendam impatiens est, quod geritur negotium. Quamvis ergo in Frisiâ septem testes in testamento requiri constet, alibi fere tabellionis testiumque duorum præsentia ac fides sufficiat, aut saltem in universum longe minor solennitas desideretur; tamen æquitate rei motus Frisiæ Senatus ratam habuit de bonis Frisicis dispositionem, Sylvæ ducis coram parocho duobusque testibus declaratam, juxta Sylvæducensis regionis usum. Et ita in praxi hæc Belgis, Germanis, Hispanis, Gallis, aliisque placuisse, auctores cujusque gentis testantur.

domicil makes a will according to the law of the place *rei sitæ*, but not according to the law of the place of his domicil, he asks the question, whether such a will is good, as to property situated elsewhere; and he answers in the negative. He next puts the case of a testator who makes his will according to the law of his place of domicil, as for example, before a notary and two witnesses; and asks, whether the will has effect upon property situate in another country, where more and other solemnities are required; and he answers in the affirmative. He then asks, if a foreigner makes his will according to the law of the place where he is merely lodging or commorant, whether the will is valid elsewhere, where he either has immovable property, or he has his domicil; and he answers in the affirmative. The only exception he makes is, where the testator, in order to evade the law, or in fraud of the law of his own domicil, goes into another country, and there makes his will [1].

§ 371 *e*. Hertius, as we have seen [2], lays down the rule, that as to the forms and solemnities of acts and contracts, they are to be governed altogether by the law of the place where the acts are done and contracts made, and not by the law of the domicil of the party or the law of the *situs rei*. *Si lex actui formam dat, inspiciendum est locus actus, non domicilii, non rei sitæ; id est, si de solennibus quæratur, si de loco, de tempore, de modo actus, ejus loci habenda est ratio, ubi actus vel negotium celebratur* [3]. He adds: *Regula hæc apud omnes, quantum quidem sciam, est indubitata;* and then says: *Valet etiamsi bona in alio territorio sint sita* [4].

§ 372. Burgundus apparently admits that generally the law of the place of the contract ought in all cases to prevail so far as respects its form, its ceremonies, and its obligation.

---

1 P. Voet, de Stat. § 9, c. 2, n. 1—4, pp. 261, 262, (edit. 1715); Id. pp.317—319, (edit. 1661).

2 Ante, § 260.

3 Hertii, Opera, De Collis, Leg. § 4, n. 10, p. 126, (edit. 1737); Id. pp. 179, 180; Ante, § 238.

4 Ibid.

The passage already cited[1] is to this effect: *In scriptura instrumenti, in solemnitatibus, et ceremoniis, et generaliter in omnibus, quæ ad formam ejusque perfectionem pertinent, spectanda est consuetudo regionis, ubi fit negotiatio. Igitur, ut paucis absolvam, quoties de vinculo obligationis vel de ejus interpretatione vel interpretatione quæritur, veluti quos, et in quantum obliget, quid sententiæ stipulationem inessæ, quid abesse credi oporteat, &c., ut id sequamur, quod in regione, in qua actum est, frequentatur*[2]. But he immediately adds, that if we would know whether the contract was valid or not, in respect to the subject-matter thereof, we must look to the law of the *situs*: *Cæterum, ut sciamus, contractus ex parte materiæ utilis sit vel inutilis, ad leges, quæ rebus, de quibus tractatur, impressæ sunt, hoc est, ad consuetudinem situs, respiciemus*[3]. He also expresses surprise, that authors, in considering contracts, should have excluded altogether the nature of the thing contracted for, and generally to have interpreted contracts according to the law of the place where they are made; for in sales, and also in letting to hire, and in other contracts, it becomes us to look to the usuage touching the subject-matter. *Quippe non solum in emptione obtinet, ut ad consuetudinem rei spectare deceat, sed in locatione præterea, et conductione, ceterisque contractibus*[4]. It must be confessed, that on this subject the distinctions and doctrines of Burgundus are open to much question.

§ 372 *a.* Dumoulin says, that it is the general opinion of jurists, that wherever the custom or law of a place prescribes the solemnities or form of an act, it binds foreigners who there do the act; and the act is valid and efficacious even in respect to immovable property beyond the territory of the custom or law. *Et est omnium doctorum sententia,*

---

[1] Ante, § 300 *a.*

[2] Burgundus, Tract. 4, n. 7, 8, p. 104.

[3] Burgundus, Tract. 4, n. 8, 9, pp. 107, 108; 2 Boullenois, Observ. 46, pp. 450—454. See J. Voet, ad Pand. lib. 1, tit. 4, Ps. 2, § 12, 13, p. 45; Post, § 433.

[4] Burgundus, Tract. 4, n. 9; Id. n. 7; Ante, § 302; Post, § 433—438.

ubicunque consuetudo, vel statutum locale, disponet de solemnitate, vel forma actus, ligari etiam exteros, ibi actum illum gerentes, et gestum esse validum, et efficacem, ubique etiam super bonis solis extra territorium consuetudinis vel statuti[1]. Gaill adopts an equally broad conclusion: *Contractus enim, celebratus cum solemnitate requisita in loco contractus, extendit se ad omnia bona, licet in loco bonorum major solemnibus requireretur*[2].

§ 372 *b*. Rodenburg, as we shall presently see, goes the full length of this doctrine, and applies it even to the cases of wills and testaments, which, he says, if made according to the law of the place where they are executed, are valid even upon property situated elsewhere[3]. There are many other jurists who maintain the same opinion, both as to contracts and other instruments, and to wills and testaments[4].

---

1 Dumoulin, Consil. 53 tom. 2, § 9, p. 965; Post, 441.

2 Gaill, Pract. Observ. 123, n. 2, p. 548.

3 Rodenburg, De Div. Stat. tit. 2, c. 3, n. 1; 2 Boullenois, App. p. 19; Post, § 475.

4 Many of them are enumerated in 1 Boullenois, Observ. 23, pp. 491—516; Ante, § 301.—M. Fœlix also has given us a long list of jurists who hold the doctrine. Indeed, he thinks the doctrine firmly and generally established. His language is: Un principe aujourd'hui généralement adopté par l'usage des nations, c'est que 'la forme des actes est réglée par les lois du lieu dans lequel ils sont faits ou passés.' C'est-à-dire que, pour la validité de tout acte, il suffit d'observer les formalités préscrites par la loi du lieu où cet acte a été dressé ou rédigé: l'acte ainsi passé exerce ses effets sur les biens meubles et immeubles situés dans un autre territoire, dont les lois établissent des formalités différentes et plus étendues (locus regit actum). En d'autres termes, les lois, qui réglent la forme des actes, étendent leur autorité tant sur les nationaux que sur les étrangers, qui contractent ou disposent dans le pays, et elles participent ainsi de la nature des lois réelles. Le droit romain ne contient aucune disposition qui consacrât le principe: locus regit actum. Dans lesquelles on a prétendu trouver cette règle, ne parlent point de la forme, mais de la matière des contrats. Dès le temps des glossateurs, la question s'est présentée par rapport aux testaments. Bartole a adopté l'affirmative: Albert de Rosate s'est prononcé pour la négative, sur le motif que la loi n'oblige que les sujets, et que ceux-ci seuls ont le droit d'employer une forme prescrite. Plus tard, Cujas a soutenu, qu'il faut suivre la loi du domicile du testateur: Fachinée exigeait l'accomplissement des formalités

§ 372 *c*. Boullenois seems to have laboured under no small embarrassment as to the question whether a contract

---

préscrites dans le lieu de la situation des biens: Burgundus, tout en admettant la régle relativement aux contrats, la rejette quant aux testaments; il regarde comme affectant la chose et comme lois réelles les solennités prescrites pour lés testaments, en invoquant l'édit de 1611 (pour les Pays-Bas), art. 12. Choppin, au contraire, soutient que le testament fait en pays étranger, d'après les formes prescrites dans le lieu de la confection, doit sortir ses affets, même à l'égard des immeubles situés dans un autre lieu, et il rapporte un arrêt du parlement de Paris, rendu en ce sens. Dumoulin, Mynsinger et Gail professent la même doctrine. Ces deux derniers auteurs attestent là jurisprudence constante de la chambre impériale (Reichskammergericht) en ce sens. Mevius, en admettant aussi la règle générale, fait remarquer que la coutume de Lubeck ne la reconnaît que sous les trois conditions suivantes; 1° maladie qui met le testateur en danger de mort; 2° décés réel en pays étranger; 3° absence de toute intention de préjudicier a aux héritiere naturels. Rodenburg et Voet, en adoptant la rêgle par rapport aux contrats comme aux testaments, la motivent sur les raisons suivantes: 1° nécessité d'éviter aux individus possédant des biens dans differents pays, l'embarras et la difficulté de rédiger autant de testaments ou de contrats qu'il y a d'immeubles situés sous l'empire de lois différentes, ou de remplir dans un même testament ou contrat toutes les solennités prescrites dans les divers lieux de la situation des biens; 2° impossibilité dans laquelle l'individu surpris à l'étranger par une maladie mortelle peut se trouver de remplir les solennités prescrites dans le pays de son domicile ou de la situation de ses biens; 3° nécessité d'empêcher que les actes faits de bonne foi soient annullés trop facilement sans la faute de la partie; 4° impossibilité pour la majecure partie des hommes de connaître les formes prescrites dans chaque localité; 5° enfin, Voet ajoute, qu'il faut appliquer ici les motifs, qui, chez les Romains, ont fait introduire la forme simple du testament militaire. En terminant, cet auteur cite presque tous ses devanciers indiques ci-dessus, en déclarant que l'opinion professée par lui a été reconnue par la jurisprudence dans les Pays-Bas, en Allemagne, en Espagne, et en France. Tel est aussi le sentiment de Zoesius, Grotius, Christin, Paul Voet, Vinnius, Jean de Sande, Vander Kessel, Vasquez, Perez, Cochin, Boullenois, Menochius, Carpzov, Huber, Hert, Hommel, Glück, Thibaut, Danz, Weber, Mansord, Muhlenbruch, Mittermaier, Tittman, Merlin, Meier, Pardessus, Story, Roçco, Hartogh, et Burge." Fœlix, Conflit des Lois Revue Etrang. et Franç. 1840, tom. 7, § 40—42, pp. 346—350. Mr. Fœlix has, however, subsequently qualified the general doctrine here stated by the following exceptions: "L'acte fait d'après les formes prescrites par la loi du lieu de sa rédaction est valable, non-seulement par rapport aux biens meubles appartenant à l'individu et qui se trouvent au lieu de son domicile, mais encore par rapport aux immeubles, en quelque endroit

was obligatory or not, merely by pursuing forms or solemnities prescribed by the law of the place where it is made.

---

qu'ils fussent situés. Cette dernière proposition, selon la nature des choses, admet une exception, dans le cas où la loi du lieu de la situation prescrit, à l'égard des actes translatifs de la propriété des immeubles, ou qui y affectent des charges réelles, des formes particulières, qui ne peuvent être remplies ailleurs que dans ce même lieu; telles sont la rédaction des actes par un notaire du même territoire, la transcription ou l'inscription aux registres tenus dans ce territoire, des actes d'aliénation, d'hypothèque, etc. L'acte fait dans un pays étranger suivant les formes qui y sont prescrites, ne perd pas sa force, quant à sa forme, par le retour de l'individu au lieu de son domicile : aucune raison de droit ne milite en faveur de l'opinion contraire. La règle, locus regit actum, ne doit pas être ètendue au delà des limites, que nous lui avons tracées au n° 40; elle ne s'applique qu'à la forme extérieure' et non pas à la matière ou substance des actes, ainsi que nous l'expliquerons encore au § suivant. Ainsi, dans un testament, la capacité de la personne et la disponibilité des biens ne se règlent point par la loi du lieu de la rédaction. Dans les dispositions entre-vifs, soit à titre oné reux, soit à titre gratuit, la loi du lieu de la rèdaction peut avoir influé, soit sur l'ensemble de l'acte, soit sur les termes employés par les parties ; et, sous ce double titre, cette loi peut être consultée par les juges comme moyen d'interprétation ; mais elle ne forme pas la loi décisive, à moins que les parties ne s'y soient soumises expressément." He afterwards adds: "La règle d'aprés laquelle la loi du lieu de la rédaction régit la forme de l'acte, admet differéntes exceptions, dont voici les principales : 1° Lorsque les contractants ou l'individu dont émane une disposition se sont rendus en pays étranger dans l'intention d'éluder une prohibition portée par la loi de leur domicile ; car la fraude fait exception à toutes les régles; 2° Lorsque la loi de la patrie défend expressément de contracter ou de disposer hors du territoire et avec des formes autres que celles prescrites par cette même loi ; car alors l'idée d'un consentement tacite de cette nation se trouve formellement exclue. Cette exception est la même que celle indiquée par M. Eichhorn, sous le n° 2; 3° En cas d'opposition expresse du statut réel Voy. supra, n° 43; Lorsque la loi du lieu de la rédaction attache à la forme qu'elle prescrit un effet, qui se trouve en opposition avec le droit public du pays où l'acte est destiné à recevoir son exécution; 5° Par rapport aux ambassadeurs ou ministres publics et à leur suite. Ces personnes ne sont pas soumises aux lois de la nation près de laquelle elles exercent leur mission diplomatique." And he finally sums up thus : "Une autre question est celle de savoir, si le contractant ou disposant, qui se trouve en pays étranger, peut se borner à employer les formes préscrites par la loi du lieu de la situation de ses immeubles, au lieu de suivre celle du lieu de la rédaction ? Nous tenons pour l'affirmative, par une raison analogue â celle donnée sur la question précédente. Le statut réel régit les immeubles ; c'est un principe résultant de la nature

He puts the case of two persons contracting, who are domiciled in one place and contract in another, and the thing

---

des choses; la permission d'user des formes établies par la loi du lieu de la rédaction de l'acte n'est qu'une exception introduite en faveur du propriétaire, et à laquelle il lui est loisible de renoncer. Tel est aussi le sentiment de Rodenburg, de Jean Voet, et de Vander Kessel; Cocceii soutient même que la forme des actes entre vifs ou testamentaires est régie exclusivement par la loi de la situation des biens. Fachinée et Burgundus (V. suprà, n° 41) partageaient cet avis, mais par rapport aux testaments seulement. En Belgique, l'édit perpétuel de 1611, art. 13, ordonnait, qu'en cas de diversité de coutume au lieu de la résidence du testateur et au lieu de la situation de ses biens, on suivrait, par rapport à la forme et à la solennité, la coutume de la situation. Paul Voet, Huber, Hert, Hommel et l'auteur de l'ancien répertoire de jurisprudence, se prononcent pour la nullité ; ce dernier invoque l'autorité de Paul de Castres, au passage rapporté au n° précédent, et le principe que la loi lie tous les individus, qui vivent dans son ressort, ne fût-ce que momentanément. Nous renvoyons à ce sujet aux observations présentées sur la question précédente. Mevius distingue entre le citoyen faisant partie de la nation dans le territoire de laquelle les biens sont situés, et entre l'étranger; il n'accorde qu'au primier la faculté de tester ou de contracter partout d'après les formes prescrites au lieu de la situation. L'auteur ne donne pas de motif de cette distinction, et nous ne pouvons la trouver fondée." Fœlix, Conflit des Lois, Revue Etrang. et Franç. tom. 7, 1840, pp. 352—360. See also the opinions of foreign jurists on the subject, 2 Burge, Comm. on Col. and For. Law, Pt. 2, ch. 9, pp. 840—871. In respect to some of these he has certainly been led into an error; and some speak so indeterminately, that it is difficult to gather what their opinion is. It is certain that M. Fœlix has misunderstood the opinion of Mr. Storey in his Conflict of Laws, (see § 364), and also the opinion of Mr. Burge. See 1 Burge, Comm. on Col. and For. Law, Pt. 1, ch. 1, pp. 21—24. His language is: "In examining all contracts, instruments, or dispositions, whether they are made inter vivos or are testamentary, our attention may be directed to four subjects: the first is, the capacity of him who makes it; the second is, the property, which is the subject or occasion of the contract or instrument; the third regards the formalities or ceremonies with which it is made; and the fourth is, the judicial process by which the rights which it confers are to be enforced. The capacity of the party to make the instrument is ascertained by consulting the law of the place of his domicil; because it is that law and that law alone which affects the person, and which gives or denies him the capacity or power to make the instrument. With respect to the property, the subject of the contract, disposition, instrument, or testament, recourse is had to the real law, being that which prevails in the place in which the property, if immovable, is actually situated; or in which, if it be movable or personal, it is presumed to be situated; that is, in the

respecting which the contract is made being situate in another, and asks, what ought to be the form and solem-

---

place of the possessor's domicil. When, however, it is necessary to ascertain whether the contract be valid, what is its true construction and effect, and whether the instrument, in which it is expressed, or whether a testament be duly and formally made, recourse is had to the law of the place in which the contract is entered into, or the instrument or testament was made; because, if it be made according to the forms prescribed by that law, it is valid everywhere. 'Aut statutum loquitur de his, quæ concernunt nudam ordinationem vel solemnitatem actus, et semper inspicitur statutum, vel consuetudo loci, ubi actus celebratur, sive in contractibus, sive in judiciis, sive in testamentis, sive in instrumentis aut aliis conficiendis, ita quod testamentum, factum coram duobus testibus in locis, ubi non requiritur major solemnitas, valet ubique.' A distinction, however, must be observed between such solemnities as are purely formal, and those which are of the substance and essence of the disposition or instrument. There are some solemnities which intrinsically affect the disposition itself, so as to render their observance essential to its validity, whilst there are others which only extrinsically regard them. An example of the former description of solemnities is given by Stockmans, in the case of a law which prohibits the husband and wife from instituting the one the heir of the other, unless by a will executed before two notaries. If the party made a will in the common form, in a place where no such law prevailed, it would be invalid, in respect of property situated in the place where it did prevail. Similar examples are afforded by the English Statute of Frauds, which denies the capacity to devise real property, otherwise than by a will attested by three or more credible witnesses; and by the law of Jamaica, which enables a married woman to convey her real estate, and a tenant in tail to bar the remainder, and acquire the fee by a simple conveyance; but it requires, at the same time, that the married woman should be examined apart from her husband, and that the conveyance should be acknowledged and recorded. The following example of that species of solemnity, which is extrinsic to the disposition, is given by Stockmans, in the case which has been cited: 'Si quis incola ditionis regiæ testetur in urbe Leodiensi, ubi testatoris subscriptio in testamentis necessaria non est, sed sufficit communis ritus, qui in aliis publicis instrumentis requiritur.' There may be said to be three species of solemnities: first, those which are requisite to enable the person, as for instance, the authority from the husband to the wife, essential, by the law of some countries, to the validity of her act. These are derived from, and must be examined with reference to the law of the domicil, or the lex loci rei sitæ. Secondly, those which form a part of, and are essential to the act, such as the delivery of the subject-matter of a gift. The third species of solemnities consists of those which are designed to establish the truth or

nities necessary to make it valid, if in each place they are different? If it is clear that the forms appertain to the solemnities of the act, he thinks that there is no difficulty in affirming, that the law of the place of the contract ought to govern. If the forms relate to the capacity of the person, then the law of the place of his domicil ought to govern. But if, on the contrary, they appertain either to the substantials of the contract, or its nature, or its accidents, or its fulfilment, (*sive ad substantialia contractus, sive ad naturalia, sive ad accidentalia, aut complementaria*), there is great difficulty, and if any general rule is established, either to follow the law of the place of the contract, or that of the *situs* of the thing, or that of the domicil of the contracting parties, a false principle will be introduced; for sometimes the formalities belong to the quality of the person, sometimes to the contract, and sometimes to other things. He therefore arrives at the conclusion, that no universal rule can be laid down applicable to all classes of cases[1]. In another place Boullenois remarks, that the French authors (*nos auteurs*) are generally of opinion, that the law of the place of the contract is to govern; *locus contractûs regit actum*[2]. And he then proceeds to lay down certain rules on the subject, which have been already cited, as the guiding principles[3]. And among them is the very important rule applicable to the subject before us, that where the law requires certain formalities which are attached to the things themselves, the law of the *situs* or situation is to govern[4].

§ 372 *d*. Mr. Burge, after suggesting that there are three

---

authenticity of the instrument, such as the proof by two or more notaries, or one notary and two witnesses, or the number, age, and quality of witnesses required for the validity of a will."

[1] 1 Boullenois, Observ. 23, pp. 464—466; 2 Boullenois, Observ. 46, p. 445.

[2] 2 Boullenois, Observ. 46, p. 456.

[3] Ante, § 240.

[4] 2 Boullenois, Observ. 46, p. 467; Ante, § 240.

species of solemnities, which he enumerates, adds: "A further distinction may be made between those solemnities which relate to contracts and instruments for the transfer of real property, and those by which it is actually transferred. With respect to the first, those are to be followed which prevail in the place where those contracts are made, or those instruments executed; but with regard to the actual transfer of such property, those are to be observed which are prescribed by the law of the place where it is situated. Thus, a contract to sell or mortgage real property will be valid, if the solemnities are observed, which are required by the law of the place where the contract is made, and will be the foundation of a personal action against the party to that contract, to compel the transport or mortgage of such property, but no transport or mortgage will be complete, nor will the *dominium* in the property have been transferred or acquired, unless those solemnities are observed which are required by the law of the place where it is situated[1]." Again he adds, in another place: "In considering the law by which the transfer of immovable property is governed, a distinction should be made between the contract to transfer, and the actual transfer of the *dominium*. There may be cases in which the law of the domicil, or that of the place of the contract, will prevail, notwithstanding it may be opposed to that of the *situs*, whilst, in other cases, the law of the *situs* will prevent the contract taking effect. Thus, instances are cited by jurists where the law of the domicil incapacitates the party from contracting; but the law of the *situs* authorizes the alienation of his immovables. Thus, by the law of Ghent, persons were minors until they had attained the age of twenty-five years; but in Hainault, a person of the age of twenty might alienate his fief situated in that country. An inhabitant of Ghent contracts to sell a fief in Hainault, of which he was the owner. The con-

---

[1] 1 Burge, Comm. on Col. and For. Law, pt. 1, ch. 1, p. 24; 2 Burge, Comm. on Col. and For. Law, pt. 2, ch. 9, pp. 844, 845.

tract, in the opinion of Burgundus, would create no obligation on him to complete this alienation. *Ut puta, civis Gandensis ætate minor, tamen vigesimum egressus annum, Hannonica feuda sine auctoritate tutoris vendidit; procul dubio in ejusmodi actu nihil agi existimandum est, et inutilem omninò contrahi obligationem; quia Gandavi, qui aliter emancipati non sunt, ante vigesimum quintum annum rebus suis intervenire prohibentur.* But if the alienation were actually made, the same jurist considers that it would be valid: *Si tamen ejusmodi feudi mancipationem fecerit venditor, tutum esse emptorem, et quod actum erit valere quotidianâ accipimus experientiâ, quando hæc sit ætas et competens, quæ in Hanonicorum feudorum alienatione requiritur. Nec enim consuetudo Gandensis potest tollere libertatem mancipationis, quia res alienas legibus suis alligare non potest; hoc enim jus dicere extra territorium.* A decision is reported by Stockman, in which the same doctrine was held. T. being of the age of twenty, and married, was according to the law of his domicil so far emancipated, as to be capable of administering, but not of alienating his estate. He alienated a property situated in Louvain, where the effect of his marriage gave him the full capacity of majority. An action was brought by his heir to recover back the purchase money, on the ground, that T. was incompetent by the law of his domicil to alienate his property, and that this law extended to, and prevented the disposition by him of his property in Louvain. But the purchaser insisted, and the Court held, that the validity of the alienation must be decided according to the law of Louvain, and dismissed the action. It follows from this doctrine, that if the person, competent by the law of his domicil, should contract to make an alienation of property situated in a country where he was incompetent to make it, his contract could not be enforced, although he might be answerable in damages to the person with whom he had contracted. On the other hand, if he were incompetent by the law of his domicil to contract, but competent to alienate by the *lex loci rei sitæ*, and an alienation was actually made by him, it would not be rescinded on the ground that he was incompetent by the law of his domicil to contract. In the cases put by Burgundus, and reported by Stockman, it will be perceived that the alienation was complete. It does not follow, that if the vendor had refused to perform his contract, the forum of the *rei sitæ* would have enforced it. The doctrine of Rodenburg is, that the contract is a nullity, and that effect cannot be given to it in any Court to compel its performance by the delivery of the property. Wesel, who concurs with Rodenburg, treats the delivery or *mancipatio* as the *simplex implementum* of the contract; and, as it is required for the validity of a sale that there should have been a preceding contract, he urges: *Cùm ergo totus venditionis contractus ob defectum ætatis sit irritus, nec sit quod mancipatione solenni impleri possit, utique nuda simplexque fundi mancipatio omninò nihil operatur, cessante causâ ad mancipandum idoneâ*[1]."

§ 372 *e.* And again, he says: "So, if those solemnities, which the *lex loci contractûs* requires, have been observed, and the contract according to that law is valid and obligatory, it will be valid everywhere else. But the latter proposition is subject to the qualification, that it does not affect immovable property, subject to a law in the country of its *situs,* which annuls a contract, because it has not been entered into with the solemnities which it requires. If the disposition of the law does not annul the contract on account of its non-observance of the solemnities which are prescribed, but gives to it a degree of authenticity or credit, which it will want if they are not observed, or if, in other words, its effect is either to dispense with a more formal proof of the instrument, if it bears on it evidence of their observance, or if in consequence of the non-observance it attaches a presumption against the execution of the instrument, and therefore requires from the parties a greater burden of proof,

---

[1] 2 Burge, Comm. on Col. and For. Law, pt. 2, ch. 20, pp. 844—846; Id. pp. 867—870.

such solemnities are to be classed amongst the proofs in the cause, which are governed neither by the *lex loci contractûs*, nor by that of the *situs*, but by that of the *forum*. This question, in the opinion of Paul Voet, regards *non tam de solemnibus, quàm probandi efficaciâ; quæ licet in uno loco sufficiens, non tamen ubique locorum; quod judex unius territorii nequeat vires tribuere instrumento, ut alibi quid operetur*[1]." There are other jurists, who maintain the same distinction[2].

---

[1] 2 Burge, Comm. on Col. and For. Law, pt. 2, ch. 9, pp. 867, 868. See also 3 Burge, Comm. pt. 2, ch. 20, pp. 751, 752.

[2] P. Voet, Ad Statut. § 4, c. 2, n. 15, 16, p. 142, (edit.1661); Ersk. Inst. b. 3, tit. 2, § 40.—Mr. Burge adds on this point: "When the question regards the property, which the law allows to be alienated, or the persons to whom, or the purposes for which its alienation may be made, it can be determined only by the law of the situs. The statutes of mortmain, the law of death-bed, the restriction of gifts inter conjuges, are strictly real laws, to which the parties to the contract must conform, although no such laws exist in the place of their domicil, or in that of the contract. In these instances the law of the situs is prohibitory, and impresses on the property a quality excluding it from the alienation. A contract, therefore, to make such an alienation as would, in any of these respects, contravene the law of the situs, would be wholly ineffectual. But when the contract does not expressly not by necessary implication contravene it, but on the contrary may be carried into effect consistently with, or by means of its provisions, although the contract itself may not give a title, yet it will be the foundation of an action by the one to compel the other to complete it in that manner, which the law of the situs requires in order to give him that title. The observation of Du Moulin, in commenting on an article of the coutume of Auvergne, illustrates this distinction. By that article all contracts or conventions respecting the succession had the effect of vesting the seisin in the person in whose favour they were made. This great jurist, whilst he thus limits its operation, de prædiis sitis sub hâc consuetudine, et non extra ejus territorium, at the same time adds, Valet quidem pactio ubique, sed translatio possessionis, quæ sit in vim consuetudinis, non valet nisi intra ejus territorium. The deed by which parties in England convey an estate in British Guiana, has no effect as a transport of it, but it operates as a contract of transport, and enables the purchaser to compel the vendor to complete the transport in the manner prescribed by the law of that settlement. Erskine has thus stated the doctrine of the law of Scotland on this subject. All personal obligations or contracts entered into according to the law of the place where they are signed, or secundum legem domicilii, vel loci contractus, are deemed as effectual, when they come to receive execution in Scotland, as if they had been perfected in the Scottish form. And this holds even in such obligations as bind

§ 372 *f*. That there may be some ground for such a distinction as is above stated, may well be admitted. But that the rule generally prevails in all nations, may well be doubted. Thus, it seems very clear that a contract made in a foreign country, for the sale of lands situate in England, Scotland, or America, would not be held a binding contract in either of those countries, to be enforced in their courts *in personam*, or *in rem*, unless the contract was in conformity to the forms prescribed by those countries [1]. At the same time, it is quite possible that the same contract might be enforced in the country where it was made, if it should conform to the law of that country touching real property [2]. But after all, looking to the great diversity of views of foreign jurists, there is much reason to be satisfied with the general rule of the common law on this whole subject; that is to say, that in respect to movables, the law of the place where the contract is made, will, with few exceptions, be allowed to govern the forms and solemnities thereof [3]; but as to immovables, no contract is obligatory or binding unless the contract is made with the forms and solemnities required by the local law where they are contracted. *(Lex sitûs)* [4].

§ 373. But, whatever may be the true rule in cases where the law of the *situs* does not prohibit the contract, as for instance a contract for the sale of land, it is very clear that, if prohibited there, it is every where invalid to all in-

---

the grantor to convey subjects within Scotland; for where one becomes bound by a lawful obligation, he cannot cease to be bound by changing places. An English deed, if so executed in point of form as validly to carry Scots heritage, will be given effect to in regard to such heritage, agreeably to the law of Scotland, notwithstanding the same deed would, by the English law under similar circumstances, be unavailable in respect of heritage situate in England." 2 Burge, Comm. on Col. and For. Law, pt. 2, ch. 9, pp. 846—848; Id. pp. 864, 865.

1 Ante, § 363—365.

2 Ante, § 76.

3 Ante, § 362—364; Post, § 379, 383, 384.

4 Ante, § 364—367, 382, 383.

tents and purposes. So the doctrine is laid down by Rodenburg. After remarking, that if a contract is made that the dotal rights shall be according to the custom of another place than that of the domicil of the husband, it will be good if there is no local law of either place which prohibits it; he adds, that the contrary, if the contract is opposed to the local, law is true *rei sitæ. Contra, si per leges loci, ubi bona constituta sunt, limitetur illud rerum immobilium doarium, &c.; eo quod nemini liceat privatâ cautione refragari legi publicæ negativæ aut prohibitoriæ*[1]. Boullenois also lays down the same rule among his general maxims: *Une convention, toute légitime qu'elle soit en elle-même, n'a pas son éxécution sur les biens, lorsqu'ils sont situés en coutumes prohibitives de la convention*[2]. Mr. Burge also lays down among his general principles the following rule: "In a conflict between a personal law of the domicil and a real law, either of the domicil or of any other place, the real law prevails over the personal law. Thus, a person who has attained his majority, and has, as incident to that *status*, the power of disposing by donation *inter vivos* of every thing he possessed, may, by the real *statute* of the place in which his property is situated, be restrained from giving the whole, or from giving it except to particular persons[3]".

---

1 2 Rodenburg, De Div. Stat. tit. 3, ch. 4, n. 1, 2; 2 Boullenois, Observ. 42, pp. 401, 402; Id. App. pp. 79, 80.

2 Boullenois, Princ. Gén. 41, pp. 9, 10; Ante, § 262.

3 1 Burge, Comm. on Col. and For. Law, pt. 1, ch. 1, p. 28, § 20; Id. p. 26, § 8, 9. It may be remarked, that some of the general principles laid down by Mr. Burge in the chapter here cited, which he says "may be adopted," admit of grave question, and are not supported by the common law.

CHAPTER IX.

PERSONAL PROPERTY.

§ 374. We next come to the consideration of the operation of foreign law in relation to personal, real, and mixed property, according to the known divisions of the common law, or to movable and immovable property, according to the known divisions of the civil law, and continental jurisprudence. For all the purposes of the present commentaries it will be sufficient to treat the subject under the heads of personal or movable property, and real or immovable property, since the class of mixed property appertains to the latter[1].

§ 375. We have already had occasion to state, that in the civil law the term, *Bona,* includes all sorts of property, movable and immovable; as the corresponding word, *Biens,* in French, also does[2]. But there are many cases in which a broad distinction is taken by foreign jurists between movable property and immovable property, as to the operation of foreign law. We have also had occasion to explain the general distinction between personal and real laws respectively, and mixed laws in the sense in which the terms are used in continental jurisprudence; personal being those which have principally persons for their object, and only treating of property incidentally; real, being those which have principally property for their object, and speaking of persons only in relation to property; and mixed, being those which concern both persons and property[3].

---

1 See on the subject of this chapter, 3 Burge, Comm. on Col. and For. Law, pt. 2, ch. 20, pp. 749—780.

2 See Liverm. Dissert. p. 81, § 106; 1 Boullenois, Observ. 2, p. 28; Id. Observ. 6, p. 127; Rodenburg, De Div. Stat. tit. 1, c. 2; 2 Boullenois, App. p. 6; Merlin, Répert. Biens, § 1.

3 Ante, § 12—16; 1 Boullenois. Princ. Gén. pp. 4—9; Id. Observ. 2,

§ 376. According to this distribution all laws respecting property, whether it be movable or immovable, would fall under the denomination of real laws; and of course upon the principles of the leading foreign jurists, would seem to be limited in their operation to the territory where the property is situate[1]. This, however, is a conclusion, which upon a larger examination will be found to be erroneous; the general doctrine held by nearly all foreign jurists being, that the right and disposition of movables is to be governed by the law of the domicil of the owner, and not by the law of their local situation[2].

§ 377. The grounds upon which this doctrine as to movables is supported, are differently stated by different jurists; but the differences are more nominal than real. Some of them are of opinion, that all laws which regard movables are real; but at the same time they maintain that by a fiction of law all movables are supposed to be in the place of the domicil of the owner, *à quo legem situmque accipiunt.* Others are of opinion that such laws are personal, because movables have in contemplation of law no *situs,* and are attached to the person of the owner wherever he is; and, being so adherent to his person, they are governed by the same laws which govern his person; that is, by the law of the place of his domicil[3]. The former opinion is maintained by Paul Voet, Rodenburg, and Boullenois; and the latter

---

p. 29; Id. Observ. 6, pp. 122—127; P. Voet, De Stat. § 4, ch. 2, n. 2, p. 117 (edit. 1715); Id. pp. 130, 131 (edit. 1661).

1 Thus Muhlenbruch (Doctrina Pandectarum, vol. 1, lib. 1, § 72, p. 167) lays down the following rule: Jura, quæ proxime rebus sunt scripta, velut quæ ad dominii causam spectant, vel ad vectigalium tributorumque onus, vel ad pignorum in judicati executionem et capiendorum et distrahendorum, tum etiam rerum apud judicem petendarum persequendarumve rationem, et quæ sunt reliqua ex hoc genere, æstimantur ex legibus ejus civitatis, ubi sitæ sunt res, de quibus agitur, atque collocatæ, nullo rerum immobilium atque mobilium habito discrimine.

2 See Ante, § 362; Post, § 377—380. See Fœlix, Conflit des Lois, Revue Etrang. et Franç. tom. 7, 1840, pp. 216—218, 221—227.

3 "Mobilia," says John Voet, "vero ex lege domicilii ipsius defuncti, vel quia semper domino presentia esse finguntur, vel ex comitate passim usu inter

by D'Argentré, Burgundus, Hertius, and Bouhier[1]. Paul Voet says: *Verum mobilia ibi censeantur esse, secundum juris intellectum, ubi is, cujus ea sunt, sedem atque larem suarum fortunarum collocavit*[2]. So Rodenburg: *Mobilia quippe illa non ideo subjacent statuto (reali), quod personale illud sit; sed quod mobilia, certo ac fixo situ carentia, ibi quemque situm velle habere, ac existere intelligimus, ubi larem ac fortunarum fixit summam, &c. In domicilii loco mobilia intelligantur existere*[3]. Again, in another place, he says: *Et quidem, de mobilibus si quæratur, cum semper ibi esse existimentur, ubi creditor foret domicilium, cujus ossibus vagæ hæ res intelliguntur adhærere*[4]. Boullenois affirms the same doctrine; and gives this reason for it: that, as movables have no such fixed and perpetual *situs* as lands have, it is necessary that their *situs* should depend upon the pleasure of the owner, and that they have the very *situs* which he wishes, when they have that of his own domicil[5].

---

gentes receptâ." J. Voet. Ad Pand. lib. 38, tit. 17, § 34, p. 596. And in another place he adds: "Sed considerandum, quadâm fictione juris, seu malis, præsumptione, hanc de mobilibus determinationem conceptam niti; cum enim certo stabilique hæc (mobilia) situ careant, nec certo sint alligata loco; sed ad arbitrium domini undiquaque in domicilii locum revocari facile ac reduci possint, et maximum domino plerumque commodum adferre soleant, cum ei sunt præsentia; visum fuit hanc inde conjecturam surgere, quod dominus velle censeatur, ut illuc omnia sua sint mobilia, aut saltem esse intelligantur, ubi fortunarum suarum larem summamque constituit; id est, in loco domicilii." J. Voet. Ad Pand. lib. 1, tit. 4, pt. 2, § 11, p. 44. Hertius says: "Nam mobiles ex conditione personæ legem accipiunt nec loco continentur." 1 Hertii, Opera, De Collis, Leg. § 4, n. 6, pp.122, 123, (edit. 1737); Id. p. 174, (edit. 1716); Fœlix. Conflit des Lois, Revue Etrang. et Franç. 1840, tom. 7, pp. 221, 222; Ante, § 362.

[1] Liverm. Dissert. pp. 128, 129; 1 Boullenois, Observ. 19, pp. 338—340; 1 Hertii, Opera, De Collis. Leg. § 4, ch. 2, n. 6, pp. 122, 123, (edit. 1737); Id. p. 174, (edit. 1716).

[2] P. Voet. De Stat. § 4, ch. 2, n. 2, p. 118, (edit. 1715); Id. § 9, ch. 1, § 8, p. 255; Id. pp. 132, 309, (edit. 1661).

[3] Rodenburg, De Div. Stat. tit. 1, ch. 2, sub finem; 2 Boullenois, App. p. 6; 1 Boullenois, Observ. 2, pp. 25, 28; Id. Observ. 6, p. 140.

[4] Rodenburg, De Div. Stat. tit. 2, ch. 5, § 16; 2 Boullenois, App. 48.

[5] 1 Boullenois, Observ. 16, pp. 223, 224; Id. Observ. 19, p. 338; Id. Prin. Gén. 33, p. 8; 3 Burge, Comm. on Col. and For. Law, pt. 2, ch. 20, pp. 750, 751.

§ 378. On the other hand, D'Argentré says: *De mobilibus aliâ censura est; quoniam per omnia ex conditione personarum legem accipiunt, et situm habere negantur, nisi affixa et cohærentia, nec loco contineri dicuntur propter habilitatem motionis et translationis. Quare statutum de bonis mobilibus vere personale est, et loco domicilii judicium sumit; et quodcumque judex domicilii de eo statuit, ubique locum obtinet. Observatio indubita est, mobilia personam sequi, nec situ judicari, aut a locis judicium accipere*[1]. Bouhier is quite as explicit. As movables (says he) have no fixed *situs*, and are easily transported from one place to another, according to the pleasure of the owner, therefore it is supposed by a sort of fiction, that they adhere to his person; and from hence comes the maxim in our customary law, that movables follow the body or person of the owner: *Meubles suivent le corps, ou la personne.—Mobilia sequuntur personam*[2].

§ 378 *a*. Burgundus puts the doctrine in the strongest form. *Puto equidem* (says he) *mobilia sequi conditionem personæ, id est, si persona fuerit servituti obnoxia, bona quoque ejus mobilia libera esse desinere, cùm apud nos servitus magis sit bonorum, quam personæ. Utputa, si quis natus in simili regione territorii Alostensis, inde postea aliò migraverit, atque decesserit, bona ejus mobilia quocumque loco reperta, cedunt natalis soli Domino. Quia perinde haberi debent, ac si per eventum nativitatis, alienæ se potestati, ac dominio defunctus subjecisset. Non aliter quàm mobilia clerici, quæ et conditionim ejus sequuntur. Sed tamen, ut existimem, bona moventia, et mobilia ita comitari personam, ut extra domici-*

---

1 D'Argentré, De Leg. Brit. tom. 1, Des Donations, art. 218, Gloss. 6, n. 30, p. 654; Liverm. Diss. § 213, pp. 128—130; 1 Boullenois, Observ. 19, p. 339.

2 Bouhier, Cout. de Bourg. ch. 25, § 2, p. 490; 1 Boullenois, Observ. 19, p. 338.—Les meubles (says Cochin) quelque sorte qu'ils soient, suivent le domicile. Cochin, Œuvres, tom. 5, p. 85, 4to. edit.; 2 Henrys, Œuvres, lib. 4, ch. 6, Quest. 105, p. 612; Id. 720; Ante, § 362; 3 Burge, Comm. on Col. and For. Law. pt. 2, ch. 20, pp. 750, 751; Fœlix, Conflit des Lois, Revue Etrang. et Fran. tom. 7, § 32, pp. 221, 222.

lium ejus censeantur existere, adduci sane non possum. Quod neque rationi, neque juri scripto congruat, sicuti nec doctorum opinionibus, aut forensi usu firmatur. Credo ego, mobilia comitari personam quamdiu domicilium non habet. Quod utique procedere poterit, si quis domicilio relicto naviget, vel iter faciat, quærens quò se conferat, atque ubi domicilium constituat[1]. Hertius says: *Nam mobiles ex conditione personæ legem accipiunt, nec loco continentur*[2].

§ 379. But, whether the one opinion or the other is adopted, it has been truly remarked by Boullenois, that the same conclusion is equally true, that movables follow the person[3]. The probability is, that the doctrine itself had not its origin in any distinction between real laws or personal laws, or in any fictitious annexation of them to the person of the owner, or in their incapacity to have a fixed *situs;* but in an enlarged policy, growing out of their transitory nature and the general convenience of nations. If the law *rei sitæ* were generally to prevail in regard to movables, it would be utterly impossible for the owner, in many cases, to know in what manner to dispose of them during his life, or to distribute them at his death; not only from the uncertainty of their situation in the transit to and from different places, but from the impracticability of knowing with minute accuracy the law of transfers *inter vivos,* or of testamentary dispositions and successions in the different countries in which they might happen to be. Any change of place at a future time might defeat the best-considered will; and any sale or donation might be rendered inoperative, from the ignorance of the parties of the law of the

---

[1] Burgundus, Tract. 2, n. 20, pp. 71, 72.

[2] 1 Hertii, Opera, De Collis. Leg. § 4, n. 6, pp. 122, 123, (edit. 1737); Id. p. 174, (edit. 1716); Ante, § 362. See J. Voet, Comm. ad Pand. vol. 2, lib. 38, tit. 17, n. 34, p. 596.

[3] 1 Boullenois, Observ. 19, p. 339. See also J. Voet, Ad Pand. lib. 38, tit. 17, § 34, p. 596; Holmes *v.* Remsen, 4 John. Ch. R. 487; 1 Burge, Comm. on Col. and For. Law, pt. 1, ch. 1, pp. 28, 29; Fœlix, Conflit des Lois, Revue Etrang. et Fran. tom. 7, (1840), pp. 204—206.

actual *situs* at the time of their acts. These would be serious evils pervading the whole community, and equally affecting the subjects and the interests of all civilized nations. But in maritime nations depending upon commerce for their revenues, their power, and their glory, the mischief would be incalculable. A sense of general utility, therefore, must have first suggested the doctrine, and as soon as it was promulgated, it could not fail to recommend itself to all nations by its simplicity, its convenience, and its enlarged policy [1].

§ 380. But, be the origin of the doctrine what it may, it has so general a sanction among all civilized nations, that it may now be treated as a part of the *jus gentium*. Lord Loughborough has stated it with great clearness and force

---

[1] See Harvey *v.* Richards, 1 Mason, R. 412; Ante, § 372 *a.*—Mr. Justice Bayley, in delivering his opinion in the case of In Re Ewin, 1 Cromp. & Jerv. 156, said, "Now, what is the rule with respect to it? It is clear, from the authority of Bruce *v.* Bruce, and the case of Somerville *v.* Somerville, that the rule is, that personal property follows the person, and it is not in any respect to be regulated by the situs; and if in any instances the situs has been adopted as the rule, by which the property is to be governed, and the lex loci rei sitæ resorted to, it has been improperly done. Wherever the domicil of the proprietor is, there the property is to be considered as situate; and in the case of Somerville *v.* Somerville, which was a case in which there was stock in the funds of this country, which were at least as far local as any of the stocks mentioned in this case are local, there was a question whether the succession to that property should be regulated by the English or by the Scotch rules of succession. The Master of the Rolls was of opinion, that the proper domicil of the party was in Scotland. And having ascertained that, the conclusion which he drew was, that the property in the English funds was to be regulated by the Scotch mode of succession; and if the executor had, as he no doubt would have, the power of reducing the property into his own possession, and putting the amount into his own pocket, it would be distributed by the law of the country in which the party was domiciled. Personal property is always liable to be transferred, wherever it may happen to be, by the act of the party to whom that property belongs; and there are authorities that ascertain this point, which bears by analogy on this case, namely, that if a trader in England becomes bankrupt, having that, which is personal property, debts, or other personal property due to him abroad, the assignment under the commission of bankrupt operates upon the property, and effectually transfers it, at least as against all those persons who owe obedience to these bankrupt laws, the subjects of this country."

in one of his most elaborate judgments. "It is a clear proposition," said he, "not only of the law of England, but of every country in the world where law has the semblance of science, that personal property has no locality. The meaning of that is, not that personal property has no visible locality, but that it is subject to that law which governs the person of the owner; both with respect to the disposition of it, and with respect to the transmission of it, either by succession or by the act of the party: it follows the law of the person. The owner in any country may dispose of his personal property. If he dies, it is not the law of the country in which the property is, but the law of the country of which he was a subject that will regulate the succession [1]." The same doctrine was recognised by Lord Chief Justice Abbott on another important occasion. "Personal property," said he "has no locality. And even with respect to that, it is not correct to say, that the law of England gives way to the law of the foreign country; but, that it is part of the law of England that personal property should be distributed according to the *jus domicilii* [2]." The same doctrine has been constantly maintained both in England and America with unbroken confidence and general unanimity [3].

---

[1] Sill *v.* Worswick, 1 H. Black. 690.

[2] Doe *d.* Birtwhistle *v.* Vardill, 5 Barn. & Cress. 438, 451, 452; S. C. 9 Bligh, R. 32—88; 2 Clarke & Fin. R. 571.

[3] The authorities on this point are very numerous. See Henry on For. Law, pp. 13—15; 4 Cowen, R. 517, note; 2 Kent, Comm. Lect. 37, p. 428, &c., 3rd edit.; Id. p. 405; Kaims on Equity, b. 3, ch. 8, § 3, 4; Ersk. Inst. b. 3, tit. 2, § 40, p. 515; Dwarris on Statutes, 649, 650; In re Ewing, 1 Tyrwhitt, R. 91; 1 Rose, Bank. Cas. 478; 5 Barn. & Cress. 451, 452; 2 Bell, Comm. pp. 2—10, 4th and 5th edit.; Piper *v.* Piper, Ambler, R. 25; Potter *v.* Brown, 5 East, R. 130; Holmes *v.* Remsen, 4 John. Ch. R. 460; Guier *v.* O'Daniel, 2 Binney, R. 349, note; Bruce *v.* Bruce, 2 Bos. & Pull. 229, note; Liverm. Diss. pp. 128—132; De Sobrey *v.* De Laistre, 2 Harr. & John. R. 191—224; Hunter *v.* Potts, 4 T. R. 182, 192; Phillips *v.* Hunter, 2 H. Black. 402, 405; Goodwin *v.* Jones, 3 Mass. R. 514, 517; Blake *v.* Williams, 6 Pick. R. 286, 314; 3 Burge, Comm. on Col. and For. Law, pt. 2, ch. 20, pp. 749—753.

§ 381. Foreign jurists are not less expressive in its favour. *Constat inter omnes*, (says Bretonnier), *que les meubles suivent les personnes, et se réglent suivant la coutume du domicile*[1]. And he speaks but the common language of the continental jurists[2]. Pothier, after remarking that movables have no locality, adds: "All things which have no locality follow the person of the owner, and are consequently governed by the law or the custom which governs his person; that is to say, by that of the place of his domicil[3]." Merlin adopts language equally general and exact. "Movables," says he, "are governed by the law of the domicil of the owner, wherever they may be situate; and this law of course changes with his change of domicil[4]." Bynkershoek asserts the principle to be so well established, that no one has dared to question it: *Adeo recepta hodie sententia est, ut nemo ausit contra hiscere*[5]. Huberus says: *Verum in mobilibus nihil esse causæ, cur aliud, quam jus domicilii sequamur; quia res mobiles non habent affectionem versus territorium, sed ad personam patrisfamilias duntaxat, qui aliud, quam quod in loco domicilii obtinebat, voluisse obtinere non potest*[6]. So that there seems a general, although not an entire harmony on this point between foreign jurists and domestic jurists[7].

---

1 2 Henrys, Œuvres, lib. 4, Quest. 127, p. 720.

2 See 1 Boullenois, Observ. 18, p. 328; Observ. 19, pp. 339, 340; Bouhier, ch. 22, p. 429, § 79, ch. 25, p. 490, § 2; 5 Cochin, Œuvres, 85; Liverm. Diss. § 212—216, pp. 129, 130; Huberus, De Confl. Leg. lib. 1, tit. 3, § 15. See Fœlix, Conflit des Lois, Revue Etrang. et Fran. tom. 7, 1840, § 32—35, pp. 221—229.

3 Pothier, Coutum. d'Orléans, ch. 1, § 2, tom. 10, p. 7, 4to edit.; Id. Traité de Choses, § 3, tom. 8, p. 109, 4to edit.

4 Merlin, Répert. Biens, § 1, n. 12; Id. Meubles, § 1; Id. Loi. § 6, n. 3.

5 2 Kent, Comm. Lect. 37, p. 429, 3rd edit.; Bynkershoek, Quest. Priv. Juris. lib. 1, cap. 16, pp. 179, 180, (edit. 1744).—Bynkershoek, in the passage here referred to, is speaking of the right of succession; but his language has been thought susceptible of a broader interpretation. See post, § 483.

6 Huberus, P. 1, lib. 3, tom. 1, De Success. ab Intest. n. 21 (s).

7 See Fœlix, Conflit. des Lois, Revue, Etrang. et Fran. tom. 7, 1840,

§ 382. When, however, we speak of movables as following the person of the owner, and as governed by the law of

---

§ 32—35, pp. 221—229. See also Mühlenbruch, Doctr. Pand. tom. 1, lib. 1, § 72, 73, pp. 166—170, who seems to make the law rei situs govern in many cases, as well with respect to movables as immovables. Jura, quæ proxime rebus sunt scripta, vel quæ ad dominii causam spectant, &c. &c. æstimantur ex legibus ejus civitatis, ubi sitæ res, de quibus agitur, atque collocatæ, nullo rerum immobilium atque mobilium habito discrimine. Id. § 72. M. Fœlix says on this subject: "Par la nature des choses, les meubles, soit corporels, soit incorporels, n'ont pas, à l'égal des immeubles, une assiette fixe dans l'endroit où ils se trouvent de fait: ils dépendent nécessairement de la personne de l'individu, à qui ils appartiennent, et ils subissent la destination, qu'il leur donne. Chaque individu étant légalement censé avoir réuni sa fortune au lieu de son domicile, c'est-à-dire au siége principal de ses affaires, on a toujours regardé en droit les meubles comme se trouvant au lieu du domicile de celui, à qui ils appartiennent; peu importe si, de fait, ils se trouvent ou non au dit lieu. Par une fiction légale, on les considère comme suivant la personne, et comme étant soumis à la même loi, qui régit l'état et la capacité de cette personne; et nous avons vu (supra, n° 21) que cette loi est celle du domicile (mobilia sequuntur personam; mobilia ossibus inhærent). En d'autres termes, le statut personnel gouverne les meubles corporels ou incorporels. Ce statut est à leur égard réel par suite de la fiction, qui les répute se trouver au lieu régi par ce même statut. Tel a toujours été le sentiment presque unanime des auteurs et des cours de justice. Témoins Dumoulin, Chopin, Bretonnier, d'Argentré, Brodeau, Lebrun, Poullain du Parc, Burgundus, Rodenburg, Abraham à Wesel, Paul Voet, Jean Voet, Sande, Christin, Gail, Carpzov, Wernher, Mevius, Franzke, Boullenois, Pothier, Struve, Leyser, Huber, Hert, Hommel, Danz, Glück, Thibaut, Merlin, MM. Mittermaier, Hauss, Meier, Favard, Duranton, Story, Wheaton, Rocca, et Burge. Trois auteurs seulement ne sont pas entièrement d'accord, en cette matiére, avec ceux que nous venons de citer: ce sont Tittmann, M. Mühlenbruch, et M. Eichhorn. Le premier, en soumettant les meubles à la même loi, qui régit les immeubles, ne s'attache qu'à l'un des cas exceptionnels, dont nous parlerons ou n° 33 ci-après, sans examiner la régle elle-même. M. Mühlenbruch repousse tout distinction entre les meubles et les immeubles par rapport à la loi, qui les régit, par le seul motif, que l'opinion contraire établirait une différence entre la succession dans les immeubles et celle dans les meubles du même individu; nous démontrerons au n° ci-après la nécessité de reconnaître cette différence. M. Eichhorn, en rejetant l'application de la loi de la situation des meubles, n'admet cependant la règle, qu'avec la modification, que, selon les circonstances, il faudra appliquer la loi du lieu où la cause se plaidera: il cite comme exemple le cas où le défendeur en revendication invoque la maxime, qu'en fait de meubles possession vaut titre." Fœlix, Conflit des Lois, Reveu Etrang. et Franç. 1840, tom. 7, § 32, pp. 222—224.

his domicil, we are to limit the doctrine to the cases in which they may be properly said to retain their original and natural character. For movables may become annexed to immovables, either by incorporation or as incidents, and then they take the character of the latter [1]. Thus, in the language of the common law, movables annexed to the freehold are deemed a part of the latter. Such are the common cases of fixtures of personal property in houses, in mills, and in other hereditaments, whether for use or for ornament. In the law of foreign countries a similar distinction is recognised; and wherever movables become thus fixed by operation of law, or by the express determination of the owner, they are deemed a part of the immovable property [2]. John Voet ranks them among immovables: *Idemque statuendum in mobilibus, per patris-familias destinationem perpetui usûs gratiâ ad certum locum, domum puta, vel fundum, delatis, ita ut perpetuo illic istius usûs causâ mansura sint, etiamsi vel nunquam immobilibus naturaliter jungenda sint, vel ex destinatione jungenda, necdum tamen inceperint immobilibus juncta esse, modo ad ipsas ædes fundosve, quibus jungenda sunt, delata fuerint* [3]. Among the class of immovables are also ranked (as we have seen) heritable bonds by the Scottish law, and ground rents, and other rents charged on lands [4].

§ 383. It follows as a natural consequence of the rule which we have been considering (that personal property has no locality), that the laws of the owner's domicil should in

---

1 Ante, § 371; Post, 447.

2 Pothier, Traité des Choses, § 1; Id. Coutum. d'Orléans, ch. 3, art. 46—48; Merlin, Répert. Biens, § 1, n. 13, § 2, n. 1; Id. Meubles, § 2, 3; 1 Bell, Comm. § 660, pp. 648—652, 4th edit.; 2 Bell, Comm. pp. 2—4, 4th edit.; 1 Bell, Comm. pp. 752—755, and 2 Bell, Comm. pp. 1—10; 1 Boullenois, Observ. 19, pp. 340, 341; 1 Kaims on Equity, b. 3, ch. 8, § 3; Ersk. Inst. b. 3, tit. 9, § 4.

3 J. Voet. Ad Pand. lib. 1, tit. 8, n. 14, p. 67.

4 1 Bell, Comm. § 660, pp. 648—652; 2 Bell, Comm. pp. 2—4, 4th edit.; Ersk. Inst. b. 2, ch. 2, § 9—20; Pothier, Traité des Choses, § 3; Ante, § 366, 367, and note; Post, § 447.

all cases determine the validity of every transfer, alienation, or disposition made by the owner, whether it be *inter vivos*, or be *post mortem*[1]. And this is regularly true, unless there is some positive or customary law of the country where they are situate, providing for special cases (as is sometimes done), or, from the nature of the particular property, it has a necessarily implied locality[2]. Lord Mansfield has mentioned as among the latter class, contracts respecting the public funds or stocks, the local nature of which requires them to be carried into execution according to the local law[3]. The same rule may properly apply to all other local stock or funds, although of a personal nature, or so made by the local law, such as Bank Stock, Insurance Stock, Turnpike, Canal and Bridge Shares, and other incorporeal property, owing its existence to, or regulated by, peculiar local laws[4]. No positive transfer can be made of such pro-

---

[1] Livermore, Diss. § 215—220, pp. 130—137.

[2] Mr. Chief Justice Tilghman on one occasion said: "The proposition (that personal property has no locality, but is transfered according to the law of the country in which the owner is domiciled), is true in general, but not to its utmost extent, nor without several exceptions. In one sense, personal property has locality, that is to say, if tangible, it has a place in which it is situated, and if invisible (consisting of debts), it may be said to be in the place where the debtor resides; and of these circumstances the most liberal nations have taken advantage, by making such property subject to regulations which suit their own convenience." "Every country has a right of regulating the transfer of all personal property within its territory; but when no positive regulation exists, the owner transfers it at his pleasure." Moreton *v.* Milne, 6 Binn. R. 361; 3 Burge, Comm. on Col. and For. Law, pt. 2, ch. 20, pp. 751, 752; Ante, § 364, and note.

[3] Robinson *v.* Bland, 2 Burr. R. 1079; S. C. 1 W. Black. R. 247; Ante, § 364.

[4] 2 Bell, Comm. pp. 4, 5, 4th edit.; Id. pp. 1—10, 5th edit.; 1 Bell, Comm. pp. 65, 67, 68, 4th edit.; Id, pp. 105—108, 5th edit.; 3 Burge, Comm. on Col. and For. Law, pt. 2, ch. 20, pp. 750—752. Mr. Burge says, that although stocks of this nature can only be transferred according to the forms of the lex rei sitæ, so as to confer a legal title on the purchaser, yet it will give the purchaser a right of action to compel the vendor to make a transfer in the manner required by the local law. Ibid.; Ante, § 364, note. Erskine, in his Institutes, (b. 3, tit. 9, § 4), puts the like ex-

perty, except in the manner prescribed by the local regulations[1]. But, nevertheless, contracts to transfer such property would be valid, if made according to the *lex domicilii* of the owner, or the *lex loci contractûs,* unless such contracts were specially prohibited by the *lex rei sitæ;* and the property would be treated as personal or as real in the course of administration, according to the local law[2].

§ 384. Subject to exceptions of this and the like nature, (such as the statutable transfer of ships, and of goods in the warehouses, or in the docks of a government, which would fall within the same predicament), the general rule is, that a transfer of personal property, good by the law of the owner's domicil, is valid, wherever else the property may be situate[3]. But it does not follow that a transfer made

---

ceptions. "We must except," says he "from this general rule, as civilians have done, certain movables, which by the destination of the deceased are considered as immovable. Among these may be reckoned the shares of the trading companies, or of the public stocks of any country, for example, the Banks of Scotland, England, and Holland, the South-Sea Company, &c., which are, without doubt, descendable according to the law of the State where such stocks are fixed. But the bonds or notes of such companies make no exception from the general rule. They are accounted part of the movable estate of the deceased." Ante, § 364, 365; Post, § 398; Robertson on Successions, pp. 94, 95. See Attor.-Gen. *v.* Dimond, 1 Cromp. & Jerv. 356, 370, 371; Attor.-Gen. *v.* Hope, 1 Cromp. Mees. & Rosc. 538; S. C. 8 Bligh, R. 44; S. C. 2 Clark & Fin. R. 84; Attor.-Gen. *v.* Bonwers, 4 Mees. & Wels. 171, 191—193; Post, 432.

1 Though stock abroad may be as to its transfer affected by the local laws, it is not to be treated as of course as partaking of the character of real estate, and descendible as such. On the contrary, if it be by the local law personal estate, it may be disposed of by an administration, as such; and the title passes, if it be made in the forms prescribed by the foreign law. See Attor.-Gen. v. Dimond, 1 Tyrwhitt, R. 243. In the matter of Ewing, 1 Tyrwhitt, R. 91; Ersk. Inst. b. 3, tit. 9, § 4; 1 Bell, Comm. p. 65; 2 Bell, Comm. pp. 4, 5, 4th and 5th edit.; Ante, 364, 365.

2 Abbott on Shipp. pt. 1, ch. 2, § 10; 1 Chitty on Comm. and Manuf. 556, 558, 566, &c.; 2 Kent, Comm. Lect. 45, pp. 145, 146, 3rd edit.

3 1 Kaims on Equity, b. 3, ch. 8, § 3.—In the case of a movable subject (says Erskine) lying in Scotland, the deed of transmission, if perfected according to the lex domicilii, is effectual to carry the property; for movables have no permanent situation. Ersk. Inst. b. 3, tit. 2, § 40, p. 515;

by the owner, according to the law of the place of its actual *situs*, would not as completely devest his title; nor even that a transfer by him in any other foreign country which would be good according to the law of that country, would not be equally effectual, although he might not have his domicil there. For purposes of this sort, his personal property may, in many cases, be deemed subject to his disposal, wherever he may happen to be at the time of the alienation. Thus, a merchant domiciled in America may, doubtless, transfer his personal property according to the law of his domicil, wherever the property may be. But, if he should direct a sale of it, or make a sale of it in a foreign country where it is situate at the time, according to the laws thereof, either in person or by an agent, the validity of such a sale would scarcely be doubted. If a merchant is temporarily abroad, he is understood to possess a general authority to transfer such personal property as accompanies his person, wherever he may be; so always, that he does not violate the law of the country where the act is done[1]. The general convenience and freedom of commerce require this enlargement of the rule; for, otherwise, the sale of personal property, actually situate in a foreign country, and made according to the forms prescribed by its laws, might be declared null and void in the country of the domicil of the owner. In the ordinary course of trade with foreign countries, no one thinks of transferring personal property according to the forms of his own domicil; but it is transferred according to the forms prescribed by the law of the place where the sale takes place.

§ 385. A question involving other considerations may be presented; and that is, whether a transfer of personal property is good which is made according to the law of the owner's domicil, but not in conformity to the law of the

---

3 Burge, Comm. on Col. and For. Law, pt. 2, ch. 20, pp. 750—752; Ante, § 364, note.

[2] See 1 Kaims on Equity, b. 3, ch. 8, § 3.

place where it is situate? And whether there is any difference in such a case between the transfer being made by the owner in his place of domicil, or its being made in the place *rei sitæ?* For instance, let us suppose, that by the law of the domicil of the owner a sale of goods is complete and perfect, to pass the title without any delivery, and that, by the law of the place of their *situs*, the sale is not complete until delivery. In such a case, if the transfer of the goods is made in the domicil of the owner, would it be valid without any delivery thereof, so as to pass the title against third persons? If it would, in such a case, what would be the effect if the transfer was made in the place where the goods were situate without any such delivery?

§ 386. The former question has been much discussed in the Courts of Louisiana, from a supposed difference between the rule of the common law and that of the civil law on this subject. By the common law, a sale of goods is, or may be, complete without delivery[1]. But by the law of Louisiana, delivery is necessary to complete the transfer, according to the well-known rule of the civil law: *Traditionibus et usucapionibus dominia rerum, non nudis pactis, transferuntur*[2]. Upon the fullest examination, and after repeated arguments, the Supreme Court of Louisiana have held the doctrine, that the transfer of personal property in

---

[1] The common law deems a sale as between the parties complete without a delivery; but not as to third persons. If, therefore, a sale is made, the purchaser, in order to complete his title against creditors and other purchasers, must take possession within a reasonable time. Where the property is at sea at the time, and is incapable of delivery, there the title is complete without delivery. But it may be lost by an omission to take possession within a reasonable time after its arrival in port. See Meeker *v.* Wilson, 1 Gall. R. 419; 1 Black. Comm. 446, 448; 2 Kent, Comm. 492, 493, 498; Id. pp. 515—522; Bohlen *v.* Cleveland, 5 Mason, R. 174; 3 Chitty on Comm. and Manuf. ch. 5, § 2, p. 272, &c.; Lanfear *v.* Sumner, 17 Mass. R. 110; Bigelow's Digest, *Sale*, A. B.; Post, § 389, note. See also Long on Sales, by Rand (edit. 1839), ch. 7, pp. 259—307.

[2] Cod. lib. 2, tit. 3, l. 20; Olivier *v.* Townes, 14 Martin, R. 93, 102; Norris *v.* Mumford, 4 Martin, R. 20; Dumford *v.* Brooks's Syndics, 3 Martin, R. 222, 225.

that State is not complete, so as to pass the title against creditors, unless a delivery is made in conformity to the laws of that State, although the transfer is made by the owner in his foreign domicil, and would be good without delivery by the laws of that domicil[1].

§ 387. The reasoning by which this doctrine is maintained, is most fully developed in a case in which a transfer of a part of a ship was made in Virginia, the ship, at the time of the sale, being locally at New Orleans; and, before any delivery thereof, she was attached by the creditors of the vendor[2]. It was, therefore, a case of conflict of rights between the creditor and the purchaser. The learned Judge[3], who delivered the opinion of the Court on that occasion, said: "The position assumed in the present case is, that by the laws of all civilized countries, the alienation of movable property must be determined according to the laws, rules, and regulations in force where the owner's domicil is situated. Hence, it is insisted, that, as by the law existing in the State where the vendor lived, no delivery was necessary to complete the sale, it must be considered as complete here; and, that it is a violation of the principle just referred to, to apply to the contract rules which are peculiar to our jurisprudence, and different from those contemplated by the parties to the contract."

§ 388. "We readily yield an assent to the general doctrine for which the appellee contends. He has supported it by a variety of authorities drawn from different systems of jurisprudence. But some of those very books furnish also the exception on which we think this case must be decided, namely, that 'when those laws clash with, and interfere with

---

[1] The point appears to have been first decided in Norris *v.* Mumford, 4 Martin, R. 20; and it has been repeatedly since adjudged in other cases, and particularly in Ramsay *v.* Stevenson, 5 Martin, R. 23; Fisk *v.* Chandler, 7 Martin, R. 24; and Olivier *v.* Townes, 14 Martin, R. 93. Mr. Livermore has contested the doctrine asserted in these decisions with great earnestness and ability. Liverm. Diss. § 220—223, pp. 137—140.

[2] Olivier *v.* Townes, 14 Martin, R. 93, 102.

[3] Mr. Justice Porter.

the rights of the citizens of the countries where the parties to the contract seek to enforce it, as one or other of them must give way, those prevailing where the relief is sought must have the preference.' Such is the language of the English books to which we have been referred; and Huberus, whose authority is more frequently resorted to on this subject than that of any other writer, because he has treated it more extensively, and with greater ability in his Treatise *De Conflictu Legum*, (n. 11), tells us, *Effecta contractuum, certo loco initorum, pro jure loci illius alibi quoque observantur, si nullum inde civibus alienis creetur prejudicium, in jure sibi quæsito.* The effects of a contract entered into at any place will be allowed, according to the law of that place, in other countries, if no inconvenience will result therefrom to the citizens of that other country, with respect to the right which they demand. This distinction appears to us founded on the soundest reasons. The municipal laws of a country have no force beyond its territorial limits; and when another government permits these to be carried into effect within her jurisdiction, she does so upon a principle of comity. In doing so, care must be taken that no injury is inflicted on her own citizens, otherwise justice would be sacrificed to courtesy. Nor can the foreigner or stranger complain of this. If he sends his property within a jurisdiction different from that where he resides, he impliedly submits it to the rules and regulations in force in the country where he places it. What the law protects it has a right to regulate. A strong evidence of this is furnished by the doctrine in regard to successions. The general principle is, that the personal property must be distributed according to the law of the State where the testator dies; but, so far as it concerns creditors, it is governed by the law of the country where the property is situated. If an Englishman or a Frenchman dies abroad, and leaves effects here, we regulate the order in which his debts are paid by our jurisprudence, not by that of his domicil[1]."

---

[1] Post, § 524.

§ 389. "We proceed to examine whether giving effect to the law of Virginia on the contract now set up would be working an injury to this State or its citizens. In doing this, we must look to the general doctrine, and the effect it would have on our ordinary transactions, as well as its operation in this particular case. If we held here, that this sale can defeat the attachment, we should on the same principle be obliged to decide, that the claimant would hold the object sold in preference to a second purchaser to whom it was delivered; the rule being, that when the debtor can sell, and give to the buyer a good title, the creditor can seize; or, in other words, where the first sale is not complete as to third persons, the creditor may attach and acquire a lien[1]. In relation to movable property, our law has provided, that delivery is essential to complete the contract of sale as to third parties. This valuable provision, by which all our citizens are bound in their dealings, protects them from the frauds to which they would be daily subjects, were they liable to be affected by previous contracts, not followed by the giving of possession. The exemption contended for here in behalf of the residents of another State, would deprive them of that protection wherever their rights, as purchasers, came in contact with strangers; a protection, which, it may be remarked, it is of the utmost importance, owing to our peculiar position, that we should carefully maintain. This city is becoming a vast storehouse for merchandize sent from abroad, owned by non-residents, and deposited here for sale, and our most important commercial transactions are in relation to property so situated. If the purchasers of it should be affected by all the previous contracts made at the owner's domicil, although unaccompanied by delivery, it is easy to see to what impositions such a doctrine would lead, to what inconvenience it would expose us, and how severely it would check and embarrass our dealings. However anxious we may be to extend courtesy, and afford protection to the people of other countries, who

---

[1] M'Neil *v.* Glass, 13 Martin, R. 261.

come themselves, or send their property within our jurisdiction, we cannot indulge our feelings so far as to give a decision that would let in such consequences as we have just spoken of. It would be giving to a foreign purchaser an advantage which the resident has not, and that, frequently, at the expense of the latter. This, in the language of the law, we think, would be a great inconvenience to the citizens of this State, and therefore we cannot sanction it[1]."

§ 390. There is certainly great force in this reasoning upon general principles; and no one can seriously doubt, that it is competent for any State to adopt such a rule in its own legislation, since it has perfect jurisdiction over all property, personal as well as real, within its own territorial limits[2]. Nor can such a rule, made for the benefit of innocent purchasers and creditors, be deemed justly open to the

---

[1] Olivier *v.* Townes, 14 Martin, R. 97—103. But see 1 Kaims on Equity, b. 3, ch. 8, § 3. The doctrine of this case seems supported by that of Lanfear *v.* Sumner, (17 Mass. R. 110), although in the latter case the Court do not found their judgment upon any supposed conflict between foreign and domestic laws. There can be little doubt, that the sale and assignment in Philadelphia, in that case, was a complete transfer by the lex loci contractûs, and there was certainly legal diligence in endeavouring to obtain possession after the sale. The Court, however, thought, that delivery was essential to perfect the transfer by the law of Massachusetts; and as there had been no delivery until the property was attached by the attaching creditor in Massachusetts, they decided in favour of the title of the latter against the vendee. The Court also said, that where each of the parties claimed the same goods by a legal title, he who first obtained possession would hold against the other, and for this principle they relied on Lamb *v.* Durant, 12 Mass. R. 54, and Caldwell *v.* Ball, 1 T. R. 205. The former case is certainly in point; but in the latter, the decision was in favour of the party who first had acquired a legal title by the prior indorsement of the bills of lading to him. "Whoever (said Ashurst, J.) was first in possession (not of the goods, but) of either of these bills of lading, had the legal title vested in him." Buller, J. said: "Both parties claim under T.; but F. & Co. have the first legal right, for two bills of lading were first indorsed to them." But see Conard *v.* Atlantic Insurance Co. 1 Peters, Sup. C. R. 386, 445; Nathan *v.* Giles, 5 Taunt. R. 558; Bohlen *v.* Cleveland, 5 Mason, R. 174.

[2] See Liverm. Diss. § 221, pp. 137, 138; Id. § 249, pp. 159—162; Hall *v.* Campbell, Cowp. R. 208; Hunter *v.* Potts, 4 T. R. 182, 192; Phillips *v.* Hunter, 2 H. Bl. 402, 405; Sill *v.* Worswick, 1 H. Bl. R. 673, 690, 691; Davis *v.* Jaquin, 5 Harr. & John. R. 100.

reproach of being founded in a narrow or a selfish policy. But, how far any Court of justice ought upon its own general authority to interpose such a limitation, independently of positive legislation, has been thought to admit of more serious question; since the doctrine which it unfolds aims a direct blow at the soundness of the policy on which the general rule, that personal property has no locality, is itself founded[1]. It is not, indeed, very easy to reconcile it with the doctrine maintained by Lord Loughborough, which has been already cited[2], or with other cases to the same effect. Nor is it easy to say to what extent it may be pressed in subversion of the general rule, since every country has so many minute regulations in regard to the transfers of personal property incorporated into its municipal code, each of which may be properly deemed beneficial to its own government, or to the interests of its citizens[3].

§ 391. Another case illustrative of the doctrine may be stated. A ship belonging to New York, and owned there, was transferred while at sea, according to the law of the owner's domicil; and the ship subsequently arrived at New Orleans, and was attached by creditors, before any delivery thereof to the vendee. The question was, whether the attachment overreached the title by the transfer. The Supreme Court of Louisiana held, that it did not; and that the transfer was valid to all intents and purposes. The Court took the distinction, that the transfer was complete before the Louisiana laws could locally attach upon it. "In the present case (said the Court) the ship, the subject of the sale, was a New York ship, and the vendor and vendee resident in New York. If, therefore, according to the *lex loci contractûs*, that of the domicil of both parties, the sale

---

[1] See Livermore, Diss. § 221—223, pp. 137—140.

[2] Ante, § 380; Sill *v.* Worswick, 1 H. Bl. 690. See also 1 Kaims on Equity, b. 3, ch. 8, § 3; Ersk. Inst. b. 3, tit. 2, § 40; Bruce *v.* Bruce, 2 Bos. & Pull. 229, note, 231; Hunter *v.* Potts, 4 T. R. 182, 192; Phillips *v.* Hunter, 2 H. Bl. 402, 405.

[3] Mr. Burge manifestly deems the decision untenable. 3 Burge, Comm. on Col. and For. Law, pt. 2, ch. 20, pp. 763, 764.

transfers the property without a delivery, it did *eo instanti*, or not at all. In transferring it, it did not work any injury to the rights of the people of another country; it did not transfer the property of a thing within the jurisdiction of another government. If two persons in any country choose to bargain as to the property which one of them has in a chattel not within the jurisdiction of the place, they cannot expect that the rights of persons in the country in which the chattel is will be permitted to be effected by their contract. But if the chattel be at sea or in any other place, if any there be, in which the law of no particular country prevails, the bargain will have its full effect, *eo instanti*, as to the whole world. And the circumstance of the chattel being afterwards brought into a country according to the laws of which the sale would be invalid, would not affect it[1]." But if the ship had been at the time of the sale in New Orleans, and she had been attached before an actual delivery to the vendee, the title of the attaching creditor would have prevailed[2].

§ 392. But, let us suppose two persons, each claiming as a purchaser under different transfers of the same personal property, one by a transfer from a partner in the place where the property is locally situate, and another by a transfer made by the other partner in the domicil of the firm,—and by the law of the latter place delivery is not essential to complete the transfer,—but by the law of the former it is; which title is to prevail? According to the doctrine held in Louisiana, the title of the purchaser in the place *rei sitæ* ought to prevail[3]. And that doctrine seems confirmed by the reasoning in certain decisions of the Supreme Court of Massachusetts, although the precise point as to the conflict of laws was not litigated, and the law of

---

1 Thuret *v.* Jenkins, 7 Martin, R. 318, 353, 354.

2 Price *v.* Morgan, 7 Martin, R. 707; Ante, § 386—389.

3 Ramsay *v.* Stevenson, 5 Martin, R. 23, 77, 78; Thuret *v.* Jenkins, 7 Martin, R. 353.

Massachusetts was supposed to require a delivery to complete the title[1].

§ 393. A case somewhat different has been put by the Supreme Court of Louisiana. "If (say the Court) A. and B. be partners in New Orleans, and C. purchases from A. a quantity of cotton in the warehouse of the firm, will his right thereto, if he take instant possession of it, be affected by a sale made a few days before by B. in Natchez or Mobile? Will not C. be listened to in his own State, when he shews, that by the *lex fori*, by that of *loci contractûs*, by that of the domicil of his vendors, and of his own, the sale and delivery vested the property[2]?" The case is certainly very strongly put. But after all it must entirely depend upon the point, whether the prior transfer at Natchez or Mobile conveyed a perfect title by the law of those places without delivery; and if so, whether the *lex rei sitæ* ought to prevail against it? If no delivery were required by the law of Louisiana to perfect the title, the Natchez or Mobile purchaser would prevail, even in the Courts of Louisiana, against the purchaser in New Orleans, whatever might be the apparent hardship of the case under all the circumstances.

§ 394. On the other hand, let us take the case of a shipment of goods from England to New Orleans, on account and risk of a merchant domiciled in England, who owes debts in New Orleans, and a subsequent transfer of the bill of lading in England to a purchaser, after their arrival at New Orleans, but before the unlading thereof. Could a creditor of the shipper at New Orleans, by an attachment, oust the title of the purchaser, because there had been no delivery to the purchaser under the bill of lading? By the law of England[3], and, indeed, by that of many other com-

---

1 See Lamb *v.* Durant, 12 Mass. R. 54; Lanfear *v.* Sumner, 17 Mass. R. 110; Ante, § 386, 389, note.

2 Thuret *v.* Jenkins, 7 Martin, R. 353.

3 Lickbarrow *v.* Mason, 2 T. R. 63; Abbott on Shipp. pt. 3, ch. 9, § 16.

mercial States, the legal title of the goods passes by the mere indorsement and delivery of the bill of lading, without any actual possession of the goods by the purchaser[1]. Would such a title, so acquired, be devested by the want of a delivery, according to the laws of Louisiana? If so, it would most materially impair the confidence which the commercial world have hitherto reposed in the universal validity of the title acquired under a bill of lading. No opinion is intended to be here expressed on the point by the Author; but it is presented, in order to shew that the doctrine is not without its embarrassments.

§ 395. If, however, the doctrine of the law *rei sitæ* is to prevail over that of the law of the place of the transfer in some cases, even in respect to movables, what is to be said in relation to assignments of choses in action, or debts due by debtors resident in a foreign country? Would an attachment before notice defeat such assignments in favour of the attaching creditor, although notice of the assignment should be afterwards given to him within a reasonable time[2]? By the law of some countries, an assignment of a debt is good without any notice to the debtor, and takes effect *instanter;* by the law of other countries, notice is necessary to perfect the title[3]. Would an assignment of a debt in the creditor's domicil, where it would be good without any such notice, be ineffectual, if the debtor resided in a country where such notice would be necessary? Suppose an attachment made by a creditor in the intervening period between the time of the assignment and the

---

[1] By the old French law, bills of lading were not negotiable, so as to pass a title in the property to the assignee, but only gave him a right of action subordinate to the rights of third persons. 1 Emérig. Assur. ch. 11, § 3. By the Code of Commerce, (art. 281), bills of lading are now negotiable, so as to pass the property to the indorsee. See 3 Pardessus, pt. 3, tit. 4, ch. 3, art. 727.

[2] See Sill *v.* Worswick, 1 H. Bl. 691, 692; Bohlen *v.* Cleveland, 5 Mason, R. 174. See Holmes *v.* Remsen, 4 John. Ch. R. 460; Lewis *v.* Wallis, Sir Thomas Jones, R. 223; 1 Kaims, Equity, b. 3, ch. 8, § 3, p. 344.

[3] 3 Burge, Comm. on Col. and For. Law, pt. 2, ch. 20, pp. 777, 778.

notice; would the assignment or the attachment be entitled to a preference[1]? By the Scottish law, a creditor may assign his debt to another person, but the transfer is not complete, so as to vest the title absolutely in the assignee, until notice of the assignment,—or, as the Scotch phrase is, until an intimation of the assignment is given to the debtor. If, therefore, an assignment is made, a creditor of the original creditor may, before such intimation, arrest or attach the debt in the hands of the debtor, and will thereby acquire a preference over the assignee. That doctrine, it would seem, has been actually applied in Scotland to debts due by Scottish debtors to foreign creditors, and assigned in the domicil of the latter[2].

§ 396. According to our law a different doctrine would

---

1 See In Re Wilson, cited 1 H. Bl. 691, 692; Post, § 399 *a*.

2 Selkrig *v.* Davis, 2 Rose, Bank. Cas., 315; Stein's Case, 1 Rose, Bank. Cas. 481; 2 Bell, Comm. pp. 21—23, 4th edit.; Id. pp. 16—23, 5th edit.; 3 Burge, Comm. on Col. and For. Law, pt. 2, ch. 20, pp. 777, 778. But see In Re Wilson, cited 1 H. Bl. 691, 692.—I have stated the law of Scotland, as I understand it to be stated in the opinion of Lord Eldon, in Selkrig *v.* Davis, (2 Rose, Bank. Cas. 315; 2 Dow, R. 230, 250), though it would seem to be exactly like the Massachusetts law stated in the next section (§ 396). And so it was understood by Lord Hardwicke and Lord Loughborough. The following passage from the judgment of the latter, in Sill *v.* Worswick, (1 H. Bl. R. 691, 692), gives a very exact view of their opinions. "A question of this nature came before Lord Hardwicke very largely in the bankruptcy of Captain Wilson. With the little explanation I am enabled to give of that case, in which the Court of Session entirely concurred with Lord Hardwicke, the distinctions will be apparent. There were three different sets of creditors who claimed, subject to the determination of the Court, on the ground that Wilson had considerable debts due to him in Scotland. By the law of Scotland debts are assignable, and an assignment of a debt notified to the debtor, which is technically called an intimation, makes a specific lien quoad that debt. An assignment of a debt not intimated to the debtor, gives a right to the assignee to demand that debt; but it is a right inferior to that of the creditor, who has obtained his assignment and intimated it. By the law of Scotland, also, there is a process for the recovery of debts, which is called an arrestment. Some of Wilson's creditors had assignments of specific debts intimated to the debtors, and completed by that intimation, prior to the act of bankruptcy. Others had assignments of debts not intimated before the bankruptcy. Others had arrested the debts due to him subsequent to the bankruptcy, and were proceeding under those arrest-

prevail; for an assignment operates, *per se*, as an equitable transfer of the debt[1]. Notice is, indeed, indispensable to charge the debtor with the duty of payment to the assignee; so that if without notice he pays the debt to the assignor, or it is recovered by process against him, he will be discharged from the debt[2]. But an arrest or attachment of the debt in his hands by any creditor of the assignor, will not entitle such creditor to a priority of right, if the debtor

---

ments to recover payment of those debts. The determination of Lord Hardwicke, and that of the Court of Session, entirely concurred. The first class I have mentioned, namely, the creditors who had specific assignments of specific debts, intimated to the debtors prior to the bankruptcy, were holden by Lord Hardwicke to stand in the same situation as creditors claiming by mortgage antecedent to the bankruptcy. All, therefore, he would do with respect to them was, that, if they recovered under that decree, they could not come in under the commission without accounting to the other creditors for what they had taken under their specific security. With respect to the next class of creditors, Lord Hardwicke was of opinion, and the Court of Session were of the same opinion, that their title being a title by assignment, was preferable to the title by arrestment; and they likewise held, that the arrestments being subsequent to the bankruptcy, were of no avail, the property being by assignment vested in the assignees under the commission. It is in this sense that an expression has been used by Lord Mansfield, in one or two cases, in which his language, rather than his decision, has been quoted, with respect to the law of Scotland, namely, that the effect of the assignment under a commission of bankruptcy was the same as a voluntary assignment. For so the law of Scotland treats it, in contradistinction to the assignment perfected by intimation, and to an assignment which the party might be compelled to make. But it does not follow that it is an assignment without consideration. On the contrary, it is for a just consideration; not, indeed, for money actually paid, nor for a consideration immediately preceding the assignment. In that respect, therefore, it is a voluntary assignment. But taking it to be so, it excludes, and is preferable to all others attaching; it is preferable to all the arresters; it is preferable to all creditors who stand under the same class; and to all who have not taken the steps to acquire a specific lien till after the act of bankruptcy committed."

1 See Ante, § 395, and note; 3 Burge, Comm. on Col. and For. Law, pt. 2, ch. 20, pp. 777, 778.

2 Foster *v.* Sinkler, 4 Mass. R. 450; Blake *v.* Williams, 13 Mass. R. 286, 307, 308, 314; Wood *v.* Partridge, 11 Mass. R. 488; Dix *v.* Cobb, 4 Mass. R. 508; Bohlen *v.* Cleveland, 5 Mason, R. 174; Holmes *v.* Remsen, 4 John. Ch. R. 460, 486. See 3 Burge, Comm. on Col. and For. Law, pt. 2, ch. 20, pp. 777, 778.

receives notice of the assignment, *pendente lite*, and in time to avail himself of it in discharge of the suit against him[1].

§ 397. In such a case of conflict of laws, the difficulty of applying any other than the general principle, that movables are transferable according to the law of the domicil of the owner, is apparent. Let us take the case of a Massachusetts creditor, assigning in that State a debt contracted there, and due to him by a person then domiciled in Scotland. The transfer is in equity complete in the place where it is made, without notice; but in the place where the debt is due, it is not complete without notice. To give effect in such a case to the law of Scotland, in opposition to that of Massachusetts, would be to give a locality to the debt, and to subject it to the exclusive operation of the law of the debtor's domicil. And it might involve this most serious difficulty, that if the debtor were afterwards found in Massachusetts, or in any other country than Scotland, he might be compelled to pay the debt to the assignee, although it might have been recovered from him in Scotland by a creditor, in a proceeding by attachment of the debt in his hands, he having had notice of the assignment, *pendente lite*.

§ 398. The reasoning of Lord Kenyon, in a celebrated case[2], would certainly lead to the conclusion, that an assignment of personal property, whether it were of goods or debts, according to the law of the owner's domicil, would pass the title in whatever country it might be, unless there were some prohibitory law in that country. His language is: "Every person having property in a foreign country, may dispose of it in this; though, indeed, if there be a law in that country directing a particular mode of conveyance that ought to be adopted. But in this case no

---

[1] Foster *v.* Sinkler, 4 Mass. R. 450; Blake *v.* Williams, 13 Mass. R. 286, 307, 308, 314; Wood *v.* Partridge, 11 Mass. R. 488; Dix *v.* Cobb, 4 Mass. R. 508; Bohlen *v.* Cleveland, 5 Mason, R. 174; Holmes *v.* Remsen, 4 John. Ch. R. 460, 486. See 3 Burge, Comm. on Col. and For. Law, pt. 2, ch. 20, pp. 777, 778.

[2] Hunter *v.* Potts, 4 T. R. 182, 192. See Liverm. Diss. pp. 140—159; Id. p. 159, § 249. See Ante, § 383.

law of that kind is stated; and we cannot conjecture that it is not competent to the bankrupt himself, prior to his bankruptcy, to have disposed of his property as he pleased." The same doctrine is maintained by Lord Hardwicke and Lord Loughborough. And all these learned judges apply it equally to the cases of assignments of goods and debts, to voluntary assignments by the party, and also (as we shall more fully see hereafter) to assignments by operation of law, as in cases of bankruptcy. The question of prior notice, or intimation, does not seem to have been thought by them material, for they treat the transfer as complete from the time of the assignment; and, if that has priority in point of time over an arrest or attachment of the property, it is to prevail. The law of England would certainly give effect to such an assignment of any goods or debts in England which were assigned by the owner in a foreign country[1].

§ 399. Lord Kaims, in commenting on the subject, says: "That, considering a debt as a subject belonging to the creditor, the natural fiction would be (if any were admissible) to place it with the creditor, as in his possession, upon the maxim, *mobilia non habent sequelam.* Others are more disposed to place it with the debtor[2]." But, in fact, a debt is not a *corpus* capable of local position, but purely a *jus incorporale*[3]. And, therefore, where the debtor and creditor live in different countries, and are subjected to different laws, Lord Kaims thinks the law of the domicil of the cre-

---

1 See Solomons *v.* Ross, and other cases cited, 1 H. Bl. 131, 132, note; Sill *v.* Worswick, 1 H. Bl. 665, 690, 691; In re Wilson, cited Ibid. pp. 691—693; Lewis *v.* Wallis, T. Jones, R. 223. See also Selkrig *v.* Davis, 2 Rose, Bank. Cas. 97; S. C. Id. 291, 315—317; Kaims on Equity, B. 3, ch. 8, § 4; Scott *v.* Allnutt, 2 Dow. & Clarke, R. 404, 412; Liverm. Diss. p. 159; Ogden *v.* Saunders, 12 Wheat. R. 364, 365. See also Merlin, Répert. Faillité, pp. 412, 414, 415.

2 Kaims on Equity, b. 3, ch. 8, § 4. See Morrison's Case, 4 T. R. 185; 1 H. Bl. 677; Ante, § 362; Rodenburg, De Div. Stat. tit. 2, c. 5, § 16; 2 Boullenois, App. pp. 47—49; Ante, § 377.

3 See Ante, § 362, 376, 384; 3 Burge, Comm. on Col. and For. Law, pt. 2, ch. 20, pp. 777—779.

ditor ought to prevail[1]. He then adds: "When the creditor makes a voluntary conveyance, it is to be expected that he should speak in the style and form of his own country; and, consequently, that the rule of his own country should be the rule here. In a word, the will of a proprietor, or of a creditor, is a good title *jure gentium* that ought to be effectual everywhere. Thus, an assignment made by a creditor in Scotland, according to our forms, of a debt due to him by a person in a foreign country, ought to be sustained in that country, as a good title for demanding payment; and a foreign assignment of a debt due here, regular according to the law of the country, ought to be sustained by our judges[2]." In another place he adds: "An equitable title, in opposition to one that is legal, can never found a real action (*actio in rem*). It cannot have a stronger effect than

---

[1] On this point I cannot do better than insert a passage from Mr. Livermore's Dissertations, (p. 162, § 251), illustrative of the same principles. "It was formerly doubted by some, whether personal actions should be considered as movables, and whether they should not be considered to have a location in the domicil of the debtor. But the common opinion seems to be well settled, that, considered actively, and with respect to the interest of the creditor and his representatives, they must be considered as attached to the person of the creditor; and this, although the payment of the debt is secured by an hypothecation upon an immovable property. Such is the doctrine of Dumoulin: Nomina et jura, et quæcumque incorporalia, non circumscribantur loco, et sic non opus est accedere ad certum locum. Tum si hæc jura alicubi esse conserentur, non reputarentur esse in re pro illis hypothecatâ, nec in debitoris personâ, sed magis in personâ creditoris, in quo activè resident, et ejus ossibus inhærent. Molin. Oper. Comm. ad Consuet. Paris. tit. 1, De fiefs. § 1, n. 9, pp. 56, 57. So also Casaregis, after saying that movables are attached to the person of the owner, and at his death, will be distributed according to the laws of his domicil, proceeds to consider what will be the rule with respect to debts, and determines that they follow the person of the creditor. An ita decendum de nominibus debitorum, actionibus, ac juribus, quæ bona neque dicuntur mobilia, neque immobilia, sed tertiam speciem bonorum componunt, et dicuntur incorporalia? Et respondeo affirmativè; nam statutum benè comprehendit nomina debitorum, licet forensium, quia eorum obligationes non circumscribuntur locis, ideoque attenditur statutum, cui subjectus est testator. Et hæc verior est sententia; nam debitorum nomina tanquam personæ cohærentia, debent regulari secundum statuta loci, cui creditor est subjectus." Casaregis, In Rubr. Stat. Cit. Genuæ de Success. ab Intest. n. 64, 65, tom. 4, pp. 42, 43.

[2] Kaims on Equity, b. 3, ch. 8, § 4.

to found an action against the proprietor to grant a more formal right, or in his default that the Court shall grant it. But in the case of a debt, where the question is not about property, but payment, an equitable title coincides in a good measure with a legal title. An assignment made by a foreign creditor, according to the formalities of his country, will be sustained here as a good title for demanding payment from the debtor; and it will be sustained though informal, provided it be good *jure gentium;* that is, provided that the creditor really granted the assignment. Such effect hath an equitable title; and a legal title can have no stronger effect[1]." This is in perfect coincidence with the law of England and America[2].

§ 399 *a.* Questions may arise upon the conflict of laws, where an assignment is validly made of personal property in one country by the owner thereof, and the property is at the time of the assignment locally in another country, by whose laws it is liable to be attached by a trustee process or garnishment, and an attachment is actually made by a creditor of the assignor before notice of the assignment. In such a case, (as we have seen[3]), if notice thereof is given before judgment in the suit, the assignee will be entitled to maintain his priority of title. But, suppose the *lex fori* enforces a different rule, and will in such a case entitle the creditor to a priority of right and a judgment against the property; will that judgment conclude the assignee, if the

---

1 Kaims on Equity, b. 3, ch. 8, § 4, sub finem. See also Huberus, De Confl. Leg. lib. 1, tit. 3, § 9.

2 See Holmes *v.* Remsen, 4 John. Ch. R. 460, 486; S. P. 20 John. R. 229, 267; Moreton *v.* Milne, 6 Binn. R. 353, 361, 369; Blake *v.* Williams, 6, Pick. R. 286, 307, 314.—It is a very different question, when an assignment of a debt is lawfully made, whether the assignee can sue the debtor in his own name, or must sue in the name of the assignor. That point has been sometimes thought to belong to the mode of remedy rather than the right, and of course is to be governed by the lex fori. See 3 Burge, Comm. on Col. and For. Law, pt. 2, ch. 20, pp. 777, 778; and see also Wolff *v.* Oxholm, 6 Maule & Selw. 92, 93. But see Alivon *v.* Furnival, 1 Cromp. Mees. & Rosc. 277, 296; Post, § 420, 566.

3 Ante, § 396.

property is afterwards found in the country where the assignment is made, by whose laws the maxim prevails, *Qui prior est in tempore, potior est in jure?* Suppose the property to be found in a different foreign country, and the assignee should sue for the same in the courts thereof, what law ought to be regarded in ascertaining the title—the law of the place of the assignment, or that of the judgment? Will it make any difference whether the assignee might or might not have intervened for his right in the first suit before judgment? or, that he happened to be in the country where the judgment was rendered at the time of the rendition thereof? These are questions more easily put than answered, and will well deserve the attention of courts of justice, when they are called upon to enforce the rights of creditors in the local tribunals, against the prior claims of title of assignees under assignments of debts or other personal property made in a foreign country[1].

§ 400. But where an attachment or garnishment has been made by a creditor according to the local law *rei sitæ*, before any assignment by the party, or by operation of law *in invitum*, there is room for a distinction; and it may well be held, that in such a case the attaching creditor is entitled to a priority over the assignee. For in such case the rule may justly prevail, *Qui prior est in tempore, potior est in jure;* and the creditor is equitably entitled to the benefits of his diligence. A case to this effect is reported by Casaregis, and reasoned out without great force upon general principles. The doctrine does not, indeed, seem in its nature susceptible of any well-founded doubt; and it is in entire conformity to the principles on the same subject recognised both in England and in America[2].

§ 401. There are some other matters connected with this

---

[1] Ante, § 395, 396.

[2] Mr. Livermore, in his Dissertations, (pp. 159—162), has given the case and the reasoning of Casaregis at large. See Selkrig *v.* Davis, 2 Rose, Bank. Cas. 291, 310; Casaregis, Il Cambista Instruito, cap. 7, tom. 3, p. 64.

subject which deserve attention. Upon the sale of goods on credit, by the law of some commercial countries, a right is reserved to the vendor to re-take them, or he has a lien upon them for the price if unpaid; and in other countries, he possesses a right of stoppage *in transitu*, only in cases of insolvency of the vendee [1]. The Roman law did not generally consider the transfer of property to be complete by sale and delivery alone, without payment or security given for the price, unless the vendor agreed to give a general credit to the purchaser; but it allowed the vendor to reclaim the goods out of the possession of the purchaser, as being still his own property. *Quod vendidi* (say the Pandects) *non aliter fit accipientis, quam si aut pretium nobis solutum sit, aut satis eo nomine datum, vel etiam fidem habuerimus emptori sine ullâ satisfactione* [2]. The present code of France gives a privilege or right of revendication against the purchaser for the price of goods sold, so long as they remain in the possession of the debtor [3]. In respect to ships, a privilege is given by the same code to certain classes of creditors (such as vendors, builders, repairers, mariners, &c.) upon the ship, which takes effect even against subsequent purchasers, until the ship has made a voyage after the purchase [4]. And, by the general maritime law, acknowledged in most if not in all commercial countries, hypothecations and liens are recognised to exist for seamen's wages, and for repairs of foreign ships, and for salvage [5].

---

[1] Abbott on Shipp. pt. 1, ch. 1, § 6; Id. pt. 3, ch. 9, § 2; 1 Domat, Civil Law, b. 1, tit. 2, § 3, n. 1, 2; Id. § 12, n. 13; Id. b. 3, tit. 1, § 5, n. 3, 4, note; Merlin, Répert. Revendication, § 1, n. 6; Code Civil, art. 2102; 4 Pardessus, Droit Comm. art. 939, 940, 1204; 2 Kent. Comm. Lect. 39, p. 540, 3rd edit.; Ante, § 322—328; 3 Burge, Comm. on Col. and For. Law, pt. 2, ch. 20, p. 770.

[2] Digest, lib. 18, tit. 1, l. 19; Id. lib. 14, tit. 4, l. 5, n. 18.—As to liens for unpaid purchase-money on lands, see ante, § 322 *b*, and Gillman *v.* Brown, 1 Mason, R. 219—221.

[3] Code Civil, art. 2102, n. 4.

[4] Code of Commerce, art. 192, 193; 3 Pardessus, Droit. Comm. art. 942, 950. See also 1 Valin, Comm. 340; Abbott on Shipp. pt. 1, ch. 1, § 6.

[5] See ante, § 322 *a*, 323; Fœlix, Conflit des Lois, Revue Etrang. et Fran. tom. 7, (1840), § 33, pp. 227, 228.

§ 402. The question, then, naturally arises, whether, if such privileges, hypothecations, or liens, are recognised in the country where the contracts or acts which give rise to them are made, they are to be deemed obligatory in every other place where the property may be found, even against innocent purchasers, or against creditors who would otherwise, by the law of *rei sitæ,* have a preference of right? Would an attachment, for instance, of foreign creditors prevail against them in the tribunals of the domicil of such creditors? Upon the general principles already stated as to the operation of contracts, and the rule that movables have no locality, it would seem that these privileges, hypothecations, and liens ought to prevail over the rights of subsequent purchasers and creditors in every other country. That having once attached rightfully *in rem,* they ought not to be displaced by the mere change of local situation of the property[1]. This doctrine was in some measure recognised in an important case in England, where the right of stoppage *in transitu* was supposed to depend upon doctrines of foreign law, materially different from the law of England. The right conferred by the foreign law was upheld against the claims of English creditors, under circumstances of that case, which were somewhat peculiar, the lien having been given by the foreign law, and enforced in the foreign country, so far as to compel the master who was in possession of the goods, to recognise it, and to agree to hold the property subject to it[2].

§ 402 *a.* Nevertheless, as we have already seen, there is no inconsiderable conflict of opinion among foreign jurists, and even among domestic jurists, as to the extent to which

---

[1] See Livermore, Dissert. p. 159, § 249; Ante, § 322.

[2] Inglis *v.* Underwood, 1 East, R. 515; Abbott on Shipp. pt. 3, ch. 9, § 3.—On that occasion Lord Kenyon said: "The decision in this case will not at all trench upon the general rule of law respecting the right of stopping goods in transitu; but giving the plaintiffs the full benefit of the argument, that the delivery of the goods on board a chartered ship was a delivery to the

the right of privilege or priority ought to be allowed in cases where such privilege or priority has arisen under foreign laws against subsequent purchasers, or against creditors in the country where the property is subsequently found[1]. Whether an exception would be allowed generally in favour of maritime liens and privileges and priorities, founded upon the public policy of giving them full effect as matters of public convenience and interest, founded upon the necessities and exigencies of commerce and naval intercourse, may admit of question. It is highly probable, however, that most, if not all commercial nations will adopt such an exception, upon the principle of comity *sub mutuæ vicissitudinis obtentu.* Indeed upon any other system bot-

---

bankrupt; still the circumstance of the Russian ordinance set forth in the case varies it very importantly, and takes it out of the general rule. By that law, the consignors, under the circumstances stated, had a right to repossess themselves of their goods; and they did so in effect, not indeed by actually taking them out of the ship on board of which they were laden, or by instituting legal process for the recovery of them; but having a right so to do, which it became unnecessary to exert, because it was in the first instance acknowledged and submitted to by the captain in whose possession the property was, they imposed terms upon him that he should sign bills of lading to their order, upon his compliance with which, they suffered the cargo to proceed to the place of its destination, disposable there as events might turn out. The goods are therefore sent with the condition attached to them. The law of Russia in this respect is a very equitable law; and I have often lamented that our own code was defective in the same particular. For every man contracting to supply another with goods acts on the presumption, that that other is in a condition to pay for them; and therefore, when the condition of the consignee is altered at the time of the delivery, and he is insolvent, and no longer capable of performing his part of the contract, honesty and good faith require that the contract should be rescinded. However, the contrary has been settled to be law, unless the consignor stop the goods in transitu before they get into the consignee's possession. But this being a transaction in a foreign country, where a more equitable law in this respect prevails, I am far from being desirous of limiting its operation; and for the reasons before given, I think that the consignors have substantially availed themselves of it, and that the defendant by delivering the goods to their order, has done no more than he was bound to do."

[1] Ante, § 322—328; Post, § 524—528.

tomry bonds, *respondentia* bonds, and other maritime hypothecations would constitute so unsafe a security, that no merchant abroad would venture to lend his money upon so fragile a title, which might be undermined or destroyed by a local law, wholly unknown and suspected by him.

§ 403. Hitherto we have been considering cases of voluntary transfers *inter vivos;* and we are now naturally led to the consideration of involuntary transfers by operation of law in the domicil of the owner, such as are statutable transfers under the bankrupt or insolvent laws of the country of his domicil. The great question here is, whether an assignment under such laws has a universal operation, so as to transfer the movable property of the bankrupt or insolvent in all other countries, to the same extent as a voluntary transfer made by him would, and thus to withdraw it from the process of the local foreign laws, by way of arrest, attachment, or otherwise, issued in favour of the foreign creditors in the country where the movable property is situate. This question has been very gravely discussed both at home and abroad; and the Courts of England and the Courts of America have arrived at opposite conclusions respecting it. The Courts of the former country uniformly maintain the doctrine of the universal operation of such an assignment upon all movable property, wherever it may be locally situate at the time of the assignment. Many (but not all) of the Courts of the latter country confine the operation of such an assignment to the territory where the party is declared bankrupt or insolvent. The question is worthy of a very full examination, and a summary of the reasoning on each side of the question will, therefore, be here brought under review.

§ 404. Those who maintain, that assignments under bankrupt or insolvent laws are, and ought to be, of universal operation to transfer movable property, in whatever country it may be locally situate, adopt reasoning to this effect[1]. The general principle certainly is, that personal

[1] Mr. Bell has examined this subject with his usual ability and accuracy;

property has no locality; but that as to its disposition, it is subject to the law which governs the person of the owner, that is to say, it is subject to the law of his domicil[1]. There can be no doubt that the owner may, by a voluntary assignment or sale, made according to the law of his domicil, transfer the title to any person, wherever the property may be locally situate[2]. Now, an assignment under the bankrupt laws of his domicil is by operation of law a valid transfer of all the bankrupt's property, as valid as if made personally by him[3]. The law upon his bankruptcy transfers his whole property to the assignees, who thus become *lege*

---

and vindicated at large the propriety of the rule, giving universal effect to assignments in bankruptcy. See 2 Bell, Comm. b. 8, ch. 2, § 1266, pp. 684—690, 4th edit.; Id. pp. 680—691, 5th edit.

1 Sill *v.* Worswick, 1 H. Black. 690, 691; Hunter *v.* Potts, 4 T. R. 182.

2 In Re Wilson cited 1 H. Black. 691, 692.

3 Sill *v.* Worswick, 1 H. Black. 691, 692; Hunter *v.* Potts, 4 T. R. 182, 192; Phillips *v.* Hunter, 2 H. Black. 402, 405; Goodwin *v.* Jones, 3 Mass. R. 517.—"It is a proposition," said the Court in Phillips *v.* Hunter, 2 H. Black. 402, 403, "not to be disputed, that previous to the bankruptcy the bankrupts themselves might have transferred or assigned this property, though abroad, as absolutely as if it had been in their own tangible possession in this country; and it seems that the assignees under their commission were entitled, by operation of law, to do with it after the bankruptcy, what the bankrupts themselves might have done." In Potts *v.* Hunter, (4 T. R. 182, 192), the Court said: "The only question here is, whether or not the property in that island (Rhode Island) passed by the assignment, in the same manner as if the owner (the bankrupt) had assigned it by his voluntary act. And that it does so pass cannot be doubted, unless there were some positive law of that country to prevent it." ... "On the general reason of the thing, if there be no positive decision to the contrary, no doubt could be entertained but that by the laws of this country, uncontradicted by the laws of any other country where personal property may happen to be, the commissioners of a bankrupt may dispose of the personal property of a bankrupt here, though such property be in a foreign country." In Goodwin *v.* Jones, (3 Mass. R. 517), Mr. Chief Justice Parsons said: "The assignment of a bankrupt's effects may be considered as his own act, as it is in the execution of laws by which he is bound, he himself being competent to make such assignment, and voluntarily committing the act which authorized the making of it." See also Livermore's Dissert. p. 159, § 249, 250. The same doctrine was affirmed by Lord Mansfield in Wadham *v.* Marlow, cited 1 H. Black. 437, 438, 439, note; S. C. and S. P. 8 East, R. 314, 316, note *a*.

loci, the lawful owners of it, and entitled to administer it for the benefit of all his creditors. The mode of transfer is wholly immaterial. The only proper question is, whether it is good according to the law of his domicil [1]. This rule is admitted and applied in all cases of the succession to movable property in cases of intestacy where the property passes by mere operation of law, in the same manner and to the same extent as where it passes by the voluntary act or transfer *inter vivos* of the owner, or where it passes by his last will or testament [2].

§ 405. The same principle applies with equal force and general convenience to the disposition of the effects of bankrupts; for the just and equal distribution of all the funds of that class of debtors becomes the common concern of the whole commercial world. In cases of intestacy it is presumed to be the intent of the intestate, that his movables, which by fiction of law have no locality independent of his person, should be brought home, and distributed according to the law of his domicil. It is equally to be presumed, as the understanding of the commercial world, that the bankrupt's effects should follow his person, and be distributed in the place of his domicil, where the credit was bestowed, or the payment expected according to the laws thereof [3]. An assignment under the bankrupt laws ought to be deemed in all respects of equal force and validity with a voluntary assignment of the party; for, by implication of law, he consents to all transfers made of his property according to the law of his domicil. Great inconveniences would follow from a different proceeding. Different commissions might issue in different countries, and have concurrent operation *simul et semel* in different countries. And thus it would be in the power of the bankrupt to throw his property under either

---

1 Ante, § 399, 420, 566.

2 Sill *v.* Worswick, 1 H. Black. 690, 691.

3 Holmes *v.* Remsen, 4 John. Ch. R. 460, 470; Hunter *v.* Potts, 4 T. R. 182, 192.

commission at pleasure, and to give local preferences to different creditors, according to his own partialities or prejudices. Such a state of things, and such conflicting systems would lead to great public inconvenience and confusion, and be the source of much fraud and injustice, and disturb the equality and equity of any bankrupt system in any country[1].

§ 406. There is great wisdom, therefore, in adopting the rule, that an assignment in bankruptcy shall operate as a complete and valid transfer of all his movable property abroad, as well as at home; and it has accordingly received a very general sanction. It is true, that any nation may adopt, if it pleases, a different system, and prefer an attaching domestic creditor to a foreign assignee or to foreign creditors. But such a course of legislation can hardly be deemed consistent with the general comity of nations, and could scarcely fail to bring on a retaliatory system of preferences in every other nation injured thereby. But, until such a legislation is positively made and interposes a direct obstruction, the true rule is, to follow out the lead of the general principle that makes the law of the owner's domicil conclusive upon the disposition of his personal property[2].

---

[1] Holmes *v.* Remsen, 4 John. Ch. R. 471: Phillips *v.* Hunter, 2 H. Black. 402.—In Phillips *v.* Hunter, (2 H. Black, 402, 403), the Court said: "The great principle of the bankrupt laws is justice founded on equality. This being the principle of those laws, it seems to follow, that the whole property of the bankrupt must be under their (the assignees') control, without regard to the locality of that property, except in cases which directly militate against the particular laws of the country in which it happens to be situated." ...."If the bankrupt laws were circumscribed by the local situation of the property, a door would be open to all the partiality and undue preferences which they were framed to prevent; it being easy to foresee how frequently property would be sent abroad with that unjust view, immediately previous to and in contemplation of bankruptcy."

[2] Holmes *v.* Remsen, 4 John. R. 471, 472; Hunter *v.* Potts, 4 T. R. 182, 192. Sill *v.* Worswick, 1 H. Black. 691, 693.—In Phillips *v.* Hunter, (2 H. Black. 402, 405), the Court said: "It is true that the laws of the country where the property is situated have the immediate control over in respect to its locality, and the immediate protection afforded to it; yet the country where the proprietor resides, in respect to another species

This reasoning applies in an especial manner to contracts made in the very country where the party is declared bankrupt[1].

§ 407. There are many authorities in favour of this doctrine. As early as 1723, Lord Talbot, then at the bar, gave an opinion that the statutes of bankruptcy of England did not extend to the plantations; yet that the personal property of an English bankrupt in the plantations passed to the assignees[2]. Lord Hardwicke, in a case in judgment before him, adopted and acted upon the doctrine that an assignment in bankruptcy in England conveyed the personal property of the bankrupt in foreign countries; and that their title would overreach that of an attaching creditor after the assignment, although at that time it was not made known to the debtor[3]. In another case, in the Court of Chancery in England, in 1704, where the property of the owner, who was domiciled in Holland, was taken under a commission of bankruptcy, and, according to the laws of Holland, the administration thereof given to and vested in persons who are called Curators of Desolate Estates, it was

---

of protection afforded to him and his property, has a right to regulate his contract relating to that property." And in Hunter *v.* Potts, (4 T. R. 182, 192), the Court said: "Every person having property in a foreign country may dispose of it in this; though, indeed if there be a law in that country, directing a particular mode of conveyance that must be adopted." "If (said Lord Loughborough) the bankrupt happens to have property which lies out of the jurisdiction of the law of England, if the country in which it lies proceeds according to the principles of well regulated justice, there is no doubt that it will give effect to the title of the assignees." . . . "But if the law of that country preferred him (a creditor) to the assignees, though I must suppose that determination wrong, yet I do not think that my holding a contrary opinion would revoke the determination of that country, however I might disapprove of the principle on which that law so decided." Sill *v.* Worswick, 1 H. Black. 691, 693.

[1] Sill *v.* Worswick, 1 H. Black. 691, 693, 694; Phillips *v.* Hunter, 2 H. Black. 404, 405; Hunter *v.* Potts, 4 T. R. 182.

[2] Livermore, Diss. 140; Beames, Lex Mercatoria, pp. 5, 6, 6th edit.

[3] In Wilson's Case, cited in 1 H. Black. 691, 692, and probably decided between 1752 and 1756. See also S. C., cited in Hunter *v.* Potts, 4 T. R. 186, 187.

decided that the Curators had immediately upon their appointment a title to recover the debts due to the bankrupt in England, in preference to the diligence of particular creditors seeking to attach those debts[1]. In another case, in 1769, the same point was decided[2]. These are cases in which the rule was asserted in favour of foreign assignees[3]. A like decision in favour of English assignees was made in the Court of Chancery in Ireland in 1763[4]. Lord Thurlow gave it the sanction of his own great name in a case decided by him in 1787[5].

§ 408. The question was most elaborately considered in England in two cases decided in 1791, in which it was solemnly held that the operation of the bankrupt laws is to vest in the assignees all the personal property of the bankrupt, wherever it may be situate; and that whenever that property shall be brought into England by any person who has obtained it, the assignees will have a right to recover it of him, for the benefit of all the creditors; and consequently, that an attachment and recovery of such property, made by a creditor in a foreign country after such assignment, will be held inoperative; upon the principle, that the title which is prior in point of time, ought to obtain preference in point of right and law[6]. Upon a writ of error the general doctrine maintained in these cases was affirmed; but in its actual application it was restricted to attachments made by British creditors against British debtors. In this state the doctrine remained until a very recent period, when in the case of a bankruptcy of an English partner in

---

1 Solomons *v.* Ross, 1 H. Bl. 131, note; Id. 691; S. C. Cooke's Bank. Laws, 306, 4th edit.

2 Jollet *v.* Deponthieu, 1 H. Bl. 132, note; Id. 691.

3 Ibid.

4 Neale *v.* Cottingham, 1 H. Bl. R. 132, note; S. C. cited in Hunter *v.* Potts, 4 T. R. 194, and Cooke's Bank. Laws, p. 303, 4th edit., (1799). See also Quelin *v.* Moisson, 1 Knapp, Appeal R. 265, note.

5 Ex parte Blakes, 1 Cox, R. 398.

6 Sill *v.* Worswick, 1 H. Bl. 665, 690, 691, 694; Hunter *v.* Potts, 4 T. R. 192; S. C. in err. 2 H. Bl. 402.

a Scotch partnership it was discussed anew. A commission of bankruptcy was issued in England; and subsequently an arrest, attachment, or sequestration, was made by a creditor, of debts due to the bankrupt in Scotland. The question then arose, whether the assignees or the attaching creditor was entitled to priority; and this depended on the question, whether an English commission of bankruptcy passed to the assignees the title to property, or debts locally situate or due in Scotland. The Court of Session in Scotland held that it did[1]; and upon appeal this judgment was affirmed by the House of Lords. "One thing," said Lord Eldon, "is quite clear, that there is not in any book any dictum or authority that would authorize me to deny, at least in this place, that an English commission passes, as with respect to the bankrupt and his creditors in England, the personal property he has in Scotland, or in any foreign country[2]."

---

1. The Court of Session in Scotland, gave very elaborate opinions on this subject in the Royal Bank of Scotland *v.* Cuthbert, commonly cited as Stein's case, 1 Rose, Bank. Cases, App. 412; 2 Rose, Bank. Cases, 91, 78. See also Smith *v.* Buchanan, 1 East, R. 6; 2 Bell, Comm. 684—687, 4th edit.; Id. pp. 680—691, 5th edit.

2. Selkrig *v.* Davis, 2 Rose, Bank. Cas. 291, 314; S. C. 2 Dow, R. 230, 250; 2 Rose, Bank. Cas. 97. See also Ex parte Dobrey, 8 Ves. 82; 2 Bell, Comm. 684—687, 4th edit.; Holmes *v.* Remsen, 4 John. Ch. R. 460; S. C. 20 John. R. 229.—The Judgment of Lord Eldon, which was affirmed apparently with entire unanimity, contains many striking remarks upon the difficulties attendant upon any other system of international jurisprudence. The following extracts are particularly valuable to be submitted to the consideration of the American Courts: "In whatever way a Scottish sequestration may be enforced, the distribution of a bankrupt's effects under it is perfectly different from what it is under an English commission of bankruptcy. The Scottish law cuts down all securities that have been made or given within a certain number of days prior to the issuing of the sequestration, whether they have been given bonâ fide, or given, as we should say, in contemplation of bankruptcy. On the other hand, in our law, though the approximation of the security to the date of the commission may be evidence that it was given in contemplation of bankruptcy; yet it is but evidence, and the security may be perfectly good. Again, in England, a man cannot become a bankrupt without committing an act of bankruptcy. The commission must be founded on that act of bankruptcy; and there are various other differences applying to the property of a bankrupt, as administered under an English commission,

§ 409. This is now, accordingly, the settled law of England, in which the following propositions are firmly estab-

---

or, vice versâ, as distributed by the rules, and according to the forms of a Scottish sequestration. If, my lords, you attempt to obviate these inconveniences by a co-existing sequestration and commission, the difficulty is tenfold greater, unless the one should be used merely as the means of assisting the distribution of the funds on the other. What personal property shall belong to the one proceeding, and what to the other proceeding, is no ordinary difficulty. The counsel for the appellant say there is no difficulty.—That a debt owing to the house in Scotland, wherever the debtor lives, ought to go to the Scotch sequestration; and, in like manner, that the debt owing to the house in England, wherever the debtor lives, should go to the commission. But the house may be constituted of persons of whom it may be difficult to say whether a man is a Scotchman or an Englishman. It may happen that a house is composed of persons, some of whom reside in Scotland, and some in England. I should wish to know, not only how the joint debts due to one firm, and the joint debts due to the other, are to be distributed; but where separate debts are due to each, whether the separate debts are to be a fund of distribution under the English commission, or under the Scottish sequestration, or what is to become of them. All these difficulties certainly belong to this case. But, notwithstanding that, one thing is quite clear; there is not in any book any dictum or authority that would authorize me to deny, at least in this place, that an English commission passes, as with respect to the bankrupt and his creditors in England, the personal property he has in Scotland or in any foreign country. It is admitted, that the assignment under the English commission, as between the bankrupt and the English and Scotch proprietors passes the Scotch property, and vests it in the assignees, when the Scotch creditors have not used legal diligence. I think the case was put at the bar thus: That the commission of bankruptcy operated so as to bring into the fund the Scotch personal property, provided that such personal property was not arrested by legal diligence in Scotland, prior to the intimation of the assignment in Scotland. It was therefore argued, that this was to be put on the same footing as the case of the assignation of a particular debt to a particular individual. Now, your lordships need not be told that, by the law of Scotland, if B. assign a debt which is due from C. to B., a creditor of B. may arrest that debt in the hands of the debtor, notwithstanding the assignment, unless the assignee has given an intimation formally to the person, by whom the debt is owing. That must be admitted. Upon that it has been insisted here, that no intimation has been given, and that this subsequent arrestment, in 1798, ought to have the preference of the title of the assignees under the commission, that was sued out in the year 1782." 2 Rose, Bank. Cas. 314—316. He afterwards proceeded to decide, that no intimation was necessary; and if necessary, it was given. Id. 318, 319. See Quelin *v.* Moisson, 1 Knapp, Rep. 265.

lished: first, that an assignment under the bankrupt law of a foreign country, passes all the personal property of the bankrupt locally situate, and debts owing in England; secondly, that an attachment of such property by an English creditor after such bankruptcy, with or without notice to him, is invalid to overreach the assignment; thirdly, that in England the same doctrine holds under assignments by her own bankrupt laws, as to personal property and debts of the bankrupt in foreign countries; fourthly, that, upon principle, all attachments made by foreign creditors after such assignment in a foreign country, ought to be held invalid; sixthly, that at all events a British creditor will not be permitted to hold the property acquired by a judgment under any attachment made in a foreign country after such assignment; and seventhly, that a foreign creditor not subjected to British laws, will be permitted to retain any such property acquired under any such judgment, if the local laws (however incorrectly upon principle) confer on him an absolute title[1]. There is no inconsiderable weight of American authority on the same side; but it must be admitted that the preponderating authority is certainly now the other way[2].

---

[1] 2 Bell, Comm. § 1266, pp. 687—690, 4th edit.; Id. pp. 680—690, 5th edit; Holmes *v.* Remsen, 4 John. Ch. R. 560; S. C. 20 John. R. 229; Dwarris on Statutes, 650, 651.

[2] Mr. Chief Justice Parsons certainly held this opinion in Goodwin *v.* Jones, 3 Mass. R. 517. And Mr. Chancellor Kent has sustained it in one of his most elaborate judgments, which will well reward a diligent perusal, Holmes *v.* Remsen, 4 John. Ch. R. 460. This is also, as we shall see, the law in France and Holland. Post, § 417. See Parish *v.* Seton, Cooper's Bank. Law, 27; Holmes *v.* Remsen, 4 John. Ch. R. 484; S. P. 20 John. R. 258; Blake *v.* Williams, 6 Pick. R. 312, 313; Merlin Répertoire, Faillité et Banqueroute, art. 10. Mr. Chancellor Kent, in his Commentaries (2 Kent, Comm. Lect. 37, pp. 404—408, 3rd edit.), has with great candour admitted, that the American doctrine is now established the other way by a preponderance of authority, although he has an undisguised distrust of the validity of its foundation. There are not a few jurists in America, each of whom may be disposed to use on this occasion the language of a great orator of antiquity, "Ego assentior Scævolæ." See Livermore's Diss. § 223—248, pp. 140—

§ 410. The reasoning which is urged in support of what may be deemed the American doctrine, is to the following effect. It is admitted that the general rule is, that personal property, including debts, has no locality, but follows, as to its disposition and transfer, the law of the domicil of the owner. But every country may by positive law regulate as it pleases the disposition of personal property found within it; and may prefer its own attaching creditors to any foreign assignee; and no other country has any right to question the determination. When there is no positive law, the general rule is to govern, with the exception of such cases as fall within the known principle of Huberus, that it is not prejudicial to the State, or to the just rights of its citizens. And this exception is the very ground upon which the objection to the ubiquity of operation of the bankrupt laws of a country, as respects the personal estate of the bankrupt, is to be rested [1].

§ 411. There is a marked distinction between a voluntary conveyance of property by the owner, and a conveyance by mere operation of law in cases of bankruptcy *in invitum*. Laws cannot force the will, nor compel any man to make a conveyance. In place of a voluntary conveyance of the owner, all that the legislature of a country can do when justice requires it, is to assume the disposition of his property *in invitum*. But a statutable conveyance, made under the authority of any legislature, cannot operate upon any property except that which is within its own territory. This makes a solid distinction between a voluntary conveyance of the owner, and an involuntary legal conveyance by the mere authority of law. The former has no relation to place; the latter, on the contrary, has the strictest relation to place. This distinction is insisted on with great force

158. There are in Mr. Henry's Appendix to his work on Foreign Law, pp. 251—258, some curious opinions given by Counsel in 1715, as to the effect of an attachment after a foreign bankruptcy.

[1] Blake *v.* Williams, 6 Pick. R. 286; Olivier *v.* Townes, 14 Martin, R. 93, 97—100; Milne *v.* Moreton, 6 Binn. 353.

by Lord Kaims[1]. It is therefore admitted, that a voluntary assignment by a party according to the law of his domicil will pass his personal estate, whatever may be its locality, abroad as well as at home. But it by no means follows that the same rule should govern in cases of assignments by operation of law.

§ 412. The true rule in such cases is to hold, that the assignees are in the same situation as the bankrupt himself in regard to foreign debts. They take the property under the assignment, subject to every equity belonging to foreign creditors, and subject to the remedies provided by the laws of the foreign country where the debt is due; and when they are permitted to sue in a foreign country, it is not as assignees having an interest, but as the representatives of the bankrupt. They stand upon the footing of administrators only, with a right to sue for the benefit of all the creditors. But our local law will not regard the choses in action of the debtor, as exclusively appropriated to the use of such assignees; and a preference can be gained by them only by pursuing the remedies which our local laws afford. This was formerly the rule in England[2].

§ 413. Nor can it be truly said, that an assignment by the bankrupt laws is with the consent of the bankrupt, because he assents by implication to such laws. This is a very unsafe and dangerous principle on which to risk the doctrine; for in the same way it may be said, that a man committing a crime, for which his estate is forfeited, voluntarily consents to its transfer. But the principle whether correct or not, can only apply to cases where the debtor and creditor belong to the same country. It is wholly inapplicable to foreign creditors.

§ 414. Besides, national comity requires us to give effect to such assignments only, so far as may be done without im-

---

[1] Kaims on Equity, b. 3, ch. 8, § 6; Remsen *v.* Holmes, 20 John. R. 258, 259; Moreton *v.* Milne, 6 Binn. 353, 369; Ante, § 351 *b.*

[2] See Mawdesley *v.* Park, cited 1 H. Black. R. 680.

pairing the remedies, or lessening the securities which our laws have provided for our own citizens. The rule is: *Quatenus sine præjudicio indulgentium fieri potest*[1]. And after all, this is mere comity, and not international law. All comity of this sort must be built up in a great measure upon the doctrine of reciprocity; and this is extremely difficult, from the known diversities in the jurisprudence of different nations[2]. It would prejudice the rights and remedies of our citizens in our own Courts, to suffer the assignments under foreign bankrupt laws to prevail over their own diligence, in seeking remedies against their debtors in our own Courts. If there is in such cases a conflict between our own laws and foreign laws, as to the rights of our citizens, and one of them must give way, our own laws ought to prevail[3]. The most convenient and practical rule is, that statutable assignments as to creditors, shall operate intra-territorially only. If our citizens conduct themselves according to our laws in regard to the property of their debtors found within our jurisdiction, it is reasonable that they should reap the fruits of their diligence, and not be sent to a foreign country to receive such a dividend of their debtors' effects, as the foreign laws allow. If each government in cases of insolvency should sequester and distribute the funds within its own jurisdiction, the general result will be favourable to the interests of creditors and to the harmony of nations. This is the rule adopted in all cases of administration of the property of deceased persons; and there is no real difference between the principle of those cases, and of cases of bankruptcy[4].

§ 415. Down to the time of the American revolution, this may fairly be deemed to have been the English doctrine.

---

1 Huberus, lib. 1, tit. 3, De Conflict. Leg. § 2.

2 Blake *v.* Williams, 6 Pick. R. 269, 313—315; Milne *v.* Moreton, 6 Binn. 353, 375; Remsen *v.* Holmes, 20 John. R. 229, 263, 264.

3 Potter *v.* Brown, 5 East, R. 131; Ante, § 326.

4 Remsen *v.* Holmes, 20 John. R. 229, 265; Milne *v.* Moreton, 6 Binn. R. 353, 361; Blake *v.* Williams, 6 Pick. R. 286.

It has since been changed. Even in England the principle has not as yet been applied in favour of any foreign countries, except such as have bankrupt laws in form or substance; and we have none in our country[1]. It can make no difference in the case, whether the debt of the attaching creditor accrued here or in foreign countries; for in either case the question is not, as to the validity of the contract, but as to a collateral matter; that is to say, the effect to be given to it in a conflict between rights growing out of our own laws, and those of a foreign country[2].

§ 416. Neither is it true, that even the voluntary conveyances of parties in all cases are to be held valid, where they are prejudicial to the rights and remedies of our own citizens. In Massachusetts, for instance, it has been held, that a voluntary assignment by a debtor of all his property, made in Pennsylvania for the benefit of creditors generally, shall not prevail over a subsequent attachment of the funds of the debtor made after the assignment; because such an assignment would be void by the laws of Massachusetts, if made in that State, as being in fraud of creditors; and it is unjust and unequal in its effects, and prejudicial to the citizens of the State. In such a case, therefore, the party, who shall by process first attach the debt, or seize the property, ought to prevail, whether creditor or assignee[3].

---

[1] Remsen *v.* Holmes, 20 John. R. 229; Blake *v.* Williams, 6 Pick. R. 286; Milne *v.* Moreton, 6 Binn. R. 353; Wallis *v.* Paterson, 1 Harr. & M'Hen. R. 463; Abraham *v.* Plestero, 3 Wendell, R. 538—550.

[2] Milne *v.* Moreton, 6 Binn. 360.

[3] Ingraham *v.* Geyer, 13 Mass. R. 146; S. C. cited 6 Pick. R. 307. See also Olivier *v.* Townes, 6 Pick. R. 97—101.—This summary of the American reasoning is principally extracted from the three leading cases of Milne *v.* Moreton, 6 Binn. R. 353; Remsen *v.* Holmes, 20 John. R. 229, and Blake *v.* Williams, 6 Pick. R. 286, where the subject is very elaborately discussed. The same doctrine will be found supported in other American cases, cited in 2 Kent, Comm. Lect. 37, p. 406—408, 3rd edit. See also Olivier *v.* Townes, 14 Martin, R. 93, 99; Harrison *v.* Sterry, 5 Cranch, R. 289; Ogden *v.* Saunders, 12 Wheaton, R. 213; Id. 360—369; Saunders *v.* Williams, 5 New Hamp. R. 213; Plestero *v.* Abraham, 1 Paige, R. 237;

§ 417. It is admitted in the reasoning in the American cases, that the old law of France and Holland is in coincidence with the British doctrine[1]. The modern law of those countries is equally decisive in its support; and very recent cases have given it a complete confirmation in their tribunals. The principal grounds of their decisions may be summed up in the following propositions: (1.) That the law of the domicil may rightfully devest the debtor of the administrator of his property, and place it under the administration of assignees or syndics. (2.) That laws, whose effects are to regulate the capacity and incapacity of persons, their personal actions, and their movables, every where belong to the category of personal statutes. (3.) That it is a matter of universal jurisprudence, and especially of that of France and the Netherlands, that the debts, actively considered, of an inhabitant against a foreigner, are deemed a part of his movable property, and have their locality in the place of domicil of the creditor[2]. At the same time it is admitted, that a purchaser from the bankrupt, in a foreign country, of property there locally situate, would be entitled to hold it against the assignees, if, at the time, he had no knowledge of any bankruptcy, or of any intent to defraud creditors[3].

§ 418. The American doctrine has been followed out to another result. Suppose (as was the fact in one case) after a commission and assignment in bankruptcy in England, the bankrupt should voluntarily make a confirmatory conveyance in aid of the commission; the question is, whether

---

S. C. 3 Wendell, R. 538; Fox *v.* Adams, 5 Greenl. R. 245; Wallis *v.* Paterson, 1 Harr. & M'Hen. R. 236, 463; Ogden *v.* Saunders, 12 Wheat. R. 213, 359—362; Ante, § 399—401.

1 Holmes *v.* Remsen, 4 John. Ch. R. 484; Remsen *v.* Holmes, 20 John. R. 258; Blake *v.* Williams, 6 Pick. R. 312, 313; Ante, § 409, note; Henry on Foreign Law, pp. 127—135; Id. pp. 153—160; Id. pp. 248—250.

2 Merlin, Répertoire, Faillité and Banqueroute, § 2, 3, art. 10, p. 412; Henry on Foreign Law, pp. 127—135; Id. 175.

3 Merlin, Id. pp. 415, 416.

it will have the effect of a voluntary assignment, so as to defeat a subsequent attachment in America? It has been held by a learned judge in New York, that it will not; because, by the law of England, the commission devests the title of the bankrupt in all his property throughout the world, and he no longer has any capacity to convey it; but in regard to that property, he is to be treated as *civiliter mortuus*[1]. There is great difficulty in maintaining this doctrine. For if the statutable assignment does, *per se*, transfer the personal property of the bankrupt in foreign countries to the assignees, and devest all his title to it, then it would seem to follow, that a subsequent attachment of it must be wholly inoperative, because he has no longer any attachable interest in it. We are not at liberty to treat the property, as still in him for one purpose, and out of him for another. The doctrine of Mr. Chancellor Kent is certainly here far more satisfactory, giving to such a voluntary assignment a full confirmatory effect[2].

§ 419. There are some other questions, arising from the operation of foreign bankrupt laws, and other analogous systems of proceeding for the benefit of creditors generally, *in invitum*, which have come under judicial cognizance, and deserve attention. In the first place, suppose a British subject is declared bankrupt, while he is on a voyage *in transitu* from England to America, and he has a large shipment of property with him; is he entitled to hold it when it arrives in America? Or, can his assignees maintain a suit against him, or against other persons holding it for his use, not being creditors? It has been held by a learned Chancellor of New York (Walworth), that the assignees are entitled to recover, upon the ground, that the assignment operates as a good conveyance to them against the bankrupt, and those holding for his use. On that occasion, the learned Judge stated the distinction

---

[1] Mr. Justice Platt, in Remsen *v.* Holmes, 20 John. R. 267.

[2] Holmes *v.* Remsen, 4 John. Ch. R. 489.

between that case, and the preceding cases. "In those cases," said he, "the contest was between foreign assignees and domestic creditors, claiming under the laws of the country where the property was situate, and where the suits were brought. The question in those cases was, whether the personal property of the debtor was to be considered as having locality, for the purpose of giving a remedy to the creditors residing in the country where the property was in fact situated, at the time of the foreign attachment. In this case, the controversy is between the bankrupt and his assignees and creditors, all residing in the country, under whose laws the assignment was made. Even the property itself at the time of assignment was constructively within the jurisdiction of that country, being on the high seas, in the actual possession of a British subject. Under such circumstances the assignment had the effect to change the property, and devest the title of the bankrupt, as if the same had been sold in England under an execution against him, or he had voluntarily conveyed the same to the assignees for the benefit of his creditors[1]." Upon an appeal, however, this doctrine was not in terms confirmed by the appellate Court; and some of the judges dissented from the doctrine of the Chancellor. But the case was ultimately reversed on another point[2].

§ 420. It is obvious that the great question involved in

---

1 Plestero *v.* Abraham, 1 Paige, R. 236; S.C. 3 Wend, R. 538.

2 Abraham *v.* Plestero, 3 Wend, 538.—It is difficult to perceive how the doctrine of the Chancellor, as to the operation of the British bankrupt laws upon British subjects, and their property in transitu, can be answered. The transfer must be admitted to be operative to devest the bankrupt's title to the extent of an estoppel, as to his own personal claim in opposition to it; for the law of America, be it what it may, had not then operated upon it. It was not locally within our jurisdiction. No one could doubt the right of the assignee to personal property locally in England at the time of the assignment. In what respect does such a case differ from a case, where it has not passed into another jurisdiction? Is there any substantial difference between its being on board of a British vessel and its being on board of an American vessel on the high seas? See Ante, § 391.

this case was, whether an assignment under a foreign bankrupt law operates as a transfer of personal property in this country? It matters not in respect to the bankrupt himself, or others claiming under him, not being creditors or purchasers, whether it operates as a legal or as an equitable transfer. In either way it will devest him of his beneficial interest. Upon this point it is impossible not to feel that the general current of American authority is in perfect coincidence with that of England, in favour of the title of the assignees[1]. In most of the cases in which assignments under foreign bankrupt laws have been denied to give a title against attaching creditors, it has been distinctly admitted, that the assignees might maintain suits in our courts under such assignments for the property of the bankrupt[2]. This is avowed in the most unequivocal manner in the leading cases in Pennsylvania and New York already cited, and it is silently admitted in those in Massachusetts[3]. And, unless the admission can be overthrown, it surrenders the principle; for no one will contend, that the assignees can sue either in law or equity in our courts, unless they possess some title

---

[1] See 1 H. Bl. 691; 6 Maule & Selw. 126; 1 East, R. 6; Coke's Bank. Laws, 4th edit. 304; Doug. R. 161, 170; Ante, § 403—410.

[2] In Alivon *v.* Furnival, 1 Cromp. Mees. & Rosc. 296, it was held, that if by the law of the foreign country the assignees or syndics of a foreign bankrupt may sue there, the same right to sue in England will be allowed by the comity of nations; and that if there are three assignees or syndics appointed under the foreign law, that two may by that law sue without joining the third, the same right to sue by two will be acknowledged and enforced by the same comity in England. Upon that occasion Mr. Baron Parke, in delivering the opinion of the Court, said: "This is a peculiar right of action created by the law of the country, and we think it may by the comity of nations be enforced in this, as much as the right of foreign assignees or curators, or foreign corporations appointed or created in a different way from that which the law of this country requires." See Ante, § 355, 399, 400; Post, § 565, 566.

[3] Holmes *v.* Remsen, 4 John. Ch. R. 485; S. C. 20 John. R. 262, 263; Milne *v.* Moreton, 6 Binn. 363, 374; Livermore's Diss. 142, 152; Blake *v.* Williams, 6 Pick. R. 305; Ingraham *v.* Gayer, 13 Mass. R. 146, 147; Goodwin *v.* Jones, 3 Mass. R. 517. But see contra, Orr *v.* Amory, 11 Mass. R. 25. See Ante, § 399, note; Post, § 566.

under the assignment. The point has hitherto been a struggle for priority and preference between parties claiming against the bankrupt under opposing titles; the assignees claiming for the general creditors, and the attaching creditors for their separate rights.

§ 421. It is true that Mr. Chief Justice Marshall, in delivering the opinion of the Court in Harrison *v.* Sterry[1], used the following language: "As the bankrupt law of a foreign country is incapable of operating a legal transfer of property in the United States, the remaining two-thirds of the funds are liable to the attaching creditors, according to the legal preference obtained by their attachments." But the very terms of this statement shew, that the Court were examining the point only as between the conflicting rights of the assignees and those of the attaching creditors, and not in relation to the bankrupt himself. And this is manifestly the light in which the doctrine was contemplated by the majority of the Court in a subsequent case[2].

§ 422. In cases of partnership, where there are different firms in different countries, or some of the partners reside in one and some in another country, there are still more embarrassing difficulties attendant upon questions of foreign bankrupt assignments. If one partner is declared bankrupt under a foreign commission, his share and interest only in the funds there can pass to his assignees, as against the partners in another country. And of course they must take, subject to an account between all the partners, and stand precisely as the bankrupt does on a settlement of all claims as between debtor and creditor[3]. Let us suppose the case of a partnership in the British West Indies and in England, and one of the partners resides in England, and becomes bankrupt, and an assignment is made, and afterwards a British West India creditor of the firm attaches a

---

1 5 Cranch, R. 289, 302. See also Ogden *v.* Saunders, 12 Wheaton, R. 61, 362—364.

2 Ogden *v.* Saunders, 12 Wheaton, R. 359—365.

3 Harrison *v.* Sterry, 5 Cranch, R. 289, 302.

debt due to the firm in the West Indies, and procures a judgment and satisfaction there. Can he be compelled to refund the same upon a suit brought by the assignees against him in England? Sir William Grant, in a case of this sort, decided in the negative; and on that occasion seemed to have great difficulty in reconciling his mind to the decisions upon the more general questions of satisfaction obtained abroad by a creditor in case of a sole bankruptcy. He held, that the bankruptcy of the partner resident in England could not affect the partners remaining in the West Indies, in a country not subject to the bankrupt law, so as to devest them of the management of the partnership concerns, or of the disposition of the partnership property. If they applied the partnership assets in the payment of the partnership debts, or, if in a legal course of proceedings against them, the debts were recovered according to the law of the country, no jurisdiction could exist in England to force the partnership, or the creditor to refund, what he had so received or so recovered. Under such circumstances the foreign partners and foreign creditors must be left to their general rights and remedies[1]. The same doctrine seems to be acknowledged in other nations, where there are partnerships and partners resident in different countries[2].

§ 423. But whatever may be the rule in relation to foreign voluntary assignments or foreign bankrupt assignments for the benefit of creditors generally, there is no doubt that there are some assignments which take effect by mere operation of law in foreign countries, and are admitted to have universal validity and effect upon personal property without respect to its locality[3]. Such is the case of a transfer of personal property arising from marriage. Thus, a marriage contracted by citizens of Massachusetts is a gift in law to the husband of all the personal tangible property of the

---

1 Brickwood *v.* Miller, 3 Merivale, R. 279.

2 See Merlin, Répertoire, Faillité et Banqueroute, § 2, art. 10, p. 414.

3 See Ante, § 398.

wife, and operates as a transfer of it to him wherever it may be situate, at home or abroad. And the right thus acquired by the law of the matrimonial domicil, will be held of perfect force and validity in every other country, notwithstanding the like rule would not arise in regard to domestic marriages by its own municipal code. This doctrine was adverted to by Lord Meadowbank in a very important case already referred to, as perfectly clear and established. "In the ordinary case," says he, "of a transference by contract of marriage, when a lady of fortune having a great deal of money in Scotland, or stock in the banks or public companies there, marries in London, the whole property is, *ipso jure*, her husband's. It is assigned to him. The legal assignment of a marriage operates without regard to territory all the world over[1]." Lord Eldon on several occasions has given this doctrine the fullest sanction of his own judgment, averring, that notice was not even necessary to give full effect to such a title[2]. The same doctrine was fully admitted in Remsen *v.* Holmes[3], and it is treated by elementary writers as beyond controversy[4]. We have already seen that foreign jurists press the doctrine to its fullest extent[5].

§ 423 *a.* It is principally in cases of voluntary assignments made by a debtor for the benefit of creditors, or of involuntary assignments under the bankrupt laws of a State against a debtor *in invitum*, that questions arise respecting the conflicting rights of creditors (*concursus creditorum*), as to the priorities and privileges in the distribution and marshalling of the assets, when they are insufficient to pay all the debts of the party. We have already had occasion to take notice,

---

[1] Ante, § 59, note; Royal Bank of Scotland *v.* Cuthbert, 1 Rose, Bank. Cas. App. 481. See Ante, § 396—398.

[2] Selkrig *v.* Davis, 2 Rose, Bank. Cas. 97, 99; Id. S. C. 291, 317.

[3] 20 John. R. 267.

[4] 2 Bell, Comm. § 1266, pp. 696, 697, 4th edit.; Id. pp. 680, 685, 686, 5th edit.; Liverm. Diss. p. 140, § 223.

[5] Ante, § 145, 146, 417.

that generally in cases of movable property the priorities and privileges are to be adjusted, and the distribution is to be made according to the law of the domicil of the debtor[1], founded upon the notion, that there all his movable property is in contemplation of law concentrated, although a part of it may be locally situated elsewhere according to the maxim: *Mobilia non habent sequelam; Mobilia tanquam ossibus affixa personæ*[2]. And in relation to immovable property, the distribution is to be made according to the *lex rei sitæ*[3]. Exceptions may doubtless exist where the law of the country in which either movable or immovable property is situate, prescribes a different rule, which must then be obeyed[4]. Similar rules will govern in cases of voluntary assignments by debtors, and of involuntary assignments under the bankrupt laws of a State. In each case the *lex loci* of the assignment, or the bankruptcy will ordinarily form the basis of the priorities and privileges attaching to his movable property, and will regulate the distribution thereof among his creditors, at least if that is the place of his domicil and of the *situs* of the property. If the property is immovable, or is situate elsewhere, the *lex loci rei sitæ* will, or at least may govern the same[5].

§ 423 *b*. Priorities and privileges are indeed generally treated as belonging to the form and order of proceedings, and are therefore properly governed by the *lex fori*, and they are not treated as belonging to the merits and matters of the decision. Rodenburg says: *Primum utamur vulgata D.D. distinctione, quâ separantur ea, quæ litis formam concernunt ac ordinationem, separantur ab iis, quæ decisionem aut materiam. Lis ordinanda secundum morem loci, in quo*

---

1 Ante, § 323—328.

2 Ante, § 362, 377, 378.

3 Ante, § 322—328; Post, § 428.

4 See Rodenburg, De Div. Stat. tit. 2, c. 5, § 5, 6; 2 Boullenois, pp. 37, 38; Post, § 550.

5 Ante, § 322, 328, 385—400, 402—416, 412—422.

ventilatur. Ut si judicati exequendi causâ bona debitoris distrahantur, qui solvendo sit, executio peragatur eo loci, ubi bona sita sunt, aut in causam judicati capiuntur. Sin cesserit foro debitor, aut propalam desierit esse solvendo, ut isti mobilium capioni, aut ulli omnino executioni non sit ultra locus, factâ jam omnium creditorum conditione pari, disputatio de privilegiis, aut concursu creditorum, veniat instituenda, ubi debitor habuerit domicilium[1].

§ 423 *c*. Matthæus (whose opinions have been already in part cited in another place[2]) holds, that hypothecations of movables are to be governed by the law of the domicil of the debtor; and hypothecations of immovables by the *lex loci rei sitæ*. In respect to priorities and privileges between hypothecary creditors upon movables, the law of the domicil of the debtor is to govern; and in respect to such priorities and privileges between hypothecary creditors upon immovables, the law of the *situs rei*, unless indeed the contest solely concerns their rights in the domicil of the debtor. *Quantum ad leges, secundum quas in disputatione de protopraxia judicandum, distinctio adhibenda est. Si bona mobilia debitoris in diversis provinciis sint, spectandæ sunt leges ejus loci, ubi debitor domicilium habet. Est enim vulgatum apud doctores, mobilia sequi personam, et idcircò censeri eo jure, quod obtinet ubi domicilium persona habet. Itaque si in loco domicilii valet pignus rei mobilis nudo pacto constitutum, manente possessione penes debitorem, potior erit in pignore is, cui ante res obligata est, licet non sit translata in eum possessio. Et si creditor aliquis in loco domicilii debitoris privilegium inter personales habeat, gaudebit eodem privilegio in ea civitate, in qua debitor tabernam habuit et merces. Contra, si in loco domicilii mobilia non habeant sequelam, nec creditor privilegium, frustra volet uti jure alterius civitatis, in qua utrumque contrario modo se habere perspicit. Quantum verò ad prædia*

---

1 Rodenburg, De Div. Stat. tit. 2, c. 5, § 16; 2 Boullenois, App. pp. 47, 48; Ante, § 325 *c*—325 *f*, and note.

2 Ante, § 325 *i*, 325 *k*.

attinet, separanda videtur hypotheca ab eo privilegio, quod quis inter hypothecarios exercet. In æstimanda hypotheca spectanda sunt ejus territorii jura, ubi prædium situm est. Itaque si in loco domicilii debitoris prædia obligari possint citra judicis auctoritatem, prædia verò sita sint in ea provincia, ubi oppigneratio judicialis desideratur, frustra obtendes locum domicilii, ad excludendum secundum creditorem, cui coram judice loci prædium pignori nexum est. Quod, si utrique fundus ritè oppigneratus sit, disputetur autem solummodò de privilegio, quod alter inter hypothecarios in loco domicilii debitoris habere se dicit, tum locus domicilii spectandus videtur: quia privilegium illud personam concernit, fundum autem pigneratum non afficit[1].

§ 423 *d*. Mr. Burge maintains a similar opinion, taking a distinction between ordinary liens and the priorities between creditors. "The vendor's lien," says he, "on the movables sold, and the right to stop them *in transitu* for the payment of the price, are privileges which attach to the subject sold, and are governed by the *lex loci contractûs*. They are distinguished from the preferences which a creditor may claim on the estate of a debtor when it is distributed under an execution sale, or general *concursus* of his creditors. The latter depend, not on the *lex loci contractûs*, but on that of the place where the movable estate is *fictione juris* considered to be situated, namely, in the domicil of its owner. The *lex loci contractûs*, although it is properly invoked as between the parties to the contract, yet it is considered unjust to give it effect against third parties, the creditors[2]".

§ 423 *e*. Mr. Bell adopts the doctrine in its fullest extent, that an assignment in bankruptcy conveys all the movable property of the bankrupt wherever it may be, and it is to be distributed according to the law of the place where the debtor has his domicil, and the proceedings in bankruptcy

---

1 Matthæus, De Auctionibus, lib. 1, c. 21, § 10, n. 35, pp. 294, 295; Id. n. 41, pp. 298, 299.

2 3 Burge, Comm. on Col. and For. Law, pt. 2, ch. 20, p. 770; Id. pp. 778, 779; Ante, § 327, note.

are had. But in relation to immovable property, that it is to be distributed and administered according to the territorial law. His language is: "The great rule on which the whole of the doctrine relative to the international effect of bankruptcy depends, has been completely fixed in all the three kingdoms upon a general principle of the law of nations; namely, that the personal estate is held as situate in that country where the bankrupt has his domicil; and that it is to be administered in bankruptcy according to the rules of the law of that country, just as if locally placed within it. The consequence of fixing this rule is, that a commission of bankruptcy in England or in Ireland, and the assignment following on it, or a sequestration in Scotland, and the conveyance to the trustee, have the effect of transferring to the trustee or assignees the whole personal estate of the bankrupt; that this transference defeats all preferences attempted to be obtained by the diligence of the law of the country where such estate happens to be placed, or by any voluntary conveyance of the bankrupt, after the period when the effect of the proceedings under the bankruptcy attaches to the funds[1]". And again: "Another great point in this doctrine is, what effect shall be allowed in Scotland to a different decision in any foreign country from that which has been adopted in these islands? Let it be supposed, for example, that effects of the bankrupt are in a country in which the sequestration and the conveyance to the trustee are held to be of no force, and where preference is given to the diligence of the country in which the effects are situate:—Is the creditor who recovers payment under such local rule obliged to pay over to the trustee in this country, for general distribution, the money he has received? And this, again, resolves into two questions:—(1.) Whether the creditor can claim for any balance without having communicated what he has received? and (2.) Whe-

---

1 2 Bell, Comm. § 1266, pp. 684, 685, 4th. edit.; Id. pp. 681, 682, 5th edit.

ther he is liable tő an action for restitution? In England, where there is no provision by statute for regulating this matter, it is held,—(1.) That an English creditor who, having notice of the bankruptcy, makes affidavit in England in order to proceed abroad, cannot retain against the assignees what he recovers. (2.) That a creditor in the foreign country would not, if preferred by the laws of that country, be obliged to refund in England; and, (3.) That, at all events, such a creditor cannot take advantage of the bankrupt laws in England without communicating the benefit of his foreign proceedings. In Scotland there is an express provision in the statute relative to payments and preferences abroad; the policy of which it is proper to explain. As the jurisdiction of the Court of Session does not reach foreign countries wherever the principle of the law of nations does not operate, or has been evaded, it is provided,—(1.) That the creditor, who, after the first deliverance on the petition for sequestration, shall obtain payment or preference abroad, shall be obliged to communicate and assign the same to the trustee for behoof of the creditors, before he can draw any dividend out of the funds in the hands of the trustee; and, (2.) That, in all events, whether he claims under the sequestration or not, he shall be liable to an action before the Court of Session, at the instance of the trustee, to communicate the said security or payment, in so far as the jurisdiction of the Court can reach him. It may, however, as already observed, be doubted, whether this enactment, in so far as it exposes a creditor to a challenge, even where he does not claim under the sequestration, might be held to include foreign creditors, not apprised of the bankruptcy and proceedings in this country, but who having recovered in the usual way the property of their debtor abroad, should have come afterwards to Scotland. Recently, the question occurred under these enactments, whether a local statute in one of our colonies abroad, which was said to proceed on views of local utility, did not so far qualify the sequestration statute of this country that the foreign creditors should be entitled to retain the preference they had obtained? But the Court held, that the preference could not be supported. As to real estate, the estate in land, or connected with land, there is a difference of principle very remarkable. The real estate is, not like the personal, regulated by the law of the domicil, but by the territorial law. A real estate in England is not held to be under the disposition of the bankrupt laws of Scotland, if the proprietor be a trader there. Nor is an heritable State in Scotland affected by the commission of the English law. And yet the spirit and policy of the laws, considered internationally, should open to the creditors of a bankrupt in either country the power of attaching his real estates[1]".

§ 423 *f.* In regard to voluntary assignments for the benefit of creditors with certain preferences, they must (as has been already stated[2]), as to their validity and operation, be governed by the *lex loci contractûs.* If they are valid there, full operation will ordinarily be given to them in every other country where the matter may come into litigation and discussion. But it is a very different question, whether they shall be permitted to operate upon property locally situate in another country, whether movable or immovable, by whose laws such a conveyance would be treated as a fraud upon the unpreferred creditors. That question was discussed in the case already alluded to, where an assignment made in Alabama, giving preferences to certain creditors, came collaterally under discussion in Louisiana, by whose laws such an assignment would be treated as a fraud. On that occasion the Court said: "We find no difficulty in assenting to the proposition, that contracts entered into in other States, as it relates to their validity and the capacity of the contracting parties, are to be tested here by the *lex loci celebrati contractûs.* This Court has often recognised

---

1 2 Bell, Comm. § 1266, pp. 689, 690, 4th edit.; Id. pp. 685, 686, 5th edit. See Lord Eldon's Remarks in Selkrig *v.* Davis, 2 Rose, R. 311.

2 Ante, § 259 *a.*

that doctrine as well settled. When a contract is entered into in Alabama, in conformity to the local law, to have its effects and execution there, it is clear the Courts of this State cannot declare its nullity on the ground, that such a contract would not be valid according to our system of jurisprudence. Such would be the case even if one of the contracting parties, or both, were not citizens of Alabama. If Andrews, for example, had been a citizen of Louisiana, having creditors and effects both here and in Alabama, had gone over to that State, and transferred a portion of his property there to certain preferred creditors, such a transaction, as to its legality, would depend upon the law of Alabama. But if such a citizen of Louisiana should immediately afterwards seek to avail himself of the benefit of our insolvent laws, a different question would present itself. Although our courts might not be authorized to annul such contracts, as to their effects between the parties, yet they might well inquire whether it was not the intention of the legislature to afford the protection of the insolvent laws to such only as shall have abstained from giving an undue preference to certain creditors, in derogation of that vital principle of our system, that the property of the debtor forms the common pledge of his creditors, and although such preferences may be tolerated by the *lex loci*. If the legislature has thought proper to declare such a condition as one upon which shall depend the right to claim the benefit of the insolvent laws, which it is not denied they had an unquestionable right to do, then there is an end to the argument, unless it can be shewn that the mere residence of the party in another State dispenses him from a compliance with the creditor[1]."

§ 423 *g*. These are by no means the only cases of a conflict of laws, or of rights growing thereout, touching personal or movable property; and which ought to admonish us of the danger and difficulty of attempting to lay

---

[1] Andrews *v.* His Creditors, 11 Louis. R. 476, 477. See also 2 Bell, Comm. § 1266, pp. 684—686, 4th edit.; Id. pp. 681—683, 5th edit.

down universal rules on such complicated subjects. By the laws of many of the nations of continental Europe, in cases of collision of ships by accident, without any fault on either side, the loss is to be sustained by a contribution by both ships[1]. By the law of England in such a case, there is no contribution whatsoever, but each party is to bear his own loss. *Res perit domino*[2]. Now, let us suppose that such a collision takes place upon the high seas, beyond any territorial jurisdiction, between an English ship and a foreign continental ship, whose laws divide the loss, and both or either of the ships is injured thereby. How is the loss to be borne? Will it make any difference whether the proceeding against the ship or owners for redress is in England, or in the proper continental Court? If the right depends upon the law of the place where the proceedings are had against the ship or the owner, then there will be no reciprocity in the operation of the rule. In a case so confessedly novel in its presentation, it will be found very difficult to affirm any ground of principle upon which the law of the one country rather than that of the other, ought to prevail.

§ 423 *h*. Considerations of an analogous nature may be presented in cases of torts committed on the high seas, and in other extra-territorial places, by the subjects of one nation, upon vessels or other movable property belonging to the subjects of another nation, where the laws of these nations are different, touching either the nature and character and consequences of the tort, or the rule of damages applicable thereto. It is not easy to say in such cases, what laws ought to govern. The most that can with any probability be stated, is, that in the absence of any general doctrine to the contrary, either each nation would, in respect to the case when pending in its own tribunals, follow its own laws[3]; or would apply the rule of reciprocity, grant-

---

1 Story on Bailm. § 608; Peters *v.* Warren Insur. Company, 14 Peters, R. 94.

2 Story on Bailm. § 608, 610.

3 See Percival *v.* Hickey, 18 John. R. 257.

ing or refusing damages, according as the law of the foreign country to which the injured ship belonged, would grant or withhold them in the case of an injured ship belonging to the other nation[1]. The rule of reciprocity is often applied in cases of the recapture of ships from the hands of a public enemy[2].

---

1 The Girelamo, 3 Hagg. Adm. R. 169.

2 The Santa Cruz, 1 Rob. R. 50; 2 Wheat. R. App. 44, 45; The Adeline, 9 Cranch, R. 244.

CHAPTER X.

REAL PROPERTY.

§ 424. Having disposed of the more important questions which have arisen respecting personal property; we are next led to the consideration of the operation of foreign law, in regard to real or immovable property. And, here the general principle of the common law is, that the laws of the place where such property is situate exclusively govern, in respect to the rights of the parties, the modes of transfer and the solemnities which should accompany them[1]. The title, therefore, to real property can be acquired, passed, and lost, only according to the *lex rei sitæ*. This is generally, although (as we shall presently see) not universally admitted by Courts and by Jurists, foreign as well as domestic. Paul Voet states the rule in a brief but clear manner: *Ut immobilia statutis loci regantur, ubi sitæ*[2]. He adds in another place: *Quid si itaque contentio de aliquo jure in re, seu ex ipsæ re descendente, vel ex contractu, vel actione personali, sed in rem scripta? An spectabitur loci statutum, ubi dominus habet domicilium, an statutum rei sitæ? Respondeo; Statutum rei sitæ*[3]. Sir Wm. Grant lays down

---

1 See on the subject of this chapter, 2 Burge, Comm. on Col. and For. Law, pt. 2, ch. 4, pp. 840—870; 4 Burge, Comm. on Col. and For. Law, pt. 2, ch. 4, § 5, p. 150, &c.; Id. ch. 5, n. 11, pp. 171, 217; Id. ch. 12, p. 576; Fœlix, Conflit des Lois, Revue Etrang, et Fran. tom. 7, (1840), § 27—37, pp. 216—230; Id. pp. 307—312.

2 P. Voet, De Stat. § 9, c. 1, n. 3, p. 253, (edit. 1715); Id. p. 307, (edit. 1661).—Yet we shall see that Paul Voet adopts some strange notions, as to the forms and solemnities of instruments of transfer of real estate, whether inter vivos or testamentary, holding that the lex loci actus, and not the lex loci rei sitæ, ought to govern. Post, § 442.

3 P. Voet, De Statut. § 9, c. 1, n. 2, p. 253, (edit. 1715); Id. p. 305, (edit. 1661).

the rule in very expressive terms: "The validity of every disposition of real estate," says he, "must depend upon the law of the country in which that estate is situated[1]." The same rule would also seem equally to apply to express liens, and to implied liens upon immovable estate[2].

§ 425. And here it may be proper to advert a little more particularly to some of the definitions of foreign jurists, in regard to personal laws and to real laws. We have already seen, that laws purely personal are those which solely affect the person, without any reference to property[3]. Laws purely real directly and indirectly regulate property and the rights of property, without intermeddling with or changing the state of the person[4]. There are other laws again, which are deemed both personal and real, containing a mixed operation upon persons and property, and which are therefore called mixed[5]. Thus, a particular law which shall authorize a minor or other person, ordinarily incapacitated to dispose of property under particular circumstances, would be deemed a mixed law; because, so far as it affects the particular capacity of a person it is personal, and so far as it enables him to do a particular act respecting property it is real[6]. In illustration of these distinctions Boullenois considers the law, known as the *Senatûs-consultum Velleianum*, prohibiting married women from making contracts, as

---

[1] Curtis *v.* Hutton, 14 Ves. jun. 537, 541; S. P. Chapman *v.* Robertson, 6 Paige, R. 627, 630; Elliott *v.* Lord Minto, 6 Madd. R. 16; Birtwhistle *v.* Vardill, 5 Barn. & Cress. 438; S. C. 9 Bligh, R. 32—88; Post, § 428—444.

[2] See 1 Boullenois, p. 683, et seq. 689, 818; Rodenburg, De Divers. Stat. tit. 2, c. 5, § 16; 2 Boullenois, App. p. 47; 1 Hertii Opera, De Collis. Leg. § 4, n. 64, p. 150; P. Voet, De Stat. § 9, c. 1, n. 2, p. 253, (edit. 1715); Id. p. 307, (edit. 1661); Ante, § 322—328; Id. § 363—374; 1 Burge, Comm. on Col. and For. Law, pt. 1, ch. 1, pp. 25, 26; Curtis *v.* Hutton, 14 Ves. jun. 537, 541; Elliott *v.* Lord Minto, 6 Madd. R. 16.

[3] 1 Boullenois, Prin. Gén. 10, p. 4.

[4] 1 Boullenois, Prin. Gén. 22, p. 6; Id. Prin. Gén. 21, p. 7. See P. Voet, De Stat. § 4, c. 2, n. 4, pp. 134, 135, (edit. 1661).

[5] 1 Boullenois, Prin. Gén. 15, 16, p. 5.

[6] Ibid.

purely personal; a law declaring that no person of full age shall devise more than a third or fourth part of his property, as purely real; and a law allowing a minor (otherwise incapacitated) when married, to make a testament or donation in favour of his wife, as mixed[1]. These distinctions are very important in examining the doctrines of foreign jurists, as they often enter very deeply into the elements of their particular opinions[2].

§ 426. Now, in regard to laws purely real, Boullenois lays down the rule, in the broadest terms, that they govern all real property within the territory, but have no extension beyond it. *Les lois réelles n'ont point d'extension directe ne indirecte hors la jurisdiction et la domination du législateur*[3]. In regard to mixed laws he lays down the rule expressively, that of right they act only upon real property within the territory to which the persons are subject; but that sometimes they act upon real property situate elsewhere; and then it is only because the laws are conformable to each other, and by a sort of kindred title only, (*à titre de paternité seulement*[4]). Rodenburg lays down a like

---

[1] 1 Boullenois, Prin. Gén. 14, 15, 26, pp. 5—7; Id. Observ. 2, pp. 25—28; Id. Observ. 16, p. 206; Observ. 23, pp. 456, 457, 477, 488; 2 Boullenois, Observ. 32, p. 11.—This definition of mixed laws is given by Boullenois, who has drawn it from Rodenburg. But it is very different (as he informs us) from the sense, in which D'Argentré, Burgundus, and Voet use the same phrase. 1 Boullenois, Prin. Gén. 16, p. 5; Id. Observ. 6, p. 122—140; Rodenburg. De Div. Stat. tit. 1, c. 2; 1 Boullenois, Observ. 2, pp. 25—29; Id. Observ. 3, pp. 29—48. See also, 1 Froland, Mém. ch. 6, p. 114.

[2] J. Voet has devoted a whole title to the subject of personal, real, and mixed laws, which will reward the diligence of the student in a thorough perusal. J. Voet, Ad Pand. tom. 1, lib. 1, tit. 4, pp. 2, 38, et seq. The same subject is elaborately discussed by Froland. 1 Froland, Mém. ch. 4, p. 49, ch. 5, p. 31, ch. 6, p. 114.

[3] 1 Boullenois, Prin. Gén. 27, p. 7; Id. 230.—Froland lays down the rule in even more brief terms. Le statut réel ne sort point de son territoire. 1 Froland, Mém. 156. And he applies the same rule to mixed statutes. Id. 157.

[4] 1 Boullenois, Prin. Gén. 20, 21, p. 6; 1 Boullenois, Observ. 16, pp. 223, 224.

rule in regard to real laws (dismissing as unnecessary the class of mixed laws): *Statuta realia inter et personalia hoc interest, quod illa, in res scripta, territorii sui concludantur metis, hæc extra eas vim et effectum protendant*[1]. Paul Voet contends, that no personal laws can regularly extend to immovable property situate in a foreign country: *Non tamen statutum personale sese regulariter extendet ad bona immobilia alibi sita*[2]; and he treats it as utterly unimportant, whether it assume to do so directly or indirectly, openly or consequentially. *Neque hic distinguam, cum lex non distinguat, an sese extendat statutum directè ad bona extra-territorium statuentium sita, an indirectè, an propalam, an per consequentiam. Cum non sint indirectè, in fraudem legis aut statuti permittenda, quæ directè sunt prohibita.*[3]

§ 426 *a.* John Voet resolutely maintains the same opinion[4]. D'Argentré holds the following language: *Quæ realia, aut mixta sunt, haud dubie locorum et rerum situm sic spectant, ut aliis legibus, quam territorii, judicari non possint*[5]. Huberus—after remarking that the foundation of the general doctrine is the subjection of every man to the laws of a country, so long as he continues to act there, which makes his act there valid or invalid according as those declare it invalid—proceeds to say, that this reasoning does not apply to immovable property which does not depend upon the mere will of the owner; but so far as certain characters are impressed upon it by the law of the country where it is situate, these characters remain indelible in that country, whatever dispositions the laws of other countries or the acts of private per-

---

1 Rodenburg, De Div. Statut. tit. 1, c. 3; 2 Boullenois, App. p, 7; 1 Boullenois, 145; Id. Observ. 9, p. 152; Id. 230.

2 P. Voet, Ad Stat. § 4, c. 2, n. 6, p. 123. (edit. 1715); Id. p. 138, (edit. 1661).

3 P. Voet, De Stat. § 4, c. 2, 6, 7. pp. 123, 124, (edit. 1715); Post, § 442.

4 J. Voet, Ad Pand. tom. 1, lib. 1, tit. 4, § 7, p. 40; Ante, § 54 *a;* Post, § 433 *a.*

5 D'Argentré De Briton. Leg. art. 218, Gloss. 6, n. 9, tom. 1, p. 650, [604]; Post, § 439; Livermore's Dissert. § 97, p. 77.

sons may ordain otherwise or contrary thereto. Nor would it be without great confusion and prejudice to the country where the immovable property is situate, that its own laws respecting it should be changed by such dispositions. *Fundamentum universæ hujus doctrinæ diximus esse, et tenemus, subjectionem hominum infra leges cujusque territorii, quamdiu illic agunt, quæ facit, ut actus ab initio validus aut nullus, alibi quoque valere aut non valere non nequeat. Sed hæc ratio non convenit rebus immobilibus, quando illæ spectantur, non ut dependentes a libera dispositione cujusque patrisfamilias, verum quatenus certæ notæ lege cujusque Reip. ubi sita sunt, illis impressæ reperiuntur; hæ notæ manent indelebiles in ista Republica, quicquid aliarum civitatum leges, aut privatorum dispositiones, secus aut contra statuant; nec enim sine magna confusione præjudicioque Reip. ubi sitæ sunt res soli, leges, de illis latæ, dispositionibus istis mutari possent*[1]. He adds in another place: *Communis et recta sententia est, in rebus immobilibus servandum est jus loci in quo bona sunt sita*[2].

§ 426 *b*. Christinæus takes the common distinction in various places between movable property and immovable property, alleging, that it is observed as a general rule, that movable property is governed by the law of the domicil, and real property by the law of the *situs rei*. *Ubi pro regula generali servatum fuit, quod bona mobilia sequi et regulari debent secundum statuti loci domicilii ejus, ad quem pertinent vel spectant, immobilia verò juxta statuta locorum, ubi illa sunt sita, ut communiter tenent Interpretes, licet dicta regula non semper locum habeat*[3].

---

1 Huberus, De Conflict Leg. lib. 1, tit. 3, § 15; Post, § 413.

2 Huberus, tom. 1, Pt. 1, lib. 3, tit. 13, 21 s. De Success. ab Intes. p. 278. See Post, § 443, 443 *a*, 476.

3 Christinæus, tom. 2, Decis. 5, n. 1—4, p. 7.—M. Fœlix on this subject says: "Cette loi réelle régit les biens situés dans l'étendue du territoire, pour lequel elle a été rendue, en excluant l'application de la loi personnelle du propriétaire, ou de celle du lieu où l'acte a été passé; (Nous parlerons plus bas de l'application de cette dernière loi); mais aussi les effets de cette loi ne s'étendent jamais au delà des limites du territoire. Telle est la régle reconnue par toutes les nations et professée par les auteurs. Nous citerons

§ 427. But it is wholly unnecessary to repeat at length the opinions of foreign jurists, since in the main proposition they generally, although not universally, concur, (for some of them insist upon certain exceptions, to which we may hereafter allude), that the law of the *situs* exclusively governs as to immovable property[1]. Pothier has laid down the rule

---

Burgundus (Tract. 1, nos 4, 11, 12 et 14), Rodenburg (tit. 1, chap. 2), Paul Voet (De Statutis, sect. 4, cap. 2, nos 4 et 6), Jean Voet (Ad. ff. Tit. de stat. no 3), Abraham à Wessel (Art. 16, no 19), Christin (Decisiones, vol. 2, tit. 1, dec. 3, no 2), Boullenois (Aux Endroits citées au no 24 ci-dessus, et tit. 1, p. 107), Hert. (Sect. 4, § 9), Huber. (No 15), Cramer (Observationes Juris Universi, tom. 5. obs. 1462), Pothier (Sur la Coutume d'Orléans, chap. 1, § 2, nos 22, 23 et 24; ch. 3, no 51), Vattel, (liv. 2, ch. 8, § 103 et 110), Gluck (Commentaire, § 76. Droit privé, § 17 et 18), Danz (Manuel, t. 1, § 53, no 1), Portalis père (Exposé des motifs du Code Civil, Locré, t. 1, p. 581; V. aussi le discours du tribun Faure ibid., p. 613), Meier (P. 17), MM. Mittermaier (§ 32), Eichhorn (§ 36), Tittmann (chap. 5), Muhlenbruch (§ 72, no 2), Brinkmann (P. 10 et 11), Story (§ 374, 424, et suiv., et surtout § 428), Wheaton (chap. 2, § 5, t. 1, p. 136), Rocca (P. 104, 110, 118 et 122), et Burge (Régle 6, t. 1, p. 25; t. 2, pp. 14, 26, 78 et 840." Fœlix, Conflit des Lois, Revue Etran. et Fran. tom. 7, § 27, pp. 217, 218.

[1] The learned reader may consult Livermore's Dissert. § 9—162, pp. 28 — 106. Hertii Opera, tom. 1, De Collis. Leg. § 4, n. 9, p. 125, (edit. 1737); Id. p. 177, (edit. 1716); Ersk. Inst. B. 3, tit. 2, § 40, p. 515; Bouhier, Cout. de Bourg. ch. 23, § 36—63, pp. 456—457; 2 Bell, Comm. § 1266, p. 690, 4th edit.; Id. p. 687, 688, 5th edit.; Fergusson on Marr. and Div. 395; Le Brun, De la Communauté, lib. 1, ch. 5, pp. 9, 10; D'Aguesseau, Œuvres, tom. 4, p. 660, 4to edit.; Cochin, Œuvres, tom. 1, p. 545, 4to edit.; Id. tom. p. 555; Henry on Foreign Law, pp. 12, 14, 15; Id. App. p. 196; J. Voet, Ad Pand. lib. 1, tit. 4, P. 2, § 3, 5, 6, pp. 39, 40; 1 Froland, Mém. ch. 4, p. 49, ch. 7, p. 155; 2 Kaims on Equity, B. 3, ch. 8, § 2.—Mr. Burge on this subject says: "The summary given in the preceding chapters exhibits a great diversity amongst the laws which regulate the modification and creation of estates and interests in real property, and the transfer and acquisition of it. The law of the place where the act making the modification or alienation is passed, frequently differs either from that of the place in which the party to the act was domiciled, or from that of the place in which the property is situated. It becomes necessary to inquire which of these conflicting laws is selected, and what are the principles on which the selection is made. There exists a difference of opinion amongst jurists as to the law which ought to govern the decisions of some of the subjects comprehended under the titles which have been just mentioned, when one of the conflicting laws affects persons as well as things, or where it ap-

in the most general form, declaring, that real laws have an exclusive dominion over all things submitted to their autho-

---

plies to the form and solemnity of the *acte* by which the modification or alienation of property is passed, as well as to things. The primary or principal object of the law, or the comparative degree in which, in the one case it affects persons or things, and in the other the form of the act or thing, affords the ground on which some jurists consider the law as real or personal, and accordingly adopt the lex loci rei sitæ, or the law of the domicil, or that of the place in which the act is passed. In the opinion of other jurists, if the law of the situs be prohibitive, it must be preferred to the personal law of the domicil, without regard to the object of that law, or its immediate effect on the status of the person. There is, however, no difference of opinion amongst them in adopting the lex loci rei sitæ in all questions regarding the modification or creation of estates or interests in immovable property. This subject does not involve any of the considerations which, in other cases, produced that difference of opinion. The law primarily and principally affects things. It is wholly independent of the status of persons, and is strictly a real law. There is the concurrence therefore, not only of those jurists who give the greatest effect to the lex loci rei sitæ; but even of those who are disposed to give such an effect to laws affecting the general status of persons, as would greatly control the operation of the lex loci rei sitæ. Thus, according to the definition of Rodenburg, 'In solas nudasque res statuti dispositio dirigitur, ut nullum intervenire necesse sit actum hominis aut aliquam concurrere personæ operam.' It is comprised in the rule laid down by Burgundus: 'Statuta realia sunt, quæ de jure, et conditione, seu qualitate rei disponunt. Statuto reali propositum est dirigere res ipsas, certisque qualitatibus dominia afficere.' The doctrine of D'Argentré is to the same effect: 'Realia sunt, ut quæ de modo dividendarum hereditatum constituuntur, in capita, in stirpes, aut talia. Item de modo rerum donandarum, et quota donationum.'...'Item illud, ne in testamento legari posset viro ab uxore, quod quidem de immobilibus constituit et rebus soli, etsi mixtam habeat de personis considerationem, quando impotentia agnatis applicatur rei soli: Nam si de mobilibus solùm quæreretur, posset videri in totum esse personale.' The doctrine of Du Moulin is, 'In his, quæ concernunt rem, vel onus rei, debet inspici consuetudo loci ubi sita res est.' Boullenois also concurs in treating those laws as real: 'Qui affecte directement les biens en fixant leur sort et leur destination, par une disposition particulière et indépendante de l'état personnel, dont l'homme est affecté pour les actes du commerce civil, encore que quelquefois ce statut ait égard à l'état personnel, que nous avons ci-devant appellé pur politique et distinctif.' Merlin maintains the same doctrine: 'Si l'objet principal, direct, immédiat de la loi, est de régler la qualité, la nature des biens, la manière d'en disposer,' it is a real law, and that, 'les effets par rapport aux personnes ne sont plus, que des conséquences éloignées de la réalité.' The estate or interest, which the law permits or prohibits to be created in immovable pro-

rity, whether the persons owning them, live within the territory, or without the territory[1]. And Vattel has laid it

perty, whether it be by substitution, entail, executory devise, condition, or any other species of limitation, may be considered as a quality impressed on, and inherent in the property. So also are the rules and limits under which the permission is given. According to the doctrine of those jurists who are the most disposed to allow personal laws, affecting the general status, to control those of the situs, the law which confers on immovable property its qualities, is strictly real, and prevails over the personal law. Thus Hertius defines the law to be real, when it impresses any certain quality on immovable property: 'Rebus fertur lex, cum certam iisdem qualitatem imprimit, vel in alienando, *e. g.* ut ne bona avita possint alienari, vel in acquirendo *e. g.* ut domini rei immobilium venditæ non aliter acquiratur, nisi facta fuerit judicialis resignatio.' The same rule is laid down by Mestertius and Burgundus, and is followed by Boullenois. These jurists, in treating of the solemnities which the law requires, should accompany certain acts, distinguish those which are 'tanquam qualitates rebus impressæ.' The existence and nature of those qualities must be determined by the law of the situs. It is conceived, therefore, to be indisputable, that the law of the situs must be adopted in all questions respecting the power of alienating immovable property, or the restrictions under which that power may be exercised. Hence, also, it follows, that the law of the situs must prevail, when the question regards the existence or validity of any substitution, the degrees to which it may be limited, the manner of computing those degrees, or the extent to which the power of alienation may be restrained, and generally the condition to which the persons substituted may be subjected. Upon the same principles, it will decide, if the question regard the acts which are essential to render the substitution or entail valid, or the respective rights and liabilities of the fiduciary, fidei commissary, or tenant in tail." 2 Burge, Comm. on Col. and For. Law, pt. 2, ch. 9, pp. 840—844. Again, alluding to the same subject in another place, he says:—"In treating of the alienations of real property by act inter vivos, it has been stated as a conclusion, sanctioned by the authority of jurists and of judicial decisions, and most consistent with admitted principles, that the capacity to make and to take under the alienation was governed by the law of the actual situs of the property if it were immovable, and by that of the domicil if it were movable. It is admitted by all jurists, that the transfer of and title to real property must be regulated by the lex loci rei sitæ; that a law, which prohibits its alienation, is a real law, and must, in whatever place the alienation is attempted, prevent the acquisition of any title. It necessarily follows from that admission, that the character and effect of the law must be the same whether its prohibition has relation to the quality of the property itself, or to the person of the owner; or whether the prohibition be general and absolute, or partial and qualified, or existing only sub

[1] Pothier, Coutume d'Orléans, ch. 1, § 2, n. 22—24, ch. 3, n. 51.

down as a principle of international law, that immovables are to be disposed of according to the laws of the country where they are situate [1].

§ 428. The consent of the tribunals acting under the common law, both in England and America, is, in a practical sense, absolutely uniform on the same subject. All the authorities, in both countries, so far as they go, recognise the principle in its fullest import, that real estate or immovable property is exclusively subject to the laws of the government within whose territory it is situate [2]. So that we may here fully adopt the language of John Voet:—*De realibus quidem, cum plerorumque consensus sit, id pluribus docere supervacuum fuerit* [3]. Indeed, so firmly is this prin-

---

modo. It is a quality impressed on the property no less when the property is prohibited to be alienated under particular circumstances than when it is prohibited to be alienated under any circumstances, or when it is prohibited to be alienated by and to persons standing in certain relations to each other, or by persons who are under a certain age, or who are in any situation which by the law precludes them from making or taking under the alienation." 4 Burge, Comm. on Col. and For. Law, pt. 2, ch. 12, p. 577; Id. pp. 580—596.

[1] Vattel, b. 2, ch. 8, § 110; Id. § 103; Chapman *v.* Robertson, 6 Paige, R. 627.

[2] The authorities are very numerous in which it has been decided or taken for granted, and among them in England are, Sill *v.* Worswick, 1 H. Black. 665; Hunter *v.* Potts, T. R. 41, 182; Phillips *v.* Hunter, 2 H. Black. 402; Selkrig *v.* Davis, 2 Rose Bank. Cas. p. 29; 2 Dow, R. 230; Coppin *v.* Coppin, 2 P. Will. 290, 293; Broadie *v.* Barry, 2 Ves. & Beames, R. 130; Birtwhistle *v.* Vardill, 5 B. & Cress. 438; 2 Bell, Comm. 690, 4th edit.; Id. p. 687, 5th edit.; and in America are, United States *v.* Crosby, 7 Cranch, 115; Clarke *v.* Graham, 6 Wheaton, R. 597; Kerr *v.* Mason, 9 Wheaton, R. 566; Harper *v.* Hampton, 1 Harr. & John. R. 687; Goodwin *v.* Jones, 3 Mass. R. 414, 518; Cutter *v.* Davenport, 1 Pick. R. 81, 86; Holmes *v.* Remsen, 4 John. Ch. R. 460; S. C. 20 John. R. 254; Hosford *v.* Nichols, 1 Paige, R. 220; Blake *v.* Williams, 6 Pick. 286; Milne *v.* Moreton, 6 Binn. R. 359. See also 4 Cowen, R. 510, 527, note; Dwarris on Stat. 649, 650; Wiles *v.* Cowper, Wilcox's Ohio Rep. 279; S.C. 2 Hammond, R. 124; Henry on Foreign Law, 8, 9; M'Cormick *v.* Sullivant, 10 Wheaton, R. 192; Darby *v.* Mayer, 10 Wheaton, R. 465; Curtis *v.* Hutton, 14 Ves. 537, 541; Elliott *v.* Lord Minto, 6 Madd. R. 16; Chapman *v.* Robertson, 6 Paige, R. 627, 630; Post, § 434; Ante, § 424.

[3] J. Voet. Ad Pand. lib. 1, tit. 5, Pt. 2, § 6, p. 40.

ciple established, that in cases of bankruptcy, the real estate of the bankrupt, situate in foreign countries, is universally admitted not to pass under the assignment, although, as we have seen, there are great diversities of opinion as to movables[1]. And Lord Eldon has gone so far as to declare, that there exists no legal or equitable obligation (although there is a moral obligation) in the bankrupt to make a conveyance thereof to his assignees; and that the creditors are without redress, unless by way of remedy *in rem*, where the real estate is situate, or by withholding a certificate of discharge until the bankrupt executes such a conveyance[2].

§ 429. Considering, however, the diversity of opinion on this subject among foreign jurists, it may be of some utility to examine into the application of the general rule in some of its more important aspects. We shall, therefore, consider it,—first, in relation to the capacity of persons to take or to transfer real estate; secondly, in relation to the forms and solemnities necessary to transfer it; thirdly, in relation to the extent of interest to be taken or transferred in it; and fourthly, in relation to the subject-matter itself, or what are properly to be deemed immovables.

§ 430. First, in relation to the capacity of persons to take or transfer real estate. It may be laid down as a general principle of the common law, that a party must have a capacity to take according to the law of the *situs*, otherwise he will be excluded from all ownership. Thus, if the laws of a country exclude aliens from holding lands, either by succession or by purchase, or by devise, such a title becomes wholly inoperative as to them, whatever may be the law of the place of their domicil[3]. On the other hand, if by the

---

1 Selkrig *v.* Davis, 2 Rose, Bank. Cas. 97; Id. 191; 2 Dow, R. 230, 250; 2 Bell, Comm. 690, 4th edit.; Id. p. 687, 5th edit.; Ante, § 403—422, 423 *a*.

2 Selkrig *v.* Davis, 2 Rose, Bank. Cas. 97; Id. 291; S. C. 2 Dow, 230, 250. But see Stein's case, 1 Rose, Bank. Cas. 462; Ante, § 423 *a*.

3 See Buchanan *v.* Deshon, 1 Gill, R. 280; Sewall *v.* Lee, 9 Mass. R 363.

local law aliens may take and hold lands, it is wholly immaterial what may be the law of their own domicil, either of origin or of choice.

§ 431. So, if a person is incapable from any other circumstance of transferring his immovable property by the law of the *situs*, his transfer will be held invalid, although by the law of his domicil no such personal incapacity exists. On the other hand, if he has capacity to transfer by the law of the *situs*, he may make a valid title, notwithstanding an incapacity may attach to him by the law of his domicil. This is the silent but irresistible result of the principle adopted by the common law, which has no admitted exception. We may illustrate the principle by an application to cases of common occurrence under the dominion of the common law. By that law a person is deemed a minor, and is incapable of conveying real estate until he has arrived at twenty-one years of age; but by the law of some foreign countries, minority continues until twenty-five, or even until thirty years of age. Let us, then, suppose a foreigner, owning lands in England or America, (where the common law prevails), who is, by the law of his domicil, in his minority, but who is over twenty-one years of age: it is clear that he may convey his real estate in England or America, notwithstanding such domestic incapacity; for he is of the age required by the local law[1]. On the other hand, let us suppose a married woman, who is domiciled in a foreign country, and by the law of that country is capable of alienating her real estate without the consent of her husband, owning real estate in England or in America where she is incapable of alienating it without such consent; she cannot alienate it without the consent of her husband; and her separate act will be held *ipso facto* void by the law of the *situs*.

§ 432. But, however clear this may seem, according to the principles of the common law on this subject, a very

---

[1] See Saul *v.* His Creditors, 17 Martin, R. 569, 597.

different doctrine is, as we have already seen, maintained by many foreign jurists on this very point[1]. They contend, that the capacity or incapacity of persons to transfer property, or to do any other act, depends altogether upon the law of the place of their domicil. If they have a capacity or incapacity there, it governs all their property elsewhere, whether movable or immovable. Thus, Boullenois maintains, that, if a man has immovable property in a place, where majority is attained at twenty-five, and by the law of his domicil he is of age at twenty, he may at twenty sell or alienate such immovable property. And, on the other hand, if by the law of the *situs* of the immovable property, he is of age at twenty, but by the law of his domicil not until twenty-five, he cannot sell or alienate such property until the age of twenty-five[2]. Rodenburg adopts the same doctrine, and maintains it with abundance of zeal[3]. After

---

[1] Ante, § 51—61, 65; 1 Burge, Comm. on Col. and For. Law, pt. 1, ch. 1, p. 21—23.

[2] Ante, § 52, 71.—There is a curious distinction maintained by many jurists on this subject, which deserves notice.—They say, that, if the local law fixes the age of majority at a particular period, and declares, that, until the party has arrived at that period, he shall not alienate immovable property,—in that case the local law governs; for it does not turn upon the mere fact of being a major or not. But if the local law only says, that no person who is not a major shall alienate, then, if the party is a major by the law of his domicil, though not by that of the rei sitæ, he may alienate the property, because the only point is majority or not, and that must be ascertained by the lex domicilii; for the state or capacity of a person by the law of his domicil extends every where. Boullenois dwells much on this distinction, and it has received the support of Merlin. 1 Boullenois, Observ. 4, p. 57; Id. Observ. 5, p. 102; Id. Observ. 12, p. 175; Id. Observ. 13, p. 183; Id. Observ. 23, p. 499; Id. Observ. 28, p. 700, 705, 720; Boullenois, Quest. Mixt. p. 19; 2 Merlin, Répertoire, Testament, § 1, 6, art. 3, p. 318, art. 2, p. 317, 318; Id. art. 3; 2 Froland, Mém. des Stat. p. 824, 825; Livermore, Diss. § 44, p. 48; Id. § 47, 48, p. 50; Id. § 59—62, p. 58—60.

[3] Rodenburg, De Div. Stat. tit. 2, c. 1; 2 Boullenois, App. p. 10; 1 Boullenois, 77, 78, 154, 155, 194, 295; 1 Hertii Opera, De Collis. Leg. § 4, n. 23, p. 133, (edit. 1737); Id. p. 175, (edit. 1716); Livermore, Dissert. § 31, p. 40; Id. § 44, p. 48, § 45, 46, p. 49; Bouhier, Cout. de Bourg. ch. 24, § 91—108, pp. 476—478; Ante, § 51, 51 *a*, 52, 52 *a*, 53.

having remarked, that, among personal statutes are to be reckoned all laws which affect the state or condition of the person, such as laws respecting majority, the paternal power over children, the marital power over the wife, and cases of prodigals, he adds: *De quibus et similibus id juris est, ut quocumque transtulerit persona statuto loci domicilii ita affecta, habilitatem aut inhabilitatem, ademptam domi, circumferat ubique, ut in universa territoria suum statutum exerceat effectum*[1]. Yet Rodenburg himself deserts this doctrine, in regard to the capacity and incapacity to make a will or testament, which he holds must be according to the *lex rei sitæ*[2]. There are many others who adhere to

---

1 Rodenburg, De Div. Stat. tit. 2, c. 1; 2 Boullenois, App. p. 11; Ante, § 51.

2 Rodenburg, De Div. Stat, tit. 2, c. 5, n. 7; 2 Boullenois, App. pp. 38, 39. His language is; Sed, ut id, quod instat, agamus: quid si nostras testetur anno ætatis decimo quarto, sortieturne effectum dispositio in rebus, quæ alterius regionis solo inhæreant, in qua major ad testandum desideratur ætas? Sit dubitandi ratio, quod de personarum ætate ac capacitate lata lex in personam concepta esse videatur, adeoque ad quæcunque producenda territoria. Verùm contra reale statutum esse inde dixeris, quod in statum ac conditionem personæ non sit scriptum, sed expressim directum in rerum alienationes aut alterationes, et quidem per solam testamenti speciem, adeoque circumscriptive ad istum alienationis actum; cujusmodi statuta realia esse traditum sæpiùs: et vel inde in proposito conspicere est, quod immoto personæ statu, quæ nulla ex parte tutelæ subducitur, auctoritate tutoris non spectante minoris testationes, tribuatur nostratibus hæc testamenti factio, adeoque cùm status non turbetur, lex personalis dici nequeat. See also 4 Burge, Comm. on Col. and For. Law, pt. 2, ch. 12, p. 578, 579. On this subject Mr. Burge has well remarked, "The difficulty of adopting such a distinction arises from the consequences to which it leads; for it seems to import, that if the law of the situs prohibits the alienation by a minor, the question whether he is a minor, or in other words, whether he is competent to make a testament, is to be determined, not by that law, but by the law of his domicil. But if the law had prohibited an alienation by a person who had not attained the age of twenty-one or twenty-five years, or any other age which was prescribed by the law as the age of majority, the law of the situs would prevail, and the competence of the person would depend on his having attained that age. But without further pursuing the inquiry, which has already been made in the former volume, it may be considered, that the opinions of Dumoulin, Burgundus, Peckius, John and Paul Voet,

the same opinion[1]. The groundwork of their argument is, that the capacity and incapacity of the person must be uni-

---

and the decision reported by Stockmans, afford authority sufficient to justify the conclusion, that the capacity to alienate by testament is that which is established by the law of the country in which the immovable property is situated, and by that of the domicil, when the testamentary disposition regards movable property." Ibid. See also 1 Burge, Comm. on Col. and For. Law, pt. 1, ch. 1, pp. 21—23; Post, § 433 *a*.

[1] Ante, § 51—54, 60; 1 Froland, Mém. des Satuts, 65, 66; Liverm. Diss. § 47, p. 54, § 55, p. 56; 2 Froland, Mém. des Stat. p. 1576—1594; Merlin, Répertoire, Testament, § 1, 5, art. 2, p. 517, 518; 1 Boullenois, Observ. 6, pp. 127—140; 1 Boullenois, Observ. 28, pp. 705—731.—This is manifestly the opinion of Mr. Livermore, (Diss. pp. 40—42; Id. pp. 48—57). So of Merlin, (Répertoire, Majorité, § 5; Autorisation Maritale, § 10, art. 2; Id. Puissance Paternelle, § 7, pp. 142—146); of Froland, (1 Froland, Mém. des Stat. p. 156, 171; 2 Froland, Mém. des Stat. p. 1595); of Bouhier, (Bouhier, Cout. de Bourg. ch. 23, § 90—96, p. 461; Id. ch. 24, § 91, &c. p. 476; Id. 1 Boullenois, Observ. 28, p. 724); of Pothier, (Pothier, Cout. d'Orléans, ch. 1, § 1, n. 7, p. 2); of Huberus, (Huberus, lib. 1, tit. 3, § 12; Ante, § 60); and of Hertius, (Hertii Opera, tom. 1, De Collis. § 4, n. 8, p. 123, 124, (edit. 1737); Id. p. 175, (edit. 1716). Merlin in another place admits that a law which prohibits a prodigal from making a testament, is personal; but that at the same time it will not prevent the prodigal from making a valid will of immovable property in a foreign country which allows it (as in Bourbourg); for which he gives two reasons: first, that a law is real, which permits one act to be done by a person who is otherwise incapable; and secondly, because a real law always prevails, when it comes in conflict with a personal law. He applies the same rule to an unemancipated son, who cannot by the law of his domicil make a testament, but yet may alienate any of his property acquired in Hainault; for its laws form an exception to the general incapacity of the son, and therefore they are real. Merlin, Répertoire, Testament, § 1, n. 5, art. 1, p. 310. This opinion seems to coincide with that of Hertius, (1 Hertii Opera, De Collis. Leg. 4, n. 22, p. 133, (edit. 1737); Id. p. 188, (edit. 1716). It seems also supported by Rodenburg, (Rodenburg, De. Div. Stat. p. 1, tit. 1, c. 2; 2 Boullenois, App. pp. 4—6, cited by Merlin, ubi supra).—But Merlin says, that, if by the laws of the country of his domicil an unemancipated son cannot make a testament, and by the laws of another country he has a general capacity; in such a case such laws are personal and in conflict, and therefore the law of the domicil is to govern. Merlin, Id. p. 311. See also 1 Boullenois, Observ. 5, pp. 77, 78. Boullenois lays down some rules upon this subject, which seem also to have received the approbation of Bouhier. (1.) When the personal statute of the domicil is in conflict with the personal statute of another place, the law of the domicil is to prevail. (2.)

formly the same every where; that the law of the domicil ought to regulate it; and that it would be utterly incongruous to make a minor in one place a major in another, thus investing him with opposite personal qualities [1].

§ 433. This notion is combated with great vigour and ability by other foreign jurists, whose opinions have been already alluded to [2]. Burgundus admits that personal laws as to capacity or incapacity govern all personal acts, such as personal contracts: *Nam, (ut Imola et Castrensis scripsere) qui inhabilis est in uno loco, etiam in alio censetur inhabilis; quod utique accipiendum est de habilitate, vel inhabilitate, quæ à statuto personali procedit, et ad actus personales dirigitur* [3]. But in regard to immovable property, he says, that it is sufficient that a person be of the age required by the law of the *situs*, to authorize him to make a valid transfer, although he may be incapable by the law of his domicil. His language is: *Quippe (sicut Bartolus existimat) habilitas personæ ad actus personales non trahit effectum ad res sitas extra territorium. Proinde, si peragendum est aliquid circa rem, jam non respiciemus personæ statum, quem foris assumpsit; sed an mancipens in eâ sit*

When the personal statute of the domicil is in conflict with the real statute of the same or another place, it yields to the real statute. (3.) When the real statute of the domicil is in conflict with the real statute of the situs of the property, each one has its own authority in its own territory. 1 Boullenois, Pr. Gén. 29—31; Id. Observ. 5, pp. 181, 182; Bouhier, Cout. de Bourg. ch. 23, § 90, 96, p. 461; Id. ch. 24, § 91, &c., p. 476; Livermore, Diss. § 59, pp. 58, 59. See the opinion of Grotius cited, Post, § 479.

1 Mr. Henry says that the personal statutes of one place may act indirectly and by comity on immovable property situate in another; as a decree of lunacy may by its effects deprive a party of a power to alienate his foreign property; and so of the disability created by bankruptcy. Henry on Foreign Law, 15. This seems inadmissible as a doctrine of the common law.

2 Ante, § 52—54, 54 *a*.

3 Burgundus, Tract. 1, n. 7, 8, p. 19. See also Rodenburg, De Div. Stat. tit. 2, c. 1; 2 Boullenois, App. pp. 11, 12; 1 Boullenois, Observ. 6, pp. 127—131; Id. pp. 199, 201, 202; Liverm. Diss. § 47—49, pp. 50—52; Bouhier, Cout. de Bourg. ch. 24, § 91, 94—107, pp. 476—478.

conditione quam bonorum situs ipse requirit[1]. And again: *Et quidem eodem modo, quoties de jure, vel servitute, aut libertate personæ quæritur, item de facultate ad res personales constituta, respondendum erit secundum conditionem personæ, quam induit in loco domicilii. Et contra, ergo si de jure ac facultate, quæ a re ipsâ proficiscitur, item de ejus servitute, atque libertate, plane ad leges situs spectare oportet. Cum enim unicuique provinciæ suæ propriæ sint leges, possessionibus injunctæ atque indictæ, sane incapacitas foris adepta in considerationem venire non potest; sed omnis, sive qualitas, sive personæ habilitas, quoad eadem bona pertinet, a loco sitûs proficiscitur*[2]. Bartolus affirms the same doctrine: *Cum est, quod de aliquo jure descendente ex re ipsa servari consuetudo vel statutum loci, ubi est res*[3]. Boullenois, after some fluctuations of opinion, comes to the result, that the capacity to make a testament, so far as it regards the person, is personal; but so far as it regards immovables, is real, and governed by the law of the *situs* of the property[4].

§ 433 *a*. Stockmans, Dumoulin, Bouhier, Paul Voet, and John Voet, maintain the same opinion[5]. Dumoulin says: *Aut statutum agit in rem, et quacumque verborum formula utatur, semper inspicitur locus ubi res est*[6]. *Si statutum dicat, quod minor xxv. annis non possit testari de immobilibus, tunc enim non respicit personam, nec agit in personam principal-*

---

1 Burgundus, Tract. 1, n. 8, p. 19; Ante, § 54; Liverm. Diss. § 47, 48, pp. 51, 52.

2 Burgundus, Tract. 1, n. 8, pp. 19, 20. See also 1 Boullenois, Observ. 6, pp. 129, 130; Id. Observ. 9, p. 150; Ante, § 372.

3 Bartol. ad Cod. lib. 1, tit. 1, n. 27; Bartol. Oper. tom. 7, p. 5.

4 1 Boullenois, Observ. 28, pp. 718—720. See Id. Observ. 5, pp. 81—84, 101, 102. See also Merlin, Répert. Testament, § 1, n. 8, art. 1, p. 310; Cochin, Œuvres, tom. 4, p. 555, 4to edit.

5 Liverm. Diss. § 49—52, pp. 52—54; 1 Froland. Mém. des Stat. pp. 65, 66; 2 Froland. des Stat, pp. 819—223; 4 Burge, Comm. on Col. and For. Law, pt. 2, ch. 12, p. 579; Ante, § 432, note.

6 Molin, Comm. ad Cod. lib. 1, tit. 1, l. 1, Conclus. de Stat. tom. 3, p. 556; Liverm. Diss. § 81, p. 69.

iter, nec in solemnitatem actus, sed agit in certas res, ad finem conservandi patrimonii, et sic est reale. Quia idem est, ac si dictum esset, immobilia non possint alienari in testamento per minores. Unde statutum loci inspicietur, sive persona subdita sit, sive non[1]. Stockmans says: *Jampridem Pragmaticorum consensa et usu fori invaluit, et ubicumque agitur de rerum soli alienatione, mancipatione, investura, successione, aliisque translationis et acquisitionis modis, inspiciuntur leges loci, ubi res sitæ sunt, sive questio sit de ætate, vel alia qualitate, habilitate, vel inhabilitate personæ, sive agatur de statuto verbis in rem, sive in personam, directè concepto; cum effectus ipse, potius quam verba, attendendus sit, qui prorsus realis est, quoties de rebus soli transferendis et mancipandis quæritur; atque proinde ab hoc effectu statutum omne, quod huc respicit, vel eò rem deducit, pro reali habendum judicandumque sit*[2]. Paul Voet adds, that personal laws do not regularly extend so as to affect immovable property in a foreign country, either directly or consequentially[3]. John Voet has gone into an elaborate consideration of the subject, and positively denies that personal laws can operate out of the territory. *Nullâ tamen ratione* (says he) *suffi-*

---

1 Molin, Comm. ad Cod. lib. 1, tit. 1, l. 1; Conclus. de Stat. tom. 3, p. 556; Post, § 475; Bouhier. Cout. de Bourg. ch. 24, § 91—102, pp. 476—478; 1 Froland. Mém. des Stat. p. 65.

2 Stockmans, Decis. 125, n. 9, p. 263; Ante, § 54; Liverm. Diss. § 50, pp. 52, 53; 2 Burge, Comm. on Col. and For. Law, pt. 2, ch. 9, pp. 863, 864.

3 P. Voet, De Stat. § 4, ch. 2, n. 7, p. 124, (edit. 1715); Id. p. 138, (edit. 1661); Ante, § 54, n. Paul Voet admits, that personal laws accompany the person every where, as to property, within the territory of the government of which he is a subject; but not as to any property elsewhere. Statutum personale ubique locorum personam comitatur, in ordine ad bona infra territorium statuentis, ubi persona affecta domicilium habet. Non tamen statutum personale sese extendit ad bona immobilia alibi sita. P. Voet, De Stat. § 4, c. 2, n. 6, p. 123, (edit. 1715); Id. p. 138, (edit. 1661). In another place he says: Immobilia statutis loci reguntur, ubi sita. P. Voet, De Stat. § 9, ch. 1, n. 4, 252, 253, (edit. 1715); Id. pp. 306, 307, (edit. 1661); Ante, § 54, note; Post, § 475, 483 *b*; Ante, § 52, 52 *a*; S. P. J. Voet, Ad Pand. lib. 1, tit. 4, § 2, 9, p. 43.

ciente, cum hæc nitantur, nec a legibus Romanis huic sententiæ patrocinium accedere possit; verius est personalia, non magis quam realia, territorium statuentis posse excedere, sive directo, sive per consequentiam. And he proceeds to put very pointed inquiries, whether any foreign country will permit its own territorial laws to be overthrown by the laws of another country, on the subject of prodigals, infamous persons, minors, illegitimacy or legitimacy, and heirship[1].

§ 433 *b.* Christinæus adopts the same opinion: *Quodcum de rebus soli, hoc est immobilibus, agitur, et diversa diversarum possessionum loca, et situs proponuntur, in acquirendis, transferendis, et asserendis, dominiis, et in controversia quo jure reguntur, certissimam in usu observationem esse noti satis juris, est, id jus de pluribus spectari, quod loci est vel situs, et suas quoque leges, statuta et consuetudines servandos fore; sic quod de talibus nulla cujusquam potestas sit præter territorii legem*[2]. Peckius is equally direct: *Etenim natura statuti est, ut non extendatur ad bona in alio territorio sita, ubi contraria stat juris dispositio*[3]. *Bona autem dicuntur esse in ejus jurisdictione, in cujus territorio sunt*[4]. And again: *Quod sive statutum loquatur in rem sive in personam, habeat locum in bonis positis in territorium statuentium, et non in aliis*[5].

§ 434. The opinion of these latter jurists is in coincidence

---

[1] J. Voet, Ad Pand. lib. 1, tit. 4, § 7, ps. 2, De Stat. p. 40, cited at large, Ante, § 54 *a*. There are some jurists who adopt an intermediate opinion, holding, that in order to transfer real property, the party must have capacity according to the lex domicilii and the lex rei sitæ. Thus, if in the country rei sitæ the age to convey is twenty-one years, and in the country of the domicil the age is twenty-five years, a party cannot convey, although he is twenty-one years of age, nor unless he is twenty-five. Ante, § 432, note; Ante, § 388.

[2] Christin. Decis. 3, vol. 2, p. 4; 1 Boullenois, Observ. 6, pp. 127—140.

[3] Peck. Oper. De Testam. Conjug. lib. 4, ch. 8, n. 5, p. 619, (edit. 1666).

[4] Ibid.

[5] Id. n. 6, 7, p. 620.

with that of the common law, as already stated; and it has been fully recognised in England in a recent case, of which we have had occasion to take notice in another place[1]. Upon that occasion Lord Chief Justice Abbott said: "The rule as to the law of domicil has never been extended to real property; nor have I found in the decisions of Westminster Hall any doctrine giving a countenance to the idea that it ought to be so extended. There being no authority for saying, that the right of inheritance follows the law of the domicil of the parties, I think it must follow that of the country where the land lies." The same doctrine was concurred in by the other Judges[2].

§ 435. Secondly, in relation to the forms and solemnities of passing the title to real estate[3]. We have already had occasion to examine the point, whether executory contracts respecting real estate must not be in the form prescribed by the local law, in order to have validity; as for instance, a contract for the sale of land in England to be in writing according to the Statute of Frauds[4]. The result of that examination was, that in countries acting under the common law, the affirmative is admitted; although foreign jurists are divided on the point[5]. It would seem clear, also, ac-

---

1 Ante, § 87.

2 Doe *d.* Birtwhistle *v.* Vardill, 5 Barn. & Cress. 438. But see S. C. 2 Clarke & Fin. 571; 9 Bligh, R. 32—38.

3 See 2 Burge, Comm. on Col. and For. Law, pt. 2, ch. 9, pp. 840—870; Id. vol. 1, pt. 1, ch. 1, pp. 21—23.

4 Ante, § 363—373. See also 2 Burge, Comm. on Col. and For. Law, pt. 2, ch. 9, pp. 867—869.

5 Ante, § 237, 363—373.—M. Fœlix, speaking on this subject, says: "Un principe aujourd'hui généralement adopté par l'usage des nations, c'est que 'la forme des actes est réglée par les lois du lieu dans lequel ils sont faits ou passés.' C'est-à-dire, que, pour la validité de tout acte, il suffit d'observer les formalités préscrites par la loi du lieu où cet acte a été dressé ou rédigé: l'acte ainsi passé exerce ses effets sur les biens meubles et immeubles situés dans un autre territoire, dont les lois établissent des formalités différentes et plus étendues (Locus regit actum). En d'autres termes, les lois, qui réglent la forme des actes, étendent leur autorité tant sur les nationaux que sur les étrangers qui contractent ou disposent dans le pays, et

cording to the common law, that no conveyance or transfer of land can be made, either testamentary or *inter vivos*,

---

elles participent ainsi de la nature des lois réelles." (Fœlix Conflit des Lois, Revue Etrang. et Fran. tom. 7, 1840, § 40, pp. 346, 347.) And again: "Parmi les écrivains modernes, nous en comptons trois, qui n'adoptent point la maxime, que la forme des actes est réglée par la loi du lieu dans lequel ils sont faits ou passés. Suivant M. Eichhorn, les actes d'une personne, qui affectent sa fortune, doivent, en régle générale, être conformes aux lois de son domicile, quant à la forme et quant à leur substance, lorsqu'on se propose de les mettre à exécution dans ce domicile : la raison en est, dit l'auteur, dans le principe de la souveraineté des nations et dans la loi 21. ff. de obl. et act. (Contraxisse unusquisque in eo loco intelligitur, in quo ut solveret, se obligavit). Cette régle, continue l'auteur, admet des exceptions : 1° lorsque l'acte a été fait sans fraude dans un pays étranger, où il y a eu impossibilité de remplir les formes préscrites au lieu du domicile de la personne, qui contracte ou qui dispose; 2° lorsque l'acte a été fait dans un pays étranger dont les lois ne protégent les actes et contrats qu'autant qu'on y a suivi une certaine forme ; 3° lorsque le statut réel exige, pour l' acquisition ou l'aliénation d'un immeuble, un acte qui précéde, la forme et le contenu de cet acte doivent se régler par ce statut réel.—Par application de la régle professée par M. Eichhorn, cet auteur soutient que le testament fait en pays étranger, d'après les formes qui y sont établies, n'aura ses effets, dans la patrie du testateur, quant à la forme, qu'autant que les lois de cette patrie reconnaissent la même forme, à moins que le testateur ne soit également décédé dans le pays de la confection du testament : dans ce dernier cas seulement, le dit testament sortirait ses effects dans sa patrie. La proposition enseignée par Eichhorn peut être vraie en droit étroit ; mais elle est contraire à l'usage des nations, attesté par le sentiment général des auteurs cités plus haut : on ne doit donc pas s'arrêter à l'opinion isolée de M. Eichhorn. D'ailleurs, les exceptions admises par cet auteur, surtout la première, ramenent son systême à celui que nous avons exposé au n° 41 ; en effet, notre systême a précisément sa base principale dans l'impossibilité ou du moins dans la difficulté de remplir à l'étranger les formalités préscrites au lieu du domicile de l'individu. Du reste, notre systême admet aussi les deux exceptions énoncées par M. Eichhorn sous les n°s 2 et 3, ainsi que nous l'ex pliquerons au° suivant. M. Mühlenbruch, en parlant des testaments, revient sur l'opinion par lui émise dans sa doctrina pandectarum ; il se range de l'avis de M. Eichhorn. Le troisième auteur qui repousse l'application de la régle locus regit actum, en ce qui concerne la forme des actes, c'est Hauss. Il regarde cette régle comme vague et inutile, et il n'en admet l'application que dans deux cas : le premier, lorsqu'il s'agit d'actes de procédure (si de processu ordinando quæritur) ; le second, lorsque les parties, en vertu de leur autonomie, se sont soumises aux lois du pays dans lequel elles ont passé un acte. L'opinion de cet auteur a sa base dans une confusion d'idées : il a cherché à appliquer la régle locus regit actum non-seulement à

except according to the formalities prescribed by the local law. Thus, in England, no instrument not under seal can operate as a conveyance of land, so as to give a perfect title thereto. An instrument therefore not under seal, executed

---

la forme des actes, mais encore à leur substance; n'ayant pu parvenir à justifier cette opinion, il a rejété entièrement la dite régle, et il a cru trouver uniquement dans la volonté expresse ou tacite des parties, la base de l'application des lois du lieu, quant à la forme et quant à la matière de l'acte. L'acte fait d'après les formes préscrites par la loi du lieu de sa rédaction est valable, non-seulement par rapport aux biens meubles appartenant à l'individu et qui se trouvent au lieu de son domicile, mais encore par rapport aux immeubles, en quelque endroit qu'ils fussent situés. Cette dernière proposition, selon la nature des choses, admet une exception, dans le cas où la loi du lieu de la situation préscrit, à l'égard des actes translatifs de la propriété des immeubles ou qui y affectent des charges réelles, des formes particulières qui ne peuvent être remplies ailleurs que dans ce même lieu; telles sont la rédaction des actes par un notaire du même territoire, la transcription ou l'inscription aux registres tenus dans ce territoire, des actes d'aliénation, d'hypothéque, etc. L'acte fait dans un pays étranger suivant lés formes qui y sont préscrites, ne perd pas sa force, quant à sa forme, par le rétour de l'individu au lieu de son domicile; aucune raison de droit ne milite en faveur de l'opinion contraire. La régle, locus regit actum, ne doit pas être étendue au-delà des limites que nous lui avons tracées au n° 40; elle ne s'applique qu'à la forme extérieure, et non pas à la matière ou substance des actes, ainsi que nous l'expliquerons encore au § suivant. Ainsi, dans un testament, la capacité de la personne, et la disposibilité des biens ne se réglent point par la loi du lieu de la rédaction. Dans les dispositions entre-vifs, soit à titre onéreux, soit à titre gratuit, la loi du lieu de la rédaction peut avoir influé, soit sur l'ensemble de l'acte, soit sur les termes employés par les parties; et, sous ce double titre, cette loi peut être consultée par les juges comme moyen d'interprétation; mais elle ne forme pas la loi décisive, à moins que les parties ne s'y soient soumises expressément. La régle indiquée au n° 40 ne s'applique pas seulement aux actes publics ou solennels, mais aussi aux actes sous signature privée comme, par exemple, les testaments olographes. Feu M. Merlin fait remarquer que 'la régle locus regit actum est générale, et il faudrait, pour la restreindre aux testaments reçus par personnes publiques, une exception autorisée par une loi expresse.' Nous ajouterons que les raisons exposées au n° 41 s'appliquent aux actes sous seing-privé comme aux actes publics. Nous régardons comme une erreur l'opinion contraire professée par M. Duranton. Nous empruntons à M. Pardessus une observation importante. C'est que, dans tous les cas où l'une des parties invoque un acte passé hors du royaume, il faut avant tout s'assurer que l'acte a été passé dans le lieu régi par les lois auxquelles on veut le soumettre." Id. § 42—47, pp. 350—354.

in a foreign country where no seal is required to pass the title to lands, would be held invalid to pass land in England[1]. The same rule is established in America, where it is held, (as we have seen), that the title to land can be acquired and lost only in the manner prescribed by the law of the place where the property is situate[2].

§ 436. Erskine in his Institutes states this to be the law of Scotland. "In the conveyance[3]," says he, "of an immovable subject, or of any right affecting heritage, the grantor must follow the solemnities established by the law, not of the country where he signs the deed, but of the State in which the heritage lies, and from which it is impossible to remove it. For though he be subject with respect to his person to the *lex domicilii*, that law can have no authority over property which hath its fixed domicil in another territory, and which cannot be tried but before the Courts, and according to the laws of that State where it is situated. And this rule is so strictly adhered to in practice, that a disposition of an heritable jurisdiction in Scotland, executed in England after the English form, was not sustained, even as an obligation to compel the grantor to execute a more

---

1 Ante, § 363, 364. See Dundas *v.* Dundas, 2 Dow & Clarke, 349; Coppin *v.* Coppin, 2 P. Will. 291, 293; 2 Fonbl. Equity, b. 5, ch. 1, § 6, note, pp. 444, 445.

2 Ante, § 427, 428; United States *v.* Crosby, 7 Cranch, 115; Cutter *v.* Davenport, 1 Pick. R. 81, 86; Hosford *v.* Nichols, 1 Page, R. 220; Wills *v.* Cowper, 2 Hamm. R. 124; S. C. Wilcox's Rep. 278; Kerr *v.* More, 9 Wheaton, R. 566; M'Cormick *v.* Sullivant, 10 Wheaton, R. 192; Darby *v.* Mayer, 11 Wheaton, R. 465.

3 Ersk. Inst. b. 3, tit. 3, § 40, p. 515; Id. § 41; 2 Kaims on Equity, b. 3, c. 8, § 2, p. 328.—But Erskine in the same section makes a distinction between contracts to convey real estate situate in Scotland and actual transfers; holding, that if the contract to convey is good by the lex loci contractus, it will be enforced in Scotland; but an actual transfer will not. "But," says he, "though obligations to convey, if they be perfected secundum legem domicilii, are binding here; yet conveyances themselves, if of subjects within Scotland, are not always effectual if they are not executed according to the solemnities of our law." The other part of the section has been already cited in a note, Ante, § 365. The common law, as we have

formal conveyance." He is well borne out in this doctrine by other authorities[1].

§ 437. Boullenois admits, that, when an incapacity to do an act, or to make a conveyance of a thing, except by certain formalities, is created by the *lex rei sitæ,* that law must be observed in regard to that thing, although the party be otherwise capable by the law of his domicil[2]. He adds, in

---

seen, with masculine vigour, and upon principle, rejects such niceties; and indeed it seems repudiated by many of the learned judges of Scotland. Ante, § 365. See Lang *v.* Whitlaw, 2 Shaw, App. Cases, p. 13; S. C. 5 Wils. & Shaw, pp. 66, 67, note; Brack *v.* Johnston, 5 Wils. & Shaw, p. 61.

[1] Ante, § 365—367; Jerningham *v.* Herbert, 1 Tamlyn, R. 103; Fergusson on Marriage and Div. pp. 395, 397.—Mr. Burge, speaking on this subject, says, "There is a perfect uniformity in all systems of jurisprudence in the adoption of this rule. Thus, a contract in England for the sale to A. of immovable property situated in England, or in those colonies which are governed by the law of England, would transfer the dominium in equity, and A. would become the owner; but if the property were situated in British Guiana, it would not transfer the dominium. On the other hand, a contract in British Guiana for the sale of immovable property situated in England, or in those colonies, would transfer the dominium on that property, but it would not transfer the dominium of property situated in British Guiana." 2 Burge, Comm. on Col. and For. Law, pt. 2, ch. 9, p. 865.

[2] 1 Boullenois, Observ. 23, pp. 476, 477, 488, 492, 498—500; Ante, § 240.—Boullenois, speaking on this subject, says: "Ces formes distinctives des contrats font, pour la plupart, dictées par le Droit commun; mais comme Me Ch. du Molin observe que chacune des villes ayant jurisdiction, peut prescrire une forme particuliere à chaque espèce de contrat, il pourroit arriver que ces formes ou formalités varieroient à l'infini; que dans le lieu du contrat, il y en auroit une; que dans le lieu du domicile, il y en auroit une autre; et que dans le lieu de la situation, il y en auroit encore une autre. Dans ces cas, si ceux qui contractent, sont domiciliés dans un lieu, qu'ils contractent dans un autre, et que la chose dont ils contractent, soit encore dans un autre quelle forme les contractants donneront-ils à l'acte, en égard à toutes ces formalités variés et multipliés? S'il étoit clair que ces formes appartinssent à la solemnité, il n'y auroit pas de difficulté qu'il faudroit suivre ce que la loi du lieu où l'acte se passeroit, prescriroit à cet égard. Si ces formalités étoient habilitantes la personne, il faudroit suivre la loi du domicile de la personne habilitée. Si au contraire elles appartenoient, sive ad substantialia contractûs, sive ad naturalia, sive ad accidentalia aut complementoria, c'est là où se rencontreroit la véritable difficulté; et si vous donnez pour principe général et indéfini, qu'il faut toujours suivre la loi du lieu où se passe le contrat, ou bien qu'il faut toujours suivre la loi de la situation, ou bien qu'il

another place, that if these formalities are attached to things and not to persons, then the laws which prescribe them are real; and, consequently, the law of the place of their situation must govern[1]. Accordingly, he lays it down as a fundamental rule: *Quand la loi exige certaines formalités, lesquelles sont attachées aux choses mêmes, il faut suivre la loi de la situation*[2]. Yet, strangely enough, he departs from this general doctrine in relation to testaments upon some subtile distinctions, which he takes between extrinsic

faut toujours suivre la loi du domicile des contractants, il est certain que vous donnerez un faux principe; parce que, comme on le verra ci-après, tantôt ces formalités appartiennent au contrat, tantôt elles appartiennent et épendent de la qualité de la personne." (1 Boullenois, Observ. 23, p. 465.) Boullenois in another place says: "Quelque variété qu'il y ait dans ce nombre considéré de différentes formalités ou solemnités, et quelque différence qu'il y ait même dans nos auteurs pour le langage, ils conviennent unanimement, que pour qu'un acte soit parfait, ex omni parte, il y a des choses requises, pour habiliter et rendre capables les personnes qui contractent, et elles sont attachées à la personne, et dépendent du domicile; qu'il y en a de requises pour la preuve et l'authenticité, et elles dépendent du lieu où se passe le contrat; qu'il y en a attachées aux choses, et elles dependent de la loi de la situation; qu'il y en a qui sont de l'essence et de la substance intérieure et viscérale des actes, et ces choses sont, selon la nature de chaque acte, communément et assez universellement les mêmes partout; qu'il y en a qui fleuent de la nature et espèce dont sont les contrats, soit qu'elles proviennent de la propre nature de ces contrats, soit qu'elles y soient liées et attachées par un usage bien constant, et une coutume invétérée, et ce sont ces choses qui peuvent faire naître le plus de contestation; qu'il y en a qui ne servent que de complément aux actes déjà formés, et elles dépendent des différentes loix; et qu'il y en a encore qui ne sont que de pure discipline, et d'autres dont l'accomplissement plus ou moins prompt dépend de la volonté des parties, et celles-ci n'entraînent pas de grandes difficultées. Mais la véritable difficulté en cette matière, est de savoir bien discerner toutes ces formalités, et les ranger chacune dans la classe qui leur appartient, afin de ne pas appliquer à une formalité d'une certaine classe des principes et des décisions, qui ne conviennent qu'à une formalité d'une autre classe. Plusieurs exemples vont faire sentir cette difficulté." 1 Boullenois, Observ. 23, pp. 456, 457; Id. pp. 488, 492, 498, 499. See Merlin, Répert. Testament, § 1, 5, art. 1—3.

[1] 1 Boullenois, Observ. 23, p. 467; Id. pp. 499, 500. See Liverm. Diss. pp. 58—60; Henry on For. Law, p. 50.

[2] 2 Boullenois, Observ. 46, p. 467, R. 4; Ante, § 240. See 1 Boullenois, Observ. 9, p. 151.

and intrinsic forms, between the solemnities required to the perfection and authenticity of an act, and those which relate to the capacity to do it, or to dispose of the thing, which is the subject of it[1].

§ 437 *a*. Sandius (John à Sandé) has given us some quite as subtile distinctions, insisting that there is a wide distinction between the solemnities of an alienation and the thing of which the alienation is the subject: *Quod multum intersit inter solennitates dispositionis et rem, de quá sit dispositio.* The solemnities respect but the form of the disposition or alienation, and the things disposed of or alienated constitute the substantial matter thereof; so that what respects the solemnities affects only the form of the act and not the things. *Solennitates sunt forma; res est subjectum dispositionis; quare tale statutum magis efficere videtur dispositionem ipsam, quam rem*[2]. Accordingly, Sandius holds, that if a foreigner makes his will according to the forms and solemnities of the law of the place where it is made, it will be valid, even as to immovables in another country, where different forms and solemnities are required. He assigns the following reason: *Ratio hujus sententiæ est, quod statutum vel consuetudo, præscribens solennitates testamenti, non afficiat res testatoris, neque ejus personam, sed ipsam dispositionem, quæ fit in loco statuti vel consuetudinis. At in cujusvis actus solennitate inspicitur consuetudo loci, ubi is celebratur, eòque in iis, quæ spectant ad formam et solennitates testamenti, inspicitur consuetudo loci, ubi illud factum est, licet testator ibi larem fixum non habeat*[3]. And again: *Deindè hæc sententia non facilè ad praxin transferri potest, uti incommoda testari volentibus, qui si habeant bona sita in diversis regionibus, quæ, quod ad testamenti solennitates attinet, diversis moribus re-*

---

1 1 Boullenois, Observ. 21, pp. 422—426.

2 1 Boullenois, Observ. 21, pp. 422, 423; Sand. Decis. Frisic. lib. 4, tit. Defin. 14, pp. 142, 143.

3 Sand. Decis. Frisic. lib. 4, tit. 1, Defin. 14, pp. 142, 143.

guntur, non possunt secundùm hanc sententiam uno testamento defungi, sed si nolint pro parte intestati decedere, coguntur contrà juris rationem plura testamenta exarare; singula scilicet juxtà consuetudinem cujusque regionis, vel in uno testamento sequi consuetudines plurium locorum, et actum per se individuum huic, et illi loco diversimodè impartiri[1].

§ 438. D'Argentré and Burgundus maintain with great clearness the general doctrine, that the law *rei sitæ* must govern as to the solemnities of alienation, *inter vivos* and testamentary[2]. D'Argentré's opinion has been already in part stated[3]. He adds in another place: *Cum de rebus soli, id est immobilibus, agitur, (qu'ils appellent d'heritage) et diversa diversarum possessionem loca, et situs proponuntur in acquirendis, transferendis, aut asserendis, dominiis, et in controversia est, quo jure regantur, certissima usu observatio est, id jus de pluribus spectari, quod loci est, et suos cuique loco, leges, statuta, et consuetudines servandos; et qui cuique mores de rebus, territorio, et potestatibus finibus sint recepti, sic ut de talibus nulla cujusquam potestas sit præter territorii legem. Sic in contractibus, sic in testamentis, sic in commerciis omnibus, et locis conveniendi constitutum; ne contra situs legem in immobilibus quidquam decerni possit privato consensu; et par est sic judicari*[4]. Burgundus, in addition to what has been already cited[5], says in another place: *Siquidem solemnitates testamenti ad jura personalia non pertinent; quia sunt quædam qualitas bonis ipsis impressa, ad quam tenetur respicere quisquis in bonis aliquid alterat. Nam, ut jura realia non porrigunt effectum extra territorium; ita et hanc præ se vir-*

---

1 Sand. Decis. Frisic. lib. 4, tit. 1, Defin. 14, p. 123.

2 1 Boullenois, Observ. 6, p. 129; Id. Observ. 9, p. 151; Id. Observ. 22, pp. 422, 425; Cujacii, Opera, tom. 3, Observ. lib. 14, c. 12, p. 399, (edit. 1758); 2 Burge, Comm. on Col. and For. Law, pt. 2, c. 9, p. 866.

3 Ante, § 426 *a*.

4 D'Argent. De Briton. Leg. art. 218, n. 2, p. 647; Ante, § 371 *a*.

5 Ante, § 372, 433, 438; Post, § 477.

tutem ferunt, quod nec alieni territorii leges in se recipiant[1]. This is also the opinion of other distinguished jurists[2].

§ 439. Froland treats as clearly real all laws which respect the alienation of immovable property, and consequently that it is governed by the *lex rei sitæ*. He lays down as a fundamental rule: *La première (chose), que le statut réel ne sort point de son territoire. Et de la vient, que dans le cas, où il s'agit de successions, &c. d'alienation d'immoveables, &c. il faut s'attacher aux coutumes des lieu, où les fonds sont situés*[3]. Cochin lays down the rule, that though the formalities of an instrument (*acte*) may be, and indeed ought to be according to the law of the place of the instrument; yet, when the clauses or contents of such an instrument are to be applied to property in another country, the law *rei sitæ* must govern. *Les formalités, dont un acte doit être revêtu, se réglent par la loi, qui exerce son empire dans le lieu, où l'acte a été passé; mais quand il s'agit d'appliquer les clauses qu'il renferme, aux biens des parties contractantes, c'est la loi de la situation de ces biens, qui doit seule être consultée*[4].

§ 440. But there are many other jurists who maintain the same opinion as Cochin, holding, that if the act or in-

---

[1] Burgundus, Tract. 6, n. 2, 3, pp. 128, 129; Post, § 477; Rodenburg, De Div. Stat. tit. 2, c. 3, § 1, 2; 2 Boullenois, App. pp. 19—21; 1 Boullenois, Observ. 6, pp. 129, 130; Id. Observ. 9, p. 151; Id. Observ. 21, pp. 422, 423, 425; Ante, § 433 *a*; 4 Burge, Comm. on Col. and For. Law, pt. 2, c. 12, pp. 581—585; Post, § 477.

[2] Ante, § 363—373. See 2 Burge, Comm. on Col. and For. Law, pt. 2, c. 9, pp. 865, 866; 1 Boullenois, Observ. 21, pp. 423, 424; Sand. Decis. Frisic. lib. 4, tit. 1, Defin. 14, p. 142, where many opinions of jurists are cited.

[3] 1 Froland, Mém. 156; Id. 65.

[4] Cochin, Œuvres, tom. 5, p. 697, 4to edit.—There is some difficulty in reconciling this passage with another cited in the note to § 440. Perhaps Cochin only means here to say, that the solemnities of the place where the act is done are to be observed; but that the interpretation of the clauses or provisions of the instrument are to be according to the law of the situs. See also 2 Burge, Comm. on Col. and For. Law, pt. 2, c. 9, p. 866.

strument have the formalities which are prescribed by the law of the place where it is made, it ought to have a universal operation[1]; and they apply it especially to the case of testamentary dispositions of real property[2]. They found themselves upon the extreme inconvenience which would otherwise result from requiring a party to make different testaments for their property, lying in different countries; and the almost utter impossibility, in many cases, of ascertaining at a critical moment what are the peculiar solemnities prescribed by the laws of each of these countries[3]. They seem wholly to have overlooked, on the other side, the inconvenience of any nation suffering property, locally and permanently situate within its own territory, to be subject to be transferred by any other laws than its own; and thus introducing into the bosom of its own jurisprudence all the innumerable diversities of foreign laws, to regulate its own titles to such property, many of which laws can be

---

1 P. Voet, De Stat. § 4, c. 2, § 6, p. 123, § 7, p. 124, (edit. 1715); Id. p. 137, (edit. 1661); J. Voet, Ad Pand. lib. 1, tit. 4, p. 2, § 5, 6, p. 39, § 10, pp. 43, 44; 1 Boullenois, Observ. 21, pp. 426—433. Mr. Livermore, in his Dissertations, sums up the opinions of different jurists. Liverm. Diss. § 78—214, pp. 69—130. So does Mr. Burge, 4 Burge, Comm. pt. 2, c. 12, pp. 581—585. Sandius, or Sandé, has also brought together the opinions of different jurists on this subject. Sand. Decis. Frisic. lib. 4, tit. 1, Defin. 14, pp. 142, 143.

2 See Rodenburg, De Div. Stat. tit. 2, c. 3; 2 Boullenois, App. p. 19; 1 Boullenois, pp. 414—421 ; Id. Observ. 21, pp. 422—433; 1 Hertii, Opera, § 4, n. 10, p. 125, (edit. 1737) ; Id. p. 179, (edit. 1716); J. Voet, Ad Pand. lib. 1, tit. 4, pp. 2, 13, 43; Bouhier, Cout. de Bourg. c. 23, § 81—89, p. 460; Vinnius ad Instit. lib. 2, tit. 10, § 14, n. 5 ; 1 Boullenois, Observ. 21, pp. 426, 427; Merlin, Rèpert. Loi. § 6, art. 6, 7.

3 Rodenburg, De Div. tit. 2, c. 3 ; 2 Boullenois, App. p. 19; 1 Boullenois, pp. 414—417; Vinnius, Ad Inst. lib. 2, tit. 10, § 14, n. 5; 1 Boullenois, Observ. 21, pp. 426, 427 ; Hertii, Opera, De Collis. Leg. § 4, n. 10, p. 126, (edit. 1737) ; Id. p. 179, (edit. 1716); Id. n. 23, p. 133, (edit. 1737); Id. p. 189, (edit. 1716); Fœlix, Conflit des Lois, Revue Etrang. et Fran. tom. 7, 1840, § 41, pp. 347, 348. John Voet has given the reasoning on this side of the question. J. Voet, Ad Pand. tom. 1, lib. 1, tit. 4, ps. 2, § 13, 15, pp. 45, 46. See also 4 Burge, Comm. on Col. and For. Law, pt. 2, c. 12, p. 590; Post, § 444 *a*.

but imperfectly ascertained, and many of which may become matters of subtile controversy[1]. Some of these jurists press their doctrine so far as to doubt, whether a transfer, made according to the solemnities of the place where the property is locally situate, would be good, if not also executed according to the law of the place where the act is done[2].

§ 441. The opinion of these jurists is supported by Dumoulin. His language is: *Et est omnium doctorum sententia, ubicumque consuetudo, vel statutum locale disponit de solemnitate, vel formâ actûs, ligari etiam exteros, ibi actum illum gerentes, et gestum esse validum, et efficacem ubique, etiam super bonis solis extra territorium consuetudinis vel statuti*[3]. In another place he says: *Aut statutum loquitur*

---

1 Cochin says, it is one of the most uniform principles, that the form of acts depends upon the law of the place where they are passed; so that, if a man is domiciled at Paris, and there has all his property (biens), but he makes his testament in another province under a different law, the law of the latter is alone to be regarded in its form, though the succession to the testator, either of heirship or testamentary, may be regulated by the law of Paris. Cochin, Œuvres, tom. 2, p. 72, 4to. edit. See Ante, § 439. D'Aguesseau treats with some sarcasm those who venture to suggest a doubt on the point. "We leave such discussions," says he, "to the ultramontanæ doctors. We say with D'Argentré, that these questions are not worthy to occupy a moment's attention. No one can doubt that the formalities of a testament ought to be governed by the law of the place where the act is done." D'Aguesseau, Œuvres, tom. 4, p. 637, 4to. edit.

2 Rodenburg, De Div. Stat. tit. 2, ch. 3; 2 Boullenois, App. p. 21; 1 Boullenois, 417; Id. Observ. 21, pp. 428—430. Grotius appears to have held the same opinion, and to have applied it to the case of wills and testaments. See Post, § 479, where his opinion is cited.

3 Molin, Oper. tom. 2, (edit. 1681); Consil. 53, § 9, p. 965; Ante, § 260, note, § 274 *a*, § 372 *a*; 1 Boullenois, Observ. 21, pp. 423, 429. Mr. Livermore manifestly entertained the opinion, that it was sufficient for a testament of immovable property to have the formalities prescribed by the law of the testator's domicil. After adverting to Dumoulin's Division of Statutes, into those which relate to the solemnities and forms of acts (nudam ordinationem vel solemnitatem actûs), and those which concern the merits and decision of causes (quæ meritum causæ vel decisionem concernunt), he added: "The statutes of the first class I do not consider to be either personal, real, or mixed. They do not act directly upon persons nor upon property, but upon the act, for the purpose of determining its authenticity. The laws of some

de his, quæ concernunt nudam ordinationem vel solemnitatem actûs, et semper inspicitur statutum vel consuetudo loci, ubi actus celebratur, sive in contractibus, sive in judiciis, sive in testamentis, sive in instrumentis, aut aliis conficiendis. Ita quod testamentum, factum coram duobus testibus in locis, ubi non requiritur major solemnitas, valet ubique. Idem in omni alio actu[1]. And yet Dumoulin, in another place, uses language not very consistent with the foregoing, unless indeed he is there to be understood as speaking, not of the forms and solemnities of testaments, but of the operation and interpretation thereof. *Sed emergit incidens quæstio, cujus loci inspiciatur, an loci testamenti, contractus, vel loci dominantis, an vero loci servientis? Et omnino dicendum inspiciendam consuetudinem loci servientis, seu rei, quæ conceditur*[2].

§ 441 *a.* Bouhier maintains, that in general the forms and solemnities of all acts done, (which of course include testaments), should be according to the law of the place where the acts are done, even when the property is situated elsewhere; at least if the custom of the *situs* is not in opposition to it[3]. He lays it down in another place among his

---

countries require that a testament shall be made in presence of seven witnesses. In other countries the law requires only the presence of a notary and two witnesses. These laws dispose of the solemnities of all testaments made within their jurisdiction; but they neither affect the capacity of the testator, nor do they dispose of his property. The law of the testator's domicil determines his capacity to make a testament; the law of the place where his immovable property is situated, determines whether it may be disposed of by testament or not; the will of the testator disposes of his property, and the sole purpose and effect of the statute, which requires a certain number of witnesses to a testament, is to shew whether that will has been expressed or not."

[1] Molin, Oper. tom. 3, ad Cod. lib. 1, tit. 1, l. 1; Conclus. des Stat. p. 554, (edit. 1681); Ante, § 260; Post, § 479 *k*; 4 Burge, Comm. on Col. and For. Law, pt. 2, ch. 12, p. 583; 1 Boullenois, Observ. 21, pp. 423, 424; Ante, § 365 *a*.

[2] Molin. Oper. tom. 1, De Fiefs, § 33, n. 86, tom. 1, p. 410, (edit. 1681); 1 Boullenois, Observ. 21, pp. 423—425; Burgundus, Tract. 6, n. 2, p. 128; Bouhier, Cout. de Bourg. ch. 23, § 39—44, pp. 454, 455.

[3] Bouhier, Cout. de Bourg. ch. 28, § 10, p. 550.

general rules: *Tout statut, qui concerne les formalités extrinceques des actes et leur authenticité, est personnel; en sorte que, quand l'acte est passé dans les formes usitées au lieu, où il est redigé, il à par-tout son exécution;* and he then applies the rule expressly to testaments[1].

§ 442. Paul Voet holds the opinion, that the solemnities of contracts and other instruments respecting the transfer of immovable property, are to be according to the laws of the place where the act is done, and not of the *rei sitæ;* for he holds laws respecting solemnities not to be either real or personal, but of a mixed nature. *Statutum quippe circa solemnia, nec est in rem, nec in personam, sed mixti generis*[2]. He therefore insists, that if a testament is made according to the solemnities of the place *rei sitæ,* but not according to that of the testator's domicil, it will not be valid as to property situate elsewhere. *Verum* (says he) *quid de solemnibus, in negotiis adhibendis, statuendum erit, si locorum statuta discrepent? Finge, quempiam testari in loco domicilii, adhibitis solemnibus rei sitæ, non sui domicilii; valebitne testamentum ratione bonorum alibi sitorum? Respondeo, quod non. Neque enim aliter testamentum valere potest, quam si ea servetur solemnitas, quam requirit locus gestionis*[3]. He further holds, that if a testament is made by a person in his own country, (*sui loci*), according to the forms and solemnities required by the laws thereof, it will be valid in respect to his immovable property in other countries where different forms and solemnities are required. And this without any distinction, whether such person has retained his original domicil, or whether he is settled in another country. *Quid, si quispiam testetur secundum solemnia sui loci, puta coram notario et duobus testibus, an vires capiet testamentum ratione bonorum*

---

1 Bouhier, Cout. de Bourg. c. 23, § 81, 82, p. 460; Id. ch. 28, § 10—20, pp. 550, 551; Id. ch. 21, § 219, p. 417.

2 P. Voet, De Stat. § 9, ch. 2, n. 3, p. 263, (edit. 1715); Id. pp. 318, 319, (edit. 1661).

3 P. Voet, De Stat. § 2, ch. 2, n. 1, p. 262, (edit. 1715); Id. p. 317, (edit. 1661).

extra territorium statuentis jacentium, puta in Frisiâ, ubi plures solemnitates requiruntur? Aff. (*affirmo*). *Idque procedit, sive testator domicilium prius retinuerit, sive alio transtulerit*[1]. And he adds, that if a foreigner makes his testament according to the law of the place where he is only temporarily abiding, it will still be valid as to his immovable property elsewhere, even in his domicil. *Quid, si forensis secundum loci statutum testamentum condat, ubi tantum hospitatur, an valebit alibi, ubi vel immobilia, vel domicilium habet? Respondeo, quod ita. Cum enim agatur de actus solemnitate, quæ quoscunque obligat, in loco negotium aliquod gerentes, etiam obligat forensem ibi disponentem, si suam dispositionem vel suum actum velit utilem, licet non præcisè liget eundem*[2]. He makes an exception, indeed, of a party's making a testament in a foreign country, with a view to a fraudulent evasion of the law of his own country. *Si tamen quispiam, ut evitaret solemnitatem loci sui domicilii, in fraudem talis statuti, extra territorium se conferat, ejus testamentum non valere existumarem*[3].

§ 443. Huberus supports the same opinion. "In Holland," says he, "a testament may be made before a notary and two witnesses. In Friezeland it is not valid unless established by seven witnesses. A Batavian made a testament in Holland, according to the local law, under which property situate in Friezeland is demanded. The question is, whe-

---

[1] P. Voet, De Stat. § 2, ch. 2, n. 2, p. 262, (edit. 1715); Id. pp. 317, 318, (edit. 1661).

[2] P. Voet, De Stat. § 9, ch. 2, n. 3, § 262, 263, (edit. 1715); Id. pp. 318, 319, (edit. 1661); Post, § 475.

[3] P. Voet, De Stat. § 9, ch. 2, n. 4, p. 264, (edit. 1715); Id. p. 319, (edit. 1661). In 4 Burge, Comm. on Col. and For. Law, pt. 2, ch. 12, p. 590, Mr. Burge supposes, that Paul Voet holds a somewhat differently modified opinion, like that of Rodenburg, that the testament will be good, if made either according to the law of the place where it is made, or according to that where he has his domicil. Post, § 444. See also Ante, § 365 *a*. I do not see anything in the passage of Paul Voet, referred to by Mr. Burge, that leads to such a conclusion. The text contains all the cases put by Paul Voet on this point, in his work De Stat. § 9, ch. 2.

ther the judges in Friezeland ought to sustain the demand under that testament. The laws of Holland cannot bind the Friezians; and therefore, by the first axiom, the testament would not be valid in Friezeland; but by the third axiom it would be valid, and according to that, judgment should be pronounced in favour of the testament. But a Friezian goes into Holland, and there makes a testament according to the local law (*more loci*), contrary to the Friezian law, and returns into Friezeland, and dies there. Is the testament valid? It is valid by the second axiom; because, while he was in Holland, although temporarily, he was bound by the local law; and an act valid in its origin ought to be valid everywhere by the third axiom; and this without any discrimination of movable or of immovable property. So the law is, and is practised[1]. On the other hand, a Friezian makes his will in his own country, before a notary and two witnesses, and it is carried into Holland, and property situate there is demanded. It will not be allowed; because the testament was from the beginning a nullity, it being made contrary to the local law. The same law will govern, if a Batavian should make a testament in Friezeland, although it would be valid if made in Holland; for in truth such an instrument would from the beginning be a nullity, for the reasons just stated[2].

§ 443 *a*. What Huberus here says may seem not very consistent with what he has said in another passage already cited[3]; but he has endeavoured to reconcile the passages by the following remarks:—But it may be asked, (says he), whether what we have already said does not give rise to an objection, that if a testament is made, which is valid by the law of the place, it ought to have the same effect even in respect to property situate elsewhere, where it is lawful to

---

1 The axioms here referred to by Huberus, are those already stated in § 29.

2 Huberus, lib. 1, tit. 3, § 4, 15.

3 Ante, § 426.

dispose thereof by will? There is no such objection; because the diversity of laws of that sort does not affect the immovable property, neither does it speak concerning the same, but only directs the act of making a testament; which, when rightly executed, the law of the country does not prohibit that act from being valid in respect to immovable property, so far as no character impressed upon that property by the law of the place is injured or diminished. This observation has a place also in contracts. Thus, if certain things or rights of the soil of Friezeland are sold to persons in Holland, in a mode prohibited in Friezeland, though valid where the sale takes place, the things are understood to be well sold. The same is true as to things not, indeed, immovable, but annexed to the soil. But if corn growing on the soil of Friezeland should be sold in Holland, according to the lasts, as it is called, the sale is void, although the law of Holland does not speak on the point; because it is prohibited in Friezeland, and it adheres to the soil, and is part thereof. *Sed an hoc non obstat ei, quod antea diximus, si factum sit testamentum jure loci validum, id effectum habere etiam in bonis alibi sitis, ubi de illis testari licet? Non obstat; quia legum diversitas in illa specie non afficit res soli, neque de illis loquitur, sed ordinat actum testandi; quo recte celebrato, Lex Reipubl. non vetat illum actum valere in immobilibus, quatenus nullus character illis ipsis a lege loci impressus læditur aut imminuitur. Hæc observatio locum etiam in contractibus habet; quibus in Hollandia venditæ res soli Frisici, modo in Frisia prohibito, licet, ubi gestus est, valido, recte venditæ intelliguntur; idemque in rebus non quidem immobilibus, at solo cohærentibus; uti si frumentum soli Frisici in Hollandia secundum lastas, ita dictas, sit venditum, non valet venditio, nec quidem in Hollandia secundum eam jus dicetur, etsi tale frumentum ibi non sit vendi prohibitum; quia in Frisia interdictum est; et solo cohæret ejusque pars est*[1].

---

[1] Huberus, De Conflict. Leg. lib. 1, tit. 3, § 15.—Whether this dis-

§ 444. Rodenburg seems at first to consider, that laws, which regulate the forms and solemnities of acts touching property, are neither strictly personal laws nor real laws; but a third sort. *Subsequitur tertium et ultimum genus, eorum nimirum statutorum, quibus lex præfigitur actui, qui à persona peragendus, eundum actum vel vetando, vel certo etiam modo circumscribendo*[1]. He afterwards proceeds to state, that the opinion commonly entertained by jurists is, that as to such acts, the law of the place where the act is done is alone to be regarded, although it respects immovable property. *Si de solemnibus quæratur, ea jampridem in foro ac pulpito prævaluit opinio, ut spectandæ sint loci cujusque leges, ubi actus conficitur*[2]. *Quare sicubi ex more loci solemnite, ordinatum fuerit testamentum, valiturum illud, ubicunque oportuerit exequi*[3]. He then remarks, that Cujacius and Burgundus had attacked this doctrine; holding, that testators are bound to observe the forms and solemnities of the *res sitæ*. He distinguishes cases of this sort from cases of contract, which bind only the person: *Cujus ossibus ubique inhæret, semel ex forma loci contractæ obligationis, nexus. De re vero alibi constituta disponendi, aut ejus in alium transcribendæ formam hæc non concernunt. Realium namque jurium eorumve actuum, quibus fit mancipatio, aut dominium transfertur, aliam esse rationem, vel quotidiana praxis edocet, et recte disputat Burgundus. Jus in re, ut nascatur, quod hic ex causa testamenti contingit, non posse id præstare alterius regionis consuetudinem, ut formâ illâ ac solemnibus circumdaret alienorum fundorum alterationes, adeoque omnino jus diceret extra territorium*[4]. He then proceeds to examine the reasoning upon which the

---

tinction is satisfactory or not, will be for the learned reader to decide. See Post, § 476.

[1] Rodenburg, De Div. Stat. tit. 2, c. 3, § 1; 2 Boullenois, App. p. 19.

[2] Ibid. [3] Ibid. [4] Ibid.

opinion is maintained, that the law of the place of the making a testament should govern as to the forms and solemnities thereof, and not the law *rei sitæ.* He admits his own view to be, that a testament made according to the forms and solemnities of the place where it is made, ought to be held valid; and also, that a testament made in such place, according to the forms of the law *rei sitæ,* ought equally to be held valid. The former he treats as an indulgence, founded in general convenience; the latter, as correct in point of strict right. *Ego potiùs utrobique pro testamento respondendum duxerim, quippe personæ qualitas ad summam rei non facit, tum factura, si Statuta illa, in solemnitates scripta, personalia forent, ut subditus iis gauderet, non gauderet exterus: sed contra constat ea mere realia esse. Quicunque enim fuerit, sive incola, sive exterus, qui rem alienare intendit, necesse habet respicere ad solemnitatem territorii, cui bona sunt obnoxia. Quare dicendum est decidendæ quæstionis rationem in modo prolatis positam esse: necessitatis nimirum rationem, summumque favorem, qui pro testamentis facit, impetrâsse, ut, quamvis illa mancipent æque atque alienationes inter vivos, ideoque consimiliter componenda forent ad normam loci, ubi res sitæ sunt, suffecerit tamen ordinâsse, secundùm leges loci, ubi actus conficitur. Proinde si quis eo, quod ad testandum expeditius suâ causâ comparatum est, noluerit uti, quod ei forte promptius sit componere suprema ad loci leges, cui bona subjaceant, quo minùs testamentum ejus valiturum sit, non video: nulla enim Juris ratio, aut æquitatis benignitas patitur, ut quæ salubriter pro utilitate hominum introducuntur, ea nos duriore interpretatione contra ipsorum commodum producamus ad severitatem; nec cùm superaddatur alia testandi forma, adimitur prior, quod novæ solemnitatis adjectionem potiùs dedisse DD. quàm priorem ac ordinariam permutâsse videantur. Unde consequens est dicere, ne disputem sine speciei appositione, Amersfurti, ubi coram trinis testibus unà cum Notario ultima conduntur elogia, viribus subsistere celebrata, coram binis testibus supra Notarium, de bonis in Hollandia, aut in alia Provinciæ nostræ parte sitis*[1]. It is hardly possible

---

[1] Rodenburg, De Div. Stat. tit. 2, ch. 3, n. 1, 2; 2 Boullenois, App. pp. 21, 22; 1 Boullenois, pp. 414—418; Id. Observ. 21, pp. 422, 423. See also 2 Burge, Comm. on Col. and For. Law, pt. 2, ch. 9, pp. 865—868. Mr. Burge says: "In selecting the law by which it is to be determined whether the acts or instruments of alienation have been made with the necessary solemnities to render the alienation valid, the distinction must be made between those which are required for the proof or authentication of the act, and those which are required to be observed as the condition on which alone the law either authorizes the alienation, or gives to it an effect which it withholds if they are not observed. The former are called sometimes solemnia probantia, and the latter solemnia habilitantia. Thus, with respect to the former, if the lex loci contractus treats as null and void every contract, the subject-matter of which exceeds in value a certain sum, if it be not reduced to writing and proved before notaries, &c., when the notarial proof is not that which is prescribed, the contract will be void in whatever place it is enforced. So if those solemnities which the lex loci contractus requires have been observed, and the contract according to that law is valid and obligatory, it will be valid everywhere else. But the latter proposition is subject to the qualification, that it does not affect immovable property subject to a law in the country of its situs which annuls a contract because it has not been entered into with the solemnities which it requires. If the disposition of the law does not annul the contract on account of its non-observance of the solemnities which are prescribed, but gives to it a degree of authenticity or credit which it will want, if they are not observed, or if, in other words, its effect is either to dispense with a more formal proof of the instrument, if it bears on it evidence of their observance, or if in consequence of their non-observance it attaches a presumption against the execution of the instrument, and therefore requires from the parties a greater burden of proof, such solemnities are to be classed amongst the proofs in the cause which are governed neither by the lex loci contractus, nor by that of the situs, but by that of the forum. This question, in the opinion of Paul Voet, regards: 'Non tam de solemnibus, quam probandi efficacia; quæ licet in uno loco sufficiens, non tamen ubique locorum; quod judex unius territorii nequeat vires tribuere instrumento, ut alibi quid operetur.' The solemnities, which are called habilitantia, and constitute the mode by which alone the alienation of immovable property is permitted to be made, or by which alone that alienation can give to the grantee or purchaser certain rights, are those which are prescribed by the lex loci rei sitæ. As that law may impose restrictions which may wholly or partially withhold the power of alienating immovable property situated within its territory, to which all persons owning that property are subject, it may prescribe the conditions on which such alienation may be made. Thus the law of Scotland does not permit a destination of heritage by a testamentary disposition, neither does it permit certain deeds to

to conceive a stronger illustration of the difficulty of undertaking to build up systems of jurisprudence upon mere

---

be made in lecto. One of the conditions may be the form or manner in which it shall be made. This solemnitas dispositionis is tanquam quædam qualitas rebus impressa, and the validity of the alienation must depend on its compliance with the prescribed solemnity. Amongst the instances illustrating the species of solemnities prescribed by the lex loci rei sitæ, and to which effect must be given in all questions respecting the validity of the alienation, may be mentioned the Statute of Frauds in England. Unless there be such an agreement in writing as is required by it, or as is sanctioned by the judicial constructions which it has received, no estate or interest in immovable property situated in England will pass, although, according to the law of the place where the agreement was made, it might be sufficient if it were by parol. The lex loci rei sitæ must be invoked, if the question regard the insinuation or registration of donations or other instruments, or the effects which are induced by the neglect of it. Dumoulin seems to treat it as a solemnity which is of the substance of the contract, and to be governed by the lex loci rei sitæ. 'Insinuatio et transcriptio in registris ordinariæ curiæ loci semper omnibus his casibus est de formâ et substantiâ: quemadmodum insinuatio donationis apud magistrum census erat de substantiâ, si excedebat quingentos aureos.' Boullenois considers that if the registration does not take place when it is prescribed by the lex loci rei sitæ, the alienation is void: 'Que si le donateur est domicilée dans un royaume, et les biens situés dans un autre, et que ces deux endroits requierent une insinuation, je dis dans ce cas contre Thésaurus, que si elle n'est pas insinuée dans les deux endroits, mais dans le seul domicile, donatio insinuatur virtute legis municipalis, non porrigit effectum suum ad bona sita extra territorium, parce que si la donation n'est pas insinuée dans le lieu de la situation, elle n'est pas revêtue de la formalité réelle qu'exige la loi de la situation.'" Vattel affirms, "that the validity of a testament, as to its form, can only be decided by the domestic judge, whose sentence, delivered in form, ought to be everywhere acknowledged." But at the same time he admits, that the validity of the bequests may be disputed, as not being according to the lex rei sitæ. (Vattel, b. 2, ch. 7, § 85; Id. § 111.) M. Fœlix seems to hold a similar opinion. He says: "Une autre question est celle de savoir, si le contractant ou disposant, qui se trouve en pays étranger, peut se borner à employer les formes préscrites par la loi du lieu de la situation de ses immeubles, au lieu de suivre celle du lieu de la rédaction? Nous tenons pour l'affirmative, par une raison analogue à celle donnée sur la question précédente. Le statut réel régit les immeubles; c'est un principe résultant de la nature des choses; la permission d'user des formes établies par la loi du lieu de la rédaction de l'acte n'est, qu'une exception introduite en faveur du propriétaire, et à laquelle il lui est loisible de renoncer. Tel est aussi le sentiment de Rodenburg, de Jean Voet, et de Vander Kessel; Cocceji soutient même, que la forme des actes entre vifs ou testamentaires est régie exclusive-

theory and private notions of general convenience. The common law has wisely adhered to the doctrine, that the title to real property can pass only in the manner, and by the forms, and to the extent allowed by the local law. It has thus cut off innumerable disputes, and given simplicity, as well as uniformity, to its operations.

§ 444 *a.* John Voet maintains in substance the same opinion as Rodenburg, and insists, that it is sufficient for the validity of testaments of immovable property, that the forms and solemnities thereof should be either according to the law of the place where the testament is made, or according to the law of the place *rei sitæ.* His language is: *Neque minus de statutis mixtis, actus cujusque solennia respicientibus, percrebuit, insuper habitis de summo cujusque jure ac potestate ratiociniis, ad validitatem actus cujusque sufficere adhibitionem solennitatum, quas lex loci, in quo actus geritur, præscripserit observandas; sic, ut quod ita gestum fuerit, sese porrigat ad bona mobilia et immobilia ubicunque sita aliis in territoriis, quorum leges longe alium, longeque pleniorem requirunt solennium interventum; quod ita placuisse videtur, tum, ne in infinitum prope multiplicarentur et testamenta et*

---

ment par la loi de la situation des biens. Fachinée et Burgundus partageaient cet avis, mais par rapport aux testaments seulement. En Belgique, l'édit perpétuel de 1611, art. 13, ordonnait, qu'en cas de diversité de coutume au lieu de la résidence du testateur et au lieu de la situation de ses biens, on suivrait, par rapport à la forme et à la solemnité, la coutume de la situation. Paul Voet, Huber, Hert, Hommel, et l'auteur de l'ancien répertoire de jurisprudence, se prononcent pour la nullité. Ce dernier invoque l'autorité de Paul de Castres, au passage rapporté au n° précédent, et le principe, que la loi lie tous les individus, qui vivent dans son ressort, ne fût-ce que momentanément. Nous renvoyons à ce sujet aux observations présentées sur la question précédente. Mevius distingué entre le citoyen faisant partie de la nation dans le territoire de laquelle les biens sont situés, et entre l'étranger; il n'accorde qu'au premier la faculté de testeur ou de contracter partout d'après les formes préscrites au lieu de la situation. L'auteur ne donne pas de motif de cette distinction, et nous ne pouvons la trouver fondée." Fœlix, Des Conflit des Lois, Revue Etrang. et Franç. tom. 7, 1840, § 50, pp. 359, 360. See also 4 Burge, Comm. on Col. and For. Law, pt. 2, ch. 12, pp. 581—587. Id. p. 590.

contractus, pro numero regionum, diverso jure circa solennia utentium; atque ita summis implicarentur molestiis, ambagibus, ac difficultatibus, quotquot actum, res plures pluribus in locis sitas concernentem, expedire voluerint: tum etiam, ne plurima bonâ fide gesta nimis facile ac prope sine culpâ gerentis conturbarentur. He afterwards adds: *Positò vero hoc generali circa solennium adhibitionem jure, excutiendum superest, quid statuendum sit, si quis, in loco aliquo actum gerens, neglectis loci istius solennibus, adhibuerit ea, quæ vel domicilii vel rei sitæ statuta requirunt, sive diversa illa sint, sive pauciora? Mynsingerus quidem et Michael Grassus actus ita gestos nullius fore momenti pronunciant, sivè actum gerens extra domicilii locum servaverit solennia domicilii, sive ea, quæ requirebantur in loco rei immobilis sitæ. Cum enim ante dictum sit, aliquem et ratione domicilii, et ratione bonorum immobilium, subditum esse magistratibus locorum, in quibus vel domicilium fixit, vel bona immobilia possidet; ac quisque magistratus secundum jus summum (de quo superius disputatum, quodque hic usum invenit) sui statuti vires non male tueatur, quo usque potest, iniquus sane esset in sibi subjectum ratione domicilii aut bonorum, si non respectu bonorum, in suo territorio jacentium, ratam haberet ultimam voluntatem aut contractum ejus, à quo sua statuta solennium intuitu servanda videt; maxime, cum hâc ratione defendens sui statuti potestatem non conturbet aut subvertat alibi bene gesta, atque adeo nequaquam alterius territorii magistratibus ullam videri possit injuriam facere*[1].

§ 444 *b*. Cujacius seems to hold, that the law of the place of the domicil of the testator ought to be regarded as to the forms and solemnities of making wills and testaments, without reference to the place where the will is made, or the property is situated. *Quæri hodie sæpenumero solet, cujus regionis aut civitatis leges moresve serviri oporteat in ordinando testamento; nam quot sunt civitates, tot fere sunt ordi-*

---

[1] J. Voet, Ad Pand. lib. 1, tit. 4, Ps. 2, § 13, 15, pp. 45, 46; 4 Burge, Comm. on Col. and For. Law, pt. 2, ch. 12, p. 590; Ante, § 440—443.

nandi testamenti leges et mores; et soleo dicere, patriam testatoris solam spectari oporte, &c. Jus igitur patriæ spectatur, potius quam jus commune Populi Romani, &c. Suæ igitur patriæ et civitatis legibus aut moribus quisquis testari debet, &c. Denique non spectari locum volo, in quo bona sunt, sed patriam testatoris, &c. Et domicilii potius quam originis spectari patriam. Possit autem quis quo loco habet bona, ejus neque originalis esse, neque incola[1]. *Nec ejus loci ulla habebitur ratio in faciendo testamento.* This might seem sufficiently explicit. On another occasion he says: *Intelligimus, inquam, in faciendo testamento, privilegium et morem patriæ testatoris, spectari oportere, non situm bonorum. Nam sola possessio bonorum non creat mihi patriam. Si possideo prædium in hac urbe, hæc urbs non est ideo mea, nisi in ea posui domicilium. Solam possessionem nec civem facere, nec incolam. Ergo in servandis solemnibus testamenti non spectabo situm bonorum, ut pro vario situ bonorum etiam varia solemnia observentur, variique mores in exequenda defuncti voluntate; sed spectabo tantum morem et privilegium patriæ testatoris*[2].

---

1 Cujac. Opera, tom. 3, Observ. lib. 14, cap. 12, p. 399, (edit. 1758); 4 Burge, Comm. on Col. and For. Law, pt. 2, c. 12, p. 582.

2 Cujac. Opera, tom. 9, Comm. ad Cod. lib. 6, tit. 23, p. 709, (edit. 1768); Bouhier, Cout. de Bourg. ch. 28, § 8, p. 549; 1 Boullenois, Observ. 21, p. 423; 2 Burge, Comm. on Col. and For. Law, pt. 2, ch. 9, p. 886; 4 Burge, Comm. pt. 2, ch. 12, p. 582; Sand. Decis. Frisic. lib. 4, tit. 8, Defin. 7, p. 194. Vinnius holds a similar opinion. He says: Quæsitum est, an testamentum juxta alicujus loci consuetudinem, aut Statutum factum, etiam vim habet extra illum locum; exempli gratiâ testator ibi testamentum fecit, ubi coram duobus testibus et Notario testari licet, ut in hac nostra Batavia; quæritur, an valeat etiam in iis locis, ubi septem testes requiruntur, uti in Frisia, ubi sequuntur jus civile. Affirmant comm. DD. in L. 1. C. C. de summ. Trinit. et secundum hanc Sententiam sæpissime judicatum. Sunt tamen qui in contrarium eant, et in quæstione proposita sic distinguendum arbitrantur, ut circa res quidem mobiles, et nomina, admittenda sit communis interpret. sententia. At circa res soli, spectandum jus ejus loci in quo sitæ sunt, &c. Mihi prior sententia videtur probabilior, multumque referre utrum Statutum disponat circa solemnitatem alicujus actus, an circa rem, puta fundum, locumve; quæ Statuta in rem concipiuntur. Qualia sunt, quæ de successione ab intestato disponunt, rem ipsam haud dubie afficiunt, ut ubicumque sit, ejus loci ubi est, legibus

§ 445. Thirdly; in relation to the extent of the interest to be taken or transferred. And here there seems a perfect coincidence between the doctrine of the common law and that maintained by foreign jurists. It is universally agreed, that the law *rei sitæ* is to prevail in relation to all dispositions of immovable property, and the nature and extent of the interest to be alienated. If the local law therefore prescribes, that no person shall dispose, by deed or by will, of more than a half, or a third, or a quarter of his immovable property; or, that he shall dispose only of a life estate in such property; such laws are of universal obligation, and no other or farther alienation thereof can be made[1]. It

---

obstringatur. Idemque habendum de Statutis, quæ circa habilitatem personarum, dispensando aliquid, disponunt. Gaill. Coras. Gomes. Quæ autem Statuta disponunt circa actus solemnitatem duntaxat, cum neque rem afficiant, neque personam actum celebrantis, sed ipsam solummodo dispositionem quæ, fit in loco Statuti, vel consuetudinis, rationi, et juri consentaneum est, ut ea vim suam exerant etiam ad bona alibi sita; quoniam actuum solemnia ad eorum spectant jurisdictionem, in quorum territorio celebrantur; et alias contra rationem juris, testato decedere volenti, plura testamenta essent condenda, aut quod absurdum est, plurium locorum consuetudines in uno testamento exquirere oporteret, actumque unum, atque individuum, qualis est testamenti, secundum diversa loca adjudicari. Ubi contraria scitè expedit, et prudenter temperat, novam quandam distinctionem Fachinei adde, quæ nos, lib. 2, Select. quest. C. 19. Plane si lex expressè testatores sequi jubeat jus loci, in quo bona sita sunt, aliud dicendum est. Talis est constitutio Principum Brabantiæ, emissa anno 1611, cujus meminerunt Burgundus, &c. Vinn. ad Inst. lib. 2, tit. 10, § 14, n. 5; 1 Boullenois, Observ. 21, pp. 426, 427. Gaill is equally explicit. Alibi statutum est, ut testamentum coram Notario et duobus testibus factum valeat. Quæsitum, utrùm tale testamentum ubique vires habeat, etiam extra territorium statuentium, ubi fortè major solennitas requiritur, vel jus Civile observantur. Conclusum quod sic; quia ex communi Doctor. opinione, statutum disponens citra solennitates testamenti, extendit se etiam extra territorium, ita ut hæres succedere possit in omnibus bonis, ubicunque sitis, et in universum jus testatoris; quia quoad solennitates attenditur consuetudo loci, in quo actus celebratur. Gaill, Pract. Observ. lib. 2, Observ. 123, p. 548. See Peckius, De Testam. Conjug. ch. 28, n. 9, p. 620, who holds a similar opinion. Fœlix, Conflit des Lois, Revue Etrang. et Fran. tom. 7, (1840), § 37, pp. 307—312; Ante, § 426—428.

[1] 1 Boullenois, Prin. Gén. 30, p. 8; Id. Observ. 16, p. 205; and 1 Froland, Mém. 156; Rodenburg, De Div. Stat. tit. 2, ch. 2, § 1; 2 Boullenois, App. p. 14; Post, § 479.

follows, that if the local law prohibits the alienation of certain kinds of immovable property, or takes from the owner the power of charging them with liens or with mortgages, that law will exclusively govern in every such case. D'Aguesseau fully assents to this doctrine, and says, that no one can be ignorant, that when the question is, what portion of immovable property may be devised, it is necessary invariably to follow the law of the place where the property is locally situate [1].

---

1 D'Aguesseau, Œuvres, tom. 4, pp. 637, 638, 4to. edit.—Mr. Burge on this subject says: "In a former part of this work it has been seen that the power to alienate immovable property by contract was a quality impressed on the property; that the law from which it was derived, or by which it was regulated, was a real law; and that the existence of this power and the validity of its exercise must be decided by the law of the country in which that property was situated. 'Rebus fertur lex, cum certam iisdem qualitatem imprimit, vel in alienando v. g. ut ne bona avita possint alienari, vel in acquirendo, v. g. ut dominium rei immobilis venditæ non aliter acquiratur, nisi facta fuerit judicialis resignatio.' The power of making the alienation by testament is no less qualitas rebus impressa, than that of making the alienation by contract. When therefore the question arises, whether the immovable property may be disposed of by testament, recourse must be had to the lex loci rei sitæ. That law must also decide, whether the full and unlimited power of disposition is enjoyed, or whether it is given under restriction. The validity of the testamentary disposition depends in the latter case on its conformity to that restriction, whether the restriction consist in limiting the extent or description of property, over which the power of disposition may be exercised, or the persons in whose favour the disposition is made, or in requiring that the testator should have survived a certain number of days after the execution of the act by which the disposition was made. The total or partial defect of the will on the ground that it did not institute heirs, or that it omitted to name the heirs, the disherison of the heirs, the grounds on which the disherison may be justified, are essentially connected with the power of disposing of immovable property by testament, and are therefore dependent on the law of its situs. Many of the restrictions on the power of disposing by testament have been considered by jurists expressly with reference to the operation of the law by which they were created. Rodenburg states the rule, 'Unde certissimâ usu ac observatione regula est, cum de rebus soli agitur, et diversa sunt diversarum possessionum loca et situs, spectari semper cujusque loci leges ac jura, ubi bona sita esse proponuntur, sic ut de talibus nulla cujusquam potestas sit, præter territorii leges.' He illustrates it by referring to a statute which prohibits a disposition of al-

§ 446. An illustration of the doctrine may be borrowed from the English jurisprudence, prohibiting alienations and

lodial property by testament. He considers such a statute a real law which renders inoperative any testamentary disposition of the property, in whatever place the testament is made. Ferriere has stated this doctrine: 'Si je legue un héritage propre, situé en coutume, que en défende la disposition, tel legs est nul, et ne peut être parfourni sur les biens situez en cette coutume, quoi qu'acquest, parce qu'à l'égard des choses, dont on peut disposer par derniere volonté, on considere la coutume où elles sont situées. Celui, quia son domicile en cette coutume peut instituer sa femme dans les biens, qu'il a dans le pais de droit écrit, comme il a été jugé par arrest du 14 Aoust, 1754 rapporté par Marion au de ses plaidoyez, ce qui doit être sans difficulté.' A testament made in a foreign country bequeathing heritable subjects situated in Scotland, is not sustained in that kingdom, though by the law of the country where the testament was made, heritage might have been settled by testament, because by the law of Scotland no heritable subject can be disposed of in that form. On this principle a Scot's personal bond taken to heirs and assignees, but 'secluding executors,' cannot be bequeathed by a foreign testament. But in all questions touching heritable subjects situate abroad, the foreign testament will be given effect to according to the lex loci. Dumoulin lays down the same doctrine respecting the restriction on the testamentary power over biens propries. 'Unde statutum loci inspicietur, sive persona sit subdita, sive non; ita si dicat, hæredia proventa ab unâ lineâ, redeant ad hæredes etiam remotiores lineæ, vel hæredes lineæ succedant in hærediis ab illâ lineâ proventis. Vel quod illi de lineâ non possunt testari de illis in totum, vel nisi ad certam partem. Hæc enim omnia et similia spectant ad caput statuti agentis in rem, et præcedentem conclusionem.' Again; the statute which prohibits a disposition to particular persons, or (which involves the same consequence) requires the disposition to be made in favour of certain persons, and therefore excludes all others, is a real law. 'Directè enim in rerum alienationem scripta hæc lex realis omnino dicenda est: nec enim statutum reale sit, an personale metiri oportet à ratione, quæ a conjugali forsan qualitate fuerit ducta, sed ab ipsâ re, quæ in prohibitione statuti ceciderit.' So also it has been held, that the law, which requires that the testator should have survived the execution of his testament, will control the disposition of property situated in the country where that law prevails, although the testament is made, or the testator domiciled in a place where no such law exists. If a testator, whose domicil and real estate were both in Normandy, made a will in some other place in which he had occasion to be present, but where the law did not require that the testator should survive forty days, it was held that the survivorship was essential to the validity of the testament, so far as it related to the real property in Normandy. If these questions arise on the power to dispose of movable property by testament, the law by which they are decided, is that of the domicil, 'pour les meubles, ils suivent la loi du domi-

devises of real estate in mortmain, or for charitable purposes. If an American citizen, owning lands in England, or a Scotchman owning lands in England, should alienate or devise such lands in violation of the mortmain acts, the instrument, whether *inter vivos* or testamentary, would be held void. And the same principle would apply to a trust created in personal property, to be invested in lands in England for the like purposes[1].

§ 447. Fourthly; in relation to the subject-matter, or what are to be deemed immovables. Here, as we have already seen, not only lands and houses, but servitudes and easements, and other charges on lands, as mortgages and rents, and trust estates, are deemed to be, in the sense of law, immovables, and governed by the *lex rei sitæ*[2]. But

---

cile, et il ne sauroit jamais y avoir de choc entre différentes coutumes, en sorte qu'il est assez inutile, quant aux meubles, d'agiter si le statut, qui permet de tester, ou qui le défend, est personnel, ou s'il est réel.' The rule is stated by Grotius, 'Ubi de formâ sive solemnitate testamenti agitur, respici locum conditi testamenti; ubi de personâ antestari possit, jus domicilii; ubi de rebus quæ testamento relinqui possunt, vel non, respici locum domicilii in mobilibus, in rebus soli situm loci.' 4 Burge, Comm. on Col. and For. Law, pt. 2, ch. 5, pp. 217—220.

[1] Attor. Gen. *v.* Mill, 3 Russell, R. 328; S. C. 2 Dow. & Clarke, 393.

[2] Ante, § 382; Poth. Cout. d'Orléans, ch. 1, § 2.—P. Voet puts on this point the very sensible distinction, that, whether rents are to be deemed personal or real, depends upon the question, whether they are charged on real property or not. "Vel enim talium redituum nomine sunt affecta immobilia, id est, super immobilibus sunt constituti, et immobilibus erunt adscribendi, adeoque statutum loci spectabitur; vel immobilia affecta non sunt illis reditibus, tumque mobilibus poterunt accenseri; atque adeo statutum loci personæ, cujus illi sunt reditus, inspici debebit." P. Voet, De Stat. § 9, ch. 1, n. 13, p. 259, (edit. 1715); Id. p. 313, (edit. 1661). And he includes among immovables all movables which are intentionally annexed permanently to the freehold. 'Nisi tamen perpetui usûs gratiâ ex destinatione patris-familias in uno loco manere debeant; quo casu immobilibus comparabuntur.' Id. n. 8, p. 255, (edit. 1715); Id. p. 309, (edit. 1661). Rodenburg speaking on this point says: De reditibus peculiaris esto consideratio. Et illi quidem, qui à re præstantur, vel cujus nomine constituta hypotheca est, collocantur à Doctoribus in immobilium numero, ita tamen, si perpetui sunt, secus si temporales, quà distinctione et Burgundus utitur. Sed vix est ut non utrobique idem sit dicendum: cùm enim ob id ipsum annumerentur

in addition to these, which may be deemed universally to partake of the nature of immovables, or (as the common law phrase is) to savor of the realty, all other things, though movable in their nature, which by the local law are deemed immovables, are, in like manner, governed by the local law. For every nation, having authority to prescribe rules for the disposition and arrangement of all the property within its own territory, may impress upon it any character which it shall choose; and no other nation can impugn or vary that character. So that the question, in all these cases, is not so much what are, or ought to be, deemed *ex suâ naturâ,* movables or not, as what are deemed so by the law of the place where they are situated. If they are there deemed part of the land, or annexed (as the common law would say) to the soil or freehold, they must be so treated in every place in which any controversy shall arise respecting their nature and character[1]. In other words, in order to ascertain what is immovable or real property or not, we must resort to the *lex loci rei*[2].

§ 448. Hitherto we have spoken of alienations and acquisitions made by the acts of the parties themselves. The question next arises, whether the same principles apply to estates and rights acquired by operation of law? It may be affirmed without hesitation that, independent of any contract, express or implied[3], no estate can be acquired by operation of law in any other manner, or to any other ex-

---

immobilibus, quod rei immobili per hypothecæ constitutionem innitantur, ponendi alioquid, vel si perpetui sint, in mobilium classe; nec hypothecæ immutetur natura, temporis aliqua ad redimendum præstitutione, nihilque ad summam rei intersit, certum an incertum luitionis sit tempus, consequens est dicere constitutos ad tempus reditus, æque atque perpetuos, immobilium nomine venire, maxime cùm per hypothecæ constitutionem, res ad summam debiti habeatur quasi alienata, quæ per solutionem redimitur. Rodenburg, De Div. Stat. tit. 2, c. 2, § 2; 2 Boullenois, App. p. 15. See also Burgundus, Tract. 2, n. 29, 30, pp. 77—79.

1 See Ersk. Institutes, b. 3, tit. 9, § 4; Ante, § 382.

2 Chapman *v.* Robertson, 6 Paige, R. 630.

3 See Livermore, Diss. § 88, 89, pp. 72, 73.

tent, or by any other means, than those prescribed by the *lex rei sitæ*. Thus, no estate in dowry, or tenancy by the curtesy, or inheritable estate, or interest in immovable property, can be acquired, except by such persons, and under such circumstances as the local law prescribes. Thus, if the law of a State where a man is domiciled at his death, should confer a title of dower on his wife, though she were an alien, that would not prevail in any other State where an alien is not dowable, and where the intestate owned real estate.

§ 449. Many questions upon this subject have arisen in the course of the discussions upon the matrimonial rights conferred by the *lex domicilii* over immovable property situate in foreign countries. In the different Italian States, and formerly in some of the provinces of France, which were governed by the Roman law, there existed various regulations with regard to dowry or dotal property, *lucrum dotis*. By the laws and customs of some places, the husband gained by survivorship the whole of the dotal effects; by others a third, by others a fourth, and by others nothing[1]. One of the questions which has been most elaborately discussed among foreign jurists, is, whether, in such a case, the law of the matrimonial domicil ought to govern the rights of the parties, as to immovable property in foreign countries, as it does in the matrimonial domicil[2]. It seems agreed on all sides, that where there is in the country *rei sitæ* a prohibitory law against any such dotal rights, and against any contract to create them, the law of the matrimonial domicil cannot prevail, if a different rule exists there[3]. But the question has been made, whether, in the absence of any such prohibitory law, or any express con-

---

1 Livermore, Diss. § 86, p. 71; 1 Domat, b. 1, tit. 9, § 1; Code Civil of France, art. 1540—1573; 2 Boullenois, 89, 90.

2 1 Boullenois, Observ. 29, pp. 732—818.

3 Livermore, Diss. § 85—91, pp. 71—75; 2 Boullenois, 89—92; Ante, § 176—180, 184, 188; P. Voet, de Stat. § 4, ch. 3, § 9, pp. 134, 135, (edit. 1715); 1 Froland, Mém. 62—64.

tract, the law of the matrimonial domicil ought not to prevail, so as to give the same dotal rights in every other place[1].

§ 450. Baldus held, that in such cases, the law or custom of the matrimonial domicil ought to govern, as to property, everywhere. *Consuetudines et statuta,* (said he), *vigentia in domicilio mariti, non curo, ubi res sint positæ, quæ in dotem datæ sunt*[2]. Dumoulin asserted the same doctrine, upon his favourite theory, that in all cases the law of the matrimonial domicil constituted a tacit contract between the parties[3]. There are many jurists who maintain the same opinion[4].

§ 451. Boullenois, as we have seen[5], does not admit the existence of any such tacit contracts as Dumoulin contends for, but he deems all laws real which respect property, making, however, a distinction in cases of laws which respect the rights of married persons in each other's property, which he treats as laws respecting the state or con-

---

1 Even Paul Voet, who is a strong advocate for the reality of statutes, admits that cases of express contract may govern, as to property locally situate in a foreign country. 'Si statuto in uno territorio contractus accesserit, seu partium conventio, etiam si in rem sit conceptum, sese extendit ad bona extra jurisdictionem statuentium sita; non ut afficiat immediatè ipsa bona, quam ipsam personam, quoad illa." P. Voet De Stat. § 4, c. 2, § 15, p. 127, (edit. 1715).

2 Livermore, Diss. § 87, pp. 71, 72; 1 Froland, Mém. 62.

3 Livermore, Diss. § 87, pp. 73, 74; 1 Froland. Mém. 61—63.—Dumoulin, in treating of the question, what law ought to prevail in fixing the rights of the husband, in regard to the dotal effects of his wife, in case of a change of domicil before the dissolution of the marriage, ultimately decides in favour of the law of the matrimonial domicil. His language is:—' Hinc infertur ad questionem quotidianam de contractu dotis et matrimonii, qui censetur fieri, non in loco, in quo contrahitur, sed in loco domicilii viri; et intelligitur, non de domicilio originis, sed de domicilio habitationis ipsius viri, de quo nemo dubitat, sed omnes consentiunt.' Molin. Oper. tom. 3, (edit. 1681), Comm. ad Cod. lib. 1, tit. 1, l. 1, Conclus. de Stat. p. 555; 1 Froland, Mém. 61; Id. 62; Ante, § 147.

4 Ante, § 145—156.

5 Ante, § 155; 1 Boullenois, Observ. 29, pp. 737—741.

dition of the person[1]. But he contends, that even if there be such a tacit contract, it does not render the laws of the place, in regard to dowry, personal; for, if that were so, (he adds), then the dowry of persons contracting at Paris would be the same in all other provinces in the realm as it is in Paris, which no one has ever yet contended for[2]. Rodenburg seems to hold, that where there is no matrimonial contract to govern the case, the law of the *situs* is to govern in respect to dowry, approving the doctrine of D'Argentré and Burgundus on this point[3]. D'Argentré says:—*Cum cautum est virum, uxore præmortua, dotem, dotisve partem lucrari; cujus loci statutum spectamus, viri, an uxoris, quod olim fuit, an quod nunc est? Nos rerum lucrandarum situm spectandum dicimus; et quid ea de re statuta singularia permittant, quid abnuant respiciendum*[4]. Burgundus boldly asserts the opinion, that the law *rei sitæ* must govern in all such cases as to immovable property[5]. *Nam si dotalitium rei immobilis in controversiam veniat, ea antiquitus obtinerit sententia, ut ad locum situs respicere oporteat; quæ cum usque ad nostra tempora, apud omnes, qui moribus reguntur, inviolabilis duret, non est committendum, ut illam dubiam faciam defensionis sollicitudine*[6]. Many jurists concur with them in opinion[7].

---

1 Ante, § 155; 1 Boullenois, Observ. 5, p. 121; Id. Observ. 29, pp. 737, 738.

2 1 Boullenois, Observ. 5, p. 121; 2 Boullenois, pp. 88—92. See Ante, § 155.

3 Rodenburg, De Div. Stat. ps. 2, tit. 2, c. 4, § 5; 2 Boullenois, App. p. 67.

4 D'Argent. ad Briton. Leg. Des Donations, art. 218, gloss. 6, n. 46, tom. 1, p. 664; Liverm. Dissert. § 92—99, pp. 75—78.

5 1 Boullenois, Observ. 5, p. 121.

6 Burgundus, Tract. 2, n. 10, pp. 63, 64; Liverm. Diss. § 104—114, pp. 80—87.

7 Ante, § 142, 148, 152, 153, 167, 168; 1 Froland, Mém. 66, 67, 156; Id. 316—323, 338, 341; 2 Froland, Mém. 816. Froland expresses himself in the following terms:—"La première (Régle) que le statut réel ne sort point de son territoire. Et delà vient que dans le cas, où il s'agit de succes-

§ 452. Similar questions have arisen in relation to the rights of community, and of mutual donations between husband and wife, whether they extended to immovable property situate elsewhere than in the matrimonial domicil or not; and the general result of the reasoning among foreign jurists turns very much upon the same considerations, which have been mentioned in relation to dowry. But this subject has been already discussed in another place, and it need not be here again examined[1].

§ 453. Similar questions have also arisen in considering the effect of mutual donations by married couples, when they are admitted by the law of the matrimonial domicil, but are unknown to or prohibited by the law of the place *rei sitæ*[2]. But they proceed upon the same general principles[3]. Cochin says, that it is not the law of the place where an act is done which determines its effect. If (says he) property is situate in a place whose laws prohibit donations *inter vivos*, or reduce them to a particular portion, no one supposes the donation to be less a nullity, or less subject to reduction, because the act is done in a place where no such prohibition exists[4].

---

sions, de la manière de les partager, de la quotité dei biens, dont il peut disposer entre vifs ou par testament, d'aliénation d'immeubles, de douaire de femme ou d'enfans, de légitime, retrait lignager, féodal ou conventionnel, de droit de puissance paternelle, de droit de viduité, et autres choses semblables, il faut s'attacher aux coutumes des lieux, où les fonds sont situez. 1 Froland, Mém. 156; Id. 49, 60—81.

[1] See Ante, § 143—158, 160—170, 174—177; 1 Froland, Mém. 66—69; Id. 177, pt. 2, ch. 1, per tot.; Cochin, Œuvres, tom. 5, p. 80, 4to edit.; Merlin, Répertoire, Testament, § 1, n. 5, art. 1, pp. 309, 310. We have already seen Boullenois's view of this subject, ante, § 155. See also ante, § 451.

[2] Ante, § 143—159.

[3] Liverm. Diss. § 181, 182, pp. 114, 115; 1 Voet, ad Pand. lib. 1, tit. 4, n. 3, p. 39; 2 Froland, Mém. ch. 18, p. 840, &c., ch. 19, p. 904; Rodenburg, De Div. Stat. tit. 2, c. 5; 2 Boullenois, App. pp. 33, 34; 1 Boullenois, 660, 661, 663; Id. Observ. 29, p. 767; 2 Boullenois, Observ. 44, pp. 430—432; Ante, § 143—159.

[4] Cochin, Œuvres, tom. 5, p. 697, 4to edit.

§ 454. The doctrine of the common law seems uniformly to be, that in all cases of this sort, touching rights in immovable property, the law of the place *rei sitæ* is to govern[1]. Hence, if persons who are married in Louisiana, where the law of community exists, own immovable property in Massachusetts, where such community is unknown, upon the death of the husband, the wife would take her dower only in the immovable property of her husband, and the husband, upon the death of the wife, would take, as tenant by the curtesy only, in the immovable property of his wife.

§ 455. Another class of cases illustrating this subject, may be derived from the known rights of fathers over the property of their children, according to the provisions of the Roman law, and the customary law of countries deriving their jurisprudence from the Roman law[2]. By the ancient Roman law all the sons were in subjection to the authority of the father, until they were emancipated by the father, or by some other mode known to that law. During such subjection they were incapable of acquiring any property for themselves by succession, or donation, or purchase, or otherwise; and whatever they thus acquired belonged of right to their father, saving only what was called the son's *peculium*, which consisted of property acquired by his service in the army, or by his skill at the bar, or in the exercise of some public employment[3]. This sort of property was therefore known by the name of *peculium castrense*, when it was acquired in war; and of *peculium quasi castrense*, when it was acquired in any other manner[4]. In the time of Justinian

---

[1] Ante, § 157—159, 174—179, 186, 187.

[2] Ante, § 139.

[3] 1 Domat, Civ. Law, Prelim. b. 2, tit. 2, § 2, p. 24, note; Id. b. 2, tit. 2, § 2, pp. 667—670, n. 1—3; Bouhier, Cout. de Bourg. ch. 16, § 8—12, p. 295; 1 Brown, Civ. Law, pp. 122, 123; 2 Froland, Mém. 806—813; 2 Henrys, Œuvres, par Bretonnier, lib. 4, Quest. 127, p. 772, &c., 717; Merlin, Répertoire, Puissance Paternelle, § 7, p. 142.

[4] 1 Domat, b. 2, § 2, p. 668.

the law was altered, and the father was no longer entitled to the property acquired by his unemancipated son; but he was entitled to the usufruct or profits thereof during his life, The rule thus modified, has found its way sometimes with and sometimes without modifications, into the jurisprudence of many provinces and states of continental Europe[1].

§ 456. Under this aspect of the law with regard to the paternal power, the question has often been discussed among foreign jurists, whether the laws respecting the paternal power are personal or real; or, in other words, whether the rights of the father allowed and secured by the law of the place of his domicil, extend to the immovable property of his sons, situate in other countries, whose jurisprudence confers no such paternal rights[2].

§ 457. Bretonnier holds the doctrine, that all laws respecting the paternal power are personal, and consequently have effect upon all real property of their children, where-ever it is situate, and especially as to the profits and usufruct of it; because the latter partake of the nature of movables. After stating the question, whether fathers, domiciled in a country using the Roman law (*dans le pays de Droit écrit*), whose sons have real property in another country, having a different customary law, are entitled to the profits of the latter; that is to say, whether the paternal power extends everywhere; he proceeds to say: *Cette question ne me semble pas susceptible d'une grande difficulté; parceque la puissance paternelle est un droit personnel, et par conséquent il ne peut être borné par aucun territoire; car c'est une maxime certaine même dans les pays de coutume, que les statuts personnels sont universels, et produisent leur effet partout. D'ailleurs, les fruits sont des choses mobiliaires. Or, constat inter omnes,*

---

[1] 1 Domat, b. 2, § 2, p. 668; Civil Code of France, art. 384—387; 1 Froland, Mém. 69; 2 Froland, Mém. ch. 17, p. 789; Bouhier, Cout. de Bourg. ch. 16, p. 294.

[2] 2 Froland, Mém. 808, 813—829.

que les meubles suivent les personnes, et se réglent suivant la coutume du domicile[1].

§ 458. Hertius seems to hold a like doctrine, as to the personality of such laws; and puts a question, whether a daughter, who is emancipated by marriage, may afterwards make a testament of property situate elsewhere; and whether the father would have a right to the usufruct of her property, situate in a place where she would be deemed unemancipated. He answers: *Questio hic duplex est; verum ex eodem principio decidenda. Jus nempe datum est personæ, quod etiam per consequentiam in bona alterius civitatis, licet immobilia, operatur*[2]. Yet Hertius, in another place, holds that an unemancipated son (*filius-familias*) who by the law of his domicil may make a testament, cannot make a testament of property situate in a foreign country. *Nam statutum est in rem conceptum, et conditio filii-familiæ non est in dispositione*[3]. *Hinc juxta regulam Puduensis filius-familias de bonis alibi sitis testari non poterit*[4]. The ground of this opinion probably is, that the general incapacity is admitted to exist by the law of the domicil, and the special exception is local and real[5]. In this opinion Hertius admits that he differs from Huberus, whom he asserts to hold the opinion, that if a Batavian, who is an unemancipated son, but has authority to make a testament in Holland, makes a testament in Holland of immovable property situate in Friezeland, that testament will be valid in Friezeland, although in Friezeland the son, however rich and of whatever age, cannot make any testament of his property[6].

---

1 Henrys, Œuvres, par Bretonnier, tom. 2, p. 720. See 2 Boullenois, Observ. 32, pp. 46, 47.

2 1 Hertii Opera, De Collis. Leg. § 4, n. 17, p. 130, (edit. 1737); Id. p. 185, (edit. 1716).

3 1 Hertii Opera, De Collis. Leg. § 4, n. 22, p. 133, (edit. 1737); Id. p. 188, (edit. 1716).

4 Ibid.

5 Merlin, Répertoire, Testament, § 1. n. 5, art. 1, p. 310.

6 Hertii Opera, De Collis. Leg. § 4, n. 22, (edit. 1737); Id. p. 188, (edit. 1716).

§ 459. Bouhier maintains with earnestness and ability, that the paternal power is altogether personal, and that it extends to the immovable property of the unemancipated child, situate in a foreign country, where the like law, as to the paternal authority, does not exist[1]. And he is supported by the opinion of Le Brun, D'Argentré, and others[2].

§ 460. On the other hand, Froland maintains that the paternal power in regard to the immovable property of a child is purely real. *Ce statut est constamment réel; il ne s'étend point sur les biens situez dans une coutume, qui n'a pas disposition pareille*[3]. Boullenois, while he admits that the laws, which give the paternal power, are personal, so far as they respect the state or condition of the parties, contends at the same time, that, so far as those laws gave rights over immovable property, they are real, and are to be governed by the law of the place where the property is situate[4]. And he proceeds to vindicate his opinion in a most elaborate manner[5].

§ 461. D'Aguesseau says; "That which characterizes a real statute, and distinguishes it essentially from a personal statute, is not that it relates to certain personal qualities, or to certain personal circumstances, or to certain personal events; otherwise we should be compelled to say, that all laws which concern the paternal power, the right of guardianship, the right of widowhood (*le droit de viduité*), and the prohibition of donations between married persons, are all personal laws. And accordingly it is beyond doubt, that in our jurisprudence all these laws are real, which are

---

1 Bouhier, Cout. de Bourg. ch. 24, § 37—87, pp. 468—475.

2 Id. ch. 24, § 41, p. 468; Le Brun, De la Communauté, lib. 1, ch. 2, n. 8; D'Argent. De Briton. Leg. Des. Donations, art. 218, Gloss. 6, n. 7, tom. 1, p. 648.

3 1 Froland, Mém. 69; Id. 39, 60, 156; 2 Froland, Mém. ch. 17, p. 789—819.

4 1 Boullenois, Observ. 4, p. 68; 2 Boullenois, Observ. 32, pp. 30—33: Id. pp. 39—47; Boullenois, Quest. Mixtes Quest. 20, p. 406.

5 Ibid.

to be governed, not according to the law of the domicil, but according to that of the place where the property is situate[1]."

§ 462. Merlin has examined the same subject in a formal discussion: and he endeavours to hold a middle course between the opinions of Bouhier and Boullenois, agreeing with the latter, that the usufruct arising under the paternal power is a real right, and governed by the *lex rei sitæ*, and at the same time holding with Bouhier, that the father cannot possess the right, unless by the law of the place of his domicil the paternal power is recognised. He then lays down three principles, which he supposes will remove all the difficulties upon this thorny subject. (1.) The law which subjects the son to the power of his father, has no need of the aid (*ministére*) of man for its execution; and it is therefore personal from the very nature of its object. (2.) The law which declares an unemancipated son (*un fils de famille*) incapable of alienating his immovable property without the authority of his father is personal, although its object is real; because it determines the state of the person in regard to what he can and cannot do. (3.) The law, which gives to a father the usufruct of the property of his son, ought to be real; because its object is real, and it makes no regulation concerning the capacity or incapacity of the unemancipated son to do anything[2]. In another

---

1 D'Aguesseau Œuvres, tom. 4, pp. 660, 4to edit.

2 Merlin, Répertoire, Puissance Paternelle, § 7, pp. 142, 144, (edit, 1827). —The reasoning of Merlin on this subject is marked with uncommon clearness and force of statement; and I have, therefore, thought that an extract from it might not be unacceptable to the reader. "Or, que trouvons-nous dans la puissance paternelle? Trois choses. Premièrement, elle détermine l'état des enfans; et à cet égard, elle forme un statut personnel, qui suit les enfans partout. Ainsi, une mère, domiciliée en Hainaut, conserve sous sa puissance les enfans, qu'elle a eus dans cette province, lors même que le hasard ou certaines circonstances les ont fait passer dans une autre coutume, qui n'accorde pas les mêmes droits aux femmes qu'aux hommes sur la personne de leurs enfans. En second lieu, la puissance paternelle imprime dans les enfans, qui y sont assujetis, une incapacité de faire certains actes: comme

place he holds, that a law which prohibits an unemancipated son to make a testament is personal; but he, at the same

---

cette incapacité est la suite de leur état, elle les suit également partout et influe sur tous leurs biens, quelle qu'en soit la situation. Ainsi, un fils de famille, né dans une coutume, où il ne peut pas contracter sans l'autorité de son père, ne peut vendre de lui-même les biens, qu'il possède dans une autre coutume, qui n'admet pas la puissance paternelle; et reciproquement un fils de famille domicilié dans une coutume, qui n'admet pas la puissance paternelle, peut, sans l'autorisation de son père, aliéner les biens qu'il possède dans une autre coutume, qui n'admet pas la puissance paternelle, peut, sans l'autorisation de son père, aliéner les biens qu'il possède dans les pays de droit écrit. Par la même raison, un fils né à Senlis, où la coutume proscrit formellement toute puissance paternelle, quoique nourri et entretenu par son père, peut acquérir pour lui-même en Hainaut et dans les pays de droit écrit. Et reciproquement, un fils de famille, né en Hainaut, ou dans un pays de droit écrit, ne peut s'approprier les biens, qu'il acquiert dans la coutume de Senlis, lorsque ses acquisitions ne réunissent pas toutes les circonstances requises, pour qu'elles tombent dans le pécule castrense, quasi-castrense, ou adventice, Troisièmement, la puissance paternelle donne au père, dans les pays de droit écrit et dans quelques coutumes, la jouissance des biens de ses enfans. Cette jouissance est, à la vérité, un accessoire de la puissance paternelle ; mais elle de forme dans les enfans ni capacité ni incapacité : le statut, qui la défére, n'a pas besoin, pour son exécution, du ministére de l'homme ; il agit seul ; l'homme n'a rien à faire. On ne peut donc pas appliquer ici les raisons, qui ont déterminé l'espéce de concordat tacite, dont nous avons parlé. Quel inconvénient y a-t-il à restreindre cette jouissance au territoire des lois ou coutumes, qui l'accordent? Quoi! parcequ'un père jouira des biens, que ses enfans ont dans une province, et qu'il ne jouira pas de ceux, qu'ils ont dans une autre, l'ordre public serait troublé, le commerce serait dérangé! Non. Il n'y a pas en cela plus de trouble ni plus de confusion, qu'à succéder à un défunt dans une coutume, et de ne pas lui succéder dans une autre. Il est donc constant que le systême du président Bouhier ne peut pas se soutenir, et que le statut, qui donne à un père l'usufruit des biens des enfans, qu'il a sous sa puissance, n'est pas personnel. Mais est-il purement réel, comme le prétend Boullenois, ou bien est-il personnel réel, c'est-à-dire, faut-il, pour qu'il produise son effet, que le père soit domicilié dans une coutume, qui admet la puissance paternelle? C'est la difficulté, qui nous reste à résoudre. Le principal peut subsister sans les accessoires: mais les accessoires ne peuvent jamais subsister sans le principal. Ce principe est aussi clair, qu'indubitable, et il nous conduit droit à la décision de notre question. Ainsi, la puissance paternelle peut avoir lieu sans l'usufruit dont nous parlons ici. La coutume de Douai nous en fournit un exemple, puisqu'elle admet l'une chap. 7, art. 2, et qu'elle exclut l'autre par son silence,

time, asserts, that this will not prevent him from making a testament of movable property in other countries where it is permitted; because this case is a mere exception from his general incapacity, and also falls within the rule, that in a conflict of real and personal laws, the latter must yield[1].

§ 463. Without going farther into an examination of the opinions of foreign jurists upon this subject, it is sufficiently obvious what difficulties they are compelled to encounter at almost every step, in order to carry into effect their favourite system of the division of laws into real and personal. The common law has avoided all these difficulties by a simple and uniform test. It declares that the law of the *situs* shall exclusively govern in regard to all rights, interests, and titles in and to immovable property. Of course it cuts down all attempts to introduce all foreign laws, whether they respect persons or things, or give or withhold the capacity to acquire or to dispose of immovable property[2].

§ 463 *a*. This subject of the nature and extent of the paternal power and rights, came recently under consideration in England, in a case somewhat complicated in its circumstances, and touching personal estate only. It may be

---

comme l'a décidé le parlement de Flandre, par un arrêt du 27 Janvier 1739, rendu au rapport de M. de Casteele de La Briarde, en faveur du Marquis de Sin, contre les sieurs et demoiselles d'Aoust. Mais l'usufruit ne peut avoir lieu sans la puissance paternelle, dont il n'est que l'accessoire. Un père ne peut donc en jouir, s'il n'a ses enfans sous sa puissance, et par conséquent s'il n'est domicilié dans une coutume, qui admet la puissance paternelle. Un père, qui émanciperait son fils au moment même de sa naissance, n'aurait certainement aucun droit à l'usufruit des biens que cet enfant acquerrait ensuite, soit dans la coutume du domicile qu'il avait alors, soit dans toute autre province. Or, ce que ce père est supposé faire, la loi le fait ellemême dans les coutumes qui n'admettent pas la puissance paternelle; elle émancipe cet enfant dès qu'il voit le jour, et conséquemment elle soustrait les biens, qu'il aura dans la suite, à l'usufruit que son père en aurait en sans cette émancipation." Merlin, Répertoire, Puissance, Paternelle, § 7, pp. 145, 146, (edit. 1827).

1 Merlin, Répertoire, Testament, § 1, n. 5, art. 1, p. 310.

2 See Brodie *v.* Barry, 2 Ves. and Beames, R. 127.

briefly stated as follows: A marriage took place in Holland between the parties. At the time of the marriage a marriage contract was there executed in the Dutch form, making certain provisions, and among other things, provision for the distribution of the wife's property in the event of her husband's surviving her. They afterwards removed to and became domiciled in England, and had children born there. The wife died, and by her death the children became entitled, under a compromise in Holland, to one-fourth of certain property of the wife in the public funds. By the French Code, which is the law of Holland also, when children are under the age of eighteen years, their surviving parent has the enjoyment of their property until they attain that age; and the father insisted, that as the children were under that age, and the marriage contract and compromise under which they took the one-fourth, were both made in Holland, the children must take it, subject to his paternal rights by the law of Holland. The Vice-Chancellor held, that the father was not so entitled. On that occasion the learned Judge said: "By the Code Napoleon, which is the law of Holland as well as of France, when children are under the age of eighteen, their surviving parent has the enjoyment of their property until they attain that age. But that is nothing more than a mere local right, given to the surviving parent by the law of a particular country, so long as the children remain subject to that law: and, as soon as the children are in a country where that law is not in force, their rights must be determined by the law of the country where they happen to be. These children were never subject to the law of Holland; they were both born in this country, and have resided here ever since. The consequence is, that this judicial decree has adjudged certain property to belong to two British-born subjects domiciled in this country; and so long as they are domiciled in this country, their personal property must be administered according to the law of this country. The claim of their father does not arise by virtue of the contract, but solely by the local law of the country where he was residing at the time of his marriage; and, therefore, this property must be considered just as if it had been an English legacy given to the children: and all that the father is entitled to is, the usual reference to the Master to inquire what allowance ought to be made to him for the past and future maintenance of his children[1]."

---

[1] Gambier *v.* Gambier, 7 Sim. R. 263, 270.

CHAPTER XI.

WILLS AND TESTAMENTS.

§ 464. Having taken these general views of the operation of foreign law in regard to movable property and immovable property, and ascertained that the general principle, at least in the common law, adopted in relation to the former is, that it is governed by the law of the domicil of the owner, and in relation to the latter, that it is governed by the law of the place where it is locally situate, we now come to make a more immediate application of these principles to two of the most important classes of cases arising constantly and uniformly, in all civilized human societies. One is, the right of a person, by an act or instrument, to dispose of his property after his death; the other is the right of succession to the same property, in case no such postmortuary disposition is made of it by the owner. The former involves the right to make last wills and testaments; and the latter the title of descent and the distribution of property *ab intestato*. We shall accordingly in this and the succeeding chapter exclusively discuss the subject of foreign law in relation to testaments, and to successions, and distributions of movable and immovable property.

§ 465. And first, in relation to testaments of movable property[1]. So far as respects the capacity or incapacity of a testator to make a will of personal or movable property, we have already had occasion to consider the subject in another place. The result of that examination was, that the law of the actual domicil of the party, at the time

---

[1] See 4 Burge, Comm. on Col. and For. Law, pt. 2, ch. 12, p. 579—581; Post, § 466, 467.

of the making of his will or testament, was to govern as to that capacity or incapacity[1]. We may therefore proceed to the consideration of the forms and solemnities by which wills of personal estates are to be governed. And here it may be stated now to be a well settled principle in the English law, that a will of personal or movable property, regularly made according to the forms and solemnities required by the law of the testator's domicil, is sufficient to pass his personal or movable property in every other country in which it is situated. But this doctrine, although now very firmly established, was, for a great length of time, much agitated and discussed in Westminster Hall[2]. On one occasion, Lord Loughborough laid down the doctrine, that, with respect to the disposition of movable property, and with respect to the transmission of it, either by succession or by the act of the party, it follows the law of the person[3]. The owner in any country may dispose of his personal property. On another occasion, Lord Thurlow asserted the same doctrine as to succession to personal property, and by implication as to wills[4]. Lord Ellenborough put it as clear in his day. He observed: "It is every day's experience to recognise the law of foreign countries as binding on personal property; as in the sale of ships, condemned as prize by the sentences of foreign courts; the succession to personal property by will,

---

1 Ante, § 52—62, § 64—78, § 101—106, § 368, 430—434. See also 2 Boullenois, App. p. 38; 4 Burge, Comm. on Col. and For. Law, pt. 2, ch. 12, p. 577—579.

2 See Brodie *v.* Barry, 2 Ves. & Beames, R. 127, 131; Bempde *v.* Johnstone, 3 Ves. R. 192, 200; Price *v.* Dewhurst, 8 Sim. R. 279, 299, 300; Moore *v.* Budd, 4 Hagg. Eccles. R. 346, 354; Robertson on Successions, p. 99, 191, 214, 215, 285, 290, 297; The case of the Goods of Marshall Bennett, before Sir H. Jenner, July, 1840, London Monthly Law Magazine, Sept. 1840, p. 264.

3 Sill *v.* Worswick, 1 H. Black. 690. See also Ommaney *v.* Bingham, cited 5 Ves. 757; 3 Hagg. Eccles. R. 414, note; Stanley *v.* Barnes, 3 Hagg. Eccles. R. 373; Hogg *v.* Lashley, 3 Hagg. Eccles. R. 415, note.

4 Bruce *v.* Bruce, 2 Bos. & Pull. 229, note.

or intestacy of the subjects of foreign countries[1]." But antecedently to this period many learned doubts and discussions had existed on the subject[2]. In the Duchess of Kingston's case, a will of personal property executed in France, but not in conformity to the laws of that country, was admitted to probate in the Ecclesiastical Courts of England in 1791, it being duly executed according to the English forms, although she was domiciled in France at the time of making the will, and also at the time of her death[3].

§ 466. Even at so late a period as 1823, Sir John Nicholl doubted whether a will of personal property, made abroad, by an English subject domiciled abroad, ought to be held valid, unless it was executed in conformity to the forms prescribed by the English law. The ground of his doubt was, whether an English subject was entitled to throw off his country (*exuere patriam*) so far as to select a foreign domicil in complete derogation of his native domicil, and thus to render his property in England distributable by succession or testament according to the foreign law. He took a distinction between testacy and intestacy, (assuming, for the sake of argument, that in the latter case the foreign law might prevail), thinking that cases of testacy might be governed by very different considerations from those of intestacy. Even if a will executed according to the law of the place of the testator's domicil, would in such a case be valid, he contended, that it by no means followed universally, and upon principle, that a will to be valid must strictly conform to that law which would have regulated the succession to the testator's property, if he had died intestate. And, therefore, he held, that a

---

1 Potter *v.* Brown, 5 East, R. 130.

2 See Bempde *v.* Johnstone, 3 Ves. 198, 200; Somerville *v.* Somerville, 5 Ves. 750; Balfour *v.* Scott, 6 Brown, Parl. Cases, 550, Tomlin's edit.; S. C. 2 Addams, Eccles. R. 15, note.

3 See Curling *v.* Thornton, 2 Addams, Eccles. R. 21. See 4 Burge, Comm. on Col. and For. Law, pt. 2, ch. 12, p. 588—590.

will of personal property, made by a British subject in France, according to the forms of the English law, was good as to such property situate in England. He admitted, that as to British subjects domiciled in any part of the United Kingdom, the law of their domicil must govern in regard to successions and wills; and so, the like law must govern in regard to successions and wills of foreigners resident abroad. The restriction which he sought to establish, was, that a British subject could not, by a foreign domicil, defeat the operation of the law of his own country, as to personal property situate in the latter[1].

§ 467. To this opinion the same learned judge firmly adhered in a still later case. But, upon an appeal, the decision was overturned by the High Court of Delegates, and the doctrine fully established, that the law of the actual foreign domicil of a British subject is exclusively to govern in relation to his testament of personal property, as it would in the case of a mere foreigner[2]. This case is the stronger, because it was the case of a will and several codicils, made according to the law of Portugal, and also of several codicils made not according to the law of Portugal, where the testator was domiciled. The will and codicils executed according to the Portuguese law were held valid; the others were held invalid[3].

§ 468. The same doctrine is now as firmly established in America. The earliest case in which it was directly in judgment, was argued in the Supreme Court of Pennsylvania, in 1808[4]; and this case may be truly said to have led the way to the positive adjudication of this important and difficult doctrine. There, a foreign testator, domiciled abroad, had made a will of his personal estate, invalid ac-

---

[1] Curling *v.* Thornton, 2 Addams, Eccles. R. p. 6, 10—25; S. C. 8 Sim. R. pp. 310, 311.

[2] Stanley *v.* Barnes, 3 Hagg. Eccles. R. p. 373—465; Moore *v.* Davell, 4 Hagg. Eccles. R. 346, 354.

[3] Ibid.

[4] Desesbats *v.* Berquiers, 1 Binney, R. 336.

cording to the law of his domicil, but valid according to the law of Pennsylvania; and the question was, whether it was competent and valid to pass personal property situate in Pennsylvania. The Court decided that it was not; and asserted the general doctrine, that a will of personal estate must, in order to pass the property, be executed according to the law of the place of the testator's domicil at the time of his death. If void by that law, it is a nullity everywhere, although it is executed with the formalities required by the law of the place where the personal property is locally situate. The Court asserted, that in this respect there was no difference between cases of succession by testament, and by intestacy[1]. The same doctrine has been since repeatedly recognised by other American courts, and may now be deemed as of universal authority here[2].

§ 469. In Scotland the doctrine was formerly involved in many doubts. By the law of Scotland, illegitimate persons are not deemed capable of making a will; and hence a will of movables in Scotland, made by such a person domiciled in England, was formerly held in Scotland to be invalid[3]. In like manner, a nuncupative will, being in Scotland invalid, was formerly held invalid to pass movables in Scotland, although the will was made in England (where such a will is valid) by a person domiciled there[4]. But the general doctrine is now the same in Scotland as in England. The law of the domicil universally prevails as to successions and wills of movables in other countries[5].

---

1 Desesbats *v.* Berquiers, 1 Binn. R. 336; S. P. Moore *v.* Budd, 4 Hagg. Eccles. R. 346, 354.

2 See Holmes *v.* Remsen, 4 John. Ch. R. 460, 469; Harvey *v.* Richards, 1 Mason, R. 381, and cases cited, p. 408, note; Dixon's Ex'ors. *v.* Ramsay's Ex'ors. 3 Cranch, R. 319; De Sobry *v.* De Laistre, 2 Harr. & John. R. 193, 224; Armstrong *v.* Lear, 12 Wheat. R. 169; Harrison *v.* Nixon, 9 Peters, R. 483, 504, 505.

3 Ersk. Inst. b. 3, tit. 2, § 41, p. 515; 2 Kaims, Equity, b. 3, ch. 8, § 3.

4 2 Kaims, Equity, b. 3, ch. 8, § 3, p. 345.

5 See Bempde *v.* Johnstone, 3 Ves. 198, 201; Somerville *v.* Somerville,

§ 470. Foreign jurists are as generally agreed as to the doctrine in regard to movables, upon the ground maintained by all of them, that *mobilia sequuntur personam*[1]. John Voet lays down the rule in the following terms: *In successionibus, testandi facultate, contractibus, aliisque, mobilia, ubicunque sita, regi debere domicilii jure, non vero legibus loci illius, in quo naturaliter sunt constituta*[2]. He adds: *Ibique D.D. (Doctores) mobilium tamen ratione in dispositionibus testamentariis, dum quæritur, an illæ in universum permittendæ sint, nec ne, uti et ab intestato successionibus, donationibus inter conjuges vetitis permissisve, et aliis similibus, de juris rigore communi quasi gentium omnium consensu laxatum est; sic ut ex comitate profecta regula praxi universali invaluerit, mobilia in dubio regi lege loci, in quo eorum dominus domicilium fovet, ubicunque illa vere exstiterint*[3].

§ 471. Vattel has spoken in terms admitting of more question, as to the extent of their meaning. After observing, that a foreigner in a foreign country has, by natural right, the liberty of making a will, he remarks: "As to the form or solemnities appointed to settle the validity of a will, it appears that the testator ought to observe those which are established in the country where he makes it,

---

5 Ves. R. 757; Brodie *v.* Barry, 2 Ves. & Beames, 127, 131, and the cases cited, Ante, § 465; Ersk. Inst. b. 3, tit. 2, § 40, 41; 2 Kaims, Equity, ch. 8, § 3.

1 See 1 Boullenois, Observ. 28, pp. 696—721; Cochin, Œuvres, tom. 5, p. 85, 4to edit.; Ante, § 362, 362 *a*, 399; 4 Burge, Comm. on Col. and For. Law, pt. 2, ch. 12, pp. 579, 580; Fœlix, Conflit des Lois, Revue Etrang. et Fran. tom. 7, (1840), § 40—50, pp. 346—360; Post, § 481.

2 J. Voet, Ad Pand. lib. 1, tit. 4, p. 2, § 11, p. 44.

3 J. Voet, Ad Pand. lib. 1, tit. 4, p. 2, § 12, p. 45. See also J. Voet, Ad Pand. lib. 28, tit. 1, n. 13, 15, 44; 4 Burge, Comm. on Col. and For. Law, pt. 2, ch. 12, pp. 579, 580, 590; P. Voet, De Stat. § 9, c. 1, n. 8, p. 255, (edit. 1715); Id. p. 309, (edit. 1661); Burgundus, Tract. 1, n. 36; Id. Tract. 6, n. 1—3; Fœlix, Conflit des Lois, Revue Etrang. et Fran. tom. 7, (1840), § 24—27, pp. 204—216; Id. § 32, 33, pp. 221—227; Ante, § 381 note, § 444 *a*; 4 Burge, Comm. on Col. and For. Law, pt. 2, ch. 5, pp. 217, 218; Id. ch. 12, pp. 576—580; Post, § 479; Sand. Decis. Frisic. lib. 4, tit. 1, Defin. 14, pp. 142, 143.

unless it be otherwise ordained by the laws of the State of which he is a member; in which case he will be obliged to observe the forms which they prescribe, if he would validly dispose of the property which he possesses in his own country. The foreign testator cannot dispose of his property, movable or immovable, which he possesses in his own country, otherwise than in a manner conformable to the laws of that country. But as to movable property, specie, and other effects which he possesses elsewhere, which he has with him, or which follow his person, we ought to distinguish between the local laws, whose effect cannot extend beyond the territory, and those laws which peculiarly affect the character of citizens. The foreigner remaining a citizen of his own country, is still bound by those last-mentioned laws, wherever he happens to be, and is obliged to conform to them in the disposal of his personal property, and all his movables whatsoever. The laws of this kind, made in the country where he resides at the time, but of which he is not a citizen, are not obligatory with respect to him. Thus, a man who makes his will, and dies in a foreign country, cannot deprive his widow of the part of his movable effects assigned to that widow by the laws of his own country. A Genevan, obliged by the laws of his country to leave a portion of his personal property to his brothers or cousins, if they are his next heirs, cannot deprive them of it by making his will in a foreign country while he continues a citizen of Geneva. But a foreigner, dying at Geneva, is not obliged in this respect to conform to the laws of the Republic. The case is quite otherwise in respect to local laws. They regulate what may be done in the territory, and do not extend beyond it. The testator is no longer subject to them when he is out of the territory, and they do not affect that part of his property which is also out of it. The foreigner is obliged to observe those laws in the country where he makes his will, with respect to the goods he possesses there[1]."

[1] Vattel, b. 2, ch. 8, § 111. See Post, § 479.

§ 472. Vattel is in this passage principally considering the effect of the law of a foreign country upon a foreigner who is resident there. And there can be no doubt that every country may by its laws prescribe whatever rules it may please, as to the disposition of the movable property of its citizens, either *inter vivos* or testamentary. But it is equally clear, that such rules are of no obligation as to movable property in any other country, and can be in force there only by the comity of nations. So that a will of such movable property, made in the foreign country where he is domiciled, and according to its laws, will be held valid, whatever may be the validity of such a will in the country to which the testator owes his allegiance by birth. But the discussion in which we are engaged, does not respect the effect of any local prohibitory laws over movable property within the particular territory, but the general principles which regulate the disposition of it, when no such prohibitory laws exist. And here, by the general consent of foreign jurists, the law of the domicil of the testator governs as to transfers *inter vivos* and testamentary[1].

§ 473. But it may be asked, what will be the effect of a change of domicil after a will or testament is made of personal or movable property, if it is valid by the law of the place where the party was domiciled when it was made, and not valid by the law of his domicil at the time of his death? The terms in which the general rule is laid down, would seem sufficiently to establish the principle, that in such a

---

1 See Ante, § 465; Hertii Opera, De Collis. Leg. § 4, n. 6, p. 112, (edit. 1737); Id. p. 174, (edit. 1710); Pothier, Cout. d'Orléans, ch. 1, § 2, n. 24; J. Voet, Ad Pand. tom. 2, lib. 38, tit. 17, § 34; Ante, § 470.—Very difficult questions, however, may still arise, as to what is to be deemed the real domicil of a party who is a native of one country, and who has yet been long resident in another. The quo animo, with which such residence has been originally taken, or subsequently upheld, often becomes a very important element in the decision. See Ante, § 44, 49; Attor.-Gen. *v.* Dunn, 6 Mees. & Welsb. 511; De Bonneval *v.* De Bonneval, 1 Curties, Eccl. R. 856; Post, § 481, note; Munro *v.* Munro, 1 Rob. R. (House of Lords) p. 493.

case the will or testament is void; for it is the law of his actual domicil at the time of his death, and not the law of his domicil at the time of making his will or testament of personal property which is to govern[1]. This doctrine is very fully recognised and laid down by John Voet. *Tamen, si quis habitans in loco, in quo minor annorum numerus in testatore requiritur, veluti in Hollandiâ, ibidem anno decimo quinto testamentum fecerit, deinde vero domicilium alio transtulerit, ubi necdum per ætatem testari licet, veluti Ultrajectum, ubi plena pubertas in masculo testatore exigitur, testamentum ejus quantum ad mobilia per talem migrationem irritum efficitur. Idemque eveniet, si Hollandus uxorem heredem instituerit, (quod ibi licitum), deinde vero ad aliam migret regionem, ibique domicilium figat, ubi gratificatio inter conjuges ne supremo quidem elogio permissa est; nam et hoc in casu mobilium intuitu in irritum deducitur voluntas ejus; cum mobilia in successione testatâ vel intestatâ regantur ex lege domicilii defuncti, adeoque res devenerit in hisce ad eum casum, à quo propter qualitatem testatoris, vel honorati, initium habere nequit. Neque enim sufficit in honorato, quod tempore facti testamenti capax sit, sed et tempore mortis testatoris eum capacem esse, necesse est*[2]. Again he adds: *Quod si is, cujus testamentum migratione ex Hollandiâ ad regionem Ultrajectinam irritum factum fuerat, ibidem ætatem expleverit in testatore requisitam, de novo quidem repetere solenniter potest priorem voluntatem, atque ita de novo testari; sed si id non fecerit, testamentum, antea anno ætatis decimo quinto in Hollandiâ conditum, ipso jure quantum ad mobilia vel immobilia Ultrajectina nequaquam convalescit; non magis, quam jure civili aut prætorio testamentum ab impubere conditum, si is pubes factus in fata concedat*[3]. If, however, he should

---

[1] See Desesbats *v.* Berquier, 1 Binn. R. 336; Potinger *v.* Wightman, 3 Meriv. R. 59, 68; Henry on Foreign Law, App. p. 196; 2 Boullenois, ch. 1, p. 2, &c.; Id. p. 7, &c.; Id. p. 54; Id. p. 57; Ante, § 55—74; 4 Burge, Comm. on Col. and For. Law, pt. 2, ch. 12, pp. 580, 581.

[2] J. Voet, Ad Pand. lib. 28, tit. 3, tom. 2, § 12, p. 292.

[3] Ibid. § 13, p. 293.

afterwards return and resume his domicil where his first will or testament was made, its original validity will revive also. *Diversum esset, si testator talis iterum postea mutatâ mente in Hollandiâ rerum ac fortunarum suarum sedem reponat; tunc enim voluntas illa, quæ migratione in irritum deducta fuerat, quasi recuperatâ pristinâ ad testandum habilitate redintegratur ex æquitate; eo modo, quo sustinetur jure prætorio testamentum, à patrefamilias conditum, quod per arrogationem irritum factum fuerat, si is iterum postea sui juris factus in eâdem perstiterit voluntate*[1].

§ 474. We next pass to the consideration of wills made of immovable property[2]. And here the doctrine is clearly established at the common law, that the law of the place where the property is locally situate, is to govern as to the capacity or incapacity of the testator, the extent of his power to dispose of the property, and the forms and solemnities to give the will or testament its due attestation and effect[3].

---

[1] J. Voet, Ad Pand. lib. 28, tit. 3, tom. 2, § 13, p. 293; 4 Burge, Comm. on Col. and For. Law, pt. 2, ch. 12, pp. 580, 591; Robertson on Succession, p. 95.

[2] See 4 Burge, on Col. and For. Law, pt. 2, ch. 12, pp. 586, 596; Fœlix, Conflit des Lois, Revue Etrang. et Fran. tom. 7, (1840), § 40—51, pp. 346—360.

[3] Coppin *v.* Coppin, 2 P. Will. 291, 293; Curtis *v.* Hutton, 14 Ves. 537, 541; Birtwhistle *v.* Vardill, 2 Fonb. Eq. pp. 444, 445, note; U. States *v.* Crosby, 7 Cranch, 115; Holmes *v.* Remsen, 4 John. Ch. R. 460; S. C. 20 John. R. 229; M'Cormick *v.* Sullivant, 10 Wheaton, R. 192, 202; Wills *v.* Cowper, 2 Hamm. R. 124; Henry on Foreign Law, pp. 13, 15; Ante, § 428, 434; 4 Burge Comm. on Col. and For. Law, pt. 2, ch. 12, pp. 576—580; Id. pt. 2, ch. 4, § 5, pp. 169, 170; Id. pt. 2, ch. 5, p. 217.—Mr. Burge speaking on this point (Id. pp. 217, 218), says: "The power of making the alienation by testament is no less qualitas rebus impressa, than that of making the alienation by contract. When therefore the question arises, whether the immovable property may be disposed of by testament, recourse must be had to the lex loci rei sitæ. That law must also decide, whether the full and unlimited power of disposition is enjoyed, or whether it is given under restriction. The validity of the testamentary disposition depends in the latter case on its conformity to that restriction, whether the restriction consists in limiting the extent or description of property, over which

§ 475. The doctrine of foreign jurists does not, as we have seen, entirely accord with that of the common law; but

the power of disposition may be exercised, or the persons in whose favour the disposition is made, or in requiring that the testator should have survived a certain number of days after the execution of the act by which the disposition was made. The total or partial defect of the will on the ground that it did not institute heirs, or that it omitted to name the heirs, the disherison of the heirs, the grounds on which the disherison may be justified, are essentially connected with the power of disposing of immovable property by testament, and are therefore dependent on the law of its situs." Again, Mr. Burge says: "By the jurisprudence of England and the United States, a will devising lands in England or the States, if the solemnities prescribed by the Statute of Frauds have not been observed, would be ineffectual to pass those lands. This doctrine is fully warranted by the qualification which has been given by jurists to the rule, lex loci regit actum. The Statute of Frauds, as regards real property situated in England and in the States of America, 'Est lex, quæ expressè testatores jubet jus loci sequi, in quo bona sita sunt.' It may be said, that the jurisprudence, which allows a testament executed according to the solemnities prescribed by the lex loci actus to affect real property situate in the country where that jurisprudence prevails, does not depart from the general principle, that the lex loci rei sitæ must determine whether the instrument is sufficient to dispose of real property. The difference between that jurisprudence and the doctrine of England and the United States is, that the effect of the latter is to require a particular form for the execution, whether it be made in England or in any other country, that is, it makes no provision for a will made in a foreign country, but the terms of its enactment are so comprehensive, as to include all wills, in whatever country they are made, if they affect real property in England. In the other systems of jurisprudence, it is a part of the lex loci rei sitæ, that its immovable property should pass by a testament executed with certain formalities, if it be made in the country where the property is situated, but that if it be made in another country, it may be executed with other solemnities, that is, with the solemnities required by the law of that country. The jurists, whose opinions have been cited in support of the rule that the testament is valid, if the testator has complied with the forms and solemnities prescribed by the law of the place in which it was made, apply it to a testament of movable as well of immovable property. The decisions of the Courts of England on the validity of testaments of personal estate made abroad are few. The two most important are on the testaments of the Duchess of Kingston and of Bernes. The former was resident in Paris; she obtained letters patent from the King of France, which gave her the same power of devising as she would have had in England. Although she died in France, she had not relinquished her English domicil. She made her testament in Paris. It was clearly null under the coutume. But she had observed the forms required by the Statute of Frauds, and the will was valid

even among them there is great weight of authority in favour

---

according to the law of England. It was the opinion of M. Turgot, an advocate of France, and his opinion was confirmed by the Court of Probate, that the testament, although made in Paris, was valid. This opinion proceeds on a principle which is admitted by jurists, that although a will made with the solemnities of the lex loci actus may be valid, yet if it were made with the solemnities of the locus rei sitæ in respect of immovables, and the locus domicilii in respect of movable property, it would also be valid. In Bernes's will it appeared that, although an Irishman by birth, he had acquired a domicil in Madeira. He made a will and several codicils in that island, some of which were not executed with the solemnities required by the law of Portugal, but with those formalities which would satisfy the law of England. The decision given by Sir John Nicholl, that the latter codicils were valid, and that it was competent to have executed them in the manner which would be consonant to the law of England, was reversed by the delegates, and they were deemed invalid. Bernes in this case had no longer a domicil in Ireland. His domicil was in Portugal. It was necessary to establish that fact to distinguish the case from that of the Duchess of Kingston. If he had still retained his domicil in Ireland, the codicils would, upon the principles referred to, and which will be presently more fully stated, have been valid. In neither of these cases did the question arise on a testament made with the solemnities required by the lex loci actus, although deficient in those required by the law of the domicil. In another case the testator was an Englishman by birth; and although he had been for many years residing in France, it did not appear that he had abandoned his English domicil. He came to England, and during his residence there made his will, which was a valid testamentary disposition in respect of forms and solemnities according to the law of England. It was contended, that it ought not to be admitted to probate, because it was not made in the manner required by the law of France. Here the Court adopted the lex loci actus; but from the report of the case, the learned Judge dwells so much on circumstances founded on the testator's domicil of origin, that it would be perhaps not correct to describe the decision as warranting the conclusion, that if the testator had not been an Englishman, his will made in England would have been valid. In Nasmyth's case, the testator was domiciled in Scotland, and his will was made and found there. He died in England in transitu. The Court of Probate in England held itself bound to defer to the law of Scotland. In giving effect to a testament made with the solemnities prescribed by the lex loci actus, jurists do not deny it to a testament made according to the forms required by the lex loci rei sitæ, if it be immovable, or the lex loci domicilii, if it be personal property, which is the subject of the disposition: "Proinde, si quis eo, quod ad testandum expeditius suâ causâ comparatum est, noluerit uti, quod ei fortè promptius sit componere suprema ad loci leges, cui bona subjaceant, quo minus testamentum ejus valiturum sit, non video." Paul Voet and John Voet adopt this

of the general principle[1]. We have already had occasion to consider the opinions of foreign jurists, as to the capacity and incapacity of the testator to make a testament of immovable property, whether it is to be governed by the law of his domicil, or by the law *rei sitæ*[2]. We have also had occasion to consider their opinions as to the law which ought to govern in respect to the forms and solemnities of testaments of immovable property, whether it is the law *rei sitæ*, or that of the domicil of the testator, or that of the place where the will was made[3]. Putting out of view these questions, as to the form and solemnities of acts, and the capacity and incapacity of the testator, (upon which we have sufficiently commented), there seems to be a general coincidence of opinion among foreign jurists, that the *lex rei sitæ* must in other respects govern as to wills and testaments of immovable property. Thus, John Voet says: *Bona defuncti immobilia, et quæ juris interpretatione pro talibus habentur, deferri secundum leges loci, in quo sita sunt*[4]. Dumoulin's opinion is to the same effect. His language is: *Aut statutum agit in rem, et quacunque verborum formula utatur, semper inspicitur locus, ubi res sita est.* And again: *Quoties ergo statutum principaliter agit in personam et in ejus consequentiam, agit in res immobiles, non extenditur ad res sitas in locis, ubi jus commune vel statutum loci diversum est*[5]. Hertius is even more direct. *Si lex directò rei im-*

---

opinion. 4 Burge, Comm. on Col. and For. Law, pt. 2, ch. 12, pp. 586—590; Robertson on Succession, p. 95. See also Harrison *v.* Nixon, 9 Peters, R. 505; Post, § 479 *g*.

1 See Ante, § 52—62, 430—435.

2 Ibid.

3 See Ante, § 363—373, § 435—446; 1 Burge, Comm. on Col. and For. Law, pt. 1, ch. 1, pp. 21—23; 4 Burge, Comm. on Col. and For. Law, pt. 2, ch. 12, pp. 576—586; Id. ch. 5, pp. 217—221. See also Fœlix, Conflit des Lois, Revue Etrang. et Fran. tom. 7, (1840), § 40—50, pp. 346—360; Sand. Decis. Frisic. lib. 4, tit. 1, Defin. 14, pp. 142, 143.

4 J. Voet, Ad Pand. lib. 38, tit. 17, § 34, p. 596; Ante, § 424.

5 Molin. Oper. Comm. Ad Cod. lib. 1, tit. 1, l. 1, De Conclus. Stat. tom. 3, p. 556, (edit. 1681); Ante, § 433; 1 Froland. Mém. 65; Id. vol. 2, p. 779.

ponitur, ea locum habet, ubicunque etiam locorum et a quocunque actus celebretur[1]. He adds in another place: *Rebus fertur lex, cum certam iisdem qualitatem imprimit, vel in aliendo,* v. g. *ut ne bona avito possint alienari, vel in acquirendo,* e. g. *ut dominium rei immobilis venditæ non aliter acquiritur, nisi facta fuerit judicialis resignatio*[2]. D'Aguesseau deems it a mere waste of time to do more than to state the general rule[3]. Paul Voet has stated the doctrine in an expressive manner: *Non tamen statutum personale sese regulariter extendit ad bona immobilia alibi sita*[4]. In another place he says: *Immobilia statutis loci, ubi sita, mobilia loci statutis, ubi testator habuit domicilium*[5]. In another place he says: *Quid, si itaque contentio de aliquo jure in re, seu ex ipsâ re descendente; vel ex contractu, vel actione personali, sed ad rem scriptâ; an spectabitur loci statutum, ubi dominus habet domicilium, an statutum rei sitæ? Respondeo; statutum rei sitæ*[6]. Boullenois cites another jurist as holding similar language: *Sive in rem sive in personam loquatur statutum, ad bona extra territorium non extenditur. Consideratur namque bonorum dominus, ut duplex homo; quoad bona nempe sita in uno territorio est unus*

---

[1] 1 Hertii Oper. De Collis. Leg. § 4, n. 9, p. 125, (edit. 1737); Id. p. 177, (edit. 1716).

[2] 1 Hertii Oper. De Collis. Leg. § 4, n. 6, p. 122, (edit. 1737); Id. p. 174, (edit. 1716); 2 Burge, Comm. p. 843; 4 Burge, Comm. p. 217.

[3] D'Aguesseau, Œuvres, tom. 4, pp. 636, 637. See Cochin, Œuvres, tom. 4, p. 555, 4to. edit.

[4] P. Voet, De Stat. § 4, c. 2, n. 6, p. 123, (edit. 1715); Id. p. 138, (edit. 1661).

[5] Id. c. 3, n. 10, p. 135, (edit. 1715); Id. p. 153, (edit. 1661); Ante, § 442.

[6] Id. § 9, c. 1, n. 2, p. 252, (edit. 1715); Id. p. 305, (edit. 1661).— We are not to confound the opinion of Paul Voet, as here expressed, with what he has said in another place, (Ante, § 442), that testaments are to be executed according to the forms and solemnities of the place where they are made, and not by those of the situs of the immovable property. He takes a distinction between the forms and solemnities of testaments, and their operation on this point. Whether there be any solid foundation for such a distinction, it is for the learned reader to decide. Ante, § 442.

homo; et quoad alterius territorii bona est alius homo[1]. Again: *Idem quod inferendum, quoad successionem testamentariam; finge enim testamentum hic fieri permissum esse, in Geldria non ita? Hinc si quispiam hic fecerit testamentum, non capiet vires, ratione bonorum, in Gelria jacentium. Tale quippe statutum spectat ipsa bona, adeoquo erit reale, non exserens vires ultra statuentis territorium*[2]. Again he adds: *Quid, si testamento bona immobilia relicta, diversis subjacent statutis? Idem dicendum; nihil enim interest, testatus quis, an intestatus, decedat, ut locus sit regulæ. Extra territorium jus dicenti impune non paretur*[3]. This is certainly the doctrine of the common law; for a man may have a capacity to take real estate in one country, when he is totally disabled to take it in another. Boullenois (as we have seen) lays it down among his general principles, that, when the personal laws of the domicil are in conflict with the real laws of the same country, or of a foreign country, the personal laws are to yield; and that when the real laws of the domicil are in conflict with the real laws of another country, both have effect within their own respective territories, according to the laws thereof[4].

§ 475 *a*. Rodenburg admits, that where the law *rei sitæ* prohibits married persons to devise their immovable estate by will or testament to each other, or where the law *rei sitæ* prohibits certain kinds of immovable property from being devised by will or testament, in such cases the law *rei sitæ* is to govern, notwithstanding the parties are domiciled or make their will or testament in a place where no such prohibition prevails; because these are real laws[5]. *Unde cer-*

---

[1] P. Voet, De Stat. § 9, ch. 1, n. 2, p. 252, (edit. 1715); Id. p. 305, (edit. 1661). 1 Boullenois, Observ. 10, p. 154.

[2] P. Voet, De Stat. § 4, ch. 3, n. 11, p. 135, (edit. 1715); Id. p. 153, (edit. 1661).

[3] P. Voet, De Stat. § 9, ch. 1, n. 4, p. 253, (edit. 1715); Id. pp. 306, 307, (edit. 1661).

[4] 1 Boullenois, Pr. Gén. 30, 31, p. 8.

[5] Rodenburg, De Div. Stat. tit. 2, ch. 5, § 1—5; 2 Boullenois, App. pp. 35—38.

tissima usu ac observatione regula est, cum de rebus soli agitur, et diversa sunt diversarum possessionum loca et situs, spectari semper cujusque loci leges ac jura, ubi bona sita esse præponuntur, sic ut de talibus nulla cujusquam potestas præter territorii leges[1].

§ 476. Huberus has expounded the subject at large. We have already had occasion to cite his remarks on the subject, so far as respects the forms and solemnities of testaments, which he insists are valid, if made according to the forms and solemnities of the place where the testament is made, although not made according to the forms and solemnities required by the law of the *situs* of the property[2]. But he takes a distinction between the forms and solemnities of testaments and the right to dispose of immovable property by testament. "The foundation," says he, "of the whole of this doctrine, which we have been speaking of and hold, is the subjection of all persons to the laws of any territory, as long as they act there, which settles it, that an act valid or invalid from the beginning will be, accordingly, valid or invalid every where else. But this reasoning does not apply to immovable property, when this is considered, not as depending upon the free disposition of the head of the family, (*pater-familias*), but as having certain marks impressed upon it by the laws of every commonwealth in which it is situate, which marks remain indelible therein, whatever the laws of other governments, or whatever the dispositions of private persons may establish to the contrary. For it would cause great confusion and prejudice to the commonwealth where immovable property is situate that the laws promulgated concerning it should be changed by any other acts. Hence, a Frizian, having lands and houses in the province of Groningen, cannot make a will thereof,

---

1 Rodenburg, De Div. Stat. tit. 2, c. 5, § 1; 2 Boullenois, App. p. 35; 4 Burge, Comm. on Col. and For. Law, pt. 2, ch. 5, p. 218; Id. ch. 12, pp. 582, 583. See also Burgundus, Tract. 1, n. 40, 41, pp. 41, 42.

2 Ante, § 443, 443 *a*.

because the laws there prohibit any will to be made of such real estate; and the Frizian laws cannot affect real estate which constitutes an integral part of a foreign territory[1]." *Fundamentum universæ hujus doctrinæ diximus esse, et tenemus, subjectionem hominum infra leges cujusque territorii, quamdiu illic agunt, quæ facit, ut actus ab initio validus aut nullus, alibi quoque valere aut non valere non nequeat. Sed hæc ratio non convenit rebus immobilibus, quando illæ spectantur, non ut dependentes a libera dispositione cujusque patrisfamilias, verum quatenus certæ notæ lege cujusque Reip. ubi sita sunt, illis impressæ reperiuntur; hæ notæ manent indelebiles in ista Republ., quicquid aliarum Civitatum Leges aut privatorum dispositiones, secus aut contra statuant; nec enim sine magna confusione præjudicioque Reip. ubi sitæ sunt res soli, Leges de illis latæ, dispositionibus istis mutari possent. Hinc Frisius habens agros et domos in provincia Groningensi, non potest de illis testari, quia Lege prohibitum est ibi de bonis immobilibus testari, non valente Jure Frisico adficere bona, quæ partes alieni territorii integrantes constituunt.* And yet, with this clear principle in view, he proceeds to declare that this does not contradict the rule which he had already laid down, that if a will is valid by the law of the place where it is made, it ought to have effect even in regard to real property situate in foreign countries, by whose laws such property may be passed by a will; because (says he) the diversity of laws in that respect does not affect the soil, neither speaks of it, but simply directs the manner of making the will, which being rightly done, the law of the commonwealth does not prohibit the instrument to have validity in regard to immovables, inasmuch as no characteristic or incident, impressed by the laws of the country, is injured or diminished[2].

§ 477. Burgundus lays down the doctrine in general terms, that in every thing which regards land and other

---

[1] Huberus, lib. 1, tit. 3, § 15.

[2] Huberus, lib. 1, tit. 3, § 15. The original is cited ante, § 443 *a*.

real inheritances, it is the law of the situation which is to decide[1]. He takes the distinction between movable and immovable property, and between real and personal statutes. *Proinde, in quantum (statutum) est reale, et immobilia dirigit, fines territorii non egreditur*[2]. And again: *Quando hoc unum generaliter obtineat, ut in immobilibus bonorum situs semper spectandus veniat; in mobilibus autem locus domicilii*[3]. And (as we have seen) he applies the rule specially to wills. *Si quidem solemnitates testamenti ad jura personalia non pertinent; quia sunt quædam qualitas bonis ipsis impressa, ad quam tenetur respicere, quisquis in bonis aliquid alterat*[4]. *Quare etiam mihi videtur consequens, juris civilis rationem exigere in testamentis exarandis adhibitionem solemnitatis, quam præscripserit consuetudo cujusque possessionis. Nam si ex solemni testamento nascitur jus in ipsâ re, quomodo id potest præstare alterius regionis consuetudo, quæ alienis fundis alterationis necessitatem imponere non potest? Hoc enim esset jus dicere extra territorium cui impune non paretur*[5]. There is a great deal of solid sense in these remarks; and they form a satisfactory answer to the distinction propounded by Huberus[6].

§ 478. The Scottish law is in perfect coincidence with the common law on this subject. Erskine, in the passage already cited, has stated, that in the conveyance of an immovable subject, or of any right affecting heritage, the owner must follow the solemnities established by the law, not of the country where he signs the instrument, but of the State in which the heritage lies[7]. And even if all due

---

1 Ante, § 433.

2 Burgundus, Tract. 1, n. 26, pp. 38, 39.

3 Burgundus, Tract. 1, n. 41, p. 43.

4 Burgundus, Tract. 6, n. 3, p. 128; Ante, § 372, 438.

5 Burgundus, Tract. 6, n. 1—3, p. 129; Id. Tract. 1, n. 36, pp. 38, 39; Ante, § 372, 433, 438; 1 Boullenois, Observ. 9, p. 151. See also Henry on For. Law, p. 97, 98.

6 Ante, § 476. See also 4 Burge, Comm. on Col. and For. Law, pt. 2, ch. 12, pp. 582—586.

7 Ante, § 436.

solemnities are observed, still no estate will pass unless in conformity with the local law. Hence, (he adds), a foreign testament bequeathing heritable subjects situate in Scotland, is not sustained in Scotland, although by the law of the country where the testament was made, a heritage might have been actually settled; because by the Scottish law no heritable subject can be disposed of in that form[1].

§ 479. Vattel (as we have seen) adopts the same rule as a general one of the *jus gentium*[2]. As to bequests, he asserts, in the most positive terms, that, when they respect immovables they must be conformable to the law of the country where they are situated[3]. He adds: In the same manner the validity of a testament, as to its form, can only be decided by the judge of the domicil, whose sentence delivered in form ought to be every where acknowledged. But without affecting the validity of the testament itself, the bequests contained in it may be disputed before the judge of the place where the effects are situated, because those effects can only be disposed of conformably to the laws of the country[4]. Grotius makes a distinction between the personal capacity of making wills and testaments and the forms and solemnities thereof, and right and power to dispose of property, whether movable or immovable, holding that the forms and solemnities are governed by the law of the place where the will or testament is made; the capacity of the person is governed by the law of his domicil; and the right to dispose of property is governed in the case of movables by the law of the domicil, and in the case of immovables by the law of the *situs rei*. *Ubi de formâ sive solemnitate testamenti agitur, respici locum conditi testamenti; ubi de persona antestari jus domicilii; ubi de rebus, quæ testamento relinqui possunt, vel non,*

---

1 Ersk. Inst. b. 3, tit. 2, § 41, pp. 515, 516; 2 Kaims, Equity, b. 3, c. 8, § 3.

2 Ante, § 471, 472.

3 Vattel, b. 2, c. 7, § 85, c. 8, § 103, 110, 111.

4 Vattel, b. 2, c. 7, § 85. See also Id. c. 8, § 110, 111; Ante, § 471.

respici locum domicilii in mobilibus in rebus soli situm loci[1]. If it were necessary, the opinions of many other foreign jurists might be cited to the same effect; but it would incumber these pages to give them a more extended review[2].

---

[1] Grotius, Epist. 467, cited 4 Burge, Comm. on Col. and For. Law, pt. 2, c. 5, p. 220.

[2] See 4 Burge, Comm. on Col. and For. Law, pt. 2, ch. 5, pp. 217, 218; Id. ch. 12, pp. 576—585.—Mr. Burge (in 4 Burge, Comm. pp. 218—220; Id. pp. 581—585) states the opinions of many foreign jurists; and among others he says (pp. 218—220): "Ferriére has stated this doctrine: 'Si je légue un héritage propre situé en coutume, qui en défende la disposition, tel legs est nul, et ne peut être parfourni sur les biens situés en cette coutume, quoi qu'acquest, parce qu'à l'égard des choses, dont on peut disposer par dernière volonté, on considére la coutume où elles sont situées. Celui qu a son domicile en cette coutume peut instituer sa femme dans les biens, qu'il a dans le pais de droit écrit, comme il a été jugé par arrest du 14 Aoust, 1754, rapporté par Marion au de ses plaidoyés, ce qui doit ètre sans difficulté.' A testament made in a foreign country, bequeathing heritable subjects situated in Scotland, is not sustained in that kingdom, though by the law of the country where the testament was made, heritage might have been settled by testament, because by the law of Scotland no heritable subject can be disposed of in that form. On this principle a Scot's personal bond taken to heirs and assignees, but 'secluding executors,' cannot be bequeathed by a foreign testament. But in all questions touching heritable subjects situate abroad, the foreign testament will be given effect to according to the lex loci. Dumoulin lays down the same doctrine respecting the restriction on the testamentary power over biens propres. 'Unde statutum loci inspicietur, sive persona sit subdita, sive non; ita si dicat, hæredia proventa ab unâ lineâ, redeant ad hæredes etiam remotiores lineæ, vel hæredes lineæ succedant in hærediis ab illâ lineâ proventis. Vel quod illi de lineâ non possunt testari de illis in totum, vel nisi ad certam partem. Hæc enim omnia et similia spectant ad caput statuti, agentis in rem, et præcedentem conclusionem.' Again; the statute, which prohibits a disposition to particular persons, or (which involves the same consequence) requires the disposition to be made in favour of certain persons, and therefore excludes all others, is a real law. 'Directè enim in rerum alienationem scripta hæc lex realis omnino dicenda est: nec enim statutum reale sit, an personale metiri oportet à ratione, quæ a conjugali forsan qualitate fuerit ducta, sed ab ipsâ re, quæ in prohibitione statuti ceciderit.' So also it has been held, that the law which requires that the testator should have survived the execution of his testament, will control the disposition of property situated in the country where that law prevails, although the testament is made, or the testator domiciled, in a place where no such law exists. If a testator, whose domicil and real estate were both in Normandy, made a will in some other place, in which he had occa-

§ 479 *a.* Passing from these considerations, as to the law by which the forms and solemnities of wills and testaments

---

sion to be present, but where the law did not require that the testator should survive forty days, it was held, that the survivorship was essential to the validity of the testament, so far as it related to the real property in Normandy. If these questions arise on the power to dispose of movable property by testament, the law by which they are decided, is that of the domicil; 'Pour les meubles, ils suivent la loi du domicile, et il ne sauroit jamais y avoir de choc entre différentes coutumes, en sorte qu'il est assez inutile, quant aux meubles, d'agiter si le statut, qui permet de tester, ou qui le défend, est personnel, ou s'il est réel.' See also Fœlix, Conflit des Lois, Revue Etrang. et Fran., tom. 7, (1840), § 37, pp. 307—312. The latter author says in this place: "Le second cas, où le statut personnel semble devoir prédominer sur le statut réel, est celui de la succession à toute la fortune d'un individu, soit ab intestat, soit par testament. Voici les arguments invoqués par les auteurs qui, dans ses deux hypothèses, prétendent faire régir la succession par la loi personelle du défunt. Lorsque, par la mort d'un individu, il s'agit de succéder à tous ses droits actifs et passifs, à toute sa fortune (universum patrimonium), on regarde en droit cette fortune comme un ensemble (universitas juris), sans égard aux objets particuliers qui la composent; et cette universalité représente de droit le défunt, même avant l'appréhension faite par l'héritier. L'héritier succéde ensuite dans cette universalité, et c'est alors seulement qu'il représente la personne du défunt. L'universalité des biens du défunt formant ainsi la continuation de la personne de ce dernier, on doit, pour tout ce qui concerne la succession à cette universalité, suivre la loi de son domicile, c'est à-dire son statut personnel; tous les objets compris dans la succession sont soumis à ce statut personnel. Ainsi la succession d'un Français est régie par le Code Civil, même à l'égard des immeubles appartenant au défunt et situés en Autriche; et on ne suit pas l'ordre des successions établi par le Code Autrichien. Cette doctrine a été professée par un grand nombre d'auteurs distingués; elle l'a été d'abord par Cujas, relativement à la succession testamentaire; ensuite la même opinion a été adoptée, quant à la succession ab intestat, par Puffendorf, Bachov, J. H. Boehmer, G. L. Boehmer, Helfeld, Glück, Hamm, Meier, par MM. Mittermaier, Eichhorn, Muhlenbruch, et Grundler. Toutefois, quatre des auteurs cités, Puffendorf, Helfeld, Glück, et Hamm, n'admettent le principe qu'avec deux restrictions: il ne sera pas applicable, lorsqu'il existe une loi prohibitive au lieu de la situation des immeubles, ou lorsqu'une qualité spéciale se trouve imprimée aux biens; par exemple, s'ils sont féodaux, stemmatiques on frappés d'un fidéicommis. En faveur de cette opinion on invoque, outre le principe que la succession représente le défunt, plusieurs considérations accessoires. D'après l'opinion commune des auteurs, la succession ab intestat repose sur la volonté présumée du défunt; le défunt n'ayant connu, en régle générale, d'autre loi que celle du lieu de son domi-

of movable property and of immovable property are to be regulated, in order to give them validity, let us proceed, in the next place, to the consideration of the rules by which such wills and testaments are to be interpreted. And, in the first place, in regard to wills and testaments of personal property. In such cases, where the will or testament is

---

cile, on doit admettre qu'il a entendu faire passer ses immeubles aux parents appelés par cette loi: si telle n'avait pas été son intention, il en aurait disposé par testament. On fait remarquer que toutes les nations admettent chez elles l'exécution des testaments consentis par un étranger dans sa patrie et dans les formes qui y sont prescrites. Ces testaments ne sont autre chose que l'expression formelle de la volanté du défunt, sanctionnée par la loi civile de sa patrie: à plus forte raison devra-t-on accorder un effet semblable à cette loi civile lorsque, sans un acte du défunt, elle prononce seule. On cite encore les inconvénients résultant de la division des patrimoines en différentes successions particulières, au préjudice des héritiers et des créanciers; enfin on fait observer que la chose publique est sans intérêt dans la question, parce que les prohibitions, les charges et impositions pesant sur l'immeuble peuvent néanmoins produire leur effet, et que, du reste, peu importe à l'état quelle est la personne, qui hérite de tel immeuble. D'autres non moins respectables n'admettent l'application du statut personnel en matière de succession, qu'en ce qui concerne les meubles, et ils la rejettent par rapport aux immeubles; ils appliquent à ceux-ci la loi de la situation, sans distinguer s'il s'agit de succéder à un immeuble particulier ou à l'universalité de la fortune d'un individu. Ils admettent autant de successions particulières qu'il y a de territoires où sont situès les immeubles provenant du défunt (Quot sunt bona diversis territoriis obnoxia, totidem patrimonia intelliguntur). Nous citerons Burgundus, Rodenburg, Paul Voet, Jean Voet, Abraham à Wesel, Christin, Sandé, Gail, Carpzov, Wernher, Mevius, Struve, Leyser, Huber, Hommel, Berger, Lauterbach, Vattel, Tittmann, Danz, Hauss, MM. Thibaut, Story, et Burge. Aucune législation positive ne s'est expliquée sur la question de savoir, si c'est la loi rèelle ou la loi personnelle, qui doit régir la succession ab intestat. Nous pensons qu'il faut appliquer le statut de la situation des immeubles. Le premier principe, en matière de conflit des lois, c'est que les lois de chaque état régissent les biens situés dans le territoire; il n'est nullement établi qu'une convention tacite s'est formée entre les nations pour l'application de la loi personnelle au cas de succession dans l'universalité des meubles et immeubles d'un individu: témoin la divergence des sentiments des auteurs. Les arguments invoqués en faveur de cette application sont fondés en partie dans le droit civil, en partie dans l'avantage commun des nations; mais on ne voit pas que l'usage des nations ait consacré cette opinion." See also Fœlix, Id. § 27, pp. 216—218; Ante, § 429—444.

made in the place of the domicil of the testator, the general rule of the common law is, that it is to be construed according to the law of the place of his domicil, in which it is made[1]. A will, therefore, made of personal estate in England, is to be construed according to the meaning of the terms used by the law of England; and this rule equally applies, whether the judicial inquiry, as to its meaning and interpretation, arises in England, or in any other country[2].

---

[1] Yates *v.* Thomson, 3 Clarke & Finell. R. 544, 570; Robertson on Successions, pp. 99, 100, 191—197, 214, 255; Post, § 490, 491.

[2] Trotter *v.* Trotter, 4 Bligh, (N. S.), 502; S. C. 3 Wils. & Shaw, R. 407.—In this case, the testator, a Scotchman, domiciled in the dominions of England in India, made his will there; he being possessed of Scotch heritable bonds, as well as of personal property there. The will was ineffectual to carry a Scotch heritage according to the law of Scotland; and the question arose, whether his heir in Scotland, who claimed the heritable bonds as heir, was also entitled to share in the movables, as a legatee under the will, without bringing in the heritable bonds, or being put to his election. It was held that the will, as to its terms, must be interpreted according to the law of England; and that, by the law of England, the terms used were not such as to import an intention to convey real estate by the testator; and therefore, that the heir was entitled to the whole heritable bonds, and also to his share of the movable property under the will. On that occasion the Lord Chancellor (Lord Lyndhurst) said:—"It was stated at the bar, and I see by the papers it was also argued below, that in cases of this description it is not unreasonable that when any technical points arise in the construction of a will of this description, the Court of Session should resort to the opinion of lawyers of the country where the will or instrument was executed, but that this applies only to technical expressions; that where a will is expressed in ordinary language, the judges of the Court of Scotland are as competent to put a proper construction upon it as judges or lawyers of the country where the will was executed. But the judges below were not of that opinion; and it is impossible, as it appears to me, that such an opinion can be reasonably entertained. A will must be interpreted according to the law of the country where it is made, and where the party making the will has his domicil. There are certain rules of construction adopted in the Courts, and the expressions which are made use of in a will, and the language of a will, have frequently reference to those rules of construction; and it would be productive, therefore, of the most mischievous consequences, and in many instances defeat the intention of the testator, if those rules were to be altogether disregarded, and the judges of a foreign court, (which it may be considered in relation to the will), without reference to that knowledge which it is desirable to obtain, of the

Thus, for example, if the question should arise, whether the terms of a will include a bequest of real estate, or shew on

---

law of the country in which the will was made, were to interpret the will according to their own rules of construction. That would also be productive of another inconvenience, namely, that the will might have a construction put upon it in the English Courts different from that which might be put upon it in the foreign country. It appears to me, that there is no solid ground for the objection; but that where a will is executed in a foreign country, by a person having his domicil in that country, with respect to that person's property the will must be interpreted according to the law of the country where it is made. It must, if it comes into question in any proceeding, have the same interpretation put upon it as would be put upon it in any tribunal of the country where it was made. It appears to me, therefore, that the Judges were perfectly right in directing the opinion to be taken of English lawyers of eminence, with respect to the import and construction of this will according to the law of England. The main question that was ultimately put to the learned persons to whom I have referred, is this: 'Whether, on the supposition of the question having arisen for trial in England, the heir would have been put to his election if he had claimed money secured by heritable bond in Scotland, as well as his share of the personal estate under the will?' The answer is in these terms: 'Considering heritable bonds in Scotland as real estates, to which the heir-at-law is entitled, unless they are conveyed away with due solemnity by his ancestor, we think the heir-at-law would be entitled in this case to claim them without being put to his election, if the question had arisen in a court of justice in England.' When that opinion was communicated to the Court in Scotland, the Court—immediately affirming that opinion—decided in favour of the heir-at-law. The heir-at-law was undoubtedly entitled to take the real estate,—that is, the heritable bond; and the sole question was, whether, when he came in to claim, under the will, his proportion of the personal estate, it was required by law that he should be put to his election, that is, whether he should take the one or the other; whether he should allow the real estate to be connected with the personal, so as to form one mass of the property, and the whole divided, or should take the real estate, and give up the personal estate? Whether he was obliged or not to do this, depended entirely on this consideration—whether upon the face of the will there was sufficient to manifest a clear intention that the testator designed by his will to dispose of his real estate; because, if he intended to dispose of his real estate, although he had not carried that intention effectually into execution, the party taking under that will would not be entitled to have the benefit of the will, and at the same time to defeat the intention of the testator. The question was, therefore, simply a question of construction. Does it appear upon the face of the will, that it was the intention of the testator to dispose of his real estate, that is, of those heritable bonds? Now, the rule of law in England with respect to subjects of this kind, is well ascertained and

the part of the testator an intention to bequeath real estate as well as personal estate, the question must be decided according to the law of the place of his domicil, and where the will was made; and the same interpretation must be put upon those terms in every other country which would be put upon them by the law of that domicil[1]. So, what is to be deemed "real estate" in the sense of a will, devising real estate to certain persons, must be decided by the law of the domicil of the testator. Thus, where a testator was domiciled in Jamaica, in which place he made his will, and the devise was in these words: "I give, devise, and bequeath one moiety of the rents, issues, and profits of my estate named Islington and Cove's Penn, in the parish of St. Mary, to be divided equally amongst my grandchildren. The other moiety of the rents, issues, and profits of my said estate and Penn I give, devise, and bequeath to my son, &c." According to the import of the words "my estate," as they are understood and used in Jamaica, not only the land, but the works, buildings, utensils, slaves, cattle, and stock on the plantation, would be included. The Court put this construction on the devise[2].

§ 479 *b*. In like manner, whether the words of a will give a legacy or create a trust in favour of a party, where the expressions used import a wish or desire, or other language of a similar sort is used, must be decided by the law of the place where the will is made and the testator has his domicil[3]. So, where a legacy is given in terms expressive of a

well defined, and it is this,—that you are not to proceed by probability or by conjecture, but that there must be a clear and manifest expression of the intention on the face of the will, to include that property which is not properly devised, before the heir can be put to his election." Ibid. See also Price *v*. Deerhurst, 8 Sim. R. 279, 299, 300; Post, § 489; Robertson on Successions, pp. 189—197.

[1] Trotter *v*. Trotter, 4 Bligh, R. (N. S.) p. 502; S. C. 3 Wils. & Shaw, p. 407.

[2] Stewart *v*. Garnett, 3 Sim. R. 298; 4 Burge, Comm. on Col. and For. Law, pt. 2, ch. 12, p. 591.

[3] Pierson *v*. Garnett, 2 Bro. Ch. R. 38; 2 Story on Eq. Jurisp. § 1068—1074.

currency in use in different countries, but of different values therein, the same rule will apply. Thus, for example, a will made in Ireland by a testator domiciled there, giving a legacy of £1000, will be interpreted to be a legacy of £1000 Irish currency, and payable accordingly, and not a £1000 English sterling currency[1]. So, legacies are deemed payable according to the law of the country, and in the currency of the country where the will is made and the testator is domiciled[2].

§ 479 *c.* In like manner the question, whether a legatee by the terms of a foreign will or testament takes an estate for life or in fee, is to be decided by the law of the place where the will is made and the testator is domiciled, and not by the law of the place where the controversy arises, or the testator was born[3]. So, if the question arises, whether it is competent to make a particular bequest of property, the validity of it must be decided by the law of the place where the will or testament is made, and the testator is domiciled[4]. So, if a legacy is given by a will or testament to a party, who dies in the lifetime of the testator, the question, whether it is an ademption of the legacy, or whether the legacy goes to his personal representatives, is to be decided by the law where the will or testament is made, and he is domiciled[5].

§ 479 *d.* Another illustration may arise under a will, which purports to direct the testator's real estate to be

---

1 Id. p. 47.

2 Ibid.; Saunders *v.* Drake, 2 Ath. 465; Pierson *v.* Garnett, 3 Bro. Ch. R. 39, 47; Malcolm *v.* Martin, 3 Bro. Ch. R. 50; Wallis *v.* Brightwell, 2 P. Will. 88; Lansdowne *v.* Lansdowne, 2 Bligh, R. 60, 88, 89, 95; 4 Burge, Comm. on Col. and For. Law, pt. 2, ch. 12, pp. 595, 596; Ante, § 259, 310—313.

3 Brown *v.* Brown, 4 Wils. & Shaw, 28, 37; Post, § 490.

4 Price *v.* Deerhurst, 8 Simons, R. 279, 299—301; 2 Boullenois, Observ. 46, pp. 505—508.

5 Anstruther *v.* Chalmer, 2 Sim. R. 1; Thornton *v.* Curling, 8 Sim. R. 310; S. C. 2 Addams, Eccles. R. 6, 10—25; Post, § 491.

sold, and the proceeds to be applied to foreign charities, which devise is good by the law of the foreign country, but is prohibited by the law of the testator's domicil. In such a case the devise will be void, because it is against the law of his domicil. This was held in a case, where a testator in England by his will directed his real estate to be sold, and the produce to be laid out in lands or in the funds, for the maintenance of a charity in Scotland. On that occasion the Master of the Rolls (Sir Wm. Grant) said: "The statute (9 Geo. 2, ch. 36) contains no express words prohibiting a bequest of money to be produced by the sale of land to charitable purposes; but it is settled by construction, that such a bequest is within the spirit and meaning of the law; and it is clear that no charity in England, not within the exception of the statute, could have derived any benefit from the produce of the real estate. The question then is, whether such produce may be given to what, in contemplation of the English law, is for a charitable purpose, when that purpose is to be carried into execution in another country? The validity of every disposition of real estate must depend upon the law of the country in which that estate is situated. The subject of this statute is real estate in England. The owners of such property are disabled from disposing of it to any charitable use, except by deed executed twelve months before the death of the owner, &c. to take effect from the execution. The words are perfectly general, 'any charitable use whatsoever,' and the object could not be to treat English charities less favourably than charities to take effect for the benefit of other countries. It would be somewhat incongruous to refuse to permit such a disposition for the most laudable and meritorious charitable institution in England; but if the party chose to carry his benevolent intention beyond England, to permit him to do so, to the effect of disinheriting his heir in his last moments. The disinheriting of the lawful heirs by languishing or dying persons, which is treated by the statute as a mischief, cannot be less so when the effect is to carry the property out of England. Therefore, neither the words of this statute, nor the presumable intention, warrant me in declaring, that it is to be confined to charitable purposes to be carried into execution in England. The statute not containing an exception in favour of the universities of Scotland, as it does with regard to the universities of England, I must consider this as a charitable disposition, by which nothing that is the produce of the testator's real estate can pass[1]."

§ 479 *e*. The same rule will apply to the ascertainment of the persons who are to take under a will or testament, when it is made by words designating a particular class or description of persons. Who are the proper persons entitled to take under the *designatio personarum*, is a point to be ascertained by the law of the place where the will is made and the testator is domiciled. Thus, for example, if a testator should bequeath his personal estate to his "heir at law," who is the person entitled to take under that description, will depend upon the law of his domicil. If domiciled in England, it will be the eldest son; if domiciled in most of the States of America, it will be all his children[2]. So, if

---

[1] Curtis *v*. Hutton, 14 Ves. 537, 541. See also 3 Peters, R. App. pp. 501—503.

[2] Harrison *v*. Nixon, 9 Peters, R. 483, 504.—On this occasion the Court said: "No one can doubt, if a testator born and domiciled in England during his whole life, should, by his will, give his personal estate to his heir at law, that the descriptio personæ would have reference to, and be governed by the import of the terms in the sense of the laws of England. The import of them might be very different, if the testator were born and domiciled in France, in Louisiana, in Pennsylvania, or in Massachusetts. In short, a will of personalty speaks according to the laws of the testator's domicil, where there are no other circumstances to control their application; and to raise the question what the testator means, we must first ascertain what was his domicil, and whether he had reference to the laws of that place or to the laws of any foreign country. Now, the very gist of the present controversy turns upon the point, who were the person or persons intended to be designated by the testator under the appellation of 'heir-at-law.' If, at the time of making his will, and at his death, he was domiciled in England, and had a reference to its laws, the designation might indicate a very different person

a person domiciled in Holland should bequeath his property to the "male children" of certain persons, and the question

---

or persons from what might be the case, (we do not say what is the case), if, at the time of making his will, and of his death, he was domiciled in Pennsylvania. In order to raise the question of the true interpretation and designation, it seems to us indispensable that the country by whose laws his will is to be interpreted, should be first ascertained; and then the inquiry is naturally presented, what the provisions of those laws are." Mr. Burge has put a number of cases from the foreign law, on the same subject. He says: "The legal effect of the expression, 'lawful heirs,' will not be controlled by words, which import an equality of distribution amongst the heirs; but those words will be understood as referring to the equality which is consistent with, and recognised by that law, which the testator is presumed to have invoked. The institution of heirs was thus expressed: 'Fratrum et sororum filios ac nepotes hæredes legitimos ex æquis partibus.' (Voet, lib. 28, tit. 5, n. 17.) If the whole inheritance were to be divided amongst those heirs in equal parts, the qualification of legitimus hæres would be disregarded, because, according to the order of succession established by law, the grandsons of one brother succeeding with the sons of another do not take per capita, but per stirpes. The equality, therefore, to be observed in the distribution, and which must be presumed to have been that contemplated by the testator, is that which the law admits, namely, an equality between the stirpes, and not between the individuals, (Neostad. Decis. 33). A case arose in the court at Brabant, of a father domiciled in Brabant, who had, in the institution of his son, desired him to allow that which he had left him to go to his lawful children. It was decided, that the grandfather's estate would devolve on those children only who would take according to the law of Brabant in the case of intestacy, namely, the children of the first, to the exclusion of those of a second marriage. (Stockmans, Curiæ Brab. Decis. 27.) Under an institution by the description of 'brothers,' brothers of the whole blood only will take, if, according to the law in the place of the lex loci domicilii, the children of the father's or mother's side only are excluded from the succession. (Christin. ad Leg. Mech. tit. 16, art. 7, n. 5, 6; Voet, lib. 28, tit. 5, n. 18; Rodenb. de Jure Quod Ori. de Stat. Divers. tit. 3, c. 2, n. 6, p. 135; Someren de Repræs. c. 5, n. 4.) If a testator institute as his heirs those whom he calls proximi, without using any expression pointing to those who would by law succeed to him in case of intestacy, and he leaves no children, it is doubtful who are entitled to the succession, whether those who would take according to the law of the place of his domicil, or those who were really and naturally the nearest to the testator in blood, although according to that law they could not be his heirs. Thus, if the testator were domiciled in a country where the relations of the deceased mother succeed in preference to the surviving father, the latter is the nearest in blood to the deceased, although he is not nearest in the order of succession. It seems that the term proximus would

should arise, as it well might, whether by "male children" be meant male descendants, that is, descendants claiming through males only, the question would be decided by the interpretation put upon those words by the law of Holland.

---

receive its natural signification, and consequently the father, as the nearest in blood, would succeed, and not the descendant in the maternal line. (Voet, lib. 28, tit. 5, n. 19, and lib. 36, tit. 1, n. 25; Someren, de Repræs. c. 6.) But it is said, that this construction is made to depend on the degree in which the law of succession deviates from the natural sense of the word proximus. And where in cases of intestacy some of the nearest are admitted to the succession with some more remote in blood, the construction would be according to the legal sense. If therefore a testator, instituting his wife as his heir, should direct that the inheritance after his death should revert to the nearest, then, according to the jus Scabinicum, [Sen-Cons-Trebellianicum,] the father would be entitled to one half, and all the brothers to the other half. (Ib. Sande, Decis. Fris. lib. 4, tit. 5, def. 6.) If the testator has called to the succession those who are nearest to him in case of intestacy, recourse must be had, not to the laws of the different countries in which his immovable property is situated, to decide who are the persons entitled to succeed, but to the lex loci domicilii. And then it may happen that those would succeed who will not be the nearest in blood. (Sande, Decis. Fris. lib. 4, tit. 5, def. 6, 8; Voet, lib. 36, tit. 1, n. 25, lib. 28, tit. 5, n. 20; Mantica, de Conj. ult. Volunt. lib. 8, tit. 14, n. 10; Van Leeuwen, Cens. For. pt. 1, lib. 3, c. 7, n. 19; Neostad, decis. 35; Jul. Clarus. § Testam. quæst. 76, n. 13; Someren, de Repræs. c. 5, n. 16; Ante, vol. 2, p. 856.) In a bequest of a pecuniary legacy, where the will affords no direct evidence of the currency in which the testator intended it to be paid, his greater familiarity with the currency of the country in which he is domiciled, than with that of any other place, justifies the presumption that he has in view that currency, when he expresses no other currency in which his bequest is to be paid. The father of a family, who was domiciled in a village in Peyrouse, in Italy, was on a visit to Ancona on business. He made his will in the latter place, and gave a legacy to one of his daughters of five hundred florins. Florins were of less value at Ancona than at Peyrouse, and the question raised was, whether the legacy should be paid according to the value of the florins at Ancona, or at Peyrouse; and it was determined it ought to be paid according to the value at Peyrouse, the place of the testator's domicil. Where a legacy consists of a certain number of modii of corn, Hertius says, that the modii ought to be according to the measure of the place of the testator's domicil, and not according to that of the place where the testament was made. So, if a testator having lands in different places devise a thousand acres without any other expression, such a devise must be understood according to the measurement prevailing in the place of his domicil." 4 Burge, Comm. on Col. and For. Law, pt. 2, ch. 12, pp. 591—594. See also 2 Burge, Comm. pt. 2, ch. 9,

§ 479 *f*. But the question may be asked, in these and the like cases, what is to be the rule of construction, if the will or testament is made by the party in the place of his domicil; but he is in fact a native of another country; or if the will or testament is made in a country of which the party is a native, and according to the forms of law in that country, and yet at the time his actual domicil is in another country, by whose laws the will or testament so made is equally good. The answer to both questions is the same. The law of the place of his actual domicil. Thus, for example, where a native of Scotland, domiciled in England, having personal property only, executed during a visit to Scotland, and deposited a will there, prepared in the Scotch form, and died in England; it was held, that the will was to be construed according to the English law[1].

---

pp. 855—860; Ante, § 271, 271 *a*, note; Post, § 484; Sand. Decis. Frisic. lib. 4, tit. 8, Defin. 7, p. 194.

[1] Anstruther *v*. Chalmer, 2 Sim. R. 1; Harrison *v*. Nixon, 9 Peters, R. 483, 504, 505, note.—Mr. Burge, on this subject, says: "The law of the place of domicil in many cases affords the rule of construction, when the testator has used expressions which are either ambiguous or of different significations in different countries. Thus, if a testator does not institute his heirs by name, but by the description of those who would succeed to his estate in case he had died intestate, and the rules of succession, where his real or immovable property is situated are different from those which prevail in the place of his domicil, or in that in which he made his will, or in that where the judicial tribunal is which adjudicates on the will, the laws of succession which prevail in the place of his domicil are those which would be adopted. And the more general opinion is, that even with respect to the succession to real or immovable property, the laws of succession in the place of domicil, and not those in loco rei sitæ, prevail. The ground on which this rule rests is, that as it becomes necessary to ascertain the sense in which the testator has used the expression, and what laws of succession he contemplated, it is presumed that they were those of the country in which he was domiciled, because it must be supposed he was familiar with those laws. There are grounds for presuming he was acquainted with them; but there exist no grounds for presuming him to be acquainted with any other laws of succession. In affixing the sense in which he has used certain words, terms, or phrases, he is presumed to have adopted that which prevailed in the place of his domicil. It has been sometimes said that they ought to be

§ 479 *g*. Another question may also be propounded. Suppose, at the time of the making of a will or testament, the testator is domiciled in the place where it is made, and he afterwards removes to another place, where he is domiciled at his death; does such removal change the rule of construction, so that if there is a difference between the law of the original domicil and that of the new domicil, as to the interpretation of the terms, the law of the new domicil is to prevail? Or, does the interpretation remain, as it was by the law of the original domicil? This question does not seem to have undergone any absolute and positive decision in the courts acting under the common law[1].

§ 479 *h*. The same rules of construction will generally apply to wills and testaments of immovable property; unless, indeed, it can be clearly gathered from the terms used in the will, that the testator had in view the law of the place of the situs, or used other language, which necessarily referred to the usages and customs or language appropriate only to that *situs*[2]. "Thus," to borrow an illustration from Mr. Burge, "in case the limitation of a deed or will were made in England, in favour of the heir of A., a person who had no children, and the settler or testator has property in England, Jamaica, and British Guiana, if the construction of the term heir was to be in conformity with the

---

understood in the sense in which they are accustomed to be used in the place where the will or contract was made; but it would be impossible to consider this as a general rule; for the residence of the party in the place may have been for so short a time as to negative the presumption that he was even acquainted with that sense." 4 Burge, Comm. on Col. and For. Law, pt. 2, ch. 12, pp. 590, 591. See also 2 Burge, Comm. on Col. and For. Law, pt. 2, ch. 9, pp. 855—857.

1 It was alluded to, and reserved for consideration in Harrison *v.* Nixon, 9 Peters, R. 483, 505. See ante, § 473; 4 Burge, Comm. on Col. and For. Law, pt. 2, ch. 4, § 5, p. 169; Yates *v.* Thomson, 3 Clarke & Finell. 544, 583—589.

2 Trotter *v.* Trotter, 3 Wills. & Shaw, 407; S. C. 4 Bligh, R. (N. S.) 502, 505; 2 Burge, Comm. on Col. and For. Law, pt. 2, ch. 9, pp. 857, 858.

law of England, the father of A. would take; if according to the law of Jamaica, the elder brother; and if according to the law of British Guiana, his father, brothers, and sisters would take his immovable property. It is not to be presumed that he used the expression in three different senses, or that he adopted the legal import given to it by the law of the one place, rather than that given to it by the law of either of the other two places. But if his domicil were in England, there is the presumption that he was acquainted with the sense attached to it by the law of England, and that he used it in this sense[1]. So, if a testator should devise his real property to his next of kin, who would be entitled, would depend upon the construction given to the words by the law of his domicil[2].

§ 479 *i*. Foreign jurists have discussed this subject on various occasions[3]. Boullenois says: When the question is respecting the interpretation of clauses expressed in a contract or a testament, it is ordinarily the circumstances of the case which are to decide it. In effect, if we sometimes find clauses or dispositions in contracts or testaments, which, from not being sufficiently developed, leave some uncertainty of knowing whether they are to be understood according to the law of the place where the acts are executed, or according to the law of the place where the goods are situated, or according to the law of the domicil of one or other of the contracting parties, or finally, according to some other law. After citing the opinions of other jurists, he declares his own opinion to be, that the law of the place where the act is executed does not always furnish the proper rule of interpretation in all cases[4]; but that the only rule which can be prescribed, is that of determining according to the different circumstances belonging

---

[1] 2 Burge, Comm. on Col. and For. Law, pt. 2, ch. 9, p. 858.
[2] Ibid.
[3] See Sand. Decis. Fris. lib. 4, tit. 8, Defin. 7, p. 194.
[4] 2 Boullenois, Observ. 46, pp. 489, 490.

to each case. These circumstances will sometimes compel us to follow the law of the place of the contract or testament, sometimes that of the *situs rei,* sometimes that of the domicil of the party, and sometimes the place where the payment or performance is to be. He adds, that he finds no doctrine more reasonable, than that which Dumoulin has laid down upon this subject[1].

---

[1] 2 Boullenois, Observ. 46, pp. 494, 503—518; Id. pp. 537, 538.—Mr. Burge has cited from 2 Boullenois, Observ. 46, p. 534 et seq. a passage illustrating Boullenois's opinion. "The terms," says Mr. Burge, "in which the contract is expressed, may receive a construction, according to the law or usage of the place where the contract is made, different from that which is given to them by the law of the situs. If, by adopting the one sense, the contract would be brought within the prohibition of the law of the situs, that construction ought to be rejected. But if this would not be the consequence, and the adoption of either meaning would not afford a ground to prevent the contract from being completed by the law of the situs, it has been a question, whether the construction given by the law or usage of the situs, or that given by the law of the place where the contract was made, ought to prevail. Thus, in some countries, the limitation by gift or devise to a person, and 'si sine liberis discesserit' to another, operates as a substitution. The children, 'positi in conditione,' are also considered as 'positi in dispositione,' and are entitled to take. Such was the law of Toulouse. But under the coutume of Paris, the expression 'si sine liberis' imported only a condition, and consequently, if there were no failure of children, there was no substitution. The following case occurred, on which M. Boullenois gave his opinion: The Comte de R., domiciled in Languedoc, made a settlement on the marriage of his son, who had resided in Paris many years, and the lady with whom he married was a native of, and domiciled in Paris. The Comte executed a general power of attorney to the Bishop of —— to arrange the marriage settlement. By this settlement he gave to his son a moiety of all his estate, movable and immovable, then belonging to him, or which should belong to him on the day of his death. 'Sous la condition que, si le futur époux décede sans enfans mâles, nés de ce mariage, la moitié des biens à lui présentement donnés, retournera à l'ainé de ses freres, ou à l'ainé des enfants mâles dudit ainé; après toutes fois que les conventions de la dite Demoiselle future épouse auront été payées et acquittées, et que déduction aura été faite de la lègitime des filles.' There were issue of the marriage a son and daughter. The real property was situated in Toulouse. The son claimed it, insisting that his father had created a substitution, and that he took as a substitute. The daughter contended that no substitution was created, that the condition had failed, and that consequently, the father having died without making any disposition, she

§ 479 *k*. We have already had occasion, in part, to refer to the opinions of Dumoulin on this subject[1]. He reproves the doctrine maintained by many jurists, that the law and custom of the place where a contract is made, is to govern the contract in all cases. *Et advertendum, quod*

---

was entitled, with her brother, as one of the heirs ab intestato. The opinion given by M. Boullenois was, that the import of the expression given by the law of Paris, where the contract was made, and where two of the parties to it were domiciled, and the donor was present by his attorney, must prevail. This opinion was confirmed by sentence des Requêtes du Palais of the 21st of August, 1734, in favour of the daughter. But this sentence was reversed on appeal, and the decision was given in favour of the son. There is great force in the arguments by which this learned jurist maintains his opinion. The principal ground on which the decision proceeded, was, that the domicil of the father, the donor, was in Toulouse, and that it must be presumed he contemplated the law with which he was acquainted, rather than that of Paris, with which he might be unacquainted, and, that in donations, the intention of the donor is principally to be considered, since the part of the donee is confined to the acceptance of the donation. But, in the present case, this consideration loses much of the weight to which it might otherwise be entitled, because the donor had granted a general power of attorney to a person resident in Paris to arrange the settlement, and had not prescribed the terms or conditions it should contain. It was not in this case insisted, nor is it the doctrine of jurists, that the situs of the property requires the application of its law to determine the legal import of any expression in the contract. The text of the civil law is, that 'In stipulationibus, et in cæteris contractibus, id sequamir, quod actum est; et si non pateat quod actum est, erit consequens, ut id sequimur, quod in regione in quâ actum est, frequentatur.' It has been justly considered, that this rule is too general; for that, if it were universally followed, the intentions of the contracting parties must be frequently defeated. It has been seen, in the passage already cited, that it was condemned by Du Moulin. In his opinion, and he is followed by Boullenois, the interpretation of expressions in a contract must depend, not on the place where it is made, but on those other circumstances, from which the will or intention of the parties may be inferred. Generally, the interpretation which it would receive in the place of their domicil is that which, it is most probable, will be conformable to their intention." 2 Burge, Comm. on Col. and For. Law, pt. 2, ch. 9, pp. 855—857; 2 Boullenois, Observ. 46, pp. 518—538; Ante, § 275. Boullenois gives other illustrations of his doctrine. 2 Boullenois, Observ. 46, pp. 495—518. Bouhier seems to hold a similar opinion. Bouhier, Cout. de Bourg. ch. 21, n. 220—222.

[1] Ante, § 274, 441.

Doctores pessime intelligunt, L. si fundus de evicti; Quia putant ruditer et indistincte, quod debeat ibi inspici locus et consuetudo, ubi fit contractus, et sic jus in loco contractus. Quod est falsum; quinimo jus est in tacita et verisimiliter mente contrahentium. And he explains himself thus: *Aut statutum loquitur de his, quæ concernunt nudam ordinationem vel solemnitatem actus, et semper inspicitur statutum vel consuetudo, ubi actus celebratur, sive in contractibus, sive in judiciis, sive in testamentis, sive in instrumentis, aut aliis conficiendis*[1]. *Aut statutum loquitur de his, quæ meritum scilicet causæ vel decisionem concernunt; et tunc aut in his, quæ pendent à voluntate partium, vel per eas immutari possunt, et tunc inspiciuntur, circumstantiæ voluntatis quarum, una est statutum loci, in quo contrahitur, et domicilii contrahentium antiqui vel recentis, et similes circumstantiæ*[2].

§ 479 *l.* Hertius lays down the rule, that the words of a testator are to be especially interpreted according to the custom of the place where the testator had his origin or domicil. *Hinc jurisconsulti verba testatoris præcipuè interpretantur secundum loci consuetudinem, ubi testator originem vel domicilium habeat*[3]. And he illustrates it by the case of a bequest of so many measures of wheat, or so many acres of land, where the question arises as to the quantity of the measures or of the acres, whether to be understood according to the *lex loci* of the testament, or the *lex domicilii* of the testator[4]. The like doctrine is adopted by John Voet, by Stockmans, by Christinæus, by Rodenburg, and by Sandius[5]. Stockmans uses the following language: *Non exigua vis est communis regula, quæ*

---

1 Molin. Opera, tom. 3, Comm. in Cod. lib. 1, tit. 1, p. 554, (edit. 1681); Ante, § 260, 274, 441; 2 Boullenois, Observ. 46, p. 495.

2 Ibid.

3 1 Hertii, Op. De Collis. Leg. § 6, n. 3, p. 222, (edit. 1716); Id. p. 158, (edit. 1737); 2 Burge, Comm. on Col. and For. Law, pt. 2, ch. 9, pp. 859, 860.

4 Ibid.; Molin. Opera, tom. 1, De Fiefs, § 33, n. 86, p. 410, (edit. 1661).

5 See Ante, § 479 *e*, note; 4 Burge, Comm. on Col. and For. Law, pt. 2, ch. 12, pp. 591—594, where the opinions of these jurists are cited.

dictat, testatorem in dubio censeri dispositionem suam aptare jure illius loci, ubi agit et testamentum condit, et consuetudinem ac leges municipales loci tacitè influere, ac temperare generales testantium locutiones et dispositiones[1]. Paul Voet says: *In specie autem consuetudo legis verba ambigua interpretatur; et si non appareat, quid actum sit inter contrahentes, ad eam, tanquam rerum ac verborum dominam, recurritur. Quam etiam in perscrutandâ testatoris voluntate*[2].

§ 479 *m.* Indeed, it may be laid down as a general rule, that wherever there are words of an ambiguous signification, or different significations in different countries are used in a will, they are to be interpreted in the sense in which they are used in the law of his domicil, with which he may be presumed either to be most familiar, or to have adopted. Sandius says: *In ambigua hac testatoris voluntate spectandum esse consuetudinem regionis, in qua testator versatus est*[3]. The same rule has been recognised in England, or rather, it has been generalized; for it has, in effect, been held, that, in the construction of ambiguous instruments or contracts, the place of executing them, the domicil of the parties, the place appointed for its execution, and other circumstances, are to be taken into consideration[4].

---

1 Stockm. Decis. 27, n. 1, p. 61.

2 P. Voet, de Stat. § 3, ch. 1, n. 2, p. 100, (edit. 1715); Id. p. 111, (edit. 1661).

3 Sand. Decis. Fris. lib. 4, tit. 8, Defin. 7, p. 195.

4 Lansdowne *v.* Lansdowne, 2 Bligh, R. 60, 87; 4 Burge, Comm. on Col. and For. Law, pt. 2, ch. 12, pp. 590, 591.

CHAPTER XII.

SUCCESSION AND DISTRIBUTION.

§ 480. Having considered the operation of foreign law in regard to testaments of movable property and of immovable property, we next proceed to the right of succession in cases of intestacy, or, as the phrase is, of succession *ab intestato*. And here the preceding discussions have left little more to be done, than to state the general principles applicable to each species of property.

§ 481. First, in relation to movable property. The universal doctrine now recognised by the common law, although formerly much contested, is, that the succession to personal property is governed exclusively by the law of the actual domicil of the intestate at the time of his death[1].

---

[1] Many of the authorities to sustain this point have been already cited, Ante, § 380—385, 465—474. But some others may be here referred to, Pipon *v.* Pipon, Ambler, R. 25; Thorne *v.* Watkins, 2 Ves. R. 35; 1 Chitty on Comm. and Manuf. 661; Sill *v.* Worswick, 1 H. Black. 690, 691; Bruce *v.* Bruce, 2 Bos. & Pull. 229, note; Hunter *v.* Potts, 4 T. R. 182; Potter *v.* Brown, 5 East, R. 130; Doe d. Birtwhistle *v.* Vardill, 5 Barn. & Cress. 438, 450—455; S. C. 9 Bligh, R. 32—88; 2 Clarke & Finell. R. 571; Yates *v.* Thomson, 3 Clarke & Finell. R. 544; Robertson on Succession, ch. 7, pp. 104—117; Id. ch. 8, pp. 118—201; Thornton *v.* Curling, 8 Sim. R. 310; Price *v.* Deerhurst, 8 Sim. R. 279, 299; Moore *v.* Budd, 4 Hagg. Eccles. R. 346, 354; 4 Burge, Comm. on Col. and For. Law, pt. 2, ch. 4, § 5, pp. 156—170; Ante, § 362, 367, 378. For a long time the law of Scotland was unsettled on this point, but it now coincides with that of England. Robertson on Succession, ubi supra; 4 Burge, Comm. ubi supra; Stairs, Instit. b. 3, tit. 8, § 35; Ersk. Inst. b. 3, tit. 9, § 4; Liverm. Dissert. 162, 163; Olivier *v.* Townes, 14 Martin, R. 99; Shultz *v.* Pulver, 3 Paige, R. 182; De Sobry *v.* De Laistre, 2 Harr. & John. R. 193, 224, 228; Holmes *v.* Remsen, 4 John. Ch. R. 460; S. C. 20 John. R. 229; De Couche *v.* Savatier, 3 John. Ch. R. 190; Erskine, Inst. b. 3, tit. 2, § 40, 41; Id. b. 3, tit. 9, § 4; 2 Kaims, Equity, b. 3, ch. 8, § 3, 4, pp. 333, 345; 1 Boullenois, Observ. 20, p. 358; 2 Boullenois, 54; Id.

It is of no consequence what is the country of the birth of the intestate, or of his former domicil, or what is the actual *situs* of the personal property at the time of his death; it devolves upon those who are entitled to take it as heirs or distributees, according to the law of his actual domicil at the time of his death[1]. Hence, if a Frenchman dies intestate in America, all his personal property, whether it be in America or in France, is distributable according to the statute of distribution of the State where he then resided, notwithstanding it may differ essentially from the distribution prescribed by the law of France.

§ 481 *a.* So the like rule prevails in the ascertainment of the person who is entitled to take as heir or distributee. The law of the domicil, therefore, is to decide whether primogeniture gives a right of preference or an exclusive right to the succession, and whether a person is legitimate or not, to take the succession. So, whether persons are to take *per capita* or *per stirpes;* and the nature and extent of the right of representation. Thus, for example, in England and in some of the American States, there is no right of representation beyond that of brothers' and sisters' children, as to the right of distribution in cases of intestacy of movable property. If, therefore, a man should die, leaving a brother and sister, and the grandchildren of a deceased brother, the latter would not take anything in virtue of a representation of the deceased brother[2].

57; Fergusson on Mar. and Divorce, 346, 361; Vattel, b. 2, § 85, 103, 110, 111; 1 Hertii Opera, De Collis. Leg. § 4, n. 26, p. 135, (edit. 1737); Id. p. 192, (edit. 1716); Huberus, De Confl. Leg. lib. 1, tit. 3, § 15; Henry on Foreign Law, pp. 13—15; Id. pp. 46, 196; J. Voet, Ad Pand. lib. 38, tit. 17, § 34, p. 596; Harvey *v.* Richards, 1 Mason, R. 418; 2 Froland. Mém. 1294; 2 Dwarris on Stat. 649.

[1] Ibid.

[2] 4 Burge, Comm. on Col. and For. Law, pt. 2, ch. 4, § 5, pp. 156—160. As in cases of movable property, the law of the domicil is thus held to regulate the succession and distribution thereof, the question may often become important, what is the actual domicil? As to this, see Ante, § 44—50. Upon this subject many difficult questions may arise. See, for example,

§ 481 *b.* This same doctrine is maintained with equal broadness by foreign jurists. It is founded in a great measure upon the doctrine that movables have no *situs,* and accompany the person of the owner; so that, *in fictione juris,* they are always deemed to be in the place of his domicil. *Mobilia sequuntur personam, et ejus ossibus adhærent*[1]. Thus Rodenburg, referring to the effect of a change of domicil on succession, takes the very distinction between movable property and immovable property, founded upon its nature and character. *Jus rebus succedendi immobilibus, semper a loco rei sitæ metiendum, huc non pertinet; succedendi mobilibus pertinet; quod ea certo loco non circumscripta, comitentur personam a domicilio ejus accipientia leges*[2]. Boullenois fully concurs in this opinion[3]. Burgundus holds

---

De Bonneval *v.* De Bonneval, 1 Curteis, R. 856; Attor.-Gen. *v.* Dunn, 6 Mees. & Welsb. R. 511. But the rule itself may require some modification, where the law of the domicil of the intestate is intended to take away the rights of persons who might otherwise succeed to movable property in another country, by a sort of hostile perversity. Thus, it has been said, that under the Berlin and Milan decrees, passed by Napoleon, Englishmen were rendered incapable of succeeding to the personal estate of intestates dying in Italy. Such a law might require England to disallow the operation of the general rule, as to personal property, of the same intestate situate in England. See Koster *v.* Sapte, 1 Curteis, Eccl. R. 691; Ante, § 472, note. Suppose a person should die in transitu from his acquired domicil, the question might then arise, whether the law of his native domicil, or of his acquired domicil, or of his intended domicil, was to govern. It seems clear, that a domicil, whether native or acquired, is not lost by a mere abandonment. It is not defeated animo merely, but animo et facto, and necessarily remains until a subsequent domicil is acquired, at least unless the party dies in transitu to his intended domicil. This last qualification of the doctrine, though stated by a learned Judge, may be exactly the point of a doubt whether it varies the rule. Munroe *v.* Douglas, 5 Madd. R. 232. See also 2 Boullenois, App. pp. 59, 60; Jennison *v.* Hapgood. 10 Pick. R. 77, 99.

[1] See Ante, § 362, 377, 378; 4 Burge, Comm. on Col. and For. Law, pt. 2, ch. 4, § 5, p. 157; Fœlix, Conflit des Lois, Revue Etrang. et Fran. tom. 7, (1840), § 32, pp. 221, 222.

[2] Rodenburg, De Div. Stat. tit. 2, pt. 2, ch. 2, § 1; 2 Boullenois, App. p. 59; 2 Boullenois, ch. 2, p. 54.

[3] 2 Boullenois, Observ. 33, pp. 57, 63, 64.

the same opinion[1]. Perhaps it might, with quite as much accuracy, be said, that the doctrine is founded in a great public policy, observed, *ex comitate*, by all nations, from a sense of its general convenience and utility, and its tendency to avoid endless embarrassments and conflicts, where personal property has often changed places, which is the view entertained by John Voet[2].

§ 482. Paul Voet has put the principle in a compendious manner. *Idem ne inferendum de statutis, quæ spectant successiones ab intestato? Respondeo, quod ita; rem enim afficiunt, non personam, ut legibus loci, ubi bona sita sunt, vel esse intelliguntur, regi debeant. Immobilia statutis loci, ubi sita; mobilia loci statutis, ubi testator habuit domicilium*[3]. And again: *Verum an, quod de immobilibus dictum, idem de mobilibus statuendum erit? Respondeo, quod non. Quia illorum bonorum nomine nemo censetur semet loci legibus subjecisse. Ut quæ res certum locum non habent, quia facile de loco in locum transferuntur; adeoque secundum loci statuta regulantur, ubi domicilium habuit defunctus*[4].

§ 482 *a*. Sandius, in speaking of successions takes the like distinction between movables and immovables. *Aliud judicium est de mobilibus, quæ ex conditione personarum legem accipiunt, nec loco continere dicuntur, sed personam sequuntur, et ab ea dependent; et ideo omnia ubicunque mobilia legibus domicilii subjiciuntur*[5]. Strykius affirms the same doctrine; as do Gaill, and Christinæus, and John Voet[6]. The latter says: *Cæterum occasione variantium in*

---

1 Burgundus, Tract. 2, n. 20, 21; Id. Tract. 1, n. 26.

2 J. Voet, Ad Pand. lib. 38, tit. 17, n. 34, tom. 2, p. 596; Post, 482 *a* note.

3 P. Voet, § 4, c. 3, n. 10, p. 135, (edit. 1716); Id. p. 153, (edit. 1661); Ante, § 475.

4 P. Voet, De Stat. § 9, c. 1, n. 8, p. 255, (edit. 1715); Id. p. 309, (edit. 1661). See also to the same point John Voet, Ad Pand. tom. 1, lib. 1, tit. 4, ps. 2, n. 11, p. 44; Ante, § 362, n. 3.

5 Sand. Decis. Frisic. lib. 4, tit. 8, Defin. 7, p. 194.

6 Strykius, De Success. Diss. 1, c. 4, n. 3; Gaill, Pract. Observ. lib. 2, Observ. 124, n. 18, p. 552; Christin. Decis. Cur. Belg. vol. 2, Decis. 3,

successionem intestatam statutorum, generaliter observandum est, bona defuncti immobilia, et quæ juris interpretatione pro talibus habentur, deferri secundum leges loci, in quo sita sunt; adeo, ut tot censeri debeant diversa patrimonia, ac tot hereditates, quot locis, diverso jure utentibus, immobilia existunt. Mobilia vero ex lege domicilii ipsius defuncti, vel quia semper domino præsentia esse finguntur, aut (ut exposui) ex comitate, passim usu[1]. Bynkershoek is equally positive. *Omnino igitur interest scire non tam, ubi quis decessit, quam ubi decedens domicilium habuit; nam si hoc sciamus, secundum leges domicilii hereditas intestati defertur, sive major, sive minor decesserit quod ad mobilia nempe, et quæ pro mobilibus habentur*[2].

§ 483. Secondly, in relation to immovable property. And here a very different principle prevails at the common law. The descent and heirship of real estate is exclusively governed by the law of the country within which it is actually situate. No person can take except those who are recognised as legitimate heirs by the laws of that country, and they take in the proportions and the order which those laws prescribe. This is the indisputable doctrine of the common law[3].

§ 483 *a*. Foreign jurists are not, indeed, universally agreed even as to this point, although certainly they differ less than in most other cases. It may truly be said that the generality of them (having a great weight of authority) unequivocally admit, that the descent and distribution of

---

n. 2, 3, p. 4; J. Voet, Ad Pand. lib. 38, tit. 17, De Success. ab Intestato. n. 34, tom. 2, p. 596; Fœlix, Conflit des Lois, Revue Etrang. et Franç. tom. 7, (1840), § 37, pp. 307—311; 4 Burge, Comm. on Col. and For. Law, pt. 2, ch. 4, § 5, pp. 156—158.

1 J. Voet, Comm. ad Pand. lib. 38, tit. 17, n. 34, tom. 2, p. 596.

2 Bynkers. Quest. Privat. Jur. lib. 1, c. 16, pp. 179, 180.

3 4 Burge, Comm. on Col. and For. Law, ch. 4, § 5, pp. 151, 152, Doe d. Birtwhistle *v.* Vardill, 5 Barn. & Cress. pp. 451, 452; S. C. 6 Bligh, R. 479, note; 9 Bligh, R. 32—88; 1 Rob. R. (House of Lords), p. 627; Ante, § 364—366, 426—429; Post, § 483 *a*, note.

real estate is, and ought to be, governed by the *lex rei sitæ*[1]. On this head it might be almost sufficient to adopt the language of John Voet, in his classification of real and personal statutes. He reduces to the class of real statutes whatever regards inheritances. *Quo pertinent jura successionum ab intestato; quo nam ordinead bona quæque ab intestato, quisque in capita, vel stirpes, vel lineas, vel jure primogenituræ admittendus sit; quâ ratione legitimi aut illegitimi, agnati, cognati vocentur; quæque his sunt similia plura*[2]. Rodenburg is equally decisive. *Jus rebus succedendi immobilibus semper a loco rei sitæ metiendum*[3]. Froland gives the rule in the most concise but energetic terms, attributing the language to Dumoulin: *Mobilia sequuntur personam; immobilia situm*[4]. Dumoulin says: *Aut statutum datur in rem;*

---

1 The authorities to this point also have been already cited, Ante, § 424—448. See Doe dem. Birtwhistle *v.* Vardill, 5 Barn. & Cress. 438; United States *v.* Crosby, 7 Cranch, R. 115; Kerr *v.* Moon, 9 Wheaton, R. 566, 570; M'Cormick *v.* Sullivant, 10 Wheaton, R. 192; Darby *v.* Mayer, 10 Wheaton, R. 469; Hosford *v.* Nichols, 1 Paige, R. 220; Cutler *v.* Davenport, 1 Pick. R. 81; Wills *v.* Cowper, 2 Hamm. R. 124; 1 Hertii Opera, De Collis. Leg. § 4, n. 26, p. 135; 1 Boullenois, 25, 223, &c.; 1 Froland, Mém. 60, 61, 65; P. Voet, De Stat. § 4, c. 2, n. 6, p. 123; J. Voet, Ad Pand. lib. 1, tit. 4, ps. 2, § 3, p. 39; Ersk. Inst. b. 3, tit. 2, § 40, 41, p. 515; D'Aguesseau, Œuvres, tom. 4, p. 637; Huberus, lib. 1, tit. 3, § 15; 2 Dwarris on Stat. p. 649; Rodenburg, pt. 2, tit. 2, c. 2; 2 Boullenois, App. p. 59, 63; 2 Boullenois, 54, 57, 383; 2 Froland, Mém. ch. 27, p. 1288; Fœlix, Conflit. des Lois Revue, Etrang. et Franç. tom. 7, (1840); § 37, pp. 307—312; 4 Burge, Comm. on Col. and For. Law, pt. 2, ch. 4, § 5, pp. 151—156.—Since the preceding sheets were worked off, I have ascertained that the case of Doe d. Birtwhistle *v.* Vardill, above cited, has been affirmed in the House of Lords. 1 Rob. R. (House of Lords), p. 627. The ground was, that by the law of England no person could inherit lands as heir who was not born after the marriage of his parents.

2 J. Voet, Ad. Pand. lib. 1, tit. 4, pt. 2, § 3, tom. 1, p. 39; Id. lib. 38, tit. 17, n. 34, tom. 2, p. 596.

3 Rodenburg, De Div. Stat. ps. 2, tit. 2, c. 2, p. 59; 2 Boullenois, App. p. 54, 57. See also Henrys, Œuvres, tom. 2, lib. 4, ch. 6, Quest. 105; Observ. Bretonnier, p. 613, 614, edit. 1771.

4 2 Froland, Mém. 1289.—I cannot find any such expressive language used by Dumoulin in the passages cited by Froland, and therefore conclude,

puta, bona descendentis veniant ad primogenitum; et tunc attenditur statutum loci, in quo sita sunt bona[1]. Bynkershoek, in his bold and uncompromising manner, asserts, that the rule is so well established that no one dares to open his mouth against it. *Immobilia enim deferri ex jure, quod obtinet in loco rei sitæ, adeo recepta hodie sententia est, ut nemo ausit contra hiscere*[2].

§ 483 *b*. Paul Voet says: *Quid si circa successionem ab Intestato, statutorum sit difformitas? Spectabitur loci statutum, ubi immobilia sita, non ubi testator moritur*[3]. Rodenburg, speaking of laws which are purely real, (*quæ quidem jure precipui merè realia sunt*), says: *Cujusmodi appellamus ea, quæ de modo dividendarum ab intestato hæreditatum tractant, territorium non egredientia; conspirant enim eò vota fere omnium, bona ut dijudicentur suâ lege loci, in quo sita sunt vel esse intelliguntur*[4]. Burgundus, after remarking that there is a diversity of opinion upon this subject among jurists, some holding that the law of the *situs* of the property is to govern, some, that the law of the domicil of the intestate, and some few, that the law of the place where the intestate happened to die, then asserts his own opinion: *Bonorum duæ sunt species; alia enim mobilia sunt, alia immobilia; illa a personâ, hæc a situ cujusque provinciæ, legem accipiunt; videlicet, ut nulla habita ratione originis, aut mortis,*

---

that it is his own concise statement of Dumoulin's opinion, in which he is certainly correct. The passages cited Molin. Opera, tom. 2, p. 701, (edit. 1681), Coutumes de Senlis, art. 140; Id. p. 747, Coutumes d'Auvergne, art. 4; Id. Consil. 53, p. 964; Id. tom. 3, p. 554, Conclus. de Statut.

1 Molin. Oper. Comm. In. Cod. lib. 1, tit. 1, l. 1, Conclus de Stat. p. 556, (edit. 1681).

2 Bynkers. Quest. Privat. Jur. lib. 1, c. 16, p. 180; Ante, § 381.

3 P. Voet, de Stat. § 9, c. 1, n. 3, 4, pp. 252, 253, (edit. 1715); Id. pp. 305—307, (edit. 1661); Ante, § 433, 475.—Paul Voet gives a long list of authorities supporting the doctrine, ut immobilia statutis loci regantur, ubi sita. P. Voet, § 9, c. 1, n. 4, ubi supra.

4 2 Rodenburg, De Div. Stat. tit. 2, c. 2, § 1, n. 1; 2 Boullenois, App. p. 14; Id. p. 74.

aut domicilii, tam hæredum, quam ipsius defuncti, dividantur secundum consuetudines locorum, ubi bona vel sunt, vel sita esse intelliguntur[1].

§ 483 *c.* Boullenois treats the subject as so entirely free from doubt, as to require no comment or explanation[2]. D'Argentré, as we have seen, resolutely maintains the same opinion[3]. Sandius says: *Contra tamen vulgo a doctoribus receptum est, statuta de bonis et successione intestati disponentia esse realia, nec egredi fines territorii. Atque ita fieri, ut secundum diversitatem statutorum diversimodè succedatur, non aliter, quam si per fictionem unius hominis diversa sunt patrimonia. Et immobilia sunt sub jurisdictione loci in quo jacent. Statutum igitur Hollandiæ non extendit se ad res immobiles in Frisia situs; sed istæ subjacent dispositione juris communis quod in Frisia obtinet*[4].

§ 483 *d.* And not to dwell upon a point which, although not without controversy among foreign jurists, is generally established, we may quote the opinion of Huberus. His language is: *Non potest heic omitti Quæstio frequens in foris hodiernis, a juris Romani tamen aliena terminis: Quia sæpe sit, ut diversum jus succedendi ab intestato in locis, ubi defunctus habuit domicilium, atque in iis locis, ubi bona sita sunt, obtineat, dubitatur, secundum utrius loci leges successio regenda sit. Communis et recta sententia est, in rebus immobilibus servandum esse jus loci, in quo bona sunt sita; quia cum partem ejusdem territorii faciant, diversæ jurisdictionis legibus adfici non possunt. Verum in mobilibus nihil esse causæ, cur aliud quam jus domicilii sequamur; quia res mobiles non habent affectionem versus territorium, sed ad personam patrisfamilias duntaxat; qui aliud quam, quod in loco domicilii obtinebat, voluisse videri non potest*[5].

---

1 Burgundus, Tract. 1, n. 36, p. 38.

2 1 Boullenois, Observ. 20, p. 358; 2 Boullenois, Observ. 41, p. 383.

3 Ante, § 438.

4 Sand. Decis. lib. 4, tit. 8, Defin. 7, p. 194.

5 Huberus, vol. 1, lib. 3, De Success. n. (s), p. 278. See also 4 Burge, Comm. on Col. and For. Law, pt. 2, ch. 4, § 5, pp. 150 — 152, 154, 155.

§ 484. We have already had occasion to state, that in the interpretation of wills of immovable property, and of movable property, if the description of persons who are to take be by some general designation, such as "heirs," or "next of kin," "issue," or "children," the rule of the common law is, that they are to be ascertained by the *lex domicilii*, both in regard to immovable property and to movable property, unless the context furnishes some clear guide for a different interpretation[1]. The same rule will apply in cases of the descent and distribution of movable property *ab intestato*, for the reason already suggested—that it is deemed by fiction of law to be in the place of his domicil, and therefore to be distributable according to the *lex domicilii;* and consequently, who are the "issue," or "children," or "heirs," or "next of kin," is a matter to be ascertained by that law[2]. But in regard to immovable property a different rule prevails, founded upon the actual *situs;* and as the succession is to be according to the *lex loci situs*, the persons who are to take by succession can be ascertained only by reference to the same law[3].

§ 484 *a*. Foreign jurists generally, although not universally, maintain the same doctrine; and accordingly hold, that in cases of succession *ab intestato* we are to ascertain the persons who are to take the inheritance by the *lex loci rei sitæ*, whether the question respect legitimacy, or primo-

---

[1] Ante, § 479 *a*, 479 *m*, 479 *n;* 2 Burge, Comm. on Col. and For. Law, pt. 2, ch. 9, pp. 855—858.

[2] See Thorne *v.* Watkins, 2 Ves. 35; Brown *v.* Brown, or Gordon *v.* Brown, 3 Hagg. Eccl. R. 455, note; S. C. 4 Wilson & Shaw, 28; P. Voet, De Stat. § 3, ch. 1, n. 2, p. 100, (edit. 1715); Id. p. 111, (edit. 1661); Elliott *v.* Lord Minto, 6 Madd. R. 16; Earl of Winchelsea *v.* Garetty, 2 Keen, R. 293, 309, 310; Ante, § 479 *e;* Post, § 490, 529.

[3] Doe d. Birtwhistle *v.* Vardill, 5 Barn. & Cress. 438; S. C. 6 Bligh, R. 749; S. C. 9 Bligh, R. 32; Ante, § 364—366, 426—429, 483; 4 Burge, Comm. on Col. and For. Law, ch. 4, § 5, pp. 150—156; Id. ch. 15, § 4, pp. 722—734; Elliott *v.* Lord Minto, 6 Madd. R. 16; Earl of Winchelsea *v.* Garetty, 2 Keen, R. 293, 309, 310; Post, § 529.

geniture, or right of representation, or proximity of blood, or next of kin. John Voet is very full and explicit on this subject. He says: *Positâ ergo varietate, si quæras, cujus loci leges in repræsentatione observandæ sint? Respondendum videtur eodem modo, quo supra in principali quæstione de successione; puta, mobilium intuitu spectandas esse leges domicilii defuncti, immobilium respectu leges cujusque loci, in quo illa sita sunt: eo quod jus repræsentationis omnino ad jus successionis intestatæ pertinet, imo successorem facit eum tanquam ex fictione legis proximum, qui vere atque naturaliter defuncto proximus non est*[1].

§ 485. But these general principles still leave behind them, even in the common law, some very embarrassing difficulties; and in the complex systems of foreign law the difficulties are greatly multiplied. Sir William Grant adverted to this subject in an important case, and said: "Where land and personal property are situated in different countries, and governed by different laws, and a question arises upon the combined effect of those laws, it is often very difficult to determine what portion of each law is to enter into the decision of the question. It is not easy to say how much is to be considered as depending on the law of real property, which must be taken from the country where the land lies, and how much upon the law of personal property, which must be taken from the law of the domicil, and to blend both together, so as to form a rule applicable to the mixed question, which neither law separately furnishes sufficient materials to decide[2]."

§ 486. Two cases of a curious nature were on the same occasion mentioned by Sir William Grant, as illustrative of

---

[1] J. Voet, Ad Pand. tom. 2, lib. 38, tit. 17, n. 35, p. 597. See Id. lib. 38, tit. 18, n. 84, p. 639, where he adds; Denique prætermittendum non est, in eo, an jus primogenituræ admittendum sit, necne; immobilium quidem intuitu spectandam esse legem loci, in quo sita sunt; mobilium vero respectu consuetudinem domicilii defuncti.

[2] Brodie *v.* Barry, 2 Ves. & Beames R. 130, 131.

his remarks, which cannot be better stated than in his own language. "I have argued," said he, "in the House of Lords cases in which difficulties of that kind occurred. Two of the most remarkable were those of Balfour *v.* Scott[1], and Drummond *v.* Drummond[2]. In the former, a person domiciled in England died intestate, leaving real estate in Scotland. The heir was one of the next of kin, and claimed a share of the personal estate. To this claim it was objected, that by the law of Scotland the heir cannot share in the personal property with the other next of kin, except on condition of collating the real estate, that is, bringing it into a mass with the personal estate, to form one common subject of division. It was determined, however, that he was entitled to take his share without complying with that obligation. There the English law decided the question[3]."

§ 487. He then added: "In Drummond *v.* Drummond, a person domiciled in England had real estate in Scotland, upon which he granted a heritable bond to secure a debt contracted in England. He died intestate; and the question was, by which of the estates this debt was to be borne. It was clear, that by the English law the personal estate was the primary fund for the payment of debts. It was equally clear, that by the law of Scotland the real estate was the primary fund for the payment of the heritable bond. Here was a direct *conflictus legum.* It was said for the heir, that the personal estate must be distributed according to the law of England, and must bear all the burthens to which it is by that law subject. On the other hand it was said, that the real estate must go according to the law of Scotland, and bear all the burthens to which it

---

1 See Robertson on Successions, pp. 202—207; 4 Burge, Comm. on Col. and For. Law, pt. 2, ch. 15, § 4, p. 731; 6 Brown, Parl. R. 731, by Tomlins.

2 6 Brown, Parl. R. (Tomlin's edit.) p. 550; 4 Burge, Comm. on Col. and For. Law, pt. 2, ch. 15, § 4, p. 729.

3 Brodie *v.* Barry, 2 Ves. & Beam. R. 130, 131.

is by that law subject. It was determined, that the law of Scotland should prevail, and that the real estate must bear the burthen[1]."

§ 488. In conclusion, he said: "In the first case, the disability of the heir did not follow him to England, and the personal estate was distributed as if both the domicil and the real estate had been in England. In the second, the disability to claim exoneration out of the personalty did follow him into England, and the personal estate was distributed as if both the domicil and the real estate had been in Scotland[2]."

§ 489. Another illustration is furnished by the very case then in judgment before Sir William Grant, which turned upon the question, whether an heir at law of heritable property in Scotland, being a legatee of personal property which was in England, under a will of the testator, which intended to dispose of all his real property in England and Scotland, but which will, not being conformable to the law of Scotland, was not capable of passing real estate there, should be put to his election to take the legacy under the will, or to surrender to the purposes of the will the Scotch heritable property. Sir William Grant decided in the affirmative, and said: "Now, what law is to determine, whether an instrument of any given nature or form is to be read against an heir at law for the purpose of putting him to an election, by which the real estate may be affected? According to Lord Hardwicke, and the Judges who have followed him, that is a question belonging to the law of real property, for they have decided it by a statute which regulates devises of land. Upon that principle, if the domicil were in Scotland and the real estate in England, an English will, imperfectly executed, ought not to be read in Scotland

---

1 Brodie *v.* Barry, 2 Ves. & Beam. R. 130, 131. See also Drummond *v.* Drummond, 6 Brown, Parl. R. (Tomlin's edit.) p. 550; Post, § 529; Robertson on Successions, pp. 209, 214; 4 Burge, Comm. on Col. and For. Law, pt. 2, ch. 15, § 4, pp. 722—734.

2 Brodie *v.* Barry, 2 Ves. & Beam. p. 132; Ante, § 266; Post, § 529.

for the purpose of putting the heir to an election; and, upon the same principle, if, by the law of Scotland no will could be read against the heir, it would follow that a will of land, situated in Scotland, ought not to be read in England to put the Scotch heir to an election. Doubting much the soundness of that principle, I am glad that the case of Cunningham *v.* Gayner[1] relieves me from the necessity of deciding the question, as whichever law is applied to the decision of the present case, the result will be the same, &c. If the law of Scotland is resorted to, the case alluded to determines that the English will may be read against the Scotch heir for the purpose of putting him to an election[2]."

§ 489 *a.* Other questions of a very difficult and embarrassing nature may arise, as to the nature and extent of the liability of the heirs to the payment of debts and other charges of the intestate, chargeable on his real estate, situate in different countries where different rules prevail, as to the nature and extent of the liability of the heirs in respect to such real estate; and the real estate descends to different persons, and in a different manner, in the respective countries. The questions may respect the exclusive or primary applicability of one or more of the real estates to the discharge of such debts or other charges, or the liability of the heirs *in solido,* or *pro portione hæreditariâ,* or the right of the heirs or devisees of the real estates in one country, to contribution or indemnity from the heirs or devisees of the real estate in another country, or the right of the creditors to proceed against them all *in solido,* or *pro portione hæreditariâ*[3].

§ 489 *b.* Many cases of this sort have been discussed by foreign jurists, and decided by foreign tribunals. Thus, for example, where one part of the succession has been situate in a country by whose laws the creditors are permitted to

---

1 1 Bligh, R. 27, note; Robertson on Successions, pp. 219—220.

2 Brodie *v.* Barry, 2 Ves. & Beam. R. 127, 133; Ante, § 479 *a,* note; Robertson on Successions, pp. 217, 218.

3 See 1 Boullenois, Observ. 17, pp. 277—288, where the subject is much discussed. Bouhier, Cout. de Bourg. ch. 21, § 213, 214, p. 416.

proceed against each heir *in solido,* and another part in the country of the domicil of the intestate, by whose laws the creditors are entitled to proceed against each heir *pro portione hæreditariâ;* there has been no small diversity of judgment as to the rule which ought to be applied in favour of the creditors, whether the rule of the law *rei sitæ,* or of the law of the domicil, as to the nature and extent of the liability of the heirs [1]. Perhaps, in such a case, the right of the creditors against the heirs respectively may most properly be deemed to be governed by the *lex rei sitæ,* and the mode of proceeding against them be regulated by the law of the place where he seeks his remedy. If he seeks to enforce his rights in the place of the domicil of the intestate, he must recover against each heir *pro portione hæreditariâ.* If he seeks to enforce them in the other country, then the heirs are there liable to him *in solido.* But this opinion is far from having the assent of several distinguished jurists. They hold, that the creditors are entitled to proceed against the heirs in either country, according to the law of the domicil of the intestate; because it is there that they suppose the heirs to have contracted the debt to the creditors. Of this opinion are Paul de Castro, Christinæus, and Bouhier, as well as the judges of several foreign tribunals [2]. On the other hand, other jurists hold, that in each country respectively the heirs contract with the creditors according to the law of the place where the succession is devolved upon, and is assumed by the heir, that is, the *lex rei sitæ.* Of this latter opinion are many distinguished jurists [3]. Merlin inclines

---

[1] 4 Burge, Comm. on Col. and For. Law, pt. 2, ch. 15, § 4, pp. 722—724, who cites several authorities upon the subject. Among them are Christin. tom. 1, Decis. 283, n. 15, 16; J. Voet, lib. 29, tit. 2, n. 31; Merlin, Répert. tit. Dette, § 4; 1 Boullenois, Observ. 17, p. 278; Bouhier, Cout. de Bourg. ch. 21, n. 213.

[2] 1 Boullenois. Observ. 17, pp. 277, 278; Bouhier, Cout. de Bourg. ch. 31, n. 213, p. 416; Christin. Decis. tom. 1, Decis. 283, n. 15, 16, p. 353. See also J. Voet, Ad Pand. lib. 29, n. 31, 32, tom. 2, p. 376; Merlin, Répert. Dette, § 4.

[3] Bouhier, Cout. de Bourg. ch. 21, n. 213, 214, p. 416.

strongly to this latter opinion[1]. Boullenois leaves the question without any expression of his own views, saying, that it is a point full of difficulty[2].

§ 489 *c.* A question of another sort may arise between the heirs or devisees of the deceased party, who, as between themselves, in cases of successions or wills of immovable property in different countries, governed by different laws, is ultimately to bear the debts of creditors or other charges for which such property is liable, and which some of the heirs have been compelled to pay. In such cases the question must first arise, which fund is primarily liable for the payment or discharge thereof *inter sese;* for it should seem, that, as between themselves, the fund primarily liable should ultimately be held chargeable therewith in exoneration of all the other funds. If there is no such priority of liability, but all the funds are equally liable *pari passu,* then it should seem reasonable that each fund, wherever it is actually situate, should contribute *pro rata,* according to its value in the hands of each heir respectively, to the discharge of the common burthen. If part of the funds are exempted from contribution, they should still possess that privilege, and the residue contribute. It will, however, be found difficult to affirm, that foreign jurists and tribunals have given any uniform support to these doctrines[3].

---

1 Merlin, Répertoire, Dette, § 4.

2 1 Boullenois, Observ. 17, p. 279.

3 Pothier appears to hold this doctrine. Pothier des Successions, ch. 5, § 1, p. 223, 4to edit. He there cites a case, of which Mr. Burge has given the substance as follows: "An inhabitant of Blois, where the coutume burthened the heir to the movable estate with all the movable debts, left in his succession biens propres situated in Blois, and others situated in Orleans. The coutume of the latter place makes all the different heirs subject to all the debts. He left an heir to his movable estate, and another heir to his biens propres, situated in Orleans and Blois. In this case Pothier says, that the heir to the biens propres must, conformably to the coutume of Orleans, where he had succeeded to that part of the succession, bear his part of all the debts of the succession, even those which are movable, regard being had to the value which the real estate at Orleans would bear to the whole succession. By this ap-

§ 490. Other illustrations of the difficulties attendant upon the administration of this branch of law, are to be found in the application of local rules to the interpretation of wills, whether arising from the *lex domicilii* or the *lex rei sitæ,* as the case may regard movable property or immovable property. We have already had occasion to discuss this subject in another place[1]. But it may not be without use to state one or two cases a little more fully than has been already done. A question of this sort was recently dis-

---

portionment effect is given to the coutume of Orleans as well as to that of Blois; for the heir to the real estate contributes only to the debts in respect of that part of the estate which is situated in Orleans, and he does not contribute in respect of that part which is situated in Blois." 4 Burge, Comm. on Col. and For. Law, pt. 2, ch. 15, § 4, pp. 724, 725. The same subject is discussed at large in 2 Froland, Mém. des. Stat. ch. 32, pp. 1547—1573, and he cites several adjudications, and among others one stated by Basnage, Coutume de Normand. tom. 2, art. 408, p. 141. See also 1 Boullenois, Observ. 17, p. 284, who cites Mornac. Comm. on Dig. lib. 5, tit. 1, l. 50, 1, De Judiciis. Mr. Burge has expressed his own opinion in the following words: "It may perhaps be stated as the correct rule, that where an obligation or an exemption is annexed to the personal estate, but no similar obligation or exemption is annexed to the real estate, the lex loci domicilii will prevail in whatever country the rights or liabilities of the heir became the subject of adjudication. But if similar obligations or exemptions are annexed to the personal and real estate by the respective laws to which the succession to these two species of property is subject, and the effect of adopting the one law rather than the other would be to throw on the one estate a burthen, or confer on it an exemption not annexed to it by the law of the country which governed the succession to it, it would be the more just and correct rule to adopt the lex loci rei sitæ, rather than the lex loci domicilii. The case of Drummond and Drummond would seem to warrant the adoption of such a rule, nor is the decision in the Bishop of Metz's succession at variance with it. The lex loci domicilii had alone annexed to the personal estate an exclusive liability to pay the debts, and no such liability was annexed to the real estate by the lex loci rei sitæ. The only liability which was annexed to the real estate by that law, was an obligation to contribute with the personal estate; but such a contribution could not take place, because the personal estate was subject to a law which made it exclusively applicable, and therefore the liability to contribute could only exist when the personal estate was subject to the same law as the real estate." 4 Burge, Comm. on Col. and For. Law, pt. 2, ch. 15, pp. 732, 733.

[1] Ante, § 479 *a*—479 *n*.

cussed in the House of Lords upon a will made in Virginia, by which the testator bequeathed to his sister, Mary Brown, "the remaining one-fourth share of the balance of his estate, at her death to be equally divided among her children, if she should have any." The question was, what estate Mary Brown took under the will, whether a life estate or an absolute property. And it appearing, that the Courts of Virginia had construed the bequest to give her an absolute estate upon the footing of that decree, the House of Lords, deeming it a question of American law, established the same construction[1].

§ 491. In another case, the same principle was adopted; and the Court laid down the rule, that in the construction of a will the *lex domicilii* must govern, unless there is sufficient on its face to show a different intention in the testator. The facts were these: A lady, a native of Scotland, was domiciled in England. On a visit to Edinburgh she made a will entirely in the Scotch form, and it was deposited with the writer at Edinburgh. She had personalty in England only, and died in England. Scotland, then, was the *domicilium originis et forum contractûs;* but, on the other hand, England was the *forum domicilii* and the *locus rei sitæ.* The question was, whether by the legatee's death in the lifetime of the testatrix the legacy lapsed according to the law of England, or survived to the legatee's representatives according to the law of Scotland. The Court decided, that being domiciled in England, it was to be presumed that she intended the law of England to be applied; and, that there was not enough in the will to repel that presumption[2].

---

[1] Gordon *v.* Brown, or Brown *v.* Brown, 3 Hagg. Eccl. R. 455, note; S. C. 4 Wils. & Shaw, p. 28; Ante, § 479 *c.*

[2] Anstruther *v.* Chalmers, 2 Simons, R. 1; 3 Hagg. Eccl. R. 444; Yates *v.* Thomson, 3 Clarke & Finell, R. 544, 570; Ante, § 479 *c.*

CHAPTER XIII.

FOREIGN GUARDIANSHIPS AND ADMINISTRATIONS.

§ 492. THE order of our subject next leads us to the consideration of the operation of foreign laws in relation to persons acting *in autre droit*, such as guardians, tutors, and curators *inter vivos*, and executors and administrators *post mortem*.

§ 493. And first, in relation to guardians[1]. By the Roman law guardianship was of two sorts, (1.) *Tutela*, and (2.) *Cura*. The first lasted in males until they arrived at fourteen years of age, and in females until they arrived at twelve years of age, which was called the age of puberty of the sexes respectively. From the time of puberty, until they were twenty-five years of age, which was their full majority, they were deemed minors, and subject to curatorship. During the first period of tutelage, their guardian was called tutor, and they were called pupils; during the second period, their guardian was called curator, and they were called minors[2]. In England, the guardian performs the offices both of a tutor and a curator under the Roman law[3]. In France, the tutorship lasts until the full age of majority[4].

§ 494. In treating of guardianship, two questions naturally arise: (1.) Whether the authority of a guardian over

---

[1] See 3 Burge, Comm. on Col. and For. Law, pt. 2, ch. 23, § 5, pp. 1001—1014.

[2] 1 Domat. Civil Law, b. 2, tit. 1, p. 260; Halifax, Analysis of Civil Law, ch. 9, pp. 15, 17, 18; 1 Brown. Civil Law, b. 1, ch. 5, pp. 129, 130. See also Ersk. Inst. b. 1, tit. 6, § 1, p. 128.

[3] Halifax, Analysis of Civil Law, ch. 9, pp. 15, 17, 18; 1 Brown, Civil Law, b. 1, ch. 5, pp. 129, 130.

[4] 1 Domat, Civil Law, b. 2, tit. 1, p. 261.

the person of his ward is local, and confined to the place of his domicil, or extends every where? (2.) Whether the authority of the guardian over the property of his ward is local, or extends every where?

§ 495. In regard to the first point, (the authority of the guardian over the person of his ward), Boullenois maintains, that the laws which regulate it are strictly personal; and, therefore, that the authority extends to the ward in foreign countries, as well as at home, and is of equal validity and right, according to the law of the domicil, in every other place. "*Je mets* (says he) *au nombre des statuts personnels, ceux, qui mettent les enfans sous la puissance de leur père, ou de leur tuteur*[1]." From this it would seem to follow, that the tutor is to be recognised as fully entitled to assert any claims over the movable property of his ward, and to sue for the debts due to his ward in foreign countries, without having any confirmation of the guardianship by the local authorities[2].

§ 496. Merlin expressly holds the same doctrine, asserting that the foreign guardian, in such a case, is competent to maintain any suit for the debts due to his ward in France and in the Netherlands, without any interposition of the local authorities to confirm the guardianship[3]. "*Il est* (says he) *de principe, que les procurations revêtues de la forme requise par la loi du lieu, où elles se passent, ont leur effet partout. Aussi ne s'est-on jamais avisé de prétendre, que le tuteur nommé à un mineur, ou à un interdit, par le juge de son domicil, ne pût agir dans un pays étranger contre les débiteurs d'un ou de l'autre, qu' après avoir fait déclarer le jugement de sa nomination exécutoire dans ce pays*[4]."

---

1 Boullenois, Observ. 4. p. 51; Id. p. 68; Ante, § 57; 2 Boullenois, Observ. 39, pp. 320, 330.

2 3 Burge, Comm. on Col. and For. Law, pt. 2, ch. 23, § 5, pp. 1002, 1003.

3 Merlin, Répertoire, Absens. ch. 3, art. 3, p. 37; Id. Faillite, § 2, n. 2, art. 9, 10, § 2, p. 412. See also, Id. Autorisation Maritale, § 10, art. 2; Ante, § 53, 54.

4 Merlin, Répertoire, Faillite, § 2, n. 2, art. 10, p. 414; Ante § 53, 54.

§ 497. Vattel lays down a similar doctrine in more comprehensive terms. "It belongs (says he) to the domestic Judge to nominate tutors and guardians for minors and idiots. The law of nations, which has an eye to the common advantage and the good harmony of nations, requires, therefore, that such nomination of a tutor or guardian be valid and acknowledged in all countries where the pupil may have any concerns[1]." This is also the opinion of Huberus, as we have already seen[2]; and it is stoutly maintained by Hertius. After having stated the rule, he adds: *Ratio hujus regulæ est evidens. Persona enim subditi quâ talis nemini alii est subjecta, quam summo imperanti, cui se submisit. Unde fit, ut leges, quæ personæ qualitatem sive characterem inquinunt comitari personam soleant, ubicunque etiam locorum versetur, tametsi in aliam civitatem migraverit, veluti si quis, mager, infamis, vel prodigus declaretur*[3]. *Hinc tutor,* (says he), *datus in loco domicilii, etiam bona alibi sita administrat.* He applies this rule, however, solely to personal rights and personal incapacities, rights of property, and power over movables. For in respect to immovables, he adds this important qualification: *Quoniam ipsi fatemur, si externa civitas circa bona immobilia aliquid directe disposuit, eam legem servari oportere*[4]. Stockmans holds a broader opinion. *Tutor etiam pupilli a Prætore authoritatem et administrationem suam extra territoriam Prætoris, et in bona ubicunque locorum sita exercet*[5]. Indeed, this same doctrine is com-

---

1 Vattel, b. 2, ch. 9, § 85.

2 Ante, § 60.

3 1 Hertii Opera, de Collis, Leg. § 4, n. 8, pp. 123, 124, (edit. 1737); Id. p. 175, (edit. 1716); Ante, § 51.

4 Ibid.

5 Stockman. Decis. 125, n. 6, p. 262. Dumoulin is thought to hold the same opinion; but it may well be doubted if it admits of that interpretation. Post, § 502 *a;* Molin. Opera, tom. 3, Comm. ad Cod. lib. 1, tit. 1, l. 1; Conclus. de Stat. p. 556, (edit. 1681). Matthæus, who has also been cited on the same side, certainly does not hold the opinion. His language is: Sed etsi silentio suo quodammodo approbare videatur curatorem a judice domicilii datum, vix tamen est, ut curator illa prædia alibi sita proscribere ac

monly asserted by all those foreign jurists, who give to personal laws an ubiquity of operation[1].

§ 498. On the other hand, there are jurists who maintain a different opinion. Paul Voet denies that laws respecting either persons or property have, in the sense of the civil jurisprudence, any extra-territorial authority, and lays down among others the following rules: (1.) that a personal statute does not affect the person beyond the territory of his domicil, so that he is not to be reputed such without the territory as he was within; (2.) that a personal statute accompanies the person every where, in regard to property within the territory of the government where the person has his domicil, and to which he is subjected[2]. He adds, that he makes no distinction in this respect, whether the statute be *in rem* or *in personam;* or, whether it purports to extend to property situate in a foreign territory or not, directly or indirectly; for the same rule applies in each case. *Quia nullum statutum, sive in rem sive in personam, si de ratione juris civilis sermo instituatur sese extendit ultra statuentis territorium*[3]. He qualifies his doctrine, however, by

---

vendere possit, sine speciali permissu ejus judiciis, in cujus territoria sita sunt. Sic enim et Tutor hodie a judice domicilii datur; nec tamen universorum negotiorum et bonorum administrationem consequitur, nisi cesset judex ejus territorii, in quo prædia sita sunt. Matthæus, de Auctionibus, lib. 1, c. 7, n. 10, p. 39. See also 3 Burge, Comm. on Col. and For. Law, pt. 2, ch. 23, § 5, pp. 1002, 1003. He says: "The appointment of tutor or guardian, committees or curators, so far as it confers the care and custody of the person of the minor or lunatic, could not, consistently with the principles of international jurisprudence, be made by any other judicial tribunal but that of the country to which the minor or lunatic was by his residence subject. According to the opinion of foreign jurists, every judicial tribunal is bound to recognise this appointment. They consider that the law which places the minor or lunatic sub tutelâ or sub curâ is a personal law, affecting the status of the person, and that the relation of tutor and ward, which it has constituted, continues to exist, notwithstanding the persons may have resorted to any other country."

[1] 3 Burge, Comm. on Col. and For. Law, pt. 2, ch. 23, § 5, pp. 1004, 1005.

[2] P. Voet, De Stat. § 4, ch. 2, n. 6, p. 123, (edit. 1716); Id. p. 137, (edit. 1661).

[3] Id. n. 7, p. 124, (edit. 1716); Id. p. 138, (edit. 1661); Ante, § 51 *b*, § 52.

admitting that movables are always deemed to be in the place of the domicil of the party, and are therefore governed by the laws thereof[1]. John Voet, as we have seen, maintains a similar opinion in the broadest and most unqualified terms[2].

§ 499. It would seem from Morrison's case[3] that the House of Lords deemed the authority of an English guardian sufficient to institute a suit for the personal property of his ward in Scotland, upon the ground that the administration of his personal estate, granted by the usual authority where he resided, must be taken to be every where of equal force with a voluntary assignment by himself. The Courts of Scotland had unequivocally decided the other way. Whether this decision has since been acted upon in England does not distinctly appear. It has certainly not received any sanction in America, in the States acting under the jurisprudence of the common law. The rights and powers of guardians are considered as strictly local; and not as entitling them to exercise any authority over the person or personal property of their wards in other States, upon the same general reasoning and policy which have circumscribed the rights and authorities of executors and administrators[4].

§ 500. In regard to the other point, whether guardians appointed in foreign countries have any authority over the property of their wards situate in other countries, foreign jurists are generally, although not universally, of opinion[5] in respect to movable property, that, since it is deemed to be in the domicil of the owner, the law of the domicil is to govern, and the rights and powers of the guardian, tutor, or curator over it, ought to be admitted to prevail every where, to the same extent as they are acknowledged by the

---

1 Ante, § 52, 377.

2 Ante, § 54 *a*.

3 Cited in 4 T. R. 140, and 1 H. Black, 677, 682.

4 Morrill *v.* Dickey, 1 John. Ch. R. 153; Kraft *v.* Vickery, 4 Gill & John. R. 332.

5 See Muhlenbruch, Doct. Pand. lib. 1, p. 1, § 72, pp. 167, 168.

law of the domicil[1]. But in respect to immovable property, foreign jurists as generally, although not universally, maintain the doctrine, (whatever may be the rule as to movable property), that the rights and authority of guardians are circumscribed by the laws of the territory of their appointment, and do not extend to other countries where the immovable property is situated. In other words, the laws *rei sitæ* are to govern; and a guardian in one country can claim nothing in another, except in the form and manner, and under the regulations prescribed by the local law. Burgundus states the doctrine with great clearness. Speaking of the capacity and incapacity of minors, he says: *Proinde confitendum est, si aliquid circa rem alterare minor velit, ut puta, alienandi vel hypothecandi facultatem exigere, ibi sane veniam impetrari debere, ubi bona sunt sita*[2]. *Nam et Constitutio Diocletiani in alienatione manifestè requirit decretum Præsidis ejus provinciæ, in quo prædium minoris est situm.* He then adds: *Nec immeritò Felinus scripsit, si facienda est dispensatio respectu rei, non ejus episcopi esse erit, cui persona subjecta est, sed ad eum spectare cui res supponitur.* He says that a different reason is given by others. *Cujus rei rationem alii tradunt, quia per ejusmodi dispensationem alteratur, et reinstatur natura ipsius beneficia et non persona*[3]. He then states a qualification of the doctrine in cases where the *venia ætatis* is obtained, saying: *Ergo, e contra, si venia ætatis in hoc dumtaxat impetretur, ut actus personales minor celebrare et peragere possit, veluti bonorum suorum administrationem consequi, contractus et obligationes inire, sane hoc casu postulare debebit a judice domicilii, cui in personas plenum jus est attributum*[4]. But whether it exists or not is immaterial, as Burgundus in an-

---

1 Ante, § 495—498; 4 Burge, Comm. on Col. and For. Law, pt. 2, ch. 23, § 5, pp. 1010, 1011.

2 Burgundus, Tract. 1, n. 12, p. 23.

3 Ibid. n. 13.

4 Ibid. n. 14, p. 24; 1 Boullenois, Observ. 9, p. 150; Id. Observ. 6, p. 129.

other passage speaks directly on the present point. *Unde ferè obtinuit, ut Judex domicilii, ubi et mobilia, rationesque et instrumenta reperiuntur, tutelam solus deferat. Sed non aliter universorum bonorum administrationem consequitur, quam si supersedente judice situs, solus ille constituatur*[1]. This, however, is a qualification by no means generally conceded or admissible.

§ 500 *a*. We have already seen that Hertius, and Matthæus, and Paul Voet, and John Voet, hold the opinion, that the guardian has not, by virtue of his appointment in the place of the domicil of his ward, any rights or authorities over the immovable property of his ward in a foreign country[2]. Paul Voet in a another place adds: *Verum à contractibus proprie sic dictis, me conferam ad quasi contractus, et quidem tutelæ, vel curatelæ. Ubi sequentia examinanda. Quid si pupillo dandus sit tutor, illene dabit, ubi pupillus domicilium habet, an ubi bona pupilli immobilia sita sunt? Respondeo; Quamvis regulariter ab illo Magistratu detur tutor, ubi pupillus domicilium habet, ubi parentes habitarunt; etiam qui dat tutorem, eum primario personæ, non rei dedisse, censeatur; adeoque is, qui simpliciter datus est, ad res omnes etiam in diversis Provinciis sitas, datus intelligatur: Id quod plerumque jure Romano obtinebat, quo diversarum Provinciarum Magistratus, uni suberant Imperatori. Ne tamen videatur Judex domicilii quid extra territorium fecisse, non præjudicabit Judici loci, ubi nonnulla pupillaria bona sita, quin et tutorem pupillo ratione illorum bonorum, scilicet immobilium, ibidem recte dederit. Unde etiam si de prædiis minorum alienandis contentio; si quidem in aliâ sita sint Provinciâ, tutius egerit tutor, qui datus est in loco domicilii, si decretum ab utroque Judice curet interponi, et domicilii pupilli, et rei sitæ*[3]. Even those jurists who contend that

---

1 Burgundus, Tract. 2, n. 18, p. 69.

2 Ante, § 497, 498.

3 P. Voet, De Stat. § 9, c. 2, n. 17; Id. n. 19, pp. 270, 271, (edit. 1715); Id. pp. 329—331, (edit. 1661).

permission ought to be given by the local judge to such a guardian to administer such foreign immovable property, at the same time concede, that without such permission the guardian cannot exercise any rights or authorities over it[1]. John Voet says: *Non autem in loco originis vel situs rerum pupillarium, sed tantum in loco domicilii pupillaris tutores à loci illius camerâ pupillari aut magistratu creari, moris est; qui hoc ipso dati intelliguntur universo pupilli patrimonio, ubicunque existenti. Quod tamen ex comitate magis, quam juris rigore sustinetur; cum in casu, quo pupillus immobilia habet sita in eo loco, qui non subest eidem magistratui supremo, cui pupillus subest ratione domicilii, magistratus loci, in quo sitâ immobilia, rebus in suo territorio existentibus peculiarem posset tutorem dare*[2].

§ 501. Boullenois, after stating that in France the principal object of guardianship is not so much the custody of the person as of property, adds, that it has in view the administration and direction of property (*biens*), and that the rights which it grants are all real rights. *La garde consiste, ou en droits de propriété, ou en droits d'usufruit; et il n'y a rien de plus réel, que ces sortes de droits. Par conséquent elle ne peut être regie, que par la loi de la situation. C'est cette loi, qui donne, ou ne donne pas; qui appelle certaines personnes, ou qui ne les appelle pas. De là il semble, qu'il faudroit nécessairement en conclure, que chaque coutume, qui admet la garde, et où il y a des biens, a seule le droit de déférer la garde, à qui bon lui semble; et qu'il n'y a que ceux, à qui elle la défére, qui puissent être gardiens, quelque domicile d'ailleurs, qu'aient ceux, qui tombent en garde, et ceux, qui sont appelés à la garde*[3]. He admits that there are jurists who assert the contrary[4].

---

1 3 Burge, on Col. and For. Law, pt. 2, ch. 23, pp. 1004—1007.

2 J. Voet, Ad Pand. lib. 26, tit. 5, § 5, tom. 2, p. 188; Id. lib. 1, tit. 4, pt. 2, § 3, 7, tom. 1, pp. 39, 40. See also other foreign jurists cited 3 Burge, Comm. on Col. and For. Law, ch. 23, pp. 1005—1007.

3 2 Boullenois, Observ. 39, pp. 320—322, 339, 340; 3 Burge, Comm. on Col. and For Law, pt. 2, ch. 23, pp. 1001, 1002.

4 Ibid.

§ 502. Hertius, as we have seen, asserts the same doctrine as to immovable property[1]. Froland arranges himself on the side of those who assert the reality of the laws which respect guardianship, distinguishing, however, as to the quality of persons entitled, the right of possessing the property, and the formalities accompanying it[2].

§ 502 *a.* Dumoulin holds the opinion, that the *lex rei sitæ* is to govern in all such cases, and explains himself with unusual fulness on the point. *Aut statutum agit in personam, et tunc non includit exteros, sive habiliter, sive inhabiliter personam, unde si statuto hujus urbis cavetur, quod contractus facti per minorem xxv annis non valeant sine consensu suorum propinquorum, et authoritate Judicis, non intelligitur, nisi de subditis suæ jurisdictioni per text. l.* 1, *in fin. ff. de curat. et tutor. dat. ab his. Unde minor dicti loci non poterit etiam extra locum prædia, in eo territorio sita, locare sine dicta solemnitate: Sed bene extra locum prædia alibi sita. Quia in quantum agit in personam, restringitur ad suos subditos; et in quantum agit in res, restringitur ad sitas intra suum territorium. Exterus autem minor annis poterit etiam de sitis intra locum dicti statuti etiam inter locum illum disponere: Quamvis is, qui datus est tutor vel curator à suo competenti judice, sit inhabilitatus propter tutelam et curam, ubique locorum pro bonis ubicumque sitis. Quia non est in vim statuti solius, sed in vim juris communis, et per passivam interpretationem legis, quæ locum habet ubique*[3]. Everhardus holds the same opinion. *Ubi ratione diversarum jurisdictionum et territoriorum diversi judices dant tutores, et unus non intromittat se de territorio alterius; semper enim inspicienda est consuetudo loci, ubi res sunt sitæ, maxime quoad immobilia*[4].

---

1 Ante, § 497; 1 Hertii Opera, De Collis. Leg. § 4, n. 8, pp. 123, 124, (edit. 1737); Id. p. 175, (edit. 1716).

2 1 Froland, Mém. c. 16, pp. 717, 749, 750, 752.

3 Molin. Opera, tom. 3, ad Cod. lib. 1, tit. 1, l. 1, Conclus. de Statut. p. 556, (edit. 1681); Ante, § 497, note. See also Rodenburg, De Div. Stat. tit. 2, c. 5, n. 16; 2 Boullenois, App. pp. 47—51.

4 Everhard. Consil. 185, n. 3, p. 406.

§ 503. Lord Kaims lays down the Scottish doctrine to be, that it is of no importance in what place curators of minors are chosen; and accordingly, a choice made in England of curators, whether English or Scotch, will be held effectual in Scotland. He admits, that the powers of a guardian of a lunatic in England are limited, extending only to his person, and not to his estate; or rather, that different guardians are, or may be, appointed by the Court of Chancery for each. But the authority of any guardian or curator, however appointed in a foreign country, is not understood by him to extend to any real estate in Scotland[1].

§ 504. There is no question whatsoever that, according to the doctrine of the common law the rights, of foreign guardians are not admitted over immovable property situate in other countries. Those rights are deemed to be strictly territorial, and are not recognised as having any influence upon such property in other countries, whose systems of jurisprudence embrace different regulations, and require different duties and arrangements[2]. No one has ever supposed that a guardian appointed in any one State of this Union had any right to receive the profits or to assume the possession of the real estate of his ward in any other State, without having received a due appointment from the proper tribunals of the State where it is situate. The case falls within the well-known principle, that rights to real property can be acquired, changed, and lost, only according to the law *rei sitæ*[3].

§ 504 *a*. The same rule is applied by the common law to movable property, and has been fully recognised both in England and in America. No foreign guardian can *virtute officii* exercise any rights, powers, functions, over the movable property of his ward, which is situated in a different

---

[1] 2 Kaims, Equity, b. 3, ch. 8, § 1, p. 325; Id. § 4, p. 348.

[2] See 3 Burge, Comm. on Col. and For. Law, pt. 2, ch. 23, § 5, pp. 1009—1011.

[3] Ante, § 424; 3 Burge, Comm. on Col. and For. Law, pt. 2, ch. 23, § 5, pp. 1005, 1006, 1009, 1010.

State or country from that in which he has obtained his letters of guardianship. But he must obtain new letters of guardianship from the local tribunals authorized to grant the same, before he can exercise any rights, powers, or functions over the same. Few decisions upon the point are to be found in the English or American authorities, probably because the principle has always been taken to be unquestionable, founded upon the close analogy of the case of foreign executors and administrators[1].

§ 505. Whether a guardian has authority to change the domicil of his ward from one country to another, seeing that it may have a most important operation, as to the succession to his movable property, in case of his death, is a matter which has been much discussed. In favour of the affirmative there are some distinguished foreign jurists, among whom we may enumerate Bynkershoek, Bretonnier, Rodenburg, and John Voet. Bynkershoek says: *Posse tutorem pupilli sui domicilium mutare, perinde ut potest parens superstes, nescio quisquam serio dubitaverit, si successionis legitimæ causa non versetur; nam si hæc versetur, multa disputatio est. Sed an hæc quoque valebunt, si superstes parens vel tutor domicilium minoris transferat, ut ejus, intestati mortui alia sit successio, quam ante fuit?* He proceeds then to discuss the question, and comes to the conclusion, that he may. *Sic puto. Scio impuberem, vel minorem proprio marte non recte domicilium suum mutare; sed quid ni posset, qui eum repræsentat, et quid ni posset cum omni effectu, nisi qua lex sit, quæ impediat*[2]*?* Rodenburg says: *Quæramus et illud quod frequentioris, est incursionis; Hollandus major viginti, minor viginti quinque annis transfert domicilium Ultrajectum, ubi vigesimo anno*

---

[1] 3 Burge, Comm. on Col. and For. Law, pt. 2, ch. 2, § 5, p. 1011; Id. p. 1010; Ante, § 499; Morrill *v.* Dickey, 1 John. Ch. R. 153; Kraft *v.* Vickery, 4 Gill & John. R. 332, 340, 341; 4 Cowen, R. 529, note; Post, § 512, 513.

[2] Bynkers. Quest. Privat. Juris. lib. 1, c. 16, pp. 174, 178, 180—186, (edit. 1744).

tutela vel cura finitur. Quid dicemus perventurum illum suam in tutelam? Respondi ex facto consultus minori hodie constituendi domicilii, facultatem non eses, tutori esse; qui ut contrahere, ita et domicilium potest constituere, quod collocetur illud per contractum, de quo mox latiùs. Proinde in proposita mihi specie, cùm mater, quæ tutrix esset, mutato à morte viri domicilio, Ultrajectum concessisset, ibique infans adolevisset: dixi ex Ultrajectinis legibus æstimandos perfectæ ætatis annos; dummodo fraus absit, aut præjudicium tertii, extra quod vix est ut non dixeris tutori, maximè matri locum ad habitandum, pupillumque educandum, eligendi Jus esse, illudque ipsum dubii veriti Batavi Jurisconsulti tutori agnato auctores fuerunt, ut stipularetur à matre illa, cùm cogitaret ex Hollandia concedere Trajectum, ne ea res infantis adspectu ullo modo domicilii mutationem induceret; quanquam fateor, si quid hoc ad rem pertinet, positâ hâc sententiâ, in potestate tutoris fore, tutelâ semet ociùs exuere, nisi tum potiùs super fraude quærendum foret[1]. John Voet says: *Plane, si etiamnum minorennis sit, patre vel matre viduâ domicilium mutante, filium etiam videri mutasse, si et ipse translatus sit, nec ex prioris sed novi domicilii, à patre matreve recenter constituti, jure censeri in dubio debere, rationis est. Utut enim haud difficulter admittendum sit, minorennem non magis posse domicilium mutare, quam contrahendo se obligare: tamen, quemadmodum contrahere auctore tutore permissum ei est, ita et domicilium cum patre matreve, tanquam tutelæ ejus aut saltem educationi præpositâ, tutoribus cæteris non contradicentibus, mutare nihil vetat: nisi ex circumstantiis manifestum esset, talem domicilii pupillaris translationem in fraudem proximorum, spem successionis ex prioris domicilii lege habentium, factam esse*[2].

§ 505 *a*. Bynkershoek thinks it impracticable to make

---

[1] Rodenburg, De Div. Stat. tit. 2, ch. 1, § 6; 2 Boullenois, App. pp. 57, 58.

[2] J. Voet. Ad Pand. lib. 5, tit. 1, § 100, tom. 1, p. 347.

any such exception of cases of fraud from the intrinsic difficulty of ascertaining what circumstances shall constitute evidence of a fraudulent change of domicil[1]. Burgundus seems to hold with Bartolus, that the domicil of the guardian is also the domicil of the minor. *Pupilli ipsi sibi constituere domicilium non possunt. Bartolus autem ibi sensit habere domicilium, ubi cum tutoribus, sive aliter habitaverint. Quæ sententia ita demum mihi vera videtur, nisi in academiam studiorum causså, vel aliò profecti, remanendi animo ibi non steterint. Qui veniam ætatis impetravit, et propriæ negotiationi commodisque subservit, ipse sibi minor domicilium instruere potest. Uxor ibi censetur habere domicilium, ubi maritus habitat. Legitimâ tori separatione factâ, ipsa sibi domicilium instruet*[2].

§ 505 *b*. Boullenois has spoken with so little clearness and precision on this subject, that it is not very easy to say, with entire exactness, what is his opinion. From the best examination, which I have been able to make of his various discussions of this subject in his different works, he seems to have thought, (1.) That the law of the actual domicil of the parents of a minor constituted the rule to regulate the succession to the minor, if he died during his minority, although it was not the domicil of his birth, but was acquired by his parents afterwards. (2.) That the like rule did not apply to the case of a minor under tutelage; and that his guardian could not by a change of domicil change the succession to the property of the minor. (3.) That, hence, if a minor, following the change of domicil of his parents, should die, his movable estate would be governed by the law of succession of the new domicil, if there was no fraud in the removal. (4.) But that there was no reason why a minor might not be reputed domiciled in the domicil of his guardian, so far as the law of that domicil would confer on him particular faculties or

---

1 Bynkers. Quest. Jur. Priv. lib. 1, ch. 16, pp. 182, 183, (edit. 1744).

2 Burgundus, Tract. 2, n. 34, pp. 80, 81.

privileges; and that, therefore, if the law of the domicil of the guardian would give him the power of making a testament of his movables, he might make one conformable to that law; for it is but just, that, in such a case, a person domiciled there, even although a minor, should be held subject to the real laws, or laws *in rem*, of the place, where he is domiciled without fraud[1].

---

[1] Boullenois, Dissert. sur Quest. de la Contrar. des Lois, Quest. 2, pp. 59—62; 2 Boullenois, Observ. 32, pp. 49—53.—It may not be unacceptable to give some extracts from Boullenois in this place. He says in his Dissertations; En effet, il y a plusieurs raisons, pour lesquelles le dernier domicile du père doit régler la succession mobiliaire du fils, lorsqu'il décéde en minorité. La première est, que le fils mineur tombant sous la puissance d'autrui, on n'a pas voulu qu'il pût dépendre d'un Tuteur de changer l'ordre de succéder au mineur en lui faisant changer de domicile; en sorte qu'on n'a pas cru qu'un Tuteur dût avoir la liberté de donner ou d'ôter aux hérities présomptifs. La seconde est, qu'un mineur à raison de sa minorité est toujours présumé grévé et chargé de fidei-commis envers les héritiers de celui de qui il a reçû les biens qui doivent composer sa succession, et un Tuteur ne doit pas avoir le pouvoir de déroger à cette espéce de fidei-commis. Again he says: Sur le changement de domicile d'un mineur en ce qui touche ses biens, il semble qu'il y auroit quelque consideration à faire. Il paroîtroit assez convenable que la succession d'un mineur au-dessous de la pleine puberté fut réglée par le domicile de ses père et mère. Que dès qu'il est pourvû par mariage, il puisse se choisir tel domicile que bon lui semblera, et que sa succession mobiliaire soit régie par ce domicile. Que le fils mineur en suivant le domicile du père, ou de la mère survivante, sa succession mobiliaire soit pareillement assujettie aux Loix de ce nouveau domicile, pourvû que d'ailleurs il n'y ait point de fraude: Que peut faire de mieux un mineur que de continuer de vivre sous l'éducation de celui de ses père et mère que Dieu lui a conservé, et dès qu'il y a prudence et justice dans cette conduite, ce nouveau domicile devient une demeure juste et légitime pour le mineur, dont la succession mobiliaire doit suivre le sort. Que le fils mineur qui fait trafic de Marchandises, et qui pour ce, s'est choisi un domicile soit pareillement en ce qui touche ses biens mobiliers, assujetti à la Loi du lieu qui a été le centre de sa fortune, et cela paroît indispensable quand le bien du mineur est un bien d'industrie. Il n'y a pas d'inconvenient qu'un mineur soit reputé domicilié au domicile de son Tuteur, quant aux facultez particulières que la Loi de ce domicile peut lui donner; c'est pour quoi si par la Loi du domicile de son Tuteur il a faculté de tester de ses meubles, il pourra tester conformément à cette Loi. Il est juste dans ce cas qu'un domicilié, même mineur, subisse les Loix pures réelles du lieu où il est domicilié sans fraude. Mais quant à son état de majeur, ou de mineur,

§ 505 *c*. On the other hand, Mornac, Christinæus, Bouhier, and Pothier, maintain the opinion in unequivocal terms, that

---

on ne sçauroit le faire dépendre que de la Loi de son origine, par les raisons qui ont été ci-devant alleguées. Boullenois, Diss. de la Contrar. des Lois, Quest. 2, pp. 59, 61, 62. In his larger Treatise, he says: Au surplus, ce que nous disons ici pour le cas de la succession mobiliaire ab intestat, doit-il avoir lieu pour le cas d'un testament? S'il s'agissoit, par exemple, de savoir si le mineur incapable de tester par la Loi de son domicile de droit, le pourroit en vertu de la Loi de son domicile de fait. L'Auteur des Observations sur Henrys, observe loco citato, que si des enfans mineurs sont mis sous la tutele d'un Lyonnois, ils pourront faire un testament, lorsqu'ils seront parvenus à la puberté parce que les mineurs suivent, à cet égard, le domicile de leur tuteur. Il dit qu'il l'a ainsi décidé en consultation, avec M. Severt, pour le testament du sieur de Servières, fait à l'âge de dix-huit ans. Son pere s'étoit marié et établi à Paris: après son décès et celui de sa semme, ses enfans, qui étoient en bas âge, furent mis sous la tutele de Charles Groflier, leur oncle parternel, domicilié en Lyonnois. Le sieur de Servières fils, avant que de partir pour l'armée, où il fut tué, fit son testament au profit d'une de ses sœurs: il fut contesté par une autre sœur, et la décision sut pour le testament. M. le P. Bouheir, ch. 21, n. 4, n'adopte pas cette décision, et j'avoue qu'elle n'est pas sans difficulté. En effet, puisque la Loi détermine le domicile du mineur, par le domicile du père, je parle d'un mineur non établi, pourquoi lui donner deux domiciles, l'un pour régler sa succession mobiliaire, et l'autre pour régler sa capacité personnelle de tester? Il n'y a, comme nous venons de le dire, que le domicile de la personne qui puisse rendre capable celui qui est incapable; et puisque le domicile du mineur est fixé au domicile du père, comment celui de fait, qu'il peut avoir par-tout ailleurs, peut-il affecter sa personne, préférablement à son domicile de droit qui est nécessairement, selon la Loi, son vrai domicile? D'ailleurs un testament apporte toujours un changement dans la succession légale du testateur, et la Loi du domicile de droit qu'a le mineur, ne lui permet pas de disposer de ses biens, et de changer rien dans sa succession. Mais pour le soutien de la décision de MM. Severt et Bretonnier, deux savans Consultans, ne peut-on pas répondre que le mineur est dans son devoir, quand il demeure avec son tuteur qui est chargé de son éducation, qu'il y demeure nécessairement et sans fraude? A la bonne heure que le domicile de son père régle sa succession ab intestat; c'est l'intérêt des héritiers qui l'a voulu ainsi, et c'est pour cela qu'il retient le domicile de son père. Mais si le mariage, si l'émancipation permettent à un mineur de changer de domicile, comme en convient M. Bouhier luimême, et que dans ce cas, le mineur puisse tester conformément à la Loi du domicile qu'il s'est choisi, pourquoi ne veut-on pas pareille chose dans le cas où le mineur passe, par nécessité, et sans fraude, dans le domicile de son tuteur? Il est vrai que dans le cas du mariage et de l'émancipation, la succession mobiliaire de ce mineur se

the domicil of a minor, so far as it regards his succession to his estate, cannot be changed by his guardian. Mornac says: *Quæsitum est, mortuo impubere, de cujus bonis mobilibus agitur, quod spectari debeat illius domicilium, utrum patris et matris, an tutoris, apud quem defunctus est; atque id, quia locus domicilii parentum, et locus domicilii tutoris contrarias, quoad successiones mobilium, diversasque consuetudines ferant. Videbatur nonnullis constituendum domicilium in ædibus tutoris, ut qui patrem referret. Prævaluit verò eorum sententia, qui domicilium minoris præsertim eo casu in loco originis, id est, in ædibus paternis ac maternis collocandum dicerent. Cum enim domicilium quatuor modis contrahi soleat, natura, ac origine, item voluntate, ac concilio, deinde conventione, aut ex necessitate muneris. Solum ex his naturale domicilium minori superest, locus scilicet, in quo ipse creverit, parentesque defecerint; absurdumque aliud fuerit affingere minori in cæteris, quod ipse per ætatem non habeat diligendi nempe domicilii consilium. Imo et præstaretur ansa interdum tutoribus fraudandi veros mobilium minoris intereuntis hæredes, transferentibus scilicet domicilium in loca, quibus successura sibi viderent ex patriis moribus, intereunte valetudinario minore desideria*[1]. Christinæus adopts the very language of Mornac on this subject[2]. Bouhier is equally direct and positive, holding that the minor retains

---

réglera par la Loi de son domicile de choix, et que je n'en dirai pas de même par rapport à un mineur qui n'est ni marié, ni émancipé; mais ce que je ne dirai pas pour le cas de la succession ab intestat, parce qu'il y a une Jurisprudence formée à cet égard, je puis le dire pour le cas du testament, parce que la Loi n'a rien décidé là-dessus, et qu'il semble juste de laisser à un mineur, que la mort prévient, une capacité que lui donne la Loi où il demeure actuellement, sans fraude. Néanmoins le premier avis me paroît le meilleur: un mineur hors le domicile de son père, avec son tuteur, habite avec lui; mais il n'est pas proprement domicilié avec lui: il séjourne en attendant sa majorité; c'est un plaideur qui attend là que le temps lui fasse gagner son procès." 2 Boullenois, Observ. 32, pp. 51—53; Ante, § 44, note 2, p. 44.

[1] Mornacci, Observ. ad Cod. lib. 3, tit. 20, tom. 3, p. 558, (edit. 1721).

[2] Christin. Decis. 176, tom. 2, p. 204.

the domicil of his parents, and that it cannot be changed by his guardian. He says, that the inviolable rule of the law in Burgundy is, that the domicil of minors in respect to the succession to their property, cannot be changed by their guardians during their minority; and he reasons out the doctrine at large[1]. Pothier takes a distinction between the case of the change of the domicil of a parent from the change of domicil of a guardian; and holds, that in the former case, if a change is made without fraud, the minor follows the domicil of his parents and of the survivor. But in the case of a guardian no such effect follows; for the minor is no part of the family of the guardian, but is like a stranger there, and only for a time (*ad tempus*)[2].

§ 506. The same question has occurred in England; and

---

[1] Bouhier, Cout. de Bourg. ch. 21, § 3, p. 383; Id. ch. 23, § 160—167, pp. 441, 442.

[2] Pothier, Coutume d'Orléans, Introd. n. 17. He uses there the following language: " Il nous suffit de dire, que les mineurs ne composent pas la famille de leur tuteur, comme les enfans composent la famille de leur père: ils sont dans la maison de leur tuteur comme dans une maison étrangere: ils y sont ad tempus, pour le temps que doit durer la tutelle; par conséquent le domicile de leur tuteur n'est pas leur vrai domicile, et ils ne peuvent être censés en avoir d'autre que le domicile paternel, jusqu'à ce qu'ils soient devenus en âge de s'en établir un eux-mêmes par leur propre choix, et qu'ils l'aient effectivement établi. Il n'en est pas de même de la mère: la puissance paternelle étant, dans notre Droit, différent en cela du Droit Romain, commune au père et à la mère, la mère, après la mort de son mari, succéde aux droits et à la qualité de chef de la famille, qu'avoit son mari vis-à-vis de leurs enfans: son domicile, quelque part qu'elle juge de le transférer sans fraude, doit donc être celui de ces enfans, jusqu'à ce qu'ils aient pu s'en choisir un, qui leur soit propre. Il y auroit fraude, s'il ne paroissoit aucune raison de sa translation de domicile, que celle de se procurer des avantages dans les successions mobiliaires de ses enfans. Les enfans suivent le domicile, que leur mère s'établit sans fraude, lorsque ce domicile lui est propre, et que, demeurant en viduité, elle conserve la qualité de chef de famille: mais lorsqu'elle se remarie, quoiqu'elle acquiere le domicile de son second mari en la famille duquel elle passe, ce domicile de son second mari ne sera pas celui de ses enfans, qui ne passent pas comme elle en la famille de leur beau-père; C'est pourquoi ils sont censés continuer d'avoir leur domicile au lieu où l'avoit leur mère avant que de se remanier, comme ils seroient censés le conserver, si elle étoit morte."

it was on that occasion held, that a guardian may change the domicil of his ward, so as to affect the right of succession, if it is done *bonâ fide* and without fraud[1]. In that case the father, a native of England, died intestate, domiciled in Guernsey, leaving a widow and infant children by her, and also by a former wife. The widow, after his death, was appointed guardian of her own children, and in conjunction with the guardian of the children of the first marriage, sold their real estate in Guernsey, and invested the amount in the English funds, and afterwards removed to England with the children. On the death of some of the children under age, the question arose, whether their shares were distributable by the law of England, or by that of Guernsey, and it was decided by the Master of the Rolls (Sir Wm. Grant), that it was to be by the law of England. On that occasion, the learned Judge said: "Here the question is, whether, after the death of the father, children remaining under the care of the mother, follow the domicil which she may acquire, or retain that which their father had at his death, until they are capable of gaining one by acts of their own. The weight of authority is certainly in favour of the former proposition. It has the sanction both of Voet and Bynkershoek; the former, however, qualifying it by a condition that the domicil shall not have been changed for the fraudulent purpose of obtaining an advantage by altering the rule of succession. Pothier, whose authority is equal to that of either, maintains the proposition as thus qualified. There is an introductory chapter to his Treatise on the Custom of Orleans, in which he considers several points that are common to all the customs of France, and, among others, the law of domicil. He holds, in opposition to the opinion of some jurists, that a tutor cannot change the domicil of his pupil; but he considers it as clear, that the domicil of the surviving mother is also the domicil of

---

1 Potinger *v.* Wightman, 3 Meriv. R. 67; Robertson on Personal Succession, 197—202.

the children, provided it be not with a fraudulent view to their succession that she shifts the place of her abode. And he says that "such fraud would be presumed, if no reasonable motive could be assigned for the change. There never was a case in which there could be less suspicion of fraud than the present. The father and mother were both natives of England. They had no long residence in Guernsey; and after the father's death there was an end of the only tie which connected the family with that island. That the mother should return to this country and bring her children with her, was so much a matter of course, that the fact of her doing so can excite no suspicion of an improper motive. I think, therefore, the Master has rightly found the deceased children to have been domiciled in England. It is consequently, by the law of this country, that the succession to their personal property must be regulated [1]." This doc-

---

[1] Potinger *v.* Wightman, 3 Meriv. R. 79, 80.—Mr. Burge on this subject remarks: "The domicil of choice being that which the person himself establishes, it can only be acquired by him who is sui juris. It cannot, therefore, be acquired by a lunatic or minor. The domicil of the father, or of the mother being a widow, is that of the child, and a change by either of those parents of their former domicil, would necessarily operate as a change of the child's domicil. It is, however, only during the mother's widowhood, that she could change the domicil of her infant. The domicil which she acquired on her second marriage, would not become that of the infant; but his domicil would continue to be that which the mother possessed previously to her second marriage. The power which the parent thus possesses of changing the domicil of his child, is assimilated by writers to that which the guardian of an infant possesses, of binding him by contracts entered into by him on behalf of the infant. But this power, it is said, must be exercised by the parent bonâ fide. If he changed the domicil of the child who was sick, with no other apparent object than that of removing him from a place, in which, according to the law of succession there prevailing, the parent would not succeed to the child's estate, to another place which admitted the parent to such succession, the removal would be deemed a fraud on the rights of those who would have succeeded if no such removal had taken place, and would not be allowed to prevail. But if the health of the child was such as to afford no expectation of his death, or if there was any reasonable motive for the removal,—or, indeed, if the child had attained an age when, by the law of the place of his domicil he had the power of making a testament—in which latter case there could be no ground for presuming any interested motive on the part of the parent in changing

trine has also been recognised as the true doctrine in America[1].

§ 507. Secondly, in relation to executors and administrators. According to the Roman law, which made no distinction in this respect between movable and immovable property, the title "heir," was indiscriminately applied to every person who was called to the succession, whether he was so called by the act of the party or by operation of law. Thus, the person who was created universal successor by a will, was called the testamentary heir (*hœres factus*), and the next of kin by blood, in cases of intestacy, was called the heir at law (*hœres natus*) or heir by intestacy. The heir, whether consisting of one or more persons, and whether testamentary or by intestacy, was entitled by succession to all the estate of the deceased, whether it was real or personal, and he was chargeable with all the burthens and debts due from him[2]. But inasmuch as the succession in either

---

his domicil, the removal could not be impeached." 1 Burge, Comm. on Col. and For. Law, pt. 1, ch. 2, pp. 38, 39. Notwithstanding this weight of authority, which, however, with one exception, is applied solely to the case of parents, or a surviving parent, there is much reason to question the principle on which the decision is founded when it is obviously connected with a change of a succession to the property of the child. In the case of a change of domicil by a mere guardian, not being a parent, it is extremely difficult to find any reasonable principle on which it can be maintained, that he can by any change of domicil change the right of succession to the minor's property. The reasoning of Bynkershoek upon the point is very unsatisfactory, while that of Mornac, Bouhier, and Pothier, has solid reason and justice to sustain it. See Robertson on Successions, pp. 196—203.

[1] Guier *v.* O'Daniel, 1 Binn. R. 349, note; Cutts *v.* Haskins, 9 Mass. R. 543; Holyoke *v.* Haskins, 5 Pick. R. 20.

[2] 1 Domat, b. 1, tit. 1, p. 557; Id. § 1, n. 1, 2, p. 558.—Domat says, that in France, in the Provinces which are governed by the testamentary law, and not by the Roman law (Droit écrit), the title of heirs is given only to the heirs by blood or heirs at law, and that the testamentary heirs are called universal legataries. But this distinction is merely nominal, and the same rules are applied to the universal legataries as to the heirs by blood. 1 Domat, b. 1, tit. 1, pp. 557, 558. Erskine in his Institutes, b. 2. tit. 2, § 3, p. 192, says, that in Scotland, "Heritable subjects are those (immovables) which, on the death of the proprietor descend to the heir; and movables those which,

case might be onerous as well as profitable, the law allowed the heir, whether he were so by testament or by intestacy, to renounce the inheritance if he pleased, or he might accept it with the benefit of an inventory, the effect of which was to exonerate the heir from any further liability than the amount of the assets or property inventoried[1]. These explanations are important in order fully to understand the reasonings of foreign jurists, and to apply them to the present subject, for the civil law distinctions every where pervade the jurisprudence of continental Europe.

§ 508. It will be at once seen, that the executor under the common law in many respects corresponds with the testamentary heir of the civil law, and that the administrator in many respects corresponds with the heir by intestacy. The principal distinction between them which is here important to be considered is, that executors and administrators have no right except to the personal estate of the deceased; whereas the Roman heir was entitled to administer both the real estate and personal estate; and all the assets were treated as of the same nature, without any distinction of equitable assets or of legal assets[2].

§ 509. From what has already been said, the heir, whether testamentary or by intestacy of immovable property, can take only according to the *lex loci rei;* or, in other words, he is not admissible as heir, so as to administer the estate in any foreign country, unless he is duly qualified according to the principles, rules, and forms of the local law[3]. In this respect, he does not differ either in regard to

---

go to executors who are on that account sometimes styled hæredes in mobilibus. It may be also observed, that those who undertake to gather in and distribute among such as are interested in the succession, the movable estate of a person deceased, in virtue of a nomination either by the testator or by the judge, frequently get the name of executors, because it is their office to execute the last will of the deceased." See Id. b. 3, tit. 9, § 1, 2, 26.

1 1 Domat, b. 1, tit. 1, § 5, n. 3, 4, p. 593.

2 1 Brown, Civil and Adm. Law, 344, note.

3 See 2 Kaims, Eq. b. 3, ch. 8, § 3, p. 332; Vattel, b. 2, ch. 8. § 109—

rights or to responsibilities from an heir or devisee, chargeable at the common law or by statute with the bond debts of his ancestor or testator. It is for the same reason, that a power to sell immovable property given to an executor, cannot be executed unless upon due probate of the will in the place where the property is situate, and showing that it may be lawfully done by the *lex loci rei sitæ*[1]. And if the party claims not under a power, but as a devisee in trust to sell it for the payment of debts, it is also necessary to have a like probate of the will. But it is not necessary in the latter case to take out letters of administration, although the devise be in trust to the party by the description of executor; for in such case he takes as devisee and not as executor, and his title is under the will, and not under the letters testamentary[2].

§ 510. But in regard to movable estate a like rule does not necessarily prevail in foreign countries, governed by a jurisprudence which is drawn from or modelled upon the civil law; for movables being treated as having no *situs*, and to be governed by the law of the domicil of the testator or intestate, the title of the heir taking its effect directly from that law is, or at least may, consistently, be held to carry the right to such property wherever it may be locally situated, in the same manner as the title would or might pass, by an assignment by the owner by an act *inter vivos*[3].

§ 511. Lord Kaims seems to take a distinction between the case of a testamentary heir and that of an heir by intestacy, asserting that the nomination of an executor (*hæres de mobilibus*, or *hæres fiduciarius*[4]) by the testator in his testament, as to his movables, is effectual all the world over, *jure gentium*, and will be sustained in Scotland; whereas

---

111; 1 Boullenois, Observ. 17, p. 242; Id. Pr. Gén. 37, p. 9; Doe dem. Lewis v. M'Farland, 9 Cranch, 151.

1 Wells v. Cowper, 2 Hamm. R. 124.

2 Doe dem. Lewis v. M'Farland, 9 Cranch, 151.

3 2 Kaims, Equity, b. 3, ch. 8, § 4.

4 Ersk. Inst. b. 3, tit. 9, § 2, 26.

letters of administration in a foreign country are strictly territorial; and, when granted in a foreign country, are not recognised in Scotland, unless they are confirmed there by a proper judicial proceeding[1]. It may be so; but Erskine lays it down as clear law, that in Scotland neither executors nor administrators, foreign or domestic, are entitled to administer the estate of the deceased, until they have been duly confirmed by the competent judge[2]. What, perhaps, Lord Kaims meant to say was, that the title of executor was a good title, *jure gentium;* and when it was established in the manner and by the process prescribed by the law of the place where it was sought to be exercised, it ought to be held of universal obligation. And so it probably is in all civilized nations, except such (if any such there now are) as adopt the *Droit d'aubaine,* and confiscate the movable property of all foreigners dying and leaving such property within their territories.

§ 512. In regard to the title of executors and administrators, derived from a grant of administration in the country of the domicil of the deceased, it is to be considered, that that title cannot, *de jure,* extend as a matter of right beyond the territory of the government which grants it, and the movable property therein. As to movable property situated in foreign countries, the title, if acknowledged at all, is acknowledged *ex comitate,* and of course it is subject to be controlled or modified as every nation may think proper, with reference to its own institutions, and its own policy, and the rights of its own subjects. And here the rule to which reference has been so often made, applies with great strength, that no nation is under any obligation to enforce foreign laws prejudicial to its own rights, or to those of its own subjects. Persons, domiciled and dying in one country, are often deeply indebted to foreign creditors,

---

1 2 Kaims, Equity b. 3, ch. 8, § 3; Id. § 4, pp. 347, 348.

2 Ersk. Inst. b. 1, tit. 9, § 27, 29. See Robertson on Succession, pp. 263—273.

living in other countries where there are personal assets of the deceased. In such cases it would be a great hardship upon such creditors to allow the original executor or administrator to withdraw those funds from the foreign country without the payment of such debts, and thus to leave the creditors to seek their remedy in the domicil of the original executor or administrator, and perhaps there to meet with obstructions and inequalities in the enforcement of their own rights from the peculiarities of the local law.

§ 513. It has hence become a general doctrine of the common law, recognised both in England and America, that no suit can be brought or maintained by any executor or administrator, or against any executor or administrator, in his official capacity, in the Courts of any other country, except that from which he derives his authority to act in virtue of the probate and letters testamentary, or the letters of administration there granted to him. But if he desires to maintain any suit in any foreign country, he must obtain new letters of administration, and give new security according to the general rules of law prescribed in that country before the suit is brought[1]. So, on the other hand, if a

---

[1] The authorities to this point are now exceedingly numerous and entirely conclusive. See Lee *v.* Moore, Palmer, R. 163; Tourton *v.* Flower, 3 P. Will. 369, 370; Thorne *v.* Watkins, 2 Ves. 35; Att.-Gen. *v.* Cockerell, 1 Price, R. 179; Burn *v.* Cole, Ambler, R. 416; Lowe *v.* Fairlie, 2 Madd. R. 101; 1 Hagg. Eccl. R. 93, 239: Mitford's Plead. 177, 4th edit.; Fenwick *v.* Sears, 1 Cranch, 259; Dixon's Executors *v.* Ramsay's Executors, 3 Cranch, 319, 323; Kerr *v.* Moon, 9 Wheaton, R. 565; Armstrong *v.* Lear, 12 Wheaton, R. 169; Thompson *v.* Wilson, 2 N. Hamp. R. 291; Dickinson's Administrators *v.* M'Craw, 4 Randolph, R. 158; Glenn *v.* Smith, 2 Gill. & John. R. 493; Stearns *v.* Burnham, 5 Greenleaf, R. 261; Goodwin *v.* Jones, 3 Mass. R. 514; Borden *v.* Borden, 5 Mass. R. 67; Stevens *v.* Gaylord, 11 Mass. R. 256; Langdon *v.* Potter, 11 Mass. R. 313; Dangerfield *v.* Thurston, 20 Martin, R. 232; Riley *v.* Riley, 3 Day, Conn. Cas. 74; Champlin *v.* Tilley, Id. 303; Trecothick *v.* Austin, 4 Mason, R. 16, 32; Ex parte Picquet, 5 Pick. 65; Holmes *v.* Remsen, 20 John. R. 229, 265; Smith, Administrator, *v.* The Union Bank of Georgetown, 5 Peters, R. 518; Campbell *v.* Tousey, 7 Cowen, R. 64; Logan *v.* Fairlie, 2 Sim. & Stu. 284; Atty *v.* Bouwens, 4 Mees. & Welsb. 171, 192,

creditor wishes a suit to be brought in any foreign country, in order to reach the effects of a deceased testator or intestate situated therein, it will be necessary that letters of administration should be there taken out in due form according to the local law, before the suit can be maintained; for the executor or administrator appointed in another country is not suable there, and has no positive right to or authority over those assets, neither is he responsible therefor. The right of a foreign executor or administrator to take out such new administration, is usually admitted as a matter of course, unless some special reasons intervene to vary or control it; and the new administration is treated as merely ancillary or auxiliary to the original foreign administration, so far as regards the collection of the effects and the proper distribution of them [1]. Still, however, the new administration is made subservient to the rights of creditors, legatees, and distributees who are resident within the country where it is granted; and the residuum is transmissible to the foreign country only, when a final account has been settled in the

---

193; Tyler v. Bell, 1 Keen, R. 826, 829; S. C. 2 Mylne & Craig, 89, 109. —On this occasion Lord Cottenham said: "That an estate cannot be administered in the absence of a personal representative, and that such personal representative must obtain his right to represent the estate from the ecclesiastical court in this country, has, I believe, never before been doubted. The cases of Tourton v. Flower, (3 P. Wms. 369); Atkins v. Smith, (2 Atk. 63); Swift v. Swift, (1 Ball & B. 326); Attorney-General v. Cockerill, (1 Price, 165); Lowe v. Fairlie, (2 Madd. 101); Logan v. Fairlie, (2 Sim. & Stu. 284); all proceed upon this, that the Courts in this country, for the security of property, will not administer the property of a person deceased, in the absence of a person authorized to represent the estate; and that they look only to the judgment of the ecclesiastical courts in this country, in granting probate or letters of administration, to ascertain who are so authorized; and it is immaterial what ecclesiastical court in this country has granted probate or letters of administration, provided the state of the property was such as to give it jurisdiction." But see Anderson v. Caunter, 2 Mylne & K. 763, which seems not a sound authority. Lord Cottenham, in Tyler v. Bell, 2 Mylne & Craig, 110, manifestly disapproved of it. 3 Burge, Comm. on Col. and For. Law, pt. 2, ch. 23, § 5, pp. 1010—1012.

[1] Harvey v. Richards, 1 Mason, R. 381; Stevens v. Gaylord, 11 Mass. R. 256; Case of Miller's Estate, 3 Rawle, R. 312.

proper tribunal where the new administration is granted, upon the equitable principles adopted by its own law, in the application and distribution of the assets found there[2].

---

[2] See Harvey *v.* Richards, 1 Mason, R. 381; Dawes *v.* Boylston, 9 Mass. R. 337; Selectmen of Boston *v.* Boylston, 2 Mass. R. 318, 384; Richards *v.* Dutch, 8 Mass. R. 506; Dawes *v.* Head, 3 Pick. R. 128; Hooker *v.* Olmstead, 6 Pick. R. 481; Davis *v.* Estey, 8 Pick. R. 475; Jennison *v.* Hapgood, 10 Pick. R. 77; Stevens *v.* Gaylord, 11 Mass. R. 256; Case of Miller's Estate, 3 Rawle, 312; Gravillon *v.* Richards, Ex'or, 13 Louis, R. 293. Many complicated questions may grow out of original and ancillary administrations, some of which have been stated in the cases of Harvey *v.* Richards, 1 Mason, R. 381, and Dawes *v.* Head, 3 Pick. R. 128.—The following extract, from the opinion of Mr. Chief Justice Parker, in the latter case, deserves an attentive perusal. The question there arose, how assets under an ancillary administration were to be disposed of in cases of insolvency, and of debts due to creditors belonging to the same country as the deceased debtor. The Chief Justice, after disposing of these particulars, said: "Thus this action is determined without touching the questions upon which it was supposed it would turn, which are of a novel and delicate nature, and though often glanced at, do not appear to have been decided either in this or any other State of the Union. We wish to avoid any thing which may be construed into a conclusive adjudication; and yet are of opinion, that it will be useful to throw out for consideration the results of our reasonings upon this subject. If the technical difficulties upon which this cause has been decided, had not occurred, but the estate had been rendered insolvent here, and a decree of distribution for a proportion had been issued, or if the debt of Lenox and Sheafe had been ascertained by a judgment, and the pleadings to a suit on the bond had been the same in that case as now, the question would be, whether the funds collected here by an ancillary administration, should be appropriated to the payment of such debts as might be regularly proved here, notwithstanding it was made to appear that the whole estate was insufficient to pay all the debts, and that the effects here were wanted by the executor abroad, to enable him duly to administer the estate. It has been contended, that this should be done; because the administrator has given bond here in the same manner as if this were the original administration, and because the statute which authorizes this administration, requires that the Judge of Probate shall settle the estate in the same way and manner as he would, if the original will had been proved here. With respect to the bond, it will be saved by a faithful administration of the estate according to law; and with respect to the settlement by the Judge of Probate, this must be understood to authorize him to require the administrator to account, and that the due course of proceedings in the probate office shall be observed. It certainly cannot be construed to mean, that in all cases a final settlement of the estate shall take place here; if it did, then if there were no debts here, and none to claim as

§ 514. But although an executor or administrator appointed in one state, is not in virtue of such appointment

---

legatees or next of kin, it would be necessary for all such to prove their right and receive their distributive shares here, notwithstanding the settlement must in such case be made according to the laws of the country where the deceased had his domicil. But we think in such case it would be very clear, that the assets collected here should be remitted to the foreign executor or administrator; for it seems to be a well settled principle, that the distribution is to be made according to the laws of the country where the deceased was domiciled; and if any part is to be retained for distribution here, it will be only by virtue of some exception to this general rule, or because the parties interested seek their remedy here; in which case it might be within the legal discretion of the court here to cause distribution, or to remit, according to the circumstances and condition of the estate. An exception to the general rule grows out of the duty of every government and its courts to protect its own citizens in the enjoyment of their property and the recovery of their debts, so far as this may be done without violating the equal rights of creditors living in a foreign country. In relation to the effects found within our jurisdiction and collected by the aid of our laws, a regard to the rights and interests of our citizens requires, that those effects should be made answerable for debts due to them, in a just proportion to the whole estate of the deceased, and all the claims upon it, whatever they may be. In the several cases which have come before this Court, where the legal character and effects of an ancillary administration have been considered, the intimations have been strong, that the administrator here shall be held to pay the debts due to our citizens. The cases Richards *v.* Dutch, Dawes, Judge, &c. *v.* Boylston, Selectmen of Boston *v.* Boylston, and Stevens *v.* Gaylord, are of this character. In all these cases, however, we must suppose the Court had reference to a solvent estate, and in such case there seems to be no question of the correctness of the principle; for it would be but an idle show of courtesy to order the proceeds of an estate to be sent to a foreign country, the province of Bengal for instance, and oblige our citizens to go or send there for their debts, when no possible prejudice could arise to the estate, or those interested in it, by causing them to be paid here; and possibly the same remark may be applicable to legacies payable to legatees living here, unless the circumstances of the estate should require the funds to be sent abroad. Whether citizens of other states claiming payment of their debts of the administrator here, are to be put upon the same footing with citizens of Massachusetts, by virtue of the privileges and immunities secured to them by the constitution of the United States, is a point which we do not now decide. But without doubt the Courts of the United States having full equity powers, would enforce payment upon the principles above stated, where there is no suggestion of insolvency of the estate. There would be no doubt, we think, that payment of debts by the administrator here, after sufficient proof that they were due, and an allowance

entitled to sue, nor is he liable to be sued, in his official capacity in any other state or country; yet there are many

---

of his account therefor by the Probate Court with proper notice, would be faithful administration according to the condition of his bond, and would be a proper way of accounting to the principal administrator abroad. In regard to effects thus collected within our jurisdiction, belonging to an insolvent estate of a deceased person having his domicil abroad, the question may be more difficult. We cannot think, however, that in any civilized country advantage ought to be taken of the accidental circumstance of property being found within its territory, which may be reduced to possession by the aid of its courts and laws, to sequester the whole for the use of its own subjects or citizens, where it shall be known that all the estate and effects of the deceased are insufficient to pay his just debts. Such a doctrine would be derogatory to the character of any government. Under the English bankrupt system, foreigners as well as subjects may prove their debts, and share in the distribution. Without doubt, in other foreign countries, where there is a cessio bonorum, or other process relating to bankrupts' estates, the same just principle is adopted. It was so under our bankrupt law while that was in force, and no reason can be suggested why so honest and just a principle should not be applied in the case of insolvent estates of deceased persons. It is always practised upon in regard to persons dying within our jurisdiction, having had their domicil here; that is, creditors of all countries have the same rights as our own citizens, to file their claims and share in the distribution. There cannot be, then, a right in any one or more of our citizens who may happen to be creditors, to seize the whole of the effects which may be found here, or claim an appropriation of them to the payment of their debts, in exclusion of foreign creditors. It is said this is no more than what may be done by virtue of our attachment law, in regard to the property of a living debtor who is insolvent. But the justness of that law is very questionable, and its application ought not to be extended to cases, by analogy, which do not come within its express provisions. What then is to be done with the effects collected here belonging to an insolvent estate in a foreign country? Shall they be sent home in order to be appropriated according to the laws of that country? This would often work great injustice, and always great inconvenience, to our own citizens, whose debts might not be large enough to bear the expense of proving and collecting them abroad; and in countries where there is no provision for an equal distribution, the pursuit of them might be wholly fruitless. As in Great Britain, our citizens whose debts would generally be upon simple contract, such as bills of exchange, promissory notes, accounts, &c., would be postponed to creditors by judgment, bond, &c., and even to other debts upon simple contract, which might be preferred by the executor or administrator. It would seem too great a stretch of courtesy to require the effects to be sent home, and our citizens to pursue them under such disadvantages. What then shall be done to avoid on the one hand the injustice

other questions which may require consideration, and in which a conflict of laws may arise in different countries.

---

of taking the whole funds for the use of our citizens, to the prejudice of foreigners, when the estate is insolvent, and on the other, the equal injustice and greater inconvenience of compelling our own citizens to seek satisfaction of their debts in distant countries? The proper course would undoubtedly be, to retain the funds here for a pro ratâ distribution according to the laws of our State, among the citizens thereof, having regard to all the assets, either in the hands of the principal administrator, or of the administrator here, and having regard also to the whole of the debts which by the laws of either country are payable out of those assets, disregarding any fanciful preference which may be given to one species of debt over another, considering the funds here as applicable to the payment of the just proportion due to our own citizens; and if there be any residue, it should be remitted to the principal administrator, to be dealt with according to the laws of his own country; the subjects of that country, if there be any injustice or inequality in the payment or distribution, being bound to submit to its laws. The only objection which can be made to this mode of adjusting an ancillary administration upon an insolvent estate, is the difficulty and delay of executing it. The difficulty would not be greater than in settling many other complicated affairs, where many persons have interests of different kinds in the same funds. The powers of a Court of Chancery are competent to embrace and settle all cases of that nature, even if the powers of our Court of Probate are not sufficiently extensive; which however is not certain. The administrator here should be held to show the condition of the estate abroad, the amount of property subject to debts, and the amount of debts; and a distribution could be made upon perfectly fair and equitable principles. The delay would undoubtedly be considerable; but this would not be so great an evil, as either sending our citizens abroad upon a forlorn hope to seek for the fragments of an insolvent estate, or paying the whole of their debts out of the property, without regard to the claims of foreign creditors. And if the Probate Court has not sufficient power to make such an equitable adjustment, a bill in equity, in which the administrator here should be the principal respondent, would probably produce the desired result; as then time and opportunity could be given to make known the whole condition of the estate, and all persons interested might be heard before any final decree; in the meantime the administrator could be restrained remitting the funds until such degree should be passed." Dawes *v.* Head, 3 Pick. R. 143—148.

The following extracts are made from the opinion of the court in Harvey *v.* Richards: "One objection urged against the exercise of the authority of the court is, that as national comity requires the distribution of the property according to the law of the domicil, the same comity requires that the distribution should be made in the same place. This consequence, however, is not admitted; and it has no necessary connexion with the preceding proposi-

In the first place, let us suppose, that an executor or administrator should go into a foreign country, and without

---

tion. The rule, that distribution shall be according to the law of the domicil of the deceased, is not founded merely upon the notion that movables have no situs, and therefore follow the person of the proprietor, even interpreting that maxim in its true sense, that personal property is subject to that law which governs the person of the owner. Nor is it, perhaps, founded upon the presumed intention of the deceased, that all his property should be distributed according to the law of the place of his domicil, with which he is supposed to be best acquainted and satisfied; for the rule will prevail even against the express intention of the deceased, unless the mode in which that intention is expressed would give it legal validity as a will. It seems, indeed, to have had its origin in a more enlarged policy, founded upon the general convenience and necessities of mankind; and in this view the maxim above stated flows from, rather than guides, the application of that policy. The only reason why any nation gives effect to foreign laws within its own territory is, the endless embarrassment which would otherwise be introduced in its own intercourse with foreign nations. The rights of its own citizens would be materially impaired, and, in many instances, totally extinguished by a refusal to recognise and sustain the doctrines of foreign law. The case now under consideration is an illustration of the perfect justice and wisdom of this general practice of nations. A person may have movable property and debts in various countries, each of which may have a different system of succession. If the law rei sitæ were generally to prevail, it would be utterly impossible for any such person to know in what manner his property would be distributed at his death, not only from the uncertainty of its situation from its own transitory nature, but from the impracticability of knowing with minute accuracy the law of succession of every country in which it might then happen to be. He would be under the same embarrassment if he attempted to dispose of his property by a testament, for he could never foresee where it would be at his death. Nay, more, it would be in the power of his debtor, by a mere change of his own domicil, to destroy the best digested will; and the accident of a moment might destroy all the anxious provisions of an excellent parent for his whole family. Nor is this all: the nation itself to which the deceased belonged, might be seriously affected by the loss of his wealth from a momentary absence, although his true home was in the centre of its own territory. These are great and serious evils, pervading every class of the community, and equally affecting every civilized nation. But in a maritime nation depending upon its commerce for its glory and its revenue, the mischief would be incalculable. The common and spontaneous consent of nations, therefore, established this rule from the noblest policy, the promotion of general convenience and happiness, and the avoiding of distressing difficulties, equally subversive of the public safety and private enterprise of all. It flowed from the same spirit that dictated judicial obedience to the foreign commissions of the admiralty.

there taking out new letters of administration, should there collect property, effects, and debts of his testator or in-

---

Sub mutuæ vicissitudinis obtentu, damus petimusque vicissim, is the language of the civilized world on this subject. There can be no pretence that the same general inconvenience or embarrassment attends the distribution of foreign effects, according to the foreign law, by the tribunals of the country where they are situate. Cases have been already stated in which great inconvenience would attend the establishment of any rule excluding such distribution. It may be admitted also, that there are cases in which it would be highly convenient to decline the jurisdiction and remit the parties to the forum domicilii. Where there are no creditors here, and no heirs or legatees here, but all are resident abroad, there can be no doubt that a court of equity would direct the remittance of the property upon the application of any competent party. The correct result of these considerations upon principle would seem to be, that whether the Court here ought to decree distribution or remit the property abroad, is a matter not of jurisdiction, but of judicial discretion, depending upon the particular circumstances of each case; that there ought to be no universal rule on this subject; but that every nation is bound to lend the aid of its own tribunals, for the purpose of enforcing the rights of all persons having a title to the fund, when such interference will not be productive of injustice or inconvenience, or conflicting equities. It is farther objected, that a rule which is to depend for its application upon the particular circumstances of each case, is too uncertain to be considered a safe guide for general practice. But this objection affords no solid ground for declining the jurisdiction; since there are an infinite variety of cases in which no general rule has been or can be laid down, as to legal or equitable relief in the ordinary controversies before judicial tribunals. In many of these, the difficulty is intrinsic in the subject-matter; and where a general rule cannot easily be extracted, each case must, and indeed ought to, rest on its own particular circumstances. The uncertainty, therefore, is neither more nor less than belongs to many other complicated transactions of human life where the law administers relief ex æquo et bono. Another objection, addressed more pointedly to a class of cases like the present, is the difficulty of settling the accounts of the estate, ascertaining the assets, what debts are sperate, what desperate, and finally, ascertaining what is the residue to be distributed, and who are the next of kin entitled to share. And to add to our embarrassment, we are told, that we cannot compel the foreign executor to render any account in our courts. I agree at once, that this cannot be done if he is not here; but I utterly deny that the administrator here cannot be compelled to account to any competent court for all the assets which he has received under the authority of our laws. And if the foreign executor chooses to lie by, and refuses to render any account of the foreign funds in his hands, so far as to enable the Court here to ascertain whether the funds are wanted abroad for the payment of debts or legacies, or not, he has no right to complain if

testate found or due there; the question might arise, whether he would not thereby, to the extent of his receipt and collection of such assets, be liable to be sued in the Courts of that country by any creditor there. Upon general principles, it would seem that he would so be liable; and, upon the principles of the common law, he would be liable as an executor *de son tort*, or person intermeddling with such assets without any rightful authority derived from the local authorities under a new grant of administra-

---

the Court refuses to remit the assets, and distributes them among those who may legally claim them. And as to settling the estate or ascertaining who are the distributees, there is no more difficulty than often falls to our lot in many cases arising under the ordinary probate proceedings. All these objections are in fact reasons for declining to exercise the jurisdiction in particular cases, rather than reasons against the existence of the jurisdiction itself. It seems, indeed, admitted by the learned counsel for the defendant, that if there be no foreign administration, it would be the duty of the Court to grant relief upon an administration taken here. Yet every objection already urged would apply with as much force in that as in the present case. The property would be to be distributed according to the foreign law of the deceased's domicil. The same difficulty would exist as to ascertaining the debts and legacies, and the assets and distributees entitled to share. But it is said in the case now put, the administration here would be the principal administration; whereas, in the case at bar, it is only an auxiliary or ancillary administration. I have no objection to the use of the terms principal and auxiliary, as indicating a distinction in fact as to the objects of the different administrations; but we should guard ourselves against the conclusion, that therefore there is a distinction in law as to the rights of parties. There is no magic in words. Each of these administrations may be properly considered as a principal one with reference to the limits of its exclusive authority; and each might, under circumstances, justly be deemed an auxiliary administration. If the bulk of the property, and all the heirs and legatees and creditors were here, and the foreign administration were only to recover a few inconsiderable claims, that would most correctly be denominated a mere auxiliary administration for the beneficial use of the parties here, although the domicil of the testator were abroad. The converse case would, of course, produce an opposite result. But I am yet to learn what possible difference it can make in the rights of parties before the Court, whether the administration be a principal or an auxiliary administration. They must stand upon the authority of the law to administer or deny relief under all the circumstances of their case, and not upon a mere technical distinction of very recent origin." Harvey *v.* Richards, 1 Mason, R. 381. See also Gravillon *v.* Richards's Ex'or, 13 Louis, R. 293.

tion there. For it would not lie in his mouth to deny that he had rightfully received such assets; and he could not rightfully receive them except as executor[1]. It would be quite a different question, whether the payment of any such debts or the delivery of any such property or effects to him by the debtors, or by other persons owing or possessing the same, would be a valid payment or discharge of such persons therefrom, or would confer any title to the same upon such executor or administrator, at least against any executor or administrator, subsequently appointed in such foreign State or country, and contesting the right or title. Upon that question there is much room for discussion and doubt, notwithstanding what has been asserted in some of the tribunals acting under the common law[2]. For it is exceedingly clear, that the probate grant of letters testamentary, or of letters of administration in one country, give authority to collect the assets of the testator or intestate only in that country, and do not extend to the collection of assets in foreign countries; for that would be to assume an extra-territorial jurisdiction or authority, and to usurp the functions of the foreign local tribunals in those matters[3]. It is no answer to the objection to say, that the

---

[1] Campbell *v.* Tousey, 7 Cowen, R. 64.

[2] Doolittle *v.* Lewis, 7 John. Ch. R. 45, 49; Post, § 515.

[3] See Attor.-General *v.* Bouwens, 4 Mees. & Welsb. 171, 190—192: —On this occasion Lord Abinger said: "Whatever may have been the origin of the jurisdiction of the ordinary to grant probate, it is clear that it is a limited jurisdiction, and can be exercised in respect of those effects only, which he would have had himself to administer in case of intestacy, and which must therefore have been so situated as that he could have disposed of them in pios usus. As to the locality of many descriptions of effects, household and movable goods for instance, there never could be any dispute. But to prevent conflicting jurisdictions between different ordinaries, with respect to choses in action and titles to property, it was established as law that judgment debts were assets for the purposes of jurisdiction where the judgment is recorded; leases, where the land lies; specialty debts, where the instrument happens to be; and simple contract debts, where the debtor resides at the time of the testator's death: and it was also decided, that, as bills of exchange and promissory notes do not alter the nature of the simple contract

effects of the testator or intestate are assets wherever they are situated, whether at home or abroad; and that such effects as are in a foreign country at the time of the death of the testator or intestate, although they remain and are wholly administered there by the executor, are equally assets. Doubtless this is true; but the question is not

---

debts, but are merely evidences of title, the debts due on these instruments were assets where the debtor lived, and not where the instrument was found. In truth, with respect to simple contract debts, the only act of administration that could be performed by the ordinary, would be to recover or to receive payment of the debt, and that would be done by him within whose jurisdiction the debtor happened to be.. These distinctions being well established, it seems to follow, that no ordinary in England could perform any act of administration within his diocese, with respect to debts due from persons resident abroad, or with respect to shares or interests in foreign funds payable abroad and incapable of being transferred here; and therefore no duty would be payable on the probate or letters of administration in respect of such effects. But, on the other hand, it is clear that the ordinary could administer all chattels within his jurisdiction; and, if an instrument is created of a chattel nature, capable of being transferred by acts done here, and sold for money here, there is no reason why the ordinary or his appointee should not administer that species of property. Such an instrument is in effect a saleable chattel, and follows the nature of other chattels as to the jurisdiction to grant probate. In this case, assuming that the foreign governments are liable to be sued by the legal holder, there is no conflict of authorities; for their governments are not locally within the jurisdiction, nor can be sued here; and no act of administration can be performed in this country except in the diocese where the instruments are, which may be dealt with, and the money received by their sale in this country. Let us suppose the case of a person dying abroad, all whose property in England consists of foreign bills of exchange, payable to order, which bills of exchange are well known to be the subject of commerce, and to be usually sold on the Royal Exchange. The only act of administration which his administrator could perform here, would be to sell the bills and apply the money to the payment of his debts. In order to make titles to the bills to the vendee, he must have letters of administration; in order to sue in trover for them, if they are improperly withheld from him, he must have letters of administration, (for even if there were a foreign administration, it is an established rule, that an administration is necessary in the country where the suit is instituted); and that these letters of administration must be stamped with a duty according to the saleable value of the bills the case of Hunt *v.* Stevens is an express authority." See also Doolittle *v.* Lewis, 7 John. Ch. R. 45—47; Morrill *v.* Dickey, 1 John. Ch. R. 153.

whether they are assets or not, but who is clothed with authority to administer them; and this must be decided by the local jurisdiction where they are situated; for the original administration has no extra-territorial operation[1].

§ 514 *a*. In the next place, let us suppose that an executor or administrator, appointed in the State where his testator or intestate died, should go into a foreign country, and should, without taking out new letters of administration, collect assets in such foreign country, and bring them home to the State from which he had received his original letters testamentary, or letters of administration; the question might arise, whether, in such a case, he would be liable to account in the Courts of the latter State for all the assets which he had so received in the foreign country, in the same way, and under the like circumstances, as he would be liable to account for them if he had received them in the home State. In other words, whether they would constitute a part of the home assets which he is bound to administer, and for which he is liable to account under the domestic administration according to the domestic laws. It has been said, that the assets so received and collected are to be so administered and accounted for as home assets by such executor or administrator. And the doctrine laid down in an ancient case is relied on for this purpose; where it is asserted to have been held by the Court, that, "if the executors have goods of the testator in any part of the world, they shall be charged in respect of them; for many merchants and other men, who have stocks and goods to a great value beyond sea, are indebted here in England: and, God forbid, that those goods should not be liable to their debts; for otherwise there would be a great defect in our law[2]". Now, this language in its broad import is certainly unmaintainable in our day; for it goes to the extent

---

[1] Att.-Gen. *v.* Dimond, 1 Cromp. & Jerv. 356, 370; Ante, § 513.

[2] Dowdale's Case, 6 Co. R. 47, 48; S. C. Cro. Jac. 55; cited and approved also in Evans *v.* Tatem, 9 Serg. & R. 252, 259.

of making a domestic executor or administrator liable for all assets of the testator or intestate which are locally situate abroad; although, as we have seen, he has not in virtue of the domestic letters of administration any authority to collect them, or to compel payment or delivery thereof to himself[1]. But the circumstances of the case called for no such doctrine. The case was of a testator who died in Ireland, and the defendant, who was his executor, collected and administered in Ireland certain property of the deceased. Afterwards he came to England, and was sued there by a creditor as executor; and the question arose, whether he was liable to the creditor in such suit for the assets collected and received by him in Ireland under the administration there. With reference, therefore, to the actual facts of the case, the more general question did arise. But according to the doctrine maintained in England in modern times, he was not all liable to be sued in Engand as executor under letters testamentary taken out in Ireland; and *à fortiori* not for the assets received and administered in Ireland under that appointment[2]. The authority of the case may, therefore, well be doubted in both of its aspects.

§ 514 *b*. Some of the American Courts have gone the length of recognising to its full extent the doctrine asserted in this case; and have held, that a foreign executor or administrator coming here, having received assets in the foreign country, is liable to be sued here, and to account for such assets, notwithstanding he has taken out no new letters of administration here, nor has the estate been positively settled in the foreign State[3]. The doctrine asserted in these Courts is, that such a foreign executor or administrator is chargeable here, as executor, for all the assets which

---

1 Ante, § 314.

2 Ibid; Post, § 515.

3 Swearingen's Ex'ors. *v*. Pendleton's Ex'ors., 4 Serg. & R. 389, 392; Evans *v*. Tatem, 9 Serg. & Rawle, 252, 259; Bryan *v*. M'Gee, 2 Wash. Cir. R. 337; Campbell *v*. Tousey, 7 Cowen, R. 64.

he still retains in his hands, or which he has expended or disposed of here, unless expended or disposed of here in the due course of administration, whether they were received here or in the foreign country, although he has not taken out any new letters of administration here[1]. There is very great difficulty in supporting these decisions to the extent of making the foreign executor or administrator liable here for assets received by him abroad in his representative character, and brought here by him. If a foreign executor or administrator cannot sue in his representative character in another State for the assets of the deceased situate there without new letters of administration, because he derives his authority solely from a foreign government which has no acthority to confer any right upon him, except to collect and receive the assets found within its own territorial jurisdiction, and to which, therefore, he is properly and directly responsible for the due administration of the assets, actually collected and received in such foreign country under its exclusive appointment, it is not easy to perceive how he can be suable in such State for such assets in his hands, received abroad by him under the sanction of the foreign administration, and by the authority of the foreign government, to which he is thus accountable for all such assets. One of the learned Courts, however, which decided the point, seems to have taken it for granted, that a foreign executor or administrator was of course suable here for all assets found in his hands. "If a foreign executor," said the Court, "is liable to be sued here, of which we apprehend there can be no question, he must, from the very nature of the case, *primâ facie*, be responsible for the assets which are shewn to have been in his possession within this State." With great deference, that was the very point to be established by some just reasoning, founded upon the principles of international jurisprudence, generally recognised by foreign

---

[1] Swearingen's Ex'ors. *v.* Pendleton's Ex'ors., 4 Serg. & R. 389, 392; Evans *v.* Tatem, 9 Serg. & Rawle, 252, 259; Bryan *v.* M'Gee, 2 Wash. Cir. R. 337; Campbell *v.* Tousey, 7 Cowen, R. 64.

jurists, or by the uniform established doctrine of the common law on this subject in modern times. It will be found exceedingly difficult to cite any modern authorities at the common law, in support of such a doctrine[1], since no authority could be shewn which supported it. On the other hand, there are other American authorities which indicate a very different doctrine[2]. The modern English authorities are to

---

1 In the cases of Swearingen's Ex'ors. *v.* Pendleton's Ex'ors., 4 Serg. & Rawle, 389, 392, and Evans *v.* Tatem, 9 Serg. & Rawle, 252, 259, the Supreme Court of Pennsylvania contented itself with merely affirming the doctrine in Dowdale's case, (6 Co. R. 47), without any general reasoning on the subject.

2 See Selectmen of Boston *v.* Boylston, 2 Mass. R. 384; Goodwin *v.* Jones, 3 Mass. R. 514; Davis *v.* Estey, 8 Pick. R. 475; Dawes *v.* Head, 3 Pick. R. 128; Doolittle *v.* Lewis, 7 John. Ch. R. 45, 47; M'Rae's Administrators *v.* M'Rae, 11 Louis. R. 571.—In the case of the Selectmen of Boston *v.* Boylston, 2 Mass. R. 384, 391, Mr. Justice Sedgwick, in delivering the opinion of the Court, after adverting to the fact, that the testator died in England, and that administration was there granted of his estate to the defendant cum testamento annexo, and that the defendant took out ancillary letters of administration in Massachusetts, where the suit was brought, and in respect whereof he was called upon to account with the plaintiffs for the assets both in England and America, said: "The Judge of Probate has in this case proceeded, and in all similar cases must proceed, according to the powers which are delegated to him by this statute. He can exercise no other powers. He has granted to the respondent administration on the estate of Thomas Boylston, lying in this government, with the will annexed. All the authority then, given to the administrator, is over the estate lying in this government. The Judge is to settle the said estate. What estate? Clearly, I think, the estate lying in this government. And it will neither consist with the intention of the legislature, nor the purposes of justice; because the administrator, with the will annexed, is here to proceed upon the fiction, that, by his relation to the testator in the same capacity in England, we ought to consider all the assets possessed by him there, as the estate of the testator lying in this government; because the estate by the statute subjected to the control of the Court of Probate, and to be settled by it, was that which was lying here before granting the letters of administration. To that, and to that only, do the words, and as I think, the meaning of the legislature, extend. The argument, from the inconveniences of admitting the construction for which the counsel for the appellants have contended, is strong and irresistible. It may reasonably be presumed, that the largest part of the testator's estate lies in the country where the original administration is granted; and that there also is the greatest portion of claims upon it. For what pur-

the same effect. They fully establish the doctrine, that, if a foreign executor or administrator brings or transmits pro-

---

pose of utility is the property to be transported to a distant region, and those to whom it belongs compelled to follow it, for the satisfaction of their demands? The expense and trouble of such a procedure, while wholly unnecessary, could not fail to be considerable. Suppose an English merchant of great property and extensive dealings to have been the testator; suppose this property to be principally in England, but portions of it to be left in several foreign countries, and that the administrator appointed there goes to collect it, and seeks the aid of the foreign governments for that purpose; and they, under pretence of giving this aid, claim an authority of drawing within their jurisdiction all the personal property of the testator, and all those who have demands upon it, or are interested in it. All these governments are independent of each other; and what is to establish a right of precedence? The commencement of a prosecution? How is this to be known? How are the other authorities to be controlled? If this is to be the construction, who will become bound for the administrator? By what means can the liability of the administrator and his sureties be known? In terms they only guaranty the settlement of the estate lying within the commonwealth; but in effect, if this construction be admitted, estate lying in every part of the globe. It is, in our opinion, impossible that such could have been the intention of the legislature. There are innumerable other inconveniences which might be, but which it is unnecessary should be pointed out." In Goodwin *v.* Jones, 3 Mass. R. 514, 519, 520, Mr. Chief Justice Parsons, in delivering the opinion of the Court, said: "When any person, an inhabitant of another State, shall die intestate, but leaving real estate within this Commonwealth, if administration should not be granted by some Judge of Probate of a county in which the estate lies, there would be no legal remedy for the creditors of the deceased to avail themselves of his real estate for the payment of the debts due to them. Therefore, to prevent a failure of justice, administration in such case must be granted by some Probate Court here; and the administrator so appointed will, by virtue of his letters of administration, and of the laws, also have the administration of all the goods, chattels, rights, and credits of the intestate which were within the State. And if a foreign administrator of that intestate should also have the administration of his personal estate here, there would exist two administrators of the same goods of the same intestate, independent of each other, and deriving their authority from different States, a consequence which cannot be admitted. But the granting of administration here, cannot divest the foreign administrator of any rights already vested in him; and the necessary inference is, that, whether administration be or be not granted in this State, an administrator appointed in another State cannot legally claim any interest in the goods of his intestate, which are subject to an administration granted in this State. And it is no objection to this reasoning, that debts due to the intestate on simple

perty here which he has received under the administration abroad, or if he is personally present, he is not, either per-

---

contract are to be considered as goods situate where he dies. For if the position be admitted, contrary to the authority of Wentworth, in his Executor, (p. 46), where it is supposed that such debts are bona notabilia where the debtor lives; yet, the administrator, if he recover judgment on such contract in this State, may satisfy it by an extent on lands, which certainly in their disposition are exclusively subject to the control of the laws of the Commonwealth. We have no particular statute relating to foreign administrators; but the manner in which an executor of a will proved without the State, may execute his trust within, is regulated by the statute of 1785, June 29, c. 12. The executor, or any person interested in any will proved without the State, may produce a copy of it, and of the probate under the seal of the foreign court which proved it, before the judge of probate of any county where the testator had real or personal estate whereon the will may operate, and request to have the same filed and recorded, which the judge, after notice, and hearing all parties, may order to be done: and he may then take bonds of the executor, or may grant administration cum testamento annexo, of the testator's estate lying in this government not administered, and may settle the estate, as in cases where the will has been proved before him. This statute needs no explanation. The executor of a will proved without the State cannot intermeddle with the effects of the testator in the State, but with the assent of a judge of probate, to whom he must first give bond. Neither can an administrator with the will annexed intermeddle, unless he is appointed by some judge within the State, who has authority to settle the whole estate within his jurisdiction. And it would be inconsistent with the manifest intent of the statute to allow an administrator of an intestate, not an inhabitant or resident within the State at his death, an authority derived from a foreign administration, which he could not have under the foreign probate of a will, of which he was the executor." In Doolittle *v.* Lewis, 7 John. Ch. R. 45, 47, Mr. Chancellor Kent said:—"It is well settled that a party cannot sue or defend in our courts as executor or administrator under the authority of a foreign Court of Probates. Our courts take no notice of a foreign administration; and before we can recognise the personal representative of the deceased, in his representative character, he must be clothed with authority derived from our law. Administration only extends to the assets of the intestate within the State where it was granted; if it were otherwise, the assets might be drawn out of the State, to the great inconvenience of the domestic creditors, and be distributed perhaps on very different terms, according to the laws of another jurisdiction. The authorities on this subject were cited by me in the case of Morrell *v.* Dickey, (1 John. Ch. R. 153), and I presume there is no dispute about the general rule; and the only difficulty lies in the application of it to this particular case."

sonally or in his representative capacity, liable to a suit here; nor is such property liable here to creditors, but they must resort for satisfaction to the forum of the original administration[1]. So, where property is remitted by a foreign executor to this country to pay legacies, no suit can be maintained for it if there is no specific appropriation of it without an administration taken out here[2].

§ 515. But, although an executor or administrator is not entitled to maintain a suit in a foreign court, in virtue of his original letters of administration, yet it has been said, that if a debtor chooses voluntarily there to pay him a debt, which he may lawfully receive under that administration, the debtor will be discharged[3]. This proposition is, or at

---

1 Currie administrator *v.* Bircham, 1 Dowl. & Ryl. R. 35; Davis *v.* Estey, 8 Pick. R. 475; Attor.-Gen. *v.* Bouwens, 4 Mees. & Wels. R. 171, 191; Tyler *v.* Bell, 1 Keen, R. 826, 829; S. C. 2 Mylne & Craig, 89, 109, 110; Attor.-Gen. *v.* Dimond, 1 Cromp. & Jerv. R. 356, 371; Spratt *v.* Harris, 4 Hagg. Eccl. R. 408; Attor.-Gen. *v.* Hope, 2 Clarke & Finell. R. 84, 90, 92; S. C. 8 Bligh, R. 44; 1 Cromp. Mees. & Rosc. 538. But see Dowdale's case, 6 Co. R. 47, and Anderson *v.* Caunter, 2 Mylne & Keen, 763; Spratt *v.* Harris, 4 Hagg. Eccl. R. 405, 408; Ante, § 513, 514 *a*. In Scrimshire *v.* Scrimshire, (2 Hagg. Consist. R. 420), Sir Edward Simson said: "If an Englishman makes a will abroad, and makes a foreigner executor, and has no effects in England, and the executor proves the will lawfully abroad, that probate or sentence of the proper court establishing the will as to effects there, of a man domiciled there, would be a bar to a discovery in Chancery of effects abroad."

2 Logan *v.* Fairlie, 2 Sim. & Stu. R. 284.

3 The proposition is thus guardedly laid down in Stevens *v.* Gaylord, 11 Mass. R. 256. But the question may also arise, whether the voluntary payment of a debt by a domestic debtor in a foreign country to a foreign administrator, when there is no domestic administrator appointed, will be a good discharge of the debtor. Debts are due not only in the domicil of the debtor, but in the domicil of the creditor; and indeed, unless a particular place of payment is appointed, they are due and may be demanded any where. If a debtor be found in the foreign country where the creditor died, and where an administrator is appointed, he would certainly be suable there, and could not protect himself by a plea that he was liable to pay only to the administrator appointed in the place of his (the debtor's) domicil. Lord Hardwicke, in Thorne *v.* Watkins, (2 Ves. 35), said that all debts follow the person, not of the debtor in respect of the right or property, but of the creditor to whom

least may be true, to the extent in which it is thus guardedly laid down and limited. For if an administration should be taken out on a creditor's estate, in the country where both the creditor and debtor resided at the time of his death, there, inasmuch as the debt is properly due in that country, and properly falls within that administration, it may be paid voluntarily by the debtor in another country, if he should afterwards change his domicil to that country, or if he should be found there: and the discharge of the administrator will be held a good discharge every where else, although no new administration be taken out; because the right to receive it primarily attached where the original administration was granted. Thus, for example, if an intestate should die in Ireland, leaving a bond debt there due by a debtor residing there at the time of his death, that bond debt would be *bona notabilia* there, and a payment afterwards, by the debtor made in England to such administrator, would, or might be a good discharge, notwithstanding no administration were taken out in England[1].

§ 515 *a*. There is, however, (as has been already stated)[2], much reason to doubt whether the doctrine be maintainable to the extent which the proposition has been sometimes understood to justify; that is to say, so as to apply it to a debt due by a debtor, who at the death of the creditor is actually domiciled in, and owes the debt in the foreign country where no administration is taken out. Suppose an administration should afterwards be granted in the foreign country, would it be any bar to an action brought by the foreign administrator against the debtor for the same debt,

---

due. In Doolittle *v.* Lewis, (7 John. Ch. R. 49), Mr. Chancellor Kent held, that a voluntary payment to a foreign executor or administrator, was a good discharge of the debt. See Shultz *v.* Pulver, 3 Paige, R. 182; Hooker *v.* Olmstead, 6 Pick. R. 481; Atkyns *v.* Smith, 2 Atk. R. 63; Trecothick *v.* Austin, 4 Mason, R. 16, 33.

1 Huthwaite *v.* Phaire, 1 Mann. & Grang. 159, and particularly what is said by Lord Chief Justice Tindal in p. 162.

2 Ante, § 514.

that the debtor had already paid it to another administrator, who had no right to demand it in virtue of his original administration, and who, therefore, might properly be deemed a stranger to the debt? Suppose a contest to arise between the original administrator and the foreign administrator, in relation to the administration of the debts so received as assets of the deceased, could the original administrator retain it against the will of the foreign administrator, or thereby subject it to a different application in the course of administration and marshalling assets from that which would otherwise exist? It seems difficult to answer these questions in the affirmative, without shaking some of the best-established principles of international law on this subject[1].

§ 516. And here it may be necessary to attend to a distinction, important in its nature and consequences. If a foreign administrator has, in virtue of his administration, reduced the personal property of the deceased there situated, into his own possession, so that he has acquired the legal title thereto, according to the laws of that country—if that property should afterwards be found in another country, or be carried away and converted there against his will, he may maintain a suit for it there in his own name and right personally, without taking out new letters of administration; for he is to all intents and purposes the legal owner thereof, although he is so in the character of trustee for other persons. In like manner, if a specific legacy of personal property is bequeathed in a foreign country, and the legatee has, under an administration there, been admitted to the full possession and ownership by the administrator, he may afterwards sue in his own name for any

---

[1] See Currie *v.* Bircham, 1 Dow. & Ryl. R. 35; Tyler *v.* Bell, 1 Keen, R. 826; S. C. 2 Mylne & Craig, 89, 109, 110; Attor.-Gen. *v.* Dimond, 1 Cromp. & Jerv. 356, 370; Contra Anderson *v.* Caunter, 2 Mylne & Keen, R. 763. But the latter case seems overruled. Ante, § 513; Post, § 518—521, 525; Huthwaite *v.* Phaire, 1 Mann. & Grang. 159, 164, 165.

injury or conversion of such property in another country where the property or wrong doer may be found, without any probate of the will there[1]. The plain reason in each of these cases is, that the executor and the legatee have, each in his own right, become full and perfect legal owners of the property by the local law; and a title to personal property, duly acquired by the *lex loci rei sitæ*, will be deemed valid, and be respected as a lawful and perfect title in every other country.

§ 517. The like principle will apply where an executor or administrator, in virtue of an administration abroad, becomes there possessed of negotiable notes belonging to the deceased, which are payable to bearer; for then he becomes the legal owner and bearer by virtue of his administration, and may sue thereon in his own name; and he need not take out letters of administration in the State where the debtor resides, in order to maintain a suit against him[2]. And for a like reason, it would seem, that negotiable paper of the deceased payable to order, actually held and indorsed by a foreign executor or administrator in the foreign country, who is capable there of passing the legal title by such indorsement, would confer a complete legal title on the indorsee, so that he ought to be treated in every other country as the legal indorsee, and allowed to sue thereon accordingly, in the same manner that he would be if it were a transfer of any personal goods or merchandize of the deceased situate in such foreign country[3].

§ 518. Where there are different administrations granted in different countries, that is deemed the principal or primary administration which is granted in the country of the

---

[1] See Commonwealth *v.* Griffith, 2 Pick. R. 11; Bollard *v.* Spencer, 7 T. R. 354; Shipman *v.* Thompson, Willes, R. 103; Slack *v.* Walcutt, 3 Mason, R. 508, 518.

[2] Robinson *v.* Crandall, 9 Wendell, R. 425. But see Stearns *v.* Burnham, 5 Greenleaf, R. 261; Thompson *v.* Wilson, 2 New Hamp. R. 291; M'Neilage *v.* Holloway, 1 B. & Ald. 218; Ante, § 354, 358, 359.

[3] Ib., and Ante, § 358, 359.

domicil of the deceased party; for the final distribution of his effects among his heirs or distributees is to be decided by the law of his domicil. Hence, any other administration which is granted in any other country, is treated as in its nature ancillary merely, and is, as we have seen, generally held subordinate to the original administration[1]. But each administration is, nevertheless, deemed so far independent of the others, that property received under one cannot be sued for under another, although it may at the moment be locally situate within the jurisdiction of the latter. Thus, if property is received by a foreign executor or administrator abroad, and it is afterwards remitted here, an executor or administrator appointed here could not assert a claim to it here, either against the person in whose hands it might happen to be, or against the foreign executor or administrator[2]. The only mode of reaching it, if necessary for the purposes of due administration in the foreign country, would be to require its transmission or distribution, after all the claims against the foreign administration had been duly ascertained and settled[3].

§ 519. But suppose a case where the personal estate of the deceased has not at the time of his decease any positive locality in the place of his domicil, or in any foreign territory; but it is strictly *in transitu* to a foreign country, and afterwards arrives in the country of its destination. It may be asked, in such case, to whom would the administration of such property rightfully belong? Would it belong to the administrator in the place of the domicil of the deceased, or to the administrator appointed in the place where it had

---

1 Ante, § 514.

2 Currie administrator *v.* Bircham, 1 Dowl. & Ryl. R. 35. See Jauncey *v.* Seeley, 1 Vern. R. 397; Ante, § 513, 515, 515 *a*. See Huthwaite *v.* Phaire, 1 Mann. & Grang. 159.

3 See Dawes *v.* Head, 3 Pick. R. 143—148; Harvey *v.* Richards, 1 Mason, R. 381; Ante, § 513, and note, § 514; Selectmen of Boston *v.* Dawes, 2 Mass. R. 384; Goodwin *v.* Jones, 3 Mass. R. 514; Dawes *v.* Boylston, 9 Mass. R. 337.

arrived? And if (as may well happen in a case of a ship and cargo sent abroad) the property or its proceeds should afterwards return to the domicil of the original owner, would the administrator there appointed be entitled to take it, and bound to account for it in the due course of administration? Practically speaking, no doubt is entertained on this subject; and the property whenever it returns to the country of the domicil of the owner, whether by remittance or otherwise, is understood to be under the administration of the administrator appointed there. Nor has there been a doubt hitherto judicially expressed, that property so sent abroad and returned might and should be so administered, and that all parties would be protected by their doings in regard to it.

§ 520. Indeed, according to the common course of commercial business, ships and cargoes and the proceeds thereof, locally situate in a foreign country at the time of the death of the owner, always proceed on their voyages, and return to the home port, without any suspicion that all the parties concerned are not legally entitled so to act; and they are taken possession of, and administered by the administrator of the *forum domicilii* with the constant persuasion that he may not only rightfully do so, but that he is bound to administer them as part of the funds appropriately in his hands. A different course of adjudication would be attended with almost inextricable difficulties, and would involve this extraordinary result, that all the personal property of the deceased must be deemed to have a fixed *situs* where it was at the moment of his death; and if removed from it, must be returned thither for the purpose of a due administration. Nay, debts due in a foreign country would be absolutely required to be retained there until a local administration was obtained, and could not without peril be voluntarily remitted to the creditor's domicil. And, if the debtor should in the mean time remove to another country, it might become matter of extreme doubt, whether a payment to a local administrator there would discharge him from the debt[1]. But it may, perhaps, after all be doubtful, whether, with a strict regard to the principles of international law, the personal property of the deceased testator or intestate, whether it consisted of goods or of debts, situate at the time of his death in a foreign country, could be lawfully disposed of, except under an administration granted in that country, although they had since been removed or transmitted to the domicil of the deceased, and had been received by his administrator appointed there[2].

§ 521. A case illustrative of these remarks has recently occurred. The personal estate of an intestate consisted in a considerable degree of stage-coaches and stage-horses, belonging to a daily line running from one State to another, and letters of administration were taken out by the same person in both States, one being that of the intestate's domicil. A question arose, under which administration the property was to be accounted for, part of it being in one State and part in the other, and part *in transitu* from one to the other at the moment of the intestate's death. The learned Chancellor of New York said, that if administration had been granted to different individuals in the two States, the property must have been considered as belonging to that administrator who first reduced it to possession within the limits of his own State. But that in the case before him, as both administrations were granted to the same person, if an account of administration were to be taken, it would be necessary to settle that, by ascertaining what had been inventoried and accounted for by him under the administration in the other State[3].

§ 522. Where administrations are granted to different persons in different States, they are so far deemed independent of each other, that a judgment obtained against one will furnish no right of action against the other, to affect

---

1 See Stevens *v.* Gaylord, 11 Mass. R. 256; Ante, § 515, 515 *a*.

2 See Ante, § 513—518; Post, § 525.

3 Orcutt *v.* Orms, 3 Paige, R. 459.

assets received by the latter in virtue of his own administration; for, in contemplation of law, there is no privity between him and the other administrator[1]. It might be different if the same person were administrator in both States[2]. On the other hand, a judgment recovered by a foreign administrator against the debtor of his intestate, will not form the foundation of an action against the debtor by an ancillary administrator appointed in another State[3]. But the foreign administrator himself might, in such a case, maintain a personal suit against the debtor in any other State; because the judgment would, as to him, merge the original debt, and make it personally due to him in his own right, he being responsible therefor to the estate[4].

§ 523. So strict is the principle, that a foreign administrator cannot do any act, as administrator, in another State, that, where the local laws convert real securities in the hands of an administrator into personal assests which he may sell or assign, he cannot dispose of such real securities, until he has taken out letters of administration in the place *rei sitæ*[5]. Thus, mortgages are declared by the laws of Massachusetts to be personal assets in the hands of administrators, and disposable by them accordingly. But the authority cannot be exercised by any, except administrators who have been duly appointed within the State[6]. On the other hand, if an administrator sells real estate for the payment of debts, pursuant to the authority given him under the local laws *rei sitæ*, he is not responsible for the proceeds as assets in any other State; but they are to

---

[1] Lightfoot *v.* Bickley, 2 Rawle, R. 431.

[2] Ibid.

[3] Talmage *v.* Chapel, 16 Mass. R. 71.

[4] Ibid. But see Smith *v.* Nicolls, 5 Bing. New Cas. p. 208; Post, § 607.

[5] Goodwin *v.* Jones, 3 Mass. R. 514, 519. See Bissell *v.* Briggs, 9 Mass. R. 467, 468. But see Doolittle *v.* Lewis, 7 John. Ch. R. 45, 47; Attor.-Gen. *v.* Bouwers, 4 Mees. & Welsb. 171, 191, 192.

[6] Cutter *v.* Davenport, 1 Pick. R. 80. But see Doolittle *v.* Lewis, 7 John Ch. R. 45, 47.

be disposed of, and accounted for, solely in the place and in the manner pointed out in the local laws[1].

§ 524. In relation to the mode of administering assets by executors and administrators, there are in different countries very different regulations. The priority of debts, the order of payments, the marshalling of assets for this purpose, and in cases of insolvency the mode of proof, as well as the mode of distribution, differ in different countries[2]. In some countries, all debts stand in an equal rank and order; and in case of insolvency the creditors are to be paid *pari passu*. In others, there are certain classes of debts entitled to a priority of payment; and they are therefore deemed privileged debts. Thus, in England, bond debts and judgment debts possess this privilege; and the like law exists in some of the States of this Union[3]. Similar provisions may be found in the law of France in favour of particular classes of creditors[4]. On the other hand, in Massachusetts, and in many other States of the Union, all debts except those due to the government possess an equal rank, and are payable *pari passu*. Let us suppose, then, that a debtor dies domiciled in a country where such priority of right and privilege exists; and he has personal assets situate in a State where all debts stand in an equal rank, and administration is duly taken out in the place of his domicil, and also in the place of the *situs* of the assets. What rule is to govern in the marshalling of the assets? The law of the domicil? or the law of the *situs*? The established rule now is, that in regard to creditors the administration of assets of deceased persons is to be governed altogether by the law of the country where the

---

1 Peck *v.* Mead, 2 Wendell, R. 471; Hooker *v.* Olmstead, 6 Pick. R. 481, 483; Goodwin *v.* Jones, 3 Mass. R. 514, 519, 520.

2 Harvey *v.* Richards, 1 Mason, R. 421; Ante, § 323—328, 401—403.

3 Smith administrator *v.* Union Bank of Georgetown, 5 Peters, R. 518.

4 Merlin, Répertoire, Privilege; Civil Code of France, art. 2092—2106.

executor or administrator acts, and from which he derives his authority to collect them, and not by that of the domicil of the deceased. The rule has been laid down with great clearness and force on many occasions[1].

§ 525. The ground upon which this doctrine has been established seems entirely satisfactory. Every nation having a right to dispose of all the property actually situate within it, has (as has often been said) a right to protect itself and its citizens against the inequalities of foreign laws which are injurious to their interests. The rule of a preference, or of an equality in the payment of debts, whether the one or the other course is adopted, is purely local in its nature, and can have no just claim to be admitted by any other nation, which in its own domestic arrangements pursues an opposite policy. And in a conflict between our own and foreign laws, the doctrine avowed by Huberus is highly reasonable, that we should prefer our own. *In tali conflictu magis est, ut jus nostrum, quam jus alienum, servemus.*[2]

§ 526. It seems that many foreign jurists, but certainly not all[3], maintain a different opinion, holding that in every case the privileges of debts, and the rank and order of payment thereof, are to be governed by the law of the

---

[1] See Harrison *v.* Sterry, 5 Cranch, 299; Milne *v.* Moreton, 4 Binn. R. 353, 361; Olivier *v.* Townes, 14 Martin, R. 93, 99; Ante, § 388; De Sobry *v.* De Laistre, 2 Harr. & John. R. 193, 224; Smith administrator *v.* Union Bank of Georgetown, 5 Peters, R. 518, 523; Dawes *v.* Head, 3 Pick. R. 128; Holmes *v.* Remsen, 20 John. R. 265; Case of Miller's Estate, 3 Rawle, R. 312; M'Elmoyle *v.* Cohen, 13 Peters, R. 312. Where there are administrations and assets in different States, and the estate is insolvent, the general principle adopted by the Courts of Massachusetts is, to place creditors there, as to the assets in the State, upon a footing of equality with other creditors in the State where the party had his domicil at his death. Davis *v.* Estey, 8 Pick. R. 475.

[2] Huberus, De Confl. Leg. lib. 1, tit. 3, § 11; See also Smith administrator *v.* Union Bank of Georgetown, 5 Peters, R. 517; Ante, § 322—327.

[3] See Ante, § 325 *a*—325 *o;* and 1 Boullenois, pp. 684—690; Rodenburg De Div. Stat. tit. 2, c. 5, § 16; 2 Boullenois, App. pp. 47—50.

domicil of the debtor at the time of his contract, or of his death. They found themselves upon the general rule, that the creditor must pursue the remedy in the domicil of the debtor, and that debts follow his person, and not that of the creditor[1]. This rule was acknowledged in matters of jurisdiction in the Roman law, in which it is said: *Juris ordinem converti postulas, ut non actor rei forum, sed reus actoris, sequatur. Nam, ubi domicilium reus habet, vel tempore contractûs habuit, licet hoc postea transtulerit, ibi tantum eum conveniri oportet*[2]. But it by no means follows, that, because this was the rule in the municipal jurisprudence of Rome, therefore it ought to be adopted as a portion of modern international law. Nor does it necessarily follow, even if the rule were admitted to govern, as to the forum where the suit should be brought against the debtor in his lifetime, that upon his death, in a conflict of the rights and

---

[1] Livermore, Diss. pp. 164—171; Ante, § 323—328. See also § 401—403.—Mr. Livermore has, in his Dissertations (pp. 164—171), controverted the correctness of the American doctrine; and he holds, that the law of the debtor's domicil, at the time when the debt was contracted, furnishes the true rule. Mr. Henry lays down the rule, that when the law of the domicil of the creditor and debtor differ, as to classing debts and rights of action among personal or real property, the law of the domicil of the debtor must prevail in suits on them. Henry on Foreign Law, 34, 35. Mr. Dwarris states the same rule, and quotes the maxims, "Actor sequitur forum rei," and "Debita sequuntur personam debitoris." He admits, indeed, that debts and rights of action attend upon the person of the creditor, "Inhærent ossibus creditoris;" but, to recover them, one must follow the forum rei, and person of the debtor. If the question regard the distribution of the creditor's estate, the law of his domicil is to be observed. If the question is, in what degree or proportion the representatives of the debtor should be charged with payment from his effects, then it is of a passive nature, and the law of the domicil of the debtor should be followed. Dwarris on Statut. 650. It would be difficult to point out, in the English law, any authority in support of this doctrine. See also Dumoulin's and Casaregis's opinions cited in Livermore's Diss. 162, 163; Molin, Opera, tom. 1. In Consuetud. Paris, de Fiefs. tit. 1, § 1, Gloss. 4, n. 9, pp. 56, 57, (edit. 1681); Casaregis in Rubr. Stat. Civ. Genuæ de Success. ab Intest. n. 64, tom. 4, pp. 42, 43; Ante, § 322—328.

[2] Cod. lib. 3, tit. 13, l. 2.

privileges of creditors (*concursus creditorum*) of different countries, the municipal law of the country of the debtor should overrule the jurisprudence of the *situs* of the effects[1].

§ 527. This, however, seems to be the doctrine of Coquille, Mævius, Carpzovius, Burgundus, Rodenburg, Matthæus, and Gaill[2]. But it is manifest, from the language used by them, that it is a matter of no small difficulty; and a diversity of laws and opinions may well be presumed to exist in regard to it. Boullenois holds the same doctrine[3]. Hertius seems in one passage to affirm it, saying: *Si de re immobili agitur, spectandas esse leges situs rei indubium est, etiamsi privilegium in ea propter qualitatem personæ tribuatur. At in rebus mobilibus, si ex contractu vel quasi agatur, locus contractus inspiciendus esset. Enimverò, quia antelatio ex jure singulari vel privilegio competit non debet in præjudicium illius civitatis, sub qua debitor degit, et res ejus mobiles contineri censeatur, extendi. Ad jura igitur domicilii debitoris, ubi fit concursus creditorum, et quo omnes cujuscunque generis lites adversus illum debitorem propter connexitatem causæ trahuntur, regulariter respiciendum erit*[4].

---

1 Ante, § 322—327.

2 Livermore, Diss. § 254—257, pp. 166—171; Rodenburg, De Div. Stat. tit. 2, c. 5, § 16; 2 Boullenois, App. p. 47; Ante, § 324—325 *o;* 1 Boullenois, pp. 684—687; Id. Observ. 30, pp. 818—834; Bouhier, Cout. de Bourg. ch. 21, § 204, ch. 22, § 151; Mævius, Comm. in Jus Lubesense, lib. 3, tit. 1, art. 11, n. 24—27, pp. 39, 40; Id. art. 10, n. 51, p. 33; Matthæus, de Auction. lib. 1, c. 21, § 35, n. 10, pp. 294, 295; Gaill. Observ. Pract. lib. 2, Observ. 130, n. 12—14, p. 563; Burgundus, Tract. 2, n. 21, p. 72, (edit. 1621); Ante, § 324—327.—Not having access to the works of Carpzovius and Coquille, I am obliged to rely on the citations which I find in Livermore's Dissertations of Coquille's opinion; and upon Rodenburg, Mævius (ubi supra), and Hertius, for the citations from Carpzovius. The other authors I have examined, and the citations are correct. Ante, § 324—327; Post, § 582.

3 1 Boullenois, p. 818; Id. Observ. 30, p. 834.

4 1 Hertii Opera, De Collis. Leg. § 4, n. 64, p. 150, (edit. 1737); Id. p. 211, (edit. 1716); Ante, § 325 *b*.

Yet he afterwards admits that cases may exist where undue preferences, given by the local laws of one state in favour of its own subjects, may be met with a just retaliation by others[1]. He cites a passage from Huberus[2], which would seem to shew that the latter was of a different opinion. A creditor (says Huberus) upon a bill of exchange, exercising his right in a reasonable time, has a preference in Holland over all other creditors upon the movable property of his debtor. He has property of the like kind in Friezeland, where no such law exists. Will such a creditor be there preferred to other creditors? By no means: since those creditors by the laws there received have already acquired a right. *Creditor ex causâ cambii, jus suum in tempore exercens, præfertur apud Batavos omnibus aliis debitoribus* [*creditoribus?*] *in bona mobilia debitoris. Hic habet ejusmodi res in Frisiâ, ubi hoc jus non obtinet. An ibi creditor etiam præferetur aliis creditoribus? Nullo modo; quoniam heic creditoribus, vi legum hic receptarum jus pridem quæsitum est*[3]. Upon this Hertius remarks: *Nimirum rectè disceret in sect. antec. non teneri Potestates sequi jus alienum in fraudem sui juris, et civium suorum. Hinc in quibusdam Germaniæ regionibus cives et incolæ in concursu creditorum antehabentur exteris, et pro consuetudine, quæ Biberaci est, ut cives chirographiarii præferantur extraneis forensibus, anteriorem hypothecam habentibus, pronunciatum in Camera Imperiali*[4]. Now this seems a virtual surrender of the main ground in all cases where there is a conflict of laws, as to the priorities and preferences of creditors, between the law

---

1 1 Hertii Opera, De Collis. Leg. § 4, n. 64, p. 150, (edit. 1737); Id. p. 211, (edit. 1716); Ante, § 325 *b*.

2 Huberus, J. P. Univers. c. 10, § 44.

3 I quote the passage as I find it in Hertius, not having access to the work of Huberus here referred to. Huberus, J. P. Univers. c. 10, § 44; 1 Hertii, Opera, De Collis. Leg. § 4, n. 64, p, 150, (edit. 1737); Id. p. 211, (edit. 1716). See Ante, § 325 *a*. Should not *debitoribus* be *creditoribus?*

4 1 Hertii Opera, De Collis, Leg. § 4, n. 64, p. 150, (edit. 1737); Id. pp. 211, 212, (edit. 1716); Ante, § 325 *b*.

of the domicil of the debtor or of the contract, and that of the *situs* of the movables.

§ 528. In the course of administrations also, in different countries, questions often arise as to particular debts, whether they are properly and ultimately payable out of the personal estate, or are chargeable upon the real estate of the deceased. In all such cases the law of the domicil of the deceased will govern in cases of intestacy; and in cases of testacy, the intention of the testator. A case illustrating this doctrine occurred in England many years ago. A testator who lived in Holland, and was seised of real estate there, and of considerable personal estate in England, devised all his real estate to one person, and all his personal estate to another whom he made his executor. At the time of his death, he owed some debts by specialty, and some by simple contract in Holland, and he had no assets there to satify those debts; but his real estate was by the laws of Holland made liable for the payment of simple contract debts, as well as specialty debts, if there were not personal assets to answer the same. The creditors in Holland sued the devisee, and obtained a decree there for the sale of the lands devised for the payment of their debts. And then the devisee brought a suit in England against the executor (the legatee of the personalty), for reimbursement out of the personal estate. The Court decided in his favour, upon the ground that in Holland, as in England, the personal estate was the primary fund for the payment of debts, and that it should come in aid of the real estate, and be in the first place charged[1].

§ 529. In the Scottish law the same doctrine is recognised, that is to say, that the fund which is primarily chargeable with the debt, shall ultimately bear it in exoneration of all other funds. But in its application under the local law to particular cases, an opposite result may be produced from that in the case just mentioned; for the per-

---

[1] Anonymous, 9 Mod. R. 66; S. P. Bowaman *v.* Reeve, Preced. ch. 511.

sonal estate is in such cases exonerated, and the real estate made to bear the debt. Thus, for example, in Scotland, heritable bonds are primarily payable out of the real estate; and, as we have seen, the personal estate of a person domiciled and dying in England, is held exonerated from the charge of such a heritable bond, made by him upon real estate in Scotland, to secure a debt contracted in England, and the Scottish estate is compellable to bear the burthen[1]. On the other hand, by the law of Scotland, movable debts (in contradistinction to heritable bonds) are primarily and properly chargeable upon the personal estate. The creditor may indeed enforce payment against the real estate in the hands of the heir; but if he does so, the heir is entitled to relief against the executor out of the personal estate. In other words, according to the law of Scotland, the real estate though subject to the payment of movable debts, is only a subsidiary fund for the purpose of payment. Payment, therefore, by the heir does not extinguish the debt in his hands, but vests in him a right to recover the amount against the personal estate[2]. The question has arisen, whether under such circumstances, the heir is entitled to enforce a payment out of the personal estate of his ancestor, not only in Scotland, but in England, (where he died domiciled), according to whose laws the personal estate is also the primary fund for the payment of debts; and it has been held that he is so entitled, upon the ground, that as between the heir and the persons entitled to the distribution of the personal estate, the primary fund must in all cases ultimately bear the burthen[3].

---

[1] Ante, § 486—488; Drummond *v.* Drummond, 6 Brown, Parl. Cases, 550 (Tomlin's edit. 1803); S. C. cited 2 Ves. & Beames, 131; Winchelsea *v.* Garetty, 2 Keen, R. 293, 310; Robertson on Succession, 209, 214; 4 Burge, Comm. on Col. and For. Law, pt. 2, ch. 15, § 4, pp. 722—734; Ante, § 266 *a*, 366, 486, 487.

[2] Earl of Winchelsea *v.* Garetty, 2 Keen, R. 293, 308.

[3] Earl of Winchelsea *v.* Garetty, 2 Keen, R. 293, 310—312. See Lord Langdale's opinion cited at large, Ante, § 266 *a*.

CHAPTER XIV.

JURISDICTION AND REMEDIES.

§ 530. We are next led to the consideration of the subject of remedies, or the modes of redress for the violation of the rights of other persons by proceedings in courts of justice. And, in the nature of things, these may well be classed into three sorts: first, those remedies which purely regard property, movable and immovable; secondly, those which purely regard persons; and, thirdly, those which regard both persons and property. The Roman jurisprudence took notice of this distinction, and accordingly divided all remedies, as to their subject, into three kinds: (1.) Real actions, otherwise called Vindications, which were those in which a man demanded something that was his own, and which were founded on dominion, or *jus in re;* (2.) Personal actions denominated also Conditions, which were those in which a man demanded what was barely due to him, and which were founded on some obligation, or *jus ad rem;* (3.) Mixed actions, which were those in which some specific thing was demanded, and where also some personal obligations were claimed to be performed [1]. The real actions of the Roman law were not, like the real actions of the common law, confined to real estate; but they included personal as well as real property. But the same distinction as to classes of remedies and actions equally pervades the common law, as it does the civil law. Thus we have in the common law, the distinct classes of real actions, personal actions, and mixed

---

1 Halifax on the Roman Law, b. 3, ch. 1, § 4, 5, pp. 85, 86; 1 Brown, Civil and Adm. Law, pp. 439, 440.—In Pothier's work on the Customs of Orleans there will be found a correspondent division of actions into the same classes. Pothier, Coutumes d'Orléans, Introd. Gén. ch. 4, art. 109—122.

actions: the first embracing those which concern real estate where the proceeding is purely *in rem;* the next embracing all suits *in personam* for contracts and torts; and the last embracing those mixed suits where the person is liable by reason of and in connexion with property [1].

§ 531. In considering the nature of actions, we are necessarily led to the consideration of the proper tribunal in which they should be brought; or, in other words, what tribunal is competent to entertain them in point of jurisdiction. And here the subject naturally divides itself into the consideration of matters of jurisdiction in regard to the administration of mere municipal and domestic justice; and matters of jurisdiction in regard to the administration of justice *inter gentes,* founded upon principles of public law.

§ 532. In the Roman jurisprudence, and among those nations which have derived their jurisprudence from the civil law, many embarrassing questions as to jurisdiction, seem to have arisen [2]. The general rule of the Roman Code is, that the plaintiff must bring his suit or action in the place where the defendant has his domicil, or where he had it at the time of the contract. *Juris ordinem* (said the Emperor Diocletian) *converti postulas; ut non actor rei forum, sed reus actoris, sequatur. Nam ubi domicilium reus habet, vel tempore contractûs habuit, licet hoc postea transtulerit, ibi tantum eum conveniri oportet* [3]. But it is not to be understood that this rule applied to all cases where the party defendant was found, without any regard to the situation of the thing sought, as if its object were to show more favour to the party defendant than to the plaintiff. Its sole object was, that the adjudication might be made where it could be enforced. Thus we find the doctrine laid down in the Code,

---

[1] 3 Black. Comm. 294; Comyns, Dig. *Action,* N.

[2] See 1 J. Voet, Ad Pand. lib. 5, tit. 1, § 303; Id. § 64, 66, 74, 91, 92; Huberus, lib. 5, tit. 1, De Foro Compet. tom. 2, § 38—52, pp. 722—730; Strykius, tom. 6, 11, 1, 8, tom. 7, 1, p. 5; 1 Boullenois, Observ. 25, pp. 601, 618, 619, 635.

[3] Cod. lib. 3, tit. 13, l. 2; Ante, § 526.

that, although the general is, that the plaintiff must bring his suit in the domicil of the defendant; yet this was dispensed with in certain suits *in rem*, which might be brought in the place *rei sitæ*. *Actor Rei forum, sive in rem, sive in personam sit actio, sequitur. Sed et in locis, in quibus res propter quas contenditur, constitutæ sunt, jubemus in rem actionem adversus possidentem moveri*[1].

§ 533. Huberus thus explains the doctrine: *Cujus ratio non tam est, quod reus sit actore favorabilior, etsi verissima; sed quod necessitatis vocandi et cogendi alium ad jus æquum, non nisi a superiore proficisci queat; superior autem cujusque non est alienus, sed proprius rector. Vocandi, inquam, et cogendi; quandoquidem sine coactione judicia forent elusoria; nec alibi forum lege stabilitur, quam ubi illa cogendi facultas adhiberi potest; non tamen, ut ubicunque illa valet, sit forum, sed ubi res et æquitas patitur. Vis illa compellendi partes ad æquum jus, imprimis est in loco domicilii, est etiam in loco rei sitæ, et rei gestæ, si Reus illic haberi possit, alias secus. Hinc tria sunt loca fori in jure nostro, Domicilii, Rei sitæ, Rei gestæ*[2]. And hence, he thinks, that the rule of the civil law *rei sitæ* applies not only to immovables, but to movables, although many jurists confine it to the former[3]. *Sed heic aliam potius rationem sequimur; quod in foro stabiliendo maxime consideretur, an in promptu sit effectum dare citationi, in cogendis partibus ad obsequium jurisdictionis; quæ facultas æque locum habet in mobilibus, ubi detinentur, quam in immobilibus, ubi sitæ sunt*[4].

§ 534. But he admits, that, as the *forum domicilii* was of universal operation, actions *in rem* might be brought in the

---

1 Cod. lib. 3, tit. 19, l. 3; 1 Boullenois, Observ. 25, pp. 618, 619; Post, § 551.

2 Huberus, lib. 5, tit. 1; De Foro Compet. § 38, tom. 2, p. 722. See also 1 Boullenois, Observ. 25, pp. 618, 619; Post, § 551.

3 The subject is a good deal controverted among the civilians; but the present work does not require me to engage in the task of discussing the various opinions which are held by them. The learned reader will find many of them referred to in J. Voet, Ad Pandect. tom. 1, lib. 5, tit. 1, § 77, &c. p. 337.

4 Huberus, tom. 2, lib. 5, tit. 1, § 48, p. 727.

forum domicilii as well as in the *forum rei sitæ*. *Videlicet, hoc semper tenendum, domicilii forum esse generale, quod in cunctis actionibus, adeoque etiam in actionibus in rem, obtinere, sciendum est, ut de dd. legibus constat*[1]. Again he says: *Summa igitur hæc esto. Domicilium in omnibus rebus et actionibus præbet forum. Res sita præterea in actionibus in rem singularibus, non excluso domicilio*[2]. And he supposes the same rule to apply in modern times in the civil law countries. *Hæc ego de foro domicilii, reique sitæ alternè conjuncto, moribus hodiernis eodem modo putem obtinere, quemadmodum jure Cæsaris præscriptum est; ut maxime in rem agatur, ubi res sita est; possit tamen omnino etiam, ubi reus habitat*[3].

§ 535. In regard to mixed actions, although there is no text of the Roman law directly in point, Huberus thinks that they may be brought, either in the place of domicil of the defendant, or of the *rei sitæ*. *De mixtis actionibus, exceptâ hæreditatis petitione, quæ partim in rem, partim in personam, esse dicuntur, non sunt textus speciales, ubi sint instituendæ. Ideoque id ex earum proprietate colligunt interpretes, cum partim imitentur naturam personalium, partim in rem actiones, illas et apud domicilium et apud rem sitam esse movendas, &c. Proinde sic est statuendum. Posse quidem illas actiones utroque loco, domicilii, sitûsque, moveri; verum, si faciendæ sunt adjudicationes manuque divisio regenda sit, partes ad judicem loci remittendas esse, res ipsa loquitur*[4].

§ 536. The civil law contemplated another place of jurisdiction, to wit, the place where a contract was made, or was to be fulfilled, or where any other act was done, if the defendant or his property could be found there, although it was not the place of his domicil. *Illud sciendum est, eum qui ita fuit obligatus, ut in Italiâ solveret, si in provinciâ*

---

1 Huberus, tom. 2, lib. 5, tit. 1, § 49, p. 728.
2 Id. § 50, p. 728.
3 Id. § 50.
4 Id. § 50, 51, p. 729.

habuit domicilium, utrobique posse conveniri, et hic, et ibi[1]. Huberus explains this thus: *Sequitur causa fori tertia, quam rem gestam esse diximus, eamque vel ex contractu vel ex delicto admisso, &c. Sed contractus ita forum tribuit, si contrahens in eodem loco reperiatur; quod convenit, requisito communi inde ab initio collocato, nullam esse fori causam, nisi cum facultate cogendi conjunctam; qualis non est ex historiâ contractûs, si vel reus ibi non inveniatur, vel bona duntaxat sita non habeat, in quæ missio fieri possit, quando Reus se in loco contractûs non sistit*[2]. These distinctions of the Roman law have found their way into the jurisprudence of most, if not of all, of the continental nations of modern Europe.

§ 537. Accordingly we find it laid down by foreign jurists generally, that there are, properly speaking, three places of jurisdiction: first, the place of domicil of the party defendant, commonly called the *forum domicilii;* secondly, the place where the thing in controversy is situate, commonly called the *forum rei sitæ;* and thirdly, the place where the contract is made or other act done, commonly called *forum rei gestæ*, or *forum contractûs. Vis illa compellandi partes ad æquum jus* (says Huberus) *imprimis est in loco domicilii; est etiam in loco rei sitæ; et rei gestæ, si reus illic haberi posse; alias secus*[3]. The same distinctions are fully laid down by John Voet and Boullenois, to whom we may generally refer for more copious information[4]. They are also recognised in the Scottish law[5]. They have been here brought into view; because they constitute the basis of the reasoning of many of the foreign jurists, in discussing the great doctrines respecting the competency of tribunals to

---

1 Dig. lib. 5, tit. 1, l. 19, § 4. See also as to all these distinctions, Pothier, Pand. lib. 5, tit. 1, n. 29—44; Cod. lib. 3, tit. 18, l. 1.

2 Huberus, tom. 2, lib. 5, tit. 1, § 53, 54, pp. 729, 730.

3 Huberus, tom. 2, lib. 5, tit. 1, De Foro Compet. § 38, p. 722.

4 J. Voet, Ad Pand. lib. 5, tit. 1, De Judiciis, p. 303, § 64—149; 1 Boullenois, Observ. 25, p. 601; Id. pp. 618, 619; Id. p. 635; Henry on Foreign Law, ch. 8, p. 54, ch. 9, p. 63.

5 Erskine, Inst. b. 1, tit. 2, § 16—22, pp. 29—39.

hold jurisdiction of causes, and the proper operation of judgments and decrees (*rei judicatæ*). They are also known as fundamental elements in the actual jurisprudence of many of the modern nations of continental Europe[1].

§ 538. In the corresponding distribution of actions by the common law into personal actions, real actions, and mixed actions[2], the two latter are, in point of jurisdiction, confined to the place *rei sitæ;* and the former are generally capable of being brought wherever the party can be found. Or, as the judicial phrase is, in the common law, real actions and mixed actions are *local*, and personal actions are *transitory*[3].

§ 539. Considered in an international point of view, jurisdiction, to be rightfully exercised, must be founded either upon the person being within the territory, or upon the thing being within the territory; for, otherwise there can be no sovereignty exerted upon the known maxim: *Extra territorium jus dicenti impune non paretur*[4]. Boullenois puts

---

1 See Code de Procédure Civile of France, b. 1, tit. 1, art. 1—4; Henry on Foreign Law, ch. 8, p. 54, ch. 9, p. 63, ch. 10, p. 71; Pardessus, Droit Comm. tom. 5, art. 1353; 1 Boullenois, Observ. 25, p. 601, 618, 619; Id. 635.—In France, jurisdiction would seem generally to belong either to the place of domicil or to the place rei sitæ. Jurisdiction in the place of the contract or of the other act done, does not seem to have been recognised under the old jurisprudence, and it does not exist in the modern Code. Code de Procédure Civile, art. 1, 2. "Le lieu," says Boullenois, "où se passent les actes, celui où les parties s'obligent de payer, et leur soumission, ne déterminent pas la justice où elles doivent plaider." 1 Boullenois, Observ. 30, pp. 829—832; 2 Boullenois, pp. 455—457. Dumoulin says: "Cæterum ex eo solo, quod quis promisit solvere certo loco, licet ibi conveniri possit de jure, sicut si ibi contraxisset; tamen hoc non observatur in hoc regno; quia in hoc regno non sortitur quis forum ratione contractûs, etiam vere et realiter facti in loco." Molin. Opera, Comm. in Decii. tom. 3, p. 837 (edit. 1681); 1 Boullenois, Observ. 30, p. 829. See also Pothier, Traité de la Procédure Civile, ch. 1.

2 3 Black. Comm. 117, 118.

3 3 Black. Comm. 294; Com. Dig. *Action*, N.; 1 Chitty on Comm. and Manuf. pp. 647—649.

4 Dig. lib. 2, tit. 1, l. 20.

this rule among his general principles. The laws of a sovereign rightfully extend over persons who are domiciled within his territory, and over property which is there situate[1]. Vattel lays down the true doctrine in clear terms: "The sovereignty," says he, "united to domain, establishes the jurisdiction of the nation in its territories, or the country which belongs to it. It is its province, or that of its sovereign, to exercise justice in all places under its jurisdiction, to take cognizance of the crimes committed, and the differences that arise in the country[2]." On the other hand, no sovereignty can extend its process beyond its own territorial limits, to subject either persons or property to its judicial decisions. Every exertion of authority of this sort beyond this limit is a mere nullity, and incapable of binding such persons or property in any other tribunals[3]. This subject, however, deserves a more exact consideration.

§ 540. In the first place, let us consider the subject of jurisdiction a little more particularly in regard to persons. These may be either citizens (native or naturalized) or foreigners. In regard to the former, while within the territory of their birth, or of their adopted allegiance, the jurisdiction of the sovereignty over them is complete and irresistible. It cannot be controlled, and it ought to be respected every where. But as to citizens of a country domiciled abroad, the extent of jurisdiction which may be lawfully exercised over them *in personam*, is not so clear upon acknowledged principles. It is true, that nations generally assert a claim to regulate the rights, and duties, and obligations, and acts of their own citizens, wherever they may be domiciled. And, so far as these rights, duties, obligations, and acts afterwards come under the cognizance of the tribunals of the sovereign power of their own country, either for enforcement, or for protection, or for remedy, there may be

---

[1] 1 Boullenois, Prin. Gén. 1, 2, p. 2, 3.
[2] Vattel, b. 2, ch. 8, § 84.
[3] Picquet *v.* Swan, 5 Mason, R. 35, 42.

no just ground to exclude this claim. But when such rights, duties, obligations, and acts come under the consideration of other countries, and especially of the foreign country where such citizens are domiciled, the duty of recognising and enforcing such a claim of sovereignty is neither clear nor generally admitted. The most that can be said is, that it may be admitted *ex comitate gentium.* But it may also be denied *ex justitiâ gentium,* whenever it is deemed injurious to the interests of such foreign nations, or subversive of their own policy or institutions. No one, for instance, would imagine that a judgment of the parent country confiscating the property, or extinguishing the personal rights or personal capacities of a native subject on account of such a foreign residence, would be recognised in any other country. And, it would be as little expected, as a matter of right, that any other country would enforce a judgment against such persons in the parent country, obtained *in invitum,* on account of a supposed contumacy in remaining abroad, to which suit he had never appeared, and of which he had received no notice, however the proceedings might be in conformity to the local laws. This is the just result deducible from the axioms of Huberus, already quoted, and especially from the first and second of those axioms[1]. Whatever authority should be given to such judgments must be purely *ex comitate,* and not as matter of absolute or positive right on one side, and of duty on the other.

§ 541. In regard to foreigners resident in a country, although some jurists deny the right of a nation generally to legislate over them, it would seem clear, upon general principles of international law, that such a right does exist; and the extent to which it should be exercised, is a matter purely of municipal arrangement and policy. Huberus lays down the doctrine in his second axiom. All persons who are found within the limits of a government, whether their residence is permanent or temporary, are to be deemed subjects

---

[1] Ante, § 29.

thereof[1]. Boullenois says, that the sovereign has a right to make laws to bind foreigners, in relation to their property within his domains, in relation to contracts and acts done therein, and in relation to judicial proceedings if they implead before his tribunals[2]. And, further, that he may of strict right make laws for all foreigners who merely pass through his domains, although commonly this authority is exercised only as to matters of police[3]. Vattel asserts the same general doctrine, and says, that foreigners are subject to the laws of a state while they reside in it[4]. And in relation to disputes which may arise between foreigners, or between a citizen and a foreigner, he holds that they are to be determined by the judge of the place, and according to the laws of the place of the defendant's domicil[5].

§ 542. There are nations, indeed, which wholly refuse to take cognizance of controversies between foreigners, and remit them for relief to their own domestic tribunals, or to that of the party defendant; and especially as to matters originating in foreign countries. Thus, in France, with few exceptions, the tribunals do not entertain jurisdiction of controversies between foreigners respecting personal rights and interests[6]. But this is a matter of mere municipal policy and convenience, and does not result from any principles of international law. In England and America, on the other hand, suits are maintainable, and are constantly maintained, between foreigners, where either of them is within the territory of the state in which the suit is brought.

§ 543. But, although every nation may thus rightfully exercise jurisdiction over all persons within its domains; yet

---

1 Ante, § 29; Huberus, tom. 2, lib. 1, tit. 3, § 2, p. 538; Ante, § 29, n. 3; Henry on For. Law, ch. 8, p. 54, ch. 9, p. 63, ch. 10, p. 71.

2 1 Boullenois, Pr. Gén. 4, 5, p. 3.

3 Id. 5, p. 3.

4 Vattel, b. 1, ch. 19, § 213; Id. b. 2, ch. 8, § 99, 101, 103.

5 Id. b. 2, ch. 8, § 103.

6 See Pardessus, Droit. Comm. tom. 5, art. 1476—1478, p. 238; Henry on For. Law, App. pp. 214—216.

we are to understand, that in regard thereto, the doctrine applies only to suits purely personal, or to suits connected with property within the same sovereignty. For although the person may be within the territorial jurisdiction; yet it is by no means true, that, in virtue thereof, every sort of suit may there be maintainable against him. A suit cannot, for instance, be maintainable against him so as absolutely to bind his property situate elsewhere; and, *à fortiori*, not so as absolutely to bind his rights and titles to immovable property situate elsewhere. It is true, that some nations do, in maintaining suits *in personam*, attempt, indirectly, by their judgments and decrees, to bind property situate in other countries; but it is always with the reserve that it binds the person only in their own courts, in regard to such property. And, certainly, there can be no pretence that such judgments or decrees bind the property itself, or the rights over it, which are established by the laws of the place where it is situate. If a Court of Chancery in England should compel a bankrupt by its decree to convey his personal and real estate, situate in foreign countries, to the assignees under the commission, (as it was at one time thought they might do, although now the doctrine is repudiated[1]); yet such a decree would not operate to transfer the property so as to affect the rights of creditors, or the regular operation of the laws of the state *rei sitæ*. So, a foreign court cannot, by its judgment or decree, pass the title to land situate in another country; neither can it bind such land by a judgment or decree, that in default of the defendants in the suit conveying it, it shall be conveyed by the deed of its own officers to the plaintiffs. Such a conveyance made by its officers would be treated, in the country where the land is situate, as a mere nullity[2].

§ 544. The doctrine of the English Courts of Chancery,

---

[1] Ex parte Blades, 1 Cox, R. 398; Selkrig *v.* Davies, 2 Rose, Bank. Cases, 97; Id. 291; S. C. 2 Dow, R. 231.

[2] Watts *v.* Waddle, 6 Peters, R. 389, 400.

on this head of jurisdiction, seems carried to an extent which may, perhaps, in some cases, not find a perfect warrant in the general principles of international public law; and, therefore, it must have a very uncertain basis as to its recognition in foreign countries, so far as it may be supposed to be founded in the comity of nations. That doctrine is, that the Court of Chancery having authority to act upon the person (*agere in personam*), may indirectly act upon real estate, situate in a foreign country, through the instrumentality of this authority over the person; and that it may compel him to give effect to its decree respecting such property, whether it goes to the entire disposition of it, or only to affect it with liens or burthens[1]. Lord Hardwicke asserted the jurisdiction in several cases[2]. At a more recent period, the Court of Chancery asserted the jurisdiction over a British creditor, who had fraudulently obtained a judgment in the British West Indies against his debtor, and had on an execution sold his debtor's real estate there, and become the purchaser thereof; and the Court set aside the purchase for the fraud[3]. It is observable, that in this last case all the parties were British subjects, and the original judgment was in a British island. The Master of the Rolls, (Sir R. P. Arden), on that occasion, said: "Upon the whole, it comes to this: that, by a proceeding in the island, an absentee's estate might be brought to sale, and for whatever interest he has, without any particular upon which they are to bid; the question is, whether any Court will permit the transaction to avail to that extent. It is said, this Court has no jurisdiction, because it is a proceeding in the West Indies. It has been argued, very sensibly, that it is strange for this Court to say, it is void by the laws of the island, or for want of notice. I admit, I am bound to say, that

---

[1] See 1 Eq. Abridg. C. p. 133; Arglasse *v.* Muschamp, 1 Vern. R. 75, 135; Kildare *v.* Eustace, 1 Vern. 75, 135, 419.

[2] See Foster *v.* Vassall, 3 Atk. 589; Penn *v.* Lord Baltimore, 1 Ves. R. 444.

[3] Cranstown *v.* Johnston, 3 Ves. Jr. 170; S. C. 5 Ves. Jr. 276.

according to those laws a creditor may do this. To that law he has had recourse, and wishes to avail himself of it; the question is, whether an English Court will permit such a use to be made of the law of that island or any other country. It is sold, not to satisfy the debt, but in order to get the estate, which the law of that country never could intend, for a price much inadequate to the real value, and to pay himself more than the debt for which the suit was commenced, and for which only the sale could be holden. It was not much litigated, that the Courts of Equity here have an equal right to interfere with regard to judgments or mortgages upon the lands in a foreign country as upon lands here. Bills are often filed upon mortgages in the West Indies. The only distinction is, that this Court cannot act upon the land directly, but acts upon the conscience of the person living here. Archer *v.* Preston, Lord Arglasse *v.* Muschamp, Lord Kildare *v.* Eustace, (1 Eqr. Abr. 133; 1 Vern. 75, 135, 419). Those cases clearly shew, that with regard to any contract made, or equity between persons in this country, respecting lands in a foreign country, particularly in the British dominions, this Court will hold the same jurisdiction as if they were situated in England. Lord Hardwicke lays down the same doctrine, (3 Atk. 589). Therefore, without affecting the jurisdiction of the Courts there, or questioning the regularity of the proceedings as in a court of law, or saying that this sale would have been set aside either in law or equity there, I have no difficulty in saying, which is all I have to say, that this creditor has availed himself of the advantage he got by the nature of those laws, to proceed behind the back of the debtor upon a constructive notice, which could not operate to the only point to which a constructive notice ought, that there might be actual notice without wilful default; that he has gained an advantage which neither the law of this nor of any other country would permit. I will lay down the rule as broad as this: this Court will not permit him to avail himself of the law of any other country to do what would be gross injustice[1]."

§ 545. To the extent of this decision perhaps there may not be any well founded objection[2]; and the same doctrine has been repeatedly acted upon by the equity courts of America[3]. But even in England the Court of Chancery will not act directly upon lands in the plantations, so as to affect the title, or the possession, or the rents and profits thereof[4]. Nor will it entertain jurisdiction over contracts with regard to lands in foreign colonies, so as to touch the title there, or to prevent a sale thereof by an injunction[5]; although it has been repeatedly held, in very general terms, that there is no doubt of the jurisdiction of the Court of Chancery as to land in the West Indies, or in other foreign places, if the persons are in England[6].

§ 546. But it is not an uncommon course for a nation by its own municipal code to provide for the institution of actions against non-resident citizens, and against not resident foreigners, by a citation *viis et modis,* (as it is called), or by an attachment of their property, nominal or real, within the limits of its own territorial sovereignty; and to proceed to judgment against the party defendant, whether he has any actual notice of the suit or not, or whether he ever appears to the suit or not. In respect to such suits *in personam,* by a mere personal citation, *viis et modis,* such as by posting up such a citation on the Royal Exchange in London, as is done in the Admiralty in England, or by an

---

1 Cranstown *v.* Johnston, 3 Ves. Jr. 170; S. C. 5 Ves. Jr. 276.

2 S. P. Jackson *v.* Petrie, 10 Ves. 164.

3 See Massie *v.* Watts, 6 Cranch, 148, 158; Ward *v.* Amedon, Hopkins, R. 213; Mead *v.* Merrett, 2 Paige, R. 402; Mitchell *v.* Burch, 2 Paige, R. 606.

4 Roberdeau *v.* Rous, 1 Atk. 543. See 1 Vern. R. 75, 135, 419; Post, § 551.

5 White *v.* Hall, 12 Ves. Jr. 321. See Massie *v.* Watts, 6 Cranch, 148, 156.

6 Jackson *v.* Petrie, 10 Ves. 165.

edictal citation, (as it is called), posted up at the quay in Leith, at the market-cross of Edinburgh, and the pier and shore of Leith, according to the practice of Scotland [1], there is no pretence to say that such modes of proceeding can confer any legitimate jurisdiction over foreigners who are non-residents, and do not appear to answer the suit, whether they have notice of the suit or not. The effects of all such proceedings are purely local; and elsewhere they will be held to be mere nullities.

§ 547. Lord Ellenborough put this doctrine with great clearness and force in a case before the Court, where a judgment was obtained in the Island of Tobago against a party stated in the proceedings to be "formerly of the City of Dunkirk, and now of the City of London, merchant," and who was cited to appear at the ensuing Court to answer the plaintiff's action by a summons which was returned served "by nailing up a copy of the declaration at the Court House door," and on which service judgment was afterwards given by default of the defendant to appear and defend it. It was attempted to maintain the judgment as authorized by the local law in cases of persons absent from the island. Lord Ellenborough, in delivering the judgment of the Court, said, "By persons absent from the island must necessarily be understood persons who have been present, and within the jurisdiction, so as to have been subject to the process of the Court; but it can never be applied to a person who, for aught appears, never was present within, or subject to the jurisdiction. Supposing, however, that the Act had said in terms, that, though a person sued in the island had

---

[1] Ersk. Instit. b. 1, tit. 2, § 17, 18; Id. b. 4, tit. 1, § 8.—After a decree is obtained in personam, in Scotland, it seems that letters of horning, as they are called, issue, requiring the defendant to comply with the decree, which may be served by personal service, or, if the party cannot be found, by application at his place of domicil, or dwelling-house; and, if he is out of the kingdom, then he is charged by a copy put up at the market-cross in Edinburgh, and at the pier and shore of Leith. Ersk. Inst. b. 2, tit. 5, § 55; Id. b. 4, tit. 3, § 9. See Douglas *v.* Forrest, 4 Bing. R. 686, 690.

never been present within the jurisdiction, yet that it should bind him upon proof of nailing up the summons at the Court door; how could that be obligatory upon the subjects of other countries? Can the Island of Tobago pass a law to bind the rights of the whole world? Would the world submit to such an assumed jurisdiction? The law itself, however fairly construed, does not warrant such an inference; for 'absent from the island' must be taken only to apply to persons who had been present there, and were subject to the jurisdiction of the Court out of which the process issued; and as nothing of that sort was in proof here to shew that the defendant was subject to the jurisdiction at the time of commencing the suit, there is no foundation for raising an assumpsit in law upon the judgment so obtained[1]."

---

[1] Buchanan v. Rucker, 9 East, R. 192, 194. See Cranstown v. Johnston, 3 Ves. Fr. 170; S. C. 5 Ves. Fr. 276; Cavan v. Stewart, 1 Starkie, R. 525; Becquet v. M'Carthy, 2 Barn. & Adolph. 951.—In Smith v. Nicolls, 4 Bing. New Cases, 208, which was an action of trover for a ship, the defendant among other things pleaded a foreign judgment and recovery by the plaintiff in the Vice-Admiralty Court at Sierra Leone for the same subject-matter. To that plea there was a replication, that the defendant was not in the Colony of Sierra Leone, or at any place within the jurisdiction of the Vice-Admiralty Court, at the commencement of, or at any time during the proceedings, or any time until after the judgment in the Colony of Sierra Leone, and had no notice thereof, &c.; and Lord Chief Justice Tindal, in delivering his opinion, adverting to this point, said: "The effect of the plaintiff's replication is this: He shews some matters, by which, at least primâ facie, the judgment relied on is a void judgment; for he says, at the time of the suit being commenced, and from that time down to the termination of the suit, not only was the defendant in that action absent from the place, but that he had no person whatever, no agent, or any other person, on whom any process or monition from the Court could be served, or who could answer for him. Till that is answered by shewing that there was some law in the colony, from which in the situation the party was, the judgment would not be a void one, we must say the plaintiff is setting up that which if unanswered, shews it to be a void judgment. In Plummer v. Woodburne, the Court says, that before you set up a foreign judgment as conclusive in the nature of an estoppel between the parties, it must appear on the record that it is decisive and binding between them in the colony where the judgment is given. That does not appear here; and therefore on both grounds I think the plea is a bad plea, as far as the foreign judgment is concerned." See also Plummer v. Woodburne, 4 Barn. & Cress.

This doctrine has been fully recognised in the American courts[1].

§ 548. In a recent case, the validity of a judgment rendered in a foreign country in a suit against persons who were non-residents, and had no actual notice of the suit, and did not appear and answer the same, came before the Court of Common Pleas in England, upon a Scottish judg-

---

625. Lord Brougham, in alluding to the same subject in Don *v.* Lippmann, 5 Clarke & Finnell. 1, 20, 21, said: "But supposing that the debt might have boen sued for in France, then comes the question, whether the French judgment cannot be sued on a substantive cause of action. It is, in fact, tendered as one of the grounds of suit here. A foreign judgment is good here for such a purpose, provided that it has not been obtained by fraud or collusion, or by a practice contrary to the principles of all law. Fraser *v.* Sinclair, (Morr. 4543), which was affirmed in this House, shewed, that we regard a foreign judgment only as primâ facie evidence of a debt. Buchanan *v.* Rucker, (1 Camp. 63; 9 East, 192), established, that the Court before which a foreign judgment is brought by a proceeding of this sort, may examine whether it has been rightly obtained or not; and the principle of the decision cannot be confined to the case of a party not being within the jurisdiction at the time the judgment is obtained. If he is a foreigner, and is not within the jurisdiction, but is by force kept out of it before the action, and is not sued by proper forms, his case is even stronger than that of the defendant in Buchanan *v.* Rucker, and he must have the same principle applied to it. The case of Douglas *v.* Forrest, (4 Bing. 686), shews how much the application of the rule is affected by circumstances. In that case, which was an action in an English Court on a Scotch judgment of horning against a Scotchman born, the Court guards itself against a general inference from the decision. The Chief Justice, in delivering the judgment of the Court says, (4 Bing. 703): , We confine our judgment to a case, where the party owed allegiance to the country in which the judgment was so given against him, and by the laws of which country his property was at the time those judgments were given protected.' Beckett *v.* M'Carthy, (2 Barn. & Ad. 951), has been supposed to go to the verge of the law: but the defendant in that case held a public office in the very colony in which he was originally sued." In the still more recent case of Ferguson *v.* Mahon, 3 Perr. & Dav. R. 143, the Court of King's Bench in England held, in an action on an Irish judgment, that it was a good plea in bar, that the defendant was never served with, nor had notice of, any process in the action.

[1] Tenton *v.* Garlick, 8 John. R. 194; Borden *v.* Fitch, 15 John. R. 121; Bissell *v.* Briggs, 9 Mass. R. 462; Mills *v.* Duryee, 7 Cranch, 481, 486; Picquet *v.* Swan, 5 Mason, R. 35, 43, 44; Buttrick *v.* Allen, 8 Mass. R. 473.

ment rendered against a Scottish absentee, upon a due attachmentof his heritable property in Scotland, and due proclamation, by what is technically called "horning," in Scotland, which judgment was rendered against the defendant by default, for his non-appearance to answer the suit. The question was, whether the judgment so rendered was void or not. It was held that the judgment was valid. This decision was founded partly upon the construction of the articles of union between Scotland and England, and partly upon the recognition of such a practice as valid by a British Act of Parliament, and partly upon the fact, that the judgment was against a Scottish subject[1]. On that occasion, Lord Chief Justice Best, in delivering the opinion of the Court, said: "A natural-born subject of any country, quitting that country, but leaving property under the protection of its laws, even during his absence, owes obedience to those laws, particularly when those laws enforce a moral obligation. The deceased, before he left his native country, acknowledged under his hand that he owed the debts; he was under a moral obligation to discharge those debts as soon as he could[2]." And after adverting to the case of Buchanan *v.* Rucker, and some others, he added: "To be sure, if attachments issued against any persons who were never within the jurisdiction of the Court issuing them, would be supported and confirmed in the country in which the person attached resided, the legislature of any country might authorize their Courts to decide on the rights of parties who owed no allegiance to the government of such country, and were under no obligation to attend its Courts or obey its laws. We confine our judgment to a case where the party owed allegiance to the country in which the judgment was so given against him, from being born in it, and by the laws of which country his property was at the time those judgments were given, protected. The debts

---

1 Douglas *v.* Forrest, 4 Bing. R. 686, 702, 703.

2 Ibid.

were contracted in the country in which the judgments were given whilst the debtor resided in it[1]."

§ 548 *a.* Another case also occurred at a later period, which presented a similar question. An action was brought and a judgment recovered in the island of Mauritius, against a party who had been a former resident in the island, but who was absent from the island during the whole course of the proceedings. By a law of the colony it was provided, that if a suit was instituted against an absent party, process should be served upon the King's Procurator-General in the colony; but it was not expressly provided that the Procurator-General should communicate with the absent party. It appeared that the process was served on the Procurator-General, but it did not appear that the absent party had any notice thereof. The Court held that the judgment was valid. Lord Tenterden on that occasion, in delivering the opinion of the Court, said: "Another objection, and not an unimportant one, was, that the testator, when the proceedings were instituted against him, was absent from the island; and it was urged that it was contrary to the principles of natural justice that any one should be condemned unheard and in his absence. Proof, however, was given, that by the law of the colony, in the case of a person formerly resident in the island, absenting himself, and not leaving any attorney upon whom process in a suit might be served, the Procurator-General or his deputy was bound to take care of the interests of such absent party. It was said, that the law of the island did not provide any means whereby the Procurator-General or his deputy might be required to hold communication with, or receive directions from an absent person. There may, perhaps, be some deficiency in the law in that respect; but as the law of the island is, that the process shall be served upon the public

---

[1] Douglas *v.* Forrest, 4 Bing. R. 686, 702, 703. See also Becquet *v.* M'Carthy, 2 Barn. & Adol. R. 951; Don *v.* Lippmann, 5 Clarke & Finell. l. 21; Plummer *v.* Woodburne, 4 Barn. & Cress. R. 625.

officer, it must be presumed that he would do whatever was necessary in the discharge of that public duty; and we cannot take upon ourselves to say that the law is so contrary to natural justice, as to render the judgment void in a case where the process was so served[1]."

§ 549. A still more common course in many states and nations is, to proceed against non-residents, whether they are citizens or whether they are foreigners, by a seizure or attachment of their property situate or found within the territory. Sometimes the seizure or attachment is purely nominal; as, for example, of a chip, or a cane, or a hat. In other cases, the seizure or attachment is *bonâ fide* of real property or personal property within the territory, or of debts due to the non-resident persons in the hands of their debtors who live within the country[2]. In such cases, for all the purposes of the suit, the existence of the property so seized or attached within the territory, constitutes a just ground of proceeding to enforce the rights of the plaintiff, to the extent of subjecting such property to execution upon the decree or judgment. But if the defendant has never appeared and contested the suit, it is to be treated to all intents and purposes as a mere proceeding *in rem,* and not as personally binding on the party as a decree or judgment *in personam;* or, in other words, it only binds the property seized or attached in the suit to the extent thereof, and is in no just sense a decree or judgment binding upon him beyond that property. In other countries it is uniformly so

---

[1] Becquet *v.* M'Carthy, 2 Barn. & Adol. 951, 958, 959.—It has been justly remarked by Lord Brougham, (in Don *v.* Lippmann, 5 Clarke & Finnell. 21), that that case "has been supposed to go to the verge of the law; but the defendant in that case held a public office in the very colony in which he was originally sued." Perhaps a stronger doubt of its correctness might, upon principles of public justice, have been pronounced. Boullenois manifestly deems an exercise of jurisdiction against an absent foreigner, to be unfounded in point of authority. 1 Boullenois, Observ. 25, p. 610.

[2] See Henry on Foreign Law, ch. 8—10, pp. 54, 63, 71; Douglas *v.* Forrest, 4 Bing. R. 686, 700, 701.

treated, and is justly considered as having no extra-territorial force or obligation[1].

---

[1] See Phelps *v.* Holker, 1 Dall. 261; Kilburn *v.* Woodworth, 5 John. R. 37; Pawling *v.* Bird's Ex'ors. 13 John. R. 192; Bissell *v.* Briggs, 9 Mass. R. 462; Robinson *v.* Ex'ors. of Ward, 8 John. R. 86; Post, § 592. But see Douglas *v.* Forrest, 4 Bing. R. 686, 702, 703; Shumway *v.* Stillman, 6 Wendell, R. 447; 1 Boullenois, Observ. 25, pp, 609, 610, 619, 620. 622—624, 628; 6 Harris & John. R. 191; Taylor *v.* Phelps, 1 Gill & John. R. 492.—Mr. Chief Justice Parsons, in his very able opinion, in Bissell *v.* Briggs, (9 Mass. R. 468), has made some pointed remarks on this subject, from which the following extract is made:—" To illustrate this position, it may be remarked, that a debtor living in Massachusetts, may have goods, effects, or credits in New Hampshire, where the creditor lives. The creditor there may lawfully attach these, pursuant to the laws of that State, in the hands of the bailiff, factor, trustee, or garnishee of his debtor; and on recovering judgment, those goods, effects, and credits, may lawfully be applied to satisfy the judgment; and the bailiff, factor, trustee, or garnishee, if sued in this State for those goods, effects, or credits, shall, in our Courts, be protected by that judgment, the Court in New Hampshire having jurisdiction of the cause for the purpose of rendering that judgment, and the bailiff, factor, trustee, or garnishee producing it, not to obtain execution of it here, but for his own justification. If, however, those goods, effects, and credits are insufficient to satisfy the judgment, and the creditor should sue an action on that judgment in this State to obtain satisfaction, he must fail; because the defendant was not personally amendable to the jurisdiction of the Court rendering the judgment. And, if the defendant, after the service of the process of foreign attachment, should either in person have gone into the State of New Hampshire, or constituted an attorney to defend the suit, so as to protect his goods, effects, or credits from the effect of the attachment, he would not thereby have given the Court jurisdiction of his person; since this jurisdiction must result from the service of the foreign attachment. It would be unreasonable to oblige any man living in one state, and having effects in another state, to make himself amenable to the courts of the last state, that he might defend his property there attached." See Post, § 584, 592, 598—618. Mr. Burge has made the following remarks on the same subject:—" In order that it may produce the effect of res judicata in the country in which it is pronounced, and à fortiori in a foreign country, the sentence must be given by a competent tribunal. It must put a final termination to the matter in litigation, and it must be certain. The want of either of these requisites is such a defect as to render the sentence null and void, and this defect is called a nullity. The judicial tribunal must be competent to entertain jurisdiction of the subject-matter of the suit. If, according to the constitution of the tribunal, the subject-matter of the sentence was excluded from its

§ 550. In the next place, let us consider the subject of jurisdiction in regard to property. It will be unnecessary to

---

cognizance, the sentence pronounced by the individuals composing, it would possess the weight, which belonging to an arbitrament made by those to whom the litigating parties had submitted their differences, but it would not possess the authority of res judicata. Where a limited tribunal takes upon itself to exercise a jurisdiction which does not belong to it, its decision amounts to nothing, and does not create any necessity for an appeal. Such a defect in the sentence cannot be cured by the appearance of the party. Another nullity in the sentence is a decision, given upon that which was not demanded or not contested, or when more has been adjudged than was demanded; for in either case the judge has exceeded his jurisdiction: 'Ultra id, quod in judicium deductum est, potestas judicis nequaquam potest excedere.' The party against whom the sentence has been obtained, must be subject to the jurisdiction of that tribunal. Such a jurisdiction is founded either in respect of the defender's domicil in the territory of the tribunal, ratione domicilii, or in respect of his being possessed of some estate or subject within it, ratione rei sitæ, or on the arrestment made by the decree of the court of the party's movable effects, arrestum causâ fundandæ jurisdictionis. A jurisdiction acquired by the arrest of the defender's property was not known to the civil law, but it was admitted in the jurisprudence of Holland, Spain, France, and Scotland, in all personal actions, in which the defender is bound, 'ad dandum, faciendum, et præstandum.' It is not allowed, in order to compel the defender to appear before any other judicial tribunal, than that of the place in which the immovable property, the subject of the suit, is situated. By the law of Scotland the jurisdiction is founded, not only on the defendant's domicil, but on his personal residence in a place for forty days. It admits jurisdiction ratione rei sitæ, unless it has for its object a question merely personal, as of status. Where a foreigner not otherwise subject to the jurisdiction of the courts of Scotland is possessed of movable property, there the jurisdiction is acquired by arresting his goods, and so fixing them within the judge's territory, or by their being already a subject of competition in a court of that kingdom. By the civil law the jurisdiction was acquired in respect of the place in which the contract was entered into, or in which it was to be performed; but the codes founded on the civil law do not admit a jurisdiction in either of these cases, unless the defendant is found in that place. The citation of the defender, the vocatio in jus, juris experiendi causâ vocatio, is essential to the validity of the sentence; because otherwise he has not had the opportunity of defending himself against the claim of his adversary. That citation need not have been served on him personally: it is sufficient, if it be left at his house. When the tribunal requires jurisdiction either ratione rei sitæ, or by arrestment in consequence of the defender having no domicil in loco fori, this citation is necessarily a merely formal act. By the Code Civil, the public

discuss the matter at large, as to personal property; since the general doctrine is not controverted, that, although movables are, for many purposes, to be deemed to have no *situs*, except that of the domicil of the owner; yet, this being but a legal fiction, it yields, whenever it is necessary for the purpose of justice that the actual *situs* of the thing should be examined. A nation, within whose territory any personal property is actually situate, has as entire dominion over it, while therein, in point of sovereignty and jurisdiction, as it has over immovable property situate there. It may regulate its transfer, and subject it to process and execution, and provide for, and control the uses and disposition of it, to the same extent, that it may exert its

---

minister is specially charged with the duty of watching over the interests of those who are presumed to be absent, and he is to be heard upon all demands which concern them. The Code de Procedure makes provision for delivering to certain public officers copies of the process which may be issued against foreigners. The jurisdiction exercised by the Courts of England is in general founded on the personal service of the process on the defendant. Indeed, according to the ancient law, the plaintiff could not proceed in an action before the defendant had actually appeared in court to answer him; and even if he pertinaciously neglected or refused to appear, the only course was to issue continued process, or to distrain upon his goods in order thereby, as it was expected, to induce him to appear, or to outlaw him, by which process he incurred a qualified forfeiture of his lands and goods, and all his civil rights as a subject were suspended. But in certain cases, after actual personal service, the plaintiff was, by the aid of certain statutes, permitted to enter an appearance for the defendant. But if the defendant were abroad, or avoided the service of process, and had no goods (the distraining of which was considered nearly equivalent to actual service, because it was supposed the defendant would hear of that proceeding), then the only course was, and still is, to proceed to outlawry, which, however, does not enable the plaintiff to proceed in his action, or to obtain judgment therein, but only causes a seizure of the lands, goods, and property of the defendant, as forfeited to the king for the defendant's contumacy and disrespect of his process. But the plaintiff may thereupon, by application to the Court of Exchequer or by petition, when his claim exceeds fifty pounds, obtain satisfaction of his debt by sale of the defendant's property seized under his outlawry, unless previously the defendant appears to the action, and enables the plaintiff to try the merits." 3 Burge, Comm. on Col. and For. Law, pt. 2, ch. 24, p. 1016, 1019.

authority over immovable property[1]. One of the grounds, upon which, as we have seen, jurisdiction is assumed over non-residents, is, through the instrumentality of their personal property, as well as of their real property, within the local sovereignty[2]. Hence it is, that whenever personal property is taken by arrest, attachment, or execution within a State, the title so acquired under the laws of the State is held valid in every other State[3]; and the same rule is applied to debts due to non-residents, which are subjected to the like process under the local laws of a State[4].

§ 551. In respect to immovable property, every attempt of any foreign tribunal to found a jurisdiction over it must, from the very nature of the case, be utterly nugatory, and its decree must be for ever incapable of execution *in rem.* We have seen, indeed, that by the Roman law a suit might in many cases be brought, either where the property was situate, or where the party had his domicil[5]. This might well be done within any of the vast domains over which the Roman empire extended; for the judgment of its tribunals would be every where respected and obeyed. But among the independent nations of modern times there would be insuperable difficulties in such a course. And hence, even in countries acknowledging the Roman law, it has become a very general principle, that suits *in rem* should be brought where the property is situate; and this principle is applied with almost universal approbation in

---

[1] See Ante, § 423 *a*.

[2] Ante, § 549.

[3] Lord Kenyon expressed his opinion to the following effect, in Ogden *v.* Folliott, (3 T. R. 733.): "I have always understood it to be clear, (said he), that all judicial acts, done in one country, over the property of the subjects within their jurisdiction, are conclusive on the property of those parties in any country."

[4] See Bissell *v.* Briggs, 9 Mass, R. 462, 468, 469. But see Folliott *v.* Ogden, 1 H. Black. R. 123, 135; S. C. 3 T. R. 726, 733. See Don *v.* Lippmann, 5 Clarke & Finnell. 1, 19.

[5] Ante, § 532, 545; Post, § 586, 591.

regard to immovable property. The same rule is applied to mixed actions, and to all suits which touch the realty[1].

§ 552. Boullenois has treated this whole subject with becoming fulness and accuracy. He has divided actions into those which are purely personal, those which are purely real, and those which are mixed and partake of the character of both, following, in these respects, as he avows, the division of Burgundus[2]. The first, (personal actions), respect the quality, state, or condition of persons, and pronounce against them judgments purely personal, *ad dandum, vel faciendum, aut non faciendum*. The next, (real actions), respect things, either the proprietary right or ownership, or the right of possession, or the right or title of a creditor, or some other right or title. The last, (mixed actions), respect both persons and things, either in adjudging the property to one, or pronouncing against him a personal judgment for the profit of the other, or adjudging the property to one, and adjudging the other to make restitution of the profits to him; so that it is the title of the action which characterizes the action[3]. Personal actions may rightfully be brought between natives in any competent tribunal of the realm; and between foreigners also, who have submitted to the jurisdiction, wherever the laws allow its exercise; and between natives and foreigners in like manner[4]. But in all these

---

1 Henry on Foreign Laws, ch. 8, § 3, p. 59, ch. 9, § 1, p. 63; 1 Boullenois, Observ. 25, p. 601, &c.; Id. pp. 618, 619; Id. p. 635, &c.; Id. p. 619.

2 The language of Burgundus is: Omnium condemnationum summa divisio, pariter in tria genera deducitur; aut enim in rem, aut in personam, aut in utramque concipiuntur. In rem, quoties alicui res asseritur, hoc est ejus esse dicitur, vel jure creditoris, aut alio modo possidenda datur. In personam, si condemnetur ad aliquid dandum aut patiendum, faciendum aut non faciendum, vel, si personæ statum afficiat. In utramque si et res, et personæ simul in condemnationem veniant. Burgundus, Tract. 3, n. 1, 2, pp. 84, 85.

3 1 Boullenois, Observ. 25, pp. 601, 602.

4 Boullenois makes a distinction in suits between natives and foreigners to this effect:—If a foreigner sues a native, then the jurisdiction is well founded against the latter in the place of his domicil; and the foreigner is bound by

cases the domicil of the party defendant is commonly supposed to be within the jurisdiction[1]. Real actions ought to be brought in the place *rei sitæ;* and this is the rule not only when the property in controversy is situate in the same kingdom; but also when the parties being domiciled in one country, engage in a litigation as to property locally situate in another country[2]. If, therefore, a judgment should be rendered in one country respecting property in another, it will be of no force in the latter. It is true, that property within a country does not make the owner generally a subject of the sovereign, where it is locally situate; but it subjects him to his jurisdiction *secundum quid, et aliquo modo*[3]. Mixed actions, so far as they regard the realty, are to be brought in the place *rei sitæ;* but if the personal damages or claims be separable in their nature and character, they may be sued for as personal actions[4]. There are many other jurists who adopt the like distinctions[5].

§ 553. Vattel explicitly avows the same doctrine. "The defendant's judge," (that is, the competent Judge), says he, "is the judge of the place where the defendant has his settled abode, or the judge of the place where the defendant is when any sudden difficulty arises, provided it does not relate to an estate in land, or to a right annexed to such an

---

the judgment. If the foreigner is defendant, and has submitted to the jurisdiction, then the same result follows. If he has not submitted, or has not appeared to the suit, then the judgment is not obligatory. 1 Boullenois, Observ. 25, pp. 609, 610. He founds himself in this opinion upon the general rule, Actor sequitur forum rei; and he quotes with approbation the remark of J. Gaill: Quis manens extra regnum non tenetur in parlamento respondere super actione personali. Id. p. 612.

[1] 1 Boullenois, Observ. 25, pp. 601—603, 606, 609, 610. See also Id. Prin. Gén. 34, pp. 8, 9.

[2] 1 Boullenois, Observ. 25, pp. 618—620, 622, 623; Id. Prin. Gén. 35, 37, p. 9.

[3] Id. Observ. 25, pp. 623—625.

[4] Id. Observ. 25, pp. 635, 636.

[5] Id. Observ. 25, pp. 601—651; 1 Hertii, Opera, De Collis. Leg. § 70 p. 132, (edit. 1737); Id. p. 215, (edit. 1716); J. Voet, Ad Pand. tom. 1, lib. 4, tit. 1, § 28, p. 241.

estate. In such a case, as property of this kind is to be held according to the laws of the country where it is situated, and as the right of granting it is vested in the ruler of the country, controversies relating to such [real] property can only be decided in the State in which it depends[1]."

§ 554. It will be perceived that in many respects the doctrine here laid down coincides with that of the common law. It has been already stated, that by the common law personal actions, being transitory, may be brought in any place where the party defendant can be found[2]; that real actions must be brought in the *forum rei sitæ;* and that mixed actions are properly referable to the same jurisdiction[3]. Among the latter are actions for trespasses and injuries to real property, which are deemed local; so that they will not lie elsewhere than in the place *rei sitæ*. This distinction was recognised as long ago as 1665, in a case[4] where the twelve Judges certified, that for torts to the per-

---

1 Vattel, b. 2, ch. 8, § 103.

2 See Mostyn *v.* Fabrigas, Cowper, R. 161, 176, 177; Robinson *v.* Bland, 2 Burr. R. 1074; S. C. 1 W. Black. 259; Ante, § 364.

3 Ante, § 364; 4 Cowen, R. 527, note.—Lord Mansfield, in Mostyn *v.* Fabrigas, (Cowper, R. 161, 176), said: "There is a formal and a substantial distinction as to the locality of trials. I state them as different things. The substantial distinction is, where the proceeding is in rem; and where the effect of judgment cannot be had, if it is laid in a wrong place. That is the case of all ejectments, &c. With regard to matters that arise out of the realm, there is a substantial distinction of locality too; for there are some cases that arise out of the realm, which ought not to be tried anywhere, but in the country where they arise. As if two persons fight in France, and both happening casually to be here, one should bring an action of assault against the other, it might be a doubt whether such an action could be maintained here; because, though it is not a criminal prosecution, it must be laid to be against the peace of the king; but the breach of the peace is merely local, though the trespass against the person is transitory." His Lordship here doubtless alluded to a case of personal trespass between foreigners; for in a subsequent part of the same opinion he expressly held, that, as between subjects, not only upon contracts, but for personal torts, an action might be maintained in England; and indeed that was the very point decided in the case then in judgment.

4 Skinner *v.* The East India Company, cited in Cowper, R. 167, 168.

son and to personal property done abroad, a remedy lay in a suit *in personam* in England; but that for torts to real property or to fixtures abroad, no suit lay. Lord Mansfield and Lord Chief Justice Eyre held at one time a different doctrine, and allowed suits to be maintained in England for injuries done by pulling down houses in foreign unsettled regions, viz., in the desert coasts of Nova Scotia and Labrador[1]. But this doctrine has been since overruled as untenable according to the actual jurisprudence of England[2]; however maintainable it might be upon general principles of international law, if the suit were for personal damages only[3].

§ 555. The grounds upon which the exclusive jurisdiction is maintained over immovable property are the same upon which the sole right to establish, regulate, and control the transfer, descent, and testamentary disposition of it have been admitted by all nations. The inconveniences of an opposite course would be innumerable, and would subject immovable property to the most distressing conflicts arising from opposing titles, and compel every nation to administer almost all other laws, except its own, in the ordinary administration of justice[4].

§ 556. Having stated these general principles in relation to jurisdiction, (the result of which is, that no nation can rightfully claim to exercise it, except as to persons and property within its own domains), we are next led to the consideration of the question, in what manner suits arising

---

1 Cited by Lord Mansfield in Mostyn *v.* Fabrigas, Cowper, R. 180, 181.

2 Doulson *v.* Matthews, 4 T. R. 503.

3 The doctrine of this last case was very fully examined and affirmed by Mr. Chief Justice Marshall, in the case of Livingston *v.* Jefferson, before the Circuit Court of Virginia, in 1811, (4 Hall's American Law Journal, p. 78). It was an action quare clausum fregit, brought against Mr. Jefferson on account of an alleged trespass to lands (the Batture) in New Orleans by his order, while he was President of the United States. The suit was dismissed for want of jurisdiction.

4 Ante § 364, 365.

from foreign causes are to be instituted, and proceedings to be had until the final judgment. Are they to be according to the law of the place where the parties or either of them live? Or are they to be according to the modes of proceeding and forms of suit prescribed by the laws of the place where the suits are brought? Fortunately, here, there is scarcely any ground left open for controversy, either at the common law or in the opinions of foreign jurists, or in the actual practice of nations. It is universally admitted and established, that the forms of remedies, and the modes of proceeding, and the execution of judgments, are to be regulated solely and exclusively by the laws of the place where the action is instituted; or, as the civilians uniformly express it, according to the *lex fori*[1].

§ 557. The reasons for this doctrine are so obvious, that they scarcely require any illustration. The business of the administration of justice by any nation is, in a peculiar and emphatic sense, a part of its public right and duty. Each nation is at liberty to adopt such forms and such a course of proceeding as best comport with its convenience and interests, and the interests of its own subjects, for whom its laws are particularly designed. The different kinds of remedies, and the modes of proceeding best adapted to enforce rights and guard against wrongs in any nation, must materially depend upon the structure of its own jurisprudence. What would be well adapted to the jurisprudence, either customary or positive, of one nation, for rights which it recognised, or for duties which it enforced, or for wrongs which it redressed, might be wholly unfit for that of another nation, either as having gross defects, or steering wide of the appropriate remedial justice. A nation acknowledging the existence of peculiar rights and privileges, either personal or real, such as seignorial rights or trusts in the realty, would naturally introduce correspondent remedies. While

---

[1] See on this point, 1 Burge, Comm. on Col. and For. Law, pt. 1, ch. 1, p. 24.

other nations, in which such rights and privileges and trusts did not exist, might well dispense with the formalities which they might require. The jurisprudence of one nation may be very refined and artificial, with a multitude of intricate and perplexed proceedings; that of another may be rude, uninformed, and harsh, consisting of an undigested mass of usages. It would be absolutely impracticable to apply the process and modes of proceeding of the one nation to the other. Besides, there would be an utter confusion in all judicial proceedings, by attempting to engraft upon the remedies of one country those of all other countries, whose subjects should be parties or be interested therein. No tribunal on earth, however learned, could hope by any degree of diligence to master the laws and processes and remedies of all other nations, and the qualifications and limitations properly belonging thereto. A whole life might be passed in obtaining little more than a few unconnected elements, and litigation would thus become immeasurably complicated, if not absolutely interminable. All that any nation can therefore be justly required to do is, to open its own tribunals to foreigners in the same manner and to the same extent as they are open to its own subjects; and to give them the same redress, as to rights and wrongs, which it deems fit to acknowledge in its own municipal code for natives and residents [1].

---

[1] Lord Brougham, in delivering his judgment in Don *v.* Lippmann, 5 Clark & Finnell. R. 1, 13, 14, made some striking remarks on this subject. "The law on this point is well settled in this country, where this distinction is properly taken, that whatever relates to the remedy to be enforced, must be determined by the lex fori, the law of the country to the tribunals of which the appeal is made. This rule is clearly laid down in the British Linen Company *v.* Drummond, (10 Barn. & Cress. 903), De la Vega *v.* Vianna, (1 Barn. & Adol. 284), and in Huber *v.* Steiner, (2 Scott, 304; 1 Hodges, 206; 2 Bing. N. C. 202; 2 Dowl. Prac. Cas. 781; and 4 Moore & Scott, 328), though the reverse had previously been recognised in Williams *v.* Jones (13 East, 439). Then, assuming that to be the settled rule, the only question in this case would be, whether the law now to be enforced is the law which relates to the contract itself, or to the remedy. When both the parties reside

§ 558. The doctrine of the common law is so fully established on this point, that it would be useless to do more than to state the universal principle which it has promulgated; that is to say, that, in regard to the merits and rights involved in actions, the law of the place where they originated is to govern: *In iis, quæ spectant decisoria causæ, et litis decisionem, inspiciuntur statuta loci, ubi contractus fuit celebratus*[1]. But the forms of remedies and the order

---

in the country where the act is done, they look of course to the law of the country in which they reside. The contract being silent as to the law by which it is to be governed, nothing is more likely than that the lex loci contractus should be considered at the time the rule; for the parties would not suppose that the contract might afterwards come before the tribunals of a foreign country. But it is otherwise when the remedy actually comes to be enforced. The parties do not necessarily look to the remedy, when they make the contract. They bind themselves to do what the law they live under requires; but as they bind themselves generally, it may be taken as if they had contemplated the possibility of enforcing it in another country. That is the lowest ground on which to place the case. The inconveniences of pursuing a different course is manifest. Not only the principles of the law, but the known course of the Courts renders it necessary that the rules of precedent should be adopted, and that the parties should take the law as they find it when they come to enforce their contract. It is true, that there may be no difficulty in knowing the law of the place of the contract, while there may be a great difficulty in knowing that of the place of the remedy. But that is no answer to the rule. The distinction which exists as to the principle of applying the remedy, exists with even greater force as to the practice of the Courts where the remedy is to be enforced. No one can say, that because the contract has been made abroad, the form of action known in the foreign Court must be pursued in the Courts where the contract is to be enforced, or the other preliminary proceedings of those Courts must be adopted, or that the rules of pleading, or the curial practice of the foreign country, must necessarily be followed. No one will assert, that before the Jury Court in Scotland the English creditor of a domiciled Scotchman would have the right to call for a trial of the case by a jury; or take the converse, that a Scotchman might refuse the intervention of a jury here, and insist on having the case tried, as in Scotland, by the judge only. No one will contend in terms, that the foreign rules of evidence should guide us in such cases; and yet it is not so easy to avoid that principle in practice, if you once admit, that though the remedy is to be enforced in one country, it is to be enforced according to the laws which govern another country.

[1] 2 Boullenois, Observ. 46, p. 462; Ante, § 260; Bank of United States

of judicial proceedings are to be according to the law of the place where the action is instituted, without any regard to the domicil of the parties, the origin of the right, or the country of the act[1].

---

v. Donnally, 8 Peters, R. 361, 372; Andrews v. Pond, 13 Peters, R. 65; Wilcox v. Hunt, 13 Peters, R. 378. See also Bouhier, Cout. de Bourg. ch. 18, n. 10; Ante, § 242, 260—273.

[1] The authorities are exceedingly numerous. Among them we may cite the following. Andrews v. Herriott, 4 Cowen, R. 408; and see Id. 528, n. (10), and authorities there cited; 2 Kent, Comm. Lect. 27, p. 118, &c. 3rd edit.; Robinson v. Bland, 2 Burr. 1084; De la Vega v. Vianna, 1 Barn. & Adol. R. 284; Trimbey v. Vignier, 1 Bing. N. Cas. 159—161; Don v. Lippmann, 5 Clark & Fin. R. 1, 13, 19, 20; Ante, § 557, n.; Fenwick v. Sears, 1 Cranch, 259; Nash v. Tupper, 1 Cain. R. 402; Pearsall v. Dwight, 2 Mass. R. 84; Smith v. Spinola, 2 John. R. 189; Van Reimsdyk v. Kane, 1 Gallis. R. 371; Lodge v. Phelps, 1 John. Cas. 412; Thrasher v. Everhart, 3 Gill & John, 234; Peck v. Hozier, 14 John. R. 346; Ohio Insur. Company v. Edmondson, 5 Louis. R. 295—300; Warren v. Lynch, 5 John. R. 239; Jones v. Hook's administrator, 2 Rand. Virg. R. 303; Wilcox v. Hunt, 13 Peters, R. 378, 379; Bank of United States v. Donnally, 8 Peters, R. 361, 370—373.—This last case was an action brought in Virginia on a promissory note made in Kentucky, not under seal, but which by the law of Kentucky was deemed a specialty. The statute of limitations of Virginia was pleaded in bar; and one question was, whether it was a good bar or not. On that occasion the Court said: "The other point, growing out of the statute of limitations, pleaded to the fourth and fifth counts (for as to the three first counts it is conceded to be a good bar) involves questions of a very different character, as to the operation and effect of a conflict of laws in cases governed by the lex loci. The statute of limitations of Virginia provides, that 'all actions of debt, grounded upon any lending or contract without specialty,' shall be commenced and sued within five years next after the cause of such action or suit, and not after. This being the language of the act, and confessedly governing the remedy in the Courts of Virginia, the bar of five years must apply to all cases of contract which are without specialty, or, in other words, are not founded on some instrument acknowledged as a specialty by the law of that State. The common law being adopted in Virginia, and the word 'specialty' being a term of art of that law, we are led to the consideration, whether the present note is deemed, in the common law, to be a specialty. And certainly it is not so deemed. It is not a sealed contract, nor does it fall under any other description of instruments or contracts or acts known in the common law as specialties. The argument does not deny this conclusion; but it endeavours to escape from its force, by affirming that the note is a specialty according to the laws of Kentucky; and if so, that this constitutes a part of its nature and obligation; and it ought, everywhere

§ 559. Nor are foreign jurists less pointed in their recognition of it. Thus Bartolus, in speaking upon contracts,

---

else, upon principles of international jurisprudence, to be deemed of the like validity and effect. The act of Kentucky of the 4th of February, 1812, provides, 'that all writings hereafter executed without a seal or seals, stipulating for the payment of money or property, or for the performance of any act, duty, or duties, shall be placed upon the same footing with sealed writings, containing the like stipulations, receiving the same consideration in all courts of justice, and to all intents and purposes having the same force and effect, and upon which the same species of action may be founded, as if sealed.' Now, it is observable that this statute does not in terms declare that such writings shall be deemed specialties, nor does it say that they shall be deemed sealed instruments. All that it affirms is, that they shall be put upon the same footing as sealed instruments, and have the same consideration, force, effect, and remedy as sealed instruments. So that it is perfectly consistent with the whole scope and object of the act, to give them the same dignity and obligation as specialties, without intending to make them such. A State legislature may certainly provide that the same remedy shall be had in a promissory note, as on a bond or sealed instrument; but it will not thereby make the note a bond or sealed instrument. It may declare that its obligation and force shall be the same as if it were sealed; but that will still leave it an unsealed contract. But, whatever may be the legislation of a State, as to the obligation or remedy on contracts, its acts can have no binding authority beyond its own territorial jurisdiction. Whatever authority they have in other States depends upon principles of international comity and a sense of justice. The general principle adopted by civilized nations is, that the nature, validity, and interpretation of contracts, are to be governed by the law of the country where the contracts are made, or are to be performed. But the remedies are to be governed by the laws of the country where the suit is brought; or, as it is compendiously expressed, by the lex fori. No one will pretend, that, because an action of covenant will lie in Kentucky on an unsealed contract made in that State, therefore, a like action will lie in another State where covenant can be brought only on a contract under seal. It is an appropriate part of the remedy which every State prescribes to its own tribunals, in the same manner in which it prescribes the times within which all suits must be brought. The nature, validity, and interpretation of the contract may be admitted to be the same in both States, but the mode by which the remedy is to be pursued, and the time within which it is to be brought, may essentially differ. The remedy, in Virginia, must be sought within the time, and in the mode, and according to the descriptive characters of the instrument known to the laws of Virginia, and not by the description and characters of it prescribed in another State. An instrument may be negotiable in one State, which yet may be incapable of negotiability by the laws of another State; and the remedy must be in the Courts of the latter on such

says: *Quæro, quid de contractibus? Pone contractum celebratum per aliquem forensem in hac civitate; litigium ortum est, et agitatur lis in loco originis contrahentis. Cujus loci statuta debent servari vel spectari? Distingue; Aut loquimur de statuto, aut de consuetudine, quæ respiciunt ipsius contractûs solennitatem, aut litis ordinationem, aut de his, quæ pertinent ad jurisdictionem ex ipso contractu evenientis executionis. Primo casu, inspicitur locus contractûs. Secundo casu, aut quæris de his, quæ pertinent ad litis ordinationem, et inspicitur locus judicii; aut de his quæ pertinent ad ipsius litis decisionem, et tunc, aut de his, quæ oriuntur secundum ipsius contractûs naturam tempore contractûs, aut de his, quæ oriuntur ex post facto, propter negligentiam vel moram; primo casu inspicitur locus contractûs, &c*[1].

§ 560. Rodenburg asserts the same distinction. *Primum utamur vulgatâ doctorum distinctione, quâ separantur ea, quæ litis formam concernunt ac ordinationem, ab iis, quæ decisionem aut materiam. Lis ordinanda secundum morem loci, in quo ventilatur*[2]. Boullenois affirms the same doctrine. *A l'ègard* (says he) *du principe de décision, quantum ad litis decisoria, il se tire, ou de la loi du contrat, ou de la loi de la situation, ou de la volonté présumée des parties, lorsqu'elles ont contracté ensemble; en un mot la loi seule de la jurisdiction n'y influe point comme telle. Diversitas fori non debet meritum causæ variare. A l'égard des formalités judiciaires, quantum ad litis ordinationem, la règle est de suivre la procédure et les usages observés dans le lieu, où l'on*

---

instrument, according to its own laws. If, then, it were admitted that the promissory note now in controversy were a specialty by the laws of Kentucky, still it would not help the case, unless it were also a specialty, and recognised as such by the laws of Virginia; for the laws of the latter must govern as to the limitation of suits in its own Courts, and as to the interpretation of the meaning of the words used in its own statutes." Post, § 567.

[1] Bartolus, Com. ad Cod. lib. 1, tit. 1, l. 1; Bart. Oper. tom. 7, p. 4, edit. 1602; 2 Boullenois, Observ. 46, pp. 455, 456; Ante, § 301.

[2] Rodenburg, De Div. Stat. tit. 2, p. 5, n. 16; 2 Boullenois, App. p. 47; 1 Boullenois, 660; Id. 685, 818; Ante, § 325 *c*, § 325 *d*, § 325 *h*, note 2.

plaide[1]. Hertius states the same point in his compendious way. *Expedita est Doctorum Responsio, Jura judicii tantum in illis observanda esse, quæ ad ordinem processûs judicialis pertinent, etsi lis sit de bonis immobilibus, in alio territorio sitis*[2].

§ 561. Strykius states it in the following language: *Quotiescunque circa judicii ordinationem controvertitur, statuta loci judicii, omnibus cæteris posthabitis, introspiciantur. In modo procedendi consuetudo judicii attendenda, ubi lis agitatur. In modo vero decidendi, seu in ipsâ causæ decisione, consuetudo litigantium, seu ubi actus est gestus, attendendus*[3]. Huberus says: *Adeoque receptum est optimâ ratione, ut in ordinandis judiciis loci consuetudo, ubi agitur, etsi de negotio alibi celebrato, spectetur*[4]. Dumoulin says: *Unde an instrumentum habeat executionem, et quo modo debeat exequi, attenditur locus ubi agitur, vel fit executio. Ratio, quia fides instrumenti concernit meritum, sed virtus executoria et modus exequendi concernit processum*[5]. Again he adds: *Quod in his, quæ pertinent ad processum judicii, vel executionem faciendam, vel ad ordinationem judicii, semper sit observanda consuetudo loci, in quo judicium agitatur*[6]. Emérigon says: *Pour tout ce, qui concerne l'ordre judiciare, on doit suivre l'usage du lieu, où l'on plaide. Pour ce, qui est de la décision du fond, on doit suivre, en règle générale, les lois du lieu, où le contrat a été passé. Cette distinction est consignée dans tous nos livres*[7].

---

[1] 1 Boullenois, Observ. 33, pp. 535—546; Id. Prin. Gén. 49, p. 11.

[2] 1 Hertii, Opera, De Collis. Leg. § 4, n. 70, pp. 152, 153, (edit. 1737); Id. p. 215, (edit. 1716).

[3] Strykii, Tract. et Disp. tom. 2, p. 27; De Jure Princ. ext. Territ. ch. 3, n. 34; Ante, § 295.

[4] Huberus, tom. 2, lib. 1, tit. 3, De Confl. Leg. § 7.

[5] 1 Boullenois, Observ. 23, pp. 523, 524; Molin. Opera, Comm. Cod. lib. 1, tit. 1, tom. 3, p. 554, (edit. 1681).

[6] 1 Boullenois, Observ. 23, pp. 523, 524; Molin. Opera, Comm. Cod. lib. 6, tit. 32, tom. 3, p. 735, (edit. 1681).

[7] 1 Emérigon, Traité des Assur. ch. 4, § 8, n. 2, p. 122; Le Roy *v.*

§ 562. We may conclude this reference to the opinions of foreign jurists by a citation from John Voet, who states at once the rule and the reason of it. *Quia vero regionum, civitatum, vicorum varia, imo contraria sæpe jura sunt, observandum est, quantum quidem ad ordinem judicii formamque attinet, judicem nullius alterius sed sui tantum fori leges sequi. Sed in litis ipsius definitione, si de solennibus contractûs, testamenti, vel negotii alterius quæstio sit, validum pronunciare debet ac solenne negotium, quoties adhibita invenit solennia loci, in quo illud gestum est, licet aliæ, aut majores, in loco judicii ad talem actum solennitates requisitæ essent*[1].

§ 563. There are many questions, however, which may arise, as to what are and what are not matters properly belonging to the remedy, (*ad litis ordinationem*), and what are and what are not matters properly belonging to the merits, (*ad litis decisionem*). Many cases of this sort may be found collected and discussed by foreign jurists upon the peculiarities of their own jurisprudence. But they could not be made intelligible to a lawyer under the common law, without occupying a space in explanations, wholly disproportionate to their importance in a treatise like the present[2].

§ 564. It may be of more utility to introduce a few illustrations of the doctrine arising peculiarly under the common law modes of proceeding: first, in regard to persons who may sue; secondly, in regard to process and proceedings; and thirdly, in regard to certain defences against actions arising from matters *ex post facto*, and founded on local law, or customary practice.

§ 565. In the first place, in regard to persons who may sue. It may be laid down, as a general rule, that all foreigners,

---

Crowninshield, 2 Mason, R. 163. See also to the same effect, P. Voet, De Stat. § 10, ch. 1, n. 1, 6, pp. 281, 285, 286, (edit. 1715); Id. pp. 339—341, (edit. 1661).

1 J. Voet, Ad Pand. tom. 1, lib. 5, tit. 1, § 51, p. 328.

2 See 1 Boullenois, Observ. 23, pp. 535—569.

sui juris, and not otherwise specially disabled by the law of the place where the suit is brought, may there maintain suits to vindicate their rights and redress their wrongs. The same doctrine applies to foreign sovereigns and to foreign corporations [1]. But questions may arise where the party suing is not the original party to the debt or claim; but he takes a derivative title only from the original party, as where he is an assignee or grantee or donee of the debt or other claim. We have already had occasion to take notice of a peculiarity of the common law, that debts and *choses in action* are not, with the exception of negotiable promissory notes and bills of exchange, assignable [2]. Hence, if any other debt or *chose in action*, such as a bond, or a covenant, or other contract, is assigned, no action can be maintained thereon in a common-law court by the assignee in his own name [3]. The same rule has been applied to assignments of debts or *choses in action*, made in foreign countries, although the assignee might be entitled to found an action thereon in such foreign country in his own name, in virtue of such assignment [4]. For (it has been said) the inquiry, in whose name a suit is to be brought, belongs not so much to the right and merit of the claim, as to the form of the remedy. No distinction seems to have been made in England, as to the right to sue, between the case of an assignee by the private voluntary act of the assignor, and an assignee by operation of law by an assignment *in invitum*

---

[1] Story, Eq. Plead. § 55; Hullett *v.* The King of Spain, 2 Bligh, R. N. S. p. 51; S. C. 1 Dow & Clarke, R. 169, 179; S. C. 1 Clark & Finnell. R. 333; Columbian Government *v.* Rothschild, 2 Sim. R. 94; South Carolina Bank *v.* Case, 8 Barn. & Cress. 427; City of Berne *v.* The Bank of England, 9 Ves. 347; Silver Lake Bank *v.* North, 4 John. Ch. R. 370; Bank of Augusta *v.* Earle, 13 Peters, R. 519, 588, 589.

[2] Ante, § 354, 355, 395—400.

[3] 3 Burge, Comm. on Col. and For. Law, pt. 2, ch. 20, pp. 777, 778; Wolff *v.* Oxholm, 6 Maule & Selw. 99; Ante, § 354, 355.

[4] Wolff *v.* Oxholme, 6 Maule & Selw. R. 99; Folliott *v.* Ogden, 1 H. Black. 131; Innes *v.* Dunlop, 8 Term. R. 595; Jeffrey *v.* M'Taggart, 6 Maule & Selw. R. 126.

under the bankrupt laws. Thus it has been held, that a Scotch assignee of a bankrupt could not maintain a suit in his own name in England for a *chose in action* of the bankrupt, which was admitted to pass under the assignment[1]. In America, contradictory decisions have been made upon the same point, some Courts affirming, and others denying the right of the assignee to sue in his own name; although the weight of authority must now be admitted to be against the right[2].

---

[1] Jeffrey *v.* M'Taggart, 6 Maule & Selw. 126, and Wolff *v.* Oxholm, 6 Maule & Selw. 99. But see in Smith *v.* Buchanan, (1 East, 11), the dictum of Lord Kenyon to the contrary. In Alivon *v.* Furnival (1 Cromp. Mees. & Rosc. 277), two out of three syndics of a French bankrupt sued a debtor of the bankrupt in their own names in England; and the objection was taken, that they had no title to sue. The Court overruled the objection. Mr. Baron Parke, in delivering the judgment of the Court, said: "Lastly, it is said, that though two may act and bring an action, yet they must sue in the name of all. Now, the effect of the testimony of Colin is, that two may sue in France without a third, and the witness for the defendant does not prove the contrary, and there seems no reason why it should not be so. The property in the effects of the bankrupt does not appear to be absolutely transferred to these syndics in the way that those of a bankrupt are in this country; but it should seem, that the syndics act as mandatories or agents for the creditors; the whole three, or any two or one of them having the power to sue for and recover the debts in their own names. This is a peculiar right of action, created by the law of that country; and we think it may by the comity of nations be enforced in this, as much as the right of foreign assignees or curators, or foreign corporations, appointed or created in a different way from that which the law of this country requires. Dutch West India Company *v.* Moses (1 Strange, 612), National Bank of St. Charles *v.* De Bernales (1 R. & Moody, 190), Solomons *v.* Ross (1 H. Black. 131, n). We do not pronounce an opinion, whether this objection is available on the plea of nil debet, or ought to have been pleaded in abatement, (though we were much struck with the argument of the learned counsel for the plaintiff), as we think it is not available at all upon the evidence in this case." See also Ante, § 419, 420.

[2] See Ante, § 358, 359, 419, 420; Milne *v.* Moreton, 6 Binn. R. 374; Goodwin *v.* Jones, 3 Mass. R. 514, 519; James *v.* Boynton, 9 Mass. R. 357; Orr *v.* Amory, 11 Mass. R. 25; Ingraham *v.* Geyer, 13 Mass. R. 146, 147; Byme *v.* Walker, 7 Serg. & Rawle, 483; Bird *v.* Caritat, 2 John. R. 342; Bird *v.* Pierpont, 1 John. R. 118; Murray *v.* Murray, 5 John. Ch. R. 60; Brush *v.* Curtis, 4 Connect. R. 312; Raymond *v.* Johnson, 11 John. R. 488; Holmes *v.* Remsen, 4 John. Ch. R. 460, 485.

§ 566. The reasoning of these decisions seems equally to apply to the case of a foreign assignee by the voluntary act of the party, even where he could sue in his own name in the country in which the assignment was made, although certainly there is room for a distinction in such a case, and it has sometimes been recognised. Thus, in a case where the assignee of an Irish judgment brought a suit in his own name in England, such a judgment being assignable in Ireland, so as to vest a title at law in the assignee, the Court of Common Pleas held, that he was entitled to recover; because (as it should seem) a legal title by the *lex loci* vested in him, and the case was not to be governed by the law of England, as the assignment was in Ireland[1]. The distinction, although nice, is at the same time clear; for the remedy is sought upon a legal right, vested *ex directo* by the local law in the assignee against the judgment debtor. There does not seem, therefore, any solid ground upon principle, why a right confessedly legal in the country where it originated, and passing a direct and positive fixed title in the assignee, should not have the same remedy in every other country, which legal fixed titles in the party are there entitled to. It is assuming the very ground in controversy to assert, that it is a mere equitable title; for the local law has adjudged it otherwise, and vested the original title *ex directo* in the assignee. In the common case, where an executor or administrator indorses negotiable paper in the country from which he derives his administrative authority, no one will doubt, that the legal title passes to the indorsee, and that he may sue thereon in any other country in his own name; and yet such an indorsement, in another country, by the executor or administrator, would not be admitted to have any such validity or effect[2]. However,

---

[1] O'Callaghan *v.* Thomond, 3 Taunt. 82, 84; Ante, § 355; 3 Burge, Comm. on Col. and For. Law, pt. 2, ch. 20, pp. 777, 778.

[2] Ante, § 353 *a*, 354, 358, 359; Trimbey *v.* Vignier, 1 Bing. N. Cas. 151, 159, 160.

the doctrine of this case has been much doubted; and, therefore, it can scarcely be thought to be unexceptionable in point of authority. There are certainly dicta and decisions which are pointedly the other way, and in which it is said, that the suit must be brought in the name of the assignor, if the *lex fori* requires it[1].

§ 567. Another illustration may be taken from the forms of action upon instruments under seal. Thus, in Virginia, a contract to pay money with a scrawl, instead of a seal, is treated as a sealed instrument, so that debt lies upon it in

---

[1] The dictum of Lord Loughborough, in Folliott *v.* Ogden, (1 H. Black. 135), and that of Lord Ellenborough, in Wolff *v.* Oxholm, (4 Maule & Sel. 92, 99), are] to this effect. But the recent case of Alivon *v.* Furnival, 1 Cromp. Mees. & Rosc. 277, 296, certainly, as far as it goes, upholds it. Ante, § 565, note. See also Robinson *v.* Campbell, 3 Wheat. R. 212. The case of Wolff *v.* Oxholm, (6 Maule & Selw. 92, 99), may perhaps be distinguishable in its circumstances as well as in the reasoning of the Court. Lord Ellenborough's language in the last case was as follows: " One of the points insisted upon in the argument for the defendant was, that this assignment and the suit instituted upon it, were a bar to the plaintiff's demand; but we think that they cannot have that effect. The assignee could not sue in the courts of this country in his own name; the action must have been brought here in the names of the original creditors, even if they had assigned the debt for a valuable consideration; and although the assignment gave the assignee a right to sue in his own name in Denmark, yet the defendant does not appear to have been prejudiced by that measure even there, nor has any material consequence resulted therefrom. And we consider the case to stand now just as it would have done if no assignment had been made, and if the suit in Denmark had been brought by the plaintiffs themselves, instead of being instituted by their trustees." See Ante, § 358, 359, 399, note. See Trasher *v.* Everhart, 3 Gill. & John. R. 234; M'Ray *v.* Mattoon, 10 Pick. R. 52; Pearsall *v.* Dwight, 2 Mass. R. 96; 3 Burge, Comm. on Col. and For. Law, pt. 2, ch. 20, pp. 777, 778. This subject is ably discussed on different sides in two articles in the American Jurist, viz., in the number for January, 1833, (9 vol. 42), and in the number for January, 1834, (11 vol. 101), to which I gladly refer, as giving a more satisfactory view of this subject than with reference to the plan of the present work I have been able to give. It may be thought that the case of foreign executors and administrators, as assignees by operation of law of the deceased's estate, stands upon a similar ground. But it appears to me to proceed on principles materially different, applicable to rights, and not merely to remedies. Ante, § 399, note; § 420, 512, 513.

that State. But in New York, where such a scrawl is not treated as a seal, the remedy must be as upon an unsealed simple contract[1]. The same doctrine has been maintained in England upon an instrument executed in Jamaica, where there was no seal, but a mark or scrawl in the place where the seal is usually affixed[2]. On the other hand, a single bill is deemed in Virginia not to be a specialty; in Maryland it is otherwise. A remedy brought in Maryland upon such a single bill, executed in Virginia, cannot be by an action of assumpsit, as upon a simple contract, but must be by action of debt, as upon a specialty[3].

§ 568. In the next place, as to process and proceedings. There is no controversy that in a general sense the mode of process constitutes a part of the remedy. But the question has arisen whether, upon contracts made in a foreign country, and which, by the laws of that country, are precluded from being enforced by a persona arrest or imprisonment, the like exemption applies in suits to enforce them in another country, where such process constitutes a part of the remedial justice. Such a contract existed, or was supposed to exist, in a case where a bond given in France and sued in England was understood to bind the property and not the person of the party in France[4]. On that occasion, Lord Chief Justice Eyre said:—"If it appears that this contract creates no personal obligation, and that it could not be sued as such by the laws of France, (on the principle of preventing arrests so vexatious as to be an abuse of the process of the Court), there seems to be a fair ground on which the Court may interpose to prevent a proceeding so oppressive as a personal arrest in a foreign country at the commence-

---

[1] Warren *v.* Lynch, 5 John. R. 239. See also Andrews *v.* Herriot, 4 Cowen, 508. But see Meredith *v.* Hindsdale, 2 Caines, R. 362.

[2] Adam *v.* Kerr, 1 Bos. & Pull. 360. See also Bank of United States *v.* Donnally, 8 Peters, R. 361; Ante, § 558, note.

[3] Trasher *v.* Everhart, 3 Gill. & John. R. 234; Bank of United States *v.* Donnally, 8 Peters, R. 361; Ante, § 558, note.

[4] Melan *v.* Fitz James, 1 Bos. & Pul. 138; 3 Burge, Comm. on Col. and For. Law, pt. 2, ch. 20, pp. 766—768.

ment of a suit, in a case which, as far as one can judge at present, authorizes no proceeding against the person in the country in which the transaction passed. If there could be none in France, in my opinion, there can be none here. I cannot conceive that what is no personal obligation in the country in which it arises can ever be raised into a personal obligation by the laws of another. If it be a personal obligation there, it must be enforced here in the mode pointed out by the law of this country. But what the nature of the obligation is must be determined by the law of the country where it was entered into; and then this country will apply its own law to enforce it[1]." And accordingly the Court discharged the party from the arrest.

§ 569. There does not seem the least reason to doubt the entire correctness of the doctrine thus laid down. If the contract creates no personal obligation, but an obligation *in rem* only, it cannot be that its nature can be changed, or its obligation varied, by a mere change of domicil. That would be to contradict all the principles maintained in all the authorities, that the validity, nature, obligation, and interpretation of a contract are to be decided by the *lex loci contractûs*[2]. A suit *in personam* in England could not be maintained, except upon some contract which bound the person. If it bound the property only, the proceeding should be *in rem;* and if in express terms the party bound his property only, and exempted himself from a personal liability, no one would doubt that a suit *in personam* would not be maintainable. The same principle would apply, if the laws of a country should declare that certain classes of contracts should not bind the person at all, but only property, or a particular species of property. Such laws do probably exist in some countries; but it does not follow, because a personal remedy is not given by the laws of a

---

1 Melan *v.* Fitz-James, 1 Bos. & Pull. 138; 3 Burge, Com. on Col. and For. Law, pt. 2, ch. 20, pp. 766—768. See also Ohio Insur. Co. *v.* Edmondson, 5 Louis, R. 295, 300.

2 Ante, § 263—273; 3 Burge, Comm. pt. 2, ch. 20, pp. 765, 766, 776.

country, that therefore there is no personal obligation in a contract[1].

§ 570. The real difficulty lies, not in the principle itself, but in its application. There is a great distinction between a contract which *ex directo* excludes personal libability and a contract made in a country which binds the party personally, but where the laws do not enforce the contract *in personam*, but only *in rem*. In the latter case, the remedy constitutes no part of the contract. The liability is general, so far as the acts of the parties go; and the mode of enforcing is a mere matter of municipal regulation. It is strictly a part of the *lex fori*, and may be changed from time to time, as the legislature may choose[2]. This was the view of the matter taken by Mr. Justice Heath, in the case alluded to; for he, in dissenting from the opinion of the Court, did not deny the principles of the decision, but held, that the contract was personal. "We all agree," said he, "that in construing contracts, we must be governed by the laws of the country in which they are made; for all the contracts have reference to such laws; but when we come to remedies it is another thing: they must be pursued by the means which the law points out where the party resides. The laws of the country where the contract was made can only have reference to the nature of the contract, not to the mode of enforcing it. Whoever comes voluntarily into a country, subjects himself to all the laws of that country, and therein to all the remedies directed by those laws on his particular engagements[3]."

§ 571. The doctrine of this case has been sometimes followed in America[4]. But the better opinion now established, both in England and America, is, that it is of no

---

[1] Talleyrand *v.* Boulanger, 3 Ves. Jr. R. 446; Flack *v.* Holm, 1 Jac. & Walk. 405.

[2] See Ogden *v.* Saunders, 12 Wheat. R. 213.

[3] Melan *v.* Fitz James, 1 Bos. & Pull. 142; Hinkley *v.* Morean, 3 Mason, R. 88; Titus *v.* Hobart, 5 Mason, R. 378.

[4] Symonds *v.* Union Insur. Co. 4 Dall. 417.

consequence whether the contract authorizes an arrest or imprisonment of the party in the country where it was made, if there is no exemption of the party from personal liability on the contract. He is still liable to arrest or imprisonment in a suit upon it in any foreign country, whose laws authorize such a mode of proceeding as a part of the local remedy[1]. In a recent case in England, where the plaintiff and defendant were both foreigners, and the debt was contracted in a country by whose laws the defendant would not have been liable to arrest, an application was made to discharge the defendant from arrest on that account; but the Court refused the application. Lord Tenterden, on that occasion, in delivering the opinion of the Court, said:—"A person suing in this country, must take the law as he finds it. He cannot, by virtue of any regulation in his own country, enjoy greater advantages than other suitors here; and he ought not, therefore, to be deprived of any superior advantage which the law of this country may confer. He is to have the same rights which all the subjects of this kingdom are entitled to[2]." The same doctrine has been solemnly promulgated by the House of Lords on a still more recent occasion[3].

§ 572. The like principles apply to the form of judgments to be rendered, and of executions to be granted in suits. They must conform to the *lex fori*, although the

---

1 See Imley *v.* Elfesson, 2 East, R. 453; Peck *v.* Hozier, 14 John, R. 346; Robinson *v.* Bland, 2 Burr. 1089; Hinkley *v.* Morean, 3 Mason, R. 88; Titus *v.* Hobart, 5 Mason, R. 378; Smith *v.* Spinolla, 2 John. R. 198, 200; De la Vega *v.* Vianna, 1 Barn. & Adol. R. 284; 3 Burge, Comm. on Col. and For. Law, pt. 2, ch. 20, pp. 766—769; Atwater *v.* Townsend, 4 Connect. R. 47; Woodbridge *v.* Wright, 3 Connect. R. 523, 526; Smith *v.* Healy, 4 Connect. R. 49.

2 De la Vega *v.* Vianna, 1 Barn. & Adol. R. 284. See also Whittemore *v.* Adams, 2 Cowen, R. 626; Willing *v.* Consequa, 1 Peters, Cir. R. 317; Courtois *v.* Carpentier, 1 Wash. Cir. R. 376; Bird *v.* Caritat, 2 John. R. 345; Wyman *v.* Soutward, 10 Wheaton, R. 1. See Henry on Foreign Law, pp. 81—86.

3 Don *v.* Lippmann, 5 Clark & Finnell. R. 1, 13—15; Ante, § 557, note.

party defendant may, in his domestic forum, have been entitled to a judgment, exempting his person from imprisonment, in virtue of a discharge under an insolvent law existing there, and of which he had there judicially obtained the benefit[1]. And it will make no difference in such case, whether the contract sued on was made in the State granting such discharge, or not, or whether the parties were citizens of that State or not. The effect of such a discharge is purely local. It is addressed solely to the courts of the State under whose authority the exemption is allowed. But it has nothing to do with the process, proceedings, or judgments of the courts of other States, which are to be governed altogether by their own municipal jurisprudence. Wherever a remedy is sought, it is to be administered according to the *lex fori;* and such a judgment is to be given as the laws of the State where the suit is brought authorize and allow, and not such a judgment as the laws of other States authorize or require[2].

§ 573. The general doctrine is stated in ample terms by Paul Voet. *Quid, si actiones sint intentandæ, et quidem personales, an sequemur, statutum domicilii debitoris, an statutum loci, ubi exigi vel intentari poterunt? Respondeo, etsi bene multi velint tales actiones certo loco non circumscribi, inspectâ tantum illâ corporali circumscriptione, ut tamen eas velint censeri de loco ubi agi et exigi possunt*[3]. Again he adds: *Sed revertar, unde fueram digressus, ad concursum statutorum variantium circa judicia. Ubi occurrunt nonnulla circa solemnia in judiciis servanda, circa tempora, cautiones, probationes, causarum decisiones, executiones, et appellationes. Finge, enim, alia servari solemnia, in loco domicilii litigatoris,*

---

1 Hinkley *v.* Morean, 3 Mason. R. 88; Titus *v.* Hobart, 5 Mason, R. 378; Atwater *v.* Townsend, 4 Connect. R. 47; Woodbridge *v.* Wright, 3 Connect. R. 523, 526; Smith *v.* Healy, 4 Connect. R. 49; 3 Burge, Comm. on Col. and For. Law, pt. 2, ch. 21, § 7, pp. 878, 879.

2 Ibid. See also Suydam *v.* Broadnax, 14 Peters, R. 67.

3 P. Voet, Ad Stat. § 10, c. 1, n. 2, p. 281, (edit. 1715); Id. p. 340, (edit. 1661).

alia in loco contractûs, alia in loco rei sitæ, alia in judicii loco. Quœnam spectanda solemnia? Respondeo; Spectanda sunt solemnia, id est, stylus judicis fori illius, ubi litigatur. Idque in genere verum est, sive loquamur de civibus, sive forensibus: statuta quippe circa solemnia meo sensu mixti erant generis; adeoque vires exserunt tam intra quam extra territorium, tam in ordine ad incolas, quam ad exteros[1].

§ 574. The same doctrine is fully confirmed by John Voet, as a received doctrine of foreign law. *Multis prœterea in locis id obtinet, ne duo ejusdem provinciœ seu territorii incolœ se invicem, aut bona, sistant in alio territorio. Sic duo Brabantini se invicem non extra Brabantiam; duo Hollandi non extra Hollandum, &c. Quod si quis, neglectâ statuti dispositione, concivem aut bona ejus alibi stiterit, litis movendœ gratiâ, non peccabunt quidem istius loci judices, si arrestum confirment; cum non ligentur alieni territorii legibus, talem arrestationem concivium vetantibus. Sed, qui ita detentus litigare coactus est, rectè petet a suo judice, condemnari concivem, ut arresti vinculum, contra statuti domicilii prohibitionem alibi impositum, remittat, litique alibi cœptœ cum impensis renunciet, ac solvat mulctam statuto dictatam*[2]. And he proceeds to add, that in some places the practice is in suits between two foreigners, belonging to one and the same country, to remit the parties to their domestic *forum;* which, however, is done, not as a matter of right or duty, but of comity, or from policy, to prevent injurious delays to the suits of their own citizens. *Quod tamen vel ex comitate magis, quam necessitate fit, vel magis ad declinandam nimiam litium frequentiam judicibus molestam, civibus, inde suarum litium protelationem patientibus, damnosam*[3].

§ 574 *a*. Dumoulin also affirms a similar doctrine in the

---

1 P. Voet, De Stat. § 10, c. 1, n. 6, p. 285, (edit. 1715); Id. pp. 345, 346, (edit. 1661).

2 J. Voet, Ad. Pand. lib. 2, tit. 4, § 45, p. 129; cited also 1 Barn. & Adol. R. 288, note; Ante, § 562.

3 Ibid.

passages already cited. *Unde, an instrumentum habeat executionem, et quomodo debeat exequi, attenditur locus, ubi agitur, vel fit executio. Ratio, quia fides instrumenti concernet meritum; sed virtus executoria et modus exequendi concernit processum*[1]. *Quod in his, quæ pertinent ad processum judicii, vel executionem faciendam, vel ad ordinationem judicii, semper sit observanda consuetudo loci, in quo judicium agitatur*[2]. Burgundus is equally expressive. *Eodem modo dicemus, in contexanda actione, fori consuetudines observandas esse, ubi contenditur, quia et in judiciis quasi contrahitur. Idem in arrestis seu manuum injectionibus tenendum est, ut scilicet consuetudinem loci spectemus, ubi facta est manus injectio; quia arrestatto apud nos ingressus est judicii, et duntaxat litis pendentiam, non executionem generet*[3]. This indeed seems, with few exceptions, to be the general doctrine maintained by foreign jurists; and Boullenois has collected their opinions at large[4]. He treats the question of imprisonment as purely one *modus exequendi;* and he applies the same principle to mesne process, and to process of execution[5]. He accordingly puts the case, where a Frenchman contracts a common debt in a country, by whose laws such a debt imparts a right to arrest the body, and says, that this right is a mere mode of enforcing the contract, *modus exequendi,* and consequently it depends upon the law of the place where the execution of it is sought; so that if it is sought in a place where no such arrest of the body is allow-

---

[1] Molin. Opera, tom. 3, Comm. ad Cod. lib. 1, tit. 1, l. 1, p. 554, (edit. 1681); Ante, § 561.

[2] Id. lib. 6, tit. 32, p. 735, [741], (edit. 1681); 1 Boullenois, Observ. 23, pp. 523, 524; Ante, § 561.

[3] Burgundus, Tract. 5, n. 1, pp. 118, 119; 1 Boullenois, Observ. 23, pp. 524, 526; 2 Boullenois, Observ. 46, p. 488. But see Burgundus, Tract. 4, n. 27, p. 116, cited Post, § 574 *c*, note.

[4] 1 Boullenois, Observ. 23, pp. 523—525, 528, 529; Id. pp. 535—543; Id. pp. 544—569. See Henry on For. Law, pp. 81—85.

[5] Id.; Henry on For. Law, pp. 55, 56; Id. pp. 81—85.

able, the creditor has no right to claim any restraint by such a rigorous course[1].

§ 574 *b*. But a distinction is taken by some foreign jurists between a contract made in a country between a stranger and a citizen thereof, or between two citizens, and a contract made in the same country between two foreigners belonging to another country, when the law of the place where the contract is made allows an arrest of the person, and the law of the place where the suit is brought, or to which the two foreigners belong, disallows such an arrest. Thus, in Brabant there is a law of Charles the Fourth, which prohibits any Brabanter from arresting another Brabanter in a foreign jurisdiction; and Peckius puts the question, whether in a case of this sort any Brabanter may arrest another Brabanter in Spain, Italy, England, France, or other foreign country. And he holds that he may not; first, because the prohibitory law is absolute, and comprehends subjects even in a foreign territory; secondly, because the power of establishing a law between subjects is not limited to the territory of the sovereign; thirdly, because if the sovereign may bind his subjects every where, this privilege equally binds them every where as a part of the law; fourthly, because a sentence of excommunication would bind the subjects in a foreign territory; and, *à fortiori*, then this privilege does bind them; and fifthly, because the incapacity of a prodigal binds him in a foreign territory, and this case of privilege is as strong or stronger. Hence he concludes, that not only the person but the movables of the Brabanter (which follow his person) also would be free from arrest. *Unde sicut persona arrestari non potest, ita nec bona mobilia ejusdem*[2].

---

1 1 Boullenois, Observ. 23, p. 525; Id. pp. 528, 529; Id. Observ. 25, p. 601, &c.

2 Peck. De Jure Sist. c. 8, n. 1—6, Peckii Opera, p. 753, (edit. 1666).

§ 574 *c*. There is great reason to doubt both the premises and the conclusion of Peckius in asserting this distinction; and certainly it now has no admitted recognition in the common law[1]. Peckius asserts another distinction, in which he has apparently the support of Christinæus and Everhardus, and some other jurists, that where the law of the place of contract allows an arrest, but the law of the place of payment does not, (and so *e contra* in the converse case), the law of the latter is to prevail. He quotes the language of Everhardus on the same point with approbation. *Quod si in loco celebrati contractus sit statutum, quod debitor possit capi et incarcerari, vel quod instrumenta notariorum habeant executionem paratam; in loco vero destinatæ solutionis, non sit simile statutum, sed servetur jus commune, attenditur, quoad hoc, mos, observantia, statutum, aut lex, destinatæ solutionis. Quippe, quod in his, quæ concernunt judicariam executionem, inspicitur locus destinatæ solutionis*[2]. He then adds in the converse case: *Quod et in arrestatione, si similis casus occurrat, locus destinatæ solutionis et judicii spectari debeat*[3]. Christinæus uses similar language[4]. The common law of England and America, however, does not recognise any such distinction[5].

---

[1] Ante, § 568—571. Mr. Henry, however, thinks the distinction sound, and deems it supported by the case of Melan *v*. The Duke of Fitz James, 1 Bos. & Pull. 138; Ante, § 568—572. Burgundus says: "Affinia solutioni sunt, præscriptio, oblatio rei debitæ, consignatio, novatio, delegatio, et ejus modi. Burgundus, Tract. 4, n. 28, p. 116.

[2] Everhard. Consil. 78, n. 22, p. 208; Peck. De Jure Sist. c. 11, p. 758, (edit. Peck. Oper. 1666).

[3] Peck. Oper. De Jure Sist. c. 11, n. 1, pp. 758, 759, (edit. 1666).

[4] Christin. tom. 1, decis. 283, n. 12, p. 355; 1 Boullenois, Observ. 23, p. 525; 2 Boullenois, Observ. 46, p. 488.

[5] Post, § 581; Campbell *v*. Steiner, 6 Dowl. R. 116; Don *v*. Lippmann, 5 Clark & Finnell. R. 1, 19, 20. In this latter case, Lord Brougham said, speaking on this point: "All the authorities, Huber (De Confl. Leg. in Div. Imp.); Voet (Dig. lib. 24, t. 3, s. 12); and Lord Kaimes, (Kaimes's Principles of Equity, 3, 8, 6, 1, 5, 3), are cited in that case. Campbell *v*. Steiner, (6 Dowl. 116), was an action for a bill of costs for business done in this house. The Court below there allowed the rule of Scotch prescription.

§ 574 *d.* Peckius then puts another case, where the contract of indebtment is made in a country where an arrest is not allowed, and the debtor has not promised to pay in another country where an arrest is allowed, but he is found there; whether in such a case he may nevertheless be arrested there, the debt being then due. He thinks he may; because to this extent it may be truly said that the law and usage of the place of the judgment ought in this matter to be observed; and that in those things which concern the proceedings in suits, foreigners are bound by the laws of the place where they are liable to be sued. *Sed quid, si quis contraxit in loco, in quo illius loci homines non utuntur arresto, neque promisit solvere in patria arresti, sed tamen illice reperitur; utrum nihilominus arrestari possit? Existimo, quod sic, si vel tempus solutionis elapsum vel in mora periculum sit; quia adhuc verum est dicere, quod statutum et consuetudo loci judicii servare debet in istius modi; et in his, quæ ad ordinationem judiciorum pertinent, forenses ligantur statutis loci, ubi conveniuntur*[1].

That judgment was affirmed by Lord Eldon, who however said that he moved it with regret. He said that it had been ruled, that the debtor being in Scotland, and the creditor in England, the debtor might plead the Scotch rule of prescription; that that was against some of the old authorities, but was in accordance with those of later date. That case cannot be reconciled with the principle that the locus solutionis is to prescribe the law. It has nothing to do with the case. Why is it then, that the law of the domicil of the debtor was there allowed to prevent the plaintiff from recovering? It was, because the creditor must follow the debtor, and must sue him where he resides; and by the necessity of that case, was obliged to sue him in Scotland. In that respect, therefore, there was in that case no difference between the lex loci solutionis and the lex fori; and it must be admitted that in such a case the rules of evidence, and if so, the rules of practice, may be varied, as they are applied in one court or the other. But governing all these cases is the principle, that the law of the country where the contract is to be enforced, must prevail in enforcing such contract, though it is conceded that the lex loci contractus may be referred to for the purpose of expounding it. If, therefore, the contract is made in one country, to be performed in a second, and is enforced in a third, the law of the last alone, and not of the other two, will govern the case."

[1] Peckii Opera, De Jure Sist. c. 11, pp. 758, 759, (edit. 1666). The

§ 575. In the next place, as to defences arising from matters *ex post facto*. These may be of the nature of counter claims or set-offs to actions, analogous to compensation in the Roman and foreign law[1]; or they may be matters of discharge, such as discharges under insolvent laws, arising at a subsequent period; or they may be laws regulating the time of instituting suits, called in the foreign law statutes of prescription, and in the common law statutes of limitations. The latter defence will deserve a very exact consideration. The former may be disposed of in a few words. The subject of discharges from the contract, either by the act of the parties or by operation of law, have been already sufficiently considered[2]. As to set-off or compensation, it is held in the courts of common law, that a set-off to any action allowed by the local law, is to be treated as a part of the remedy; and that therefore it is admissible in claims between persons belonging to different states or countries, although it may not be admissible by the law of the country where the debt which is sued was contracted[3]. The liens and implied hypothecations, and priorities of satisfaction given to creditors by the law of particular countries, and the order of payment of their debts, are, as we have already seen[4], generally treated as belonging to the proceedings in suits, *ad litis ordinationem*, and not to the merits of the claim[5].

§ 576. In regard to statutes of limitation or prescription

---

same point was held in Don *v.* Lippmann, 5 Clark & Finnell. R. 1, 20; Ante, § 574 *c*, note.

1 Pothier, Oblig. n. 587, 588.

2 Ante, § 330—352. See also 3 Burge, Comm. on Col. and For. Law, pt. 2, ch. 21, § 7, pp. 874—886.

3 Gibbs *v.* Howard, 2 New Hamp. R. 296; Ruggles *v.* Keeler, 3 John. R. 263. See Pothier on Oblig. n. 641, 642.

4 Ante, § 322 *b*—328, 423 *a*.

5 Rodenburg, De Div. Stat. tit. 2, c. 5, n. 15, 16; 2 Boullenois, App. pp. 47, 49; 1 Boullenois, Observ. 25, pp. 634, 635, 639; Id. p. 685; Id. p. 818. See also P. Voet, De Stat. § 10, c. 1, n. 2—6, pp. 282—289, (edit. 1715); Id. pp. 340—346, (edit. 1661).

of suits, there is no doubt that they are strictly questions affecting the remedy, and not questions upon the merits. They go *ad litis ordinationem*, and not *ad litis decisionem*, in a just juridical sense[1]. The object of them is to fix certain periods, within which all suits shall be brought in the Courts of a State, whether they are brought by or against subjects, or by or against foreigners. And there can be no just reason, and no sound policy, in allowing higher or more extensive privileges to foreigners, than are allowed to subjects. Laws, thus limiting suits, are founded in the noblest policy. They are statutes of repose, to quiet titles, to suppress frauds, and to supply the deficiency of proofs, arising from the ambiguity and obscurity, or the antiquity of transactions. They proceed upon the presumption, that claims are extinguished, or ought to be held extinguished, whenever they are not litigated in the proper forum, within the prescribed period. They take away all solid grounds of complaint; because they rest on the negligence or *laches* of the party himself. They quicken diligence, by making it in some measure equivalent to right. They discourage litigation, by burying in one common receptacle all the accumulations of past times, which are unexplained, and have now, from lapse of time, become inexplicable. It has been said by John Voet with singular felicity, that controversies are limited to a fixed period of time, lest they should be immortal, while men are mortal: *Ne autem lites immortales essent, dum litigantes mortales sunt*[2].

§ 577. It has accordingly become a formulary in international jurisprudence, that all suits must be brought within the period prescribed by the local law of the country where the suit is brought, (*lex fori*), otherwise the suits will be barred; and this rule is as fully recognised in foreign jurisprudence as it is in the common law[3]. Not, indeed,

---

[1] 1 Boullenois, Observ. 23, p. 530.

[2] J. Voet, Ad Pand. lib. 5, tit. 1, § 53, p. 328.

[3] The authorities in the common law are very numerous. A considerable

that there are no diversities of opinion upon this subject; but the doctrine is established by a decisive current of well-considered authorities[1]. Thus, Huberus lays down the doctrine in clear terms, applying it to the very case of a prescription; and he assigns the reason: *Ratio hæc est, quod præscriptio et executio non pertinent ad valorem contractûs, sed ad tempus et modum actionis instituendæ, quæ per se, quasi contractum, separatum negotium constituit. Adeoque receptum est optimâ ratione, ut ordinandis judiciis, loci consuetudo, ubi agitur, etsi de negotio, alibi celebrato, spectatur, ut docet Sandius, ubi tradit, etiam in executione sententiæ alibi latæ, servari jus loci, in quo fit executio, non ubi res judicata est*[2]. Paul Voet says: *Ubi quoad actionis intentationem, occurrit illa difficultas, an si diversa sint statuta circa actionis finitionem seu terminum, spectandus sit terminus statuti debitoris, an creditoris? Respondeo; quia actor sequitur forum rei, ideo extraneus petens à reo, quod sibi debetur, sequetur terminum statuti præscriptum actioni in foro rei. Et quia hoc statutum non exserit vires extra*

number of them are cited in 4 Cowen, R. 528, note 10; Id. 530; Van Reimsdyk *v.* Kane, 1 Gallis. R. 371; Le Roy *v.* Crowninshield, 2 Mason, R. 351; British Linen Company *v.* Drummond, 10 Barn. & Cresw. 903; De la Vega *v.* Vianna, 1 Barn. & Adol. R. 284; Huber *v.* Steiner, 2 Bing. New Cases, 202, 209—212; Don *v.* Lippmann, 5 Clark & Finnell. R. 1, 13—17; Medbury *v.* Hopkins, 3 Connect. R. 472; Woodbridge *v.* Wright, 3 Connect. R. 523; Bank of U. S. *v.* Donnally, 8 Peters, R. 361; Bulger *v.* Roche, 11 Pick, 36; De Couche *v.* Savatier, 3 John. Ch. R. 190; Lincoln *v.* Battelle, 6 Wend. R. 475.

[1] See Ersk. Inst. b. 3, tit. 7, n. 49, pp. 633, 634.

[2] Huberus, tom. 2, lib. 1, tit. 3, De Conflict. Leg. § 7; 1 Hertii, Opera, De Collis. § 4, n. 65, pp. 150, 151, (edit. 1737); Id. p. 312, (edit. 1716). Hertius seems of a different opinion; saying, that if the prescription only of the place where the suit is brought, could prevail, the times of prescription would be very uncertain; for a man might frequently be sued in different places. 1 Hertii, Opera, De Collis. Leg. § 4, n. 65, p. 150, (edit. 1737); Id. p. 212, (edit. 1716). See also the opinions of other jurists to the same point in 1 Boullenois, Observ. 23, pp. 528—530; 2 Boullenois, Observ. 46, pp. 487, 488; Erskine's Inst. b. 3, tit. 7, § 48, pp. 633, 634; J. Voet, Ad Pand. tom. 2, lib. 44, tit. 3, § 10, 12; 3 Burge, Comm. on Col. and For. Law, pt. 2, ch. 21, § 7, pp. 878, 879.

territorium statuentis, ideo, etiam reo alibi convento, tale statutum objicere non poterit[1]. Boullenois holds a similar doctrine, asserting, that the bar of prescription is a part of the *modus procedendi*[2]. It is in vain, he adds, to assert, that the bar of prescription is a peremptory exception, (*exceptio peremptoria*), and that, according to Baldus, *exceptio peremptoria pertinet ad decisionem causæ*:—That remark properly applies to a peremptory exception, which falls upon the contract, and not to one which falls only upon the action or proceedings in a suit[3]. Many other jurists might be cited in support of this doctrine, if it were necessary to go at large into the subject[4]. The doctrine of the Scottish courts is in precise conformity to that of the common law[5].

§ 578. But if the question were entirely new, it would be difficult upon principles of international justice or policy to establish a different rule. Every nation must have a right to settle for itself the times, and modes, and circumstances, within and under which suits shall be litigated in its own Courts. There can be no pretence to say, that foreigners are entitled to crowd the tribunals of any nation with suits of their own, which are stale and antiquated, to the exclusion of the common administration of justice between its own subjects. As little right can foreigners have to insist, that the times and modes of proceeding in

---

1 P. Voet, De Stat. § 10, c. 1, n. 1, p. 281, (edit. 1715); Id. p. 340, (edit. 1661).

2 1 Boullenois, Observ. 23, p. 530; Post, § 579.

3 Ibid.

4 See 1 Boullenois, Observ. 23, pp. 530, 550; 2 Boullenois, Observ. 46, pp. 455, 456; Casaregis Disc. 179, § 59, 60; P. Voet, De Stat. § 10, c. 1, § 1, p. 281, (edit. 1715); Id. pp. 339, 340, (edit. 1661). See 3 Burge, Comm. on Col. and For. Law, pt. 2, ch. 10, § 5, pp. 122—124; Id. ch. 21, § 7, pp. 878—880; Erskine, Inst. b. 3, tit. 7, § 48, pp. 633, 634.

5 Erskine, Inst. b. 3, tit. 7, § 48, p. 633; Le Roy *v.* Crowninshield, 2 Mason, R. 174; Kaims on Equity, b. 3, ch. 8, § 4, 6; P. Voet, De Stat. § 10, c. 1, n. 1, pp. 280, 281, (edit. 1715); Id. pp. 339, 340, (edit. 1661).

suits, provided by the laws of their own country, shall supersede those of the nation in which they have chosen to litigate their controversies, or in whose tribunals they are properly parties to any suit.

§ 579. The reasoning sometimes insisted upon by foreign jurists, in opposition to this plain and intelligible doctrine, is, in the first place, that the statute of limitations or prescription really operates as a preremptory bar, and therefore does not, in fact, touch the mode of proceeding, but the merits of the case: *Non tangit modum simplicem procedendi; sed tangit meritum causæ*[1]; and, in the next place, that it subjects the party to different prescriptions in different places, and therefore leaves his rights in uncertainty[2]. The latter objection may be answered by the obvious consideration, that, if the party chooses to reside within any particular territory, he thereby subjects himself to the laws of that territory, as to all suits brought by or aginast him. It may be added, that, as the law of prescription of a particular country, even in case of a contract made in such country, forms no part of the contract itself, but merely acts upon it *ex post facto* in case of a suit, it cannot properly be deemed a right stipulated for, or included in the contract. Even these foreign jurists do not pretend that the prescription of a country, where a contract is made, constitutes a part of the contract. What they contend for amounts at most only to this, that the prescription of the *lex loci contractûs* acts upon, and appertains to, the decision of the cause. *Hoc pertinet ad decisionem causæ,* says Baldus. *Prescriptio utique ad contractum et meritum causæ pertinet, non ad processum,* says Gerhard Titius[3]. This objection, indeed, is fully and satisfactorily answered by Boullenois in the passage above cited[4].

---

[1] 1 Boullenois, Observ. 23, pp. 529, 530; Ante, § 577.

[2] 1 Hertii Opera, De Col. Leg. § 4, n. 65, pp. 150, 151, (edit. 1737); Id. p. 212, (edit. 1716).

[3] 1 Boullenois, Observ. 23, pp. 529, 530; Ersk. Inst. b. 3, tit. 7, § 48, pp. 633, 634.

[4] Ante, § 577.—Lord Brougham also, in delivering his judgment in Don

§ 580. The other objection is well founded in its form, but it does not shake the ground of the general doctrine. It is true, as Baldus contends, that the statute of limitations or prescription does go to the decision of the cause; *exceptio peremptoria pertinet ad decisionem causæ*. But that is not the question. The question is, whether it is a matter of the original merits, as for example, a question of the original validity, or interpretation, or discharge of a contract, or whether it is a matter touching the time and mode of remedial justice, which is provided by law to redress grievances, or to prevent wrongs, or to suppress vexatious litigation. Suppose a nation were to declare, (as France has done in regard to foreigners in some cases), that no suits should be maintained in its own Courts between foreigners[1]. This would be a peremptory exception. But could it be denied, that France had a right so to regulate the jurisdiction of its own tribunals? Or that it was an enactment touching remedies? Considered in their true light, statutes of limitation or prescription are ordinarily simple regulations of suits and not of rights. They regulate the

---

v. Lippmann, 1 Clark & Finnell. pp. 1, 15, 16, met the very objection. His language on that occasion was (it being the case of a bill of exchange accepted and payable in France, and sued afterwards in Scotland, and the Scottish prescription set up as a bar): "It is said, that the limitation is of the very nature of the contract. First, it is said, that the party is bound for a given time, and for a given time only. That is a strained construction of the obligation. The party does not bind himself for a particular period at all, but merely to do something on a certain day, or on one or other of certain days. In the case at the bar, the obligation is to pay a sum certain at a certain day; but the law does not suppose, that he is at the moment of making the contract contemplating the period at which he may be freed by lapse of time from performing it. The argument, that the limitation is of the nature of the contract, supposes that the parties look only to the breach of the argreement. Nothing is more contrary to good faith than such a supposition, that the contracting parties look only to the period at which the Statute of Limitations will begin to run. It will sanction a wrong course of conduct, and will turn a protection against laches into a premium for evasiveness."

[1] Ante, § 542.

times in which rights may be asserted in courts of justice, and do not purport to act upon those rights. Boullenois has truly said: *L'exception ne tombe, que sur l'action et la procédure intentée*[1]. Pothier very properly treats prescription, (*fin de non recevoir*), not so much as an extinguishment of the debt or claim, as an extinguishment of the right of action thereon[2]. And this is precisely the manner in which the subject is contemplated at the common law[3], as well as by many foreign jurists[4].

§ 581. And here, again, upon the same mistaken foundation already discussed, some foreign jurists (as we have seen[5]) maintain the doctrine in relation to contracts, (a doctrine repudiated by the common law[6]), that, if they are made in one place, and to be performed or paid in another place, the law of prescription of the latter place is to govern. Such is the opinion of Everhardus. *Aut quærimus* (says he), *quis locus inspiciatur, quoad extinctionem actionis propter præscriptionem statutoriam, vigentem in uno loco, et non in alio, ubi statuta locorum sunt diversa. Et certum est, quod inspicitur locus destinatæ solutionis*[7]. Bartolus, Burgundus, and Christinæus hold the same opinion[8]. Of course

---

1 1 Boullenois, Observ. 23, p. 530; Ante, § 577; Ersk. Inst. b. 3, tit. 7, § 48, pp. 633, 634.

2 Pothier on Oblig. n. 640—642.

3 Sturgis *v.* Crowninshield, 4 Wheat. R. 122, 200, 207.

4 J. Voet, Ad Pand. lib. 44, tit. 3, § 10; D'Aguesseau, Œuvres, tom. 5, p. 374, 4to. edit.; Le Roy *v.* Crowninshield, 2 Mason, R. 170, 171; Merlin, Répert. tit. Prescription, sect. I. § 3, n. 7.—Corporations are deemed to be domiciled in the country from which they derive their act or charter of incorporation; and therefore the same rule applies to them as applies to private persons in cases of prescription. 3 Burge, Comm. on Col. and For. Law, pt. 2, ch. 21, § 7, pp. 881, 882.

5 Ante, § 574 *c.*

6 Ibid.

7 Everhard. Consil. 78, p. 208; 2 Boullenois, Observ. 46, p. 488.

8 2 Boullenois, Observ. 46, p. 488.—It is surprising that Mr. Henry should have cited this doctrine of foreign authors, as sound law, (apparently copying it from Boullenois), without considering that the whole course of English opinions on this subject disclaimed it. (Henry on Foreign Law, ch.

the doctrine of these authors must be understood to be limited to prescription in personal actions; for, as to prescription in cases of immovable property, it is beyond reasonable doubt, that it is and ought to be governed purely by the *lex loci rei sitæ*[1]. Dumoulin has laid down the distinction in broad but exact terms: *Aut statutum disponit de præscriptione, vel usucapione rerum corporalium, sive mobilium, sive immobilium, et tunc indistincte inspicitur locus, ubi res est. Idem in rebus sive Juribus incorporalibus limitatis ad res corporales, sive quatenus ad illas res limitantur; Secus si de Juribus, vel actionibus personalibus, sive momentaneis, sive annuis personæ adherentibus, id est non limitatis ad certas res, etiamsi illis actionibus adhæreat hypotheca generalis, vel accessoria rerum corporalium*[2]. Paul Voet takes the like distinction: *Quid, si itaque contentio de aliquo jure in re, seu ex ipsâ re descendente? vel ex contractu, vel actione personali, sed in rem scriptâ? An spectabitur loci statutum, ubi dominus habet domicilium, an statutum rei sitæ? Respondeo; Statutum rei sitæ. Ut tamen actio etiam intentari possit, ubi*

8, § 1, 2, pp. 54, 55). Pardessus says, that when a debtor pleads a statute of prescription, the right to use this plea, and the time within which it should be pleaded, will be regulated by the law of the place where he has promised to pay; or, if this place has not been determined, then at the domicil of the debtor, at the time when he contracted the obligation; because, prescription being a plea given to the debtor against the demand of his creditor, it is naturally in the domicil of the debtor, or of his government, that he should find this protection. Pardessus, tom. 5, p. 6, tit. 9, ch. 2, § 2, art. 1445, p. 275; Henry on Foreign Law, Appendix, p. 237. Pardessus goes on to state, that these rules apply to the case where several sureties for the same debt reside in jurisdictions where the laws respecting prescription are different. Each, in becoming a surety, must be supposed to have intended to enjoy all the real pleas or exceptions existing in favour of the principal debtor, without renouncing the particular prescription in his own favour to extinguish his obligation as surety, which is regulated by the law of his domicil at the moment when he signed the contract. Pardessus, Id. art. 1495, pp. 275, 276; Henry on Foreign Law, 238. This is certainly pressing the doctrine to a very great extent.

[1] 1 Boullenois, Observ. 20, p. 350; J. Voet. Ad Pand. lib. 44, tit. 3, § 12.

[2] Molin. Opera, tom. 3, Comm. ad Cod. lib. 1, tit. 1, l. 1, p. 557, De Præscript. (edit. 1681); 1 Boullenois, Observ. 20, p. 350.

reus habet domicilium. Idque obtinet, sive forensis sit ille, de cujus re controversia est, sive incola loci, ubi res est sita[1]. John Voet maintains the same doctrine: *Si præscriptioni implendæ alia præfinita sint tempora in loco domicilii actoris, alia in loco ubi reus domicilium fovet, spectandum videtur tempus, quod obtinet ex statuto loci, in quo reus commoratur, nisi de immobilium præscriptione quæstio sit; quo casu neque leges domicilii præscribentis, neque leges domicilii ejus, in cujus præjudicium præscriptio sit, sed magis leges loci, in quo sita immobilia, spectandæ sunt; cum tralatitium sit, immobilia regi lege loci, in quo sita sunt*[2]. Pothier and Merlin fully recognise the same doctrine[3]. The common law has firmly fixed its own doctrine, that the prescription of the *lex fori* must prevail in all cases of personal actions. In all cases of real actions, and of actions touching things savouring of the realty, the prescription of the law *rei sitæ* is also to prevail. And as, by the common law, no actions of this sort can be brought *ex directo,* except in the place *rei sitæ;* it follows that the *lex fori* governs as a universal rule, applicable to all cases[4].

§ 582. But although statutes of limitation or prescription

---

[1] P. Voet, De Stat. § 9, ch. 1, n. 2, p. 251, (edit. 1715); Id. p. 305, (edit. 1661).

[2] J. Voet, Ad Pand. tom. 2, lib. 44, tit. 3, n. 12, p. 877; 3 Burge, Comm. on Col. and For. Law, pt. 2, ch. 10, § 5, pp. 122, 125; J. Voet, Ad Pand. tom. 1, lib. 5, tit. 1, n. 77.

[3] Pothier, Traité de la Prescript. n. 247; Merlin, Répert. tit. Prescription, sect. I. § 3, n. 7; 3 Burge, Comm. on Col. and For. Law, pt. 2, ch. 10, § 5, pp. 123, 124.

[4] See British Linen Company *v.* Drummond, 10 Barn. & Cress. 903; Huber *v.* Steiner, 2 Bing. N. Cas. 202, 209—216; Don *v.* Lippmann, 5 Clark & Finnell. R. 1, 13—17; Bulger *v.* Roche, 11 Pick. R. 36; De Couche *v.* Savatier, 3 John. Ch. R. 190, 218, 219; De la Vega *v.* Vianna, 1 Barn. & Adol. 284; Lincoln *v.* Battelle, 6 Wend. R. 475; Ante, § 552—555; Broh *v.* Jenkins, 9 Martin, R. 526; 3 Burge, Comm. on Col. and For. Law, pt. 2, ch. 10, § 5, pp. 123—125.—The Roman law seems to have given an election to the plaintiff to bring his action in the domicil of the defendant (reus) or of the rei sitæ. Ante, § 532; 1 Boullenois, Observ. 25, pp. 618, 619.

of the place where a suit is brought may thus properly be held to govern the rights of parties in such suit, or, as the proposition is commonly stated, the recovery must be sought, and the remedy pursued, within the times prescribed by the *lex fori*, without regard to the *lex loci contractûs*, or the origin or merits of the cause; yet there is a distinction which deserves consideration, and which has been often propounded. It is this:—Suppose the statutes of limitation or prescription of a particular country do not only extinguish the right of action, but the claim or title itself, *ipso facto*, and declare it a nullity after the lapse of the prescribed period; and the parties are resident within the jurisdiction during the whole of that period, so that it has actually and fully operated upon the case; under such circumstances the question might properly arise, whether such statutes of limitation or prescription may not afterwards be set up in any other country to which the parties may remove, by way of extinguishment, or transfer of the claim or title. This is a point which does not seem to have received as much consideration in the decisions of the common law as it would seem to require. That there are countries in which such regulations do exist, is unquestionable. There are States which have declared that all right to debts, due more than a prescribed term of years, shall be deemed extinguished; and that all titles to real and personal property, not pursued within the prescribed time, shall be deemed for ever fixed in the adverse possessor[1]. Suppose, for instance, (as has occurred), personal property is adversely held in a State for a period beyond that prescribed by the laws of that State, and after that period has elapsed the possessor should remove into another State which has a longer period of pre-

[1] See J. Voet, Ad Pand. lib. 44, tit. 3, § 5, 6, 9; Ersk. Inst. b. 3, tit. 7, § 1, 2, 7, 8; Beckford *v.* Wade, 17 Ves. 86; Lincoln *v.* Battelle, 6 Wend. R. 475.—A statute of this sort, extinguishing the title to real estate after an adverse possession, and transferring the title to the adverse possessor, actually exists in the State of Rhode Island. Act of 1822, Digest of Rhode Island Laws, pp. 363, 364, (edit. 1822).

scription, or is without any prescription; could the original owner assert a title there against the possessor, whose title, by the local law, and the lapse of time, had become final and conclusive before the removal? It has certainly been thought, that, in such a case, the title of the possessor cannot be impugned [1]. If it cannot, the next inquiry is, whether the bar of a statute extinguishment of a debt, *lege loci*, ought not equally to be held a peremptory exception in every other country? This subject may be deemed by some persons still open for future discussion. It has, however, the direct authority of the Supreme Court of the United States in its favour [2]; and its correctness has been recently recognised by the Court of Common Pleas in England [3].

In the American Courts, other than the Supreme Court, it does not seem, hitherto, to have obtained any direct approval or recognition. But, in all the cases in which the question might have been incidentally discussed in these Courts, the statutes under consideration did not purport to extinguish the right, but merely the remedy [4].

§ 582 *a*. A question of a kindred character has been discussed of late years, both in England and America; and that is, whether the statute of limitations or prescription of the country where a suit is brought, is a good defence

---

1 See Beckford *v*. Wade, 17 Ves. 88; Newby *v*. Blakeley, 3 Hen. & Mum. R. 57; Brent *v*. Chapman, 5 Cranch, R. 358; Shelby *v*. Grey, 11 Wheat. R. 361, 371, 372. But see Lord Dudley *v*. Warde, Ambler, R. 113.

2 Shelby *v*. Grey, 11 Wheat. R. 361, 371, 372.

3 Huber *v*. Steiner, 2 Bing. N. Cases, 202, 211. See also Don *v*. Lippmann, 5 Clark & Finnell. 1, 16, 17; 3 Burge, Comm. on Col. and For. Law, pt. 2, ch. 10, § 5, pp. 883, 884.

4 On this subject, see De Couche *v*. Savatier, 3 John. Ch. R. 190, 218, 219; Van Reimsdyk *v*. Kane, 1 Gallis. R. 371; Le Roy *v*. Crowninshield, 2 Mason, R. 151, and the cases there cited; Lincoln *v*. Battelle, 6 Wend. R. 475; 1 Domat, b. 3, § 4, art. 1, p. 464; Id. art. 10, p. 466. John Voet says in one place: "Si præscriptioni implendæ alia prefinita sint tempora in loco domicilii actoris, alia in loco, ubi reus domicilium fovet, spectandum videtur tempus, quod obtinet ex statuto loci, in quo reus commoratur." J. Voet, Ad Pand. lib. 44, tit. 3, § 12, p. 877.

and bar to a suit brought there to enforce a foreign judgment. In both countries it has been held, that it is a good defence and bar [1]. In America the case was stronger than it was as presented in England, for it was a judgment rendered in one of the United States, which was sought to be enforced in another State of the Union; and, therefore, fell within the clause of the constitution, which declares that full faith, and credit, and effect shall be given in each State to the judicial proceedings of every other. It was thought that this clause did not in the slightest degree vary the application of the general principle, that in all matters of proceedings in Courts the *lex loci* was to govern [2].

---

[1] Don *v.* Lippmann, 5 Clark & Finnell. R. 1. 19—21; M'Elmoyle *v.* Cohen, 13 Peters, R. 312.

[2] M'Elmoyle *v.* Cohen, 13 Peters, R. 312, 327, 328.—Mr. Justice Wayne, in delivering the opinion of the Court, after adverting to the clause of the constitution of the United States, and the interpretation thereof, said: "Such being the faith, credit, and effect, to be given to a judgment of one State in another by the Constitution and the act of Congress, the point under consideration will be determined by settling what is the nature of a plea of the statute of limitations. Is it a plea that settles the right of a party on a contract or judgment, or one that bars the remedy? Whatever diversity of opinion there may be among jurists upon this point, we think it well settled to be a plea to the remedy, and consequently, that the lex fori must prevail. Higgins *v.* Scott, 2 Barn. & Adol. 413; 4 Cowen, R. 528, note 10; Id. 530; Van Reimsdyk *v.* Kane, 1 Gallis. R. 371; Le Roy *v.* Crowninshield, 2 Mason, R. 351; British Linen Company *v.* Drummond, 10 Barn. & Cress. 903; De la Vega *v.* Vianna, 1 Barn. & Adol. 284; De Couche *v.* Savatier, 3 Johns. Ch. R. 190; Lincoln *v.* Battelle, 6 Wend. R. 475; Gulick *v.* Lodes, Green's New Jersey Rep. 68; 3 Burge, Comm. on Col. and For. Law, p. 883. The statute of Georgia is, 'that actions of debt on judgments obtained in Courts, other than the Courts of this State, must be brought within five years after the judgment obtained.' It would be strange, if in the now well-understood rights of nations to organize their judicial tribunals according to their notions of policy, it should be conceded to them in every other respect, than that of prescribing the time within which suits shall be litigated in their Courts. Prescription is a thing of policy, growing out of the experience of its necessity; and the time after which suits or actions shall be barred, has been, from a remote antiquity, fixed by every nation, in virtue of that sovereignty by which it exercises its legislation for all persons and property within its jurisdiction. This being the foundation of the right to pass statutes of prescrip-

§ 582 *b*. It may be important, then, carefully to distinguish between cases where the statute of limitations is strictly a mere bar to the remedy, and cases where it goes directly to the extinguishment of the debt, claim, or right. Where it professes to dispose of the latter, it would seem difficult to say, that a mere removal to another country can revive an extinguished debt, claim, or right, or change the positive title of property acquired and perfected under the local law of the place where the parties and property are situated[1]. But where it professes to deny, or control, or extinguish the remedy only, other considerations may pro-

---

tion or limitation, may not our States, under our system, exercise this right in virtue of their sovereignty? Or is it to be conceded to them in every other particular, than that of barring the remedy upon judgments of other States by the lapse of time? The States use this right upon judgments rendered in their own Courts; and the common law raises the presumption of the payment of a judgment after the lapse of twenty years. May they not then limit the time for remedies upon the judgments of other States, and alter the common law by statute, fixing a less or larger time for such presumption, and altogether barring suits upon such judgments, if they shall not be brought within the time stated in the statute? It certainly will not be contended, that judgment creditors of other States shall be put upon a better footing, in regard to a State's right to legislate in this particular, than the judgment creditors of the State in which the judgment was obtained. And if this right so exists, may it not be exercised by a State's restraining the remedy upon the judgment of another State, leaving those of its own Courts unaffected by a statute of limitations, but subject to the common law presumption of payment after the lapse of twenty years? In other words, may not the law of a State fix different times for barring the remedy in a suit upon a judgment of another State, and for those of its own tribunals? We use this mode of argument to shew the unreasonableness of a contrary doctrine. But the point might have been shortly dismissed with this safe declaration, that there is no direct constitutional inhibition upon the States, nor any clause in the Constitution from which it can be even plausibly inferred, that the States may not legislate upon the remedy in suits upon the judgments of other States, exclusive of all interference with their merits. It being settled, that the statute of limitations may bar recoveries upon foreign judgments; that the effect intended to be given under our Constitution to judgments is, that they are conclusive only as regards the merits; the common law principle then applies to suits upon them, that they must be brought within the period prescribed by the local law, the lex fori, or the suit will be barred."

[1] Don *v*. Lippmann, 5 Clark & Finnell. R. 1, 15—17.

perly apply. It has, indeed, been decided upon a recent occasion, in one of the American Courts, that in cases falling within the latter predicament, it will make no difference, whether both parties have remained domiciled in the same country where the original cause of action arose, during the whole period required by the local statute of limitations to bar the remedy thereon, or whether they have changed their domicil after it has begun to run[1]. But the reasoning which thus repels any such distinction is not so clear or decisive as has been supposed. Every nation has a complete and exclusive sovereignty to enact laws, which shall limit all rights of action to certain prescribed periods within its own tribunals; and to declare, that after that period all rights of action shall be extinguished; and if the parties remain domiciled within the territorial jurisdiction during that whole period, the law *ipso facto* operates on the case, and the rights of action are completely extinguished there. But the same doctrine is not true, or rather may not be true, where, before the prescribed period has arrived, one or both of the parties have changed their national domicil; for by such change they have ceased to be under the exclusive dominion of the nation whose statute of limitations has begun to operate upon their rights of action, but has not as yet extinguished them. The laws thereof can no longer operate on those rights, at least not operate except within the territorial limits of the nation. Elsewhere they can be deemed as having only an inchoate and imperfect effect; and the change of domicil suspends their power to extinguish the rights of action in future, since they can have no binding extra-territorial force. It is no answer to say, that when once the statute of limitations begins to run, no subsequent impediment stops it from continuing to run. That is true in the nation whose laws contain such provisions, or inculcate such a doctrine. But no other nation is bound to give effect to such provisions or to such a doctrine.

---

[1] Bulger *v.* Roche, 11 Pick. R. 36.

They are strictly intra-territorial regulations and interpretations of the *lex fori,* which other nations are not bound to observe or keep. While the parties were domiciled there, the statute of limitations continued to run against them; but it had not then extinguished any rights of action. When they changed their domicil, the statute as to them or their rights of action, in respect to personal property, or personal claims, was no longer operative or obligatory; but the statutes only of their new domicil. It would, or at least might, then require a very different consideration, where the local law had before the change of domicil actually extinguished all rights of action; for then to revive them is to create new rights, and not to enforce old rights subsisting at the time of the removal[1].

---

[1] In Bulger *v.* Roche, 11 Pick. R. 36, the very case arose of a cause of action extinguished by the local law of the country, (Nova Scotia), where both parties resided during the whole period of the running of the Statute of Limitations; and the Supreme Court of Massachusetts held, that the right of action, after a change of domicil of the defendant by a removal to Massachusetts, was not thereby extinguished in the State tribunals, but might be pursued within the period prescribed by the Statute of Limitations of Massachusetts. On that occasion, Mr. Chief Justice Shaw, in delivering the opinion of the Court, said:—"The facts, so far as they are material, are these; that the cause of action accrued in 1821, more than six years before the commencement of this action; that the plaintiff and defendant were both domiciled at Halifax, in Nova Scotia, and were subjects of the king of Great Britain; and that by the law of that country, an action of assumpsit is barred in six years. It is stated in the replication, and admitted by the rejoinder, that the plaintiff came into this commonwealth for the first time in 1829, and that the action was commenced within six years from that time. That the law of limitation in a foreign country cannot of itself be pleaded as a bar to an action in this commonwealth seems conceded, and is indeed too well settled by authority to be drawn in question. Byrne *v.* Crowninshield, 17 Mass. R. 55. The authorities, both from the civil and the common law, concur in fixing the rule, that the nature, validity, and construction of contracts, is to be determined by the law of the place where the contract is made; and that all remedies for enforcing such contracts are regulated by the law of the place where such remedies are pursued. Whether the law of prescription, or Statute of Limitation, which takes away every legal mode of recovering a debt, shall be considered as affecting the contract like payment, release, or judgment, which in effect extinguish the contract, or whether they are to be con-

§ 583. What has been thus far stated on this head, may be concluded by quoting a passage from John Voet, the correctness and force of which, in point of principle, are submitted to the consideration of the reader. *Quod, si restitutio concedenda sit non ex causâ, quæ ipsum negotium ab initio comitabatur, (uti comitatur metus, dolus, error) sed ex eâ, quæ post supervenit, (qualis est Usucapio rerum, aut*

---

sidered as affecting the remedy only by determining the time, within which a particular mode of enforcing it shall be pursued, were it an open question, might be one of some difficulty. It was ably discussed upon general principles in a late case (Le Roy *v.* Crowninshield, 2 Mason's R. 151) before the Circuit Court, in which however it was fully conceded by the learned Judge, upon a full consideration and review of all the authorities, that it is now to be considered a settled question. A doubt was intimated in that case, whether, if the parties had remained subjects of the foreign country until the term of limitation had expired, so that the plaintiff's remedy would have been extinguished there, such a state of facts would not have presented a stronger case, and one of more serious difficulty. Such was the case in the present instance. But we think it sufficient to advert to a well-settled rule, in the construction of the statute of limitations, to shew that this circumstance can make no difference. The rule is this, that where the statute has begun to run, it will continue to run, notwithstanding the intervention of any impediment, which if it had existed when the cause of action accrued, would have prevented the operation of the statute. For instance, if this action accrued in Nova Scotia in 1821, and the plaintiff or defendant had left that country in 1825, within six years, in 1828, after the lapse of six years the action would be as effectually barred, and the remedy extinguished there, as if both had continued to reside in Halifax down to the same period. So that when the parties met here in 1829, so far as the laws of that country, by taking away all legal remedy, could affect it, the debt was extinguished, and that equally whether they had both remained under the jurisdiction of those laws till the time of limitation had elapsed, or whether either or both had previously left it. The authorities referred to, therefore, must be held applicable to a case where both parties were subject to the jurisdiction of a foreign state, when the bar arising from its statute of limitations attached. The same conclusion results from the reason upon which these cases proceed, which is, that statutes of limitation affect only the time within which a legal remedy must be pursued, and do not affect the nature, validity, or construction of the contract. This reason, whether well founded or not, applies equally to cases where the term of limitation has elapsed, when the parties leave the foreign State, as to those where it has only begun to run before they have left the State, and elapses afterwards." But see Don *v.* Lippmann, 5 Clark & Finnell. R. 1, 15—17.

Præscriptio jurium et actionum, propter absentiam non interrupta) ita generaliter definiendum existimo, illius loci leges in restitutione faciendâ attendendas esse, secundum cujus loci leges impleta summo jure fuit per absentiam Usucapio vel Præscriptio. Quid enim, obsecro, aut justius aut æquius, quam ut ex eorundem legislatorum præscripto remedium adversus læsionem indulgeatur, ex quorum præscripto et summo jure primitus læsio nata fuit? Quibus consequens est, ut, si immobilium rerum Usucapio impleta sit, serventur in restitutione faciendâ jura regionis, in quâ immobiles res sitæ sunt: adeoque, ut in amittendo, sic et in recuperando dominio, regantur immobilia ex sitûs sui lege, juxta vulgatam regulam in materiâ statutariâ. Sin mobilia usucapta fuerint, in restitutione magis erit, ut serventur leges domicilii ejus, qui per usucapionem dominium amiserat; ut ita mobilia, quæ censentur illic esse, ubi domicilium fovet dominus, ex lege domicilii redeant, uti fuerant amissa. Sed si actiones in personam temporis lapsu, per absentiam contingente, extinctæ sint; probabilius fuerit, in illis restituendis ob justam absentiæ causam spectandum esse jus loci, in quo debitor commoratur, contra quem restitutio petitur: cum etiam ex istius loci lege Præscriptio implenda fuerit[1].

---

[1] J. Voet, Ad Pand. lib. 4, tit. 1, § 29, p. 241; Henry on Foreign Law, pp. 56, 59.

CHAPTER XV.

FOREIGN JUDGMENTS.

§ 584. We come, in the next place, to the consideration of foreign judgments, or of the force and effect of foreign sentences, *exceptio rei judicatæ*. As to the effect to be given to foreign judgments, there has been much diversity of practice as well as of opinion among jurists and nations. We do not speak here of cases where the point was, whether the Court pronouncing the judgment had jurisdiction or not; but, assuming the jurisdiction to be unquestionable, what force and effect ought to be given to such judgment? Ought it to be held conclusive upon the parties? or ought it to be open to impeachment by new evidence, or to be re-examined upon the original merits? The subject may be considered in two general aspects: first, in regard to judgments *in rem;* and secondly, in regard to judgments *in personam*[1]. The latter is again divisible into several heads: first, where the judgment is set up by way of defence to a suit in a foreign tribunal; and secondly, where the judgment is sought to be enforced in a foreign tribunal against the original defendant or his property; and thirdly, where the judgment is between subjects, or between fo-

---

[1] Burgundus divides judgments (sententiæ) into three classes: (1.) in rem; (2.) in personam; (3.) mixed, in rem et in personam. "Omnium condemnationum summa divisio, pariter in tria genera deducitur. Aut enim in rem, aut in personam, aut in utramque concipiuntur. In rem, quoties alicui res asseritur, hoc est ejus esse dicitur, vel jure creditoris, aut alio modo possidenda datur. In personam, si condemnetur ad aliquid dandum aut patiendum, faciendum aut non faciendum, vel si personæ statum afficiat. In utramque, si et res et personæ simul in condemnationem veniant." Burgundus, Tract. 3, n. 1, 2, pp. 84, 85; 1 Boullenois, Observ. 25, p. 602.

reigners, or between foreigners and subjects. These divisions will in some degree require a separate examination[1].

§ 585. Vattel has said with great force, that it is the province of every sovereignty to administer justice in all places within its own territory and under its own jurisdiction, to take cognizance of crimes committed there, and of the controversies that arise within it. Other nations ought to respect this right; and as the administration of justice necessarily requires that every definitive sentence regularly pronounced, be esteemed just, and executed as such; when once a cause in which foreigners are interested, has been decided in form, the sovereign of the defendants ought not to hear their complaints. To undertake to examine the justice of a definitive sentence, is an attack upon the jurisdiction of the sovereign who has passed it[2]. Hence Vattel deduces the general rule, that in consequence of this right of jurisdiction, the decision made by the judge of the place within the extent of his authority, ought to be respected, and to take effect even in foreign countries[3].

§ 586. Reasonable as this doctrine seems to be, it is difficult to affirm that it has obtained the general assent of civilized nations in modern times in their intercourse with each other. The support which it has received from the common law, is far more extensive and uniform than it has received in the jurisprudence of continental Europe. In order, however, to found a proper ground of recognition of any foreign judgment in another country, it is indispensable to establish, that the Court pronouncing judgment should have a lawful jurisdiction over the cause, over the thing, and over the parties[4]. If the jurisdiction fails as to either, it is, (as we have already seen), treated as a mere nullity, having no obligation, and entitled to no respect beyond the

---

[1] See on this subject, 3 Burge, Comm. on Col. and For. Law, pt. 2, ch. 24, pp. 1014—1080.

[2] Vattel, b. 2, ch. 7, § 84.

[3] Id. § 85.

[4] See 1 Boullenois, Observ. 25, pp. 618—620.

domestic tribunals [1]. And this is equally true, whether the proceedings be *in rem*, or *in personam*, or *in rem* and also *in personam* [2].

§ 587. This subject was a good deal considered in a celebrated case, (a proceeding *in rem*), before the Supreme Court of the United States, where the principal point was, whether there had been a change of the ownership of the property by the sentence of a foreign court in a suit there pending *in rem*. Upon that occasion Mr. Chief Justice Marshall, in delivering the opinion of the Court, used the following language: "The power of the (foreign) Court, then, is of necessity examinable to a certain extent by that tribunal which is compelled to decide whether its sentence has changed the right of property. The power under which it acts must be looked into; and its authority to decide questions which it professes to decide, must be considered.

§ 588. "But although the general power, by which a Court takes jurisdiction of causes must be inspected, in order to determine whether it may rightfully do what it professes to do, it is still a question of serious difficulty; whether the situation of the particular thing on which the sentence has passed, may be inquired into for the purpose of deciding whether that thing was in a state which subjected it to the jurisdiction of the Court passing the sentence. For example, in every case of a foreign sentence condemning a vessel as prize of war, the authority of the tribunal to act as a prize court must be examinable. Is the question, whether the vessel condemned was in a situation to subject her to the jurisdiction of that court, also examinable? This question, in the opinion of the Court, must be answered in the affirmative.

---

1 Ante, § 539, 546, 547; Buchanan *v.* Rucker, 9 East, R. 192; Bissell *v.* Briggs, 9 Mass. R. 462; Shumway *v.* Stillman, 6 Wend. R. 447; Don *v.* Lippmann, 5 Clark & Finnell. 1, 20, 21; 4 Cowen, R. 524, n.; 1 Starkie on Evid. pt. 2, § 68, p. 214; Henry on Foreign Law, 18, n.; Id. 23; Id. 73; Cavan *v.* Stuart, 1 Stark. 525; Hall *v.* Williams, 6 Pick. 232; Wood *v.* Tremere, 6 Pick. R. 354.

2 Ibid.

§ 589. "Upon principle, it would seem that the operation of every judgment must depend on the power of the Court to render that judgment; or, in other words, on its jurisdiction over the subject-matter which it has determined. In some cases, that jurisdiction unquestionably depends as well on the state of the thing as on the constitution of the Court. If by any means whatever a prize court should be induced to condemn, as prize of war, a vessel which was never captured, it could not be contended that this condemnation operated a change of property. Upon principle, then, it would seem, that, to a certain extent, the capacity of the Court to act upon the thing condemned, arising from its being within or without their jurisdiction as well as the constitution of the Court, may be considered by that tribunal which is to decide on the effect of the sentence.

§ 590. "Passing from principle to authority, we find, that in the Courts of England, whose decisions are particularly mentioned, because we are best acquainted with them, and because, as is believed, they give to foreign sentences as full effect as are given to them in any part of the civilized world, the position, that the sentence of a foreign Court is conclusive with respect to what it professes to decide, is uniformly qualified with the limitation, that it has, in the given case, jurisdiction of the subject-matter[1]."

§ 591. Let us now consider the operation of judgments in the different classes of cases which have been already adverted to. And first, in relation to judgments *in rem.* If the matter in controversy is land, or other immovable property, the judgment pronounced in the *forum rei sitæ* is held to be of universal obligation as to all the matters of right and title which it professes to decide in relation thereto[2]. This results from the very nature of the case; for no other Court can have a competent jurisdiction to inquire into, or settle such right or title. By the general consent of nations,

---

[1] Rose *v.* Himely, 4 Cranch, 269, 270.

[2] Ante, § 532, 545, 551.

therefore, in cases of immovables, the judgment of the *forum rei sitæ* is held absolutely conclusive[1]. *Immobilia ejus jurisdictionis esse reputantur, ubi sita sunt*[2]. On the other hand, a judgment in any foreign country, touching such immovables, will be held of no obligation. John Voet is explicit on this point: *Licet autem regulariter judex requisitus non cognoscat de justitiâ sententiæ per alterum judicem latæ, nec eam ad examen penitius revocet, sed pro justitiâ ejus ac æquitate præsumat. Tamen si animadvertat, eam directo contra sui territorii statuta latam esse circa res immobiles, in suo territorio sitas, eandem non exsequitur; uti nec, si alias absque prolixâ causæ cognitione constet, sententiam nullam esse*[3].

§ 592. The same principle is applied to all other cases of proceedings *in rem*, against movable property within the jurisdiction of the Court pronouncing the judgment[4]. Whatever the Court settles as to the right or title, or whatever disposition it makes of the property by sale, revendication, transfer, or other act, will be held valid in every other country where the same question comes directly or indirectly in judgment before any other foreign tribunal. This is very familiarly known in the cases of proceedings *in rem* in foreign Courts of Admiralty, whether they are causes of prize, or of bottomry, or of salvage, or of forfeiture, or of any the like nature, over which such Courts have a rightful jurisdiction, founded on the actual or constructive possession of the subject-matter (*res*)[5]. The same rule is applied to other courts

---

[1] 1 Boullenois, Observ. 25, pp. 618, 619, 623.

[2] Id. p. 619; 1 Hertii, Opera, De Collis, § 4, n. 73, pp. 153, 154, (edit. 1737); Id. p. 216, (edit. 1716.) See also J. Voet, Ad Pand. tom. 1, lib. 1, tit. 4, ps. 2, n. 11, p. 44, and Ante, § 362, n. 3.

[3] J. Voet, Ad Pand. tom. 2, lib. 42, tit. 1, n. 41, p. 788.

[4] See Kaims on Equity, b. 3, ch. 8, § 4.

[5] Croudson *v.* Leonard, 4 Cranch, 434; Williams *v.* Armroyd, 7 Cranch, R. 423; Rose *v.* Himley, 4 Cranch, 241; Hudson *v.* Guestier, 4 Cranch, 293; The Mary, 9 Cranch, 126, 142—146; 1 Starkie on Evidence, pt. 2, § 81, p. 238, &c.; Marshall on Insur. b. 1, ch. 9, § 6, pp. 412, 435; Cases cited in 4 Cowen, R. 520, n. 3; Grant *v.* M'Lachlin, 4 John. R. 34; Peters *v.* The Warren Insur. Co. 3 Sumner, Rep. 389; S. C. 1 Chand. Law Re-

proceeding *in rem*, such as to the Court of Exchequer in England, and to other Courts exercising a like jurisdiction *in rem* upon seizures[1]. And in cases of this sort it is wholly immaterial whether the judgment be of acquittal or of condemnation. In both cases it is equally conclusive[2]. But the doctrine, however, is always to be understood with this limitation, that the judgment has been obtained *bonâ fide* and without fraud; for if fraud has intervened, it will doubtless avoid the force and validity of the sentence[3]. So it must appear, that there have been regular proceedings to found the judgment or decree; and that the parties in interest *in rem* have had notice, or an opportunity to appear and defend their interests, either personally or by their proper representatives, before it was pronounced; for the common justice of all nations requires that no condemnation should be pronounced before the party has an opportunity to be heard[4].

§ 592 *a*. Proceedings also by creditors against the personal property of their debtor in the hands of third persons, or against debts due to him by such third persons, (commonly called the process of foreign attachment or garnishment, or trustee process), are also treated as in some sense proceedings *in rem*, and are deemed entitled to the same

---

porter, 222; Blad *v.* Bamfield, 3 Swanst. R. 604, 605; Bradstreet *v.* Neptune Insur. Co. 2 Chand. Law Rep. 262, 264, 265; S. C. 3 Sumner, Rep. 600; Magoun *v.* New England Insur. Co. 3 Chand. Law Rep. 127, 130, 131.

1 Ibid. and Starkie on Evid. pt. 2, § 67, 80, 81, p. 336; Gelston *v.* Hoyt, 3 Wheaton, R. 246; Williams *v.* Armroyd, 7 Cranch, 423.

2 Ibid.

3 See Post, § 597; Duchess of Kingston's Case, 11 State Trials, pp. 261, 262; S. C. 20 Howell, State Trials, p. 355; Id. p. 538, the opinion of the Judges; Bradstreet *v.* The Neptune Insur. Co. 2 Chand. Law Rep. 262, 264, 265; S. C. 3 Sumner, R. 600; Magoun *v.* The New England Insur. Co. 3 Chand. Law Rep. 127, 130, 131.

4 Sawyer *v.* Maine Fire and Mar. Insur. Co. 12 Mass. R. 291; Bradstreet *v.* The Neptune Insur. Co. 2 Chand. Law Rep. 263; S. C. 3 Sumner, R. 600; Magoun *v.* New England Insur. Co. 3 Chand. Law Rep. 127, 130.

consideration[1]. But in this last class of cases we are especially to bear in mind, that to make any judgment effectual the Court must possess and exercise a rightful jurisdiction over the *res*, and also over the person, at least so far as the *res* is concerned, otherwise it will be disregarded. And if the jurisdiction over the *res* be well founded, but not over the person, except as to the *res*, the judgment will not be either conclusive or binding upon the party *in personam*, although it may be *in rem*[2].

§ 593. In all these cases the same principle prevails, that the judgment, acting *in rem*, shall be held conclusive upon the title and transfer and disposition of the property itself, in whatever place the same property may afterwards be found, and by whomsoever the latter may be questioned; and whether it be directly or incidentally brought in ques-

---

1 See cases cited in 4 Cowen, R. 520, 521, n.; Ante, § 549; Holmes *v.* Remsen, 20 John. R. 229; Hull *v.* Blake, 13 Mass. R. 153; M'Daniel *v.* Hughes, 3 East, R. 366; Phillips *v.* Hunter, 2 H. Black, 402, 410.

2 Ante, 549, and note; Bissell *v.* Briggs, 9 Mass. R. 468. See also 3 Burge, Comm. on Col. and For. Law, pt. 2, ch. 24, pp. 1014—1019.—Some very important questions may arise in cases of foreign attachment or garnishment. Suppose A., a creditor of B., should bring a suit by foreign attachment or garnishment in a foreign country against C., as garnishee of the property or credits of B., will a judgment rendered in that suit conclude D., who claims the same property or credit by a prior title in another suit therefor in the same country, or in another country? Will it make any difference, that A., before obtaining his judgment, had notice of D.'s claim and right? Will it make any difference, that D. might by the lex fori have intervened in the first suit to vindicate his title, and to support it, if he was not domiciled in the country at the time, although he had notice of the same suit? Another case may be put involving similar considerations. Suppose a suit is brought in a foreign country by A. against B. to recover property there situate, to which C., who is domiciled in a foreign country, also claims title; and by the law of the country where the suit is brought, C. might intervene for his title; but he does not, although he has notice of the suit. If A. obtains judgment in the suit for the property against B., will that judgment bind C. in the courts of that country in a subsequent suit brought there by C. against A. for the same property? If it will bind him there, will it bind him in a suit brought in the country of his own domicil, or in another foreign country? These questions are propounded for the consideration of the learned reader, without any attempt to discuss or solve them.

tion. But it is not so universally settled, that the judgment is conclusive of all the points which are incidentally disposed of by the judgment, or of the facts or allegations upon which it professes to be founded. In this respect different rules are adopted by different States, both in Europe and in America. In England such judgments are held conclusive, not only *in rem*, but also as to all the points and facts which they professedly or incidentally decide[1]. In some of the American States the same doctrine prevails. While in other American States the judgments are held conclusive only *in rem*, and may be controverted as to all the incidental grounds and facts on which they profess to be founded[2].

§ 594. A similar doctrine has been contended for, and in many cases successfully, in favour of sentences of a peculiar character; such as those which touch the general capacity of persons, and those which concern marriage and divorce. Thus, foreign jurists strongly contend, that the decree of a foreign Court, declaring the state (*status*) of a person, and placing him as an idiot, or minor, or prodigal under guardianship, ought to be deemed of universal authority and obligation[3]. And so it ought, and doubtless would be deemed,

---

1 In Blad *v.* Bamfield, decided by Lord Nottingham, and reported in 3 Swanst. R. 604, a perpetual injunction was awarded to restrain certain suits of trespass and trover for seizing the goods of the defendant (Bamfield) for trading in Ireland, contrary to certain privileges granted to the plaintiff and others. The property was seized and condemned in the Danish Courts; Lord Nottingham held the sentence conclusive against the suits, and awarded the injunction accordingly.

2 See 4 Cowen, R. 522, n. and cases cited; Vandenheuvel *v.* U. Insur. Co. 2 Cain. Cases in Err. 217; 2 John. Cases, 451; Id. 481; Robinson *v.* Jones, 8 Mass. R. 536; Maley *v.* Shattuck, 3 Cranch, 488; 2 Kent, Comm. Lect. 37, pp. 120, 121, 3rd edit. and cases there cited; Tarleton *v.* Tarleton, 4 M. & Selw. 20. See Peters *v.* Warren Insur. Co. 3 Sumner, R. p. 389; S.C. 1 Chand. Law Reporter, 281; Gelston *v.* Hoyt, 3 Wheat. R. 246.

3 1 Boullenois, Observ. 25, p. 603, Burgundus's opinion. Indeed Burgundus seems to have been of opinion, that the only judgments which ought to have any force or operation extra-territorially, are those which respect the state and condition of persons. Sed quoniam omnis propositi nostri summa eò spectat, ut sciatur, utrùm suum sententia egrediatur territorium, excutia-

in regard to all acts done, and authority exercised within the jurisdiction of the sovereign, whose tribunals have pronounced the sentence. But the necessity of giving it universal effect, so as to make the guardianship operative and effectual in all other countries, in regard to the person and his property in those countries, is not so obvious. But we have already had occasion to consider this subject in another place [1].

§ 595. As to sentences confirming marriages, or granting divorces, they may well stand upon a distinct ground. If they are pronounced by competent tribunals in regard to persons within the jurisdiction, there is great reason to say, that they ought to be held of universal conclusiveness, force, and effect, in all other countries. Lord Hardwicke is reported to have said in a case before him, in which the validity of a marriage in France was asserted to have been established by the sentence of a Court in France, having the proper jurisdiction thereof; "It is true, that if so, it is conclusive, whether in a foreign Court or not, from the law of nations in such cases; otherwise the rights of mankind would be very precarious [2]."

§ 596. On the other hand Lord Stowell, in a case before him, in which the validity of a foreign sentence of divorce was set up as a bar to proceedings in the English Ecclesiastical Courts between the same parties, said: "Something has been said on the doctrine of law, regarding the respect due to foreign judgments; and undoubtedly a sentence of separation in a proper Court for adultery would be entitled to credit and attention in this Court. But I think the conclusion is carried too far, when it is said that a sentence of

---

mus itaque naturam singularum. Nam mihi sola (says he) illa sententia, quæ de statu personæ fertur, explicare vires extra territorii limites videtur. Burgundus, Tract. 3, n. 11, 12, p. 90; 1 Boullenois, Observ. 25, p. 603.

[1] Ante, § 495—504.

[2] Roast *v.* Garvin, 1 Ves. 157. See also a case in the time of Charles II., cited by Lord Hardwicke in Boucher *v.* Lawson, Cas. T. Hard. 89; and also in Kennedy *v.* Earl of Cassilis, 2 Swanst. R. 326, note.

nullity of marriage is necessarily and universally binding on other countries. Adultery and its proofs are nearly the same in all countries. The validity of marriage, however, must depend, in a great degree, on the local regulations of the country where it is celebrated. A sentence of nullity of marriage, therefore, in the country where it was solemnized, would carry with it great authority in this country. But I am not prepared to say that a judgment of a third country on the validity of a marriage not within its territories, nor had between subjects of that country, would be universally binding. For instance, the marriage alleged by the husband, is a French marriage; a French judgment on that marriage would have been of considerable weight; but it does not follow that the judgment of a Court at Brussels, on a marriage in France, would have the same authority, much less on a marriage celebrated here in England. Had there been a sentence against the wife for adultery in Brabant, it might have prevented her from proceeding with any effect against her husband here; but no such sentence anywhere appears [1]."

§ 597. This subject, however, has already been considered at large in the preceding discussions relative to divorces. The result of the doctrine therein stated is, that the English Courts seem not to be disposed to admit, that any valid sentence of divorce can be pronounced in any foreign country, which shall amount to the dissolution of a marriage celebrated in England between English subjects, at least so far as such a divorce is to have any force or operation in England. At the same time it may be remarked, that the doctrine, so apparently held, has undergone very elaborate discussions at a very recent period; and the grounds upon which it rests have been greatly shaken [2]. But in Scotland, and in America, a different doctrine is maintained; and it

---

[1] Sinclair *v.* Sinclair, 1 Hagg. Consist. Rep. 297. See also Scrimshire *v.* Scrimshire, 2 Hagg. Consist. Rep. 397, 410.

[2] Ante, § 215, 225—228.

is firmly held, that a sentence of divorce pronounced between parties actually domiciled in the country, whether natives or foreigners, by a competent tribunal, having jurisdiction over the case, is valid, and ought to be held everywhere a complete dissolution of the marriage, in whatever country it may have been originally celebrated[1]. Of course we are to understand that the sentence is obtained *bonâ fide* and without fraud; for fraud in this case, as in other cases, will vitiate any judgment, however well founded in point of jurisdiction[2].

§ 598. In the next place, as to judgments *in personam*. And here a distinction is commonly taken between suits brought by a party to enforce a foreign judgment, and suits brought against a party who sets up a foreign judgment in bar of the suit by way of defence. In the former case it is often urged that no sovereign is bound *jure gentium* to execute any foreign judgment within his dominions; and, therefore, if execution of it is sought in his dominions, he is at liberty to examine into the merits of the judgment, and to refuse to give effect to it, if upon such examination it should appear unjust and unfounded. He acts in executing it upon the principles of comity; and has, therefore, a right to prescribe the terms and limits of that comity[3]. But it is otherwise, (it is said), where the defendant sets up a foreign judgment as a bar to proceedings; for if it has been pronounced by a competent tribunal, and carried into effect, the losing party has no right to institute a new suit else-

---

1 See Ante, § 212, 215—230.

2 See Starkie on Evid. pt. 2, § 77, 79, 83; Duchess of Kingston's case, 11 State Trials, 261, 262; S. C. 20 Howell, State Trials, 355, and the opinion of the Judges; Id. p. 538, note. See also Mr. Hargrave's learned argument in this case, as to the conclusiveness of res adjudicata, especially in cases of jactitation of marriage and divorce, and of the effect of fraud in procuring such sentences. Harg. Law Tracts, 449, 479, 483. See also Bowles *v.* Orr, 1 Younge & Coll. 464.

3 2 Kent, Comm. Lect. 37, pp. 119, 120, 3rd edit.; and the cases there cited. See also 1 Boullenois, Observ. 25, p. 601; Post, § 611—618.

where, and thus to bring the matter again into controversy; and the other party is not to lose the protection which the foreign judgment gave him. It is then *res judicata*, which ought to be received as conclusive evidence of right; and the *exceptio rei judicatæ*, under such circumstances, is entitled to universal conclusiveness and respect [1]. This distinction has been very frequently recognised as having a just foundation in international justice [2].

§ 599. Lord Chief Justice Eyre has stated it with his usual force in an elaborate judgment. "If we had the means," said he, "we could not examine a judgment of a Court in a foreign State brought before us in this manner, (that is, by the defendant as a bar). It is in one way only that the sentence or judgment of the Court of a foreign State is examinable in our Courts, and that is, when the party who claims the benefit of it applies to our Courts to enforce it. When it is thus voluntarily submitted to our jurisdiction we treat it not as obligatory to the extent to which it would be obligatory, perhaps, in the country in which it was pronounced, nor as obligatory to the extent to which, by our law, sentences and judgments are obligatory; not as conclusive, but as matter *in pais;* as a consideration *primâ facie* sufficient to raise a promise. We examine it as we do all other considerations of promises; and for that purpose we receive evidence of what the law of the foreign State is, and whether the judgment is warranted by that law. In all other cases we give entire faith and credit to the sentences of foreign Courts, and consider them as conclusive upon us [3]." The same distinction is found applied in the same manner in the jurisprudence of Scotland [4].

§ 599 *a*. The view which was thus taken by Lord Chief

---

1 2 Kent, Comm. Lect. 37, pp. 119, 120, 3rd edit.; and cases there cited.

2 Id. and cases there cited; Burrows *v.* Jemino, 2 Str. R. 733; S. C. cited cas. T. Hard. 87; Boucher *v.* Lawson, cas. T. Hard. 89; 2 Swanst. R. 326, note; Tarleton *v.* Tarleton, 4 M. & Selw. 20; Taylor *v.* Phelps, 1 Gill & John. R. 492; Griswold *v.* Pitcairn, 4 Connect. R. 85.

3 Phillips *v.* Hunter, 2 H. Black. R. 410.

4 Erskine, Inst. b. 4, tit. 3, § 4.

Justice Eyre does not appear to have been acted upon to its full extent in subsequent times. It would seem a natural result from that view that if a suit was brought for the same cause of action in an English Court, which had already been decided in favour of either party in a foreign Court of competent jurisdiction, and was final and conclusive there, that judgment might be well pleaded in bar of the new suit upon the original cause of action, and would, if *bonâ fide*, be conclusive. It may be doubted, however, whether the same doctrine is at present entertained in England. In a recent case the Court seem to have thought, that, if a plaintiff has recovered judgment in a foreign country upon any original cause of action, he may, notwithstanding, sue in England upon that original cause of action, or may sue upon the judgment there obtained, at his option; because the original cause of action is not merged in such a judgment[1]. Now, if the original cause of action is not merged in a case where the judgment is in favour of the plaintiff, it seems difficult to assert that it is merged by a judgment in the foreign Court in favour of the defendant.

§ 600. Lord Kaims has marked out and supported another distinction between suits sustaining and suits dismissing a claim. "In the last place," says he, "come foreign decrees, which are of two kinds, one sustaining the claim, and one dismissing it. A foreign decree sustaining the claim is not one of those universal titles which ought to be made effectual everywhere. It is a title that depends on the authority of the Court whence it issued, and, therefore, has no coercive authority *extra territorium*. And yet, as it would be hard to oblige the person, who claims on a decree, to bring a new action against his party in every country to

---

[1] Smith *v.* Nicolls, 5 Bing. N. Cases, 208, 221—224. There were peculiar circumstances in the case, and, therefore, the point was not positively decided. The same doctrine seems to have been asserted in Hall *v.* Odber, 11 East, R. 118; but there also it was not directly decided. But see Plummer *v.* Woodhouse, 4 Barn. & Cresw. R. 625; Ante, § 547, note; Becquet *v.* M'Carthy, 2 Barn. & Adol. 951; Ante, § 548 *a*.

which he may retire; therefore, common utility, as well as regard to a sister Court, have established a rule among all civilized nations, that a foreign decree shall be put in execution, unless some good exception be opposed to it in law or in equity; which is making no wider step in favour of the decree than to presume it just, till the contrary be proved. But this includes not a decree decerning for a penalty, because no Court reckons itself bound to punish, or to concur in punishing, any delict committed *extra territorium.*"

§ 601. "A foreign decree, which, by dismissing the claim, affords an *exceptio rei judicatæ* against it, enjoys a more extensive privilege. We not only presume it to be just, but will not admit any evidence of its being unjust. The reasons follow. A decreet-arbitral is final by mutual consent. A judgment-condemnator ought not to be final against the defendant because he gave no consent. But a decreet-absolvitur ought to be final against the plaintiff, because the judge was chosen by himself; with respect to him, at least, it is equivalent to a decreet-arbitral. Public utility affords another argument extremely cogent. There is nothing more hurtful to society than that lawsuits be perpetual. In every lawsuit there ought to be a *ne plus ultra;* some step ought to be ultimate; and a decree dismissing a claim is in its nature ultimate. Add a consideration, that regards the nature and constitution of a Court of justice. A decree dismissing a claim may, it is true, be unjust, as well as a decree sustaining it. But they differ widely in one capital point; in declining to give redress against a decree dismissing a claim the Court is not guilty of authorizing injustice, even supposing the decree to be unjust; the utmost that can be said is, that the Court forbears to interpose in behalf of justice. But such forbearance, instead of being faulty, is highly meritorious in every case where private justice clashes with public utility. The case is very different with respect to a decree of the other kind; for, to award execution upon a foreign decree, without admitting any objection against it, would be, for aught the Court can know, to support and promote injustice. A Court, as well as an individual, may, in certain circumstances, have reason to forbear acting or executing their office; but, the doing injustice, or the supporting it, cannot be justified in any circumstances[1]."

§ 602. It does not appear that this distinction of Lord Kaims, between judgments sustaining suits, and judgments dismissing them, has been recognised in the common law[2]. And there seems quite as much reason that a defendant should be protected against a new litigation, after there has been a final sentence in his favour, as there is, that a plaintiff should be protected in the enjoyment of any right which is established by a sentence in his favour. The sentence for the defendant may, in its legal operation, as completely establish a right in him, or as completely establish the non-existence of any right in the plaintiff, as the contrary sentence would establish an adverse right in the plaintiff, and the non-existence of any repugnant right in the defendant.

§ 603. In the next place, as to judgments *in personam*, which are sought to be enforced by a suit in a foreign tribunal. There has certainly been no inconsiderable fluctuation of opinion in the English courts upon this subject. It is admitted on all sides, that in such cases, the foreign judgments are *primâ facie* evidence to sustain the action, and are to be deemed right until the contrary is established[3]; and of course they may be avoided, if they are founded in fraud, or are pronounced by a Court not having any competent

---

1 2 Kaims on Equity, p. 365, 3rd edit. 1778.

2 See the cases cited in Starkie on Evid. pt. 2, § 80; Hoyt *v.* Gelston, 13 John. R. 561; S. C. 3 Wheat. R. 246; The Bennett, 1 Dodson, R. 175, 180.

3 See Walker *v.* Witter, Doug. R. 1, and cases there cited; Arnold *v.* Redfern, 3 Bing. R. 353; Sinclair *v.* Fraser, cited Doug. R. 4, 5, note; Houlditch *v.* Donegal, 2 Clark & Finnell. R. 470; S. C. 8 Bligh, R. 301; Don *v.* Lippmann, 5 Clark & Finnell. 1, 19, 20; Price *v.* Dewhurst, 8 Sim. R. 279; Alivon *v.* Furnival, 1 Cromp. Mees. & Rosc. 277; Hall *v.* Odber, 11 East, R. 118; Ripple *v.* Ripple, 1 Rawle, R. 386.

jurisdiction over the cause[1]. But the question is, whether they are to be deemed conclusive, or whether the defendant is at liberty to go at large into the original merits, to shew that the judgment ought to have been different upon the merits, although obtained *bonâ fide*. If the latter course be the correct one, then a still more embarrassing consideration is, to what extent, and in what manner, the original merits can be properly inquired into.

§ 604. Lord Nottingham, in a case where an attempt was made to examine a foreign sentence of divorce in Savoy, in the reign of Charles the Second, held, that it was conclusive, and its merits not examinable. "We know not," said he, "the laws of Savoy. So, if we did, we have no power to judge by them. And, therefore, it is against the law of nations not to give credit to the sentences of foreign countries till they are reversed by the law, and according to the form of those countries wherein they were given. For what right hath one kingdom to reverse the judgment of another? And how can we refuse to let a sentence take place, until it be reversed? And what confusion would follow in Christendom, if they should serve us so abroad, and give no credit to our sentences[2]." Lord Hardwicke manifestly held the same opinion, saying: "That where any Court, foreign or domestic, that has the proper jurisdiction of the cases, makes the determination, it is conclusive to all other Courts[3]."

§ 605. On the other hand, Lord Mansfield thought, that foreign judgments gave a ground of action, but that they were examinable[4]. The same doctrine was held by Lord

---

[1] See Bowles *v.* Orr, 1 Younge & Coll. 464; Ante, § 544—550; Ferguson *v.* Mahon, 3 Perry & Dav. 143; Price *v.* Dewhurst, 8 Simons, R. 279, 302; Don. *v.* Lippmann, 5 Clark & Finnell. R. 1, 19—21.

[2] Kennedy *v.* Earl of Cassilis, 2 Swanst. R. note, 326, 327.

[3] Boucher *v.* Lawson, Cas. T. Hard. 89. See also Roach *v.* Garvan, 1 Ves. 157.

[4] Walker *v.* Witter, Doug. 1; Id. 6, note 3; Herbert *v.* Cooke, Willes, R. 36, note; S. P. Hall *v.* Odber, 11 East, R. 118; B. P. Bayley *v.* Edwards, 3 Swanst. R. 703, 711, 712.

Chief Baron Eyre[1] and Mr. Justice Buller[2], the latter relying upon a decision of the House of Lords, as giving the true line of distinction between foreign and domestic judgments. In that case the House of Lords reversed a decision of the Court of Session of Scotland, in which the latter Court held the plaintiff bound in a suit upon a foreign judgment, to prove before the Court the general nature and extent of the demand on which the judgment had been obtained. The reversal expressly declared, that the judgment ought to be received as evidence, *primâ facie,* of the debt; and that it lay upon the defendant to impeach the justice thereof, or to shew the same to have been irregularly, or wrongfully obtained[3]. But it may be remarked of this last decision, that it does not go to the extent of establishing the doctrine, that the merits of the judgments *ab origine* are re-examinable *de novo;* but only that its justice may be impeached, or its irregularity or fraud shewn[4].

§ 606. Lord Kenyon seems clearly to have been of a different opinion, and expressed serious doubts, whether foreign judgments were not binding upon the parties here[5]. And Lord Ellenborough, upon an occasion in which the argument was pressed before him, that a foreign judgment was re-examinable, and that the defendant might impeach the justice of it, pithily remarked, that he thought he did not sit at *Nisi Prius* to try a writ of error upon the proceedings

---

1 Phillips *v.* Hunter, 2 H. Black. 410; Ante, § 2.

2 Galbraith *v.* Neville, cited Doug. R. 6, note 3.

3 Sinclair *v.* Fraser, Doug. R. 4, 5, note 1.

4 Ante, § 544—550, 603.—In Alivon *v.* Furnival, 1 Cromp. Mees. & Rosc. 277, it seems to have been held, although not expressly so laid down by the Court, that the proceedings of foreign courts must be presumed to be consistent with the foreign law until the contrary is distinctly shewn; and that, therefore, the principle adopted by a foreign court in assessing damages cannot be impugned, unless contrary to natural justice, or proved not to be conformable to the foreign law. The same point was adjudged in Martin *v.* Nicolls, 3 Sim. R. 458, and Becquet *v.* M'Carthy, 2 Barn. & Adol. 951.

5 Galbraith *v.* Neville, Doug. R. 5, note 3. See also Guinness *v.* Carwell, 1 Barn. & Adol. 459.

of the Court abroad[1]. In a more recent case, Sir L. Shadwell, (the Vice-Chancellor), upon a full examination of the authorities, held the opinion, that the true doctrine was, that foreign judgments were conclusive evidence, and not re-examinable; that this was the true result of the old authorities; and therefore in a suit brought in England to enforce a foreign judgment, he held the judgment to be conclusive[2]. The present inclination of the English Courts seems to be to sustain the conclusiveness of foreign judgments[3], although certainly there yet remains no inconsiderable diversity of opinion among the learned judges of the different tribunals[4].

§ 607. It is indeed very difficult to perceive what could be done, if a different doctrine were maintainable to the full extent of opening all the evidence and merits of the cause anew, on a suit upon the foreign judgment. Some of the witnesses may be since dead; some of the vouchers may be lost or destroyed. The merits of the case, as formerly before the Court upon the whole evidence, may have been decidedly in favour of the judgment; upon a partial possession of the original evidence they may now appear otherwise. Suppose a case purely sounding in damages, such as an action for an assault, for slander, for conversion of property, for a malicious prosecution, or for a criminal conversation; is the defendant to be at liberty to re-try the

---

[1] Tarleton *v.* Tarleton, 4 Maule & Selw. 21. But see Hall *v.* Odber, 11 East, R. 118.

[2] Martin *v.* Nicolls, 3 Simons, R. 458.

[3] See Guinness *v.* Carroll, 1 Barn. & Adol. 459; Becquet *v.* M'Carthy, 2 Barn. & Adol. R. 951.

[4] In Houlditch *v.* Donegal, 8 Bligh, R. 301, 337—340, Lord Brougham held a foreign judgment to be only *primâ facie* evidence, and gave his reasons at large for that opinion. On the other hand, Sir L. Shadwell, in Martin *v.* Nicolls, held the contrary opinion, that it was conclusive; and also gave a very elaborate judgment on the point, in which he reviewed the principal authorities. Of course, the learned Judge meant to except, and did except, in a later case, Price *v.* Dewhurst, 8 Sim. R. 279, 302, judgments which were produced by fraud. See also Don. *v.* Lippmann, 5 Clark & Finnell. 1, 20, 21; Ante, § 545—550, 605; Alivon *v.* Furnival, 1 Cromp. Mees. & Rosc. 277, 284.

whole merits, and to make out, if he can, a new case upon new evidence[1]? Or is the Court to review the former decision, like a court of appeal, upon the old evidence? In a case of covenant, or of debt, or of a breach of contract, are all the circumstances to be re-examined anew? If they are, by what laws and rules of evidence and principles of justice is the validity of the original judgment to be tried? Is the Court to open the judgment, and to proceed *ex æquo et bono?* Or is it to administer strict law, and stand to the doctrines of the local administration of justice? Is it to act upon the rules of evidence acknowledged in its own jurisprudence, or upon those of the foreign jurisprudence? These and many more questions might be put to shew the intrinsic difficulties of the subject. Indeed, the rule, that the judgment is to be *primâ facie* evidence for the plaintiff, would be a mere delusion, if the defendant might still question it by opening all or any of the original merits on his side; for under such circumstances it would be equivalent to granting a new trial. It is easy to understand, that the defendant may be at liberty to impeach the original justice of the judgment, by shewing that the Court had no jurisdiction; or that he never had any notice of the suit; or that it was procured by fraud; or that upon its face it is founded in mistake; or that it is irregular, and bad by the local law *fori rei judicatæ*. To such an extent the doctrine is intelligible and practicable. Beyond this, the right to impugn the judgment is in legal effect the right to re-try the merits of the original cause at large, and to put the defendant upon proving those merits[2].

§ 608. The general doctrine maintained in the American Courts in relation to foreign judgments certainly is, that they are *primâ facie* evidence; but that they are impeach-

---

[1] See Alivon *v.* Furnival, 1 Cromp. Mees. & Rosc. 277.

[2] See Arnot *v.* Redfern, 2 Carr. & Payne, 88; S. C. 3 Bing. R. 353; Novelli *v.* Rossi, 2 Barn. & Adol. 757; Douglas *v.* Forrest, 4 Bing. R. 686; Obicini *v.* Bligh, 8 Bing. R. 335; Martina *v.* Nicolls, 3 Sim. R. 458; Alivon *v.* Furnival, 1 Cromp. Mees. & Rosc. 277. See also Starkie on Evi-

able[1]. But how far, and to what extent this doctrine is to be carried, does not seem to be definitely settled. It has been declared, that the jurisdiction of the Court, and its power over the parties and the things in controversy, may be inquired into; and that the judgment may be impeached for fraud[2]. Beyond this no definite lines have as yet been drawn.

§ 609. By the constitution of the United States it is declared, that full faith and credit shall be given in each State to the public acts, records, and judicial proceedings of every other State. And Congress, in pursuance of the power given them by the Constitution in a succeeding clause, have declared that the judgments of State Courts shall have the same faith and credit in other States, as they have in the State where they are rendered[3]. They are, therefore, put upon the same footing as domestic judgments. But this does not prevent an inquiry into the jurisdiction of the Court in which the original judgment was rendered, to pronounce the judgment, nor an inquiry into the right of the State to exercise authority over the parties, or the subject-

---

dence, pt. 2, § 67; Phillips & Amos on Evidence (8th edit.), pp. 537, 538, (1838); Buttrick *v.* Allen, 8 Mass. R. 273; Huberus, tom. 2, lib. 1, tit. 3, De Conflictu, § 6.

1 Many of the cases are collected: 2 Kent, Comm. Lect. 27, p. 118, &c., 3d edit.; in 4 Cowen, R. 520, note 3; and in Mr. Metcalf's notes to his valuable edition of Starkie on Evidence, pt. 2, § 67, 68, (edit. 1830), pp. 214—216. See also Bissell *v.* Briggs, 9 Mass. R. 462; Borden *v.* Fitch, 15 John. R. 121; Green *v.* Sarmiento, 1 Peters, Circ. R. 74; Field *v.* Gibbs, 1 Peters, Circ. R. 155; Aldrich *v.* Kinney, 4 Connect. R. 380; Shumway *v.* Stillman, 6 Wend. R. 447; Hall *v.* Williams, 6 Pick. 247; Starbuck *v.* Murray, 5 Wend. R. 148; Davis *v.* Peckars, 6 Wend. R. 327; Buttrick *v.* Allen, 8 Mass. R. 273; Pawling *v.* Bird's Ex'rs. 13 John. R. 192; Hitchcock *v.* Aicken, 1 Cain. R. 460; Warton's Dig. Judgment, I.; Bigelow's Dig. Judgment, H.; Johnson's Digest, Debt, H.; Coxe's Digest, Judgment; Hoxie *v.* Wright, 2 Vermont Rep. 263; Bellows *v.* Ingraham, 2 Vermont R. 575; Barney *v.* Patterson, 6 Harris & John. 182.

2 Ibid.

3 Constitution, Art. 3, § 4; Act of Congress of 26th May, 1790, ch. 11; 3 Story's Comm. on Constit. ch. 29, § 1297—1307.

matter, nor an inquiry, whether the judgment is founded in, and impeachable for a manifest fraud[1]. The Constitution did not mean to confer any new power upon the States; but simply to regulate the effect of their acknowledged jurisdiction over persons and things within their territory[2]. It did not make the judgments of other States domestic judgments to all intents and purposes; but only gave a general validity, faith, and credit to them as evidence. No execution can issue upon such judgments without a new suit in the tribunals of other States. And they enjoy not the right of priority, or privilege, or lien, which they have in the State where they are pronounced, but that only which the *lex fori* gives to them by its own laws in their character of foreign judgments[3].

§ 610. In the next place, as to judgments *in personam* in suits between citizens, in suits between foreigners, and in suits between citizens and foreigners. The common law recognises no distinction whatever as to the effect of foreign judgments, whether they are between citizens, or between foreigners, or between citizens and foreigners. In all cases they are deemed of equal obligation, whoever are the parties. The cases which have been already cited, refer to no such distinction; but the same rules are indiscriminately applied to all persons.

§ 611. We have hitherto been principally considering the doctrines of the common law. But it cannot be affirmed, that the same doctrines are generally maintained, either by

---

1 Taylor *v.* Bryden, 8 John R. 173.

2 See Story's Comment. on the Constit. ch. 29, § 1297—1307, and cases there cited:—Hall *v.* Williams, 6 Pick. R. 237; Bissell *v.* Briggs, 9 Mass. R. 462; Shumway *v.* Stillman, 6 Wend. R. 447; Evans *v.* Tarleton, 9 Sergt. & R. 260; Benton *v.* Burgot, 10 Sergt. & R. 240; Hancock *v.* Barrett, 1 Hall, Sup. Ct. R. 155; S. C. 2 Hall, Sup. Ct. R. 302; Wilson *v.* Niles, 2 Hall, Sup. Ct. R. 358; Hoxie *v.* Wright, 2 Vermont, R. 263; Bellows *v.* Ingraham, 2 Vermont, R. 573; Aldrich *v.* Kinney, 4 Connect. R. 380.

3 M'Elmoyle *v.* Cohen, 13 Peters, R. 312, 328, 329; Ante, § 582 *a*, note.

foreign Courts, or by foreign jurists. Many foreign jurists contend for the doctrine of Vattel, that the judgments of a foreign competent tribunal are to be held of equal validity in every other country[1]. Thus, Huberus lays down the rule: *Cuncta negotia et acta, tam in judicio quam extra judicium, seu mortis causâ, sive inter vivos, secundum jus certi loci rite celebrata, valent, etiam ubi diversa juris observatio viget, ac ubi sic inita, quemadmodum facta sunt, non valerunt*[2]. And again: *Similem usum habet hæc observatio in rebus judicatis. Sententia in aliquo loco pronunciata, vel delicti venia, ab eo, qui jurisdictionem illam habet, data, ubique habet effectum; nec fas est alterius Reipublicæ magistratibus, Reum alibi absolutum, veniave donatum, licet absque justa causa persequi, aut iterum permittere recusandum, &c. Idem obtinet in sententiis rerum civilium*[3]. The same doctrine seems equally well founded in the expressive language of the Roman law. *Res judicata pro veritate accipitur*[4].

§ 612. D'Argentré holds the like opinion. *Nam de omni personali negotio, judicis ejus cognitionem esse, cui persona subsit, sic, ut quocunque persona abeat, id jus sit, quod ille statuerit*[5]. Gaill asserts, that any other rule would involve absurdity. *Absurdum enim fore, si post sententiam definitivam alia esset ferenda sententia, et processum in infinitum extrahi litemque ex lite oriri debere*[6]. John Voet maintains a similar opinion in all suits except those respecting immovables. *Licet autem regulariter Judex requisitus non cognoscat de justitiâ sententiæ per alterum*

1 Henry on Foreign Law, 75, 76.

2 Huberus, tom. 2, lib. 1, tit. 3, De Conflict. Leg. § 3.

3 Idem, § 6.

4 Dig. lib. 1, tit. 5, l. 25.

5 D'Argentr. Comm. ad Leg. Briton. art. 218, Gloss. 6, n. 47, p. 665, (edit. 1640); Henry on Foreign Law, p. 74; 1 Boullenois, Observ. 25, p. 605.

6 Henry on Foreign Law, pp. 74, 75; Gaill, Pract. Observ. lib. 1, Observ. 113, n. 11, p. 201; 1 Boullenois, Observ. 25, pp. 605, 606.—There is an error in the reference of Boullenois to Gaill. It should be to Observ. 113, instead of 123.

Judicem latæ, nec eam ad examen penitius revocet; sed pro justitia ejus ex æquitate præsumat; tamen, si animadvertat, eam directo contra sui territorii statuta latam esse circa res immobiles in suo territorio sitas, eandem non exsequetur[1].

§ 613. There are, however, other foreign jurists, who maintain a very different opinion[2]. We have already had occasion to take notice of the doctrines of Boullenois upon the right of jurisdiction[3]; and he applies them in an especial manner to the authority of foreign judgments. In regard to judgments *in rem*, or partly *in rem* and partly *in personam*, he deems the jurisdiction to belong exclusively to the tribunals of the place *rei sitæ;* and, consequently, that the judgment rendered there, ought to be of universal obligation[4]. But, in regard to judgments in personal actions, he makes the following distinctions:—If the foreign judgment is in a suit between natives of the same country in which it is pronounced, and it is rendered by a competent tribunal, in such a case it ought to be executed in every other country without any new inquiry into the merits[5]. The reason assigned is, that the judgment has emanated from a lawful authority, and has been rendered between persons who are subject to that authority; and consequently, the judgment ought not to be submitted to examination or discussion in any other tribunal, which for such purposes must be wholly incompetent. If the foreign judgment is rendered in a suit between mere strangers, who are foreigners found within the territorial authority of the Court rendering it, and the jurisdiction is rightfully exercised over the parties, in such a case the judgment is equally conclusive, and not examinable by any other tri-

---

[1] J. Voet, Ad Pand. tom. 2, lib. 42, tit. 1, n. 41, p. 788.

[2] See 1 Boullenois, Observ. 25, pp. 601—650; 3 Burge, Comm. on Col. and For. Law, pt. 2, ch. 24, p. 1050; Id. pp. 1050—1060; Id. pp. 1062—1076.

[3] Ante, § 552.

[4] 1 Boullenois, Observ. 25, pp. 618—624; Id. pp. 635, 636.

[5] 1 Boullenois, Observ. 25, pp. 603, 605.

bunal[1]. But he thinks, that the jurisdiction cannot be rightfully exercised, merely because the foreigners are there, unless they are domiciled, and have made themselves subject to the laws, or have made some contract there, or some contract to be executed there, which is the subject-matter of the suit[2]. Lastly, if the judgment is rendered in a suit between a native of the country where the judgment is pronounced and a foreigner, in such a case, if the foreigner be the plaintiff, then the judgment ought to be conclusive, and not examinable, whether the foreigner has been successful or unsuccessful in his claim; for, in such a case, the suit is brought before the proper forum, according to the maxim, *Actor sequitur forum rei*, and then, *Standum est in judicio;* and the execution of the judgment ought to be every where held perfect and entire without any new examination[3]. But if the foreigner be the defendant, and he has not entered into any contract in the place where the suit is brought, or into any contract which is to be performed there, and which is the subject-matter of the suit; in such a case the judgment is not conclusive against the defendant[4].

§ 614. Boullenois concludes his remarks upon this subject, in the following manner: "When, then, some of our authors say, that foreign judgments are not to be executed in France, and that it is necessary to commence a new action, that is true without any exception, in all matters touching the realty. It is also true in personal matters, when the defendant is a Frenchman who has not contracted in the foreign country, nor promised to pay there, nor submitted himself voluntarily to the foreign jurisdiction; for in such a case a new action should be brought, saving the

---

1 1 Boullenois, Observ. 25, pp. 606, 607.
2 1 Boullenois, Observ. 25, pp. 606—610.
3 1 Boullenois, Observ. 25, p. 609.
4 1 Boullenois, Observ. 25, pp. 610, 617.

right to demand a provisional execution of the foreign judgment. But, in the other cases above mentioned, the judgment ought to be executed without a new action[1]."

§ 615. There was in France an ancient Ordinance, (in 1629), one article of which expressly declared, that judgments rendered in foreign countries for any cause whatever, should not executed within the realm, and that subjects, against whom they were rendered, might contest their rights anew throughout France[2].

§ 616. Emérigon says, that judgments rendered in foreign countries against Frenchmen, are not of the slightest weight in France; and that the causes must be there litigated anew. In support of this statement, he quotes the remark of D'Aguesseau, that it is an inviolable maxim, that a Frenchman can never be transferred to a foreign court: *C'est une maxime inviolable, qu'un Français ne peut jamais être traduit devant un juge étranger*[3]. Immediately afterwards Emérigon adds, that it is the same as to foreign judgments, rendered in favour of a foreigner against a foreigner domiciled in France. He then proceeds to remark, that it is only in suits between foreigners not domiciled in France that a foreign judgment will be executed in France. The rule equally applies whether the Frenchman be plaintiff or be defendant in the cause. But, on the other hand, a Frenchman may sustain a suit in the French Courts against a foreigner, and the judgment rendered by such foreigner may be executed against his property in France. Emérigon, however, admits that the rule is not exempt from doubt, and has been much controverted; for the

---

[1] 1 Boullenois, Observ. 25, p. 646.—Toullier has commented upon and denied the distinctions of Boullenois, as not being well founded in French jurisprudence. 10 Toullier, Droit Civ. Fran. ch. 6, § 3, p. 83.

[2] 1 Boullenois, Observ. 25, p. 646; 2 Kent, Comm. Lect. 37, pp. 121, 122, note, 3rd edit. See 10 Toullier, Droit Civ. Fran. ch. 6, § 3, n. 82, 83.

[3] D'Aguesseau, Œuvres, tom. 5, p. 87, 4to edit.

maxim, *Actor sequitur forum rei,* belongs to the law of nations[1]. Vattel affirms the same maxim in explicit terms[2].

§ 617. The doctrine thus promulgated by Emérigon has continued down to a very recent period[3]. But by the present Code of France, the Ordinance of 1629 seems to be abolished; and foreign judgments are now deemed capable of execution in that country[4]. But the merits of the judgment are examinable; and no distinction seems to be made whether the judgment is in a suit between foreigners, or between Frenchmen, or between a foreigner and a Frenchman; or whether it is in favour of one party or of the other; or whether it is rendered upon default, or upon confession, or upon a full trial and contestation of the merits[5]. Toullier considers it as now the established jurisprudence of France, that no foreign judgment can be rendered executory in France, but upon a full cognizance of the cause before the French tribunals, in which all the original grounds of the action are to be debated and considered anew[6]. And he adds, that the same principle is applied to cases where foreign judgments are set up by the defendant by way of bar to a new action. The judgments are equally re-examinable upon the merits[7].

---

1 Emérigon, Traité des Ass. tom. 1, ch. 4, § 8, n. 2, pp. 122, 123; 2 Kent, Comm. Lect. 37, pp. 121, 122, n. 3rd edit.—The same doctrine is explicitly avowed to be the law of France in many other authorities. See Henry on Foreign Law, App. 209.

2 Vattel, b. 2, ch. 8, § 103.

3 Merlin, Répertoire, Jugement, § 6; Id. Etranger. § 2—5; Id. Questions de Droit, Jugement, § 14; 2 Kent, Comm. Lect. 37, pp. 121, 122, note, 3rd edit.; 10 Toullier, Droit Civ. Fran. ch. 6, § 3, pp. 76, 81, 82, 86.

4 Code de Procédure Civile, art. 546; Code Civil, art. 2123, 2128; 10 Toullier, Droit Civ. Fran. ch. 6, § 3, n. 76—78, 84—86.

5 10 Toullier, Droit Civ. Fran. ch. 6, § 3. n. 76—78, 80, 81, 84—86; Pardessus, Droit Comm. tom. 5, art. 1488; 3 Burge, Comm. on Col. and For. Law, pt. 2, ch. 24, pp. 1048, 1049.

6 Id. n. 85, 86; 2 Kent, Comm. Lect. 37, pp. 121, 122, note, 3rd edit.; Pardessus, Droit, Comm. tom. 5, art. 1488.

7 10 Toullier, Droit Civ. Fran. ch. 6, § 3, n. 76—86; Merlin, Réper-

§ 618. It is difficult to ascertain what the prevailing rule is in regard to foreign judgments in some of the other nations of continental Europe; whether they are deemed conclusive evidence, or only *primâ facie* evidence. Holland seems at all times, upon the general principle of reciprocity, to have given great weight to foreign judgments; and in many cases, if not in all cases, to have given to them a weight equal to that given to domestic judgments, wherever the like rule of reciprocity with regard to Dutch judgments has been adopted by the foreign country whose judgment is brought under review. This is certainly a very reasonable rule, and may perhaps hereafter work itself firmly into the structure of international jurisprudence[1].

---

toire, Jugement, § 6; Id. Questions de Droit, Jugement, § 14; Pardessus, Droit Comm. tom. 5, art. 1488; 2 Kent, Comm. Lect. 37, pp. 118—121, 3rd edit.

[1] Henry on Foreign Law, ch. 10, § 2, pp. 75, 76; Id. App. pp. 209—214.

CHAPTER XVI.

PENAL LAWS AND OFFENCES.

§ 619. WE are next led to the consideration of the operation of foreign laws in regard to penalties and offences. And this will not require any expanded examination, as the topics are few, and the doctrines maintained by foreign jurists and by tribunals acting under the common law, involve no intricate inquiries into the peculiar jurisprudence of different nations.

§ 620. The common law considers crimes as altogether local, and cognizable and punishable exclusively in the country where they are committed. No other nation, therefore, has any right to punish them, or is under any obligation to take notice of, or to enforce any judgment rendered in such cases by the tribunals having authority to hold jurisdiction within the territory where they are committed [1]. Hence it is, that a criminal sentence of attainder in the courts of one sovereign, although it there creates a personal disability to sue, does not carry the same disability with the person into other countries. Foreign jurists, indeed, maintain on this particular point a different opinion, holding that the state or condition of a person in the place of his domicil accompanies him every where [2]. Lord Loughbo-

---

[1] Rutherf. Inst. b. 2, ch. 9, § 12; Martens, Law of Nations, b. 3, ch. 3, § 22—25; Merlin, Répertoire, Souveraineté, § 5, n. 5, 6, pp. 379—382; Commonwealth *v.* Green, 17 Mass. R. 515, 545—548.

[2] Ante, § 91, 92; 1 Hertii Opera, de Collis. Leg. § 4, n. 8, p. 124, (edit. 1737); Id. p. 175, (edit. 1716); 1 Boullenois, Obs. 4, pp. 64, 65.—Boullenois states this doctrine in strong terms:—"A l'égard des statuts, qui prononcent une morte civile pour crimes, ou une note d'infamie, l'état de ces misérables se porte par tout, indépendamment de tout domicile; et cela par un concert et un concours général des nations, ces sortes de peines étant une

rough, in declaring the opinion of the Court on one occasion, said: "Penal laws of foreign countries are strictly local, and affect nothing more than they can reach and can be seized by virtue of their authority. A fugitive who passes hither, comes with all his transitory rights. He may recover money held for his use, and stock, obligations, and the like; and cannot be affected in this country by proceedings against him in that which he has left, beyond the limits of which such proceedings do not extend[1]." Mr. Justice Buller, in the same case, on a writ of error, said: "It is a general principle, that the penal laws of one country cannot be taken notice of in another[2]." The same doctrine was affirmed by Lord Ellenborough in a subsequent case[3]. And it has been recently promulgated by Lord Brougham, in very clear and authoritative terms: "The *lex loci* (says he) must needs govern all criminal jurisdiction, from the nature of the thing and the purpose of the jurisdiction[4]."

§ 621. The same doctrine has been frequently recognised in America. On one occasion, where the subject underwent a good deal of discussion, Mr. Chief Justice Marshall, in delivering the opinion of the Supreme Court, said: "The Courts of no country execute the penal laws of another[5]." On another occasion, in New York, Mr. Chief Justice Spencer said: "We are required to give effect to a law (of Connecticut) which inflicts a penalty for acquiring a right to a *chose in action*. The defendant cannot take advantage of, nor expect the Court to enforce, the criminal laws of another State. The penal acts of one State can have no operation in another State. They are strictly local, and

---

tache, une plaie incurable, dont le condamné est affligé, et qui l'accompagne en tous lieux. C'est ce que dit D'Argentré." 1 Boullenois, Observ. 4, pp. 64, 65.

1 Folliott *v*. Ogden, 1 H. Black. p. 135.

2 Ogden *v*. Folliott, 3 T. R. 733, 734.

3 Wolff *v*. Oxholm, 6 M. & Selw. R. 99.

4 Warrender *v*. Warrender, 9 Bligh, 119, 120.

5 The Antelope, 10 Wheat. R. 66, 123.

affect nothing more than they can reach[1]." Upon the same ground, also, the Supreme Court of Massachusetts have held, that a person convicted of an infamous offence in one State, is not thereby rendered incompetent as a witness in other States[2].

§ 622. The same doctrine is stated by Lord Kaims as the doctrine in Scotland. "There is not," says he, "the same necessity for an extraordinary jurisdiction to punish foreign delinquencies. The proper place for punishment is where the crime is committed. And no society takes concern in any crime but what is hurtful to itself[3]."

§ 623. The same doctrine is laid down by Martens as a clear principle of the law of nations. After remarking that the criminal power of a country is confined to the territory, he adds: "By the same principles a sentence which attacks the honour, rights, or property of a criminal, cannot extend beyond the courts of the territory of the sovereign who has pronounced it. So that he who has been declared infamous, is infamous in fact, but not in law. And the confiscation of his property cannot affect his property situate in a foreign country. To deprive him of his honour and property judicially there also, would be to punish him a second time for the same offence[4]."

§ 624. Pardessus has affirmed a similar principle. "In all the States of Christendom," says he, "by a sort of general consent and uniformity of practice, the prosecution and punishment of penal offences are left to the tribunals of the country where they are committed. The principle of the French Legislation, that the laws of police and bail are obligatory upon all who are within the territory, is a principle of common right in all nations[5]." Bouhier also admits the

---

1 Scoville *v.* Canfield, 14 John. R. 338, 340. See also The State *v.* Knight, Taylor's N. C. Rep. 65.

2 Commonwealth *v.* Green, 17 Mass. R. 515, 540, 541, 546, 547.

3 Kaims on Equity, b. 3, ch. 8, § 1. See also Ersk. Inst. b. 1, tit. 2, 23.

4 Martens, Summary of the Law of Nations, b. 3, ch. 3, § 24, 25.

5 Pardessus, Droit Comm. 5, art. 1467. See also Merlin, Répertoire, Souveraineté, § 5, n. 5, 6, pp. 379—382.

locality, or, as he terms it, the reality, of penal laws; and of course he limits their operation to the territory of the sovereignty within which they are committed[1].

§ 625. On the other hand, Hertius and Paul Voet seem to maintain a different doctrine, holding that crimes committed in one state may, if the criminal is found in another state, be upon demand punished there[2]. Paul Voet says: *Statutum personale ubique locorum personam comitatur, &c., etiam in ordine ad pœnam a cive petendam, si pœna civibus sit imposita*[3]. And he, as well as some others of the foreign jurists, enters into elaborate discussions of the question, whether, if a foreign fugitive criminal is arrested in another country, he is to be punished according to the law of his domicil, or according to the law of the place where the offence was committed[4]. If any nation should suffer its own Courts to entertain jurisdiction of offences committed by foreigners in foreign countries, the rule of Bartolus would seem to furnish the true answer. *Delicta puniuntur juxta mores loci commissi delicti, et non loci ubi de crimine cognoscitur*[5].

---

1 Bouhier, Cout. de Bourg. c. 34, p. 588. See also Matthæi Comm. ad Pand. lib. 48, tit. 20, § 17, 18, 20.—Mr. Hallam has remarked: "The death of Servetus has, perhaps, as many circumstances of aggravation as any execution for heresy that ever took place. One of these, and among the most striking, is, that he was not the subject of Geneva, nor domiciled in the city, nor had the *Christianissima Restitutio* been published there, but at Vienna. According to our laws, and those, I believe, of most civilized nations, he was not answerable to the tribunals of the republic." Hallam's Introduction to the Literature of Europe, vol. 2, (Lond. edit. 1839), cap. 2, § 27, p. 109.

2 Hertii Opera, De Collis. Leg. § 4, n. 18—21, pp. 130—132, (edit. 1737); Id. pp. 185—188, (edit. 1716).

3 P. Voet, De Stat. § 4, c. 2, n. 6, p. 123, (edit. 1715); Id. p. 138, (edit. 1661). See Id. § 11, c. 1, n. 4, 5, pp. 294—296, (edit. 1715); Id. pp. 355—360, (edit. 1761).

4 See 1 Hertii Opera, De Collis. Leg. § 4, n. 19—21, pp. 131, 132, (edit. 1737); Id. pp. 185—188, (edit. 1716); P. Voet, De Stat. § 11, c. 1, § 1, 4, 5, pp. 291—297, (edit. 1715); Id. pp. 355—360, (edit. 1661).

5 Henry on For. Law, p. 47.—I quote the passage as I find it in Henry. Upon examining Bartolus in the place apparently intended to be cited by Mr.

§ 626. There is another point which has been a good deal discussed of late; and that is, whether a nation is bound to surrender up fugitives from justice who escape into its territories and seek there an asylum from punishment. The practice has, beyond question, prevailed as a matter of comity, and sometimes of treaty, between some neighbouring states, and sometimes also between distant states having much intercourse with each other[1]. Paul Voet remarks, that under the Roman Empire this right of having a criminal remitted for trial to the proper *forum criminis* was unquestionable. It resulted from the very nature of the universal dominion of the Roman Laws. *Jure tamen civili notandum, remissionibus locum fuisse de necessitate, ut reus ad locum ubi deliquit, sic petente judice, fuerit mittendus, quod omnes judices uni subessent imperatori. Et omnes provinciæ Romanæ unitæ essent accessoriè, non principaliter*[2]. But he remarks, that according to the customs of almost all Christendom (except Saxony) the remitter of criminals, except in cases of humanity, is not admitted; and, when done, it is to be upon letters rogatory, so that there may be no prejudice to the local jurisdiction. *Moribus nihilominus (non tamen Saxonicis) totius fere Christianismi, nisi ex humanitate, non sunt admissæ remissiones. Quo casu, remittenti magistratui cavendum per litteras reversoriales, ne actus jurisdictioni remittentis ullum pariat præjudicium. Id quod etiam*

Henry (Bartolus, Comm. ad Cod. lib. 1, tit. 1, l. 1, n. 20, 21; Id. n. 44; Id. n. 47, tom. 7, p. 4, (edit. 1602), I have not been able to find any such language used by Bartolus. Martens deems it clear, that a sovereign in whose dominions a criminal has sought refuge, may, if he chooses, punish him for the offence, though committed in a foreign country; though he admits that the more common usage in modern times is to remand the criminal to the country where the crime was committed. Martens, Law of Nations, b. 3, ch. 3, § 22, 23. See also Vattel, b. 2, ch. 2, § 76; Grotius, De Jure Belli et Pac. b. 2, c. 21, § 2—5; Burlemaqui, p. 4, c. 3, § 24—26. See Lord Brougham's opinion in Warrender *v.* Warrender, 9 Bligh, R. 118—120.

[1] See Vattel, b. 2, ch. 6, § 76.

[2] P. Voet, De Stat. § 11, c. 1, n. 6, p. 297, (edit. 1715); Id. p. 358, (edit. 1661).

in nostris Provinciis Unitis est receptum[1]. And he adds: *Neque enim Provinciæ Fœderatæ uni supremo parent*[2]; a remark strictly applicable to the American States. It is manifest, that he treats it purely as a matter of comity and not of national duty.

§ 627. It has, however, been treated by other distinguished jurists as a strict right, and as constituting a part of the law and usage of nations, that offenders charged with a high crime, who have fled from the country in which the crime has been committed, should be delivered up and sent back for trial by the sovereign of the country where they are found. Vattel manifestly contemplates the subject in this latter view, contending that it is the duty of the government where the criminal is, to deliver him up, or to punish him; and if it refuses so to do, then it becomes responsible, as in some measure an accomplice in the crime[3]. This opinion is also maintained with great vigour by Grotius, by Heineccius, by Burlemaqui, and by Rutherforth[4]. There is no inconsiderable weight of common law authority on the same side; and Mr. Chancellor Kent has adopted the doctrine in a case which called directly for its decision[5].

§ 628. On the other hand, Puffendorf explicitly denies it as a matter of right[6]. Martens is manifestly of the same

---

1 P. Voet, De Stat. § 11, c. 1, n. 6, p. 297, (edit. 1715); Id. p. 358, (edit. 1661).

2 Id. See also Matthæi Comm. de Criminibus, Dig. lib. 48, tit. 14, l. 1, § 3.

3 Vattel, b. 2, ch. 6, § 76.

4 Grotius, De Jure Belli et Pacis, c. 21, § 2—5; Heineccii Prælect. in Grot. h. t.; Burlemaqui, pt. 4, ch. 3, § 23—29, pp. 258, 259, (edit. 1763); Ruthërf. Inst. b. 2, ch. 9, § 12.

5 In the matter of Washburn, 4 John. Ch. R. 106; 1 Kent. Comm. Lect. 2, p. 36, 3rd edit.; Rex *v.* Hutchinson, 3 Keble, 785; Rex *v.* Kimburley, 2 Strange, R. 848; East India Company *v.* Campbell, 1 Ves. Sen. 246; Mure *v.* Kaye, 4 Taunton, R. 34, Per Heath J.; Wynne's Eunomus, Dialog. 3, § 67; Lundy's Case, 2 Vent. R. 314; Rex *v.* Ball, 1 Amer. Jurist, 287.

6 For this reference to Puffendorf's opinion, I must rely on Burlemaqui (pt. 4, ch. 3, § 23, 24), not having been able to find it in his Treatise on the Law of Nations. The only reference to the point which I have met with in that work is in b. 8, ch. 3, § 23, 24.

opinion, contending that, with respect to crimes committed out of his territories, no sovereign is obliged to punish the criminal who seeks shelter in his dominions, or to execute a sentence pronounced against his person or his property[1]. Lord Coke expressly maintains, that the sovereign is not bound to surrender up fugitive criminals from other countries, who have sought a shelter in his dominions[2]. Mr. Chief Justice Tilghman has adhered to the same doctrine in a very elaborate judgment[3]. The reasoning of Mr. Chief Justice Parker in a leading case[4], leads to a similar conclusion; and it stands indirectly confirmed by the opinion of a majority of the Judges of the Supreme Court of the United States in a very recent case of the deepest interest[5].

---

1 Martens, Law of Nations, b. 3, ch. 3, § 23.

2 3 Coke, Inst. 180.

3 Commonwealth *v.* Deacon, 10 Serg. & R. 125; 3 Story, Comm. on Constit. § 1802. See also Merlin, Rèpertoire, Souverainetè, § 5, n. 5, 6, pp. 379—382.

4 Commonwealth *v.* Green, 17 Mass. R. 515, 540, 541, 546—548.

5 Holmes *v.* Jennison, 14 Peters, R. 540.—Mr. Justice Barbour maintained the same opinion in the case of Jose Ferreira de Santos, 2 Brock. R. 493. Most of the reasoning on each side will be found very fully collected in the case of the matter of Washburn, 4 John. Ch. R. 106; that of Commonwealth *v.* Deacon, 10 Serg. & Rawle, 123; Holmes *v.* Jennison, 14 Peters, R. 540—598; and that of Rex. *v.* Ball, 1 Amer. Jurist, 297. The latter case is the decision of Mr. Chief Justice Reid of Canada. See also 1 Amer. State Papers, 175; Commonwealth *v.* De Longchamps, 1 Dall. 111, 115; U. States *v.* Davis, 2 Sumner, R. 482, 486.

CHAPTER XVII.

EVIDENCE AND PROOFS.

§ 629. We come, in the last place, to the consideration of the operation of foreign laws, in relation to evidence and proofs. And here, independently of other more complicated questions, two of a very general nature may arise. In the first place, what rule is to prevail, as to the competency or incompetency of witnesses? Is the rule of the law of the country where the transaction to which the suit relates had its origin, to govern, or the law of the country where the suit is brought? In the next place, what is the rule which is to prevail in the proof of written instruments? In other words, in what manner are contracts, instruments, or other acts made or done in other countries to be proved? Is it sufficient to prove them in the manner and by the solemnities and proofs which are deemed sufficient by the law of the place where the contracts, instruments, or other acts were executed? Or is it necessary to prove them in the manner and according to the law of the place where the action or other judicial proceeding is instituted?

§ 630. Various cases may be put to illustrate these questions. A contract or other instrument is executed and recorded before a Notary Public in a foreign country, in which by law a copy of the contract or other instrument certified by him is sufficient to establish its existence and genuineness; would that certificate be admissible in the Courts of common law of England or America to establish the same facts?[1] Again, persons who are interested, and even parties

[1] See Mascardus, De Probat. vol. 2, Conclus. 927, n. 4—8, p. 336, (455, edit. 1731).

in the very suit, are in some foreign countries admissible witnesses to prove contracts, instruments, and other acts, material to the merits of the suit; would they be admissible as witnesses in suits brought in the course of common law in England and America, to prove the like facts in relation to contracts, instruments, or other acts, made or done in such foreign countries, material to the suit? These are questions more easily put, than satisfactorily answered upon principles of international jurisprudence.

§ 630 *a*. Similar considerations may arise in respect to the rules as to presumptions *de facto* and *de jure*, which may be different in different countries. Thus, for example, the title to movable property may depend upon the question of survivorship of one of two persons who both died under the like circumstances; as, for example, on board a ship which foundered at sea, or was totally lost with all her crew by shipwreck. Now, different countries may, and probably do, adopt different presumptions as to the survivorship in such calamitous circumstances, founded upon considerations of the age, or sex, or other natural or even artificial grounds of belief or presumption[1]. What rule then is to be adopted? the law of the place of domicil of the parties, or the law of the forum where the suit is instituted? On one occasion, when a question of this very nature was before him, a late learned Judge (Sir William Grant) said: "There are many instances in which principles of law have been adopted from the Civilians by our English Courts of Justice; but none that I know of in which they have adopted presumptions of fact from the rules of the civil law[2]."

§ 630 *b*. There are certain rules of evidence which may be affirmed to be generally, if not universally, recognised. Thus, in relation to immovable property, inasmuch as the rights and titles thereto are generally admitted to be governed by the law of the *situs*, and as suits and controversies

[1] See Fearne's Posthum. Works, 38; The Case of Gen. Stanwix and Daughter; Code Civil of France, art. 720—722; 4 Burge, Comm. on Col. and For. Law, pt. 1, ch. 4, § 5, pp. 152, 153.

[2] Mason *v*. Mason, 1 Meriv. R. 308, 312.

touching the same *ex directo* properly belong to the forum of the *situs*, and not elsewhere, it would seem a just and natural, if not an irresistible, conclusion, that the law of evidence of the *situs* touching such rights, titles, suits, and controversies, must and ought exclusively to govern in all such cases. So in cases relating to the due execution of wills and testaments of immovables, the proofs must and ought to be according to the law of the *situs*. So in respect to the due execution of wills and testaments of movables, as they are governed by the law of the domicil of the testator, the proofs must and ought to be according to the law of his domicil. By the present law of England, a will or testament of movable property, in order to be valid, must be executed in the presence of two witnesses. If, then, an Englishman, domiciled in England, should make his will in England, in the presence of one witness only, that will could not be admitted to proof in Scotland to govern movable property situate there[1]. The like rule would apply to a case where the will was executed in the presence of two witnesses, both or either of whom were incompetent by the law of England, although competent by the law of Scotland.

§ 631. Similar principles may well be applied to many other cases. There are certain formalities of proof, which are required by the laws of foreign countries in regard to contracts, instruments, and other acts, which are indispensable to their validity there; and these are therefore held to be of universal obligation; and must be duly proved in every foreign tribunal, in which they are in litigation, before any right can be founded on them[2]. An illustration of this doctrine may be drawn from the known rule of the common law, that a bill of exchange, upon its dishonour, must be protested before a notary; and if not proved to be so protested,

---

[1] Yates *v.* Thomson, 3 Clark & Finnell, 544, 576, 577.

[2] See Trasher *v.* Everhart, 3 Gill. & John. R. 234, 242; Ante, § 260—263.

no remedy can be had against the drawer or indorsers[1]. Another illustration may be drawn from the registration of deeds and other instruments, which cannot be given in evidence, unless proved to be duly registered according to the *lex loci rei sitæ*. Another illustration may be drawn from cases of contract under the Statute of Frauds, which must be in writing, and must state a good consideration, in order to be valid in point of legal obligation or evidence[2]. Another illustration may be drawn from the known doctrine as to stamps, by which it is held, that no instrument can be given in evidence unless it is properly stamped[3]. In all these cases the proper proofs must doubtless be given in conformity with the local law[4]. And if the proofs are given in the mode which the local law requires, there is some difficulty in asserting that such proofs ought not to be deemed every where a full authentication of the instrument[5].

§ 632. Boullenois divides the formalities of acts into several classes: those which are required before the act, *quæ requiruntur ante factum;* those which are required at the time of the act, *quæ requiruntur in facto;* and those which are required afterwards, *quæ requiruntur ex post facto*[6]. But a more important distinction in his distribution is of the formalities at the time of the act, which he denominates the formalities of proof, (*formalites probantes*), and those which are substantial and intrinsic formalities[7]. Among the former he includes those which respect the number of witnesses who are to witness the execution of the act, their age, quality, and residence, and the date and place of the act. And here he holds, that as to the formalities of proof the

---

1 See Boyden *v.* Taylor, 2 Harr. & John. 396; Ante, § 260 *a*, 360, 361; Wilcox *v.* Hunt, 13 Peters, R. 378.

2 Ante, § 262, 262 *a*.

3 Ante, § 260.

4 Ante, § 260, 260 *a*, 360, 361, 363—373.

5 See Ersk. Inst. b. 3, tit. 2, § 39, 40.

6 1 Boullenois, Observ. 23, p. 491.

7 1 Boullenois, Observ. 23. pp. 492, 498, 506, &c.

maxim applies: *Solemnitates testimoniales non sunt in potestate contrahentium, sed in potestate juris*[1]. *Solemnitates sumendæ sunt ex consuetudine loci, in quo res et actus geritur*[2].

§ 632 *a*. Mascardus holds a similar opinion; and says, that an act executed before a notary in any place, if duly executed according to the law of that place, and valid as a notarial act, ought to be held of the same obligation and validity in every other place. *Unde jus probationis, ortum a principio, non tollitur mutatione loci*[3]. Paul Voet appears to enter tain a different opinion; and he puts the case, whether, if an instrument were executed in one place before a notary who by the *lex loci* is competent for that purpose, the validity or force of that instrument would extend to another place where the notary would be deemed incompetent, so that he could not there give public authenticity to the instrument. *Quid si tamen in uno loco factum sit instrumentum coram notario qui ibidem est habilis, an extendetur vis illius instrumenti ad alium locum ubi censetur inhabilis, sic ut publicum ibidem nequeat facere instrumentum*[4]*?* After giving the opinions of several jurists in the affirmative, he proceeds to give his own to this effect: that it is not so much a question of solemnities, as of the efficacy of proof, which, although it may be sufficient in one place, may not be so every where; and that the tribunal of one country cannot give such validity and force to any instrument, as that it shall have operation elsewhere[5].

---

[1] 1 Boullenois, Observ. 23, pp. 492, 493; Ante, § 260.

[2] Ibid.

[3] Mascard. De Probat. Conclus. 927. tom. 2, pp. 336, 337, [454, 455, edit. 1731], n. 4—14; Ante, § 260 *a*.

[4] P. Voet, De Stat. § 10, c. 1, n. 11, pp. 287, 288, (edit. 1715); Id. p. 347, (edit. 1661).

[5] P. Voet, De Stat. § 10, c. 1, n. 11, pp. 287, 288, (edit. 1715); Id. p. 347, (edit. 1661). His language is: Quid si tamen in uno loco factum sit instrumentum coram notario qui ibidem est habilis, an extendetur vis illius instrumenti ad alium locum ubi censetur inhabilis, sic ut publicum ibidem nequeat facere instrumentum? Sunt qui id adfirmant. Quasi loci consuetudo, dans robur scripturæ, etiam obtineat extra territorium. Sunt qui id

§ 633. Paul Voet, also, in another place, speaking upon the subject of the operation of the *lex fori* as to the modes of proceeding in suits, uses the following language: *Si de probationibus et quidem testibus; sic eas adhibebit, sic examinabit hosce, prout exigit forum judicis ubi producuntur. Si de instrumentis; sic exhibenda, sic edenda, ut fert loci statutum, ubi exhibentur, vel eduntur*[1]. The generality of these expressions must lead us to the conclusion, that he was of opinion that the modes of proof and the law of evidence of the *lex fori* ought to regulate the proceedings in all suits, whether these suits arose from foreign contracts, or instruments, or other acts or not. But perhaps he may have intended to give them a more limited application[2].

§ 634. Bouhier states a case where a suit was brought in France, by an Englishman, against another person for money supposed to be lent by him to the latter; and he offered proof thereof by witnesses. It was objected, that by the Ordinance of Moulins, (art. 54), such parol proof was in-

---

ideo adfirmant, quod non tam de habilitate et inhabilitate notarii laboremus, quam de solemnibus. Quod si verum foret, res extra dubitationis aleam esset collocata. Verum, ut quod res est dicam, existumem hic agi, non tam de solemnibus, quam probandi efficaciâ, quæ licet in uno loco sufficiens, non tamen ubique locorum; quod judex unius territorii nequeat vires tribuere instrumento, ut alibi quid operetur. Hinc etiam mandatum ad litesc oram notario et testibus hic sufficienter factum, non tamen erit validum in Gelriæ partibus, ubi notarii non admittuntur, ut coram lege loci, hic confectum esse oporteat, quo in Geldriâ sortiatur effectum. Quemadmodum enim personam non subditam, non potest quis alibi inhabilitare; ita nec personam subditam potest alibi facere habilem. P. Voet, ubi supra.

[1] P. Voet, De Stat § 10, ch. 9, n. 10, p. 287, (edit. 1715); Id. p. 347, (edit. 1661).

[2] Erskine in his Institutes says, that in suits in Scotland with foreigners upon obligations made in a foreign country, they may prove payment or extinguishment lege loci. If, for instance, the law of the foreign country allows the payment of a debt constituted by writing, to be proved by witnesses, that manner of proof will also be allowed by the Scottish Courts as sufficient for extinguishing such debt, although by the Scottish law obligations formed by writing are not extinguishable by parol evidence. (Ersk. Inst. b. 3, tit. 5, § 7.) This seems a mixed case of the law of the place governing as to the discharge of contracts, and also of the mode of proof of the discharge.

admissible. But the Court admitted it upon the ground, that the law of England where the contract was made admitted such parol proof, and therefore it was admissible in a controversy on the contract in France. Bouhier holds the decision to be correct, if the contract was made, as he supposes it to have been, in England[1].

§ 634 *a*. Upon this subject it is perhaps not possible to lay down any rules which ought to be, or even which can be, applied to all cases of evidence. Generally speaking, it seems true, that neither the *lex loci contractûs*, nor the *lex loci domicilii*, is applicable to the course of procedure; but the course of procedure ought to be according to the law of the forum where the suit is instituted[2]. And perhaps it may be stated as a general truth, that the admission of evidence and the rules of evidence are rather matters of procedure, than matters attaching to the rights and titles of parties under contracts, deeds, and other instruments; and therefore they are to be governed by the law of the country where the Court sits. But then, (as has been well observed by an eminent judge), in all questions of international jurisprudence it is easy to say, how things are here and there, when there is very great difference between the points; but when we come to the confines, and when one province runs into the other, then arises the difficulty, and then we get *inter apices juris*[3]. There may be cases

---

1 Bouhier, Cout. de Bourg. ch. 21, § 205, p. 415. See also Strykius, tom. 2, Diss. 1, ch. 3, § 18—25, pp. 21, 27.

2 See Yates *v.* Thomson, 3 Clark & Finnell. R. 577, 580; Don *v.* Lippmann, 5 Clark & Finnell. R. 1, 14—16.

3 Lord Brougham in Yates *v.* Thomson, 3 Clark & Finnell, 577, 580.—Lord Brougham on this occasion said (it being a case where a question arose in Scotland upon the interpretation of a will made in England): "It is on all hands admitted, that the whole distribution of Mr. Yates's personal estate must be governed by the law of England where he had his domicil through life, and at the time of his decease, and at the dates of all the instruments executed by him. Had he died intestate, the English statute of distributions, and not the Scotch law of succession in movables, would have regulated the whole course of the administration. His written declarations must, therefore, be taken with respect to the English law. I think it follows from hence, that

which at once partake of the nature of the law of evidence,

---

those declarations of intention touching that property, must be construed as we should construe them here by our principles of legal interpretation. Great embarrassment may, no doubt, arise from calling upon a Scotch Court to apply the principles of English law to such questions, many of those principles being among the most nice and difficult known in our jurisprudence. The Court of Session may, for example, be required to decide, whether an executory devise is void as being too remote, and to apply, for the purpose of ascertaining that question, the criterion of the gift passing or not passing, what would be an estate in the realty, although in the language of the Scotch law there is no such expression as executory devise, and within the knowledge of Scotch lawyers no such thing as an executory estate tail. Nevertheless, this is a difficulty which must of necessity be grappled with; because in no other way can the English law be applied to personal property situated locally within the jurisdiction of the Scottish forum; and the rule which requires the law of the domicil to govern succession to such property, could in no other way be applied and followed out. Nor am I aware, that any distinction in this respect has ever been taken between testamentary succession and succession ab intestato, or that it has been held either here or in Scotland, that the Court's right to regard the foreign law was excluded, wherever a foreign instrument had been executed. It is therefore my opinion, that in this, as in other cases of the like description, the Scotch Court must inquire of the foreign law as a matter of fact, and examine such evidence as will shew how in England such instruments would be dealt with as to construction. I give this as my opinion upon principle, for I am not aware of the question ever having received judicial determination in either country. But here I think the importing of the foreign code (sometimes incorrectly called the comitas) must stop. What evidence the Courts of another country would receive, and what reject, is a question into which I cannot at all see the necessity of the Courts of any one country entering. Those principles, which regulate the admission of evidence, are the rules by which the Courts of every country guide themselves in all their inquiries. The truth with respect to men's actions, which form the subject-matter of their inquiry, is to be ascertained according to a certain definite course of proceeding, and certain rules have established, that in pursuing this investigation some things shall be heard from witnesses, others not listened to; some instruments shall be inspected by the judge, others kept from his eye. This must evidently be the same course, and governed by the same rules, whatever be the subject-matter of investigation. Nor can it make any difference, whether the facts concerning which the discussion arises, happened at home or abroad; whether they related to a foreigner domiciled abroad, or a native living and dying at home. As well might it be contended that another mode of trial should be adopted, as that another law of evidence should be admitted in such cases. Who would argue, that in a question like the present the Court of Session should try the

and also of the substance of the weightier matters of international jurisprudence[1].

---

point of fact by a jury according to the English procedure, or should follow the course of our dispositions or interrogatories in Courts of Equity, because the testator was a domiciled Englishman, and because those methods of trial would be applied to his case, were the question raised here? The answer is, that the question arises in the Court of Session, and must be dealt with by the rules which regulate inquiry there. Now, the law of evidence is among the chief of these rules; nor let it be said, that there is any inconsistency in applying the English rules of construction and the Scotch ones of evidence to the same matter, in investigating facts by one law and intention by another. The difference is manifest between the two inquiries; for a person's meaning can only be gathered from assuming, that he intended to use words in the sense affixed to them by the law of the country he belonged to at the time of framing his instrument. Accordingly, where the question is, what a person intended by an instrument relating to the conveyance of real estate situated in a foreign country, and where the lex loci rei sitæ must govern, we decide upon his meaning by that law, and not by the law of the country where the deed was executed; because we consider him to have had that foreign law in his contemplation. The will of April 1828 has not been admitted to probate here; it has not even been offered for proof, so that there is no sentence of any Court of competent jurisdiction upon it either way. But in England it would never be received in evidence nor seen by any Court; neither would it have been seen if it had been proved ever so formally. Our law holds the probate as the only evidence of a will of personalty, or of the appointment of executors; in short, of any disposition which a testator may make, unless it regards his real estate. Can it be said, that the Scotch Court is bound by this rule of evidence, which, though founded upon views of convenience, and for anything I know well devised, is yet one which must be allowed to be exceedingly technical, and which would exclude from the view of the Court a subsequent will, clearly revoking the one admitted to probate. The English Courts would never look at this will, although proof might be tendered, that it had come to the knowledge of the party on the eve of the trial. A delay might be granted to enable him to obtain a revocation of the probate of the former will. It is absurd to contend, that the Court of Session shall admit all this technicality of procedure into its course of judicature, as often as a question arises upon the succession of a person domiciled in England. Again, there are certain rules just as strict, and many of them not less technical, governing the admission of parol evidence with us. Can it be contended, that, as often as an English succession comes in question before the Scotch Court, witnesses are to be admitted or rejected upon the practice of the English Courts; nay, that examination and cross-examination are to proceed upon

---

[1] Ibid.

§ 635. There are very few traces to be found, in the Reports of the common law, of any established doctrines

---

those rules of our practice, supposing them to be (as they may possibly be) quite different from the Scotch rules? This would be manifestly a source of such inconvenience as no Court ever could get over. Among other embarrassments equally inextricable there would be this; that a host of English lawyers must always be in attendance on the Scotch Courts, ready to give evidence, at a moment's notice, of what the English rules of practice are, touching the reception or refusal of testimony, and the manner of obtaining it; for those questions which, by the supposition, are questions of mere fact in the Scotch Courts, must arise unexpectedly during each trial, and must be disposed of on the spot, in order that the trial may proceed. The case which I should however put, as quite decisive of this matter, comes nearer than any other to the one at bar; and it may, with equal advantage to the elucidation of the argument, be put as arising both in an English and in a Scotch Court. By our English rules of evidence no instrument proves itself, unless it be thirty years old, or is an office copy authorized by law to be given by the proper officer, or is the London Gazette, or is by some special act made evidence, or is an original record of a Court under its seal, or an exemplification under seal, which is quasi a record. By the Scotch law all instruments prepared and witnessed according to the provisions of the act of 1681 are probative writs, and may be given in evidence without any proof. Now, suppose a will of personalty or any other instrument relating to personal property, attested by two witnesses and executed in England according to the provisions of the Scotch act, is tendered in evidence before the Court of Session; it surely never will be contended, that the learned Judges, on being satisfied that the question relates to English personal succession, ought straightway to examine what is the English law of evidence, and to require the attendance of one or other of the subscribing witnesses, where the instrument is admissible by the Scotch law as probative. Of this I can have no doubt. But suppose the question to arise in England, and that a deed is executed in Scotland according to the Act of 1681 by one domiciled here, would any Court here receive it as proving itself, being only a year old, without calling the attesting witnesses? It would have a strange effect to hear the circumstance of there being two subscribing witnesses to the instrument, which makes it prove itself in the Parliament House of Edinburgh, urged in Westminster Hall as the ground of its admission without any parol testimony. The Court would inevitably answer, 'Two witnesses;—then, because there are witnesses, it cannot be admitted, but they must, one or other of them, be called to prove it.' The very thing that makes the instrument prove itself in Scotland, makes it in England necessary to be proved by witnesses. I have, therefore, no doubt whatever, that the rules of evidence form no part of the foreign law, according to which you are to proceed in disposing of English questions arising in Scotch Courts."

on this subject. We have already seen in regard to witnesses generally, that their competency is governed in common cases by the *lex fori*[1]. But, suppose the only witness to a contract, written or verbal, was incompetent on account of interest by the common law, but competent by the law of the place of the contract; in a suit in a tribunal of the common law on the contract, ought his testimony to be rejected? Again, suppose that the books of account of merchants, which (as is well known[2]) are by the laws of some states admissible, and by those of other states inadmissible, as evidence, are offered in the forum of the latter to establish debts contracted in the former; ought they to be rejected[3]?

§ 635 *a*. Cases, *vice versâ*, may easily be put, which will present questions quite as embarrassing. Thus, for example, let us suppose the case of a crime, committed on board an American ship on the high seas by a white man, or upon a white man, and the principal witnesses of the offence are black men, either free or slaves; and suppose, (as is or may be the fact), that in the slaveholding States black men are competent witnesses only in cases in which black men are parties, and not in cases where white men are parties; and in the non-slaveholding States black men are in all cases competent witnesses. If the offender is apprehended and tried for that offence before a Court of the United States in a slaveholding State, would the black men be witnesses or not? If not there, would they be

---

1 Ante, § 621—623.

2 See Pothier on Oblig. p. 4, ch. 1, art. 2, § 4, n. 719; Cogswell *v.* Dolliver, 2 Mass. R. 217; 1 Starkie on Evid. pt. 2, § 130, 131; Strykius, tom. 7, Diss. 1, ch. 4, § 5.

3 Upon this very point foreign jurists have delivered opposite opinions, as appears from Hertius, who, however, abstains from giving any opinion on the subject. 1 Hertii Opera, De Collis. Leg. § 4, n. 68, p. 152, (edit. 1737); Id. p. 214, (edit. 1716); 4 Burge, Comm. on Col. and For. Law, pt. 2, ch. 3, § 5, p. 153. Paul Voet thinks they are to be deemed primâ facie evidence, but not conclusive. P. Voet, De Stat. § 5, c. 2, n. 9, p. 160, (edit. 1715); Id. p. 183, (edit. 1661).

witnesses in the case if the trial were in a non-slaveholding State? In other words, will the rules of evidence in such a case, in the Courts of the United States, depend upon the rules of evidence in the State where the trial is had? If not, then what rules of evidence are to prevail? The answer in the present State of our law cannot be given with entire confidence, as to its accuracy and universality of adoption.

§ 635 *b*. Lord Brougham, in a recent case, where the question was much considered, both as to the law of procedure and the rules of evidence on foreign contracts, sued in another country, used the following language: "No one will contend in terms, that the foreign rules of evidence should guide us in such cases; and yet it is not so easy to avoid that principle in practice, if you once admit, that though the remedy is to be enforced in one country, it is to be enforced according to the laws which govern another country. Look to the rules of evidence, for example. In Scotland, some instruments are probative; in England, until after the lapse of thirty years, they do not prove themselves. In some countries forty years are required for such a purpose; in others, thirty are sufficient. How, then, is the law to be ascertained which is to govern the particular case? In one Court there must be a previous issue of fact; in another, there need be no such issue. In the latter, then, the case must be given up as a question of evidence. Then come to the law. The question, whether a parol agreement is to be given up, or can be enforced, must be tried by the law of the country in which the law is set in motion to enforce the agreement. Again, whether payment is to be presumed or not, must depend on the law of that country, and so must all questions of the admissibility of evidence; and that clearly brings us home to the question on the Statute of Limitations. Until the Act of Lord Tenderden, a parol agreement or promise was sufficient to take the case out of the Statute of Limitations; but that has never been the case in Scotland. It is not contended here, that the practice of England is applicable to Scotland; but these are illustrations of the inconvenience of applying one set of rules of law to an instrument, which is to be enforeed by a law of a different kind[1].

§ 635 *c.* In many foreign countries original contracts, deeds, conveyances, and other solemn instruments, are often written in the public books of notaries public, and executed, registered, and kept there, and are not allowed to be given out to the parties; but certified copies only thereof are delivered to the parties, and these copies are deemed in such countries admissible evidence in all suits to establish and prove such original papers and documents. The question has arisen in England, whether such copies so certified are admissible, either as original or as secondary evidence, in suits pending in the English Courts. It has been held, that they are not; at least, not without proof that they were made at the time of entering and registering the original paper, and in the presence of the parties, although they were admissible in the country where the originals were executed. The ground of this decision seems to have been, that the rules of evidence of the foreign country were not to be followed, but the rules of evidence of England; and by the law of England copies of original documents were not admissible under such circumstances, unless proved by some witnesses who had compared them with the original, as in common cases[2]. So, upon the like ground, it has been held, that copies of a judgment of the Supreme Court of Jamaica, signed by the clerk thereof, are not admissible evidence in a suit in England, although such copies would be admissible in Jamaica[3].

§ 635 *d.* By the old law of Louisiana, in case the party

---

[1] Don *v.* Lippmann, 5 Clark & Finnell. p. 15; Id. p. 17.

[2] Brown *v.* Thornton, 6 Barn. and Adol. 185.

[3] Appleton *v.* Lord Braybrook, 6 Maule & Selw. 34; Black *v.* Lord Braybrook, 6 Maule & Selw. 39.

formally disavowed his signature to an instrument, proof thereof was required to be made by experts[1]. In a case where a written paper or receipt was executed in the State of Mississippi, and a suit brought thereon in Louisiana, and the signature was disavowed, the question arose, whether the proof of the signature in such a case was to be made by experts, or might be made by witnesses, as was the law of Mississippi. The Court on that occasion said: "In treating of the third and last question," that is the question now under consideration, "it is proper to observe, that we believe it to be admitted as a principle in all tribunals, that the *lex loci*, or law of the country where the contract is made, ought to govern its suits commenced in any other country on such contracts; and it does appear by a law of the *Partidas*, that this principle extends even to the proof of the contract, expressed in general terms, which might perhaps be applied to the mode of proving facts as well as to the amount of evidence necessary to their verification. But it is unnecessary to determine this point absolutely in the present case, because there is sufficiently found in the determination of the first and second questions on which to decide against the opinion of the Judge of the District Court[2]." From this language, it would seem to have been the inclination of the Court to admit the evidence.

§ 636. In regard to wills of personal property made in a foreign country, it would seem to be almost a matter of necessity to admit the same evidence to establish their validity and authenticity abroad, as would establish them in the domicil of the testator; for otherwise, the general rule, that personal property shall pass every where by a will made according to the law of the place of the testator's domicil, might be sapped to its very foundation, if the law of evidence in any country where such property was situate, was

---

1 Code of Louis. 1809, art. 226.

2 Clark's Ex'or. *v.* Cochran, 3 Martin, R. 353, 361, 362. See also Wilcox *v.* Hunt, 13 Peters. R. 378.

not precisely the same as in the place of his domicil. And, therefore, parol evidence has been admitted in courts of common law to prove the manner in which the will is made and proved in the place of the testator's domicil, in order to lay a suitable foundation to establish the will elsewhere[1].

§ 637. Passing from this most embarrassing, and as yet (in a great measure) unsettled class of questions, let us consider in what manner courts of justice arrive at the knowledge of foreign laws. Are they to be judicially taken notice of? or are they to be proved as matters of fact? The established doctrine now is, that no court takes judicial notice of the laws of a foreign country, but they must be proved as facts[2].

§ 638. But it may be asked, whether they are to be proved as facts to the jury if the case is a trial at the common law, or as facts to the Court. It would seem as facts to the latter; for all matters of law are properly referable to the Court, and the object of the proof of foreign laws is to enable the Court to instruct the jury, what, in point of law, is the result of the foreign law to be applied to the matters in controversy before them. The Court are, therefore, to decide what is the proper evidence of the laws of a foreign country; and when evidence is given of those laws, the Court are to judge of their applicability, when proved, to the case in hand[3].

---

1 De Sobry *v.* De Laistre, 2 Harr. and John. 191, 195. See Yates *v.* Thomson, 3 Clark & Finnell. 544, 574.

2 See Mostyn *v.* Fabrigas, Cowp. 174; Male *v.* Roberts, 3 Esp. R. 163; Douglas *v.* Brown, 2 Dow & Clark, R. 171; De Sobry *v.* De Laistre, 2 Harr. & John. R. 193; Trasher *v.* Everhart, 3 Gill. & John. R. 234; Brackett *v.* Norton, 4 Connect. R. 517; Talbot *v.* Seeman, 1 Cranch, 38; Church *v.* Hubbart, 2 Cranch, 187, 236, 237; Andrews *v.* Herriott, 4 Cowen, R. 515, 516, note; Starkie on Evid. pt. 2, § 33; Id. § 92; Id. pt. 4, p. 569; Conseequa *v.* Willings, Peters' Cir. R. 229; Legg *v.* Legg, 8 Mass. R. 99; Hosford *v.* Nichols, 1 Paige, R. 220.

3 De Sobry *v.* De Laistre, 2 Harr. & John. 193, 219. But see Brackett *v.* Norton, 4 Connect. R. 517.—In Trasher *v.* Everhart (3 Gill & John. 234, 242), the Court said: "It is in general true that foreign laws are facts

§ 639. As to the manner of proof, this must vary according to circumstances. The general principle is, that the best testimony or proof shall be produced, which the nature of the thing admits of; or, in other words, that no testimony shall be received, which presupposes better testimony behind, and attainable by the party who offers it. This rule applies to the proof of foreign laws, as well as of other facts. But to require proof of such laws by such a species of testimony as the institutions and usages of the foreign country do not admit of, would be unjust and unreasonable. In this, as in all other cases, no testimony is required which can be shewn to be unattainable[1].

§ 640. Generally speaking, authenticated copies of the written laws, or of other public instruments of a foreign government, are expected to be produced; for it is not to be presumed, that any civilized nation will refuse to give such copies duly authenticated, which are usual and necessary for the purposes of administering justice in other countries. It cannot be presumed, that an application to a foreign government to authenticate its own edict or law

---

which are to be found by the jury. But this general rule is not applicable to a case in which foreign laws are introduced for the purpose of enabling the Court to determine whether a written instrument is evidence. In such the evidence always goes in the first instance to the Court, which, if the evidence be clear and uncontradicted, may and ought to decide what the foreign law is, and, according to its determination on that subject, admit or reject the instrument of writing as evidence to the jury. It is offered to the Court to determine a question of law,—the admissibility or inadmissibility of certain evidence to the jury. It is true, that if, what the foreign law is be a matter of doubt, the Court may decline deciding it, and may inform the jury, that if they believe the foreign law attempted to be proved exists as alleged, then they ought to receive the instrument in evidence. On the contrary, if they should believe that such is not the foreign law, they should reject the instrument as evidence." Is not foreign law offered in all cases to instruct the Court in matters of law material to the point in issue? Can the Court properly leave it to the jury to find out what the law is, and apply it to the case? Lord Mansfield in Mostyn *v.* Fabrigas, (Cowper, R. 174), said: "The way of knowing foreign laws is by admitting them to be proved as facts, and the Court must assist the jury in ascertaining what the law is."

[1] Church *v.* Hubbart, 2 Cranch, R. 237.

will be refused; but the fact of such a refusal must, if relied on, be proved. But if such refusal is proved, then inferior proofs may be admissible[1]. Where our own government has promulgated any foreign law or ordinance of a public nature as authentic, that may of itself be sufficient evidence of the actual existence and terms of such law or ordinance[2].

§ 641. In general, foreign laws are required to be verified by the sanction of an oath, unless they can be verified by some other high authority, such as the law respects not less than it respects the oath of an individual[3]. The usual mode of authenticating foreign laws (as it is of authenticating foreign judgments) is by an exemplification of a copy under the great seal of a state; or by a copy proved to be a true copy by a witness who has examined and compared it with the original; or by the certificate of an officer properly authorized by law to give the copy, which certificate must itself also be duly authenticated[4].

§ 642. But foreign unwritten laws, customs, and usages, may be proved, and indeed must ordinarily be proved, by parol evidence. The usual course is to make such proof by the testimony of competent witnesses, instructed in the laws, customs, and usages, under oath[5]. Sometimes, however, certificates of persons in high authority have been allowed as evidence without other proof[6].

§ 643. It seems, that the public seal of a foreign sovereign affixed to a writing, purporting to be a written edict, or law,

---

1 Church *v.* Hubbart, 2 Cranch, R. 237, 238.

2 Talbot *v.* Seeman, 1 Cranch, R. 38.

3 Church *v.* Hubbart, 2 Cranch, R. 237; Brackett *v.* Norton, 4 Connect. R. 517; Hempstead *v.* Reed, 6 Connect. R. 480; Dyer *v.* Smith, 12 Connect. R. 384.

4 Church *v.* Hubbart, 2 Cranch, R. 238; Packard *v.* Hill, 2 Wend. R. 411; Lincoln *v.* Battelle, 6 Wend. R. 475.

5 Church *v.* Hubbart, 2 Cranch, R. 237; Dalrymple *v.* Dalrymple, 2 Hagg. R. App. pp. 15—144; Brush *v.* Wilkins, 4 John. Ch. R. 520; Mostyn *v.* Fabrigas, Cowper, R. 174.

6 In Re Dormay, 3 Hagg. Eccl. R. 767, 769; Rex *v.* Picton, 30 Howell's State Trials, 515—573; The Diana, 1 Dods. R. 95, 101, 102.

or judgment is, of itself, the highest evidence of its authority; and the Courts of other countries will judicially take notice of such public seal, which is therefore considered as proving itself[1]. But the seal of a foreign Court does not prove itself, and therefore it must be established as such by competent testimony[2]. There is an exception to this rule in favour of Courts of Admiralty, which being Courts of the law of nations, the Courts of other countries will judicially take notice of their seal without positive proof of its authenticity[3].

§ 644. The mode by which the laws, records, and judgments of the different States composing the American Union are to be verified, has been prescribed by Congress, pursuant to an authority given in the Constitution of the United States. It is, therefore, wholly unnecessary to dwell upon this subject, as these regulations are properly a part of our own municipal law, and do not strictly belong to a treatise on international law[4].

§ 645. And here these Commentaries on this interesting branch of public law are brought to a close. It will occur to the learned reader, upon a general survey of the subject, that many questions are still left in a distressing state of uncertainty, as to the true principles which ought to regulate and decide them. Different nations entertain different doctrines and different usages in regard to them. The

---

1 Lincoln *v.* Battelle, 6 Wend. R. 475; Griswold *v.* Pittcairn, 2 Conn. R. 85; Church *v.* Hubbart, 2 Cranch, 238, 239; Anon. 7 Mod. R. 66; United States *v.* Johnson, 4 Dall. 416; Appleton *v.* Lord Braybrook, 6 Maule & Selw. 34; Black *v.* Lord Braybrook, 6 Maule & Selw. 39.

2 Starkie on Evid. pt. 2, § 92; Delafield *v.* Hurd. 3 John. R. 310; De Sobry *v.* De Laistre, 2 Harr. & John. R. 193; Henry *v.* Adey, 3 East, R. 221; Andrews *v.* Herriott, 4 Cowen, R. 526, note.

3 See Yeaton *v.* Fry, 5 Cranch, 335; Thompson *v.* Stewart, 3 Conn. R. 171.

4 See on this subject the Act of Congress of 26th of May, 1790, ch. 11, and the Act of Congress of the 27th of March, 1804, ch. 56; 3 Story, Comm. on Const. § 1297—1307; Andrews *v.* Herriott, 4 Cowen, R. 526, 527, note.

jurists of different countries hold opinions opposite to each other, as to some of the fundamental principles which ought to have a universal operation; and the jurists of the same nation are sometimes as ill agreed among themselves. Still, however, with all these deductions, it is manifest, that many approximations have been already made towards the establishment of a general system of international jurisprudence, which shall elevate the policy, subserve the interests, and promote the common convenience of all nations. We may thus indulge the hope that, at no distant period, the comity of nations will be but another name for the justice of nations; and that the noble boast of the great Roman Orator may be in some measure realized:—*Non erit alia lex Romæ, alia Athenis, alia nunc, alia posthac; sed et omnes gentes et omni tempore una lex, et sempiterna, et immortalis, continebit*[1].

---

[1] Cicero, Fragm. de Repub.

INDEX.

*** *The Figures refer to the* Sections *of the Work.*

FINIS.

LONDON:
W. M'DOWALL, PRINTER, PEMBERTON-ROW,
GOUGH-SQUARE.

www.ingramcontent.com/pod-product-compliance
Lightning Source LLC
LaVergne TN
LVHW100021220926
848483LV00002BA/263
* 9 7 8 1 5 8 4 7 7 1 4 5 6 *